Seventh Edition

SERVICES MARKETING

PEOPLE, TECHNOLOGY, STRATEGY

Global Edition

Christopher Lovelock
Yale University

Jochen Wirtz
National University of Singapore

PEARSON

Boston Columbus Indianapolis New York San Francisco Upper Saddle River Amsterdam
Cape Town Dubai London Madrid Milan Munich Paris Montréal Toronto
Delhi Mexico City Sao Paulo Sydney Hong Kong Seoul Singapore Taipei Tokyo

Editorial Director: Sally Yagan
Editor in Chief: Eric Svendsen
Acquisitions Editor: James Heine
Senior Acquisitions Editor, Global Edition: Steven Jackson
Editorial Project Manager: Kierra Kashickey
Editorial Assistant: Karin Williams
Director of Marketing: Patrice Lumumba Jones
Senior Marketing Manager: Anne K. Fahlgren
Marketing Manger, International: Dean Erasmus
Marketing Assistant: Melinda Jensen
Senior Managing Editor: Judy Leale
Project Manager: Clara Bartunek
Senior Operations Supervisor: Arnold Vila
Operations Specialist: Ilene Kahn
Senior Art Director: Jayne Conte
Cover Designer: Jodi Notowitz
Manager, Visual Research: Beth Brenzel
Photo Researcher: Kathy Ringrose
Manager, Rights and Permissions: Zina Arabia
Image Permission Coordinator: Debbie Latronica
Manager, Cover Visual Research & Permissions: Karen Sanatar
Cover Art: © BC photography/Alamy
Media Editor: Ashley Lulling
Media Production Project Manager: Lisa Rinaldi
Full-Service Project Management: Elm Street Publishing Services
Cover Printer: Courier Kendallville

Pearson Education Limited
Edinburgh Gate
Harlow
Essex CM20 2JE
England

and Associated Companies throughout the world

Visit us on the World Wide Web at:
www.pearsoned.co.uk

Authorised adaptation from the United States edition, entitled Services Marketing: People, Technology, Strategy, 7th edition, ISBN 978-0-13-61-0721-7 by Christopher Lovelock *and* Jochen Wirtz, *published by Pearson Education, publishing as Prentice Hall © 2011.*

Credits and acknowledgments borrowed from other sources and reproduced, with permission, in this textbook appear on appropriate page within text (or on page 625).

British Library Cataloguing-in-Publication Data
A catalogue record for this book is available from the British Library

10 9 8 7 6 5 4 3 2
14 13

ISBN 13: 978-0-27-375606-4
ISBN 10: 0-27-375606-0

Typeset in 10/12 Palatino by Integra Software Services Pvt. Ltd.
Printed and bound by Courier Kendallville in The United States of America

The publisher's policy is to use paper manufactured from sustainable forests.

With gratitude and in loving memory of Christopher Lovelock,
One of the guiding lights of services marketing.

Co-author, mentor, and friend,
And above all, an inspiration.

—JW

ABOUT THE AUTHORS

As a team, Christopher Lovelock and Jochen Wirtz provide a blend of skills and experience that's ideally suited to writing an authoritative and engaging services marketing text. Since first meeting in 1992, they've worked together on a variety of projects, including cases, articles, conference papers, two Asian adaptations of earlier editions of *Services Marketing,* and the new text book *Essentials of Services Marketing.* In 2005, both were actively involved in planning the American Marketing Association's biennial Service Research Conference, hosted by the National University of Singapore and attended by participants from 22 countries on five continents.

The late **Christopher Lovelock** was one of the pioneers of services marketing. He consulted and gave seminars and workshops for managers around the world, with a particular focus on strategic planning in services and managing the customer experience. From 2001 to 2008, he had been an adjunct professor at the Yale School of Management, where he taught services marketing in the MBA program.

After obtaining a BCom and an MA in economics from the University of Edinburgh, he worked in advertising with the London office of J. Walter Thompson Co. and then in corporate planning with Canadian Industries Ltd. in Montreal. Later, he obtained an MBA from Harvard and a PhD from Stanford, where he was also a postdoctoral fellow.

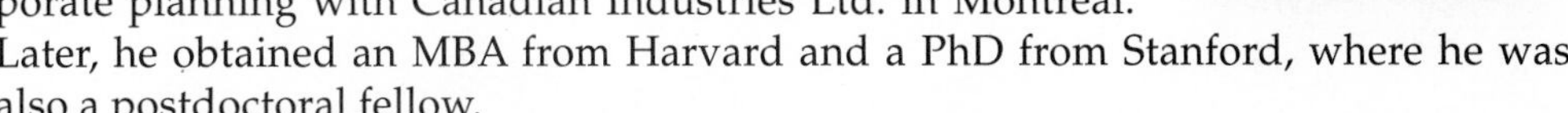

Professor Lovelock's distinguished academic career included 11 years on the faculty of the Harvard Business School and two years as a visiting professor at IMD in Switzerland. He has held faculty appointments at Berkeley, Stanford, and the Sloan School at MIT as well as visiting professorships at INSEAD in France and The University of Queensland in Australia.

Author or co-author of over 60 articles, more than 100 teaching cases, and 27 books, Professor Lovelock has seen his work translated into 14 languages. He served on the editorial review boards of the *Journal of Service Management, Journal of Service Research, Service Industries Journal, Cornell Hospitality Quarterly,* and *Marketing Management,* and served as an ad hoc reviewer for the *Journal of Marketing.*

Widely acknowledged as a thought leader in services, Christopher Lovelock has been honored with the American Marketing Association's prestigious Award for Career Contributions in the Services Discipline. His article with Evert Gummesson, "Whither Services Marketing? In Search of a New Paradigm and Fresh Perspectives" won the AMA's Best Services Article Award in 2005. Earlier, he received a best article award from the *Journal of Marketing.* Recognized many times for excellence in case writing, he has twice won top honors in the *BusinessWeek* European Case of the Year award. For further information, see www.lovelock.com.

Jochen Wirtz holds a Ph.D. in services marketing from the London Business School and has worked in the field of services for over 20 years. He is a tenured associate professor at the National University of Singapore (NUS) where he teaches services marketing in executive, MBA, and undergraduate programs. He is also the founding director of the dual degree UCLA – NUS Executive MBA Program, a Fellow of the NUS Teaching Academy, and an Associate Fellow of Executive Education at Saïd Business School, University of Oxford.

Professor Wirtz's research focuses on service marketing and has been published in over 80 academic journal articles, 100 conference presentations, and some 30 book chapters. He is a co-author of more than 10 books, including his latest—*Essentials of Services Marketing* (Prentice Hall, 2009) and *Flying High in a Competitive Industry: Secrets of the World's Leading Airline* (McGraw Hill, 2009).

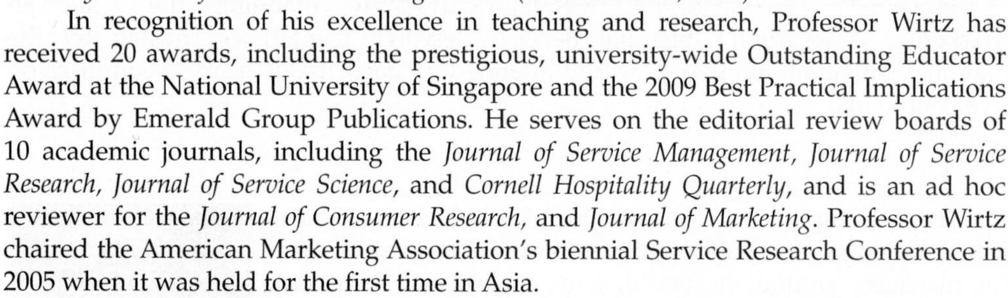

In recognition of his excellence in teaching and research, Professor Wirtz has received 20 awards, including the prestigious, university-wide Outstanding Educator Award at the National University of Singapore and the 2009 Best Practical Implications Award by Emerald Group Publications. He serves on the editorial review boards of 10 academic journals, including the *Journal of Service Management, Journal of Service Research, Journal of Service Science*, and *Cornell Hospitality Quarterly*, and is an ad hoc reviewer for the *Journal of Consumer Research,* and *Journal of Marketing*. Professor Wirtz chaired the American Marketing Association's biennial Service Research Conference in 2005 when it was held for the first time in Asia.

Professor Wirtz has been an active management consultant, working with international consulting firms, including Accenture, Arthur D. Little, and KPMG, and major service firms in the areas of strategy, business development, and customer feedback systems. Originally from Germany, Professor Wirtz spent seven years in London before moving to Asia. For further information, see www.JochenWirtz.com.

ABOUT THE CONTRIBUTORS OF THE CASES

Benjamin Edelman is an assistant professor at Harvard Business School

Lorelle Frazer is a professor at Griffith University, Australia

James L. Heskett is Baker Foundation Professor at Harvard Business School

Roger Hallowell is an affiliated professor of strategy at HEC Paris and a former professor at Harvard Business School

Sheryl E. Kimes is a professor at the School of Hotel Administration, Cornell University

Jill Klein is an associate professor of marketing, INSEAD, France

Youngme Moon is Donald K. David Professor of Business Administration at Harvard Business School

John A. Quelch is Senior Associate Dean and Lincoln Filene Professor of Business Administration at Harvard Business School

Stowe Shoemaker is Associate Dean of Research and Donald Hubbs Distinguished Professor at Conrad Hilton College of Hotel and Restaurant Management, University of Houston

Lauren Wright is a professor of marketing, California State College, Chico

BRIEF CONTENTS

CONTENTS

PREFACE

Services dominate the expanding world economy as never before, and technology continues to evolve in dramatic ways. Nothing is standing still. Established industries and their often famous and old companies decline and may even disappear as new business models and industries emerge. Competitive activity is fierce, with firms often employing new strategies and tactics in response to customers' ever-changing needs, expectations, and behaviors. This book has been written in response to the global transformation of our economies to services. Clearly, the skills in marketing and managing services have never been more important!

As the field of services marketing has evolved, so too has this book, with each successive edition representing a significant revision over its predecessor. The new, 7th edition is no exception. You can be confident that it captures the reality of today's world, incorporates recent academic and managerial thinking, and illustrates cutting-edge service concepts.

WHAT'S NEW IN THIS EDITION?

The 7th edition includes insights on ongoing developments in the service economy, new research findings, and enhancements to the structure and presentation of the book in response to feedback from reviewers and adopters.

New Structure, New Topics

- The chapter text is organized around a revised framework for developing effective service marketing strategies that seamlessly builds on topics learned in a principles or marketing management course. The framework is introduced in Figure I.1 and on pages 50–52. Let's look at coverage in the book's four parts.
  - *Part I* explains the nature of services, how to understand services, how consumer behavior relates to services, and how to position services. It lays the building blocks for studying services and for learning how one can become an effective service marketer.
  - *Part II* covers the development of the service concept and its value proposition, and it explains the product, distribution, pricing, and communications strategies that are needed for developing a successful business model. Part II revisits the 4 Ps of the traditional marketing mix (Product, Place, Price, and Promotion) and expands them to account for the specific characteristics of services that make them different from goods marketing.
  - *Part III* focuses on managing the interface between customers and the service organization. It covers the additional 3 Ps (Process, Physical environment, and People) that are specific to services marketing.
  - *Part IV*, the longest and most challenging part of the text, addresses four key issues in implementing and managing effective services marketing. They are building customer loyalty, complaint handling and service recovery, improving service quality and productivity, and striving for service leadership.
- Each of the 15 chapters has been revised. All chapters incorporate new examples and references to recent research, and some have been re-titled to reflect important changes in emphasis.
- Based on reviewer feedback, the 7th edition no longer contains separate readings. Rather, the key issues from the readings and latest research are now synthesized, conceptualized, and integrated into the relevant chapters. Furthermore, removing the readings from the text gave us the space to add new topics and learning aids, such as succinct but comprehensive chapter summaries in point format.

- Chapter 1, "New Perspectives on Marketing in the Service Economy," has been rewritten. It more deeply explores the nature of the modern service economy and presents a crisp, new conceptualization of the nature of services, based on award-winning research by one of the authors. In addition, it introduces the seven key elements of the services marketing mix (collectively referred to as the 7 Ps) and presents the organizing framework for the book.
- New applications of technology—from Internet-based strategies and biometrics to search-engine optimization, Twitter, and M-commerce—and the opportunities and challenges they pose for customers and service marketers alike, are woven into the text at relevant points across virtually all chapters, as well as illustrated in boxed inserts.
- You will also find that all chapters have been streamlined, with minimum redundancies within and between chapters (with cross-referencing to other parts of the book where necessary). This has significantly enhanced the clarity and structure of the text.
- Many chapters are now structured around strong organizing frameworks such as the three-stage model of consumer behavior related to services (Chapter 2), the flower of service (Chapter 4), the service talent cycle (Chapter 11), the wheel of loyalty (Chapter 12), and the service-profit chain (Chapter 15).
- In rewriting and restructuring the chapters, we have worked hard to create a text that is clear, readable, and focused. Opening vignettes and boxed inserts within the chapters are designed to capture student interest and provide opportunities for in-class discussions. They describe significant research findings, illustrate practical applications of important service marketing concepts, and describe best practices by innovative service organizations from around the world.

New and Updated Cases

- *Services Marketing, 7th edition* features an exceptional selection of 18 up-to-date, classroom-tested cases of varying lengths and levels of difficulty. We wrote a majority of the cases ourselves. Others are drawn from the case collections of Harvard, INSEAD, and Yale.
- Three cases are completely new to this edition (Banyan Tree Hotels & Resorts, Distribution at American Airlines, and Revenue Management of Gondolas). Ten of the remaining cases carried over from the previous edition have been updated. Copyright dates for most cases are 2008 or 2010.
- The new case selection provides even broader coverage of service marketing issues and application areas, with cases featuring a wide array of industries and organizations, ranging in size from multinational giants to small entrepreneurial start-ups, and from nonprofit organizations to professional service firms.

You'll find that this text takes a strongly managerial perspective, yet it is rooted in solid academic research, complemented by strong frameworks. Our goal is to bridge the all-too-frequent gap between theory and the real world. Practical management applications are reinforced by numerous examples within the 15 chapters.

Preparing this new edition has been an exciting challenge. Services marketing, once a tiny academic niche championed by just a handful of pioneering professors, has become a thriving area of activity for both research and teaching. There's growing student interest in taking courses in this field, which makes good sense from a career standpoint, because most business school graduates will go on to work in service industries. We designed this new edition to serve you as a practical resource during your education and career. We hope that you will enjoy reading this text as much as we enjoyed writing it!

Teaching Aids within the Text

We hope you will find that these features work well in your course.

- An opening vignette to each chapter that highlights the key issues and questions addressed.
- Learning objectives and chapter summaries in bullet-point format that allow students to gain a quick overview of the core concepts and messages of each chapter.

- Three types of boxed inserts found throughout the chapters, which lend themselves well to in-class discussions:
  - *Best Practice in Action* (demonstrations of the application of best practices)
  - *Research Insights* (summaries of relevant and often provocative academic research)
  - *Service Perspectives* (in-depth examples that illustrate key concepts)
- Interesting graphics, photographs, and reproductions of advertisements that guide student learning, provide opportunities for discussion, and add visual appeal.
- Review Questions and Applications Exercises, located at the end of each chapter, that closely follow the chapter structure and cover all key learning objectives.

Pedagogical Materials Available from the Publisher

An exceptional instructor's resource manual features:

- Detailed course design and teaching hints, plus sample course outlines.
- Chapter-by-chapter teaching suggestions, plus discussion of learning objectives and sample responses to study questions and exercises.
- Suggested student exercises and comprehensive projects (designed for either individual or team use).
- Detailed case teaching notes, which include teaching objectives, suggested study questions, in-depth analysis of each question, and helpful hints on teaching strategy designed to aid student learning, create stimulating class discussions, and help instructors create end-of-class wrap-ups and "takeaways."
- A table suggesting which cases to pair with which chapters.
- An updated and extended test bank.
- PowerPoint slides, keyed to each chapter and featuring both word-slides and graphics. All slides have been redesigned to be clear, comprehensible, and easily readable.

FOR WHAT TYPES OF COURSES CAN THIS BOOK BE USED?

This text is designed for advanced undergraduates, MBA students, and EMBA students. *Services Marketing, 7th edition* places marketing issues within a broader general management context. The book will appeal both to full-time students headed for a career in management and to EMBAs and executive program participants who are combining their studies with ongoing work in managerial positions.

Whatever a manager's specific job may be, we argue that he or she has to understand and acknowledge the close ties that link the marketing, operations, and human resource functions. With that perspective in mind, we've designed this book so that instructors can make selective use of chapters, readings, and cases to teach courses of different lengths and formats in either services marketing or service management.

WHAT ARE THE BOOK'S DISTINGUISHING FEATURES?

Key features of this highly readable book include:

- A strong managerial focus supported by the latest academic research. It not only addresses the need for service marketers to understand customer needs and behavior, but also considers how to use these insights to develop effective strategies for competing in the marketplace.
- The text is organized around an integrated framework, which students immediately relate to as it seamlessly builds on topics covered in principles and marketing management courses.

- Use of memorable organizing frameworks for most chapters that have been classroom-tested for relevance and effectiveness. Examples include the three-stage model of consumer behavior related to services, the flower of service, the wheel of loyalty, the service talent cycle, and the service-profit chain.
- Each chapter takes a systematic learning approach that is clear and easy to follow. Each chapter has:
  - An opening vignette, which introduces the concepts taught in the chapter.
  - Clear learning objectives.
  - Chapter summaries in bullet form that condense the core concepts and messages of each chapter.
  - Interesting examples and illustrations from a wide range of industries and geographies that link theory to practice.
  - Review questions designed to consolidate understanding of key concepts through discussion and study.
  - Application exercises that extend understanding beyond the question-and-answer format and focus on application and internalization of the concepts, theories, and key messages of each chapter.
- Inclusion of 18 carefully selected American, European, and Asian cases that offer a global perspective.
- Extensive and up-to-date references at the end of each chapter.

We've designed *Services Marketing, 7th edition* to complement the materials found in traditional marketing management and principles texts. Recognizing that the service sector of the economy can best be characterized by its diversity, we believe that no single conceptual model suffices to cover marketing-relevant issues among organizations ranging from huge international corporations (in fields such as airlines, banking, insurance, telecommunications, freight transportation, and professional services) to locally owned and operated small businesses, such as restaurants, laundries, taxis, optometrists, and many business-to-business services. In response, the book offers a carefully designed "toolbox" for service managers, teaching students how different concepts, frameworks, and analytical procedures can best be used to examine and resolve the varied challenges faced by managers in different situations.

ACKNOWLEDGMENTS

Over the years, many colleagues in both the academic and business worlds have provided us with valued insights into the management and marketing of services through their publications, in conference or seminar discussions, and through stimulating individual conversations. In addition, both of us have benefited enormously from in-class and after-class discussions with our students and executive program participants.

We're much indebted to those researchers and teachers who helped to pioneer the study of services marketing and management, and from whose work we continue to draw inspiration. Among them are John Bateson of SHL Group; Leonard Berry of Texas A&M University; Mary Jo Bitner and Stephen Brown of Arizona State University; Richard Chase of the University of Southern California; Pierre Eiglier of Université d'Aix-Marseille III; Raymond Fisk of the University of New Orleans; Christian Grönroos of the Swedish School of Economics in Finland; Stephen Grove of Clemson University; Evert Gummesson of Stockholm University; James Heskett and Earl Sasser of Harvard University; and Benjamin Schneider of the University of Maryland. We salute, too, the contributions of the late Eric Langeard and Daryl Wyckoff.

A particular acknowledgment is due to six individuals who have made exceptional contributions to the field, not only in their role as researchers and teachers but also as journal editors, in which capacity they facilitated publication of many of the important articles cited in this book. They are Bo Edvardsson, University of Karlstad and editor, *Journal of Service Management (JOSM)*; Robert Johnston, University of Warwick and founding editor of *JOSM*; Jos Lemmink, Maastricht University and former editor, *JOSM*; Roland Rust of the University of Maryland, and founding editor, *Journal of Service Research (JSR)*; A. "Parsu" Parasuraman, University of Miami and former editor, *JSR*; and Katherine Lemon, Boston College, current editor of *JSR*.

Although it's impossible to mention everyone who has influenced our thinking, we particularly want to express our appreciation to the following: Tor Andreassen, Norwegian School of Management; David Bowen of Thunderbird Graduate School of Management; John Deighton, Theodore Levitt, and Leonard Schlesinger, all currently or formerly of Harvard Business School; Loizos Heracleous of University of Warwick; Douglas Hoffmann of Colorado State University; Sheryl Kimes of Cornell University; Jean-Claude Larréché of INSEAD; David Maister of Maister Associates; Anna Mattila of Pennsylvania State University; Anat Rafaeli of Technion-Israeli Institute of Technology; Frederick Reichheld of Bain & Co; Bernd Stauss of Katholische Universität Eichstät; Charles Weinberg of the University of British Columbia; Lauren Wright of California State University, Chico; George Yip of London Business School; and Valarie Zeithaml of the University of North Carolina.

We've also gained important insights from our co-authors on international adaptations of *Services Marketing*, and we are grateful for the friendship and collaboration of Guillermo D'Andrea of Universidad Austral, Argentina; Harvir Singh Bansal of Wilfrid Laurier University, Canada; Jayanta Chatterjee of Indian Institute of Technolgy at Kanpur, India; Patricia Chew of UniSIM, Singapore; Luis Huete of IESE Business School, Spain; Keh Hean Tat of Peking University, China; Laura Iacovone of Università Bocconi, Italy; Denis Lapert of INT-Management, France; Barbara Lewis of Manchester School of Management, UK; Lu Xiongwen of Fudan University, China; Annie Munos of Euromed Marseille École de Management, France; Javier Reynoso of Tec de Monterrey, Mexico; Paul Patterson of the University of New South Wales, Australia; Sandra Vandermerwe of Imperial College, UK; Rhett Walker of LaTrobe University, Australia; and Shirai Yoshio of Takasaki City University of Economics, Japan.

IBM Cooperation has been a major catalyst in developing the new field of service science, and we would like to especially thank James Spohrer, Paul Maglio, and Wendy Murphy of the IBM's Almaden Research Center for advancing services thinking across functional and disciplinary boundaries.

It's a pleasure to acknowledge the insightful and helpful comments of reviewers of this and previous editions: David M. Andrus of Kansas State University; Charlene Bebko of Indiana University of Pennsylvania; Michael L. Capella of Villanova University; Susan Carder of Northern Arizona University; Frederick Crane of the University of New Hampshire; Harry Domicone of California Lutheran University; Lukas P. Forbes of Western Kentucky University; Bill Hess of Golden Gate University; Ben Judd of the University of New Haven; P. Sergius Koku of Florida Atlantic University; Robert P. Lambert of Belmont University; Martin J. Lattman of Johns Hopkins University; Daryl McKee of Louisiana State University; Terri Rittenburg of the University of Wyoming; Cynthia Rodriguez Cano of Augusta State University; and Lisa Simon of California Polytechnic State University. They challenged our thinking and encouraged us to include many substantial changes. In addition, we benefited from the valued advice of Sharon Beatty of the University of Alabama and Karen Fox of Santa Clara University, who provided thoughtful suggestions for improvement.

It takes more than authors to create a book and its supplements. Warm thanks are due to our three research assistants, Valerie Phay, Lisa Tran, and Nicole Wong, who provided excellent support with various aspects of writing this book. And we're very appreciative of all the hard work put in by the editing and production staff who worked to transform our manuscript into a handsome published text. They include James Heine, Acquisitions Editor; Kierra Kashickey, Editorial Project Manager; Karin Williams, Editorial Assistant; Judy Leale, Senior Managing Editor; Clara Bartunek, Production Project Manager; and Emily Winders of Elm Street Publishing Services. Thanks also to Gavin Fox of Texas Tech University, author of the Seventh Edition test bank.

Finally, we'd like to thank you, our reader, for your interest in this exciting and fast-evolving field of services marketing. If you have interesting research, examples, stories, cases, videos, or any other materials that would look good in the next edition of this book, or any feedback, please do contact us via www.JochenWirtz.com. We'd love to hear from you!

Christopher Lovelock
Jochen Wirtz

Pearson gratefully acknowledges and thanks the following people for their work on the Global Edition:

Naila Aaijaz, Faculty of Entrepreneurship and Business, University of Malaysia Kelantan, Malaysia.

Dr. Mohammad A Al-hawari, Assistant Professor, Management, Marketing, and Public Administration Department, Business Administration College, Sharjah University, United Arab of Emirates.

Dr. Melodena Stephens Balakrishnan, Associate Professor, University of Wollongong in Dubai, Dubai.

Adjunct Associate Professor Gerard Gonzales, Division of Marketing & International Business, Nanyang Business School, Nanyang Technological University, Singapore.

Dr. Osman G¨ok, Faculty of Economics and Administrative Sciences, Yasar University, Turkey

Prof. Raija Komppula, Lecturer of Tourism Business, Centre for Tourism Studies, University of Joensuu, Finland.

Winnie Quah-Leow, Senior Lecturer of Marketing and Retail, School of Business, Singapore Polytechnic, Singapore.

Helen Reijonen, Senior Assistant, Economics and Business Administration, University of Joensuu, Finland.

Quah Kheng Siong, Faculty of Management and Information Technology, UCSI University, Malaysia.

Jon and Diane Sutherland.

Services Marketing

People, Technology, Strategy

Global Edition

PART ONE

Understanding Service Products, Consumers, and Markets

Part One explains the nature of services, how to understand services, how consumer behavior relates to services and how to position services. It lays the building blocks for studying services and for learning how one can become an effective service marketer. It consists of the following three chapters:

CHAPTER 1 NEW PERSPECTIVES ON MARKETING IN THE SERVICE ECONOMY

Chapter 1 highlights the importance of services in our economies. We also define the nature of services and how they create value for customers without transfer of ownership. The chapter highlights some distinctive challenges involved in marketing services and introduces the 7 Ps of services marketing.

The framework shown in Figure I.1 on the facing page will accompany us throughout as it forms the basis for each of the four parts in this book. It describes in a systematic manner of what is involved in developing marketing strategies for different types of services. The framework is introduced and explained in Chapter 1.

CHAPTER 2 CUSTOMER BEHAVIOR IN A SERVICES CONTEXT

Chapter 2 provides a foundation for understanding consumer needs and behavior in both high-contact and low-contact services. The chapter is organized around the three-stage model of service consumption that explores how customers search for and evaluate alternative services, make purchase decisions, experience and respond to service encounters, and finally, evaluate service performance.

CHAPTER 3 POSITIONING SERVICES IN COMPETITIVE MARKETS

Chapter 3 discusses how a value proposition should be positioned in a way that creates competitive advantage for the firm. The chapter shows how firms can segment a service market, position their value proposition and finally focus on attracting their target segment.

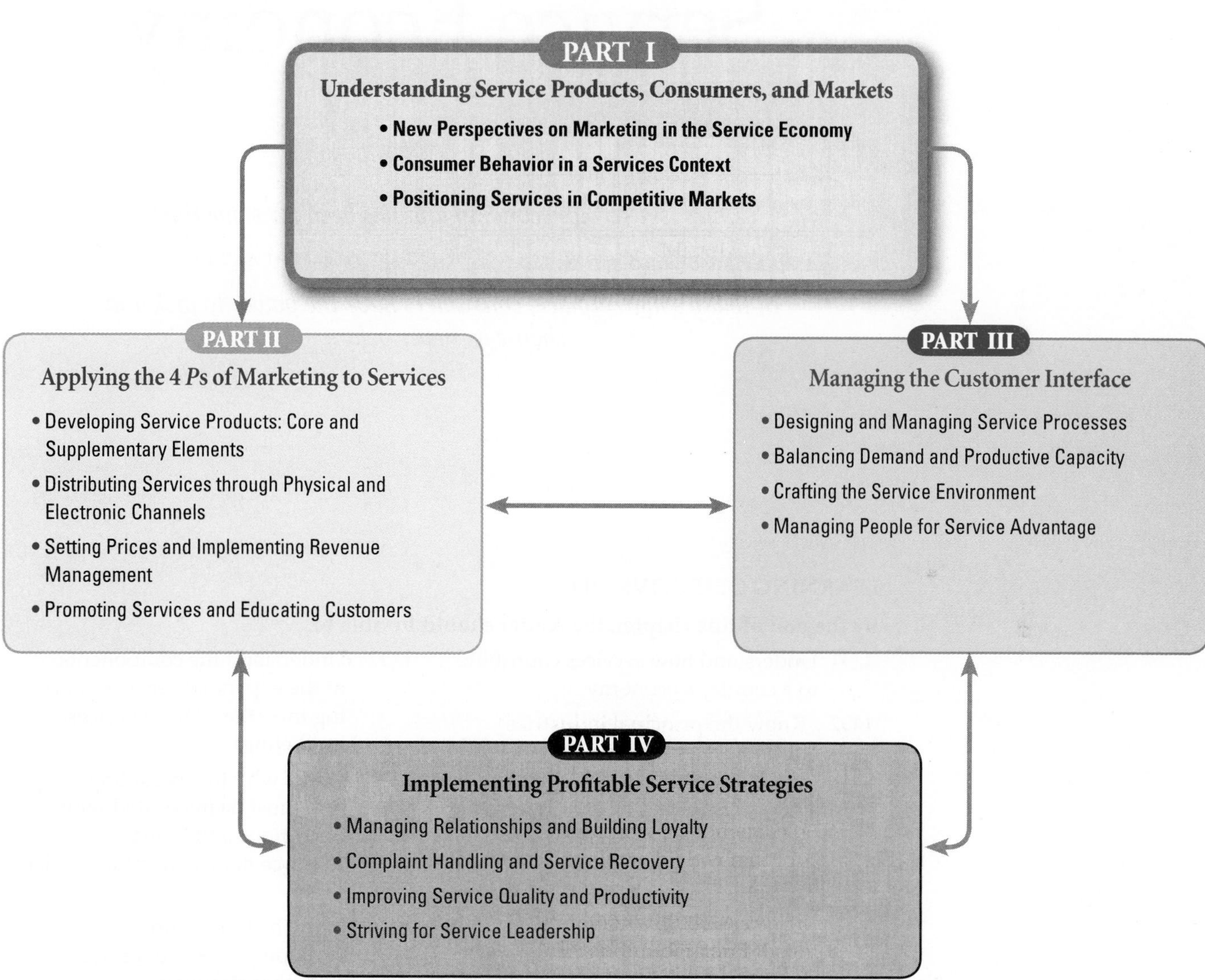

FIGURE I.1 Organizing Framework for Services Marketing

CHAPTER 1

New Perspectives on Marketing in the Service Economy

Ours is a service economy and has been for some time.

KARL ALBRECHT AND RON ZEMKE

In today's marketplace, consumers have the power to pick and choose as never before.

THE ECONOMIST

LEARNING OBJECTIVES (LOs)

By the end of this chapter, the reader should be able to:

LO1 Understand how services contribute to a country's economy

LO2 Know the principal industries of the service sector

LO3 Identify the powerful forces that are transforming service markets

LO4 Define services using the nonownership service framework

LO5 Identify the four broad "processing" categories of services

LO6 Be familiar with the characteristics of services and the distinctive marketing challenges they pose

LO7 Understand the components of the expanded services marketing mix (the 7 Ps of services marketing)

LO8 Know why the marketing function must be integrated with operations and human resource management in service firms

LO9 Know the framework for developing effective service marketing strategies

Introduction to the World of Services Marketing

Like every reader of this book, you're an experienced service consumer. You use an array of services every day, although some—like talking on the phone, using a credit card, riding a bus, or withdrawing money from an ATM—may be so routine that you hardly notice them unless something goes wrong. Other service purchases may involve more forethought and be more memorable—for instance, booking a cruise vacation, getting financial advice, or having a medical examination. Enrolling in college or graduate school may be one of the biggest service purchases you will ever make. The typical university is a complex service organization that offers not only educational services, but also libraries, student accommodations, healthcare, athletic facilities, museums, security, counseling, and career services. On campus, you may find a bookstore, a post office, photocopying services, Internet access, a bank, food, entertainment, and more. Your use of these services are examples of service consumption at the individual, or business-to-consumer (B2C), level.

Companies and nonprofit organizations use a wide array of business-to-business (B2B) services, varying to some degree according to the nature of their industry, but usually involving purchases on a much larger scale than those made by individuals or families. Nowadays, firms are outsourcing more and more tasks to external service providers in order to focus on their core business. Without being able to buy these services at a good value, these companies can't hope to succeed.

Unfortunately, consumers are not always happy with the quality and value of the services they receive. Sometimes, you may be delighted with your service experiences, but there have probably been instances where you were very disappointed. Both individual and corporate purchasers complain about broken promises, poor value for money, lack of understanding of their needs, rude or incompetent personnel, inconvenient service hours, bureaucratic procedures, wasted time, malfunctioning self-service machines, complicated websites, and a host of other problems.

Suppliers of services, often facing stiff competition, sometimes appear to have a very different set of concerns. Many owners and managers complain about how difficult it is to keep costs down and make a profit, to find skilled and motivated employees, or to satisfy customers who, they sometimes grumble, have become unreasonably demanding. Fortunately, some service companies do know how to please their customers while also running a productive and profitable operation.

You probably have a few favorite service organizations you like to patronize. Have you ever stopped to think about how they succeed in delivering service that meets your needs and sometimes even exceeds your expectations? This book will teach you how service businesses should be managed to achieve customer satisfaction and profitability. In addition to studying key concepts, organizing frameworks, and tools of services marketing, you'll also be introduced to a wide array of organizations examples from across the United States and around the world. From their experiences, you can draw important lessons on how to succeed in increasingly competitive service markets.

In this opening chapter, we present an overview of today's dynamic service economy, define the nature of services, and highlight some distinctive challenges involved in marketing services. We conclude the chapter by presenting a framework for developing and implementing service marketing strategies. This framework provides the structure for this book.

WHY STUDY SERVICES?

Here's a paradox: We live in a service economy, but at most business schools the academic study and teaching of marketing still is dominated by a manufacturing perspective. If you took a marketing course previously, you most likely learned more about marketing manufactured products, especially consumer goods, than about services marketing. Fortunately, a growing and enthusiastic group of scholars, consultants, and teachers—including the authors of this text—have chosen to focus on services marketing. Together, they build on the extensive research conducted in this field over the past three decades.[1] You can be confident that this book will provide you with the knowledge and skills that are highly relevant in tomorrow's business environment.

Services Dominate the Economy in Most Nations

The size of the service sector is increasing in virtually all countries around the world. As a national economy develops, the relative share of employment between agriculture, industry (including manufacturing and mining), and services changes dramatically.[2] Even in emerging economies, the service output is growing rapidly and often represents at least half of the gross domestic product (GDP). Figure 1.1 shows how the

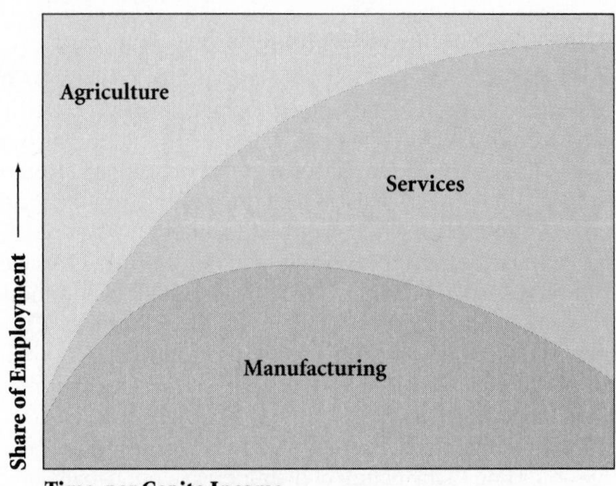

FIGURE 1.1 Changing Structure of Employment as an Economy Develops

Source: Adapted from International Monetary Fund, 1997.

evolution to a service-dominated economy likely will take place over time as per capita income rises. In developed economies, knowledge-based services—defined as those that are intensive users of high technology and/or have relatively skilled workforces—have been proving the most dynamic component.[3] Figure 1.2 shows that the service sector already accounts for almost two-thirds of the value of the GDP globally.

For-profit and nonprofit services differ in their underlying goals, although both want to create value for their various stakeholders. For-profit businesses seek to achieve *financial* profits subject to *social* constraints, whereas nonprofit service suppliers seek to achieve *social* profits subject to *financial* constraints.[4] Many public agencies and nonprofit organizations charge a price for their services that partially covers their costs, but often they depend on donations, grants, or tax-based subsidies to cover the rest. (For simplicity, we will use the terms *business, company, corporation, firm*, and *organization* to apply generically to all types of service providers.)

As in the United States, most emerging and developed countries have seen their service economies grow rapidly. Figure 1.3 shows the relative size of the service sector in an array of both large and small economies. In most of the more highly developed nations, services account for between two-thirds and three-fourths of the GDP, although manufacturing-oriented South Korea (58 percent) is an exception. Which are the world's most service-dominated economies? One is the Cayman Islands (95 percent), a group of small, British-administered islands in the western Caribbean, known for both tourism and offshore financial and insurance services. Jersey, the Bahamas, and Bermuda—all small islands with a similar economic mix—are equally service dominated. Luxembourg (86 percent) has the most service-dominated economy in the European Union. Panama's strong showing (78 percent) reflects not only the operation of the Panama Canal—widely used by cruise ships as well as freight vessels—but also such related services as container ports, flagship registry, and a free port zone, as well as financial services, insurance, and tourism (Figure 1.4).

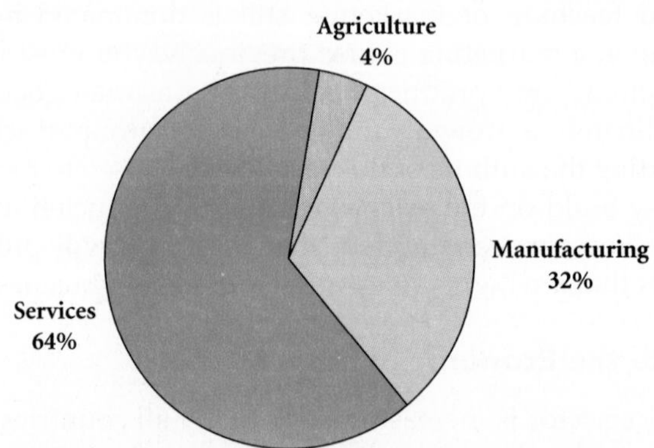

FIGURE 1.2 Contribution of Service Industries to GDP globally, 2008

Source: The World Factbook 2008, Central Intelligence Agency, https://www.cia.gov/library/publications/the-worldfactbook/fields/2012.html accessed March 26, 2009.

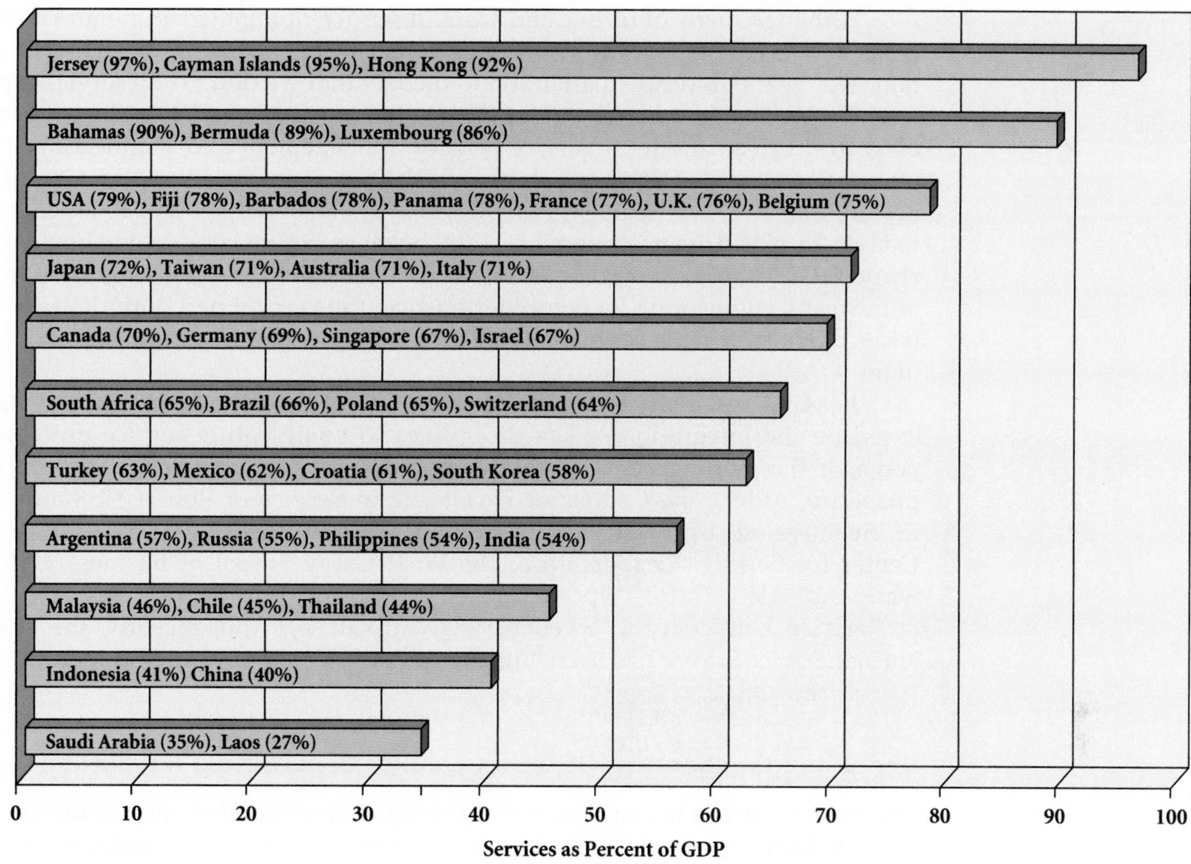

FIGURE 1.3 Estimated Size of Service Sector in Selected Countries as a Percentage of GDP

Source: The World Factbook 2008, Central Intelligence Agency, https://www.cia.gov/library/publications/the-world-factbook/fields/2012.html accessed March 26, 2009.

Near the opposite end of the scale is China (40 percent), whose emerging economy is dominated by a substantial agricultural sector and booming manufacturing and construction industries. However, China's economic growth is now leading to increased demand for business and consumer services. China's government is investing heavily in service infrastructure, including shipping facilities and new airport terminals. Shanghai, the country's major commercial center, even boasts the world's fastest airport train service, featuring German-designed vehicles powered by magnetic levitation and capable of speeds of up to 260 mph (420 km/h). Last among relatively affluent countries is Saudi Arabia, with its oil-dominated economy to which services contribute only 35 percent of the GDP.

FIGURE 1.4 The Panama Canal Forms the Backbone of This Country's Service Economy

Most New Jobs Are Generated by Services

Employment is predicted to continue shrinking in manufacturing, mining, and agriculture in the United States. Like most developed economies, the United States will look to service industries for new job creation. And, contrary to popular belief, many new service jobs likely will demand significant training and educational qualifications, and employees often are highly compensated.[5] Some of the fastest growth is expected in knowledge-based industries—such as professional and business services,[6] education, and health services.

Although many of us live and work in service-dominated economies, most students still graduate from universities steeped in management or technical education.[7] For years, IBM called attention to the fact that we don't train service economy workers. Reflecting the ever tighter integration of value creation in the service economy, IBM coined the term Service Science, Management and Engineering (SSME), often called *service science* for short, which integrates key disciplines required to design, improve, and scale service systems. To achieve this—and to be effective in today's service-driven economies—IBM believes future graduates should be "T" shaped. That is, they should have a deep understanding of their own discipline such as business, engineering, or computer science (the vertical part of the T) as well as a basic understanding of service-related topics in other disciplines (the horizontal part of the T).[8]

Leading research centers have followed IBM's call and are increasingly focused on the integration of key disciplines to equip future service professionals. Some of the leading centers that have embraced service science include (in alphabetical order): the Center for Excellence in Service of Robert H. Smith School of Business at University of Maryland (see www.rhsmith.umd.edu/ces); the Center for Services Leadership at the W. P. Carey School of Business at Arizona State University (http://wpcarey.asu.edu/csl); and The Service Research Center at Karlstad University in Sweden (www.ctf.kau.se). And, recently, the academic journal *Service Science* has been launched to provide a publication outlet for service science research.[9]

Understanding Services Offers a Personal Competitive Advantage

This book is written in response to the global transformation of our economies toward services. Learning about the distinctive characteristics of services and how they affect both customer behavior and marketing strategy will give you important insights—and perhaps create a competitive advantage for your own career. Unless you're predestined to work in a family manufacturing or agricultural business, the probability is high that you'll spend most of your working life in service organizations. You may also find yourself serving as a volunteer or board member for a nonprofit organization. Maybe the knowledge gained from studying this book will even stimulate you to think about starting your own service business!

WHAT ARE THE PRINCIPAL INDUSTRIES OF THE SERVICE SECTOR?

What industries make up the service sector, and which are the biggest? The latter may not be the ones you first imagine, because this diverse sector includes many services targeted at business customers, some of which are not highly visible unless you happen to work in that industry. National economic statistics are a useful starting point. To provide a better understanding of today's service-dominated economy, government statistical agencies have developed new ways to classify industries. In the United States, the manufacturing-oriented Standard Industrial Classification (SIC) system, developed in the 1930s, has been replaced by the new North American Industry Classification System (NAICS).[10] Canada and Mexico adopted it, too. (For details, see Research Insights 1.1.)

Contribution to Gross Domestic Product

To see how much value each of the major service industry groups contributes to the U.S. GDP, take a look at Figure 1.5. Would you have guessed that real estate and rental and leasing would be the largest for-profit service industry sector in the United States, accounting for 12.5 percent in 2007, almost one-eighth of the GDP? Over 90 percent of this figure comes from such activities as renting residential or commercial property; managing properties on behalf of their owners; providing realty services to facilitate purchases, sales, and rentals; and appraising property to determine its condition and value. The balance is accounted for by renting or leasing a wide variety of other manufactured

RESEARCH INSIGHTS 1.1

NAICS: A NEW WAY TO CLASSIFY THE ECONOMIES OF NORTH AMERICA

The North American Industry Classification System—developed jointly by the statistical agencies of Canada, Mexico, and the United States—offers a new approach to classifying industries in the economic statistics of the three North American Free Trade Agreement (NAFTA) countries. It replaces previous national systems, such as the SIC codes formerly used in the United States.

NAICS (pronounced "nakes") includes many new service industries that have emerged in recent decades and also reclassifies as services "auxiliary" establishments that provide services to manufacturing industries—examples include accounting, catering, and transportation. Every sector of the economy has been restructured and redefined. NAICS includes 358 new industries that the SIC did not identify, 390 that are revised from their SIC counterparts, and 422 that continue substantially unchanged. These industries are grouped into sectors and further subdivided into subsectors, industry groups, and establishments.

Among the new sectors and subsectors devoted to services are: *Information*, which recognizes the emergence and uniqueness of businesses in the "information economy"; *Health Care and Social Assistance; Professional, Scientific and Business Services; Educational Services;* and *Accommodation and Food Services; and Arts, Entertainment and Recreation* (which includes most businesses engaged in meeting consumers' cultural, leisure, or entertainment interests).

NAICS uses a consistent principle for classification, grouping businesses that use similar production processes. Its goal is to make economic statistics more useful and to capture developments that encompass applications of high technology (e.g., cellular telecommunications), new businesses that previously did not exist (e.g., environmental consulting), and changes in the way business is done (e.g., warehouse clubs).

The NAICS codes are set up in such a way that researchers can drill down within broad industry sectors to obtain information on tightly defined types of service establishments. For instance, NAICS code 71 designates arts, entertainment, and recreation. Code 7112 designates spectator sports, and code 711211 designates sports teams and clubs. By looking at changes over time in "real" dollars (adjusted for inflation), it's possible to determine which industries have been growing and which have not. The NAICS codes are also being used to categorize employment statistics and numbers of establishments within a particular industry. And a new North American Product Classification System (NAPCS) defines thousands of service products. If you want to research service industries and service products, NAICS data is a great place to start.

Sources: Economic Classification Policy Committee, "NAICS—North American Industry Classification System: New Data for a New Economy." Washington, DC: Bureau of the Census, October 1998; North American Industry Classification System, United States 2002 [Official NAICS manual], Washington, DC: National Technical Information Service, PB2002101430*SS, 2002. http://www.census.gov/eos/www/naics/, accessed June 29, 2009.

products, ranging from heavy construction equipment (with or without operators) to office furniture, tents, and party supplies. Another large cluster of services provides for distribution of physical products. Wholesale and retail trade, plus freight transportation and warehousing, collectively account for about 12.3 percent of the GDP.

Other substantial industry sectors or subsectors are professional and business services (12.3 percent), finance and insurance (7.9 percent), and healthcare (7.9 percent). Part of the "other services" category (6.1 percent), accommodation and food services, constitute only 2.7 percent, while the arts, entertainment, and recreation subsector—which includes such high-profile consumer services as spectator sports, fitness centers, skiing facilities, museums and zoos, performing arts, casinos, golf courses, marinas, and theme parks—collectively represents a mere 1.0 percent of the GDP. Nevertheless, in an economy with an output of more than $25.8 trillion, this last group of services was still valued at an impressive $207 billion in 2007.

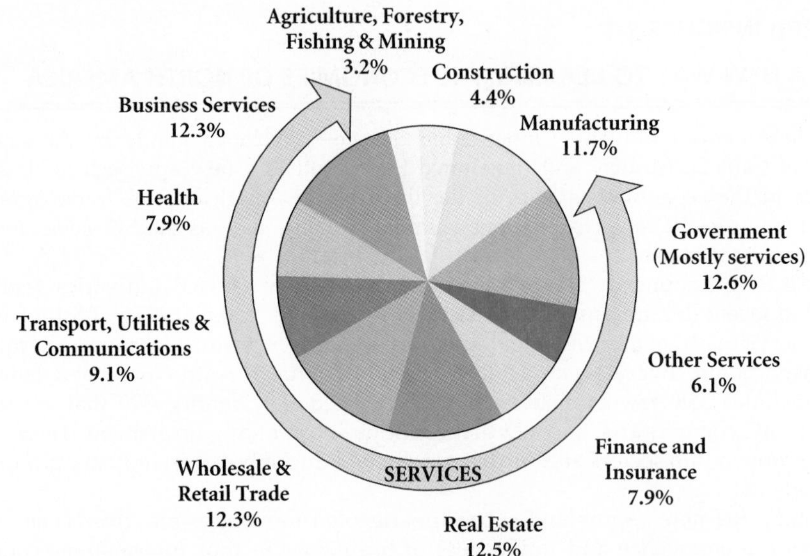

FIGURE 1.5 Value Added by Service Industry Categories to U.S. Gross Domestic Product

Note: "Other services" include arts, entertainment, recreation, accommodation, education, and food services.

Source: US Bureau of Economic Analysis, Industry Economics Accounts, Gross-Domestic-Product-by-Industry Accounts for 2007, http://www.bea.gov/industry/gpotables/gpo_action.cfm?anon=89618&table_id=23975&format_type=0; accessed March 29, 2009.

POWERFUL FORCES ARE TRANSFORMING SERVICE MARKETS

What is driving the rapid growth of the service sector? Government policies, social changes, business trends, advances in information technology, and globalization are among the powerful forces transforming today's service markets (Figure 1.6). Collectively, these forces are reshaping demand, supply, the competitive landscape, and even customers' styles of decision making. The Internet transfers power from suppliers to customers, especially in consumer markets.[11] For example, the travel industry will never be the same again now that travelers can easily research alternatives and make their own bookings. Electronic distribution is changing relationships and roles between suppliers, intermediaries, and customers as traditional channel members (such as local travel agencies) are replaced by innovative newcomers such as Orbitz, Travelocity, and Priceline.[12] Table 1.1 shows specific examples of each of these forces and its impact on the service economy; collectively, they are reshaping demand, supply, the competitive landscape, and even the way customers buy and use services.

Will service jobs be lost to lower-cost countries? New communications technology means that some service work can be carried out far from where customers are located (Figure 1.7, See page 36). A study by the international consulting firm McKinsey & Co. estimated that 11 percent of service jobs around the world could be carried out remotely. But in practice, McKinsey predicted the percentage of service jobs actually "offshored" will prove much more limited, only 1 percent of all service employment in developed countries in 2008.[13] Of course, loss of even that small percentage will still affect a large number of workers, including some well-paid professionals whose work can be performed much more cost-effectively by, say, highly-qualified engineers working in India.[14]

WHAT ARE SERVICES?

Thus far, our discussion of services has focused on different types of service industries. But now it's time to ask the question: What exactly is a *service*?

The Historical View

Attempts to describe and define services go back more than two centuries. In the late-eighteenth and early-nineteenth centuries, classical economists focused on the creation and possession of wealth. They contended that goods (initially referred to as "commodities") were objects of value over which ownership rights could be established and

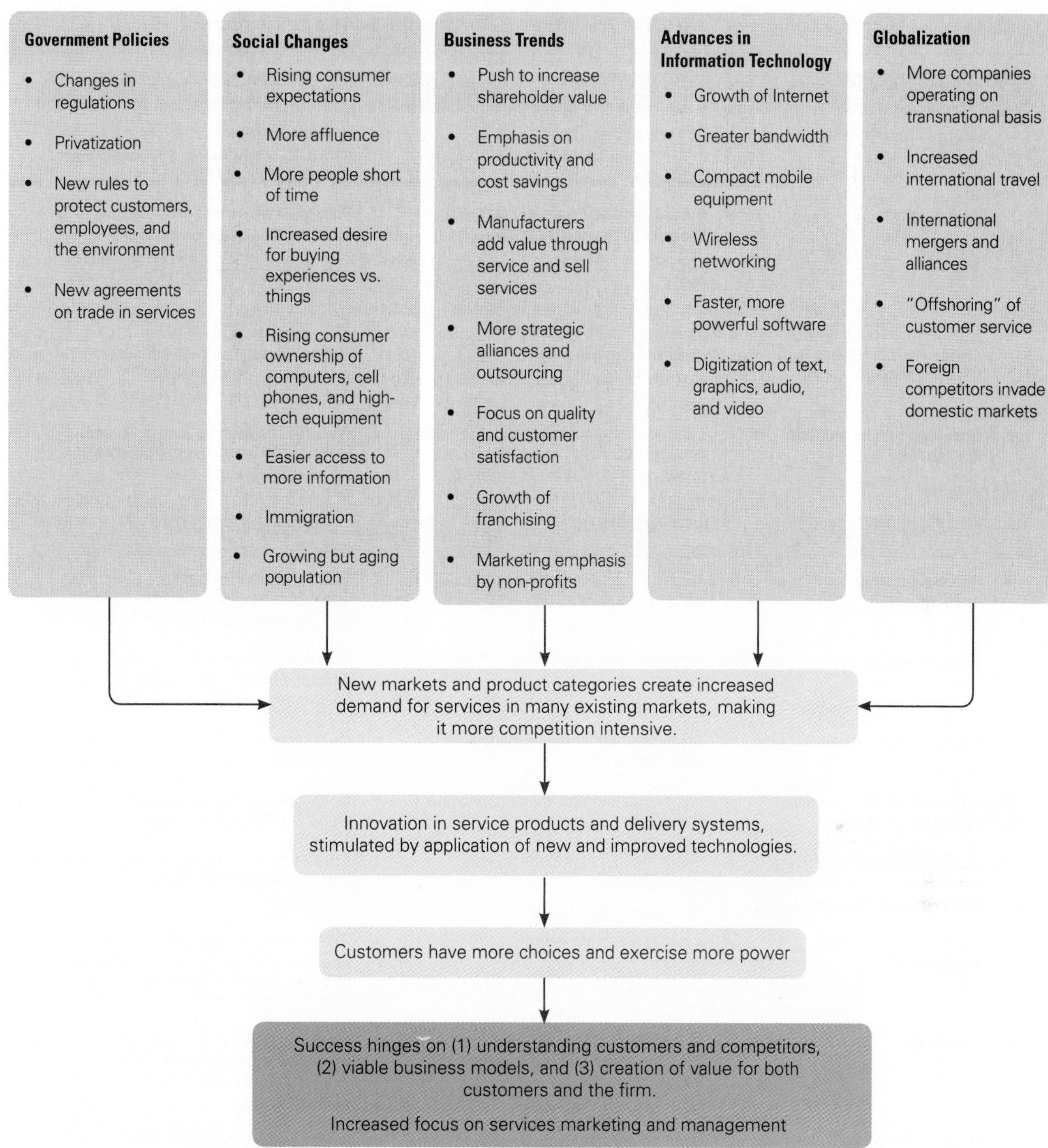

FIGURE 1.6 Factors Stimulating the Transformation of the Service Economy

exchanged. Ownership implied tangible possession of an object that had been acquired through purchase, barter, or gift from the producer or a previous owner and was legally identifiable as the property of the current owner.

Adam Smith's famous book, *The Wealth of Nations*, published in Great Britain in 1776, distinguished between the outputs of what he termed "productive" and "unproductive" labor.[15] The former, he stated, produced goods that could be stored after production and subsequently exchanged for money or other items of value. But unproductive labor, however "honourable,…useful, or…necessary" created services that *perished* at the time of production and therefore didn't contribute to wealth. Building on this theme, French economist Jean-Baptiste Say argued that production and consumption were inseparable in services, coining the term "immaterial products" to describe them.[16]

TABLE 1.1 Specific Examples of Forces that Transform and Impact the Service Economy

Government Policies	Example	Impact on Service Economy
• **Changes in regulations**	• Ban on smoking in restaurants, and limitation of transfats in food preparation	• Improved customer comfort and health measures in restaurants will encourage people to dine out more often
• **Privatization**	• Privatization of infrastructure services like utilities and transportation	• Potential retrenchment of existing suppliers in a more competitive environment, but job creation and investments by new players entering the market
• **New regulations to protect customers, employees, and the environment**	• Increased taxes to aviation industry for harmful gas emission	• Increased costs of air travel may dampen demand; policy stimulates development of jet engines that are more fuel efficient and less polluting
• **New agreements on trade in services**	• Companies from foreign countries can take over basic services like water, health, transportation, and education	• Transfer of expertise across borders. New investments result in improved infrastructure and better quality
Social Changes	**Example**	**Impact on Service Economy**
• **Rising consumer expectations**	• Higher expectation of service quality and convenience	• Training of service staff to deliver good service; extended hours offer more part-time job opportunities
• **More affluence**	• Higher spending on tourism	• Creation of a wider variety of offerings; development of new services in new locations boosts local economies
• **Personal outsourcing**	• Home cleaning services, baby and child care services	• New service providers include both local firms and national/regional chains
• **Increased desire for buying experiences vs. things**	• Higher spending on luxury services like spa treatments	• New players emerge; existing health clubs and resort hotels add spas
• **Rising consumer ownership of computers, cell phones, and high-tech equipment**	• Higher demand for laptops and 3G mobile phones	• Greater need for designers, engineers and marketers for these types of equipment
• **Easier access to more information**	• Internet and podcasting	• Allows firms to build closer, more focused relationships with customers and new opportunities to reach them on the move in real time
• **Migration**	• Many Indian nationals who have migrated to the USA now move back to home country	• Transfers talent to home country but may create a vacuum in the employment market of developed economies
• **Growing but aging population**	• Matured European countries	• More services catering to the needs of elderly, including health care and, construction of retirement communities
Business Trends	**Example**	**Impact on Service Economy**
• **Push to increase shareholder value**	• Shareholders pressure company boards to deliver higher returns	• Search for new revenue sources such as additional fees, higher prices, adoption of revenue management strategies, plus cuts in customer service to reduce costs
• **Emphasis on productivity and cost savings**	• Move to self-service technologies	• Rethink service delivery system, invest in new technologies that replace employees
• **Manufacturers add value through service and sell services**	• IBM's consulting and IT services for financial markets	• Competition with service providers from other industries, such as traditional management consulting firms

• **More strategic alliances**	• Airlines form alliances such as Star Alliance and Oneworld	• Routes are rationalized to avoid duplications, schedules and ticketing are coordinated; marketing is leveraged and operating efficiency improved
• **Focus on quality and customer satisfaction**	• Hotels and motels at all levels define standards more tightly and seek to meet them consistently	• Training programs to equip service staff with necessary skills; investment in modernization of existing facilities and construction of new ones offering better amenities
• **Growth of franchising**	• Fast food chains expand around the world	• Challenge of maintaining consistent service standards worldwide while adapting to local food preferences and cultures
• **Marketing emphasis by nonprofits**	• Museums seek to expand audiences and generate more frequent repeat visits	• Fund raising for improved facilities; addition of new revenue generating services like restaurants and facilities rental

Advances in Information Technology	Example	Impact on Service Economy
• **Growth of Internet**	• Information at the fingertips of the customers, making them more knowledgeable and informed	• Creation of new services that gather the various sources of information and repackage them to provide value to customers
• **Greater bandwidth**	• Allows for delivery of sophisticated and interactive educational content	• Service delivery processes need to be redesigned
• **Compact mobile equipment**	• 3G mobile phones that integrate many high tech functions	• Advanced marketing and maintenance services needed
• **Wireless networking**	• Public libraries, cafes, and hotels provide this service (free or at a price) to attract customers	• More brick and mortar service firms are expected to provide similar benefits to stay competitive
• **Faster, more powerful software**	• Customized software development by software consulting firms like Infosys	• Increase in training software engineers to develop packaged services instead of piece meal services
• **Digitization of text, graphics, audio, and video**	• Online download service providers	• Need for service providers to invest in maintaining a secure and credible website and guarantee virus-free files for download

Globalization	Example	Impact on Service Economy
• **More companies operating on transnational basis**	• MNCs such as banks and "Big 4" accounting firms have numerous operations around the world	• Increase in the scope of service that can be provided; training of staff in local markets to upgrade skills, capabilities, and servicestandards
• **Increased international travel**	• More services offered to more places; new travel options for business and pleasure	• More services provided by airlines, ferries and cruise ships, coach tours, international trains, leading to greater competition
• **International mergers and alliances**	• Merger between international airlines (e.g. KLM and Air France), banks, insurance companies, etc.	• Greater market leverage and operational efficiency but consolidation may lead to job losses
• **"Offshoring" of customer service**	• Call center operations relocated to India, Philippines, etc.	• Investment in technology and infrastructure stimulates local economies, raises living standards, and attracts related industries
• **Foreign competitors invade domestic markets**	• International banks such as HSBC and ING do business in the USA	• Build branch network by purchasing one or more regional banks; invest heavily in new and improved branches and in electronic delivery channels

FIGURE 1.7 Many Services Today Can Be Outsourced to Lower Cost Destinations

Source: © Randy Glasbergen. www.glasbergen.com

Today, we know that production and consumption are indeed *separable* for many services (think of dry cleaning, lawn mowing, and weather forecasting) and that not all service performances are perishable (consider video recordings of concert performances and sports events). Very significantly, many services are designed to create *durable value* for their recipients (your own education is a case in point!). But the distinction between ownership and *nonownership*, which we will discuss in the next section, remains a valid one, emphasized by several leading service marketing scholars.[17]

A Fresh Perspective: Benefits without Ownership

Suppose you stayed at a hotel last weekend, or went to a physical therapist who worked on your injured knee, or attended a concert. Naturally, none of these purchases resulted in actual ownership of any of these services. But if you didn't receive a transfer of ownership the last time you purchased a service, then what did you buy? What do you have to show for your money, time, and effort? What are, or were, the benefits? What problems did the service help you solve? In short: Where's the value?

Christopher Lovelock and Evert Gummesson contend that services involve a form of *rental* through which customers can obtain benefits.[18] What customers value and are willing to pay for are desired experiences and solutions. We use the term *rent* as a generic term to denote the payment made for using or accessing something—typically for a defined period of time—instead of buying it outright. You can't own people, but you can rent their labor and expertise.

Paying for temporary use of an object or for access to a physical facility is a way for customers to enjoy things they cannot afford to buy, cannot justify purchasing, or prefer not to retain and store after use. In addition, renting—in the form of access and usage fees—offers a means to participate in network systems that individuals and most organizations couldn't possibly afford to own and operate themselves.

We can identify five broad categories within the nonownership framework:

- ***Rented goods services.*** These services enable customers to obtain the temporary right to use a physical good that they prefer not to own. Examples include boats, fancy dress costumes, and combine harvesters.
- ***Defined space and place rentals.*** Here, customers obtain use of a defined portion of a larger space in a building, vehicle, or other area. Examples include a suite in an office building, a seat in an aircraft, or a table in a restaurant. The space typically is designated by location, but its purpose may vary widely. In other words, renting space may either be an end in its own right (e.g., a storage container in a warehouse) or simply a means to an end (e.g., a table in a restaurant or a seat in a theatre).
- ***Labor and expertise rentals.*** Customers hire other people to perform work that they either choose not to do for themselves (e.g., cleaning a house) or are unable to do because they lack the necessary expertise, tools, or skills. In many instances, customers may effectively rent the services of an entire team as in car repair, surgery, and management consultancy.
- ***Access to shared physical environments.*** These environments may be located indoors or outdoors—or a combination of both. Examples include museums, theme parks, trade shows, gyms, ski resorts, golf courses, and toll roads. In return for a fee, customers rent the right to share use of the environment with other customers.
- ***Access to and usage of systems and networks.*** Here, customers rent the right to participate in a specified network such as telecommunications, utilities, banking, insurance, or specialized information services. Service providers often create a veritable menu of terms for access and use in response to varying customer needs and differing abilities to pay.

In many instances, two or more of these categories may be combined. When you take a taxi, you're hiring both a driver and a vehicle. If you undergo surgery, you are, in essence, hiring a skilled team of medical personnel, led by the surgeon, as well as renting temporary (but exclusive) use of specialized equipment in a dedicated operating facility at a hospital or clinic.

Defining Services

Services cover a vast array of different and often very complex activities, making them difficult to define.[19] The word *service* originally was associated with the work servants did for their masters. In time, a broader association emerged, captured in the dictionary definition of "the action of serving, helping, or benefiting; conduct tending to the welfare or advantage of another."[20] Early marketing definitions of services contrasted them against goods and described services as "acts, deeds, performances, or efforts" and argued that they had different characteristics from goods—defined as "articles, devices, materials, objects, or things."[21] In these early definitions, intangibility and perishability were the two most cited characteristics that critically distinguished services from goods.

But we believe services should be defined in their own right, not in relation to goods. A short and snappy definition, like the oft-repeated "something which can be bought and sold but which cannot be dropped on your foot"[22] is amusing and memorable, but may not be particularly helpful as a guide to marketing strategy. Instead, we offer the following, comprehensive definition:

> **DEFINITION OF SERVICES**
>
> Services are economic activities offered by one party to another. Often time-based, performances bring about desired results to recipients, objects, or other assets for which purchasers have responsibility.
>
> In exchange for money, time, and effort, service customers expect value from access to goods, labor, professional skills, facilities, networks, and systems; but they do not normally take ownership of any of the physical elements involved.[23]

Note that we define services as *economic activities* between two parties, implying an exchange of value between seller and buyer in the marketplace. We describe services as *performances* that are most commonly *time-based.* We emphasize that purchasers buy services because they are looking for *desired results.* In fact, many firms explicitly market their services as "solutions" to prospective customers' needs. And finally, our definition emphasizes that while customers *expect value* from their service purchases *in exchange for money, time, and effort*, this value comes from *access to a variety of value-creating elements rather than transfer of ownership.* (Spare parts installed during repairs and restaurant-prepared food and beverages are among the few exceptions, but the value added by these items usually is less than that of the accompanying service elements.)

Intangible Elements Dominate Value Creation

Services often include important tangible elements, such as hotel beds, restaurant meals, and bank cards and checkbooks. However, as the nonownership perspective and our definition of services implies, it is the intangible elements—including the labor and expertise of service employees—that dominate the creation of value in service performances. Intangibility can consist of both mental and physical dimensions. *Mental intangibility* cannot be easily visualized and understood, while *physical intangibility* cannot be touched or experienced by the other senses.[24] A useful way to distinguish between goods and services, first suggested by Lynn Shostack, is to place them on a continuum, ranging from tangible-dominant to intangible-dominant (see Figure 1.8).[25]

Clearly, there are some potentially ambiguous products toward the center of this scale. One suggested economic test of whether a product should be regarded as a good or a service is whether more than half the value comes from the service elements.[26] At a full-service restaurant, for example, the cost of the food itself may account for as little as

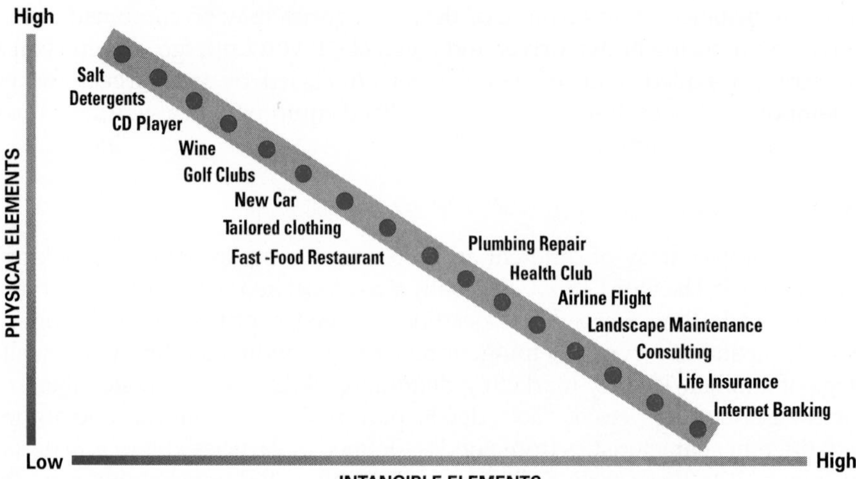

FIGURE 1.8 Value Added by Tangible versus Intangible Elements in Goods and Services

20–30 percent of the price of the meal. Most of the value added comes from food preparation and cooking, table service, the restaurant environment, and facilities such as valet parking and restroom and coatroom attendants. The notion of service as a performance that cannot be wrapped up and taken away links directly to the nonownership framework. When buying a service, customers rarely acquire ownership of the elements that create most of the value.

Service Products versus Customer Service and After-Sales Service

The growth of the service economy, along with the emphasis on adding value-enhancing services to manufactured goods, sometimes blurs the line between services and manufacturing. Many manufacturing firms—from carmaker Toyota and aerospace engine producers GE and Rolls-Royce to high-tech equipment manufacturers IBM and Xerox—are moving aggressively into service businesses.[27] Theodore Levitt long ago observed that "There are no such things as service industries. There are only industries whose service components are greater or less than those of other industries. Everybody is in service."[28] More recently, Roland Rust suggested that manufacturing firms understood this message when he noted that "most goods businesses now view themselves primarily as services."[29] An even more radical view has been advanced by Stephen Vargo and Robert Lusch in their award-winning article on a new mindset, the service-dominant logic. This concept suggests that all products are valued for the services they provide and that the value derived from a physical good, for example, is not the good itself, but the service it provides during consumption.[30] Nevertheless, for a marketing professional it's important to clarify the distinction between *service products* and what often is termed *customer service* (or customer support). Every business should have a customer service orientation, but not every business markets what NAICS data categorizes as a service product.

In this book, we describe a firm's market offerings as divided into *core product* elements and *supplementary service* elements—those activities or amenities that facilitate and enhance use of the core offering. We draw a clear distinction between *marketing of services*—where a service itself is the core product—and *marketing through service.* Certainly, good service often helps to sell a physical good and even make it more useful—and thereby valuable—to the buyer. Many firms in manufacturing, agricultural, natural resource, or construction industries now base their marketing strategies on a philosophy of serving customers well and adding supplementary service elements to the core product. But that core product still remains a physical good (a term we use here to include structures and commodities) when marketing's goal is to sell the item and transfer ownership. Supplementary services may include consultation, finance, shipping, installation, customization, training, maintenance, upgrades, removal, and environmentally responsible disposal. These services may be offered "free" (i.e., the cost is bundled with the price of the initial product purchase) or charged separately.

Many manufacturing firms have transitioned from simply bundling supplementary services with their physical products to reformulating and enhancing certain elements so that they can be marketed as stand-alone services (see the example of Gulfstream in Figure 1.9). At that point, the firm may target new customers who haven't previously purchased its manufactured products—and may even have no interest in doing so. As the organization's expertise builds, it may add new service products and move from just bundling supplementary services with their physical products to marketing certain elements as stand-alone services.[31] IBM, once known mainly as a manufacturer of computers and business machines, offers four main groups of services today as part of IBM Global Services: strategic outsourcing, business consulting, integrated technology services, and maintenance. Another success story is Rolls-Royce, featured in Best Practice in Action 1.1.

You'll find that the same distinction between customer service and service products exists for consumer goods, especially durables. Purchasers of a luxury car, like those marketed under Toyota's Lexus brand, receive not only excellent warranty coverage but also an exceptional level of service from the Lexus-trained dealer, a franchisee running a service business. However, cars are manufactured products, and we must distinguish between marketing that product at the time of sale and marketing services that customers will pay for to maintain their car for several years after the sale. Lexus dealers don't compete with Jaguar or BMW for service sales; instead, they compete with the best independent repair garages that not only offer excellent repair and maintenance service, but may also be more conveniently located to many Lexus owners' homes or offices.

Source: Courtesy of Gulfstream, Inc.

FIGURE 1.9 Gulfstream Advertises Its Award-Winning Maintenance and Support Services

BEST PRACTICE IN ACTION 1.1

Rolls-Royce Sells Power by the Hour

Rolls-Royce has prospered by relentlessly pursuing technical innovation and making world class aircraft engines—Rolls-Royce engines power about half of the latest wide-bodied passenger jets and a quarter of all single-aisle aircrafts entering service. A crucial ingredient for its success has been the move from manufacturing to selling "power by the hour"—a complex offering of services and manufacturing that keeps the engines of its customers burning.

Imagine this, high above the Pacific, passengers doze on a long haul flight from Tokyo to Los Angeles. Suddenly, a bolt of lightning cleaves the air. Those startled by the flash will soon settle back into their dreams. But on the other side of the world, in Derby in England, engineers at Rolls-Royce get busy. Lightning strikes on jets are common and usually harmless, but this one has caused a cough in one of the engines. The aircraft will land safely and could do so even with the engine shut down. The question is whether it will need a full engine inspection in Los Angeles, which would be normal practice but inconvenience hundreds of passengers waiting in the departure lounge.

A torrent of data is beamed from the plane to Derby. Numbers dance across screens, graphs are drawn and engineers scratch their heads. Before the aircraft lands word comes that the engine is running smoothly and the plane can take off on time.

Industry experts estimate that manufacturers of jet engines can make some seven times the revenue from servicing and selling spare parts than they do from selling the engines. These juicy margins have attracted a swarm of independent servicing firms, which can offer spare parts for as low as one third of the price charged by the original manufacturers. This is where Rolls-Royce has integrated its technology with service which makes it more difficult for competitors to pinch its clients. Instead of selling engines and then later parts and service, Rolls-Royce has created an attractive bundle, which it branded TotalCare®, that charges for every hour that an engine runs. Its website advertises it as a solution ensuring "peace of mind" for the lifetime of an engine. Rolls-Royce promises to maintain the engine and replace it if it breaks down. The operations room in Derby continuously monitors the performance of some 3,500 engines, enabling it to predict when engines are likely to fail and let airlines schedule engine changes efficiently and reduce repairs and unhappy passengers. Today, about 80% of engines shipped to its clients are covered by such contracts!

Sources: The Economist, "Briefing Rolls-Royce. Britain's Lonely High Flyer" January 10, 2009, p. 58–60; www.rolls-royce.com, accessed April 3, 2009.

FOUR BROAD CATEGORIES OF SERVICES—A PROCESS PERSPECTIVE

Even if we accept that services typically do not involve transfer of ownership, major differences still exist among services depending on what is being processed. In services, people, physical objects, and data can be processed, and the nature of the processing can be tangible or intangible. Tangible actions are performed on people's bodies or to their physical possessions. Intangible actions are performed on people's minds or to their intangible assets. This gives rise to the classification of services into four broad categories. They are *people processing, possession processing, mental stimulus processing,* and *information processing* (Figure 1.10).[32] Although the industries within each category may at first appear very different, analysis will show that they share important process-related characteristics. As a result, managers from different industries within the same category may obtain useful insights by studying another and then create useful innovations for their own organization. Let's examine why these four different types of processes often have distinctive implications for marketing, operations, and human resource management.

People Processing

From ancient times, people have sought out services directed at themselves—being transported, fed, lodged, restored to health, or made more beautiful. To receive these types of services, customers must physically enter the service system. Why? Because they are an integral part of the process and cannot obtain the desired benefits by dealing at arm's length with service suppliers. In short, they must enter the *service factory*, a physical location where people or machines (or both) create and deliver service benefits to customers. Sometimes, of course, service providers are willing to come to customers, bringing the necessary tools of their trade to create the desired benefits at the customers' preferred location.

Nature of the Service Act	Who or What Is the Direct Recipient of the Service? People	Possessions
Tangible Actions	**People-processing** (services directed at people's bodies): • Passenger Transportation, Lodging • Health care	**Possession-processing** (services directed at physical possessions): • Freight transportations, Repair and maintenance • Laundry and dry cleaning
Intangible Actions	**Mental stimulus processing** (services directed at people's mind): • Education • Advertising / PR • Psychotherapy	**Information processing** (services directed at intangible assets): • Accounting • Banking • Legal services

FIGURE 1.10 Four Categories of Services

If you, as a customer, want the benefits of a people-processing service, you must be prepared to cooperate actively with the service operation. For example, if you want a manicure, you would have to cooperate with the manicurist by specifying what you want, sitting still, and presenting each hand for treatment when requested. If you needed an eye exam, the optometrist would ask you to submit to a number of tests and, for those that checked the acuity of your vision, to report back what you saw on the chart or other display.

The amount of time required of customers in people-processing services varies widely, ranging from boarding a city bus for a short ride to undergoing a lengthy course of treatments at a hospital. In between these extremes are such activities as ordering and eating a meal; having hair washed, cut, and styled; and spending several nights in a hotel room. The output from these services (after a period of time that can vary from minutes to months) is a customer who has reached her destination or satisfied his hunger or is now sporting clean and stylishly cut hair or has had a good night's sleep away from home or is now in physically better health.

Managers should be thinking about process and output from the standpoint of what happens to the customer. Reflecting on the service process helps to identify not only what benefits are created at each point in the process but also the nonfinancial costs incurred by the customer in terms of time, mental and physical effort, and even fear and pain.

Possession Processing

Often, customers ask a service organization to provide tangible treatment for some physical possession—a house invaded by insects, an overgrown hedge, a malfunctioning elevator, a package that needs to be delivered to another city, dirty clothes, or a sick pet.

Many such activities are quasi-manufacturing operations and do not involve simultaneous production and consumption. Examples include cleaning, maintaining, storing, improving, or repairing physical objects—both living and inanimate—that belong to the customer in order to extend their usefulness. Additional possession-processing services include transport and storage of goods; wholesale and retail distribution; and installation, removal, and disposal of equipment—in short, the entire value-adding chain of activities that may take place during the lifetime of the object in question.

Customers are less physically involved with this type of service than with people-processing services. Consider the difference between passenger and package transportation. In the former, you have to go along for the ride to obtain the benefit of traveling from one location to another. But with a package, you drop it off at a mailbox or post office (or request a courier to pick it up from your home or office) and wait for it to be delivered to the recipient.

In most possession-processing services, the customer's involvement usually is limited to dropping off the item that needs treatment, requesting the service, explaining the problem, and later returning to pick up the item and pay the bill. In such instances, production and consumption can be described as *separable*. However, in some instances, the customer may prefer to be present during service delivery, perhaps

FIGURE 1.11 A Car Maintenance Service Is a Possession-Processing Service, Typically with Limited Customer Involvement

wishing to supervise the hedge cutting or comfort the family dog while it receives an injection at the veterinary clinic (Figure 1.11).

Mental Stimulus Processing

Services directed at people's minds include education, news and information, professional advice, psychotherapy, entertainment, and certain religious activities. Anything touching people's minds has the power to shape attitudes and influence behavior. So, when customers are in a position of dependency or potential for manipulation exists, strong ethical standards and careful oversight are required. Obtaining the full benefit of such services requires an investment of time and a degree of mental effort on the customer's part. However, recipients don't necessarily have to be physically present in a service factory—just mentally in communication with the information presented. There's an interesting contrast with some people-processing services. Passengers can sleep through a flight and still arrive at their desired destination. But if you fall asleep in class or during an educational TV broadcast, you won't be any wiser at the end!

Services like entertainment and education often are created in one place and transmitted by television, radio, or the Internet to individual customers in distant locations. However, they can also be delivered to groups of customers at the originating location in a facility such as a theater or lecture hall. As you probably know, watching a live concert on television is not the same experience as watching it in a concert hall in the company of hundreds or even thousands of other people. Managers of concert halls face many of the same challenges as their colleagues in people-processing services. Similarly, participating in a discussion-based class through interactive cable television lacks the intimacy of people debating one another in the same room.

Because the core content of services in this category is information based (whether music, voice, or visual images), it can be converted to digital bits or analog signals; recorded for posterity; and transformed into a manufactured product, such as a CD or DVD, which may then be packaged and marketed much like any other physical good. For instance, a concert can be attended live, viewed or heard live, prerecorded on TV, or sold as digital recordings. Services in this category can thus be "inventoried" for consumption at a later date; in fact, the same performance can be consumed repeatedly. For some customers, purchasing an educational video to play at home may be a better solution than taking a class. Increasingly, customers can download electronic content on demand through their computers or cell phones from a supplier such as Apple's music/video online shop.

Information Processing

Information processing has been revolutionized by information technology, but not all information is processed by machines. Professionals in a wide variety of fields also use their brains to perform information processing and packaging. Information is the most intangible form of service output, but it may be transformed into more enduring, tangible forms as letters, reports, plans, CD-ROMs, or DVDs. Among the services that are highly dependent on the effective collection and processing of information are financial services and professional services like accounting, law, marketing research, management consulting, and medical diagnosis.

The line between information processing and mental stimulus processing may be blurred. For instance, a stockbroker may use an analysis of a client's brokerage transactions to recommend the most appropriate type of investment strategy for the future. An attorney in a corporate law firm may spot patterns that pose legal risks for clients and advise them accordingly. And market researchers may see opportunities to publish useful insights they have gained from reviewing trends over time. For simplicity, we will periodically combine our coverage of mental stimulus-processing services and information-processing services under the umbrella term of *information-based services.*

SERVICES POSE DISTINCT MARKETING CHALLENGES

Are the marketing concepts and practices developed in manufacturing companies directly transferable to service organizations where no transfer of ownership takes place? The answer is often "no." Table 1.2 lists eight common differences between services and goods. Together, these differences cause marketing management tasks in the service sector to differ from those in the manufacturing sector in several important respects. It's important to recognize that these differences, while useful generalizations, *do not apply equally to all services.* In fact, large differences exist between the four categories of services we discussed in the previous section. For example, people tend to be part of the service experience only if the customer has contact with service employees, which typically is the case for people-processing services but not for many information-processing service

TABLE 1.2 Managerial Implications of Eight Common Features of Services

Difference	Implications	Marketing-Related Topics
Most service products cannot be inventoried	• Customers may be turned away or have to wait	• Smooth demand through promotions, dynamic pricing, and reservations • Work with operations to adjust capacity
Intangible elements usually dominate value creation	• Customers cannot taste, smell, or touch these elements and may not be able to see or hear them • Harder to evaluate service and distinguish from competitors	• Make services tangible through emphasis on physical clues • Employ concrete metaphors and vivid images in advertising, branding
Services are often difficult to visualize and understand	• Customers perceive greater risk and uncertainty	• Educate customers to make good choices, explain what to look for, document performance, offer guarantees
Customers may be involved in co-production	• Customers interact with provider's equipment, facilities, and systems • Poor task execution by customers may hurt productivity, spoil service experience, curtail benefits	• Develop user-friendly equipment, facilities, and systems • Train customers to perform effectively; provide customer support
People may be part of the service experience	• Appearance, attitude and behavior of service personnel and other customers can shape the experience and affect satisfaction	• Recruit, train, and reward employees to reinforce the planned service concept • Target the right customers at the right times, shape their behavior
Operational inputs and outputs tend to vary more widely	• Harder to maintain consistency, reliability, and service quality or to lower costs through higher productivity • Difficult to shield customers from results of service failures	• Set quality standards based on customer expectations; redesign product elements for simplicity and failure-proofing • Institute good service recovery procedures • Automate customer-provider interactions; perform work while customers are absent
The time factor often assumes great importance	• Customers see time as a scarce resource to be spent wisely; dislike wasting time waiting, want service at times that are convenient	• Find ways to compete on speed of delivery, minimize burden of waiting, offer extended service hours
Distribution may take place through non-physical channels	• Information-based services can be delivered through electronic channels such as the Internet or voice telecommunications, but core products involving physical activities or products cannot	• Seek to create user-friendly, secure web sites and free access by telephone • Ensure that all information-based service elements can be downloaded from site

transactions such as online banking. You will recognize these differences as we discuss the marketing mix for services later in this chapter and throughout this text.

The 7 Ps of Services Marketing

When developing strategies to market manufactured goods, marketers usually address four basic strategic elements: product, price, place (or distribution), and promotion (or communication). As a group, these usually are referred to as the "4 Ps" of the marketing mix.[33] As shown in Table 1.2, the nature of services poses distinct marketing challenges. Hence, the 4 Ps of goods marketing are not adequate to deal with the issues arising from marketing services and have to be adapted and extended. We will therefore revisit the traditional 4 Ps of the marketing mix in this book to focus on service-specific issues.

Furthermore, the traditional marketing mix does not cover managing the customer interface. We therefore need to extend the marketing mix by adding three Ps associated with service delivery—*process*, *physical environment*, and *people*.[34] Collectively, these seven elements—the "7 Ps" of services marketing—represent the ingredients required to create viable strategies for meeting customer needs profitably in a competitive marketplace. You can think of these elements as the seven strategic levers of services marketing. Now, let's look briefly at each of the 7 Ps.

THE TRADITIONAL MARKETING MIX APPLIED TO SERVICES

Product Elements

Service products lie at the heart of a firm's marketing strategy. If a product is poorly designed, it won't create meaningful value for customers, even if the rest of the 7 Ps are well executed. Planning the marketing mix begins with creating a service concept that will offer value to target customers and satisfy their needs better than competing alternatives. Working to transform this concept into reality involves design of a cluster of different, but mutually reinforcing elements. Service products consist of (1) a core product that responds to the customers' primary need and (2) an array of supplementary service elements that are mutually reinforcing value-added enhancements that help customers to use the core product more effectively.

Place and Time

Service distribution may involve physical or electronic channels (or both), depending on the nature of the service (see Table 1.2). For example, today's banks offer customers a choice of distribution channels, including visiting a branch, using a network of ATMs, doing business by telephone, or conducting banking transactions over the Internet. Many information-based services can be delivered almost instantaneously to any location in the world that has Internet access. Furthermore, firms may deliver service directly to end-users or through intermediary organizations—such as retail outlets that receive a fee or commission—to perform certain tasks associated with sales, service, and customer contact. To deliver service elements to customers, decisions need to be made on where and when as well as the methods and channels used.[35]

DISTRIBUTION OF CORE VERSUS SUPPLEMENTARY SERVICES. The Internet is reshaping distribution strategy for a broad array of industries. But we need to distinguish between its potential for delivering information-based *core products* (those that respond to customers' primary requirements) and simply providing *supplementary services* that facilitate the purchase and use of physical goods. Examples of the former include the online educational programs offered by the University of Phoenix and automobile insurance coverage from Progressive Casualty Co.

Contrast these two web-enabled services with the website of REI (Recreational Equipment Inc.), a renowned supplier of specialty outdoor gear and clothing, which has over 80 retail stores across the United States. By visiting www.rei.com, you can learn about the pros and cons of different camping gear, obtain online live help, and place orders and pay for specific products online. Similarly, without leaving your home, let alone the country, you can review British Airways' worldwide schedules at www.ba.com, check out how fares vary according to time of day and day of the week (you'll find huge variations in economy fares on some routes within Europe), make a reservation, indicate any special needs, and pay for the electronic ticket. But in both cases, delivery of the core product itself must take place through physical channels. The tent and sleeping bag you bought from REI will be delivered to your home by UPS, FedEx, or the U.S. Postal Service (your choice). And you'll have to go to the airport in person to board your BA flight. Much e-commerce activity concerns supplementary services based on *transfer of information and payments relating to the product*, as opposed to downloading the core product itself. Figure 1.12 displays an example of supplementary service websites.

THE TIME FACTOR FREQUENTLY ASSUMES GREAT IMPORTANCE. Speed and convenience of place and time have become important determinants of effective distribution and delivery of services (see Table 1.2). Many services are delivered in real time while customers are physically present. Today's customers are the most time sensitive in history, are in more of a hurry, and see wasted time as a cost to avoid.[36] (You probably do, too.) They may be willing to pay extra to save time, such as taking a taxi when a city bus serves the same route, or to get a needed task performed faster. Increasingly, busy customers expect service when it suits them, rather than when it suits the supplier. If one firm responds by offering extended hours, its competitors often feel obliged to follow suit. Nowadays, a growing number of services are available 24/7, and via more and more distribution channels, including retail branches, self-service machines like ATMs, call centers, and the Internet.

Price and Other User Outlays

Like product value, the value inherent in payments is central to marketing's role in facilitating a value exchange between the firm and its customers. For suppliers, pricing strategy is the financial mechanism though which income is generated to offset

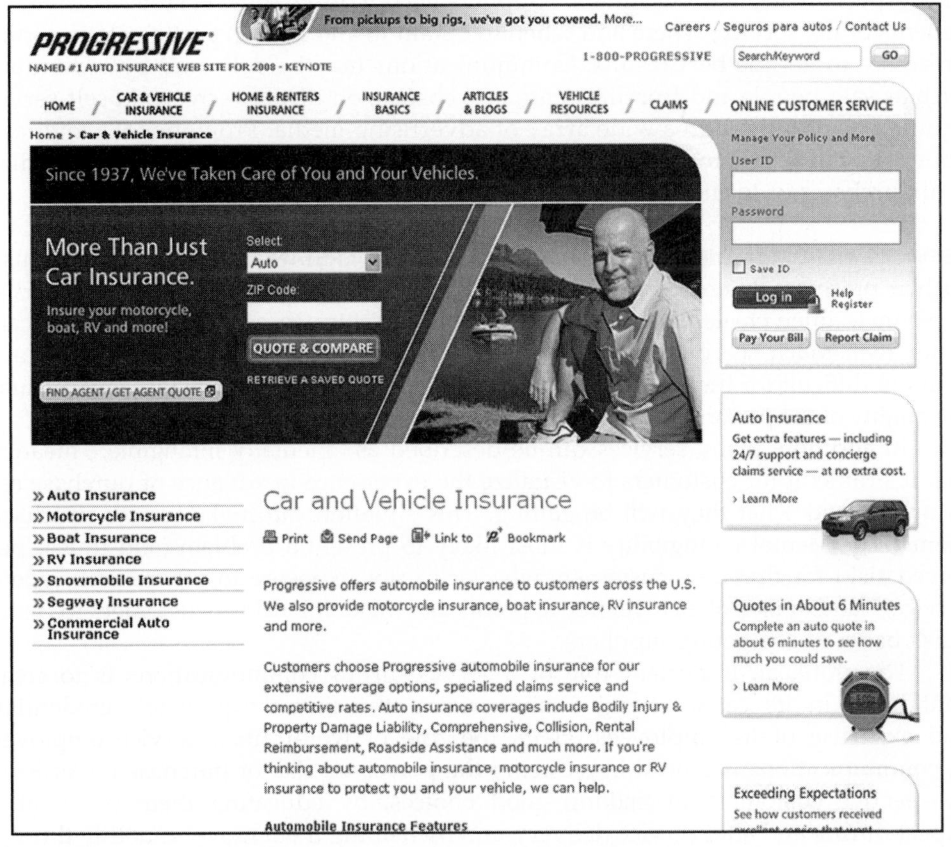

Source: Copyright © 2009 Progressive Insurance. Used with permission.

FIGURE 1.12 Web Sites Can Deliver Progressive Insurance's Services Directly.

the costs of providing service and to create a surplus for profits. Pricing strategy often is highly dynamic, with price levels adjusted over time according to such factors as type of customer, time and place of delivery, level of demand, and available capacity.

Customers, by contrast, see price as a key part of the costs they must incur to obtain desired benefits. To calculate whether a particular service is "worth it," they may go beyond just money and assess the outlays of their time and effort. Service marketers, therefore, must not only set prices that target customers are willing and able to pay, but also understand—and seek to minimize, where possible—other burdensome outlays that customers incur in using the service. These outlays may include additional monetary costs (such as travel expenses to a service location), time expenditures, unwanted mental and physical effort, and exposure to negative sensory experiences.

MOST SERVICE PRODUCTS CANNOT BE INVENTORIED. Because services involve actions or performances, they are ephemeral—transitory and perishable—and so typically cannot be stocked as inventory following production (see Table 1.2). Although facilities, equipment, and labor can be held in readiness to create the service, each represents productive capacity, not the product itself. If there's no demand, unused capacity is wasted and the firm loses the chance to create value from these assets. During periods when demand exceeds capacity, customers may be sent away disappointed or asked to wait until later. A key task for service marketers, therefore, is to find ways of smoothing demand levels to match available capacity using dynamic pricing strategies.

Promotion and Education

What should we tell customers and prospects about our services? No marketing program can succeed without effective communications. This component plays three vital roles: providing needed information and advice, persuading target customers of the merits of a specific brand or service product, and encouraging them to take action at specific times. In services marketing, much communication is educational in nature, especially for new customers. Suppliers need to teach these customers about the benefits of the service, where and when to obtain it, and how to participate in service processes to get the best results. Communications may be delivered by individuals such as salespeople and frontline staff, at websites, on display screens in self-service equipment, and through a wide array of advertising media. Promotional activities—which may include a monetary incentive—often are designed to stimulate immediate trial purchases or to encourage consumption when demand is low.

SERVICES ARE OFTEN DIFFICULT TO VISUALIZE AND UNDERSTAND. Intangible elements—such as processes, Internet-based transactions, and the expertise and attitudes of service personnel—often create the most value in service performances. When customers can't taste, smell, touch, see, or hear these elements (i.e., they are physically intangible), it may be more difficult for them to assess important service features in advance and evaluate the quality of the performance itself (see Table 1.2).

In addition, many services can be described as "mentally intangible," meaning that it's difficult for customers to visualize the experience in advance of purchase and to understand what they will be getting. This situation can make service purchases seem risky. Mental intangibility is most likely to present a problem (and thus a perceived risk) for first-time customers who lack prior exposure to a particular type of service;[37] and, a lack of easy reference points can make it hard for customers to distinguish between competing suppliers.

Therefore, an important role of a service firm's communications is to create confidence in its capabilities by emphasizing the firm's experience, credentials, and expertise of its employees. Here, the role of well-trained service employees in communications is crucial in reducing the perceived risk of purchase by assisting prospective customers in making good choices, by educating them on what to expect during and after service delivery, and by helping them move smoothly through the service process. Documenting performance, explaining what was done and why, and offering guarantees are additional ways to reassure customers and reduce anxiety.

CUSTOMERS NEED TO BE EDUCATED ON HOW TO BEST USE A SERVICE. Service firms have much to gain from helping customers become more competent and productive.[38] And so do customers. After all, if you know how to use a service well, you'll not only have a better service experience and outcome, but your greater efficiency may boost the firm's productivity, lower its costs, and even enable it to reduce the price you pay (see Table 1.2). An important role of a service firm's communications and promotions is to educate and train customers on how to use its service delivery channels effectively.

CUSTOMER-CUSTOMER INTERACTIONS AFFECT THE SERVICE EXPERIENCE. When you encounter other customers at a service facility, you know that they, too, can affect your satisfaction. How they're dressed, who they are, and how they behave can all serve to reinforce or negate the image a firm is trying to project and the experience it's trying to create. Were you annoyed by the customer at the movie theatre talking loudly on her phone about problems at work or by the hurried businessman cutting in line at the ticket counter? One of the authors of this text has never forgotten staying at a hotel where half the guests were attending an academic conference and the rest were football fans who had come for the weekend to support their team. We differed in our expectations of what constituted a good experience! Other customers should enhance the experience, not detract from its value. The implications are clear: Marketing communications needs to be careful to attract the right segment to the service facility, and once there, it needs to educate them on the proper behavior.

THE EXTENDED SERVICES MARKETING MIX FOR MANAGING THE CUSTOMER INTERFACE

Process

Smart managers know that where services are concerned, *how* a firm does things—the underlying processes—often are as important as *what* it does. So, creating and delivering product elements requires design and implementation of effective processes. Badly designed service processes lead to slow, bureaucratic, and ineffective service delivery; wasted time; and a disappointing experience. They also make it difficult for front line employees to do their jobs well, resulting in low productivity and increased likelihood of service failure.

OPERATIONAL INPUTS AND OUTPUTS CAN VARY WIDELY. Manufactured goods can be produced at a distant factory, under controlled conditions, and checked for conformance with quality standards long before they reach the customer. For services, however, operational inputs and outputs tend to vary more widely and make customer service process management a challenge (see Table 1.2). But when a service is delivered face-to-face and consumed as it is produced, final "assembly" must take place in real time, and operations are distributed often across many thousands of sites or branches. Distributed operations (rather than a central factory) make it difficult for service organizations to ensure reliable delivery, control quality, and improve productivity. As a former packaged goods marketer once observed after moving to a new position at Holiday Inn:

> We can't control the quality of our product as well as a Procter and Gamble control engineer on a production line can... When you buy a box of Tide, you can reasonably be 99 and 44/100ths percent sure that this stuff will work to get your clothes clean. When you buy a Holiday Inn room, you're sure at some lesser percentage that it will work to give you a good night's sleep without any hassle, or people banging on the walls and all the bad things that can happen in a hotel.[39]

FIGURE 1.13 Co-Producing the Service: Working Out at the Gym Under the Direction of a Personal Trainer

Nevertheless, the best service firms have made significant progress in reducing variability by carefully designing customer service processes, adopting standardized procedures, implementing rigorous management of service quality, training employees more carefully, and automating tasks previously performed by humans.

CUSTOMERS ARE OFTEN INVOLVED IN CO-PRODUCTION. Some services require customers to participate actively in co-producing the service product (see Table 1.2 and Figure 1.13). For instance, you're expected to cooperate with service personnel in settings such as fast food restaurants and libraries. In fact, service scholars argue that customers often function as *partial employees*.[40] (How do you feel about being described this way?) Increasingly, your involvement takes the form of self-service, often using self-service technologies (SSTs) facilitated by smart machines, telecommunications, and the Internet.[41] Whether customers co-produce or use SSTs, well-designed customer service processes are required to facilitate service delivery.

DEMAND AND CAPACITY NEED TO BE BALANCED. Manufacturing can ensure a smooth process flow through buffering materials or parts. For services, buffering means customers are waiting in the service process! Therefore, closely related topics to service process management are the balancing of demand and capacity, the design of waiting systems and queues configurations, and the management of the customer's psychology of waiting.

Physical Environment

If your job is in a service business that requires customers to enter the service factory, you'll also have to spend time thinking about design of the physical environment or "servicescape."[42] The appearance of buildings, landscaping, vehicles, interior furnishings, equipment, staff members' uniforms, signs, printed materials, and other visible cues provide tangible evidence of a firm's service quality, facilitate service delivery, and guide customers through the service process. Service firms need to manage "servicescapes" carefully, since they can have a profound impact on customer satisfaction and service productivity.

FIGURE 1.14 Hospitality Is Shown Through Employees Wearing Smart Outfits and a Ready Smile

People

Despite technology advances, many services will always require direct interaction between customers and service employees (see Table 1.2). You must have noticed many times how the difference between one service supplier and another lies in the attitudes and skills of their employees. Service firms need to work closely with their human resources (HR) departments and devote special care in selecting, training, and motivating their service employees (see Figure 1.14). In addition to possessing the technical skills required by the job, these individuals also need good interpersonal skills and positive attitudes. HR managers who think strategically recognize that loyal, skilled, motivated employees who can work well independently or together in teams represent a key competitive advantage.

MARKETING MUST BE INTEGRATED WITH OTHER MANAGEMENT FUNCTIONS

In the previous section, we described the 7 Ps as the strategic levers of services marketing. As you think about these different elements, it should quickly become clear that marketers working in a service business can't expect to operate successfully in isolation from managers in other functions. In fact, three management functions play central and interrelated roles in meeting the needs of service customers: marketing, operations, and human resources. Figure 1.15 illustrates this interdependency. One of top management's responsibilities is to ensure that managers and other employees in each of these three functions don't operate in departmental silos.

Operations is the primary line function in a service business, responsible for managing service delivery through equipment, facilities, systems, and many tasks performed by customer-contact employees. In most service organizations, you can also expect to see operations managers actively involved in product and process design, many aspects of the physical environment, and implementation of productivity and quality improvement programs.

HR often is seen as a staff function, responsible for job definition, recruitment, training, reward systems, and quality of work life—all of which are, of course, central to the people element. But in a well-managed service business, HR managers view these activities from a strategic perspective by (1) engaging in design and monitoring of all service delivery processes that involve employees, (2) working with marketers to ensure that employees have the skills and training to deliver promotional messages and educate customers, and (3) designing aspects of the physical environment that directly feature employees—including uniforms, personal appearance, and stage-managed behavior.

For these reasons, we don't limit our coverage exclusively to marketing in this book. In many chapters, we also refer to service operations and human resources management. Some firms deliberately rotate their managers among different job functions, especially between marketing and operations positions, precisely so they will learn to appreciate different perspectives. Your own career in services might follow a similar path.

Imagine you are the manager of a small hotel. Or, if you like, think big and picture yourself as the chief executive officer (CEO) of a major bank. In both instances, you need to be concerned about satisfying your customers on a daily basis, running your operational systems smoothly and efficiently, and making sure your employees

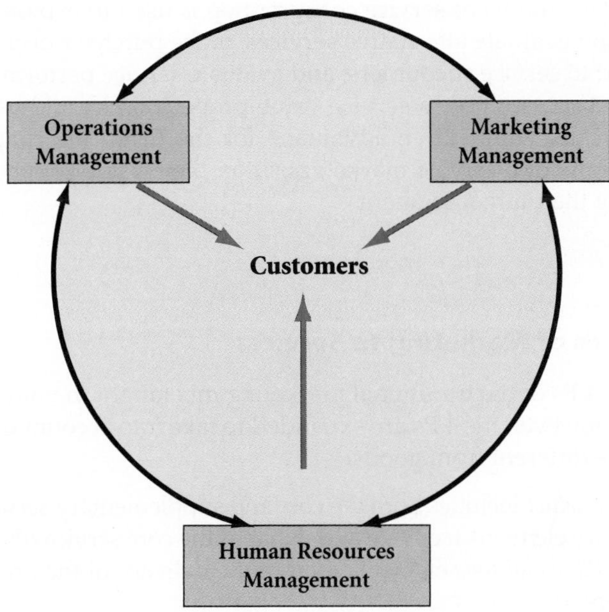

FIGURE 1.15 Marketing, Operations, and Human Resources Functions Must Collaborate to Serve the Customer

not only work productively, but also deliver good service. In short, integration of activities between these three functions is the name of the game in services. Problems in any one of these three areas can negatively affect execution of tasks in the other functions and result in dissatisfied customers. Only a minority of people who work in a service firm are employed in formal marketing positions. But, argues Evert Gummesson, all those whose work affects the customer in some way—either through direct contact or design of processes and policies that shape customers' experiences—need to think of themselves as *part-time marketers*.[43]

A FRAMEWORK FOR DEVELOPING EFFECTIVE SERVICE MARKETING STRATEGIES

The 7 Ps are integrated into the wider organizing framework of this book, combining it with the consumer and competitor analysis, as well as implementation. It shows how each of the chapters fits together with the others as they address related topics and issues. Figure 1.16 presents the organizing framework for this book, which is divided into four parts: (1) *understanding service products, consumers and markets;* (2) *applying the 4 Ps of marketing to services;* (3) *managing the customer interface;* and (4) *implementing profitable service strategies.* Note the arrows linking the different boxes in the model: They stress the interdependences between the different parts and make it clear that the process of creating a strategy is not like stopping at a series of points along a one-way street. Instead, it's an iterative process, that is, one whose components may have to be revisited more than once because they are interdependent. Decisions in one area must be consistent with those taken in another, so that each strategic element will mutually reinforce the rest.

The key contents of the four parts of this book are:

PART I

Understanding Service Products, Consumers, and Markets

Part I of the book lays the building blocks for studying services and learning how to become an effective services marketer.

- Chapter 1—defines services and shows how we can create value without transfer of ownership.
- Chapter 2—discusses consumer behavior in both high- and low-contact services. The three-stage model of service consumption is used to explore how customers search for and evaluate alternative services, make purchase decisions, experience and respond to service encounters, and evaluate service performance.
- Chapter 3—discusses how a service value proposition should be positioned in a way that creates competitive advantage for the firm. The chapter shows how firms can segment a service market, position their value proposition, and focus on attracting their target segment.

PART II

Applying the 4 *Ps* of Marketing to Services

Part II revisits the 4 Ps of the traditional marketing mix taught in your marketing management course. However, the 4 Ps are expanded to take into account the characteristics of services that are different from goods.

- Chapter 4—*Product* includes both the core and supplementary service elements. The supplementary elements facilitate and enhance the core service offering.
- Chapter 5—*Place and time* elements refer to the delivery of the product elements to the customers.

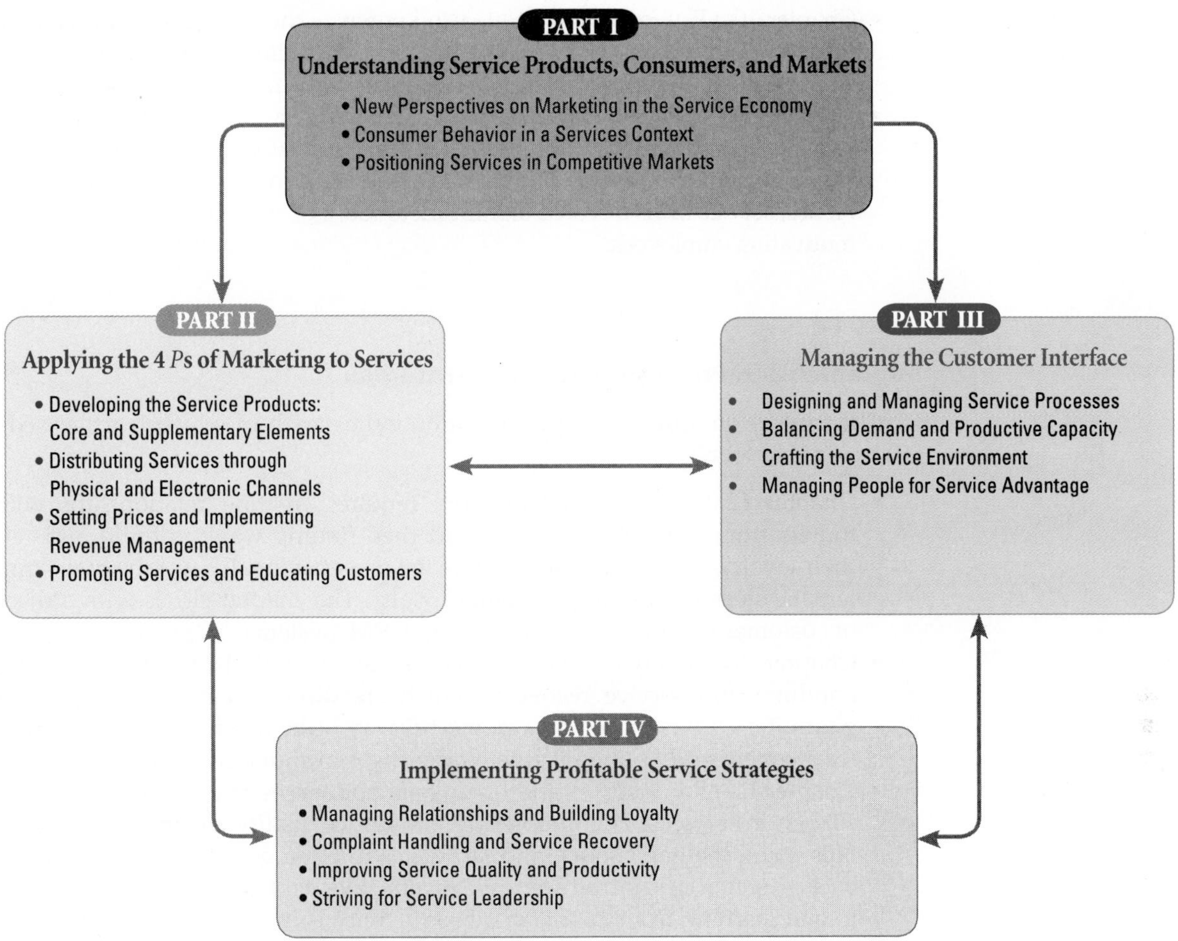

FIGURE 1.16 Organizing Framework for Services Marketing

- Chapter 6—*Prices* of services need to be set with reference to costs, competition and value, and revenue management considerations.
- Chapter 7—*Promotion and education* explains how firms should inform customers about their services. In services marketing, much communication is educational in nature to teach customers how to effectively move through service processes.

PART III

Managing the Customer Interface

Part III of the book focuses on managing the interface between customers and the service firm. It covers the additional 3 Ps unique to services marketing and not found in goods marketing.

- Chapter 8—*Processes* create and deliver the product elements. The chapter begins with the design of effective delivery processes, specifying how the operating and delivery systems link together to create the value proposition. Very often, customers are involved in these processes as co-producers, and well-designed processes need to account for that.
- Chapter 9—This chapter also relates to process management and focuses on managing fluctuating demand and balancing that against capacity. It includes understanding the patterns and determinants of demand. Marketing strategies for managing demand involve smoothing demand fluctuations, inventorying demand through reservation systems, and formalized queuing. Managing customer waiting is also explored in this chapter.

- Chapter 10—*Physical environment*, also known as the *servicescape*, needs to be engineered to create the right impression and facilitate effective service process delivery. The servicescape provides tangible evidence of a firm's image and service quality.
- Chapter 11—*People* play a very important role in services marketing. Many services require direct interaction between customers and service personnel. The nature of these interactions strongly influences how customers perceive service quality. Hence, service firms devote a significant amount of effort to recruiting, training, and motivating employees.

PART IV

Implementing Profitable Service Strategies

Part IV focuses on four key implementation issues, each of which is discussed in the following chapters:

- Chapter 12—Achieving profitability requires creating relationships with customers from the right segments and then finding ways to build and reinforce their loyalty. This chapter introduces the wheel of loyalty, which shows three systematic steps in building customer loyalty. The chapter closes with a discussion of customer relationship management (CRM) systems.
- Chapter 13—A loyal customer base often is built from effective complaint handling and service recovery, which are discussed in this chapter. Service guarantees are explored as a powerful way of institutionalizing effective service recovery and as an effective marketing tool signaling high-quality service.
- Chapter 14—Productivity and quality are both necessary and related for financial success in services. This chapter covers service quality, diagnosing quality shortfalls using the gap model, and strategies to close quality gaps. Customer feedback systems are introduced as an effective tool for systematically listening to and learning from customers. Productivity is introduced as closely related to quality, and it is emphasized that in today's competitive markets, firms need to simultaneously improve both quality and productivity—not one at the expense of the other.
- Chapter 15—The service profit chain is used as an integrative model to demonstrate the strategic linkages involved in running a successful service organization. Implementing the service profit chain requires integration of the three key functions of marketing, operations, and human resources. We discuss how to move a service organization to higher levels of performance in each functional area. The chapter closes with a discussion about the role of leadership in both evolutionary and turnaround environments and in creating and maintaining a climate for service.

CONCLUSION

Why study services? Because modern economies are driven by individual service businesses operating within a remarkable array of industries. Collectively, services are responsible for the creation of a substantial majority of all new jobs, both skilled and unskilled, around the world. Many of these industries are undergoing dramatic transformations, driven by advances in technology, globalization, changes in government policies, evolving consumer needs, and lifestyles. In such an environment, effective marketing plays a vital role in determining whether an individual organization survives and thrives—or declines and fails.

In this chapter, we've demonstrated that services require a distinctive approach to marketing, because the context and the tasks often differ in important aspects from those in the manufacturing sector. Succeeding as a marketing manager in a service business requires you not only to understand key marketing concepts and tools, but also know how to use them effectively. Each of the 7 Ps—the strategic levers of services marketing—has a role to play, but it's how well you tie them together that will make the difference. As you study this book, attend classes, and undertake projects, remember that the winners in today's highly competitive service markets succeed by continually rethinking the way they do business, by looking for innovative ways to serve their customers better, by taking advantage of new developments in technology, and by embracing a disciplined and well-organized approach to developing and implementing services marketing strategy.

Chapter Summary

LO1 Services represent an important and growing contribution to most economies in the world. As economies develop, services form the largest part of the GDP of those economies. Globally, most new jobs are generated in the service sector.

LO2 The principal industries of the service sector include
- Business and professional services
- Finance, insurance, and real estate services
- Wholesale and retail trade
- Transport, utilities, and communications services
- Health care services
- Arts, entertainment recreation, accommodation, and food services
- Government services

LO3 Many forces are transforming our economies, making them more *services oriented.* They include government policies, social changes, business trends, advances in information technology, and globalization.

LO4 What exactly is a service? The key distinguishing feature of a service is that it is a form of rental rather than ownership. Service customers obtain the rights to use a physical object or space; hire the labor and expertise of personnel; or pay for access to shared physical environments, facilities, and networks. Services are performances that bring about the desired results or experience for the customer.

LO5 Services vary widely and can be categorized according to the nature of the underlying process: Is the service directed at customers or their possessions? Are service actions tangible or intangible in nature? These distinctions have important marketing implications and lead to four broad categories of services:
- People processing
- Possession processing
- Mental stimulus processing
- Information processing

Mental stimulus and information processing can be combined into what is called information-based services.

LO6 Services have unique characteristics that make them different from products:
- Most service products cannot be inventoried
- Intangible elements usually dominate value creation
- Services often are difficult to visualize and understand
- Customers may be involved in co-production
- People may be part of the service experience
- Operational inputs and outputs tend to vary widely
- Time factor often assumes great importance
- Distribution may take place through nonphysical channels

LO7 Due to the unique characteristics of services, the traditional marketing mix of the 4 Ps needs to be amended. Some important amendments include:
- *Product elements* include more than the core elements. They also include supplementary service elements.
- *Place and time* elements refer to the delivery of the product elements to the customer; many information-processing elements are delivered electronically.
- *Pricing* includes nonmonetary costs to the consumer and revenue management considerations.
- *Promotion* is also viewed as a form of communication and education guiding customers through service processes, rather than just advertising and promotions.

Services marketing requires three additional Ps covering management of the customer interface:
- *Process* refers to the design and management of customer service processes, including managing demand and capacity and related customer waits.
- *Physical environment*, also known as the *servicescape*, provides tangible evidence of a firm's image and service quality and facilitates process delivery.
- *People* covers the recruiting, training, and motivating of service employees to deliver service quality and productivity.

LO8 The extended services marketing mix shows that the marketing, operations, and human resources (HR) management functions all have a direct influence on the customer experience. Therefore, the three functions must be tightly integrated in service firms.

LO9 A framework for services marketing strategy forms the underlying structure of this book. The framework consists of the following four interlinked parts:
- Part I begins with the need for service firms to understand their markets, customers, and competition.
- Part II shows us how to apply the traditional 4 Ps to services marketing.

- Part III covers the 3 Ps of the extended services marketing mix and shows how to manage the customer interface.
- Part IV illustrates how to implement profitable service strategies and discusses how to build customer relationships, manage complaints and service recovery, and how to improve service quality and productivity. This part closes with a discussion on how change management and leadership can propel a firm to become a service leader.

Review Questions

1. Is it possible for an economy to be entirely based on services? Is it a sign of weakness when a national economy manufactures few of the goods it consumes?
2. What are the main reasons for the growing share of the service sector in all major economies of the world?
3. What are the five powerful forces transforming the service landscape, and what impact do they have on the service economy?
4. "A service is rented rather than owned." Explain what this statement means, and use examples to support your explanation.
5. Describe the four broad "processing" categories of services, and provide examples for each.
6. What is so distinctive about services marketing that it requires a special approach, set of concepts, and body of knowledge?
7. "The 4Ps are all a marketing manager needs to create a marketing strategy for a service business!" Prepare a response that argues the contrary and justify your conclusions.
8. What types of services do you think are (a) most affected and (b) least affected by the problem of variable inputs and outputs? Why?
9. Why is time so important in services?
10. How has the development of self-service technologies affected services marketing strategy? What factors determine whether customers make use of them or not?
11. Why do marketing, operations, and human resources have to be closely linked in services but less so in manufacturing? Give examples.
12. The term "marketing mix" could suggest that marketing managers are mixers of ingredients. Is that perspective a recipe for success when employing the 7 Ps to develop a services marketing strategy?

Application Exercises

1. Visit the websites of the following national statistical bureaus: U.S. Bureau of Economic Analysis (www.bea.gov); Statistics Canada (www.statcan.ca); Eurostat (http://europa.eu.int/en/comm/eurostat/); Japanese Statistics Bureau (/www.stat.go.jp); Central Bureau of Statistics (Indonesia) (www.bps.go.id); Statistics South Africa (www.statssa.gov.za); and the respective website for your country if it is not covered here. In each instance, obtain data on the latest trends in services as (a) a percentage of the GDP; (b) the percentage of employment accounted for by services; (c) breakdowns of these two statistics by type of industry; and (d) service exports and imports. Looking at these trends, what are your conclusions for the main sectors of these economies, and within services, for specific service sectors.
2. Review IBM's annual report, www.ibm.com/annual report; recent quarterly reports, www.ibm.com/investor; and other information on its website describing its different businesses. What conclusions do you draw about future opportunities in different markets? What do you see as competitive threats?
3. Legal and accounting firms now advertise their services in many countries. Search for a few advertisements and review the following: What do these firms do to cope with the intangibility of their services? What could they do better? How do they deal with consumer quality and risk perceptions, and how could they improve this aspect of their marketing?
4. Give examples of how Internet and telecommunications technologies (e.g., Interactive Voice Response Systems [IVRs] and mobile commerce [M-Commerce]) have changed some of the services you use.
5. Choose a service company you are familiar with, and show how each of the 7 Ps of services marketing applies to a specific product.

Endnotes

1. Henry Chesbrough, "Towards a New Science for Services," *Harvard Business Review*, February 2005, 43–44.
2. Organisation for Economic Co-operation and Development, *The Service Economy*. Paris: OECD, 2000.
3. Michael Peneder, Serguei Kaniovsky, and Bernhard Dachs, "What Follows Tertiarisation? Structural Change and the Rise of Knowledge-Based Industries," *The Service Industries Journal*, 23, March 2003, 47–66.
4. Christopher H. Lovelock and Charles B. Weinberg, *Public and Nonprofit Marketing*, 2nd ed. Redwood City, CA: The Scientific Press, 1989; Paul Flanagan, Robert Johnston, and Derek Talbot, "Customer Confidence: The Development of 'Pre-Experience' Concept," *International Journal of Service Industry Management*, 16, No. 4, 2005, 373–384.
5. "The Great Jobs Switch," *The Economist*, October 1, 2005, 11, 14.
6. Marion Weissenberger-Eibl and Daniel Jeffrey Koch, "Importance of Industrial Services and Service Innovations," *Journal of Management and Organization*, 13, No. 2, 2007, 88–101.
7. Mary Jo Bitner and Stephen W. Brown, "The Service Imperative," *Business Horizons*, 51, 2008, 39–46.
8. For more information on SSME, see IFM and IBM, *Succeeding through Service Innovation: A Discussion Paper.* Cambridge, UK: University of Cambridge Institute for Manufacturing, 2007; Paul P. Maglio and Jim Spohrer, "Fundamentals of Service Science," *Journal of the Academy of Marketing Science*, 36, No. 1, 2008 18–20.
9. See the website of Service Science for the latest research in this field: http://www.sersci.com/Service Science, accessed June 2, 2009.
10. U.S. Department of Commerce, *North American Industry Classification System—United States.* Washington, DC: National Technical Information Service, # PB 2002-101430, 2002.
11. "Crowned at last," *The Economist*, April 2, 2005, 3–6.
12. Bill Carroll and Judy Siguaw, "The Evolution of Electronic Distribution: Effects on Hotels and Intermediaries," *Cornell Hotel and Restaurant Administration Quarterly*, 44, August 2003, 38–51.
13. Diana Farrell, Martha A. Laboissière, and Jaeson Rosenfeld, "Sizing the Emerging Global Labor Market," *The McKinsey Quarterly*, No. 3, 2005, 93–103.
14. Thomas H. Davenport and Bala Iyer, "Should You Outsource Your Brain?" *Harvard Business Review*, February 2009, 38.
15. Smith, Adam (1776), *The Wealth of Nations, Books I-III*, with an Introduction by Alan B. Krueger. London: Bantam Classics, 2003.
16. Say, Jean Baptiste (1803), *A Treatise on Political Economy: The Production Distribution and Consumption of Wealth.* Translated by and with notes from C.R. Prinsep. M.A, Scholarly Publishing Office, University of Michigan Library, 2005.
17. Robert C. Judd, "The Case for Redefining Services," *Journal of Marketing*, 28, January 1964, 59; John M. Rathmell, *Marketing in the Service Sector.* Cambridge, MA: Winthrop, 1974; Christopher H. Lovelock and Evert Gummesson, "Whither Services Marketing? In Search of a New Paradigm and Fresh Perspectives," *Journal of Service Research*, 7, August 2004, 20–41.
18. Lovelock and Gummeson, op. cit.
19. Robin G. Qiu, "Service Science: Scientific Study of Service Systems," *Service Science.* Retrieved at http://www.sersci.com/ServiceScience/paper_details.php?id=1, published on November 22, 2008.
20. Lesley Brown (ed.), *Shorter Oxford English Dictionary*, 5th ed., 2002.
21. John M. Rathmell, "What is Meant by Services?" *Journal of Marketing*, 30, October 1966, 32–36.
22. Evert Gummesson (citing an unknown source), "Lip Service: A Neglected Area in Services Marketing," *Journal of Consumer Services*, No. 1, Summer 1987, 19–22.
23. Adapted from a definition by Christopher Lovelock (identified anonymously as Expert 6, Table II, p. 112) in Bo Edvardsson, Anders Gustafsson, and Inger Roos, "Service Portraits in Service Research: A Critical Review," *International Journal of Service Industry Management*, 16, No. 1, 2005, 107–121.
24. John E. G. Bateson, "Why We Need Service Marketing" in O. C. Ferrell, S. W. Brown, and C. W. Lamb Jr., eds. *Conceptual and Theoretical Developments in Marketing.* Chicago: American Marketing Association, 1979: 131–146.
25. G. Lynn Shostack, "Breaking Free from Product Marketing," *Journal of Marketing*, April 1977.
26. W. Earl Sasser, R. Paul Olsen, and D. Daryl Wyckoff, *Management of Service Operations: Text, Cases, and Readings.* Boston: Allyn & Bacon, 1978.
27. Rogelio Oliva and Robert L. Kallenberg, "Managing the Transition from Products to Services," *International Journal of Service Industry Management*, 14, No. 2, 2003, 160–172; Mohanbir Sawhney, Sridhar Balasubramanian, and Vish V. Krishnan, "Creating Growth with Services," *MIT Sloan Management Review*, 45, Winter 2004, 34–43; Wayne A. Neu and Stephen A. Brown, "Forming Successful Business-to-Business Services in Goods-Dominant Firms," *Journal of Service Research*, 8, August 2005.
28. Theodore Levitt, *Marketing for Business Growth.* New York: McGraw-Hill, 1974, 5.
29. Roland Rust, "What is the Domain of Service Research?" (Editorial), *Journal of Service Research*, 1, November 1998, 107.
30. Stephen L. Vargo and Robert R. Lusch, "Evolving to a New Dominant Logic for Marketing," *Journal of Marketing*, 9, No. 2, 2004, 1–21; Stephen L. Vargo and Robert R. Lusch, "Service-dominant Logic: Continuing the Evolution," *Journal of the Academy of Marketing Science*, 36, No. 1, 2008, 1–10.
31. For recommendations for manufacturing firms to successfully offer services see Werner Reinartz and Wolfgang Ulaga, "How to Sell Services Profitably," *Harvard Business Review*, May 2008, 90–96.
32. These classifications are derived from Christopher H. Lovelock, "Classifying Services to Gain Strategic Marketing Insights," *Journal of Marketing*, 47, Summer 1983: 9–20.
33. The 4 Ps classification of marketing decision variables was created by E. Jerome McCarthy, *Basic Marketing: A Managerial Approach* (Homewood, IL: Richard D. Irwin, Inc., 1960). It was a refinement of the long list of ingredients included in the marketing mix concept, created by

Professor Neil Borden at Harvard in the 1950s. Borden got the idea from a colleague who described the marketing manager's job as being a "mixer of ingredients."

34. An expanded 7 Ps marketing mix was first proposed by Bernard H. Booms and Mary J. Bitner, "Marketing Strategies and Organization Structures for Service Firms," in J. H. Donnelly and W.R. George, eds. *Marketing of Services.* Chicago: American Marketing Association, 1981, 47–51).
35. Philip J. Coelho and Chris Easingwood, "Multiple Channel Systems in Services: Pros, Cons, and Issues," *The Service Industries Journal*, 24, September 2004, 1–30.
36. Gary Stix, "Real Time," *Scientific American*, September 2002, 36–39.
37. Paul Flanagan, Robert Johnston, and Derek Talbot, op. cit., "Customer Confidence: The Development of 'Pre-Experience' Concept, *International Journal of Service Industry Management*, 16, No. 4, 2005, 373–384.
38. Bonnie Farber Canziani, "Leveraging Customer Competency in Service Firms," *International Journal of Service Industry Management*, 8, No. 1, 1997, 5–25.
39. Gary Knisely, "Greater Marketing Emphasis by Holiday Inns Breaks Mold," *Advertising Age*, January 15, 1979.
40. The term "partial employee" was coined by P. K. Mills and D. J. Moberg, "Perspectives on the Technology of Service Operations," *Academy of Management Review*, 7, No. 3, 467–478. For recent research on this topic, see: Karthik Namasivayam, "The Consumer as Transient Employee: Consumer Satisfaction through the Lens of Job-performance Models, *International Journal of Service Industry Management*, 14, No. 4, 2004, 420–435. An-Tien Hsieh, Chang-Hua Yen, and Ko-Chien Chin, "Participative customers as partial employees and service provider workload, *International Journal of Service Industry Management*, 15, No. 2, 2004, 187–200.
41. For research on SST, see Matthew L. Meuter, Mary Jo Bitner, Amy L. Ostrom, and Stephen W. Brown, "Choosing Among Alternative Delivery Modes: An Investigation of Customer Trial of Self Service Technologies," *Journal of Marketing*, 69, April 2005, 61–84. A. Parasuraman, Valarie Zeithaml, and Arvind Malhotra, "E-S-QUAL: A Multiple Item Scale for Assessing Electronic Service Quality," *Journal of Service Research*, 7, February 2005, 213–233. Devashish Pujari, "Self-service with a Smile: Self-service Technology (SST) Encounters among Canadian Business-to-business," *International Journal of Service Industry Management*, 15, No. 2, 2004, 200–219. Angus Laing, Gillian Hogg, and Dan Winkelman, "The Impact of the Internet on Professional Relationships: The Case of Health Care," *The Service Industries Journal*, 25, July 2005, 675–688.
42. The term "servicescape" was coined by Mary Jo Bitner, "Servicescapes: The Impact of Physical Surroundings on Customers and Employees," *Journal of Marketing*, 56, April 1992, 57–71.
43. The term "part-time marketer" was coined by Evert Gummesson, "The New Marketing: Developing Long-Term Interactive Relationships," *Long Range Planning*, 4, 1987. See also Christian Grönroos, *Service Management and Marketing*, 2nd ed. Chichester, UK: John Wiley & Sons, Ltd, 2001 and Evert Gummesson, *Total Relationship Marketing*, 2nd ed., Oxford: Butterworth Heinemann, 2002.

CHAPTER 2

Consumer Behavior in a Services Context

I can't get no satisfaction.

MICK JAGGER

An individual who seeks out the necessary information and chooses wisely has a better chance of getting satisfaction than Mick Jagger.

CLAES FORNELL

All the world's a stage and all the men and women merely players; they have their exits and their entrances and one man in his time plays many parts.

WILLIAM SHAKESPEARE
AS YOU LIKE IT

LEARNING OBJECTIVES (LOs)

By the end of this chapter, the reader should be able to:

LO1 Understand the three-stage model of service consumption.

LO2 Learn how consumers evaluate and choose between alternative service offerings and why they have difficulty making those evaluations.

LO3 Know the perceived risks that customers face in purchasing services and the strategies firms can use to reduce consumer risk perceptions.

LO4 Understand how customers form service expectations and the components of these expectations.

LO5 Contrast how customers experience and evaluate high versus low contact services.

LO6 Be familiar with the servuction model and understand the interactions that together create the service experience.

LO7 Obtain insights from viewing service encounter as a form of theater.

LO8 Know how role and script theory contribute to a better understanding of service experiences.

LO9 Know how customers evaluate services and what determines their satisfaction.

Susan Munro, Service Customer[1]

After morning classes, Susan Munro, a final-year business student, and her friends had lunch at the recently renovated student union. It featured a variety of small kiosks from local suppliers to brand-name fast food chains that offered choices of sandwiches, health foods, and a variety of desserts. Although she wanted a sandwich, there was a long line of customers at the sandwich shop. Thus, Susan joined her friends at Burger King and then splurged on a café latte from the adjacent Have-a-Java coffee stand. The food court was unusually crowded that day, perhaps because of the rain pouring down outside. When they finally found a table, they had to clear away the dirty trays. "Lazy slobs!" commented her friend Mark, referring to the previous customers.

After lunch, Susan stopped at the cash machine and withdrew some money. When she remembered she had a job interview at the end of the week, she telephoned her hairdresser and counted herself lucky to be able to make an appointment for later. This was because of a cancellation by another client.

Susan looked forward to her visit to the hairdresser. The salon had a bright, trendy décor and was staffed by friendly hairdressers. Unfortunately, the stylist was running late and Susan had to wait for 20 minutes. She used that time to review a human resources course. Some of the other waiting customers were reading magazines provided by the salon. Eventually, it was time for a shampoo, after which the stylist proposed a slightly different cut. Susan agreed, although she drew the line at the suggestion to lighten her hair color as she had never done it before and was unsure how it would look. She did not want to take the risk. She sat very still, watching the hair-cutting process in the mirror and turning her head when requested. She was very pleased with the result and complimented the stylist on her work. Then she tipped her and paid for the haircut at the reception desk.

On the way home, she stopped by the cleaners to pick up some clothes. The store was rather gloomy, smelled of cleaning solvents, and the walls badly needed repainting. She was annoyed to find that although her silk blouse was ready as promised, the suit that she needed for the interview was not. The assistant, who had dirty fingernails, mumbled an apology in an insincere tone. Although the store was convenient and the quality of work was quite good, Susan considered the employees unfriendly and not very helpful and was unhappy with their service. However, she had no choice but to use them as there were no other dry cleaners around.

FIGURE 2.1 Food for Thought—Susan Munro Is Just Another Customer Facing a Large Selection of Services Out There

Back at her apartment building, she opened the mailbox in the lobby. Her mail included a bill from her insurance company; however, it required no action since payment was deducted automatically from her bank account. She was about to discard the junk mail when she noticed a flyer promoting a new dry-cleaning store, which included a discount coupon. She decided to try the new store and pocketed the coupon.

Since it was her turn to cook dinner, she looked in the kitchen to see what food was available. Susan sighed when she realized there was nothing much. Maybe she would make salad and call for delivery of a large pizza.

THE THREE-STAGE MODEL OF SERVICE CONSUMPTION

The story of Susan Munro depicts consumer behavior in a variety of situations and stages. Understanding customer behavior lies at the heart of marketing. We need to understand how people make decisions about buying and using a service and what determines their satisfaction with it after consumption. Without this understanding, no organization can hope to create and deliver services that will result in satisfied customers.

Service consumption can be divided into three principal stages: prepurchase, service encounter, and postencounter. Figure 2.2 shows that each stage consists of two or more steps. The prepurchase stage includes four steps: (1) awareness of need, (2) information search, (3) evaluation of alternatives, and (4) making a purchase decision. During the service encounter stage, the customer initiates, experiences, and consumes the service.

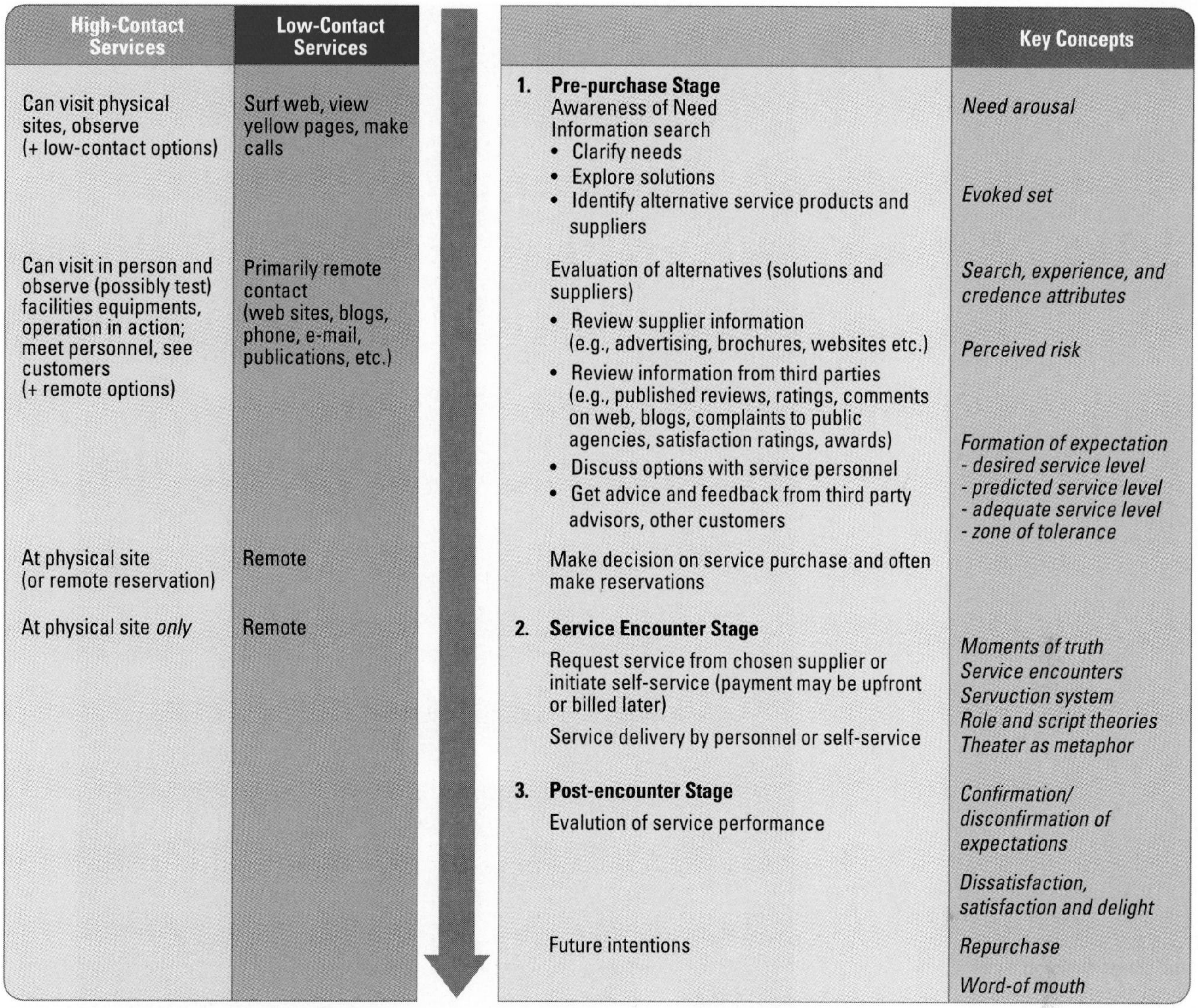

High-Contact Services	Low-Contact Services		Key Concepts
Can visit physical sites, observe (+ low-contact options)	Surf web, view yellow pages, make calls	**1. Pre-purchase Stage** Awareness of Need	*Need arousal*
		Information search • Clarify needs • Explore solutions • Identify alternative service products and suppliers	*Evoked set*
Can visit in person and observe (possibly test) facilities equipments, operation in action; meet personnel, see customers (+ remote options)	Primarily remote contact (web sites, blogs, phone, e-mail, publications, etc.)	Evaluation of alternatives (solutions and suppliers) • Review supplier information (e.g., advertising, brochures, websites etc.)	*Search, experience, and credence attributes* *Perceived risk*
		• Review information from third parties (e.g., published reviews, ratings, comments on web, blogs, complaints to public agencies, satisfaction ratings, awards) • Discuss options with service personnel • Get advice and feedback from third party advisors, other customers	*Formation of expectation* *- desired service level* *- predicted service level* *- adequate service level* *- zone of tolerance*
At physical site (or remote reservation)	Remote	Make decision on service purchase and often make reservations	
At physical site *only*	Remote	**2. Service Encounter Stage** Request service from chosen supplier or initiate self-service (payment may be upfront or billed later) Service delivery by personnel or self-service	*Moments of truth* *Service encounters* *Servuction system* *Role and script theories* *Theater as metaphor*
		3. Post-encounter Stage Evalution of service performance	*Confirmation/ disconfirmation of expectations* *Dissatisfaction, satisfaction and delight*
		Future intentions	*Repurchase* *Word-of mouth*

FIGURE 2.2 The Three-Stage Model of Service Consumption

The postencounter stage includes evaluation of the service performance, which determines future intentions such as wanting to buy again from the same firm and recommending the service to friends.

As shown on the left-hand side of Figure 2.2, the nature of these steps varies depending on whether the service is high-contact (great degree of interaction between service employees and customers, typical of people-processing services) or low-contact (little to no face-to-face contact between service employees and customers, common for many information-processing services that can be delivered at arm's length). Furthermore, at each stage, different concepts offer insights that can help us understand, analyze, and manage what is taking place. Key chapter concepts are located on the right-hand side of Figure 2.2; the rest of this chapter is organized around the three stages and key concepts of service consumption.

PREPURCHASE STAGE

The prepurchase stage begins with *need arousal*—the prospective customer's awareness of a need—and continues through information search and evaluation of alternatives to a deciding whether or not to buy a particular service.

FIGURE 2.3 Prudential Financial's Advertising Aims to Stimulate Thinking About Retirement Needs

Source: Courtesy of Prudential Financial. Photography © Dale Wilson/ masterfile.com

Need Awareness

The decision to buy or use a service is triggered by a person's or an organization's underlying need or *need arousal.* The awareness of a need will drive an information search and evaluation of alternatives before a decision is reached. Needs may be triggered by:

- Unconscious minds (e.g., personal identity and aspirations).
- Physical conditions (e.g., Susan Munro's hunger need drove her to Burger King).
- External sources (e.g., a service firm's marketing activities) (see Figure 2.3).

When a need is recognized, people are likely to be motivated to take action to resolve it. In the story of Susan Munro, her need for the services of a hairdresser was triggered by remembering a job interview she had scheduled for the end of the week. She wanted to look her her best for the interview. In developed economies, consumers now have a greater need than ever before to spend on more elaborate vacations, entertainment, and other service experiences. This shift in consumer behavior and attitudes provides opportunities for those service providers that understand and meet changing needs. For example, some service providers have taken advantage of the increased interest in extreme sports by offering guided mountain climbs, paragliding, white-water rafting trips, and mountain biking adventures (see Figure 2.4 on page 61). The idea of the service *experience* also extends to business and industrial situations, for example, modern trade shows where exhibitors engage potential clients' interest through interactive presentations and entertainment.[2]

Information Search

FIGURE 2.4 As Extreme Sports Enthusiasts Increase Worldwide, More Service Providers Offer Rough-and-Tumble Activities Like White Water Rafting

Once a need or a problem has been recognized, customers are motivated to search for solutions to satisfy the need. Alternative solutions might involve deciding between different approaches to address the same problem, such as hiring a landscaping firm to cut down a dying tree in your yard as opposed to renting a chainsaw and doing it yourself. Or choosing between going out to a movie theater, renting a video or DVD, or downloading an on-demand movie from your cable service company. And, of course, there's always the alternative of doing nothing—at least for the time being.

Several alternatives may come to mind, and these form the *evoked set* (also called the *consideration set*), the set of products or brands a customer may consider in the decision-making process. For Susan Munro, the first choice in her evoked set was a sandwich shop but, due to the long line, she settled for the second choice in her evoked set, Burger King. The evoked set can be derived from past experience or external sources such as advertising, retail displays, news stories, online searches, and recommendations from service personnel, friends, and family. Once an evoked set is in place, the different alternatives need to be evaluated before a final choice can be made.

Evaluating Alternatives

SERVICE ATTRIBUTES. When faced with several alternatives, customers need to compare and evaluate the different service offerings. Many services, however, are difficult to evaluate before purchase. Ease or difficulty of evaluating a product before purchase is a function of its attributes where we distinguish between three types.[3] They are:

- ***Search attributes*** are tangible characteristics customers can evaluate before purchase. Style, color, texture, taste, and sound are examples of such features that allow prospective consumers to try out, taste, or "test drive" the product prior to purchase. These tangible attributes help customers understand and evaluate what they will get in exchange for their money and reduces the sense of uncertainty or risk associated with the purchase. Clothing, furniture, cars, electronic equipment, and foods are among the manufactured products high in search attributes. Search attributes are found in many services, too. For example, you can assess many attributes before visiting a particular restaurant, including type of food, location, type of restaurant (e.g., fine dining, casual, family-friendly, etc.), and price. Or you can ask to view alternative rooms in a hotel, check out a golf course before actually playing a round, or take a tour of a health club and sample one or two pieces of equipment.
- ***Experience attributes*** are those that cannot be evaluated before purchase. Customers must "experience" the service before they can assess attributes such as reliability, ease of use, and customer support. In our restaurant example, you won't know how much you actually like the food, the service provided by your waiter, and the atmosphere in the restaurant until you are actually consuming the service.

Vacations, live entertainment performances, and even many medical procedures all have high experience attributes. Although people can examine brochures, scroll through websites describing a specific holiday destination, view travel films, or read reviews by travel experts, they can't really evaluate or feel the dramatic beauty associated with, say, hiking in the Canadian Rockies or snorkeling in the Caribbean until they experience these activities. Nor can customers always rely on information from friends, family, or other personal sources when evaluating these and similar services, because different people may interpret or respond to the same stimuli in different ways. Consider your own experiences in following up on recommendations from friends to see a particular movie. Perhaps you can recall an occasion when you walked into the theater with high expectations, but felt disappointed after viewing the film because you didn't like it as much as your friends had.

Finally, reviews and recommendations cannot possibly account for all situation-specific circumstances, for example, the excellent chef may be on vacation or a boisterous birthday party at the neighboring table may spoil the romantic candlelight dinner you came for to celebrate an anniversary.

- ***Credence Attributes.*** Product characteristics that customers find hard to evaluate even after consumption are known as credence attributes. Here, the customer is forced to believe or trust that certain tasks have been performed at the promised level of quality. In our restaurant example, credence attributes include the hygiene conditions of the kitchen and the healthiness of the cooking ingredients.

  It's not easy for a customer to determine the quality of repair and maintenance work performed on a car, and patients can't usually evaluate how well their dentists have performed complex dental procedures. And consider the purchase of professional services. People seek such services precisely because they lack the necessary training and expertise themselves—think about counseling, surgery, legal advice, and consulting services. How can you really be sure that the best possible job was done? Sometimes it comes down to a matter of having confidence in the provider's skills and professionalism.

All products can be placed on a continuum ranging from "easy to evaluate" to "difficult to evaluate," depending on whether they are high in search, experience, or credence attributes. As shown in Figure 2.5, most physical goods are located somewhere toward the left of the spectrum because they are high in search attributes. In contrast, most services tend to be located from the center to the right of the continuum as they tend to be high in experience and credence attributes. However, when discussing these three types of attributes, we should be careful not to overgeneralize because, for example, there may be a big difference between an experienced customer's ability to evaluate a service and that of a first time user.

The more difficulty a customer has in evaluating a service before purchase, the higher the perceived risk associated with that decision. We review perceived risk next.

PERCEIVED RISK. When evaluating competing services, customers try to assess the likely performance of each service on service attributes that are important to them

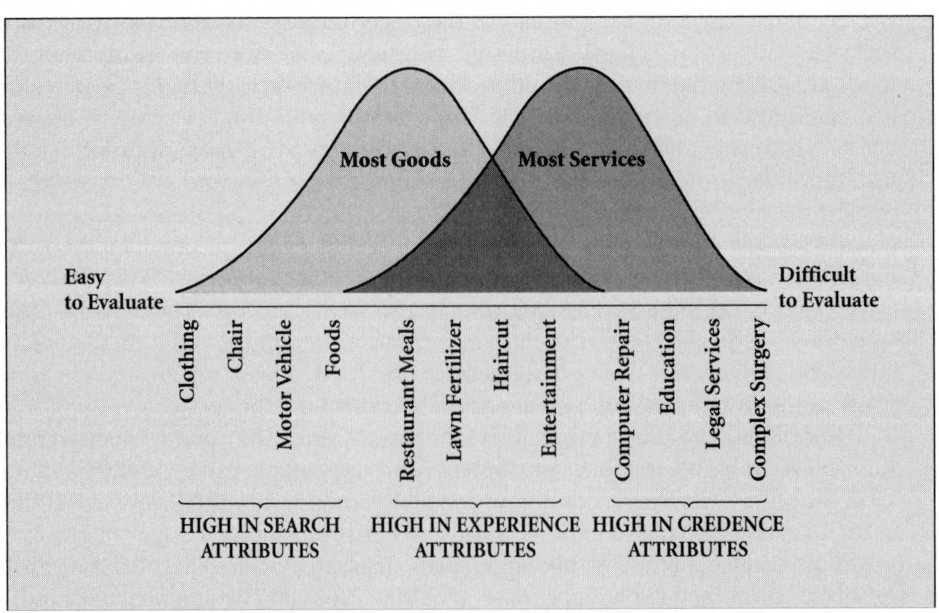

FIGURE 2.5 How Product Characteristics Affect Ease of Evaluation

Source: Adapted from Valarie A. Zeithaml, "How Consumer Evaluation Processes Differ Between Goods and Services," in J.H. Donnelly and W. R. George, Marketing of Services (Chicago: American Marketing Association, 1981).

and choose the service that is expected to best meet their needs. Because of the high proportion of experience and credence attributes, customers may worry about the risk of making a purchase that subsequently proves disappointing. If you buy a physical good that is unsatisfactory, you can usually return or replace it. This option is not as readily available with services. Susan Munro had not tried coloring her hair before and was uncertain how it would turn out. Hence, when the hairdresser suggested she lighten her hair color, Susan was worried and therefore declined.

Although some services can be repeated, such as recleaning clothes that have not been laundered satisfactorily, this is not a practical solution in the case of a poorly performed play or a badly taught course (e.g., do you really want to take Financial Accounting again next semester?).

Perceived risk is especially relevant for services that are difficult to evaluate before purchase and consumption, and first-time users are likely to face greater uncertainty. Think about how you felt the first time you had to make a decision about an unfamiliar service, especially one with important consequences such as buying a health insurance or choosing a college. It's likely that you worried about the probability of a negative outcome. The worse the possible outcome and the more likely it is to occur, the higher the perception of risk. Table 2.1 outlines seven categories of perceived risks.

How might consumers handle perceived risk? People typically feel uncomfortable with perceived risks and use a variety of methods to reduce them, including:

- Seeking information from trusted and respected personal sources such as family, friends, and peers.
- Using the Web to compare service offerings and to search for independent reviews and ratings.

TABLE 2.1 Perceived Risks of Purchasing and Using Services

Type of Risk	Examples of Customer Concerns
Functional (unsatisfactory performance outcomes)	• Will this training course give me the skills I need to get a better job? • Will this credit card be accepted wherever and whenever I want to make a purchase? • Will the dry cleaner be able to remove the stains from this jacket?
Financial (monetary loss, unexpected costs)	• Will I lose money if I make the investment recommended by my stockbroker? • Could my identity be stolen if I make this purchase on the Internet? • Will I incur a lot of unanticipated expenses if I go on this vacation? • Will repairing my car cost more than the original estimate?
Temporal (wasting time, consequences of delays)	• Will I have to wait in line before entering the exhibition? • Will service at this restaurant be so slow that I will be late for my afternoon meeting? • Will the renovations to our bathroom be completed before our friends come to stay with us?
Physical (personal injury or damage to possessions)	• Will I get hurt if I go skiing at this resort? • Will the contents of this package get damaged in the mail? • Will I fall sick if I travel abroad on vacation?
Psychological (personal fears and emotions)	• How can I be sure that this aircraft will not crash? • Will the consultant make me feel stupid? • Will the doctor's diagnosis upset me?
Social (how others think and react)	• What will my friends think of me if they learnt that I stayed at this cheap motel? • Will my relatives approve of the restaurant I have chosen for the family reunion dinner? • Willl my business colleagues disapprove of my selection of an unknown law firm?
Sensory (unwanted effects on any of the five senses)	• Will I get a view of the parking lot rather than the beach from my restaurant table? • Will the hotel bed be uncomfortable? • Will I be kept awake by noise from the guests in the room next door? • Will my room smell of stale cigarette smoke? • Will the coffee at breakfast taste disgusting?

FIGURE 2.6 This Doctor Displays Many Accreditations to Communicate His Credentials

- Relying on a firm with a good reputation.
- Looking for guarantees and warranties.
- Visiting service facilities or trying aspects of the service before purchasing, and examining tangible cues or other physical evidence such as the feel and look of the service setting or awards won by the firm.
- Asking knowledgeable employees about competing services.

Customers are risk averse and—everything else equal—will choose the service with the lower perceived risk. Therefore, firms need to proactively work on reducing customer risk perceptions. Suitable strategies vary according to the nature of the service and may include all or some of the following:

- Encourage prospective customers to preview the service through brochures, websites, and videos.
- Encourage prospective customers to visit the service facilities in advance of purchase.
- Offer free trials that are suitable for services with high experience attributes. Some providers of online computer services have adopted this strategy. For example, AOL (America Online) offers potential users free software and the chance to try its services without charge for a limited period of time. This strategy reduces customers' concerns about entering into a paid contract without first testing the service. AOL hopes consumers will be "hooked" on its Web services by the end of the free trial.
- Advertise. This provides consumers with an interpretation and value of any product or service. For services with high credence qualities and high customer involvement, firms should focus on key service dimensions and provide tangible information about service performance outcomes.
- Display credentials. Professionals such as doctors, architects, and lawyers often display their degrees and other certifications because they want customers to "see" the credentials that qualify them to provide expert service (see Figure 2.6). Many professional firms' websites inform prospective clients about their services, highlight their expertise, and even showcase successful past engagements.
- Use *evidence management*, an organized approach where customers are presented with coherent evidence of the company's targeted image and its value proposition. This includes the appearance of furnishings, equipment, and facilities as well as employees' dress and behavior.[4] For example, the pleasing decor at the hairdressing salon that Susan Munro visited may have initially helped her choose this particular salon and now probably contributes to her feeling satisfied in the end—even though her stylist kept her waiting for 20 minutes.
- Institute visible safety procedures that build confidence and trust.
- Give customers access to online information about the status of an order or procedure. Many courier service providers use this (e.g., FedEx, DHL, and UPS).
- Offer service guarantees such as money-back guarantees and performance warranties.

When a company does a good job of managing potential customers' risk perceptions, uncertainty is reduced, thereby increasing the chances that they will be the service provider chosen. Another important input to consumer choice (and later satisfaction) are expectations, discussed next.

SERVICE EXPECTATIONS. Expectations are formed during the search and decision-making process, and they are heavily shaped by information search and evaluation of attributes. If you have no relevant prior experience, you may base your prepurchase expectations on word-of-mouth comments, news stories, or the firm's own marketing efforts. Expectations can even be situation-specific. For example, if it is a

SERVICE PERSPECTIVES 2.1

PARENTS SEEK INVOLVEMENT IN MEDICAL DECISIONS AFFECTING THEIR CHILDREN

Many parents want to participate actively in decisions relating to their children's medical treatment. Thanks in part to in-depth media coverage of medical advances and health-related issues, as well as the educational efforts of consumer advocates, parents are better informed and more assertive than in previous generations, no longer willing simply to accept the recommendations of medical specialists. In particular, parents whose child has been born with congenital defects or has developed a life-threatening illness are often willing to invest immense amounts of time and energy to learn everything they can about their child's condition. Some have even founded nonprofit organizations centered on a specific disease to bring together other families facing the same problems and to help raise money for research and treatment.

The Internet has made it much easier to access health care information and research findings. A study by the Texas-based Heart Center of 160 parents who had Internet access and children with cardiac problems found that 58 percent obtained information related to their child's diagnosis. Four out of five users searching for cardiology-related information stated that locating the information was easy; of those, half could name a favorite cardiology web site. Almost all felt that the information was helpful in further understanding their child's condition. The study reported that six parents even created interactive personal web sites specifically related to their child's congenital heart defect.[5]

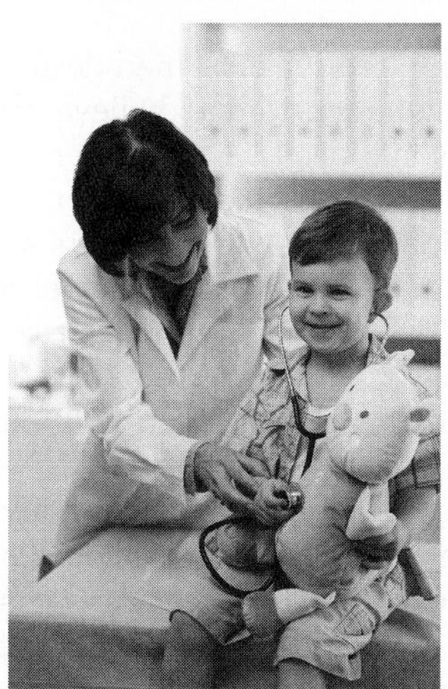

Commenting on the phenomenon of highly-informed parents, Norman J. Siegel, MD, former chair of pediatrics at Yale New Haven Children's Hospital, observed:

> *It's a different practice today. The old days of "trust me, I'm going to take care of this" are completely gone. I see many patients who come in carrying a folder with printouts from the Internet and they want to know why Dr. So-and-So wrote this. They go to chat rooms, too. They want to know about the disease process, if it's chronic. Some parents are almost as well informed as a young medical student or house officer.*

Dr. Siegel said he welcomed the trend and enjoyed the discussions but admitted that some physicians found it hard to adapt.

Source: Christopher Lovelock and Jeff Gregory "Yale New Haven Children's Hospital" New Haven, CT: Yale School of Management, 2003.

peak period, expectations of service delivery timing will be lower than during a nonpeak period. Expectations change over time, too, and are influenced by supplier-controlled factors—such as advertising, pricing, new technologies, and service innovation—as well as social trends, advocacy by consumer organizations, and increased access to information through the media and the Internet. For instance, today's health-care consumer is well-informed and often seeks a participative role in decisions relating to medical treatment. Service Perspectives 2.1 describes a new assertiveness among parents of children with serious illnesses.

What are the components of customer expectations? Expectations embrace several elements, including desired, adequate, and predicted service, and a zone of tolerance

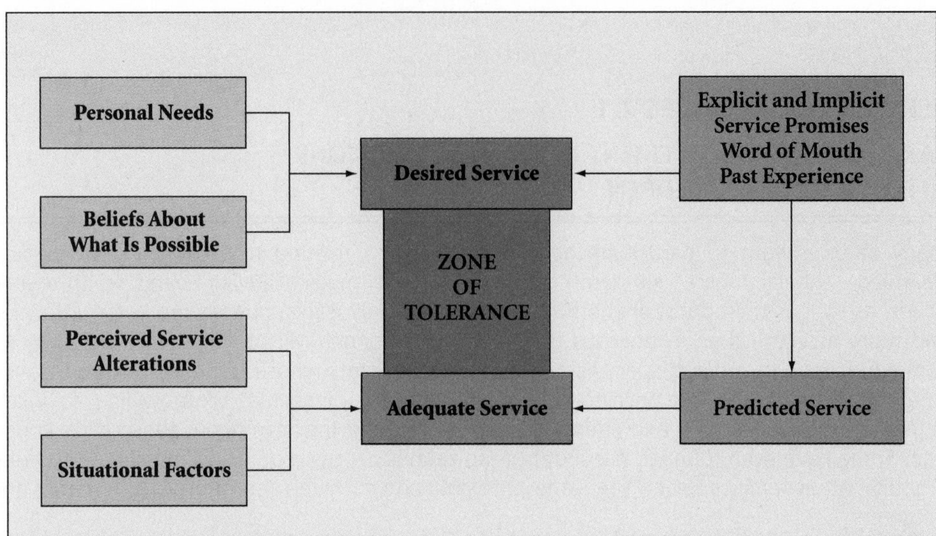

FIGURE 2.7 Factors Influencing Customer Expectations of Service

Source: Adapted from Valarie A. Zeithaml, Leonard L. Berry, and A. Parasuraman, "The Nature and Determinants of Customer Expectations of Service," Journal of the Academy of Marketing Science, 21, No. 1, 1993, 1–12.

that falls between the desired and adequate service levels.[6] The model in Figure 2.7 shows the factors that influence the different levels of customer expectations. These factors are:

- **Desired service.** The type of service customers hope to receive is termed desired service. It's a "wished for" level—a combination of what customers believe can and should be delivered in the context of their personal needs. Desired service could also be influenced by explicit and implicit promises made by service providers, word of mouth, and past experience.[7] However, most customers are realistic. Recognizing that a firm can't always deliver the "wished for" level of service, they also have a threshold level of expectations, termed *adequate service*, and a predicted service level.
- **Adequate service.** The minimum level of service customers will accept without being dissatisfied.
- **Predicted service.** This is the level of service customers actually anticipate receiving. Predicted service can also be affected by service provider promises, word of mouth, and past experiences. The predicted service level directly affects how customers define "adequate service" on that occasion. If good service is predicted, the adequate level will be higher than if poorer service is predicted. Customer predictions of service often are situation specific. From past experience, for example, customers visiting a museum on a summer day may expect to see larger crowds if the weather is poor than if the sun is shining. So, a 10-minute wait to buy tickets on a cool, rainy day in summer might not fall below their adequate service level. Another factor that may set this expectation is the service level anticipated from alternative suppliers.
- **Zone of tolerance.** It can be difficult for firms to achieve consistent service delivery at all touchpoints across many service delivery channels, branches, and often thousands of employees. Even the performance by the same service employee is likely to vary over the course of a day and from one day to another. The extent to which customers are willing to accept this variation is called the zone of tolerance. Performing too low causes frustration and dissatisfaction, whereas exceeding the desired service level should surprise and delight customers. Another way of looking at the zone of tolerance is to think of it as the range of service within which customers don't pay explicit attention to service performance.[8] When service falls outside this range, customers will react—either positively or negatively.

The size of the zone of tolerance can be larger or smaller for individual customers, depending on such factors as competition, price, or importance of specific service attributes—each of which can influence the level of adequate service levels. By contrast, desired service levels tend to move up very slowly in response to accumulated customer experiences. Consider a small business owner who needs some advice from her accountant. Her ideal level of professional service may be receiving a thoughtful response by the following day. However, if she makes her request at the time of year when all accountants are busy preparing corporate and individual tax returns, she will probably know from experience not to expect a fast reply. Although her ideal service level probably won't change, her zone of tolerance for response time may be broader because she has a lower adequate service threshold at busy times of the year.

It's important for firms to understand the width of their customers' zones of tolerance. For example, a study of guests at four-star, five-star, and resort hotels in Northern Cyprus (located in the eastern Mediterranean) found a relatively narrow zone of tolerance between desired and adequate service levels.[9] Examination of individual attributes showed that guests were more sensitive about intangibles such as prompt service, employee courtesy, and convenience of operating hours than about tangibles such as physical facilities and modern-looking equipment.

The predicted service level is probably the most important level for the consumer choice process, which we discuss in the next section. Desired and adequate levels and the zone of tolerance become important determinants to customer satisfaction, which we will discuss in the postencounter stage section.

Purchase Decision

After consumers have evaluated possible alternatives, by, for example, comparing the performance of important attributes of competing service offerings; assessed the perceived risk associated with each offering; and developed their desired, adequate, and predicted service level expectations—they are ready to select the option they like best.

Many purchase decisions for frequently purchased services are quite simple and can be made quickly, without too much thought—the perceived risks are low, the alternatives are clear, and, because they have been used before, their characteristics are easily understood. If the consumer already has a favorite supplier, he or she will probably choose it again in the absence of a compelling reason to do otherwise.

In many instances however, purchase decisions involve trade-offs. Price often is a key factor. For example, is it worth paying more for faster service, as in choosing between a taxi and a bus? Or for a larger rental car that will give family members more room on a long vacation drive? For more complex decisions, trade-offs can involve multiple attributes: In choosing an airline, convenience of schedules, reliability, seat comfort, attentiveness of cabin crew, and availability of meals may well vary among different carriers, even at the same fares.

Once a decision is made, the consumer is ready to move to the service encounter stage. This next step may take place immediately, as in deciding to enter a fast-food restaurant, or it may first involve an advance reservation, as usually happens with taking a flight or attending a live theater performance.

SERVICE ENCOUNTER STAGE

After making a purchase decision, customers move on to the core of the service experience: the service encounter stage, which usually includes a series of contacts with the chosen service firm. This stage often begins with placing an order, requesting a reservation, or even submitting an application (consider the process of obtaining a loan, seeking insurance coverage, or getting into college or graduate school). Contacts may take the form of personal exchanges between customers and service employees or impersonal interactions with machines or websites. During service delivery, many customers start evaluating the quality of service they are receiving and decide whether it meets their expectations. High-contact services usually supply a greater array of clues to service quality than low-contact services.

A *service encounter* is a period of time during which a customer interacts directly with a service provider.[10] Although some of these encounters are very brief and consist of just a few steps—consider what is involved in a taxi ride or a phone call—others may extend over a longer time frame and involve multiple actions of varying degrees of complexity. A leisurely restaurant meal might stretch over a couple of hours; a visit to a hospital might last several days.

We use a number of models and frameworks to better understand consumers' behavior during the service encounter experience. First, the "moments of truth" metaphor shows the importance of effectively managing touchpoints. A second framework, the high/low contact service model, helps us to better understand the extent and nature of points of contact. A third concept, the servuction model, focuses on the various types of interactions that together create the customer's service experience. Finally, the theater metaphor communicates effectively how one can look at "staging" service performances to create the experience customers desire.

Service Encounters Are "Moments of Truth"

Richard Normann borrowed the "moment of truth" metaphor from bullfighting to show the importance of contact points with customers (Figure 2.8):

> [W]e could say that the perceived quality is realized at the moment of truth, when the service provider and the service customer confront one another in the arena. At that moment they are very much on their own.... It is the skill, the motivation, and the tools employed by the firm's representative and the expectations and behavior of the client which together will create the service delivery process.[11]

In bullfighting, the life of either the bull or the matador (or possibly both) is at stake. The moment of truth is the instant at which the matador deftly slays the bull with his sword—hardly a comfortable analogy for a service organization intent on building long-term relationships with its customers! Normann's point, of course, is that it's the life of the relationship at stake. Contrary to bullfighting, the goal of relationship marketing—which we explore in depth in Chapter 12—is to prevent one unfortunate (mis)encounter from destroying what is already, or has the potential to become, a mutually valued, long-term relationship.

Jan Carlzon, the former chief executive of Scandinavian Airlines System (SAS), used the "moment of truth" metaphor as a reference point for transforming SAS from an operations-driven business into a customer-driven airline. Carlzon made the following comments about his airline:

> Last year, each of our 10 million customers came into contact with approximately five SAS employees, and this contact lasted an average of 15 seconds each time. Thus, SAS is "created" 50 million times a year, 15 seconds at a time. These 50 million "moments of truth" are the moments that ultimately determine whether SAS will succeed or fail as a company. They are the moments when we must prove to our customers that SAS is their best alternative.[12]

Each service business faces similar challenges in defining and managing the moments of truth its customers will encounter.

FIGURE 2.8 The Service Provider Is the Matador Who Skillfully Manages the Service Encounter

Service Encounters Range from High Contact to Low Contact

Services involve different levels of contact with the service operation. Some of these encounters can be very brief and may consist of a few steps, such as when a customer calls a customer contact center. Others may extend over a longer time frame and involve multiple interactions of varying degrees of complexity. For example, a visit to a theme park might last all day. In Figure 2.9, we group services into three levels of customer contact. These represent the extent of interaction with service personnel, physical service elements, or both. You'll notice that traditional retail banking, person-to-person phone banking, and Internet banking are each located in different parts of the chart. While recognizing that level of customer contact covers a spectrum, it's useful to examine the differences between organizations at the high and low ends, respectively.

- **High-contact Services.** Using a high-contact service entails interaction throughout service delivery between customers and the organization. The customer's exposure to the service provider takes on a physical and tangible nature. When customers visit the facility where service is delivered, they enter a service "factory"—something that rarely happens in a manufacturing environment. Viewed from this perspective, a motel is a lodging factory, a hospital is a health treatment factory, an airplane is a flying transportation factory, and a restaurant is a food service factory. Because each of these industries focuses on "processing" people rather than inanimate objects, the marketing challenge is to make the experience appealing for customers in terms of both the physical environment and their interactions with service personnel. During the course of service delivery, customers usually are exposed to many physical clues about the organization—the exterior and interior of its buildings, equipment and furnishings, appearance and behavior of service personnel, and even other customers.
- **Low-contact Services.** At the opposite end of the spectrum, low-contact services involve little, if any, physical contact between customers and service providers. Instead, contact takes place at arm's length through the medium of electronic or physical distribution channels—a fast-growing trend in today's convenience-oriented

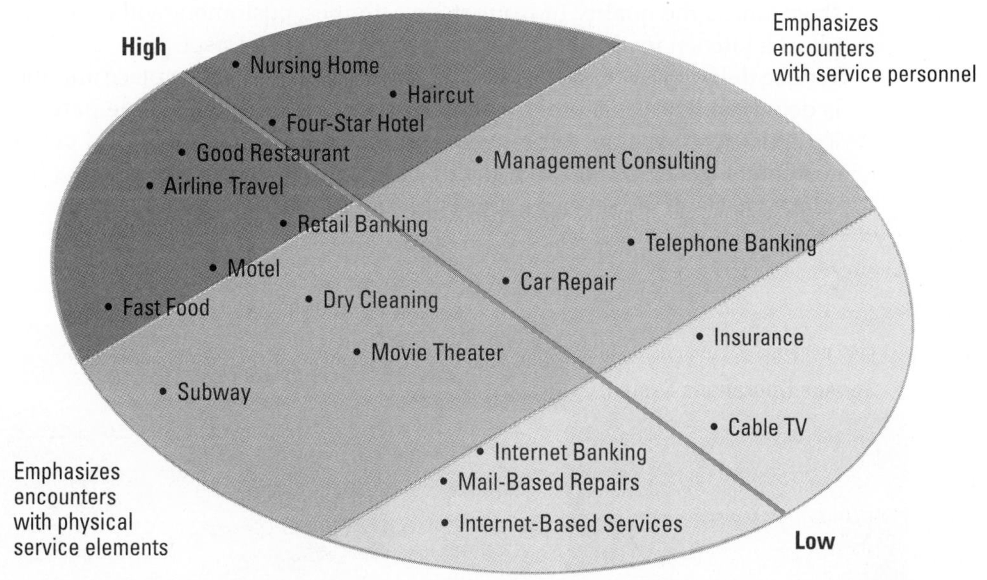

FIGURE 2.9 Levels of Customer Contact with Service Organizations

society. Many high-contact and medium-contact services are transforming into low-contact services as customers undertake more self-service; conduct their insurance and banking transactions by mail, telephone and Internet; or purchase a host of information-based services by visiting websites rather than brick-and-mortar facilities.

If you're like many people, you may alternate between high-contact and low-contact delivery channels in your use of retail banking services. The nature of your encounters with the bank varies accordingly.

The Servuction System

French researchers Pierre Eiglier and Eric Langeard were the first to conceptualize the service business as a system that integrated marketing, operations, and customers. They coined the term *servuction system* (combining the terms service and production) to describe that part of the service organization's physical environment that is visible to and experienced by customers.[13]

Consumers purchase a service for its bundle of benefits or value. Very often, the value of a service is derived from the experience created for the customer. The servuction model in Figure 2.10 shows all the interactions that together make up a typical customer experience in a high-contact service. Customers interact with the service environment, service employees, and even other customers present during the service encounter. Each type of interaction can create value (e.g., a pleasant environment, friendly and competent employees, and other customers who are interesting to observe) or destroy value (e.g., another customer blocking your view in a movie theatre). Firms have to "engineer" all interactions to make sure their customers get the service experience they came for.

The servuction system consists of a technical core *invisible* to the customer and the service delivery system *visible* to and experienced by the customer.

- **Technical core**—where inputs are processed and the elements of the service product are created. This technical core typically is in the back-stage and invisible to the customer (e.g., think of the kitching in a restaurant). Like in the theater, the visible components can be termed "front-stage" or "front office," while the invisible components can be termed "back-stage" or "back office."[15] What goes on back-stage usually is not of interest to customers. However, if what goes on back-stage affects the quality of front-stage activities, customers will notice. For example, if a kitchen reads orders wrongly, diners will be upset.
- **Service delivery system**—where the final "assembly" takes place and the product is delivered to the customer. This subsystem includes the visible part of the service operations system—buildings, equipment and personnel—and possibly other customers. Using the theater analogy, the visible front office is like a live theater where we stage the service experience for our customers.

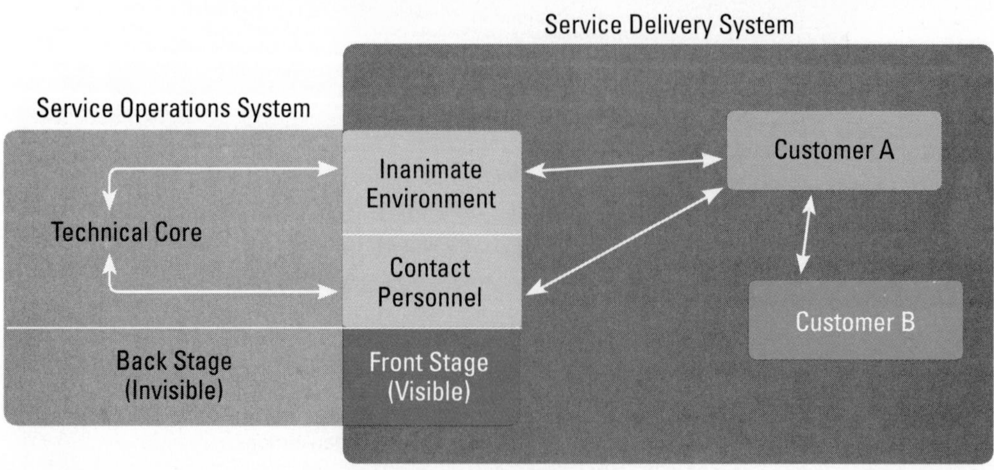

FIGURE 2.10 The Servuction Model

Source: Adapted and expanded from an original concept by Eric Langeard and Pierre Eiglier[14]

The proportion of the overall service operation visible to customers varies according to the level of customer contact. Because high-contact services directly involve the physical person of the customer, the visible component of the entire service operations tends to be substantial, and many interactions—or moments of truth—have to be managed. In contrast, low-contact services usually have most of the service operations system back-stage with front-stage elements limited to mail and telecommunications contacts. Here, customers normally do not see the "factory" where the work is performed, making the design and management of such facilities much easier. For example, credit card customers may never have to visit a physical bank—they only talk to the service provider on the phone if there is a problem, and there is very little left of the "theater" performance.

We will explore the three core components of the service delivery system in detail in later chapters of this book—Chapter 7 focuses on educating customers on how to move through the service delivery process so they can play their part in the service performance, Chapter 10 discusses the process of engineering the service environment, and Chapter 11 explores how to manage service employees.

Theater as Metaphor for Service Delivery: An Integrative Perspective

Because service delivery consists of a series of events that customers experience as a *performance,* the theater is a good metaphor for services and the creation of service experiences through the servuction system.[16] This metaphor is a particularly useful approach for high-contact service providers, such as physicians and hotels, and for businesses that serve many people simultaneously, such as professional sports, hospitals, and entertainment. Let us discuss the stages (i.e., service facilities) and the members of the cast (i.e., the front-line personnel):

- **Service facilities.** Imagine service facilities as containing the *stage* on which the drama unfolds. Sometimes the setting changes from one act to another (e.g., when airline passengers move from the entrance to the terminal to the check-in stations and then on to the boarding gate and finally step inside the aircraft). Some stages have minimal "props," like a taxi for instance. In contrast, other stages have more elaborate "props," like resort hotels that have elaborate architecture, interior design, and landscaping.
- **Personnel.** The front-stage personnel are like the members of a cast, playing roles as *actors* in a drama, and supported by a back-stage production team. In some instances, service personnel are expected to wear special costumes when on stage (such as the the fanciful uniforms often worn by hotel doormen, or the more basic brown ones worn by UPS drivers), whereby the choice of uniform design and colors is carefully integrated with other corporate design elements. Front-line employees often are required to conform to both a dress code and grooming standards (such as Disney's rule that employees can't wear beards, except as required in costumed roles).

The theater metaphor also includes the roles of the players on stage and the scripts they have to follow, which we discuss next.

Role and Script Theories

The servuction model is static and describes a single service encounter, or moment of truth. Service processes, however, usually consist of a series of encounters, such as your experiences with airline travel, from making a reservation to checking in, taking the flight, and retrieving your bags on arrival. Like actors in a theater, organizations must have knowledge of role and script theories to better understand, design, and manage both employee and customer behaviors during service encounters.

ROLE THEORY. If we view service delivery from a theatrical perspective, then both employees and customers act out their parts in the performance according to predetermined roles. Stephen Grove and Ray Fisk define a role as "a set of behavior patterns learned through experience and communication, to be performed by an individual in a certain social interaction in order to attain maximum effectiveness in goal accomplishment."[17] Roles have also been defined as combinations of social cues, or expectations of society, that guide behavior in a specific setting or context.[18] In service encounters, employees and customers each have roles to play. The satisfaction and productivity of both parties depend on role congruence, or the extent to which each person acts out his or her prescribed role during a service encounter. Employees must perform their roles with reference to customer expectations, or they risk dissatisfying their customers. And as a customer you, too, must "play by the rules," or you risk causing problems for the firm, its employees, and even other customers.

SCRIPT THEORY. Much like a movie script, a service script specifies the sequences of behavior that employees and customers are expected to learn and follow during service delivery. Employees receive formal training; customers learn scripts through experience, communication with others, and designed communications and education.[19] The more experience a customer has with a service company, the more familiar that particular script becomes. Unwillingness to learn a new script may be a reason not to switch to a competing organization. Any deviations from this known script may frustrate both customers and employees and can lead to dissatisfaction. If a company decides to change a service script (e.g., by using technology to transform a high-contact service into a low-contact one), service personnel and customers need to be educated about the new approach and the benefits it provides.

Many service dramas are tightly scripted (consider the formal style of service in some upscale restaurant settings), which reduces variability and ensures uniform quality. However, not all services involve tightly scripted performances. Scripts tend to be more flexible for providers of highly customized services—designers, educators, consultants—and may vary by situation and by customer.

Depending on the nature of their work, employees may have to learn and repeat specific lines, ranging from announcements in several languages in a location attracting a diverse audience to a sing-song sales spiel (just think of the last telemarketer who called you) to a parting salutation of "Have a nice day!" And just like the theater, companies often use scripting to define actors' behavior as well as their lines—eye contact, smiles, and handshakes may be required in addition to a spoken greeting. Other rules of conduct, welcomed by many customers, may include bans on smoking, eating, drinking, chewing gum, or using cell phones while on duty.

Figure 2.11 shows a script for teeth cleaning and a simple dental examination, involving three players—the patient, the receptionist, and the dental hygienist. Each has a specific role to play, reflecting what he or she brings to the encounter. The role of the customer (who is probably not looking forward to this encounter) is different from that of the two service providers, and the receptionist's role differs from the hygienist's, reflecting their distinctive jobs. This script is driven partly by the need to run an efficient dental office, but even more importantly by the need to perform a technical task proficiently and safely (note the mask and gloves). The core service of examining and cleaning teeth can only be accomplished satisfactorily if the patient cooperates in delivery of the service.

Several elements in this script relate to information flows. Confirming and honoring appointments avoids delays for customers and ensures effective use of dental professionals' time. Obtaining patient histories and documenting analysis and treatment is vital for maintaining complete dental records and also for accurate billing. Payment on receipt of treatment improves cash flow and avoids the problem of bad debts. And finally, adding greetings, statements of thanks, and goodbyes displays friendly good manners and helps to humanize what most people see as, at best, a slightly unpleasant experience.

ROLE AND SCRIPT THEORY COMPLEMENT EACH OTHER. Role theory and script theory govern both consumer and employee behavior during an encounter. Think, for example, of professor and student *roles* in the classes you've attended. What is the role of the professor? Typically, it's to deliver a well-structured lecture, focusing on the key topics assigned for that day, making them interesting, and engaging the students in discussion. What is the role of a student? Basically, it's to come to class prepared and on time, listen attentively, participate in discussions, and not disrupt the class. By contrast, the opening portion of the *script* for a lecture describes specific actions to be taken by each party. For instance, students should arrive at the lecture hall before class starts, select a seat, sit down, and open

Patient	Receptionist	Dental Hygienist
1. Phone for appointment		
	2. Confirm needs and set date	
3. Arrive at dental office		
	4. Greet patient; verify purpose; direct to waiting room; notify hygienist of arrival	
		5. Review notes on patient
6. Sit in waiting room		
		7. Greet patient and lead way to treatment room
8. Enter rooms; sit in dental chair		
		9. Verify medical and dental history; ask about any issues since previous visit
10. Respond to hygienist's questions		
		11. Place protective cover over patient's clothes
		12. Lower dental chair; put on own protective face mask; gloves and glasses
		13. Inspect patient's teeth (option to ask questions)
		14. Place suction device in patient's mouth
		15. Use high-speed equipment and hand tools to clean teeth in sequence
		16. Remove suction device; complete cleaning process
		17. Raise chair to sitting position; ask patient to rinse
18. Rinse mouth		
		19. Remove and dispose of mask and gloves; remove glasses
		20. Complete notes on treatment; return patient file to receptionist
		21. Remove cover from patient
		22. Give patient free toothbrush; offer advice on personal dental care for future
23. Rise from chair		
		24. Thank patient and say goodbye
25. Leave treatment room		
	26. Greet patient; confirm treatment received; present bill	
27. Pay bill		
	28. Give receipt; agree on date for next appointment; document agree-on date	
29. Take appointment card		
	30. Thank patient and say good-bye	
31. Leave dental office		

FIGURE 2.11 Script for Teeth Cleaning and Simple Dental Examination

their labtops; the professor enters, puts notes on the table, turns on the laptops and LCD projector, greets the class, makes any preliminary announcements needed, and starts the class on time. As you can see, the frameworks offered by the two theories are complementary and describe behavior during the encounter from two different perspectives. Excellent service marketers understand both perspectives and proactively define, communicate, and train their employees and customers in their roles and service scripts to achieve performance that yields high customer satisfaction and service productivity.

We will revisit how to design scripts and roles in Chapter 8, "Designing and Managing Service Processes" and how to educate and "train" customers in their roles and scripts in Chapter 7, "Promoting Services and Educating Customers."

POSTENCOUNTER STAGE

In the postencounter stage of service consumption, customers evaluate the service performance they have experienced and compare it with their prior expectations. Let's explore in more detail how satisfaction evaluations are formed.

Customer Satisfaction with Service Experiences

Satisfaction is as an attitude-like judgment following a consumption experience. Most research confirms that the confirmation or disconfirmation of preconsumption expectations is the essential determinant of satisfaction.[20] This means that customers have a certain predicted service level in mind prior to consumption. This predicted level typically is the outcome of the search and choice process, when customers decided to buy a particular service. During the service encounter, customers experience the service performance and compare it to their predicted service levels. Satisfaction judgments are then formed based on this comparison. The resulting judgment is labeled *positive disconfirmation* if the service is better than expected, *negative disconfirmation* if it is worse than expected, and simple *confirmation* if it is as expected.[21] In short, customers evaluate service performance by comparing what they expected with what they perceive they received from a particular supplier.

Customers will be reasonably satisfied as long as perceived performance falls within the zone of tolerance, that is, above the adequate service level. As performance perceptions approach or exceed desired levels, customers will be very pleased; these customers are more likely to make repeat purchases, remain loyal to that supplier, and spread positive word of mouth. However, if the service experience does not meet their expectations, customers may complain about poor service quality, suffer in silence, or switch providers in the future.[22] In highly competitive service markets, customers may expect service providers to even anticipate their unexpressed needs and deliver on them.[23]

Service Expectations

Where do service expectations in our satisfaction model come from? During the decision-making process, customers assess attributes and risks related to a service offering. In the process, they develop expectations about how the service they choose will perform (i.e., our predicted, desired and adequate service levels as discussed in the consumer decision-making section). The zone of tolerance can be narrow and firm if they are related to attributes that were important in the choice process. For example, if a customer paid a premium of $350 for a direct flight rather than one that has a four-hour stopover, then the customer will not take it lightly if there is a six-hour flight delay. A customer will also have high expectations if he paid a premium for high-quality service and will be deeply disappointed when the service fails to deliver. Smart firms manage customers' expectations at each step in the service encounter so that customers expect what the firm can deliver.[24]

Are Expectations Always the Right Comparison Standard?

Comparing performance to expectations works well in reasonably competitive markets in which customers have sufficient knowledge to choose a service that meets their needs and wants. Then, when expectations are met, customers are satisfied. However, in noncompetitive markets or in situations in which customers do not have free choice (e.g., because switching costs would be prohibitive, or because of time or location constraints), there are risks in defining customer satisfaction relative to their prior expectations. For example, if customer expectations are low and actual service delivery meets the dismal level that was expected, customers will hardly feel they are receiving good service quality. In such situations, it is better to use needs or wants as comparison standards and to define satisfaction as meeting or exceeding customer wants and needs rather than expectations.[25]

Much satisfaction research assumes customers are dealing with products high in search and experience attributes. However, a problem arises when customers are asked to evaluate the quality of services high in credence characteristics, such as complex legal cases or medical treatments, which they find difficult to evaluate even after delivery is completed. Here, customers may be unsure what to expect in advance and may not know for years—if ever—how good a job the professional actually did. A natural tendency in such situations is for clients or patients to use tangible cues and their experience as proxies to evaluate quality. Experience factors include customers' feelings about the personal style of individual providers and satisfaction levels with those service elements they feel competent to evaluate (e.g., the tastiness of hospital meals). As a result, customers' perceptions of service quality may be strongly influenced by their evaluation of process attributes and tangible elements of the service—a halo effect.[26] Firms therefore have to understand how customers evaluate their service to proactively manage those aspects of their operations that have a strong effect on customer satisfaction, even if these attributes may be unrelated to the core attributes (e.g., the correctness of a diagnosis and the quality of a surgery).

Customer Delight

Findings from a research project by Richard Oliver, Roland Rust, and Sajeev Varki suggest that customer delight is a function of three components: (1) unexpectedly high levels of performance, (2) arousal (e.g., surprise, excitement), and (3) positive affect (e.g., pleasure, joy, or happiness).[27] By contrast, high satisfaction alone is a function of positively disconfirmed expectations (better than expected) and positive affect. So, achieving delight requires focusing on what is currently unexpected by the customer. It's more than just avoiding problems—the "zero defects" strategy.

The researchers asked: "If delight is a function of surprisingly unexpected pleasure, is it possible for delight to be manifest in truly mundane services and products, such as newspaper delivery or trash collecting?" Furthermore, once customers have been delighted, their expectations are raised. They will be dissatisfied if service levels return to previous levels, and it may take more effort to "delight" them in the future.[28] Based on analysis of 10 years of data from the American Customer Satisfaction Index (ACSI), Claes Fornell and his colleagues caution against trying to exceed customer expectations on a continual basis, arguing that reaching for unobtainable objectives may backfire. They note that such efforts often come close to the point of diminishing returns.[29]

Nevertheless, a few innovative and customer-centric firms seem to be able to delight customers, even in highly customized and complex service encounters (see Best Practice in Action 2.1). This discussion also shows that firms must think carefully about whether certain delightful service offerings should be charged, which is discussed more in Chapter 6 on service pricing.

Links between Customer Satisfaction and Corporate Performance

Why is satisfaction so important to service managers? There's convincing evidence of strategic links between the level of customer satisfaction with a company's services and that firm's overall performance. Researchers from the University of Michigan found that on average, every 1 percent increase in customer satisfaction is associated with a 2.37 percent increase in a firm's return on investment (ROI).[30] And, analysis of companies' scores on the ACSI shows that, on average, among publicly traded firms, a 5 percent change in the ACSI score is associated with a 19 percent change in the market value of common equity.[31] In other words, by creating more value for the customer, as measured by increased satisfaction, the firm creates more value for its owners.

BEST PRACTICE IN ACTION 2.1

Turkish Delight: Back-Up Company Offers Customers Surprisingly Innovative Solutions

Has your child had a high fever in the middle of the night? Have you had a car accident and now you need a car rental service? Or do you want to organize a special birthday party for your partner? If so, then call Back-Up Company for an instant solution.

Back-Up is a membership company founded in 2003 to provide comprehensive service solutions for almost any problem. The company offers several alternative membership options, each with different prices, service offerings, and utilization limits. Back-Up's founders initially intended to combine services that are traditionally provided by different organizations like credit card, insurance, and automotive companies. With time, their service offerings have expanded, and now this unique Turkish company offers members a broad variety of services, including road assistance, home repair services, private drivers, medical support, and delivery services as well as tickets for events and consultancy for almost every issue, such as weddings, pet care, gifts, travel, or fashion. Back-Up can drive your car to the mechanic, deliver your medication from the pharmacy, or pick up your suits from the dry cleaner. The company even provides ideas for an unforgettable marriage proposal or answers to strange questions from your children, such as "Why is the sky blue?" At no cost to its members, Back-Up even finds the best rates on airline flights.

Back-Up provides surprising services and its customer testimonials signal the company's amazing service performances abilities. If a customer wants to order a birthday cake for a surprise party at midnight, the staff can find the cake and have it delivered to the customer's apartment. When a customer arrives at the airport realizing that he has forgotten his passport at home, a Back-Up staff member can run to his home and bring the passport to the airport. Unbelievably, when a customer's child is hungry but stuck on a school bus as a result of backed-up Istanbul traffic, Back-Up can deliver an emergency hamburger to the bus. Naturally, this level of "customer delight" cannot be free, and the company charges its members for these special solutions, considering the expenses of a particular service.

Back-Up positions itself as a close friend; someone its member customers can call even in the dead of night to resolve a problem. Its motto? "If you don't know who to call, call Back-Up." Thanks to its surprising and delighting service solutions, the company continues to grow and now "backs up" more than 250,000 members nationwide.

Susan Fournier and David Mick state:

> Customer satisfaction is central to the marketing concept...[I]t is now common to find mission statements designed around the satisfaction notion, marketing plans and incentive programs that target satisfaction as a goal, and consumer communications that trumpet awards for satisfaction achievements in the marketplace.[32]

CONCLUSION

The three-stage model of service consumption—prepurchase, service encounter, and postencounter—helps us to understand how individuals recognize their needs; search for alternative solutions; address perceived risks; choose, use, and experience a particular service; and finally, evaluate their service experience resulting in a customer satisfaction outcome. The various models we explored for each of the stages are complementary and together provide a rich and deep understanding of consumer behavior in a services context. In all types of services, managing customer behavior in the three stages of service consumption effectively is central to creating satisfied customers who will be willing to enter into long-term relationships with the service provider. As such, gaining a better understanding of customer behavior should lie at the heart of all services marketing strategies, which we discuss in much of the remainder of this book.

Chapter Summary

LO1 Service consumption can be divided into the following stages: (1) the prepurchase stage, (2) the service encounter stage, and (3) the postencounter stage.

The prepurchase stage consists of the following four steps: (1) awareness of need, (2) information search, (3) evaluation of alternative solutions and suppliers, and (4) making a purchase decision.

The following theories help us to better understand consumer behavior in this stage:

LO2
- *Service attributes.* People often have difficulty in evaluating the services because services tend to have a high proportion of experience and credence attributes that make it difficult for consumers to evaluate services before purchase.
- *Perceived risk.* Because many services are hard to evaluate, consumers perceive higher risk. As customers do not like to take risks and prefer safe choices, firms should employ risk reduction strategies such as offering free trials and guarantees.

LO3
- *Service expectations.* These are shaped by the information search and evaluation of service attributes. The components of expectations include desired, adequate, and predicted service levels. Between the desired and adequate service levels is the zone of tolerance, within which customers are willing to accept variation in service levels.
- *Purchase decision.* The outcome of the prepurchase stage is a purchase decision, based largely on attribute performance expectations and risk perceptions of alternative solutions. Many decisions involve complex tradeoffs along several attributes, typically including price.

In the service encounter stage, the customer initiates, experiences, and consumes the service. A number of concepts and models help us to better understand customer behavior in this stage:

LO4
- The *moment-of-truth metaphor* refers to customer touchpoints that can make or break a customer relationship.

LO5
- We distinguish between *high-* and *low-contact services.* High-contact services are challenging as they have many points of contact and moments of truth that have to be managed. In contrast, low-contact services are mostly delivered via websites, equipment (e.g., ATMs), or call centers with relatively few customer interfaces.

LO6
- The *servuction model* encompasses a technical core and a service delivery system.
- The *technical core* is back-stage and *invisible* to the customers, but what happens back-stage can affect the quality of front-stage activities. Therefore, back-stage activities have to be coordinated with front-stage activities.
- The *service delivery system* is front-stage and visible to the customer. It encompasses all the interactions that together create the service experience, which in a high-contact service includes customer interactions with the service environment, its service employees, and with other customers. Each type of interaction can create or destroy value. Firms have to orchestrate all these interactions to create a satisfying service experience.

LO7
- *Theater can be used as a metaphor* for service delivery, and firms can view their service as "staging" a performance with props and actors, and manage them accordingly. The props are the service facilities and equipment. The actors are the service employees and customers.

LO8
- Each of the actors needs to understand their roles and scripts in order to perform their part of the service well. Firms can make use of the *role* and *script theories* to better design, train, communicate, and manage both employee and customer scripts and roles.

LO9 In the postencounter stage, customers evaluate the service performance and compare it with their prior expectations.

- Satisfaction is a continuum from very high satisfaction to deep dissatisfaction. As long as perceived performance falls within the zone of tolerance, that is, above the adequate service level, customers will be reasonably satisfied. As performance perceptions approach or exceed desired levels, customers will be very satisfied.
- Customer delight occurs when positive disconfirmation is coupled with pleasure and surprise.
- Very satisfied customers are more likely to make repeat purchases, remain loyal to that supplier, and spread positive word of mouth. Dissatisfied customers, however, may complain or switch service providers.

Review Questions

1. Explain the three-stage model of service consumption.
2. Describe search, experience, and credence attributes, and give examples of each.
3. Explain why services tend to be harder for customers to evaluate than goods.
4. Why does consumer perception of risk constitute an important aspect in selecting, purchasing, and using services? How can firms reduce consumer risk perceptions?
5. How are customers' expectations formed? Explain the difference between desired service and adequate service with reference to a service experience you've had recently.
6. What are "moments of truth"?
7. Describe the difference between high-contact and low-contact services, and explain how the nature of a customer's experience may differ between the two.
8. Choose a service you are familiar with, and create a diagram that represents the servuction system. Define the "front-stage" and "back-stage" activities.
9. How do the concepts of theatrical perspective, role theory, and script theory help to provide insights into consumer behavior during the service encounter?
10. Describe the relationship between customer expectations and customer satisfaction.

Application Exercises

1. Select three services: one high in search attributes, one high in experience attributes, and one high in credence attributes. Specify what product characteristics make them easy or difficult for consumers to evaluate, and suggest specific strategies that marketers can adopt in each case to facilitate evaluation and reduce perceived risk.
2. Develop a simple questionnaire designed to measure the key components of customer expectations (i.e., desired, adequate, and predicted service and the zone of tolerance). Conduct 10 interviews with key target customers of a service of your choice to understand the structure of their expectations. Based on your findings, develop recommendations for firms offering this service.
3. What are the back-stage elements of (a) a car repair facility, (b) an airline, (c) a university, and (d) a consulting firm? Under what circumstances would it be appropriate or even desirable to allow customers to see some of these back-stage elements, and how would you do it?
4. What roles are played by front-stage service employees in low-contact organizations? Are these roles more or less important to customer satisfaction than in high-contact services?
5. Visit the facilities of two competing service firms in the same industry (e.g., banks, restaurants, or gas stations) that you believe have different approaches to service. Compare and contrast their approaches using suitable frameworks from this chapter.
6. Apply the script and role theories to a service of your choice. What insights can you give that would be useful for management?
7. Develop two different customer scripts, one for a highly standardized service and one for a highly customized service. Map all key customer steps of this script across the three stages of service consumption. What are the key differences between the standardized and customized service?
8. Describe an unsatisfactory encounter you experienced recently with (a) a low-contact service provider via email, mail, or phone and (b) a high–contact, face-to-face service provider. What were the key drivers of your dissatisfaction with these encounters? In each instance, what could the service provider have done to improve the situation?

Endnotes

1. Adapted from Christopher Lovelock and Lauren Wright, *Principles of Services Marketing and Management*, 2nd ed. Prentice Hall, 2001.
2. B. Joseph Pin and James H. Gilmore, "Welcome to the Experience Economy," *Harvard Business Review*, 76, July–August 1998, 97–108.
3. Valarie A. Zeithaml, "How Consumer Evaluation Processes Differ Between Goods and Services," in J. A. Donnelly and W. R. George, eds. *Marketing of Services*, Chicago: American Marketing Association, 1981, 186–190.
4. Leonard L. Berry and Neeli Bendapudi, "Clueing in Customers," *Harvard Business Review*, 81, February 2003, 100–107.
5. C. M. Ikemba et al., "Internet Use in Families with Children Requiring Cardiac Surgery for Congenital Heart Disease," *Pediatrics*, 109, No. 3, 2002, 419–422.
6. Valarie A. Zeithaml, Leonard L. Berry, and A. Parasuraman, "The Behavioral Consequences of Service Quality," *Journal of Marketing*, 60, April 1996, 31–46; R. Kenneth Teas and Thomas E. DeCarlo, "An Examination and Extension of the Zone-of-Tolerance Model: A Comparison of Performance-Based Models on Perceived Quality," *Journal of Service Research*, 6, No. 3, 2004, 272–286.
7. Cathy Johnson and Brian P. Mathews, "The Influence of Experience on Service Expectations," *International Journal of Service Industry Management*, 8, No. 4, 1997, 46–61.
8. Robert Johnston, "The Zone of Tolerance: Exploring the Relationship between Service Transactions and Satisfaction with the Overall Service," *International Journal of Service Industry Management*, 6, No. 5, 1995, 46–61.
9. Halil Nadiri and Kashif Hussain, "Diagnosing the Zone of Tolerance for Hotel Services," *Managing Service Quality*, 15, No. 5, 2005, 259–277.
10. Lynn Shostack, "Planning the Service Encounter," in J. A. Czepiel, M. R. Solomon, and C. F. Surprenant, eds. *The Service Encounter.* Lexington, MA: Lexington Books, 1985, 243–254.
11. Normann first used the term "moments of truth" in a Swedish study in 1978; subsequently it appeared in English in Richard Normann, *Service Management: Strategy and Leadership in Service Businesses*, 2nd ed. Chichester, UK: John Wiley & Sons, 1991, 16–17.
12. Jan Carlzon, *Moments of Truth,* Cambridge, MA: Ballinger Publishing Co., 1987, 3.
13. Pierre Eiglier and Eric Langeard, "Services as Systems: Marketing Implications," in Pierre Eiglier, Eric Langeard, Christopher H. Lovelock, John E. G. Bateson, and Robert F. Young, eds. *Marketing Consumer Services: New Insights.* Cambridge, MA: Marketing Science Institute, Report # 77–115, November 1977, 83–103; Eric Langeard, John E. Bateson, Christopher H. Lovelock, and Pierre Eiglier, *Services Marketing: New Insights from Consumers and Managers,* Marketing Science Institute, Report # 81–104, August 1981.
14. Adapted from Pierre Eiglier and Eric Langeard, "Services as Systems: Marketing Implications," in Pierre Eiglier, Eric Langeard, Christopher H. Lovelock, John E. G. Bateson, and Robert F. Young, eds. *Marketing Consumer Services: New Insights.* Cambridge, MA: Marketing Science Institute, Report # 77-115, November 1977, 83–103; Eric Langeard, John E. Bateson, Christopher H. Lovelock, and Pierre Eiglier, *Services Marketing: New Insights from Consumers and Managers,* Marketing Science Institute, Report # 81-104, August 1981.
15. Richard B. Chase, "Where Does the Customer Fit in a Service Organization?" *Harvard Business Review*, 56, November–December 1978, 137–142. Stephen J. Grove, Raymond P. Fisk, and Joby John, "Services as Theater: Guidelines and Implications," in Teresa A. Schwartz and Dawn Iacobucci, eds. *Handbook of Services Marketing and Management,* Thousand Oaks, CA: Sage, 2000, 21–36.
16. Stephen J. Grove, Raymond P. Fisk, and Joby John, "Services as Theater: Guidelines and Implications," in Teresa A. Schwartz and Dawn Iacobucci, eds. *Handbook of Services Marketing and Management,* Thousand Oaks, CA: Sage, 2000, 21–36; Steve Baron, Kim Harris, and Richard Harris, "Retail Theater: The 'Intended Effect' of the Performance," *Journal of Service Research*, 4, May 2003, 316–332; Richard Harris, Kim Harris, and Steve Baron, "Theatrical Service Experiences: Dramatic Script Development with Employees," *International Journal of Service Industry Management*, 14, No. 2, 2003, 184–199.
17. Stephen J. Grove and Raymond P. Fisk, "The Dramaturgy of Services Exchange: An Analytical Framework for Services Marketing," in L. L. Berry, G. L. Shostack, and G. D. Upah, eds. *Emerging Perspectives on Services Marketing,* Chicago, IL: The American Marketing Association, 1983, 45–49.
18. Michael R. Solomon, Carol Suprenant, John A. Czepiel, and Evelyn G. Gutman, "A Role Theory Perspective on Dyadic Interactions: The Service Encounter," *Journal of Marketing*, 49, Winter 1985, 99–111.
19. See R. P. Abelson, "Script Processing in Attitude Formation and Decision-Making," in J. S. Carrol and J. W. Payne, eds. *Cognitive and Social Behavior.* Hillsdale, NJ: Erlbaum, 1976, 33–45; Richard Harris, Kim Harris, and Steve Baron, "Theatrical Service Experiences: Dramatic Script Development with Employees," *International Journal of Service Industry Management*, 14, No. 2, 2003, 184–199.
20. Richard L. Oliver, "Customer Satisfaction with Service," in Teresa A. Schwartz and Dawn Iacobucci, eds. *Handbook of Service Marketing and Management,* Thousand Oaks, CA: Sage Publications, 2000, 247–254; Jochen Wirtz and Anna S. Mattila, "Exploring the Role of Alternative Perceived Performance Measures and Needs-Congruency in the Consumer Satisfaction Process," *Journal of Consumer Psychology*, 11, No. 3, 2001, 181–192.
21. Richard L. Oliver, *Satisfaction: A Behavioral Perspective on the Consumer,* New York: McGraw-Hill, 1997.
22. Jaishankar Ganesh, Mark J. Arnold, and Kristy E. Reynolds, "Understanding the Customer Base of Service Providers: An Examination of the Differences Between Switchers and Stayers," *Journal of Marketing*, 64, No. 3, 2000, 65–87.
23. Uday Karmarkar, "Will You Survive the Service Revolution?" *Harvard Business Review*, June 2004, 101–108.
24. Ray W. Coye, "Managing Customer Expectations in the Service Encounter," *International Journal of Service Industry Management*, 15, No. 4, 2004: 54–71.
25. Jochen Wirtz and Anna S. Mattila, "Exploring the Role of Alternative Perceived Performance Measures and

Needs-Congruency in the Consumer Satisfaction Process," *Journal of Consumer Psychology*, 11, No. 3, 2001, 181–192.

26. Jochen Wirtz, "Halo in Customer Satisfaction Measures—The Role of Purpose of Rating, Number of Attributes, and Customer Involvement," *International Journal of Service Industry Management*, 14, No. 1, 2003, 96–119.
27. Richard L. Oliver, Roland T. Rust, and Sajeev Varki, "Customer Delight: Foundations, Findings, and Managerial Insight," *Journal of Retailing*, 73, Fall 1997, 311–336.
28. Roland T. Rust and Richard L. Oliver, "Should We Delight the Customer?" *Journal of the Academy of Marketing Science*, 28, No. 1, 2000, 86–94.
29. Claes Fornell, David VanAmburg, Forrest Morgeson, Eugene W. Anderson, Barbara Everitt Bryant, and Michael D. Johnson, *The American Customer Satisfaction Index at Ten Years—A Summary of Findings: Implications for the Economy, Stock Returns and Management*. Ann Arbor, MI: National Quality Research Center, University of Michigan, 2005, 54.
30. Eugene W. Anderson and Vikas Mittal, "Strengthening the Satisfaction-Profit Chain," *Journal of Service Research*, 3, November 2000, 107–120.
31. Claes Fornell, David VanAmburg, Forrest Morgeson, Eugene W. Anderson, Barbara Everitt Bryant, and Michael D. Johnson, *The American Customer Satisfaction Index at Ten Years—A Summary of Findings: Implications for the Economy, Stock Returns and Management*. Ann Arbor, MI: National Quality Research Center, University of Michigan, 2005, 40.
32. Susan Fournier and David Glen Mick, "Rediscovering Satisfaction," *Journal of Marketing*, 63, October 1999, 5–23.

CHAPTER 3

Positioning Services in Competitive Markets

To succeed in our overcommunicated society, a company must create a position in the prospect's mind, a position that takes into consideration not only a company's own strengths and weaknesses, but those of its competitors as well.

AL REIS AND JACK TROUT

The essence of strategy is choosing to perform activities differently than rivals do.

MICHAEL PORTER

LEARNING OBJECTIVES (LOs)

By the end of this chapter, the reader should be able to:

LO1 Know positioning strategy in a services context.

LO2 Understand the four focus strategies to achieve competitive advantage.

LO3 Learn how to identify and select target segments.

LO4 Distinguish between important and determinant attributes for consumer choice and positioning services.

LO5 Understand how to use service levels for positioning services.

LO6 Understand how to develop an effective positioning strategy using market, internal, and competitor analysis.

LO7 Demonstrate how positioning maps help to analyze and respond to the dynamics of competitive positioning.

Positioning a Chain of Child Care Centers away from the Competition

Roger Brown and Linda Mason met at business school, following previous experience as management consultants. After graduation, they operated programs for refugee children in Cambodia and then ran a "Save the Children" relief program in East Africa. When they returned to the U.S., they saw a need for child-care centers that would provide caring, educational environments and give parents confidence in their children's well-being.

Through research, they discovered an industry that had many weaknesses. There were no barriers to entry, profit margins were low, the industry was labor intensive, there were low economies of scale, there was no clear brand differentiation, and there was a lack of regulation in the industry. Brown and Mason developed a service concept that would allow them to turn these industry weaknesses into strengths for their own company, Bright Horizons (BH). Instead of marketing their services directly to parents—a one-customer-at-a-time sale—BH formed partnerships with companies seeking to offer an on-site day-care center for employees with small children. The advantages included:

- A powerful, low-cost marketing channel.
- A partner/customer who supplied the funds to build and equip the center and would therefore want to help BH to achieve its goal of delivering high-quality care.
- Benefits for parents, who would be attracted to a BH center (rather than competing alternatives) because of its nearness to their own workplace, thus lowering traveling time and offering greater peace of mind.

BH offered a high pay and benefits package to attract the best staff, so that they could provide quality service, one aspect that was lacking in the other providers. Since traditional approaches to child care either did not have a proper teaching plan, or had strict, cookie-cutter lesson plans, BH developed a flexible teaching plan. It was called "World at Their Fingertips," and had a course outline, but gave teachers control over daily lesson plans.

The company sought accreditation for its centers from the National Association for the Education of Young Children (NAEYC) and actively promoted this. BH's emphasis on quality meant that it could meet or exceed the highest local/state government licensing standards. As a result, lack of regulation became an opportunity, not a threat for BH and gives it a source of competitive advantage.

With the support and help from its clients, which include many hi-tech firms, BH has developed innovative technologies such as streaming video of its classrooms to the parents' desktop computers; digitally scanned or photographed artwork; electronic posting of menus, calendars, and student assessments; as well as online student assessment capabilities. All of these serve to differentiate BH and help it to stay ahead of the competition.

BH sees labor as a competitive advantage. It seeks to recruit and retain the best people. It has been named by FORTUNE magazine for the ninth time as among the "100 Best Companies to Work for" in the U.S. in 2008. In the UK, Bright Horizons has been recognized as one of the 2007 *Financial Times* 50 Best Workplaces. By mid-2009, Bright Horizons had some 20,000 employees worldwide, and was operating more than 600 centers in the U.S., Canada, and Europe for over 700 of the world's leading employers, including corporations, hospitals, universities, and government offices. Clients want to hire BH as a partner because they know they can trust the staff.

Source: Roger Brown, "How We Built a Strong Company in a Weak Industry," *Harvard Business Review*, February 2001, 51–57; www.brighthorizons.com, accessed June 2, 2009.

WHAT IS REQUIRED FOR POSITIONING SERVICES EFFECTIVELY?

In an industry with low barriers of entry and a lot of competition, Bright Horizons managed to find a niche position and differentiated itself from the competition. They linked up with employers instead of individual parents, emphasized service quality, and used accreditation as a selling point. As competition intensifies in the service sector, it is becoming ever more important for service organizations to differentiate their products in ways that are meaningful to customers. This is especially true for many mature service industries (e.g., banking, insurance, hospitality, and education) where, for a firm to grow, it has to take share from its competitors or expand into new markets. However, ask a group of managers from different service businesses how they compete, and the chances are high that many will say simply, "on service." Press them a little further, and they may add words and phrases such as "value for money," "service quality," "our people," or "convenience." None of this is very helpful to a marketing specialist trying to develop a meaningful value proposition and a viable business model for a service product that will enable it to compete profitably in the marketplace.

At issue is what makes consumers or institutional buyers select—and remain loyal to—one supplier over another. Terms such as "service" typically subsume a variety of specific characteristics, ranging from the speed with which a service is delivered to the quality of interactions between customers and service personnel; and from avoiding errors to providing desirable "extras" to supplement the core service. Likewise, "convenience" could refer to a service that's delivered at a convenient location, available at convenient times, or easy to use. Without knowing which product features are of specific interest to customers, it's hard for managers to develop an appropriate strategy. In a highly competitive environment, there's a risk that customers will perceive little real difference between competing alternatives and so make their choices based on who offers the lowest price.

Positioning strategy is concerned with creating, communicating, and maintaining distinctive differences that will be noticed and valued by those customers with whom the firm would most like to develop a long-term relationship. Successful positioning requires managers to understand their target customers' preferences, their conception of value, and the characteristics of their competitors' offerings. Price and product attributes are two of the 4 Ps of marketing that are most commonly associated with positioning strategy. For services, however, positioning often relates also to other Ps of the services marketing mix, including service processes (e.g., their convenience, ease of use), distribution systems, service schedules, locations, the service's environment, and service personnel. Competitive strategy can take many different routes. George Day observes:

> The diversity of ways a business can achieve a competitive advantage quickly defeats any generalizations or facile prescriptions... First and foremost, a business must set itself apart from its competition. To be successful, it must identify and promote itself as the best provider of attributes that are important to target customers.[1]

This means that managers need to think systematically about all facets of the service offering and emphasize competitive advantage on those attributes that will be valued by customers in their target segment(s). Achieving a competitive advantage typically requires a firm to focus, which we will discuss next.

ACHIEVE COMPETITIVE ADVANTAGE THROUGH FOCUS

It's usually not realistic for a firm to try to appeal to all potential buyers in a market, because customers are varied in their needs, purchasing behavior, and consumption patterns and often too numerous and geographically widely spread. Service firms also vary widely in their abilities to serve different types of customers well. Hence, rather than trying to compete in an entire market, each company needs to focus its efforts on those customers it can serve best. In marketing terms, *focus* means providing a relatively narrow product mix for a particular market segment—a group of buyers who share common characteristics, needs, purchasing behavior, or consumption patterns. Nearly all successful service firms apply this concept. They have identified the strategically important elements in their service operations and concentrate their resources on them.

The extent of a company's focus can be described along two dimensions: market focus and service focus.[2] *Market focus* is the extent to which a firm serves few or many markets, while *service focus* describes the extent to which a firm offers few or many services. These two dimensions define the four basic focus strategies shown in Figure 3.1. The four focus strategies are:

- ***Fully focused.*** A fully focused organization provides a limited range of services (perhaps just a single core product) to a narrow and specific market segment. Developing recognized expertise in a well-defined niche may provide protection against would-be competitors and allows a firm to charge premium prices. An example of a fully focused firm is Shouldice Hospital, featured in Case 10. The hospital performs only a single surgery (hernia) on otherwise healthy patients (mostly men in their 40s to 60s). Because of their focus, their surgery and service quality are superb.
- ***Market focused.*** A market focused company concentrates on a narrow market segment, but has a wide range of services. Best Practice in Action 3.1 features the example of Rentokil Initial, a provider of business-to-business services. Rentokil has profited from the growing trend in outsourcing of services related to facilities maintenance, which has enabled it to develop a large range of services for its clients.
- ***Service focused.*** Service focused firms offer a narrow range of services to a fairly broad market. However, as new segments are added, firms need to develop knowledge and skills in serving each segment. Lasik eye surgery clinics and Starbucks coffee shops follow this strategy, serving a broad customer base with a largely standardized product.
- ***Unfocused.*** Finally, many service providers fall into the unfocused category, because they try to serve broad markets and provide a wide range of services. The danger with this strategy is that unfocused firms often are "jacks of all trades and masters of none." In general, that's not a good idea, although public utilities and government agencies may be obliged to do so. A few departmental stores followed this strategy, and as a result have been struggling against more focused competitors (e.g., hypermarkets and specialty stores).

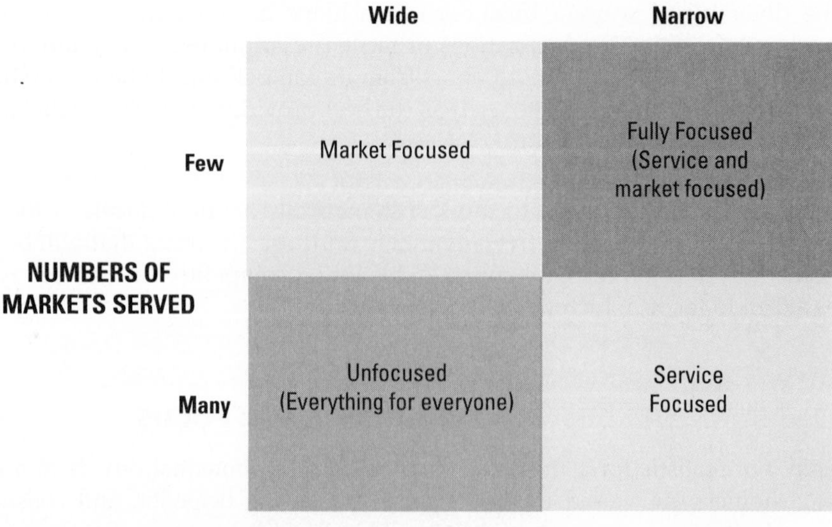

FIGURE 3.1 Basic Focus Strategies for Services

Source: Robert Johnston, "Achieving Focus in Service Organizations." *The Service Industries Journal*, 16 (January 1996): 10–20.

BEST PRACTICE IN ACTION 3.1

Positioning a Brand Across Multiple Services at Rentokil Initial

With revenue for the first quarter of 2009 at £635 million (USD 1.05 billion), Rentokil Initial is one of the world's largest business support service companies. The company has about 78,000 employees in over 50 countries where the "Rentokil" and "Initial" brands have come to represent innovation, deep expertise, and consistent quality of service. The UK-based firm has evolved substantially from its origins as a manufacturer of rat poison and a pesticide for killing wood-destroying beetles. When the firm realized it could make more money by providing a service to kill rodents than by selling products customers would use themselves to target these pests, it shifted to pest control and extermination services.

Through organic growth and acquisitions, Rentokil Initial has developed an extensive product range that includes testing and safety services, security, package delivery, interior plants landscaping (including sale or rental of tropical plants), specialized cleaning services, pest control, uniform rental and cleaning, clinical waste collection and disposal, personnel services, and a washroom attendant service that supplies and maintains a full array of equipment, dispensers, and consumables.

The firm sees its core competence as "the ability to carry out high-quality services on other people's premises through well-recruited, well-trained, and motivated staff." In the United States, Rentokill's Buffalo Grove, Illinois-headquartered subsidiary, Ambius, serves 25,000 customers coast-to-coast and in Canada. Its 1,400 employees manage 1.6 million office plants, producing annual revenues of $112 million. It is the only national supplier of such services in a highly fragmented industry in which competition is local in character.

Promoting use of additional services to existing customers is an important aspect of the firm's strategy. Initial Integrated Services offers clients the opportunity to move beyond the established concept of "bundling" services—bringing together several free-standing support services contracts from one provider—to full integration of services. Clients purchase sector-specific solutions that deliver multiple services but feature just "one invoice, one account manager, one help desk, one contract, and one motivated service team."

According to former chief executive, Sir Clive Thomson:

> Our objective has been to create a virtuous circle. We provide a quality service in industrial and commercial activities under the same brand-name, so that a customer satisfied with one Rentokil Initial Service is potentially a satisfied customer for another. . . . Although it was considered somewhat odd at the time, one of the reasons we moved into [providing and maintaining] tropical plants [for building interiors] was in fact to put the brand in front of decision makers. Our service people maintaining the plants go in through the front door and are visible to the customer. This contrasts with pest control where no one really notices unless we fail. . . . The brand stands for honesty, reliability, consistency, integrity and technical leadership.

Investment in R&D ensures constant improvement in its many service lines. For example, the company has built the RADAR intelligent rodent trap. RADAR attracts rats and mice into a sealable chamber and kills them humanely by injecting carbon dioxide. Using Rentokil's unique "pestconnect" technology, the trap causes emails to be sent to the customer and the local branch when a rodent is caught, and a Rentokil technician receives a text message identifying which unit has been activated at which customer's premises, and its precise location. Pestconnect checks each individual RADAR unit every 10 minutes, 24/7. Getting information in real time enables technicians to remove dead rodents promptly and to control future infestation better.

Rentokil Initial's success lies in its ability to position each of its many business services in terms of the company's core brand values, which include providing superior standards of customer care and utilizing the most technologically advanced services and products. The brand image is reinforced through physical evidence in terms of distinctive uniforms, vehicle color schemes, and use of the corporate logo.

Source: Clive Thompson, "Rentokil Initial: Building a Strong Corporate Brand for Growth and Diversity," in F. Gilmore (ed.) *Brand Warriors* (London: HarperCollinsBusiness, 1997), p. 123–124; TXT Technology 4 Pest Control, press release, December 6, 2005, www.rentokil-initial.com, accessed May 5, 2009.

It is recommended that firms have some sort of focus, whether on market segments or on services. Firms should not use the unfocused strategy as this will only dilute their efforts and cause them to spread their resources too thin when they try to do many things at the same time. How then should a firm select which of the three alternative "focused" strategies to pursue?

Each strategy has opportunities (as discussed above), but also risks. The biggest risk of the fully focused strategy is that the market may be too small to get the volume of business needed for financial success. Other risks of the fully focused strategy include the danger that demand for the service may decrease because of alternative products, new technologies offered by other providers, or that purchasers in the chosen segment may be affected by an economic downturn.

To hedge against such risks, some firms with a narrow product line elect to serve multiple segments and create a portfolio of customers (i.e., pursue a service-focused strategy). However, as new segments are added, the firm needs to develop expertise in serving each segment, which may require a broader sales effort and greater investment in marketing communication—particularly in B2B markets.

Finally, offering a broad product line to a narrowly defined target segment (i.e., a market focused strategy) often looks attractive, because it offers the potential of selling multiple services to a single purchaser. However, before choosing a market focused strategy, managers need to be sure their firms have the operational capability to do an excellent job of delivering each of the different services selected. They also need to understand customer purchasing practices and preferences. In a B2B context, when trying to cross-sell additional services to the same client, many firms have been disappointed to find that decisions on purchasing the new service are made by an entirely different group within the client company.

MARKET SEGMENTATION FORMS THE BASIS FOR FOCUSED STRATEGIES

Segmentation is one of the most important concepts in marketing. Service firms vary widely in their abilities to serve different types of customers. Hence, rather than trying to compete in an entire market, perhaps against superior competitors, each firm should adopt a strategy of market segmentation, identifying those parts, or segments, of the market that it can serve best. Firms in tune with customer requirements may choose to employ a needs-based segmentation approach, focusing on those customers who value specific attributes.[3]

Identifying and Selecting Target Segments

A *market segment* is composed of a group of buyers who share common characteristics, needs, purchasing behavior, or consumption patterns. Effective segmentation groups buyers into segments in ways that result in as much similarity as possible on the relevant characteristics within each segment, but dissimilarity on those same characteristics between segments.

A *target segment* is one that a firm has selected from among those in the broader market and may be defined on the basis of several variables. For instance, a department store in a particular city might target residents of the metropolitan area (geographic segmentation), who have incomes within a certain range (demographic segmentation), value personal service from knowledgeable staff, and are not highly price sensitive (both reflecting segmentation according to expressed attitudes and behavioral intentions). Because at least some competing retailers in the city will be targeting the same customers, the department store has to create a distinctive appeal (appropriate characteristics to highlight might include a wide array of merchandise categories, breadth of selection within each product category, and the availability of such supplementary services as advice and home delivery). Service firms that are developing strategies based on use of technology recognize that customers can also be segmented according to their degree of competence and comfort in using technology-based delivery systems.[4]

Some market segments offer better sales and profit opportunities than others. Marketers should select not only on the basis of their sales and profit potential, but also with reference to the firm's ability to match or exceed competing offerings directed at the same segment. Sometimes research will show that certain market segments are "underserved," meaning that their needs are not well met by existing suppliers. Such markets often are surprisingly large. For example, in many emerging-market economies, huge numbers of consumers have incomes that are too small to attract the interest of service businesses accustomed to focus on the needs of more affluent customers. Collectively, however, small wage earners represent a very big market and may offer even greater potential for the future, provided we can tap them and create more value. Service Perspective 3.1 describes an innovative approach to providing financial services to lower-income households in the emerging markets like UAE, the Philippines, and India.

SERVICE PERSPECTIVE 3.1

MOBILE REMITTANCE

Of the 4 million residents in the United Arab Emirates (UAE), more than 80 percent are expatriates. UAE is the third-largest remittance source in the world and second in the Gulf after Saudi Arabia, with more than USD $7 billion being remitted annually. The World Bank estimates that remittances in 2008 reached USD $397 billion, and the unofficial remittances could be double that estimate. A study by Adams and Page (2005) finds that, for every dollar remitted from abroad compared with every dollar generated by domestic economic activity, poverty alleviation in the home country was much higher for money remitted.

The migrant labor segment, which is at the bottom half of the economic pyramid, is very regular in remittance payments, sending up to 80 percent of their individual salaries monthly to support family in their home countries. These micro-transactions (small value amounts) are often routed through unofficial, or *hawala,* channels. Price sensitivity is very high for this segment. They would like to monitor foreign exchange rates to get the best rates but are often limited from remitting money on lucrative days due to work responsibilities or inability to access a service as work or lodging is far from the main city. From a country perspective, *hawala* is to be discouraged as the money becomes untraceable and can be used for illegal activities like terrorism.

UAE Exchange, one of the largest exchange houses in the Middle East, with a presence in more than 64 countries, has more than 20 percent of the UAE population registered as customers. In 2005, it introduced the UAE Exchange Wallet, which allows UAE Exchange customers to remit money using their existing mobile phones anywhere and at any time. In 2008, Western Union brought in a similar service between UAE and the Philippines, which had the fourth highest remittances in 2008. The Philippines already had more than 6,000 merchant locations where mobile phone payment was accepted; hence, adoption of this new service is higher. Etisalat, UAE's largest telecom provider, entered the remittance market in 2008 focussing on India, which had the world's highest remittance in 2008, by partnering with Mashreq Bank, Tata Communications, Idea Cellular, and HSBC India, though, due to regulatory issues from India, it was still getting operationalized in 2009.

Though this service is able to target a neglected segment and offer convenience and better rates, there are still adoption problems. Perhaps comfort level with technology and auxiliary services, like merchant acceptance of mobile payment, are issues. Rural coverage is vital, as these lower-income segments are spread over remote areas, where mobile reception could be low. Visit the sites of the mobile remittance companies mentioned, and see how well they are doing.

Sources: Adams, Jr., R. H., and Page, J. (2005), "Do International Migration and Remittances Reduce Poverty in Developing Countries?" *World Development,* Vol. 33, No. 10, pp. 1645–1669; Saleem, N. (2008), "Etisalat Gears Up to Offer Mobile Remittance Services," April 2, 2008, www.gulfnews.com/; Sudhir, N. (2009), "Remit Money Using Your Phone Soon," May 21, 2009, www.business24-7.ae/; "UAE Exchange Launches UAE Exchange Wallet," January 10, 2005, www.ameinfo.com/; World Bank (2009), "Remittances Prices Worldwide," remittanceprices.worldbank.org/; Walid, T. (2008), "UAE Pilots Mobile Money Transfer System," November 11, 2008, www.arabianbusiness.com/.

SERVICE ATTRIBUTES AND LEVELS

Once a target segment has been selected, firms need to provide their market with the right service concept. For this, formal research often is needed to identify which attributes of a given service are important to specific segments and how well prospective customers perceive competing organizations as performing against these attributes. However, you need to recognize that the same individuals may set different priorities for attributes according to:

- The purpose of using the service.
- Who makes the decision.
- The timing of use (time of day/week/season).
- Whether the customer is using the service alone or with a group, and if the latter, the composition of that group.

Consider the criteria you might use when choosing a restaurant for lunch when you are (1) on vacation with friends or family, (2) meeting with a prospective business client, or (3) going for a quick meal with a coworker. Given a reasonable selection of alternatives, it's unlikely that you would choose the same type of restaurant in each instance, let alone the same one. It's possible, too, that if you left the decision to another person in the party, he or she would make a different choice. It is therefore important to be quite specific about the occasion and context a service is purchased for.

Important versus Determinant Attributes

Consumers usually make their choices among alternative service offerings on the basis of perceived differences between them. However, the attributes that distinguish competing services from one another are not always the most important ones. For instance, many travelers rank "safety" as their number one consideration in air travel. They may avoid traveling on unknown carriers or on an airline that has a poor safety reputation, but after eliminating such alternatives from consideration, a traveler flying on major routes still is likely to have several choices of carriers perceived as equally safe. Hence, safety usually is not an attribute that influences the customer's choice at this point.

Determinant attributes (i.e., those that actually determine buyers' choices between competing alternatives) often are way down on the list of service characteristics important to purchasers, but they are the attributes on which customers see significant differences among competing alternatives. For example, convenience of departure and arrival times, availability of frequent flyer miles and related loyalty privileges, quality of inflight service, or the ease of making reservations might be determinant characteristics for business travelers when selecting an airline. For budget-conscious vacation travelers, on the other hand, price might assume primary importance.

The marketing researchers' task, of course, is to survey customers in the target segment, identify the relative importance of various attributes, and then ask which ones have been determinant during recent decisions involving a choice of service suppliers. Researchers also need to be aware of how well each competing service is perceived by customers as performing on these attributes. Findings from such research form the necessary basis for developing a positioning (or repositioning) campaign.[5]

Establishing Service Levels

Although we need to understand the difference between important and determinant attributes for our target customers, creating a positioning strategy requires more than just identifying those attributes. Decisions must be also be made on what level of performance to offer on each attribute.[6] Some service attributes are easily quantified, while others are qualitative. Price, for instance, is a quantitative attribute. Punctuality of transport services can be expressed in terms of the percentage of trains, buses, or flights arriving within a specified number of minutes from the scheduled time. Both of these attributes are easy to understand and therefore quantifiable. However, characteristics such as the quality of personal service or a hotel's degree of luxury are more qualitative and therefore subject to individual interpretation. To facilitate both service design and performance measurement, each attribute needs to be operationalized and standards must be established. For instance, if customers say they value physical comfort, what does that mean for a hotel or an airline, beyond the size of the room or the seat? In a hotel context, does it refer to ambient conditions, such as absence of noise? Or to visible, tangible elements such as the bed? In practice, hotel managers need to address both ambient conditions and tangible elements.

Customers often can be segmented according to their willingness to trade off price versus service level across a broad array of attributes within the service concept. Price-insensitive customers are willing to pay a relatively high price to obtain an elevated level of service on each of the attributes important to them. In contrast, price-sensitive customers will look for an inexpensive service that offers a relatively low level of performance on many key attributes (see Service Perspective 3.2)—although there may be others, such as safety, on which they are unwilling to compromise.

SERVICE PERSPECTIVE 3.2

CAPSULE HOTELS

Capsule hotels consist of small rooms almost the size of large cupboards. Some of these cupboard-like rooms cost only about $18 a night. The main benefits of these hotels are convenience and price. They started in space-constrained Japan in the 1980s but did not take off in other parts of the world until recently. Now, capsule hotel chains have been launched in many countries and include Pod Hotel in New York, Yotel in London, Citizen M and Qbic in Amsterdam, and StayOrange.com Hotel in Kuala Lumpur, Malaysia.

These new chains have also modified their service offerings, differentiating themselves from the early capsule hotels in Japan. For example, the Yotel group offers different classes of rooms they call cabins. This concept was derived from the capsule hotels of Japan and the first-class cabins in British Airways airplanes. For example, the premium room includes a double bed that can be converted into a couch at the touch of a button; tables that accommodate hand luggage; a luxury bathroom; and a study desk that unfolds and has all the techno points available, including free Internet access, a flat-screen TV, and 24-hour in-cabin service. The cost of that premium room at the London Heathrow Airport is £80 a night, and the cost for a standard room per day is only £55, a fraction of the typical price for a hotel room in London.

Yotel and Qbic have aggressive growth plans, and we can expect capsule hotels to become a mainstream choice for travelers in the future.

FIGURE 3.2 Yotel Capsule Hotel at Heathrow Airport Terminal 4

Sources: http://www.stayorange.com/; www.yotel.com; http://www.thepodhotel.com/index.html; http://en.wikipedia.org/wiki/Capsule_hotel accessed May 5, 2009; *The Economist*, "Capsule Hotel: Thinking Small," November 17, 2007.

POSITIONING DISTINGUISHES A BRAND FROM ITS COMPETITORS

Once we have segmented the market, and understood determinant attributes and related service levels, we need to see how we can best position our service in a competitive market. Competitive positioning strategy is based on establishing and maintaining a distinctive place in the market for an organization and/or its individual product offerings. Jack Trout distilled the essence of positioning into the following four principles[7]:

1. A company must establish a position in the minds of its targeted customers.
2. The position should be singular, providing one simple and consistent message.
3. The position must set a company apart from its competitors.
4. A company cannot be all things to all people—it must focus its efforts.

These principles apply to any type of organization that competes for customers. Understanding the principles of positioning is key to developing an effective competitive posture. The concept of positioning is certainly not limited to services—indeed, it had its origins in packaged-goods marketing—but it offers valuable insights by forcing service managers to analyze their firm's existing offerings and to provide specific answers to the following six questions:

1. What does our firm currently stand for in the minds of current and prospective customers?
2. What customers do we serve now, and which ones would we like to target in the future?
3. What is the value proposition for each of our current service offerings and what market segments is each one targeted at?
4. How does each of our service products differ from those of our competitors?
5. How well do customers in the chosen target segments perceive our service offerings as meeting their needs?
6. What changes do we need to make to our service offerings in order to strengthen our competitive position within our target segment(s)?

One of the challenges in developing a viable positioning strategy is to avoid the trap of investing too heavily in points of difference that can easily be copied. As researchers Kevin Keller, Brian Sternthal, and Alice Tybout note: "Positioning needs to keep competitors out, not draw them in."[8] When Roger Brown and Linda Mason, founders of the Bright Horizons chain of child-care centers featured in the opening vignette of this chapter, were developing their service concept and business model, they took a long, hard look at the industry.[9] Discovering that for-profit child-care companies had adopted low-cost strategies, Brown and Mason selected a different approach that competitors would find very difficult to copy.

Similarly, it used to be that when large companies were looking for auditing services, they typically turned to one of the Big Four accounting firms, prestigious players offering global coverage. But a growing number of clients are now switching to so-called "Tier Two" accounting firms in a search for better service, a lower bill, or both.[10] Grant Thornton, the fifth largest firm in the industry has successfully positioned itself as offering easy access to partners and having "a passion for the business of accounting." Its advertising promotes an award from J. D. Powers ranking it as achieving "Highest Performance Among Audit Firms Serving Companies with up to $12 billion in Annual Revenue" (Figure 3.3).

DEVELOPING AN EFFECTIVE POSITIONING STRATEGY

After we now understand the importance of focus and the principles of positioning, let us discuss how to develop a positioning strategy. Positioning involves decisions on attributes important to customers. To improve a product's appeal to a specific target segment, it may be necessary to change product features and its available times and locations, or to change the forms of delivery offered. Positioning plays a pivotal role in marketing strategy, because it links market analysis and competitive analysis to internal corporate analysis. From these three, a position statement can be developed that enables the service organization to answer the questions, "What is our product (or service concept), what do we want it to

Source: Courtesy Grant Thornton, LLP.

FIGURE 3.3 Grant Thornton Links Its Passion for Accounting to High Client Satisfaction with Its Auditing Services

become, and what actions must we take to get there?" Table 3.1 summarizes the principal uses of positioning analysis as a diagnostic tool, providing input to decisions relating to product development, service delivery, pricing, and communication strategy.

Developing a positioning strategy can take place at several different levels, depending on the nature of the business in question. Among multisite, multiproduct service businesses, a position might be established for the entire organization, for a given service outlet, or for a specific service offered at that outlet. There must be consistency between the positioning of different services offered at the same location, because the image of one may spill over into the others, especially if perceived to be related. For instance, if a hospital has an excellent reputation for warm and competent obstetrical services, that may enhance perceptions of its services in gynecology and pediatrics. By contrast, it would be detrimental to all three services if their positioning was conflicting.

Because of the intangible, experiential nature of many services, an explicit positioning strategy is valuable in helping prospective customers to get a mental "fix" on what to expect. Failure to select a desired position in the marketplace—and to develop a marketing action plan designed to achieve and hold this position—may result in one of several possible outcomes, all undesirable:

- The organization (or one of its products) is pushed into a position where it faces head-on competition from a stronger competitor.

TABLE 3.1 Principal Uses of Positioning Analysis as a Diagnostic Tool

1. Provide a useful diagnostic tool for defining and understanding the relationships between products and markets:
   - How does the product compare with competitive offerings on specific attributes?
   - How well does product performance meet consumer needs and expectations on specific performance criteria?
   - What is the predicted consumption level for a product with a given set of performance characteristics offered at a given price?
2. Identify market opportunities for
   a. Introducing new products
      - What segments to target?
      - What attributes to offer relative to the competition?
   b. Redesigning (repositioning) existing products
      - Appeal to the same segments or to new ones?
      - What attributes to add, drop, or change?
      - What attributes to emphasize in advertising?
   c. Eliminating products that
      - Do not satisfy consumer needs
      - Face excessive competition
3. Make other marketing mix decisions to preempt or respond to competitive moves:
   a. Distribution strategies
      - Where to offer the product (locations, types of outlet)?
      - When to make the product available?
   b. Pricing strategies
      - How much to charge?
      - What billing and payment procedures to use?
   c. Communication strategies
      - What target audience(s) are most easily convinced that the product offers a competitive advantage on attributes that are important to them?
      - What message(s)? Which attributes should be emphasized and which competitors, if any, should be mentioned as the basis for comparison on those attributes?
      - Which communication channels: personal selling versus different advertising media? (Selected for their ability not only to convey the chosen message(s) to the target audience(s) but also to reinforce the desired image of the product.)

- The organization (product) is pushed into a position nobody else wants, because little customer demand exists.
- The organization's (product's) position is so blurred that nobody really knows its distinctive competence.

Market, Internal, and Competitor Analyses

Positioning links market analysis and competitor analysis to internal corporate analysis. From these three, a position statement can be developed that allows the service organization to answer six questions for developing an effective positioning strategy. Figure 3.4 identifies the basic steps involved in identifying a suitable market position and developing a strategy to reach it.

MARKET ANALYSIS. Market analysis addresses such factors as the overall level and trend of demand and the geographic location of this demand. Is demand increasing or decreasing for the benefits offered by this type of service? Are there regional or international variations in the level of demand? Alternative ways of segmenting the market should be considered and an appraisal made of the size and potential of different market segments. Research may be needed to gain a better understanding not only of customer needs and preferences within each of the different segments, but also of how each perceives the competition.

INTERNAL CORPORATE ANALYSIS. In international corporate analysis, the objective is to identify the organization's resources (financial, human labor and know-how, and physical assets), limitations or constraints, goals (profitability, growth, professional preferences, etc.), and how its values shape the way it does business. Using insights from this analysis, management should be able to select a limited number of target market segments that can be served with either existing or new services.

COMPETITOR ANALYSIS. Identification and analysis of competitors can provide a marketing strategist with a sense of competitors' strengths and weaknesses that may, in

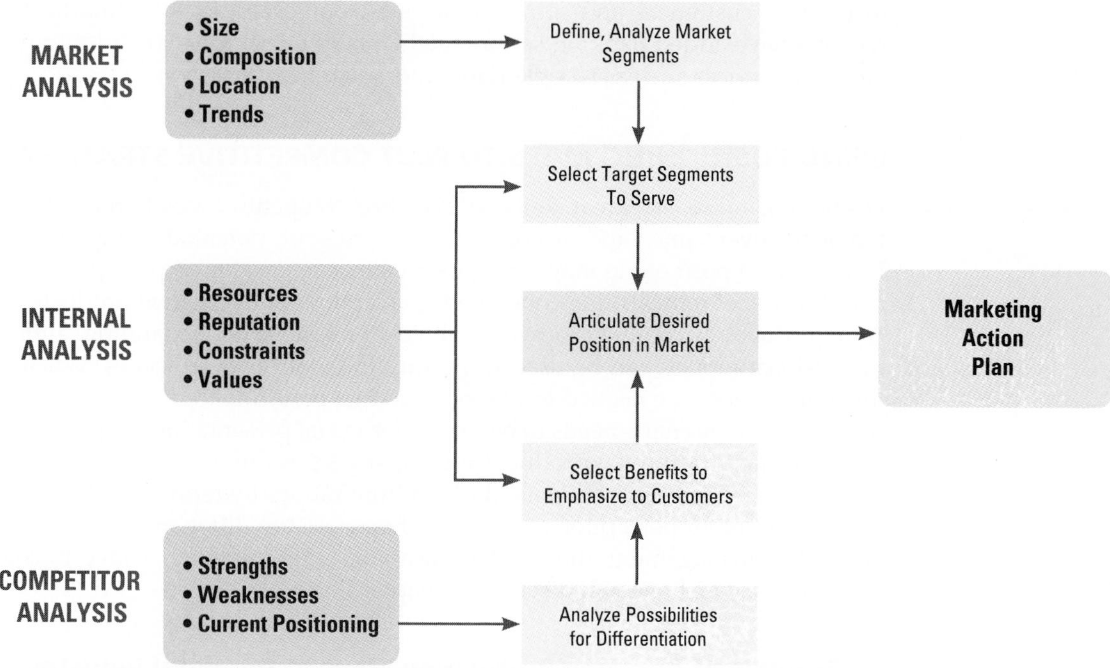

FIGURE 3.4 Developing a Market Positioning Strategy

Sources: Developed from an earlier schematic by Michael R. Pearce.

turn, suggest opportunities for differentiation. Relating these insights back to the internal corporate analysis should suggest what might be viable opportunities for differentiation and competitive advantage, thereby enabling managers to decide which benefits should be emphasized to which target segments. This analysis should consider both direct and indirect competition.

Before deciding on a specific positioning, management should also anticipate responses to potential positioning strategies. For example, management should consider the possibility that one or more competitors might pursue the same market position. Perhaps another service organization has independently conducted the same positioning analysis and arrived at similar conclusions? Or an existing competitor may feel threatened by the new strategy and take steps to reposition its own service to compete more effectively. Alternatively, a new entrant to the market may decide to play "follow the leader," yet offer customers a higher service level on one or more attributes and/or a lower price.

The best way to anticipate possible competitive responses is to identify all current or potential competitors and conduct an internal corporate analysis for each of these competitors.[11] Coupling the insights from the analysis with data from existing market and competitive analysis (with one's own firm cast in the role of competitor) should provide a good sense of how competitors may be likely to act. If chances seem high that a stronger competitor will move to occupy the same niche with a superior service concept, then it would be wise to reconsider the positioning strategy.

POSITION STATEMENT. The outcome of integrating these three forms of analysis (i.e., market analysis, internal corporate analysis, and competitor analysis) is a statement that articulates the desired position of the organization in the marketplace (and, if desired, that of each of the services it offers). Armed with this understanding, marketers can now develop a specific plan of action. The cost of implementing this plan must, of course, be related to the expected payoff.

Such a positioning analysis and its implementation have to be done periodically as positions usually change over time. They change in response to changing market structures, technology, competitive activity, and the evolution of the firm itself. Typically, repositioning includes adding or removing services and target segments. Some companies decrease their offerings and discontinue certain lines of business or services in order to be more focused. Others expanded their offerings to increase sales to existing customers and attract new ones. For example, supermarkets and other retailers have added banking services, while online providers are adding new and innovative services such as Google Earth and YouTube.

USING POSITIONING MAPS TO PLOT COMPETITIVE STRATEGY

Positioning maps are great tools to visualize competitive positioning, to map developments over time, and to develop scenarios of potential competitor responses. Developing a positioning map—a task sometimes referred to as perceptual mapping—is a useful way of representing consumers' perceptions of alternative products graphically. A map usually is confined to two attributes for ease of understanding, although three-dimensional models can be used to portray three of these attributes. When more than three dimensions are needed to describe product performance in a given market, then a series of separate charts needs to be drawn for visual presentation purposes.

Information about a product (or company's position relative to any one attribute) can be inferred from market data, derived from ratings by representative consumers, or both. If consumer perceptions of service characteristics differ sharply from "reality" as defined by management, then communications efforts may be needed to change these perceptions, which we will discuss in Chapter 7.

An Example of Applying Positioning Maps to the Hotel Industry

The hotel business is highly competitive, especially during seasons when the supply of rooms exceeds demand. Within each class of hotels, customers visiting a large city may find several alternatives to choose from. The degree of luxury and comfort in physical amenities will be one choice criterion; research shows that business travelers are concerned not only with the comfort and facilities offered in their rooms (where they may wish to work as well as sleep), but also with other physical spaces, ranging from the reception area to meeting rooms, a business center, restaurants, a swimming pool, and exercise facilities.

The quality and range of services offered by hotel staff is another key criterion: Can a guest get 24-hour room service? Can clothes be laundered and pressed overnight? Is there a knowledgeable concierge on duty? Are there staff available to offer professional business services? There are other choice criteria, too, perhaps relating to the ambiance of the hotel (modern architecture and decor are favored by some customers; others may prefer "Old World" charm and antique furniture). Additional attributes include factors such as quietness, safety, cleanliness, and special rewards programs for frequent guests.

Let's look at an example, based on a real-world situation, of how to apply positioning maps. Managers of the Palace, a successful four-star hotel, developed a positioning map of their own and competing hotels to develop a better understanding of future threats to their established market position in a large city that we will call Belleville.

Located on the edge of the booming financial district, the Palace was an elegant old hotel that had been extensively renovated and modernized a few years earlier. Its competitors included eight four-star establishments, and the Grand, one of the city's oldest hotels, which had a five-star rating. The Palace had been very profitable in recent years and boasted an above average occupancy rate. For many months of the year, it was sold out on weekdays, reflecting its strong appeal to business travelers, who were very attractive to the hotel because of their willingness to pay a higher room rate than tourists or conference delegates. However, the general manager and his staff saw problems on the horizon. Planning permissions had recently been granted for four large new hotels in the city, and the Grand had just started a major renovation and expansion project, which included construction of a new wing. There was a risk that customers might see the Palace as falling behind.

To better understand the nature of the competitive threat, the hotel's management team worked with a consultant to prepare charts that displayed the Palace's position in the business traveler market both before and after the advent of new competition. Four attributes were selected for study: room price, level of personal service, level of physical luxury, and location.

DATA SOURCES. In this instance, management did not conduct new consumer research; instead, they inferred customer perceptions from various sources:

- Published information.
- Data from past surveys the hotel had commissioned.
- Reports from travel agents and knowledgeable hotel staff members who frequently interacted with guests.

Information on competing hotels was not difficult to obtain, because the locations were known. Information was obtained through:

- Visiting and evaluating the physical structures.
- Sales staff kept themselves informed on pricing policies and discounts.
- To evaluate service level, they used the ratio of rooms per employee, a convenient surrogate measure. It is easily calculated from the published number of rooms and employment data provided to the city authorities.
- Data from surveys of travel agents conducted by the Palace provided additional insights on the quality of personal service at each competitor.

SCALES AND HOTEL RATINGS. Scales were then created for each attribute and each hotel was rated on each of the attributes so the positioning maps could be drawn:

- Price was simple because the average price charged to business travelers for a standard single room at each hotel was already quantified.
- The rooms-per-employee ratio formed the basis for a service level scale, with low ratios equated to high service. This rating was then fine-tuned because of what was known about the quality of service actually delivered by each major competitor.
- Level of physical luxury was more subjective. The management team identified the hotel that members agreed was the most luxurious (the Grand) and then the four-star hotel that they viewed as having the least luxurious physical facilities (the Airport Plaza). All other four-star hotels were then rated on this attribute relative to these two benchmarks.
- Location was defined with reference to the stock exchange building in the heart of the financial district, because past research had shown that a majority of the Palace's business guests were visiting destinations in this area. The location scale plotted each hotel in terms of its distance from the stock exchange. The competitive set of 10 hotels lay within a four-mile, fan-shaped radius, extending from the exchange through the city's principal retail area (where the convention center was also located) to the inner suburbs and the nearby airport.

Two positioning maps were created to portray the existing competitive situation. The first (Figure 3.5) showed the 10 hotels on the dimensions of price and service level; the second (Figure 3.6) displayed them on location and degree of physical luxury.

FINDINGS. Some findings were intuitive, but others provided valuable insights:

- A quick glance at Figure 3.5 shows a clear correlation between the attributes of price and service: Hotels that offer higher levels of service are relatively more expensive. The shaded bar running from upper left to lower right highlights this relationship, which is not a surprising one (and can be expected to continue diagonally downward for three-star and lesser-rated establishments).
- Further analysis shows that there appear to be three clusters of hotels within what is already an upscale market category. At the top end, the four-star Regency is close to the five-star Grand; in the middle, the Palace is clustered with four other hotels, and at the lower end, there is another cluster of three hotels. One surprising insight from this map is that the Palace appears to be charging significantly more (on a relative basis) than its service level would seem to justify. Because its occupancy rate is very high, guests are evidently willing to pay the going rate.
- Figure 3.6 shows how the Palace is positioned relative to the competition on location and degree of luxury. We don't expect these two variables to be related, and

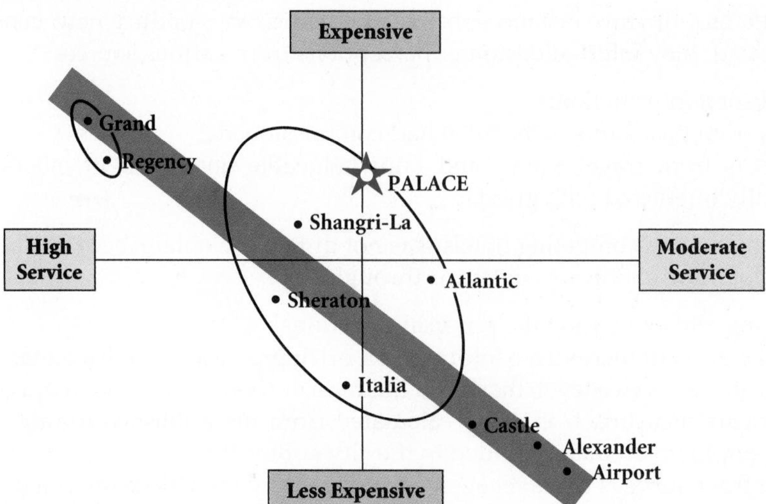

FIGURE 3.5 Positioning Map of Belleville's Principal Business Hotels: Service Level Versus Price Level (Before New Competition)

they don't appear to be so. A key insight here is that the Palace occupies a relatively empty portion of the map. It is the only hotel in the financial district—a fact that probably explains its ability to charge more than its service level (or degree of physical luxury) seems to justify.

- There are two clusters of hotels in the vicinity of the shopping district and convention center (Figure 3.6). There is a relatively luxurious group of three, led by the Grand, and a second group of two offering a moderate level of luxury.

Mapping Future Scenarios to Identify Potential Competitive Responses

What of the future? The Palace's management team next sought to anticipate the positions of the four new hotels being constructed in Belleville as well as the probable repositioning of the Grand (see Figures 3.6 and 3.8). Predicting the positions of the four new hotels was not difficult for experts in the field, especially as preliminary details of the new hotels had already been released to city planners and the business community.

The construction sites were already known; two would be in the financial district and two in the vicinity of the convention center, under expansion. Press releases distributed by the Grand had already declared its management's intentions: The "New" Grand would be not only larger, the renovations would be designed to make it even more luxurious, and there were plans to add new service features. Three of the newcomers would be affiliated with international chains and their strategies could be guessed by examining recent hotels opened in other cities by these same

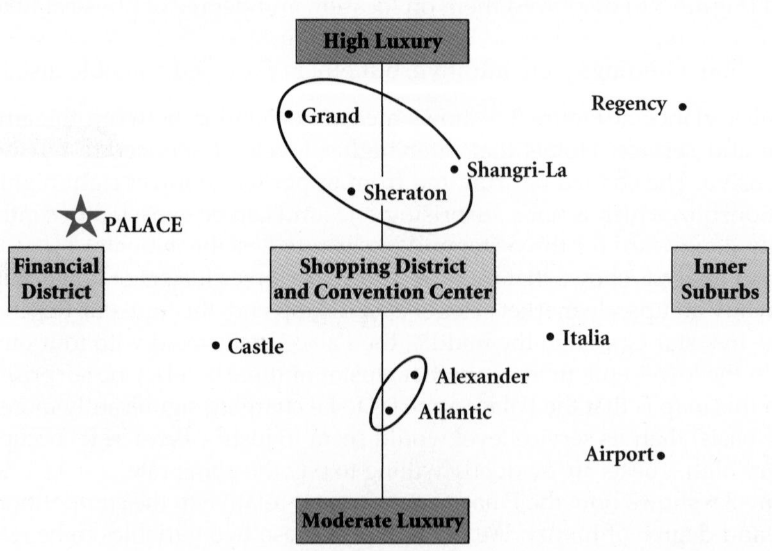

FIGURE 3.6 Positioning Map of Belleville's Principal Business Hotels: Location Versus Physical Luxury (Before New Competition)

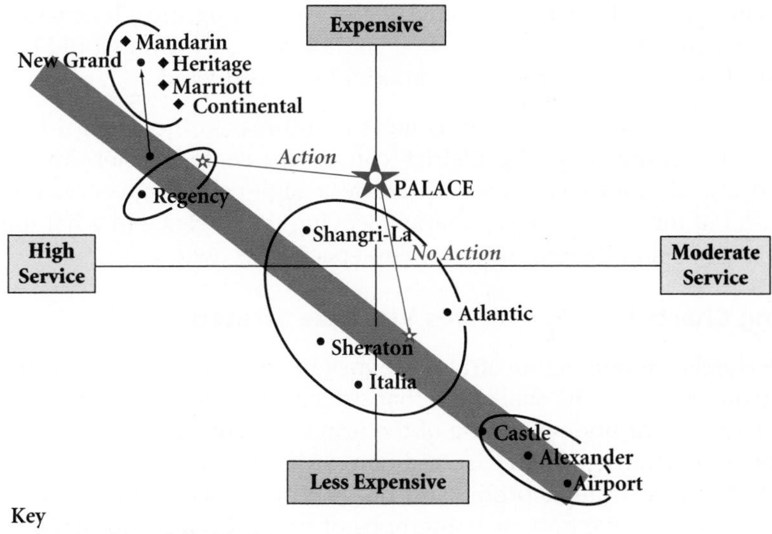

FIGURE 3.7 Future Positioning Map of Belleville's Business Hotels: Service Level Versus Price Level

chains. The owners of two of the hotels had declared their intentions to seek five-star status, although this might take a few years to achieve.

Pricing was also easy to project. New hotels use a formula for setting posted room prices (the prices typically charged to individuals staying on a weeknight in high season). This price is linked to the average construction cost per room at the rate of $1 per night for every $1,000 of construction costs. Thus, a 200-room hotel that costs $80 million to build (including land costs) would have an average room cost of $400,000 and would need to set a price of $400 per room per night. Using this formula, Palace managers concluded that the four new hotels would have to charge significantly more than the Grand or Regency, in effect establishing what marketers call a *price umbrella* above existing price levels and thereby giving competitors the option of raising their own prices. To justify their high prices, the new hotels would have to offer customers very high standards of service and luxury. At the same time, the New Grand would need to raise its own prices to recover the costs of renovation, new construction, and enhanced service offerings (see Figure 3.7).

Assuming no changes by either the Palace or other existing hotels, the effect of the new competition in the market clearly posed a significant threat to the Palace:

- It would lose its unique location advantage and in future be one of three hotels in the immediate vicinity of the financial district (Figure 3.8).

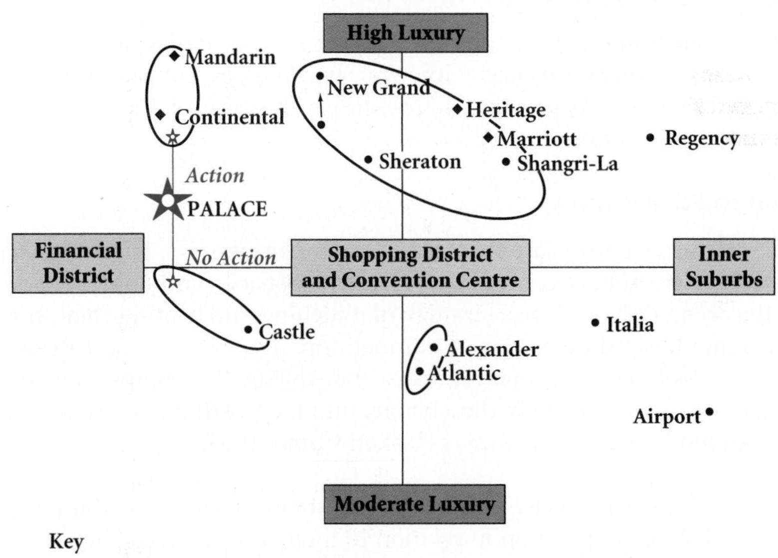

FIGURE 3.8 Future Positioning Map of Belleville's Business Hotels: Location Versus Physical Luxury

- The sales staff believed that many of the Palace's existing business customers would be attracted to the Continental and the Mandarin and would be willing to pay the higher rates to obtain the superior benefits offered.

The other two newcomers were seen as more of a threat to the Shangri-La, Sheraton, and New Grand in the shopping district/convention center cluster. Meanwhile, the New Grand and the newcomers would create a high-price/high-service (and high-luxury) cluster at the top end of the market, leaving the Regency in what might prove to be a distinctive—and therefore defensible—space of its own.

Positioning Charts Help Executives Visualize Strategy

The Palace Hotel example demonstrates the insights that come from visualizing competitive situations. One of the challenges that strategic planners face is to ensure that all executives have a clear understanding of the firm's current situation before moving to discuss changes in strategy. Chan Kim and Renée Mauborgne argue that graphic representations of a firm's strategic profile and product positions are much easier to grasp than tables of quantitative data or paragraphs of prose. Charts and maps can help to achieve a "visual awakening." By enabling senior managers to compare their business with that of competitors and understand the nature of competitive threats and opportunities, visual presentations can highlight gaps between how customers (or prospects) see the organization and how management sees it, and thus help confirm or dispel beliefs that a service or a firm occupies a unique niche in the marketplace.[12]

By examining how anticipated changes in the competitive environment would literally redraw the current positioning map, the management team at the Palace could see that the hotel could not hope to remain in its current market position once it lost its locational advantage. Unless they moved proactively to enhance its level of service and physical luxury, raising its prices to pay for such improvements, the hotel was likely to find itself pushed into a lower price bracket that might even make it difficult to maintain current standards of service and physical upkeep.

CHANGING COMPETITIVE POSITIONING

Markets are constantly changing, creating both threats and opportunities among competing firms. As a result, firms sometimes have to make significant changes in an existing position. Such a strategy, known as repositioning, could mean revising service characteristics or redefining target market segments. At the firm level, repositioning may entail abandoning certain products and withdrawing completely from some market segments.

Changing Perceptions through Advertising

Improving negative brand perceptions may require extensive redesign of the core product and/or supplementary services. However, weaknesses are sometimes perceptual rather than real. Service Perspective 3.3 describes the case of UPS changing market perceptions about its service offering.

Innovation in Positioning

Many successful service firms are imitated by their competitors. Firms that try to compete in a space where intense competition already exists can end up in a "bloody" fight that stains the ocean red, because a strategy of matching and beating rivals tends to emphasize the same basic dimensions of competition. The way out is to use the "blue ocean" strategy, looking for a market space that makes the competition irrelevant.[13] The challenge is to introduce new dimensions into the positioning equation that other firms cannot immediately match. James Heskett frames the issue nicely:

> The most successful service firms separate themselves from "the pack" to achieve a distinctive position in relation to their competition. They differentiate themselves . . . by altering typical characteristics of their respective industries to their competitive advantage.[14]

SERVICE PERSPECTIVE 3.3

UPS REPOSITIONS ITSELF TO DELIVER

Founded as a messenger company in the United States in 1907, UPS has become one of the world's top service brands, developing new services and expanding into new markets around the globe. In recent years, the company has had to develop communication strategies to change the perceptions of both current and potential customers. Although recognized as a leader in the ground shipping business, the company wanted wider awareness of its other services like supply chain management, multi-modal transportation, and financial services. So it started a rebranding and repositioning exercise to make sure that all UPS services were closely identified with the UPS name.

Research showed that UPS was strongly associated with the color brown, used on its trucks and employee uniforms. This color also gave UPS an image of trustworthiness and reliability. Seeking to clarify that UPS could do more for customers than just deliver packages, UPS adopted the tag line "What Can Brown Do For You?" and combined it with a new slogan, "Synchronizing the World of Commerce."

The company understood that changing the perception of a brand had to start with the employees first. Although it can be difficult to change people's mindsets about a company's vision, UPS succeeded. Employees accepted the new brand positioning strategy and learned to work with each other across business units. Working together, they were able to serve customers better.

Today, the company operates in more than 200 countries and territories worldwide. In 2009, it served some 8 million customers daily and had operating revenues of over $50 billion. UPS has a very strong retail presence in the United States, with 4,700 retail stores, 1,300 mailboxes, 1,000 customer centers, 16,000 authorized outlets, and 40,000 drop boxes. Their website has an average of 18.5 million tracking requests daily, and the UPS jet aircraft fleet is the eighth largest in the world!

Source: Vivian Manning-Schaffel. "UPS and FedEx Compete to Deliver," http://www.brandchannel.com/features_effect.asp?pf_id=210, May 17, 2004, accessed May 6, 2009; http://www.ups.com/content/sg/en/about/facts/worldwide.html, accessed May 6, 2009.

CONCLUSION

Most service businesses face active competition. Marketers need to find ways of creating meaningful value propositions for their products that stake a distinctive and defensible *position* in the market against competing alternatives. The nature of services introduces a number of distinctive possibilities for competitive differentiation, going beyond price and physical product features to include: location and scheduling, performance levels such as speed of service delivery and the caliber of service personnel, and a range of options for customer involvement in the production process.

Nearly all successful service firms pursue a focus strategy. They identify the strategically important elements in their service operations and concentrate their resources on them. They target segments they can serve better than other providers, offering and promoting a higher level of performance on those attributes particularly valued by their target customers.

Chapter Summary

LO1 *Positioning strategy* is concerned with creating, communicating, and maintaining distinctive differences valued by those customers with whom the firm aims to develop long-term relationships. Positioning services often is associated with:

- Price and product attributes (e.g., terms and conditions of a mortgage product).
- Customer service processes (e.g., their convenience and ease of use).
- Service distribution and delivery systems, service schedules, and locations (e.g., coverage and density of branch and ATM networks).
- Service environment (e.g., its functionality and level of luxury).

- Service personnel (e.g., their competence and customer service orientation).

LO2 In competitive service industries, most firms need to focus to achieve competitive advantage. There are three focused strategies firms can follow to be able to achieve a competitive advantage. They are:
- *Fully focused*: a firm provides a limited range of services (perhaps only one) to a narrow target segment (e.g., Shouldice Hospital).
- *Market focused*: a firm concentrates on a narrow market segment, but offers a wide range of services to address the many diverse needs to that segment (e.g., Rentokil).
- *Service focused*: a firm offers a narrow range of services to a fairly broad market (e.g., Lasik eye surgery clinics or Starbucks coffee shops).
- There is a fourth, the unfocused strategy. However, it generally is not advisable for firms to choose an unfocused strategy as this will mean that they spread themselves too thin to remain competitive (e.g., some departmental stores).

LO3 *Market segmentation* forms the basis for the three focused strategies. In market segmentation, a firm needs to identify and select target segments it can serve best.

LO4 It is crucial for positioning a service in its target segment to understand the difference between important and determinant attributes for consumer choice.
- *Important attributes.* They are important to the consumer, but that may not be important for the buying decisions (e.g., safety is important, but all airlines a traveler considers are seen as safe). If that is the case, such an attribute should not be used as a basis for segmentation.
- *Determinant attributes.* They often are way down on the list of service characteristics important to customers, but they are attributes on which customers see significant differences between competing alternatives (e.g., frequency of flights to a destination and resultant convenience of departure times, or quality of in-flight service).

LO5 Once the important and determinant attributes are understood, management needs to decide which *service level* the firm should offer on each of the attributes. Service levels often are used to segment customers according to their willingness to trade off price and service level across a broad variety of attributes.

LO6 Effective positioning required firms to *link market and competitor analysis to internal corporate analysis.* The outcome of these analyses is the position statement that articulates the desired position of the firm's offering in the marketplace.

LO7 *Positioning maps* are an important tool to help firms develop their positioning strategy. They provide a visual way of summarizing customer perceptions of how different services are performing on determinant attributes.

Review Questions

1. Why should service firms focus their efforts? Describe the basic focus strategies, and give examples of how these work.
2. Why is market segmentation important to service firms?
3. How do you identify and select target market segments?
4. What is the distinction between important and determinant attributes in consumer purchase decisions? How can research help you to understand which is which?
5. How are service levels of determinant attributes related to positioning services?
6. What are the six questions for developing an effective positioning strategy?
7. Describe what is meant by positioning strategy and how do the market, internal, and competitive analyses relate to positioning strategy?
8. How can positioning maps help managers better understand and respond to competitive dynamics?

Application Exercises

1. Find examples of companies that illustrate each of the four focus strategies discussed in this chapter.
2. Travel agencies are losing business to passengers booking their flights directly on airline websites. Identify some possible focus options open to travel agencies wishing to develop new lines of business that would make up for the loss of airline ticket sales.
3. Provide two examples of service firms that use service levels (other than airlines, hotels, and car rentals) to differentiate their products. Explain the determinant

attributes and service levels used to differentiate the positioning of one service from another?

4. Choose an industry you are familiar with (such as cell phone service, credit cards, or online music stores), and create a perceptual map showing the competitive positions of different service providers in that industry. Use attributes you believe are determinant attributes. Identify gaps in the market, and generate ideas for a potential "blue ocean" strategy.

5. Imagine you have been hired as a consultant to give advice to the Palace Hotel. Consider the options facing the hotel based on the four attributes in the positioning charts (Figures 3.5 and 3.6). What actions do you recommend the Palace take? Explain your recommendations.

Endnotes

1. George S. Day, *Market Driven Strategy,* New York: The Free Press, 1990, 164.
2. Robert Johnston, "Achieving Focus in Service Organizations," *The Service Industries Journal*, 16, January 1996, 10–20.
3. A best-practice example in a B2B context is discussed in: Ernest Waaser, Marshall Dahneke, Michael Pekkarinen, and Michael Weissel, "How You Slice It: Smarter Segmentation for Your Sales Force," *Harvard Business Review*, 82, No. 3, 2004, 105–111.
4. Shun Yin Lam, Jeongwen Chiang, and A. Parasuraman, "The Effects of the Dimensions of Technology Readiness on Technology Acceptance: An Empirical Analysis," *Journal of Interactive Marketing*, 22, No. 4, 2008, 19–39; Jonas Matthing, Per Kristensson, Anders Gustafsson, and A. Parasuraman, "Developing Successful Technology-Based Services: The Issue of Identifying and Involving Innovative Users," *Journal of Services Marketing*, 20, No. 5, 2006, 288–297.
5. For further insights into multiattribute modeling, see William D. Wells and David Prensky, *Consumer Behavior.* New York: John Wiley & Sons, 1996, 321–325.
6. Frances X. Frei, "The Four Things a Service Business Must Get Right," *Harvard Business Review*, April 2008, 70–80.
7. Jack Trout, *The New Positioning: The Latest on the World's #1 Business Strategy.* New York: McGraw-Hill, 1997.
8. Kevin Lane Keller, Brian Sternthal, and Alice Tybout, "Three Questions You Need to Ask about Your Brand," *Harvard Business Review*, 80, September 2002, 84.
9. Roger Brown, "How We Built a Strong Company in a Weak Industry," *Harvard Business Review*, 79, February 2001, 51–57.
10. Nanette Byrnes, "The Little Guys Doing Large Audits," *BusinessWeek*, August 22/29, 2005, 39.
11. For a detailed approach, see Michael E. Porter, "A Framework for Competitor Analysis, Chapter 3" in *Competitive Strategy*, New York: The Free Press, 1980 47–74.
12. W. Chan Kim and Renée Mauborgne, "Charting Your Company's Future," *Harvard Business Review*, 80, June 2002, 77–83.
13. W. Chan Kim and Renée Mauborgne, *Blue Ocean Strategy: How to Create Uncontested Market Space and Make Competition Irrelevant.* Boston: Harvard Business School Press, 2005.
14. James L. Heskett, *Managing in the Service Economy*, Boston: Harvard Business School Press, 1984, 45.

PART TWO

Applying the 4 *P*s of Marketing to Services

A value proposition consists of the whole cluster of benefits that a firm promises to deliver to its target market, whereby service marketers need to create a coherent offering in which each element is compatible with the others, and all are mutually reinforcing. Part Two of the book covers the development of the service concept and its value proposition, the product, distribution, pricing, and communications strategies that are needed for developing a successful business model. Part Two revisits the 4 *P*s of the traditional marketing mix (***P***roduct, ***P***lace, ***P***rice, and ***P***romotion) and expands, them to account for the specific characteristics of services that makes them different from goods marketing. It consists of the following four chapters:

CHAPTER 4 DEVELOPING SERVICE PRODUCTS: CORE AND SUPPLEMENTARY ELEMENTS

Chapter 4 discusses the meaningful service product that includes both the core and supplementary elements. The supplementary elements both facilitate and enhance the core service offering.

CHAPTER 5 DISTRIBUTING SERVICES THROUGH PHYSICAL AND ELECTRONIC CHANNELS

Chapter 5 examines the time and place elements. Manufacturers usually require physical distribution channels to move their products. Some service businesses however, are able to use electronic channels to deliver all (or at least some) of their service elements. For services delivered in real time with customers physically present, speed and convenience of place and time have become important determinants of effective service delivery.

CHAPTER 6 SETTING PRICES AND IMPLEMENTING REVENUE MANAGEMENT

Chapter 6 provides an understanding of pricing from both the firm and customer's point of view. For firms, the pricing strategy determines income generation. Service firms need to implement revenue management to maximize the revenues that can be generated from available capacity at any given time.

From the customer's perspective, price is a key part of the costs they incur to obtain the desired benefits. However, the cost to the customer also often includes significant non-monetary costs which have important marketing implications.

CHAPTER 7 PROMOTING SERVICES AND EDUCATING CUSTOMERS

Chapter 7 deals with how firms should communicate with their customers about their services through promotion and education. Since customers are co-producers and contribute to how others experience service performances, much communication in services marketing is educational in nature to teach customers how to effectively move through a service process.

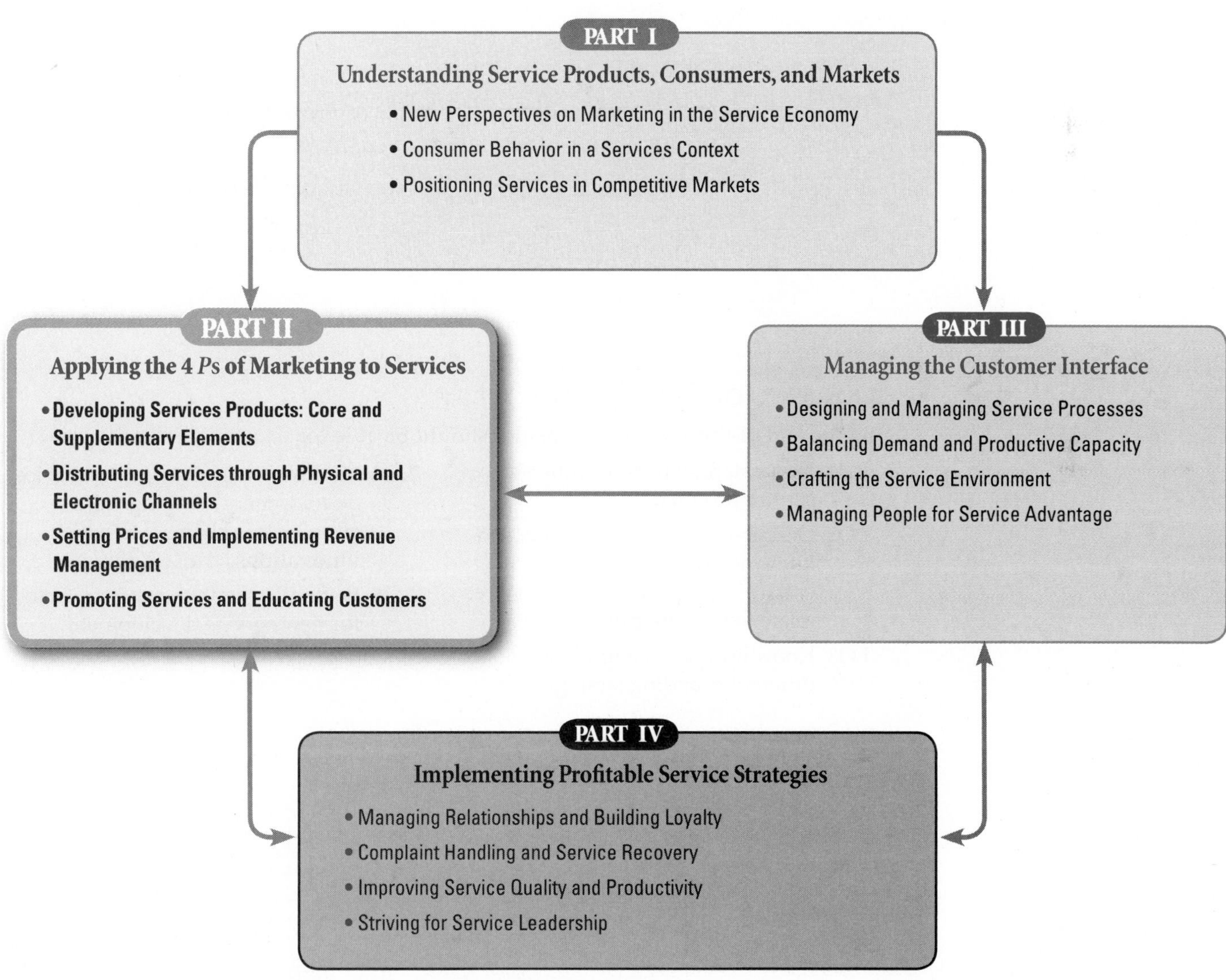

FIGURE II.1 Organizing Framework for Services Marketing

CHAPTER 4

Developing Service Products: Core and Supplementary Elements

Each and every one of you will make or break the promise that our brand makes to customers.

AN AMERICAN EXPRESS MANAGER SPEAKING TO HIS EMPLOYEES

LEARNING OBJECTIVES (LOs)

By the end of this chapter, the reader should be able to:

LO1 Understand what constitutes a service product.

LO2 Describe the *Flower of Service,* and know how facilitating and enhancing supplementary services relate to the core product.

LO3 Know how service firms use different branding strategies.

LO4 List the categories of new service development, ranging from simple style changes to major innovations.

LO5 Be familiar with the success factors for new service development.

Santa Holidays: Christmas in Lapland

Christmas in Lapland is an experience-based tourist product based on the Finnish belief that Santa Claus lives in Lapland. The British tour operator, Goodwood Travel, arranged the first Concorde flight to Finnish Lapland during the Christmas season of 1984. This exclusive one-day journey offered winter activities and a meeting with Santa for 100 tourists. Today, this product is sold by several tour operators in the United Kingdom, Spain, and Russia. More than 100 charter flights bring Santa tourists to Lapland every December. There are several versions of the product, ranging from one-day, all-inclusive trips to one-week trips with optional activities.

The tourist product includes three components: service concept, service process, and service system (see Figure 4.2). The core, *the service concept,* focuses on the kind of experience the customer expects. It is expressed in catchphrases like "in search of Father Christmas" and "Winter Wonderland," which evoke mental images of the kind of value the customer expects. The peak experience is meeting Santa Claus.

The *service process* includes the formal product that is shown to the customer in the form of a brochure or an offer. *Christmas in Lapland* is understood as a package, essential service modules of which include direct flights from the country of departure to Lapland, accommodations, meals, outdoor activities typical for Lapland, and meeting Santa. The *service system* includes the resources needed in the service process to realize the service concept. These include the involvement of the staff, the customers, the physical and technical environment, the organization, and the control of these resources. The hospitality element of the product is mainly produced by the staff and customers. In addition, the product is highly place specific: The region of the implementation of the services is situated in Finnish Lapland. Santa has his office in Rovaniemi, where tourists can visit him every day of the year.

FIGURE 4.1 Christmas in Lapland Would not be Complete without a Visit to Santa's Grotto

PLANNING AND CREATING SERVICE PRODUCTS

All service organizations face choices concerning the types of products to offer and how to deliver them to customers. To better understand the nature of services, it's useful to distinguish between the core product and the supplementary elements that facilitate its use and enhance its value for customers. Designing a service product is a complex task that requires an understanding of how the core and supplementary services should be combined, sequenced, delivered, and scheduled to create a value proposition that meets the needs of target segments.

Service Product

What do we mean by a service "product"? Service performances are experienced rather than owned. Even when there are physical elements to which the customer takes title—such as a cooked meal (which is promptly consumed), a surgically implanted pacemaker, or a replacement part for a car—a significant portion of the price paid is for the value added by the service elements, including expert labor and the use of specialized equipment. A service product comprises all of the elements of the service performance, both physical and intangible, that create value for customers.

Designing the Service Concept

How should you go about designing a service concept? Experienced service marketers recognize the need to take a holistic view of the entire performance they want customers to experience. The value proposition must address and integrate three components: (1) *core product*, (2) *supplementary services*, and (3) *delivery processes*.

CORE PRODUCT. Services usually are defined with reference to a particular industry—for instance, health care or transportation—based on the core set of benefits and solutions delivered to customers. The core product is the central component that supplies the principal, problem-solving benefits customers seek. For example, transport services solve the need to move a person or a physical object from one location to another, management consulting should yield expert advice on what actions a client should take, and repair services restore a damaged or malfunctioning machine to good working order.

SUPPLEMENTARY SERVICES. Delivery of the core product usually is accompanied by a variety of other service-related activities referred to collectively as *supplementary services*. These services augment the core product, facilitating its use and enhancing its value and appeal to the customer's overall experience.[1] Core products tend to become commodified as an industry matures and competition increases, so the search for competitive advantage often emphasizes supplementary services. Adding supplementary elements or increasing their level of performance should be done in ways that enhance the perceived value of the core product and enable the service provider to charge a higher price.

DELIVERY PROCESSES. The third component in designing a service concept concerns the processes used to deliver both the core product and each of the supplementary services. The design of the service offering must address the following issues:

- How the different service components are delivered to the customer.
- The nature of the customers' role in those processes.
- How long delivery lasts.
- The prescribed level and style of service to be offered.

The integration of the core product, supplementary services, and delivery processes is captured in Figure 4.2, which illustrates the components of the service offering for an overnight stay at a luxury hotel. The core product—overnight rental of a bedroom—dimensioned by service level, scheduling (how long the room may be used before another payment becomes due), the nature of the process (in this instance, people processing), and the role of the customers in terms of what they are expected to do for themselves and what the hotel will do for them, such as making the bed, supplying bathroom towels, and cleaning the room.

Surrounding the core product is a variety of supplementary services. These range from reservations to meals, to in-room service elements. Delivery processes must be specified for each of these elements. The more expensive the hotel is, the higher the level of service required of each element. For example, very important guests might be received at the airport and transported to the hotel in a limousine. Check-in arrangements can be done on the way to the hotel. By the time the guests arrive at the hotel, they are ready to be escorted to their rooms, where a butler is on hand to serve them.

DOCUMENTING THE DELIVERY SEQUENCE OVER TIME. A crucially important part of the process design is the sequence in which customers will use each of the core and

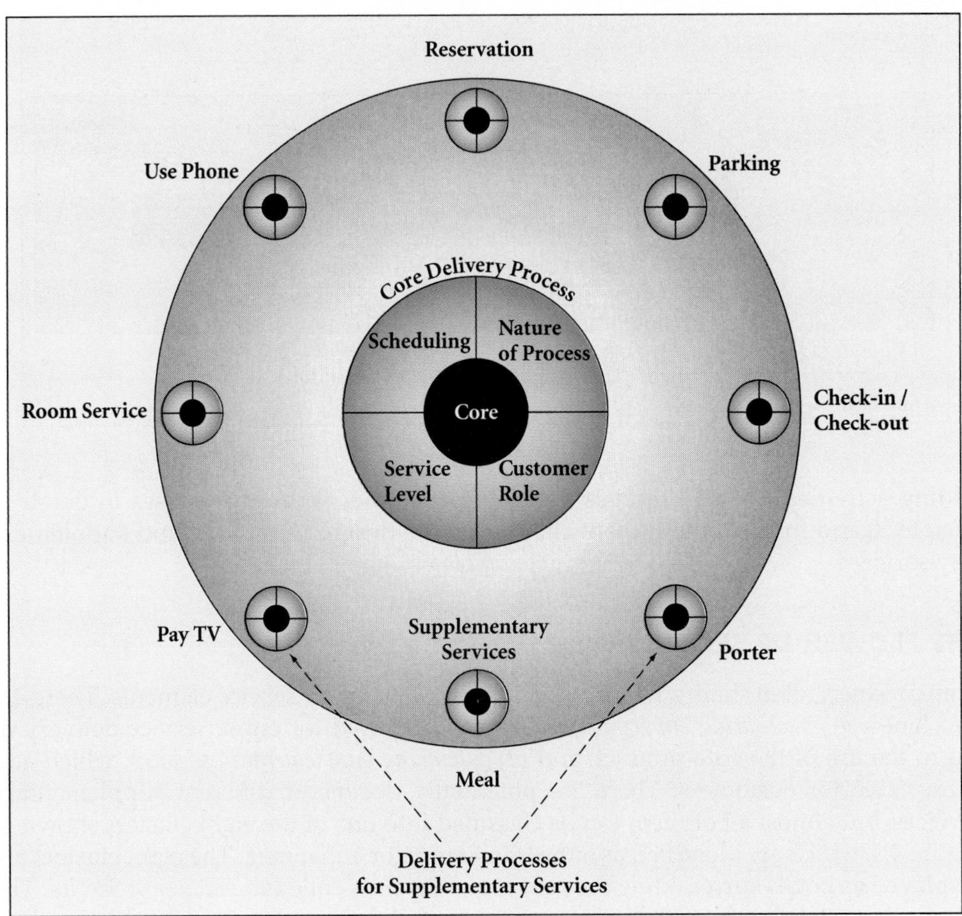

FIGURE 4.2 Depicting the Service Offering for an Overnight Hotel Stay

supplementary services and the approximate length of time required in each instance. This information, which should reflect a good understanding of customer needs, habits, and expectations, is necessary not only for marketing purposes but also for facilities planning, operations management, and allocation of personnel. In some instances, as in the script for teeth cleaning services at the dentist (see Figure 2.11 in Chapter 2), certain service elements must be delivered in a prescribed sequence. In other instances, there may be some flexibility.

Time plays a key role in services, not only from an operational standpoint as it relates to allocating and scheduling purposes, but also from the perspective of customers. In the hotel industry, neither the core service nor its supplementary elements are delivered continuously throughout the duration of the service performance. Certain services must necessarily be used before others. In this industry, as in many services, consumption of the core product is sandwiched between use of supplementary services needed earlier or later in the delivery sequence. Figure 4.3 adds a temporal dimension to the different elements of the luxury hotel service concept (as depicted in Figure 4.2), identifying when and for how long they are likely to be consumed by a typical guest from a given segment. Not every guest uses every service, of course, and schedules may vary.

An important aspect of service planning is determining the amount of time customers may spend on different service elements. In some instances, research may show that customers from a given segment expect to budget a specific amount of time for a given activity that has value for them and would not wish to be rushed (for instance, eight hours for sleeping, an hour and a half for a business dinner, 20 minutes for breakfast). In other instances, such as making a reservation, checking in and out, or waiting for a car to be retrieved from valet parking, customers may wish to minimize or even eliminate time spent on what they perceive as nonvalue

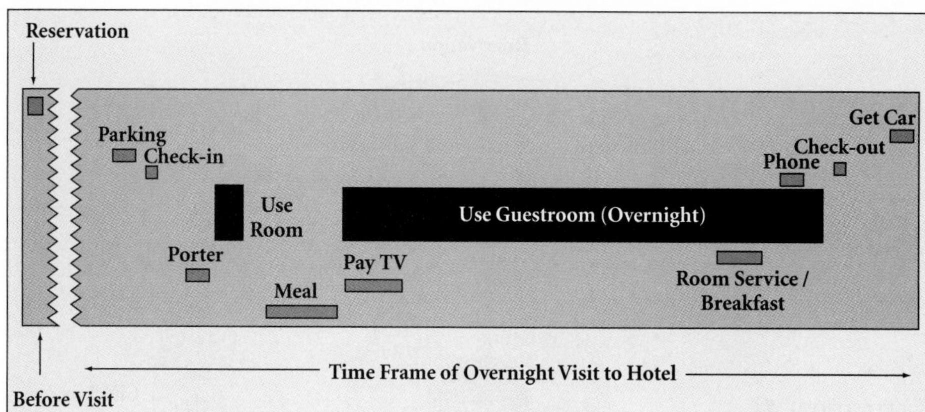

FIGURE 4.3 Temporal Dimension to Augmented Hotel Product

adding activities. We will discuss designing customer service processes in detail in Chapter 8 and focus in the present chapter on the design of the core and supplementary services.

THE FLOWER OF SERVICE[2]

Core products often share a range of similar supplementary service elements. There are two kinds: (1) *facilitating supplementary services*, required for either service delivery or aid in the use of the core product, and (2) *enhancing supplementary services*, which add extra value for customers. There are potentially dozens of different supplementary services, but almost all of them can be classified into one of the eight clusters shown in Figure 4.4, which are identified as either facilitating or enhancing. The eight clusters are displayed as petals surrounding the center of a flower—called the *Flower of Service*. The petals are arranged in a clockwise sequence, following how they are likely to be encountered by customers (although this sequence may vary—for instance, payment may have to be made before service is delivered rather than afterwards). The flower

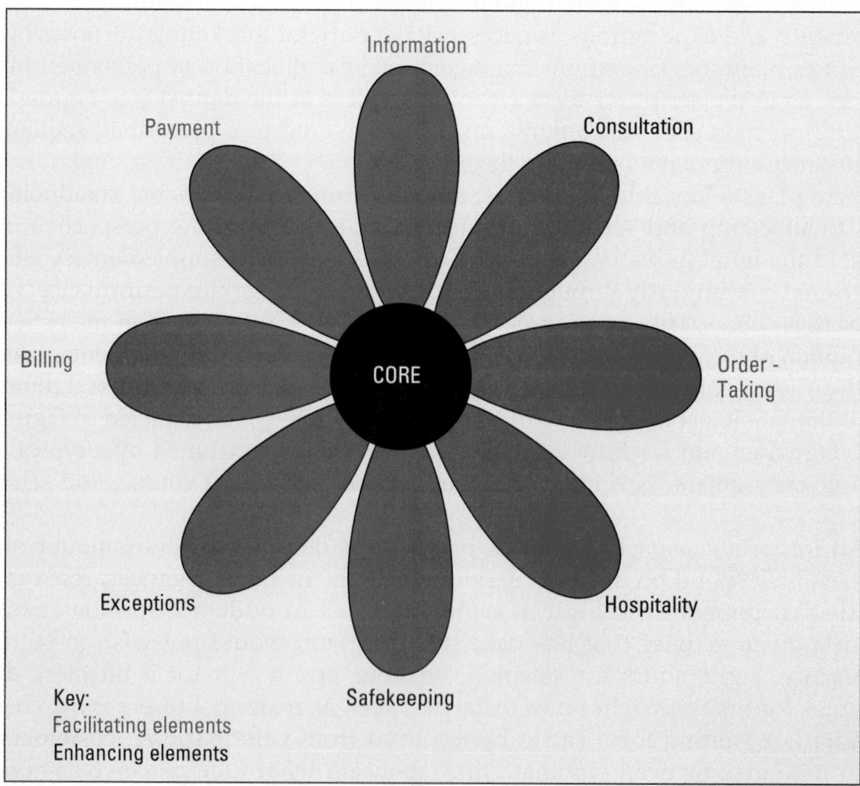

FIGURE 4.4 The Flower of Service: Core Product Surrounded by Cluster of Supplementary Services

Facilitating Services	Enhancing Services
• Information	• Consultation
• Order-taking	• Hospitality
• Billing	• Safekeeping
• Payment	• Exceptions

analogy can help us understand the need for consistent performance on all supplementary elements, so that a weakness in one element doesn't spoil the overall impression. In a well-designed and well-managed service product, the petals and core are fresh and well formed. A badly designed or poorly executed service is like a flower with missing, wilted, or discolored petals. Even if the core is perfect, the overall impression of the flower will be unattractive. Think about your own experiences as a customer (or when purchasing on behalf of an organization). When you were dissatisfied with a particular purchase, was it the core that was at fault, or was it a problem with one or more of the petals?

Supplementary elements often are common to several industries. For example, a wide range of services use "reservations," from car rental, conference organizers to theme parks and opera houses. Here, managers should be studying businesses outside their own industries in a search for "best-in-class" performers on specific supplementary services.

Facilitating Supplementary Services

1. *Information* To obtain full value from any good or service, customers need relevant information (Figure 4.5). The types of information range from train and airline schedules to assistance in locating specific retail outlets, to information on the services of professional firms. New customers and prospects are especially information-hungry. Customers' needs may include directions to the site where the product is sold (or details of how to order it), service hours, prices, and instructions for use. Further information, sometimes required by law, might include conditions of sale and use, warnings, reminders, and notification of changes. Customers also appreciate advice on how to get the most value from a service and how to avoid problems. Finally, customers may want documentation of what has already taken place, such as confirmation of reservations, receipts and tickets, or monthly summaries of account activity. Companies should make sure the information they provide is both timely and accurate. If not, it is likely to make customers feel irritated or cause them inconvenience.

Traditional ways of providing information include using front-line employees (who are not always as well-informed as customers might like), printed notices, brochures, and instruction books. Information can also be provided through videos

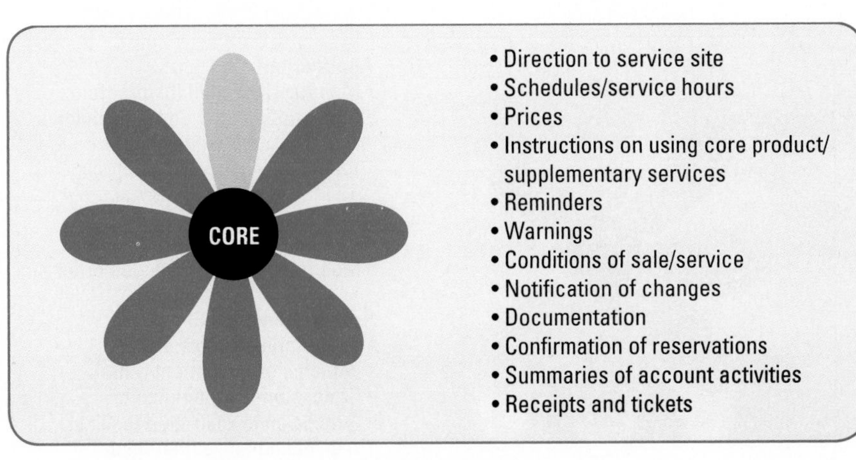

FIGURE 4.5 Examples of Information Elements

FIGURE 4.6 Shipments Can Be Tracked Around the World with Their Identity Code

or software-driven tutorials, touch-screen video displays, or through company websites. Many business logistics companies offer shippers the opportunity to track the movements of their packages—each of which has been assigned a unique identification number (Figure 4.6). For example, Amazon.com provides its customers with a reference number that allows tracking of the goods so that customers know when to expect them.

2. ***Order-Taking*** Once customers are ready to buy, a key supplementary element comes into play—accepting applications, orders, and reservations (Figure 4.7). Order-taking includes applications, order entry, and reservations or check-ins. Banks, insurance companies, and utilities require prospective customers to go through an application process designed to gather relevant information and to screen out those who do not meet basic enrollment criteria (such as a bad credit record or serious health problems). Universities also require prospective students to apply for admission.

Reservations (including appointments and check-in) represent a special type of order-taking that entitles customers to a specified unit of service—for example, an airline seat, a restaurant table, a hotel room, time with a qualified professional, or admission to a facility such as a theater or sports arena with designated seating. Accuracy in scheduling is vital—reserving seats for the wrong day will likely be unpopular with customers.

Order entry can be received through a variety of sources such as through sales personnel, phone and email, or online (Figure 4.8). The process of order-taking should be polite, fast, and accurate so that customers do not waste time and endure unnecessary mental or physical effort. Technology can be used to make order-taking easier and faster for both customers and suppliers—the key lies in minimizing the time and effort required of both parties, while also ensuring completeness and accuracy. For example, airlines now make use of ticketless systems, based on telephone or website reservations. Customers receive a confirmation number when they make the reservation and need only show identification at the airport to claim their seats and receive a boarding pass.

3. ***Billing*** Billing is common to almost all services (unless the service is provided free of charge). Inaccurate, illegible, or incomplete bills risk disappointing customers who may, up to that point, have been quite satisfied with their experience, or worse, such failures add insult to injury if the customer is already dissatisfied. Billing should also be timely, because it stimulates faster payment. Procedures range from verbal statements

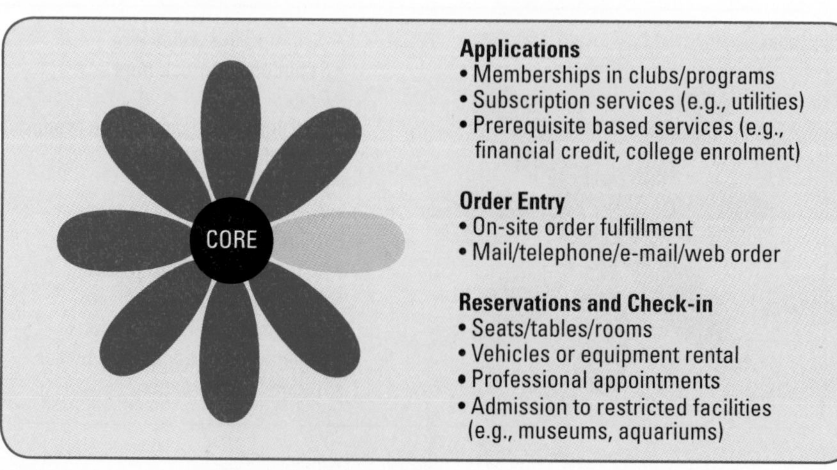

FIGURE 4.7 Examples of Order-Taking Elements

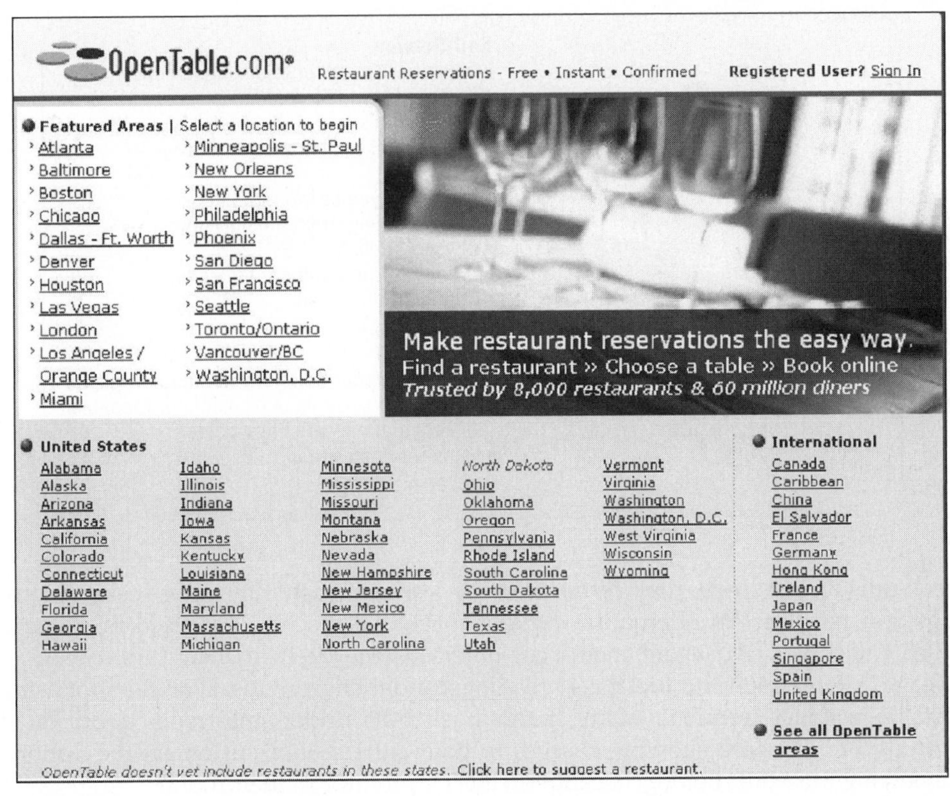

Source: Courtesy of OpenTable, Inc.

FIGURE 4.8 OpenTable Takes Dining Reservations to a Whole New Level by Allowing Diners to Bypass the Traditional Call-and-Hope Reservation Experience with a Mere Click

to a machine-displayed price, and from handwritten invoices to elaborate monthly statements of account activity and fees (Figure 4.9). Perhaps the simplest approach is self-billing, by which the customer tallies up the amount of an order and authorizes a card payment or writes a check. In such instances, billing and payment are combined into a single act, although the seller may still need to check for accuracy.

Customers usually expect bills to be clear and informative, and itemized in ways that make it clear how the total was computed. Unexplained, arcane symbols that have all the meaning of hieroglyphics on an Egyptian monument (and are decipherable only by the high priests of accounting and data processing) do not create a favorable impression of the supplier. Nor does fuzzy printing or illegible handwriting. Laser printers, with their ability to switch fonts and typefaces, to box and to highlight, can produce statements that are not only more legible but also organize information in useful ways. Marketing research can help here, by asking customers what information they want and how they would like it to be organized and presented.

Busy customers hate to be kept waiting for a bill to be prepared in a hotel, restaurant, or rental car lot. Many hotels and car rental firms have now created express check-out options, taking customers' credit card details in advance and documenting charges later by mail. However, accuracy is essential: Even though customers use the express

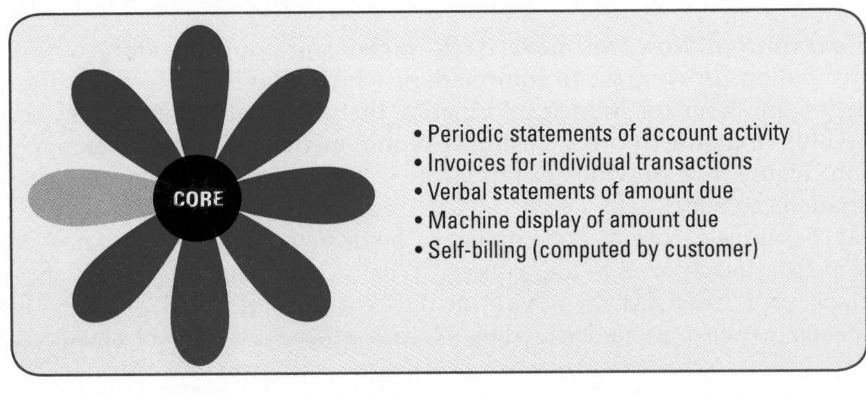

FIGURE 4.9 Examples of Billing Elements

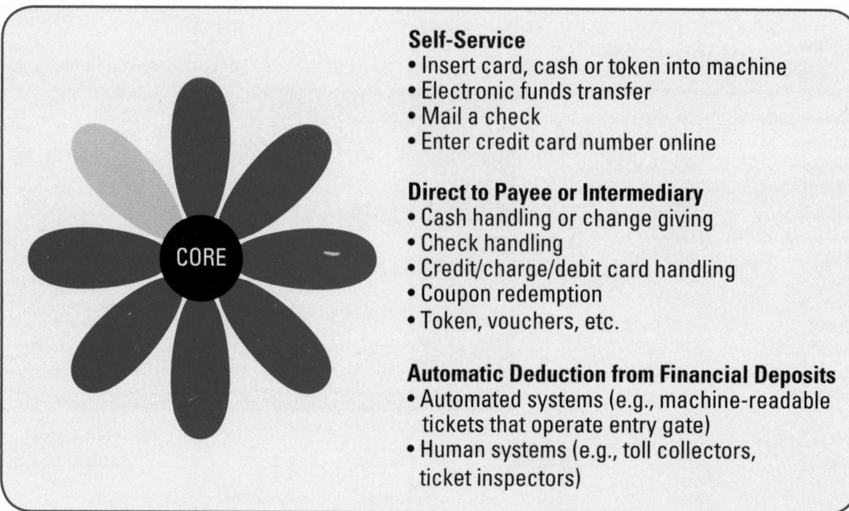

FIGURE 4.10 Examples of Payment Elements

check-outs to save time, they certainly don't want to waste time later seeking corrections and refunds. An alternative express check-out procedure is used by some car rental companies. An agent meets customers as they return their cars, checks the mileage/kilometrage and fuel gauge readings, and then prints a bill on the spot using a portable wireless terminal. Many hotels push bills under guestroom doors on the morning of departure showing charges to date; others offer customers the option of previewing their bills before checkout on the TV monitor in their room.

4. *Payment* In most cases, a bill requires the customer to take action on payment (and such action may be very slow in coming!). Exceptions include bank statements and other direct debit paid services, which detail charges that will be deducted from a custome's account.

A variety of payment options exist, but all customers expect ease and convenience. (Figure 4.10). Self-service payment systems, for instance, require insertion of coins, banknotes, tokens, or cards in machines. Equipment breakdowns will destroy the whole purpose of such a system, so good maintenance and rapid-response troubleshooting are essential. Most payment still takes the form of cash or credit cards. Other alternatives include vouchers, coupons, or prepaid tickets and other electronic means such as PayPal, which offers a fuss-free and secure way to make payments especially since increasingly more shopping is done online. Firms benefit from prompt payment, because it reduces the amount of accounts receivable.

To ensure that people actually pay what is due, some service businesses have instituted control systems, such as ticket checks before entering a movie theater or on board a train. However, inspectors and security officers must be trained to combine politeness with firmness in performing their jobs, so that honest customers do not feel harassed. To reinforce good behavior, NStar, a Massachusetts electrical utility, periodically sends "thank you" notes to customers who have consistently paid on time.

Enhancing Supplementary Services

1. *Consultation* Now we move on to enhancing supplementary services, led by consultation. In contrast to information, which suggests a simple response to customers' questions (or printed information that anticipates their needs), consultation involves a dialog to probe customer requirements and then develop a tailored solution. Figure 4.11 provides examples of several supplementary services in the consultation category.

At its simplest, consultation consists of immediate advice from a knowledgeable service person in response to the request: "What do you suggest?" For example, you might ask your hairstylist for advice on different hairstyles and products. Effective consultation requires an understanding of each customer's current situation, before

FIGURE 4.11 Examples of Consultation Elements

suggesting a suitable course of action (Figure 4.12). Good customer records can be a great help in this respect, particularly if relevant data can be retrieved easily from a remote terminal.

Counseling represents a more subtle approach to consultation because it involves helping customers better understand their situations so that they can come up with their "own" solutions and action programs. This approach can be a particularly valuable supplement to services such as health treatment, in which part of the challenge is to get customers to take a long-term view of their personal situation and to adopt more healthful behaviors, often involving significant lifestyle changes. For example, diet centers like Weight Watchers use counseling to help customers change behaviors so that weight loss can be sustained after the initial diet is completed.

More formalized efforts to provide management and technical consulting for corporate customers include the "solution selling" associated with expensive industrial equipment and services. The sales engineer researches a customer's situation and then offers advice about what particular package of equipment and systems will yield the best results. Some consulting services are offered free of charge in the hope of making a sale. In other instances, however, the service is "unbundled" and customers are expected to pay for it (e.g., for diagnostic tests before a surgery, or a feasibility study before a solution is being proposed). Advice can also be offered through tutorials, group training programs, and public demonstrations.

2. *Hospitality* Hospitality-related services should, ideally, reflect pleasure at meeting new customers and greeting old ones when they return. Well-managed businesses try, at least in small ways, to ensure their employees treat customers as guests. Courtesy and consideration for customers' needs apply to both face-to-face encounters and telephone interactions (Figure 4.13). Hospitality finds its fullest expression in face-to-face encounters. In some cases, it starts (and ends) with an offer of transport to and from the service site on courtesy shuttle buses. If customers must wait outdoors before the service can be delivered, then a thoughtful service provider will offer weather protection. If customers have to wait indoors, a waiting area with seating and even entertainment (TV, newspapers, or magazines) may be provided to pass the time. Recruiting employees who are naturally warm, welcoming, and considerate for customer-contact jobs helps to create a hospitable atmosphere. Shoppers at Giordano, an international clothing retailer with markets in Asia-Pacific and

FIGURE 4.12 A Tax Advisor Provides a Human Touch During the Process of Consultation

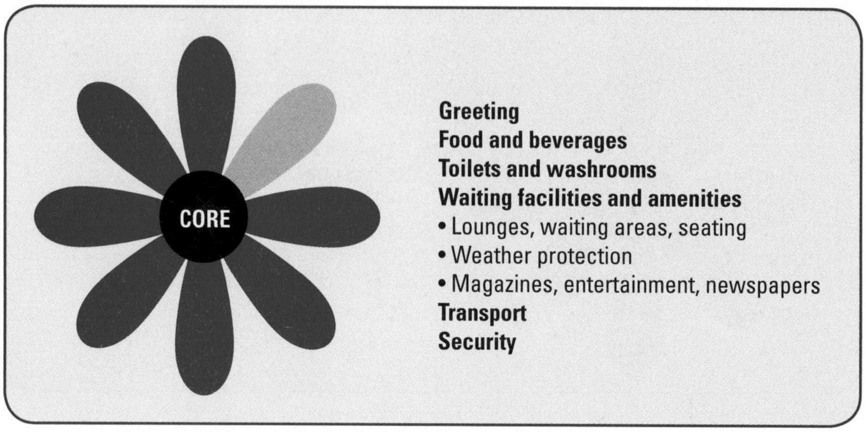

CORE

Greeting
Food and beverages
Toilets and washrooms
Waiting facilities and amenities
- Lounges, waiting areas, seating
- Weather protection
- Magazines, entertainment, newspapers

Transport
Security

FIGURE 4.13 Examples of Hospitality Elements

the Middle East, are given a cheerful "hello" and "thank you" when they enter and leave the store, even if they did not buy anything (see Case 5 on Giordano).

The quality of the hospitality services offered by a firm plays an important role in determining customer satisfaction. This is especially true for people-processing services, because one cannot easily leave the service facility until delivery of the core service is completed. Private hospitals often seek to enhance their appeal by providing the level of room service that might be expected in a good hotel. This includes the provision of quality meals. Some airlines seek to differentiate themselves from their competitors with better meals and a more attentive cabin crew; Singapore Airlines is well recognized on both counts.[3]

Although preflight and inflight hospitality is important, an airline journey doesn't really end until passengers reach their final destination. Air travelers have come to expect departure lounges, but British Airways (BA) came up with the novel idea of an arrivals lounge for its terminals at London's Heathrow and Gatwick airports to serve passengers arriving early in the morning after a long, overnight flight from the Americas, Asia, Africa, and Australia. The airline offers holders of first- and business-class tickets or a BA Executive Club gold card (awarded to the airline's most frequent flyers) the opportunity to use a special lounge where they can take a shower, change, use the spa, have breakfast, make phone calls, and check email before continuing to their final destination feeling a lot fresher. It's a nice competitive advantage, which BA actively promotes. Other airlines have since felt obliged to copy this innovation, although few can match the array of services offered by BA.

3. ***Safekeeping*** When customers are visiting a service site, they often want assistance with their personal possessions. In fact, unless certain safekeeping services are provided (such as safe and convenient parking for their cars), some customers may not come at all. On-site safekeeping services includes coatrooms; baggage transport, handling and storage; safekeeping of valuables; and even child care and pet care (Figure 4.14). Responsible

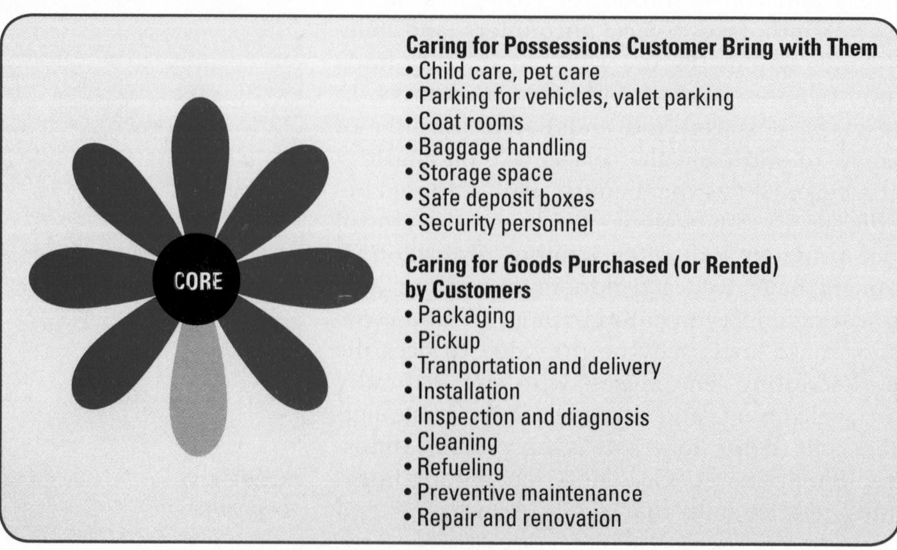

FIGURE 4.14 Examples of Safekeeping Elements

businesses pay close attention to safety and security issues for customers visiting the firm's premises. Wells Fargo Bank mails a brochure with its bank statements containing information about using its ATM machines safely, educating its customers about how to protect both their ATM cards and themselves from theft and personal injury. And the bank makes sure that its machines are in brightly lit, highly visible locations.

Additional safekeeping services may involve physical products that customers buy or rent. They may include packaging, pick-up and delivery, assembly, installation, cleaning, and inspection. These services may be offered free or for an additional fee.

4. *Exceptions* *Exceptions* involve supplementary services that fall outside the routine of normal service delivery (Figure 4.15). Astute businesses anticipate exceptions and develop contingency plans and guidelines in advance. That way, employees will not appear helpless and surprised when customers ask for special assistance. Well-defined procedures make it easier for employees to respond promptly and effectively. There are several types of exceptions:

1. *Special requests.* A customer may request service that requires a departure from normal operating procedures. Advance requests often relate to personal needs, including care of children, dietary requirements, medical needs, religious observance, and personal disabilities. Such requests particularly are common in the travel and hospitality industries.
2. *Problem solving.* Sometimes normal service delivery (or product performance) fails to run smoothly as a result of accident, delay, equipment failure, or a customer having difficulty in using a product.
3. *Handling of complaints/suggestions/compliments.* This activity requires well-defined procedures. It should be easy for customers to express dissatisfaction, offer suggestions for improvement, or pass on compliments, and service providers should be able to make an appropriate response quickly (see Chapter 13 on complaint handling and service recovery).
4. *Restitution.* Many customers expect compensation for serious performance failures; it may take the form of repairs under warranty, legal settlements, refunds, an offer of free service, or other form of payment-in-kind.

Managers need to keep an eye on the level of exception requests. Too many requests may indicate that standard procedures need revamping. For instance, if a restaurant frequently receives requests for special vegetarian meals since there are none on the menu, it may be time to revise the menu to include at least one or two such dishes. A flexible approach to exceptions generally is a good idea, because it reflects

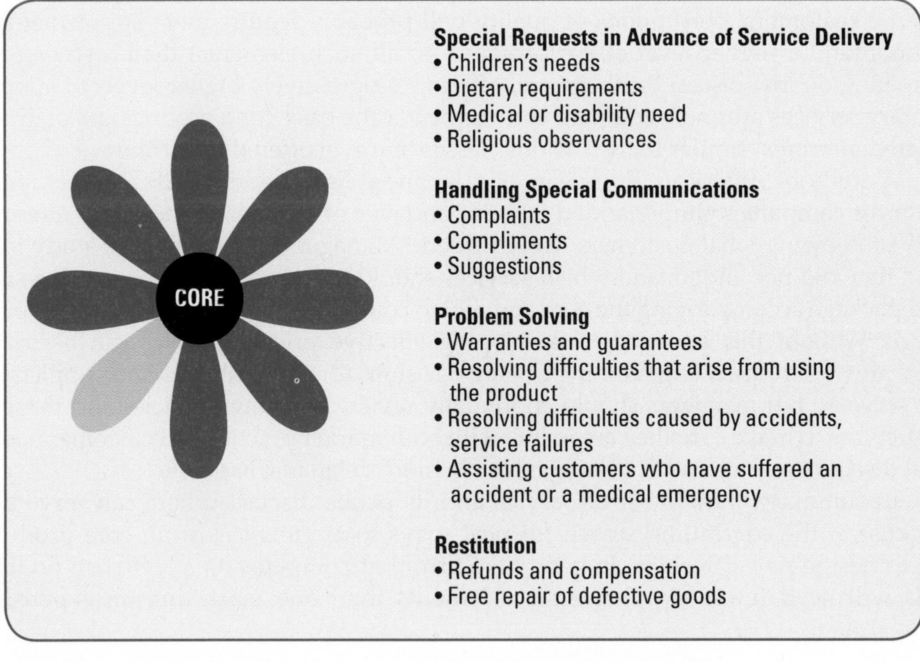

FIGURE 4.15 Examples of Exception Elements

responsiveness to customer needs. On the other hand, too many exceptions may compromise safety, negatively impact other customers, and overburden employees.

Managerial Implications

The eight categories of supplementary services that form the "Flower of Service" collectively provide many options for enhancing core products. Most supplementary services do (or should) represent responses to customer needs. As noted earlier, some are facilitating services—such as information and reservations—that enable customers to use the core product more effectively. Others are "extras" that enhance the core or even reduce its nonfinancial costs (e.g., meals, magazines, and entertainment are hospitality elements that help pass the time). Some elements—notably billing and payment—are, in effect, imposed by the service provider. Even if they are not actively desired by the customer, they still form part of the overall service experience. Any badly handled element may negatively affect customers' perceptions of service quality. The "information" and "consultation" petals illustrate the emphasis in this book on the need for education as well as promotion in communicating with service customers (see Chapter 7 on communications and customer education).

Not every core product is surrounded by supplementary elements from all eight petals of the Flower of Service. Each of the four categories of processes introduced in Chapter 2—people, possession, mental stimulus, and information processing—has different implications for operational procedures, the degree of customer contact with service personnel and facilities, and requirements for supplementary services. The nature of the product helps to determine which supplementary services must be offered and which might usefully be added to enhance value and make the organization easy to do business with. As you might anticipate, people-processing services tend to be the most demanding in terms of supplementary elements—especially hospitality—since they involve close (and often extended) customer contact; similarly, high-contact services usually have more customer interaction than low-contact services. When customers don't visit the service factory, the need for hospitality may be limited to simple courtesies in letters and telecommunications. Possession-processing services sometimes place heavy demands on safekeeping elements, but there may be no need for this particular "petal" when providing information-processing services in which customers and suppliers deal entirely at arm's length. Financial services provided electronically are an exception, however, as these companies must ensure that their customers' intangible financial assets and privacy are carefully safeguarded in transactions that occur via phone or the Web.

A company's market positioning strategy helps to determine which supplementary services should be included (see Chapter 3). A strategy of adding benefits to increase customers' perceptions of quality will probably require more supplementary services (and a higher level of performance on all such elements) than a strategy of competing on low prices. Furthermore, offering progressively higher levels of supplementary services around a common core may offer the basis for a product line of differentiated offerings, similar to the various classes of travel offered by airlines.

A study of American, European, and Japanese firms serving B2B markets found that most companies simply added layer upon layer of services to their core offerings without knowing what customers really valued.[4] Managers surveyed in the study indicated they did not understand which services should be offered to customers as a standard package accompanying the core and which could be offered as options for an extra charge. Without this knowledge, developing effective pricing policies can be tricky. There are no simple rules governing pricing decisions for core products and supplementary services, but managers should continually review their own policies and those of competitors to make sure they are in line with both market practice and customer needs. We'll discuss these and other pricing issues in more detail in Chapter 6.

In summary, the Flower of Service and its petals discussed here can serve as a checklist in the continuing search for new ways to augment existing core products and to design new offerings. In general, a firm that competes on a low-cost, no frills basis will need fewer supplementary elements than one marketing an expensive, high-value-added product. Regardless of which supplementary services a firm decides to offer, all of the elements in each petal should receive the care and attention needed to consistently meet defined service standards. That way, the resulting "flower" will always have a fresh and appealing appearance.

BRANDING SERVICE PRODUCTS AND EXPERIENCES

In recent years, more and more service businesses have started talking about their *products*—a term previously associated with manufactured goods. Some even speak of their "products and services," an expression also used by service-driven manufacturing firms. What is the distinction between these two terms in today's business environment?

A *product* implies a defined and consistent "bundle of output" as well as the ability to differentiate one bundle of output from another. In a manufacturing context, the concept is easy to understand and visualize. Service firms can also differentiate their products in similar fashion to the various "models" offered by manufacturers. For example, fast-food restaurants display a menu of their products, which are, of course, highly tangible. If you are a burger connoisseur, you can easily distinguish Burger King's Whopper from a Whopper with Cheese, as well as a Whopper from a Big Mac.

Providers of more intangible services, also offer a "menu" of products, representing an assembly of carefully prescribed value-added supplementary services built around the core product. For instance, insurance companies offer different types of policies, and universities offer different degree programs; each is composed of a mix of required and elective courses. One bundle of output can be differentiated from another bundle of output. Another example is Banyan Tree Hotels & Resorts (featured in Case 4), which carefully crafted specified products for its various target segments branded such as "Heavenly Honeymoon," "Spa Indulgence," or "Intimate Moments."[5] The latter is a product especially created for couples celebrating their wedding anniversary. It is presented as a surprise to the spouse when guests find their villas decorated with lit candles; incense burning; flower petals spread throughout the room; satin sheets on the decorated bed; chilled champagne or wine; and a private, outdoor pool decorated with flowers, candles, and bath oils. The couple is presented with a variety of aromatic massage oils to further inspire those intimate moments. Having "packaged" and "branded" this product allows Banyan Tree to sell it via its website, distributors, and reservations centers and to train it at the individual hotels. Without specifying exactly what this product means and giving it a name, marketing, selling, and delivery would not be effective. Let's next look at alternative branding strategies for services.

Branding Strategies for Services

Most service organizations offer a line of products rather than just a single product. As a result, they must choose among four broad branding alternatives: Branded house (i.e., using a single brand to cover all products and services), house of brands (i.e., using a separate stand-alone brand for each offering), or subbrands and endorsed brands which are both some combination of these two extremes.[6] These alternatives are represented as a spectrum in Figure 4.16, and are discussed in the following sections.

BRANDED HOUSE. David Aaker and E. Joachimsthaler use the term *branded house* to describe a company, such as the Virgin Group, that applies its brand name to multiple offerings in often unrelated fields.[7] The danger of such a branding strategy is that the brand gets overextended and weakened.

SUBBRANDS. Next on the spectrum are *subbrands*, for which the corporate or the master brand is the primary frame of reference but the product itself also has a distinctive name (examples are Singapore Airlines Raffles Class, denoting the company's business class and Singapore Airlines Suits, its "beyond" first-class service on the A380).

FedEx has been successfully using a subbranding strategy. When Federal Express changed its trading name to the more modern "FedEx," it also changed its logo to feature the new name in a distinctive logo. Consistent applications of this design were

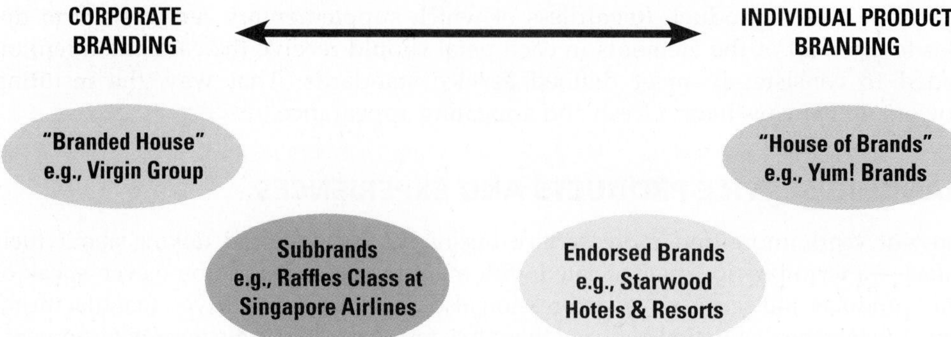

FIGURE 4.16 The Spectrum of Branding Alternatives

Source: Adapted from James Devlin "Brand Architecture in Services: The Example of Retail Financial Services." Journal of Marketing Management 19, 2003, 1046. Copyright © 2003. Reprinted by permission of Westburn Publishers Ltd.

developed for use in settings ranging from business cards to boxes and from employee caps to aircraft exteriors. When the company decided to rebrand a ground delivery service it had purchased, it chose the name FedEx Ground and developed an alternative color treatment of the standard logo (purple and green rather than purple and orange). Its goal was to transfer the positive image of reliable, on-time service associated with its air services to its less expensive, small-package ground service. The well-known air service was then rebranded as FedEx Express.

Other subbrands in what the firm refers to as "the FedEx family of companies" include FedEx Home Delivery (delivers to U.S. residential addresses), FedEx Freight (regional, less-than-truckload transportation for heavyweight freight), FedEx Custom Critical (nonstop, door-to-door delivery of time-critical shipments), FedEx Trade networks (customs brokerage, international freight forwarding, and trade facilitation), Fedex Supply Chain Services (comprehensive suite of solutions that synchronize the movement of goods), and Fedex Kinko's (office and printing services, technology services, shipping supplies, and packing services located in both city and suburban retail stores).

ENDORSED BRANDS. For *endorsed brands* the product brand dominates, but the corporate name is still featured. Many hotel corporations adopt this approach—the hotel industry in the United States has more than 200 brands competing for business, more than any other product category. Many hotel chains offer a family of subbrands and/or endorsed brands. For instance, Hilton Hotels Corporation, Intercontinental, and Starwood each has eight to ten subbrands, whereas Marriott International has 16 (including the wholly-owned Ritz-Carlton chain which, to protect its exclusive image, is not normally identified for marketing purposes as part of the Marriott Group).

For a multibrand strategy to succeed, each brand must promise a distinctive value proposition, targeted at a different customer segment. Because accommodations vary by service level (and thus price), room configurations and amenities also vary. Certain brands are targeted at guests who are making an extended stay, and finally, there are resort brands that primarily target vacationers. In some instances, segmentation is situation-based: The same individual may have different needs (and willingness to pay) under other circumstances, such as when vacationing with family or traveling on business. A strategy of brand extension is aimed at encouraging customers to continue patronizing units within the brand family and often are reinforced by loyalty programs. A study of the brand-switching behavior of 5,400 hotel customers found that brand extensions seem to encourage customer retention, but that the strategy may be less effective in discouraging switching when the number of brands reaches four or more.[8]

HOUSE OF BRANDS. At the far end of the spectrum is the *house of brands* strategy, exemplified by Procter and Gamble, with about 80 packaged goods products, each actively promoted under its own brand name. Yum! Brands Inc. adopts the house of brands strategy, with more than 35,000 restaurants in 110 countries. While many may not have heard of Yum! Brands, people certainly are familiar with their restaurant brands—A&W, Kentucky Fried Chicken, Pizza Hut, Taco Bell, and Long John's Silver. Each of these brands is actively promoted under their own name (Figure 4.17).

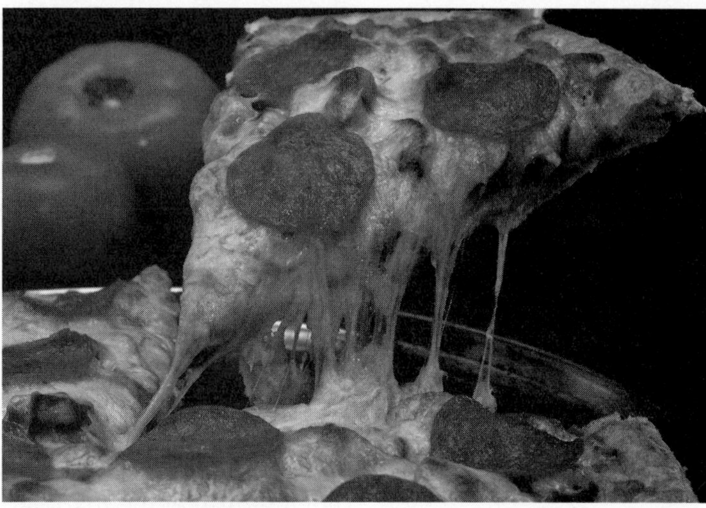

FIGURE 4.17 KFC and Pizza Hut Are Just Some of the Few Popular Fast Food Brands Fronting Yum! Brands

Tiering Service Products with Branding

In a number of service industries, branding is not only used for core services, but also to clearly differentiate different service levels. Often based on offering several price-based classes of service concept, each is based on packaging a distinctive level of service performance across many attributes. This phenomenon, known as *service tiering*, is particularly evident in industries such as hotels, airlines, car rentals, and computer hardware and software support. Table 4.1 displays examples of the key tiers within each of these industries. Other examples of tiering include health-care insurance, cable television, and credit cards.

Please note that we will discuss a different but related concept of tiering of the customer base in Chapter 12, where higher levels of performance on various service attributes usually requires participation in membership programs and high usage.

In the car rental industry, the size and type of car forms the primary basis of tiering. In the airline industry, individual carriers decide what levels of performance should be included with each class of service. Pressures to save money often result in a financially troubled airline reducing its service level standards. However, innovative carriers, such as British Airways, Singapore Airlines, and Virgin Atlantic, are continually trying to add new service features—particularly in business class—that will create a competitive advantage and enable them to sell more seats at full fare. Unlike these three carriers, each of which offers business class seats that fold flat into beds for overnight travel, many airlines have not yet matched this feature. As a result, there is inconsistency within tiers among competing airlines. In other industries, tiering often reflects an individual firm's strategy of bundling service elements into a limited number of packages, rather

TABLE 4.1 Examples of Service Tiering

Industry	Tiers	Key Service Attributes and Physical Elements Used in Tiering
Lodging	Star or diamond ratings (5 to 1)	Architecture; landscaping; room size, furnishings, and décor; restaurant facilities and menus; room service hours; array of services and physical amenities; staffing levels; caliber and attitudes of employees
Airline	Classes (intercontinental): first, business, premium economy, economy[a]	Seat pitch (distance between rows), seat width, and reclining capability; meal and beverage service; staffing ratios; check-in speed; departure and arrival lounges; baggage retrieval speed
Car rental	Class of vehicle[b]	Based on vehicle size (from subcompact to full size), degree of luxury, plus special vehicle types (minivan, SUV, convertible)
Hardware and software support	Support levels[c]	Hours and days of service; speed of response; speed of delivering replacement parts; technician-delivered service versus advice on self-service; availability of additional services

[a]Only a few airlines offer as many as four classes of intercontinental service; domestic services usually feature one or two classes.

[b]Avis and Hertz offer seven classes based on size and luxury, plus several special vehicle types.

[c]Sun Microsystems offers four support levels.

than offering a broad *a la carte* menu of options, each priced separately. Let's examine a few examples next.

BRITISH AIRWAYS SUBBRANDS. A comprehensive example of strong subbranding of service tiers in the airline industry comes from British Airways, which offers seven distinct air travel products. There are four intercontinental offerings—First (deluxe service), Club World (business class), World Traveller Plus (premium economy class), and World Traveller (economy class); two intra-European subbrands—Club Europe (business class) and Euro-Traveller (economy class); and, within the United Kingdom, Shuttle, offering frequent, economy-class service between London and major British cities. Each BA subbrand represents a specific service concept and a set of clearly stated product specifications for preflight, inflight, and on-arrival service elements. To provide additional focus on product, pricing, and marketing communications, responsibility for managing and developing each service is assigned to a separate management team. Through internal training and external communications, staff and passengers alike are kept informed of the characteristics of each service. Except for the domestic shuttle and nonjet services, most aircrafts in BA's fleet are configured in several classes. For instance, the airline's intercontinental fleet of Boeing 747s and 777s is equipped to serve First, Club World, World Traveller Plus, and World Traveller passengers.

On any given route, all passengers traveling on a particular flight receive the same core product—say, a 10-hour journey from Los Angeles to London—but the nature and extent of most of the supplementary elements differ widely, both on the ground and in the air. Passengers in Club World, for instance, not only benefit from better tangible elements, they also receive more personalized service from airline employees and benefit from faster service on the ground at check-in, passport control in London (special lines), and baggage retrieval (priority handling). First-class passengers are even more pampered. The higher the service level, of course, the higher the price!

SUN MICROSYSTEMS HARDWARE AND SOFTWARE SUPPORT. For an example of branding different tiers in a high-tech, business-to-business product line, consider Sun Microsystems. The company offers a comprehensive hardware and software support program branded as "SunSpectrum Support."[9] Four different levels of support are available, subbranded from platinum to bronze (Figure 4.18). The

FIGURE 4.18 Sun System Service Plans for Solaris Clearly Differentiate Service Levels

Source: Courtesy of Sun Systems, Inc.

objective is to give buyers the flexibility to choose a level of support consistent with their own organization's needs (and willingness to pay), ranging from expensive, mission-critical support at the enterprise level (Platinum Service Plan) to relatively inexpensive assistance with self-service maintenance support (Bronze Service Plan):

- Platinum: Mission-critical support with onsite service 24/7 and a two-hour response time.
- Gold: Business critical support with onsite service from Monday to Friday, 8 a.m. to 8 p.m., telephone service 24/7 and a four-hour response time.
- Silver: Basic support with onsite service from Monday to Friday, 8 a.m. to 5 p.m., telephone service from Monday to Friday, 8 a.m. to 8 p.m., and a four-hour response time.
- Bronze: Self support with phone service 8 a.m. to 5 p.m.

Offering a Branded Experience

Branding can be employed at both the corporate and product levels by almost any service business. In a well-managed firm, the corporate brand is not only easily recognized but also has meaning for customers, standing for a particular way of doing business. Applying distinctive brand names to individual products enables the firm to communicate to the target market the distinctive experiences and benefits associated with a specific service concept. In short, it helps marketers to establish a mental picture of the service in customers' minds and to clarify the nature of the value proposition.

The Forum Corporation, a consulting firm, differentiates between (1) a random customer experience with high variability; (2) a generic branded experience by suppliers who offer a consistently similar experience, differentiated only by the presence of the brand name (ATMs are a good example); and (3) a "branded customer experience" in which the customer's experience is shaped in specific and meaningful ways.[10] (See Service Perspective 4.1 for Forum's recommendations on how to achieve this.)

SERVICE PERSPECTIVE 4.1

MOVING TOWARD THE BRANDED CUSTOMER EXPERIENCE

Forum Corporation identified the following basic steps to develop and deliver the Branded Customer Experience:

1. Target profitable customers, employing behavior rather than demographic segmentation as behavior is a more accurate indicator of tastes and preferences.
2. Achieve a superior understanding of what your targeted customers value.
3. Create a brand promise—an articulation of what target customers can expect from their experience with your organization—that is of value to customers, addresses a need, and is actionable and can be incorporated into standards, and provides focus for the organization and its employees.
4. Apply that understanding to shape a truly differentiated customer experience.
5. Give employees the skills, tools, and supporting processes needed to deliver the defined customer experience.
6. Make everyone a brand manager who is behind the brand and supports the brand.
7. Make promises that your processes can exceed.
8. Measure and monitor: Consistency of delivery is paramount.

Source: "Forum Issues #17," Boston: The Forum Corporation, 1997; Joe Wheeler and Shaun Smith, "Loyalty by Design," Forum Corporation, 2003.

Around the world, many financial service firms continue to create and register brand names to distinguish the different accounts and service packages they offer. Their objective is to transform a series of service elements and processes into a consistent and recognizable service experience, offering a definable and predictable output at a specified price. Unfortunately, there often is little discernible difference—other than name—between one bank's branded offering and another's, and their value proposition may be unclear. Don Shultz emphasizes that "The brand promise or value proposition is not a tag line, an icon, or a color or a graphic element, although all of these may contribute. It is, instead, the heart and soul of the brand. . . ."[11]

An important role for service marketers is to become brand champions, familiar with and responsible for shaping every aspect of the customer's experience. We can relate the notion of a branded service experience to the "Flower of Service" metaphor (discussed earlier) by emphasizing the need for consistency in the color and texture of each "petal." Unfortunately, many service experiences remain haphazard and create the impression of a flower stitched together with petals drawn from many different plants! (We return to a discussion of branding in the context of marketing communications strategy in Chapter 7.)

NEW SERVICE DEVELOPMENT

Competitive intensity and customer expectations are increasing in nearly all service industries. Thus, success lies not only in providing existing services well, but also in creating new approaches to service. Because the outcome and process aspects of a service often combine to create the experience and benefits obtained by customers, both aspects must be addressed in new service development.

A Hierarchy of New Service Categories

There are many different ways for a service provider to innovate. Below, we identify seven categories of new services, ranging from simple style changes to major innovations.

1. *Style changes* represent the simplest type of innovation, typically involving no changes in either processes or performance. However they often are highly visible, create excitement, and may serve to motivate employees. Examples include repainting retail branches and vehicles in new color schemes, outfitting service employees in new uniforms, introducing a new bank check design, or minor changes in service scripts for employees.
2. *Service improvements* are the most common type of innovation. They involve modest changes in the performance of current products, including improvements to either the core product or to existing supplementary services.
3. *Supplementary service innovations* take the form of adding new facilitating or enhancing service elements to an existing core service or of significantly improving an existing supplementary service. FedEx Kinkos now offers customers high-speed Internet access round-the-clock at most of its locations in the United States and Canada. Low-tech innovations for an existing service can be as simple as adding parking at a retail site or agreeing to accept credit cards for payment. Multiple improvements may have the effect of creating what customers perceive as an entirely new experience, even though it is built around the same core. Theme restaurants such as the Rainforest Café enhance the core food service with new experiences. The cafés are designed to keep customers entertained with aquariums, live parrots, waterfalls, fiberglass monkeys, talking trees that spout environmentally related information, and regularly timed thunderstorms, complete with lightning.[12]
4. *Process line extensions* are less innovative than process innovations but often represent distinctive new ways of delivering existing products, either with the intent of offering more convenience and a different experience for existing customers or of attracting new customers who find the traditional approach unappealing. Most commonly, they involve adding a lower-contact distribution channel to an existing high-contact channel, such as creating telephone-based or Internet-based

banking service. Barnes and Noble, the leading bookstore chain in the United States, added Internet retailing through BarnesandNoble.com to help compete against Amazon.com Such dual-track approaches are sometimes referred to as "click and mortar." Creating self-service options to complement delivery by service employees is another form of process line extension.

5. *Product line extensions* are additions to a company's current product lines. The first company in a market to offer such a product may be seen as an innovator; the others are merely followers, often acting defensively. These new services may be targeted at existing customers to serve a broader array of needs or designed to attract new customers with different needs (or both). Delta Airlines is one of several major carriers to attempt the launch of a separate low-cost operation designed to compete with discount carriers such as JetBlue and Southwest Airlines, but none of these ventures has been successful. In banking, many banks now retail insurance products in the hope of increasing the number of profitable relationships with existing customers.
6. *Major process innovations* consist of using new processes to deliver existing core products in new ways with additional benefits. For example, the University of Phoenix competes with other universities by delivering undergraduate and graduate degree programs in a nontraditional way. It has no permanent central campus, but offers courses either online or in rented facilities. Its students get most of the benefits of a college degree in half the time and at a much lower price than at other universities.[13] Often, such Internet-based business models add new, information-based benefits such as greater customization, the opportunity to visit chatrooms with fellow customers, and suggestions for additional products that match well with what has already been purchased.
7. *Major service innovations* are new core products for markets that have not been previously defined. They usually include both new service characteristics and radical new processes. Examples include FedEx's introduction of overnight, nationwide, express package delivery in 1971 and eBay's launch of online auction services.

Service innovation can occur at many different levels; not every type of innovation has an impact on the characteristics of the service product or is experienced by the customer.

Reengineering Service Processes

The design of service processes has implications not only for customers but also for the cost, speed, and productivity with which the desired outcome is achieved. Improving productivity in services often requires speeding up the overall process (or cycle time), because the cost of creating a service usually is related to how long it takes to deliver each step in the process, plus any dead time between each step. *Reengineering* involves analyzing and redesigning processes to achieve faster and better performance.[14] To reduce overall process time, analysts must identify each step, measure how long it takes, look for opportunities to speed it up (or even eliminate it altogether), and cut out dead time. Running tasks in parallel rather than in sequence is a well-established approach to speeding up processes (a simple household example is to cook the vegetables for a meal while the main dish is in the oven). Service companies can use blueprinting (discussed in Chapter 8) to diagram these aspects of service operations in a systematic way.

Examination of processes may also lead to creation of alternative delivery methods that are so radically different as to constitute entirely new service concepts. Options may include eliminating certain supplementary services, adding new ones, instituting self-service procedures, and rethinking where and when service is delivered. Figure 4.19 illustrates this principle with simple flowcharts of four alternative ways to deliver meal service, as compared to a full-service restaurant. Take a look and contrast what happens front-stage at a fast-food restaurant, a drive-in restaurant, home delivery, and home catering. From the customer's perspective, what has been added to or deleted from the scenario at a full-service restaurant? And, in each instance, how do these changes affect back-stage activities?

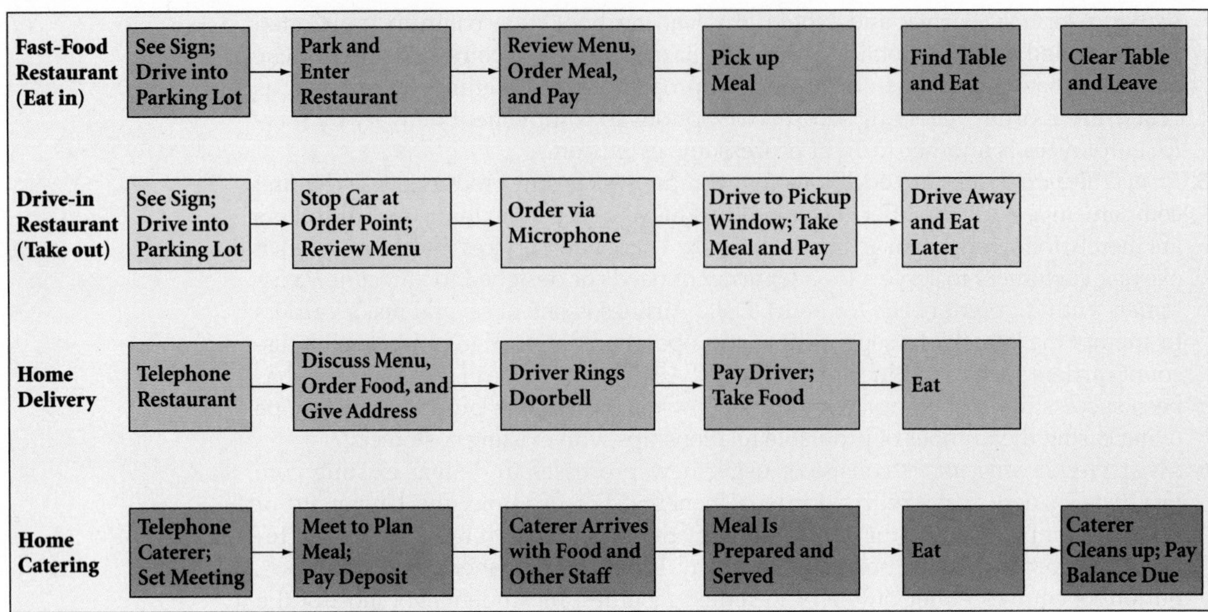

FIGURE 4.19 Alternative Service Concepts for Meal Delivery

Physical Goods as a Source of New Service Ideas

Goods and services may be competitive substitutes when they offer the same key benefits. For example, if your lawn needs mowing, you could buy a lawn mower and do it yourself, or you could contract with a lawn maintenance service to take care of the chore, effectively avoiding ownership and renting both labor and machines. Such decisions may be shaped by the customer's skills, physical capabilities, and time budget as well as such factors as cost comparisons between purchase price (plus operating costs) and service fees, storage space for purchased products, and anticipated frequency of need.

Many services can be built around providing an alternative to owning a physical good and enabling customers to do the work themselves. Figure 4.20 shows four possible delivery alternatives each for car travel and word processing, respectively. Three of these alternatives present service opportunities. Each alternative is based on choosing between ownership and rental of the necessary physical goods and between performing self-service and hiring another person to perform the necessary tasks. Additional services can be added to enhance the value proposition.

Any new physical product has the potential to create a need for related possession-processing services (particularly if the product is a high-value, durable item). Industrial equipment may require servicing throughout its lifespan, beginning with financing and insurance, then shipping (and possibly installation), and continuing with maintenance, cleaning, repair, consulting advice and problem solving, upgrading, and ultimate disposal. Historically, such after-sales services have generated important revenue streams for many years after the initial sale for products like trucks, factory machinery, locomotives, computers, and jet engines.

	OWN A PHYSICAL GOOD	RENT THE USE OF A PHYSICAL GOOD
PERFORM THE WORK ONESELF	• Drive Own Car • Type on Own Word Processor	• Rent a Car and Drive It • Rent a Word Processor and Type on It
HIRE SOMEONE TO DO THE WORK	• Hire a Chauffeur to Drive Car • Hire a Typist to Use Word Processor	• Hire a Taxi or Limousine • Send Work Out to a Secretarial Service

FIGURE 4.20 Services as Substitutes for Goods Ownership and Task Performance

Caterpillar, the well-known manufacturer of heavy-duty earthmoving and construction equipment, has developed a portfolio of service businesses to complement its highly cyclical manufacturing business.[15] These services include:

- *Cat Financial*—extends credit for three-quarters of all Caterpillar sales.
- *Cat Insurance*—serves both dealers and customers, protecting equipment against physical damage and offering extended warranty coverage.
- *Cat Rental Stores*—a network of dealer-owned facilities that offer daily, weekly, and monthly rentals of Caterpillar products and related equipment.
- *Cat Logistics*—undertakes supply chain management for customers around the world, offering both planning and program management.
- *Equipment Training Solutions Group*—offers courses for operators to help them select the right equipment for the job and use it skillfully to improve productivity, decrease downtime, reduce operating costs, and enhance safety.
- *Maintenance and Support*—creates individualized customer support agreements tailored to each customer's specific needs and can range from simple preventive maintenance kits to sophisticated total cost performance guarantees.
- *Remanufacturing*—uses proprietary technologies to salvage, clean, restore and rebuild used equipment from both Caterpillar and other original equipment manufacturers.

Using Research to Design New Services

If a company is designing a new service from scratch, how can it figure out what features and price will create the best value for target customers? It's hard to know without asking customers—hence the need for research. Research Insights 4.1 presents a classic example of how the Marriott Corporation used market research experts to help with new service development in the hotel industry.

Marriott was sufficiently encouraged by the findings to build three prototype Courtyard by Marriott hotels. After testing the concept under real-world conditions and making some refinements, the company developed a large chain whose advertising slogan became "Courtyard by Marriott—the hotel designed by business travelers." Marriott continues to use this theme, with recent advertising for Courtyard headlined "Architects Design Most Hotels, Road Warriors Designed Ours" and promoting free high-speed Internet access and 24-hour business services.

The new service concept filled a gap in the market with a product that represented the best balance between the price customers were prepared to pay and the physical and service features they most desired. The success of the Courtyard concept led Marriott to use the same research methodology to develop additional customer-driven products. These include Fairfield Inn, a moderately-priced chain whose rooms are supported by only limited hotel services, and SpringHill Suites, a moderately-priced all-suites hotel targeted at both business and pleasure travelers and offering separate working, sleeping and eating areas, including a pantry with sink, microwave, and coffee-maker.

Achieving Success in New Service Development

Consumer goods are notorious for their high failure rates, with more than 90 percent of the 30,000 new products introduced each year ending in failure.[16] Services are not immune to the high failure rates that plague new manufactured products. The advent of the Internet stimulated entrepreneurs to create numerous new "dot com" companies to deliver Internet-based services, but the vast majority failed within just a few years. The reasons for failure ranged widely, including not meeting a demonstrable consumer need, inability to cover costs from revenues, and poor execution. In the restaurant business, H. T. Parsa and his colleagues found a failure rare of about 26 percent during the first year rising to close to 60 percent within three years. Interestingly, the rate varied widely by type of food served, ranging from 33 percent for seafood and burger restaurants to 76 percent for subsandwich shops and bakeries and 86 percent for restaurants serving Mexican food.[17]

RESEARCH INSIGHTS 4.1

DESIGNING THE COURTYARD BY MARRIOTT CONCEPT

When Marriott was designing a new chain of hotels for business travelers (which eventually became known as Courtyard by Marriott), it hired marketing research experts to help establish an optimal design concept. Because there are limits to how much service and how many amenities can be offered at any given price, Marriott needed to know how customers would make trade-offs in order to arrive at the most satisfactory compromise in terms of value for money. The intent of the research was to get respondents to trade off different hotel service features to see which ones they valued most. Marriott's goal was to determine if a niche existed between full-service hotels and inexpensive motels, especially in locations where demand was not high enough to justify a large full-service hotel. If such a niche existed, executives wanted to develop a product to fill that gap.

A sample of 601 consumers in four metropolitan areas participated in the study. Researchers used a sophisticated technique known as conjoint analysis, which asks survey respondents to make trade-offs among different groupings of attributes. The objective was to determine which mix of attributes at specific prices offered them the highest degree of utility. The 50 attributes in the Marriott study were divided into the following seven factors (or sets of attributes), each containing a variety of different features based on detailed studies of competing offerings:

1. *External factors*—building shape, landscaping, pool type and location, hotel size.
2. *Room features*—room size and décor, climate control, location and type of bathroom, entertainment systems, other amenities.
3. *Food-related services*—type and location of restaurants, menus, room service, vending machines, guest shop, in-room kitchen.
4. *Lounge facilities*—location, atmosphere, type of guests.
5. *Services*—reservations, registration, check-out, airport limousine, bell desk (baggage service), message center, secretarial services, car rental, laundry, valet.
6. *Leisure facilities*—sauna, whirlpool, exercise room, racquetball and tennis courts, game room, children's playground.
7. *Security*—guards, smoke detectors, 24-hour video camera.

For each of these seven factors, respondents were presented with a series of stimulus cards displaying different levels of performance for each attribute. For instance, the "Rooms" stimulus card displayed nine attributes, each of which had three to five different levels. Thus, amenities ranged from "small bar of soap" to "large soap, shampoo packet, shoeshine mitt" to "large soap, bath gel, shower cap, sewing kit, shampoo, special soap" and then to the highest level, "large soap, bath gel, shower cap, sewing kit, special soap, toothpaste, etc."

In the second phase of the analysis, respondents were shown a number of alternative hotel profiles, each featuring different levels of performance on the various attributes. They were asked to indicate on a 5-point scale how likely they would be to stay at a hotel with these features, given a specific room price per night. Fifty different profiles were developed for this research, with each respondent asked to evaluate five of them.

The research yielded detailed guidelines for the selection of almost 200 features and service elements, representing those attributes that provided the highest utility for the customers in the target segments, at prices they were willing to pay. An important aspect of the study was that it focused not only on what business travelers wanted, but also identified what they liked but weren't prepared to pay for (there's a difference, after all, between wanting something and being willing to pay for it!). Using these inputs, the design team was able to meet the specified price while retaining the features most desired by the target market.

Source: Jerry Wind et al., "Courtyard by Marriott: Designing a Hotel Facility with Customer Based Marketing Models," *Interfaces*, January–February 1989, 25–47; Paul E. Green, Abba M. Krieger, and Yoram (Jerry) Wind, "Thirty Years of Conjoint Analysis: Reflections and Prospects," *Interfaces* 31, May–June 2001, S56–S73.

Chris Storey and Christopher Easingwood argue that in developing new services, the core product is of only secondary importance. The quality of the total service offering and the marketing support that goes with it are vital. Underlying success in these areas, they emphasize, is market knowledge: "Without an understanding of the marketplace, knowledge about customers, and knowledge about competitors, it is very unlikely that a new product will be a success."[18] Stephen Tax and Ian Stuart contend that new services should be defined in terms of the extent of change required to the existing service system, relative to the interactions between participants (people), processes, and physical elements (e.g., facilities and equipment).[19]

To what extent can rigorously conducted and controlled development processes for new services enhance their success rate? A study by Scott Edgett and Steven Parkinson focused on discriminating between successful and unsuccessful new financial services.[20] They found that the three factors contributed most to success were, in order of importance:

1. *Market synergy*—The new product fit well with the existing image of the firm, provided a superior advantage to competing products in terms of meeting customers' known needs, and received strong support during and after the launch from the firm and its branches; further, the firm had a good understanding of its customers' purchase decision behavior.
2. *Organizational factors*—There was strong interfunctional cooperation and coordination; development personnel were fully aware of why they were involved and of the importance of new products to the company.
3. *Market research factors*—Detailed and scientifically designed market research studies were conducted early in the development process with a clear idea of the type of information to be obtained; a good definition of the product concept was developed before undertaking field surveys were undertaken.

Another survey of financial service firms to determine what distinguished successful from unsuccessful products yielded similar findings.[21] In this instance, the key factors underlying success were determined as *synergy* (the fit between the product and the firm in terms of needed expertise and resources present) and *internal marketing* (the support given to staff prior to launch to help them understand the new product and its underlying systems, plus details about direct competitors, and support). Yet another study found similar factors—marketing synergy and human resource issues like meeting customer needs and having a human resource strategy that links to the development of service processes—are keys to success.[22]

Courtyard by Marriott's success in a very different industry—a people-processing service with many tangible components—supports the notion that a highly structured development process will increase the chances of success for a complex service innovation. However, it's worth noting that there may be limits to the degree of structure that can and should be imposed. Swedish researchers Bo Edwardsson, Lars Haglund, and Jan Mattson reviewed new service development in telecommunications, transport, and financial services. They concluded:

> [C]omplex processes like the development of new services cannot be formally planned altogether. Creativity and innovation cannot only rely on planning and control. There must be some elements of improvization, anarchy, and internal competition in the development of new services. . . . We believe that a contingency approach is needed and that creativity on the one hand and formal planning and control on the other can be balanced, with successful new services as the outcome.[23]

An important conclusion from subsequent research in Sweden concerns the role of customers in service innovation. Researchers found that in the idea-generation stage, the nature of submitted ideas differed significantly depending on whether they were created by professional service developers or by the users themselves. Users' ideas were judged more original and to have a higher perceived value for customers. However, on average, these ideas were harder to convert into commercial services.[24]

CONCLUSION

A service product comprises all the elements of the service performance that create value for the customer, and it consists of a core product bundled with a variety of supplementary service elements and their delivery processes. In mature industries, in which the core service tends to become commoditized, the search for competitive advantage often centers on creating new supplementary services or significantly improving performance on existing ones. Another important differentiator can be the way the product is delivered, that is the service delivery processes. It is not the outcome of a service delivery, but the way this outcome is achieved that often differentiates one service provider from another.

Designing a service product is a complex task that requires an understanding of how the core and supplementary services should be combined, sequenced, delivered, and branded to create a value proposition that meets the needs of target market segments. To do this, we discussed the "Flower of Service," branding strategies, and new service development as key tools for product development.

Chapter Summary

LO1 A service product consists of three components:

- Core product delivers the principle benefits and solutions customers seek.
- Supplementary services facilitate and enhance the core product.
- Delivery processes determine how the core and supplementary service elements are delivered to the customer.

The core product often becomes commoditized, and differentiation then centers on supplementary services and service delivery processes.

LO2 The Flower of Service concept categorizes supplementary services into facilitating and enhancing supplementary services. *Facilitating supplementary services* are needed for service delivery or help in the use of the core product. They are: information, order-taking, billing, and payment. *Enhancing supplementary services* add value for the customer and include consultation, hospitality, safekeeping, and dealing with exceptions. The use of the flower metaphor helps us to understand that all the supplementary elements must be performed well. A weakness in one element will spoil the overall impression.

LO3 Most service firms offer a line of products, with each service product having a different combination of service attributes and their respective performance levels. Branding of individual services products is used to increase tangibility of the service offering and value proposition. Firms can use a variety of branding strategies, including

- *Branded house*: applying a brand to multiple, often unrelated services (e.g., Virgin Group).
- *Subbrands*: using a master brand (often the firm name) together with a specific service brand (e.g., British Airways Club World service) or to identify specific service levels (e.g., Sun Microsystems' Platinum Service Plan).
- *Endorsed brands*: here, the product brand dominates but the corporate brand is still featured (e.g., Starwood Hotels & Resorts).
- *House of brands*: individual services are promoted under their own brand name without the corporate brand (e.g., KFC of Yum! Brands).

LO4 Firms need to improve and develop new services to maintain a competitive edge. The seven levels in the hierarchy of new service development are

- *Style changes*: highly visible, create excitement (e.g., repainting retail branches and vehicles in a new color scheme), but typically do not involve changes in performance or processes.
- *Service improvements*: involve modest changes in the performance of current products.
- *Supplementary service innovations*: significantly improving or adding new facilitating or enhancing service elements.
- *Process line extensions*: new ways of delivering existing services products, such as creating self-service options.
- *Product line extensions*: adding new services that typically deliver the same core service but specified to satisfy different needs (e.g., adding a budget service to a full-service airline's offering).
- *Major process innovations*: using new processes to deliver current product, such as adding online courses to traditional class-room delivered lectures.

- *Major service innovations*: development of new core products, such as eBay's launch of online auction service.

  Major service innovations are relatively rare. More common is the use of new technologies to deliver existing services in new ways, enhancing or creating new supplementary services, and greatly improving performance on existing ones through process redesign.

LO5 Factors that enhance the chances of success in new service development are listed in order of importance:

- *Market synergy*: the new product fits well with the firm's existing image, expertise and resources, and provides a superior advantage in terms of meeting customers' needs over competing services.
- *Organizational factors*: well-supported by coordinated efforts between the different functional areas in a firm.
- *Market research:* customer ideas and research is already incorporated early in the new service design process.

Review Questions

1. Explain what is meant by core product and supplementary services.
2. Explain the *Flower of Service* concept and identify each of its *petals*. What insights does this concept provide for service marketers?
3. Explain the distinction between enhancing and facilitating supplementary services. Give several examples of each, relative to services you have used recently.
4. How is branding used in services marketing? What is the distinction between a corporate brand such as Marriott and the names of its various inn and hotel chains?
5. What are the approaches firms can take to create new services?
6. Why do new services often fail? What factors are associated with successful development of new services?

Application Exercises

1. Select a specific service product you are familiar with and identify its core product and supplementary services. Then, select a competing service and analyze the differences in terms of core product and supplementary services between the two services.
2. Identify two examples of branding in financial services (e.g., specific types of retail bank accounts or insurance policies), and define their characteristics. How meaningful are these brands likely to be to customers?
3. Using a firm you are familiar with, analyze what opportunities it might have to create product line extensions for its current and/or new markets. What impact might these extensions have on its present services?
4. Identify two failed new service developments. Analyze the causes for their failure.

Endnotes

1. The notion of a core service enhanced by supplementary services was advanced by Pierre Eiglier and Eric Langeard, "Services as Systems: Marketing Implications," in P. Eiglier, E. Langeard, C. H. Lovelock, J. E. G. Bateson, and R. F. Young, eds. *Marketing Consumer Services: New Insights.* Cambridge, MA: Marketing Science Institute, 1977, 83–103. Note: An earlier version of this article was published in French in *Révue Française de Gestion,* March–April 1977, 72–84; G. Lynn Shostack, "Breaking Free from Product Marketing," *Journal of Marketing,* 44, April 1977, 73–80; Christian Grönroos, *Service Management and Marketing.* Lexington, MA: Lexington Books, 1990, 74.
2. The "Flower of Service" concept was first introduced in Christopher H. Lovelock, "Cultivating the Flower of Service: New Ways of Looking at Core and Supplementary Services," in P. Eiglier and E. Langeard, eds. *Marketing, Operations, and Human Resources: Insights into Services.* Aix-en-Provence, France: IAE, Université d'Aix-Marseille III, 1992, 296–316.
3. Loizos Heracleous, Jochen Wirtz, and Nitin Pangarkar, *Flying High in a Competitive Industry— Secrets of the World's Leading Airline.* Singapore: McGraw Hill, 2009.
4. James C. Anderson and James A. Narus, "Capturing the Value of Supplementary Services," *Harvard Business Review,* 73, January–February 1995, 75–83.

5. See /www.banyantree.com, accessed June 3, 2009.
6. James Devlin, "Brand Architecture in Services: The Example of Retail Financial Services," *Journal of Marketing Management*, 19, 2003, 1043–1065.
7. David Aaker and E. Joachimsthaler, "The Brand Relationship Spectrum: The Key to the Brand Challenge," *California Management Review*, 42, No. 4, 2000, 8–23.
8. Weizhong Jiang, Chekitan S. Dev, and Vithala R. Rao, "Brand Extension and Customer Loyalty: Evidence from the Lodging Industry," *Cornell Hotel and Restaurant Administration Quarterly*, 43, August 2002, 5–16.
9. http://www.sun.com/service/serviceplans/sunspectrum/index.jsp accessed May 7, 2009.
10. Joe Wheeler and Shaun Smith, *Managing the Experience.* Upper Saddle River, NJ: Prentice Hall, 2003.
11. Don E. Shultz, "Getting to the Heart of the Brand," *Marketing Management*, 10, September–October 2001, 8–9.
12. Chad Rubel, "New Menu for Restaurants: Talking Trees and Blackjack," *Marketing News*, 30, July 29, 1996, 1. www.rainforestcafe.com, accessed June 12, 2009.
13. See James Traub, "Drive-Thru U.," *The New Yorker*, October 20 and 27, 1997 and Joshua Macht, "Virtual You," *Inc. Magazine*, January 1998, 84–87.
14. See, for example, Michael Hammer and James Champy, *Reengineering the Corporation.* New York: HarperBusiness, 1993.
15. Michael Arndt, "Cat Sinks Its Claws Into Services," *Business Week*, December 5, 2005, 56–58.
16. Clayton M. Christenson, Scott Cook, and Taddy Hall," Marketing Malpractice: The Cause and the Cure," *Harvard Business Review,* December 2005, 4–12.
17. H. T. Parsa, John T. Self, David Njite, and Tiffany King, "Why Restaurants Fail," *Cornell Hotel and Restaurant Administration Quarterly*, 46, August 2005, 304–322.
18. Chris D. Storey and Christopher J. Easingwood, "The Augmented Service Offering: A Conceptualization and Study of Its Impact on New Service Success," *Journal of Product Innovation Management*, 15, 1998, 335–351.
19. Stephen S. Tax and Ian Stuart, "Designing and Implementing New Services: The Challenges of Integrating Service Systems," *Journal of Retailing*, 73, No. 1, 1997, 105–134.
20. Scott Edgett and Steven Parkinson, "The Development of New Financial Services: Identifying Determinants of Success and Failure," *International Journal of Service Industry Management*, 5, No. 4, 1994, 24–38.
21. Christopher Storey and Christopher J. Easingwood, "The Impact of the New Product Development Project on the Success of Financial Services," *Service Industries Journal*, 13, No. 3, July 1993, 40–54.
22. Michael Ottenbacher, Juergen Gnoth, and Peter Jones, "Identifying Determinants of Success in Development of New High-Contact Services," *International Journal of Service Industry Management*, 17, No. 4, 2006, 344–363.
23. Bo Edvardsson, Lars Haglund, and Jan Mattsson, "Analysis, Planning, Improvisation and Control in the Development of New Services," *International Journal of Service Industry Management*, 6, No. 2, 1995, 24–35 (p. 34). See also Bo Edvardsson and Jan Olsson, "Key Concepts for New Service Development," *The Service Industries Journal*, 16, April 1996, 140–164.
24. Peter R. Magnusson, Jonas Matthing, and Per Kristensson, "Managing User Involvement in Service Innovation: Experiments with Innovating End Users," *Journal of Service Research*, 6, November 2003, 111–124; Jonas Matthing, Bodil Sandén, and Bo Edvardsson, "New Service Development: Learning from and with Customers," *International Journal of Service Industry Management*, 15, No. 5, 2004, 479–498.

CHAPTER 5

Distributing Services Through Physical and Electronic Channels

Companies best equipped for the twenty-first century will consider investment in real time systems as essential to maintaining their competitive edge and keeping their customers.

REGIS MCKENNA

Think globally, act locally.

JOHN NAISBITT

LEARNING OBJECTIVES (LOs)

By the end of this chapter, the reader should be able to:

LO1 List the four questions that form the foundation of any service distribution strategy.

LO2 Know *what* is being distributed, given the nonownership and experiential nature of many services.

LO3 Understand the importance of distinguishing between distributing core and supplementary services.

LO4 Know the three main modes of distribution of services and *how* they can be distributed.

LO5 Understand determinants of customers' channel preferences.

LO6 Describe the *where* (place) and *when* (time) decisions of physical channels.

LO7 Recognize the issues of delivering services through electronic channels.

LO8 Understand the part played by intermediaries in distributing services.

LO9 Appreciate the special challenges of distributing services internationally.

Being Global in an Instant?. . . Or Does It Take Forever?

Some services spread like wildfire and ramp up with incredible speed. For example, Lauren Luke's *panacea81* has become one of the world's most popular YouTube channels in less than 12 months. Luke has become an Internet celebrity with her short video tutorials showing viewers how to apply make up for various occasions. Related services, including the British make-up artist's website, have been phenomenally successful.[1]

Other services however, may take decades to achieve global distribution. Think of how long it took Starbucks or global supply chain solutions providers such as UPS or DHL to achieve a global presence! These contrasting examples demonstrate both the diversity of the service sector and the importance of distinguishing information processing and people or possession processing services. The former can be scaled rapidly, whereas the latter require the building of facilities in every market where they want presence, requiring the growing firm to deal with local labor, building, food hygiene regulations, and more. That requires deep pockets and lots of management time!

DISTRIBUTION IN A SERVICES CONTEXT

What? How? Where? When? Responses to these four questions form the foundation of any service distribution strategy. The customer's service experience and types of encounters (if any) with service employees are a function of how the different elements of the "flower of service" are distributed and delivered through selective physical and electronic channels.

What Is Distributed?

If you mention distribution, many people are likely to think of moving boxes through physical channels to distributors and retailers for sale to end users. In services though, often there's nothing to move. Experiences, performances, and solutions are not physically shipped and stored. Meanwhile, informational transactions are increasingly conducted via electronic channels. How then does distribution work in a services context? In a typical sales cycle, distribution embraces three interrelated flows, which partially address the question of *what* is distributed:

- **Information and promotion flow**—distribution of information and promotion materials relating to the service offer. The objective is to get the customer interested in buying the service.
- **Negotiation flow**—reaching an agreement on the service features and configuration, and the terms of the offer, so that a purchase contract can be closed. The objective is to sell the *right* to use a service (e.g., sell a reservation or a ticket).
- **Product flow**—many services, especially those involving people processing or possession processing, require physical facilities for delivery. Here, distribution strategy requires development of a network of local sites. For information-processing services, such as Internet banking, distance learning, broadcast news, and entertainment, the product flow can be undertaken via electronic channels, employing one or more centralized sites.

DISTINGUISHING BETWEEN DISTRIBUTION OF SUPPLEMENTARY AND CORE SERVICES. The flow perspective on what is distributed can relate to the core service as well as to supplementary services and can be mapped back to the "flower of service." Information flow relates to the information and potentially consultation petals; negotiations flow to the order taking and potentially billing and payment petals; and products flow to the remaining petals and core service. Distinguishing between core and supplementary services is important, as many core services require a physical location, which severely restricts distribution. For instance, you can only consume Club Med holidays at Club Med Villages, and a live performance of a Broadway show must take place at a theater in Manhattan (until it goes on tour). However, many of the supplementary services are informational in nature and can be distributed widely and cost-effectively via other means. Prospective Club Med customers can get information and consultation from a travel agent, either face-to-face, online, by phone or by email, and then make a booking through one of these same channels. Similarly, you can purchase theater tickets through an agency without the need for an advance trip to the facility itself.

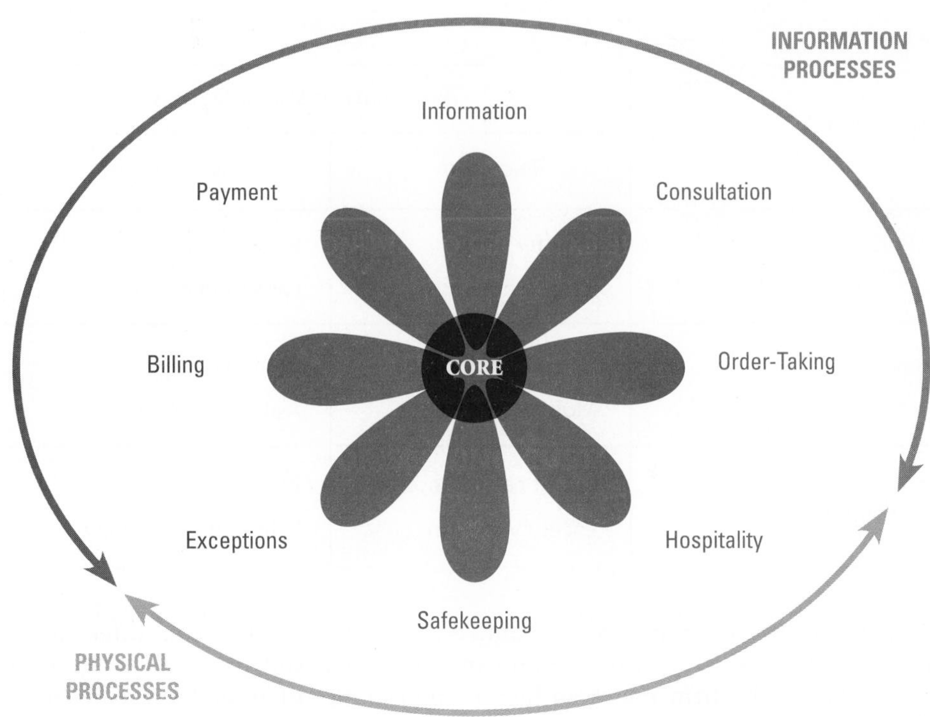

FIGURE 5.1 Information and Physical Processes of the Augmented Service Product

When you look at the eight petals of the "flower of service," you can see that no fewer than five supplementary services are information based (Figure 5.1). Information, consultation, order-taking, billing, and payment (e.g., via credit card) can all be transmitted using the digital language of computers. Even service businesses that involve physical core products, such as retailing and repair, are shifting delivery of many supplementary services to the Internet, closing physical branches, and relying on speedy business logistics to enable a strategy of arm's-length transactions with their customers.

The distribution of information, consultation, and order-taking (or reservations and ticket sales) has reached extremely sophisticated levels in some global service industries, requiring a number of carefully integrated channels targeted at key customer segments. For instance, Starwood Hotels & Resorts Worldwide—whose approximately 900 hotels include such brands as St. Regis, W Hotel, Westin, Le Méridien, and Sheraton—had more than 30 global sales offices (GSOs) around the world to manage customer relationships with key global accounts, offering a one-stop solution to corporate travel planners, wholesalers, meeting planners, incentive houses, and major travel organizations.[2] The company also operated 12 customer servicing centers (CSCs) strategically placed around the globe to cover all time zones and key language requirements to provide one-stop customer service for its guests, covering worldwide hotel reservations, enrolment and redemption of Starwood's loyalty program, and general customer service. You only need to call one toll-free number to book any Starwood hotel. Alternatively, you can reserve rooms through electronic channels, including www.starwoodhotels.com, or the individual hotel websites.

DISTRIBUTION OPTIONS FOR SERVING CUSTOMERS: DETERMINING THE TYPE OF CONTACT

How should services be distributed? Here, a key question is: Does the service or the firm's positioning strategy require customers to be in direct physical contact with its personnel, equipment, and facilities? (As we saw in Chapter 1, this is inevitable for people-processing services, but optional for other categories.) If so, do customers have to visit the facilities of the service organization, or will the latter send personnel and equipment to customers' own sites? Alternatively, can transactions between provider and customer be completed at arm's length through the use of either

TABLE 5.1 Six Options for Service Delivery

Nature of Interaction Between Customer and Service Organization	Availability of Service Outlets	
	Single Site	Multiple Sites
Customer goes to service organization	Theater Barbershop	Bus service Fast-food chain
Service organization comes to customer	House painting Mobile car wash	Mail delivery Auto club road service
Customer and service organization transact remotely (mail or electronic communications)	Credit card company Local TV station	Broadcast network Telephone company

telecommunications or physical channels of distribution? (The three possible options are shown in the first column of Table 5.1.) And for each of these three options, should the firm maintain just a single outlet or offer to serve customers through multiple outlets at different locations?

Customers Visit the Service Site

The convenience of service factory locations and operational schedules assume great importance when a customer has to be physically present—either throughout service delivery or even just to initiate and terminate the transaction. Elaborate statistical analysis, in the form of retail gravity models, is sometimes used to aid decisions on where to locate supermarkets and similar large stores relative to prospective customers' homes and workplaces. Traffic and pedestrian counts help to establish how many prospective customers pass by certain locations in a day. Construction of an expressway or the introduction of a new bus or rail service may have a significant effect on travel patterns and, in turn, determine which sites are now more desirable—and which are less so.

Service Providers Go to Their Customers

For some types of services, the supplier visits the customer. Aramark, which provides food services to a wide array of customers—from schools and hospitals to sports stadiums and prisons—must necessarily bring its equipment, food products, and personnel to the customer's site, because the need is location specific. In remote areas like Alaska or Canada's Northwest Territory, service providers often fly to visit their customers, because the latter find it so difficult to travel. Australia is famous for its Royal Flying Doctor Service, in which physicians fly into farms and sheep stations in the Outback. The question then is, when should service providers go to their customers?

Going to the customer's site is unavoidable whenever the object of the service is some immovable physical item, such as a tree to be pruned, installed machinery to be repaired, or a house that requires pest-control treatment. In other instances, going to the customer is optional. Because it's more expensive and time consuming for the service firm to send personnel and their equipment to travel to the customer rather than vice versa, the trend has been toward requiring customers to come to the service provider instead (fewer doctors make housecalls nowadays!).

In general, service providers are more likely to visit corporate customers at their premises than to visit individuals in their homes, reflecting the larger volume associated with business-to-business (B2B) transactions. However, there may be a profitable niche in serving individuals willing to pay a premium for the convenience of receiving personal visits. One young veterinary doctor has built her business around making housecalls to

SERVICE PERSPECTIVE 5.1

POWER AND TEMPERATURE CONTROL FOR RENT

You probably think of electricity as coming from a distant power station and of air conditioning and heating as fixed installations. So how would you deal with the following challenges?

- Luciano Pavarotti, the famous tenor, is giving an open-air concert in Münster, Germany, and the organizers require an uninterruptible source of electrical power for the duration of the concert, independent of the local electricity supply.
- A tropical cyclone has devastated the small mining town of Pannawonica in Western Australia, destroying everything in its path, including power lines, and electrical power must be restored as soon as possible so that the town and its infrastructure can be rebuilt.
- In Amsterdam, organizers of the World Championship Indoor Windsurfing competition need to power 27 wind turbines that will be installed along the length of a huge indoor pool to create winds of 20–30 mph (32–48 km/h).
- A U.S. Navy submarine needs a shore-based source of power when it is docked at a remote Norwegian port.
- Sri Lanka faces an acute shortage of electricity-generating capability after water levels fall dangerously low at major hydro electric dams, a result of insufficient monsoon rains two years in a row.
- Hotels in Florida need to be dried out following water damage in a hurricane.
- A large, power-generating plant in Oklahoma urgently seeks temporary capacity to replace one of its cooling towers, destroyed in a tornado the previous day.
- The Caribbean island of Bonaire requires a temporary power station to stabilize its grid after fire damages the main power plant and results in widespread blackouts.

These are all challenges that have been faced and met by a company called Aggreko, which describes itself as "The World Leader in Temporary Utility Rental Solutions." Aggreko operates from more than 133 locations using more than $1 billion of rental equipment to serve customers in over 100 countries. It rents a "fleet" of mobile electricity generators, oil-free air compressors, and temperature control devices ranging from water chillers and industrial air conditioners to giant heaters and dehumidifiers.

Aggreko's customer base is dominated by large companies and government agencies. Although much of its business comes from predicted needs, such as backup operations during planned factory maintenance or the filming of a James Bond movie, the firm is poised to resolve problems that arise unexpectedly from emergencies or natural disasters.

Much of the firm's rental equipment is contained in soundproofed, boxlike structures that can be shipped anywhere in the world to create the specific type and level of electrical power output or climate-control capability required by the client. Consultation, installation, and ongoing technical support add value to the core service. Emphasis is placed on solving customer problems rather than just renting equipment. Some customers have a clear idea of their needs in advance, others require advice on how to develop innovative and cost effective solutions to what may be unique problems, and still others are desperate to restore power that has been lost because of an unexpected disaster. In the last-mentioned instance, speed is essential because downtime can be extremely expensive and lives may depend on the promptness of Aggreko's response.

Delivering service requires Aggreko to ship its equipment to the customer's site. Following the Pannawonica cyclone, Aggreko's West Australian team swung into action, rapidly setting up some 30 generators ranging from 60–750 kVA, plus cabling, refueling tankers, and other equipment. The generators were transported by four "road trains," each comprising a giant tractor unit pulling three 40-foot (13 m) trailers. Technicians and additional equipment were flown in on two Hercules aircraft. The Aggreko technicians remained on site for six weeks, providing 24/7 service while the town was rebuilt.

Sources: Aggreko's "International Magazine," 1997, www.aggreko.com, accessed June 1, 2009.

care for sick pets. She has found that customers are glad to pay extra for a service that not only saves them time, but is also less stressful for their pets than waiting in a crowded veterinary clinic. Other consumer services of this nature include mobile car washing, office and in-home catering, and made-to-measure tailoring services for businesspeople.

A growing service activity involves the rental of both equipment and labor for special occasions or in response to customers who need to expand their productive capacity during busy periods. Service Perspective 5.1 describes the B2B services of Aggreko, an international company that rents generating and cooling equipment around the world.

The Service Transaction Is Conducted Remotely

When you deal with a service firm through remote transactions, you may never see the service facilities and meet service personnel face-to-face. There tend to be service encounters, and those encounters that you do have with service personnel are more likely to be made via a call center or, even more remotely, by mail or email.

Repair services for small pieces of equipment sometimes require customers to ship the product to a maintenance facility where it is serviced and then returned by mail (with the option of paying extra for express shipment). Many service providers offer solutions with the help of integrated logistics firms such as FedEx or UPS. These solutions range from storage and express delivery of spare parts for aircraft (B2B delivery), to pickup of defective cell phones from customers' homes and subsequent return of the repaired phone to the customer (B2C pickup and delivery, also called "reverse logistics").

Any information-based product can be delivered almost instantaneously through the Internet to almost any point on the globe. As a result, telecommunications services are now directly competing with physical logistics services.

Channel Preferences Vary among Consumers

The use of different channels to deliver the same service not only has different cost implications for a service organization, but it also drastically affects the nature of the service experience for the customer. Banking services, for instance, can be delivered remotely via computer or mobile phone, a voice response system, a call center, and ATMs; or face-to-face in a branch, or, in the case of private banking, through a direct visit to a wealthy customer's home.

Although electronic self-service channels tend to be the most cost-effective, not all customers like to use them. This means migration of customers to new electronic channels may require different strategies for different segments[3] as well as recognition that some proportion of customers will never voluntarily depart from their preferred high-contact delivery environments. An alternative that appeals to many people, perhaps because it uses a familiar technology, is conducting banking and other service transactions by telephone; however, automated phone services can be another matter. How do you feel about voicemail transactions, with their sometimes lengthy messages promoting other services, trying to drive you to the company's website, and then, if you persist, requiring you to "press 1" for this and "press 2" for that several times before you finally reach the transaction you actually want to make? Recent research has explored how customers choose among personal, impersonal, and self-service channels and has identified the following key drivers:[4]

- For complex and high perceived risk services, people tend to rely on personal channels. For example, customers are happy to apply for credit cards using remote channels, but prefer a face-to-face transaction when obtaining a mortgage.
- Individuals with higher confidence and knowledge about a service and/or the channel are more likely to use impersonal and self-service channels

- Customers who look for the functional aspects of a transaction prefer more convenience. This often means the use of impersonal and self-service channels. Customers with social motives tend to use personal channels.
- Convenience is a key driver of channel choice for the majority of consumers. Service convenience means saving time and effort rather than saving money. A customer's search for convenience is not just confined to the purchase of core products but also extends to convenient times and places. People want easy access to supplementary services, too—especially information, reservations, and problem solving.

Service providers have to be careful when channels are priced differently—increasingly, sophisticated customers take advantage of price variation among channels and markets, a strategy known as channel arbitrage.[5] For example, customers can ask the expensive full-service broker for advice (and perhaps place a small order) and then conduct the bulk of their trades via the much lower-priced discount broker. Service providers need to develop effective strategies that will enable them to deliver value and capture it through the appropriate channel.

PLACE AND TIME DECISIONS

How should service managers make decisions on the places *where* service is delivered and the times *when* it is available? The answer: Start by understanding customer needs and expectations, competitive activity, and the nature of the service operation. As we noted earlier, the distribution strategies employed for some of the supplementary service elements may differ from those used to deliver the core product itself. For instance, as a customer, you're probably willing to go to a particular location at a specific time to attend a sporting or entertainment event. But you probably want greater flexibility and convenience when reserving a seat in advance, so you may expect the reservations service to be open for extended hours, to offer booking and credit card payment by phone or the Web, and to deliver tickets through postal or electronic channels.

Where Should Service Be Delivered in a Brick-and-Mortar Context?

Deciding where to locate a service facility for customers involves very different considerations from locating the back-stage elements where cost, productivity, and access to labor often are key determinants. In the first instance, customer convenience and preference are key. Firms should make it easy for people to access frequently purchased services, especially those that face active competition.[6] Examples include retail banks and fast-food restaurants. However, customers may be willing to travel further from their homes or workplaces to reach specialty services.

People Get Upset When Electronic Distribution Systems Let Them Down
Source: Reprinted from Christopher Lovelock, Product Plus (New York: McGraw-Hill, 1994), p. 283.

MINISTORES. An interesting innovation among multisite service businesses involves creating numerous small service factories to maximize geographic coverage. Automated kiosks represent one approach. ATMs offer many of the functions of a bank branch within a compact, self-service machine that can be located within stores, hospitals, colleges, airports, and office buildings. Another approach results from separating the front- and back-stages of the operation. Taco Bell's innovative K-Minus strategy involves restaurants without kitchens.[7] Food preparation takes place in a central commissary from which meals are shipped to restaurants (which can now devote more of their expensive floor-area to customer use) and to other "points of access" (such as mobile foodcarts), where the food can be reheated before serving.

Increasingly, firms offering one type of service business are purchasing space from another provider in a complementary field. Perhaps you've noticed small bank branches inside supermarkets and food outlets such as Dunkin Donuts and Subway sharing space with a fast-food restaurant such as Burger King.

LOCATING IN MULTIPURPOSE FACILITIES. The most obvious locations for consumer services are close to where customers live or work. Modern buildings often are designed to be multipurpose, featuring not only office or production space but also such services as a bank (or at least an ATM), a restaurant, a hair salon, several stores, and maybe a health club. Some companies even include a children's day-care facility to make life easier for busy working parents.

Interest is growing in locating retail and other services on transportation routes and in bus, rail, and air terminals. Most major oil companies have developed chains of small retail stores to complement the fuel pumps at their service stations, thus offering customers the convenience of one-stop shopping for fuel, vehicle supplies, food, and a selection of basic household products. Truckstops on major highways often include laundry centers, restrooms, ATMs, Internet access, restaurants, and inexpensive accommodation in addition to a variety of vehicle maintenance and repair services. Airport terminals—designed as part of the infrastructure for air transportation services—have been transformed into vibrant shopping malls—a big change from the nondescript areas where passengers and their bags used to be processed (see Service Perspective 5.2).

LOCATIONAL CONSTRAINTS. Although customer convenience is important, the need for economies of scale is an operational issue that may restrict choice of locations. Major hospitals offer many different health-care services at a single location, requiring a very large facility. Customers requiring complex, in-patient treatment must go to the service factory, rather than be treated at home. However, an ambulance—or even a helicopter—can be sent to pick them up. Medical specialists, as opposed to general practitioners, often find it convenient to locate their offices close to a hospital because it saves them time when they need to treat their patients.

Furthermore, operational requirements set tight constraints for some services. Airports, for instance, often are inconveniently located relative to travelers' homes, offices, or destinations. Because of noise and environmental factors, finding suitable sites for construction of new airports or expansion of existing ones is a very difficult task. (A governor of Massachusetts was once asked what would be an acceptable location for a second airport to serve Boston; he thought for a moment and then responded, "Nebraska!") One way to make airport access more convenient is to install fast rail links, such as San Francisco's BART service, or London's Heathrow Express. A different type of location constraint is imposed by other geographic factors, such as terrain and climate. By definition, ski resorts have to be in the mountains and ocean beach resorts on the coast.

When Should Service Be Delivered?

In the past, most retail and professional services in industrialized countries followed a traditional schedule of being available about 40 or 50 hours a week. In large measure, this routine reflected social norms (and even legal requirements or union agreements) as to what were appropriate hours for people to work and for enterprises to sell

SERVICE PERSPECTIVE 5.2

FROM AIRPORTS TO AIR MALLS

Large airports used to be places where thousands of people spent time waiting with little to keep them occupied. Airports were often bound by contract to a single food operator, which translated into low-quality food at high prices. Other than visiting stores selling newspapers, magazines, and paperback books, there wasn't much opportunity for travelers to shop unless they wanted to spend money on expensive (and often tawdry) souvenirs. The one exception was the tax-free shop at international airports, where opportunities to save money created a brisk trade in alcohol, perfume, tobacco, and consumer products such as cameras. Today however, some airports have terminals that have been transformed into shopping malls. London's Heathrow Airport even has a branch of Harrods, the famous department store.

Three factors make investments in airport retailing very appealing. One is the upscale demographics of airline passengers, whose numbers continue to grow rapidly. A second is that many passengers have time to spare while waiting for their flights. Tighter security requirements mean that passengers must now check in very early for their flights. Finally, many existing terminal interiors have free space that can be put to profitable use. As terminals are expanded, new retail sites can be included as an integral part of the design.

The first (and still the most successful) custom-built airport retail complex in the United States is the Pittsburgh Air Mall, created as part of a new airport terminal and operated under a 10-year contract by BAA International, the largest global airport operator. Pittsburgh is an important hub airport serving some 10 million passengers a year, most of whom are domestic travelers. Goods and services available in the Air Mall's more than 100 stores and restaurants range from tasty take-out sandwiches for passengers who don't expect a meal on their discount-priced flight, to $30 massages for tired travelers with aching backs. Perhaps the most striking statistic is that sales per square foot are four to five times those of typical U.S. regional shopping centers.

BAA also operates long-term retail contracts at Baltimore-Washington and Boston-Logan in the U.S. as well as at seven airports in the U.K. It has equity investments in six Australian airports and one in Naples, Italy.

Source: BAA International www.baa.com and www.pitairport.com, accessed June 2, 2009.

things. The situation inconvenienced working people who had to shop either during their lunch break or on Saturdays. Historically, Sunday opening was strongly discouraged in most Christian cultures and often was prohibited by law, reflecting a long tradition based on religious practice.

Today, the situation has changed. For some highly responsive service operations, the standard has become "24/7" service—24 hours a day, 7 days a week, around the world. (For an overview of the factors behind the move to more extended hours, see Service Perspective 5.3.) Some firms, however, have resisted the trend to seven-day operations. Atlanta-based Chick-fil-A, a highly successful restaurant chain, declares that "being closed on Sunday is part of our value proposition" and claims that giving managers and crews a day off is a factor in the firm's extremely low turnover rate.

DELIVERING SERVICES IN CYBERSPACE

Developments in telecommunications and computer technology have spurred many new approaches to service delivery. In the hospitality industry, reservations are increasingly handled via firms' websites. For example, Swissôtel Hotels & Resorts

SERVICE PERSPECTIVE 5.3

FACTORS THAT ENCOURAGE EXTENDED OPERATING HOURS

At least five factors are driving the move toward extended operating hours and seven-day operations. The trend that originated in the United States and Canada, has since spread to many other countries around the world.

- *Economic pressure from consumers.* The growing number of two-income families and single wage earners who live alone need time outside normal working hours to shop and use other services. Once one store or firm in any given area extends its hours to meet the needs of these market segments, competitors often feel obliged to follow. Chain stores have frequently led the way.
- *Changes in legislation*. Support has declined for the traditional religious view that a specific day (Sunday in predominantly Christian cultures) should be legislated as a day of rest for one and all, regardless of religious affiliation. In a multicultural society, of course, it's a moot point which day should be designated as special—for observant Jews and Seventh Day Adventists, Saturday is the Sabbath; for Muslims, Friday is the holy day; and agnostics or atheists are presumably indifferent. There has been a gradual erosion of such legislation in Western nations in recent years.
- *Economic incentives to improve asset utilization.* A great deal of capital is often tied up in service facilities. The incremental cost of extending hours tends to be relatively modest, and if it reduces crowding and increases revenues, then it is economically attractive. There are costs involved in shutting down and reopening a facility such as a supermarket, yet climate control and some lighting must be left running all night, and security personnel must be paid 24/7. So, even if the number of extra customers served is minimal, there are both operational and marketing advantages to remaining open 24 hours.
- *Availability of employees to work during "unsocial" hours.* Changing lifestyles and a desire for part-time employment have created a growing labor pool of people willing to work evenings and nights. They include students looking for part-time work outside classroom hours, people working a second job, parents juggling child-care responsibilities, and others who simply prefer to work by night and relax or sleep by day.
- *Automated self-service facilities.* Self-service equipment has become increasingly reliable and user friendly. Many machines now accept card-based payments in addition to coins and banknotes. Installing unattended machines may be economically feasible alternative for locations that cannot support a staffed facility. Unless a machine requires frequent servicing or is particularly vulnerable to vandalism, the incremental cost of going from limited hours to 24-hour operation is minimal. In fact, it may be simpler to leave machines running continuously than to turn them on and off.

executed an entire campaign to increase online bookings, especially among the important business traveler segment. Within seven months of launch, its revamped website (www.swissotel.com) more than doubled online revenues.[8] Apart from the enhanced express reservation functions (with fewer clicks), user-friendly navigation, and online promotions and incentives, the hotel company's "Best Rate Guarantee" was a key driver of its success. Guests booking via its website were guaranteed the best rate for their booking. If they found another website with a lower rate, Swissôtel not only matched this rate, it also offered an additional 50 percent discount in the first night of the guest's stay. The guarantee gave customers peace of mind. Swissôtel's logo (see Figure 5.2) now includes its website address to drive its guests toward online reservations and services.

Service Delivery Innovations Facilitated by Technology

More recently, entrepreneurs have taken advantage of the Internet to create new services. Four innovations of particular interest are:

- Development of "smart" mobile telephones and PDAs (personal digital assistants) and Wi-Fi high-speed Internet technology that can link users to the Internet—wherever they may be.
- Usage of voice recognition technology that allows customers to give information and request service simply by speaking into a phone or microphone.
- Creation of websites that provide information, take orders, and even serve as a delivery channel for information-based services.
- Commercialization of "smart cards" containing a microchip that can store detailed information about the customer and act as an electronic purse containing digital money. The ultimate in self-service banking will be when you can not only use a smart card as an electronic wallet for a wide array of transactions, but also refill it from a special card reader connected to your PC.

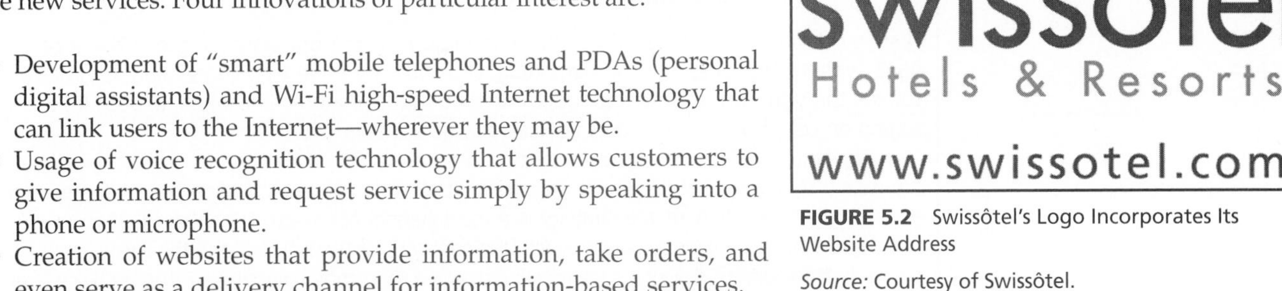

FIGURE 5.2 Swissôtel's Logo Incorporates Its Website Address

Source: Courtesy of Swissôtel.

Singly or in combination, electronic channels offer a complement or alternative to traditional physical channels for delivering information-based services. Best Practice in Action 5.1 describes a multichannel application for electronic banking.

E-Commerce: The Move to Cyberspace

As a distribution channel, the Internet can facilitate distribution of information-based services and all the information petals of the "flower of service" of people- and possession-processing services. In addition, the Internet enables researchers to (1) collect data on consumer information-seeking and search behaviors, (2) obtain feedback quickly from consumers, and (3) create online communities to help market services.[9] Amazon.com pioneered the concept of the virtual store, but now thousands exist all over the world. Among the factors luring customers into virtual stores are convenience, ease of search (obtaining information and searching for desired items or services), a broader selection, and the potential for better prices. Enjoying 24/7 service with prompt delivery is particularly appealing to customers whose busy lives leave them short of time (see Service Perspective 5.4). Think about the products that you, your family, and friends have purchased lately through the Internet. Why did you select this channel in preference to alternative forms of service delivery?

Many retailers, such as giant bookstore chain Barnes and Noble, have a strong Internet presence to complement their physical stores in an effort to counter competition from "cyberspace retailers" such as Amazon.com, which have no stores. However, adding an Internet channel to an already established physical channel is a double-edged strategy. It requires high capital set-up costs, and no one can be sure whether the investment will lead to long-term profits and high growth.[10]

Websites are becoming increasingly sophisticated, but also more user friendly. They often simulate the services of a well-informed sales assistant in steering customers toward items that are likely to be of interest. Some even provide the opportunity for "live" email or chat dialog with helpful customer service personnel. Facilitating searches is another useful service on many sites, ranging from looking at what books are available by a particular author to finding schedules of flights between two cities on a specific date.

Particularly exciting are recent developments that link websites, customer relationship management (CRM) systems, and mobile telephony. Integrating mobile devices into the service delivery infrastructure can be used as a means to (1) *access* services, (2) *alert* customers to opportunities or problems by delivering the right information or interaction at the right time, and (3) *update* information in real time to

BEST PRACTICE IN ACTION 5.1

Multi-Channel Banking Without Branches at First Direct

First Direct, a division of HSBC, has become famous as the originator of the concept of a retail bank without branches. At the beginning of 2008, it was serving more than 1.2 million customers throughout the United Kingdom (and abroad) through call centers, a website, text messaging on cell phones, and access to HSBC's large network of ATMs.

In January 2000, First Direct—by that time describing itself as "the largest virtual bank in the world"—announced it would transform itself into an e-bank and set the standard for e-banking. At the heart of the strategy is a multichannel approach to banking that combines First Direct's telephone banking experience with the strengths of the Internet and the versatility of the cell phone technologies to deliver a superior service at fiercely competitive prices. As noted by chief executive Alan Hughes: "We are the first bank in the world to reengineer our entire business for the e-age. The scale of the initiative creates a new category of e-banking and sets a benchmark for the industry around the globe. More than a bank, firstdirect.com will be the first Internet banking store."

By 2008, 80 percent of all customer contact with First Direct and 43 percent of sales were via e-channels. Some 885,000 customers were using Internet banking and 390,000 were using SMS (short message service) text messaging. The bank sent out some 2.6 million text messages a month.

A central element in this strategy is to offer Britain's most comprehensive cell phone banking service, recognizing that almost all adults in the United Kingdom either own or use a cell phone. Through SMS text messages, First Direct customers have access to mini-statements for up to three accounts and can be advised when credits or debits enter or leave the account. In addition, they are alerted automatically if their accounts go into the red. First Direct was the first bank to adapt its online banking so that it worked well with the iPhone.

Although person-to-person voice telephone still remains the backbone of the bank's relationship with its customers, in August 2005 the bank launched a new Webchat service, enabling customers to "talk" with banking reps through a keyboard and mouse rather than by phone. It promotes this service as offering the immediacy of a phone conversation with the convenience of email.

Is this nontraditional strategy working? The evidence suggests a resounding "yes." An independent global survey of 25,000 customers of financial organizations worldwide found that, among all banks surveyed, First Direct had the greatest proportion of customers prepared to recommend their own bank. For the past 16 years, First Direct had the highest customer satisfaction rating of banks in the United Kingdom.

FIGURE 5.3 View of One of the First Direct Call Centers

Source: http://www.firstdirect.com/press/photos_premises.shtml.

Source: Anne-Marie Cagna and Jean-Claude Larréché, "First Direct 2005: The Most Recommended Bank in the World." Fontainebleau, France: INSEAD, 2005; press releases distributed on www.firstdirect.com, accessed May 15, 2009.

SERVICE PERSPECTIVE 5.4

ONLINE VS. BRICK-AND-MORTAR: THE MALAYSIAN SHOPPING ADVENTURE

Malaysia offers a bewildering range of shopping establishments, catering to every taste and budget, which includes shopping malls, department stores, hypermarkets, specialty stores, handicraft centers, duty-free shops, bazaars, and night markets. In a test of comparative shopping speed, price, mode of payment, and service offering, a company appointed three college students to conduct product market research for *tudungs,* a local name for headscarves widely worn by Malaysian women. These students were given a budget of $250 to purchase five branded *tudungs* from three different retailers, using whatever form of payment that is most convenient. The first student surfed the Internet from her home, the second surveyed shops at the big shopping mall, and the third visited the night market, traditionally called *pasar malam* in Malay, to purchase the branded *tudungs.* The *pasar malam* is a local marketplace where traders trade from evening until midnight. These open-air markets feature hawker stalls that sell a variety of local produce, foodstuffs, clothing, and cakes. It's a bargain-hunter's paradise, where things are available for cash payment in the local currency only. The results: The online shopper stood first; within an hour, she had ordered, through a business blog, five branded designer *tudungs* for $125 with express delivery; she paid with her credit card. However, she admitted that the *tudungs* that she received were not the color that she ordered. The mall shopper took nearly three hours to purchase her *tudungs,* paying $170 (with festive discount) via her debit card at the exclusive *tudung* boutique. The *pasar malam* shopper purchased the *tudungs* after haggling for a bargain price of $100 in two hours, but she could not get the actual branded *tudungs.* Hence, the online shopper got the best deal.

Sources: "Market Research Experience," Afruz Reality Adventure, posted September 17, 2008; http://travelmalaysiaguide.com/night-markets-pasar-malam-shopping-kuala-lumpur/ – September 17, 2004.

ensure it is continuously accurate and relevant.[11] For example, customers can set stock alerts on their broker's website and get an email or SMS alert when a certain price level is reached (or breached) or when a particular transaction has been conducted, or they can obtain real-time information on stock prices. Customers can respond by accessing the brokerage and trade directly by voice or via an SMS interface, as they prefer.

THE ROLE OF INTERMEDIARIES

Many service organizations find it cost-effective to outsource certain tasks. Most frequently, this delegation concerns supplementary service elements. For instance, despite their increased use of telephone call centers and the Internet, cruise lines and resort hotels still rely on travel agents to handle a significant portion of their customer interactions such as giving out information, taking reservations, accepting payment, and ticketing.

How should a service provider work in partnership with one or more intermediaries to deliver a complete service package to customers? In Figure 5.4 we use the "flower of service" framework to show an example in which the core product is delivered by the originating supplier, together with certain supplementary elements in the informational, consultation, and exceptions categories, but delivery of other supplementary services is delegated to an intermediary to complete the offering as experienced by the customer. In other instances, several specialist outsourcers might be involved as intermediaries for specific elements. The challenge for the original supplier is to act as guardian of the overall process, ensuring that each element offered by intermediaries fits the overall service concept to create a consistent and seamless branded service experience.

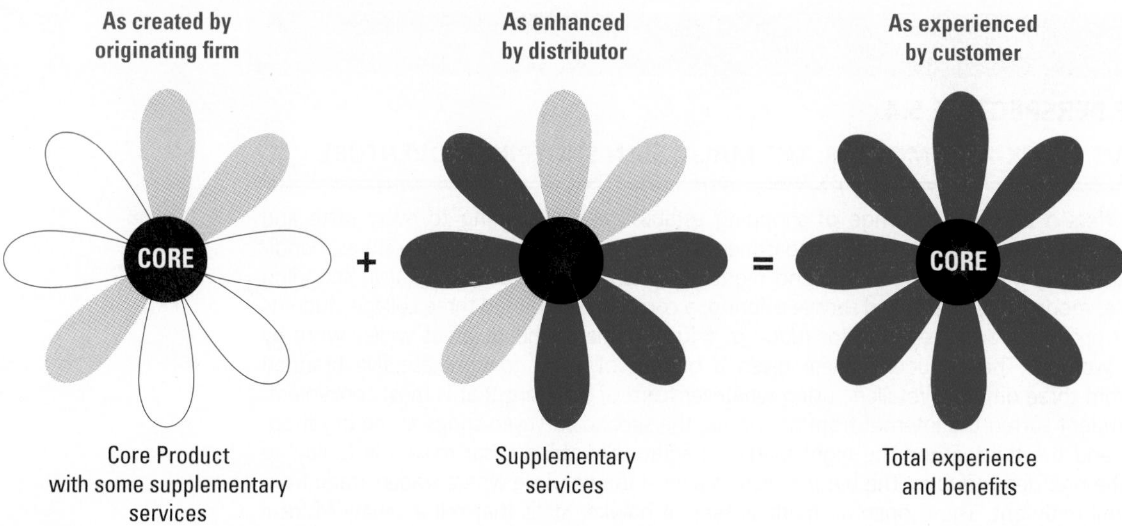

FIGURE 5.4 Splitting Responsibilities for Service Delivery

Franchising

Even delivery of the core product can be outsourced to an intermediary. Franchising has become a popular way to expand delivery of an effective service concept, embracing all of the 7 Ps (see Chapter 1), to multiple sites, without the level of investment capital that would be needed for rapid expansion of company-owned and -managed sites. A franchisor recruits entrepreneurs who are willing to invest their own time and equity in managing a previously developed service concept. In return, the franchisor provides training in how to operate and market the business, sells necessary supplies, and provides promotional support at a national or regional level to augment local marketing activities that are paid for by the franchisee, but must adhere to copy and media guidelines prescribed by the franchisor.

Franchising is an appealing strategy for growth-oriented service firms because franchisees are highly motivated to ensure customer orientation and high-quality service operations.[12] Although franchising is most commonly associated with fast-food restaurants (for an example, see Figure 5.5), the concept has been applied to a very wide array of both consumer and B2B services and now spans some 75 different product categories. New concepts are created and commercialized all the time in countries around the world. From 2003 to 2006, some 1,200 new franchise concepts were launched in the United States alone. The fastest-growing categories of concepts are related to health and fitness, publications, security, and consumer services.[13] In your own role as a consumer, you probably patronize more franchises than you realize. New types of franchises are created and commercialized continuously around the world.[14]

FIGURE 5.5 Dunkin' Brands Uses Franchising to Distribute Its Branded Service Concepts, Dunkin' Donuts (Coffee and Baked Goods), Baskin Robbins (Ice Cream), and Togo's (Sandwiches)

According to the International Franchise Association, some 760,000 franchise businesses in the United States provide jobs for more than 18 million people and create more than $1.5 trillion in economic activity—about 9.5 percent of the private sector's total output.[15] Among the cases featured in this book is "Aussie Pooch Mobile," which describes a successful Australian-based franchised dog washing service (see page 516).

Nevertheless, a significant attrition rate exists among franchisors in the early years of a new franchise system, with one-third of all systems failing within the first four years and no less than three quarters of all franchisors ceasing to exist after 12 years.[16] Success factors for franchisors include the ability to achieve a larger size with a more recognizable brand name, offering franchisees fewer supporting services but longer-term contracts, and having lower overhead per outlet. Because growth is very important to achieve an efficient scale, some franchisors adopt a strategy known as "master franchising," which involves delegating the responsibility for recruiting, training, and supporting franchisees within a given geographic area. Master franchisees often are individuals who have already succeeded as operators of one or several individual franchise outlets.

A disadvantage of delegating activities to franchisees is that it entails some loss of control over the delivery system and, thereby, over how customers experience the actual service. Ensuring that an intermediary adopts exactly the same priorities and procedures as prescribed by the franchisor is difficult, yet it's vital to effective quality control. Franchisors usually seek to exercise control over all aspects of the service performance through a contract that specifies adherence to tightly defined service standards, procedures, scripts, and physical presentation. Franchisors control not only output specifications, but also the appearance of the servicescape, employee performance, and such elements as service timetables.

An ongoing problem is that as franchisees gain experience, they may start to resent the various fees they pay the franchisor and believe that they can operate the business better without the constraints imposed by the agreement. The resulting disputes often lead to legal fights between the two parties.

An alternative to franchising is licensing another supplier to act on the original supplier's behalf to deliver the core product. Trucking companies regularly make use of independent agents, instead of locating company-owned branches in each of the different cities they serve. They may also choose to contract with independent "owner-operators" who drive their own trucks.[17]

Other service distribution agreements include financial services. Banks seeking to move into investment services often will act as the distributor for mutual fund products created by an investment firm that lacks extensive distribution channels of its own. Many banks also sell insurance products underwritten by an insurance company. They collect a commission on the sale, but normally are not involved in handling claims.

THE CHALLENGE OF DISTRIBUTION IN LARGE DOMESTIC MARKETS

There are important differences between marketing services within a compact geographic area and marketing services in a federal nation covering a large geographic area such as the United States, Canada, or Australia. In these cases, physical logistics immediately become more challenging for many types of services, because of the distances involved and the existence of multiple time zones. Multiculturalism is also an issue, due to the growing proportion of immigrants and the presence of indigenous peoples. Firms that market across Canada have to work in two official languages, English and French (the latter is spoken throughout Quebec, where it is the only official language; in parts of New Brunswick, which is officially bilingual; and in northeastern Ontario). Finally, there are differences within each country between the laws and tax rates of the various states or provinces and those of the respective federal governments. The challenges in Australia and Canada, however, pale in comparison to those facing service marketers in the mega-economy of the United States.

Visitors from overseas who tour the United States often are overwhelmed by the immense size of the country, surprised by the diversity of its people, astonished by the climatic and topographic variety of the landscape, and impressed by the scale and scope of some of its business undertakings. Consider some of the statistics: Marketing at a national level in the "lower 48" states of the United States involves dealing with a population of some 300 million people and transcontinental distances that exceed 2,500 miles (4,000 km). If Hawaii and Alaska are included, the market embraces even greater distances, covering six time zones, incredible topographic variety, and all climatic zones from arctic to tropical. From a logistical standpoint, serving customers in all 50 states might seem at least as complex as serving customers throughout, say, Europe, North Africa, and the Middle East, were it not for the fact that the United States has an exceptionally well developed communications, transportation, and distribution infrastructure.

The United States is less homogeneous than stereotypes might suggest. As a federal nation, the United States has a diverse patchwork of government practices. In addition to observing federal laws and paying federal taxes, service businesses operating nationwide may also need to conform to relevant state and municipal laws and plan for variations in tax policies from one state to another. However, U.S. law firms operating in multiple states may find this exposure an advantage when expanding overseas (Figure 5.6). Because cities, counties, and special districts (such as regional transit authorities) have taxing authority in many states, there are also thousands of variations in sales tax across the United States. Some states deliberately seek out new business investments by promoting their lower tax rates or offering tax incentives to encourage firms to establish or relocate factories, call centers, or back-office operations.

As the U.S. population becomes increasingly mobile and multicultural, market segmentation issues have become more complex for U.S. service marketers operating on a national scale as they encounter growing populations of immigrants (as well as visiting tourists) who speak many languages, led by Spanish. U.S. economic statistics show a wider range of household incomes and personal wealth (or lack thereof) than almost anywhere else on earth. Corporate customers, too, present considerable diversity, although the relevant variables may be different.

Faced with an enormous and diverse domestic marketplace, most large U.S. service companies simplify their marketing and management tasks by targeting specific market segments (refer to Chapter 3). Some firms segment on a geographic basis. Others target certain groups based on demographics, lifestyle, needs, or—in a corporate context—on industry type and company size. Smaller firms wishing to operate nationally usually seek out narrow market niches, a task made easier today by the growing use of websites and email. However, the largest national service operations face tremendous challenges as they seek to serve multiple segments across a huge geographic area. They must strike a balance between standardization of strategies across all the elements embraced by the 7 Ps and adaptation to different segments and local market conditions—decisions especially challenging when they concern high-contact services in which customers physically visit the delivery site.

DISTRIBUTING SERVICES INTERNATIONALLY

Many service companies have an international presence, and quite a number of American service brands are global, including Starbucks, Hertz, AMEX, McKinsey, and Google. What are the driving forces pushing these firms to go international or even global?

Factors Favoring Adoption of Transnational Strategies

Several forces or *industry drivers* influence the trend toward globalization and the creation of transnationally integrated strategy.[18] As applied to services, these forces are market drivers, competition drivers, technology drivers, cost drivers, and government drivers. Their relative significance may vary by type of service.

FIGURE 5.6 The Giant U.S. Law Firm of Wilmer Cutler Pickering Hale and Dorr LLP Now Operates in Five Countries on Three Continents

Source: Copyright © WilmerHale. Used with permission.

MARKET DRIVERS. Market factors that stimulate the move toward transnational strategies include common customer needs across many countries, global customers who demand consistent service from suppliers around the world, and the availability of international channels in the form of efficient physical supply chains or electronic networks.

As large corporate customers become global, they often seek to standardize and simplify the suppliers used in different countries for a wide array of B2B services. For instance, they may seek to minimize the number of auditors they use around the world, expressing a preference for "Big Four" accounting firms (i.e., PricewaterhouseCoopers, Deloitte Touche Tohmatsu, Ernst & Young, and KPMG) that can apply a consistent approach (within the context of the national rules prevailing within each country of operation). Use of globalized corporate banking, insurance, and management consulting are further examples. Similarly, the development of global logistics and supply chain management capabilities among such firms as DHL, FedEx, and UPS has encouraged many manufacturers to outsource responsibility for their logistics function to a single firm (Figure 5.7). In each instance, real advantages exist in consistency, ease of access, consolidation of information, and accountability. Similarly, international business travelers and tourists often feel more comfortable with predictable international standards of performance for such travel-related services as airlines and hotels.

COMPETITION DRIVERS. The presence of competitors from different countries, interdependence of countries, and the transnational policies of competitors themselves

FIGURE 5.7 DHL Combines Multiple Transport Modes to Create Integrated Logistics Solutions for Its Global Customer Base

are among the key competition drivers that exercise a powerful force in many service industries. Firms may be obliged to follow their competitors into new markets in order to protect their positions elsewhere. Similarly, once a major player moves into a new foreign market, a scramble for territory among competing firms may ensue.

TECHNOLOGY DRIVERS. Technology drivers tend to center around advances in information technology—such as enhanced performance and capabilities in telecommunications, computerization, and software; miniaturization of equipment; and the digitization of voice, video, and text—so that all can be stored, manipulated, and transmitted in the digital language of computers. For information-based services, the growing availability of broadband telecommunication channels, capable of moving vast amounts of data at great speed, is playing a major role in opening up new markets.[19] Access to the Internet is accelerating around the world. Significant economies may be gained by centralizing "information hubs" on a continent-wide or even global basis. Firms can take advantage of favorable labor costs and exchange rates by consolidating operations of supplementary services (such as reservations) or back-office functions (such as accounting) in just one or a few selected countries.

COST DRIVERS. Big is sometimes beautiful from a cost standpoint. Economies of scale may be gained from operating on an international or even global basis, plus sourcing efficiencies as a result of favorable logistics and lower costs in certain countries. Lower operating costs for telecommunications and transportation, accompanied by improved performance, facilitate entry into international markets. The effect of these drivers vary according to the level of fixed costs required to enter an industry and the potential for cost savings. Barriers to entry caused by the upfront cost of equipment and facilities may be reduced by such strategies as equipment leasing (as many airlines do), seeking investor-owned facilities such as hotels and then obtaining management contracts, or awarding franchises to local entrepreneurs. However, cost drivers may be less applicable for services that are primarily people based. When most elements of the service factory are replicated in multiple locations, scale economies tend to be lower and experience curves flatter.

GOVERNMENT DRIVERS. Government policies can serve to encourage or discourage development of a transnationally integrated strategy. Among these drivers are favorable trade policies, compatible technical standards, and common marketing regulations. For instance, the actions taken by the European Commission to create a single market throughout the European Union (EU) are a stimulus to creation of pan-European service strategies in numerous industries.

Furthermore, the World Trade Organization (WTO) and its focus on the internationalization of services has pushed governments around to world to create more favorable regulatory environments for transnational service strategies. The power of the drivers for internationalization can be seen in the case of a Qantas airliner arriving in Hong Kong (described in Service Perspective 5.5).

Many of the factors driving internationalization and the adoption of transnational strategies also promote the trend to have nationwide operations. The market, cost, technological, and competitive forces that encourage creation of nationwide service

SERVICE PERSPECTIVE 5.5

FLIGHT TO HONG KONG: A SNAPSHOT OF GLOBALIZATION

A white and red Boeing 747, sporting the flying kangaroo of Qantas, banks low over Hong Kong's dramatic harbor, crowded with merchant vessels, as it nears the end of its 10-hour flight from Australia. Once landed, the aircraft taxis past a kaleidoscope of tail-fins, representing airlines from more than a dozen different countries on several continents—just a sample of all the carriers that offer service to this remarkable city.

The passengers include business travelers and tourists, as well as returning residents. After passing through immigration and customs, most visitors will be heading first for their hotels, many of which belong to global chains (some of them, Hong Kong-based). Some travelers will be picking up cars, reserved earlier from Hertz, or one of the other well-known rental car companies with facilities at the airport. Others will take the fast train into the city. Tourists on packaged vacations are actively looking forward to enjoying Hong Kong's renowned Cantonese cuisine. Parents, however, are resigned to having their children demand to eat at the same fast-food chains found back home. Many of the more affluent tourists are planning to go shopping, not only in distinctive Chinese jewelry and antiques stores, but also in the internationally branded luxury stores found in most world-class cities.

What brings the business travelers to this SAR ("special administrative region") of China? Many are negotiating supply contracts for manufactured goods ranging from clothing to toys to computer components, whereas others have come to market their own goods and services. Some are in the shipping or construction businesses, others in an array of service industries ranging from telecommunications to entertainment and international law. The owner of a large Australian tourism operation has come to negotiate a deal for package vacations on Queensland's famous Gold Coast. The Brussels-based, Canadian senior partner of a Big Four accounting firm is half-way through a grueling round-the-world trip to persuade the offices of an international conglomerate to consolidate all its auditing business on a global basis with his firm alone. An American executive and her British colleague, both working for a large Euro-American telecom partnership, are hoping to achieve similar goals by selling a multinational corporation on the concept of employing their firm to manage all of its telecommunications activities worldwide. And more than a few of the passengers either work for international banking and financial service firms or have come to Hong Kong, one of the world's most dynamic financial centers, to seek financing for their own ventures.

In the Boeing's freight hold are not only passengers' bags, but also cargo for delivery to Hong Kong and other Chinese destinations. The freight includes mail, Australian wine, some vital spare parts for an Australian-built high-speed ferry operating out of Hong Kong, a container full of brochures and display materials about the Australian tourism industry for an upcoming trade promotion, and a variety of other high-value merchandise. Waiting at the airport for the aircraft's arrival are local Qantas personnel, baggage handlers, cleaners, mechanics and other technical staff, customs and immigration officials, and, of course, people who have come to greet individual passengers. A few are Australians, but the great majority are local Hong Kong Chinese, many of whom have never traveled very far afield. Yet in their daily lives, they patronize banks, fast-food restaurants, retail stores, and insurance companies whose brand names—promoted by global advertising campaigns—may be equally familiar to their expatriate relatives living in countries such as Australia, Britain, Canada, Singapore, and the United States. They can watch CNN on cable TV, listen to the BBC World Service on the radio, make phone calls through Hong Kong Telecom (part of a worldwide operation), and watch movies from Hollywood either in English or dubbed into the Chinese dialect of Cantonese. Welcome to the world of global services marketing!

businesses or franchise chains often are the same as those that subsequently drive some of the same firms to operate transnationally.

How Does the Nature of a Service Affect International Distribution?

Are some types of services easier to internationalize than others? What are the alternative ways a service company can tap the potential of international markets? Depending in part on the nature of the service, international distribution strategies have vastly different requirements. Table 5.2 summarizes important variations in the impact of each of the five groups of globalization drivers on three broad categories of services: people-processing services, possession-processing services, and information-based services.

PEOPLE-PROCESSING SERVICES. People-processing services require direct contact with the customer. The service provider needs to have a local geographic presence as well as the necessary personnel, buildings, equipment, vehicles, and supplies within reasonably easy reach of target customers. There are three options for people-processing services:

- *Export the service concept.* Acting alone or in partnership with local suppliers, the firm establishes a service factory in another country. The objective may be to reach out to new customers or to follow existing corporate or individual customers to new locations (or both). This approach is commonly used by chain restaurants, hotels, car rental firms, and weight-reduction clinics, for which a local presence is essential to be able to compete. Best Practice in Action 5.2 describes some of the ways in which Groupe Accor, a major international hotel chain, has developed a global presence.

TABLE 5.2 Impact of Globalization Drivers on Various Service Categories

Globalization Drivers	People Processing	Possession Processing	Information Based
Competition	Simultaneity of production and consumption limits leverage of foreign-based competitive advantage in front stage of service factory, but advantage in anagement systems an be basis for globalization.	Lead role of technology creates driver for globalization of competitors with technical edge (e.g., Singapore Airlines' technical servicing for other carriers' aircraft).	Highly vulnerable to global dominance by competitors with monopoly or competitive advantage in information (e.g., BBC, Hollywood, CNN), unless restricted by governments.
Market	People differ economically and culturally, so needs for service and ability to pay may vary. Culture and education may affect willingness to do self-service.	Less variation for service to corporate possessions, but level of economic development affects demand for services to individually owned goods.	Demand for many services is derived to a significant degree from economic and educational levels. Cultural issues may affect demand for entertainment.
Technology	Use of IT for delivery of supplementary services may be a function of ownership and familiarity with technology, including telecommunications and intelligent terminals.	Need for technology-based service delivery systems is a function of the types of possessions requiring service and the cost tradeoffs in labor substitution.	Ability to deliver core services through remote terminals may be a function of investments in computerization, quality of telecommunications infrastructure, and education levels.
Cost	Variable labor rates may affect pricing in labor-intensive services (consider self-service in high-cost locations).	Variable labor rates may favor low-cost locations if not offset by shipment costs. Consider substituting equipment for labor.	Major cost elements can be centralized and minor cost elements localized.
Government	Social policies (e.g., health care) vary widely and may affect labor costs, role of women in front-stage jobs, and hours/days on which work can be performed.	Tax laws, environmental regulations, and technical standards may decrease/increase costs and encourage/discourage certain types of activity.	Policies on education, censorship, public ownership of communications, and infrastructure standards may affect demand and supply and distort pricing.

BEST PRACTICE IN ACTION 5.2

Groupe Accor: Hotel Innovation in a Global Setting

Paris-based Groupe Accor is one of the world's leaders in the lodging industry. It recently sold its investments in the travel agency and contract food service businesses in order to focus on its core activities. According to industry experts, Accor is one of a few truly global hotel companies with some 4,000 hotels containing 480,000 rooms in 100 countries. Over the years, the group has proved to be a highly innovative service provider, as reflected by its in-depth market opportunity analysis, integrated offerings, and international growth strategies.

Accor has gone from being the first truly European hotel chain to one of the largest hotel chains in the world. It operates several distinct categories of hotels, such as the four/five-star Sofitel brand, three/four-star Novotel, three/four-star Mercure, and two/three-star Ibis. Accor has also pioneered an easily prefabricated replicable budget hotel concept known as the Formule 1 chain. In the United States, Accor operates the Motel 6 chain of budget motels and has plans for other acquisitions. Care is given to maintaining the distinctive identities of each of its hotel brands. Some 1,000 of its hotels are operated by franchisees. Accor plans to invest heavily in the economy and budget hotel categories, many of which will be opened in emerging markets.

Accor's former chairman, Jean-Marc Espalioux, sought to give the company the integrated structure it needed to operate and compete on a global basis. Under his leadership, hotel activities were restructured into three strategic segments, reflecting their market positioning. There are also two functional divisions. The first, a global services division, was created to spearhead the major functions common to all hotel activities: information systems, reservation systems, maintenance and technical assistance, purchasing, key accounts, and partnerships and synergy between hotel and other activities. The second, the hotel development division, is structured by brand and by region and is responsible for working with the management of each hotel to develop marketing, service development, and growth strategies. Espalioux was a strong believer in economies of scale:

> In view of the revolution in the service sector which is now taking place, I do not see any future for purely national hotel chains—except for very specific niche markets with special architecture and locations, such as Raffles in Singapore or the Ritz in Paris. National chains can't invest enough money.

The group is continuing its internationalization drive, focusing on further consolidating and integrating its network, as well as building a presence in such emerging markets as Poland, Hungary, and other ex-Soviet bloc countries. Espalioux is also very aware that the underlying obstacle to successful globalization in services was—and continues to be—people.

> Globalization brings considerable challenges which are often underestimated. The principal difficulty is getting our local management to adhere to the values of the group. [They] must understand our market and culture, for example, and we have to learn about theirs.

Because international cooperation, communication, and teamwork are integral to achieving global consistency, Accor has eliminated, as much as possible, hierarchy, rigid job descriptions and titles, and even organizational charts. Its 158,000 associates are encouraged to interact as much as possible both with their colleagues and with guests. They define the limits of their jobs within the context of the overall "customer experience" and are recognized and rewarded on how well they meet these definitions. In addition to these structural and organizational initiatives, videoconferencing and other technologies are used extensively to create and reinforce a common, global culture among Accor employees around the world. All of the group's European hotels are linked together through a sophisticated IT network, and Accor hotels worldwide are linked to a 24/7 global reservation system.

Sources: Andrew Jack, "The Global Company: Why There Is No Future for National Hotel Chains," _Financial Times_, October 10, 1997; W. Chan Kim and Renee Mauborgne, "Value Innovation: The Strategic Logic of High Growth," _Harvard Business Review_, January–February 1997, 121–123; and the firm's website, www.accor.com, accessed May 22, 2009.

For corporate customers, the industries are likely in fields such as banking, professional services, business logistics, and more. If the customers are mobile, as in the case of business travelers and tourists, then the same customers may patronize a company's offerings in many different locations and make comparisons between them.

- *Import customers.*[20] Customers from other countries are invited to come to a service factory with distinctive appeal or competences in the firm's home country. People will travel from abroad to ski at outstanding North American resorts such as

Whistler-Blackholm in British Columbia or Vail in Colorado. If they can afford it, they may also travel for specialized medical treatment at famous hospitals and clinics, such as Massachusetts General Hospital or the Mayo Clinic in Rochester, Minnesota. Increasingly, two-way traffic is developing in health care, with a growing number of patients from North America, Europe, and Australasia traveling to custom-built modern hospitals in Asian countries for an array of medical interventions by Western-trained specialists, ranging from hip replacements to cosmetic surgery. Even after paying for travel and accommodation, the total cost usually amounts to far less than patients would pay in their home countries, with the added attraction of recuperating under vacation-like conditions at an often exotic location.

POSSESSION-PROCESSING SERVICES. Possession-processing services may also be geographically constrained in many instances. This category involves services to the customer's physical possessions and includes repair and maintenance, freight transport, cleaning, and warehousing. Most services in this group require an ongoing local presence, regardless of whether customers drop off items at a service facility or if personnel visit the customer's site. Sometimes, expert personnel may be flown in from another country. However, small transportable items can be shipped to distant service centers for repair, cleaning, and maintenance. Certain types of service processes can be applied to physical products through electronic diagnostics and transmission of "remote fixes."

INFORMATION-BASED SERVICES. This group includes *mental-processing services* (services to the customer's mind, such as news and entertainment) and *information-processing services* (services to customers' intangible assets, such as banking and insurance). They are, perhaps, the most interesting category of services from the point of view of global strategy development. This is because data is transmitted or changed to create value. Information-based services can be distributed internationally in one of three ways:

- *Exporting the service to a local service factory*. The service can be made available in a local facility that customers visit. For instance, a film made in Hollywood can be shown in movie theaters around the world, or a college course can be designed in one country and then be offered by approved teachers elsewhere.
- *Importing customers.* Customers may travel abroad to visit a specialist facility, in which case the service takes on the characteristics of a people-processing service. For example, large numbers of foreign students study in U.S. and Canadian universities.
- *Exporting the information via telecommunications and transforming it locally.* Rather than ship object-based services stored on physical media such as CDs or DVDs from their country of origin, the data are increasingly downloaded at that country for physical production in local markets (even by customers).

In theory, none of these information-based services require face-to-face contact with customers, because all can potentially be delivered at arm's length through telecommunications or mail. Banking and insurance are good examples of services that can be delivered from other countries. Bank customers requiring cash in another country need only visit a local ATM connected to a global network such as VISA. In practice, however, a local presence may be necessary to build personal relationships, conduct on-site research (as in consulting or auditing), or even to fulfill legal requirements.

In addition to such industries as financial services, insurance, news, and entertainment, education is becoming a likely candidate for globalized distribution using a combination of channels. Many universities already have international campuses, extension courses delivered by both local and traveling faculty, and long-established correspondence programs. On a national basis, the University of Phoenix in the United States and the Open University in the United Kingdom are among the national leaders in electronically distributed programs. A truly globalized service is the next logical step.

Barriers to International Trade in Services

The marketing of services internationally has been the fastest-growing segment of international trade.[21] Transnational strategy involves the integration of strategy formulation and its implementation across all countries in which the company elects to do business in. Barriers to entry, historically a serious problem for foreign firms wishing to do business abroad, are slowly diminishing. The passage of free trade legislation in recent years has been an important facilitator of transnational operations. Notable developments include NAFTA, linking Canada, Mexico, and the United States; Latin American economic blocs such as Mercosur and Pacto Andino; and the European Union, now 27 countries strong and expected to expand its membership in the coming years (see Service Perspective 5.6).

However, operating successfully in international markets remains difficult for some services. Despite the efforts of the WTO and its predecessor, GATT (General Agreement on Trade and Tariffs), there are many hurdles to overcome. Airline access is a sore point—many countries require bilateral (two-country) agreements on establishing new routes. If one country is willing to allow entry by a new carrier, but the other is not, then access will be blocked. Compounding government restrictions of this nature are capacity limits at certain major airports, which lead to denial of new or additional landing rights for foreign airlines. Both passenger and freight transport are affected by such restrictions.

Other constraints may include administrative delays, refusals by immigration offices to provide work permit applications for foreign managers and workers, heavy taxes on foreign firms, domestic preference policies designed to protect local suppliers, legal restrictions on operational and marketing procedures (including international data flows), and the lack of broadly agreed accounting standards for services. Different languages and cultural norms may require expensive changes in the nature of a service and how it is delivered and promoted. The cultural issue has been particularly significant for the entertainment industry. Many nations are wary of seeing their own culture swamped by U.S. imports.

SERVICE PERSPECTIVE 5.6

THE EUROPEAN UNION: MOVING TO BORDERLESS TRADE

Many of the challenging strategic decisions facing service marketers in pan-European markets are extensions of decisions already faced by firms operating on a national basis in the United States. Although geographically more compact than the United States, the 27-country European Union (EU) has an even larger population (500 million versus 307 million) and is culturally and politically more diverse, with distinct variations in tastes and lifestyles, plus the complication of 23 official national languages and a variety of regional tongues, from Catalan to Welsh. As new countries join the EU, the "single market" will become even larger. The admission of several Eastern European countries such as Romanian and Bulgaria and the possibility of a formal link to Turkey (whose land area straddles Europe and Asia) added further cultural diversity and brought the EU market closer to Russia and the countries of Central Asia.

Within the EU, the European Commission has made huge progress in harmonizing standards and regulations to level the competitive playing field and discourage efforts by individual member countries to protect their own service and manufacturing industries. The results are already evident, with many service firms operating across Europe as well as overseas.

Another important economic step facilitating transnational marketing on a pan-European basis is monetary union. In January 1999, the exchange values of 11 national European currencies were linked to a new currency, the Euro, which completely replaced all European currencies in 2002. Today, services are priced in Euros from Finland to Portugal. Other European countries, including Britain and Sweden, may eventually decide to switch to Euros, although this issue remains contentious.

However, although the potential for freer trade in services within the EU continues to increase, "Greater Europe"—ranging from Iceland to Russia west of the Ural Mountains—includes many countries that are likely to remain outside the Union for some years to come. Some of these countries, such as Switzerland and Norway (which both rejected membership), tend to enjoy much closer trading relations with the EU than others. Whether there will ever be full political union—a "United States of Europe"—remains a hotly debated and contested issue. However, from a services marketing standpoint, the EU certainly is moving toward the U.S. model in terms of both scale and freedom of movement. See http://europa.eu.int and http://en.wikipedia.org/wiki/EU for more information on the EU.

CONCLUSION

What? How? Where? When? Responses to these four questions form the foundation of any service distribution strategy. The customer's service experience is a function of how the different elements of the "flower of service" are distributed and delivered through selective physical and electronic channels. In addition to "what" and "how," service marketing strategy must address issues of place and time, paying at least as much attention to speed, scheduling, and electronic access as to the more traditional notion of physical location. Here, the rapid growth of the Internet and broadband mobile communications is especially exciting for service firms, and many elements of service are informational in nature. Furthermore, in the heat of globalization, important questions are raised concerning the design and implementation of international service distribution strategies.

Chapter Summary

LO1 *What? How? Where? When?* Responses to these four questions form the foundation of any service distribution strategy.

LO2 *What* is distributed? The flow model of distribution can be mapped onto the "flower of service" concept and includes the following flows of service distribution:

- Information and promotion flows (includes the information and potentially consultation petals).
- Negotiation flow (includes the order-taking and potentially also billing and payment petals).
- Product flow (includes the remaining petals of the "flower of service" and the core product).

A service distribution strategy encompasses all three flows.

LO3 Some core services require a physical location (e.g., people-processing services), which severely restricts their distribution. However, information-based core services and many supplementary services can be distributed and delivered remotely.

LO4 *How* can services be distributed? Services can be distributed through three main modes:

- Customers visit the service site (e.g., for people-processing services such as an MRI scan).
- Service providers go to their customers (e.g., as for high net-worth private banking services).
- Service transactions conducted remotely (i.e., at arm's length such as for Skype or buying a travel insurance online).

LO5 Customer preferences drive channel choice. Customers often prefer remote channels because of their convenience and when they have high confidence and knowledge about the product and are technology savvy. However, consumers rely more on personnel channels when the perceived risk is high and when there are social motives behind the transaction.

LO6 *Where* and *when* should service be delivered? The place and time decisions must reflect customer needs and expectations.

- Customer convenience and operational requirements are main factors to consider.
- Recent location trends include mini stores, sharing retail space with complementary providers, and locating in multipurpose facilities (e.g., ATMs in office buildings).
- There is a move toward extended operating hours, with the ultimate goal of 24/7 service every day of the year, often achieved through the use of self-service technology.

LO7 Information-based core and supplementary services can be offered 24/7 on the Internet. Recent technological developments link CRM systems, mobile telephones, and websites to provide increasingly convenient and sophisticated services.

LO8 Service firms frequently use intermediaries to distribute some of the supplementary services (e.g., cruise lines still use travel agencies to provide information, take reservations, and collect payment).

- Service organizations may find it cost effective to outsource certain tasks.
- The challenge for the service firm is to ensure that overall service is seamless and experienced as desired.

Franchising is frequently used to distribute the core service. There are advantages and disadvantages to franchising:

- It allows fast growth, and franchisees are highly motivated to ensure customer orientation, high-quality service operations, and cost-effective operations.
- Disadvantages of franchising include the loss of control over the delivery system and the customers' service experience. Hence, franchisors often enforce strict quality controls over all aspects of the operation.

LO9 Five important forces drive service firms to go international. They are:

- Market drivers (e.g., customers expect a global presence).
- Competitive drivers (e.g., competitors become global and put pressure on domestic firms).
- Technology drivers (e.g., the Internet allows global distribution and cost arbitrage).
- Cost drivers (e.g., economies of scale push toward adding markets).
- Government drivers (e.g., countries joining the WTO have to open many service sectors to international competition).

LO10 How does the nature of service affect international distribution? People-processing, possession-processing, and information-based services have very different requirements.

- People-processing services require direct contact with the customer. There are several options, including (1) export the service concept, and (2) import customers.
- Most possession-processing services require an ongoing local presence. However, in some instances, the crew and equipment can be flown to the customer's site, or the customer's possessions can be transported to the provider's location.
- Information-based services are the most flexible as they don't require face-to-face contact or contact with possessions or equipment. They can be distributed in several ways: (1) export the service to a local service factory, (2) import customers, and (3) export the service via telecommunications and, if required, transform it locally.

Review Questions

1. What is meant by "distributing services?" How can an experience or something intangible be distributed?
2. Why is it important to consider the distribution of core and supplementary services both separately and jointly?
3. What are the different options for service delivery? For each of the options, what factors do service firms need to take into account when using that option?
4. What are the key factors driving place and time decisions of service distribution?
5. What risks and opportunities are entailed for a retail service firm in adding electronic channels of delivery (a) paralleling a channel involving physical stores, or (b) replacing the physical stores with a combined Internet and call center channel? Give examples.
6. Why should service marketers be concerned with new developments in mobile communications?
7. What marketing and management challenges are raised by the use of intermediaries in a service setting?
8. Why is franchising a popular way to expand distribution of an effective service concept? What are some disadvantages of franchising, and how can they be mitigated?
9. What can service marketers who are planning transnational strategies learn from studying existing practices within the United States?
10. What are the key drivers for increasing globalization of services?
11. How does the nature of the service affect the opportunities for globalization?

Application Exercises

1. An entrepreneur is thinking of setting up a new service business (you can choose any specific business). What advice would you give regarding the distribution strategy for this business? Address the *What? How? Where? When?* of service distribution.
2. Think of three services you buy or use either mostly or exclusively via the Internet. What is the value proposition of this channel over alternative channels (e.g., phone, mail, or branch network)?
3. What advice would you give to (a) a weight reduction clinic, (b) a pest control company, and (c) a university offering undergraduate courses about going international?
4. Select three different service industries, one each for people-processing, possession-processing, and information-based services. For each, assess the five globalization drivers and their impact on these three industries.
5. Obtain recent statistics for international trade in services for the United States and another country of your choice. What are the dominant categories of service exports and imports? What factors do you think are driving trade in specific service categories? What differences do you see between the countries?

Endnotes

1. http://en.wikipedia.org/wiki/Lauren_Luke and www.bylaurenluke.com, accessed February 18, 2009.
2. Jochen Wirtz and Jeannette P. T. Ho, "Westin in Asia: Distributing Hotel Rooms Globally," in Jochen Wirtz and Christopher H. Lovelock, eds. *Services Marketing in Asia—A Case Book*. Singapore: Prentice Hall, 2005, 253–259. www.starwoodhotels.com, accessed February 16, 2009.
3. Recent research on the adoption of self-service technologies includes: Matthew L. Meuter, Mary Jo Bitner, Amy L. Ostrom, and Stephen W. Brown, "Choosing Among Alternative Service Delivery Modes: An Investigation of Customer Trial of Self-Service Technologies," *Journal of Marketing*, 69, April 2005, 61–83; James M. Curran and Matthew L. Meuter, "Self-Service Technology Adoption: Comparing Three Technologies," *Journal of Services Marketing*, 19, No. 2, 2005, 103–113.
4. The section was based on the following research: Nancy Jo Black, Andy Lockett, Christine Ennew, Heidi Winklhofer, and Sally McKechnie, "Modelling Consumer Choice of Distribution Channels: An Illustration from Financial Services," *International Journal of Bank Marketing*, 20, No. 4, 2002, 161–173; Jinkook Lee, "A Key to Marketing Financial Services: The Right Mix of Products, Services, Channels and Customers," *Journal of Services Marketing*, 16, No. 3, 2002, 238–258; and Leonard L Berry, Kathleen Seiders, and Dhruv Grewal, "Understanding Service Convenience," *Journal of Marketing*, 66, No. 3, July 2002, 1–17. Jiun-Sheng C. Lin and Pei-ling Hsieh, "The Role of Technology Readiness in Customers' Perception and Adoption of Self-Service Technologies," *International Journal of Service Industry Management*, 17, No. 5, 2006, 497–517.
5. Paul F. Nunes and Frank V. Cespedes, "The Customer has Escaped," *Harvard Business Review*, 81, No. 11, 2003, 96–105.
6. Michael A. Jones, David L. Mothersbaugh, and Sharon E. Beatty, "The Effects of Locational Convenience on Customer Repurchase Intentions across Service Types," *Journal of Services Marketing*, 17, No. 7, 2004, 701–712.
7. James L. Heskett, W. Earl Sasser Jr., and Leonard A. Schlesinger, *The Service Profit Chain*. New York: The Free Press, 1997, 218–220.
8. www.swissotel.com and http://www.eyefortravel.com/node/9187, accessed May 23, 2009.
9. See also P. K. Kannan, "Introduction to the Special Issue: Marketing in the E-Channel," *International Journal of Electronic Commerce*, 5, No. 3, 2001, 3–6; Customer satisfaction and loyalty can be built with electronic channels that build "digital proximity," see Sonja M. Salmen and Andrew Muir, "Electronic Customer Care: The Innovative Path to E-Loyalty," *Journal of Financial Services Marketing*, 8, No. 2, 2003, 133–144.
10. Inge Geyskens, Katrijn Gielens, and Marnik G. Dekimpe, "The Market Valuation of Internet Channel Additions," *Journal of Marketing*, 66, No. 2, April 2002, 102–119. For a study showing that customer perception of greater integration of physical and online channels is important in a multichannel strategy and is associated with higher loyalty, see Elliot Bendoly, James D. Blocher, Kurt M. Bretthauer, Shanker Krishnan, and M. A. Venkataramanan, "Online/In-Store Integration and Customer Retention," *Journal of Service Research*, 7, No. 4, 2005, 313–327.
11. Katherine N. Lemon, Frederick B. Newell, and Loren J. Lemon, "The Wireless Rules for e-Service," in Roland T. Rust and P. K. Kannan, eds. *New Directions in Theory and Practice*. Armonk, New York: M.E. Sharpe, 2002, 200–232.
12. James Cross and Bruce J. Walker, "Addressing Service Marketing Challenges Through Franchising," in Teresa A. Swartz and Dawn Iacobucci, eds. *Handbook of Services Marketing & Management*. Thousand Oaks, CA: Sage Publications, 2000, 473–484; Lavent Altinay, "Implementing International Franchising: The Role of Intrapreuneurship," *International Journal of Service Industry Management*, 15, No. 5, 2004, 426–443.
13. International Franchise Association Educational Foundation Inc., "Franchise Industry Gains 300 Concepts in One Year," November 19, 2007 in http://www.franchise.org/Franchise-News-Detail.aspx?id=36416, accessed May 24, 2009.
14. Richard C. Hoffman and John F. Preble, "Global Franchising: Current Status and Future Challenges," *Journal of Services Marketing*, 18, No. 2, 2004, 101–113.
15. "Extending the Front Lines of Franchising," *Business Week Online*, accessed September 19, 2005.
16. Scott Shane and Chester Spell, "Factors for New Franchise Success," *Sloan Management Review*, 39, Spring 1998, 43–50.
17. For a discussion on what to watch for when parts of the service are outsourced, see Lauren Keller Johnson, "Outsourcing Postsale Service: Is Your Brand Protected? Before You Spin Off Repairs, or Parts Distribution, or Customer Call Centers, Consider the Cons as well as the Prof," *Harvard Business Review Supply Chain Strategy*, July 2005, 3–5.
18. John K. Johansson and George S. Yip, "Exploiting Globalization Potential: US and Japanese Strategies," *Strategic Management Journal*, 15, October 1994, 579–601; Christopher H. Lovelock and George S. Yip, "Developing Global Strategies for Service Businesses," *California Management Review*, 38, Winter 1996, 64–86; May Aung and Roger Heeler, "Core Competencies of Service Firms: A Framework for Strategic Decisions in International Markets," *Journal of Marketing Management*, 17, 2001, 619–643; Rajshkhar G. Javalgi and D. Steven White, "Strategic Challenges for the Marketing of Services Internationally," *International Marketing Review*, 19, No. 6, 2002, 563–581.
19. Rajshekhar G. Javalgi, Charles L. Martin, and Patricia R. Todd, "The Export of E-Services in the Age of Technology Transformation: Challenges and Implications for International Service Providers," *Journal of Services Marketing*, 18, No. 7, 2004, 560–573.
20. This term was coined by Curtis P. McLauglin and James A. Fitzsimmons, "e-Service: Strategies for Globalizing Service Operations," *International Journal of Service Industry Management*, 7, No. 4, 1996, 43–57.
21. Rajshkhar G. Javalgi and D. Steven White, "Strategic Challenges for the Marketing of Services Internationally," *International Marketing Review*, 19, No. 6, 2002, 563–581.

CHAPTER 6

Setting Prices and Implementing Revenue Management

What is a cynic? A man who knows the price of everything and the value of nothing.

OSCAR WILDE

There are two fools in any market: One does not charge enough. The other charges too much.

RUSSIAN PROVERB

LEARNING OBJECTIVES (LOs)

By the end of this chapter, the reader should be able to:

LO1 Recognize that effective pricing is central to the financial success of service firms.

LO2 Outline the foundations of a pricing strategy as represented by the pricing tripod.

LO3 Define different types of financial costs and explain the limitations of cost-based pricing.

LO4 Understand the concept of net value and how gross value can be enhanced through value-based pricing and reduction of related monetary and nonmonetary costs.

LO5 Describe competition-based pricing and situations where service markets are less price-competitive.

LO6 Define revenue management and describe how it works.

LO7 Understand the role of rate fences in effective revenue management.

LO8 Be familiar with the issues of ethics and consumer concerns related to service pricing.

LO9 Understand how fairness can be designed into revenue management policies.

LO10 Know the seven questions marketers need to answer to design an effective pricing schedule.

Dynamic Pricing at Easy Internet Cafe[1]

easyInternetcafe is part of the easyGroup of companies headed by Stelios Haji-Ioannou, the Greek entrepreneur who received knighthood from Queen Elizabeth II for his contribution to entrepreneurship. This Internet café is entirely self-service and is unmanned. Vending machines dispense credit to customers. There are currently 25 easyInternetcafes in countries including the United Kingdom, the United States, Italy, Turkey, Greece, and France with a total of some 5,200 PCs.

easyInternetcafe has many features that allow revenue management to be used successfully. First, the capacity is perishable. Once no one uses the Internet access time, that hour is gone and cannot be resold. Second, there is relatively fixed capacity and high fixed costs. The equipment, software, bandwidth, and rental are fixed costs that are incurred whether or not a customer is in the café. Third, demand varies by time of the day, day of the week, months, and seasons. Finally, different customers are willing to pay different amounts for one hour of Internet access time.

FIGURE 6.1 The New York easyInternetcafe

To cater to the different price sensitivities of its customers, easyInternetcafe offers two different types of passes. Customers can either buy premium-priced passes that allow unlimited access during a set period of time or passes at the going rate. Passes sold at the going rate are priced using dynamic pricing. The variation in price does not come from the price of the pass (it is the same for both passes), but from the number of minutes on that pass. As the number of customers in the store increases, the number of minutes of individual surfing time decreases. The fewer customers in the store, the longer a pass will last. In this way, when it is very busy, the line will move faster as each user has a shorter time and when it is less busy, each user has a longer time and demand is allowed to build up. As a result, waiting time is also moderated. Price sensitive customers can use the café when they see that many terminals are available, and those customers willing to pay more know that even during busy periods, the wait is not that long. The concept has been very successful as a high percentage of customers feel that easyInternetcafe offers good value.

EFFECTIVE PRICING IS CENTRAL TO FINANCIAL SUCCESS

Importantly, marketing is the only function that brings operating revenues into the organization. All other management functions incur costs. A *business model* is the mechanism whereby, through effective pricing, sales are transformed into revenues, costs are covered, and value is created for the owners of the business. As noted by Joan Magretta:

> A good business model answer Peter Drucker's age-old questions: Who is the customer? And what does the customer value? It also answers the fundamental questions that every manager must ask: How do we make money in this business? What is the underlying economic logic that explains how we can deliver value to customers at an appropriate cost?[2]

Creating a viable service requires a business model that allows for the costs of creating and delivering the service, plus a margin for profits, to be recovered through realistic pricing and revenue management strategies.

Pricing of services, however, is complicated. Consider the bewildering fee schedules of many consumer banks or cell phone service providers, or try to understand the fluctuating fare structure of a full-service airline. Service organizations even use different terms to describe the prices they set. Universities talk about tuition, professional firms collect fees, banks impose interest and service charges, brokers charge commissions, some expressways impose tolls, utilities set tariffs, and insurance companies determine premiums—the list goes on. Consumers often find service pricing difficult to understand (insurance products or hospital bills), risky (when you make a hotel reservation on three different days, you may be offered three different prices), and sometimes even unethical (many bank customers complain about an array of fees and charges they perceive as unfair). Examine your own purchasing behavior. How did you feel the last time you had to decide on booking a vacation, reserving a rental car, or opening a new bank account? In this chapter, you will learn how to set an effective pricing and revenue management strategy that fulfills the promise of the value proposition so that a value exchange takes place (i.e., the consumer decides to buy your service).

In many service industries of the past, pricing was traditionally driven by a financial and accounting perspective, which often used cost-plus pricing. Price schedules often were tightly constrained by government regulatory agencies—and some still are. Today, however, most service businesses enjoy significant freedom in setting prices and have a good understanding of value-based and competitive pricing. These developments have led to creative pricing schedules and sophisticated revenue management systems. In this chapter, we review the role of pricing in services marketing and provide guidelines on how to develop an effective pricing strategy.

Objectives for Establishing Prices

Any pricing strategy must be based on a clear understanding of a company's pricing objectives. The most common pricing objectives are related to revenues and profits as well as building demand and developing a user base (Table 6.1).

GENERATING REVENUES AND PROFITS. Within certain limits, profit-seeking firms aim to maximize long-term revenue, contributions, and profits. Perhaps top management is eager to reach a particular financial target or seeks a specific percentage return on investment. Revenue targets may be broken down by division, geographic unit, type of service, and even by key customer segments. This practice requires prices to be set based on a good knowledge of costing, competition, and price elasticity of market segments and their value perceptions, all of which we will discuss later in this chapter.

In capacity-constrained organizations, financial success often is a function of ensuring optimal use of productive capacity at any given time. Hotels, for instance, seek to fill their rooms because an empty room is an unproductive asset. Similarly, professional firms want to keep their staff members occupied. Thus, when demand is low, such organizations may offer special discounts to attract additional business. Conversely, when demand exceeds capacity, these types of businesses may increase their prices and focus on segments willing to pay a high price premium. We'll discuss these practices in detail in the section on revenue management.

TABLE 6.1 Objectives for Pricing of Services

Revenue and Profit Objectives

Seek Profit

- Make the largest possible contribution or profit.
- Achieve a specific target level, but do not seek to maximize profits.
- Maximize revenue form a fixed capacity by varying prices and target segments over time. This is done typically using revenue management systems.

Cover costs

- Cover fully allocated costs, including corporate overhead.
- Cover costs of providing one particular service, excluding overhead.
- Cover incremental costs of selling one extra unit or to one extra customer.

Patronage and User Base-Related Objectives

Build Demand

- Maximize demand (when capacity is not a restriction), provided a certain minimum level of revenue is achieved.
- Achieve full capacity utilization, especially when high capacity utilization adds to the value created for all customers (e.g.'full-house' adds excitement to a theater play or basket ball game).

Build a User Base

- Encourage trail and adoption of a service. This is especially important for new service with high infrastructure costs, and for membership-type services that provide a large amount of revenues from their continued usage after adoption (e.g. cell phone service subscriptions, or life insurance plans).
- Build market share and/or a large user base, especially if there are a lot of economies of scale that lead to a competitive cost advantage (e.g. if development or fixed costs are high).

BUILDING DEMAND AND DEVELOPING A USER BASE. In some instances, maximizing patronage, subject to achieving a certain minimum level of profits, may be more important than profit maximization. Getting a full house in a theater, sports stadium, or race track usually creates excitement that enhances the customer's experience. It also creates an image of success that attracts new patrons.

New services, in particular, often have trouble attracting customers. Yet, in order to create the impression of a successful launch, and to enhance the image of the firm, it's important that the firm is seen to be attracting a good volume of business from the right types of customers. Introductory price discounts often are used to stimulate trial and sign up customers, sometimes in combination with promotional activities such as contests and giveaways. For example, to compete with rival UPS and build sales for its network of more than 1,300 FedEx Kinko's Office and Print Center (now called FedEx Office) locations in the United States, FedEx promoted savings of up to 30 percent on express shipments from these stores.

In industries that require large investments in infrastructure (e.g., broadband services), it's often important to build a critical mass of users quickly. Market leadership often means low cost per user, so volume is necessary to generate sufficient revenue for future investments such as upgrading technology and infrastructure. As a result, penetration pricing is frequently used in such industries.

PRICING STRATEGY STANDS ON THREE FOUNDATIONS

Once the pricing objectives are understood, we can focus on the pricing strategy. The foundations underlying pricing strategy can be described as a tripod, with *costs* to the provider, *competitors'* pricing, and *value* to the customer as the three legs (Figure 6.2). In many service industries, pricing used to be viewed from a financial and accounting standpoint; therefore, cost-plus pricing often was used. Today however, most services have a good understanding of value-based and competitive pricing. In the pricing tripod, the costs a firm needs to recover usually sets a minimum price, or floor, for a specific service offering, and the customer's perceived value of the offering sets a maximum, or ceiling.

The price charged by competing services typically determines where, within the floor-to-ceiling range, the price can be set. The pricing objectives of the organization then determine where actual prices should be set given the feasible range provided by the pricing tripod analysis. Let's look at each leg of the pricing tripod in more detail, starting with cost to the provider.

Cost-Based Pricing

Pricing typically is more complex in services than in manufacturing. Because there's no ownership of services, it's usually harder to determine the financial costs of creating a

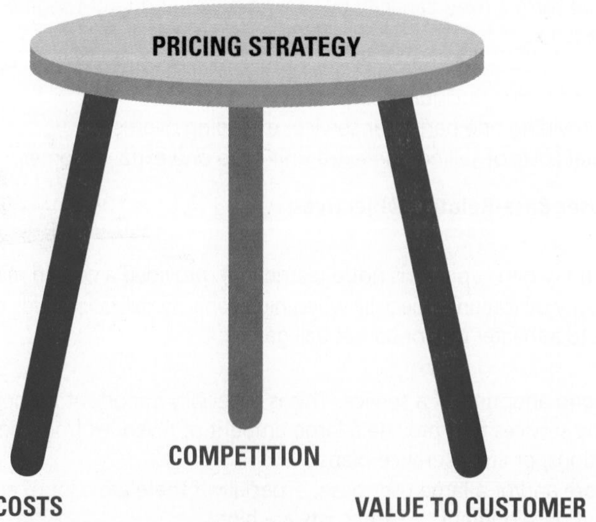

FIGURE 6.2 The Pricing Tripod

process or intangible real-time performance for a customer than it is to identify the labor, materials, machine time, storage, and shipping costs associated with producing and distributing a physical good. In addition, because of the labor and infrastructure needed to create performances, many service organizations have a much higher ratio of fixed costs to variable costs than is typical in manufacturing firms (Figure 6.3). Service businesses with high fixed costs include those with expensive physical facilities (such as hospitals or colleges), or a fleet of vehicles (such as airlines or trucking companies), or a network (such as railroads or telecommunications and gas pipeline companies).

FIGURE 6.3 Train Services Have Very High Infrastructure Costs; Variable Costs of Transporting an Additional Customer Are Insignificant

ESTABLISHING THE COSTS OF PROVIDING SERVICE. Even if you have already taken a marketing course, you may find it helpful to review how service costs can be estimated, using fixed, semi-variable, and variable costs, as well as how the notions of contribution and break-even analysis can help in pricing decisions (see Marketing Review box on p. 162). These traditional cost-accounting approaches work well for service firms with significant variable costs and/or semi-variable costs (e.g., many professional services). For complex product lines with shared infrastructure (e.g., retail banking products), it may be worthwhile to consider the more complex activity-based costing (ABC) approach.

ACTIVITY-BASED COSTING.[3] A growing number of organizations have reduced their dependence on traditional cost accounting systems and developed activity-based cost management systems (ABC), which recognize that virtually all activities taking place within a firm directly or indirectly support the production, marketing, and delivery of goods and services. Moreover, ABC systems link resource expenses to the variety and complexity of goods and services produced—not just to the physical volume. A set of activities is combined that comprise the processes needed to create and deliver the service. Each step in a flowchart constitutes an activity with which costs can be associated. This approach makes ABC ideally suited for use in a service organization.

If implemented well, the ABC approach yields reasonably accurate cost information about service business activities and processes—and about the costs of creating specific types of services, performing activities in different locations (even different countries), or serving specific customers.[4] The net result is a management tool that can help companies to pinpoint the profitability of different services, channels, market segments, and even individual customers.[5]

It's essential to distinguish between those activities that are mandatory for operation within a particular service business and those that are discretionary. The traditional approach to cost control often results in reducing the value generated for customers, because the activity being pruned is, in fact, mandatory to provide a certain level and quality of service. For instance, many firms have created marketing problems for themselves when they try to save money by firing large numbers of customer service employees in an attempt to save money. However, this strategy often has boomeranged, resulting in a rapid decline in service levels that spurred discontented customers to take their business elsewhere.

PRICING IMPLICATIONS OF COST ANALYSIS. To make a profit, a firm must set its price high enough to recover the full costs of producing and marketing the service and add a sufficient margin to yield the desired profit at the predicted sales volume.

Managers in businesses with high fixed and marginal variable costs may feel they have tremendous pricing flexibility and be tempted to set low prices to boost sales. Some firms promote *loss leaders*—services sold at less than full cost to attract customers—who (it is hoped) will then be tempted to buy profitable service offerings from the same organization

MARKETING REVIEW

Understanding Costs, Contribution, and Break-Even Analysis

Fixed costs are economic costs a supplier would continue to incur (at least in the short run) even if no services were sold. These costs are likely to include rent, depreciation, utilities, taxes, insurance, salaries and wages for managers and long-term employees, security, and interest payments.

Variable costs refer to the economic costs associated with serving an additional customer, such as making an additional bank transaction or selling an additional seat on a flight. In many services, such costs are very low. For instance, very little labor or fuel cost is involved in transporting an extra passenger on a flight. In a theater, the cost of seating an extra patron is close to zero. More significant variable costs are associated with such activities as serving food and beverages or installing new parts when undertaking repairs, because they often include providing costly physical products in addition to labor. Just because a firm has sold a service at a price that exceeds its variable cost doesn't mean the firm is now profitable, for there are still fixed and semi-variable costs to be recouped.

Semi-variable costs fall in between fixed and variable costs. They represent expenses that rise or fall in a stepwise fashion as the volume of business increases or decreases. Examples include adding an extra flight to meet increased demand on a specific air route or hiring a part-time employee to work in a restaurant on busy weekends.

Contribution is the difference between the variable cost of selling an extra unit of service and the money received from the buyer of that service. It goes to cover fixed and semi-variable costs before creating profits.

Determining and allocating economic costs can be a challenging task in some service operations because of the difficulty of deciding how to assign fixed costs in a multiservice facility, such as a hospital. For instance, certain fixed costs are associated with running the emergency department in a hospital. Beyond that, there are fixed costs of running the hospital. So, how much of the hospital's fixed costs should be allocated to the emergency department? A hospital manager might use one of several approaches to calculate the emergency department's share of overhead costs. These could include (1) the percentage of total floor space it occupies, (2) the percentage of employee hours or payroll it accounts for, or (3) the percentage of total patient contact hours involved. Each method is likely to yield a totally different fixed-cost allocation. One method might show the emergency department to be very profitable, while the other might make it seem like a big loss-producing operation.

Break-even analysis allows managers to know at what sales volume a service will become profitable. This is called the break-even point. The necessary analysis involves dividing the total fixed and semivariable costs by the contribution obtained on each unit of service. For example, if a 100-room hotel needs to cover fixed and semivariable costs of $2 million a year, and the average contribution per room-night is $100, then the hotel will need to sell 20,000 room-nights per year out of a total annual capacity of 36,500. If prices are cut by an average of $20 per room-night (or variable costs rise by $20), then the contribution will drop to $80, and the hotel's break-even volume will rise to 25,000 room-nights. The required sales volume needs to be related to *price sensitivity* (Will customers be willing to pay this much?), *market size* (Is the market large enough to support this level of patronage after taking competition into account?), and *maximum capacity* (the hotel in our example has a capacity of 36,500 room-nights per year, assuming no rooms are taken out of service for maintenance or renovation).

in the future. However, there will be no profit at the end of the year unless all relevant costs have been recovered. Many service businesses have gone bankrupt because they ignored this fact. Hence, firms that compete on low prices need to have a very good understanding of their cost structure and of the sales volumes needed to break even.

As a service marketer, you will need to move beyond seeing costs from an accounting perspective. Rather, you should regard them as an integral part of the company's efforts to create value for its customers. Antonella Carù and Antonella Cugini clarify the limitations of traditional cost measurement systems and recommend relating the costs of any given activity to the value generated:

> Costs have nothing to do with value, which is established by the market and, in the final analysis, by the degree of customer acceptance. The customer is not interested *a priori* in the cost of a product. . . but in its value and price.
>
> Management control which limits itself to cost monitoring without interesting itself in value is completely one-sided. . . . The problem of businesses is not so much that of cost control as it is the separation of value activities from other activities. The market only pays for the former. Businesses which carry out unnecessary activities are destined to find themselves being overtaken by competitors which have already eliminated these.[6]

Value-Based Pricing

Another leg of the pricing tripod is value to the customer. No customer will pay more for a service than he or she thinks it is worth. So, marketers need to understand how customers perceive service value in order to set an appropriate price.[7]

UNDERSTANDING NET VALUE. When customers purchase a service, they are weighing the perceived benefits of the service against the perceived costs they will incur. As we saw in Chapter 4, companies sometimes create several tiers of service, recognizing the different tradeoffs that customers are willing to make between these various costs. Customer definitions of value may be highly personal and idiosyncratic. Valarie Zeithaml proposes four broad expressions of value:

- Value is low price.
- Value is whatever I want in a product.
- Value is the quality I get for the price I pay.
- Value is what I get for what I give.[8]

In this book, we focus on the fourth category and use the term *net value*, which is the sum of all perceived benefits (gross value) minus the sum of all the perceived costs of service. The greater the positive difference between the two, the greater the net value. Economists use the term *consumer surplus* to define the difference between the price customers pay and the amount they would actually have been willing to pay to obtain the desired benefits (or "utility") offered by a specific product.

If the perceived costs of a service are greater than the perceived benefits, then the service in question will possess negative net value, and the consumer will not buy. You can think of calculations customers make in their minds as similar to weighing materials on a pair of old-fashioned scales, with product benefits in one tray and the costs associated with obtaining those benefits in the other tray (Figure 6.4). When customers evaluate competing services, they are basically comparing the relative net values. As we discussed in Chapter 4, a marketer can increase the value of a service by adding benefits to the core product and by improving supplementary services.

MANAGING THE PERCEPTION OF VALUE.[9] Service pricing strategies often are unsuccessful because they lack a clear association between price and value.[10] Value is subjective, and not all customers have the expertise to assess the quality and value they receive. This is true in particular for credence services (discussed in Chapter 2), for which customers cannot assess the quality of a service even after consumption.[11] Marketers of services such as strategy consulting and specialized hospitals must find ways to communicate the time, research, professional expertise, and attention to detail that go into, for example, completing a best practice consulting project. Why? Because the invisibility of back-stage facilities and labor makes it hard for customers to see what they're getting for their money.

Consider a homeowner who calls an electrician to repair a defective circuit. The electrician arrives, carrying a small bag of tools. He disappears into the closet where the circuit board is located, locates the problem, replaces a defective circuit breaker, and presto! Everything works. A mere 20 minutes have elapsed. A few days later, the homeowner is horrified to receive a bill for $90, most of it for labor charges. Just think what the couple could have bought for that amount of money—new clothes, several DVDs, a nice dinner. Not surprisingly, customers are often left feeling exploited—take a look at Blondie's reaction to the plumber in Figure 6.5.

To manage the perception of value, effective communications and even personal explanations are needed to help customers understand the value they receive. What they often fail to recognize are the fixed costs that business owners need to recoup: the office, telephone, insurance, vehicles, tools, fuel, and office support staff. The variable costs of a home visit are also higher than they appear. To the 20 minutes spent at the house, 15 minutes of driving each way might be added, plus 5 minutes each to unload and reload needed tools and supplies from the van, thus effectively tripling the labor time to a total of 60 minutes devoted to this call. And the firm still has to add a margin in order to make a profit.

More recently, auctions and dynamic pricing have become increasingly popular as a way to price according to value perceptions of customers. Our story on easyInternetcafe in the opening vignette is one such example of dynamic pricing. See Service Perspective 6.1 for other examples of dynamic pricing in the Internet environment.

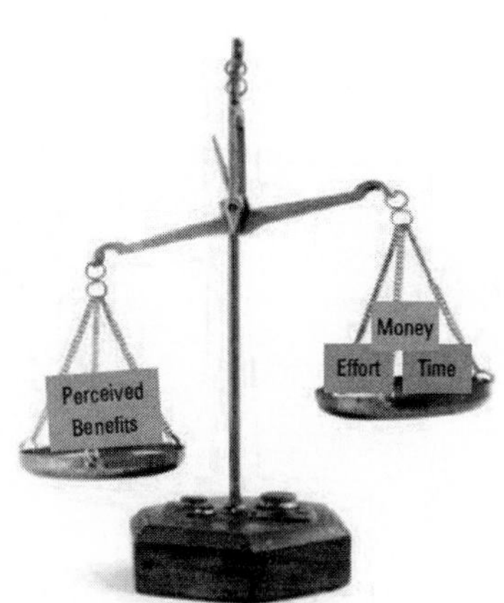

FIGURE 6.4 Net Value Equals Benefits Minus Costs

FIGURE 6.5 Blondie Seeks Her Money's Worth from the Plumber

Source: BLONDIE © King Features Syndicate.

REDUCING RELATED MONETARY AND NONMONETARY COSTS. When we consider customer net value, we need to understand the customers' perceived costs. From a customer's point of view, the price charged by a supplier is only part of the costs involved in buying and using a service. There are other *costs of service*, which are made up of the *related monetary* and *nonmonetary costs.*

Related Monetary Costs. Customers often incur significant financial costs in searching for, purchasing, and using the service, above and beyond the purchase price paid to the supplier. For instance, the cost of an evening at the theater for a couple with young children usually far exceeds the price of the two tickets, because it can include such expenses as hiring a babysitter, travel, parking, food, and beverages.

Nonmonetary Costs. Nonmonetary costs reflect the time, effort, and discomfort associated with search, purchase, and use of a service. Like many customers, you may refer to them collectively as "effort" or "hassle." Nonmonetary costs tend to be higher when customers are involved in production (which is particularly important in people-processing services and in self-service) and must travel to the service site. Services high on experience and credence attributes may also create psychological costs, such as anxiety. There are four distinct categories of nonmonetary costs: time, physical, psychological, and sensory costs.

- *Time costs* are inherent in service delivery. Today's customers often are time-constrained and may use similar terms to define time usage as they do for money; for instance, consumers talk about budgeting, spending, investing, wasting, losing, and saving time. Time spent on one activity represents an opportunity cost because it could be spent more profitably in other ways. Internet users often are frustrated by the amount of time they spend looking for information on a website. Many people loathe visiting government offices to obtain passports, driving licenses, or permits, not because of the fees involved, but because of the time "wasted."
- *Physical costs* (like fatigue, discomfort) may be incurred in obtaining services, especially if customers must go to the service factory, if waiting is involved, and if delivery entails self-service.
- *Psychological costs* such as mental effort, perceived risk, cognitive dissonance, feelings of inadequacy, or fear sometimes are attached to buying and using a particular service.
- *Sensory costs* relate to unpleasant sensations affecting any of the five senses. In a service environment, these costs may include putting up with crowding, noise, unpleasant smells, drafts, excessive heat or cold, uncomfortable seating, and visually unappealing environments.

As shown in Figure 6.6, service users can incur costs during any of the three stages of the service consumption model as introduced in Chapter 2. Consequently, firms have to consider (1) *search costs*, (2) *purchase and service encounter costs*, and (3) *postconsumption* or *after costs.* When you were looking at colleges and universities, how much money, time, and effort did you spend before deciding where to apply? How much time and effort would you put into selecting a new cell phone service provider or a bank, or planning a vacation? A strategy of minimizing those nonmonetary and related monetary costs to increase consumer value can create competitive advantage for a firm. Possible approaches include:

- Working with operations experts to reduce the time required to complete service purchase, delivery and consumption; become "easy-to-do-business-with."

SERVICE PERSPECTIVE 6.1

DYNAMIC PRICING ON THE INTERNET

Dynamic pricing—also known as customized or personalized pricing—is a new version of the age-old practice of price discrimination. It is popular with service suppliers because of its potential to increase profits and at the same time provide customers with what they value. E-tailing, or retailing over the Internet, lends itself well to this strategy because changing prices electronically is a simple procedure. Dynamic pricing enables e-tailers to charge different customers different prices for the same product based on information collected about their purchase history, preferences, price sensitivity, and so on. Tickets.com gained up to 45 percent more revenue per event when pricing of concerts and events was adjusted to meet demand and supply. However, customers may not be happy.

E-tailers often are uncomfortable about admitting to use of dynamic pricing because of the ethical and legal issues associated with price discrimination. Customers of Amazon.com were upset when they learned the online megastore was not charging everyone the same price for the same movie DVDs. A study of online consumers by the University of Pennsylvania's Annenberg Public Policy Center found that 87 percent of respondents did not think dynamic pricing was acceptable.

Reverse Auctions

Travel e-tailers such as Priceline.com, Hotwire.com, and Lowestfare.com follow a customer-driven pricing strategy known as a reverse auction. Each firm acts as an intermediary between prospective buyers who request quotations for a product or service and multiple suppliers who quote the best price they're willing to offer. Buyers can then review the offers and select the supplier that best meets their needs. Although the offer usually describes product attributes, it frequently doesn't provide brand information. Priceline has moved to correct this deficiency. Says a spokesperson "Customers can now choose the exact brand name and product from a published list price, whereas before they could only use our name-your-own-price [service]. As a result, people were never sure what hotel they would get until they made their purchase. So, if you were traveling with friends, you wouldn't know if you'd get the same hotel."

Different business models underlie these services. Although some are provided free to end users, most e-tailers either receive a commission from the supplier or do not pass on the whole savings. Others charge customers either a fixed fee or one based on a percentage of the savings.

Traditional Auctions

Other e-tailers, such as eBay and Yahoo! Auctions, follow the traditional online auction model in which bidders place bids for an item and compete with each other to determine who buys it. Marketers of both consumer and industrial products use such auctions to sell obsolete or overstock items, collectibles, rare items, and second-hand merchandise. This form of retailing has become immensely successful since eBay launched it first in 1995.

Shopbots Help Consumers to Benefit from Dynamic Pricing

Consumers now have tools of their own to combat the potentially exploitive practices of dynamic pricing. One approach involves using shopbots to track competitive prices. *Shopbots*, or shopping robots, basically are intelligent agents that automatically collect price and product information from multiple online vendors. A customer has only to visit a shopbot site, such as Dealtime.com, and run a search for the desired item. The shopbot instantly queries all the associated retailers to check availability, features, and price, then presents the results in a comparison table.

There's little doubt that dynamic pricing is here to stay. With further advances in technology and wider applications, its reach will extend to more and more service categories.

Sources: Stephan Biller, Lap Mui Ann Chan, David Simchi-Levi, and Julie Swann, "Dynamic Pricing and Direct-to-Customer Model in the Automotive Industry," *Electronic Commerce Research*, 5, No. 2, April 2005, 309–334; Melissa Campanelli, "Getting Personal: Will Engaging in Dynamic Pricing Help or Hurt Your Business?," *Entrepreneur*, 33, No. 10, October 2005, 44–46; Mikhail I. Melnik and James Alm, "Seller Reputation, Information Signals, and Prices for Heterogeneous Coins on eBay," *Southern Economic Journal*, 72, No. 2, 2005, 305–328; "Dynamic Pricing Schemes—Value Led" *Managing Change: Strategic Interactive Marketing*, www.managingchange.com/dynamic/valueled.htm, accessed April 21, 2009.

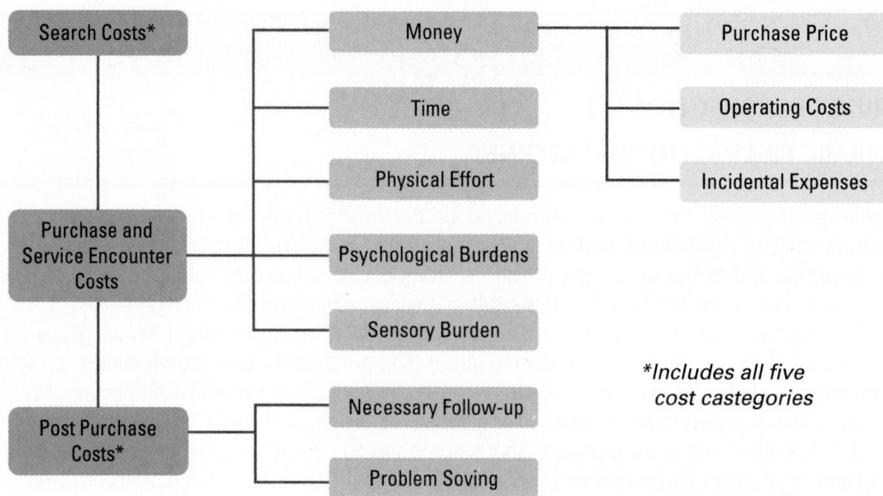

FIGURE 6.6 Defining Total User Costs

- Minimizing unwanted psychological costs of service at each stage by eliminating or redesigning unpleasant or inconvenient procedures, educating customers on what to expect, and retraining staff to be friendlier and more helpful.
- Eliminating or minimizing unwanted physical effort, notably during search and delivery processes. Improve signage and "road mapping" in facilities and on webpages to improve way-finding and avoid customers getting lost and frustrated.
- Decreasing unpleasant sensory costs of service by creating more attractive visual environments, reducing noise, installing more comfortable furniture and equipment, curtailing offensive smells, and the like.
- Suggesting ways in which customers can reduce associated monetary costs, including discounts with partner suppliers (e.g., parking) or offering mail or online delivery of activities that previously required a personal visit.

Perceptions of net value may vary widely among customers and from one situation to another for the same customer. Most segments have at least two segments—one segment that spends time to save money, and another that spends money to save time. Therefore, many service markets can be segmented by sensitivity to time savings and convenience versus sensitivity to price savings.[12] Consider Figure 6.7, which identifies a choice of three clinics available to an individual who needs to obtain a routine chest X-ray. In addition to varying dollar prices for the service, different time and effort costs are associated with using each service. Depending on the customer's priorities, nonmonetary costs may be as important, or even more important, than the price charged by the service provider.

Competition-based Pricing

The last leg of the pricing tripod is competition. Firms with relatively undifferentiated services need to monitor what competitors are charging and should to try to price accordingly. When customers see little or no difference between competing offerings, they may just choose what they perceive to be the cheapest. In such a situation, the firm with the lowest cost per unit of service enjoys an enviable market advantage and often assumes *price leadership*. Here, one firm acts as the price leader, with others taking their cue from this company. You can sometimes see this phenomenon at the local level when several gas stations compete within a short distance of one another. As soon as one station raises or lowers its prices, the others follow suit.

Price competition intensifies with (1) an increasing number of competitors, (2) an increasing number of substituting offers, (3) a wider distribution of competitor and/or substitution offers, and (4) an increasing surplus capacity in the industry. Although some service industries can be fiercely competitive (e.g., airlines or online banking), not all are, especially when one or more of the following circumstances reduce price competition:

Which Clinic Would You Patronize if You Needed a Chest X-ray (Assuming That All Three Clinics Offer Good Technical Quality)?		
Clinic A	**Clinic B**	**Clinic C**
• Price $65 • Located 1 hour away by car or transit • Next available appointment is in 3 weeks • Hours: Monday – Friday, 9am – 5pm • Estimated wait at clinic is about 2 hours	• Price $125 • Located 15 min away by car or transit • Next available appointment is in 1 week • Hours: Monday – Friday, 8am – 10pm • Estimated wait at clinic is about 30 to 45 minutes	• Price $185 • Located next to your office building (or college) • Next available appointment is in 1 day • Hours: Monday – Saturday, 8am – 10pm • By appointment – estimated wait at clinic is about 0 to 15 minutes

FIGURE 6.7 Which Clinic Would You Patronize if You Needed a Chest X-ray

- **Nonprice-related costs of using competing alternatives are high.** When saving time and effort are of equal or greater importance to customers than price in selecting a supplier, the intensity of price competition is reduced.
- **Personal relationships matter.** For services that are highly personalized and customized, such as hair styling or family medical care, relationships with individual providers often are very important to customers, thus discouraging them from responding to competitive offers.
- **Switching costs are high.** When it takes time, money, and effort to switch providers, customers are less likely to take advantage of competing offers. Cell phone providers often require one- or two-year contracts from their subscribers and enforce significant financial penalties for early cancellation of service.
- **Time and location specificity reduce choice.** When people want to use a service at a specific location or at a particular time (or perhaps both, simultaneously), they usually find they have fewer options.[13]

Firms that always react to competitors' price changes run the risk of pricing *lower* than might really be necessary. Managers should be aware of falling into the trap of comparing competitors' prices dollar for dollar and then seeking to match them. A better strategy is to take into account the entire cost to customers of each competitive offering, including all related financial and nonmonetary costs, plus potential switching costs, and then compare this total with that of the provider's own service. Managers should also assess the impact of distribution, time and location factors, as well as estimating competitors' available capacity before deciding what response is appropriate.

REVENUE MANAGEMENT: WHAT IT IS AND HOW IT WORKS

Many service businesses now focus on strategies to maximize the revenue (or contribution) that can be derived from available capacity at any given point in time. Revenue management is important in value creation as it ensures better capacity utilization, and it reserves capacity for higher-paying segments. It's a sophisticated approach to managing supply and demand under varying degrees of constraint. Airlines, hotels, and car rental firms, in particular, have become adept at varying their prices in response to the price sensitivity and needs of different market segments at different times of the day, week, or season. More recently hospitals, restaurants, golf courses, on-demand IT services, data processing centers, and even nonprofit organizations have increasingly used revenue management.[14]

Revenue management is most effective when applied to service businesses characterized by:

- High fixed cost structure and relatively fixed capacity, which result in perishable inventory.
- Variable and uncertain demand.
- Varying customer price sensitivity.

Reserving Capacity for High-yield Customers

In practice, revenue management (also known as yield management) involves setting prices according to predicted demand levels among different market segments. The least price sensitive segment is the first to be allocated capacity, paying the highest price; other segments follow at progressively lower prices. Because higher-paying segments often book closer to the time of actual consumption, firms need a disciplined approach to save capacity for them instead of simply selling on a first-come, first-served basis. For example, business travelers often reserve airline seats, hotel rooms, and rental cars at short notice, but vacationers may book leisure travel months in advance, and convention organizers often block hotel space years in advance of a big event.

A well-designed revenue management system can predict with reasonable accuracy how many customers will use a given service at a specific time at each of several different price levels. This information can be used to increase usage through incentives and schemes, gain a competitive market share, or create value. In the case of telecommunication providers, it is far more likely to see these models integrate massive historical databases on past usage to forecast demand. The objective is to maximize the revenues on a day-to-day basis. Holidays typically see a drop in commercial usage, and, hence, incentives are focused on the individual. Best Practice in Action 6.1 shows how pricing and promotional incentives have been used by Du, a UAE telecommunications company, to increase revenues, gain market share, and create customer value.

HOW DOES COMPETITORS' PRICING AFFECT REVENUE MANAGEMENT? Because revenue management systems monitor booking pace, they indirectly pick up the effect of competitors' pricing. If a firm prices too low, it will experience a higher booking pace, and its cheaper seats fill up quickly. That generally is not good, as it means a higher share of late-booking but high fare-paying customers will not be able to get their seats confirmed and will therefore fly on competing airlines. If the initial pricing is too high, the firm will get too low a share of early booking segments (which still tend to offer a reasonable yield) and may later have to offer deeply discounted "last-minute" prices to sell excess capacity. Some of these sales may take place through reverse auctions, using intermediaries such as Priceline.com.

Price Elasticity

For revenue management to work effectively, there need to be two or more segments that attach different value to the service and have different price elasticities. To allocate and price capacity effectively, the revenue manager needs to determine how sensitive demand is to price and what net revenues will be generated at different prices for each target segment. The concept of elasticity describes how sensitive demand is to changes in price and is computed as follows:

$$\text{Price elasticity} = \frac{\text{Percentage change in demand}}{\text{Percentage change in price}}$$

When price elasticity is at "unity," sales of a service rise (or fall) by the same percentage that price falls (or rises). If a small change in price has a big impact on sales, demand for that product is said to be *price elastic.* If a change in price has little effect on sales, demand is described as *price inelastic.* The concept is illustrated in the simple chart presented in Figure 6.8, which shows the price elasticity for two segments, one with a highly elastic demand (a small change in price results in a big change in the amount demanded) and the other with a highly inelastic demand (even big changes in price have little impact on the amount demanded).

BEST PRACTICE IN ACTION 6.1

A Tale of Two Telecoms: Using Price to Give Customer Value

Until 2006, the UAE telecommunication sector was dominated by one provider—Emirates Telecommunications Corporation—Etisalat. Etisalat was established in 1976 and is the sixth largest company in terms of revenue and capital in the Middle East. Etisalat is known for its products and coverage (it has roaming agreements with more than 520 operators in more than 190 countries) and claims to have a 100 percent penetration in the UAE market. With the introduction of Du in 2006, a war of "value" began. The UAE market is unique as it's a saturated market with a mobile penetration of 122 percent. In 2009, Du had achieved a penetration of 30 percent in the UAE market. It still has a long way to go, but considering Etisalat had a head start, Du has done a remarkably good job understanding its customer. The rivalry ultimately benefits the customer, and, to prevent a price war that could affect organization profitability, all incentives have to be run through the watchful eyes of the Telecommunication Regulatory Authority.

One example of this price value war is that of the iPhone. Etisalat was first to introduce the iPhone, and its customers were willing to pay a premium for the iconic status symbol; however, when Du acquired the rights to also offer iPhone service, it chose to offer a huge discount on the data packages, a savings of 22 percent over Etisalat (though there are limits on the amount that can be downloaded). Du is preferred by the price-sensitive and younger segment of the population. For example, in 2009, Du's "Business Super Plan" offered a 50 percent discount on international calls and 300 minutes of free international calls. This was targeted at the small and medium-sized enterprises, which are 90 percent of all businesses in UAE. Because UAE is a trading hub and 80 percent of its population are expatriates, this is an important incentive. Identifying with the culture of UAE and the region is another important part of Du's strategy. It has taken the form of special rates for customers taking the Hajj pilgrimage between November 21 and December 12. This allows Du subscribers in Saudi Arabia to receive calls free of charge and to pay for outgoing calls from Saudi Arabia to UAE at a rate of about AED 3.00/minute $1/minute at a 60-second pulse rate. Another incentive is the National Day promotion, which allows everyone in UAE to decorate their cars for National Day, load the pictures online at www.du.ae/uae38, and thereby enter a chance to win one of 38 Du BlackBerry® 8900 smartphones.

Where is this long-term turf war going? In the interests of both telecommunication regulators and the possibility of this sector being deregulated (estimated for 2015), and having more foreign investors, perhaps the only way forward is collaboration. We are seeing some of that with number portability, which has gained momentum since 2006.

Sources: "Du Announces Special Roaming Tariffs for Hajj Pilgrims," November 19, 2009, www.du.ae/en; Etisalat Corporate Information, available: http://etisalat.ae/; Gale, I. (2006). "Du and Etisalat in Talks over Mobile Number Portability," August 5, 2006, http://gulfnews.com/; Gale, I. (2006), "Du Ready to Take on Goliath Etisalat," August 5, 2006, http://gulfnews.com/; Gara, T. (2009), "Mobile Broadband Price War Begins, or Please Du, May I Have an iPhone?" October 15, 2009, http://blogs.thenational.ae/; John, I. (2009) "Du Slashes International Call Rates by 50%," *Khaleej Times,* August 10, 2009, www.khaleejtimes.com/; Sambidge, A. (2009), "UAE Mobile Phone Network Choice to Launch in Nov," October 21, 2009, www.arabianbusiness.com; "Share in the Spirit of Patriotism with Du This UAE National Day," November 23, 2009, www.du.ae/en/; Sudhir, N. (2009), "Etisalat and Du's Customer Base to Reach 235 Percent," *Emirates Business 24/7,* June 14, 2009, http://www.zawya.com.

Designing Rate Fences

Inherent in revenue management is the concept of *price customization*—that is, charging different customers different prices for what is, in effect, the same product. As noted by Hermann Simon and Robert Dolan,

> The basic idea of price customization is simple: Have people pay prices based on the value they put on the product. Obviously you can't just hang out a sign saying "Pay me what it's worth to you," or "It's $80 if you value it that much but only $40 if you don't." You have to find a way to segment customers by their valuations. In a sense, you have to "build a fence" between high-value customers and low-value customers so the "high" buyers can't take advantage of the low price.[15]

How can a firm ensure that customers for whom the service offers high value are unable to take advantage of lower price buckets? Properly designed rate fences allow

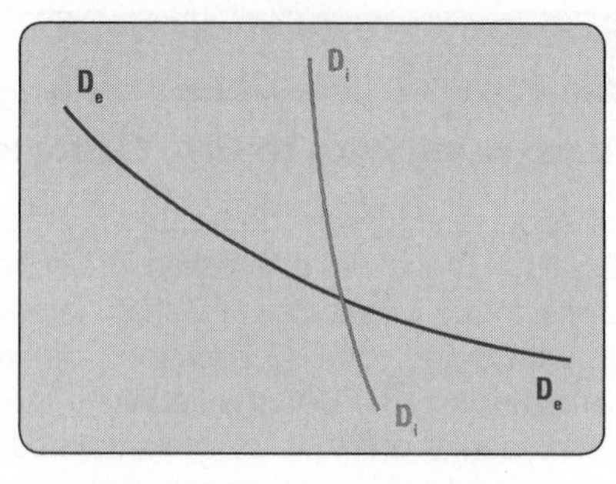

Price Elasticity = $\frac{\text{Percentage change in demand}}{\text{Percentage change in price}}$

D_e : Demand is *price elastic*. Small changes in price lead to big changes in demand
D_i : Demand for service is *price inelastic*. Big changes have little impact on demand

FIGURE 6.8 Illustrations of Price Elasticity

TABLE 6.2 Key Categories of Rate Fences

RATE FENCES	EXAMPLES
Physical (product-related) fences	
• Basic product	• Class of travel (business/economy class) • Size of rental car • Size and furnishing of a hotel room • Seat location in a theater or stadium
• Amenities	• Free breakfast at a hotel, airport pick up, etc. • Free golf cart at a golf course • Valet parking
• Service level	• Priority wait-listing, separate check-in counter with no or only short queues • Improved food and beverage selection • Dedicated service hotlines • Personal butler • Dedicated account management team
Non-Physical Fences *Transaction Characteristics*	
• Time of booking or reservation	• Discounts for advance purchase
• Location of booking or reservation	• Passengers booking air-tickets for an identical route in different countries are changed different prices. • Customers making reservation online are changed a lower price than chose making reservation by phone
• Flexibility of ticket usage	• Fees/penalties for canceling or changing a reservation (up to loss of entire ticket price) • Non-refundable reservation fees
Consumption Characteristics	
• Time or duration of use	• Early bird special in a restaurant before 6:00pm • Must stay over a Saturday night for an hotel booking. • Must stay at least for five nights
• Location of consumption	• Price depends on departure location, especially in international travel. • Prices vary by location (between cities, city center versus edges of the city)
Buyer Characteristics	
• Frequency of volume of consumption	• Member of certain loyalty-tier with the firm (e.g. Platinum member) get priority pricing, discounts or loyalty benefits
• Group membership	• Child, student, senior citizen discounts • Affiliation with certain groups (e.g. Alumni) • Corporate rates
• Size of consumer group	• Group discounts based on size of group
• Geographic location	• Local customers are changed lower rates than tourists • Customers from certain countries are changed higher prices

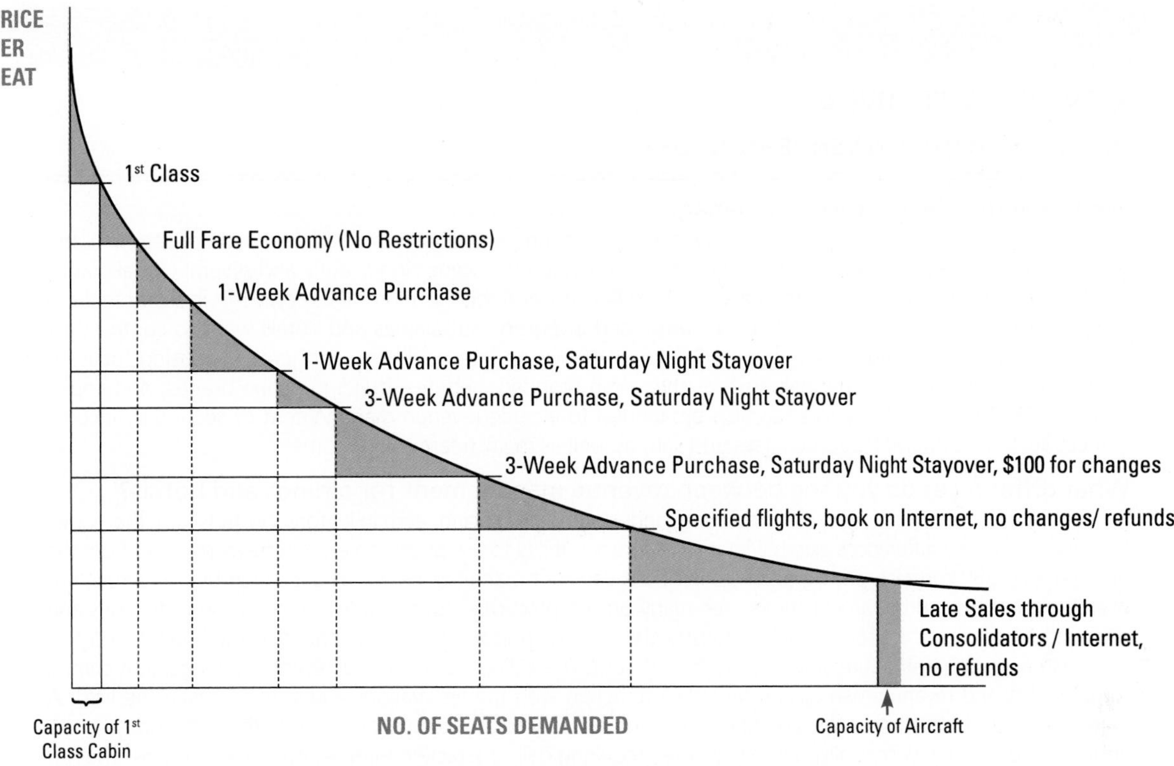

FIGURE 6.9 Relating Price Buckets to the Demand Curve

customers to self-segment on the basis of service characteristics and willingness to pay and help companies to restrict lower prices to customers willing to accept certain restrictions on their purchase and consumption experiences.

Fences can be either *physical* or *nonphysical. Physical fences* refer to tangible product differences related to the different prices, such as the seat location in a theatre, the size and furnishing of a hotel room, or the product bundle (e.g., first class is better than economy). In contrast, *nonphysical fences* refer to consumption, transaction or buyer characteristics, but otherwise they actually refer to the same basic service (e.g., there is no difference in economy class service whether a person bought a ticket really cheaply or paid full fare for it). Examples include having to book a certain length of time ahead, not being able to cancel or change a booking (or having to pay cancellation or change penalties), or having to stay over a weekend night. Examples of common rate fences are shown in Table 6.2.

In summary, using a detailed understanding of customer needs, preferences, and willingness to pay, product and revenue managers can jointly design effective products comprising the core service, physical product features (physical fences), and nonphysical product features (nonphysical fences). A good understanding of the demand curve is needed so that "buckets" of inventory can be assigned to the various products and price categories. An example from the airline industry is shown in Figure 6.9, and Service Perspective 6.2 provides insights to the thinking and work of a revenue manager. And lastly, the design of revenue management systems needs to incorporate safeguards for consumers as we will discuss in the next section on Ethical Concerns in Service Pricing.

ETHICAL CONCERNS IN SERVICE PRICING

Do you sometimes have difficulty understanding how much it's going to cost you to use a service? Do you believe that many prices are unfair? If so, you're not alone.[16] The fact is, service users can't always be sure in advance what they will receive in return for their money. There's an implicit assumption among many customers that a higher priced service should offer more benefits and greater quality than a lower priced one. For example, a professional—say a lawyer—who charges very high fees is assumed

SERVICE PERSPECTIVE 6.2

INTERVIEW WITH A REVENUE MANAGER

What is your role as a revenue manager?

When I started in 1993, the primary focus was on forecasting, inventory control, pricing, market segment and geographic mix, and allotment control. The Internet changed the scene significantly and several global giants, like Expedia and Travelocity, emerged after 9/11 when travel bookings plummeted and the industry realized the power of the Internet to help them sell distressed inventory. But airlines and hotels want to control their own inventory and pricing to cut costs and reduce reliance on intermediaries, so there's increasing focus on driving bookings via direct channels such as their own branded websites, building online brands, and implementing CRM programs. My role has also broadened to include revenue management of secondary income sources such as restaurants, golf courses and spa, as well as mainstream hotel rooms.

What differences do you see between revenue management for airlines and hotels?

Fundamentally, the techniques of forecasting and optimizing pricing and inventory controls are the same. However, some key differences exist. Airlines have a larger ability to use pricing to expand travel demand from the home market. By contrast, pricing practices in hotels can shift market share within a location but, as a rule, not overall market size. Although consumers see many pricing practices—such as advance purchase restrictions and discounts—as fair practice for the airline industry, they see them as less fair when applied by the hotel industry.

Organizational structure also tends to be different. The airlines adopt central revenue management control for all flights and revenue managers have little interaction with the reservations and sales teams in the field. A more precise and statistical application of pricing and inventory control is thus the focus. In the hotel industry, revenue management is decentralized to every hotel, requiring daily interaction with reservations and sales. The human element is key for successful implementation in hotels, requiring acceptance of pricing and inventory decisions not only by consumers but also by internal departments such as reservations, sales, and even front office.

What skills do you need to succeed as a revenue manager?

Strong statistical and analytical skills are essential, but to be really successful, revenue managers need to have equally strong interpersonal and influencing skills in order for their decisions to be accepted by other departments. Traditional ways of segmenting customers via their transactional characteristics such as booking lead time, channel of reservation, and type of promotion are insufficient. Both behavioral characteristics (such as motive for travel, products sought, spending pattern, and degree of autonomy) and emotional characteristics (such as self-image, conspicuous consumer or reluctant traveler, impulse or planned) need to be incorporated into revenue management considerations.

How are revenue management practices perceived by customers?

The art of implementation is not to let the customers feel that your pricing and inventory control practices are unfair and meant primarily to increase the top and bottom line of the company. Intelligent and meaningful rate fences have to be used to allow customers to self-segment so that they retain a feeling of choice.

Daily Nature of the Job

The market presents a lot of demand changes and you need to monitor your competitors' price as it fluctuates daily across the various distribution channels. It's definitely a prerequisite to be quick in analysis and decisive. One needs to feel comfortable taking calculated risks and choose from a plethora of revenue management and pricing tools to decide on the best fit for the situation.

Source: We thank Jeannette Ho, who was Vice President Distribution Marketing & Revenue Management at Raffles International Limited when this interview was conducted on January 6, 2006. Jeannette was responsible for spearheading and implementing the revenue management initiatives for the group. Her team drove the company's global distribution strategy and oversaw its e-commerce channels and central reservations system. Jeannette is presently Vice President Marketing and Sales for Raffles Hotels & Resorts. Over the past 15 years, Jeannette has been working in revenue management with various international companies such as Singapore Airlines, Banyan Tree, and Westin Hotels & Resorts.

more skilled than one who is relatively inexpensive. Although price can serve as a surrogate for quality, it is sometimes hard to be sure if the extra value is really there.

Service Pricing Is Complex

Pricing schedules for services tend to be complex and hard to understand. Comparison across providers may even require intricate spreadsheets or even mathematical formulas. Consumer advocates sometimes charge that this complexity represents a deliberate choice on the part of service suppliers who don't want customers to determine who offers the best value for money and therefore reduce price competition. In fact, complexity makes it easy (and perhaps more tempting) for firms to engage in unethical behavior. The quoted prices typically used by consumers for price comparisons may be only the first of several charges they can be billed.

For example, cell phone companies have a confusing variety of plans to meet the distinct needs and calling patterns of different market segments. Plans can be national, regional, or purely local in scope. Monthly fees vary according to the number of minutes selected in advance, which typically include separate allowances for peak and off-peak minutes. Overtime minutes and "roaming minutes" on other carriers are charged at higher rates. Some plans allow unlimited off-peak calling, others allow free incoming calls. Some providers charge calls per second, per 6-second block, or even per-minute block, resulting in vastly different costs per call. Family plans let parents and children pool their monthly minutes for use on several phones as long as the total for everyone's calling doesn't exceed the monthly quota.

In addition, baffling new fees have started to appear on bills, ranging from "paper bill fee" to pay for the bill itself to obscure sounding fees such as "property tax allotment," "single bill fee," and "carrier cost recovery fee." Bundled plans that include mobile, landline, and Internet services compound the confusion further, in that the various surcharges can increase the total bill by up to 25 percent. Phone bills include real taxes (e.g., sales tax), but on many bills the majority of surcharges, which users often misread as taxes, go directly to the phone company. For instance, the "property tax allotment" is nothing more than a factor for the property taxes the carrier pays, the "single bill fee" charges for consolidated billing of the mobile and land line service, and the "carrier cost recovery fee" is a catch-all for all sorts of operating expenses. In an editorial entitled "Cell Hell," Jim Guest, Consumer Union's president, observed:

> In the 10 years since *Consumer Reports* started rating cell phones and calling plans, we've never found an easy way to compare actual costs. From what our readers tell us, they haven't either. Each carrier presents its rates, extra charges, and calling areas differently. Deciphering one company's plan is hard enough, but comparing plans from various carries is nearly impossible.[17]

Many people find it difficult to forecast their own usage, which makes it hard to compute comparative prices when evaluating competing suppliers whose fees are based on a variety of usage-related factors. It's no coincidence that the humorist Scott Adams (creator of Dilbert) used exclusively service examples when he "branded" the future of pricing as "confusiology." Noting that firms—such as telecommunication companies, banks, insurance firms, and other financial service providers—offer nearly identical services, Adams remarks:

> You would think this would create a price war and drive prices down to the cost of providing it (that's what I learned between naps in my economic classes), but it isn't happening. The companies are forming efficient confusopolies so customers can't tell who has the lowest prices. Companies have learned to use the complexities of life as an economic tool.[18]

One of the roles of effective government regulation, says Adams, should be to discourage this tendency for certain service industries to evolve into "confusopolies."

Piling on the Fees

Not all business models are based on generating income from sales. There is a growing trend today to impose fees that sometimes have little to do with usage. In the United States, the car rental industry has attracted some notoriety for advertising bargain rental prices and then telling customers on arrival that other fees like collision and personal insurance are compulsory. Also, staff sometimes fails to clarify certain "small print" contract terms such as (say) a high mileage charge that is added once the car exceeds a very low threshold of free miles. The "hidden extras" phenomenon for car rentals in some Florida resort towns got so bad at one point that people were joking: "The car is free, the keys are extra!"[19]

There has also been a trend to adding (or increasing) fines and penalties. Banks have been heavily criticized for using penalties as an important revenue-generating tool as opposed to using them merely to educate customers and achieve compliance with payment deadlines. Chris Keeley, a New York University student, used his debit card to buy $230 worth of Christmas gifts. His holiday mood soured when he received a notice from his bank that he had overdrawn his checking account. Although his bank authorized each of his seven transactions, it charged him $31 per payment, totaling $217 for only $230 in purchases. Keeley maintained that he had never requested the so-called overdraft protection on his account and wished his bank had rejected the transactions, because he would then simply have paid by credit card. He fumed, "I can't help but think they wanted me to keep spending money so that they could collect these fees."[20]

The importance of fees as a proportion of profits has increased dramatically—for some banks they now exceed earnings from mortgages, credit cards, and all other lending combined. None of the fees is more controversial than "bounce protection" (i.e., the practice of allowing you to overdraw your account beyond an agreed credit line), which generates some $8 billion in income for banks, and making up almost 30 percent of all their service fees. Critics feel that some banks market bounce protection too aggressively. Regulators are particularly worried about bounce protection offered via ATMs. For example, a customer with a balance of $300 in his account, but a $500 bounce protection could be told at the ATM that he has $800 available. If he withdrew $400, the ATM would still show available funds of $370 (after charging a fee of, for example, $30 for using the bounce protection balance).

Some banks don't charge for overdraft protection. Said Dennis DiFlorio, president for retail banking at Commerce Bancorp Inc. in Cherry Hill, N.J.: "It's outrageous. It's not about customer convenience. It's just a way for banks to make money off customers." Some banks now offer services that cover overdrafts automatically from savings accounts, other accounts, or even the customer's credit card, and don't charge fees for doing so.[21]

It's possible to design fees and even penalties that do not seem unfair to customers. Research Insights 6.1 describes what drives customers' fairness perceptions with service fees and penalties.

Designing Fairness into Revenue Management

Like pricing plans and fees, revenue management practices can be perceived as highly unfair, and customer perceptions have to be carefully managed. Therefore, a well-implemented revenue management strategy cannot mean blind pursuit of short-term yield maximization. Rather, the following approaches can help to reconcile yield management practices with customers' fairness perceptions and satisfaction, trust, and goodwill:[22]

- **Design Price Schedules and Fences That Are Clear, Logical, and Fair.** Firms should proactively spell out all fees and expenses (e.g., no-show or cancellation charges) clearly in advance so there are no surprises. A related approach is to

RESEARCH INSIGHTS 6.1

CRIME AND PUNISHMENT: HOW CUSTOMERS RESPOND TO FINES AND PENALTIES

Various types of "penalties" are part and parcel of many pricing schedules, ranging from late fees for DVD rentals to cancellation charges for hotel bookings and charges for late credit card payments. Customer responses to penalties can be highly negative, and can lead to switching providers and poor word of mouth. Young Kim and Amy Smith conducted an online survey using the Critical Incident Technique (CIT) in which the 201 respondents were asked to recall a recent penalty incident, describe the situation, and then complete a set of structured questions based on how the respondents felt and how they responded to that incident. Their findings showed that negative consumer responses can be reduced significantly by following three guidelines:

1. Make Penalties Relative to the Crime Committed. The survey showed that customers' negative reaction to a penalty increased drastically when they perceived that the penalty was out of proportion to the "crime'"committed. Customers' negative feelings were further aggravated if they were "surprised" by the penalty being suddenly charged to them and they had not been aware of the fee or the magnitude of the fee. These findings suggest that firms can reduce negative customer responses significantly by exploring which amounts are seen as reasonable or fair for a given "customer laps," and the fines/fees are communicated effectively even before a chargeable incident happens that gets charged (e.g., in a banking context through a clearly explained fee schedule, and through front line staff that explains at the point of opening an account or selling additional services the potential fines or fees that are associated with various "violations," such as overdrawing beyond the authorized limits, bounced checks, or late payments).

2. Consider Causal Factors and Customize Penalties. The study showed that customers' perceptions of fairness were lower and negative responses were higher when they perceived the causes that led to the penalty to be out of their control ("I mailed the check on time—there must have been a delay in the postal system"), rather than when they felt it was within their control and really their fault (e.g., "I forgot to mail the check"). To increase the perception of fairness, firms may want to identify common penalty cases that typically are out of the control of the customer and allow the frontline to waive or reduce such fees.

In addition, it was found that customers who generally observe all the rules, and therefore have not paid fines in the past, react particularly negatively if they are fined. One respondent said, "I have always made timely payments and have never been late with a payment—they should have considered this fact and waived the fee." Service firms should take into account customers' penalties history in dealing with penalties, and offer differential treatments based on past behavior—perhaps waiving the first fine for the first incident, while at the same time communicating that the fee will be charged for subsequent incidents, could improve fairness perceptions.

3. Focus on Fairness and Manage Emotions during Penalty Situations. Consumers' responses are heavily driven by their perception of fairness perceptions. Customers are likely to perceive penalties as excessive and respond negatively if they find that a penalty is out of proportion compared to the damage or extra work caused by the penalized incident to the service firm. One consumer complained, "I thought this particular penalty [credit card late payment] was excessive. You are already paying high interest; the penalty should have been more in line with the payment. The penalty was more than the payment!" Considering customers' perceptions of fairness might mean, for example, that the late fee for a keeping a DVD should not exceed the potentially lost rental fees during that period.

Service companies can also make penalties seem fairer by providing adequate explanations and justifications for the penalty. Ideally, penalties should be imposed for the good of other customers (e.g., "We kept the room for you which we could have given to another guest on our wait list") or community, but not as a means for generating significant profit. Finally, front-line employees should be trained in how to handle customers who have become angry or distressed and complain about penalties (see Chapter 13 for some recommendations on how to deal with such situations).

In sum, this study shows how firms can reduce customer unhappiness related to penalties.

Source: Young "Sally" K. Kim and Amy K. Smith, "Crime and Punishment: Examining Customers' Responses to Service Organizations' Penalties," *Journal of Service Research*, 8, No. 2, 2005, 162–180.

develop a simple fee structure so customers can more easily understand the financial implications of a specific usage situation. For a rate fence to be perceived as fair, customers must understand them easily (i.e., fences have to be transparent and upfront), see the logic in them, and be convinced they are difficult to circumvent and therefore fair.

- **Use High Published Prices and Frame Fences as Discounts.** Rate fences framed as customer gains (i.e., discounts) generally are perceived as fairer than those framed as customer losses (i.e., surcharges) even if the situations are economically equivalent. For example, a customer who patronizes her hair salon on Saturdays may perceive the salon as profiteering if she finds herself facing a weekend surcharge. However, she is likely to find the higher weekend price more acceptable if the hair salon advertises its peak weekend price as the published price and offers a $5 discount for weekday haircuts. Furthermore, having a high published price also helps to increase the reference price and potentially quality perceptions in addition to the feeling of being rewarded for the weekday patronage.
- **Communicate Consumer Benefits of Revenue Management.** Marketing communications should position revenue management as a win–win practice. Providing different price and value balances allows a broader spectrum of customers to self-segment and enjoy the service. It allows each customer to find the price and benefits (value) balance that best satisfies his or her needs. For example, charging a higher price for the best seats in the theater recognizes that some people are willing and able to pay more for a better location and makes it possible to sell other seats at a lower price. Perceived fairness is affected by what customers perceive as normal. Hence, when customers become more familiar with particular revenue management practices, the unfairness perceptions are likely to decrease over time.[23]
- **Use Bundling to "Hide" Discounts.** Bundling a service into a package effectively obscures the discounted price. When a cruise line includes the price of air travel or ground transportation in the cruise package, the customer knows only the total price, not the cost of the individual components. Bundling usually makes price comparisons between the bundles and its components impossible and thereby side-steps potential unfairness perceptions and reductions in reference prices.[24]
- **Take Care of Loyal Customers.** Firms should build in strategies for retaining valued customers, even to the extent of not charging the maximum feasible amount on a given transaction. After all, customer perceptions of price gouging do not build trust. Yield management systems can be programmed to incorporate "loyalty multipliers" for regular customers, so that reservations systems can give them "special treatment" status at peak times, even when they are not paying premium rates.
- **Use Service Recovery to Compensate for Overbooking.** Many service firms overbook to compensate for anticipated cancellations and no-shows. Profits increase but so, too, does the incidence of being unable to honor reservations. Being "bumped" by an airline or "walked" by a hotel can lead to a loss of customer loyalty[25] and adversely affect a firm's reputation. So it's important to back up overbooking programs with well-designed service recovery procedures, such as:
  1. Give customers a choice between retaining their reservation and receiving compensation (e.g., many airlines practice voluntary offloading at check-in against cash compensation and a later flight).
  2. Provide sufficient advance notice that customers are able to make alternative arrangements (e.g., preemptive offloading and rescheduling to another flight on the day before departure, often in combination with cash compensation).

3. If possible, offer a substitute service that delights customers (e.g., upgrading a passenger to business or first class on the next available flight, often in combination with options 1 and 2 above).

A Westin beach resort found that it can free up capacity by offering guests who are departing the next day the option of spending their last night in a luxury hotel near the airport or in the city at no cost. Guest feedback on the free room, upgraded service, and a night in the city after a beach holiday has been very positive. From the hotel's perspective, this practice trades the cost of securing a one-night stay in another hotel against that of turning away a multiple-night guest arriving that same day.

PUTTING SERVICE PRICING INTO PRACTICE

Although the main decision in pricing usually is seen as how much to charge, there are other decisions to be made. Table 6.3 summarizes the questions that service marketers need to ask themselves as they prepare to create and implement a well-thought out pricing strategy. Let's look at each in turn.

How Much to Charge?

Realistic decisions on pricing are critical for financial solvency. The pricing tripod model, discussed earlier (refer to Figure 6.2), provides a useful starting point. The three elements involve determining the relevant economic costs to be recovered at different sales volumes and setting the relevant floor price; assessing the elasticity of demand of the service from both the providers' and customers' perspectives, as it helps to set a "ceiling" price for any given market segment; and analyzing the intensity of price competition among the providers.

A specific figure must be set for the price itself. This task involves several considerations, including the need to consider the pros and cons of setting a rounded price and the ethical issues involved in setting a price exclusive of taxes, service charges, and other extras.

What Should Be the Specified Basis for Pricing?

It's not always easy to define a unit of service as the specified basis for pricing. Many options may exist. For instance, should price be based on completing a promised service task—such as repairing a piece of equipment or cleaning a jacket? Should it be based on admission to a service performance—such as an educational program, a concert, or a sports event? Should it be time based—for instance, using an hour of a lawyer's time or occupying a hotel room for a night? Alternatively, should it be related to a monetary value associated with service delivery, as when an insurance company scales its premiums to reflect the amount of coverage provided, or a realtor takes a commission that is a percentage of the selling price of a house?

Some service prices are tied to the consumption of physical resources such as food, drinks, water, or natural gas. In the hospitality industry, rather than charging customers an hourly rate for occupying a table and chairs, restaurants put a sizable markup on the food and drink items consumed. Recognizing the fixed cost of table service—such as a clean tablecloth for each party—restaurants in some countries impose a fixed cover charge that is added to the cost of the meal. Others may establish a minimum meal charge per person. Transport firms have traditionally charged by distance, with freight companies using a combination of weight or cubic volume and distance to set their rates. Such a policy has the virtue of consistency and reflects calculation of an average cost per mile (or kilometer). However, it ignores relative market strength on different routes, which should be included when a yield management system is used. Simplicity may suggest a flat rate, as with postal charges for

TABLE 6.3 Some Pricing Issues

1. **How much should be charged for this service?**
   - What costs are the organization attempting to recover? Is the organization trying to achieve a specific profit margin or return on investment by selling this service?
   - How sensitive are customers to various prices?
   - What prices are charged by competitors?
   - What discount(s) should be offered from basic prices?
   - Are psychological pricing points (e.g., $4.95 versus $5.00) customarily used?
2. **What should be the basis of pricing?**
   - Execution of a specific task
   - Admission to a service facility
   - Units of time (hour, week, month, year)
   - Percentage commission on the value of the transaction
   - Physical resources consumed
   - Geographic distance covered
   - Weight or size of object serviced
   - Should each service element be billed independently?
   - Should a single price be charged for a bundled package?
3. **Who should collect payment?**
   - The organization that provides the service
   - A specialist intermediary (travel or ticket agent, bank, retailer, etc.)
   - How should the intermediary be compensated for this work—flat fee or percentage commission?
4. **Where should payment be made?**
   - The location at which the service is delivered
   - A convenient retail outlet or financial intermediary (e.g., bank)
   - The purchaser's home (by mail or phone)
5. **When should payment be made?**
   - Before or after delivery of the service
   - At which times of day
   - On which days of the week
6. **How should payment be made?**
   - Cash (exact change or not?)
   - Token (where can these be purchased?)
   - Stored value card
   - Check (how to verify?)
   - Electronic funds transfer
   - Charge card (credit or debit)
   - Credit account with service provider
   - Vouchers
   - Third-party payment (e.g., insurance company or government agency)?
7. **How should prices be communicated to the target market?**
   - Through what communication medium? (advertising, signage, electronic display, salespeople, customer service personnel)
   - What message content (how much emphasis should be placed on price?)

domestic letters below a certain weigh, or a rate for packages that groups geographic distances into broad zones.

For some services, prices may include separate charges for access and for usage. Recent research suggests that access or subscription fees are an important driver of adoption and customer retention, whereas usage fees are much more important drivers of actual usage.[26]

PRICE BUNDLING. An important question for service marketers is whether to charge an inclusive price for all elements (referred to as a "bundle") or to price component elements separately. If customers prefer to avoid making many small payments, then bundled pricing may be preferable. However, if they dislike being charged for product elements they do not use, itemized pricing may be preferable.

Bundled prices offer firms a certain level of guaranteed revenue from each customer, while providing customers a clear idea in advance of how much they can expect to pay. Unbundled pricing provides customers with the freedom to choose what to buy and pay for.[27] For instance, many U.S. airlines now charge economy class passengers for meals, drinks, and check-in baggage on their domestic flights. However, customers may be angered if they discover the actual price of what they consume, inflated by all the "extras," is substantially higher than the advertised base price that attracted them in the first place.

DISCOUNTING. Selective price discounting targeted at specific market segments can offer important opportunities to attract new customers and fill capacity that would otherwise go unused. However, unless it is used with effective rate fences that allow a clean targeting of specific segments, a strategy of discounting should be approached cautiously. It reduces the average price and contribution received and may attract customers whose only loyalty is to the firm that can offer the lowest price on the next transaction. Volume discounts are sometimes used to cement the loyalty of large corporate customers who might otherwise spread their purchases among several different suppliers.

Who Should Collect Payment?

As discussed in Chapter 4, supplementary services include information, order-taking, billing, and payment. Customers appreciate it when a firm makes it easy to obtain price information and make reservations. They also expect well-presented billing and convenient procedures for making payment. Sometimes, firms delegate these tasks to intermediaries such as travel agents who make hotel and transport bookings and collect payment from customers and ticket agents who sell seats for theaters, concert halls, and sports stadiums. Although the original supplier pays a commission, the intermediary usually is able to offer customers greater convenience in terms of where, when, and how payment can be paid. Using intermediaries may also result in a net savings in administrative costs. Nowadays, however, many service firms are promoting their websites with best rate or price guarantees as direct channels for customer self-service, thus bypassing traditional intermediaries and avoiding payment of commissions.

Where Should Payment Be Made?

Service delivery sites are not always conveniently located. Airports, theaters, and stadiums, for instance, often are situated some distance from where potential patrons live or work. When consumers have to purchase a service before using it, there are obvious benefits to using intermediaries that are more conveniently located, or allowing payment by mail or bank transfer. A growing number of organizations now accept Internet, telephone, and email bookings with payment by credit card.

When Should Payment Be Made?

Two basic options are to ask customers to pay in advance (as with an admission charge, airline ticket, or postage stamps) or to bill them once service delivery has been completed, as with restaurant bills and repair charges. Occasionally, a service provider may ask for an initial payment in advance of service delivery, with the balance due later (Figure 6.10). This approach is quite common for expensive repair and maintenance jobs, when the firm—often a small business with limited working capital—must buy materials upfront.

Asking customers to pay in advance means the buyer is paying before the benefits are received. However, prepayments may be advantageous to the customer as well as to the provider. Sometimes it is inconvenient to pay each time a regularly patronized service—such as the Postal Service or public transport—is used. To save time and effort, customers may prefer the convenience of buying a book of stamps or a monthly travel pass.

"Unless we receive the outstanding balance within ten days, we will have no choice but to destroy your credit rating, ruin your reputation, and make you wish you were never born. If you have already sent the seven cents, please disregard this notice."

FIGURE 6.10 Some Firms Do Not Leave Their Customers with Much Flexibility in Dealing with Late Payment

Source: © Randy Glasbergen

Performing arts organizations with heavy upfront financing requirements offer discounted subscription tickets in order to bring in money before the season begins.

Finally, the timing of payment can determine usage pattern. From an analysis of the payment and attendance records of a Colorado-based health club, John Gourville and Dilip Soman found that members' usage patterns were closely related to their payment schedules. When members made payments, their use of the club was highest during the months immediately following payment and then declined steadily until the next payment; members with monthly payment plans used the health club much more consistently and were more likely to renew, perhaps because each month's payment encouraged them to use what they were paying for.

Gourville and Soman conclude that the timing of payment can be used more strategically to manage capacity utilization. For instance, if a golf club wants to reduce the demand during its busiest time, it can bill its fees long before the season begins (e.g., in January rather than in May or June), as the member's pain of payment will have faded by the time the peak summer months come, and thereby reduces the need to get his or her "money's worth." A reduction in demand during the peak period would then allow the club to increase its membership.[28]

How Should Payment Be Made?

As shown earlier in Table 6.3, there are many different forms of payment. Cash may appear to be the simplest method, but it raises security problems and is inconvenient when exact change is required to operate machines. Accepting payment by check for all but the smallest purchases is now fairly widespread and offers customer benefits, although it may require controls to discourage bad checks, such as a hefty charge for returned checks ($15–$20 on top of any bank charges is not uncommon at retail stores).

Credit and debit cards can be used around the world. As their acceptance has become almost universal, businesses that refuse to accept them increasingly find themselves at a competitive disadvantage. Many companies also offer customers the convenience of a credit account, which generates a membership relationship between the customer and the firm (see Chapter 12).

Other payment procedures include tokens or vouchers as supplements to (or instead of) cash. Vouchers are sometimes provided by social service agencies to elderly or low-income citizens. Such a policy achieves the same benefits as discounting, but avoids the need to publicize different prices and to require cashiers to check eligibility.

Now coming into broader usage are prepayment systems based on cards that store value on a magnetic strip or in a microchip embedded within the card. Service firms that want to accept payment in this form, however, must first install card readers. Service marketers should remember that the simplicity and speed with which payment is made may influence the customer's perception of overall service quality. To save its customers time and effort, Chase bank has introduced credit cards with what it calls "blink," an embedded technology that can be read by a point-of-sale terminal without physically touching it.

Interestingly, a recent study found that the payment mechanism has an effect on the total spending of customers, especially for discretionary consumption items such as spending in cafes.[29] The less tangible or immediate the payment mechanism, the more consumers tend to spend. Cash is the most tangible (i.e., consumers will be more careful and spend less), followed by credit cards, prepayment cards, and finally more sophisticated and even less tangible and immediate mechanisms such as payment via one's cell phone service bill.

How Should Prices Be Communicated to the Target Markets?

The final task, once each of the other issues has been addressed, is to decide how the organization's pricing policies can best be communicated to its target market(s). People need to know the price for some product offerings well in advance of purchase. They may also need to know how, where, and when that price is payable. This information must be presented in intelligible and unambiguous ways so that customers will not be misled and question the ethical standards of the firm. Dismayed by the complexity of cell phone calling plans in the United States, Consumers Union has called for a simple, standardized summary of the features of each calling plan that would simplify the process for consumers to compare competing offers. This would be similar in style to the government-mandated box printed on all credit card solicitations that lays out, in standard format and readable type, the offer's essential rates and terms.[30]

When the price is presented in the form of an itemized bill, marketers should ensure that it is both accurate and intelligible. Hospital bills, which may run to several pages and contain dozens or even hundreds of items, have been much criticized for inaccuracy. Hotel bills, despite containing fewer entries, are also notoriously inaccurate. One study estimated that business travelers in the United States may be overpaying for their hotel rooms by half-a-billion dollars a year, with 11.6 percent of all bills incorrect, resulting in an average overpayment of $11.36.[31]

CONCLUSION

To determine an effective pricing strategy, a firm has to have a good understanding of its costs, the value created for customers, and competitor pricing. In addition, revenue management is a powerful tool that helps to manage demand and to price different segments closer to their value perceptions. A pricing strategy must address the central issue of what price to charge for a given unit of service at a particular point in time (however that unit may be defined). Because services often combine multiple elements, pricing strategies can be highly creative.

Finally, firms need to be careful lest pricing schedules become so complex and hard to compare that they simply confuse customers and can lead to accusations of unethical behavior, loss of trust, and customer dissatisfaction. Therefore, great care has to be taken in the way service pricing and revenue management are implemented to ensure that customer satisfaction and perceived fairness are not compromised.

Chapter Summary

LO1 Effective pricing is central to the financial success of service firms. The objectives for establishing prices can be to generate profits, cover costs, build demand, and develop a user base. Once a firm sets its pricing objectives, it needs to decide on its pricing strategy.

LO2 The foundations of a pricing strategy are the three legs of the pricing tripod:
- The *costs* the firm needs to recover set the minimum or floor price.
- The customer's *perceived value* of the offering sets a maximum or ceiling price.
- The price charged for *competing services* determines where, within the floor-to-ceiling range, the price can be set.

LO3 The first leg of the pricing tripod is the cost to the firm.
- Costing services often is complex. Services frequently have high fixed costs, varying capacity utilization, and large shared infrastructures that make it difficult to establish unit costs.
- If services have a large proportion of variable and/or semivariable costs, cost-accounting approaches work well (e.g., using contribution and break-even analysis).
- However, for complex services with shared infrastructure, activity-based costing (ABC) often is more appropriate.

LO4 The second leg of the pricing tripod is value to the customer.
- Net value is the sum of all perceived benefits (gross value) minus the sum of all the perceived costs of a service. Customers will only buy if the net value is positive. The net value can be enhanced by increasing value and reducing costs.
- Since value is perceived and subjective, it can be enhanced through communication and education

to help customers understand the value they receive.

- In addition to the price customers pay for the service, costs include related monetary costs (e.g., the taxi fare to the service location) and nonmonetary costs (e.g., time, physical, psychological, and sensory costs) during the search, purchase and service encounter, and postconsumption stages. Firms can enhance net value by reducing these related monetary and nonmonetary costs.

LO5 The third leg of the pricing tripod is competition.

- Price competition can be fierce in markets with relatively undifferentiated services. Here, firms need to closely observe what competitors are charging and price accordingly.
- However, services tend to be location- and time-specific, and competitor services have their own set of related monetary and nonmonetary costs, sometimes to the extent that the actual prices charged become secondary for competitive comparisons.

LO6 Revenue management (RM) increases revenue for the firm through better capacity utilization and reserving capacity for higher paying segments. Specifically, RM:

- Designs products using physical and nonphysical rate fences, and prices them for different segments according to their specific reservation prices.
- Sets prices according to predicted demand levels of different customer segments.
- Works best in service businesses characterized by (1) high fixed costs and perishable inventory, (2) several customer segments with different price elasticities, and (3) variable and uncertain demand.

LO7 Well-designed rate fences are needed to define "products" for each target segment so that customers with high value for a service offer are unable to take advantage of lower price buckets. Rate fences can be physical and nonphysical:

- Physical fences refer to tangible product differences related to different prices (e.g., seat location in a theatre, size of a hotel room, or service level).
- Nonphysical fences refer to consumption (e.g., stay must be over a weekend), transaction (e.g., two weeks advance booking with cancellation and change penalties), or buyer characteristics (e.g., student and group discounts). The service experience is identical across fence conditions although different prices are charged.

LO8 Customers often have difficulties understanding service pricing (e.g., RM practices and their many fences and fee schedules). Service firms need to be careful that their pricing does not become so complex and with hidden fees that customers perceive them as unethical and unfair.

LO9 The following ways help firms to improve customers' fairness perceptions:

- Design price schedules and fences that are clear, logical, and fair.
- Use published prices and frame fences as discounts.
- Communicate consumer benefits of revenue management.
- Use bundling to "hide" discounts.
- Take care of loyal customers.
- Use service recovery to deal with overbooking.

LO10 To put service pricing into practice, service marketers need to consider seven questions to have a well-thought-out pricing strategy. The questions are:

1. How much to charge?
2. What should be the specified basis for pricing?
3. Who should collect payment?
4. Where should payment be made?
5. When should payment be made?
6. How should payment be made?
7. How should prices be communicated to the target markets?

Review Questions

1. What is the role of service pricing and revenue management in a business model?
2. Why is the pricing of services more difficult compared to the pricing of goods?
3. How can the pricing tripod approach to service pricing be useful to come to a good pricing point for a particular service?
4. How can a service firm compute its unit costs for pricing purposes? How does predicted and actual capacity utilization affect unit costs and profitability?
5. Why can't we compare competitor prices dollar-for-dollar in a service context?
6. Why is the price charged by the firm only one, and often not the most important component of the total cost to the consumer? When should we cut non-price-related costs to the bone, even if that incurs higher costs and a higher price to be charged?
7. What is the role of nonmonetary costs in a business model, and how do they relate to the consumer's value perceptions?

8. What is revenue management, how does it work, and what type of service operations benefit most from good revenue management systems and why?
9. Why are ethical concerns and fairness perception important issues when designing service pricing schedules and revenue management strategies? What are potential consumer responses to service pricing schedules or policies perceived as unfair?
10. How can we charge different prices to different segments without customers feeling cheated? How can we even charge the same customer different prices at different times, contexts, and/or occasions, and at the same time be seen as fair?
11. What are the seven key decisions managers need to make when designing an effective pricing schedule?

Application Exercises

1. Select a service organization of your choice, and find out what its pricing policies and methods are. In what respects are they similar to or different from what has been discussed in this chapter?
2. From the customer perspective, what serves to define value in the following services: (a) a hair salon, (b) a legal firm specializing in business and taxation law, and (c) a nightclub?
3. Explore two highly successful business models based on innovative service pricing and/or revenue management strategies, and identify two business models that failed because of major issues in their pricing strategy. What general lessons can you learn from your analysis?
4. Review recent bills you have received from service businesses, such as those for telephone, car repair, cable TV, and credit cards. Evaluate each one against the following criteria: (a) general appearance and clarity of presentation, (b) easily understood terms of payment, (c) avoidance of confusing terms and definitions, (d) appropriate level of detail, (e) unanticipated ("hidden") charges, (f) accuracy, and (g) ease of access to customer service in case of problems or disputes.
5. How might revenue management be applied to (a) a professional service firm (e.g., consulting), (b) a restaurant, and (c) a golf course? What rate fences would you use and why?
6. Collect the pricing schedules of three leading cell phone service providers. Identify all the pricing dimensions (e.g., airtime, subscription fees, free minutes, per second/6 seconds per minute billing, air time roll-over, etc.) and pricing levels for each dimension (i.e., the range offered by the players in the market). Determine the usage profile for a particular target segment (e.g., a young executive who uses the phone mostly for personal calls or a full-time student). Based on the usage profile, determine the lowest-cost provider. Next, measure the pricing schedule preferences of your target segment (e.g., via conjoint analysis). Finally, advise the smallest of the three providers how to redesign its pricing schedule to make it more attractive to your target segment.
7. Consider a service of your choice, and develop a comprehensive pricing schedule. Apply the seven questions marketers need to answer for designing an effective pricing schedule.

Endnotes

1. "Dynamic Pricing—EasyInternetCafe Case Study," Managing Change: Strategic Interactive Marketing, http://www.managingchange.com/dynamic/easyic.htm; http://www.stelios.com; http://www.easyinternetcafe.com accessed April 21, 2009.
2. Joan Magretta, "Why Business Models Matter," *Harvard Business Review*, 80, May 2002, 86–92.
3. This section is based on: Robin Cooper and Robert S. Kaplan, "Profit Priorities from Activity-Based Costing," *Harvard Business Review*, 69, May–June 1991, 130–135; Craig A. Latshaw and Teresa M. Cortese-Daniele, "Activity-Based Costing: Usage and Pitfalls," *Review of Business*, 23, Winter 2002, 30–32; Robert S. Kaplan and Steven R. Anderson, "Time-Driven Activity Based Costing," *Harvard Business Review*, 82, November 2004, 131–138.
4. Daniel J. Goebel, Greg W. Marshall, and William B. Locander, "Activity Based Costing: Accounting for a Marketing Orientation," *Industrial Marketing Management*, 27, No. 6, 1998, 497–510; Thomas H. Stevenson and David W. E. Cabell, "Integrating Transfer Pricing Policy and Activity-Based Costing," *Journal of International Marketing*, 10, No. 4, 2002, 77–88.
5. Robin Cooper and Robert S. Kaplan, "Profit Priorities from Activity-Based Costing," *Harvard Business Review*, 69, No. 3, May–June 1991, 130–135.
6. Antonella Carù and Antonella Cugini, "Profitability and Customer Satisfaction in Services: An Integrated Perspective between Marketing and Cost Management Analysis," *International Journal of Service Industry Management*, 10, No. 2, 1999, 132–156.

7. Gerald E. Smith and Thomas T. Nagle, "How Much Are Customers Willing to Pay?" *Marketing Research*, Winter 2002, 20–25.
8. Valarie A. Zeithaml, "Consumer Perceptions of Price, Quality, and Value: A Means-End Model and Synthesis of Evidence," *Journal of Marketing*, 52, July 1988, 2–21. A recent paper exploring alternative conceptualizations of value is: Chien-Hsin Lin, Peter J. Sher, and Hsin-Yu Shih, "Past Progress and Future Directions in Conceptualizing Customer Perceived Value," *International Journal of Service Industry Management*, 16, No. 4, 2005, 318–336.
9. Parts of this section are based on Leonard L. Berry and Manjit S. Yadav, "Capture and Communicate Value in the Pricing of Services," *Sloan Management Review*, 37, Summer 1996, 41–51.
10. Hermann Simon, "Pricing Opportunities and How to Exploit Them," *Sloan Management Review*, 33, Winter 1992, 71–84.
11. Anna S. Mattila and Jochen Wirtz, "The Impact of Knowledge Types on the Consumer Search Process – An Investigation in the Context of Credence Services," *International Journal of Service Industry Management*, 13, No. 3, 2002, 214–230.
12. Leonard L. Berry, Kathleen Seiders, and Dhruv Grewal, "Understanding Service Convenience," *Journal of Marketing*, 66, July 2002, 1–17.
13. Kristina Heinonen, "Reconceptualizing Customer Perceived Value: The Value of Time and Place," *Managing Service Quality*, 14, No. 3, 2004, 205–215.
14. For application of yield management to industries beyond the traditional airline, hotel and car rental contexts see: Frédéric Jallat and Fabio Ancarani, "Yield Management, Dynamic Pricing and CRM in Telecommunications," *Journal of Services Marketing*, 22, No. 6, 2008, 465–478; Sheryl E. Kimes and Jochen Wirtz, "Perceived Fairness of Revenue Management in the US Golf Industry," *Journal of Revenue and Pricing Management*, 1, No. 4, 2003, 332–344; Sheryl E. Kimes and Jochen Wirtz, "Has Revenue Management Become Acceptable? Findings from an International Study and the Perceived Fairness of Rate Fences," *Journal of Service Research*, 6, November 2003, 125–135; Richard Metters and Vicente Vargas, "Yield Management for the Nonprofit Sector," *Journal of Service Research*, 1, February 1999, 215–226; Sunmee Choi and Anna S. Mattila, "Hotel Revenue Management and Its Impact on Customers' Perception of Fairness," *Journal of Revenue and Pricing Management*, 2, No. 4, 2004, 303–314; Alex M. Susskind, Dennis Reynolds, and Eriko Tsuchiya, "An Evaluation of Guests' Preferred Incentives to Shift Time-Variable Demand in Restaurants," *Cornell Hotel and Restaurant Administration Quarterly*, 44, No. 1, 2004, 68–84; Parijat Dube, Yezekael Hayel, and Laura Wynter, "Yield Management for IT Resources on Demand: Analysis and Validation of a New Paradigm for Managing Computing Centres," *Journal of Revenue and Pricing Management*, 4, No. 1, 2005, 24–38; and Sheryl E. Kimes and Sonee Singh, "Spa Revenue Management," *Cornell Hospitality Quarterly*, 40, No. 1, 2009, 82–95.
15. Hermann Simon and Robert J. Dolan, "Price Customization," *Marketing Management*, 7, Fall 1998, 11–17.
16. Lisa E. Bolton, Luk Warlop, and Joseph W. Alba, "Consumer Perceptions of Price (Un)Fairness," *Journal of Consumer Research*, 29, No. 4, 2003, 474–491; Lan Xia, Kent B. Monroe, and Jennifer L. Cox, "The Price is Unfair! A Conceptual Framework of Price Fairness Perceptions," *Journal of Marketing*, 68, October 2004, 1–15. Christian Homburg, Wayne D. Hoyer, and Nicole Koschate, "Customer's Reactions to Price Increases: Do Customer Satisfaction and Perceived Motive Fairness Matter?" *Journal of the Academy of Marketing Science*, 33, No. 1, 2005, 36–49.
17. Jim Guest, "Cell Hell" (p. 3) and "Complete Cell-Phone Guide," *Consumer Reports*, February 2003, 11–27; Ken Belson, "A Monthly Mystery," *New York Times*, August 27, 2005.
18. Scott Adams, *The Dilbert^{TM} Future - Thriving on Business Stupidities in the 21st Century.* New York: Harper Business, 1997, 160.
19. Ian Ayres and Barry Nalebuff, "In Praise of Honest Pricing," *Sloan Management Review*, 45, Fall 2003, 24–28.
20. Dean Foust, "Protection Racket? As Overdraft and Other Fees Become Huge Profit Sources for Banks, Critics See Abuses," *Business Week*, 5, February 2005, 68–89.
21. The banking examples and data in this section were from Dean Foust, "Protection Racket? As Overdraft and Other Fees Become Huge Profit Sources for Banks, Critics See Abuses," *Business Week*, 5, February 2005, 68–89.
22. Parts of this section are based on Jochen Wirtz, Sheryl E. Kimes, Jeannette P. T. Ho, and Paul Patterson, "Revenue Management: Resolving Potential Customer Conflicts," *Journal of Revenue and Pricing Management*, 2, No. 3, 2003, 216–228.
23. Jochen Wirtz and Sheryl E. Kimes, "The Moderating Role of Familiarity in Fairness Perceptions of Revenue Management Pricing," *Journal of Service Research*, 9, No. 3, 2007, 229–240.
24. Judy Harris and Edward A. Blair, "Consumer Preference for Product Bundles: The Role of Reduced Search Costs," *Journal of the Academy of Marketing Science*, 34, No. 4, 2006, 506–513.
25. Florian v. Wangenheim and Tomas Bayon, "Behavioral Consequences of Overbooking Service Capacity," *Journal of Marketing*, 71, No. 4, October 2007, 36–47.
26. Peter J. Danaher, "Optimal Pricing of New Subscription Services: An Analysis of a Market Experiment," *Marketing Science*, 21. Spring 2002, 119-129; Gilia E. Fruchter and Ram C. Rao, "Optimal Membership Fee and Usage Price Over Time for a Network Service," *Journal of Services Research*, 4, No. 1, 2001, 3-14.
27. Avery Johnson, "Northwest to Charge Passengers in Coach for Meals," *Wall Street Journal*, February 16, 2005.
28. John Gourville and Dilip Soman, "Pricing and the Psychology of Consumption," *Harvard Business Review*, 9, September 2002, 90–96.
29. Dilip Soman, "The Effect of Payment Transparency on Consumption: Quasi-Experiments from the Field," *Marketing Letters*, 14, No. 3, 2003, 173–183.
30. "Needed: Straight Talk about Cellphone Calling Plans," *Consumer Reports*, February 2003, 18.
31. See, for example, Anita Sharpe, "The Operation Was a Success; The Bill Was Quite a Mess," *Wall Street Journal*, September 17, 1997, 1; Gary Stoller, "Hotel Bill Mistakes Mean Many Pay Too Much," *USA Today*, July 12, 2005.

CHAPTER 7

Promoting Services and Educating Customers

Life is for one generation; a good name is forever.

JAPANESE PROVERB

Education costs money, but then so does ignorance.

SIR CLAUS MOSER

LEARNING OBJECTIVES (LOs)

By the end of this chapter, the reader should be able to:

LO1 Learn the role of marketing communications in services.

LO2 Understand the challenges of service communications.

LO3 Know the 5 Ws of marketing communications planning.

LO4 Be familiar with the marketing communications mix in a services context.

LO5 Know the communications mix elements of the traditional marketing channels.

LO6 Understand the role of the Internet, cellular, and other electronic media in service marketing communications.

LO7 Know the communications mix elements available via service delivery channels.

LO8 Understand communications mix elements that originate from outside the firm.

LO9 Appreciate ethical and consumer privacy related issues in marketing communications.

LO10 Understand the role of corporate design in communications.

LO11 Know the importance of integrating marketing communications to deliver a strong brand identity.

Westin's "This Is How You Should Feel" Campaign to Reposition Its Brand[1]

Imagine this. After a long tiring day at work, you head for the subway to take you home. When you ride down on the escalator, you suddenly feel as if you were in the middle of a rushing waterfall—the escalator is wrapped in a design that wonderfully simulates that! Somehow, you feel a little less tired and more refreshed. When you step onto the train, you are stunned for a moment—the car features a striking blue design and you feel as if you were in an underwater world theme park. You wonder what this is all about. Since all the seats are taken, you walk further along and step into a white, snow-covered mountainous environment. Curious, you decide to explore the other cars to see what you will find. You discover that you can be in a green rainforest (Figure 7.1), or even a sauna. It is almost like taking a holiday around the world! After your "round the world trip," you decide to take a seat at Iceland. That is when something else catches your attention. As the train moves, you see the effects of a flower slowly blooming as the train passes by a portion of wall along the tunnel. As you journey further, you see waves crashing. By the time you leave the subway, you feel as if you have lived a lifetime of experiences that leave you feeling refreshed even though it is just the end of a long work day! You have just been through the Westin experience.

Westin spent $30 million on this campaign, called "This Is How it Should Feel." The campaign used a range of traditional and nontraditional media such as print, radio, online, and multiplatform. There were more than 270 different visuals and 2,754 media placements. The various experiences in the train were part of the shuttle wrap. Apart from that, Westin also used escalator and column wraps. The blooming flower was part of the submedia, which used the motion of the train to cause the images on the wall of the tunnel to move like a giant flipbook. Westin also used image shifting lenticulars (ads that change as you move) that may, for example, change from an emergency exit door to a forest. Outdoors, Westin positioned larger-than-life, three-dimensional billboards spread over five major cities in the United States. In Boston, for instance, three-dimensional skydivers were placed in front of a beautifully printed sky.

FIGURE 7.1 The Sleepy Routine of Commuters Across Major Cities in the U.S. Was Given a Bit of Pep by the Westin Experience

Starwood, the parent company of Westin, aimed to reposition and redefine the brands of hotels in its portfolio and embarked on this creative campaign to reposition staying at a Westin as rejuvenating and destressing. Westin's website asked: "What will you experience at a Westin? Will you get away from it all, or will you explore the world around you? Reignite a romance or bond with your family? Whatever escape you can imagine, we have a Westin Experience Package for you."

THE ROLE OF MARKETING COMMUNICATIONS

Through communications, marketers explain and promote the value proposition their firm is offering. The Westin campaign used experiential advertising to communicate an experience of renewal. It is a promise of what customers can expect if they stay at a Westin hotel.

Communication is the most visible or audible—some would say intrusive—of marketing activities, but its value is limited unless it is used intelligently in conjunction with other marketing efforts. An old marketing axiom says that the fastest way to kill a poor product is to advertise it heavily. By the same token, an otherwise well-researched and planned marketing strategy is likely to fail if prospects don't learn of a service firm's existence, what it has to offer them, the value proposition of each of its products, and how to use them to best advantage. Customers might be more easily lured away by competitors and competitive offerings, and there would be no proactive management and control of the firm's identity. Marketing communications, in one form or another, are essential to a company's success.

There is a lot of confusion over the scope of service marketing communications, with many people still defining it too narrowly. Communications must be viewed more broadly than as just media advertising, public relations, and professional salespeople. There are many other ways for a service business to communicate with current and prospective customers. The location and atmosphere of a service delivery facility, corporate design features such as the consistent use of colors and graphic elements, the appearance and behavior of employees, the design of a website—all contribute to an impression in the customer's mind that reinforces or contradicts the specific content of formal communication messages. The past few years have seen the emergence of new and exciting opportunities for reaching prospects through the Internet, with degrees of targeting and message specificity previously unimaginable. All these media must be effectively synchronized to attract new customers and to reconfirm the choice of existing customers while educating them on how to proceed through a service process. It is for good reason that we define the marketing communication element of the 7 Ps as *Promotion and Education.* Let us now look at some specific roles performed by marketing communications.

Position and Differentiate the Service

Companies use marketing communications to persuade target customers that their service product offers the best solution to meet those customers' needs, relative to the offerings of competing firms. See Figure 7.2 for an advertisement on how Wausau conveys

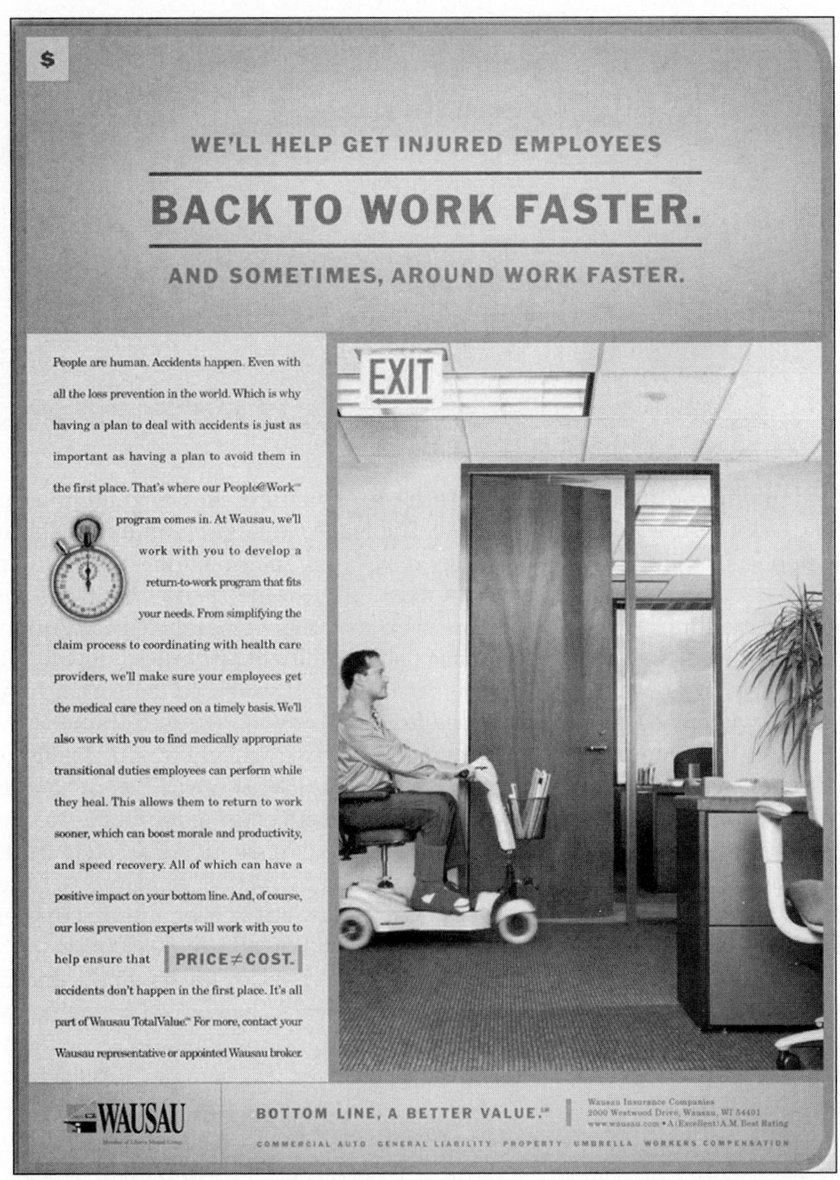

Source: Courtesy of Wausau Insurance.

FIGURE 7.2 Wausau Promotes Its Innovative People @ Work℠ Program Targeted at Employers

FIGURE 7.3 The National Guard Communicates Its Service to the Public

this, building on its in-depth expertise on preventing and managing accidents in the workplace. Figure 7.3 illustrates how The National Guard communicates its service to the public. Communication efforts serve not only to attract new users but also to maintain contact with an organization's existing customers and build relationships with them. Marketing communications is used to convince potential and current customers about the firm's superior performance on determinant attributes (see Chapter 3).

Even if customers understand what a service is supposed to do, they may find it hard to tell the difference between offerings from different suppliers. Companies may use concrete clues to communicate service performance by highlighting the quality of equipment and facilities and by emphasizing employee characteristics such as qualifications, experience, commitment, and professionalism. Some performance attributes are easier or more appropriate to communicate than others. Airlines do not advertise safety because even the suggestion that things might go wrong makes many passengers nervous. Instead, they approach this ongoing customer concern indirectly by advertising the expertise of their pilots, the newness of their aircraft, and the skills and training of their mechanics.

To document the superior quality and reliability of its small package delivery services, a FedEx advertisement showed the awards it received for being rated as highest in customer satisfaction for air, ground, and international delivery from J. D. Power and Associates, widely known and respected for its customer satisfaction research in numerous industries.[2]

Promote the Contribution of Service Personnel and Backstage Operations

High-quality, frontline staff and back-stage operations can be important service differentiators. In high-contact services, frontline personnel are central to service delivery. Their presence makes the service more tangible and, in many cases, more personalized. An ad that shows employees at work helps prospective customers understand the nature of the service encounter and implies a promise of the personalized attention they can expect to receive.

Advertising, brochures, and websites can also show customers the work that goes on "back-stage" to ensure good service delivery. Highlighting the expertise and commitment of employees whom customers normally never encounter may enhance trust in the organization's competence and commitment to service quality. For example, Starbucks has publicity materials and web pages that show customers what service personnel do behind the scenes. Starbucks shows how coffee beans are cultivated, harvested, and produced—highlighting its use of the finest and freshest.

Advertising messages set customer expectations, so advertisers must be reasonably realistic in their depictions of service personnel. They should also inform employees about the content of new advertising campaigns or brochures that promise specific attitudes and behaviors so that employees know what is expected of them.

Add Value through Communication Content

Information and consultation represent important ways to add value to a product. Prospective customers may need information and advice about what service options are available to them; where and when these services are available; how much they cost; and what specific features, functions, and service benefits are on hand. (See the "flower of service" framework in Chapter 4 for more on how this information can add value.)

Facilitate Customer Involvement in Service Production

When customers are actively involved in service production, they need training to help them perform well—just as employees do. Improving productivity often involves making innovations in service delivery. However, the desired benefits won't be achieved if customers resist new, technologically based systems or avoid self-service alternatives.

Marketers often use sales promotions as incentives to encourage customers to make the necessary changes in their behavior. For example, giving price discounts is one way to encourage customers to try and switch to self-service. And, if necessary, well-trained service personnel can provide one-on-one tutoring to help customers adapt to new procedures.

One approach to training customers, recommended by advertising experts, is to show service delivery in action. Television and videos are effective because of their ability to engage the viewer and display a seamless sequence of events in visual form. Some dentists show their patients videos of surgical procedures before the surgery takes place so that customers know what to expect. Shouldice Hospital in Toronto, featured in Case 10 (page 529) specializes exclusively in hernia repair. It offers prospective patients an opportunity to view an online simulation on hernia and explains the hospital experience on its website (see www.shouldice.com). This educational technique helps patients prepare mentally for the experience and shows them what role they need to play in service delivery to ensure a successful surgery and fast recovery.

Stimulate or Dampen Demand to Match Capacity

Many live service performances—a seat at the theater for Friday evening's performance or a haircut at Supercuts on Tuesday morning—are time specific and can't be stored for resale at a later date. Advertising and sales promotions can help to change the timing of customer use and thus help to match demand with the available capacity at a given time.

Demand management strategies include shifting usage during peak demand periods and stimulating it during off-peak periods. Low demand outside peak periods poses a serious problem for service industries with high fixed costs, such as hotels. One strategy is to run promotions that offer extra value—such as room upgrades or free breakfasts—in an attempt to stimulate demand without decreasing price. When demand increases, the number of promotions can be reduced or eliminated (see also Chapter 6 on revenue management and Chapter 9 on managing demand and capacity).

CHALLENGES OF SERVICES COMMUNICATIONS

Now that we've discussed the role of market communications, let's explore some of the communications challenges service firms face. Traditional marketing communication strategies were shaped largely by the needs and practices associated with marketing manufactured goods. However, several of the differences that distinguish services from goods also have a significant effect on the ways we approach the design of service marketing communication programs.

Problems of Intangibility

Because services are performances rather than objects, their benefits can be difficult to communicate to customers, especially when the service in question does not involve tangible actions to customers or their possessions.[3] Intangibility creates four problems for marketers seeking to promote its attributes or benefits: abstractness, generality, nonsearchability, and mental impalpability.[4] Banwari Mittal and Julie Baker highlight the implications of each of these four problems as follows:[5]

- *Generality* refers to items that comprise a class of objects, persons, or events—for instance, airline seats, flight attendants, and cabin service. These general classes have physical analogues, and most consumers of the service know what they are. However, a key task for marketers seeking to create a distinctive value proposition is to communicate what makes a specific offering distinctly different from—and superior to—competing offerings.
- *Abstractness.* Because abstract concepts such as financial security, expert advice, or safe transportation do not have one-to-one correspondence with physical objects, it can be challenging for marketers to connect their services to those concepts. Figure 7.3 illustrates how The National Guard communicates its services to the public.
- *Nonsearchability* refers to the fact that intangibles cannot be searched or inspected before they are purchased. Physical service attributes, such as the appearance of a health club and the type of equipment installed, can be checked in advance, but the experience of working with the trainers can only be determined through extended personal involvement. And as noted in Chapter 2, credence attributes, such as surgeon expertise, must be taken on faith.
- *Mental impalpability.* Many services are sufficiently complex, multidimensional, or novel that it is difficult for consumers—especially new prospects—to understand what the experience of using them will be like and what benefits will result.

Banwari Mittal and Julie Baker suggest that to create messages that clearly communicate intangible service attributes and benefits to potential consumers, service marketers can follow specific communications strategies for dealing with them (see Table 7.1).

Overcoming the Problems of Intangibility

Tangible cues and metaphors can be effective in overcoming the challenges of intangibility.

TANGIBLE CUES. Commonly used strategies in advertising include the use of tangible cues whenever possible, especially for low-contact services that involve few tangible elements. It's also helpful to include "vivid information" that catches the audience's attention and produces a strong, clear impression on the senses, especially for services that are complex and highly intangible.[6] For example, many business schools feature successful alumni to

TABLE 7.1 Advertising Strategies for Overcoming Intangibility

Intangibility Problem	Advertising Strategy	Description
Incorporeal Existence	Physical Representation	Show Physical Components of Service
Generality:		
• For objective claims	System documentation	Objectively document physical system capacity
	Performance documentation	Document and cite past performance statistics
• For subjective claims	Service performance episode	Present an actual service delivery incident
Nonsearchability	Consumption documentation	Obtain and present customer testimonials
	Reputation documentation	Cite independently audited performance
Abstractness	Service consumption episode	Capture and display typical customers benefiting from the service
Impalpability	Service process episode	Present a vivid documentary on the step-by-step service process
	Case history episode	Present an actual case history of what the firm did for a specific client
	Service consumption episode	An articulate narration or depiction of a customer's subjective experience

Source: Banwari Mittal and Julie Baker, "Advertising Strategies for Hospitality Services," *Cornell Hotel and Restaurant Administration Quarterly, 43*, April 2002, 53. Copyright © 2002. Used by permission of Sage Publications.

make the benefits of its education tangible and communicate what its education could do for prospective students in terms of career advancement and salary increases.

Research Insights 7.1 shows how visualization and comparative advertising affect consumer perceptions of both hedonic services (those that bring pleasure and enjoyment) and utilitarian services (those consumed for practical or functional purposes).

USE METAPHORS. Some companies have created metaphors that are tangible in nature to help communicate the benefits of their service offerings and to emphasize key points of difference relative to competing alternatives. Insurance companies often use this approach to market their highly intangible products. Thus Allstate advertises that "You're in Good Hands" and Prudential uses the Rock of Gibraltar as a symbol of corporate strength. Professional service firms sometimes use metaphors to communicate their value propositions more dramatically. Consider the advertising campaign created by Accenture, an international consulting firm, to dramatize the abstract notion of helping clients capitalize on innovative ideas in a fast-moving world. It features champion golfer Tiger Woods in eye-catching situations to highlight the firm's ability to help clients "develop the reflexes of a high-performance business" (Figure 7.4).

Where possible, advertising metaphors should highlight *how* service benefits are actually provided.[7] Consulting firm AT Kearney emphasizes that it includes all management levels in seeking solutions, not just higher-level management. Its clever advertisement, showing bear traps across the office floor, draws attention to the way in which the company differentiates its service through careful work with all levels in its client organizations, thus avoiding the problems left behind by other consultants who work only with top management (Figure 7.5).

MARKETING COMMUNICATIONS PLANNING

Now that we've discussed the role of market communications and how to overcome the challenge of intangibility of service offerings, we now turn our discussion to how to plan and design an effective marketing communications strategy.

RESEARCH INSIGHTS 7.1

VISUALIZATION AND COMPARATIVE ADVERTISING FOR SERVICES

Experts often recommend using visual stimuli to convey a vivid mental picture and documenting facts and figures in order to overcome service intangibility and better communicate the value proposition of a service. To test the effectiveness of visualization and documentation strategies for hedonic and utilitarian services, four academics conducted a laboratory experiment.

They showed the 160 participating student subjects one print advertisement each, and then measured their responses. An ad for a spring-break travel service was used as the hedonic service, and one for a bank with specific student offers was used for the utilitarian service. In the visualization condition, one picture of the hotel and one of young adults in an oceanside pool were added to the text for the hedonic service. For the bank, photos of the exterior of the bank building and an ATM were shown. The text-only documentation condition used an indirect comparative advertising copy stating the high performance of the service provider along the three most important attributes for the respective two services. The study then compared the text-only documentation condition with the ad that contained the pictures (visualization condition).

The findings showed that for both types of services, ads based on a visualization strategy were perceived as more informative than text-only ads. Participants who viewed the visualization ads perceived the services as higher quality and were more likely to say they intended to use these services. Documentation worked well for the hedonic service, but not the utilitarian one (further research is needed to explain why). The study has two important managerial implications:

1. **Use pictures to increase tangibility of the value proposition.** Whether you market a hedonic or a utilitarian service, use pictures and photos to communicate the potential benefits of your service. For example, Hilton Hotels Corp. started using photos to market its Chef's Signature Catering Collection, replacing its more traditional method of sending text-only menu information to clients who wanted to plan a dinner at the hotel. One Hilton executive noted, "people eat with their eyes, and when they see something they can relate to, something they can recognize, it develops a level of confidence and comfort level for the customer."
2. **Comparative data help readers to visualize especially hedonic services.** The study indicated that hedonic services can benefit from adding comparative information into its ads. For example, if Six Flags Great America advertises that its Déjà Vu roller coaster is 196 feet tall compared to only 120 feet of other top roller coasters, and that its speed is up to 65 mph (104 km/h), compared to only 50 to 60 mph for other roller coasters, then one should expect readers to better visualize the Déjà Vu as one of the tallest and fastest roller coasters in the world. Simply listing the height and speed alone wouldn't be as effective—readers need the benchmarking provided by the comparative information.

Source: Donna J. Hill, Jeff Blodgett, Robert Baer, and Kirk Wakefield, "An Investigation of Visualization and Documentation Strategies in Service Advertising," *Journal of Service Research*, 7, No. 2, 2004, 155–166.

Planning a marketing communications campaign should reflect a good understanding of the service product and how well prospective buyers can evaluate its characteristics in advance of purchase. It's essential to understand target market segments and their exposure to different media as well as consumers' awareness of the product and their attitudes toward it. Decisions include determining the content, structure, and style of the message to be communicated, its manner of presentation, and the media most suited to reaching the intended audience. Additional considerations include the budget available for execution; timeframes, defined by such factors as seasonality, market opportunities, and anticipated competitive activities; and methods of measuring and evaluating performance.

Source: Courtesy of Accenture.

FIGURE 7.4 Accenture Promotes Its Ability to Help Clients Turn Innovative Ideas into Results

What role should communications play in helping a service firm achieve its marketing goals? A useful checklist for marketing communications planning is provided by the "5 Ws" model:

Who is our target audience?

What do we need to communicate and achieve?

How should we communicate this?

Where should we communicate this?

When do the communications need to take place?

Let's first consider the issues of defining the target audience and specifying communication objectives. Then we'll review the wide array of communication tools available to service marketers. Issues relating to the location and scheduling of communication activities tend to be highly situation specific, and so we will not address them here.

Defining the Target Audience

Prospects, users, and employees represent broad target audiences for any service communications strategy:

- *Prospects*—Because marketers of consumer services do not usually know prospects in advance, they typically need to employ a traditional communications mix,

FIGURE 7.5 AT Kearney Uses Bear Traps as a Metaphor for Problems

Source: Courtesy of AT Kearney.

comprising such elements as media advertising, public relations, and use of purchased lists for direct mail or telemarketing.

- *Users*—In contrast to prospects, more cost-effective channels may be available to reach existing users, including cross- or up-selling efforts by frontline employees, point-of-sale promotions, and other information distributed during service encounters. If the firm has a membership relationship with its customers and has a database containing contact and profiling information, it can distribute highly targeted information through email, text messages, direct mail, or telephone. These channels may serve to complement and reinforce communications' broader channels or simply replace them.
- *Employees*—Employees serve as a secondary audience for communication campaigns through public media. A well-designed campaign targeted at users, nonusers, or both can also be motivating for employees, especially those in frontline roles. In particular, it may help to shape employees' behavior if the advertising content shows them what is promised to customers. However, there's a risk of generating cynicism among employees and actively demotivating them if the communication in question promotes levels of performance that employees regard as unrealistic or even impossible to achieve.

Communications directed specifically at staff typically are part of an internal marketing campaign, using company-specific channels, and so are not accessible to customers. We will discuss internal communications in Chapter 11.

Specifying Communication Objectives

After we are clear about our target audience, we need to now specify what exactly we want to achieve with this target audience. Communications objectives answer the question of what we need to communicate and achieve. Marketers need to be clear about their goals; otherwise, it will be difficult to formulate specific communications objectives and select the most appropriate messages and communication tools to achieve them. Objectives may include shaping and managing customer behavior in any of the three stages of the purchase and consumption process we discussed in Chapter 2 (i.e., the prepurchase, service encounter, and postconsumption stages). Common educational and promotional objectives for service organizations include:

- Create memorable images of companies and their brands.
- Build awareness and interest in an unfamiliar service or brand.
- Compare a service favorably with competitors' offerings.
- Build preference by communicating the strengths and benefits of a specific brand.
- (Re)position a service relative to competitive offerings.
- Reduce uncertainty and perceived risk by providing useful information and advice.
- Provide reassurance, such as by promoting service guarantees.
- Encourage trial by offering promotional incentives.
- Familiarize customers with service processes in advance of use.
- Teach customers how to use a service to their best advantage.
- Stimulate demand in low-demand periods and shift demand during peak periods.
- Recognize and reward valued customers.

THE MARKETING COMMUNICATIONS MIX

After understanding our target audience and our specific communications objectives, we now need to select a mix of cost-effective communications channels. Most service marketers have access to numerous forms of communication, referred to collectively as the *marketing communications mix*. Different communication elements have distinctive capabilities relative to the types of messages they can convey and the market segments most likely to be exposed to them. As shown in Figure 7.6, the mix includes personal

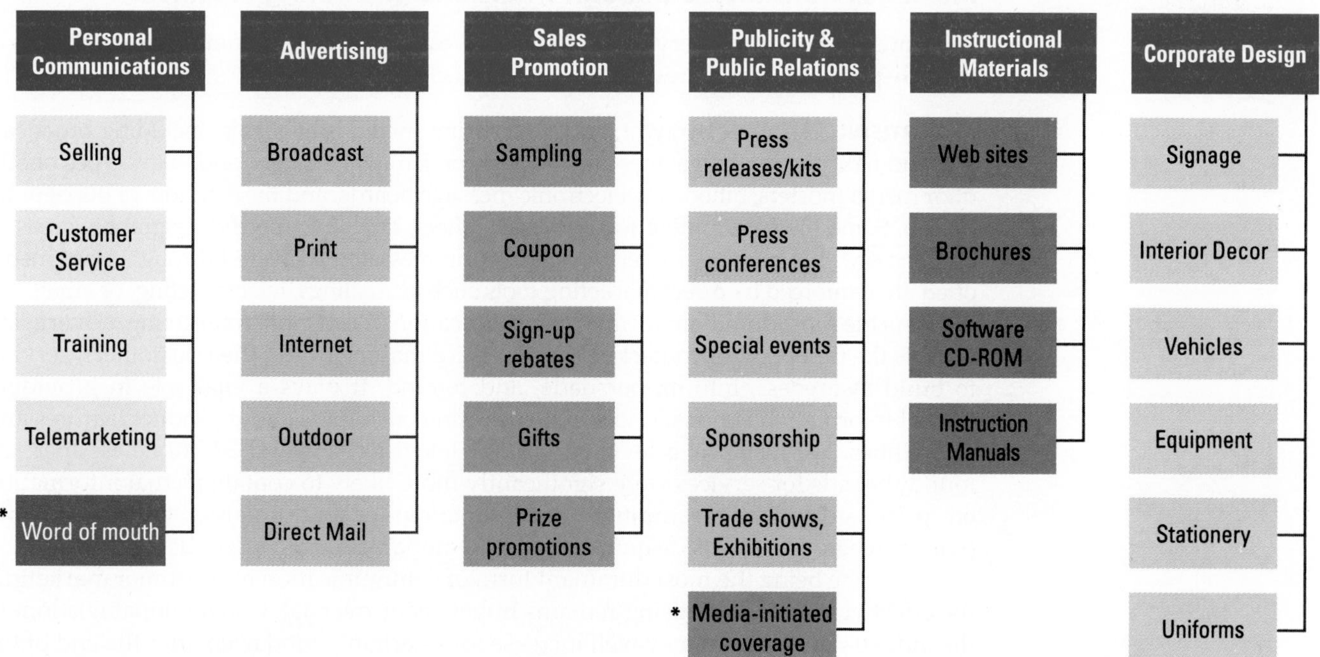

FIGURE 7.6 The Marketing Communications Mix for Services

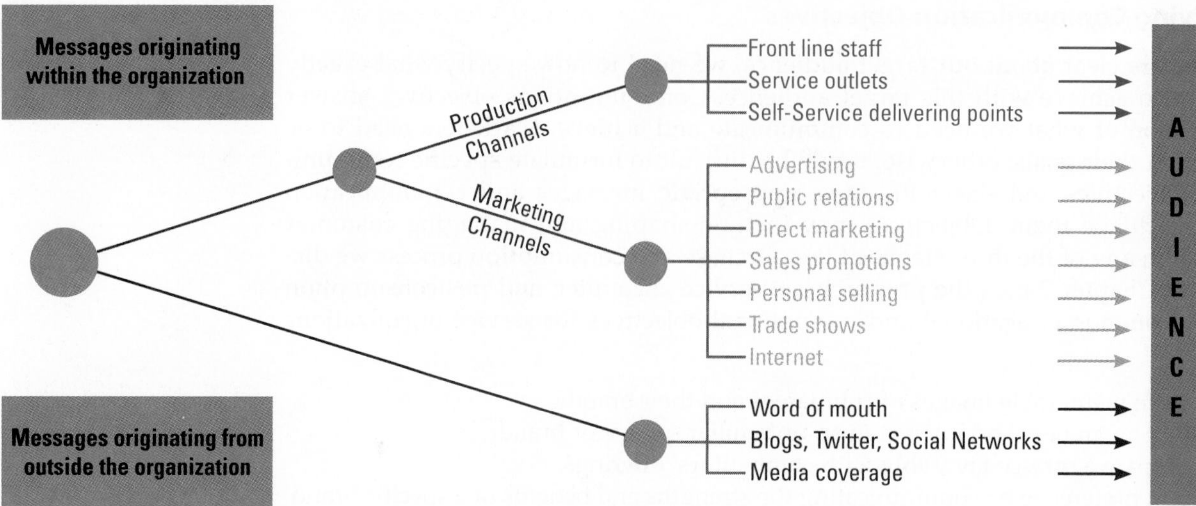

FIGURE 7.7 Sources of Messages Received by a Target Audience

Source: Adapted from a diagram by Adrian Palmer, *Principles of Services Marketing*, London: McGraw-Hill, 4th ed., 2005, p. 397.

communications, advertising, sales promotion, publicity and public relations, instructional materials, and corporate design.

Communications Originate from Different Sources

As shown in Figure 7.6, the traditional communications mix shown in Figure 7.7 can also be categorized into two main channels—those controlled by the organization and those that are not. Not all communications messages originate from the service provider. Rather, some messages originate from outside the organization. Furthermore, Figure 7.6 shows that messages from an internal source can be further divided into those transmitted through marketing channels (traditional media and the Internet) and those transmitted through the service firm's own service delivery channels. Let's look at the options within each of these three originating sources.

Messages Transmitted through Traditional Marketing Channels

As shown in Figure 7.6, service marketers have a wide array of communication tools at their disposal. We briefly review the principal elements.

ADVERTISING. A wide array of paid advertising media is available, including broadcast (TV and radio), print (magazines and newspapers), movie theaters, and many types of outdoor media (posters, billboards, electronic message boards, and the exteriors of buses or bicycles). Some media are more focused than others, targeting specific geographic areas or audiences with a particular interest. Advertising messages delivered through mass media often are reinforced by direct marketing tools such as mailings, telemarketing, or email.

As the most dominant form of communication in consumer marketing, advertising often is the first point of contact between service marketers and their customers, serving to build awareness, inform, persuade, and remind. It plays a vital role in providing factual information about services and educating customers about product features and capabilities. For instance, a review of 11,543 television ads and 30,940 newspaper ads found that ads for services were significantly more likely to contain factual information on price, guarantees/warranties, documentation of performance, and availability (where, when, and how to acquire products) compared to ads for goods.[8]

Despite being the most dominant form of communication in consumer marketing, the effectiveness of advertising remains hugely controversial. Conventional wisdom in the industry is that sales may well increase for a certain period even after the end of the advertising campaign. However, there comes a point when sales start to decline and it becomes extremely expensive to rebuild the brand. Robert Shaw of Cranfield School of

Management runs a forum in which large companies try to monitor the "marketing payback" from advertising. According to Shaw, the results were "never terribly good," with less than half of the ads generating a positive return on their investment.[9]

One of the challenges facing advertisers is how to get their messages noticed. In general, people are tiring of ads in all their forms. A recent study by Yankelovich Partner, a U.S. marketing services consulting firm, says that consumer resistance to the growing intrusiveness of advertising has reached an all-time high. The study found that 65 percent of people feel "constantly bombarded" by ad messages, and 59 percent feel that ads have very little relevance to them.[10] Television and radio broadcasts are cluttered with commercials, while newspapers and magazines sometimes seem to contain more ads than news and features.

FIGURE 7.8 Avatars Crowd in Front of Sony BMG's Media Island. Virtual Video Game Worlds Like Second Life Lead the New Wave of Dynamic In-Game Advertising

Source: Second Life ® used by permission of Linden Labs.

How can a firm hope to stand out from the crowd? Longer, louder commercials and larger format ads are not necessarily the answer. Marketers are trying to be more creative with their advertising to allow their messages to be more effective. For example, when customers have low involvement with a service, firms should focus on more emotional appeals and the service experience itself.[11] Some advertisers stand out by employing striking designs or a distinctively different format. Others, like Comcast, seek to catch the audience's attention through use of humor as it seeks to show how slow competing services are compared to its own high-speed Internet cable access. Or firms are now placing advertisements in video games, which can be dynamic advertisements if the games are connected to the Internet (Figure 7.8).[12]

PUBLIC RELATIONS. Public relations (PR) involves efforts to stimulate positive interest in an organization and its products by sending out news releases, holding press conferences, staging special events, and sponsoring newsworthy activities put on by third parties. A basic element in PR strategy is the preparation and distribution of press releases (including photos and/or videos) that feature stories about the company, its products, and its employees.

Other widely used PR techniques include recognition and reward programs, obtaining testimonials from public figures, community involvement and support, fundraising, and obtaining favorable publicity for the organization through special events and *pro bono* work. These tools can help a service organization build its reputation and credibility; form strong relationships with its employees, customers, and the community; and secure an image conducive to business success.

Firms can also win wide exposure through sponsorship of sporting events and other high-profile activities like the Olympics and World Cup for soccer where banners, decals, and other visual displays provide continuing repetition of the corporate name and symbol. Furthermore, unusual activities can present an opportunity to promote a company's expertise. FedEx gained significant favorable publicity when it safely transported two giant pandas from Chengdu, China, to the National Zoo in Washington, D.C. The pandas flew in specially designed containers aboard a FedEx aircraft renamed "FedEx PandaOne." In addition to press releases, the company also featured information about the unusual shipment on a special page on its website.

DIRECT MARKETING. This category embraces such tools as mailings, email, and text messaging. These channels offer the potential to send personalized messages to highly targeted microsegments. Direct strategies will most likely succeed when marketers possess a detailed database of information about customers and prospects. Commercial services are available that combine company-collected data with rich, third-party online and offline data sources. Experian, one of the globally leading providers in this market, states on its website: "We can help you to build a richer picture of your customers' behavior so you can predict and engineer how they behave in the future. Using internal and external data sources, our proven customer management tools allow you to tailor strategies to an individual.... Powered by up to 6,000 variables... uses lifestyle, demographic, transaction, permissible credit and consumer classification data."[13]

Advances in on-demand technologies such as email spam filters, TiVo, podcasting, and pop-up blockers empower consumers to decide how and when they prefer to be reached and by whom. Because a 30-second television spot interrupts a viewer's favorite program and a telemarketing call interrupts a meal, customers increasingly use such technologies to protect their time, thereby reducing the effectiveness of mass media. These developments give rise to *permission marketing*, where customers are encouraged to "raise their hands" and agree to learn more about a company and its products in anticipation of receiving useful marketing information or something else of value. Instead of annoying prospects by interrupting their personal time, permission marketing allows customers to self-select into the target segments.

In the permission marketing model, the goal is to persuade consumers to volunteer their attention. By reaching out only to individuals who have expressed prior interest in receiving a certain type of message, permission marketing enables service firms to build stronger relationships with their customers. In particular, email in combination with websites, can be integrated into a one-to-one permission-based medium.[14] For instance, people can be invited to register at the firm's website and specify what type of information they would like to receive via email. These emails can be designed as the start of a more interactive, multilayered communication process, in which customers can request regular information about topics of their interest. In addition, if they are particularly excited about a new service or piece of information, they can click through a URL link embedded in the email to more in-depth information and even video materials. Finally, they can subscribe online for additional services, recommend their friends, and the like.

The greater effectiveness of permission-based communications combined with the falling prices and improving quality of customer relationship management (CRM) and online technology, which together power permission-based marketing, has led many service firms to increase their focus on permission-based marketing strategies. To see how some firms have implemented excellent permission-based marketing strategies, visit Amazon.com or Hallmark.com and register at these websites.

SALES PROMOTION. A useful way of looking at sales promotions is as a communication attached to an incentive. Sales promotions usually are specific to a time period, price, or customer group—sometimes all three. Typically, the objective is to accelerate the purchasing decision or motivate customers to use a specific service sooner, in greater volume with each purchase, or more frequently.[15] Sales promotions for service firms may take such forms as samples, coupons and other discounts, gifts, and competitions with prizes. Used in these forms, sales promotions add value, provide a "competitive edge," boost sales during periods when demand would otherwise be weak, speed the introduction and acceptance of new services, and generally get customers to act faster than they would in the absence of any promotional incentive.[16] Sales promotions need to be used with care because research shows that customers acquired through sales promotions may have lower repurchase rates and lower lifetime values.[17]

Some years ago, SAS International Hotels devised an interesting sales promotion targeted at older customers. If a hotel had vacant rooms, guests over 65 years of age could get a discount equivalent to their years (e.g., a 75-year-old could save 75 percent of the normal room price). All went well until a Swedish guest checked into one of the SAS chain's hotels in Vienna, announced his age as 102, and asked to be paid 2 percent of the room rate in return for staying the night. This request was granted, whereupon the spry centenarian challenged the general manager to a game of tennis—and got that, too. (The results of the game, however, were not disclosed!) Events like these are the stuff of dreams for public relations people. In this case, a clever promotion led to a humorous, widely reported story that placed the hotel chain in a favorable light.

PERSONAL SELLING. Interpersonal encounters in which efforts are made to educate customers and promote preference for a particular brand or product are referred to as personal selling. Many firms, especially those marketing B2B services, maintain a dedicated sales force or employ agents and distributors to undertake personal selling efforts on their behalf.

Relationship marketing strategies often are based on account management programs, under which customers are assigned to a designated account manager who acts as an interface between the customer and the supplier. Account management is commonly practiced in industrial and professional firms that sell relatively complex services, resulting in an ongoing need for advice, education, and consultation. Examples of account management for individual consumers can be found in insurance, investment management, and medical services. Likewise, for infrequently purchased services such as property or funeral services, the firm's representative may act as a consultant to help buyers make their selections.

"Before you hang up, Mrs. Johnson, are you aware that you can lose up to 50 pounds a year by listening to telemarketers instead of eating your dinner?"

FIGURE 7.9 Telemarketers Often Call in the Evenings

Source: © Randy Glasbergen.

However, face-to-face selling to new prospects is expensive. A lower-cost alternative is *telemarketing*, involving use of the telephone to reach prospective B2C as well as B2C customers. At the consumer level, there is growing frustration with the intrusive nature of telemarketing, which often is timed to reach people when they are home in the evening or on weekends (Figure 7.9). Today, many people in the United States subscribe to a "Do Not Call Registry" which has dramatically reduced the number of solicitor calls that reach their prospects.

TRADE SHOWS. In the business-to-business marketplace, trade shows are a popular form of publicity that also includes important personal selling opportunities.[18] In many industries, trade shows stimulate extensive media coverage and offer business customers an opportunity to find out about the latest offerings from a wide array of suppliers in the field. Service vendors provide physical evidence in the form of exhibits, samples, and demonstrations and brochures to educate and impress these potential customers. Trade shows can be very productive promotional tools, because they are among the few opportunities in which large numbers of prospective buyers come to the marketer rather than the other way around. A sales representative who usually reaches four to five prospective clients per day may be able to generate five qualified leads per hour at a show.

Messages Transmitted through the Internet

Advertising on the Web allows companies to supplement conventional communications channels at a reasonable cost. However, like any of the elements of the marketing communications mix, Internet advertising should be part of an integrated, well-designed communications strategy.[19] Firms can market through their own websites or through online advertising.

COMPANY'S WEBSITE. Marketers use their own websites for a variety of communications tasks, including promoting consumer awareness and interest, providing information and consultation, facilitating two-way communications with customers through email and chat rooms, stimulating product trial, enabling customers to place orders, and measuring the effectiveness of specific advertising or promotional campaigns.

Innovative companies continually are looking for ways to improve the appeal and usefulness of their sites. The appropriate communication content varies widely from one type of service to another. A B2B site may offer visitors access to a library of technical information (e.g., Siebel or SAP both provide substantial information on their customer relationship management solutions at their respective websites at www.siebel.com and www.sap.com). By contrast, a website for an MBA program website might include attractive photographs

FIGURE 7.10 easyJet Paints Its Web Site Address on Each of Its More Than 200 Aircraft

featuring the location, the facilities, and past students and short videos showing the university, its professors and facilities, student testimonials, and even the graduation ceremony.

Marketers must also address other attributes such as downloading speed that affect website "stickiness" (i.e., whether visitors are willing to spend time on the site and will revisit it in the future). A sticky site is:

- **High in quality content.** Relevant and useful content is king. A site needs to contain what visitors are looking for on that site.
- **Easy to use.** Easy to use means good navigation, a site structure that is neither overcomplicated nor too big, and well signposted. Customers do not get lost in good sites!
- **Quick to download.** Viewers don't want to wait and will often give up if it takes too long for pages to download from a site. Good sites download quickly, and bad sites are slow.
- **Updated frequently.** Good sites look fresh and up-to-date. They include recently posted information that visitors find relevant and timely.[20]

A memorable Web address helps to attract visitors to a site. Ideally, they are based on the company's name (e.g., www.citibank.com or www.aol.com), although sometimes an alternative must be found if the simple form of the name has already been taken by a similarly named company in another industry. Ensuring that people are aware of the address requires displaying it prominently on business cards, letterhead stationery, email templates, brochures, advertising, promotional materials, and even vehicles. One of the largest of the European discount airlines, easyJet, has painted its address in huge orange letters on each of its aircraft (Figure 7.10).

ONLINE ADVERTISING. There are two main options, banner advertising and search engine advertising. A key advantage of online advertising is that it provides a very clear and measurable return on investment, especially when compared to other forms of advertising. Particularly in performance-priced online advertising (e.g., pay-per-click), the link between advertising costs and the customers who were attracted to a company's website or offer is trackable. Contrast this to traditional media advertising on TV or in magazines where it is notoriously difficult to assess the success and return of investment of an advertisement.

- **Banner Advertising.** Many firms pay to place advertising banners and buttons on portals like Yahoo or CNN as well as on other firms' websites. The usual goal is to draw online traffic to the advertiser's own site. In many instances, websites include advertising messages from other marketers with related but noncompeting services. For example, Yahoo's stock quotes page features a sequence of advertisements for various financial service providers.

  Simply obtaining a large number of exposures ("eyeballs") to a banner (a thin horizontal ad running across all or part of a web page), a skyscraper (a long skinny ad running vertically down one side of a website), or a button doesn't necessarily lead to increases in awareness, preference, or sales for the advertiser. One consequence is that the practice of paying a flat monthly rate or by number of impressions for banner advertising is falling out of favor. Even when visitors click through to the advertiser's site, this action doesn't necessarily result in sales. Consequently, there's now more emphasis on advertising contracts that tie fees to marketing-relevant behavior by these visitors, such as providing the advertiser with some information about themselves or making a purchase. Internet advertisers increasingly pay only if a visitor to the host site clicks through on the link to the advertisers' site. This is the equivalent of paying for the delivery of junk mail only to households that read it.[21]

- **Search Engine Advertising.** Search engines are a form of a reverse broadcast network. Instead of advertisers broadcasting their messages to consumers, search engines let advertisers know exactly what consumers want through their keyword search, and advertisers can then target relevant marketing communications directly at these consumers.[22] One of the phenomenal success stories of search engine advertising has been Google (see Service Perspective 7.1), with firms like Yahoo!, AOL, MSN, and most recently Blink seeking to become major players in this field.

Advertisers have several options. They can pay for the targeted placement of ads to keyword searches relevant to the advertising firm; they can sponsor a short text message with a click-through link, located parallel to the search results; or they can buy top rankings in the display of search results through a "pay-for-placement" option. This last approach is somewhat controversial because it conflicts with users' expectations that the rankings will

SERVICE PERSPECTIVE 7.1

GOOGLE—THE ONLINE MARKETING POWERHOUSE

Larry Page and Sergey Brin, who were both fascinated by mathematics, computers, and programming from an early age, founded Google in 1998 while they were Ph.D. students at Stanford University. Seven years later, following Google's successful public offering, they became multibillionaires, and Google became one of the world's most valuable companies.

The company has the grand vision "To organize the world's information and make it universally accessible and useful." The utility and ease of its search engine has made it immensely successful, almost entirely through word of mouth from satisfied users. Few company names become verbs, but to "google" has now entered common use in English.

Its popularity has enabled Google to become a new and highly targeted advertising medium, allowing advertisers two important ways to reach their customers—through sponsored links and through content ads, which are highly targeted display ads next to search results or on websites of Google's partners.

Sponsored links appear at the top of search results on Google's website and are identified as "sponsored links." Google prices its sponsored links service as "cost per click", using a sealed-bid auction (i.e., where advertisers submit bids for a search term without knowing the bids of other advertisers for the same term). This means prices depend on the popularity of the search terms with which the advertiser wants to be associated. Heavily used terms such as "MBA" are more expensive than less popular terms such as "MSc in Business." Advertisers can easily keep track of their ad performance using the reports in Google's online account Control Center.

Google allows *content ads* to be highly targeted through a number of means via its Google AdWords service. Ads can be placed next to search results on Google.com (they are, for example, displayed as banner ads, which is very different from the sponsored link approach), allowing businesses to connect with potential customers at the precise moment when looking at related topics or even specific product categories. Here, firms buy the opportunity to be associated with particular search categories or terms. To explore this aspect of Google's advertising business model, just "google" a few words and observe what appears on your screen in addition to the search results.

AdWords also allows advertisers to display their ads at websites that are part of the Google content network rather than only on Google.com. This means these ads are not initiated by a search, but simply get displayed when a user browses a website. Such ads are called "placement targeted ads." Advertisers can specify either individual websites or website content (e.g., about travel or baseball). Placement targeting allows advertisers to handpick their target audiences, which can be really large (e.g., all baseball fans in the United States or even in the world) or small and focused (e.g., people interested in fine dining in the Boston area). Google places the ads alongside relevant content of a Google partner's websites. For example, if you read an article on a partner website, you will see an ad block at the foot of the article. These ads have been dynamically targeted to the content of that article by Google. They can be the same ads that appear on Google.com alongside searches, but they are distributed in a different way here and appear on websites of publishers of all sizes in the Google partner network.

FIGURE 7.11 One of the Large Welcome Signs for Googleplex, Google's Headquarters in Mountain View, Silicon Valley, California

AdWords is complemented by a second service, called AdSense, which represents the other side of Google's advertising model. AdSense is used by website owners who wish to make money by displaying ads on their websites. In return for allowing Google to display relevant ads on their content pages, these website owners receive a share of the advertising revenue generated. An important side-effect of AdSense has been that it has created advertising income streams for thousands of small and medium online publishers and blog sites, making those businesses sustainable. Although big media companies like the *New York Times* and CNN also use AdSense, it generates a smaller portion of their total online advertising revenue compared to the typical niche web- or blog site.

Google's ability to deliver an advertising medium that is highly targeted, contextual, and results-based has been highly attractive to advertisers and led to rapid revenue growth and profits. It's no surprise that Google's success frightens other advertising media.

Sources: Roben Farzad and Ben Elgin, "Googling for Gold," *Business Week*, December 5, 2005, 60–70; www.google.com and http://en.wikipedia.org/wiki/Adwords, both accessed June 6, 2009.

reflect the best fit with the keywords employed in the search. Google's policy is to shade paid listings that appear at the top of the rankings column and identify them as "sponsored links." Pricing for these ads and placements can be based on either the number of impressions (i.e., eyeballs) or click-throughs. One company that has built a successful business model around highly targeted Internet advertising is Pinstorm (see Service Perspective 7.2).

MOVING FROM IMPERSONAL TO PERSONAL COMMUNICATIONS. Communication experts divide impersonal communications—where messages move in only one direction and generally are targeted at a large group of customers and prospects rather than at a single individual—and personal communications such as personal selling, telemarketing, and word of mouth. However, technology has created a gray area between personal and

SERVICE PERSPECTIVE 7.2

PINSTORM—THE SEARCH ENGINE OPTIMIZATION SPECIALIST

Pinstorm is a leading search engine marketing and optimization company based in India with offices around the globe. Its clients range from Kodak, HP, and Accenture to eBay, Disney, and INSEAD. Its value proposition is to design and execute online marketing campaigns on Google or Yahoo! that achieve better results for the same amount of dollars than conventional buying of search terms.

Common search terms for sponsored links are expensive. To cut costs for its clients, Pinstorm applies the Long Tail phenomenon to keyword searches. This phenomenon is one where search terms that are low in demand or infrequently used can together make up a significant share of search terms. Pinstorm has the technology to look for the long tail of low-priced keywords relevant to their clients' offering.

Pinstorm's business model guarantees results. Clients only pay for pre-agreed definitions of results such as measured visits, unique visitors, online actions, leads, or even sales. Hence, Pinstorm does everything to make sure it gets the desired results. Apart from picking effective words that are low-priced, they also develop effective online ads for their clients. These are tested again and again during a campaign until they find one that performs best. Pinstorm tracks millions of searches and understands demand for a particular product category and even geographical region. As a result, they are able to microtarget and micromarket. The leads they deliver to their clients are therefore self-selected and high quality. Clients will be able to know where the leads came from, the time they visited, and the search terms used. All these kinds of information provide clients with a lot more understanding about their customers.

Sources: http://www.pinstorm.com, accessed June 5, 2009; "The Long Tail," *Wikipedia*, http://en.wikipedia.org/wiki/The_Long_Tail, accessed June 5, 2009.

impersonal communications. Think about the email messages you've received, containing a personal salutation and perhaps some reference to your specific situation or past use of a particular product. Similarly, interactive software can simulate a two-way conversation. For example, a few firms are beginning to experiment with Web-based agents—on-screen simulations that move, speak, and even change expression.

Furthermore, with the advances of on-demand technologies, consumers are increasingly empowered to decide how and when they like to be reached. This development is transforming marketing communications not only on the Internet but also on TV and radio (see Service Perspective 7.3).

Messages Transmitted through Service Delivery Channels

Unlike most goods marketers, service firms typically control the point-of-sale and service delivery channels, which offer service firms particularly powerful and cost-effective communications opportunities. Specifically, messages can be transmitted through service outlets, frontline employees, self-service delivery points, and even customer training.

SERVICE OUTLETS. Both planned and unintended messages reach customers through the medium of the service delivery environment. Impersonal messages can be distributed in the form of banners, posters, signage, brochures, video screens, and audio. As we will discuss in Chapter 10, "Crafting the Service Environment," the physical design of the service outlet—what we call the *servicescape*—sends important messages to customers.[23] Interior architects and corporate design consultants can help to design the servicescape to coordinate the visual elements of both interiors and exteriors so that they communicate and reinforce the positioning of the firm and shape the nature of the customers' service experiences in desired ways.

FRONTLINE EMPLOYEES. Employees in frontline positions may serve customers face-to-face, by telephone, or via email. Communication from front line staff takes the form of the core service and a variety of supplementary services, including providing information, taking reservations, receiving payments, and solving problems. New customers, in particular, often rely on customer service personnel for help in learning to use a service effectively and to solve problems.

When several different products are available from the same supplier, firms encourage their customer service staff to cross-sell additional services, or to up-sell to higher value services. However, this approach is likely to fail if strategies are not properly planned and executed.[24] In the banking industry, for example, a highly competitive marketplace and new technologies have forced banks to add more services in an attempt to increase their profitability. In many banks, tellers who traditionally provided customer service are now expected to cross-sell new services to their customers as well. Despite training, many employees feel uncomfortable in this role and don't perform as effectively as salespeople. (This issue is raised in Case 12, p. 543 on Menton Bank.) We will discuss training frontline employees in more depth in Chapter 11, "Managing People for Service Advantage."

SELF-SERVICE DELIVERY POINTS. ATMs, vending machines, and web sites are all examples of self-service delivery points. Promoting self-service delivery requires clear signage, step-by-step instructions (perhaps through diagrams or animated videos) on how to operate the equipment, and user-friendly design. Self-service delivery points often can be effectively used in communications with current and potential customers and to cross-sell services and promote new services.

CUSTOMER TRAINING. Some companies, especially those that sell complex B2B services, offer formal training courses to familiarize customers with the service product and to teach them how to use it to their best advantage. Alternatively (or additionally), this task may be assigned to the same frontline personnel who handle service delivery.

In the telecommunications industry, many firms offer customer education training programs to personal users to stimulate adoption and increased use of their services. Customers learn how to use and benefit from the full potential of service offerings.

SERVICE PERSPECTIVE 7.3

NEW MEDIA AND THEIR IMPLICATIONS FOR MARKETING COMMUNICATIONS

Technology has created some exciting new communications channels that offer important opportunities for targeting. Among the key developments are TiVo, podcasting, mobile advertising, Web 2.0 technology, YouTube, and social networks.

TiVo

TiVo (also known as Digital Video Recorder (DVR) or personal video) can record many hours of television programs digitally on its hard disk very much like a VCR. However, unlike a VCR, TiVo is "always on" and continuously stores some 30 minutes of the channel that is currently being watched. This means that TiVo users can pause or rewind live TV. In fact, many users begin watching a TV program after the broadcast has started so that they can fast-forward and skip the commercials. This is worrysome for advertisers. Interestingly, while customers liked TiVo because it can be commercial free, TiVo is attracting marketers and advertisers as well with its promise of interactivity, measurability, and long-form advertising. In June 2004, Charles Schwab & Co. became the first financial services company to use TiVo's new interactive technology, employing a 30-second spot featuring golfer Phil Mickelson. The spot allowed viewers to move from the commercial into a four-minute video to watch three segments hosted by the golf pro. Viewers could also order information on Schwab's golf-rewards program at the same time. The effectiveness of ads can be immediately measured based on viewer responses.

Podcasting

Podcasting comes from the words "iPod" and "broadcasting." It refers to a group of technologies for distributing audio or video programs over the Internet using a publisher/subscriber model. Podcasting enables independent producers to create self-published, syndicated "shows" and gives broadcast radio or television programs a new distribution method. Once someone has subscribed to a certain feed, they will automatically receive new "episodes" that become available.

Podcasting is so popular that it now has several variations, including video podcasting for delivery of video clips, mobilecast for downloads onto a cell phone, and blogcast for attachment of an audio or video file to a blog. It is beneficial to include podcasting as part of a firm's marketing communications program because once a listener has subscribed to a specific show, this means the listener is interested in the topic. Hence, podcasts can reach a wide audience of listeners that have a narrow focus, more like "narrowcasting" than broadcasting. When the advertising message is more targeted, this leads to a higher return on investment for the advertising dollars spent.

Mobile Advertising

Mobile advertising is a form of advertising through cell phones and other mobile wireless devices. Mobile advertising is quite complex as it can involve the Internet, video, text, gaming, music, and much more. For example, advertisements can come in the form of an SMS, MMS, advertisements in mobile games, or videos or even some music before a voicemail recording. Through mobile advertising and the use of a global positioning system, customers can walk into shopping malls and receive advertisements from those malls where they can activate coupons or get discounts if they visited a particular store within the mall. What will this mean for the consumer? It might be greater convenience, more targeted advertising—or does it mean the invasion of privacy?

Web 2.0

Web 2.0 technology facilitates the rise of user-generated content and combining it with the power of peer-to-peer communications, and it is an umbrella term for various media including Wikipedia, Flickr, YouTube, Twitter, and other social networks. In Web 2.0, content is generated, updated, and fine-tuned by multiple users and shared freely, and marketers cannot control what is said. Marketers need to understand Web 2.0 and carefully integrate it into its marketing mix and selectively even participate in conversations.

YouTube

YouTube was founded in February 2005, and the company was bought by Google in late 2006. YouTube is a trendy video sharing website where registered users can upload videos, and unregistered users can watch most videos and post responses to those videos. In 2006, some 100 million YouTube video clips were viewed daily, and, by 2008, some 200,000 new videos were uploaded every day.

Advertisers were quick to see the advantages of using YouTube as a marketing communications channel.

The CEO of Red Hat, Matthew Szulik, used a video called "Truth Happens" to open a keynote address four years ago. That video has been viewed more than 50,000 times on YouTube. Today, the company uses YouTube, blogs, and its own magazines as marketing communications tools. By mid-2009, people were watching hundreds of millions of videos a day on YouTube and uploading 15 hours of video to YouTube every minute, the equivalent of Hollywood releasing 90,000 new full-length movies each week.

FIGURE 7.12 YouTube's Headquarters Is in This Office Building at 901 Cherry Avenue, San Bruno, California

Social Networks and Communities

Internet-based virtual worlds like Second Life and social networks like Facebook and LinkedIn offer communication and learning opportunities for marketers. Second Life has virtual advertising forms and campaigns in different communities, with business functions just like in the real world.

As social networks have gained in popularity, marketers have begun to use applications to analyze the networks within the communities to enable them to identify those who may be influential in spreading word-of-mouth about specific services. Marketers who want to take advantage of these rich networks need to remember, though, that they are in a community where people would not welcome the intrusion of marketers. Hence, marketers must come up with creative ways to engage participants in these networks.

Even the U.S. Army launched a fan page on Facebook and started on Twitter. Spokesperson Lindy Kyzer says: "Young people today don't watch the evening news. Their friends are sharing information through Twitter or Facebook. If we have no presence on those spaces, then we're not telling the army's story." However, the Defense Department computer security restrictions pose an obstacle to the social networking campaign, as soldiers often are barred from accessing Facebook or Twitter on military bases, even as some senior commanders write blogs and maintain a Facebook page. For example, General Ray Odierno, who commands U.S. forces in Iraq, has more than 5,000 friends on his Facebook page, which shows photos from his trips around Iraq but does not contain gossip from the battlefield. According to Kyzer, the security restrictions have not killed blogging by soldiers, but the rules require that blogs are not written without the knowledge of their superiors. She explained: "The commander needs to know what you're up to. If you're blogging in a deployed setting, as a soldier, writing as a soldier, you should let your commander know that."

Sources: D. Fichter, "Seven Strategies for Marketing in a Web 2.0 World," *Marketing Library Services*, 21, No. 2, March/April 2007 in http://www.infotoday.com/mls/mar07/Fichter.shtml, accessed April 24, 2009; S. Silverthorne, "TiVo Ready to Fast Forward?" *HBS Working Knowledge*, November 2004, 15; TiVo, http://www.en.wikipedia.org/wiki/TiVo, accessed April 24, 2009; Podcast, http://en.wikipedia.org/wiki/Podcast, accessed April 24, 2009; R. Rumford, "What You Don't Know About Podcasting Could Hurt Your Business: How to Leverage & Benefit From This New Media Technology," Podcasting White Paper, The Info Guru LLC, June 2005; B. Smith, "Mobile Advertising Reaches for the Sky," *Wireless Week*, August 15, 2008, http://www.wirelessweek.com/Mobile-Advertising.aspx, accessed April 24, 2009; Mobile Advertising http://en.wikipedia.org/wiki/Mobile_advertising accessed April 24, 2009; "YouTube Serves Up 1,000 Million Videos a Day Online," *USA Today*, Gannett Co. Inc, July 16, 2006; C. Daniels, "Animated Conversation," *PRweek*, New York,10, No. 25, June 25, 2007, 15; For YouTube statistics see http://ksudigg.wetpaint.com/page/ YouTube+Statistics?t=anon, accessed June 2, 2009. View also a talk by Michael Wesch, "An Introduction to YouTube," presented at the Library of Congress on June 23, 2009, at: http://www.youtube.com/watch?v=TPAO-lZ4_hU&feature=channel_page, accessed June 2, 2009; "US Army Enlists Facebook, Twitter," on http://www.physorg.com/news160077300.html, published on April 27, 2009, accessed June 2, 2009.

Mid-River Telephone Cooperative, based in Circle, Montana, holds customer appreciation days and Internet workshops at which it provides free food and high-speed Internet connections. Customer service representatives (CSRs) then interact with customers and answer any questions. The firm's member service coordinator, Dick Melvin, says "More tech-savvy customers generally ask more advanced questions, about Web design, for example. They have been very receptive to this type of training because of the individual attention they receive." He added that the CSRs not only teach Internet usage from basic to advanced levels, they even explain the features customers encounter on their monthly bills.[25]

Messages Originating from Outside the Organization

Some of the most powerful messages about a company and its products come from outside the organization and are not controlled by the marketer. They include word of mouth, blogs, Twitter, and media coverage.

WORD OF MOUTH. Recommendations from other customers are generally viewed as more credible than firm-initiated promotional activities and can have a powerful influence on people's decisions to use (or avoid using) a service. In fact, the greater the risk customers perceive in purchasing a service, the more actively they will seek and rely on word of mouth (WOM) to guide their decision making.[26] Customers less knowledgeable about a service rely more on WOM than do expert consumers.[27] WOM even takes place during service encounters. When customers talk with each other about some aspect of service, this information can influence both their behavior and their satisfaction with the service[28] and is an important predictor of top-line growth.[29]

Research shows that the extent and content of WOM is related to satisfaction levels. Customers who hold strong views are likely to tell more people about their experiences than those with milder views, and extremely dissatisfied customers tell more people than those who are highly satisfied.[30] Interestingly, even customers initially dissatisfied with a service can end up spreading positive WOM if they are delighted with the way the firm handled service recovery[31] (more on this in Chapter 13, "Complaint Handling and Service Recovery").

Positive WOM is particularly important for service firms, as services tend to have a high proportion of experience and credence attributes and are therefore associated with high perceived risk by potential buyers. In fact, many successful service firms such as Starbucks and Mayo Clinic built powerful brands largely by relying on WOM of their satisfied customers. Because WOM can act as such a powerful and highly credible selling agent, some marketers employ a variety of strategies to stimulate positive and persuasive comments from existing customers.[32] These include:

- Creating exciting promotions that get people talking about the great service the firm provides. Richard Branson of Virgin Atlantic Airways has repeatedly generated global news that got people talking about his airline. Examples include Branson abseiling off a 407-foot Las Vegas hotel in a tuxedo ala James Bond to promote his, then new, Virgin America airline, and inviting college student Kyla Ebbert to its maiden first flight from San Francisco to Las Vegas. Ebbert gained notoriety when she was asked to leave a Southwest Airlines flight because her outfit was deemed as too revealing (she was later allowed to board the plane after adjusting her outfit). More and more firms are running creative promotions on social media that can get global attention in a few days.
- Offering promotions that encourage customers to persuade others to join them in using the service (for instance "bring two friends, and the third eats for free" or "subscribe to two cell phone service plans, and we'll waive the monthly subscription fee for all other immediate family members").
- Developing referral incentive schemes, such as offering an existing customer units of free service, a voucher, or even cash for introducing new customers to the firm.
- Referencing other purchasers and knowledgeable individuals, for instance: "We have done a great job for ABC Corp., and if you wish, feel free to talk to Mr. Cabral, their MIS manager, who oversaw the implementation of our project."
- Presenting and publicizing testimonials that simulate WOM. Advertising and brochures sometimes feature comments from satisfied customers.

WOM in cyberspace is becoming increasingly powerful. The ubiquity of the Internet has accelerated the spread of personal influence, causing it to evolve into a "viral marketing" phenomena that businesses can ill afford to ignore.[33] Research Insights 7.2 discusses research on why and how people pass on emails. In fact, viral marketing, which takes advantage of networks among customers and prospects to influence attitudes and behaviors, has now become an industry in itself. One of the very early success stories of

RESEARCH INSIGHTS 7.2

PASS ALONG EMAILS—CONSUMERS' MOTIVATIONS, ATTITUDES, AND BEHAVIORS

How can firms make better use of pass-along emails and viral marketing? First, managers need to understand how consumers respond when they receive pass-along emails, what senders write in such messages, and what motivates recipients to forward them. The following three studies sought answers to these questions.

Study 1 explored how recipients responded to pass-along emails and how these communications differed from undesirable spam. Eight focus groups were conducted, involving a total of 66 individuals. Respondents considered emails as spam when the sender wasn't known. By contrast, the recipient typically knew who had sent them a pass-along email. When questioned about the types of viral messages they receive, there was consistent mention of jokes, followed by virus alerts, inspirational stories, religious messages, requests to vote on certain issues, lost children, chain letters, poems, animated clips, links to specific web sites, and urban legends.

The positive emotions recipients experienced when receiving what they viewed as meaningful messages ranged from simply good (e.g., "someone is thinking about me") and brightens my day ("when it's someone I haven't heard from in a while") to excited ("it's like seeing a letter in the mail...") and rewarded ("when I get something from the church."). Negative emotions included irritation (e.g., when the message seemed irrelevant, felt like a waste of time, or when an individual kept sending too many messages), anger (e.g., when an individual had asked to be taken off a list), disappointment (e.g., when a person wanted a more personal note from someone), to skeptical (if an offer looked too good to be true), burdened (e.g., when the recipient had too much work, felt overwhelmed, or obligated to answer).

In *Study 2*, the researchers conducted a content analysis of 1,259 pass-along messages sent by 34 focus group participants in order to better understand what type of messages were forwarded. The analysis revealed that 40 percent of messages were actually forwarded to others. The main reasons for not doing so involved messages that were perceived to be out of date, uninteresting, or inappropriate. Alternatively, respondents were in a rush and did not have time to forward messages. About one-third of the forwarded emails were sent with a personalized note, mostly to motivate the recipient to read the message. When recipients forwarded pass-along emails, the great majority did not change the subject line. Only a few of the forwarded emails concerned products, services, or companies—suggesting that either firms are not making much use of pass-along emails or they are not using them effectively.

Study 3 focused on the reasons why people forward pass-along emails. The six top-rated reasons centered on enjoyment and entertainment (e.g., "it's fun," "I enjoy it," and "it's entertaining") and social motivations (e.g., "to help others," and "to let others know I care about their feelings"). The findings also showed that for a message to be forwarded, it must be important or contain something the sender believes the recipient will like.

This research demonstrates the untapped potential of service marketers to use pass-along emails in their communications efforts. However, the findings also suggest that (1) firms need to be careful in crafting messages their target segments will find relevant enough to forward; (2) the message content should spark emotion (e.g., humor, fear, or inspiration) and appeal to the desire for fun, entertainment, and social connection; and (3) firms should think carefully about the wording of the subject line as it is likely to be forwarded in unchanged format.

Source: Joseph E. Phelps, Regina Lewis, Lynne Mobilio, David Perry, and Niranjan Raman, "Viral Marketing or Electronic Word-of-Mouth Advertising: Examining Consumer Responses and Motivations to Pass Along Emails," *Journal of Advertising Research*, December 2004, 333–348.

viral marketing was the Hotmail free email service, which grew from zero to 12 million users in 18 months on a miniscule advertising budget, thanks mostly to the inclusion of a promotional message including Hotmail's URL in every email sent by its users.[34] eBay and other firms that engage in electronic auctions rely on users to rate sellers and buyers in order to build trust in the items offered on their web sites thereby facilitating transactions between strangers who, without access to such peer ratings, might be reluctant to transact on these sites.

In addition to traditional email, WOM is amplified by chat, social media, and online communities that have potential for global reach in a matter of days! Refer back to

Service Perspective 7.3 on Web 2.0 and social networks in our section on messages transmitted through the Internet. Here, we will add blogs and Twitter to this discussion.

BLOGS—A TYPE OF ONLINE WOM.[35] Web logs, usually referred to as blogs, have become ubiquitous. Blogs are frequently modified web pages in which entries are listed in reverse chronological sequence. They can be best described as online journals, diaries, or news listings where people can post anything about whatever they like. Their authors, known as bloggers, usually focus on narrow topics, and quite a few have become de facto watchdogs and self-proclaimed experts in certain fields. Blogs can be about anything, ranging from baseball and sex to karate and financial engineering. There are a growing number of travel-oriented sites, ranging from Hotelchatter.com (focused on boutique hotels), CruiseDiva.com (reporting on the cruise industry), and pestiside.hu ("the daily dish of cosmopolitan Budapest"). Some sites, such as the travel-focused tripadvisor.com, allow users to post their own reviews or ask questions that more experienced travelers may be able to answer.[36]

Marketers' are interested in the way blogs have evolved into a new form of social interaction on the Web: a massively distributed but completely connected conversation covering every imaginable topic, including consumers' experiences with service firms and their recommendations on avoiding or patronizing certain firms. A byproduct of this online communication is the set of hyperlinks made between weblogs in the exchange of dialog. These links allows customers to share information with others and influence opinions of a brand or product—just search for the terms "Citibank and blog," or "Charles Schwab and blog," and you will see an entire list of blogs or blog entries relating to these service firms. Increasingly, service firms monitor blogs and view them as a form of immediate market research and feedback. Some service companies have even started their own blogs, for example, see Google's blog at http://googleblog.blogspot.com.

TWITTER.[37] Twitter is a social networking and microblogging service that allows its users to send and read other users' updates, which are up to 140 characters in length and can send and receive via the Twitter web site, Short Message Service (SMS), or external applications. Created in 2006 by Jack Dorsey, Twitter has gained in popularity worldwide and was the fastest-growing social networking service in 2009. Service firms have started using Twitter in various ways. Comcast, the U.S. cable service provider, has set up @comcastcares to answer customer queries in real-time. Zappos's CEO interacts with his customers as if they were friends; celebrity Ashton Kutcher interacts with his fans while on the move; and airline branding firm SimpliFlying used Twitter to help establish itself as a though leader in its niche by holding special trivia and competitions for its "followers" around the world.

MEDIA COVERAGE. Although the online world is rapidly increasing in importance, coverage on traditional media cannot be neglected, especially as newsworthy events often are first discussed in the online world, but then are picked up and reported in the traditional media that then reach the broad masses. Media coverage of firms and their services is frequently stimulated by PR activity, but broadcasters and publishers also often initiate their own coverage. In addition to news stories about a company and its services, editorial coverage can take several other forms. For example, journalists responsible for consumer affairs often contrast and compare service offerings from competing organizations, identifying their strong and weak points, and offering advice on "best buys." In a more specialized context, *Consumer Reports*, the monthly publication of Consumers' Union, periodically evaluates services offered on a national basis, including financial services and telecommunications, and commenting on the strengths and weaknesses of different service providers and seeking to determine the true cost of their often confusing fee schedules and pricing plans.

Furthermore, investigative reporters may conduct an in-depth study of a company, especially if they believe it is putting customers at risk, cheating them, employing deceptive advertising, damaging the environment, or exploiting poor workers in developing countries. Some columnists specialize in helping customers who have been unable to get complaints resolved.

Ethical and Consumer Privacy Issues in Communications

We have been focusing on the various communications tools and channels of communication where customers receive information about a firm. However, firms also need to consider the ethical and privacy issues associated with communications, especially as few aspects of marketing lend themselves so easily to misuse (and even abuse) as advertising, selling, and sales promotion. The fact that customers often find it hard to evaluate services makes them more dependent on marketing communication for information and advice. Communication messages frequently include promises about the benefits that customers will receive and the quality of service delivery. When promises are made and then broken, customers are disappointed because their expectations have not been met.[38]

Some unrealistic service promises result from poor internal communications between operations and marketing personnel concerning the level of service performance that customers can reasonably expect. In other instances, unethical advertisers and salespeople deliberately make exaggerated promises to secure sales. Finally, deceptive promotions lead people to think they have a much higher chance of winning prizes or awards than is really the case. Fortunately, many consumer watchdog groups are on the lookout for these deceptive marketing practices. They include consumer protection agencies, trade associations within specific industries, and journalists seeking to expose fraud and misrepresentation.

A different type of ethical issue concerns unwanted intrusion by aggressive marketers into people's personal lives. The increase in telemarketing, direct mail, and email is frustrating for those who receive unwanted sales communications. How do you feel when your dinner at home is interrupted by a telephone call from a stranger trying to interest you in buying services in which you have no interest? Even if you are interested, you may feel, as many do, that your privacy has been violated (see Research Insights 7.3).

To address growing hostility toward these practices, both government agencies and trade associations have acted to protect consumers. In the United States, the Federal Trade Commission's National Do Not Call Registry enables consumers to remove their home and mobile numbers from telemarketing lists for a five-year period. People who continue to receive unauthorized calls from commercial telemarketers can file a complaint, and the telemarketing firm may be subject to heavy fines for such violations.[39] Similarly, the Direct Marketing Association helps consumers remove their names from mailing, telemarketing, and email lists.[40]

THE ROLE OF CORPORATE DESIGN

So far, we have focused on communications media and content, but not much on design. Corporate design is key to ensure a consistent style and message is communicated through all of a firm's communications mix channels. Corporate design is particularly important for companies operating in competitive markets where it's necessary to stand out from the crowd and to be instantly recognizable in different locations. Have you noticed how some companies stand out in your mind because of the colors they use, the widespread application of their logos, the uniforms worn by their employees, and the design of their physical facilities?

Many service firms employ a unified and distinctive visual appearance for all tangible elements to facilitate recognition and reinforce a desired brand image. Corporate design strategies usually are created by external consulting firms and include such features as stationery and promotional literature, retail signage, uniforms, and color schemes for painting vehicles, equipment, and building interiors. The objective is to provide a unifying and recognizable theme linking all the firm's operations in a branded service experience through the strategic use of physical evidence. Companies can do that in several ways:

RESEARCH INSIGHTS 7.3

CONSUMER CONCERNS ABOUT ONLINE PRIVACY

Technological advances have made the Internet a threat to consumer privacy. Information is collected on not just people who register and shop or use email but also on those who just surf the Internet, participate in social networks, or contribute to blogs! Individuals are increasingly fearful of databases and concerned about their online privacy. Hence, they use several ways to protect themselves, including:

- Providing false information about themselves (e.g., disguising their identity).
- Using technology like antispam filters, email shredders, and cookie-busters to hide the identity of their computers from websites.
- Refusing to provide information and avoid websites that require personal information to be disclosed.

Such consumer responses will make information used in CRM systems inaccurate and incomplete, and thereby reduce the effectiveness of a firm's customer relationship marketing and its efforts to provide more customized, personalized, and convenient service. Firms can take several steps to reduce consumer privacy concerns, including:

- Customers' fairness perceptions are key—marketers need to be careful about how they use the information they collect and whether consumers perceive their treatment and outcomes as fair. In particular, marketers should continually provide the customer with enhanced value such as customization, convenience, and improved offers and promotions to enhance fairness perceptions of the information exchange.
- Especially if highly sensitive, the information asked for should be perceived to be related to the transaction. Therefore, firms should clearly communicate why the information is needed and how information disclosure will benefit the consumer.
- Firms should have a good privacy policy in place that can be readily found on the websites, is in an easy to understand language, and is comprehensive enough to be effective.
- Fair information practices need to be embedded in the work practices of all service employees to prevent any situation whereby an employee may allow personal customer information to be misused.
- Firms should have high ethical standards of data protection. They can use third party endorsements like TRUSTe or the Better Business Bureau and have recognizable privacy seals displayed clearly on their website.

Sources: Jochen Wirtz and May O. Lwin, "Regulatory Focus Theory, Trust and Privacy Concern," *Journal of Service Research*, 12 (2), 2009, 190–207.

- Use of colors in corporate designs. If we look at gasoline retailing, we see BP's bright green and yellow service stations; Texaco's red, black and white; and Sunoco's blue, maroon, and yellow.
- Companies in the highly competitive express delivery industry tend to use their names as a central element in their corporate designs. When Federal Express changed its trading name to the more modern "FedEx," it featured the new name in a distinctive, new logo.
- Many companies use a trademarked symbol, rather than a name, as their primary logo. Shell makes a pun of its English name by displaying a yellow scalloped shell on a red background, which has the advantage of making its vehicles and service stations instantly recognizable. McDonald's "Golden Arches" is said to be the most widely recognized corporate symbol in the world and is featured at all touchpoints, including its restaurants, on employee uniforms and packaging, and in all the company's communications materials.
- Some companies have succeeded in creating tangible, recognizable symbols to associate with their corporate brand names. Animal motifs are common physical symbols for services. Examples include the eagles of the U.S. Postal Service and

AeroMexico, the lions of ING Bank and the Royal Bank of Canada, the ram of the investment firm T. Rowe Price, and the Chinese dragon of Hong Kong's Dragonair.

INTEGRATING MARKETING COMMUNICATIONS

Have you ever seen a new, exciting service promotion touted on a firm's website, only to find when you then visited a branch office that the counter staff was not aware of this promotion and couldn't sell it to you? What went wrong? In many service firms, different departments look after different aspects of a firm's market communications. For example, the marketing department is in charge of advertising, the PR department of public relations, functional specialists look after a company's website and its direct marketing and promotions activities, operations of customer service, and human resources of training. The service failure described above is a consequence of these various departments not coordinating their efforts effectively.

With so many channels delivering messages to customers and prospects, it becomes more and more important for firms to adopt the concept of integrated marketing communications (IMC). IMC ties together and reinforces all communications to deliver a strong brand identity. It means that a firm's various media deliver the same messages and have the same look and feel, and the communications from the different media and communications approaches all become part of a single, overall message about the service firm and its products. Firms can achieve this by giving ownership of IMC to a single department (e.g., marketing) or by appointing a marketing communications director who has overall responsibility for all of the firm's market communications.

CONCLUSION

The *promotion and education* element of the 7 Ps requires a somewhat different emphasis from the communication strategy used to market goods. The communication tasks facing service marketers include emphasizing tangible clues for services that are difficult to evaluate, clarifying the nature and sequence of the service performance, highlighting the performance of customer contact personnel, and educating the customer about how to effectively participate in service delivery. A key point for you to take away from this chapter is that effective service marketers are good educators who can use a variety of communication media in cost-efficient ways, not only to promote their firm's value propositions but also to teach both prospects and customers what they need to know about selecting and using the firm's services.

Chapter Summary

LO1 The role of service marketing communication is to:

- Position and differentiate the service.
- Help customers to evaluate service offerings.
- Promote the contribution of service personnel.
- Add value through communication content.
- Facilitate customer involvement in production.
- Stimulate or dampen demand to match capacity.

LO2 The intangibility of services presents challenges for communications. Two ways to overcome the problem of intangibility are:

- Emphasize tangible clues like its employees, facilities, certificates and awards, or its customers.
- Use metaphors to communicate the value proposition.

LO3 After understanding the challenges of service communications, service marketers need to plan and design an effective communications strategy. They can use the 5 Ws model to guide service communications planning. The 5 Ws are:

- Who is our target audience? Are they prospects, users, and/or employees?
- What do we need to communicate and achieve? Do the objectives relate to consumer behavior in the prepurchase, service encounter, or postencounter stage?
- How should we communicate this? Which media mix should we use?
- Where should we communicate this?
- When do the communications need to take place?

LO4 To achieve the communications objectives, we can use a variety of communications channels, including:

- Traditional marketing channels (e.g., advertising and PR).
- Internet (e.g., the firm's website and online advertising) and new media (e.g., Web 2.0, including YouTube and social networks).
- Service delivery channels (e.g., service outlets and frontline employees).
- Messages originating from outside the organization (e.g., word of mouth and media coverage).

LO5 The traditional marketing channels include advertising, public relations, direct marketing (including permission marketing), sales promotions, personal selling, and tradeshows. These communication elements typically are used to help companies create a distinctive position in the market and reach prospective customers.

LO6 Internet communications channels include the firm's websites and online advertising (e.g., banner advertising and search engine advertising and optimization).

- Developments in Internet technology are driving innovations such as permission marketing and exciting possibilities of highly targeted online advertising.
- New media communications that blur the line between impersonal and personal communications include TiVo, podcasting, YouTube, mobile advertising, Web 2.0, and social networks and communities.

LO7 Service firms usually control service delivery channels and point-of-sale environments that offers them cost-effective ways of reaching their current customers (e.g., via its customer service employees, service outlets, and self-service delivery points).

LO8 Some of the most powerful messages about a company and its services originate from outside the organization and are not controlled by the marketer. They include word of mouth, blogs, Twitter, social media, and coverage in traditional media.

- Recommendations from other customers generally are viewed as more credible than firm-initiated communications and are sought by prospects, especially for high-risk purchases.
- Firms can stimulate word of mouth from its customers through a number of means including creating exciting promotions, referral incentive programs, and referencing customers that are increasingly shifted to the online environment.

LO9 When designing their communication strategy, firms need to bear in mind ethical and privacy issues in terms of promises made, intrusion into private lives (e.g., through telemarketing or email campaigns), and protecting the privacy and personal data of customers and prospects.

LO10 Besides communication media and content, corporate design is key to achieving a unified image in customers' minds. Good corporate design uses a unified and distinctive visual appearance for tangible elements including all market communications mix elements, stationery, retail signage, uniforms, vehicles, equipment, and building interiors.

LO11 With so many channels delivering messages to customers and prospects, it becomes crucial for firms to adopt the concept of integrated marketing communications (IMC).

Review Questions

1. In what ways do the objectives of services communications differ substantially from those of goods marketing? Describe four common educational and promotional objectives in service settings, and provide a specific example for each of the objectives you list.
2. What are some challenges in service communications and how can they be overcome?
3. Why is the marketing communications mix larger for service firms compared to firms that market goods?
4. What roles do personal selling, advertising, and public relations play in (a) attracting new customers to visit a service outlet and (b) retaining existing customers?
5. What are the different forms of online marketing? Which do you think would be the most effective online marketing strategies for (a) an online broker and (b) a new nightclub in Los Angeles?
6. Why is permission-based marketing gaining so much focus in service firms' communications strategies?
7. Why is word of mouth important for the marketing of services? How can a service firm that is the quality leader in its industry induce and manage word of mouth?
8. How can companies use corporate design to differentiate themselves?
9. What are the potential ways to implement IMC?

Application Exercises

1. Which elements of the marketing communications mix would you use for each of the following scenarios? Explain your answers.
   - A newly established hair salon in a suburban shopping center.
   - An established restaurant facing declining patronage because of new competitors.
   - A large, single-office accounting firm in a major city that serves primarily business clients and that wants to aggressively grow its client base.
2. Identify one advertisement (or other means of communication) that aims mainly at managing consumer behavior in the (a) choice, (b) service encounter, and (c) postconsumption stage. Explain how they try to achieve their objectives and discuss how effective they may be.
3. Discuss the significance of search, experience, and credence attributes for the communications strategy of a service provider. Assume the objective of the communications strategy is to attract new customers.
4. If you were explaining your current university or researching the degree program you are now in, what could you learn from blogs and any other online word of mouth you can find? How would that information influence the decision of a prospective applicant to your university? Given that you are an expert about the school and degree you are pursuing, how accurate is the information you found online?
5. Identify an advertisement that runs the risk of attracting mixed segments to a service business. Explain why this may happen, and state any negative consequences that could result.
6. Describe and evaluate recent public relations efforts made by service organizations in connection with three or more of the following: (a) launching a new offering, (b) opening a new facility, (c) promoting an expansion of existing services, (d) announcing an upcoming event, or (e) responding to a negative situation that has arisen. (Pick a different organization for each category.)
7. What tangible cues could a diving school or a dentistry clinic use to position itself as appealing to upscale customers?
8. Explore the websites of a management consulting firm, an Internet retailer, and an insurance company. Critique them for ease of navigation, content, and visual design. What, if anything, would you change about each site?
9. Register at Amazon.com and Hallmark.com and analyze their permission-based communications strategy. What are their marketing objectives? Evaluate their permission-based marketing for a specific customer segment of your choice—what is excellent, what is good, and what could be further improved?
10. Conduct a Google search for (a) MBA programs and (b) vacation (holiday) resorts. Examine two or three contextual ads triggered by your searches. Critique these ads—what are they doing right, and what can be improved?

Endnotes

1. Westin Turns Traditional Hotel Advertising on its Head, http://www.hotelmarketing.com/index.php/content/print/070802_westin_turns_traditional_hotel_advertising_on_its_head, August 6, 2007 (article downloaded on February 23, 2009). Source for photo: http://www.westinadvertising.com/, accessed February 23, 2009; http://www.starwoodhotels.com/promotions/promo_landing.html?category=WI_SUM06_PICKER&IM=WI_HP_TL_EN_EXPERIENCE08, accessed February 23, 2009, and www.westin.com, accessed February 23, 2009.
2. JD Power's Consumer Center website includes ratings of service providers in finance and insurance, health care, telecommunications, and travel, plus useful information and advice; see http://www.jdpower.com/, accessed June 4, 2009.
3. For a useful review, see Kathleen Mortimer and Brian P. Mathews, "The Advertising of Services: Consumer Views v. Normative Dimensions," *The Service Industries Journal*, 18, July 1998, 14–19. See also James F. Devlin and Sarwar Azhar, "Life Would be a Lot Easier if We Were a Kit Kat: Practitioners' Views on the Challenges of Branding Financial Services Successfully," *Brand Management*, 12, No. 1, 2004, 12–30.
4. Banwari Mittal, "The Advertising of Services: Meeting the Challenge of Intangibility," *Journal of Service Research*, 2, August 1999, 98–116.
5. Banwari Mittal and Julie Baker, "Advertising Strategies for Hospitality Services," *Cornell Hotel and Restaurant Administration Quarterly*, 43, April 2002, 51–63.
6. Donna Legg and Julie Baker, "Advertising Strategies for Service Firms," in C. Surprenant, ed., *Add Value to Your Service*. Chicago: American Marketing Association, 1987, 163–168. See also Donna J. Hill, Jeff Blodgett, Robert Baer, and Kirk Wakefield, "An Investigation of Visualization and Documentation Strategies in Service Advertising," *Journal of Service Research*, 7, November 2004, 155–166; Debra Grace and Aron O'Cass, "Service Branding: Consumer Verdicts on Service Brands," *Journal of Retailing and Consumer Services*, 12, 2005, 125–139.

7. Banwari Mittal, "The Advertising of Services: Meeting the Challenge of Intangibility," *Journal of Service Research*, 2, August 1999, 98–116.
8. Stephen J. Grove, Gregory M. Pickett, and David N. Laband, "An Empirical Examination of Factual Information Content among Service Advertisements," *The Service Industries Journal*, 15, April 1995, 216–233.
9. "The Future of Advertising–The Harder Hard Sell," *The Economist*, June 24, 2004.
10. "The Future of Advertising–The Harder Hard Sell," *The Economist*, June 24, 2004.
11. Penelope J. Prenshaw, Stacy E. Kovar, and Kimberly Gladden Burke, "The Impact of Involvement on Satisfaction for New, Nontraditional, Credence-based Service Offerings," *Journal of Services Marketing*, 20, No. 7, 2006, 439–452.
12. "Got Game: Inserting Advertisements into Video Games Holds Much Promise," *The Economist*, June 9, 2007, 69.
13. Experian, www.experian.co.uk, accessed January 14, 2009.
14. Seth Godin and Don Peppers, *Permission Marketing: Turning Strangers into Friends and Friends into Customers*. New York: Simon & Schuster, 1999; Ray Kent and Hege Brandal, "Improving Email Response in a Permission Marketing Context," *International Journal of Market Research*, 45, Quarter 4, 2003, 489–503.
15. Gila E. Fruchter and Z. John Zhang, "Dynamic Targeted Promotions: A Customer Retention and Acquisition Perspective," *Journal of Service Research*, 7, August 2004, 3–19.
16. Ken Peattie and Sue Peattie, "Sales Promotion–a Missed Opportunity for Service Marketers," *International Journal of Service Industry Management*, 5, No. 1, 1995, 6–21.
17. M. Lewis, "Customer Acquisition Promotions and Customer Asset Value," *Journal of Marketing Research*, XLIII, May 2006, 195–203.
18. Dana James, "Move Cautiously in Trade Show Launch," *Marketing News*, November 20, 2000, 4, 6; Elizabeth Light, "Tradeshows and Expos—Putting Your Business on Show," *Her Business*, March–April 1998, 14–18; and Susan Greco, "Trade Shows versus Face-to-Face Selling," *Inc.*, May 1992, 142.
19. Stefan Lagrosen, "Effects of the Internet on the Marketing Communication of Service Companies," *Journal of Services Marketing*, 19, No. 2, 2005, 63–69.
20. Paul Smith and Dave Chaffey, *eMarketing Excellence*. Oxford, UK: Elsevier Butterworth-Heinemann, 2005, 173.
21. "The Future of Advertising–The Harder Hard Sell," *The Economist*, June 24, 2004.
22. Catherine Seda, "Search Engine Advertising: Buying Your Way to the Top to Increase Sales (Voices That Matter),"Indianapolis, IN: New Riders Press, 2004, 4–5.
23. Mary Jo Bitner, "Servicescapes: The Impact of Physical Surroundings on Customers and Employees," *Journal of Marketing*, 56, April 1992, 57–71.
24. David H. Maister, "Why Cross Selling Hasn't Worked," *True Professionalism*. New York: The Free Press, 1997, 178–184.
25. Megan O'Donnell, "Why Type of Training or Education Do You Provide to Customers for New Technology Offerings?" *Rural Communications*, July–August 2005, 12.
26. Harvir S. Bansal and Peter A. Voyer, "Word-of-Mouth Processes Within a Services Purchase Decision Context," *Journal of Service Research*, 3, No. 2, November 2000, 166–177. Malcom Gladwell explains how different types of epidemics, including word-of-mouth epidemics, develop. Malcom Gladwell, *The Tipping Point*, NY: Little, Brown and Company, 2000, 32.
27. Anna S. Mattila and Jochen Wirtz, "The Impact of Knowledge Types on the Consumer Search Process—An Investigation in the Context of Credence Services," *International Journal of Research in Service Industry Management*, 13, No. 3, 2002, 214–230.
28. Kim Harris and Steve Baron, "Consumer-to-Consumer Conversations in Service Settings," *Journal of Service Research*, 6, No. 3, 2004, 287–303.
29. Frederick F. Reichheld, "The One Number You Need to Grow," *Harvard Business Review*, 81, No. 12, 2003, 46–55.
30. Eugene W. Anderson, "Customer Satisfaction and Word of Mouth," *Journal of Service Research*, 1, August 1998, 5–17; Magnus Sőderlund, "Customer Satisfaction and Its Consequences on Customer Behaviour Revisited: The Impact of Different Levels of Satisfaction on Word of Mouth, Feedback to the Supplier, and Loyalty, *International Journal of Service Industry Management*, 9, No. 2, 1998, 169–188. Srini S. Srinivasan, Rolph Anderson, and Kishore Ponnavolu, "Customer Loyalty in e-Commerce: An Exploration of its Antecedents and Consequences," *Journal of Retailing*, 78, No. 1, 2002, 41–50. For a meta analysis of research on word of mouth see Celso Augusto de Matos and Carlos Alberto Vargas Rossi, "Word-of-Mouth Communications in Marketing: A Meta-Analytic Review of the Antecedents and Moderators," *Journal of the Academy of Marketing Science*, 36, No. 4, 2008, 578–596.
31. Jeffrey G. Blodgett, Kirk L. Wakefield, and James H. Barnes, "The Effects of Customer Service on Consumers Complaining Behavior," *Journal of Services Marketing*, 9, No. 4, 1995, 31–42; Jeffrey G. Blodgett and Ronald D. Anderson, "A Bayesian Network Model of the Consumer Complaint Process," *Journal of Service Research*, 2, No. 4, May 2000, 321–338; Stefan Michel, "Analyzing Service Failures and Recoveries: A Process Approach," *International Journal of Service Industry Management*, 12, No. 1, 2001, 20–33; James G. Maxham III and Richard G. Netemeyer, "A Longitudinal Study of Complaining Customers' Evaluations of Multiple Service Failures and Recovery Efforts," *Journal of Marketing*, 66, No. 4, 2002, 57–72.
32. Jochen Wirtz and Patricia Chew, "The Effects of Incentives, Deal Proneness, Satisfaction and Tie Strength on Word-of-Mouth Behaviour," *International Journal of Service Industry Management*, 13, No. 2, 2002, 141–162; Tom J. Brown, Thomas E. Barry, Peter A. Dacin, and Richard F. Gunst, "Spreading the Word: Investigating Antecedents of Consumers' Positive Word-of-Mouth Intentions and Behaviors in a Retailing Context," *Journal of the Academy of Marketing Science*, 33, No. 2, 2005, 123–138; John E. Hogan, Katherine N. Lemon, and Barak Libai, "Quantifying the Ripple: Word-of-Mouth and Advertising Effectiveness," *Journal of Advertising Research*, September 2004, 271–280.
33. Renee Dye, "The Buzz on Buzz," *Harvard Business Review*, November–December 2000, 139–146; Joseph E. Phelps, Regina Lewis, Lynne Mobilio, David Perry, and Niranjan Raman, "Viral Marketing or Electronic Word-of-Mouth Advertising: Examining Consumer Responses and Motivations to Pass Along Emails," *Journal of Advertising Research*, 44, December 2004, 333–348; P. R.

Datta, D. N. Chowdhury, and B. R. Chakraborty, "Viral Marketing: New Form of Word-of-Mouth Through Internet," *The Business Review*, 3, No. 2, Summer, 2005, 69–75.

34. Steve Jurvetson, "What Exactly Is Viral Marketing?" *Red Herring*, 78, 2000, 110–112.
35. This section draws from Lev Grossman, "Meet Joe Blog," *Time*, June 21, 2004, 65; S. C. Herring, L. A. Scheidt, E. Wright, and S. Bonus, "Weblogs as a Bridging Genre," *Information, Technology & People*, 18, No. 2, 2005, 142–171; C. Marlow, "Audience, Structure and Authority in the Weblog Community," paper presented at International Communication Association Conference, New Orleans, LA, 2004, web.media.mit.edu/∼cameron/cv/pubs/04-01.pdf, accessed December 19, 2005; Ericka Menchen Trevino, "Blogger Motivations: Power, Pull, and Positive Feedback," paper presented at AoIR 6.0, October 9, 2005, http://blog.erickamenchen.net/MenchenBlogMotivations.pdf, accessed December 19, 2005.
36. Steven Kurutz, "For Travelers, Blogs Level the Playing Field," *New York Times*, August 7, 2005, TR-3.
37. http://en.wikipedia.org/wiki/Twitter, accessed April 24, 2009.
38. Louis Fabien, "Making Promises: The Power of Engagement," *Journal of Services Marketing*, 11, No. 3, 1997, 206–214.
39. www.donotcall.gov/default.aspx, accessed April 25, 2009.
40. http://www.dmachoice.org, accessed April 25, 2009.

PART THREE

Managing the Customer Interface

Part III of the book focuses on managing the interface between customers and the service organization. It covers the additional 3 Ps (***P***rocess, ***P***hysical environment, and ***P***eople) that are specific to services marketing. Part III consists of the following four chapters:

CHAPTER 8 DESIGNING AND MANAGING SERVICE PROCESSES

It begins with design of an effective *service delivery process,* specifying how operating and delivery systems link together to create the promised value proposition. Very often, customers are actively involved in service creation, especially if acting as co-producers, and the process becomes their experience.

CHAPTER 9 BALANCING DEMAND AND PRODUCTIVE CAPACITY

Chapter 9 still relates to process management and focuses on the widely fluctuating demand and how to balance the level and timing of customer demand against available productive capacity. Well-managed demand and capacity leads to smooth processes with less waiting time for customers. Marketing strategies for managing demand involve smoothing demand fluctuations and inventorying demand through reservation systems and formalized queuing. Understanding customer motivations in different segments is one of the keys to successful demand management.

CHAPTER 10 CRAFTING THE SERVICE ENVIRONMENT

Chapter 10 focuses on the physical environment, which is also known as the servicescape. It needs to be engineered to create the right impression and facilitate effective delivery of service processes. The servicescape needs to be managed carefully, because it can have a profound impact on customers' impressions, guide their behavior throughout the service process, and provide tangible clues of a firm's service quality and positioning.

CHAPTER 11 MANAGING PEOPLE FOR SERVICE ADVANTAGE

Chapter 11 introduces people, who are a defining element of many services. Many services require direct interaction between customers and contact personnel. The nature of these interactions strongly influences how customers perceive service quality. Hence, service firms devote a significant amount of effort to recruiting, training and motivating their employees. Happy employees who perform well are often a source of competitive advantage for a firm as the effective management of frontline employees is key to delivering customer satisfaction and productivity.

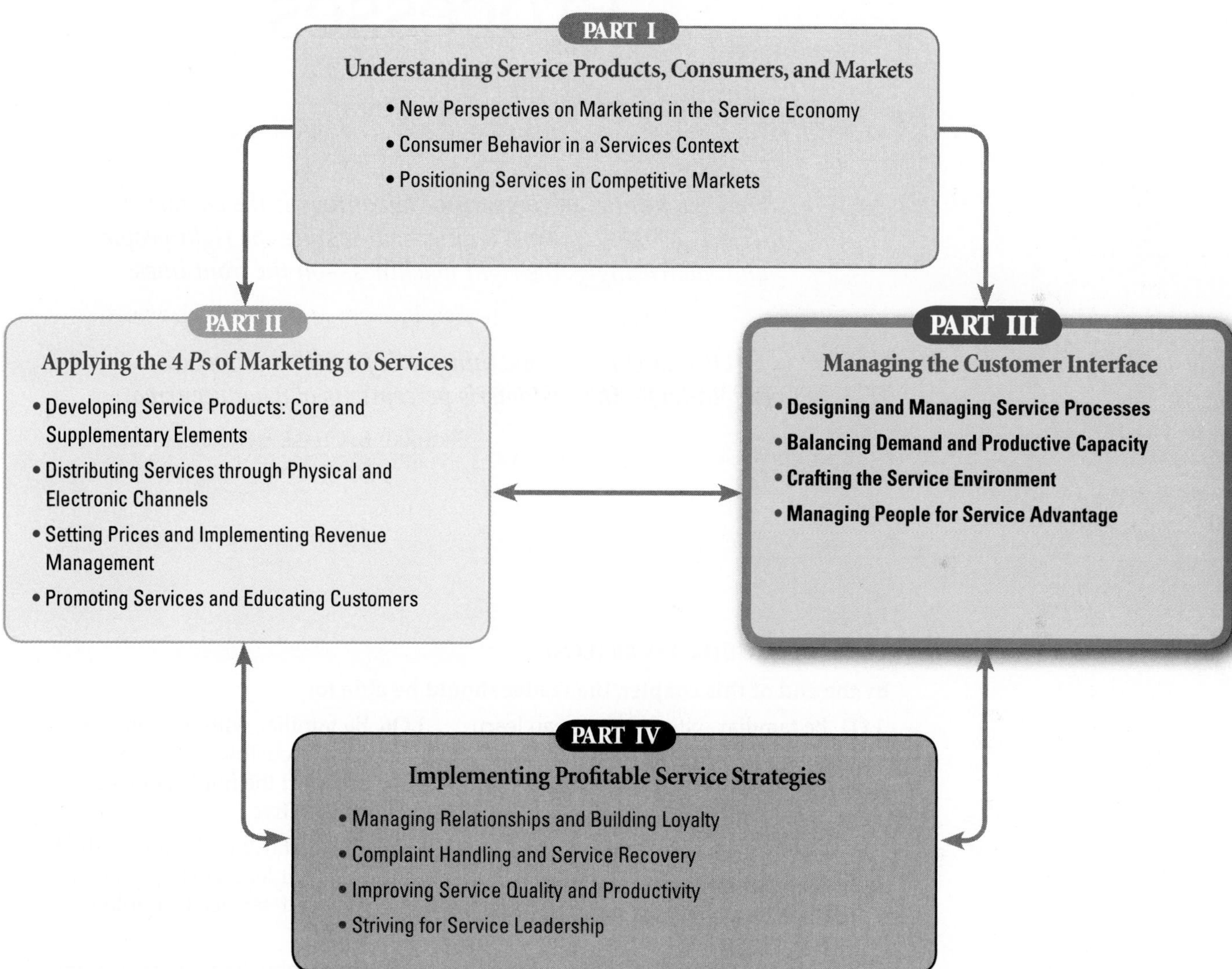

FIGURE III.1 Organizing Framework for Services Marketing

CHAPTER 8

Designing and Managing Service Processes

The new frontier of competitive advantage is the customer interface. Making yours a winner will require the right people and, increasingly, the right machines—on the front lines.

JEFFREY RAYPORT AND BERNARD JAWORSKI

Ultimately, only one thing really matters in service encounters—the customer's perceptions of what occurred.

RICHARD B. CHASE AND SRIRAM DASU

LEARNING OBJECTIVES (LOs)

By the end of this chapter, the reader should be able to:

LO1 Be familiar with what we can learn from flowcharting a service and know how flowcharts are drawn.

LO2 Tell the difference between flowcharting and blueprinting.

LO3 Develop a blueprint for a service process with all the necessary elements in place.

LO4 Understand how to use failure proofing to design fail points out of service processes.

LO5 Know how service redesign can help improve both service quality and productivity.

LO6 Be familiar with the concept of service customers as "co-producers" and the implications of this perspective.

LO7 Understand and manage the factors that lead customers to accept new self-service technologies (SSTs).

LO8 Know how to manage customers' reluctance to change their behaviors in service processes, including adoption of SSTs.

Process Redesign in Singapore's Libraries[1]

In this digital age, libraries have suffered from reduced usage. The National Library Board of Singapore (NLB) had to work hard to change people's view that the library was a place with rows of shelves full of old books and unfriendly staff. NLB managed to transform its library services through clever use of the latest technologies to expand its services, go virtual, encourage use of the libraries and promote lifelong learning of its members, all while dramatically increasing productivity. Core of that transformation was the radical redesign of its service processes.

One of the many examples how NLB used advanced technology to redesign processes is its electronic library management system (ELiMS) based on radio-frequency identification (RFID). In fact, NLB was the first public library in the world to prototype RFID, an electronic system for automatically identifying items. It uses RFID tags, or transponders, which are contained in smart labels consisting of a silicon chip and coiled antenna. They receive and respond to radio-frequency queries from an RFID transceiver, which enables remote automatic storage, retrieval, and sharing of information. Unlike barcodes, which need to be manually scanned, RFID simply broadcasts its presence and automatically sends data about the item to electronic readers. This technology is already in use in mass-transit cashless ticketing systems, ski resort lift passes, and security badges for controlled access to buildings.

NLB installed RFID tags in its over 10 million books making it one of the largest users of RFID tags in the world. After redesigning the processes with RFID, customers don't have to spend time waiting anymore; book issuing is automatic as customers walk out of the library, and books can be returned simply at any book drop at any library in its system. From the outside, the book drop looks like an ATM, but with a large hole covered by a flap. A user simply places the book in the box below the flap, the book is scanned using RFID, and a message on the screen instantly confirms that the book has been recorded as "returned" in the user's account.

To go one step further, NLB pioneered "smart bookshelves." When a book was either removed or placed on a bookshelf, the RFID technology took note of it. Therefore, if a book was put in the wrong place, the bookshelf "knew" and alerted staff. With a hand-held device, the librarian could then locate the book within moments. This allowed books to be traced easily, and both staff and customers saved time in not having to search for specific books. To enhance convenience and productivity further, NLB has been moving toward completely side-stepping the handling of physical books—library members can now download for free some 800,000 e-books and 600 e-magazines from its website. Another recent innovation was a dispensing machine for some of its most popular books (Figure 8.1).

FIGURE 8.1 NLB's National Library Building Is a Prominent Landmark Located in the Heart of the Cultural, Entertainment, and Civic District of Singapore

The result of the rigorous redesigning of service processes? A world-class library, winner of Singapore Quality Award, highly regarded by librarians around the world, and featured in teaching case studies at top business schools such as Harvard Business School and INSEAD.

FLOWCHARTING CUSTOMER SERVICE PROCESSES

From the customer's perspective, services are experiences (e.g., calling a customer contact center or visiting a library). From the organization's perspective, services are processes that have to be designed and managed to create the desired customer experience. This makes processes the architecture of services. Processes describe the method and sequence in which service operating systems work and specify how they link together to create the value proposition promised to customers. In high-contact services, customers are an integral part of the operation, and the process becomes their experience. Badly designed processes are likely to annoy customers because they often result in slow, frustrating, and poor-quality service delivery. Similarly, poor processes make it difficult for frontline employees to do their jobs well, result in low productivity, and increase the risk of service failures.

Flowcharting Is a Simple Tool to Document Service Processes

Flowcharting, a technique for displaying the nature and sequence of the different steps involved in delivering service to customers, offers an easy way to understand the totality of the customer's service experience. By flowcharting the sequence of encounters customers have with a service organization, we can gain valuable insights into the nature of an existing service. Recognizing that a value proposition may embrace all or part of the whole cluster of benefits a firm offers to its target market, service marketers need to create a coherent offering in which each element is compatible with the others and all are mutually reinforcing.

Marketers find that creating a flowchart for a specific service is particularly useful for distinguishing between those steps at which customers use the core service and those involving service elements that supplement the core product as we discussed in the "flower of service" model in Chapter 4. For instance, for restaurants, food and beverages constitute the core product, but supplementary services may include reservations, valet parking, a coat room, being escorted to a table, ordering from the menu, billing, payment, and use of restrooms. If you prepare flowcharts for a variety of services, you will soon notice that although the core products may differ widely, common supplementary elements—from information to billing and from reservations/order-taking to problem resolution—keep recurring.

Flowcharting will help you to understand how the nature of the customer's involvement with the service organization varies among each of the four categories of services introduced in Chapter 1—people-, possession-, mental stimulus-, and information-processing. Let's take one example of each category—staying in a motel, getting a DVD player repaired, obtaining a weather forecast, and purchasing health insurance. Figure 8.2 displays a simple flowchart that demonstrates what's involved in each of the four scenarios. Imagine you are the customer in each instance, and think about the extent and nature of your involvement in the service delivery process and the types of encounters with the organization that take place.

- *Stay at a motel (people processing).* It's late evening. You're driving on a long trip and getting tired. Spotting a motel displaying a vacancy sign, you decide it's time to stop for the night. On closer inspection, however, the building exterior looks run down, there are weeds growing through cracks in the asphalt parking lot, and the grass needs cutting. You decide to continue and soon come to another motel which, in addition to a vacancy sign, also displays a price that seems very reasonable. You park your car, noting that the grounds are clean and the buildings seem freshly painted. On entering the reception area, you're greeted by a friendly clerk who checks you in and gives you the key to a room. You move your car to the space in front of your assigned unit and let yourself in. After using the bathroom, you go to bed. Following a good night's sleep, you rise the next morning, shower, dress, and pack. Then you walk to the reception area where you take advantage of the free coffee, juice, and donuts; return your key to a different clerk; pay for the room; and drive away.
- *Repair a DVD player (possession processing).* When you use your DVD player, the picture quality on the TV screen is poor. Fed up with the situation, you search the online Yellow Pages to find an appliance repair store in your area. At the store, the neatly dressed technician checks your machine carefully yet quickly and declares that it needs to be adjusted and cleaned. His professional manner inspires confidence. The estimated price seems realistic, and you're reassured to learn that repairs are guaranteed for three months. So you agree to the work and are told

PEOPLE PROCESSING - STAY AT MOTEL

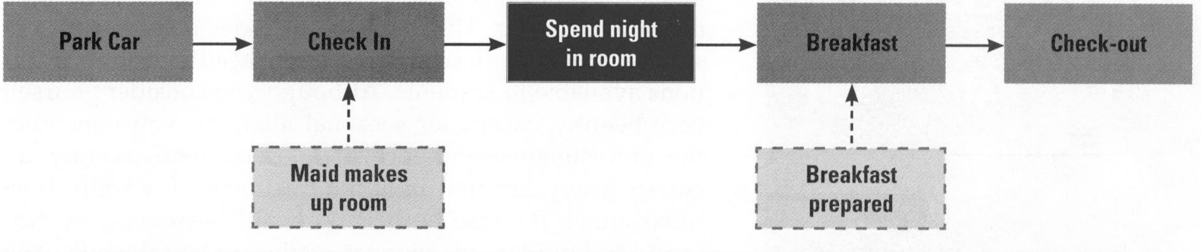

POSSESSION PROCESSING - REPAIR A DVD PLAYER

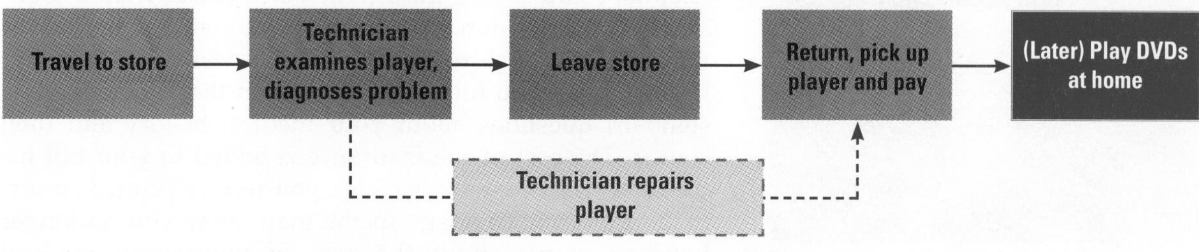

MENTAL STIMULUS PROCESSING - WEATHER FORECAST

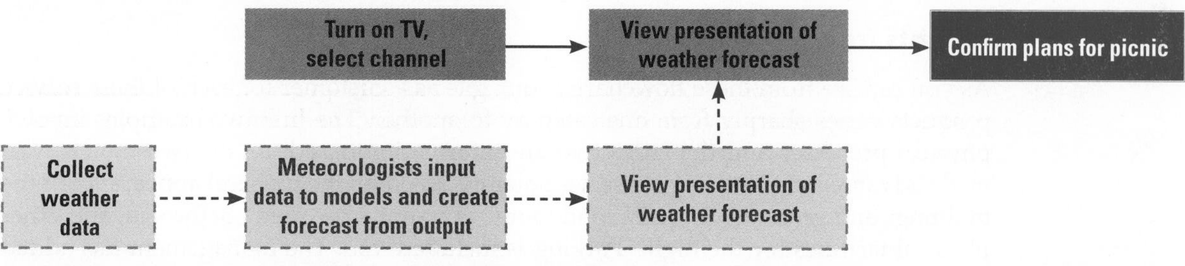

INFORMATION PROCESSING - HEALTH INSURANCE

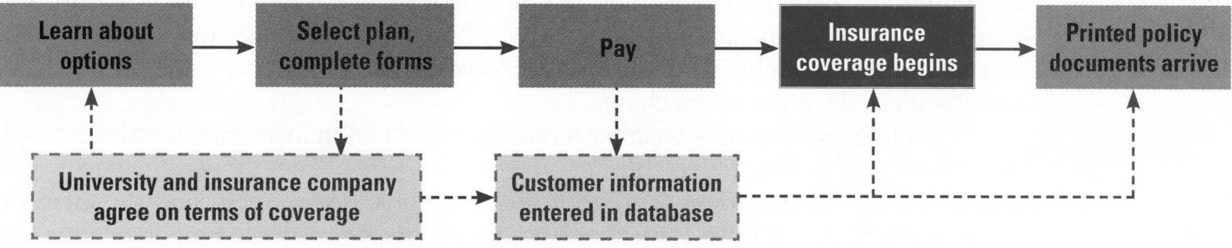

FIGURE 8.2 Simple Flowcharts for Delivery of Various Types of Services

that the player will be ready in three days' time. The technician disappears into the back office with your machine, and you leave the store. On the appointed day, you return to pick up the product, the technician explains the work he did, and demonstrates that the machine is now working well. You pay the agreed price and leave the store with your machine. Back home, you plug in the player, insert a DVD, and find that the picture is now much improved.

- *Weather forecast (mental stimulus processing).* You're planning a picnic trip to the lake, but one of your friends says she's heard that it's going to be really cold this weekend. Back home that evening, you check the weather forecast on TV. The meteorologist shows animated charts indicating the probable path of a cold front over the next 72 hours and states that the latest National Weather Service computer projections suggest the front will remain well to the north of your area. Armed with this information, you call your friends to tell them that the picnic is on.

FIGURE 8.3 Weather Forecasting Is a Service Directed at People's Minds

- *Health insurance (information processing).* Your university mails you a package of information before the beginning of the new semester. This package includes a student health service brochure describing several health insurance options available to students. Although you consider yourself very healthy, except for seasonal allergies, you remember the unfortunate experience of a friend who recently incurred heavy hospital bills for treatment of a badly fractured ankle. Because he had no health insurance, he was forced to liquidate his modest savings to pay the bills. You don't want to pay for more coverage than you need, so you telephone and ask for information and advice from a counselor. At registration, you select an option that will cover the cost of hospital treatment as well as visits to the student health center. You fill in a printed form that includes some standard questions about your medical history and then sign it. The cost of the insurance is added to your bill for the semester. A few weeks later, you receive printed confirmation of your coverage in the mail. Now you no longer have to worry about the risk of unexpected medical expenses.

Insights from Flowcharting

As you can see from these flowcharts, your role as a customer for each of these service products varies sharply from one category to another. The first two examples involve physical processes and the latter two are information based. At the two motels, you made advance judgments about service quality based on the physical appearance of the buildings and grounds. At the second motel, you rent a bedroom, bathroom, and other physical facilities for the night. Parking is included, too. The management has added value by offering a simple breakfast as part of the package.

Your role at the appliance repair store, however, is limited to briefly explaining the symptoms, leaving the machine, and returning several days later to pick it up. You have to trust the technician's competence and honesty in executing the service in your absence. However, inclusion of a guarantee lowers the risk. You enjoy the benefits later when you use the repaired machine.

The other two services, weather forecasting and health insurance, involve intangible actions and a less active role for you as consumer. The TV station you watch competes with other stations (and with radio stations, newspapers, and the Internet) for an audience, so it must appeal on the design of its graphics, the personality and presentation skills of its meteorologist, convenience of its schedule, and reputation for accuracy. You incur no financial cost to obtain the forecast, but you may have to watch some ads first, because advertising revenues constitute the business model that funds the station's operations. Delivery of the information you need takes only a couple of minutes, and you can act on it immediately. Obtaining health insurance, by contrast, takes more time and mental effort, because you have to evaluate several options and complete a detailed application. Then you may have to wait for the policy to be issued and coverage to begin. Your choice of health plans will reflect the cost relative to the benefits offered. How clearly these benefits are explained may influence your decision. If their brand names mean anything to you, you may also be influenced by the reputation of the companies providing the insurance.

BLUEPRINTING SERVICES TO CREATE VALUED EXPERIENCES AND PRODUCTIVE OPERATIONS

A key tool we use to design new services (or redesign existing ones) is known as *blueprinting*. It's a more sophisticated version of *flowcharting*. As we distinguish between these terms in a service context, a flowchart describes an existing process, often in fairly simple form; a blueprint specifies in detail how a service process should be constructed and includes details as to what is visible to the customer and where there are potential fail points in the service process.

It's no easy task to create a service, especially one that must be delivered in real time with customers present in the service factory. To design services that are both satisfying for customers and operationally efficient, marketers and operations specialists need to work together, and a blueprint can provide a common perspective and language to the various departments involved.

Perhaps you're wondering where the term blueprinting comes from and why we're using it here. The design for a new building or a ship usually is captured on architectural drawings called blueprints, so called because reproductions have traditionally been printed on special paper on which all the drawings and annotations appear in blue. These blueprints show what the product should look like and detail the specifications to which it should conform. In contrast to the physical architecture of a building or piece of equipment, service processes have a largely intangible structure. That makes them all the more difficult to visualize. As Lynn Shostack has pointed out, the same is true of processes such as logistics, industrial engineering, decision theory, and computer systems analysis, each of which employs blueprint-like techniques to describe processes involving flows, sequences, relationships, and dependencies.[2]

Developing a Blueprint

How should you get started on developing a service blueprint? First, you need to identify all the key activities involved in creating and delivering the service in question and then specify the linkages between these activities.[3] Initially, it's best to keep activities relatively aggregated in order to define the "big picture." You can later refine any given activity by "drilling down" to obtain a higher level of detail. In an airline context, for instance, the passenger activity of "boards aircraft" actually represents a series of actions and can be decomposed into such steps as "wait for seat rows to be announced, give agent boarding pass for verification, walk down jetway, enter aircraft, let flight attendant verify boarding pass, find a seat, stow carry-on bag, sit down."

A key characteristic of service blueprinting is that it distinguishes between what customers experience "front-stage" and the activities of employees and support processes "back-stage," where customers can't see them. Between the two lies what is called the *line of visibility.* Operationally oriented businesses are sometimes so focused on managing back-stage activities that they neglect the customer's purely front-stage perspective. Accounting firms, for instance, often have elaborately documented procedures and standards for how to conduct an audit, but may lack clear standards for hosting a meeting with clients or how staff members should answer the telephone.

Service blueprints clarify the interactions between customers and employees, and how these are supported by back-stage activities and systems. By clarifying interrelationships among employee roles, operational processes, information technology, and customer interactions, blueprints can facilitate the integration of marketing, operations, and human resource management within a firm. Although there's no single, required way to prepare a service blueprint, we recommend that a consistent approach be used within any one organization. To illustrate blueprinting later in this chapter, we adapt and simplify an approach proposed by Jane Kingman-Brundage.[4]

Blueprinting also gives managers the opportunity to identify potential *fail points* in the process, points where there is a significant risk of things going wrong and diminishing service quality. When managers are aware of these fail points, they are better able to take preventive measures, prepare contingency plans, or both. They can also pinpoint stages in the process at which customers commonly have to wait. Armed with this knowledge, marketing and operational specialists can then develop standards for execution of each activity, including times for completion of a task, maximum customer wait times in between tasks, and scripts and role definitions (as discussed in Chapter 2) to guide interactions between staff members and customers.

A blueprint complements service scripts, which provide a step-by-step description of the service encounter from the perspectives of the various players involved. A script can help to identify potential or existing problems in a specific service process. Recall from Chapter 2 the script for teeth cleaning and a simple dental examination involving three players—the patient, the receptionist, and the dental hygienist. Each of these players may be invited to review the script and to identify either missing or superfluous steps, to suggest changes in sequence, or to highlight ways in which developments in either information technology or dental equipment and treatment might require changes in the procedures. By examining existing scripts, service managers may discover ways to modify the service blueprint in order to improve service delivery, increase productivity, and enhance the nature of the customer's experience.

Blueprinting the Restaurant Experience: A Three-Act Performance

To illustrate blueprinting of a high-contact, people-processing service, we examine the experience of dinner for two at Chez Jean, an upscale restaurant that enhances its core food service with a variety of other supplementary services (Figure 8.4). A rule of thumb in full-service restaurants is that the cost of purchasing the food ingredients represents about 20 to 30 percent of the price of the meal. The balance can be seen as the fees that customers are willing to pay for "renting" a table and chairs in a pleasant setting, the services of food preparation experts and their kitchen equipment, and serving staff to wait on them in the dining room.

The key components of the blueprint, reading from top to bottom, are:

1. Definition of standards for each front-stage activity (only a few examples are actually specified in the figure).
2. Physical and other evidence for front-stage activities (specified for all steps).
3. Principal customer actions (illustrated by pictures).
4. Line of interaction.
5. Front-stage actions by customer-contact personnel.
6. Line of visibility.
7. Back-stage actions by customer-contact personnel.
8. Support processes involving other service personnel.
9. Support processes involving information technology.

Reading from left to right, the blueprint prescribes the sequence of actions over time. In Chapter 2, we likened service performances to theater. To emphasize the involvement of human actors in service delivery, we've followed the practices adopted by some service organizations using pictures to illustrate each of the 14 principal steps involving our two customers, beginning with making a reservation and concluding with departure from the restaurant after the meal. Like many high-contact services involving discrete transactions—as opposed to the continuous delivery found in, say, utility or insurance services—the "restaurant drama" can be divided into three "acts" that represent activities that take place before the core product is encountered, delivery of the core product (in this case, the meal), and subsequent activities while still involved with the service provider.

The "stage," or *servicescape*, includes both the exterior and interior of the restaurant. Front-stage actions take place in a very visual environment; restaurants often are quite theatrical in their use of physical evidence (such as furnishings, décor, uniforms, lighting, and table settings) and may employ background music in their efforts to create a themed environment that matches their market positioning.

ACT 1—PROLOGUE AND INTRODUCTORY SCENES. In this particular drama, Act I begins with a customer making a reservation by telephone. This action could take place hours or even days in advance of visiting the restaurant. In theatrical terms, the telephone conversation can be likened to a radio drama, with impressions created by the nature of the respondent's voice, speed of response, and style of the conversation. When our customers arrive at the restaurant, a valet parks their car, they leave their coats in the coatroom, and they enjoy a drink in the bar while waiting for their table. The act concludes when they are escorted to a table and seated.

These five steps constitute the couple's initial experience of the restaurant performance, with each involving an interaction with an employee—by phone or face to face. By the time the two of them reach their table in the dining room, they've been exposed to several supplementary services and have encountered a sizeable cast of characters, including five or more contact personnel, as well as other customers.

Standards can be set for each service activity, but should be based on a good understanding of guest expectations (remember our discussion in Chapter 2 of how expectations are formed). Below the line of visibility, the blueprint identifies key actions to ensure that each front-stage step is performed in a manner that meets or exceeds those expectations. These actions include recording reservations, handling customers' coats, delivery and preparation of food, maintenance of facilities and equipment, training and assignment of staff for each task, and use of information technology to access, input, store, and transfer relevant data.

ACT II—DELIVERY OF THE CORE PRODUCT. As the curtain rises on Act II, our customers are finally about to experience the core service they came for. For simplicity, we've condensed the meal into just four scenes. In practice, reviewing the menu and placing the order are two separate activities; meantime, meal service proceeds on a course-by-course basis. If you were actually running a restaurant, you'd need to go into greater detail to identify each of the many steps involved in what often is a tightly scripted drama. Assuming all goes well, the two guests will have an excellent meal, nicely served in a pleasant atmosphere, and perhaps a fine wine to enhance it. But if the restaurant fails to satisfy their expectations (and those of its many other guests) during Act II, it's going to be in serious trouble. There are numerous potential fail points. Is the menu information complete? Is it intelligible? Is everything listed on the menu actually available this evening? Will explanations and advice be given in a friendly, noncondescending manner for guests who have questions about specific menu items or are unsure about which wine to order?

After our customers decide on their meals, they place their orders with the server, who must then pass on the details to personnel in the kitchen, bar, and billing desk. Mistakes in transmitting information are a frequent cause of quality failures in many organizations. Bad handwriting or unclear verbal requests can lead to incorrect preparation or delivery of the wrong items altogether.

In subsequent scenes of Act II, our customers may evaluate not only the quality of food and drink—the most important dimension of all—but also how promptly it is served (not too promptly, for that might suggest frozen foods cooked by microwave!) and the style of service. A technically correct performance by the server can still be spoiled by such human failures as a disinterested, cold, or ingratiating manner or by displaying overly casual behavior.

ACT III—THE DRAMA CONCLUDES. The meal may be over, but much is still taking place both front-stage and back-stage as the drama moves to its close. The core service has now been delivered, and we'll assume that our customers are happily digesting it. Act III should be short. The action in each of the remaining scenes should move smoothly, quickly, and pleasantly, with no shocking surprises at the end. We can hypothesize that in a North American environment, most customers' expectations would probably include the following:

- An accurate, intelligible bill is presented promptly as soon as the customer requests it.
- Payment is handled politely and expeditiously (with all major credit cards accepted).
- The guests are thanked for their patronage and invited to come again.
- Customers visiting the restrooms find them clean and properly supplied.
- The right coats are promptly retrieved from the coatroom.
- The customer's car is brought promptly to the door in the same condition as when it was left; the attendant thanks them again and bids them a good evening.

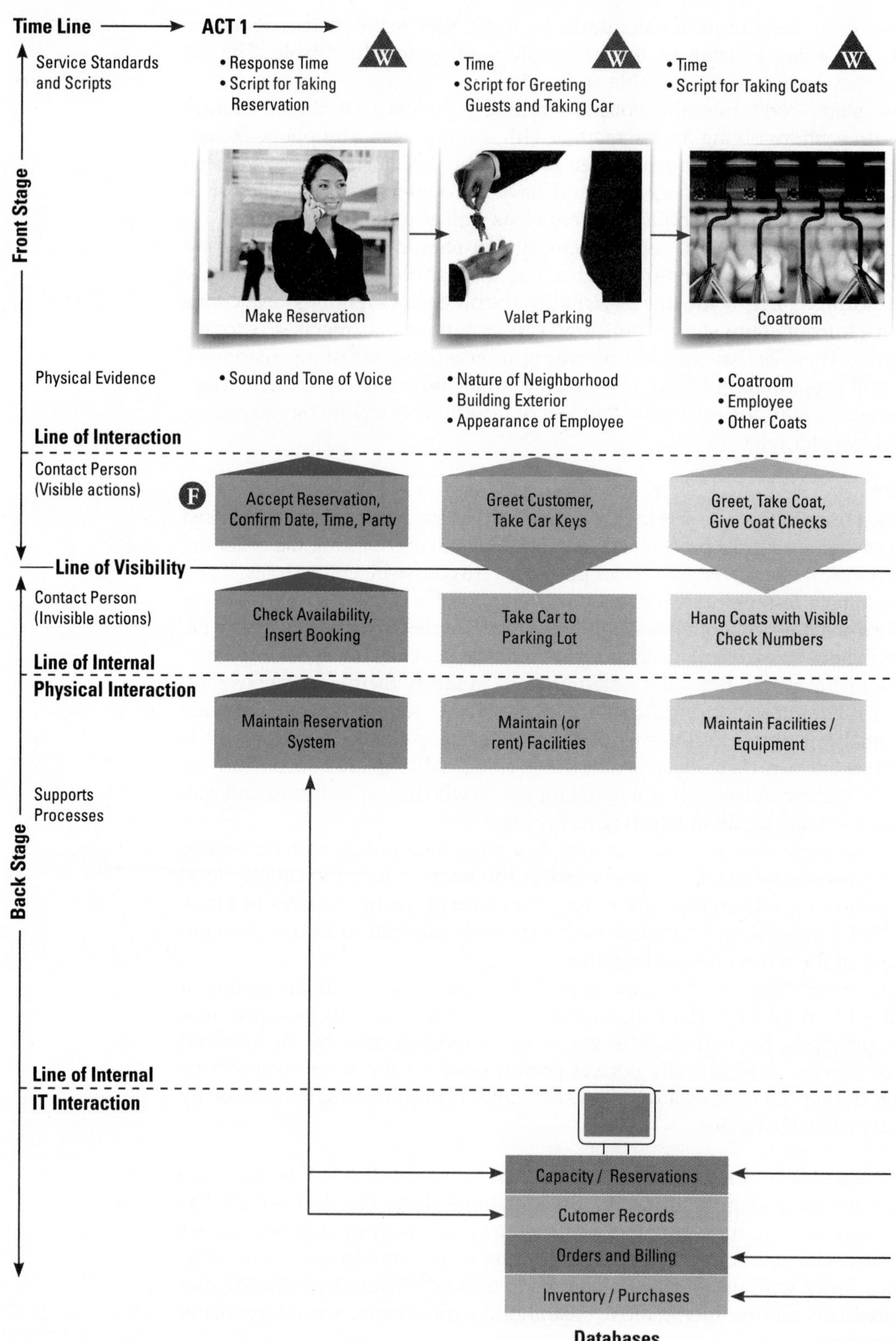

FIGURE 8.4 Blueprinting a Full-Service Restaurant Experience

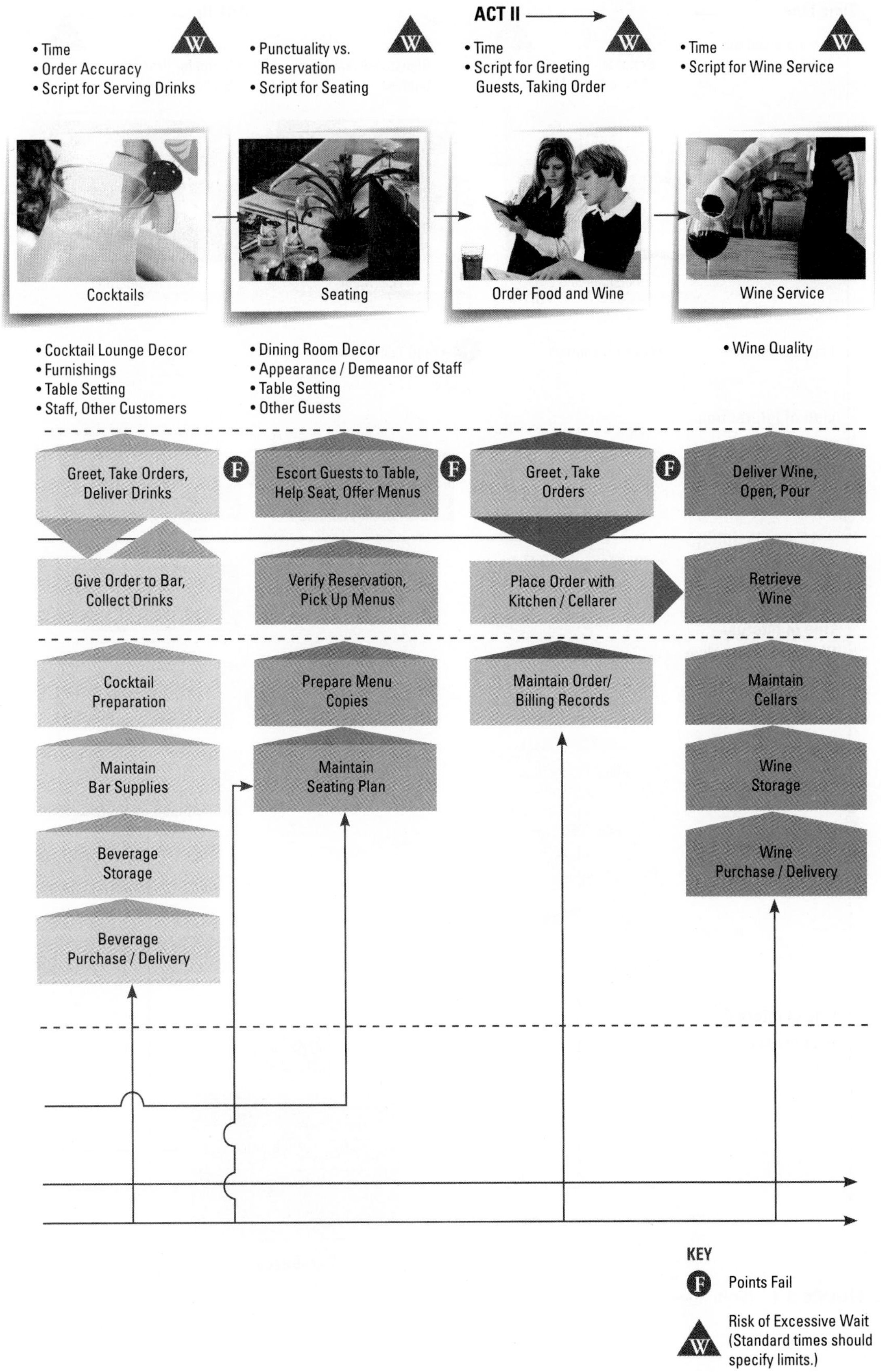

FIGURE 8.4 *(Continued)*

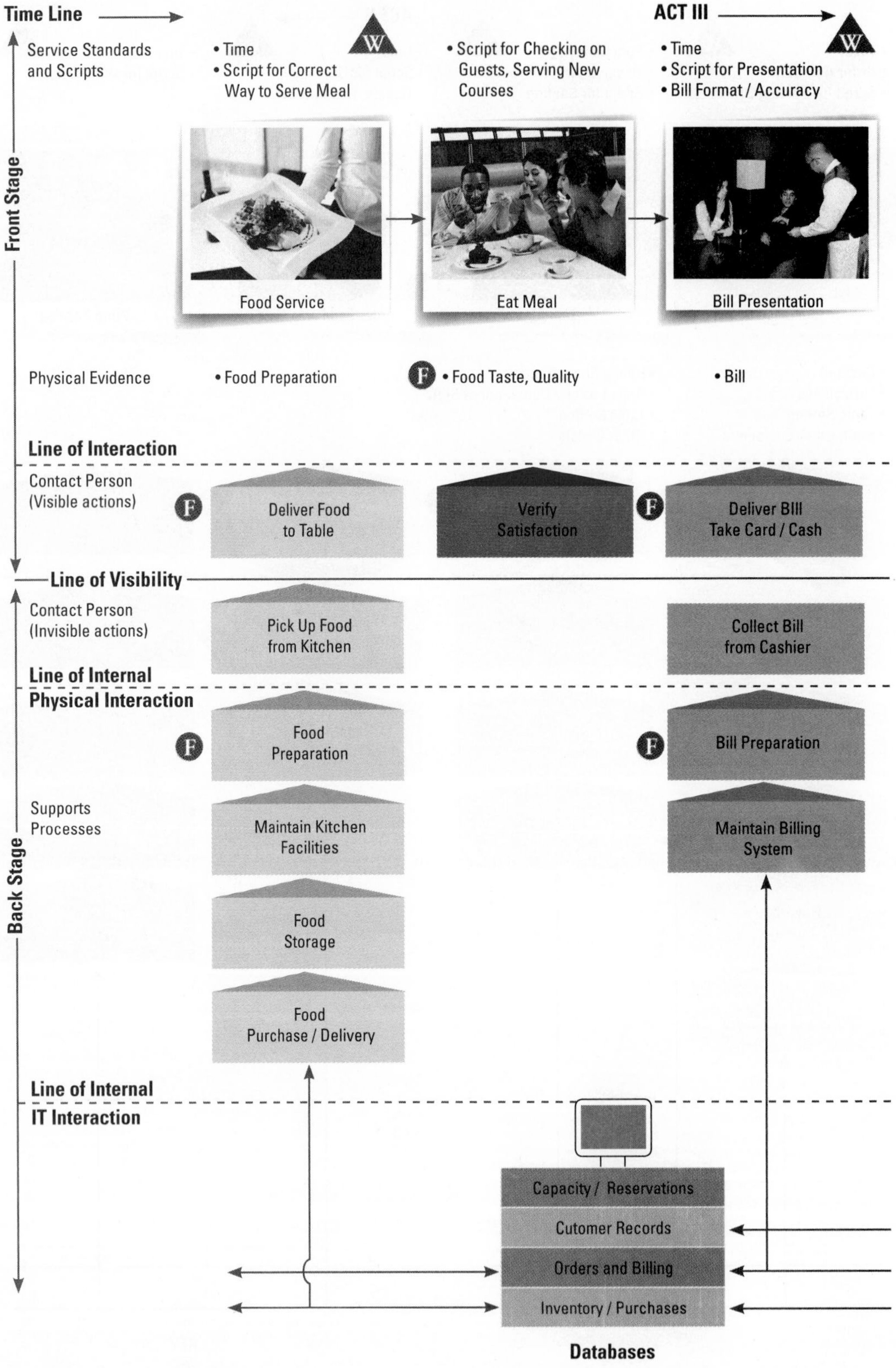

Time Line →

ACT III →

Front Stage

Service Standards and Scripts

- Time
- Script for Correct Way to Serve Meal

- Script for Checking on Guests, Serving New Courses

- Time
- Script for Presentation
- Bill Format / Accuracy

Food Service → Eat Meal → Bill Presentation

Physical Evidence

- Food Preparation
- Food Taste, Quality
- Bill

Line of Interaction

Contact Person (Visible actions)

Deliver Food to Table | Verify Satisfaction | Deliver Bill Take Card / Cash

Line of Visibility

Back Stage

Contact Person (Invisible actions)

Pick Up Food from Kitchen | Collect Bill from Cashier

Line of Internal Physical Interaction

Food Preparation | Bill Preparation

Supports Processes

Maintain Kitchen Facilities | Maintain Billing System

Food Storage

Food Purchase / Delivery

Line of Internal IT Interaction

Capacity / Reservations

Cutomer Records

Orders and Billing

Inventory / Purchases

Databases

FIGURE 8.4 *(Continued)*

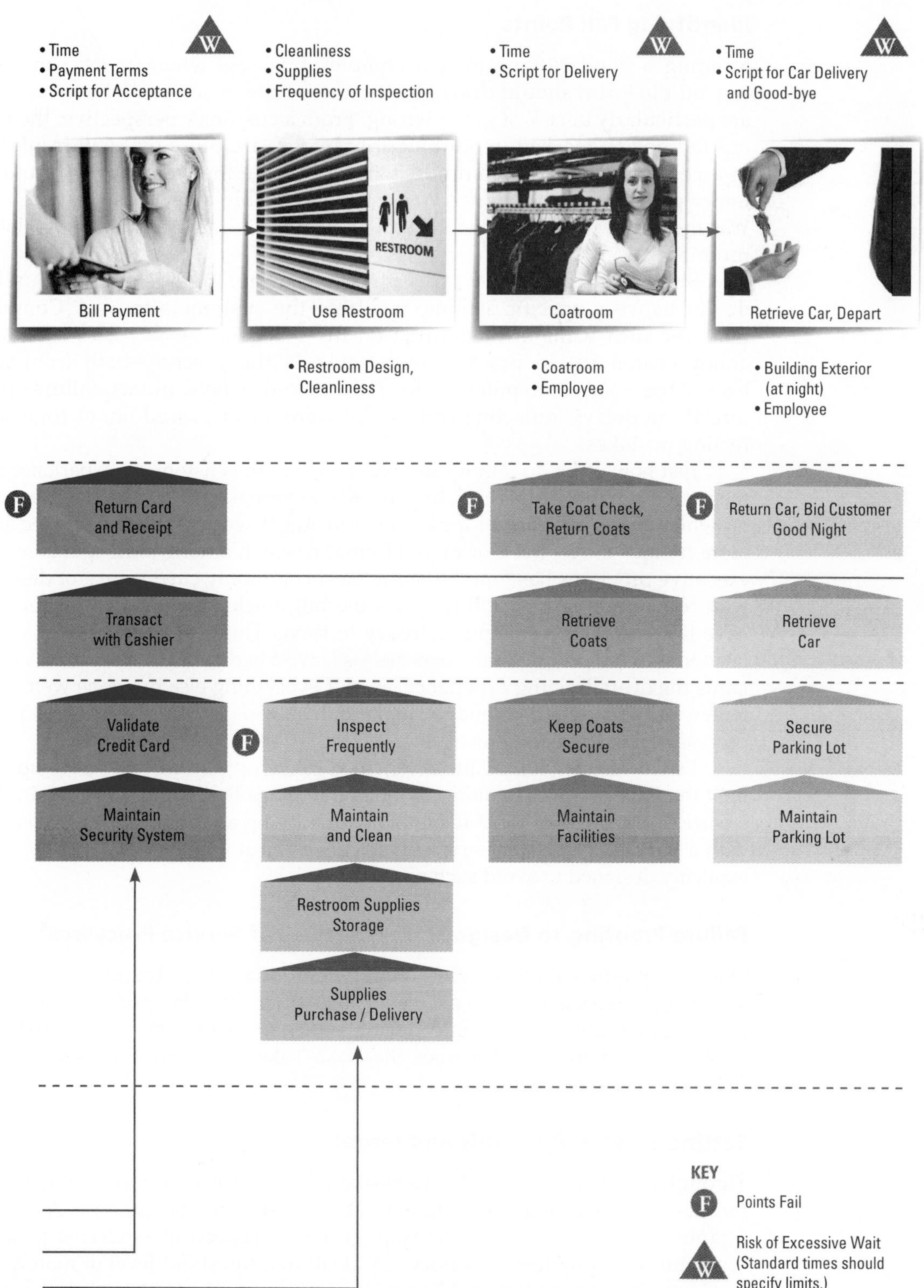

FIGURE 8.4 *(Continued)*

Identifying Fail Points

Running a good restaurant is a complex business where much can go wrong. A good blueprint should draw attention to points in service delivery where things are particularly at risk of going wrong. From a customer perspective, the most serious fail points, marked in our blueprint by (F) are those that will result in failure to access or enjoy the core product. They involve the reservation (Could the customer get through by phone? Was a table available at the desired time and date? Was the reservation recorded accurately?) and seating (Was a table available when promised?).

Since service delivery takes place over time, there is also the possibility of delays between specific actions, requiring the customers to wait. Common locations for such waits are identified on the blueprint by (W). Excessive waits will annoy customers. In practice, every step in the process—both front-stage and back-stage—has some potential for failures and delays. In fact, failures often lead directly to delays, reflecting orders that were never passed on, or time spent correcting mistakes.

Just how often do failures intervene to ruin the customers' experience and spoil their good humor? Think back to your own experience. Can you remember occasions on which the experience of a nice meal in Act II was completely spoiled by one or more failures in Act III? Our own informal research among participants in dozens of executive programs has found that the most commonly cited source of dissatisfaction with restaurants is an inability to get the bill quickly at lunchtime, after customers have finished their meal and are ready to leave. This seemingly minor failing, unrelated to the core product, can nevertheless leave a bad taste in a customer's mouth that taints the overall dining experience, even if everything else has gone well. When customers are on a tight time budget, making them wait unnecessarily at any point in the process is akin to stealing their time.

David Maister coined the acronym OTSU ("opportunity to screw up") to highlight the importance of thinking about all the things that might go wrong in delivering a particular type of service.[5] It's only by identifying all the possible OTSUs associated with a particular task that service managers can put together a delivery system that's explicitly designed to avoid such problems.

Failure Proofing to Design Fail Points Out of Service Processes[6]

Once fail points have been identified, careful analysis of the reasons for failure in service processes is necessary. This analysis often reveals opportunities for "failure proofing" certain activities in order to reduce or even eliminate the risk of errors. Service Perspective 8.1 describes the Poka-Yoke technique that is widely used to fail-safe service processes.

Setting Service Standards and Target

Through both formal research and on-the-job experience, service managers can learn the nature of customer expectations at each step in the process. As outlined in Chapter 2, customers' expectations range across a spectrum—referred to as the zone of tolerance—from desired service (an ideal) to a threshold level of merely adequate service (refer back to Figure 2.7on p. 66. Service providers should design standards for each step sufficiently high to satisfy and even delight customers; if that's not possible, then they will need to modify customer expectations. These standards might include time parameters, the script for a technically correct performance, and prescriptions for appropriate style and demeanor.

As the axiom goes, "What is not measured is not managed," standards must be expressed in ways that permit objective measurement. Process performance needs to be monitored against standards, and compliance targets need to be determined. The service blueprint combined with discussions with customers and frontline employees help to determine the service quality attributes important to customers at each

SERVICE PERSPECTIVE 8.1

POKA-YOKES—AN EFFECTIVE TOOL TO DESIGN FAIL POINTS OUT OF SERVICE PROCESSES

One of the most useful Total Quality Management (TQM) methods in manufacturing is the application of poka-yoke, or fail-safe, methods to prevent errors in manufacturing processes. Richard Chase and Douglas Steward introduced this concept to fail-safe service processes.

Part of the challenge of implementing poka-yokes in a services context is the need to address not only server errors, but also customer errors. Server poka-yokes ensure that service employees do things correctly, as requested, in the right order and at the right speed. Examples include surgeons whose surgical instrument trays have indentations for each instrument. For a given operation, all of the instruments are nested in the tray so it is clear if the surgeon has not removed all instruments from the patient before closing the incision (Figure 8.5).

Some service firms use poka-yokes to ensure that certain steps or standards in the customer-staff interaction are adhered to. A bank ensures eye contact by requiring tellers to record the customer's eye color on a checklist at the start of a transaction. Some firms place mirrors at the exits of staff areas to foster a neat appearance; frontline staff can then automatically check their appearance before greeting a customer. At one restaurant, servers place round coasters in front of those diners who have ordered a decaffeinated coffee and square coasters in front of the others.

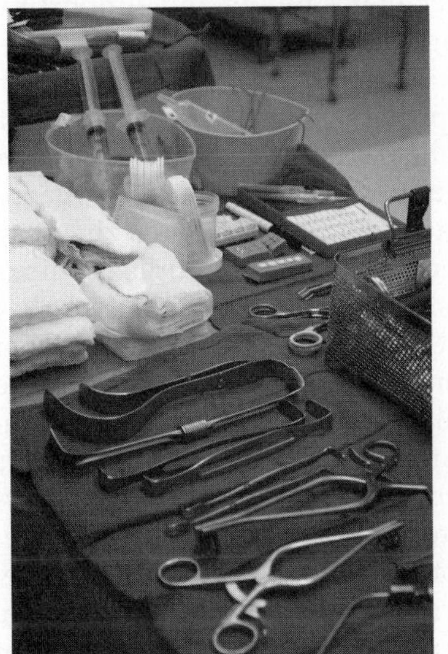

FIGURE 8.5 The Practice of Poka-Yoke Is Observed in the Operating Room

Customer poka-yokes usually focus on preparing the customer for the encounter (including getting them to bring the right materials for the transaction and to arrive on time, if applicable), understanding and anticipating their role in the service transaction, and selecting the correct service or transaction. Examples that prepare the customer for the encounter include printing dress code requests on invitations, sending reminders of dental appointments, and printing guidelines on customer cards (e.g., "Please have your account and pin number ready before calling our service reps"). Poka-yokes that address customer errors during the encounter include beepers at ATMs so that customers do not forget to take their cards, and locks on aircraft lavatory doors that must be engaged in order for the lights to go on.

Designing poka-yokes is part art and part science. Most of the procedures seem trivial, but this actually is a key advantage of this method. It can be used to design frequently occurring service failures out of service processes and to ensure adherence to certain service standards or service steps.

Source: Adapted from Richard B. Chase and Douglas M. Stewart, "Make Your Service Fail-Safe," *Sloan Management Review*, Spring 1994, 35–44.

touchpoint. Those aspects that require the attention of management (i.e., attributes most important to customers and most difficult to manage) should be the basis for setting standards.

Important service quality attributes can be operationalized via service quality indicators and create a basis for monitoring process performance. For example, the attribute "responsiveness" can be operationalized (based on customer interviews) as "processing time to approve a loan application." Service standards are then based on customer expectations, moderated by policy decisions about how to meet these needs cost effectively. In cases where standards deviate from customer needs, expectations need to be managed (e.g., application approval times can be communicated in brochures and application forms). Finally, performance targets define specific process and/or team performance targets (e.g., 80 percent of all applications within 24 hours) for which staff will be held accountable for. Figure 8.6 shows the relationship between indicators, standards, and targets.[7]

The distinction between standards and performance targets is important because of their subsequent use in evaluating staff, branch, and/or team performance. This makes the setting of standards and targets highly political. By separating standards and targets, the firm can be "hard" about reflecting customer expectations in the performance standards (i.e., making sure that what customers expect is captured in the standards) but "realistic" about what the teams actually can deliver. In practice, management can stand firm on setting the right standards (i.e., according to customer needs and expectations) and go easy on negotiating performance targets that reflect operational reality (i.e., it may not be possible to consistently achieve the standards). This separation of standards and targets can be important for three reasons. First, the correct (i.e., customer driven) standards get internalized by the organization. Second, when implemented well, process owners and department or branch managers can raise performance targets gradually over time to bring them more in line with customer expectations. Third, it facilitates buy-in and support for the service standards by providing latitude to management and staff.

Ideally, service firms should try to provide consistently high performance at each step. In reality however, many service performances are inconsistent. Therefore, it is particularly important to start and finish strong. The opening scenes of a service drama are particularly important, because customers' first impressions can affect their evaluations of quality during later stages of service delivery. Perceptions of their service experiences tend to be cumulative.[8] If a couple of things go badly wrong at the outset, customers may simply walk out. Even if they stay, they may now be looking for other things that aren't quite right. On the other hand, if the first steps go really well, customers' zones of tolerance may increase so that they are more willing to overlook minor mistakes later in the service performance. Research by Marriott Hotels indicates that four of the five top factors contributing to customer loyalty come into play during the first 10 minutes of service delivery.[9] And research into the design of doctor's offices and medical procedures suggests that unfavorable initial impressions can lead patients to cancel surgery or even change doctors.[10] However, performance standards should not be allowed to fall off toward the end of service delivery. Other research findings point to the importance of a strong finish and suggest that a service encounter perceived to start poorly but then builds in quality will be better rated than one that starts

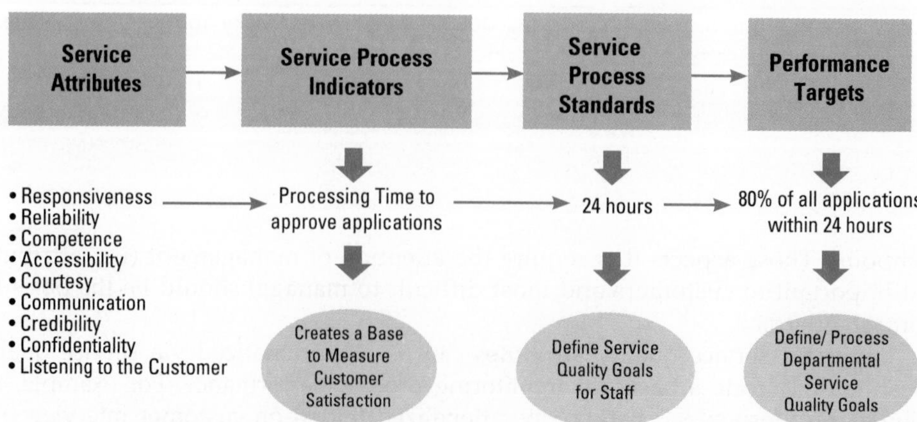

FIGURE 8.6 Setting Standards and Targets for Customer Service Processes

well but declines to end poorly.[11] Research Insights 8.1 provides some additional food for thought.

Our restaurant example was deliberately chosen to illustrate a high-contact, people-processing service with which you and other readers are likely to be familiar. However, many possession-processing services (such as repair or maintenance) and information-processing services (such as insurance or accounting) involve far less contact with customers, because much of the action takes place back-stage. In these situations, a failure committed front-stage is likely to represent a higher proportion of the customer's service encounters with a company and may therefore be viewed even more seriously, also because there are fewer subsequent opportunities to create a favorable impression.

SERVICE PROCESS REDESIGN

Service process redesign revitalizes processes that have become outdated. However that doesn't necessarily mean the processes were poorly designed in the first place. Rather, changes in technology, customer needs, added service features, and new offerings may have made existing processes crack and creak.[12] Mitchell T. Rabkin MD, former president of Boston's Beth Israel Hospital (now Beth Israel-Deaconess Medical Center), characterized the problem as "institutional rust" and declared: "Institutions are like steel beams—they tend to rust. What was once smooth, shiny and nice tends to become rusty."[13] He suggested two main reasons for this situation. The first involves changes in the external environment that make existing practices obsolete and require redesign of the underlying processes—or

RESEARCH INSIGHTS 8.1

LEARNING FROM STUDIES OF SEQUENTIAL SERVICE ENCOUNTERS

A laboratory study by Hansen and Danaher explored how respondents judged hypothetical service encounters in three different service categories—a weekend car rental, an international flight, and a retail purchase. Within each category, one of three scenarios was presented to participants. In the first, the initial service events were performed well, the core service adequately, and the concluding steps poorly, thus creating a deteriorating trend. In the second, the situation was reversed, to create an improving trend, and in the third, a consistently adequate service was delivered from start to finish. The findings showed that a weak start that built toward a strong finish received more favorable judgments than the other scenarios. A conclusion drawn from this research is that managers who are not immediately able to raise all elements of the service encounter should begin by focusing on improving the concluding events in the process rather than the opening steps.

Another laboratory study by Hamer, Liu, and Sudharshan simulated a visit to a restaurant. Respondents were presented with two scenarios in which they were going out to eat with a group of friends and were given information at certain key steps during the service encounter. The findings showed that respondents continuously updated their expectations during service delivery and that these evolving expectations had a larger effect on their perceptions of service quality than perceived service performance. A key managerial insight from this study is that it's very important for managers to shape and control customers' expectations as service delivery proceeds.

An exploratory study of sequential service encounters in a real-world setting was conducted by Verhoef, Antonides, and de Hoog. It examined inbound telephone calls by customers to the call center of a large financial service provider. The findings suggested that customer satisfaction was not created solely by the average quality of the events in the service process but could be enhanced by a positive peak experience at some point in the process.

Sources: David E. Hansen and Peter J. Danaher, "Inconsistent Performance During the Service Encounter," *Journal of Service Research*, 1, February 1999, 227–235; Lawrence O. Hamer, Ben Shaw-Ching Liu, and D. Sudharshan, "The Effects of Intraencounter Changes in Expectations on Perceived Service Quality Models," *Journal of Service Research*, 1, February 1999, 275–289; Peter C. Verhoef, Gerrit Antonides, and Arnoud N. de Hoog, "Service Encounters as a Sequence of Events: The Importance of Peak Experiences," *Journal of Service Research*, 7, August 2004, 53–64.

even creation of brand-new processes—in order for the organization to remain relevant and responsive. In health care, such changes may reflect new forms of competition, legislation, technology, health insurance policies, and evolving customer needs.

The second reason for institutional rusting occurs internally. Often, it reflects a natural deterioration of internal processes, creeping bureaucracy, or the evolution of spurious, unofficial standards (see Service Perspective 8.2). Symptoms such as extensive information exchange, data redundancy, a high ratio of checking or control activities to value-adding activities, increased exception processing, and growing numbers of customer complaints about inconvenient and unnecessary procedures often indicate that a process is not working well and requires redesign.

Examining blueprints of existing services may suggest opportunities for product improvement that might be achieved by reconfiguring delivery systems, adding or deleting specific elements, or repositioning the service to appeal to other segments. Each year, Avis determines a set of factors that car renters care about the most. The company breaks down the car rental process into more than 100 incremental steps, including making reservations, finding the pickup counter, getting to the car, driving it, returning it, paying the bill, and so forth.[14] Because Avis knows customers' key concerns, it claims it can quickly identify ways to improve their satisfaction. What travelers most desire is to get their rental car quickly and drive away, so the firm has designed its processes to achieve that goal. "We're constantly making little enhancements around the edges," says Scott Deaver, the company's executive vice president of marketing. Obviously, Avis is living up

SERVICE PERSPECTIVE 8.2

ROOTING OUT UNOFFICIAL STANDARDS IN A HOSPITAL

One of the distinctive characteristics of Mitchell T. Rabkin's 30-year tenure as president of Boston's Beth Israel Hospital was his policy of routinely visiting all areas of the hospital. He usually did so unannounced and in a low-key fashion. No one working at the hospital was surprised to see Dr. Rabkin drop by at almost any time of the day or night. His natural curiosity gave him unparallel insights into how effectively service procedures were working and the subtle ways in which things could go wrong. As the following story reveals, he discovered that there is often a natural deterioration of messages over time.

> One day, I was in the EU [emergency unit], chatting with a house officer [physician] who was treating a patient with asthma. He was giving her medication through an intravenous drip. I looked at the formula for the medication and asked him, "Why are you using this particular cocktail?" "Oh," he replied, "that's hospital policy." Since I was certain that there was no such policy, I decided to investigate.
>
> What had happened went something like this. A few months earlier, Resident [physician] A says to Intern B, who is observing her treat a patient: "This is what I use for asthma." On the next month's rotation, Intern B says to new Resident C: "This is what Dr. A uses for asthma." The following month, Resident C says to Intern D, "This is what we use for asthma." And finally, within another month, Intern D is telling Resident E, "It's hospital policy to use this medication."
>
> As a result of conversations like these, well-intentioned but unofficial standards keep cropping up. It's a particular problem in a place like this, which isn't burdened by an inhuman policy manual where you must look up the policy for everything you do. We prefer to rely on people's intelligence and judgment and limit written policies to overall, more general issues. One always has to be aware of the growth of institutional rust and to be clear about what is being done and why it is being done.

Source: Christopher Lovelock, *Product Plus.* New York: McGraw-Hill, 1994: 355.

to its tagline, "We Try Harder," which the company has employed for some 40 years. "It's not a slogan," says Deaver. "It's in the DNA of the place."

Service Process Redesign Should Improve Both Quality and Productivity

Managers in charge of service process redesign projects should look for opportunities to achieve a quantum leap in both productivity and service quality at the same time. Reengineering the ways in which tasks are performed has significant potential to increase output, especially in many back-stage jobs.[15] Redesign efforts typically focus on achieving the following key performance measures:

1. Reduced number of service failures.
2. Reduced cycle time from customer initiation of a service process to its completion.
3. Enhanced productivity.
4. Increased customer satisfaction.

Ideally, redesign efforts should achieve all of the four measures simultaneously.

Service process redesign encompasses reconstitution, rearrangement, or substitution of service processes. These efforts can be categorized into a number of types, including:[16]

- **Eliminating nonvalue-adding steps**—Often, activities at the front-end and back-end processes of services can be streamlined with the goal of focusing on the benefit-producing part of the service encounter. For example, a customer wanting to rent a car is not interested in filling out forms or processing payment and check of the returned car. Service redesign streamlines these tasks by trying to eliminate nonvalue adding steps. Now, some car rental companies offer customers to rent a car online and pick it up from a designated car park (a large electronic board lists the name of the customer, the car, and the parking lot numbers). The ignition key is in the car, and the only interaction with a car rental employee is at the exit when driving the car out of the car lot where the customer's driver's license is checked and the contract signed (including the customer confirming the condition of the car). When returning the car, it is simply parked at a designated area on the rental company's car lot, the key is returned to a safe deposit box, the final bill is mailed to a predetermined billing address and deducted from the customer credit card, and the customer does not have to come into contact with service personnel. The outcomes of such process redesigns typically include increased productivity and customer satisfaction at the same time.
- **Shifting to self-service**—Significant productivity and sometimes even service quality gains can be achieved by increasing self-service. For example, FedEx succeeded in shifting more than 50 percent of its transactions from its call centers to its website, thus reducing the number of employees in its call centers by some 20,000.
- **Delivering direct service**—This type of redesign involves bringing the service to the customer instead of bringing the customer to the service firm. This often is done to improve convenience for the customer, but can also result in productivity gains if companies can do away with expensive locations.
- **Bundling services**—Bundling services involves bundling, or grouping, multiple services into one offer, focusing on a well-defined customer segment. Bundling can help increase productivity (the bundle is already tailored for a particular segment, making the transaction faster, and reducing the marketing costs of each individual service), while at the same time adding value to the customer through lower transaction costs. It often has a better fit to the needs of the target segment.
- **Redesigning the physical aspects of service processes**—Physical service redesign focuses on the tangible elements of a service process and includes changes to the service facilities and equipment to improve the service experience. This leads to convenience and productivity and often enhances the satisfaction and productivity of frontline employees.

TABLE 8.1 Five Types of Service Redesign

Approach and Concept	Potential Company Benefits	Potential Customer Benefits	Challenges/Limitations
Elimination of non value-added steps (streamlines process)	• Improves efficiency • Increases productivity • Increases ability to customize service • Differentiates company	• Improves efficiency, speed • Shifts tasks from customer to service firm • Separates service activation from delivery • Customizes service	• Requires customer education and employee training to implement smoothly and effectively
Self-service (customer assumes role of producer)	• Lowers cost • Improves productivity • Enhances technology reputation • Differentiates company	• Increases speed of service • Improves access • Saves money • Increases perception of control	• Must prepare customers for the role • Limits face-to-face interaction and opportunities to build relationships • Harder to get customer feedback
Direct service (service delivered to the customer's location)	• Eliminates store location limitations • Expands customer base • Differentiates company	• Increases convenience • Improves access	• Imposes logistical burdens • May be costly • Needs credibility and trust
Bundled service (combines multiple services into a package)	• Differentiates company • Aids customer retention • Increases percapita service use	• Increases convenience • Customizes service	• Requires extensive knowledge of targeted customers • May be perceived as wasteful
Physical service (manipulation of tangibles associated with the service)	• Improves employee satisfaction • Increases productivity • Differentiates company	• Increases convenience • Enhances function • Generates interest	• Easily imitated • Requires expense to effect and maintain • Raises customer expectations for the industry

Source: Adapted from Leonard L. Berry and Sandra K. Lampo, "Teaching an Old Service New Tricks: The Promise of Service Redesign." *Journal of Service Research*, 2, no. 3 (2000): 265–275.

Table 8.1 summarizes five types of service redesign, provides an overview of their potential benefits for the firm and its customers, and highlights potential challenges or limitations. You should note that these redesigns often are used in combination. For example, central to Amazon.com's success is the combined appeal of self-service, direct service, and minimization of nonvalue-added steps through the effective capture of customer preferences, plus shipping and payment data.

Another dimension of service redesign concerns decisions on who should be responsible for delivery of each of the component elements in the blueprint. Increasingly, companies are outsourcing noncore activities to specialist suppliers which allows them to focus on high value-adding activities within the firm's core competencies.[17] IBM employs the term *componentization* to describe the deconstruction (or unbundling) of a company's activities and subsequent reconstruction into *value nets* (as opposed to a value chain) in which value is created by businesses and their suppliers, buyers, and partners by combining and enhancing the component services collectively provided by participants.[18] "Businesses," argue Luba Cherbakov and her colleagues at IBM, "should view themselves as a federation of capabilities that collaborate with other enterprises within a business ecosystem."[19]

THE CUSTOMER AS CO-PRODUCER

Blueprinting helps to specify the role of customers in service delivery and to identify the extent of contact between them and service providers. Blueprinting also clarifies whether the customer's role in a given service process is primarily that of passive recipient or entails active involvement in creating and producing the service.

Levels of Customer Participation

Customer participation refers to the actions and resources supplied by customers during service production and/or delivery, including mental, physical, and even emotional inputs.[20] Some degree of customer participation in service delivery is inevitable in people-processing services and in many other services involving real-time contact between customers and providers. However, as Mary Jo Bitner and her colleagues show, the extent of such participation varies widely and can be divided into three broad levels.[21]

LOW PARTICIPATION LEVEL. With a low participation level, employees and systems do all the work. Products tend to be standardized. Payment may be the only required customer input. In situations in which customers come to the service factory, all that is required is the customers' physical presence. Visiting a movie theater or taking a bus are such examples. In possession-processing services such as routine cleaning or maintenance, customers can remain entirely uninvolved with the process other than providing access to service providers and making payment.

MODERATE PARTICIPATION LEVEL. With a moderate participation level, customer inputs are required to assist the firm in creating and delivering service and in providing a degree of customization. These inputs may include provision of information, personal effort, or even physical possessions. When getting their hair washed and cut, customers must let the stylist know what they want and cooperate during the different steps in the process. If a client wants an accountant to prepare a tax return, she must first pull together information and physical documentation the accountant can use to prepare the return correctly and then be prepared to respond to any questions the latter may have.

HIGH PARTICIPATION LEVEL. With a high participation level, customers work actively with the provider to co-produce the service. Service cannot be created without the customer's active participation. In fact, if customers fail to assume this role effectively and don't perform certain mandatory production tasks, they will jeopardize the quality of the service outcome. Marriage counseling and some health-related services fall into this category, especially those related to improvement of the patient's physical condition, such as rehabilitation or weight loss, in which customers work under professional supervision. Successful delivery of many B2B services requires customers and providers to work closely together as members of a team, such as for management consulting and supply chain management services.

Reducing Service Failures Caused by Customers

Stephen Tax, Mark Colgate, and David Bowen found that customers cause about one-third of all service problems.[22] Recovering from instances of customer failure, they argue, is difficult—not least because customers and the company may have different views of what caused the problem. Instead, they recommend that firms focus on preventing customer failures by collection data on problem occurrence, analyzing the root causes, and establishing preventive solutions (see Research Insights 8.2)

Customers as Partial Employees

Some researchers even argue that firms should view customers as "partial employees" who can influence the productivity and quality of service processes and outputs.[23] This perspective requires a change in management mindset, as Benjamin Schneider and David Bowen make clear:

> If you think of customers as partial employees, you begin to think very differently about what you hope customers will bring to the service encounter. Now they must bring not only expectations and needs but also relevant service production competencies that will enable them to fill the role of partial employees. The service management challenge deepens accordingly.[24]

RESEARCH INSIGHTS 8.2

A THREE-STEP APPROACH TO PREVENTING CUSTOMER FAILURES

Fail-safe methods (or poka-yokes) need to be designed not only for employees but also for customers, especially in services in which the latter participate actively in the creation and delivery processes. A good way is to employ the following three-step approach to prevent customer-generated failures.

1. Systematically collect information on the most common failure points.
2. Identify their root causes. It is important to note that an employee's explanation may not be the true cause. Instead, the cause must be investigated from the customer's point of view. Human causes of customer failure include lack of needed skills, failure to understand their role, and insufficient preparation. Shortcomings in processes often involve excessive complexity and lack of clarity. Other causes may include weaknesses in design of the servicescape and self-service technology (e.g., "un-friendly" user machines and websites).
3. Create strategies to prevent the failures identified. The five strategies listed below may need to be combined for maximum effectiveness.
   a. Redesign processes (e.g., redesign customers' role as well as processes). For example, customer identification with cards and PINs at ATMs could be replaced using biometric identification (e.g., retina reading combined with voice recognition) and thereby designing lost card or forgotten PIN problems out of the process and increasing customer convenience.
   b. Use technology. For example, hospitals can use automated systems that send short text messages or emails to patients to confirm and remind them of their appointments and informs them how to reschedule an appointment if required.
   c. Manage customer behavior (e.g., remind customers when payment is due, reward them for avoiding failure).
   d. Encourage "customer citizenship" (e.g., customers help one another to prevent failure, like in weight-loss programs).
   e. Improve the servicescape. Many firms forget that customers need user-friendly directional signs to help them find their way around, failing which they might become very frustrated.

Helping customers to avoid failure can become a source of competitive advantage, especially when companies increasingly deploy self-service technologies.

Source: Stephen S. Tax, Mark Colgate, and David E. Bowen, "How to Prevent Customers from Failing," *MIT Sloan Management Review*, 47, Spring 2006, 30–38.

Managing customers effectively as partial employees is another way to enhance customer performance in service processes and to reduce customer-induced service failures. This task requires using the same human resource strategy as managing a firm's paid employees and should follow these steps:

1. Effective human resource management starts with *recruitment and selection*. The same approach should hold true for "partial employees." So if co-production requires specific skills, firms should target their marketing efforts to recruit new customers who have the competency to perform the necessary tasks.[25] (Many colleges do just this in their student selection process!)
2. Conduct a "*job analysis*" of customers' present roles in the business and compare it against the roles that the firm would like them to play. Determine if customers are aware of how they are expected to perform and have the skills needed to perform as required.
3. Next come *education and training*, especially if the job analysis identified significant misalignment of customers' role perceptions. The more work customers are expected to do, the greater their need for information about how to perform for best results. The necessary education can be provided in many different

FIGURE 8.7 Tourists Appreciate Easy-to-Understand Instructions When Traveling Abroad

ways. Advertising for new services often contains significant educational content, and brochures and posted instructions are two widely used approaches. Automated machines often contain user-friendly operating instructions (Figure 8.7). Many websites include an FAQ (frequently asked questions) section. eBay's website provides detailed instructions for getting started, including how to submit an item for auction and how to bid for items you might want to buy.

Benjamin Schneider and David Bowen recommend providing a realistic service preview in advance of service delivery so that customers have a clear picture of the role they're expected to play in co-production.[26] For example, a company might show a video presentation to help customers understand their role in the service encounter. Think of videos shown to tourists before adventure tours to help customers understand what they are about to experience and how they should cooperate to help make things go smoothly and safely.

In many businesses, customers look to employees for advice and assistance and are frustrated if they can't obtain it. Service providers, ranging from sales assistants and customer service representatives to flight attendants and nurses, must be trained to "educate" customers on how to do their part of service delivery. As a last resort, people may turn to other customers for help. Think about your own experiences in unfamiliar surroundings when you were grateful for the friendly advice or assistance provided by a fellow customer. And you've probably reached out yourself to assist someone who seemed to be having difficulties in a service setting where you already knew the ropes.

4. *Motivate* customers by ensuring that they will be rewarded for performing well (e.g., satisfaction from better quality and more customized output, enjoyment of participating in the actual *process*, a belief that their own productivity speeds the *process* and keeps costs down).[27]
5. *Appraise* customers' performance regularly. If it is unsatisfactory, improve customer education and training and/or seek to change their roles and the service processes in which they are involved.
6. When a relationship is not working out, *ending* it remains an option of last resort. Physicians have a legal and ethical duty to help their patients, but the relationship will succeed only if it is mutually cooperative. Sooner or later, most doctors encounter a patient so abusive, noncompliant (in terms of following a prescribed treatment), dishonest, or troublesome that the physician simply has to ask that individual to seek care elsewhere.[28] Of course, "terminating"

customers has to be done nicely (see the section on "jaycustomers" in Chapter 13). Having to terminate customer relationships may indicate problems in the recruitment process that needs to be addressed.

SELF-SERVICE TECHNOLOGIES

The ultimate form of involvement in service production is for customers to undertake a specific activity, using facilities or systems provided by the service supplier. In effect, the customer's time and effort replaces that of a service employee. In the case of telephone and Internet-based service, customers even provide their own terminals.

Consumers are faced with an array of self-service technologies (SSTs) that allow them to produce a service independent of direct service employee involvement.[29] SSTs include automated banking terminals, self-service scanning at supermarket checkouts, self-service gasoline pumps, automated telephone systems such as phone banking, automated hotel checkout, and numerous Internet-based services.

Information-based services lend themselves particularly well to the use of SSTs and include not only such supplementary services as getting information, placing orders and reservations, and making payment, but also delivery of core products in fields such as banking, research, entertainment, and self-paced education. Even the consultation and sales process has been transformed to self-service with the use of electronic recommendation agents,[30] and recent academic research suggest ways to make them more effective (Research Insights 8.3). Many companies have developed strate-

RESEARCH INSIGHTS 8.3

MAKING ELECTRONIC RECOMMENDATION AGENTS MORE EFFECTIVE

Consumers often face a bewildering array of choices when purchasing goods and services from online vendors. One way in which "e-tailers" try to assist consumers is to offer electronic recommendation agents as part of their service. Recommendation agents are low-cost "virtual salespeople" designed to help customers make their selections among large numbers of competing offerings by generating rank-ordered alternative lists based on consumer preferences. However, research by Lerzan Aksoy for her doctoral dissertation showed that many existing recommendation agents rank options in different ways than the customers they are designed to help. First, they weight product attributes differently from customers; second, they may use alternative decision strategies that do not match the simple rules of thumb used by customers.

The research simulated selection of a cellular phone from among 32 alternatives, described on a website as each having different features relating to price, weight, talk time, and standby time. The study results demonstrated that it helps consumers to use a recommendation agent that thinks like them, either in terms of attribute weights or decision strategies. When the ways in which agents work are completely dissimilar, then consumers may be no better off—and sometimes even worse served—than if they simply used a randomly ordered list of options. Even though the subjects in this research tended to defer to the agent's recommendations, those who felt it had a dissimilar decision strategy and dissimilar attribute weights from their own were less likely to come back to the website, recommend it to friends, or believe that the site had met their expectations well.

In conclusion, to make recommendation agents add value to the customer and enhance sales and repeat business, firms need to closely understand their customers' decision-making strategies, attributes, and attribute weightings (refer back to Chapter 2 on consumer decision making, and Chapter 3 on determinant attributes).

Source: Lerzan Aksoy, Paul N. Bloom, Nicholas H. Lurie, and Bruce Cooil, "Should Recommendation Agents Think Like People?" Journal of Service Research, 8 (May 2006): 297–315. Copyright © 2006 Sage Publications, Inc. Used with permission.

gies designed to encourage customers to undertake self-service through the Internet. They hope to divert customers from using more expensive alternatives such as direct contact with employees, use of intermediaries such as brokers and travel agents, or voice-to-voice telephony.

Nevertheless, not all customers take advantage of SSTs. Matthew Meuter and his colleagues observe: "For many firms, often the challenge is not managing the technology but rather getting consumers to try the technology."[31]

Psychological Factors in Customer Self-Service

The logic of self-service historically relied on an economic rationale, emphasizing the productivity gains and cost savings that result when customers take over work previously performed by employees. In many instances, a portion of the resulting savings is shared with customers in the form of lower prices as an inducement for them to change their behavior.

Given the significant investment in time and money required for firms to design, implement, and manage SSTs, it's critical for service marketers to understand how consumers decide between using an SST option and relying on a human provider. Firms need to recognize that SSTs present both advantages and disadvantages for their customers. In addition to benefiting from time and cost savings, flexibility, convenience of location, greater control over service delivery, and a higher perceived level of customization, customers may also derive fun, enjoyment, and even spontaneous delight from SST usage.[32] However, there's evidence that some consumers feel uncomfortable using SSTs and see the introduction of SSTs into the service encounters as something of a threat, causing anxiety and stress.[33]

Research by James Curran, Matthew Meuter, and Carol Surprenant found that multiple attitudes drive customer intentions to use a specific SST, including overall attitudes toward related service technologies, global attitudes toward the specific service firm, and attitudes toward its employees.[34] Also, some consumers view service encounters as social experiences and prefer to deal with people.

What Aspects of SSTs Please or Annoy Customers?

Research suggests that customers both love and hate SSTs.[35] They love SSTs when they bail them out of difficult situations, often because SST machines are conveniently located and accessible 24/7. And of course, a website is as close as the nearest computer, making this option much more accessible than the company's physical sites. Customers also love SSTs when they perform better than the alternative of being served by a service employee, enabling users to get detailed information and complete transactions faster than they could through face-to-face or telephone contact. Experienced travelers rely on SSTs to save time and effort at airports, rental car facilities, and hotels. As a *Wall Street Journal* article summarized the trend, "Have A Pleasant Trip: Eliminate Human Contact."[36] Success at the customer interface requires an understanding of what target customers want from an interaction. Sometimes a well-designed SST can deliver better service than a human. Said one customer about the experience of purchasing convenience store items from a new model of automated vending machine, "A guy in the store can make a mistake or give you a hard time, but not the machine. I definitely prefer the machine."[37] In short, many customers are still in awe of technology and what it can do for them—when it works well and especially when customers have to use them frequently.

However, customers hate SSTs when they fail. Users get angry when they find that machines are out of service, their PINs are not accepted, websites are down, or tracking numbers do not work. Even when SSTs do work, customers are frustrated by poorly designed technologies that make service processes difficult to understand and use. A common complaint is difficulty in navigating one's way around a website or completing online registrations and forms that keep rejecting their entries.

Users also get frustrated when they themselves mess up, due to such errors as forgetting their passwords, failing to provide information as requested, or simply hitting the wrong buttons. Self-service logically implies that customers can cause their own dissatisfaction. However, even when it is the customers' own fault, they may still blame the service provider for not providing a simpler and more user-friendly system and then, on the next occasion, revert to the traditional human-based system.[38]

Designing a website to be virtually failure proof is no easy task and can be very expensive, but it is through such investments that companies create loyal users and active word-of-mouth. Best Practice in Action 8.1 describes the emphasis on user-friendliness of TLContact's CarePages service (Note: this innovative company is profiled in-depth in Case 16 on page 586).

BEST PRACTICE IN ACTION 8.1

TLContact Creates an Exceptional User Experience with Its CarePages Service

When his sister Sharon's five-day-old baby underwent surgery at the University of Michigan Medical Center in early 1998 to correct a life-threatening heart defect, Mark Day was more than a thousand miles away at Stanford, studying for a PhD in engineering. Feeling isolated, knowing nothing about the heart, and wanting to do something useful, Mark turned for medical information to the Internet, which was just beginning to hit its stride. Within a few weeks, he had created a simple website that family and friends could access. He edited the information he had gathered and loaded it on the site, together with bulletins on Matthew's condition and how the baby was responding to treatment. "It was a very simple site," Mark declared later. "If I had paid somebody else to do it for me, it probably wouldn't have cost more than a few hundred dollars." To minimize the need for emailing, Mark added a bulletin board so that people could send messages to Sharon and her husband, Eric.

To everyone's surprise, the site proved exceptionally popular. News spread by word-of-mouth and the site recorded hundreds of daily visitors, with more than 200 different people leaving messages for the family. People who confessed they had never before used the Internet found a way to access the site, follow baby Matthew's progress, and send messages.

Two years and three operations later, Matthew was a happy healthy toddler. His parents, Eric and Sharon Langshur, decided to create a company, TLContact.com, to commercialize Mark's concept as a service for patients and their families. They invited Mark to join the company as chief technology officer. To ensure quality control and retain intellectual capital, Mark decided to build the necessary software systems in-house, rather than subcontracting the task to outside vendors. He hired a skilled technical team, including programmers and graphic designers.

Recognizing that TLC's patient sites, known as CarePages, would be accessed by a wide array of individuals, many of whom would be under stress and even having their first experience of using the Internet, Mark and his team placed a premium on ease of use. He commented: "It's very difficult to create a piece of software that's really user friendly. It takes an incredible amount of skill, effort, and time to develop something that's usable, functional, and scalable—meaning that it can be expanded and built upon without failing." The total cost of creating the initial functioning website was close to half a million dollars.

As the company grew, continued investments were made to expand the functionality of the service for patients, visitors, and sponsoring hospitals; to eliminate any problems that users had reported; and to further improve user friendliness. Enhancements included an option for user feedback, addition of an email notification tool to announce updated news on a CarePage, and the ability to access CarePages through a hospital's own website. Receiving feedback that users encountered problems when they mistyped a CarePage name and failed to gain access, TLC added software logic to fix common mistakes, thereby reducing the volume of customer service inquiries. By 2006, TLC had turned the corner financially and was growing rapidly. Heartwarming tributes from satisfied users were pouring in. But work continued to enhance the CarePage experience, with software changes and improvements made every six to eight weeks.

Source: Christopher Lovelock, "CarePages.com (A)" 2007 (case reproduced on page 586); http://www.carepages.com, accessed April 26, 2009.

A key problem with SSTs is that so few of them incorporate service recovery systems. In too many instances, when the process fails, there is no simple way to recover on the spot. Typically, customers are forced to telephone or make a personal visit to resolve the problem, which may be exactly what they were trying to avoid in the first place. Mary Jo Bitner suggests that managers should put their firms' SSTs to the test by asking the following basic questions:[39]

FIGURE 8.8 Fail-Safe Measures Are Crucial for Self-Service Technologies to Be Adopted by Customers

- *Does the SST work reliably?* Firms must ensure that SSTs work as dependably as promised and that the design is user friendly for customers. Southwest Airlines' online ticketing services have set a high standard for simplicity and reliability. It boasts the highest percentage of online ticket sales of any airline—clear evidence of customer acceptance.
- *Is the SST better than the interpersonal alternative?* If it doesn't save time or provide ease of access, cost savings, or some other benefit, then customers will continue to use familiar conventional processes. Amazon.com's success reflects its efforts to create a highly personalized, efficient alternative to visiting a retail store.
- *If it fails, what systems are in place to recover?* It's critical for firms to provide systems, structures, and recovery technologies that will enable prompt service recovery when things go wrong (Figure 8.8). Most banks display a phone number at their ATMs, giving customers direct access to a 24-hour customer service center where they can talk to a "real person" if they have questions or run into difficulties. Supermarkets with self-service checkout lanes usually assign one employee to monitor the lanes; this practice combines security with customer assistance. In telephone-based service systems, well-designed voicemail menus include an option for customers to reach a customer service representative.

Managing Customers' Reluctance to Change

Increasing the customers' participation level in a service process or shifting the process entirely to self-service using SSTs requires the firm to change customer behavior—often a difficult task as customers resent being forced to use SST.[40] Service Perspective 8.3 identifies ways of addressing customer resistance to change, particularly when the innovation is a radical one. Once the nature of the changes has been decided, marketing communications can help prepare customers for the change, explaining the rationale, the benefits, and what customers will need to do differently in the future.

CONCLUSION

In this chapter, we emphasized the importance of designing and managing service processes—central in creating the service product and significantly shaping the customer experience. We covered in-depth blueprinting as a powerful tool to understand, document, analyze, and improve service processes. Blueprinting helps to identify and reduce service fail points and provides important insights for service process redesign.

An important part of process design is to define the roles customers should play in the production of services. Their level of desired participation needs to be determined, and customers need to be motivated and taught to play their part in the service delivery to ensure customer satisfaction and firm productivity.

SERVICE PERSPECTIVE 8.3

MANAGING CUSTOMERS' RELUCTANCE TO CHANGE

Customer resistance to changes in familiar processes and long-established behavior patterns can thwart attempts to improve productivity and even quality. Failure to examine proposed changes from the customer's perspective may spur resistance. The following six steps can help smooth the path of change.

1. **Develop customer trust.** It's more difficult to introduce productivity-related changes when people are basically distrustful of the initiator, as they often are in the case of large, seemingly impersonal institutions. Customers' willingness to accept change may be closely related to the degree of goodwill they bear toward the organization.
2. **Understand customers' habits and expectations.** People often get into a routine of using a particular service, with certain steps taken in a specific sequence. In effect, they have their own individual service script or flowchart in mind. Innovations that disrupt ingrained routines are likely to face resistance unless consumers are carefully briefed as to what changes to expect.
3. **Pretest new procedures and equipment.** To determine probable customer response to new procedures and equipment, marketing researchers can employ concept and laboratory testing and/or field testing. If service personnel are going to be replaced by automatic equipment, it's essential to create designs that customers of almost all types and backgrounds will find easy to use. Even the phrasing of instructions needs careful thought. Ambiguous, complex, or authoritarian instructions may discourage customers with poor reading skills as well as those used to personal courtesies from the service personnel whom the machine replaces.
4. **Publicize the benefits.** Introduction of self-service equipment or procedures requires consumers to perform part of the task themselves. Although this additional "work" may be associated with such benefits as extended service hours, time savings, and (in some instances) monetary savings, these benefits are not necessarily obvious—they have to be promoted. Useful strategies may include use of mass media advertising, on-site posters and signage, and personal communications to inform people of the innovation, arouse their interest in it, and clarify the specific benefits to customers of changing their behavior and using new delivery systems.
5. **Teach customers to use innovations and promote trial.** Assigning service personnel to demonstrate new equipment and answer questions—providing reassurance as well as educational assistance—is a key element in gaining acceptance of new procedures and technology. The costs of such demonstration programs can be spread across multiple outlets by moving staff members from one site to another if the innovation is rolled out sequentially across the various locations. For Web-based innovations, it's important to provide access to email, chat, or even telephone-based assistance. Promotional incentives such as price discounts, loyalty points, or lucky draws may also serve to stimulate initial trial. Once customers have tried a self-service option (particularly an electronically based one) and find that it works well, they will be more likely to use it regularly in the future.
6. **Monitor performance and continue to seek improvements.** Introducing quality and productivity improvements is an ongoing process, especially for SSTs. If customers are displeased by new procedures, they may revert to their previous behavior, so it's important to monitor utilization, frequency of transaction failures (and their fail points), and customer complaints over time. Service managers must work hard to continuously improve SSTs and keep up the momentum so that SSTs can achieve their full potential and are not allowed to flag and become white elephants.

Chapter Summary

LO1 Flowcharting is a technique for displaying the nature and sequence of the different steps in delivering a service to the customer. It is a simple way to visualize the total customer service experience.

LO2 Blueprinting is a more detailed form of flowcharting, allowing detailed design and redesign of customer service processes. A blueprint typically shows:

- The front-stage activities that map the overall customer experience, the desired inputs and outputs, and the sequence in which delivery of that output should take place. Specific times can be set for the completion of each task and the acceptable wait between each customer activity.
- The back-stage activities that must be performed to support a particular front-stage step.
- The required supplies that need to be made available for both front- and back-stage steps.
- The information needed at each point in the step, typically provided by information systems.
- Service standards should be established for each activity, reflecting customer expectations.

LO3 A good blueprint identifies fail points where things can go wrong. Fail-safe methods, also called poka-yokes, can then be designed to prevent and/or recover such failures for both employees and customers. A three-step approach can be used to develop poka-yokes:

1. Collect information on the most common fail points
2. Identify the root causes of those failures.
3. Create strategies to prevent the failures that have been identified.

LO4 Changes in technology, customer needs, and service offerings require customer service processes to be redesigned periodically. Such service process redesign efforts aim to:

1. Increase customer satisfaction.
2. Improve productivity.
3. Reduce number of service failures.
4. Reduce cycle time.

There are five types of service process redesign. They are:

1. Elimination of nonvalue-adding steps (streamlining processes).
2. Shifting to self-service.
3. Delivering direct service (services delivered to the customer's location).
4. Bundling services (combining multiple services into a package).
5. Redesigning the physical aspects of service processes (service environment and equipment).

LO5 Customers often are involved in service processes as co-producers and therefore can be thought of as "partial employees." Their performance affects the quality and productivity of output. Therefore, service firms need to educate and train customers so that they have the skills and motivation needed to perform their tasks well.

LO6 The ultimate form of customer involvement is self-service. Most people welcome SSTs that offer more convenience (i.e., more locations, 24/7 availability, faster service), better control and information, customization, and even enjoyment. However, poorly designed technology and inadequate education in how to use SSTs can cause customers to reject SSTs.

Three basic questions can be used to assess the potential for success of an SST:

- Does the SST work reliably?
- Is the SST better for customers compared to other service delivery alternatives?
- If the SST fails, are there systems in place to recover the service?

LO7 Increasing the customers' participation level in a service process or shifting the process entirely to self-service requires the firm to change customer behavior. There are six steps to guide this process and reduce customer reluctance to change:

- Develop customer trust.
- Understand customers' habits and expectations.
- Pretest new procedures and equipment.
- Publicize the benefits of changes.
- Teach customers to use innovations and promote trial.
- Monitor performance and continue to seek improvements.

Review Questions

1. How does flowcharting help us to understand the difference between people-, possession-, mental- and information-processing services?
2. How does blueprinting help in designing, managing, and redesigning service processes?
3. How can fail-safe procedures be used to reduce service failures?
4. How does the creation and evaluation of a service blueprint help managers understand the role of time in service delivery?
5. Why is periodic process redesign necessary, and what are the main types of service process redesign?
6. Why does the customer's role as a co-producer need to be designed into service processes? What are the implications of considering customers as partial employees?
7. Explain what factors make customers like and dislike self-service technologies (SSTs).
8. How can you test whether a SST has the potential to be successful, and what can a firm do to increase its chances of customer adoption?

Application Exercises

1. Review the blueprint of the restaurant visit in Figure 8.4. Identify several possible "OTSUs" ("opportunity to screw up") for each step in the front-stage process. Consider possible causes underlying each potential failure and suggest ways to eliminate or minimize these problems.
2. Prepare a blueprint for a service with which you are familiar. On completion, consider (a) the tangible cues or indicators of quality from the customers perspective, considering the line of visibility; (b) whether all steps in the process are necessary; (c) the extent to which standardization is possible and advisable throughout the process; (d) the location of potential fail points and how they could be designed out of the process and what service recovery procedures could be introduced; and (e) the potential measures of process performance.
3. Think about what happens in a doctor's office when a patient comes for a physical examination. How much participation is needed from the patient in order for the process to work smoothly? If a patient refuses to cooperate, how can that affect the process? What can the doctor do in advance to ensure the patient cooperates in the delivery of the process?
4. Observe supermarket shoppers who use self-service checkout lanes, and compare them to those who use the services of a checker. What differences do you observe? How many of those conducting self-service scanning appear to run into difficulties, and how do they resolve their problems?
5. Identify three situations in which you use self-service delivery. For each situation, what is your motivation for using self-service delivery, rather than having service personnel do it for you?
6. What actions could a bank take to encourage more customers to bank by phone, mail, Internet, or through ATMs rather than visiting a branch?
7. Identify one website that is exceptionally user friendly and another that is not. What are the factors that make for a satisfying user experience in the first instance and a frustrating one in the second? Specify recommendations for improvements in the second website.

Endnotes

1. Kah Hin Chai, Jochen Wirtz, and Robert Johnston, "Using Technology to Revolutionize the Library Experience of Singaporean Readers," in Christopher Lovelock, Jochen Wirtz, and Patricia Chew, eds. *Essentials of Services Marketing*. Singapore: Prentice Hall, 2009, 534–536, http://www.nlb.gov.sg, accessed June 6, 2009.
2. See G. Lynn Shostack, "Understanding Services through Blueprinting," in T. Schwartz et al., eds. *Advances in Services Marketing and Management*. Greenwich, CT: JAI Press, 1992, 75–90.
3. G. Lynn Shostack, "Designing Services That Deliver," *Harvard Business Review*, 62, January–February 1984, 133–139.
4. Jane Kingman-Brundage, "The ABCs of Service System Blueprinting," in M. J. Bitner and L. A. Crosby, eds. *Designing a Winning Service Strategy*. Chicago: American Marketing Association, 1989. For a recent method developed for blueprinting service experiences, see Lia Patrício, Raymond P. Fisk, and João Falcãe Cunha, "Designing Multi-Interface Service Experiences: The Service

Experience Blueprint," *Journal of Service Research*, 10, No. 4, 2008, 318–334.

5. David Maister, now president of Maister Associates, coined the term OTSU while teaching at Harvard Business School in the 1980s.
6. This section is based in part on Richard B. Chase and Douglas M. Stewart, "Make Your Service Fail-Safe," *Sloan Management Review*, 35, Spring 1994, 35–44.
7. This section was adapted from Jochen Wirtz and Monica Tomlin, "Institutionalizing Customer-driven Learning through Fully Integrated Customer Feedback Systems," *Managing Service Quality*, 10, No. 4, 2000, 205–215.
8. See for example, Eric J. Arnould and Linda L. Price, "River Magic: Extraordinary Experience and the Extended Service Encounter," *Journal of Consumer Research*, 20, June 1993, 24–25; Eric J. Arnould and Linda L. Price, "Collaring the Cheshire Cat: Studying Customers' Services Experience Through Metaphors," *The Service Industries Journal*, 16, October 1996, 421–442; and Nick Johns and Phil Tyas, "Customer Perceptions of Service Operations: Gestalt, Incident or Mythology?" *The Service Industries Journal*, 17, July 1997, 474–488.
9. "How Marriott Makes a Great First Impression," *The Service Edge*, 6, May 1993, 5.
10. Lisa Bannon, "Plastic Surgeons Are Told to Pay More Attention to Appearances," *Wall Street Journal*, March 15, 1997, B1.
11. David E. Hansen and Peter J. Danaher, "Inconsistent Performance during the Service Encounter: What's a Good Start Worth?" *Journal of Service Research*, 1, Feburary 1999, 227–235; Richard B. Chase and Sriram Dasu, "Want to Perfect Your Company's Service? Use Behavioral Science," *Harvard Business Review*, 79, June 2001, 79–84.
12. Jochen Wirtz and Monica Tomlin, "Institutionalizing Customer-driven Learning Through Fully Integrated Customer Feedback Systems," *Managing Service Quality*, 10, No. 4, 2000, 205–215.
13. Mitchell T. Rabkin, MD, cited in Christopher H. Lovelock, *Product Plus*. New York: McGraw-Hill, 1994, 354–355.
14. Thomas Mucha, "The Payoff for Trying Harder," *Business 2.0*, July 2002, 84–86.
15. See, for example, Michael Hammer and James Champy, *Reengineering the Corporation*. New York: Harper Business, 1993.
16. This section is partially based on Leonard L. Berry and Sandra K. Lampo, "Teaching an Old Service New Tricks – The Promise of Service Redesign," *Journal of Service Research*, 2, No. 3, 2000, 265–275. Berry and Lampo identified the five service redesign concepts: self-service, direct service, pre-service, bundled service, and physical service. We expanded some of these concepts in this section to embrace more of the productivity enhancing aspects of process redesign.
17. Jochen Wirtz and Michael Ehret, "Creative Restruction—How Business Services Drive Economic Evolution," *European Business Review*, 21, No. 4, 2009, 380–394.
18. D. Bovet and J. Martha, *Breaking the Supply Chain to Unlock Hidden Profits*. New York: John Wiley& Sons, 2000.
19. L. Cherbakov, G. Galambos, R. Harishankar, S. Kalyana, and G. Rackham, "Impact of Service Orientation at the Business Level," *IBM Systems Journal*, 44, No. 4, 2005, 653–668.
20. Amy Risch Rodie and Susan Schultz Klein, "Customer Participation in Services Production and Delivery," in T. A. Schwartz and D. Iacobucci, eds. *Handbook of Service Marketing and Management*. Thousand Oaks, CA: Sage Publications, 2000, 111–125.
21. Mary Jo Bitner, William T. Faranda, Amy R. Hubbert, and Valarie A. Zeithaml, "Customer Contributions and Roles in Service Delivery," *International Journal of Service Industry Management*, 8, No. 3, 1997, 193–205.
22. Stephen S. Tax, Mark Colgate, and David E. Bowen, "How to Prevent Customers from Failing," *MIT Sloan Management Review*, 47, Spring 2006, 30–38.
23. David E. Bowen, "Managing Customers as Human Resources in Service Organizations," *Human Resources Management*, 25, No. 3, 1986, 371–383.
24. Benjamin Schneider and David E. Bowen, *Winning the Service Game*. Boston: Harvard Business School Press, 1995, 85.
25. Bonnie Farber Canziani, "Leveraging Customer Competency in Service Firms," *International Journal of Service Industry Management*, 8, No. 1, 1997, 5–25.
26. Benjamin Schneider and David E. Bowen, *Winning the Service Game*. Boston: Harvard Business School Press, 1995, 92.
27. See also Noah J. Goldstein, Robert B. Cialdini, and Vladas Griskevicius, "A Room With a Viewpoint: Using Social Norms to Motivate Environmental Conservation in Hotels," *Journal of Consumer Research*, 35, No. 3, 2008, 472–482.
28. Kim Painter, "Cutting Ties to Vexing Patients," *USA Today*, January 14, 2003, 8D.
29. Matthew L. Meuter, Amy L. Ostrom, Robert I. Roundtree, and Mary Jo Bitner, "Self-Service Technologies: Understanding Customer Satisfaction with Technology-Based Service Encounters," *Journal of Marketing*, 64, July 2000, 50–64.
30. Gerard Haübl and Kyle B. Murray, "Preference Construction and Persistence in Digital Marketplaces: The Role of Electronic Recommendation Agents," *Journal of Consumer Psychology*, 13, No. 1, 2003, 75–91; Lerzan Aksoy, Paul N. Bloom, Nicholas H. Lurie, and Bruce Cooil, "Should Recommendation Agents Think Like People?" *Journal of Service Research*, 8, May 2006, 297–315.
31. Matthew L. Meuter, Mary Jo Bitner, Amy L. Ostrom, and Stephen W. Brown, "Choosing Among Alternative Service Delivery Modes: An Investigation of Customer Trial of Self-Service Technologies," *Journal of Marketing*, 69, April 2005, 61–83.
32. Pratibha A. Dabholkar, "Consumer Evaluations of New Technology-Based Self-Service Options: An Investigation of Alternative Models of Service Quality," *International Journal of Research in Marketing*, 13, 1996, 29–51; Mary Jo. Bitner, Stephen W. Brown, and Matthew L. Meuter, "Technology Infusion in Service Encounters," *Journal of the Academy of Marketing Science*, 28, No. 1, 2000, 138–149; Pratibha A. Dabholkar, L. Michelle Bobbitt, and Eun-Ju Lee, "Understanding Consumer Motivation and Behavior Related to Self-Scanning in Retailing," *International Journal of Service Industry Management* 14, No. 1, 2003, 59–95.

33. David G. Mick and Susan Fournier, "Paradoxes of Technology: Consumer Cognizance, Emotions, and Coping Strategies," *Journal of Consumer Research*, 25, September 1998, 123–143.
34. James M. Curran, Matthew L. Meuter, and Carol G. Surprenant, "Intentions to Use Self-Service Technologies: A Confluence of Multiple Attitudes," *Journal of Service Research*, 5, February 2003, 209–224.
35. Matthew L. Meuter, Amy L. Ostrom, Robert I. Roundtree, and Mary Jo Bitner, "Self-Service Technologies: Understanding Customer Satisfaction with Technology-Based Service Encounters," *Journal of Marketing*, 64, July 2000, 50–64; Mary Jo Bitner, "Self-Service Technologies: What Do Customers Expect?" *Marketing Management*, Spring 2001, 10–11.
36. Kortney Stringer, "Have a Pleasant Trip: Eliminate All Human Contact," *Wall Street Journal*, October 31, 2002, p. 5.
37. Jeffrey F. Rayport and Bernard J. Jaworski, "Best Face Forward," *Harvard Business Review*, 82, December 2004, 47–58.
38. Neeli Bendapudi and Robert P. Leone, "Psychological Implications of Customer Participation in Co-Production," *Journal of Marketing*, 67, January 2003, 14–28.
39. Mary Jo Bitner, "Self-Service Technologies: What Do Customers Expect?" *Marketing Management*, 10, Spring 2001, 10–11.
40. Machiel J. Reinders, Pratibha A. Dabholkar, and Ruud T. Frambach, "Consequences of Forcing Consumers to Use Technology-Based Self-Service," *Journal of Service Research*, 11, No. 2, 2008, 107–123.

CHAPTER 9

Balancing Demand and Productive Capacity

Balancing the supply and demand sides of a service industry is not easy, and whether a manager does it well or not makes all the difference.

EARL SASSER

They also serve who only stand and wait.

JOHN MILTON

LEARNING OBJECTIVES (LOs)

By the end of this chapter, the reader should be able to:

LO1 Understand what is meant by "capacity" in a service context.

LO2 Know the different demand-supply situations that fixed capacity firms may face.

LO3 Use capacity management techniques to match variations in demand.

LO4 Recognize that demand varies by segment, and predict segment-specific variations in demand and their causes.

LO5 Be familiar with the five basic ways to manage demand.

LO6 Use marketing mix elements to smooth out fluctuations in demand.

LO7 Know how to inventory demand through waiting lines and queuing systems.

LO8 Understand how customers perceive waits and how to make waiting less burdensome for them.

LO9 Know how to inventory demand through reservations systems.

LO10 Be familiar with the data requirements for designing effective strategies to manage demand and capacity.

A Park for All Seasons?

Established in 2003, Cairngorms National Park is the largest in Britain. It covers a vast area of nearly 1,500 square miles of northeast Scotland. Some 16,000 people live and work in the towns and villages within the park. Major centers such as Aviemore are closely associated with skiing, but to ensure that the park attracts tourists year-round, other activities have been developed. With tourism accounting for some 80 percent of the local economy and the park attracting 1.4 million visitors a year, walking, fishing, shooting, and stalking have all become important outdoor activities for the area. Climbing, school trips, mountain biking, canoeing and kayaking, sightseeing, and photography are now commonplace tourism activities, none of which relies on the snow.

There has been investment in tourism infrastructure and the development and maintenance of the park. In addition, the park management has actively encouraged greater exploration, longer stays, increased spending, responsible behavior, and repeat visits. One of the major challenges has been to try to spread tourism opportunities across the year. Disruption and congestion in peak times has a negative effect for tourists, locals, and the natural environment; furthermore, it focuses income from tourism to a limited part of the year.

The long-term sustainability of the park is reliant on supporting a diverse economy. Tourism is worth some $280 million per year across the park and provides jobs for 5,000 people. In many respects, tourism is vital, but it needs to be sustainable despite the park's goal to increase tourism revenues by 50 percent by 2015. The only way in which this can be achieved without detrimentally affecting the park and its unique selling proposition is to restructure the tourism industry itself.

Sustainability is seen as one of the keys, but other incentives are under way. Strengthening awareness and spending on local crafts through better branding, providing support for business development, and the marketing of produce grown in the park are all prime examples. Collating parkwide information is problematic, but more recently vehicle counters, car park usage, visitor attraction numbers, and people counters have all been implemented to help keep track of visitor numbers. Another key initiative has been to encourage the development of events and festivals out of season.

FIGURE 9.1 Tourists Tend to Visit the Cairngorns in the Summer for Walking and the Winter for Skiing

Source: Cairngorms National Park Plan 2007, Cairngorms National Park Authority 2007 (http://www.cairngorms.co.uk).

FLUCTUATIONS IN DEMAND THREATEN PROFITABILITY

Fluctuating demand is a major challenge for many types of capacity-constrained service organizations, including airlines, restaurants, vacation resorts, courier services, consulting firms, theaters, and call centers. These demand fluctuations may range in frequency from as long as a season of the year as discussed in the opening vignette to as short as an hour, and they play havoc with efficient use of productive assets, thus eroding profitability. By working collaboratively with managers in operations and human resources, service marketers may be able to develop strategies to bring demand and capacity into balance in ways that create benefits for customers as well as improving financial returns for the business.

Defining Productive Capacity

What do we mean by productive capacity? The term refers to the resources or assets that a firm can employ to create goods and services. In a service context, productive capacity can take several forms:

1. *Physical facilities designed to contain customers* and used for delivering people-processing services or mental stimulus processing services. Examples include

medical clinics, hotels, passenger aircrafts, and college classrooms. The primary capacity constraint is likely to be defined in terms of such furnishings as beds, rooms, or seats. In some cases, for health or safety reasons, local regulations may set an upper limit to the number of people allowed in for health or safety reasons.

2. *Physical facilities designed for storing or processing goods* that either belong to customers or are being offered to them for sale. Examples include pipelines, warehouses, parking lots, and railroad freight wagons.
3. *Physical equipment used to process people, possessions, or information* may embrace a huge range of items and may be very situation specific—diagnostic equipment, airport security detectors, toll gates, bank ATMs, and "seats" in a call center are among the many items whose absence in sufficient numbers for a given level of demand can bring service to a crawl (or even a complete stop).
4. *Labor* is a key element of productive capacity in all high-contact services and many low-contact ones. Staffing levels for restaurant servers, and nurses and call center staff need to be sufficient to meet anticipated demand—otherwise customers are kept waiting or service is rushed. Professional services are especially dependent on highly skilled staff to create high value-added, information-based output. Abraham Lincoln captured it well when he remarked that "A lawyer's time and expertise are his stock in trade."
5. *Infrastructure.* Many organizations are dependent on access to sufficient capacity in the public or private infrastructure to be able to deliver quality service to their own customers. Capacity problems of this nature may include congested airways that lead to air traffic restrictions on flights, traffic jams on major highways, and power failures (or "brown outs" caused by reduced voltage).

Financial success in capacity-constrained businesses is, in large measure, a function of management's ability to use productive capacity—labor, equipment, and facilities—as efficiently and as profitably as possible. In practice, however, it's difficult to achieve this ideal all the time. Not only do demand levels vary, often randomly, but the time and effort required to process each person or thing may vary widely at any point in the process. In general, processing times for people are more variable than for objects or things, reflecting varying levels of preparedness ("I've lost my credit card"), argumentative versus cooperative personalities ("If you won't give me a table with a view, I'll have to ask for your supervisor"), and so forth. Furthermore, service tasks are not necessarily homogeneous. In both professional services and repair jobs, diagnosis and treatment times vary according to the nature of the customers' problems.

From Excess Demand to Excess Capacity

Most services are perishable and normally cannot be stockpiled for sale at a later date, posing a challenge for any capacity-constrained service that faces wide swings in demand. The problem is most acute for organizations that engage in physical processes such as people or possession processing, but it also affects labor-intensive, information-processing services that face cyclical shifts in demand. Accounting and tax preparation are cases in point.

For fixed capacity firms, the problem is a familiar one. "It's either feast or famine for us!" sighs the manager. "In peak periods, we're disappointing prospective customers by turning them away. And in low periods, our facilities are idle, our employees are standing around looking bored, and we're losing money." In other words, demand and supply are not in balance.

Effective use of productive capacity is one of the secrets of success in such businesses. The goal should not be to utilize staff, labor, equipment, and facilities as much as possible, but rather to use them as *productively* as possible. At the same time, the search for productivity must not be allowed to undermine service quality and degrade the customer experience.

At any given moment, a fixed-capacity service may face one of four conditions (see Figure 9.2):

- *Excess demand*—The level of demand exceeds maximum available capacity with the result that some customers are denied service and business is lost.

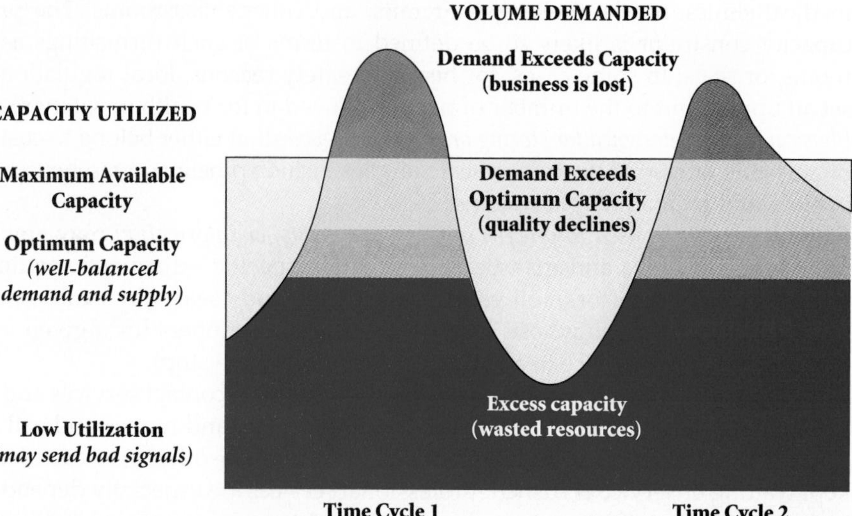

FIGURE 9.2 Implications of Variations in Demand Relative to Capacity

- *Demand exceeds optimum capacity*—No one is turned away, but conditions are crowded and customers are likely to perceive a deterioration in service quality and may feel dissatisfied.
- *Demand and supply are well balanced* at the level of optimum capacity. Staff and facilities are busy without being overworked and customers receive good service without delays.
- *Excess capacity*—Demand is below optimum capacity and productive resources are underutilized, resulting in low productivity. Low usage also poses a risk that customers may find the experience disappointing or have doubts about the viability of the service.

Sometimes optimum and maximum capacities are one and the same. At a live theater or sports performance, a full house is grand, since it stimulates the players and creates a sense of excitement and audience participation. The net result? A more satisfying experience for all. With most other services, however, you probably feel that you get better service if the facility is not operating at full capacity. The quality of restaurant service, for instance, often deteriorates when every table is occupied, because the staff is rushed and there is a greater likelihood of errors or delays. And if you are traveling alone in an aircraft with high-density seating, you tend to feel more comfortable if the seat next to you is empty. When repair and maintenance shops are fully scheduled, delays may result if there is no slack in the system to allow for unexpected problems in completing particular jobs.

There are two basic approaches to the problem of fluctuating demand. One is to adjust the level of capacity to meet variations in demand. This approach requires an understanding of what constitutes productive capacity and how it may be increased or decreased on an incremental basis. The second approach is to manage the level of demand, using marketing strategies to smooth out the peaks and fill in the valleys so as to generate a more consistent flow of requests for service. Many firms use a mix of both approaches.[1]

Measures of capacity utilization include: the number of hours (or percentage of total available time) that facilities, labor and equipment are productively employed in revenue operation, and the units or percentage of available space (e.g., seats, cubic freight capacity, telecommunications bandwidth) that is utilized in revenue operations. Human beings tend to be far more variable than equipment in their ability to sustain consistent levels of output over time. One tired or poorly trained employee staffing a single station in an assembly-line service operation like a cafeteria restaurant or a motor vehicle license bureau can slow the entire service to a crawl.

Many services, such as health care or repair and maintenance, involve multiple actions delivered sequentially. What this means is that a service organization's capacity to satisfy demand is constrained by one or more of its physical facilities, equipment, personnel, and the number and sequence of services provided. In a well-planned, well-managed service operation, the capacity of the facility, supporting equipment and service personnel will be in balance. Similarly, sequential operations will be designed to minimize the likelihood of bottlenecks at any point in the process.

MANAGING CAPACITY

Although service firms may encounter capacity limitations because of varying demand, there are a number of ways in which capacity can be adjusted to reduce the problem. Capacity can be stretched or shrunk, and the overall capacity can be adjusted to match demand.

Capacity Levels Can Sometimes Be Stretched or Shrunk

Some capacity is elastic in its ability to absorb extra demand. Here, the actual level of capacity remains unchanged, and more people are being served with the same level of capacity. For example, the normal capacity for a subway car may offer 40 seats and allow standing room for another 60 passengers with adequate handrail and floor space for all. Yet at rush hours perhaps up to 200 standees can be accommodated under sardine-like conditions. Similarly, the capacity of service personnel can be stretched and may be able to work at high levels of efficiency for short periods of time. However, staff would quickly tire and begin providing inferior service, if they had to work that fast all day long.

Another strategy for stretching capacity is to utilize the facilities for longer periods. For example, some banks extend their opening hours during weekdays and even open on weekends. Universities may offer evening classes, and weekend and summer semester programs.

Lastly, the average amount of time customers (or their possessions) spend in process may be reduced. Sometimes, this is achieved by minimizing slack time. For example, a restaurant can buzz tables, seat arriving diners and present menus fast, and the bill can be presented promptly to a group of diners relaxing at the table after a meal.[2] In other instances, it may be achieved by cutting back the level of service—say, offering a simpler menu at busy times of the day.

Adjusting Capacity to Match Demand

Unlike the previous option, this set of options involves tailoring the overall level of capacity to match variations in demand—a strategy that is also known as *chasing demand*. There are several actions that managers can take to adjust capacity as needed.[3] These actions start from the easiest to implement, to the more difficult.

- *Schedule downtime during periods of low demand.* To ensure that 100 percent of capacity is available during peak periods, maintenance, repair, and renovations should be conducted when demand is expected to be low. Employee vacations should be taken during such periods.
- *Cross-train employees.* Even when the service delivery system appears to be operating at full capacity, certain physical elements—and their attendant employees—may be underutilized. If employees can be cross-trained to perform a variety of tasks, they can be shifted to bottleneck points as needed, thereby increasing total system capacity. In supermarkets, for instance, the manager may call on stockers to operate cash registers when lines become too long. Likewise, during slow periods, the cashiers may be asked to help stock shelves.
- *Use part-time employees.* Many organizations hire extra workers during their busiest periods. Examples include postal workers and retail store associates during the Christmas season, extra staff for tax preparation service firms in the spring, and additional hotel employees during vacation periods and for major conventions.
- *Invite customers to perform self-service.* If the number of employees is limited, capacity can be increased by involving customers in co-production of certain tasks. One way to do this is by adding self-service technologies such as electronic kiosks at the airport for airline ticketing and check-in (Figure 9.3) or automated check-out stations at supermarkets.

FIGURE 9.3 Airlines Boost Check-in Capacity by Installing Self-Service Ticketing Machines at Airports

- *Ask customers to share.* Capacity can be stretched by asking customers to share a unit of capacity normally dedicated to one individual. For instance, at busy airports and train stations, where the supply of taxis is sometimes insufficient to meet demand, travelers going in the same direction may be given the option of sharing a ride at a reduced rate.
- *Create flexible capacity.* Sometimes, the problem lies not in the overall capacity but in the mix available to serve the needs of different market segments. One solution lies in designing physical facilities to be flexible. For example, the tables in a restaurant can be all two-seaters. When necessary, two tables can be combined to seat four, or three tables combined to seat six. In the airline context, an airline may have too few seats in economy even though there are empty seats in the business class cabin on a given flight. Boeing, facing stiff competition from Airbus, received what were described, tongue-in-cheek, as "outrageous demands" from prospective customers when it was designing its 777 airliner. The airlines wanted an aircraft in which galleys and lavatories could be relocated, plumbing and all, almost anywhere in the cabin within a matter of hours. Boeing gulped but solved this challenging problem. Airlines can rearrange the passenger cabin of the "Triple Seven" within hours, reconfiguring it with varying numbers of seats allocated among different classes.
- *Rent or share extra facilities and equipment.* To limit investment in fixed assets, a service business may be able to rent extra space or machines at peak times. Firms with complementary demand patterns may enter into formal sharing agreements.

ANALYZE PATTERNS OF DEMAND

Now let's look at the other side of the equation. In order to effectively manage demand for a particular service, managers need to understand that demand often differs by market segment.

Demand Varies by Market Segment

Random fluctuations usually are caused by factors beyond management's control. However, analysis will sometimes reveal that a predictable demand cycle for one segment is concealed within a broader, seemingly random pattern. This fact illustrates the importance of breaking down demand on a segment-by-segment basis. For instance, a repair and maintenance shop that services industrial electrical equipment may already know a certain proportion of its work consists of regularly scheduled contracts to perform preventive maintenance. The balance may come from "walk-in" business and emergency repairs. Although it might seem hard to predict or control the timing and volume of such work, further analysis might show that walk-in business was more prevalent on some days of the week than others and that emergency repairs were frequently requested following damage sustained during thunderstorms (which tend to be seasonal in nature and often forecast a day or two in advance). Understanding demand patterns allows the firm to schedule less preventive maintenance work on days with high anticipated demand of typically more profitable emergency repairs.

No strategy for smoothing demand is likely to succeed unless it is based on an understanding of why customers from a specific market segment choose to use the service when they do. It's difficult for hotels to convince business travelers to remain on Saturday nights since few executives do business over the weekend. Instead, hotel managers may do better to promote weekend use of their facilities for conferences or pleasure travel. Attempts to get commuters to shift their travel to off-peak periods will probably fail, since such travel is determined by people's employment hours. Instead, efforts should be directed at employers to persuade them to adopt flextime or staggered working hours. These firms recognize that no amount of price discounting is likely to develop business out of season. However, summer resort areas like Cape Cod may have good opportunities to build business during the "shoulder seasons" of spring and fall (which some consider the most attractive times to visit the Cape) by promoting different attractions—such as hiking, birdwatching, visiting museums, and looking for bargains in antique stores—and altering the mix and focus of services to target a different type of clientele.

Understanding Patterns of Demand

To understand the patterns of demand by segment, research should begin by getting some answers to a series of important questions about the patterns of demand and their underlying causes[4] (Table 9.1).

As you think about some of the seemingly "random" causes, consider how rain and cold affect the use of indoor and outdoor recreational or entertainment services. Then reflect on how heart attacks and births affect the demand for hospital services. Imagine what it is like to be a police officer, firefighter, or ambulance driver—you never know exactly where your next call will come from or what the nature of the emergency will be. Finally, consider the impact of natural disasters such as earthquakes, tornadoes, and hurricanes, not only on emergency services but also for disaster recovery specialists and insurance firms.

Most periodic cycles influencing demand for a particular service vary in length from one day to 12 months. In many instances, multiple cycles may operate simultaneously. For example, demand levels for public transport may vary by time of day (highest during commute hours), day of week (less travel to work on weekends but more leisure travel), and season of year (more travel by tourists in summer). The demand for service during the peak period on a Monday in summer is likely very different from the level during the peak period on a Saturday in winter, reflecting day-of-week and seasonal variations jointly.

Keeping good records of each transaction helps enormously when it comes to analyzing demand patterns based on past experience. Best practice queuing systems supported by sophisticated software can track customer consumption patterns by date and time of day automatically. Where it is relevant, it's also useful to record weather conditions and other special factors (a strike, an accident, a big convention in town, a price change, launch of a competing service, etc.) that might have influenced demand.

TABLE 9.1 Questions about Demand Patterns and Their Underlying Causes

1. ***Do demand levels follow a predictable cycle?***
   If so, is the duration of the **demand cycle**
   - One *day* (varies by hour)
   - One *week* (varies by day)
   - One *month* (varies by day or by week)
   - One *year* (varies by month or by season or reflects annual public holidays)
   - Another period
2. ***What are the underlying causes of these cyclical variations?***
   - Employment schedules
   - Billing and tax payment/refund cycles
   - Wage and salary payment dates
   - School hours and vacations
   - Seasonal changes in climate
   - Occurrence of public or religious holidays
   - Natural cycles, such as coastal tides
3. ***Do demand levels seem to change randomly?***
   If so, could the underlying causes be
   - Day-to-day changes in the weather
   - Health events whose occurrence cannot be pinpointed exactly
   - Accidents, fires, and certain criminal activities
   - Natural disasters (e.g., earthquakes, storms, mudslides, and volcanic eruptions)
4. ***Can demand for a particular service over time be disaggregated by market segment to reflect such components as***
   - Use patterns by a particular type of customer or for a particular purpose
   - Variations in the net profitability of each completed transaction

MANAGING DEMAND

Once we have understood the demand patterns of the different market segments, we can manage demand. There are five basic approaches to managing demand. The first, which has the virtue of simplicity but little else, involves *taking no action and leaving demand to find its own levels.* Eventually, customers learn from experience or word-of-mouth when they can expect to stand in line to use the service and when it will be available without delay. The trouble is, they may also learn to find a more responsive competitor, and low off-peak utilization cannot be improved unless action is taken. More interventionist approaches involve influencing the level of demand at any given time by taking active steps to *reduce demand in peak periods* and to *increase demand when there is excess capacity.*

Two more approaches to managing demand involve *inventorying demand until capacity becomes available.* A firm can accomplish this either by *creating formalized wait and queuing systems*, or by introducing a booking or *reservations system* that promises customers access to capacity at specified times (or by a combination of the two).

Table 9.2 links these five approaches to the two problem situations of excess demand and excess capacity. Many service businesses face both situations at different points in the cycle of demand and should consider use of the interventionist strategies described. Next in this section we will discuss how marketing mix elements can help to shape demand levels, followed by two sections on how to inventory demand first through waiting lines and queuing systems and then through reservation systems.

Marketing Mix Elements Can Be Used to Shape Demand Patterns

Several marketing mix variables have roles to play in stimulating demand during periods of excess capacity and in decreasing or shifting demand during periods of insufficient capacity. Price often is the first variable to be proposed for bringing demand

TABLE 9.2 Alternative Demand-Management Strategies for Different Capacity Situations

	Capacity Situation	
Approaches to Manage Demand	**Insufficient Capacity (Excess Demand)**	**Excess Capacity (Insufficient Demand)**
Take no action	• Unorganized queuing results (may irritate customers and discourage future use)	• Capacity is wasted (customers may have a disappointing experience for services such as theater)
Reduce demand	• Higher prices will increase profits • Communication can encourage use in other time slots (can this effort be focused on less profitable and less desirable segments?)	• Take no action (but see preceding)
Increase demand	• Take no action unless opportunities exist to stimulate (and give priority to) more profitable segments	• Lower prices selectively (try to avoid cannibalizing existing business; ensure that all relevant costs are covered) • Use communications and variation in products and distribution (but recognize extra costs, if any, and make sure that appropriate trade-offs are made between profitability and use levels)
Inventory demand by formalized wait and queuing system	• Match appropriate queue configuration to service process • Consider priority system for most desirable segments and make other customer shift to off-peak period • Consider separate queues based on urgency, duration, and premium pricing of service • Shorten customer's perceptions of waiting time and make their waits more comfortable	• Not applicable
Inventory demand by reservation system	• Focus on yield and reserve capacity for less price sensitive customers • Consider a priority system for important segments • Make other customer shift to off-peak period	• Clarify that capacity is available and let customers make reservation at their preferred time slot

and supply into balance, but changes in product, distribution strategy, and communication efforts can also play an important role. Although each element is discussed separately, effective demand management efforts often require changes in two or more elements jointly.

USE PRICE AND NONMONETARY COSTS TO MANAGE DEMAND. One of the most direct ways to balance supply and demand is the use of pricing. Nonmonetary costs, too, may have a similar effect. For instance, if customers learn they are likely to face increased time and effort costs during peak periods, those who dislike spending time waiting in crowded and unpleasant conditions will try to come during less busy times. Similarly, the lure of cheaper prices and an expectation of no waiting may encourage at least some people to change the timing of their behavior, whether it is for shopping, travel, or sending in equipment for repair.

For the monetary price of a service to be effective as a demand management tool, managers must have some sense of the shape and slope of a product's demand curve—that is, how the quantity of service demanded responds to increases or decreases in the price per unit at a particular point in time. It's important to determine whether the demand curve for a specific service varies sharply from one time period to another. For instance, will the same person be willing to pay more for a weekend stay in a hotel on Cape Cod in summer than in winter (when the weather can be freezing)? The answer is probably "yes." If so, significantly different pricing schemes may be needed to fill capacity in each time period.

Complicating matters further, separate demand curves typically exist for different segments within each time period (e.g., business travelers usually are less price sensitive than tourists). (Figure 9.4 shows a sample demand curve for two segments in different seasons.)

One of the most difficult tasks facing service marketers is determining the nature of all the different demand curves. Historical data (often from revenue management systems), research, trial and error, and analysis of parallel situations in other locations or in comparable services, are all ways of obtaining an understanding of the situation. Many service businesses explicitly recognize the existence of different demand curves by designing distinct products with physical and nonphysical design elements (or rate fences) for their key segments, each priced at levels appropriate to the demand curve of a particular segment. In essence, each segment receives a variation of the basic product, with value added to the core service through supplementary services to appeal to higher paying segments. For instance, in computer and printing service firms, product enhancement takes the form of faster turnaround and more specialized services. In each case, the objective is to maximize the revenues received from each segment.

When capacity is limited, however, the goal in a profit-seeking business should be to ensure that as much capacity as possible is utilized by the most profitable segments available at any given time. Airlines, for instance, hold a certain number of seats for business passengers paying full fare and place restrictive conditions on excursion fares for tourists (using nonphysical rate fences such as requiring advance purchase and a Saturday night stay) in order to prevent business travelers from taking advantage of

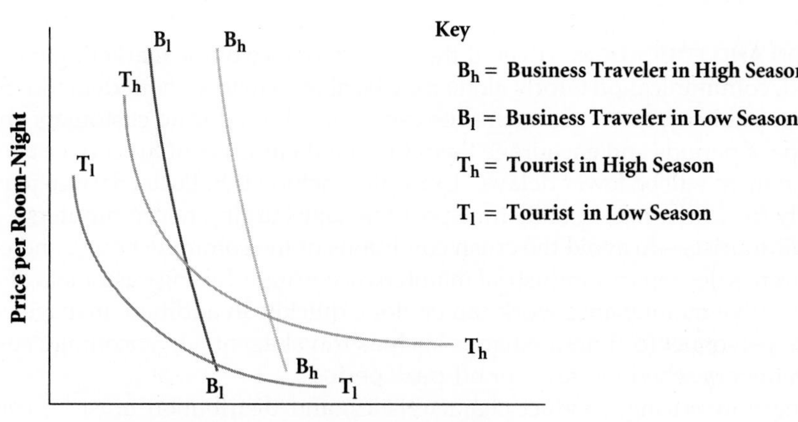

FIGURE 9.4 Hotel Demand Curves by Segment and by Season

cheap fares designed to attract tourists who can help fill the aircraft. Pricing strategies of this nature are known as *revenue management* and are discussed in Chapter 6.

CHANGE PRODUCT ELEMENTS. Sometimes, pricing alone will be ineffective in managing demand. The opening vignette is a good point in case—in the absence of skiing opportunities, no skiers would buy lift tickets for use on a midsummer day at any price. Similar thinking prevails at a variety of other seasonal businesses. Thus, educational institutions offer weekend and summer programs for adults and senior citizens, and small pleasure boats offer cruises in the summer and a dockside venue for private functions in winter months. These firms recognize that no amount of price discounting is likely to develop business out of season, and a new service product targeted at different segments is needed to encourage demand.

During the course of a 24-hour period, there can be product variations. Some restaurants provide a good example of this, marking the passage of the hours with changing menus and levels of service, variations in lighting and decor, opening and closing of the bar, and the presence or absence of entertainment. The goal is to appeal to different needs within the same group of customers, to reach out to different customer segments, or to do both, according to the time of day.

MODIFY PLACE AND TIME OF DELIVERY. Rather than seeking to modify demand for a service that continues to be offered at the same time in the same place, firms can also respond to market needs by modifying the time and place of delivery. The following basic options are available:

- *No change.* Regardless of the level of demand, the service continues to be offered in the same location at the same times.
- *Varying the times when the service is available.* This strategy reflects changing customer preference by day of week, by season, and so forth. Theaters and cinema complexes often offer matinees on weekends when people have more leisure time throughout the day; during the summer, cafes and restaurants may stay open later because of the general inclination of people to enjoy long, balmy evenings outdoors; and shops may extend their hours in the lead-up to Christmas or during school holiday periods.
- *Offering the service to customers at a new location.* One approach is to operate mobile units that take the service to customers, rather than requiring them to visit fixed-site service locations. Traveling libraries, mobile car wash services, in-office tailoring services, home-delivered meals and catering services, and vans equipped with primary care medical facilities are examples of this. A cleaning and repair firm that wishes to generate business during low demand periods might offer free pickup and delivery of portable items that need servicing. Alternatively, service firms whose productive assets are mobile may choose to follow the market when that, too, is mobile. For instance, some car rental firms establish seasonal branch offices in resort communities. In these new locations, they often change the schedule of service hours (as well as certain product features) to conform to local needs and preferences.

PROMOTION AND EDUCATION. Even if the other variables of the marketing mix remain unchanged, communication efforts alone may be able to help smooth demand. Signage, advertising, publicity, and sales messages can be used to educate customers about the timing of peak periods and encourage them to avail themselves of the service at off-peak times when there will be fewer delays.[5] Examples include U.S. Postal Service requests to "Mail Early for Christmas," public transport messages urging noncommuters—such as shoppers or tourists—to avoid the crush conditions of the commute hours, and communications from sales reps for industrial maintenance firms advising customers of periods when preventive maintenance work can be done quickly. In addition, management can ask service personnel (or intermediaries such as travel agents) to encourage customers with discretionary schedules to favor off-peak periods.

Changes in pricing, product characteristics, and distribution must be communicated clearly. If a firm wants to obtain a specific response to variations in marketing mix elements it must, of course, inform customers fully about their options. As discussed in

Chapter 7, short-term promotions, combining both pricing and communication elements as well as other incentives, may provide customers with attractive incentives to shift the timing of service usage.

Not all demand is desirable. Road traffic management is one example of where increased demand affects quality of life (time, congestion, likelihood of an accident), support services (emergency services like ambulances and police), and environment (pollution). As discussed in Best Practice in Action 9.1, the government can take a proactive role in discouraging road traffic, but it requires creating support services, better infrastructure, education through marketing campaigns, and product strategies to deter road traffic and add value to other public transport systems.

BEST PRACTICE IN ACTION 9.1

Road Transport Authority: Managing Traffic

The city of Dubai, in the United Arab Emirates, is one of the fastest growing cities in the world. One of the disadvantages of this rapid growth is traffic. The number of cars is increasing at a rate of 17 to 20 percent, compared with the average for developed countries of 2 to 3 percent. Traffic affects quality of life, so, from a service perspective, how do you manage the traffic better? The job of discouraging private car usage was entrusted to the Roads and Transport Authority (RTA) in 2005. The RTA used a two-prong strategy. It discouraged traveling on feeder roads through the use of toll gates called *Salik*. Then it encouraged traveling on the improved public transportation service.

The Dubai Metro was launched on September 9, 2009, with the objective of getting 17 percent of Dubai's 1.5 million residents to rely on the Metro by 2020. This would help alleviate the congestion Dubai foresees due to the 15 million tourists expected in 2015. In the two years prior to the Metro launch, city transportation was integrated seamlessly using road, rail, and water transport modes. This involved increasing the number of buses, increasing bus coverage and frequency, and regulating traffic flow through infrastructure development. Other facilities like taxi stands, park-and-ride facilities, and intercity connections were started, and a multi-transport, single rechargeable pay card called *Nol* was introduced to encourage Dubai Metro usage.

Because it is a new product, consumer education began using social campaigns about Metro etiquette and information campaigns about schedules, ticketing, and service. The online journey planner *wojhati* facilitated using the Metro. One kilogram of gasoline (energy equivalent) per person allows a car to travel 12 miles, a bus for 24 miles, and a train for 30 miles, making the Metro the most energy efficient, and the Dubai Metro has 0 percent carbon emissions. By indirectly discouraging the demand for cars, the RTA adds to quality of life, prevents congestion, allows emergency services to have a faster response, and improves the environment.

FIGURE 9.5 Dubai is One of the Fastest Growing Cities in the World and Reducing Road Traffic is a Key Priority for the Government

Sources: Ahmed, A. (2007), "'Rapid changes' delay road to smooth traffic by one year," *Gulf News*, September 25, 2007, http://archive.gulfnews.com/; RTA available at: http://www.rta.ae/wpsv5/wps/portal; Salik available at: http://www.salik.ae/; Yaqoob, T. (2009), "My city, My Metro, My slogan," *The National*, September 5, 2009, www.thenational.ae/; Marrian, N. (2008), "Tapping Mass Market Will Boost Dubai's Visitors to 15 m by 2015," *Gulf News*, August 24, 2008, www.gulfnews.com/; Journey Planner: http://wojhati.rta.ae/; About Dubai Metro: http://dubaimetro.eu/about-dubai-metro.

INVENTORY DEMAND THROUGH WAITING LINES AND QUEUING SYSTEMS

One of the challenges of services is that they cannot normally be stored for later use. A hairstylist cannot prepackage a haircut for the following day: it must be done in real time. In an ideal world, nobody would ever have to wait to conduct a service transaction. However, firms cannot afford to provide extensive extra capacity that would go unutilized most of the time. As we have seen, there are a variety of procedures for bringing demand and supply into balance. But what's a manager to do when the possibilities for shaping demand and adjusting capacity have been exhausted and yet supply and demand are still out of balance? Not taking any action and leaving customers to sort things out is no recipe for customer satisfaction. Rather than allowing matters to degenerate into a random free-for-all, customer-oriented firms try to develop strategies for ensuring order, predictability, and fairness. In businesses in which demand regularly exceeds supply, managers often can take steps to inventory demand. This task can be achieved in one of two ways: (1) by asking customers to wait in line—usually on a first-come, first-served basis—or by offering customers more advanced queuing systems and (2) by offering customers the opportunity of reserving or booking space in advance. We will discuss the wait line and queuing systems in this section and reservation systems in the next.

Waiting Is a Universal Phenomenon

It's estimated that Americans spend 37 billion hours a year (an average of almost 150 hours each) waiting in lines, "during which time they fret, fidget, and scowl," according to *The Washington Post.*[6] Similar (or worse) situations seem to prevail around the world. Nobody likes to be kept waiting (Figure 9.6). It's boring, time-wasting, and sometimes physically uncomfortable, especially if there is nowhere to sit or you are outdoors. And yet waiting for a service process is an almost universal phenomenon: Almost every organization faces the problem of waiting lines somewhere in its operation. People are kept waiting on the phone, listening to recorded messages like "your call is important to us"; they line up with their supermarket carts to check out their grocery purchases; and they wait for their bills after a restaurant meal. They sit in their cars waiting to enter drive-in car washes and to pay at toll booths.

A national survey of 1,000 adults in the United States revealed that the waiting lines most dreaded by Americans are those in doctors' offices (cited by 27 percent) and in government departments that issue motor vehicle registrations and drivers' licenses (26 percent), followed by grocery stores (18 percent) and airports (14 percent).[7] Situations that make it even worse at retail check-outs include slow or inefficient cashiers, someone changing their mind about an item that has already been rung up, and a person who leaves the line to run back for an item. It doesn't take long before people start to lose their cool: One third of Americans say they get frustrated after waiting in line for 10 minutes or less, although women report more patience than men and are more likely to chat with others to pass the time while waiting.

Physical and inanimate objects wait for processing, too. Customers' emails sit in customer service staff's inboxes, appliances wait to be repaired, and checks wait to be cleared at a bank. In each instance, a customer may be waiting for the outcome of that work—an answer to an email, an appliance that is working again, and a check credited to a customer's balance.

Why Waiting Lines Occur

Waiting lines—known to operations researchers (and the British) as "queues"—occur whenever the number of arrivals at a facility exceeds the capacity of the system to process them. In a very real sense, queues basically are a symptom of unresolved capacity management problems. Analysis and modeling of queues is a well-established branch of operations management. Queuing theory has been traced back to 1917, when a Danish telephone engineer was charged with determining how large the switching unit in a telephone system had to be to keep the number of busy signals within reason.[8]

FIGURE 9.6 Hertz Helps Its Customers to Avoid the Time and Hassle of Waiting in Line

Source: © 2003 The Hertz Corporation. All Rights Reserved.

As the telephone example suggests, not all queues take the form of a physical waiting line in a single location. When customers deal with a service supplier at arm's length, as in information-processing services, they call from home, office, or college using telecommunication channels such as voice telephone or the Internet. Typically, calls are answered in the order received, often requiring customers to wait their turn in a virtual line. Some physical queues are geographically dispersed. Travelers wait at many different locations for the taxis they have ordered by phone to arrive and pick them up.

Many websites now allow people to do things for themselves, such as obtaining information or making reservations that formerly required making telephone calls or visiting a service facility in person. Companies often promote the time savings that can be achieved. Although accessing the Web can be slow sometimes, at least the wait is conducted while the customer is comfortably seated and able to attend to other matters.

Managing Waiting Lines

The problem of reducing customer waiting time often requires a multipronged strategy, as evidenced by the approach taken by a Chicago bank (Best Practice in Action 9.2). Increasing capacity simply by adding more space or more staff is not always the optimal solution in situations in which customer satisfaction must be balanced against

BEST PRACTICE IN ACTION 9.2

Cutting the Wait for Retail Banking Customers

How should a big retail bank respond to increased competition from new financial service providers? A large bank in Chicago decided that enhancing service to its customers would be an important element in its strategy. One opportunity for improvement was to reduce the amount of time customers spent waiting in line for service in the bank's retail branches—a frequent source of complaints. Recognizing that no single action could resolve the problem satisfactorily, the bank adopted a three-pronged approach.

First, technological improvements were made to the service operation, starting with introduction of an electronic queuing system that not only routed customers to the next available teller station but also provided supervisors with online information to help match staffing to customer demand. Meantime, computer enhancements provided tellers with more information about their customers, enabling them to handle more requests without leaving their stations. And new cash machines for tellers saved them from selecting bills and counting them twice (yielding a time savings of 30 seconds for each cash withdrawal transaction).

Second, changes were made to human resource strategies. The bank adopted a new job description for teller managers that made them responsible for customer queuing times and for expediting transactions. It created an officer-of-the-day program, under which a designated officer was equipped with a beeper and assigned to help staff with complicated transactions that might otherwise slow them down. A new job category of peak-time teller was introduced, paying premium wages for 12–18 hours of work a week. Existing full-time tellers were given cash incentives and recognition to reward improved productivity on predicted high-volume days. Lastly, management reorganized meal arrangements. On busy days, lunch breaks were reduced to half-hour periods and staff received catered meals; in the meantime, the bank cafeteria was opened earlier to serve peak-time tellers.

A third set of changes centered on customer-oriented improvements to the delivery system. Quick-drop desks were established on busy days to handle deposits and simple requests, while newly created express teller stations were reserved for deposits and check cashing. Lobby hours were expanded from 38 to 56 hours a week, including Sundays. A customer brochure, *How to Lose Wait*, alerted customers to busy periods and suggested ways of avoiding delays.

Subsequently, internal measures and customer surveys showed that the improvements had not only reduced customer wait times but also increased customer perceptions that this bank was "the best" bank in the region for minimal waits in teller lines. The bank also found that adoption of extended hours had deflected some of the "noon rush" to before-work and after-work periods.

Source: Leonard L. Berry and Linda R. Cooper, "Competing with Time-Saving Service," *Business*, .40, No. 2, 1990, 3–7.

cost considerations. Like the bank, managers should consider a variety of alternatives, including:

1. Rethinking the design of the queuing system.
2. Installing a reservations system.
3. Tailoring the queuing system to different market segments.
4. Managing customers' behavior and their perceptions of the wait.
5. Redesigning processes to shorten the time of each transaction.

Points 1 to 4 are discussed in subsequent sections of this chapter, and for point 5, refer to Chapter 8 on customer service process redesign.

Different Queue Configurations

There are a variety of different types of queues and the challenge for managers is to select the most appropriate procedure. Figure 9.7 shows diagrams of several types you have probably experienced yourself.

- In *single line, sequential stages*, customers proceed through several serving operations, as in a cafeteria. Bottlenecks may occur at any stage where the process takes longer to execute than at previous stages. Many cafeterias have lines at the cash

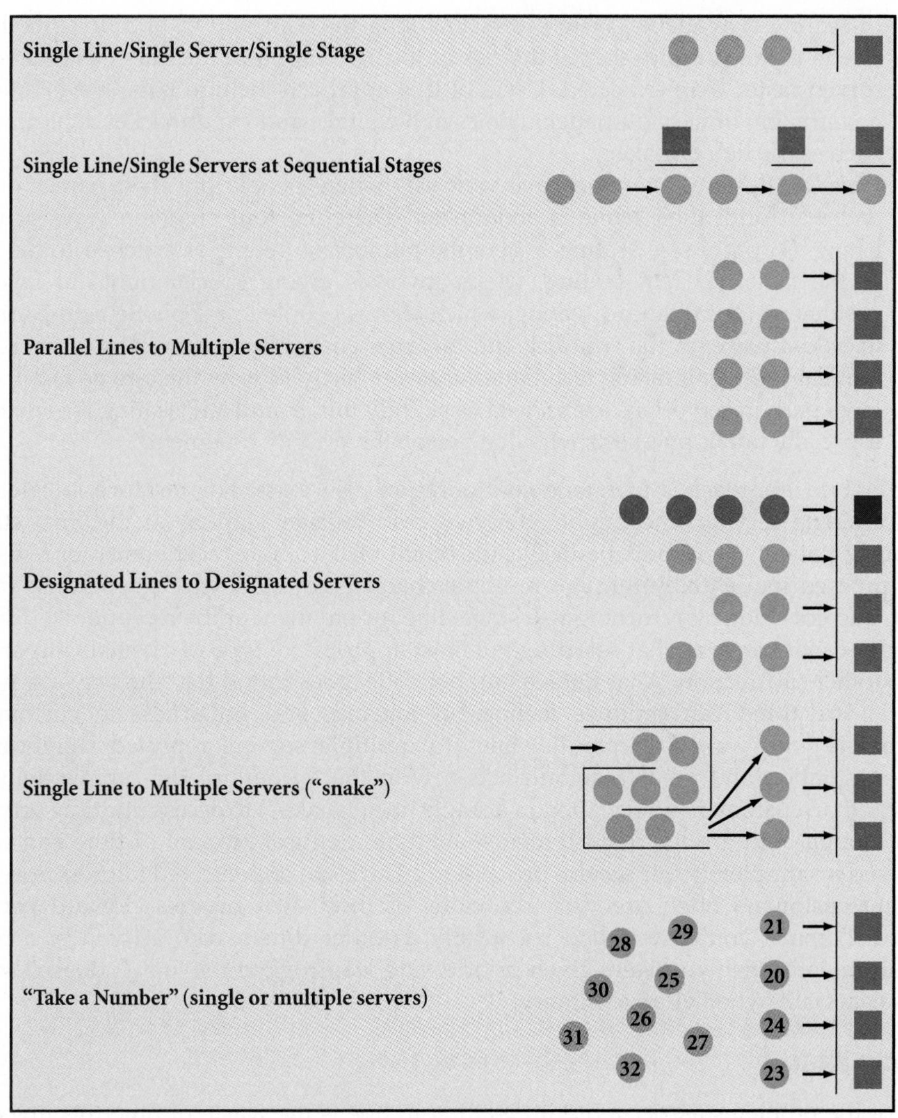

FIGURE 9.7 Alternative Queue Configurations

register because the cashier takes longer to calculate how much you owe and to make change than the servers take to slap food on your plate.

- *Parallel lines to multiple servers* offer more than one serving station, allowing customers to select one of several lines in which to wait. Banks and ticket windows are common examples. Fast food restaurants usually have several serving lines in operation at busy times of day, with each offering the full menu. A parallel system can have either a single stage or multiple stages. The disadvantage of this design is that lines may not move at equal speed. How many times have you chosen what looked like the shortest line only to watch in frustration as the lines either side of you moved at twice the speed of yours, because someone in your line has a complicated transaction?
- A *single line to multiple servers,* commonly known as a "Snake." This type of waiting line solves the problem of the parallel lines to multiple servers moving at different speeds. This approach is encountered frequently at post offices and airport check-ins.
- *Designated lines* involve assigning different lines to specific categories of customer. Examples include express lines (for instance, 12 items or less) and regular lines at supermarket check-outs, and different check-in stations for first class, business class, and economy class airline passengers.
- *Take a number* saves customers the need to stand in a queue, because they know they will be called in sequence. This procedure allows them to sit down and relax

(if seating is available) or to guess how long the wait will be and do something else in the meantime—but at the risk of losing their place if earlier customers are served faster than expected. Users of this approach include large travel agents, government offices, outpatient clinics in hospitals, and supermarket departments such as the deli or bakery.

- *Wait list.* Restaurants often have wait lists where people put their names down and wait until their name is announced. There are four common ways of wait listing: (1) party size seating, where the number of people is matched to the size of the table; (2) VIP seating, which involves giving special rights to favored customers; (3) call-ahead seating, which allows people to telephone before arrival to hold a place on the wait list; and (4) large party reservations. If customers are familiar with wait listing techniques, they are likely to view them to be fair. If not, large party reservations are viewed as slightly unfair, and VIP seating is viewed as especially unfair by guests who don't enjoy the priority treatment.[9]

Hybrid approaches to queue configuration also exist. For instance, a cafeteria with a single serving line might offer two cash register stations at the final stage. Similarly, patients at a small medical clinic might visit a single receptionist for registration, proceed sequentially through multiple channels for testing, diagnosis, and treatment, and conclude by returning to a single line for payment at the receptionist's desk.

Research suggests that selecting the most appropriate type of queue is important to customer satisfaction. Anat Rafaeli and her colleagues found that the way a waiting area is structured can produce feelings of injustice and unfairness in customers. Customers who waited in parallel lines to multiple servers reported significantly higher agitation and greater dissatisfaction with the fairness of the service delivery process than customers who waited in a single line ("snake") to access multiple servers, even though both groups of customers waited an identical amount of time and were involved in completely fair service processes.[10] The issue of perceived fairness arises as waiting customers often are very conscious of their own progress toward getting served. Perhaps you've watched resentfully as other diners who arrived at a busy restaurant later than you were given priority and leapfrogged the line. It doesn't seem fair—especially when you are hungry!

Virtual Waits

One of the problems associated with waiting in line is the waste of time this involves for customers. The "virtual-queue" strategy is an innovative way of taking the physical waiting out of the wait altogether. Instead, customers register their place in line on a computer, which estimates the time at which they will reach the front of the virtual line and should return to claim their place.[11] Best Practice in Action 9.3 describes the virtual queuing systems used in two very different industries: a theme park and a call center.

The concept of virtual queues has many potential applications. Cruise ships, all-inclusive resorts, and restaurants can all use this strategy if customers are willing to provide their cell phone numbers or remain within buzzing range of a firm-operated pager system.

Queuing Systems Can Be Tailored to Market Segments

Although the basic rule in most queuing systems is "first come, first served," not all queuing systems are organized on this basis. Market segmentation is sometimes used to design queuing strategies that set different priorities for different types of customers. Allocation to separate queuing areas may be based on any of the following:

- ***Urgency of the job.*** At many hospital emergency units, a triage nurse is assigned to greet incoming patients and decide which ones require priority medical treatment and which can safely be asked to register and then sit down while they wait their turn.
- ***Duration of service transaction.*** Banks, supermarkets, and other retail services often institute "express lanes" for shorter, less complicated tasks.

BEST PRACTICE IN ACTION 9.3

Waiting in a Virtual Queue

Disney is well known for its efforts to give visitors to its theme parks information on how long they may have to wait to ride a particular attraction and for entertaining guests while they are waiting in line. However, the company found that the long waits at its most popular attractions still represented a major source of dissatisfaction and so created an innovative solution.

The virtual-queue concept was first tested at Disney World. At the most popular attractions, guests were able to register their place in line with a computer and were then free to use the wait time visiting other places in the park. Surveys showed that guests who used the new system spent more money, saw more attractions, and had significantly higher satisfaction. After further refinement, the system—now named FASTPASS—was introduced at the five most popular attractions at Disney World and subsequently extended to all Disney parks worldwide. It is now used by more than 50 million guests a year.

FASTPASS is easy to use. When guests approach a FASTPASS attraction, they are given two clear choices: Obtain a FASTPASS ticket there and return at a designated time, or wait in a standby line. Signs indicate how long the wait is in each instance. The wait time for each line tends to be self-regulating, because a large difference between the two will lead to increasing numbers of people choosing the shorter line. In practice, the virtual wait tends to be slightly longer than the physical one. To use the FASTPASS option, guests insert their park admission ticket into a special turnstile and receive a FASTPASS ticket specifying a return time. Guests have some flexibility because the system allows them a 60-minute window beyond the printed return time.

Just like the FASTPASS system, call centers also use virtual queues. Many vendors sell different types of virtual queuing systems designed for call centers. The first-in, first-out queuing system is very common. When callers call in, they will hear a message that informs them of the estimated wait time for the call to be taken by an agent. The caller can (1) wait in the queue and get connected to an agent when his turn arrives, or (2) choose to receive a call back. When the caller chooses this option, he has to enter his telephone number and tell his name. He then hangs up the phone. However, his virtual place in the queue is maintained. When he is nearly at the head of the queue, the system calls the customer back and puts him at the head of the queue where an agent will attend to him next. In both situations, the customer is unlikely to complain. In the first situation, it is their choice to wait in the queue, and the person can still do something else as he already knows the estimated wait time. In the second situation, the person does not have to wait for very long before reaching an agent. The call center also benefits because there are fewer frustrated customers that may take up the valuable time of the agents by complaining about how long they have to wait. In addition, firms also reduce aborted or missed calls from customers.

Source: Duncan Dickson, Robert C. Ford, and Bruce Laval, "Managing Real and Virtual Waits in Hospitality and Service Organizations," *Cornell Hotel and Restaurant Administration Quarterly* 46, February 2005, 52–68; "Virtual Queue," Wikipedia, www.en.wikipeidao.org/wiki/virtual_queuing, accessed June 2, 2009.

- ***Payment of a premium price.*** Airlines usually offer separate check-in lines for first-class and economy-class passengers, with a higher ratio of personnel to passengers in the first-class line, resulting in reduced waits for those who have paid more for their tickets. At some airports, premium passengers may also enjoy faster lanes for the security check.
- ***Importance of the customer.*** A special area may be reserved for members of frequent user clubs. Airlines often provide lounges, offering newspapers and free refreshments, where frequent flyers can wait for their flights in greater comfort.

CUSTOMER PERCEPTIONS OF WAITING TIME

Research shows that people often think they have waited longer for a service than they actually did. Studies of public transportation use, for instance, have shown that travelers perceive time spent waiting for a bus or train as passing one and a half to seven times more slowly than the time actually spent traveling in the vehicle.[12] People don't like wasting their time on unproductive activities any more than they like wasting money. Customer dissatisfaction with delays in receiving service often can stimulate strong emotions, even anger.[13]

The Psychology of Waiting Time

The noted philosopher William James observed, "Boredom results from being attentive to the passage of time itself." When increasing capacity or shifting demand is simply not possible or sufficient, service firms should try to be creative and look for ways to make waiting more palatable for customers. Doctors and dentists stock their waiting rooms with piles of magazines for people to read while waiting. Car repair facilities may have a television for customers to watch. One tire dealer goes even further, providing customers with free popcorn, soft drinks, coffee, and ice cream while they wait for their cars to be serviced.

An experiment at a large bank in Boston found that installing an electronic news display in the lobby led to greater customer satisfaction, but it didn't reduce the perceived time spent waiting for teller service.[14] In some locations, transit operators erect heated shelters equipped with seats to make it less unpleasant for travelers to wait for a bus or train in cold weather. Restaurants solve the waiting problem by inviting dinner guests to have a drink in the bar until their table is ready (that approach makes money for the house as well as keeping the customer occupied). In similar fashion, guests waiting in line for a show at a casino may find themselves queuing in a corridor lined with slot-machines.

The doorman at one Marriott Hotel has taken it upon himself to bring a combination barometer/thermometer to work each day, hanging it on a pillar at the hotel entrance where guests waiting can spend a moment or two examining it while they wait for a taxi or for their car to be delivered from the valet parking.[15] Theme park operators cleverly design their waiting areas to make the wait look shorter than it really is, finding ways to give customers in line the impression of constant progress, and make time seem to pass more quickly by keeping customers amused or diverted while they wait.

Does it help to tell people how long they are likely to have to wait for service? Common sense would suggest that this is useful information for customers, because it allows them to make decisions as to whether they can afford to take the time to wait now or come back later. It also enables them to plan the use of their time while waiting. An experimental study in Canada looked at how students responded to waits while conducting transactions by computer—a situation similar to waiting on hold on the telephone, in that there are no visual clues as to the probable wait time.[16] The study examined dissatisfaction with waits of 5, 10, or 15 minutes under three conditions: (1) the student subjects were told nothing, (2) they were told how long the wait was likely to be, or (3) they were told what their place in line was. The results suggested that for 5-minute waits, it was not necessary to provide information to improve satisfaction. For waits of 10 or 15 minutes, offering information appeared to improve customers' evaluations of service. However, for longer waits, the researchers suggest that it may be more positive to let people know how their place in line is changing rather than letting them know how much time remains before they will be served. One conclusion we might draw is that when the wait is longer, people prefer to see (or sense) that the line is moving, rather than to watch the clock.

Savvy service marketers recognize that customers experience waiting time in different ways, depending on the circumstances. David Maister and other researchers have the following suggestions on how to use the psychology of waiting to make waits less stressful and unpleasant:[17]

- ***Unoccupied time feels longer than occupied time.*** When you are sitting around with nothing to do, time seems to crawl. The challenge for service organizations is to give customers something to do or to distract them while waiting. For example, BMW car owners can wait in comfort in BMW service centers where waiting areas are furnished with designer furniture, plasma TVs, Wi-Fi hotspots, magazines, and freshly brewed cappuccino. Many customers even bring their own entertainment in the form of a cell phone with messaging and games, an MP3 player, or a personal play station.

- ***Solo waits feel longer than group waits.*** Waiting with one or more people you know is reassuring. Conversation with friends can help to pass the time, but not everyone is comfortable talking to a stranger.
- ***Physically uncomfortable waits feel longer than comfortable waits.*** "My feet are killing me!" is one of the most frequently heard comments when people are forced to stand in line for a long time. And whether they are seated or standing, waiting seems more burdensome if the temperature is too hot or too cold, if it's drafty or windy, or if there's no protection from rain or snow.
- ***Pre- and post-process waits feel longer than in-process waits.*** Waiting to buy a ticket to enter a theme park is different from waiting to ride on a roller coaster once you're in the park.
- ***Unfair waits are longer than equitable waits.*** Perceptions about what is fair or unfair sometimes vary from one culture or country to another. In the United States, Canada, or Britain, for example, people expect everybody to wait their turn in line and are likely to get irritated if they see others jumping ahead or given priority for apparently no good reason.
- ***Unfamiliar waits seem longer than familiar ones.*** Frequent users of a service know what to expect and are less likely to worry while waiting. New or occasional users, by contrast, often are nervous, wondering not only about the probable length of the wait but also about what happens next.
- ***Uncertain waits are longer than known, finite waits.*** Although any wait may be frustrating, we usually can adjust mentally to a wait of a known length. It's the unknown that keeps us on edge. Imagine waiting for a delayed flight and not being told how long the delay is going to be. You don't know whether you have the time to get up and walk about in the terminal or whether to stay at the gate in case the flight is called any minute.
- ***Unexplained waits are longer than explained waits.*** Have you ever been in a subway or an elevator that has stopped for no apparent reason, without anyone telling you why? In addition to uncertainty about the length of the wait, there's added worry about what is going to happen. Has there been an accident on the line? Will you be stuck for hours in close proximity with strangers?
- ***Anxiety makes waits seem longer.*** Can you remember waiting for someone to show at a rendezvous, and worrying about whether you had gotten the time or location correct? While waiting in unfamiliar locations, especially outdoors and at night, people often worry about their personal safety.
- ***The more valuable or important the service, the longer people will wait.*** People will queue up overnight under uncomfortable conditions to get good seats to a major concert or sports event expected to sell out fast.

INVENTORY DEMAND THROUGH RESERVATIONS SYSTEMS

As an alternative, or in addition to, waiting lines, reservations systems can be used to inventory demand. Ask someone what services come to mind when you talk about reservations and most likely they will cite airlines, hotels, restaurants, car rentals, and theater seats. Use synonyms like "bookings" or "appointments" and they may add haircuts, visits to professionals such as doctors and consultants, vacation rentals, and service calls to fix anything from a broken refrigerator to a neurotic laptop. There are many benefits in having a reservations system:

- Customer dissatisfaction due to excessive waits can be avoided. One aim of reservations is to guarantee that service will be available when customers want it. Customers who hold reservations should be able to count on avoiding a queue, because they have been guaranteed service at a specific time.

- Reservations allow demand to be controlled and smoothed out in a more manageable way. A well-organized reservations system allows the organization to deflect demand for service from a first-choice time to earlier or later times, from one class of service to another ("upgrades" and "downgrades"), and even from first-choice locations to alternative ones, and thereby overall contributing to higher capacity utilization.
- Reservations systems enable revenue management and serve to presell a service to different customer segments (see Chapter 6 on revenue management). For example, requiring reservations for normal repair and maintenance allows management to make sure that some time will be kept free for handling emergency jobs. Since these are unpredictable, higher prices can be charged and these bring with them higher margins.
- Data from reservation systems also help organizations to prepare operational and financial projections for future periods. Systems vary from a simple appointments book for a doctor's office, using handwritten entries, to a central, computerized data bank for an airline's global operations.

The challenge in designing reservation systems is to make them fast and user friendly for both staff and customers. Many firms now allow customers to make their own reservations on a self-service basis via their websites. Whether customers talk with a reservations agent or make their own bookings, they want quick answers to questions about whether a service is available at a preferred time and at what price. They also appreciate it if the system can provide further information about the type of service they are reserving. For instance, can a hotel assign a specific room on request? Or can it at least assign a room with a view of the lake rather than a view of the parking lot or the nearby power station? Some businesses now charge a fee for making reservations (see Service Perspective 9.1). Malaysia Airlines encourages passengers to log on to their website, www.malaysiaairlines.com, to avail all the special fares for Malaysian hospitality like assigned seats, baggage allowance, and 5-star refreshments packages, which

SERVICE PERSPECTIVE 9.1

PAY TO GET FREE2ROAM WHEN WAITING IN LINE

Waiting in line is a waste of the consumer's time and a loss of profit to a business. It is said that an average person spends more than two years of his or her life waiting in line. An entrepreneur in Malaysia proposes to begin a unique paid service for saving customers from long waits. Initially, customers will register for this service.

1. Easy to use: Customers can use their mobile phones (via SMS or Interactive Voice Response, IVR) to ask the service provider to hold their spots in line while they are free to roam.
2. On-demand update: The agent says that this system will keep track and remind customers of their wait times.
3. Database a gold mine: The agent boasts of collecting a wealth of information into a customer database. The companies can request reports on their customers' traffic each day and can view their customers' line in real time from a web browser. Free2Roam will be linked with applications on social networking sites like Facebook or Friendster to drive more traffic and attract advertisers. Free2Roam can talk on what's hot and what's not.
4. No hardware or software is required as it will be a hosted solution. The customers will only need a mobile phone, and the merchants will need a browser.

The entrepreneur proposing this solution adds that it will revolutionize the service industry in Malaysia in the near future. The target market for Free2Roam will be food and beverage, cinemas, clinics, hospitals, theme parks, shopping malls, banks, airlines, and government agencies.

Source: http://www.kickstart.com.my/program/entrepreneur/participants/Christy.htm

are only available online. Northwest Airlines charges customers $15 if they want to reserve the more desirable economy class seats, and Air Canada charges $12 for advanced seat reservations on certain flights.[18]

Of course, problems arise when customers fail to show or when service firms over-book. Marketing strategies for dealing with these operational problems include requiring a deposit, canceling nonpaid reservations after a certain time, and providing compensation to victims of over-booking were discussed in Chapter 6 on revenue management.

Reservations Strategies Should Focus on Yield

Service organizations often use percentage of capacity sold as a measure of operational efficiency. Transport services talk of the "load factor" achieved, hotels of their "occupancy rate," and hospitals of their "census." Similarly, professional firms can calculate what proportion of a partner's or an employee's time is classified as billable hours, and repair shops can look at utilization of both equipment and labor. By themselves, however, these percentage figures tell us little of the relative profitability of the business attracted, since high utilization rates may be obtained at the expense of heavy discounting—or even outright giveaways.

More and more, service firms are looking at their "yield"—that is, the average revenue received per unit of capacity. The aim is to maximize this yield in order to improve profitability. As noted in Chapter 6, revenue management strategies designed to achieve this goal are widely used in such capacity-constrained industries as passenger airlines, hotels, and car rentals. Revenue management systems based on mathematical modeling are of greatest value for service firms that find it expensive to modify their capacity but incur relatively low costs when they sell another unit of available capacity.[19] Other characteristics encouraging use of such programs include fluctuating demand levels, ability to segment markets by extent of price sensitivity, and sale of services well in advance of usage.

Yield analysis forces managers to recognize the opportunity cost of selling capacity for a given date to a customer from one market segment when another might subsequently yield a higher rate. Consider the following problems facing sales managers for different types of capacity-constrained service organizations:

- Should a hotel accept an advance booking from a tour group of 200 room nights at $140 each when some of these same room nights might possibly be sold later at short notice to business travelers at the full posted rate of $300?
- Should a railroad with 30 empty freight cars at its disposal accept an immediate request for a shipment worth $1,400 per car or hold the cars idle for a few more days in the hope of getting a priority shipment that would be twice as valuable?
- Should a print shop process all jobs on a first-come, first-served basis, with a guaranteed delivery time for each job, or should it charge a premium rate for "rush" work, and tell customers with "standard" jobs to expect some variability in completion dates?

Decisions on problems deserve to be handled with a little more sophistication than just resorting to the "bird in the hand is worth two in the bush" formula. Good information, based on detailed recordkeeping of past usage and supported by current market intelligence, is the key to allocating the inventory of capacity among different segments. The decision to accept or reject business should be based on realistic estimates of the probabilities of obtaining higher rated business and awareness of the need to maintain established (and desirable) customer relationships. Managers who decide on the basis of guesswork and "gut feel" are little better than gamblers who bet on rolls of the dice.

Figure 9.8 illustrates capacity allocation in a hotel setting, where demand from different types of customers varies not only by day of the week but also by season. These allocation decisions by segment, captured in reservation databases that are accessible worldwide, tell reservations personnel when to stop accepting reservations at certain prices, even though many rooms may still remain unbooked. Loyalty program members, primarily business travelers, are obviously a particularly desirable segment.

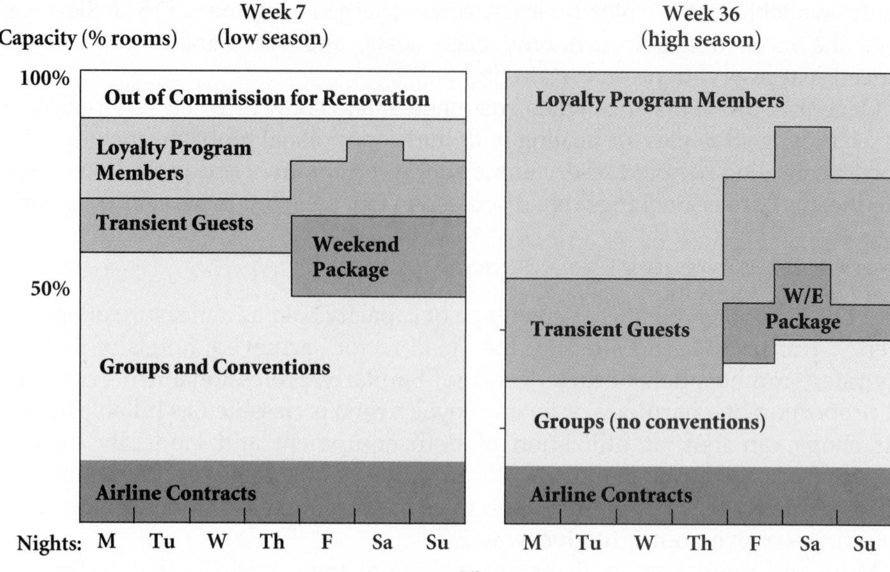

FIGURE 9.8 Setting Capacity Allocation Targets by Segment for a Hotel

Similar charts can be constructed for most capacity-constrained businesses. In some instances, capacity is measured in terms of seats for a given performance, seat-miles, or room nights; in others, it may be in terms of machine time, labor time, billable professional hours, vehicle miles, or storage volume—whichever is the scarce resource. Unless it's easy to divert business from one facility to a similar alternative, allocation planning decisions will have to be made at the level of geographic operating units. So each hotel, repair and maintenance center, or computer service bureau may need its own plan. On the other hand, transport vehicles represent a mobile capacity that can be allocated across any geographic area the vehicles are able to serve.

Create Alternative Use for Otherwise Wasted Capacity

Even after professional management of capacity and demand, most service firms will still experience periods of excess capacity. However, not all unsold productive capacity has to be wasted as alternative "demand" can be created by innovative firms. Many firms take a strategic approach to disposition of anticipated surplus capacity, allocating it in advance to build relationships with customers, suppliers, employees, and intermediaries.[20] Possible uses for free capacity include:

- *Use capacity for service differentiation.* When capacity utilization is low, service employees can go all the way to truly "wow" their customers. A firm that wants to build customer loyalty and market share should use spare time in operations to focus on outstanding customer service. This can include extra attention paid to the customer, allocation of preferred seating, and the like.
- *Reward your best customers and build loyalty.* This can be done through special promotions as part of a loyalty program, while ensuring that existing revenues are not cannibalized.
- *Customer and channel development.* Provide free or heavily discounted trials for prospective customers and for intermediaries who sell to end customers.
- *Reward employees.* In certain industries such as restaurants, beach resorts, or cruise lines, capacity can be used to reward employees and their families to build loyalty. This can improve employee satisfaction and provide employees an understanding of the service as experienced from the customer's perspective, thereby raising performance.
- *Barter free capacity.* Service firms often can save costs and increase capacity utilization by bartering capacity with their own suppliers. Among the most widely bartered services are advertising space or airtime, airline seats, and hotel rooms.

Effective Demand and Capacity Management Requires Information

Managers require substantial information to help them develop effective strategies to manage demand and capacity and then monitor subsequent performance in the marketplace. The following are some important categories of information for this purpose.

- *Historical data* on the level and composition of demand over time, including responses to changes in price or other marketing variables.
- *Forecasts* of the level of demand for each major segment under specified conditions.
- *Segment-by-segment data* to help management evaluate the impact of periodic cycles and random demand fluctuations.
- *Cost data* to enable the organization to distinguish between fixed and variable costs and to determine the relative profitability of incremental unit sales to different segments and at different prices.
- *Meaningful variations in demand levels and composition* on a location-by-location basis (in multisite organizations).
- *Customer attitudes* toward queuing under varying conditions.
- *Customer opinions* on whether the quality of service delivered varies with different levels of capacity utilization.

Where might all this information come from? Many large organizations with expensive fixed capacity have implemented revenue management systems (discussed in Chapter 6). For organizations without such systems, much of the needed data probably are already being collected within the organization—not necessarily by marketers—and new studies can be conducted to obtain additional data. A stream of information comes into most service businesses, notably concerning individual customer transactions. Sales receipts alone often contain vast detail. Service businesses need to collect detailed information for operational and accounting purposes and can frequently associate specific customers with specific transactions.

Unfortunately, the marketing value of such data often is overlooked, and they are not always stored in ways that permit easy retrieval and analysis by marketers. Nevertheless, collection and storage of customer transaction data can be reformatted to provide at least some of the desired information, including how existing segments have responded to past changes in marketing mix variables.

Other information may have to be collected through special studies, such as customer surveys or reviews of analogous situations. It may also be necessary to collect information on competitive performance, because changes in the capacity or strategy of competitors may require corrective action.

When new strategies are under consideration, operations researchers often can contribute useful insights by developing simulation models of the effect of changes in different variables. Such an approach is particularly useful in service "network" environments, such as theme parks and ski resorts, where customers can choose between multiple activities at the same site. Madeleine Pullman and Gary Thompson modeled customer behavior at a ski resort, where skiers can choose between different lifts and ski runs of varying lengths and levels of difficulty. Through analysis, they were able to determine the potential future effect of lift capacity upgrades (bigger or faster chair lifts), capacity expansion in the form of extended skiing terrain, industry growth, day-to-day price variations, customer response to information about wait times at different lifts, and changes in the customer mix.[21]

CONCLUSION

Because many capacity-constrained service organizations have heavy fixed costs, even modest improvements in capacity utilization tend to have a significant effect on the bottom line. In this chapter, we have shown how managers can manage productive capacity and demand and improve customers' waiting and queuing experience. Managing capacity and demand for a service at a particular place and time closely links back to what we've learned in past chapters, including decisions on *product elements and tiering of service* (Chapter 4), *place and time of service delivery* (Chapter 5), *revenue management* (Chapter 6), and *promotion and education* (Chapter 7).

Chapter Summary

LO1 There are several different forms of productive capacity in services: physical facilities for processing customers; physical facilities for processing goods; physical equipment for processing people, possessions or information; and labor and infrastructure.

LO2 At any one time, a firm with limited capacity can face different demand-supply situations: excess demand, demand that's more than ideal capacity, well-balanced demand and supply, or excess capacity.
- When demand and supply are not in balance, firms will have idle capacity during low periods, but have to turn away customers during peak periods. This situation impedes the efficient use of productive assets and erodes profitability.
- Firms therefore need to try and balance demand and supply through adjusting capacity and/or demand.

LO3 *Capacity* can be managed in a number of ways, including:
- Stretching capacity—some capacity is elastic and more people can be served with the same capacity through crowding (e.g., in a subway car), extending operating hours, or speeding up customer processing times.
- Scheduling downtime during low periods.
- Cross-training employees, use part-time employees.
- Inviting customers to perform self-service.
- Asking customers to share capacity.
- Designing capacity to be flexible.
- Renting or sharing extra facilities and equipment.

LO4 To manage *demand* effectively, firms need to understand demand patterns and drivers by market segment. Different segments often exhibit different demand patterns (e.g., routine maintenance versus emergency repairs). Once firms have an understanding of the demand patterns of their market segments, they can use marketing strategies to reshape those patterns.

LO5 Demand can be managed in the following five basic ways:
- Take no action, and leave demand to find its own levels.
- Reduce demand during peak periods.
- Increase demand during low periods.
- Inventory demand through waiting lines and queuing systems.
- Inventory demand through reservation systems.

LO6 The following marketing mix elements can be used to help smooth out fluctuations in demand:
- Use price and nonmonetary customer costs to manage demand.
- Change product elements to attract different segments at different times.
- Modify the place and time of delivery (e.g., through extended opening hours).
- Promotion and education (e.g., "mail early for Christmas").

LO7 When designing *waiting line and queuing systems*, firms need to bear in mind that there are different types of queues with their respective advantages and applications. Queuing systems include single line with sequential stages, parallel lines to multiple servers, single line to multiple servers, designated lines, taking a number, and wait list.

Not all queuing systems are organized on a "first come, first served" basis. Rather, good systems often segment waiting customers by:
- Urgency of the job (e.g., hospital emergency units).
- Duration of the service transaction (e.g., express lanes).
- Premium service based on a premium price (e.g., first-class check-in counters).
- Importance of the customer (e.g., frequent travelers get priority check-in).

LO8 Customers don't like wasting their time waiting. Firms need to understand the psychology of waiting and take active steps to make waiting less frustrating. We discussed 10 possible steps, including keeping customers occupied or entertained while waiting, informing customers how long the wait is likely to be, providing them with an explanation of why they have to wait, and avoiding perceptions of unfair waits.

LO9 Effective *reservations systems* inventory demand and offer several benefits. They:
- Help to reduce or even avoid customers waiting in queues and thereby avoid dissatisfaction due to excessive waits.
- Allow the firm to control demand and smooth it out.
- Enable the use of revenue management to focus on increasing yield by reserving scarce capacity for higher-paying segments, rather than just selling off capacity.

LO10 Substantial information is required for designing effective strategies to manage demand and capacity including historical data, forecasts, segment-by-segment data, cost data, location or branch-specific variations in demand, and customer attitudes toward waiting and different utilization levels.

Review Questions

1. What is meant by productive capacity in services?
2. Why is capacity management particularly important for service firms?
3. What is the difference between ideal capacity and maximum capacity? Provide examples of a situation where (a) the two might be the same and (b) the two are different.
4. What actions can firms take to adjust capacity to more closely match demand?
5. How can firms identify the factors that affect demand for their services?
6. What actions can firms take to adjust demand to more closely match capacity?
7. How can marketing mix elements be used to reshape demand patterns?
8. What do you see as the advantages and disadvantages of the different types of queues for an organization serving large numbers of customers? For which type of service might each of the queuing types be more suitable?
9. How can firms make waiting more pleasant for their customers?
10. What are the benefits of having an effective reservation system?

Application Exercises

1. Explain how flexible capacity can be created in each of the following situations: (a) a local library, (b) an office-cleaning service, (c) a technical support helpdesk, (d) an Interflora franchise.
2. Identify some specific examples of firms in your community (or region) that significantly change their product and/or marketing mix in order to increase patronage during low demand periods.
3. Select a service organization of your choice, and identify its particular patterns of demand with reference to the checklist provided in Table 9.1 and answer: (a) What is the nature of this service organization's approach to capacity and demand management? (b) What changes would you recommend in relation to its management of capacity and demand and why?
4. Review the 10 suggestions on the psychology of waiting. Which are the most relevant in (a) a supermarket; (b) a city bus stop on a rainy, dark evening; (c) a doctor's office; and (d) a ticket line for a football game expected to be a sell-out.
5. Give examples, based on your own experience, of a reservation system that worked really well and of one that worked really badly. Identify and examine the reasons for the success and failure of these two systems. What recommendations would you make to both firms to improve (or further improve in the case of the good example) their reservation systems?

Endnotes

1. Kenneth J. Klassen and Thomas R. Rohleder, "Combining Operations and Marketing to Manage Capacity and Demand in Services," *The Service Industries Journal*, 21, April 2001, 1–30.
2. Breffni M. Noone, Sheryl E. Kimes, Anna S. Mattila, and Jochen Wirtz, "The Effect of Meal Pace on Customer Satisfaction," *Cornell Hospitality Quarterly*, 48, No. 3, 2007, 231–245.
3. Based on material in James A. Fitzsimmons and M. J. Fitzsimmons, *Service Management: Operations, Strategy, and Information Technology*, 6th ed. New York: Irwin McGraw-Hill, 2008; W. Earl Sasser, Jr., "Match Supply and Demand in Service Industries," *Harvard Business Review*, 54, November–December 1976, 133–140
4. Christopher H. Lovelock, "Strategies for Managing Capacity-Constrained Service Organisations," *Service Industries Journal*, 4, November 1984, 12–13
5. Kenneth J. Klassen and Thomas R. Rohleder, "Using Customer Motivations to Reduce Peak Demand: Does It Work?" *The Service Industries Journal*, 24, September 2004, 53–70.
6. Malcolm Galdwell, "The Bottom Line for Lots of Time Spent in America," *The Washington Post*, syndicated article, February 1993.

7. "Chase 'Just in the Blink of Time' Index—National Results." Chase Bank News Release, May 19, 2005, accessed on www.chaseblink.com, June 5, 2009.
8. Richard Saltus, "Lines, Lines, Lines, Lines...The Experts Are Trying to Ease the Wait," *The Boston Globe*, October 5, 1992, 39, 42.
9. Kelly A. McGuire and Sheryl E. Kimes, "The Perceived Fairness of Waitlist-Management Techniques for Restaurants," *Cornell Hotel and Restaurant Administration Quarterly*, 47, May 2006, 121–134.
10. Anat Rafaeli, G. Barron, and K. Haber, "The Effects of Queue Structure on Attitudes," *Journal of Service Research*, 5, November 2002, 125–139.
11. Duncan Dickson, Robert C. Ford, and Bruce Laval, "Managing Real and Virtual Waits in Hospitality and Service Organizations," *Cornell Hotel and Restaurant Administration Quarterly*, 46, February 2005, 52–68.
12. Jay R. Chernow, "Measuring the Values of Travel Time Savings," *Journal of Consumer Research*, 7, March 1981,360–371. Note: this entire issue of Journal of Consumer Research was devoted to the consumption of time.
13. Ana B. Casado Diaz and Francisco J. Más Ruiz, "The Consumer's Reaction to Delays in Service," *International Journal of Service Industry Management*, 13, No. 2, 2002, 118–140.
14. Karen L. Katz, Blaire M. Larson, and Richard C. Larson, "Prescription for the Waiting-in-Line Blues: Entertain, Enlighten, and Engage," *Sloan Management Review* 32, Winter 1991, 44–53.
15. Bill Fromm and Len Schlesinger, *The Real Heroes of Business and Not a CEO Among Them.* New York: Currency Doubleday, 1994, 7.
16. Michael K. Hui and David K. Tse, "What to Tell Customers in Waits of Different Lengths: An Integrative Model of Service Evaluation," *Journal of Marketing*, 80, No. 2, April 1996, 81–90.
17. This section is based on David H. Maister, "The Psychology of Waiting Lines," in J. A. Czepiel, M. R. Solomon, and C. F. Surprenant, eds. *The Service Encounter.* Lexington, MA: Lexington Books/D.C. Heath, 1986, 113–123; M. M. Davis and J. Heineke, "Understanding the Roles of the Customer and the Operation for Better Queue Management," *International Journal of Service Industry Management*, 7, No. 5, 1994, 21–34; and Peter Jones and Emma Peppiat, "Managing Perceptions of Waiting Times in Service Queues," *International Journal of Service Industry Management*, 7, No. 5, 1996, 47–61. Also, see the findings for wait situations in stressful service encounters such as dental appointments by Elizabeth Gelfand Miller, Barbarah E. Kahn, and Mary Frances Luce, "Consumer Wait Management Strategies for Negative Service Events: A Coping Approach," *Journal of Consumer Research*, 34, No. 5, 2008, 635–648.
18. Susan Carey, "Northwest Airlines to Charge Extra for Aisle Seats," *The Wall Street Journal*, March 14, 2006.
19. Sheryl E. Kimes and Richard B. Chase, "The Strategic Levers of Yield Management," *Journal of Service Research*, 1, November 1998, 156–166; Anthony Ingold, Una McMahon-Beattie, and Ian Yeoman, eds., *Yield Management Strategies for the Service Industries*, 2nd edn. London: Continuum, 2000.
20. Irene C. L. Ng, Jochen Wirtz, and Khai Sheang Lee, "The Strategic Role of Unused Service Capacity," *International Journal of Service Industry Management*, 10, No. 2, 1999, 211–238.
21. Madeleine E. Pullman and Gary M. Thompson, "Evaluating Capacity- and Demand-Management Decisions at a Ski Resort," *Cornell Hotel and Restaurant Administration Quarterly*, 43, December 2002, 25–36; Madeleine E. Pullman and Gary Thompson, "Strategies for Integrating Capacity with Demand in Service Networks," *Journal of Service Research*, 5, February 2003, 169–183.

CHAPTER 10

Crafting the Service Environment

Managers . . . need to develop a better understanding of the interface between the resources they manipulate in atmospherics and the experience they want to create for the customer.

JEAN-CHARLES CHEBAT AND LAURETTE DUBÉ

Restaurant design has become as compelling an element as menu, food and wine . . . in determining a restaurant's success.

DANNY MEYER

LEARNING OBJECTIVES (LOs)

By the end of this chapter, the reader should be able to:

LO1 Recognize the four core purposes service environments fulfill.

LO2 Know the theoretical underpinning from environmental psychology that helps us to understand customer as well as employee responses to service environments.

LO3 Be familiar with the integrative servicescape model.

LO4 Know the dimensions of the service environment.

LO5 Understand the key ambient conditions and their effects on customers.

LO6 Understand the roles of spatial layout and functionality.

LO7 Understand the roles of signs, symbols, and artifacts.

LO8 Know how service employees and other customers are part of the servicescape.

LO9 Explain why designing an effective servicescape has to be done holistically and from the customer's perspective.

Guggenheim Museum in Bilbao[1]

When the Guggenheim Museum in Bilbao in northern Spain opened its doors to the public, praise poured in from all over the world. Hailed as "the greatest building of our time," its fascinating architecture was designed by Philip Johnson, the influential and world-famous American architect, and it put Bilbao on the world map as a tourist destination. Before that, most people had never heard of Bilbao, once an industrial area with a shipyard and large warehouse districts and a river that had been filled with a century of waste from the factories that lined its shores. The entire city was transformed with the museum as the first step of the city's redevelopment plan. Such a transformation is now even called the "Bilbao effect," and is being studied to understand how this kind of wow-effect architecture can help to transform a city.

The design features of the museum link to a number of meanings and messages. It is shaped like a ship and blends in with the environment of the river. The museum is a mixture of regular forms built in stone, curved forms made of titanium, and huge glass walls that allow natural light to penetrate the museum and provide visitors inside the building with a view of the surrounding hills. Outside, titanium panels have been arranged to look like fish scales, in keeping with the nearby Nervion River. A 43-foot-tall terrier topiary made of pots of fresh pansies and a huge spider sculpture—"Maman" by twentieth-century leading sculptor Louise Bourgeoris—greets visitors.

From the museum's huge, metal-domed atrium, patrons can visit 19 other galleries connected by curved walkways, glass lifts, and stairways. Even the design of the galleries is meant to hint at what visitors can expect inside. The rectangular shaped galleries have limestone covered walls. The rectangle is a more conventional shape, and these galleries hold the classic art collections. The irregularly shaped galleries hold collections of selected living artists. There are also special galleries with no columns within the museum so that large artworks can be displayed. The structures of these galleries are also a work of art that comes from a specially designed and planned servicescape.

While not all servicescapes are great works of architecture, the Guggenheim Museum in Bilbao is. It is an attention-drawing medium that shapes the expectations of its visitors. They can look forward to an awesome experience at the museum.

FIGURE 10.1 The Extraordinary Design of the Guggenheim Museum has Drawn Large Amounts of Praise and Crowds

WHAT IS THE PURPOSE OF SERVICE ENVIRONMENTS?

The physical service environment customers experience plays a key role in shaping the service experience and enhancing (or undermining) customer satisfaction, especially so in high-contact, people-processing services. Disney theme parks often are cited as vivid examples of service environments that make customers feel comfortable and highly satisfied and leave a long-lasting impression. In fact, organizations from hospitals to hotels and from restaurants to the offices of professional service firms have come to recognize that the service environment is an important component of their service's marketing mix and overall value proposition.

Designing the service environment is an art that takes a lot of time and effort, and it can be expensive to implement. Service environments, also called servicescapes, relate to the style and appearance of the physical surroundings and other experiential elements encountered by customers at service delivery sites.[2] Once designed and built, service environments are not easy to change.

Let's examine why many service firms take so much trouble to shape the environment in which their customers and service personnel will interact. For the Guggenheim Museum in Bilbao, it was to address several of the city's problems and to create a tourist attraction. For the museum and many service firms, there are four core purposes of servicescapes: (1) engineer the customers' experiences and shape their behavior; (2) convey the planned image of the firm and support its positioning and differentiation strategy; (3) be part of the value proposition; and (4) facilitate the service encounter and enhance both service quality and productivity. We elaborate on these key purposes in the next four sections.

Shape Customers' Experiences and Behavior

For organizations that deliver high-contact services, the design of the physical environment and the way in which tasks are performed by customer-contact personnel jointly play a vital role in creating a particular corporate identity and shaping the nature of customers' experiences. This environment and its accompanying atmosphere affect buyer behavior in three important ways:

1. *As a message-creating medium*—using symbolic cues to communicate to the intended audience about the distinctive nature and quality of the service experience.
2. *As an attention-creating medium*—to make the servicescape stand out from that of competing establishments and to attract customers from target segments.
3. *As an effect-creating medium*—employing colors, textures, sounds, scents, and spatial design to enhance the desired service experience and/or to heighten an appetite for certain goods, services, or experiences.

For Image, Positioning, and Differentiation

Services often are intangible, and customers cannot assess their quality well. So customers use the service environment as an important quality proxy, and firms take great pains to signal quality and portray the desired image.[3] Perhaps you've seen the reception area of successful professional firms such as investment banks or management consulting firms, where the decor and furnishings tend to be elegant and designed to impress. In retailing, the store environment affects how customers perceive the quality of its merchandise. However, if poorly designed, the service environment can drive away customers (see Research Insights 10.1).

Like other people, you probably infer higher merchandise quality if the goods are displayed in an environment with a prestige image rather than in one that creates a discount feel.[4] Consider Figure 10.2, which shows the lobbies of the Orbit Hotel and Hostel in Los Angeles and the St. Regis Grand Hotel in Rome, two different types of hotels that cater to two very different target segments. The Orbit caters to younger guests who love fun and have low budgets, and the St. Regis to a more mature, affluent, and prestigious clientele that includes upscale business travelers. Each of these two servicescapes clearly communicates and reinforces its hotel's respective positioning and sets service expectations as guests arrive.

Many servicescapes are purely functional. Firms seeking to convey the impression of low-price service do so by locating in inexpensive neighborhoods; occupying buildings with a simple appearance; minimizing wasteful use of space; and dressing their employees in practical, inexpensive uniforms. However, servicescapes do not always shape customer perceptions and behavior in ways intended by their creators. Customers often make creative use of physical spaces

RESEARCH INSIGHTS 10.1

COSMETIC SURGEONS' OFFICES TURN OFF PATIENTS

It appears that plastic surgeons could use some service marketing training along with their other courses in medical school. That's the diagnosis of two experts, Kate Altork and Douglas Dedo, who did a study of patients' reactions to doctors' offices. They found that many patients will cancel a surgery, change doctors, or refuse to consider future elective surgery if they feel uneasy in the doctor's office. The study results suggested that patients don't usually "doctor-jump" because they don't like the doctor but because they don't like the context of the service experience. The list of common patient dislikes includes graphic posters of moles and skin cancers decorating office walls; uncomfortable plastic identification bracelets for patients; claustrophobic examining rooms with no windows or current reading material; bathrooms that aren't clearly marked; and not enough wastebaskets and water coolers in the waiting room.

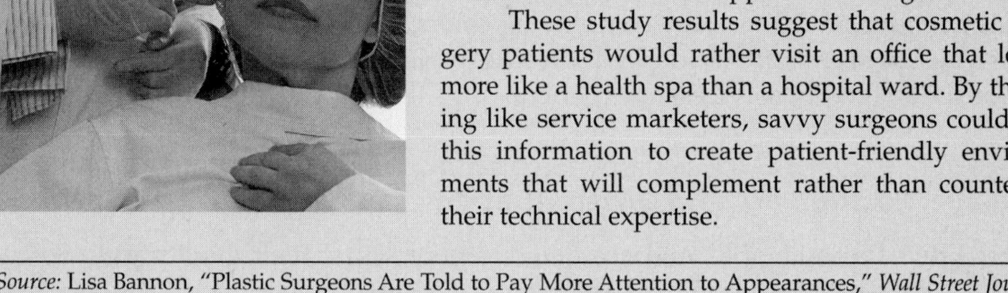

What do patients want? Most requests are surprisingly simple and involve creature comforts such as tissues, water coolers, telephones, plants, and bowls of candy in the waiting room and live flower arrangements in the lobby. Patients also want windows in the examining rooms and gowns that wrap around the entire body. They would like to sit on a real chair when they talk to a doctor instead of perching on a stool or examining table. Finally, pre-operative patients prefer to be separated from post-operative patients, because they don't want to be disturbed by sitting next to someone in the waiting room whose head is wrapped in bandages.

These study results suggest that cosmetic surgery patients would rather visit an office that looks more like a health spa than a hospital ward. By thinking like service marketers, savvy surgeons could use this information to create patient-friendly environments that will complement rather than counteract their technical expertise.

Source: Lisa Bannon, "Plastic Surgeons Are Told to Pay More Attention to Appearances," *Wall Street Journal*, March 15, 1997, B1.

and objects for different purposes. For instance, businesspeople may set aside a restaurant table for use as a temporary office desk, with papers spread around and a laptop computer and mobile phone positioned on its surface, competing for space with the food and beverages.[5] Students meeting for a study date in a restaurant or coffee shop often do the same with their textbooks and notepads. Smart designers keep an eye open for such trends—they may even lead to the creation of a new service concept!

The Servicescape as Part of the Value Proposition

Physical surroundings help to shape appropriate feelings and reactions in customers and employees.[6] Consider how effectively many amusement parks use the servicescape concept to enhance their service offerings. The clean environment of Disneyland or Denmark's Legoland, plus employees in colorful costumes, all contribute to the sense of fun and excitement visitors encounter on arrival and throughout their visit.

FIGURE 10.2 Comparison of Hotel Lobbies

Resort hotels illustrate how servicescapes can become a core part of the value proposition. Club Med's villages, designed to create a totally carefree atmosphere, may have provided the original inspiration for "getaway" holiday environments. New destination resorts are not only far more luxurious than Club Med, but also draw inspiration from theme parks to create fantasy environments, both inside and outside. Perhaps the most extreme examples can be found in Las Vegas. Facing competition from numerous casinos in other locations, Las Vegas has repositioned itself away from a somewhat unsavory adult destination once described in a London newspaper as "the electric Sodom and Gomorrah," to a more wholesome resort where families, too, can have fun. The gambling is still there, of course, but many of the huge hotels recently built (or rebuilt) have been transformed into visually striking entertainment centers that feature such attractions as erupting "volcanoes," mock sea battles, and striking reproductions of Paris, the Pyramids, and Venice and its canals.

Even movie theaters are discovering the power of servicescapes. Attendance at movies has been falling in the United States, and some of the big chains are hurting. However a few upstart boutique chains are trying a different approach. By building extravagant theaters and offering plush amenities, including lavishly decorated bars and restaurants and supervised playrooms for children, chains such as Florida-based Muvico are successfully enticing moviegoers to abandon their home entertainment centers—despite charging sharply higher admission prices. Says Muvico CEO Hamid Hashemi of his competitors: "At the end of the day, you all get the same 35-mm tape.... What sets you apart is how you package it."[7] At one Egyptian-themed Muvico cinema, moviegoers follow a purple-tiled pattern representing the Nile into the lobby, passing between hieroglyphics-covered pillars. Inside the auditorium, they find wide aisles and seats upholstered in red velvet. It's a very different experience from the megaplex at the local mall.

Facilitate the Service Encounter and Enhance Productivity

Finally, service environments often are designed to facilitate the service encounter and to increase productivity. Richard Chase and Douglas Stewart highlighted ways in which fail-safe methods embodied in the service environment can help reduce service failures and support a fast and smooth service delivery process.[8] For example, child-care centers use toy outlines on walls and floors to show where toys should be placed after use. In fast-food restaurants and school cafeterias, strategically located tray-return stands and notices on walls remind customers to return their trays. Service Perspective 10.1 illustrates how the design of hospitals helps patients recover and employees perform better.

SERVICE PERSPECTIVE 10.1

THE HOSPITAL SERVICESCAPE AND ITS EFFECTS ON PATIENTS AND EMPLOYEES[9]

Thankfully, most of us do not have to stay in a hospital. If it should happen, we hope our stay will allow us to recover in a suitable environment. But what is considered suitable in a hospital?

Patients may contract infections while hospitalized, feel stressed by contact with many strangers yet bored without much to do, dislike the food, and be unable to rest well. All these factors may delay a patients' recovery. Medical workers usually work under demanding conditions and may contract infectious diseases, be stressed by the emotional labor of dealing with difficult patients, or be at risk of injury when exposed to various types of medical equipment. Research has shown that more care in designing the hospital servicescape reduces these risks and contributes to patient well-being and recovery as well as staff welfare and productivity. The recommendations include:

- ***Provide single-bed rooms.*** These can lower infections caught in the hospital, improve rest and sleep quality by lessening disturbance caused by other patients sharing the room, increase patient privacy, facilitate social support by families, and even improve communication between staff and patients.
- ***Reduce noise levels.*** This leads to decreased stress levels for staff, and improved sleep for patients.
- ***Provide distractions for patients***, including areas of greenery and nature that they can see. This can aid patient recovery.
- ***Improve lighting***, especially access to natural light. A lighted environment increases cheerfulness in the building. Natural lighting can lead to reduced length of stay for patients. Staff work better under proper lighting and make fewer errors.
- ***Improve ventilation*** and air filtration to reduce the transmission of airborne viruses and improve air quality in the building.
- ***Develop user-friendly "wayfinding" systems.*** Hospitals are complex buildings, and it is very frustrating for the many first-time and infrequent visitors to get lost, especially when rushing to see a loved one who has been hospitalized.
- ***Design the layout*** of patient care units and the location of nurse stations to reduce unnecessary walking within the building and the tiredness and waste of time that can result. In this way, the quality of care to patients can be improved. Well designed layouts also enhance staff communication and activities.

Source: R. Ulrich, X. Quan, C. Zimring, A. Joseph, and R. Choudhary, "The Role of the Physical Environment in the Hospital of the 21st Century: A Once-in-a-Lifetime Opportunity," *Report to the center for health design for the Designing the 21st Century Hospital Project,* funded by the Robert Wood Johnson Foundation, 2004, September.

THE THEORY BEHIND CONSUMER RESPONSES TO SERVICE ENVIRONMENTS

We now understand why service firms take so much effort to design the service environment. But why does the service environment have such important effects on people and their behaviors? The field of environmental psychology studies how people respond to specific environments, and we can apply the theories from this field to better understand and manage how customers behave in different service settings.

Feelings Are a Key Driver of Customer Responses to Service Environments

Two important models help us better understand consumer responses to service environments. The first, the Mehrabian-Russell Stimulus-Response Model holds that our feelings are central to how we respond to the many environmental stimuli we are exposed to. The second, Russell's Model of Affect, focuses on how we can better understand those feelings and their implications on response behaviors.

THE MEHRABIAN-RUSSELL STIMULUS-RESPONSE MODEL. Figure 10.3 displays a simple yet fundamental model of how people respond to environments. The model holds that the conscious and unconscious perception and interpretation of the environment influences how people feel.[10] People's feelings in turn drive their responses to that environment. Feelings are central to the model, which posits that feelings—rather than perceptions or thoughts—drive behavior. For example, we don't avoid an environment simply because there are a lot of people around us; rather, we are deterred by the unpleasant feeling of crowding, of people being in our way, of lacking perceived control, and of not being able to get what we want as fast as we wish. If we had all the time in the world, felt excited about being part of the crowd during seasonal festivities, then exposure to the same number of people might lead to feelings of pleasure and excitement that would lead us to want to stay and explore that environment.

In environmental psychology, the typical outcome variable is "approach" or "avoidance" of an environment. Of course, in services marketing, we can add a long list of additional outcomes that a firm may want to manage, including how much money people spend and how satisfied they are with the service experience after they have left the firm's premises.

RUSSELL'S MODEL OF AFFECT. Given that affect or feelings are central to how people respond to an environment, we need to understand those feelings better. Russell's model of affect (see Figure 10.4) is widely used to help understand feelings in service environments and suggests that emotional responses to environments can be described along two main dimensions, pleasure and arousal.[11] Pleasure is a direct, subjective response to the environment, depending on how much the individual likes or dislikes the environment. Arousal refers to how stimulated the individual feels, ranging from deep sleep (lowest level of internal activity) to highest levels of adrenaline in the bloodstream, for example, when bungee-jumping (highest level of internal activity). The arousal quality of an environment is much less subjective than its pleasure quality. Arousal quality depends largely on

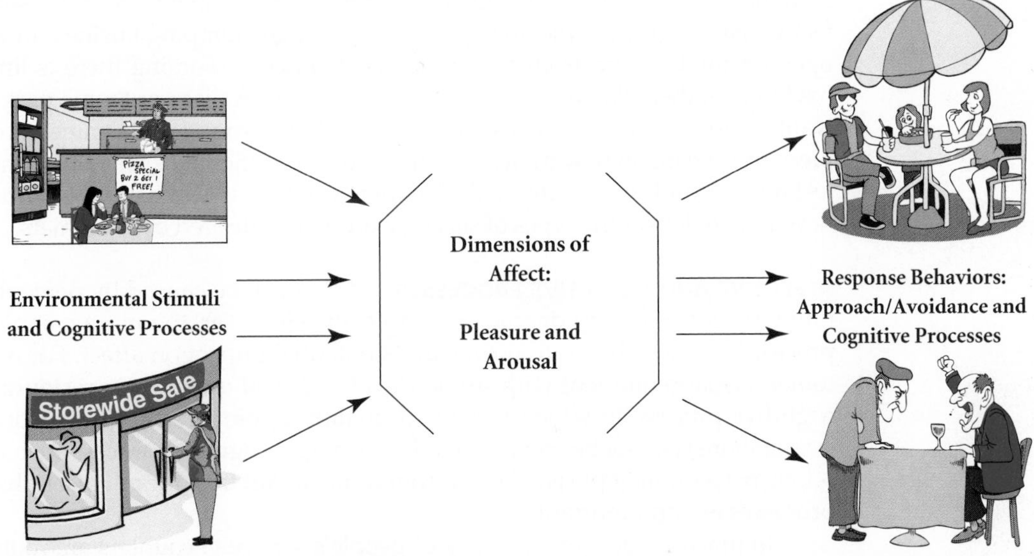

FIGURE 10.3 Model of Environmental Responses

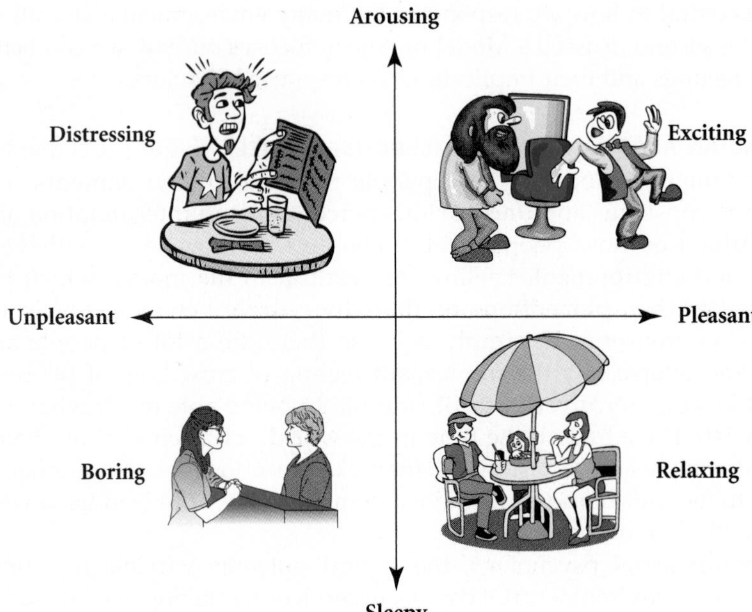

FIGURE 10.4 The Russell Model of Affect

the information rate or load of an environment. For example, environments are stimulating (i.e., have a high information rate) when they are complex, include motion or change, and have novel and surprising elements. A low rate, relaxing environment has the opposite characteristics.

You may wonder how all your feelings and emotions can be explained by only two dimensions. Russell separated the cognitive or thinking part of emotions from these two basic underlying emotional dimensions. Thus, the emotion of anger about a service failure could be modeled as high arousal, and high displeasure, which would locate it in the distressing region in our model, combined with a cognitive attribution process. When a customer attributes a service failure to the firm (i.e., he thinks it is the firm's fault that this has happened, that it is under the firm's control, and that the firm is not doing much to avoid it happening again), then this powerful cognitive attribution process feeds directly into high arousal and displeasure. Similarly, most other emotions can be dissected into their cognitive and affective components.

The strength of Russell's model of affect is its simplicity as it allows a direct assessment of how customers feel while in the service environment. Firms can set targets for affective states. For example, the operator of a bungee-jumping business or a roller coaster operator might want its customers to feel aroused (assuming there is little pleasure in having to gather all one's courage before jumping). A disco or theme park operator may want customers to feel excited (a relatively high arousal environment combined with pleasure), a bank may want its customers to feel confident, a spa may want customers to feel relaxed, and so on. Later in this chapter, we discuss how service environments can be designed to deliver the types of service experiences desired by customers.

AFFECTIVE AND COGNITIVE PROCESSES. Affect can be caused by perceptions and cognitive processes of any degree of complexity. However, the more complex a cognitive process becomes, the more powerful its potential impact on affect. For example, a customer's disappointment with service level and food quality in a restaurant (a complex cognitive process, in which perceived quality is compared to previously held service expectations) cannot be compensated by a simple cognitive process such as the subconscious perception of pleasant background music. Yet this doesn't mean that such simple processes are unimportant.

In practice, the large majority of people's service encounters are routine, with little high level cognitive processing. We tend to function on "auto pilot" and follow our service scripts when doing routine transactions such as using a bus or subway or entering a fast-food restaurant or a bank. Most of the time, it is the simple cognitive processes that determine how people feel in the service setting. Those include the conscious and even unconscious perceptions of space, colors, scents, and so on. However, should higher levels of cognitive processes be triggered—for instance, through something surprising in the service environment—then it's the interpretation of this surprise that determines people's feelings.[12]

BEHAVIORAL CONSEQUENCES OF AFFECT. At the most basic level, pleasant environments tend to draw people in, whereas unpleasant ones result in avoidance behaviors. Arousal acts as an amplifier of the basic effect of pleasure on behavior. If the environment is pleasant, increasing arousal can generate excitement, leading to a stronger positive consumer response. Conversely, if a service environment is inherently unpleasant, managers should avoid increasing arousal levels, as this would move customers into the "distressed" region. For example, loud, fast-beat music would increase the stress levels of shoppers when they are trying to make their way through crowded aisles on a pre-Christmas Friday evening. In such situations, managers need to find ways to lower information load of the environment.

Finally, customers have strong affective expectations of some services. Think of such experience as a romantic, candlelit dinner in a restaurant; a relaxing spa visit; or an exciting time at a stadium or a nightclub. When customers have strong affective expectations, it is important that the environment be designed to match those expectations.[13]

The Servicescapes Model—An Integrative Framework

Building on the basic models in environmental psychology, Mary Jo Bitner developed a comprehensive model that she named the "servicescape."[14] Figure 10.5 shows the main dimensions she identified in service environments: ambient conditions, space/functionality, and signs, symbols, and artifacts. Because individuals tend to perceive these dimensions holistically, the key to effective design is how well each individual dimension fits together with everything else.

Bitner's model shows that there are customer and employee-response moderators. This means that the same service environment can have different effects on

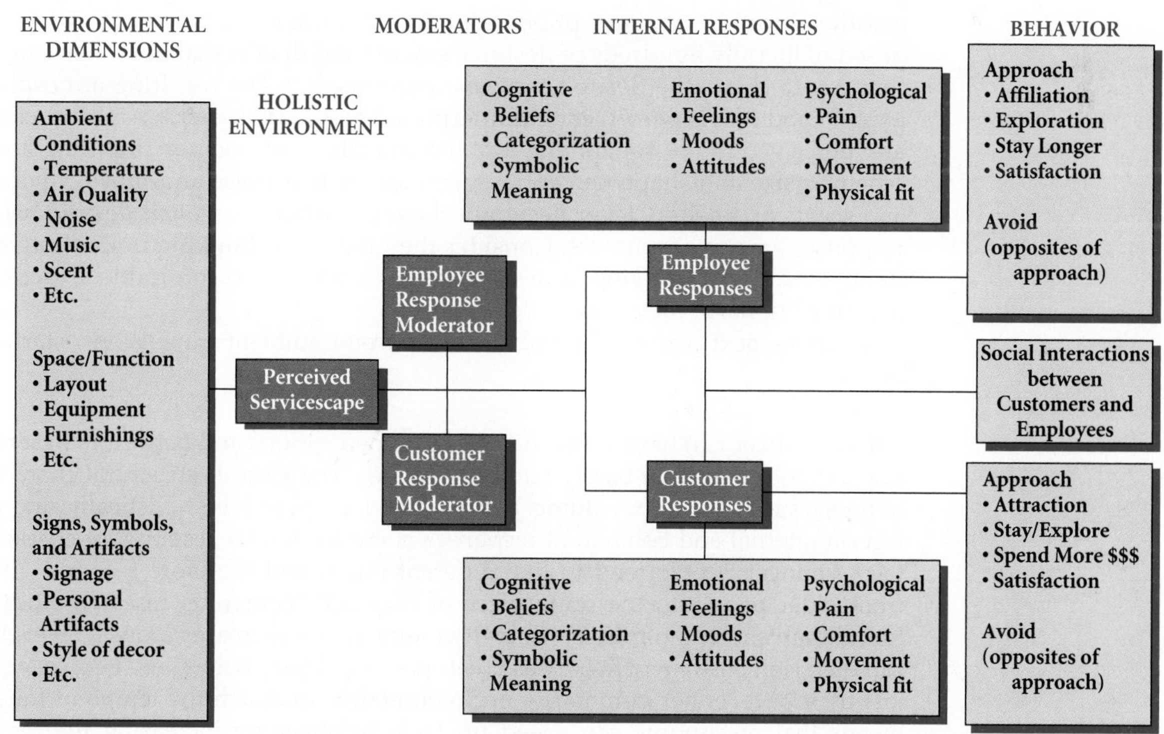

FIGURE 10.5 The Servicescapes Model

Source: Mary Jo Bitner, "Servicescapes: The Impact of Physical Surroundings on Customers and Employees," *Journal of Marketing, 56* (April 1992), 57–71. Copyright © 1992 American Marketing Association. Used with permission.

different customers, depending on who that customer is and what she or he likes—beauty lies in the eyes of the beholder, and is subjective. For example, rap music may be sheer pleasure to some customer segments—and sheer torture to others.

An important contribution of Bitner's model is inclusion of employee responses to the service environment. After all, employees spend much more time there than customers, and it's crucial that designers become aware of how a particular environment enhances (or at least does not reduce) the productivity of frontline personnel and the quality of service they deliver.

Internal customer and employee responses can be categorized into cognitive responses (e.g., quality perceptions and beliefs), emotional responses (e.g., feelings and moods), and psychological responses (e.g., pain and comfort). These internal responses lead to overt behavioral responses such as avoiding a crowded department store or responding positively to a relaxing environment by remaining there longer and spending extra money on impulse purchases. It's important to understand that the behavioral responses of customers and employees must be shaped in ways that facilitate production and purchase of high-quality services. Consider how the outcomes of service transactions may differ in situations where both customers and frontline staff feel agitated and stressed rather than relaxed and happy.

DIMENSIONS OF THE SERVICE ENVIRONMENT

Service environments are complex and have many design elements. In Table 10.1, for example, you can see an overview of the design elements that might be encountered in a retail outlet. In this section, we focus on the main dimensions of the service environment in the servicescape model: the ambient conditions, space and functionality, and signs, symbols, and artifacts.[15]

The Effect of Ambient Conditions

Ambient conditions refer to those characteristics of the environment that pertain to your five senses. Even when they're not noted consciously, they may still affect your emotional well-being, perceptions, and even attitudes and behaviors. They are composed of literally hundreds of design elements and details that must work together if they are to create the desired service environment.[16] The resulting atmosphere creates a mood that is perceived and interpreted by the customer.[17] Ambient conditions are perceived both separately and holistically and include lighting and color schemes, size and shape perceptions, sounds such as noise and music, temperature, and scents or smells. Clever design of these conditions can elicit desired behavioral responses among consumers. Consider the innovative thinking underlying the new trend to transform flying into a more relaxing and comfortable experience, as described in Best Practice in Action 10.1.

Let us next discuss a number of important ambient dimensions, starting with music.

MUSIC. Music can have powerful effects on perceptions and behaviors in service settings, even if played at barely audible volumes. The various structural characteristics of music such as tempo, volume, and harmony are perceived holistically, and their effect on internal and behavioral responses is moderated by respondent characteristics (e.g., younger people tend to like different music and therefore respond differently from older people to the same piece of music).[18] Numerous research studies have found that fast tempo music and high volume music increases arousal levels,[19] which can then lead customers to increase their pace of various behaviors. People tend to adjust their pace, either voluntarily or involuntarily, to match the tempo of music. This means that restaurants can speed up table turnover by increasing the tempo and volume of the music and serve more diners during the course of an evening, or slow diners down with slow beat music and softer volume to keep them longer in the restaurant and increase beverage revenues as shown in a number of field experiments.

TABLE 10.1 Design Elements of a Retail Store Environment

DIMENSIONS	DESIGN ELEMENTS	
Exterior facilities	• Architectural style • Height of building • Size of building • Color of building • Exterior walls and exterior signs • Storefront • Marquee • Lawns and gardens	• Window displays • Entrances • Visibility • Uniqueness • Surrounding stores • Surrounding areas • Congestion • Parking and accessibility
General interior	• Flooring and carpeting • Color schemes • Lighting • Scents • Odors (e.g., tobacco smoke) • Sounds and music • Fixtures • Wall composition • Wall textures (paint, wallpaper) • Ceiling composition	• Temperature • Cleanliness • Width of aisles • Dressing facilities • Vertical transportation • Dead areas • Merchandise layout and displays • Price levels and displays • Cash register placement • Technology, modernization
Store layout	• Allocation of floor space for selling, merchandise, personnel, and customers • Placement of merchandise • Grouping of merchandise • Workstation placement • Placement of equipment • Placement of cash register	• Waiting areas • Traffic flow • Waiting queues • Furniture • Dead areas • Department locations • Arrangements within departments
Interior displays	• Point-of-purchase displays • Posters, signs, and cards • Pictures and artwork • Wall decorations • Themesetting • Ensemble	• Racks and cases • Product display • Price display • Cut cases and dump bins • Mobiles
Social dimensions	• Personnel characteristics • Employee uniforms • Crowding	• Customer characteristics • Privacy • Self-service

Sources: Barry Berman and Joel R. Evans, Retail Management—A strategic approach, 8th ed. Upper Saddle River, NJ: Prentice Hall, 2001, p. 604; L. W. Turley and Ronald E. Milliman, "Atmospheric Effects on Shopping Behavior. A review of the experimental literature." *Journal of Business Research*, 49 (2000): 193–211.

For example, a restaurant study conducted over eight weeks showed that beverage revenue increased substantially when slow-beat music was played. Customers who dined in a slow-music environment spent longer in the restaurant than individuals in a fast-music condition.[20] Likewise, shoppers walked less rapidly when slow music was played and increased their level of impulse purchases. Playing familiar music in a store was shown to stimulate shoppers and thereby reduce their browsing time, whereas playing unfamiliar music induced shoppers to spend more time there.[21]

In situations that require waiting for service, effective use of music may shorten perceived waiting time and increase customer satisfaction. Relaxing music proved effective in lowering stress levels in a hospital's surgery waiting room. And pleasant music has even been shown to enhance customers' perceptions of service personnel.[22]

BEST PRACTICE IN ACTION 10.1

Emirates Airline Delights Its Customers

Emirates Airline is one of the world's youngest but largest airlines. Back in October 1985, it had just two leased aircraft, but today it has more than 137 that fly to more than 100 destinations in 60 countries. Its growth has never been lower than 20 percent per year, and some 40 percent of all flight movement in the Dubai airport is by Emirates Airline.

Delighting customers means offering them the unexpected. When Emirates launched the Dubai–Toronto flight toward the end of 2008, it offered all first-class passengers a complimentary stay in the Atlantis Hotel, Dubai.

Delighting customers also means looking at upgrading technology. Emirates Airlines's in-flight entertainment program has won six awards in a row for Best Airline In-flight Entertainment. Emirates was also the first airline to introduce in-flight mobile phone usage for its passengers across its entire fleet, at a cost of more than $27 million in 2008.

The airline prides itself on providing what it terms an exceptional journey. The airline has carefully constructed a blend of service, comfort, and technology to improve the travel experience. A primary part of this has been not only to provide a comfortable, relaxing environment but also to ensure that all passengers, regardless of class, arrive refreshed. Notable innovations include a unique lighting system designed to simulate the time of day at the destination of the flight. This aids in offsetting jetlag. First-class customers enjoy a tranquil environment; it is luxurious, peaceful, and quiet. First-class passengers can enjoy private suites with amenities, additional space, and comfort. Business-class customers have the advantage of a flat bed on selected routes, and even economy seating has more leg room and seats that recline for a more comfortable journey. A major part of the overall relaxation package for all travelers is the award-winning in-flight meals that are created by internationally renowned chefs.

The relaxing environment begins in the departure lounges. The first-class lounges offer gourmet dining and spas. Each of the departure lounges is designed around separate areas to help travelers to relax and unwind before their flight.

Many of the innovations can be linked to the former head of marketing, Mike Simon, who retired in 2009. He once admitted that he did not like flying, but he liked the process of getting there.

Sources: www.emirates.com; www.thenational.ae.

Providing the right mix of music to restaurants, retail stores, and even call centers has become an industry in its own right. For example, Texas-based DMX provides music to over 300 corporate clients through creating signature mixes of between 200 to 800 licensed songs and pipes the music into their clients' outlets. These music mixes are updated remotely about once a month.[23]

Would it surprise you to learn that music can also be used to deter the wrong type of customers? Many service environments, including subway systems, supermarkets, and other publicly accessible locations, attract individuals who are not bona fide customers. Some are jaycustomers (see Chapter 13) whose behavior causes problems for management and customers alike. In the United Kingdom, an increasingly popular strategy to drive such individuals away is to play classical music, which is apparently painful to vandals' and loiterers' ears. Co-op, a UK grocery chain, has been experimenting with playing music outside its outlets to stop teenagers from hanging around and intimidating customers. Its staff are equipped with a remote control and, as reported by Steve Broughton of Co-op, "can turn the music on if there's a situation developing and they need to disperse people."[24]

The London Underground (subway) system has probably made the most extensive use of classical music as a deterrent. Thirty stations pump out Mozart and Haydn to discourage loitering and vandalism. A London Underground spokesperson reports that the most effective deterrents are anything written by Mozart or sung by Pavarotti. According to Adrian North, a psychologist researching the link between music and behavior at Leicester University, unfamiliarity is a key factor in driving people away. When the target individuals are unused to strings and woodwinds, Mozart will do

(Figure 10.6). However, for the musically literate loiterer, an atonal barrage is likely to work better. For instance, North tormented Leicester's students in the local bar with what he describes as "computer-game music." It cleared the place!

FIGURE 10.6 Classical Music Can Be Used to Deter Vandals and Loiterers

SCENT. Scent is another important ambient dimension. Ambient scent or smell, which pervades an environment, may or may not be consciously perceived by customers and is not related to any particular product. The presence of scent can have a strong impact on mood, affective and evaluative responses, and even purchase intentions and in-store behaviors.[25] We are experiencing the power of smell when we are hungry and get a whiff of freshly baked croissants long before we pass a local bakery. This smell makes us aware of our hunger and points us to the solution (i.e., walk into the bakery and get some food). Other examples include the smell of freshly baked cookies on Main Street in Disney's Magic Kingdom to relax customers and provide a feeling of warmth, or the smell of potpourri in Victoria's Secret stores to create the ambiance of a lingerie closet.

Olfaction researcher Alan R. Hirsch, M.D. of the Smell & Taste Treatment and Research Foundation based in Chicago, is convinced that at some point in the future we will understand scents so well that we will be able to use them to manage people's behaviors.[26] Service marketers will be interested in how to make you hungry and thirsty in the restaurant, relax you in a dentist's waiting room, and energize you to work out harder in a gym. In aromatherapy, it is generally accepted that scents have distinct characteristics and can be used to solicit certain emotional, physiological, and behavioral responses. Table 10.2 shows the generally assumed effects of specific scents on people as prescribed by aromatherapy. In service settings, research has shown that scents can have significant impact on customer perceptions, attitudes, and behaviors. For example:

- Gamblers plunked 45 percent more quarters into slot machines when a Las Vegas casino was scented with a pleasant artificial smell. When the intensity of the scent was increased, spending jumped by 53 percent.[27]
- People were more willing to buy Nike sneakers and pay more for them—an average of $10.33 more per pair—when they tried on the shoes in a floral-scented room. The same effect was found even when the scent was so faint that people could not detect it, that is, the scent was perceived unconsciously.[28]

TABLE 10.2 Aromatherapy—The Effects of Selected Fragrances on People

Fragrance	Aroma Type	Aromatherapy Class	Traditional Use	Potential Psychological Effect on People
Eucalyptus	Camphoraceous	Toning, stimulating	Deodorant, antiseptic, soothing agent	Stimulating and energizing
Lavender	Herbaceous	Calming, balancing, soothing	Muscle relaxant, soothing agent, astringent	Relaxing and calming
Lemon	Citrus	Energizing, uplifting	Antiseptic, soothing agent	Soothing energy levels
Black pepper	Spicy	Balancing, soothing	Muscle relaxant, aphrodisiac	Balancing people's emotions

Sources: www.Fragrant.demon.co.uk, www.naha.org/WhatisAromatherapy; Dana Butcher, "Aromatherapy-Its Past & Future," *Drug and Cosmetic Industry*, 16, No. 3, 1998, 22–24; Shirley Price and Len Price, *Aromoatherapy for Health Professionals*, 3rd edn.; A. S. Mattila and J. Wirtz, "Congruency of Scent and Music as a Driver of In-store Evaluations and Behavior," *Journal of Retailing*, 77, 2001, 273–289.

Service firms have recognized the power of scent and increasingly make it part of their brand experience. For example, Westin Hotels uses a white tea fragrance throughout its lobbies, and Sheraton scents its lobbies with a combination of fig, clove, and jasmine. As a response to the trend of scenting servicescapes, professional service firms have entered the scent marketing space. For example, Ambius, a Rentokil Initial company, offers scent-related services such as "sensory branding," "ambient scenting" and "odor remediation" for retail, hospitality, health care, financial services, and other services. Firms can outsource their servicescape scenting to Ambius, which offers one-stop solutions ranging from consulting and designing exclusive signature scents for a service firm to managing the ongoing scenting of all the outlets of a chain.[29]

COLOR. In addition to music and scent, researchers have found that colors have a strong impact on people's feelings.[30] Color is "stimulating, calming, expressive, disturbing, impressional, cultural, exuberant, symbolic. It pervades every aspect of our lives, embellishes the ordinary, and gives beauty and drama to everyday objects."[31]

The de facto system used in psychological research is the Munsell System, which defines colors in the three dimensions of hue, value, and chroma.[32] *Hue* is the pigment of the color (i.e., the name of the color: red, orange, yellow, green, blue, or violet). *Value* is the degree of lightness or darkness of the color, relative to a scale that extends from pure black to pure white. *Chroma* refers to hue-intensity, saturation or brilliance; high chroma colors have a high intensity of pigmentation in them and are perceived as rich and vivid, whereas low chroma colors are perceived as dull.

Hues are classified into warm colors (red, orange, and yellow hues) and cold colors (blue and green), with orange (a mix of red and yellow) the warmest and blue the coldest of the colors. These colors can be used to manage the warmth of an environment. For example, if a violet is too warm, you can cool it off by reducing the amount of red. Or if a red is too cold, warm it up by giving it a shot of orange.[33] Warm colors are associated with elated mood states and arousal, but also heightened anxiety, whereas cool colors reduce arousal levels and can elicit emotions such as peacefulness, calmness, love, and happiness.[34] Table 10.3 summarizes common associations and responses to colors.

Research in a service environment context has shown that despite differing color preferences, people generally are drawn to warm color environments. However, paradoxically, findings show that red-hued retail environments are seen as negative, tense,

TABLE 10.3 Common Associations and Human Responses to Colors

Color	Degree of Warmth	Nature Symbol	Common Association and Human Responses to Color
Red	Warm	Earth	High energy and passion; can excite, stimulate emotions, expressions, and warmth
Orange	Warmest	Sunset	Emotions, expression, and warmth
Yellow	Warm	Sun	Optimism, clarity, and intellect, and mood-enhancing
Green	Cool	Growth, grass, and trees	Nurturing, healing, and unconditional love
Blue	Coolest	Sky and ocean	Relaxation, serenity, and loyalty
Indigo	Cool	Sunset	Meditation and spirituality
Violet	Cool	Violet flower	Spirituality; reduces stress, can create an inner feeling of calm

Sources: Sara O. Marberry and Laurie Zagon, *The Power of Color—Creating Healthy Interior Spaces.* New York: John Wiley, 1995, 18; Sarah Lynch, *Bold Colors for Modern Rooms: Bright Ideas for People Who Love Color.* Gloucester, MA: Rockport Publishers, 2001, 24–29.

and less attractive than cool color environments. Warm colors encourage fast decision making and in service situations are best suited for low-involvement decisions or impulse purchases. Cool colors are favored when consumers need time to make high-involvement purchase decisions.[35]

Although we have an understanding of the general effects of colors, their use in any specific context should be approached with caution. For example, when a transportation company in Israel painted its buses green as part of an environmentalism public relations campaign, reactions to this seemingly simple act were unexpectedly negative. Some customers found the green color hampered service performance because the green buses blended in with the environment and were difficult to see; some felt it esthetically unappealing and inappropriate as it represented undesirable notions such as terrorism or opposing sports teams. [36]

A good example of using color schemes to enhance the service experience is provided by the HealthPark Medical Center in Fort Meyers, Florida, which has combined full-spectrum color in its lobby with unusual lighting to achieve a dreamlike setting. The lobby walls are awash in rainbow colors by an arrangement of high-intensity lamps in blue, green, violet, red, orange, and yellow. Craig Roeder, the lighting designer for the hospital, explained: "It's a hospital. People walk into it worried and sick. I tried to design an entrance space that provides them with light and energy—to 'beam them up' a little bit before they get to the patient rooms."[37]

Spatial Layout and Functionality

In addition to ambient conditions, spatial layout and functionality are other key dimensions of the service environment. As a service environment generally has to fulfill specific purposes and customer needs, spatial layout and functionality are particularly important.

Spatial layout refers to the floor plan, size, and shape of furnishings, counters, and potential machinery and equipment and the ways in which they are arranged. *Functionality* refers to the ability of those items to facilitate the performance of service transactions. Spatial layout and functionality create the visual and functional servicescape for delivery and consumption to take place. Both dimensions determine user friendliness and the facility's ability to service customers well; and, they not only affect the efficiency of the service operation, they also shape the customer experience (Figure 10.7). Tables that are too close in a café, counters in a bank that lack privacy, uncomfortable chairs in a lecture theatre, and lack of car

FIGURE 10.7 The Spacious Kuala Lumpur International Airport in Malaysia Is Designed to Help Travelers Find Their Way

FIGURE 10.8 Signs Are Frequently Used to Teach and Reinforce Behavioral Rules in Service Settings
Note: Fines are in Singapore Dollars (equivalent to roughly US$300).

parking space can all leave negative impressions on customers, affect service experience and buying behavior, and consequently the business performance of the service facility.

Signs, Symbols, and Artifacts

Many things in the service environment act as explicit or implicit signals to communicate the firm's image, help customers find their way, and to convey the service script. In particular, first-time customers will automatically try to draw meaning from the environment to guide them through the service processes.

Examples of explicit signals include signs that can be used (1) as labels (e.g., to indicate the name of the department or counter); (2) for giving directions (e.g., to certain service counters, entrance, exit, the way to elevators and toilets); (3) for communicating the service script (e.g., take a number and wait for it to be called or clear the tray after your meal); and (4) behavioral rules (e.g., switch off or turn your mobile devices to silent mode during the performance, or smoking/no-smoking areas). Signs frequently are used to teach and reinforce behavioral rules in service settings. Singapore, which strictly enforces rules in many service settings, especially in public buildings and public transport, is sometimes referred to ironically as a "fine" city (Figure 10.8).

The challenge for servicescape designers is to use signs, symbols, and artifacts to guide customers clearly through the process of service delivery and to teach the service script in as intuitive a manner as possible. This task assumes particular importance in situations in which there is a high proportion of new or infrequent customers and/or a high degree of self-service with no or only few service employees available to guide customers through the process.

Customers become disoriented when they cannot derive clear signals from a servicescape, leading to anxiety and uncertainty about how to proceed and how to obtain the desired service. Customers can easily feel lost in a confusing environment and experience anger and frustration as a result. Think about the last time you were in a hurry and tried to find your way through an unfamiliar hospital, shopping center, or airport where the signs and other directional cues were not intuitive to you. At many service facilities, customers' first point of contact is likely to be the location where they park their cars. As emphasized in Best Practice in Action 10.2, the principles of effective environment design apply even in this very mundane environment.

People are Part of the Service Environment, Too

The appearance and behavior of both service personnel and customers can reinforce or detract from the impression created by a service environment. Within the constraints imposed by legal obligations and skill requirements, service firms may seek to recruit staff to fill specific roles, costume them in uniforms consistent with the servicescape in which they will be working, and script their speech and movements. Dennis Nickson and his colleagues use the term "aesthetic labor" to capture the importance of the physical imagery of service personnel who serve customers directly.[39] Employees at Disney theme parks are called cast members. Whether the staff is acting as Cinderella, one of the seven dwarfs, or as park cleaner or the person managing Buzz Lightyear's Tomorrowland booth, these cast members must dress up and look the part. Once dressed up, they must "perform" for the guests.

BEST PRACTICE IN ACTION 10.2

Guidelines for Parking Design

Car parks play an important role at many service facilities. Effective use of signs, symbols, and artifacts in a parking lot or garage helps customers find their way, manages their behavior, and portrays a positive image for the sponsoring organization.

- ***Friendly warnings***—All warning signs should communicate a customer benefit. For instance, "Fire lane—for everyone's safety, we ask you not to park in the fire lane."
- ***Safety lighting***—Good lighting that penetrates all areas makes life easier for customers and enhances safety. Firms may want to draw attention to this feature with notices stating that "Parking lots have been specially lit for your safety."
- ***Help customers remember where they left their vehicle***—Forgetting the location of the family car in a huge lot or parking structure can be a nightmare. Many parking garages have adopted color-coded floors to help customers remember which level they parked on. Boston's Logan Airport goes two steps further—each level has been assigned a theme associated with Massachusetts such as Paul Revere's Ride, Cape Cod, or the Boston Marathon. An image is attached to each theme: a male figure on horseback, a lighthouse, or a woman runner. And while waiting for the elevator, travelers hear a few bars of music tied to the theme for that level; in the case of the Boston Marathon floor, it's the theme music from *Chariots of Fire*, an Oscar-winning movie about an Olympic runner.
- ***Maternity parking***—Handicapped spaces often are required by law but require special stickers on a vehicle. A few thoughtful organizations have designated "expectant mother" parking spaces, painted with a blue/pink stork. This strategy demonstrates a sense of caring and understanding of customer needs.
- ***Fresh paint***—Curbs, crosswalks, and lot lines should be repainted regularly, before any cracking, peeling, or disrepair become evident. Pro-active and frequent painting give positive cleanliness cues and projects a positive image.[38]

Likewise, marketing communications may seek to attract customers who will not only appreciate the ambience created by the service provider but will actively enhance it by their own appearance and behavior. In hospitality and retail settings, newcomers often survey the array of existing customers before deciding whether to patronize the establishment. Consider Figure 10.9, which shows the interior of two restaurants. Imagine you have just entered each of these two dining rooms. How is each positioning itself within the restaurant industry? What sort of meal experience can you expect? And what clues do you employ to make your judgments? In particular, what inferences do you draw from looking at the customers already seated in each restaurant?

PUTTING IT ALL TOGETHER

Although individuals often perceive particular aspects or individual design features of an environment, it is the total configuration of all those design features that determines consumer responses. That is, consumers perceive service environments holistically.[40]

Design with a Holistic View

Whether a dark, glossy wooden floor is the perfect flooring depends on everything else in that service environment, including the type, color scheme, and materials of the furniture, the lighting, the promotional materials, and the overall brand perception and

FIGURE 10.9 Distinctive Servicescapes—From Table Settings to Furniture and Room Design—Create Different Customer Expectations of These Two Restaurants

positioning of the firm. Servicescapes have to be seen holistically, which means no one dimension of the design can be optimized in isolation, because everything depends on everything else. Research Insight 10.2 shows that even the arousal elements of scent and music interact and need to be considered in conjunction to elicit the desired customer responses.

The holistic characteristic of environments makes designing service environments an art, so much so that professional designers tend to focus on specific types of servicescapes. For example, a handful of famous interior designers do nothing but create hotel lobbies around the world. Similarly, there are design experts, who focus exclusively on restaurants, bars, clubs, cafes and bistros, or retail outlets, or healthcare facilities, and so forth.[41]

Design from a Customer's Perspective

Many service environments are built with an emphasis on esthetic values, and designers sometimes forget the most important factor to consider when designing service environments: the customers who will be using them. Ron Kaufman, the founder of Up Your Service! College, experienced the following design flaws in two, new high-profile service environments:

- "A new Sheraton Hotel just had opened in Jordan without clear signage that would guide guests from the ballrooms to the restrooms. The signs that did exist were etched in muted gold on dark marble pillars. More 'obvious' signs were apparently inappropriate amidst such elegant décor. Very swish, very chic, but who were they designing it for?"
- "At a new airport lounge in a major Asian city, a partition of colorful glass hung from the ceiling. My luggage lightly brushed against it as I walked inside. The entire partition shook and several panels came undone. A staff member hurried over and began carefully reassembling the panels. (Thank goodness nothing broke.) I apologized profusely. 'Don't worry,' she replied, 'This happens all the time.'" An airport lounge is a heavy traffic area. People are always moving in and out. Kaufman keeps asking, "What were the interior designers thinking? Who were they designing it for?"

"I am regularly amazed," declared Kaufman, "by brand new facilities that are obviously user 'unfriendly'! Huge investments of time and money…but who are they designing it for? What were the architects thinking about? Size? Grandeur? Physical

RESEARCH INSIGHT 10.2

MATCH AND MISMATCH OF SCENT AND MUSIC IN THE SERVICESCAPE

Whether a certain type of background enhances consumer responses depends on the ambient scent of the service environment. Using a field experiment, Anna Mattila and Jochen Wirtz manipulated two types of pleasant music and pleasant scent in a gift store, which differed in their arousing qualities. Consumer impulse purchasing and satisfaction were measured for the various music and scent conditions.

The experiment used two compact discs from the *Tune Your Brain*™ series by Elizabeth Miles, an ethnomusicologist. The low arousal music was the Relaxing Collection featuring slow-tempo music, while the high arousal music consisted of the Energizing Collection, featuring fast-tempo music. Similarly, scent was manipulated to have high or low arousal quality. Lavender was used for the low arousal scent because of its relaxing and calming properties. Grapefruit was used for the high arousal scent because of its stimulating properties, which can refresh, revive, and improve mental clarity and alertness and can even enhance physical strength and energy.

The results of this experiment show that when the arousal qualities of music and ambient scent were matched, consumers responded favorably. The figures below show these effects clearly. For instance, scenting the store with low arousal scent (lavender) combined with slow tempo music led to higher satisfaction and more impulse purchases than using that scent with high arousal music. Playing fast tempo music had a more positive effect when the store was scented with grapefruit (high arousal scent) rather than with lavender. This study showed that when environmental stimuli act together to provide a coherent atmosphere, consumers in that environment will respond more positively.

These findings suggest that bookstores might induce people to linger longer and buy more by playing slow tempo music combined with a relaxing scent, or event managers might consider using arousing scents aromas to enhance excitement.

FIGURE 10.10 The Effect of Scent and Music on Satisfaction

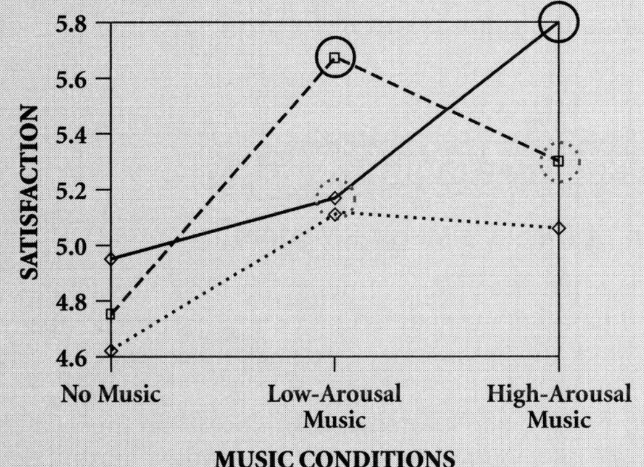

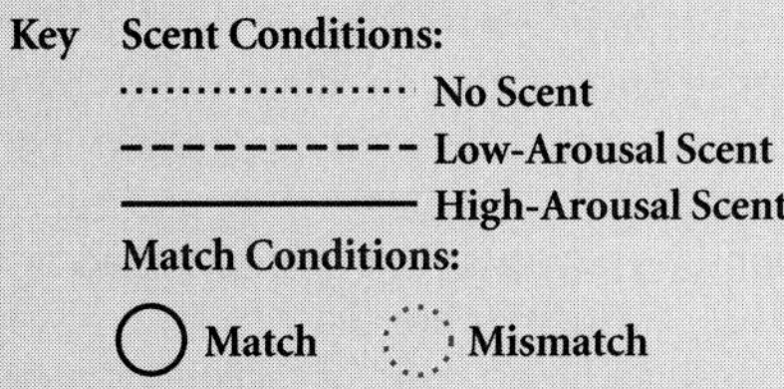

FIGURE 10.11 The Effect of Scent and Music on Impulse Purchases

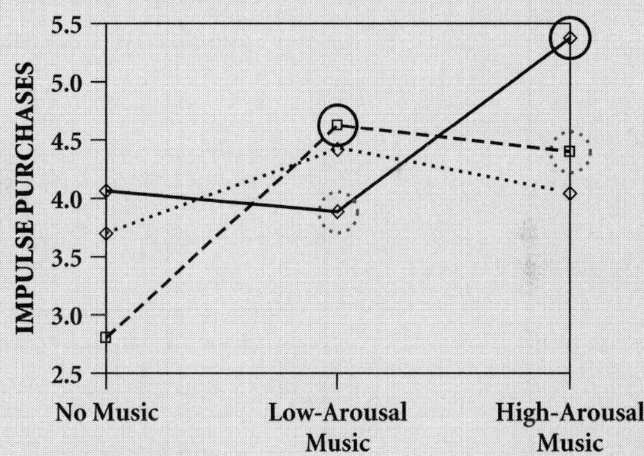

**Note:* Both charts are on a scale from 1 to 7, with 7 being the extreme positive response. The solid-line circles show the match conditions, where both music and scent are either stimulating or relaxing, and the intermitted-line circles show the mismatch conditions, in which one stimulus is relaxing and the other is stimulating (i.e., relaxing music and stimulating scent or stimulating music and relaxing scent).

Source: Anna S. Mattila and Jochen Wirtz, "Congruency of Scent and Music as a Driver of In-Store Evaluations and Behavior," *Journal of Retailing* 77 (2001): 273–289.

exercise?" He draws the following key learning point: "It's easy to get caught up in designing new things that are 'cool' or 'elegant' or 'hot.' But if you don't keep your customer in mind throughout, you could end up with an investment that's not."[42]

Alain d'Astous explored environmental aspects that irritate shoppers. His findings highlighted the following problems:

- *Ambient Conditions* (ordered by severity of irritation):
  - Store is not clean.
  - Too hot inside the store or the shopping center.
  - Music inside the store is too loud.
  - Bad smell in the store.
- *Environmental Design Variables*:
  - No mirror in the dressing room.
  - Unable to find what one needs.
  - Directions within the store are inadequate.
  - Arrangement of store items has been changed.
  - Store is too small.

Now, contrast Kaufman's experiences and d'Astou's findings with the Disney example in Best Practice in Action 10.3. What conclusions do you draw?

Tools to Guide Servicescape Design

As a manager, how might you determine which aspects of the servicescape irritate customers and which they like? Among the tools you can use are:

- ***Keen observation*** of customers' behavior and responses to the service environment by management, supervisors, branch managers, and frontline staff.
- ***Feedback and ideas from frontline staff and customers*** using a broad array of research tools ranging from suggestion boxes to focus groups and surveys. (The

BEST PRACTICE IN ACTION 10.3

Design of Disney's Magic Kingdom

Walt Disney was one of the undisputed champions of designing service environments. His tradition of amazingly careful and detailed planning has become one of his company's hallmarks and is visible everywhere in its theme parks. For example, Main Street is angled to make it seem longer upon entry into the Magic Kingdom than it actually is. With myriad facilities and attractions strategically inclined and located at each side of the street, this makes people look forward to the relatively long journey to the Castle. However, looking down the slope from the Castle back toward the entrance makes Main Street appear shorter than it really is, relieving exhaustion and rejuvenating guests. It encourages strolling, which minimizes the number of people who take buses and so eliminates the threatening problem of traffic congestion.

Meandering sidewalks with multiple attractions keep guests feeling entertained by both the planned activities and by watching other guests; trash bins are plentiful and always in sight to convey the message that littering is prohibited; and repainting of facilities is a routine procedure that signals a high level of maintenance and cleanliness.

Disney's servicescape design and upkeep help to script customer experiences and create pleasure and satisfaction for guests, not only in its theme parks but also in its cruise ships and hotels.

Sources: Lewis P. Carbone and Stephen H. Haeckel, "Engineering Customer Experiences," *Marketing Management*, 3, No. 3, Winter 1994, 10–11; Kathy Merlock Jackson, *Walt Disney, A Bio-Bibliography.* Westport: Greenwood Press, 1993, 36–39; Andrew Lainsbury, *Once Upon An American Dream: The Story of Euro Disneyland.* Lawrence, KS: University Press of Kansas, 2000, 64–72. See also Disney Institute, *Be Our Guest: Perfecting the Art of Customer Service.* Disney Enterprises, 2001.

latter often are called environmental surveys if they focus on the design of the service environment.)

- ***Photo audit*** is a method of asking customers (or mystery shoppers) to take photographs of their service experience. These photographs can be used later as a basis for further interviews of their experience or included as part of a survey about the service experience.[43]
- ***Field experiments*** that can be used to manipulate specific dimensions in an environment so that the effects can be observed. For instance, you might experiment with the use of various types of music and scents and then measure the time and money customers spend in the environment and their level of satisfaction. Laboratory experiments, using slides or videos or other ways to simulate real-world service environments (such as computer-simulated virtual tours), can be used effectively to examine the effect of changes in design elements that cannot easily be manipulated in a field experiment. Examples include testing of alternative color schemes, spatial layouts, or styles of furnishing.
- ***Blueprinting*** or flowcharting (described in Chapter 8) can be extended to include the physical evidence in the environment. Design elements and tangible cues can be documented as the customer moves through each step of the service delivery process. Photos and videos can supplement the map to make it more vivid.

Table 10.4 shows an analysis of a customer's visit to a movie theater, identifying how different environmental elements at each step exceeded or failed to meet expectations. The service process was broken up into increments, steps, decisions, duties, and

TABLE 10.4 A Visit to the Movies: The Service Environment as Perceived by the Customer

	Design of the Service Environment	
STEPS IN THE SERVICE ENCOUNTER	EXCEEDS EXPECTATIONS	FAILS EXPECTATIONS
Locate a parking lot	Ample room in a bright place near the entrance, with a security officer protecting your valuables	Insufficient parking spaces, so patrons have to park in another lot
Queuing up to obtain tickets	Strategic placement of mirrors, posters of upcoming movies, and entertainment news to ease perception of long wait, if any; movies and time slots easily seen; ticket availability clearly communicated	A long queue and having to wait for a long while; difficult to see quickly what movies are being shown at what time slots and whether tickets are still available
Checking of tickets to enter the theater	A very well maintained lobby with clear directions to the theater and posters of the movie to enhance patrons' experience	A dirty lobby with rubbish strewn and unclear or misleading directions to the movie theater
Go to the restroom before the movie starts	Sparkling clean, spacious, brightly lit, dry floors, well stocked, nice decor, clear mirrors wiped regularly	Dirty, with an unbearable odor, broken toilets; no hand towels, soap, or toilet paper; overcrowded; dusty and dirty mirrors
Enter the theater and locate your seat	Spotless theater; well designed with no bad seats; sufficient lighting to locate your seat; spacious, comfortable chairs, with drink and popcorn holders on each seat; and a suitable temperature	Rubbish on the floor, broken seats, sticky floors, gloomy and insufficient lighting, burnedout exit signs
Watch the movie	Excellent sound system and film quality, nice audience, an enjoyable and memorable entertainment experience overall	Substandard sound and movie equipment, uncooperative audience that talks and smokes because of lack of "No Smoking" and other signs; a disturbing and unenjoyable entertainment experience overall
Leave the theater and return to the car	Friendly service staff greet patrons as they leave; an easy exit through a brightly lit and safe parking area back to the car with the help of clear lot signs	A difficult trip, as patrons squeeze through a narrow exit, unable to find the car because of no or insufficient lighting

Source: Adapted from Steven Albrecht, "See Things from the Customer's Point of View—How to Use the 'Cycles of Service' to Understand What the Customer Goes Through to Do Business with You." *World's Executive Digest* (December 1996): 53–58.

activities—all designed to take the customer through the entire service encounter. The more a service company can see, understand, and experience the same things as its customers, the better-equipped it will be to realize errors in the design of its environment and to further improve what is already functioning well.

CONCLUSION

The service environment plays a major part in shaping customers' perception of a firm's image and positioning. As service quality often is difficult to assess, customers frequently use the service environment as an important quality signal. A well-designed service environment makes customers feel good and boosts their satisfaction and allows the firm to influence their behavior (e.g., adhering to the service script and impulse purchasing) while enhancing the productivity of the service operation.

Chapter Summary

LO1 Service environments fulfill four core purposes. Specifically, they:

- Shape customers' experiences and their behavior.
- Play an important role in determining customer perceptions of the firm and its image and positioning. Customers often use the service environment as an important quality signal.
- Can be a core part of the value proposition (e.g., as for theme parks and resort hotels).
- Facilitate the service encounter and enhance productivity.

LO2 The theoretical underpinning for understanding the effects of service environments on customers and service employees comes from environmental psychology. There are two key models:

- The Mehrabian-Russell Stimulus-Response model holds that environments influence peoples' affective state (or emotions and feelings), which in turn drives their behavior.
- Russell's Model of Affect holds that affect can be modeled with the two interacting dimensions of pleasure and arousal, which together determine whether people approach, spend time and money in an environment, or whether they avoid it.

LO3 The servicescape model, which builds on the above theories, represents an integrative framework that explains how customers and service staff respond to key environmental dimensions.

LO4 The servicescape model emphasizes three dimensions of the service environment:

- Ambient conditions (including music, scents, and colors).
- Spatial layout and functionality.
- Signs, symbols, and artifacts.

LO5 Ambient conditions refer to those characteristics of the environment that pertain to our five senses. Even when not consciously perceived, they still can affect internal and behavioral responses. Important ambient dimensions include:

- *Music.* Its tempo, volume, harmony, and familiarity shape behavior by eliciting emotions and moods. People tend to adjust their pace to match the tempo of the music.
- *Scent.* Ambient scent can elicit powerful emotions and relax or simulate customers.
- *Color.* Colors can have strong effects on people's feelings with differential impact of warm (a mix of red and orange) versus cold colors (blue). The former are associated with elated mood states and the latter with peacefulness and happiness.

LO6 Effective spatial layout and functionality are important to enable service operation and enhance user-friendliness.

- Spatial layout refers to the floor plan, size, and shape of furnishing, counters, potential machinery, and equipment and the ways in which they are arranged.
- Functionality refers to the ability of those items to facilitate service operations.

LO7 Signs, symbols, and artifacts help customers to draw meaning from the environment and guide them through the service process. They can be used to:

- Label facilities, counters or departments.
- Show directions (e.g., to entrance, exit, elevator, restroom).
- Communicate the service script (e.g., take a number and watch it to be called).
- Reinforce behavioral rules (e.g., "please turn your cell phones to silent").

LO8 The appearance and behavior service employees and other customers in a servicescape can be part of the value proposition and can reinforce (or detract from) the positioning of the firm.

LO9 Service environments are perceived holistically. Therefore, no individual aspect can be optimized without considering everything else, making designing service environments an art rather than a science.

- Because of this challenge, professional designers tend to specialize in specific types of environments such as hotel lobbies, clubs, health-care facilities, and so on.
- Beyond esthetic considerations, the best service environments are designed with the customer's perspective in mind, guiding them smoothly through the service process.
- Tools that can be used to design and improve servicescapes include careful observation, feedback from employees and customers, photo audits, field experiments, and blueprinting.

Review Questions

1. What are the four main purposes service environments fulfill?
2. Compare and contrast the strategic and functional roles of service environments within a service organization.
3. Describe how the Mehrabian-Russell Stimulus-Response Model and Russell's Model of Affect explain consumer responses to a service environment.
4. What is the relationship or link between the Russell Model of Affect and the servicescape model?
5. Why can it happen that different customers and service staff respond vastly differently to the same service environment?
6. Explain the dimensions of ambient conditions and how each can influence customer responses to the service environment.
7. What are the roles of signs, symbols, and artifacts?
8. What are the implications of the fact that environments are perceived holistically?
9. What tools are available for aiding our understanding of customer responses and for guiding the design and improvement of service environments?

Application Exercises

1. Identify firms from three different service industries where the service environment is a crucial part of the overall value proposition. Analyze and explain in detail the value delivered by the service environment in each of the three industries.
2. Visit a service environment, and have a detailed look around. Experience the environment, and try to feel how the various design parameters shape what you feel and how you behave in that setting.
3. Select a bad and a good waiting experience, and contrast the two situations with respect to the aesthetics of the surroundings, diversions, and other people waiting.
4. Visit a self-service environment, and analyze how the design dimensions guide you through the service process. What do you find most effective, and what seems least effective? How could that environment be improved to further ease the "way finding" for self-service customers?
5. With a digital camera, conduct an environmental audit of a specific servicescape. Photograph examples of excellent and very poor design features. Develop concrete suggestions for how this environment could be improved.

Endnotes

1. Beatriz Plaza, "The Bilbao Effect," *Museum News*, September/October 2007, 13–15, 68; Denny Lee, "Bilbao, 10 Years Later," *The New York Times*, September 23, 2007 in http://travel.nytimes.com/2007/09/23/travel/23bilbao.html, accessed June 8, 2009. http://en.wikipedia.org/wiki/Guggenheim_Museum_Bilbao, accessed June 8, 2009.
2. The term *servicescape* was coined by Mary Jo Bitner in her paper "Servicescapes: The Impact of Physical Surroundings on Customers and Employees," *Journal of Marketing*, 56, 1992, 57–71.
3. Anja Reimer and Richard Kuehn, "The Impact of Servicescape on Quality Perception," *European Journal of Marketing*, 39, No. 7/8, 2005, 785–808.

4. Julie Baker, Dhruv Grewal, and A. Parasuraman, "The Influence of Store Environment on Quality Inferences and Store Image," *Journal of the Academy of Marketing Science*, 22, No. 4, 1994, 328–339.
5. Véronique Aubert-Gamet, "Twisting Servicescapes: Diversion of the Physical Environment in a Reappropriation Process," *International Journal of Service Industry Management*, 8, No. 1, 1997, 26–41.
6. Madeleine E. Pullman and Michael A. Gross, "Ability of Experience Design Elements to Elicit Emotions and Loyalty Behaviors," *Decision Sciences*, 35, No. 1, 2004, 551–578.
7. Lisa Takeuchi Cullen, "Is Luxury the Ticket?" *Time*, August 22, 2005, 38–39.
8. Richard B. Chase and Douglas M. Stewart, "Making Your Service Fail-Safe," *Sloan Management Review*, 35, 1994, 35–44.
9. For a review of the literature on hospital design effects on patients, see Karin Dijkstra, Marcel Pieterse, and Ad Pruyn, "Physical Environmental Stimuli That Turn Healthcare Facilities into Healing Environments Through Psychologically Mediated Effects: Systematic Review," *Journal of Advanced Nursing*, 56, No. 2, 2006, 166–181. See also the painstaking effort the Mayo Clinic extends to lowering noise levels in their hospitals: Leonard L. Berry and Kent D. Seltman, *Management Lessons from Mayo Clinic: Inside One of the World's Most Admired Service Organization.* McGraw Hill, 2008, 171–172. For a study on the effects of servicescape design in a hospital setting on service workers' job stress and job satisfaction, and subsequently, their commitment to the firm see Janet Turner Parish, Leonard L. Berry, and Shun Yin Lam, "The Effect of the Servicescape on Service Workers," *Journal of Service Research*, 10, No. 3, 2008, 220–238.
10. Robert J. Donovan and John R. Rossiter, "Store Atmosphere: An Environmental Psychology Approach," *Journal of Retailing*, 58, No. 1, 1982, 34–57.
11. James A. Russell, "A Circumplex Model of Affect," *Journal of Personality and Social Psychology*, 39, No. 6, 1980, 1161–1178.
12. Jochen Wirtz and John E. G. Bateson, "Consumer Satisfaction with Services: Integrating the Environmental Perspective in Services Marketing into the Traditional Disconfirmation Paradigm," *Journal of Business Research*, 44, No. 1, 1999, 55–66.
13. Jochen Wirtz, Anna S. Mattila, and Rachel L. P. Tan, "The Moderating Role of Target-Arousal on the Impact of Affect on Satisfaction – An Examination in the Context of Service Experiences," *Journal of Retailing*, 76, No. 3, 2000, 347–365. Jochen Wirtz, Anna S. Mattila, and Rachel L. P. Tan, "The Role of Desired Arousal in Influencing Consumers' Satisfaction Evaluations and In-Store Behaviours," *International Journal of Service Industry Management*, 18, No. 2, 2007, 6–24.
14. Mary Jo Bitner, "Service Environments: The Impact of Physical Surroundings on Customers and Employees," *Journal of Marketing*, 56, April 1992, 57–71.
15. For a comprehensive review of experimental studies on the atmospheric effects refer to: L. W. Turley and Ronald E. Milliman, "Atmospheric Effects on Shopping Behavior: A Review of the Experimental Literature," *Journal of Business Research*, 49, 2000, 193–211.
16. Patrick M. Dunne, Robert F. Lusch, and David A. Griffith, *Retailing*, 4th ed, Orlando, FL: Hartcourt, 2002, 518.
17. Barry Davies and Philippa Ward, *Managing Retail Consumption*, West Sussex, UK: John Wiley & Sons, 2002, 179.
18. Steve Oakes, "The Influence of the Musicscape Within Service Environments," *Journal of Services Marketing*, 14, No. 7, 2000, 539–556.
19. Morris B. Holbrook and Punam Anand, "Effects of Tempo and Situational Arousal on the Listener's Perceptual and Affective Responses to Music," *Psychology of Music*, 18, 1990, 150–162; S. J. Rohner and R. Miller, "Degrees of Familiar and Affective Music and Their Effects on State Anxiety," *Journal of Music Therapy*, 17, No. 1, 1980, 2–15.
20. Laurette Dubé and Sylvie Morin, "Background Music Pleasure and Store Evaluation Intensity Effects and Psychological Mechanisms," *Journal of Business Research*, 54, 2001, 107–113.
21. Clare Caldwell and Sally A. Hibbert, "The Influence of Music Tempo and Musical Preference on Restaurant Patrons' Behavior," *Psychology and Marketing*, 19, No. 11, 2002, 895–917.
22. For a review of the effects of music on various aspects of consumer responses and evaluations see Steve Oakes and Adrian C. North, "Reviewing Congruity Effects in the Service Environment Musicscape," *International Journal of Service Industry Management*, 19, No. 1, 2008, 63–82.
23. See www.dmx.com for in-store music solutions provided by DMX; see also Leah Goodman, "Shoppers Dance to Retailers' Tune," *Financial Times*, August 21, 2008, 10.
24. This section is based on "Classical Music and Social Control: Twilight of the Yobs," *The Economist*, January 8, 2005, 48.
25. Eric R. Spangenberg, Ayn E. Crowley, and Pamela W. Henderson, "Improving the Store Environment: Do Olfactory Cues Affect Evaluations and Behaviors?" *Journal of Marketing*, 60. April 1996, 67–80; Paula Fitzerald Bone and Pam Scholder Ellen, "Scents in the Marketplace: Explaining a Fraction of Olfaction," *Journal of Retailing*, 75, No. 2, 1999, 243–262; Jeremy Caplan, "Sense and Sensibility," *Time*, 168, No. 16, 2006, 66, 67.
26. Alan R. Hirsch, *Dr. Hirsch's Guide to Scentsational Weight Loss.* UK: Harper Collins, January 1997, 12–15.
27. Alan R. Hirsch, "Effects of Ambient Odors on Slot Machine Usage in a Las Vegas Casino," *Psychology and Marketing*, 12, No. 7, 1995, 585–594.
28. Alan R. Hirsch and S. E. Gay, "Effect on Ambient Olfactory Stimuli on the Evaluation of a Common Consumer Product," *Chemical Senses*, 16, 1991, 535.
29. See Ambius's website for details of its scent marketing, ambient scenting and sensory branding services on http://www.ambius.com/services/microfresh.aspx, accessed on June 3, 2009.
30. Gerald J. Gorn, Amitava Chattopadhyay, Tracey Yi, and Darren Dahl, "Effects of Color as an Executional Cue in Advertising: They're in the Shade," *Management Science*, 43, No. 10, 1997, 1387–1400; Ayn E. Crowley, "The Two-Dimensional Impact of Color on Shopping," *Marketing Letters*, 4, No. 1, 1993, 59–69; Gerald J. Gorn, Amitava Chattopadhyay, Jaideep Sengupta, and Shashank Tripathi, "Waiting for the Web: How Screen Color Affects Time Perception," *Journal of Marketing Research*, XLI, May 2004, 215–225; Iris Vilnai-Yavetz and Anat Rafaeli, "Aesthetics

and Professionalism of Virtual Servicescapes," *Journal of Service Research* 8, No. 3, 2006, 245–259.

31. Linda Holtzschuhe, *Understanding Color – An Introduction for Designers*, 3rd ed. New Jersey: John Wiley, 2006, 51.
32. Albert Henry Munsell, *A Munsell Color Product.* New York: Kollmorgen Corporation, 1996.
33. Linda Holtzschuhe, *Understanding Color – An Introduction for Designers*, 3rd ed. New Jersey: John Wiley & Sons, Inc., 2006.
34. Heinrich Zollinger, *Color: A Multidisciplinary Approach.* Zurich: Verlag Helvetica Chimica Acta (VHCA) Weinheim, Wiley-VCH, 1999, 71–79.
35. Joseph A. Bellizzi, Ayn E. Crowley, and Ronald W. Hasty, "The Effects of Color in Store Design," *Journal of Retailing*, 59, No. 1, 1983, 21–45.
36. Anat Rafaeli and Iris Vilnai-Yavetz, "Discerning Organizational Boundaries Through Physical Artifacts," in N. Paulsen and T. Hernes, eds. *Managing Boundaries in Organizations: Multiple Perspectives.* Basingstoke, Hampshire: Macmillan, 2003; Anat Rafaeli and Iris Vilnai-Yavetz, "Emotion as a Connection of Physical Artifacts and Organizations," *Organization Science*, 15, No. 6, 2004, 671–686; Anat Rafaeli and Iris Vilnai-Yavetz, "Managing Organizational Artifacts to Avoid Artifact Myopia," in A. Rafaeli and M. Pratt, eds. *Artifacts and Organization: Beyond Mere Symbolism.* Mahwah, NJ: Lawrence Erlbaum Associates Inc., 2005, 9–21.
37. Sara O. Marberry and Laurie Zagon, *The Power of Color – Creating Healthy Interior Spaces.* New York: John Wiley & Sons, 1995, 38.
38. Lewis P. Carbone and Stephen H. Haeckel, "Engineering Customer Experiences," *Marketing Management*, 3, No. 3, Winter 1994, 9–18; Lewis P. Carbone, Stephen H. Haeckel, and Leonard L. Berry, "How to Lead the Customer Experience," *Marketing Management*, 12, No. 1, January/February 2003, 18; Leonard L. Berry and Lewis P. Carbone, "Build Loyalty Through Experience Management," *Quality Progress*, 40, No. 9, September 2007, 26–32.
39. Dennis Nickson, Chris Warhurst, and Eli Dutton, "The Importance of Attitude and Appearance in the Service Encounter in Retail and Hospitality," *Managing Service Quality*, 2, 2005, 195–208.
40. Anna S. Mattila and Jochen Wirtz, "Congruency of Scent and Music as a Driver of In-store Evaluations and Behavior," *Journal of Retailing*, 77, 2001, 273–289.
41. Christine M. Piotrowski and Elizabeth A. Rogers, *Designing Commercial Interiors.* New York: John Wiley & Sons, Inc., 1999; Martin M. Pegler, *Cafes & Bistros.* New York: Retail Reporting Corporation, 1998; Paco Asensio, *Bars & Restaurants.* New York: HarperCollins International, 2002; Bethan Ryder, *Bar and Club Design.* London: Laurence King Publishing, 2002.
42. Ron Kaufman, "Service Power: Who Were They Designing it For?" *Newsletter*, May 2001, http://Ron Kaufman.com.
43. Madeleine E. Pullman and Stephani K. A. Robson, "Visual Methods: Using Photographs to Capture Customers' Experience with Design," *Cornell Hotel and Restaurant Administration Quarterly*, 48, No. 2, 2007, 121–144.

CHAPTER 11

Managing People for Service Advantage

*The old adage 'People are your most important asset' is wrong. The **right** people are your most important asset.*

JIM COLLINS

Customer satisfaction results from the realization of high levels of value compared to competitors . . . Value is created by satisfied, committed, loyal, and productive employees.

JAMES L. HESKETT, W. EARL SASSER, JR., AND LEONARD L. SCHLESINGER

LEARNING OBJECTIVES (LOs)

By the end of this chapter, the reader should be able to:

LO1 Explain why service employees are crucially important to the success of a firm.

LO2 Understand the factors that make the work of frontline staff demanding, challenging, and often difficult.

LO3 Describe the cycles of failure, mediocrity, and success in HR for service firms.

LO4 Understand the key elements of the Service Talent Cycle and know how to get HR right in service firms.

LO5 Know how to attract, select, and hire the right people for service jobs.

LO6 Explain the key areas in which service employees need training.

LO7 Understand why empowerment is so important in many frontline jobs.

LO8 Explain how to build high-performance service delivery teams.

LO9 Know how to motivate and energize service employees so they will deliver service excellence and productivity.

LO10 Understand the role of service leadership and culture in developing people for service advantage.

Cora Griffith—The Outstanding Waitress[1]

Cora Griffith, a waitress for the Orchard Café at the Paper Valley Hotel in Appleton, Wisconsin, is superb in her role, appreciated by first-time customers, famous with her regular customers, and revered by her coworkers. Cora loves her work—and it shows. Comfortable in a role she believes is right for her, Cora follows nine rules of success:

1. **Treat Customers Like Family.** First-time customers are not allowed to feel like strangers. Cheerful and proactive, Cora smiles, chats, and includes everyone at the table in the conversation. She is as respectful to children as she is to adults and makes it a point to learn and use everyone's name. "I want people to feel like they're sitting down to dinner right at my house," she says. "I want them to feel they're welcome, that they can get comfortable, that they can relax. I don't just serve people, I pamper them."
2. **Listen First.** Cora has developed her listening skills to the point that she rarely writes down customers' orders. She listens carefully and provides a customized service: "Are they in a hurry?" "Do they have a special diet?" "Do they like their selection cooked in a certain way?"
3. **Anticipate Customers' Wants.** Cora replenishes beverages and brings extra bread and butter in a timely manner. One regular customer, who likes honey with her coffee, gets it without having to ask. "I don't want my customers to have to ask for anything," says Cora, "so I always try to anticipate what they might need."
4. **Simple Things Make the Difference.** Cora manages the details of her service, monitoring the cleanliness of the utensils and their correct placement. The fold for napkins must be just right. She inspects each plate in the kitchen before taking it to the table, and she provides crayons for small children to draw pictures while waiting for the meal. "It's the little things that please the customer," she says.
5. **Work Smart.** Cora scans all her tables at once, looking for opportunities to combine tasks. "Never do just one thing at a time," she advises. "And never go from the kitchen to the dining room empty-handed. Take coffee or iced tea or water with you." When she refills one water glass, she refills others. When clearing one plate, she clears others. "You have to be organized, and you have to keep in touch with the big picture."
6. **Keep Learning.** Cora makes an ongoing effort to improve existing skills and learn new ones.
7. **Success Is Where You Find It.** Cora is content with her work. She finds satisfaction in pleasing her customers, and she enjoys helping other people enjoy. Her optimistic attitude is a positive force in the restaurant. She is hard to ignore. "If customers come to the restaurant in a bad mood, I'll try to cheer them up before they leave," she says. Her definition of success: "To be happy in life."
8. **All for One, One for All.** Cora has been working with many of the same coworkers for more than eight years. The team supports one another on the crazy days when 300 conventioneers come to the restaurant for breakfast at the same time. Everyone pitches in and helps. The wait staff cover for one another, the managers bus the tables, the chefs garnish the plates. "We are like a little family," Cora says. "We know each other very well and we help each other out. If we have a crazy day, I'll go in the kitchen toward the end of the shift and say, 'Man, I'm just proud of us. We really worked hard today.'"
9. **Take Pride in Your Work.** Cora believes in the importance of her work and in the need to do it well: "I don't think of myself as 'just a waitress' . . . I've chosen to be a waitress. I'm doing this to my full potential, and I give it my best. I tell anyone who's starting out: 'take pride in what you do.' You're never just an anything, no matter what you do. You give it your all . . . and you do it with pride."

FIGURE 11.1 A Waitress' Pride in Her Professionalism Earns Her Admiration and Respect from Customers and Co-Workers

Cora Griffith is a success story. She is loyal to her employer and dedicated to her customers and coworkers. A perfectionist who seeks continuous improvement, Cora's enthusiasm for her work and unflagging spirit creates an energy that radiates through the restaurant. She is proud of being a waitress, proud of "touching lives." Says Cora: "I have always wanted to do my best. However, the owners really are the ones who taught me how important it is to take care of the customer and who gave me the freedom to do it. The company always has listened to my concerns and followed up. Had I not worked for the Orchard Café, I would have been a good waitress, but I would not have been the same waitress."

Source: Leonard L. Berry, *Discovering the Soul of Service—The Nine Drivers of Sustainable Business Success.* New York: The Free Press, 1999, pp. 156–159.

SERVICE EMPLOYEES ARE CRUCIALLY IMPORTANT

Among the most demanding jobs in service businesses are the so-called frontline jobs. Employees working in these customer-facing jobs span the boundary between inside and outside the organization. They are expected to be fast and efficient in executing operational tasks as well as courteous and helpful in dealing with customers. In fact, frontline employees are a key input for delivering service excellence and competitive advantage.

Therefore, behind most of today's successful service organizations stands a firm commitment to effective management of human resources (HR) including recruitment, selection, training, motivation, and retention of employees. Organizations that display this commitment understand the economic payoff from investing in their people. These firms are also characterized by a distinctive culture of service leadership and role modeling by top management. It is probably harder for competitors to duplicate high-performance human assets compared to any other corporate resource.

Service Personnel as a Source of Customer Loyalty and Competitive Advantage

Almost everybody can recount some horror story of a dreadful experience they have had with a service business. If pressed, many of these same people can also recount a really good service experience. Service personnel usually feature prominently in such dramas. They either feature in roles as uncaring, incompetent villains or as heroes who went out of their way to help customers by anticipating their needs and resolving problems in a helpful and empathetic manner. You probably have your own set of favorite stories, featuring both villains and heroes—and if you're like most people, you probably talk more about the former than the latter.

From a customer's perspective, the encounter with service staff is probably the most important aspect of a service. From the firm's perspective, the service levels and the way service is delivered by the frontline personnel can be an important source of differentiation as well as competitive advantage. Service employees are so important to customers and the firm's competitive positioning because the frontline:

- **Is a core part of the product.** Often, the service employees is the most visible element of the service, delivers the service, and significantly determines service quality.
- **Is the service firm.** Frontline employees represent the service firm, and from a customer's perspective, they are the firm.
- **Is the brand.** Frontline employees and the service they provide often are a core part of the brand. The employees determine whether the brand promise is delivered.
- **Affects sales.** Service personnel often are crucially important for generating sales, cross-sales, and up-sales.
- **Determine productivity.** Frontline employees have heavy influence on the productivity of frontline operations.

Furthermore, frontline employees play a key role in anticipating customers' needs, customizing the service delivery, and building personalized relationships with customers.[2] Effective performance of these activities should ultimately lead to customer loyalty. How attentive employees can be in anticipating customers' needs was shown in the opening vignette citing Cora Griffith as an example. This and many other success stories of employees showing discretionary effort that made a difference have reinforced the truism that highly motivated people are at the core of service excellence.[3] They are increasingly a key variable for creating and maintaining competitive positioning and advantage.

The intuitive importance of the effect of service employees on customer loyalty was integrated and formalized by James Heskett and his colleagues in their pioneering research on what they call the *service profit chain* (Chapter 15 illustrates the chain in more detail). It demonstrates the chain of relationships among (1) employee satisfaction, retention, and productivity; (2) service value; (3) customer satisfaction and loyalty; and (4) revenue growth and profitability for the firm.[4] These themes were developed further in their book, *The Value Profit Chain: Treat Employees Like Customers and Customers like Employees.*[5] Unlike manufacturing, "shop-floor workers" in services (i.e., frontline staff) are in constant contact with customers, and solid evidence shows that employee satisfaction and customer satisfaction are highly correlated.[6] Therefore, this chapter focuses on how to retain satisfied, loyal, and productive service employees.

The Frontline in Low-Contact Services

Most research in service management and many of the best practice examples featured in this chapter relate to high-contact services. This is not entirely surprising, of course, because the people in these jobs are so visible. They are the actors who appear front-stage in the service drama when they serve the customer. So, it is obvious why the frontline is so crucially important to customers and therefore to the competitive position of the firm. However, there's a growing trend across virtually all types of services toward low-contact delivery channels such as call centers and self-service options. Many routine transactions are now conducted without involving frontline staff at all. Examples include the many types of self-service technologies (SSTs) provided via websites, automatic teller machines (ATMs), and interactive voice response (IVR) systems (see Chapter 8 for a more detailed discussion of SSTs). In light of these trends, are frontline employees really all that important?

Although the quality of SSTs and their customer interface can reach very high levels—and SSTs' importance has been elevated drastically to the core engine for service delivery in many industries—the quality of frontline employees still remains imperative. Most people do not call the service hotline or visit the service center of their cell phone service provider, or their credit card company more than once or twice a year. However, these occasional service encounters are absolutely critical—they are the "moments of truth" that drive a customer's perceptions of the service firm (see Figure 11.2). Also, it is likely that these interactions are not about routine transactions, but about service problems and special requests. These very few contacts determine whether a customer thinks, "Customer service is excellent! When I need help, I can call you, and this is one important reason why I bank with you," or "Your service stinks. I don't like interacting with you, and I am going to spread the word about how bad your service is!"

Given that technology is relatively commoditized, the service delivered by the front line, whether it is face to face, "ear to ear," or via email, Twitter, or chat, is highly visible and important to customers, and therefore a critical component of a service firm's marketing strategy.

FIGURE 11.2 A Friendly Employee at a San Diego Bank Delivering a 'Moment of Truth'

FRONTLINE WORK IS DIFFICULT AND STRESSFUL

The service-profit chain requires high-performing, satisfied employees to achieve service excellence and customer loyalty. However, these customer-facing employees work in some of the most demanding jobs in service firms. Perhaps you have worked in one or more of such jobs, which are particularly common in the health care, hospitality, retailing, and travel industries. Let's discuss the main reasons why these jobs are so demanding (and you can relate these to your own experience, while recognizing there may be differences between working part-time for short periods and full-time as a career).

Boundary Spanning

The organizational behavior literature refers to service employees as *boundary spanners.* They link the inside of an organization to the outside world, operating at the boundary of the company. Because of the position they occupy, boundary spanners often have conflicting roles. In particular, customer contact personnel must attend to both operational and marketing goals. This multiplicity of roles in service jobs often leads to role conflict and role stress among employees,[7] which we will discuss next.

Sources of Conflict

There are three main causes of role stress in frontline positions: organization/client, person/role, and inter-client conflicts.

ORGANIZATION/CLIENT CONFLICT. Customer contact personnel must attend to both operational and marketing goals. They are expected to delight customers, which takes time, yet they have to be fast and efficient at operational tasks. On top of that, they often are expected to do selling, cross-selling, and up-selling, for instance, "Now would be a good time to open a separate account to save for your children's education" or "For only 25 dollars more per night, you can upgrade to the executive floor."

Finally, sometimes customer contact personnel are even responsible for enforcing rate integrity and pricing schedules that might be in direct conflict with customer satisfaction (e.g., "I am sorry, but we don't serve ice water in this restaurant, but we have an excellent selection of still and carbonated mineral waters" or "I am sorry, but we cannot waive the fee for the bounced check for the third time this quarter." This type of conflict is also called the two-bosses dilemma where service employees have the unpleasant choice of whether to enforce the company's rules or satisfy customer demands. The problem is especially acute in organizations that are not customer oriented. In these cases, staff frequently has to deal with customer needs and requests that are in conflict with organizational rules, procedures, and productivity requirements.

PERSON/ROLE CONFLICT. Service staff may have conflicts between what their job requires and their own personalities, self-perception, and beliefs. For example, the job may require staff to smile and be friendly even to rude customers (see the section on jaycustomers in Chapter 12). V. S. Mahesh and Anand Kasturi note from their consulting work with service organizations around the world that thousands of frontline staff consistently tend to describe customers with a pronounced negative flavor—frequently using phrases such as "overdemanding," "unreasonable," "refuse to listen," "always want everything their way, immediately," and "arrogant."[8]

Providing quality service requires an independent, warm, and friendly personality. These traits are most likely found in people with high self-esteem. However, many frontline jobs are often perceived as low-level jobs that require little education, offer low pay, and often lack prospects. If an organization is not able to "professionalize" their frontline jobs and move away from this image, these jobs may be inconsistent with staff's self-perception and lead to person/role conflicts.

INTER-CLIENT CONFLICT. Conflicts between customers are not uncommon (e.g., smoking in nonsmoking sections, jumping queues, talking on a cell phone in a movie theater, or being excessively noisy in a restaurant), and it usually is the service staff that are summoned to call the offending customer to order. This is a stressful and unpleasant task, as it is difficult and often impossible to satisfy both sides.

In short, frontline employees may perform triple roles: satisfying customers, delivering productivity, and generating sales. In combination, playing such roles often leads to role conflict and role stress for employees.[9] Although employees may experience conflict and stress, they still are expected to have a pleasant disposition toward the customer. We call this emotional labor, which in itself is an important cause of stress. Let's look at emotional labor in more detail in the next section.

Emotional Labor

The term *emotional labor* was coined by Arlie Hochschild in her book *The Managed Heart*.[10] Emotional labor arises when a discrepancy exists between the way frontline staff feel inside and the emotions that management requires them to show in front of customers. Frontline staff are expected to be cheerful, genial, compassionate, sincere, or even self-effacing—emotions that can be conveyed through facial expressions, gestures, tone of voice, and words. Although some service firms make an effort to recruit employees with such characteristics, there will inevitably be situations when employees do not feel such positive emotions, yet are required to suppress their true feelings in order to conform to customer expectations. As Pannikkos Constanti and Paul Gibbs point out, "the power axis for emotional labor tends to favor both the management and the customer, with the front line employee . . . being subordinate," thus creating a potentially exploitative situation.[11]

The stress of emotional labor is nicely illustrated in the following, probably apocryphal story: A flight attendant was approached by a passenger with: "Let's have a smile." She replied with: "Okay. I'll tell you what. First you smile and then I'll smile, okay?" He smiled. "Good," she said. "Now hold that for 15 hours," and walked away.[12] Figure 11.3 captures emotional labor with humor.

FIGURE 11.3 Dilbert Encounters Emotional Labor at the Bank

Source: DILBERT: © Scott Adams/Dist. by permission of United Syndicate, Inc.

Firms need to be aware of ongoing emotional stress among their employees[13] and to devise ways of alleviating it, which should include training on how to deal with emotional stress and how to cope with pressure from customers. For example, because of Singapore Airlines' reputation for service excellence, its customers tend to have very high expectations and can be very demanding. This puts considerable pressure on its frontline employees. The commercial training manager of Singapore Airlines (SIA) explained,

> We have recently undertaken an external survey and it appears that more of the "demanding customers" choose to fly with SIA. So the staff are really under a lot of pressure. We have a motto: "If SIA can't do it for you, no other airline can." So we encourage staff to try to sort things out, and to do as much as they can for the customer. Although they are very proud, and indeed protective of the company, we need to help them deal with the emotional turmoil of having to handle their customers well, and at the same time, feel they're not being taken advantage of. The challenge is to help our staff deal with difficult situations and take the brickbats. This will be the next thrust of our training programs.[14]

Service Sweat Shops?

Rapid developments in information technology are permitting service businesses to make radical improvements in business processes and even completely reengineer their operations. These developments sometimes result in wrenching changes in the nature of work for existing employees. In some instances, deployment of new technology and methods can dramatically change the nature of the work environment (see Service Perspective 11.1). In other instances, face-to-face contact is replaced by use of the Internet or call center-provided services, and firms have redefined and relocated jobs, created new employee profiles for recruiting purposes, and sought to hire employees with a different set of qualifications.

As a result of the growing shift from high-contact to low-contact services, a large and increasing number of customer contact employees work by telephone or email, never meeting customers face to face.[15] For example, a remarkable 3 percent plus of the total U.S. workforce is now employed in call centers as "customer service representatives" or CSRs.

At best, when well designed, such jobs can be rewarding, and often offer parents and students flexible working hours and part-time jobs (some 50 percent of call center workers are single mothers or students). In fact, it has been shown that part-time workers are more satisfied with their work as CSRs than full-time staff, and perform just as well.[16] At worst, these jobs place employees in an electronic equivalent of the old-fashioned sweat shop. Even in the best managed call centers (also often called "customer contact centers"), the work is intense (see Figure 11.4), with CSRs expected to deal with up to two calls a minute (including trips to the restroom and breaks) and under a high level of monitoring. There is also significant stress from customers themselves, because many are irate at the time of contact.

Mahesh and Anand's research on call centers found that intrinsically motivated agents suffered less customer stress.[17] As we will discuss in this chapter, some of the keys to success in this area involve screening applicants to make sure they already know how to present themselves well on the telephone and have the potential to learn additional skills, training them carefully, and giving them a well-designed working environment.[18]

SERVICE PERSPECTIVE 11.1

COUNTING THE SECONDS—PERFORMANCE MEASUREMENT OF FRONTLINE EMPLOYEES

Retailers have come under tremendous pressure to cut costs, and labor is their biggest controllable expense. It is no wonder then that business is booming for the Operations Workforce Optimization (OWO) unit that was recently acquired by Accenture, the global consulting firm. The consulting and software company adapted time-motion concepts developed for manufacturing operations to service businesses, where it breaks down tasks such as working a cash register in a supermarket into quantifiable units and develops standard times to complete each unit or task. The firm then implements software to help its clients to monitor employee performance.

A spokesperson of a large retailer explained that they "expect employees to be at 100% performance to the standards, but we do not begin any formal counseling process until the performance falls below 95%." If a staff falls below 95% of the baseline score too many times, he or she is likely to be bounced to a lower-paying job or be fired. Employee responses to this approach can be negative. Interviews with cashiers of that large retailer suggest that the system has spurred many to hurry up and experience increased stress levels. Hanning, 25 years old, took a job a cashier in one of the chain's stores in Michigan for $7.15 per hour in July 2007. She said she was "written up" three or four times for scores below 95% and was told that she had to move to another department at a lower pay if her performance did not improve. She recalled being told, "Make sure you're just scanning, grabbing, bagging." She resigned after almost one year on the job.

The customers' experience can also be negatively affected. Gunter, 22 years old, says he recently told a longtime customer that he could not chat with her anymore as he was being timed. He said, "I was told to get people in and out." Other cashiers said that they avoided eye contact with shoppers and hurried along those customers who may take longer to unload carts or make payment. A customer reported, "Everybody is under stress. They are not as friendly. I know elderly people have a hard time making change because you lose your ability to feel. They're so rushed at checkout that they don't want to come here."

OWO recommends that retailers adjust time standards to account for customer service and other variables that can affect how long a particular task should take, but the interviews seem to suggest that quite a number of firms are focusing on productivity first. One clothing and footwear chain calculated that they could save $15,000 per annum for every second cut from the checkout process, and another installed fingerprint readers directly at the cash registers so that cashiers can sign in directly at their individual workplaces and not at a central time clock, which saves minutes of wasted time according to a former director of a major retailer. OWO says that its methods can cut labor costs by 5 to 15%.

Source: Vanessa O'Connell, "Seconds Counts as Stores Trim Costs," *The Wall Street Journal*, November 17, 2008, http://www.nwanews.com/adg/Business/244489, accessed June 5, 2009.

CYCLES OF FAILURE, MEDIOCRITY, AND SUCCESS

Having discussed the importance of frontline employees and how difficult their work is, let's look at the big picture—how poor, mediocre, and excellent firms set up their frontline employees for failure, mediocrity, or success. All too often, poor working environments translate into dreadful service, with employees treating customers the way their managers treat them. Businesses with high employee turnover frequently are stuck in what has been termed the *cycle of failure*. Others, which offer job security but little scope for personal initiative, may suffer from an

FIGURE 11.4 Work in Customer Contact Centers Is Intense! Yet How Customer Service Representatives Perform Often Determines How a Firm's Service Quality Is Perceived by Customers

equally undesirable *cycle of mediocrity*. However, if the working environment is managed well, there is potential for a virtuous cycle in service employment, the *cycle of success*.[19]

The Cycle of Failure

In many service industries, the search for productivity is carried out with a vengeance. One solution takes the form of simplifying work routines and hiring workers as cheaply as possible to perform repetitive work tasks that require little or no training. Among consumer services, department stores, fast-food restaurants, and call center operations often are cited as examples in which this problem abounds (although there are notable exceptions). The cycle of failure captures the implications of such a strategy, with its two concentric but interactive cycles: one involving failures with employees; the second, with customers (Figure 11.5).

The *employee cycle of failure* begins with a narrow design of jobs to accommodate low skill levels, an emphasis on rules rather than service, and the use of technology to control quality. A strategy of low wages is accompanied by minimal effort in selection or training. Consequences include bored employees who lack the ability to respond to customer problems, who become dissatisfied, and who develop a poor service attitude. Outcomes for the firm are low service quality and high employee turnover. Because of weak profit margins, the cycle repeats itself with the hiring of more low-paid employees to work in this unrewarding atmosphere. Some service firms can reach such low levels of employee morale that frontline staff become hostile toward customers and may even engage in "service sabotage" as described in Research Insights 11.1.

The *customer cycle of failure* begins with heavy organizational emphasis on attracting new customers who become dissatisfied with employee performance and the lack of continuity implicit in continually changing faces. These customers fail to develop any loyalty to the supplier and turn over as rapidly as the staff. This situation requires an ongoing search for new customers to maintain sales volume. The departure of discontented customers is especially disturbing in light of what we now know about the greater profitability of a loyal customer base.

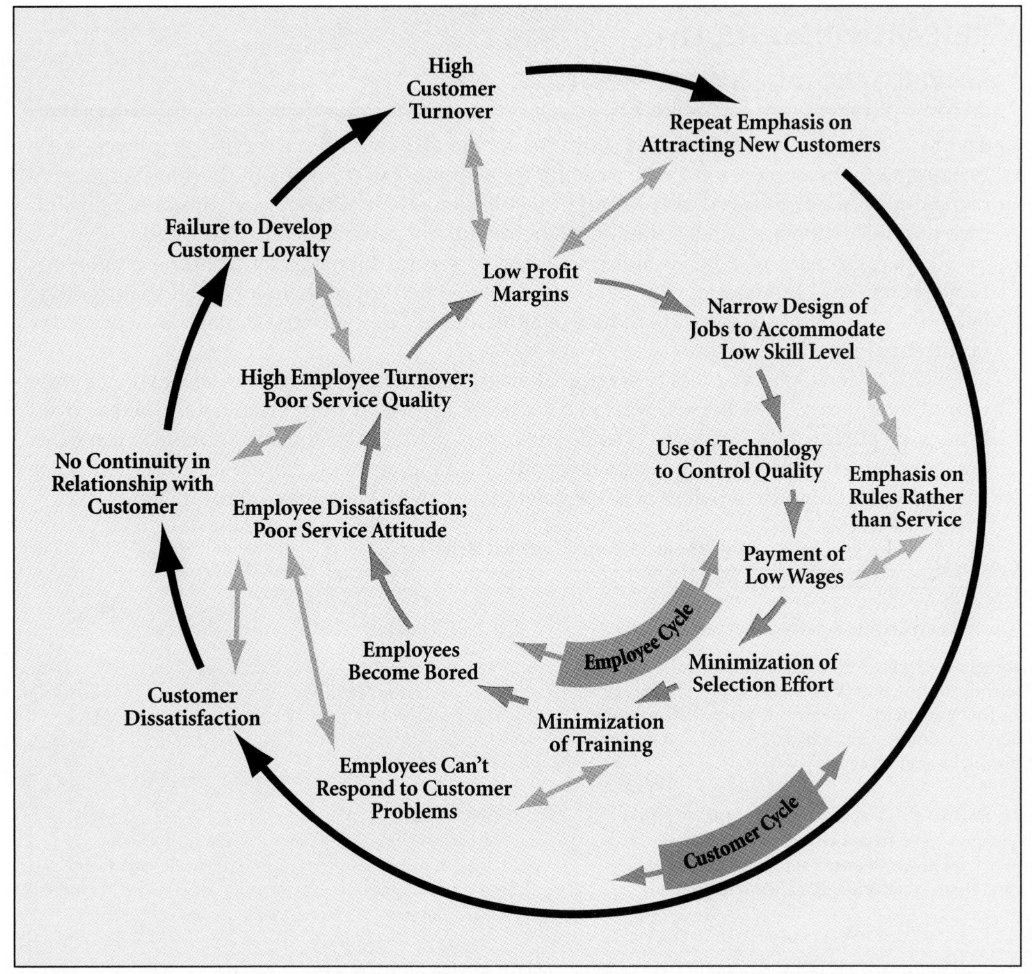

FIGURE 11.5 The Cycle of Failure

Source: Leonard L. Schlesinger and James L. Heskett "Breaking the Cycle of Failure in Services" *Sloan Management Review 31* (Spring1991): 17–28.

Managers' excuses and justifications for perpetuating the cycle of failure tend to focus on employees:

- You just can't get good people nowadays.
- People today just don't want to work.
- To get good people would cost too much and you can't pass on these cost increases to customers.
- It's not worth training our frontline people when they leave you so quickly.
- High turnover is simply an inevitable part of our business. You've got to learn to live with it.[20]

Too many managers ignore the long-term financial effects of low-pay/high turnover human resource strategies. James Heskett, Earl Sasser, and Leonard Schlesigner argue that companies need to measure employee lifetime value, just as they seek to calculate customer lifetime value.[21] Part of the problem is the failure to measure all relevant costs.

Three key cost variables often are omitted: (1) the cost of constant recruiting, hiring, and training (as much a time cost for managers as a financial cost); (2) the lower productivity of inexperienced new workers; and (3) the costs of constantly attracting new customers, which requires extensive advertising and promotional discounts. Also ignored are two revenue variables: (1) future revenue streams that might have continued for years but are lost when unhappy customers take their business elsewhere and (2) the potential income lost from prospective customers turned off by negative word of mouth. Finally, there are less easily quantifiable costs of disruptions to service while a job remains unfilled and loss of the departing employee's knowledge of the business (and potentially his or her customers as well).

RESEARCH INSIGHTS 11.1

SERVICE SABOTAGE BY THE FRONTLINE

The next time you are dissatisfied with the service provided by a service employee—in a restaurant, for example—it's worth pausing for a moment to think about the consequences of complaining about the service. You might just become the unknowing victim of a malicious case of service sabotage, such as having something unhygienic added to your food.

There actually is a fairly high incidence of service sabotage by frontline employees. Lloyd Harris and Emmanuel Ogbonna found that 90 percent of them accepted that frontline behavior with malicious intent to reduce or spoil the service—service sabotage is an everyday occurrence in their organizations.

Harris and Ogbonna classify service sabotage along two dimensions: covert-overt and routinized-intermittent behaviors. Covert behaviors are concealed from customers, whereas overt actions are purposefully displayed often to coworkers as well as customers. Routinized behaviors are ingrained into the culture, whereas intermittent actions are sporadic and less common. Some true examples of service sabotage classified along these two dimensions appear in Figure 11.6.

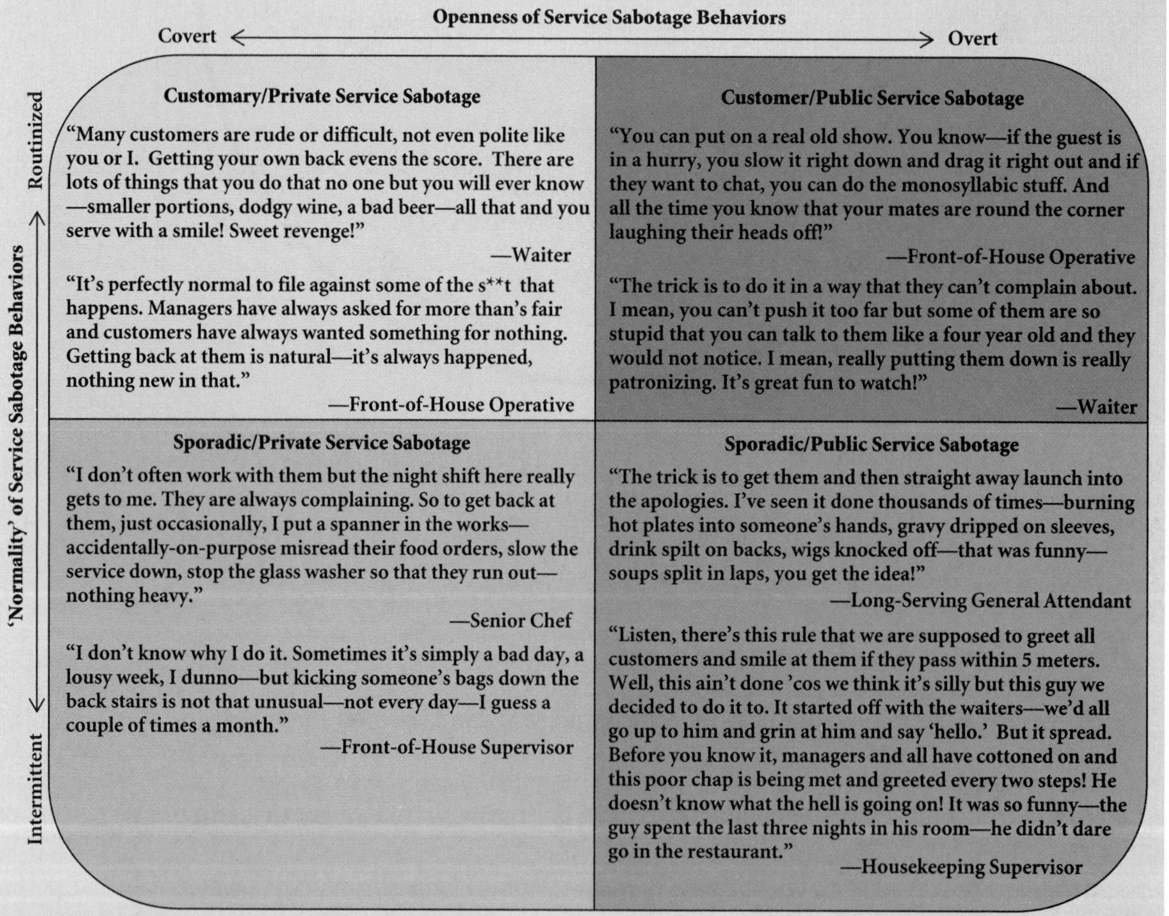

Openness of Service Sabotage Behaviors

Covert ⟵⟶ Overt

'Normality' of Service Sabotage Behaviors: Routinized ⟷ Intermittent

Covert	Overt
Customary/Private Service Sabotage "Many customers are rude or difficult, not even polite like you or I. Getting your own back evens the score. There are lots of things that you do that no one but you will ever know—smaller portions, dodgy wine, a bad beer—all that and you serve with a smile! Sweet revenge!" —Waiter "It's perfectly normal to file against some of the s**t that happens. Managers have always asked for more than's fair and customers have always wanted something for nothing. Getting back at them is natural—it's always happened, nothing new in that." —Front-of-House Operative	**Customer/Public Service Sabotage** "You can put on a real old show. You know—if the guest is in a hurry, you slow it right down and drag it right out and if they want to chat, you can do the monosyllabic stuff. And all the time you know that your mates are round the corner laughing their heads off!" —Front-of-House Operative "The trick is to do it in a way that they can't complain about. I mean, you can't push it too far but some of them are so stupid that you can talk to them like a four year old and they would not notice. I mean, really putting them down is really patronizing. It's great fun to watch!" —Waiter
Sporadic/Private Service Sabotage "I don't often work with them but the night shift here really gets to me. They are always complaining. So to get back at them, just occasionally, I put a spanner in the works—accidentally-on-purpose misread their food orders, slow the service down, stop the glass washer so that they run out—nothing heavy." —Senior Chef "I don't know why I do it. Sometimes it's simply a bad day, a lousy week, I dunno—but kicking someone's bags down the back stairs is not that unusual—not every day—I guess a couple of times a month." —Front-of-House Supervisor	**Sporadic/Public Service Sabotage** "The trick is to get them and then straight away launch into the apologies. I've seen it done thousands of times—burning hot plates into someone's hands, gravy dripped on sleeves, drink spilt on backs, wigs knocked off—that was funny—soups split in laps, you get the idea!" —Long-Serving General Attendant "Listen, there's this rule that we are supposed to greet all customers and smile at them if they pass within 5 meters. Well, this ain't done 'cos we think it's silly but this guy we decided to do it to. It started off with the waiters—we'd all go up to him and grin at him and say 'hello.' But it spread. Before you know it, managers and all have cottoned on and this poor chap is being met and greeted every two steps! He doesn't know what the hell is going on! It was so funny—the guy spent the last three nights in his room—he didn't dare go in the restaurant." —Housekeeping Supervisor

FIGURE 11.6 Examples of Services Sabotage

Source: Lloyd C. Harris and Emmanuel Ogbonna, "Exploring Service Sabotage: The Antecedents, Types and Consequences of Frontline, Deviant, Antiservice Behaviors," *Journal of Service Research, Vol. 4, No. 3,* 2002, pp. 163–183. Copyright © 2002 Sage Publications. Used with permission.

The Cycle of Mediocrity

The cycle of mediocrity is another potentially vicious employment cycle (see Figure 11.7). You are most likely to find it in large, bureaucratic organizations. These often are typified by state monopolies, industrial cartels, or regulated oligopolies in which there's little market pressure from more agile competitors to improve performance and in which fear

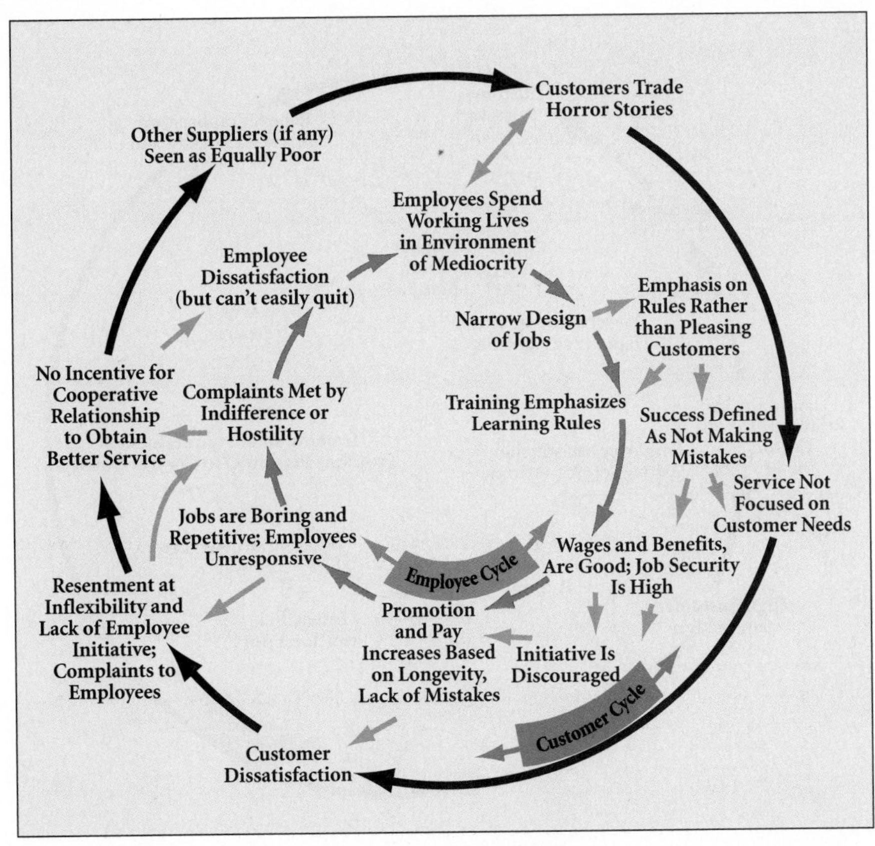

FIGURE 11.7 The Cycle of Mediocrity

Source: Christopher Lovelock,"Managing Services: The Human Factor" in *Understanding Service Management,* ed. W.J. Glynn and J.G. Barnes (Chichester, UK John Wiley, 1995), 228.

of entrenched unions may discourage management from adopting more innovative labor practices.

In such environments, service delivery standards tend to be prescribed by rigid rulebooks and oriented toward standardized service, operational efficiencies, and prevention of both employee fraud and favoritism toward specific customers. Job responsibilities tend to be narrowly and unimaginatively defined, tightly categorized by grade and scope of responsibilities, and further rigidified by union work rules. Salary increases and promotions are largely based on longevity. Successful performance in a job often is measured by absence of mistakes, rather than by high productivity or outstanding customer service. Training focuses on learning the rules and the technical aspects of the job, not on improving human interactions with customers and coworkers. Because there are minimal allowances for flexibility or employee initiative, jobs tend to be boring and repetitive. However, in contrast to the cycle of failure, most positions provide adequate pay and often good benefits combined with high security. Thus, employees are reluctant to leave. This lack of mobility is compounded by an absence of marketable skills that would be valued by organizations in other fields.

Customers find such organizations frustrating to deal with. Faced with bureaucratic hassles, lack of service flexibility, and unwillingness of employees to make an effort to serve them well, customers can become resentful. It's not surprising that dissatisfied customers sometimes display hostility toward service employees who feel trapped in their jobs and powerless to improve the situation. Perhaps you've been provoked by bad service and poor attitudes into reacting this way yourself. However, customers often continue to be "held hostage" by the organization because there is nowhere else for them to go, either because the service provider holds a monopoly, or because all other available players are perceived as equally bad or worse.

Employees may then protect themselves through such mechanisms as withdrawal into indifference, playing overtly by the rulebook, or countering rudeness with rudeness. The net result is a vicious cycle of mediocrity in which unhappy customers continually complain to sullen employees (and to other customers) about poor service and bad attitudes, generating greater defensiveness and lack of caring on the part of the

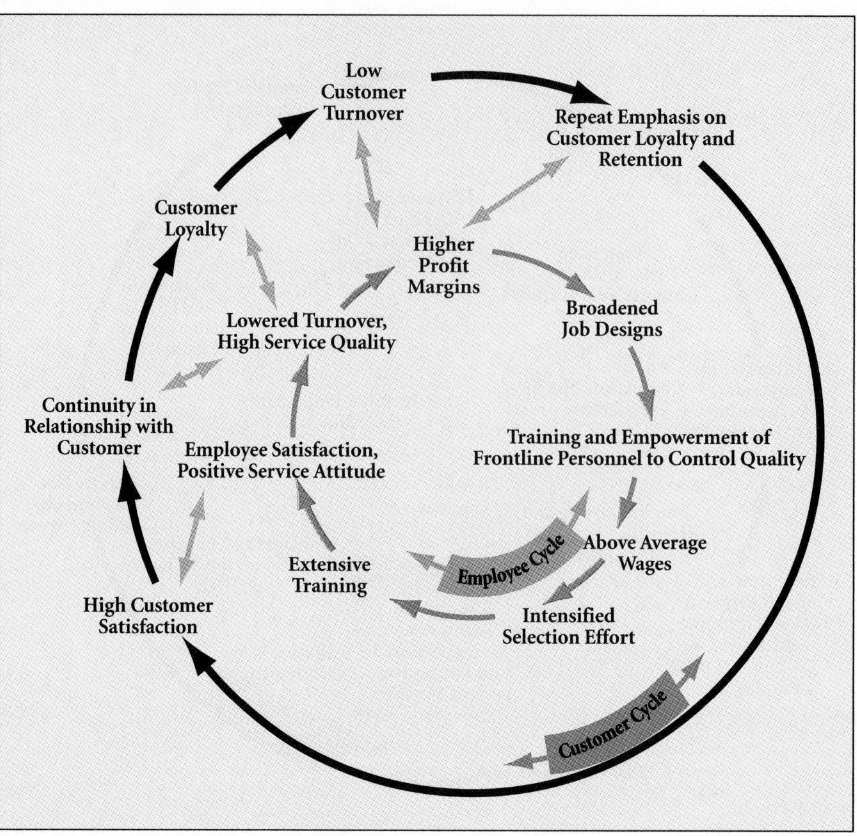

FIGURE 11.8 The Cycle of Success

Source: Leonard L. Schlesinger and James L. Heskett "Breaking the Cycle of Failure in Services" *Sloan Management Review 31* (Spring1991): 17-28.

staff. Under such circumstances, there's little incentive for customers to cooperate with the organization to achieve better service.

The Cycle of Success

Some firms reject the assumptions underlying the cycles of failure or mediocrity. Instead, they take a longer term view of financial performance, seeking to prosper by investing in their people in order to create a cycle of success (Figure 11.8).

As with failure or mediocrity, success applies to both employees and customers. Attractive compensation packages are used to attract good quality staff. Broadened job designs are accompanied by training and empowerment practices that allow frontline staff to control quality. With more focused recruitment, intensive training, and better wages, employees are likely to be happier in their work and to provide higher quality, customer-pleasing service. Regular customers also appreciate the continuity in service relationships resulting from lower turnover and so are more likely to remain loyal. Profit margins tend to be higher, and the organization is free to focus its marketing efforts on reinforcing customer loyalty through customer retention strategies. These strategies usually are much more profitable than strategies for attracting new customers.

A powerful demonstration of a frontline employee working in the cycle of success is waitress Cora Griffin (featured in the opening vignette of this chapter). Even public service organizations in many countries are increasingly working toward creating their cycles of success, too, and offer their users good quality service at a lower cost to the public.[22]

HUMAN RESOURCES MANAGEMENT—HOW TO GET IT RIGHT

Any rational manager would like to operate in the cycle of success. In this section, we'll discuss HR strategies that can help service firms to move toward that goal. Specifically, we'll discuss how firms can hire, motivate, and retain engaged service employees willing and able to deliver service excellence, productivity, and sales. Figure 11.9 shows the

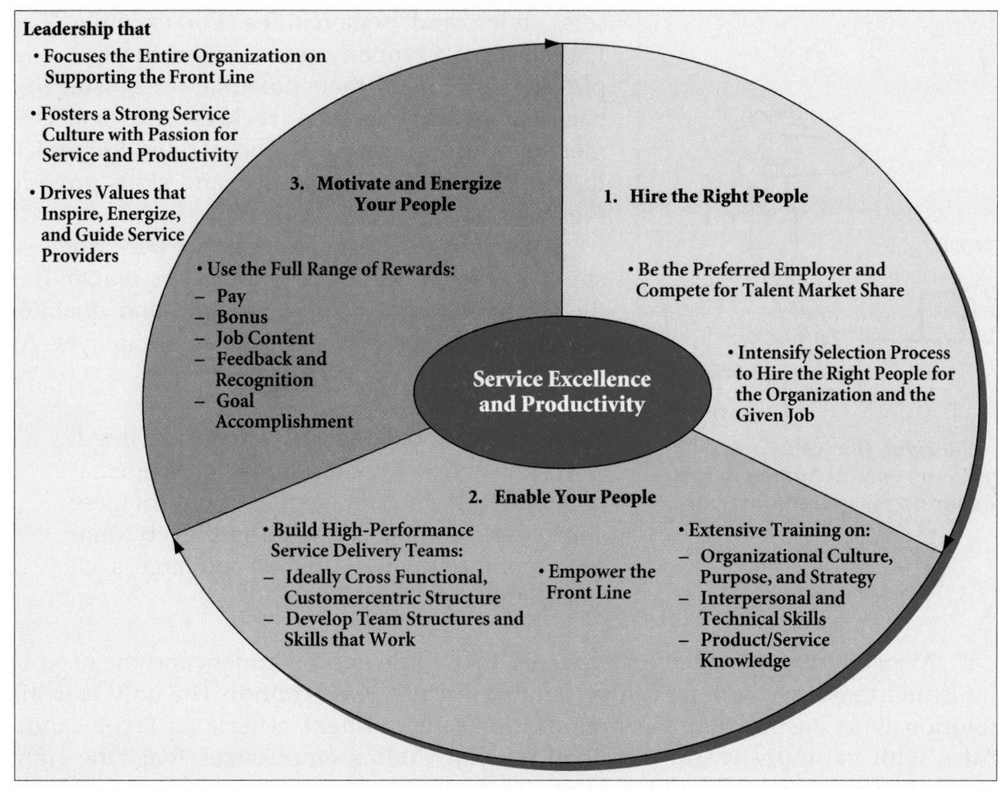

FIGURE 11.9 The Service Talent Cycle – Getting HR Right in Service Firms

service talent cycle that is our guiding framework for successful HR practices in service firms. We will then discuss the recommended practices one by one in this section.

Hire the Right People

It it is naïve to think that it's sufficient to satisfy employees. Employee satisfaction should be seen as necessary but not sufficient for having high performing staff. For instance, a recent study showed that employee effort was a strong driver of customer satisfaction over and above employee satisfaction.[23] As Jim Collins said, "The old adage 'People are the most important asset' is wrong. The *right* people are your most important asset.'" We would like to add to this: "...and the wrong people are a liability that is often difficult to get rid of." Getting it right starts with hiring the right people.

Hiring the right people includes competing for applications from the best employees in the labor market, then selecting from this pool the best candidates for the specific jobs to be filled.

BE THE PREFERRED EMPLOYER. To be able to select and hire the best people, they first have to apply for a job with you and then accept your job offer over others (the best people tend to be selected by several firms). That means a firm has to first compete for talent market share,[24] engaging in, as McKinsey & Company called it "the war for talent."[25] Competing in the labor market means having an attractive value proposition for prospective employees and includes factors such as having a good image in the community as a place to work for as well as delivering high-quality products and services that make employees feel proud to be part of the team.

Furthermore, the compensation package cannot be below average—top people expect above average packages. In our experience, it takes a salary in the range of the 60th to 80th percentile of the market to attract top performers to top companies. However, a firm does not have to be a top paymaster, if other important aspects of the value proposition are attractive. In short, understand the needs of your target-employees and get your value proposition right.

SELECT THE RIGHT PEOPLE. There's no such thing as the perfect employee (see Figure 11.10). Different positions often are best filled by people with different skill

FIGURE 11.10 There's No Such Thing as a Perfect Employee
Source: © Randy Glasbergen

sets, styles, and personalities. For example, The Walt Disney Company assesses prospective employees in terms of their potential for on-stage or backstage work. On-stage workers, known as cast members, are assigned to those roles for which their appearance, personalities, and skills provide the best match.

What makes outstanding service performers so special? Often it is things that *cannot* be taught. It is the qualities intrinsic to the people and qualities they would bring with them to any employer. As one study of high performers observed:

> Energy . . . cannot be taught, it has to be hired. The same is true for charm, for detail orientation, for work ethic, for neatness. Some of these things can be enhanced with on-the-job training . . . or incentives. . . . But by and large, such qualities are instilled early on.[26]

Also, HR managers have discovered that while good manners and the need to smile and make eye contact can be taught, warmth itself cannot. The only realistic solution is to ensure that the organization's recruitment criteria to favor candidates with naturally warm personalities. Jim Collins emphasizes that "the right people are those who would exhibit the desired behaviors anyway, as a natural extension of their character and attitude, regardless of any control and incentive system."[27]

The logical conclusion is that service firms should devote great care to attracting and hiring the right candidates. Let's next review tools that can help identify the right candidates for a given firm and job, and perhaps even more importantly, reject those candidates that don't fit.

Tools to Identify the Best Candidates

Excellent service firms use a number of approaches to identify the best candidates in their applicant pool. These approaches include interviewing applicants, observing behavior, conducting personality tests, and providing applicants with a realistic job preview.[28]

USE MULTIPLE, STRUCTURED INTERVIEWS. To improve hiring decisions, successful recruiters like to employ structured interviews built around job requirements and to use more than one interviewer. People tend to be more careful in their judgments when they know that another individual is also evaluating the same applicant. Another advantage of using two or more interviewers is that it reduces the risk of "similar to me" biases—we all like people similar to ourselves.

OBSERVE BEHAVIOR. The hiring decision should be based on the behavior that recruiters observe, not just the words they hear. As John Wooden said: "Show me what you can do, don't tell me what you can do. Too often, the big talkers are the little doers."[29] Behavior can be directly or indirectly observed by using behavioral simulations or assessment center tests that use standardized situations in which applicants can be observed to see whether they display the kind of behaviors the firms' clients would expect. Also, past behavior is the best predictor of future behavior: Hire the person who has won service excellence awards, received many complimentary letters, and has great references from past employers.

CONDUCT PERSONALITY TESTS. Personality tests help to identify traits relevant for a particular job. For example, willingness to treat customers and colleagues with courtesy, consideration, and tact; perceptiveness of customer needs; and ability to communicate accurately and pleasantly are measurable traits. Hiring decisions based on such tests tend to be accurate.

For example, the Ritz-Carlton Hotels Group uses personality profiles on all job applicants. Employees are selected for their natural predisposition for working in a service context. Inherent traits such as a ready smile, a willingness to help others, and an affinity for multitasking enable them to go beyond learned skills. An applicant to Ritz-Carlton shared about her experience of going through the personality test for a job as a junior-level concierge at the Ritz-Carlton Millenia Singapore. Her best advice: "Tell the truth. These are experts; they will know if you are lying," and then she added:

> "On the big day, they asked if I liked helping people, if I was an organized person and if I liked to smile a lot." Yes, yes and yes, I said. But I had to support it with real life examples. This, at times, felt rather intrusive. To answer the first question for instance, I had to say a bit about the person I had helped—why she needed help, for example. The test forced me to recall even insignificant things I had done, like learning how to say hello in different languages which helped to get a fix on my character."[30]

It's better to hire upbeat and happy people, because customers report higher satisfaction when served by more satisfied staff.[31] Apart from intensive interview-based psychological tests, cost-effective Internet-based testing kits are available. Here, applicants enter their test responses to a Web-based questionnaire, and the prospective employer receives the analysis, the suitability of the candidate, and a hiring recommendation. Developing and administering such tests has become a significant service industry in its own right. A leading global supplier of such assessment products, the SHL Group, serves some 15,500 organizations in 30 languages in over 50 countries. Have a look at its website at www.shl.com to see the tests that are available.

GIVE APPLICANTS A REALISTIC PREVIEW OF THE JOB. During the recruitment process, service companies should let candidates know the reality of the job,[32] thereby giving them a chance to "try on the job" and assess whether it's a good fit or not. At the same time, recruiters can observe how candidates respond to the job's realities. This approach allows some candidates to withdraw if they determine the job is not suitable for them. At the same time, the company can manage new employees' expectations of their job. Many service companies adopt this approach. For example, Au Bon Pain, a chain of French bakery cafes, lets applicants work for two paid days in a café prior to the final selection interview. Here, managers can observe candidates in action, and candidates can assess whether they like the job and the work environment.[33]

See Best Practice in Action 11.1 to learn how the Americana Group uses a combination of interviews and other selection tools to identify the right candidates with the right attitude and a personality that fits the Americana culture from its vast pool of applicants. Not only must the group be trained, but it also must work well to deliver the final service and be able to interact with the customers to create a positive experience.

Train Service Employees Actively

If a firm has good people, investments in training can yield outstanding results. Service champions show a strong commitment to training in words, dollars, and action. As Benjamin Schneider and David Bowen put it, "The combination of attracting a diverse and competent applicant pool, utilizing effective techniques for hiring the

BEST PRACTICE IN ACTION 11.1

Human Resources at Americana Group: Getting It Right

Americana Group began in 1964 in Kuwait and today operates more than 1,000 restaurants with more than 35,000 employees across 17 countries between the Atlantic Ocean and Caspian Sea. It has several international franchises like Hardee's, TGIF's, Krispy Kreme, KFC, and Pizza Hut, and its portfolio also includes a wide range of consumer foods manufactured in 18 factories in five countries. Some challenges in the markets of operation for Americana are the strong talent war from competitors, inadequate employment pool, poor technical education, and the absence of national vocational qualification systems. Unskilled and unhappy employees lead to dissatisfied customers and increased costs to the organization.

Because the local talent pool is inadequate, Americana staffs restaurants with employees from outside the region. It also recruits three times as many employees as its nearest competitor in the region. Americana needs to make sure these employees respect cultural sensitivities. Americana recruits 15,000 employees per year. Except for Egypt, most Gulf Cooperation Council (GCC) countries have a dearth of labor. Eighty percent of their expatriate labor force is hired from Egypt, the Philippines, India, and Bangladesh. The remaining workers come from Nepal, Indonesia, and China. More recently, Americana has broadened its talent search to Kenya and Burma. It is common within the GCC to recruit foreign workers, yet what is unique about Americana is its approach.

The lead time from search, identification, and final selection of an employee is approximately four to five months. An incorrect identification of an employee becomes costly not only in time but money spent. To ensure that this process is as efficient as possible, Americana works with partner recruitment firms in these countries, as they have access to these talent pools. Americana must first align these recruitment companies with its needs and expectations. This involves first training the recruiters on the skills required in candidates, including their ability to work in very conservative societies. A recruitment schedule and expectation of potential employees is given. Most of these potential employees must have had some experience with the quick service restaurant (QSR) industry. Recruiters shortlist potential employees, and then Americana will select the final employees. An efficient process should decrease costs and optimize selection.

On selection, employees are brought to a central location, where Americana invests an additional 40 to 50 hours on cultural training (most industries will spend 8 to 12 hours); for example, the customs and culture of the Middle East are very different from those in China, from which some employees are recruited. Concurrently, because the highest emphasis is on the service standards, workplace training, such as in food safety, is done. Then, employees are allocated to their places of employment, where additional training takes place; this is routine training to introduce new products or new skills and to keep them abreast of corporate culture.

Because the expatriate employees live far from home, many in dormitories, the company needs to ensure that they are happy, even outside of work. The employees generally live in gender-segregated dormitories based on their home country so that the food that is served is to their liking. The company conducts annual climate surveys on workplace, dormitories, company transportation to and from work, and infrastructure. Feedback is used to motivate employees and create an environment that is familial and operational. Games and sports are organized, and festivals (home country and host country) are celebrated. Most service QSR industries worldwide have a turnover of 100 percent in a year; Americana has a turnover of 30 percent. By giving employees a way to improve their income, using constantly evolving HR best practices, Americana has created a work environment that is motivating and productive.

Source: http://www.americana-group.net/Default.aspx?Id=1297; industry sources.

most appropriate people from that pool, and then training the heck out of them would be gangbusters in any market."[34] Service employees need to learn:

- **The Organizational Culture, Purpose, and Strategy.** Start strong with new hires; focus on getting emotional commitment to the firm's core strategy; and promote core values such as commitment to service excellence, responsiveness, team spirit, mutual respect, honesty, and integrity. Use managers to teach, and focus on "what", "why" and "how" rather than on the specifics of the job.[35] For example, new recruits at Disneyland attend the "Disney University Orientation." It starts with a detailed discussion of the company history and philosophy, the service standards expected of cast members, and a comprehensive tour of Disneyland's operations.[36]

- **Interpersonal and Technical Skills.** Interpersonal skills tend to be generic across service jobs and include visual communications skills such as making eye contact, attentive listening, body language, and even facial expressions. Technical skills encompass all the required knowledge related to processes (e.g., how to handle a merchandise return), machines (e.g., how to operate the terminal), and rules and regulations related to customer service processes. Both technical and interpersonal skills are *necessary* but neither alone is *sufficient* for optimal job performance.[37]
- **Product/Service Knowledge.** Knowledgeable staff are a key aspect of service quality. They must be able to explain product features effectively and position the product correctly. For instance, in Best Practice in Action 11.2, Jennifer Grassano of Dial-A-Mattress coaches individual staff members on how to paint pictures in the customer's mind.

Of course, training has to result in tangible changes in behavior. If staff do not apply what they have learned, the investment is wasted. Learning is not only about becoming smarter, but about changing behaviors and improving decision making. To achieve this, practice and reinforcement are needed. Supervisors can play a

BEST PRACTICE IN ACTION 11.2

Coaching at Dial-A-Mattress

Coaching is a common method employed by services leaders to train and develop staff. Dial-A-Mattress' Jennifer Grassano is a bedding consultant (BC) for three days a week and a coach to other BCs for one day a week. She focuses on staff whose productivity and sales performance are slumping.

Her first step is to listen in on the BCs telephone calls with customers. She will listen for about an hour and take detailed notes on each call. The BCs understand that their calls may be monitored, but they receive no advance notice as that would defeat the purpose.

Grassano conducts a coaching session with the staff member, in which strengths and areas for improvements are reviewed. She knows how difficult it is to maintain a high energy level and convey enthusiasm when handling some 60 calls per shift. She likes to suggest new tactics and phrasings "to spark up their presentation." One BC was not responding effectively when customers asked why one mattress was more expensive than another. Here, she stressed the need to paint a picture in the customer's mind:

Customers are at our mercy when buying bedding. They don't know the difference between one coil system and another. It is just like buying a carburetor for my car. I don't even know what a carburetor looks like. We have to use very descriptive words to help bedding customers make the decision that is right for them. Tell the customer that the more costly mattress has richer, finer padding with a blend of silk and wool. Don't just say the mattress has more layers of padding.

About two months after the initial coaching session, Grassano conducts a follow-up monitoring session with that BC. She then compares the BC's performance before and after the coaching session to assess the effectiveness of the training.

Grassano's experience and productivity as a BC give her the credibility as a coach. "If I am not doing well as a BC, then who am I to be a coach? I have to lead by example. I would be much less effective if I was a full-time trainer." She clearly relishes the opportunity to share her knowledge and pass on her craft.

Source: Reprinted with the permission of The Free Press, a division of Simon & Schuster, Inc., from *Discovering the Soul of Service: The Nine Drives of Sustainable Business Success* by Leonard L. Berry.

FIGURE 11.11 Morning Briefings by a Supervisor Offer Effective Training Opportunities

crucial role by following up regularly on learning objectives, for instance, meeting with staff to reinforce key lessons from recent complaints and compliments (Figure 11.11).

Training and learning professionalizes the frontline, moving these individuals away from the common (self)-image of being in low-end jobs that have no significance. Well-trained employees feel and act like professionals. A waiter who knows about food, cooking, wines, dining etiquette, and how to effectively interact with customers (even complaining ones) feels professional, has a high self-esteem, and is respected by his customers. Training is therefore extremely effective in reducing person/role stress.

Empower the Frontline

After selecting the right candidates and training them well, the next step is to empower the frontline. Virtually all breakthrough service firms have legendary stories of employees who recovered failed service transactions or walked the extra mile to make a customer's day or avoid some kind of disaster for that client (for an example, see Best Practice in Action 11.3).[38] To allow this to happen, employees have to be empowered. Nordstrom trains and trusts its employees to do the right thing and empowers them to do so. Its employee handbook

BEST PRACTICE IN ACTION 11.3

Empowerment at Nordstrom

Van Mensah, a men's apparel sales associate at Nordstrom, received a disturbing letter from one of his loyal customers. The gentleman had purchased some $2,000 worth of shirts and ties from Mensah and mistakenly washed the shirts in hot water. They all shrank. He was writing to ask Mensah's professional advice on how he should deal with his predicament (the gentleman did not complain and readily conceded the mistake was his).

Mensah immediately called the customer and offered to replace those shirts with new ones—at no charge. He asked the customer to mail the other shirts back to Nordstrom—at Nordstrom's expense. "I didn't have to ask for anyone's permission to do what I did for that customer," said Mensah. "Nordstrom would rather leave it up to me to decide what's best.

Middlemas, a Nordstrom's veteran, said to employees, "You will never be criticized for doing too much for a customer; you will only be criticized for doing too little. If you're ever in doubt as to what to do in a situation, always make a decision that favors the customer before the company." Nordtrom's Employee Handbook confirms this. It reads:

Welcome to Nordstrom

We're glad to have you with our Company.

Our number one goal is to provide outstanding customer service.

Set both your personal and professional goals high.

We have great confidence in your ability to achieve them.

Nordstrom Rules:

Rule #1: Use your good judgment in all situations.

There will be no additional rules.

Please feel free to ask your department manager, store manager, or division general manager any question at any time.

Source: Robert Spector and Patrick D. McCarthy, *The Nordstrom Way.* New York: John Wiley & Sons, Inc., 2000, 15–16, 95.

has only one rule: "Use good judgment in all situations." Employee self-direction has become increasingly important, especially in service firms, because frontline staff frequently operate on their own, face to face with their customers, and it tends to be difficult for managers to closely monitor their behavior.[39] Research also linked high empowerment to higher customer satisfaction.[40]

For many services, providing employees with greater discretion (and training in how to use their judgment) enables them to provide superior service on the spot, rather than taking time to get permission from supervisors. Empowerment looks to frontline staff to find solutions to service problems and to make appropriate decisions about customizing service delivery.

IS EMPOWERMENT ALWAYS APPROPRIATE? Advocates claim that the empowerment approach is more likely to yield motivated employees and satisfied customers than the "production-line" alternative in which management designs a relatively standardized system and expects workers to execute tasks within narrow guidelines. However, David Bowen and Edward Lawler suggest that different situations may require different solutions, declaring that "both the empowerment and production-line approaches have their advantages . . . and . . . each fits certain situations. The key is to choose the management approach that best meets the needs of both employees and customers." Not all employees are necessarily eager to be empowered, and many employees do not seek personal growth within their jobs and would prefer to work to specific directions rather than to use their own initiative. Research has shown that a strategy of empowerment is most likely appropriate when most of the following factors are present within the organization and its environment:

- The firm's business strategy is based on competitive differentiation and on offering personalized, customized service.
- The approach to customers is based on extended relationships rather than on short-term transactions.
- The organization uses technologies that are complex and nonroutine in nature.
- The business environment is unpredictable, and surprises are to be expected.
- Existing managers are comfortable with letting employees work independently for the benefit of both the organization and its customers.
- Employees have a strong need to grow and deepen their skills in the work environment, are interested in working with others, and have good interpersonal and group process skills.[41]

CONTROL VERSUS INVOLVEMENT. The production-line approach to managing people is based on the well-established *control* model of organization design and management. There are clearly defined roles, top-down control systems, hierarchical pyramid structures, and an assumption that the management knows best. Empowerment, by contrast, is based on the *involvement* (or *commitment*) model, which assumes that employees can make good decisions and produce good ideas for operating the business if they are properly socialized, trained, and informed. This model also assumes that employees can be internally motivated to perform effectively and that they are capable of self-control and self-direction.

Schneider and Bowen emphasize that "empowerment isn't just 'setting the frontline free' or 'throwing away the policy manuals.' It requires systematically redistributing four key ingredients throughout the organization, from the top downwards."[42] The four features are:

- *Information* about organizational performance (e.g., operating results and measures of competitive performance).
- *Knowledge* that enables employees to understand and contribute to organizational performance (e.g., problem-solving skills).
- *Power* to make decisions that influence work procedures and organizational direction (e.g., through quality circles and self-managing teams).
- *Rewards* based on organizational performance such as bonuses, profit sharing, and stock options.

In the control model, the four features are concentrated at the top of the organization, while in the involvement model these features are pushed down through the organization.

LEVELS OF EMPLOYEE INVOLVEMENT. The empowerment and production-line approaches are at opposite ends of a spectrum that reflects increasing levels of employee involvement as additional information, knowledge, power, and rewards are pushed down to the front line. Empowerment can take place at several levels:

- *Suggestion Involvement* empowers employees to make recommendations through formalized programs. McDonald's, often portrayed as an archetype of the production-line approach, listens closely to its frontline. Did you know that innovations, ranging from Egg McMuffin to methods of wrapping burgers without leaving a thumbprint on the bun, were invented by employees?
- *Job Involvement* represents a dramatic opening up of job content. Jobs are redesigned to allow employees to use a wider array of skills. In complex service organizations such as airlines and hospitals, in which individual employees cannot offer all facets of a service, job involvement often is accomplished through the use of teams. To cope with the added demands accompanying this form of empowerment, employees require training, and supervisors need to be reoriented from directing the group to facilitating its performance in supportive ways.
- *High Involvement* gives even the lowest-level employees a sense of involvement in the company's overall performance. Information is shared. Employees develop skills in teamwork, problem solving, and business operations, and they participate in work-unit management decisions. There is profit sharing, often in the form of bonuses.

Southwest Airlines illustrates a high-involvement company, promoting common sense and flexibility. It trusts its employees and gives them the latitude, discretion, and authority they need to do their jobs. The airline has eliminated inflexible work rules and rigid job descriptions so its people can assume ownership for getting the job done and enabling flights to leave on time, regardless of whose "official" responsibility it is. This gives employees the flexibility to help each other when needed. As a result, they adopt a "whatever it takes" mentality.

Southwest mechanics and pilots feel free to help ramp agents load bags. When a flight is running late, it's not uncommon to see pilots helping passengers in wheelchairs to board the aircraft, assisting operations agents by taking boarding passes, or helping flight attendants clean the cabin between flights. All of these actions are their way of adapting to the situation and taking ownership for getting customers on board more quickly. In addition, Southwest employees apply common sense, not rules, when it's in the best interests for the customer.

Rod Jones, assistant chief pilot, recalls a captain who left the gate with a senior citizen who had boarded the wrong plane. The customer was confused and very upset. Southwest asks pilots not to go back to the gate with an incorrectly boarded customer. In this case, the captain was concerned about this individual's well-being. "So, he adapted to the situation." says Jones. "He came back in to the gate, deplaned the customer, pushed back out, and gave us an irregularity report. Even though he broke the rules, he used his judgment and did what he thought was best. And we said, 'Attaboy!'"[43]

Build High-Performance Service-Delivery Teams

A team can be defined as "a small number of people with complementary skills committed to a common purpose, set of performance goals, and approach for which they hold themselves mutually accountable."[44] The nature of many services requires people to work in teams, often across functions, in order to offer seamless customer service processes.

Traditionally, many firms were organized by functional structures, under which, for example, one department is in charge of consulting and selling (e.g., selling a subscription contract with a cell phone), another, in charge of customer service (e.g., activation of value-added services, changes of subscription plans), and still a third is in charge of billing. This structure prevents internal service teams from viewing end customers as their own, and this structure can also mean poorer teamwork across functions, slower service, and more errors between functions. When customers have service problems, they easily fall between the cracks.

Empirical research has confirmed that frontline employees themselves regard lack of interdepartmental support as an important factor in hindering them from satisfying their customers.[45] Because of these problems, service organizations in many industries need to create cross-functional teams with the authority and responsibility to serve customers from beginning of the service encounter to the end. Such teams are also called self-managed teams.[46]

THE POWER OF TEAMWORK IN SERVICES. Teams, training, and empowerment go hand-in-hand. Teams facilitate communication among team members and the sharing of knowledge. By operating like a small, independent unit, service teams take on more responsibility and require less supervision than more traditional functionally organized customer service units. Furthermore, teams often set higher performance targets for themselves than supervisors would. Within a good team, pressure to perform is high.[47] Best Practice in Action 11.4 shows not only how Singapore Airlines uses teams to provide emotional support and to mentor its cabin crew, but also how the company effectively assesses, rewards, and promotes staff.

Some academics even feel that too much emphasis is placed on hiring "individual stars," and too little attention is paid to hiring staff with good team abilities and motivation to work cooperatively. Stanford professors Charles O'Reilly and Jeffrey Pfeffer emphasize that how well people work in teams often is as important as how good people are, and that stars can be outperformed by others through superior teamwork.[48]

At Customer Research Inc. (CRI), a progressive and successful marketing research firm, team members' feelings are illustrated in the following quotes:

- "I like being on the team. You feel like you belong. Everyone knows what's going on."
- "We take ownership. Everyone accepts responsibility and jumps in to help."
- "When a client needs something in an hour, we work together to solve the problem."
- "There are no slugs. Everyone pulls their weight."[49]

Team ability and motivation are crucial for effective delivery of many types of services, especially those involving individuals who are each playing specialist roles. For example, health care services depend heavily on effective teamwork of many specialists (see Figure 11.12).

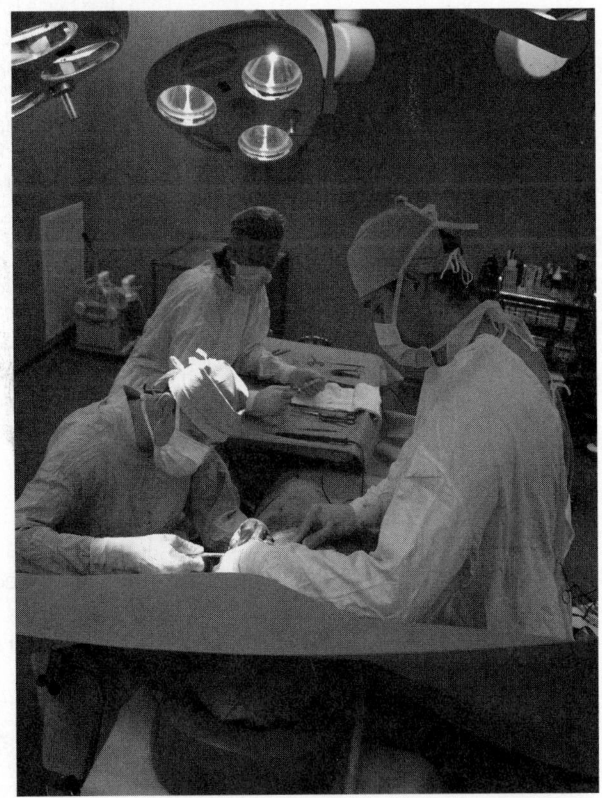

FIGURE 11.12 Surgical Teams Work under Particularly Demanding Conditions

CREATING SUCCESSFUL SERVICE-DELIVERY TEAMS. It's not easy to make teams function well. If people are not prepared for teamwork, and the team structure isn't set up right, a firm risks having initially enthusiastic volunteers who lack the competencies that teamwork requires. The skills needed include not only cooperation, listening to others, coaching and encouraging one another, but also an understanding of how to air differences, tell one another hard truths, and ask tough questions. All these require training.[50] Management also needs to set up a structure that will steer the teams toward success. A good example is

BEST PRACTICE IN ACTION 11.4

Singapore Airlines' Team Concept

Singapore Airlines (SIA) understands the importance of teamwork in the delivery of service excellence and has been focusing on creating an *esprit de corps* among its cabin crew. This is made more difficult by the fact that many crew members are scattered around the world. SIA's answer is the "team concept."

Choo Poh Leong, Senior Manager Cabin Crew Performance, explained:

"In order to effectively manage our 6,600 crew, we divide them into teams, small units, with a team leader in charge of about 13 people. We will roster them to fly together as much as we can. Flying together, as a unit, allows them to build up camaraderie, and crew members feel like they are part of a team, not just a member. The team leader will get to know them well, their strengths and weaknesses, and will become their mentor and their counsel, and someone to whom they can turn if they need help or advice. The 'check trainers' oversee 12 or 13 teams and fly with them whenever possible, not only to inspect their performance, but also to help their team develop."

"The interaction within each of the teams is very strong. As a result, when a team leader does a staff appraisal, they really know the staff. You would be amazed how meticulous and detailed each staff record is. So, in this way, we have good control, and through the control, we can ensure that the crew delivers the promise. They know that they're being constantly monitored and so they deliver. If there are problems, we will know about them and we can send them for re-training. Those who are good will be selected for promotion."

According to Toh Giam Ming, Senior Manager Crew Performance, "What is good about the team concept is that despite the huge number of crew, people can relate to a team and have a sense of belonging. 'This is my team.' And they are put together for 1–2 years and they are rostered together for about 60–70 percent of the time, so they do fly together quite a fair bit . . . So especially for the new people, I think they find that they have less problems adjusting to the flying career, no matter what their background is. Because once you get familiar with the team, there is support and guidance on how to do things." Choo Poh Leong adds: "The individual, you see, is not a digit or a staff number, because if you don't have team-flying, you have 6,000 odd people, it can be difficult for you to really know a particular person."

SIA also has a lot of seemingly unrelated activities in the cabin crew division. For example, there is a committee called the Performing Arts Circle made up of talented employees with an interest in the arts. During a recent bi-annual Cabin Crew Gala Dinner, members of SIA raised over half a million dollars for charity. In addition to the "Performing Arts Circle," SIA also has a gourmet circle, language circles (such as a German and French speaking group), and even sports circles (such as football and tennis teams). As mentioned by Sim Kay Wee, "SIA believes that all these things really encourage camaraderie and teamwork."

Sources: Jochen Wirtz, Loizos Heracleous, and Nitin Pangarkar, "Managing Human Resources for Service Excellence and Cost Effectiveness at Singapore Airlines," *Managing Service Quality,* 18, No. 1, 2008, 4–19; Loizos Heracleous, Jochen Wirtz, and Nitin Pangarkar, *Flying High in a Competitive Industry: Secrets of the World's Leading Airline.* Singapore: McGraw-Hill, 2009.

American Express Latin America, which developed the following rules for making its teams work:

- Each team has an "owner"—a person who owns the team's problems.
- Each team has a leader who monitors team progress and team process. Team leaders are selected for their strong business knowledge and people skills.
- Each team has a quality facilitator—someone who knows how to make teams work and who can remove barriers to progress and train others to work together effectively.[51]

Motivate and Energize People

Once a firm has hired the right people, trained them well, empowered them, and organized them into effective service delivery teams, how can it ensure that they will deliver? Staff performance is a function of ability and motivation.[52] Effective hiring, training, empowerment, and teams give a firm able people; and reward systems are key to motivating them. Service staff must get the message that providing quality service holds the key for them to be rewarded. Motivating and rewarding strong service performers are some of the most effective ways of retaining them. Staff pick up quickly if those who get promoted are the truly outstanding service providers, and if those who get fired are those that do not deliver at the customer level.

A major way service businesses fail is not utilizing the full range of available rewards effectively. Many firms think in terms of money as reward, but it does not pass the test of an effective reward. Receiving a fair salary is a hygiene factor rather than a motivating factor. Paying more than what is seen as fair only has short-term motivating effects and wears off quickly. On the other hand, bonuses contingent on performance have to be earned again and again and therefore tend to be more lasting in their effectiveness. Other, more lasting rewards are the job content itself, recognition and feedback, and goal accomplishment.

JOB CONTENT. People are motivated and satisfied simply by knowing that they are doing a good job. They feel good about themselves and like to reinforce that feeling. This is true especially if the job also offers a variety of different activities, requires the completion of "whole" and identifiable pieces of work, is seen as significant in the sense that it has an impact on the lives of others, comes with autonomy, and provides direct and clear feedback about how well employees did their work (grateful customers and sales performance).

FEEDBACK AND RECOGNITION. Humans are social beings, and they derive a sense of identity and belonging to an organization from the recognition and feedback they receive from the people around them—their customers, colleagues, and bosses. If employees are recognized and thanked for service excellence, they will want to continue achieving it. If done well, star employee of the month-type of awards recognize excellent performances and can be highly motivating.

GOAL ACCOMPLISHMENT. Goals focus people's energy. Goals that are specific, difficult but attainable, and accepted by the staff are strong motivators. They result in higher performance than no goals or vague goals ("do your best") or goals impossible to achieve.[53] In short, goals are effective motivators.

The following are important points to note for effective goal setting:

- When goals are seen as important, achieving the goals is a reward in itself.
- Goal accomplishment can be used as a basis for giving rewards, including pay, feedback, and recognition. Feedback and recognition from peers can be given faster, more cheaply and effectively than pay, and have the additional benefit of gratifying an employee's self-esteem.
- Service employee goals that are specific and difficult must be set publicly to be accepted. Although goals must be specific, they can be something intangible like improved employee courtesy ratings.
- Progress reports about goal accomplishment (feedback) and goal accomplishment itself must be public events (recognition) if they are to gratify employees' esteem need.
- It is mostly unnecessary to specify the means to achieve goals. Feedback on progress while pursuing the goal serves as a corrective function. As long as the goal is specific, difficult but achievable, and accepted, goal pursuit will result in goal accomplishment, even in the absence of other rewards.

Successful firms recognize that people issues are complex. Hewitt Associates, a professional firm delivering human capital management services, captures the challenge of employee complexity in its advertising (Figure 11.13). Charles O'Reilly and Jeffrey Pfeffer conducted in-depth research on why some companies can succeed over long

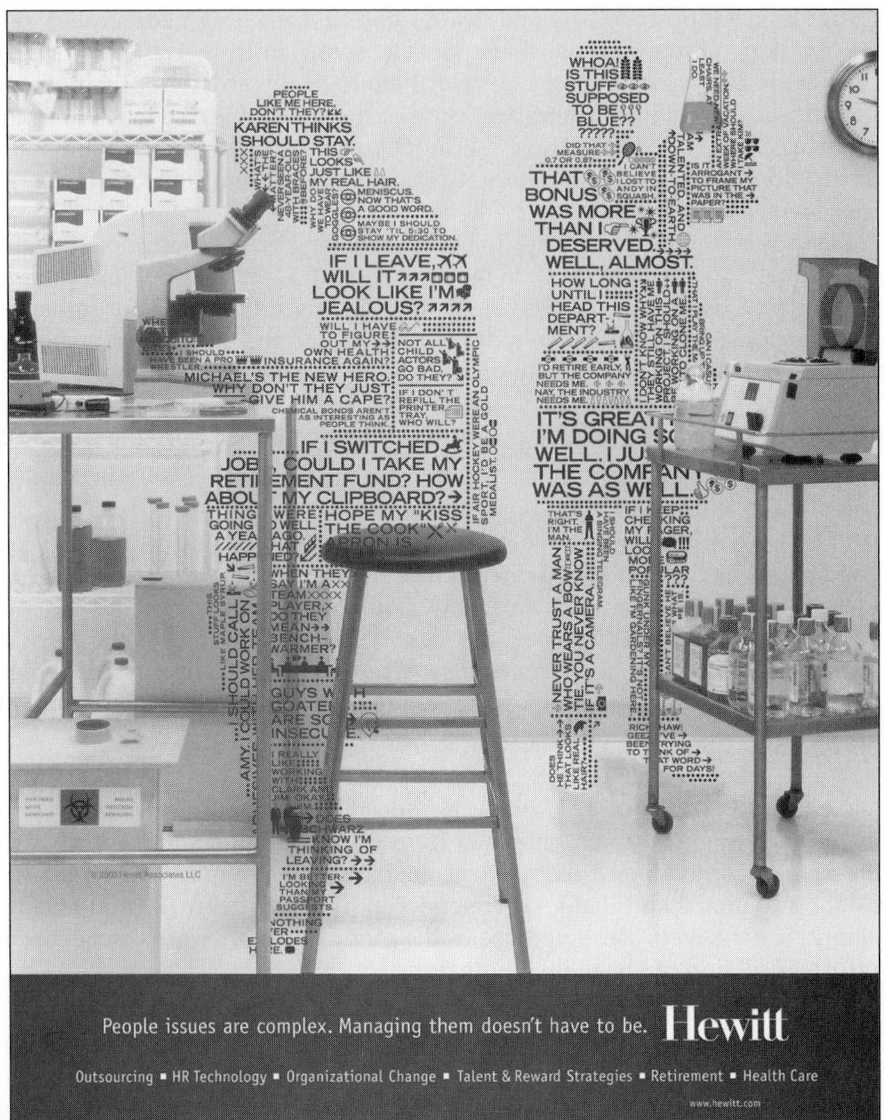

FIGURE 11.13 "People Issues Are Complex: Managing Them Doesn't Have to Be" Declares Hewitt Associates

Source: Copyright © 2003 Hewitt Associates LLC

periods of time in highly competitive industries without having the usual sources of competitive advantage such as barriers of entry or proprietary technology. They concluded that these firms did not succeed by winning the war for talent (although these firms were hiring extremely carefully for fit), "but by fully using the talent and unlocking the motivation of the people" they already had in their organizations.[54]

The Role of Labor Unions

Labor unions and service excellence do not seem to gel. The power of organized labor is widely cited as an excuse for not adopting new approaches in both service and manufacturing businesses. "We'd never get it past the unions," managers say, wringing their hands and muttering darkly about restrictive work practices. Unions often are portrayed as villains in the press, especially when high-profile strikes inconvenience millions. Many managers seem to be rather antagonistic toward unions.

Contrary to the negative view presented above, many of the world's most successful service businesses are highly unionized—Southwest Airlines is one example.

The presence of unions in a service company is not an automatic barrier to high performance and innovation, unless there is a long history of mistrust, acrimonious relationships, and confrontation.

Jeffrey Pfeffer has observed wryly that "the subject of unions and collective bargaining is... one that causes otherwise sensible people to lose their objectivity."[55] He urges a pragmatic approach to this issue, emphasizing that "the effects of unions depend very much on what *management* does." The higher wages, lower turnover, clearly established grievance procedures, and improved working conditions often found in highly unionized organizations can yield positive benefits in a well-managed service organization. Furthermore, management consultation and negotiation with union representatives are essential if employees are to accept new ideas (conditions equally valid in nonunionized firms). The challenge is to jointly work with unions, to reduce conflict, and to create a climate for service.[56]

SERVICE LEADERSHIP AND CULTURE

So far, we have discussed the key strategies that help to move an organization toward service excellence. However, to truly get there, we need a strong service culture that is continuously reinforced and developed by management to achieve alignment with the firm's strategy.[57] *Charismatic leadership*, also called *transformational leadership*, fundamentally changes the values, goals, and aspirations of the frontline to be consistent with that of the firms.' With this kind of leadership, staff are more likely to perform their best and "above and beyond the call of duty," because it is consistent with their own values, beliefs, and attitudes.[58]

Leonard Berry advocates a value-driven leadership that inspires and guides service providers. Leadership should bring out the passion for serving. It should also tap the creativity of service providers, nourish their energy and commitment, and give them a fulfilled working life. Some of the core values Berry found in excellent service firms included excellence, innovation, joy, teamwork, respect, integrity, and social profit.[59] These values are part of the firm's culture. A *service culture* can be defined as:

- Shared perceptions of *what* is important in an organization, and
- Shared values and beliefs of *why* those things are important.[60]

Employees rely heavily on their perceptions of what is important by noting what the company and their leaders do, not so much what they say. Employees gain their understanding of what is important through the daily experiences they have with the firm's human resource, operations, and marketing practices and procedures.

A strong service culture is one where the entire organization focuses on the frontline, understanding that it is the lifeline of the business. The organization understands that today's as well as tomorrow's revenues are driven largely by what happens at the service encounter. Figure 11.14 shows the inverted pyramid, which highlights the importance of the frontline and shows that the role of top management and middle management is to support the frontline in their task of delivering service excellence to their customers.

In firms with a passion for service, top management show by their actions that what happens at the frontline is crucially important to them, by being informed and actively involved. They achieve this by regularly talking to and working with frontline staff and customers. Many actually spend significant amounts of time at the frontline serving customers. For example, Disney World's management spends two weeks every year in frontline staff job such as sweeping streets, selling ice cream, or working as the ride attendant to gain a better appreciation and understanding of what really happens on the ground.[61]

Service leaders are not only interested in the big picture, but they focus on the details of service, they see opportunities in nuances that competitors might consider trivial, and they believe the way the firm handles little things sets the tone for how it handles everything else.

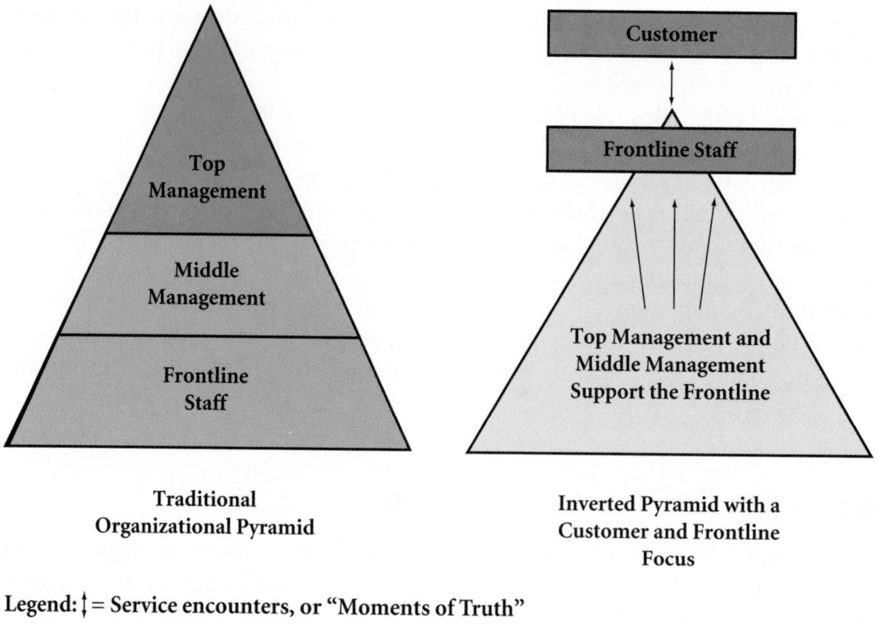

FIGURE 11.14 The Inverted Organizational Pyramid

Internal Marketing

In addition to a strong leadership that focuses on the frontline, it takes a strong communications effort to shape the culture and get the message to the troops. Service leaders use multiple tools to build their service culture, ranging from internal marketing and training to core principles and company events and celebrations.

Internal communications from senior managers to their employees play a vital role in maintaining and nurturing a corporate culture founded on specific service values. Well-planned internal marketing efforts are especially necessary in large service businesses that operate in widely dispersed sites, sometimes around the world. Even when employees are working far from the head office in the home country, they still need to be kept informed of new policies, changes in service features, and new quality initiatives. Communications may also be needed to nurture team spirit and support common corporate goals across national frontiers. Consider the challenge of maintaining a unified sense of purpose at the overseas offices of companies such as Citibank, Air Canada, Marriott, or Starbucks where people from different cultures who speak different languages must work together to create consistent levels of service.

Effective internal communications can help ensure efficient and satisfactory service delivery; achieve productive and harmonious working relationships; and build employee trust, respect, and loyalty. Commonly used media include internal newsletters and magazines, videos, private corporate television networks like those owned by FedEx and Merrill Lynch, Intranets (private networks of websites and email inaccessible to the general public), face-to-face briefings, and promotional campaigns using displays, prizes, and recognition programs.

For example, Ritz-Carlton translated the key product and service requirements of its customers into the Ritz-Carlton Gold Standards, which include a credo, motto, three steps of service, and 12 service values (see Best Practice in Action 11.5). An important aspect of the service values is their hierarchical structure. Service values 10, 11, and 12 represent functional values such as safety, security, and cleanliness. Ritz-Carlton refers to the next level of excellence as emotional engagement, which covers values 4 through 9. They relate to learning and professional growth of its employees, teamwork, service, problem solving and service recovery, innovation, and continuous improvement. Beyond the guests' functional needs and emotional engagement is the third level, which relates to values 1, 2, and 3 and is called "the Ritz-Carlton Mystique." This level aims to create unique, memorable, and personal

BEST PRACTICE IN ACTION 11.5

Ritz-Carlton's Gold Standards

Gold Standards

Our Gold Standards are the foundation of The Ritz-Carlton Hotel Company, L.L.C. They encompass the values and philosophy by which we operate and include:

The Credo

The Ritz-Carlton Hotel is a place where the genuine care and comfort of our guests is our highest mission.

We pledge to provide the finest personal service and facilities for our guests who will always enjoy a warm, relaxed, yet refined ambience.

The Ritz-Carlton experience enlivens the senses, instills well-being, and fulfills even the unexpressed wishes and needs of our guests.

Motto

At The Ritz-Carlton Hotel Company, L.L.C., "We are Ladies and Gentlemen serving Ladies and Gentlemen." This motto exemplifies the anticipatory service provided by all staff members.

Three Steps Of Service

1. A warm and sincere greeting. Use the guest's name.
2. Anticipation and fulfillment of each guest's needs.
3. Fond farewell. Give a warm good-bye, and use the guest's name.

Service Values: I Am Proud to Be Ritz-Carlton

1. I build strong relationships and create Ritz-Carlton guests for life.
2. I am always responsive to the expressed and unexpressed wishes and needs of our guests.
3. I am empowered to create unique, memorable and personal experiences for our guests.
4. I understand my role in achieving the Key Success Factors, embracing Community Footprints and creating The Ritz-Carlton Mystique.
5. I continuously seek opportunities to innovate and improve The Ritz-Carlton experience.
6. I own and immediately resolve guest problems.
7. I create a work environment of teamwork and lateral service so that the needs of our guests and each other are met.
8. I have the opportunity to continuously learn and grow.
9. I am involved in the planning of the work that affects me.
10. I am proud of my professional appearance, language and behavior.
11. I protect the privacy and security of our guests, my fellow employees and the company's confidential information and assets.
12. I am responsible for uncompromising levels of cleanliness and creating a safe and accident-free environment.

The 6th Diamond

Mystique
Emotional Engagement
Functional

The Employee Promise

At The Ritz-Carlton, our Ladies and Gentlemen are the most important resource in our service commitment to our guests.

By applying the principles of trust, honesty, respect, integrity and commitment, we nurture and maximize talent to the benefit of each individual and the company.

The Ritz-Carlton fosters a work environment where diversity is valued, quality of life is enhanced, individual aspirations are fulfilled, and The Ritz-Carlton Mystique is strengthened.

Source: ©1992–2006 The Ritz-Carlton Hotel Company, L. L. C. All Rights Reserved. Reprinted with the permisson of The Ritz-Carlton Hotel Company, L. L. C.

guest experiences that Ritz-Carlton believes can only occur when employees delivery on the guests' expressed and unexpressed wishes and needs and when they strive to build lifetime relationships between Ritz-Cartlon and its guests.[62] The three levels are reflected in the Sixth Diamond in Ritz-Carton's gold standards as "a new benchmark in the hospitality industry and the three levels for achieving both employee and customer engagement."[63]

Tim Kirkpatrick, Director of Training and Development of Ritz-Carlton's Boston Common Hotel said, "The Gold Standards are part of our uniform, just like your nametag. But remember, it's just a laminated card until you put it into action."[64] To reinforce these standards, every morning briefing includes a discussion directly related to the standards. The aim of these discussions is to keep the Ritz-Carlton philosophy at the center of its employees' minds.

Another great example of a firm with a strong culture is Southwest Airlines, which uses continuously new and creative ways to strengthen its culture. Southwest's Culture Committee members are zealots when it comes to the continuation of Southwest's family feel. The committee represents everyone from flight attendants and reservationists to top executives. As one participant observed, "The Culture Committee is not made up of Big Shots; it is a committee of Big Hearts." Culture Committee members are not out to gain power. They use the power of the Southwest spirit to better connect people to the cultural foundations of the company. The committee works behind the scenes to foster Southwest's commitment to its core values. The following are examples of events held to reinforce Southwest's cultures.

- **Walk a Mile in My Shoes.** This program helped Southwest employees gain an appreciation for other people's jobs. Employees were asked to visit a different department on their day off and to spend a minimum of six hours on the "walk." These participants were rewarded not only with transferable roundtrip passes, but also with goodwill and increased morale.
- **A Day in the Field.** This activity is practiced throughout the company all year long. Barri Tucker, then a senior communications representative in the executive office, for example, once joined three flight attendants working a three-day trip. Tucker gained by experiencing the company from a new angle and by hearing directly from customers. She was able to see how important it is for corporate headquarters to support Southwest's frontline employees.
- **Helping Hands.** Southwest sent out volunteers from around the system to lighten the load of employees in the cities where Southwest was in direct competition with United's Shuttle. This not only built momentum and strengthened the troops for the battle with United, it also helped rekindle the fighting spirit of Southwest employees.[65]

Empirical research in the hotel industry demonstrates why it is important for management to walk the talk. Judi McLean Park and Tony Simons conducted a study of 6,500 employees at 76 Holiday Inn hotels to determine whether workers perceived that hotel managers showed behavioral integrity using measures such as "My manager delivers on promises" and "My manager practices what he preached." These statements were correlated with employee responses to questions such as "I am proud to tell others I am part of this hotel," and "My coworkers go out of the way to accommodate guests' special requests," and then to revenues and profitability.

The results were stunning. They showed that behavioral integrity of a hotel's manager was highly correlated to employees' trust, commitment, and willingness to go the extra mile. Furthermore, of all manager behaviors measured, it was the single most important factor driving profitability. In fact, a mere one-eighth point increase in a hotel's overall behavioral integrity score on a five-point scale was associated with a 2.5 percent increase in revenue and a $250,000 increase in profits per year per hotel.[66]

CONCLUSION

The quality of a service firm's people—especially those working in customer-facing positions—plays a crucial role in determining market success and financial performance. That's why the *People* element of the 7 Ps is so important. Successful service organizations are committed to effective management of human resources and work closely with marketing and operations managers to balance what might otherwise prove to be conflicting goals. They recognize the value of investing in HR and understand the costs resulting from high levels of turnover. In the long run, offering better wages and benefits may be a more financially viable strategy than paying less to employees who have no loyalty and soon defect.

The market and financial results of managing people effectively for service advantage can be phenomenal. Good HR strategies allied with strong management leadership at all levels often lead to a sustainable competitive advantage. It is probably harder to duplicate high-performance human assets than any other corporate resource.

Chapter Summary

LO1 Service employees are extremely important to the success of a service firm because they are:

- A source of competitive positioning because they are (1) a core part of the service product, (2) they represent the service firm in the eyes of the customer, and (3) are a core part of the brand as they deliver the brand promise.
- Often crucially important for generating sales, cross-sales, and up-sales.
- A key driver of the productivity of the frontline operations.
- A source of customer loyalty.
- Even in low-contact services, frontline employees are the ones who leave an impression on the customer in those few but critical "moments of truth" encounters.

LO2 The work of frontline employees is difficult and stressful because they are in boundary-spanning positions which often entail:

- Organization/client conflicts.
- Person/role conflict.
- Interclient conflicts.
- Emotional labor and emotional stress.

LO3 We used three types of cycles involving frontline employees and customers to describe how firms can be set up for failure, mediocrity, and success:

- The *cycle of failure* involves a low-pay and high-employee turnover strategy and, as a consequence, results in high-customer dissatisfaction and defections that depress profit margins.
- The *cycle of mediocrity* typically is found in large bureaucracies, offering job security but not much scope in the job itself. There is no incentive to serve customers well.
- Successful service firms operate in the *cycle of success* where employees are satisfied with their jobs and are productive; as a consequence, customers are satisfied and loyal. High profit margins allow investment in the recruitment, development, and motivation of the right frontline employees.

LO4 The Service Talent Cycle is a guiding framework for successful HR strategies in service firms, helping them to move their firms into the cycle of success. Implementing the service talent cycle correctly will give firms highly motivated employees willing and able to deliver service excellence and go the extra mile for their customers and are highly productive at the same time. It has four key prescriptions:

- Hire the right people.
- Enable frontline employees.
- Motivate and energize them.
- Have a leadership team that emphasizes and supports the frontline.

LO5 To hire the right people, firms need to attract, select, and hire the right people for their firm and any given service job. Best-practice HR strategies start with recognition that in many industries the labor market is highly competitive. Competing for talent by being the preferred employer requires:

- Work on being seen as a preferred employer, and as a result, receive a large number of applications from the best potential candidates in the labor market.
- Careful selection ensures that new employees fit both job requirements and the organization's culture. Select the best-suited candidates using screening methods such as observation, personality tests, structured interviews, and providing realistic job previews.

LO6 To enable their frontline employees, firms need to:

- Conduct painstaking extensive training on (1) the organizational culture, purpose, and strategy; (2) interpersonal and technical skills; and (3) product/service knowledge.

LO7 Empower the frontline so they can respond with flexibility to customer needs and nonroutine encounters and service failures. Empowerment and training will give employees the authority, skills, and self-confidence to use their own initiative in delivering service excellence.

LO8 Organize frontline employees into effective service delivery teams (often cross-functional) that can serve their customers from end-to-end.

LO9 Finally, energize and motivate employees with a full set of rewards, ranging from pay, satisfying job content, recognition, and feedback to goal accomplishment.

LO10 Top and middle managers, including frontline supervisors, need to continuously reinforce a strong culture that emphasizes service excellence and productivity. Effective service leadership involves:

- Focusing the entire organization on supporting the front line.
- Reinforcing a strong service culture that emphasizes service excellence and productivity and builds employee understanding and support for the organization's goals.
- Driving values that inspire, energize, and guide service providers, and give them a fulfilled working life.

Review Questions

1. Why are service personnel so important for service firms?
2. There is a trend of service delivery moving from high contact to low contact. Are service employees still important in low-contact services? Explain your answer.
3. What is emotional labor? Explain the ways in which it may cause stress for employees in specific jobs. Illustrate with suitable examples.
4. What are the key barriers for firms to break the cycle of failure and move into the cycle of success? And how should an organization trapped in the cycle of mediocrity proceed?
5. List five ways in which investment in hiring and selection, training, and ongoing motivation of employees will pay dividends in customer satisfaction for such organizations as (a) a restaurant, (b) an airline, (c) a hospital, and (d) a consulting firm.
6. Describe the key components of the service talent cycle.
7. What can a service firm do to become a preferred employer and, as a result, receive a large number of applications from the best potential candidates in the labor market?
8. How can a firm select the best-suited candidates from a large number of applicants?
9. What are the key types of training service firms should conduct?
10. What are the factors that favor a strategy of employee empowerment?
11. Identify the factors needed to make service teams successful in (a) an airline, (b) a restaurant, and (c) a customer contact center.
12. How can frontline employees be effectively motivated to deliver service excellence and productivity?
13. How can a service firm build a strong service culture that emphasizes service excellence and productivity?

Application Exercises

1. An airline runs a recruiting advertisement for cabin crew that shows a picture of a small boy sitting in an airline seat and clutching a teddy bear. The headline reads: "His mom told him not to talk to strangers. So what's he having for lunch?" Describe the types of personalities you think would be (a) attracted to apply for the job by that ad and (b) discouraged from applying.
2. Consider the following jobs: emergency department nurse, bill collector, computer repair technician, supermarket cashier, dentist, kindergarten teacher, prosecuting attorney, server in a family restaurant, server in an expensive French restaurant, stockbroker, and undertaker. What type of emotions would you expect each of them to display to customers in the course of doing their job? What drives your expectations?
3. Use the service talent cycle as a diagnostic tool on a successful and an unsuccessful service firm you are familiar with. What recommendations would you prescribe to each of these two firms?

4. Think of two organizations you are familiar with, one that has a very good and one that has a very poor service culture. Describe the factors that contributed to shaping those organizational cultures. What factors do you think contributed most? Why?
5. As a human resources manager, which issues do you see as most likely to create boundary spanning problems for employees in a customer contact center at a major Internet service provider? Select four issues and indicate how you would mediate between operations and marketing to create a satisfactory outcome for all three groups.

Endnotes

1. Adapted from Leonard L. Berry, *Discovering the Soul of Service—The Nine Drivers of Sustainable Business Success.* New York: The Free Press, 1999, 156–159.
2. Liliana L. Bove, and Lester W. Johnson, "Customer Relationships with Service Personnel: Do We Measure Closeness, Quality or Strength?" *Journal of Business Research*, 54, 2001, 189–197; Magnus Söderlund and Sara Rosengren, "Revisiting the Smiling Service Worker and Customer Satisfaction," *International Journal of Service Industry Management*, 19, No. 5, 2008, 552–574; Anat Rafaeli, Lital Ziklik, and Lorna Doucet, "The Impact of Call Center Employees' Customer Orientation Behaviors and Service Quality," *Journal of Service Research*, 10, No. 3, 2008, 239–255.
3. Recent research established the link between extra-role effort and customer satisfaction; e.g., Carmen Barroso Castro, Enrique Martín Armario, and David Martín Ruiz, "The Influence of Employee Organizational Citizenship Behavior on Customer Loyalty," *International Journal of Service Industry Management*, 15, No. 1, 2004, 27–53.
4. James L. Heskett, Thomas O. Jones, Gary W. Loveman, W. Earl Sasser, Jr., and Leonard A. Schlesinger, " Putting the Service Profit Chain to Work," *Harvard Business Review*, 72, March–April 1994, 164–174.
5. James L. Heskett, W. Earl Sasser, Jr., and Leonard L. Schlesinger, *The Value Profit Chain: Treat Employees Like Customers and Customers Like Employees.* New York: The Free Press, 2003.
6. Benjamin Schneider and David E. Bowen, "The Service Organization: Human Resources Management is Crucial," *Organizational Dynamics*, 21, No. 4, Spring 1993, 39–52.
7. David E. Bowen and Benjamin Schneider, "Boundary-Spanning Role Employees and the Service Encounter: Some Guidelines for Management and Research." In J. A. Czepiel, M. R. Solomon, and C. F. Surprenant, eds., The Service Encounter. Lexington, MA: Lexington Books, 1985, pp. 127–148.
8. Vaikakalathur Shankar Mashesh and Anand Kasturi, "Improving Call Centre Agent Performance: A UK-India Study Based on the Agents' Point of View," *International Journal of Service Industry Management,* 17, No. 2, 2006, 136–157. On potentially conflicting goals see also Detelina Marinova, Jun Ye, and Jagdip Singh, "Do Frontline Mechanisms Matter? Impact of Quality and Productivity Orientations on Unit Revenue, Efficiency, and Customer Satisfaction," *Journal of Marketing*, 72, No. 2, 2008, 28–45.
9. David E. Bowen and Benjamin Schneider, "Boundary-Spanning Role Employees and the Service Encounter: Some Guidelines for Management and Research," in J. A. Czepiel, M. R. Solomon, and C. F. Surprenant, eds., *The Service Encounter.* Lexington, MA: Lexington Books, 1985, 127–148.
10. Arlie R. Hochschild, *The Managed Heart: Commercialization of Human Feeling.* Berkeley: University of California Press, 1983.
11. Panikkos Constanti and Paul Gibbs, "Emotional labor and Surplus Value: The Case of Holiday 'Reps'," *The Service Industries Journal*, 25, January 2005, 103–116.
12. Arlie Hochschild, "Emotional Labor in the Friendly Skies," *Psychology Today,* June 1982. 13–15. Cited in Valarie A. Zeithaml, Mary Jo Bitner, and Dwayne D. Gremler, *Services Marketing: Integrating Customer Focus Across the Firm*, 4th ed. New York: McGraw-Hill, 2006, 359. See also Aviad E. Raz, "The Slanted Smile Factory: Emotion Management in Tokyo Disneyland," *Studies in Symbolic Interaction*, 21, 1997, 201–217.
13. See also Michel Rod and Nicholas J. Ashill, "Symptoms of Burnout and Service Recovery Performance," *Managing Service Quality*, 19, No. 1, 2009, 60–84; Jody L. Crosno, Shannon B. Rinaldo, Hulda G. Black, and Scott W. Kelley, "Half Full or Half Empty: The Role of Optimism in Boundary-Spanning Positions," *Journal of Service Research*, 11, No. 3, 2009, 295–309.
14. Jochen Wirtz and Robert Johnston, "Singapore Airlines: What It Takes to Sustain Service Excellence - A Senior Management Perspective," *Managing Service Quality*, 13, No. 1, 2003, 10–19; Loizos Heracleous, Jochen Wirtz, and Nitin Pangarkar, *Flying High in a Competitive Industry: Secrets of the World's Leading Airline.* Singapore: McGraw-Hill, 2009.
15. "The Bangalore Paradox," *The Economist*, April 23, 2005, 67–69.
16. Dan Moshavi and James R. Terbord, "The Job Satisfaction and Performance of Contingent and Regular Customer Service Representatives – A Human Capital Perspective," *International Journal of Service Industry Management*, 13, No. 4, 2002, 333–347.
17. Vaikalathur Shankar Mahesh and Anand Kasturi, "Improving Call Centre Agent Performance," *International Journal of Service Industry Management*, 17, No. 2, 2006, 136–157.
18. See also Vaikalathur Shankar Mahesh and Anand Kasturi, "Improving Call Centre Agent Performance," *International Journal of Service Industry Management*, 17, No. 2, 2006, 136–157.
19. The terms "cycle of failure" and "cycle of success" were coined by Leonard L. Schlesinger and James L. Heskett,

"Breaking the Cycle of Failure in Services," *Sloan Management Review* 32, Spring 1991, 17–28. The term, "cycle of mediocrity" comes from Christopher H. Lovelock, "Managing Services: The Human Factor," in W. J. Glynn and J. G. Barnes, eds. *Understanding Services Management.* Chichester, UK: John Wiley & Sons, 1995, 228.

20. Leonard Schlesinger and James L. Heskett, "Breaking the Cycle of Failure," *Sloan Management Review* 32, Spring 1991, 17–28.
21. James L. Heskett, W. Earl Sasser, Jr., and Leonard A. Schlesinger (2003), The Value Profit Chain, Free Press, pp. 75–94
22. Reg Price and Roderick J. Brodie, "Transforming a Public Service Organization from Inside out to Outside in," *Journal of Service Research*, 4, No. 1, 2001, 50–59.
23. Mahn Hee Yoon, "The Effect of Work Climate on Critical Employee and Customer Outcomes," *International Journal of Service Industry Management*, 12, No. 5, 2001, 500–521.
24. Leonard L. Berry and A. Parasuraman, *Marketing Services—Competing Through Quality.* New York: The Free Press, 1991, 151–152.
25. Charles A. O'Reilly III and Jeffrey Pfeffer, *Hidden Value—How Great Companies Achieve Extraordinary Results with Ordinary People.* Boston, MA: Harvard Business School Press, 2000, 1.
26. Bill Fromm and Len Schlesinger, *The Real Heroes of Business.* New York: Currency Doubleday, 1994, 315–316.
27. Jim Collins, "Turning Goals into Results: The Power of Catalytic Mechanisms," *Harvard Business Review,* July–August 1999, 77.
28. This section was adapted from Benjamin Schneider and David E. Bowen, *Winning the Service Game.* Boston: Harvard Business School Press, 1995, 115–126.
29. John Wooden, *A Lifetime of Observations and Reflections On and Off the Court.* Chicago: Lincolnwood, 1997, 66.
30. Serene Goh, "All the Right Staff," and Arlina Arshad, "Putting Your Personality to the Test," *The Straits Times,* September 5, 2001, H1.
31. For a review of this literature, see Benjamin Schneider, "Service Quality and Profits: Can You Have Your Cake and Eat It, Too?" *Human Resource Planning,* 14, No. 2, 1991, 151–157.
32. This section was adapted from Leonard L. Berry, *On Great Service—A Framework for Action.* New York: The Free Press, 1995, 181–182.
33. Leonard Schlesinger and James L. Heskett, "Breaking the Cycle of Failure," *Sloan Management Review* 32, Spring 1991, 26.
34. Benjamin Schneider and David E. Bowen, *Winning the Service Game.* Boston, MA: Harvard Business School Press, 1995, 131.
35. Leonard L. Berry, *Discovering the Soul of Service—The Nine Drivers of Sustainable Business Success.* New York: The Free Press, 1999, 161.
36. Disney Institute, *Be Our Guest: Perfecting the Art of Customer Service.* Disney Enterprises, 2001.
37. David A. Tansik, "Managing Human Resource Issues for High Contact Service Personnel," in D. E. Bowen, R. B. Chase, T. G. Cummings, and Associates, eds. *Service Management Effectiveness.* San Francisco: Jossey-Bass, 1990, 152–176.
38. Parts of this section are based on David E. Bowen and Edward E. Lawler, III, "The Empowerment of Service Workers: What, Why, How and When," *Sloan Management Review* 33, Spring 1992, 32–39.
39. Dana Yagil, "The Relationship of Customer Satisfaction and Service Workers' Perceived Control—Examination of Three Models," *International Journal of Service Industry Management*, 13, No. 4, 2002, 382–398.
40. Graham L. Bradley and Beverley A. Sparks, "Customer Reactions to Staff Empowerment: Mediators and Moderators," *Journal of Applied Social Psychology*, 30, No. 5, 2000, 991–1012.
41. David E. Bowen and Edward E. Lawler, III, "The Empowerment of Service Workers: What, Why, How and When," *Sloan Management Review* 33, Spring 1992, 32–39.
42. Benjamin Schneider and David E. Bowen, *Winning the Service Game.* Boston, MA: Harvard Business School Press, 1995, 250.
43. This paragraph is based on Kevin Freiberg and Jackie Freiberg, *Nuts! Southwest Airlines' Crazy Recipe for Business and Personal Success.* New York: Broadway Books, 1997, 87–88.
44. Jon R. Katzenbach and Douglas K. Smith, "The Discipline of Teams," *Harvard Business Review* 71, March–April, 1993, 112.
45. Andrew Sergeant and Stephen Frenkel, "When Do Customer Contact Employees Satisfy Customers?" *Journal of Service Research,* 3, No. 1, August 2000, 18–34.
46. For a recent study that on self-managed team performance see Ad de Jong, Ko de Ruyter, and Jos Lemmink, "Antecedents and Consequences of the Service Climate in Boundary-Spanning Self-Managing Service Teams," *Journal of Marketing,* 68. April 2004. 18–35.
47. Leonard L. Berry, *On Great Service—A Framework for Action.* New York: The Free Press, 1995, 131.
48. Charles A. O'Reilly III and Jeffrey Pfeffer, *Hidden Value—How Great Companies Achieve Extraordinary Results with Ordinary People.* Boston, MA: Harvard Business School Press, 2000,9.
49. Leonard L. Berry, *Discovering the Soul of Service—The Nine Drivers of Sustainable Business Success.* New York: The Free Press, 1999, 189.
50. Benjamin Schneider and David E. Bowen, *Winning the Service Game.* Boston, MA: Harvard Business School Press, 1995, 141; Leonard L. Berry, *On Great Service—A Framework for Action.* New York: The Free Press, 1995, 225.
51. Ron Zemke, "Experience Shows Intuition Isn't the Best Guide to Teamwork," *The Service Edge,* 7, No. 1 January 1994, 5.
52. This section is based on Benjamin Schneider and David E. Bowen, *Winning the Service Game.* Boston, MA: Harvard Business School Press, 1995, 145–173.
53. A good summary of goal setting and motivation at work can be found in Edwin A. Locke and Gary Latham, *A Theory of Goal Setting and Task Performance.* New Jersey: Englewood Cliffs, Prentice Hall, 1990.
54. Charles A. O'Reilly III and Jeffrey Pfeffer, *Hidden Value—How Great Companies Achieve Extraordinary Results with Ordinary People*, Boston, MA: Harvard Business School Press, 2000, 232.

55. Jeffrey Pfeffer, *Competitive Advantage Through People.* Boston: Harvard Business School Press, 1994, 160–163.
56. Jody Hoffer Gittell, Andrew von Nordenflycht, and Thomas A. Kochan, "Mutual Gains for Zero Sum? Labor Relations and Firm Performance in the Airline Industry," *Industrial and Labor Relations Review*, 57, No. 2, 2004, 163–180.
57. The authors of the following paper emphasize the role of alignment between tradition, culture and strategy that together form the basis for the firms HR practices: Benjamin Schneider, Seth C. Hayes, Beng-Chong Lim, Jana L. Raver, Ellen G. Godfrey, Mina Huang, Lisa H. Nishii, and Jonathan C. Ziegert, "The Human Side of Strategy: Employee Experiences of a Strategic Alignment in a Service Organization," *Organizational Dynamics*, 32, No. 2, 2003, 122–141.
58. Scott B. MacKenzie, Philip M. Podsakoff, and Gregory A. Rich, "Transformational and Transactional Leadership and Salesperson Performance," *Journal of the Academy of Marketing Science*, 29, No. 2, 2001, 115–134.
59. Leonard L. Berry, *On Great Service – A Framework for Action.* New York: The Free Press, 1995, 236–237; Leonard L. Berry and Kent D. Seltman, *Management Lessons from Mayo Clinic: Inside One of the World's Most Admired Service Organization.* McGraw Hill, 2008. The following study emphasized the importance of the perceived ethical climate in driving service commitment of service employees: Charles H. Schwepker Jr. and Michael D. Hartline, "Managing the Ethical Climate of Customer-Contact Service Employees," *Journal of Service Research,* 7, No. 4, 2005, 377–397.
60. Benjamin Schneider and David E. Bowen, *Winning the Service Game.* Boston, MA: Harvard Business School Press, 1995, 240.
61. Catherine DeVrye, *Good Service is Good Business.* Upper Saddle River, NJ: Prentice Hall, 2000, 11.
62. Joseph A. Mitchelli, *The New Gold Standard: 5 Leadership Principles for Creating a Legendary Customer Experience Courtesy of The Ritz-Carton Hotel Company.* McGraw Hill, 2008, 61–66, 191–197.
63. http://careers.ritzcarltonclub.com/standards.asp, accessed June 3, 2009.
64. Paul Hemp, "My Week as a Room-Service Waiter at the Ritz," *Harvard Business Review*, 80, June 2002, 8–11.
65. Adapted from Kevin Freiberg and Jackie Freiberg, *Nuts! Southwest Airlines' Crazy Recipe for Business and Personal Success.* New York: Broadway Books, 1997, 165–168.
66. Tony Simons, "The High Cost of Lost Trust," *Harvard Business Review* 80, September 2002, 2–3.

PART FOUR

Implementing Profitable Service Strategies

Part IV focuses on four key issues in the implementation of effective services marketing strategies. Part IV consists of the following four chapters:

CHAPTER 12 MANAGING RELATIONSHIPS AND BUILDING LOYALTY

Chapter 12 focuses on achieving profitability through creating relationships with customers from the right segments and then finding ways to build and reinforce their loyalty using the wheel of loyalty as an organizing framework. This chapter closes with a discussion of customer relationship management (CRM) systems.

CHAPTER 13 COMPLAINT HANDLING AND SERVICE RECOVERY

Developing a strategy for effective complaint handling and service recovery often determines whether a firm can build a loyal customer base or has to watch its customers take their business elsewhere. Chapter 13 examines how effective complaint handling and professional service recovery can be implemented. It starts with a review of consumer complaining behavior and principles of effective service recovery systems. Service guarantees are discussed as a powerful way of institutionalizing effective service recovery and as a marketing tool signaling high quality service. The chapter also discusses how to deal with jaycustomers who take advantage of service recovery policies and abuse the service in other ways.

CHAPTER 14 IMPROVING SERVICE QUALITY AND PRODUCTIVITY

Chapter 14 deals with productivity and quality. Both productivity and quality are necessary and related ingredients for financial success in services. Chapter 14 covers service quality, diagnosing quality shortfalls using the gaps model, and reviewing strategies to close quality gaps. Customer feedback systems are introduced as an effective tool for systematically listening to and learning from customers. Productivity is concerned with bringing down costs, and key approaches for increasing productivity are discussed.

CHAPTER 15 STRIVING FOR SERVICE LEADERSHIP

The final chapter addresses the challenge of remaining competitive and forward-looking, which will require change not only in the firm's marketing but also its operations and human resources management. Chapter 15 uses the service profit chain as an integrative model to demonstrate the strategic linkages involved in running a successful service organization. Implementing the service profit chain requires integration of the three key functions of marketing, operations, and human resources. We discuss how to move a service organization to higher levels of performance in each functional area.

The caliber of its leadership determines whether a firm can be a service leader in its industry. The chapter closes with the role of leadership in both evolutionary and turnaround environments, and in creating and maintaining a climate for service.

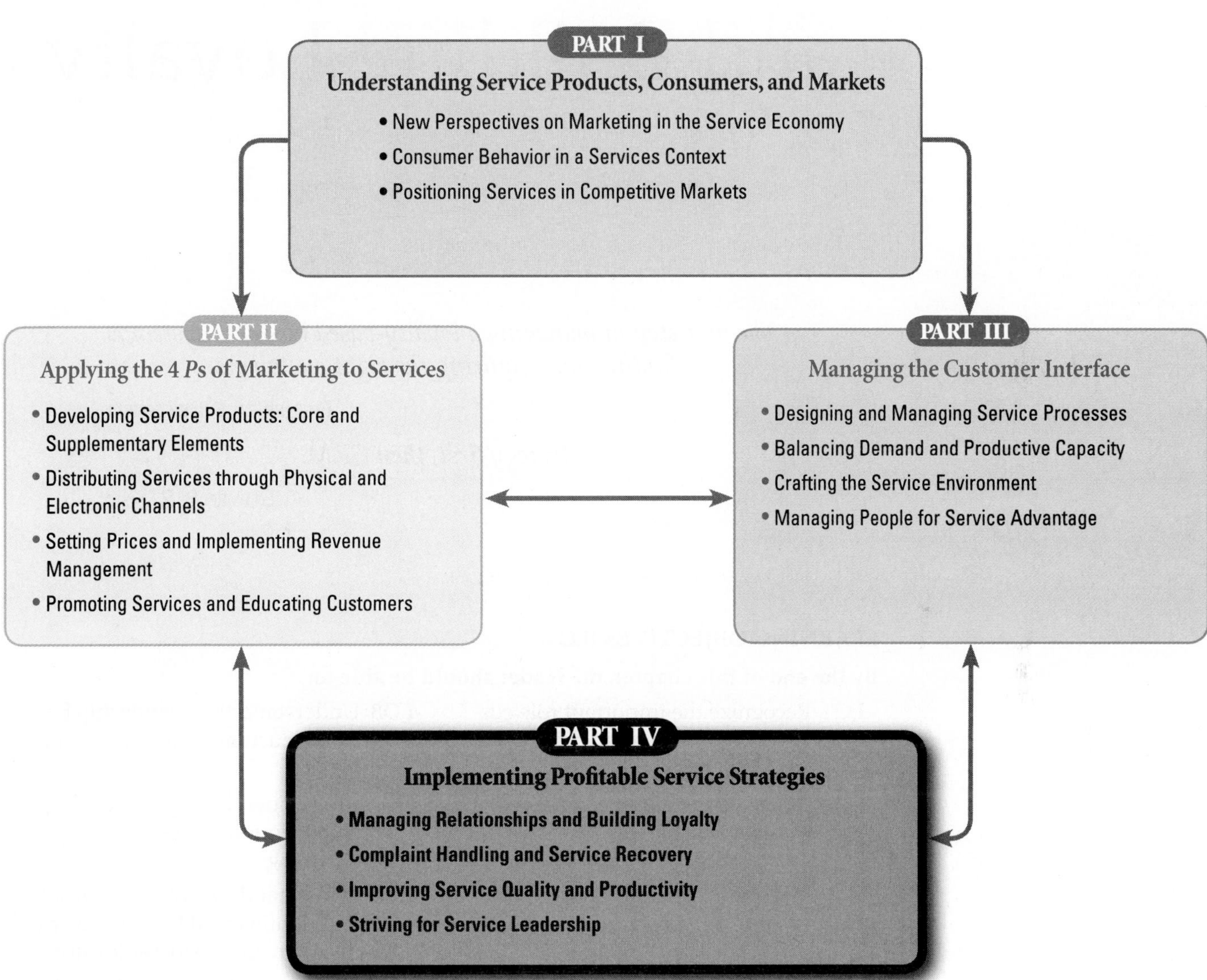

FIGURE IV.1 Organizing Framework for Services Marketing

CHAPTER 12

Managing Relationships and Building Loyalty

The first step in managing a loyalty-based business system is finding and acquiring the right customers.

FREDERICK F. REICHHELD

Strategy first, then CRM.

STEVEN S. RAMSEY

LEARNING OBJECTIVES (LOs)

By the end of this chapter, the reader should be able to:

LO1 Recognize the important role customer loyalty plays in driving a service firm's profitability.

LO2 Calculate the lifetime value (LTV) of a loyal customer.

LO3 Understand why customers are loyal to a particular service firm.

LO4 Explain the different types of marketing relating to the customer-firm relationship and understand how membership relationships can be created.

LO5 Know the core strategies of the Wheel of Loyalty that explain how to develop a loyal customer base.

LO6 Appreciate why it is so important for service firms to target the "right" customers.

LO7 Use service tiering to manage the customer base and build loyalty.

LO8 Understand the relationship between customer satisfaction and loyalty.

LO9 Know how to deepen the relationship through cross-selling and bundling.

LO10 Understand the role of financial and nonfinancial loyalty rewards in enhancing customer loyalty.

LO11 Appreciate the power of social, customization, and structural bonds in enhancing loyalty.

LO12 Understand what factors cause customers to switch to a competitor and how to reduce such switching.

LO13 Understand the part played by customer relationship management (CRM) systems in delivering customized services and building loyalty.

A Little Extra

Tesco is a UK-based international grocery and other merchandise retail chain. It is the third largest global retailer after Wal-Mart and Carrefour. With annual profits of some $4.95 billion, it is ahead of Carrefour. Tesco launched its Clubcard customer loyalty card in 1995 after two years of research. Customers receive one Clubcard point for every $1.65 they spend in-store. The points generate vouchers, which are worth 1 percent of the spending when spent in-store and 4 percent when spent on special deals such as holidays. Since 1995, the loyalty scheme has rewarded Tesco customers with nearly $5 billion in vouchers.

In 2007, the Clubcard was introduced to Malaysia on a similar basis. The card proved so popular that there were more than 800,000 applications in the first two weeks after the launch. In the UK alone, there are 17 million Clubcard members, compared with 11.7 million Barclaycard holders. Tesco has recently launched Clubcard in Poland, Thailand, and Slovakia. This added 3 million new Clubcard holders in just seven weeks, bringing the total number of Clubcard members outside the UK to 12.5 million.

When Tesco launched the Clubcard 2 in the UK in May 2009, it managed to add another 1 million members, with customers signing up at a rate of six per minute. The key to the success of the card is its personalization and infinite variability. There are 9 million variations of the Clubcard statement to ensure that customers get extra rewards that are relevant to them. According to Tesco, no more than three customers ever get exactly the same statement. The net effect of the relaunch was to increase spending by 5 percent.

In the early 1990s, Tesco was considered to be down market. The middle class shopped at Sainsbury or at Waitrose. As the British have come to perceive themselves as being more middle class, Tesco has followed them up market. The Clubcard is a prime example of how technology was used to find out what their customers want. The customer loyalty scheme allows Tesco to record what people are buying. In 2005, when there were some 12 million Clubcard users each buying on average 20 items per week, this created 12 billion pieces of data every year. It allows Tesco to explore the links between purchases of different products. Tesco may have one of the largest databases anywhere in the world. It allows Tesco to adjust its shelves to suit the profile of local areas or even times of day. A Tesco located in an immigrant area can focus on products such as plantains favored by those from the Caribbean. A store in the center of a city can sell office workers sandwiches at lunch time and ready-made meals for the evening.

On a truly vast scale, Tesco has been able to use the Clubcard to combine the local knowledge of a small corner store, where the owner has intimate knowledge of the purchases of every single customer, and to enjoy the economies of scale and logistical advantages of a multinational. The information loop means that Tesco can respond to immediate changes in buying habits. Tesco has also expanded to sell financial services and clothes, giving it an even broader information base upon which to monitor customer buying behavior and shape future habits.

FIGURE 12.1 Tesco Have Cemented Their Market Position with the Innovative Use of Customer Loyalty Programs

Sources: "This Sceptered Aisle," *The Economist*, August 4, 2005; Thomas, J., "Tesco Point Scoring: Initial Data Suggests Clubcards Relaunch May Be Working," *Marketing Magazine*, September 22, 2009; Tesco (www.tesco.com).

THE SEARCH FOR CUSTOMER LOYALTY

Targeting, acquiring, and retaining the "right" customers is at the core of many successful service firms. In Chapter 3, we discussed segmentation and positioning. In this chapter, we emphasize the importance of focusing carefully on desirable, loyal customers within the chosen segments and then taking pains to build and maintain their loyalty through well-conceived relationship marketing strategies. The objective is to build relationships and to develop loyal customers who will do a growing volume of business with the firm in the future.

Loyalty is an old-fashioned word traditionally used to describe fidelity and enthusiastic devotion to a country, a cause, or individual. More recently, it has been used in a business context, to describe a customer's willingness to continue patronizing a firm over the long term, preferably on an exclusive basis, and recommending the firm's products to friends and associates. Customer loyalty extends beyond behavior and includes preference, liking, and future intentions. Ask yourself: What service companies are you loyal to? And why are you loyal to these firms?

"Few companies think of customers as annuities," says Frederick Reichheld, author of *The Loyalty Effect*, and a major researcher in the field of customer loyalty.[1] And yet that is precisely what a loyal customer can mean to a firm—a consistent source of revenue over a period of many years. The active management of the customer base and customer loyalty is also referred to as *customer asset management*.[2]

"Defector" was a nasty word during wartime. It describes disloyal people who sell out their own side and go over to the enemy. Even when they defected toward "our" side, rather than away from it, they are still suspect. Today, in a marketing context, the term defection is used to describe customers who drop off a company's radar screen and transfer their brand loyalty to another supplier. Reichheld and Sasser popularized the term *zero defections*, which they describe as keeping every customer the company can serve profitably.[3] Not only does a rising defection rate indicate that something is wrong with quality (or that competitors offer better value), it may also be a leading indicator signaling a fall in profits. Big customers don't necessarily disappear overnight; they often may signal their mounting dissatisfaction by steadily reducing their purchases and shifting part of their business elsewhere.

Why Is Customer Loyalty Important to a Firm's Profitability?

How much is a loyal customer worth in terms of profits? In a classic study, Reichheld and Sasser analyzed the profit per customer in different service businesses, as categorized by the number of years a customer had been with the firm.[4] They found that customers became more profitable the longer they remained with a firm in each of these industries. Annual profits per customer, indexed over a five-year period for easier comparison, are summarized in Figure 12.2. The industries studied (with average profits from a first-year customer shown in parentheses) were credit cards ($30), industrial laundry ($144), industrial distribution ($45), and automobile servicing ($25). A study of Internet firms showed similar loyalty effects. It took typically more than a year to recoup customer acquisition costs, and profits then increased as customers stayed longer with the firm.[5]

Underlying this profit growth, say Reichheld and Sasser, are four factors that work to the supplier's advantage to create incremental profits. In order of magnitude at the end of seven years, these factors are:

1. ***Profit derived from increased purchases (or, in a credit card and banking environment, higher account balances).*** Over time, business customers often grow larger and so need to purchase in greater quantities. Individuals may also purchase more as their families grow or as they become more affluent. Both types of customers may be willing to consolidate their purchases with a single supplier who provides high-quality service.
2. ***Profit from reduced operating costs.*** As customers become more experienced, they make fewer demands on the supplier (for instance, they have less need for information and assistance and make more use of self-service options). They may

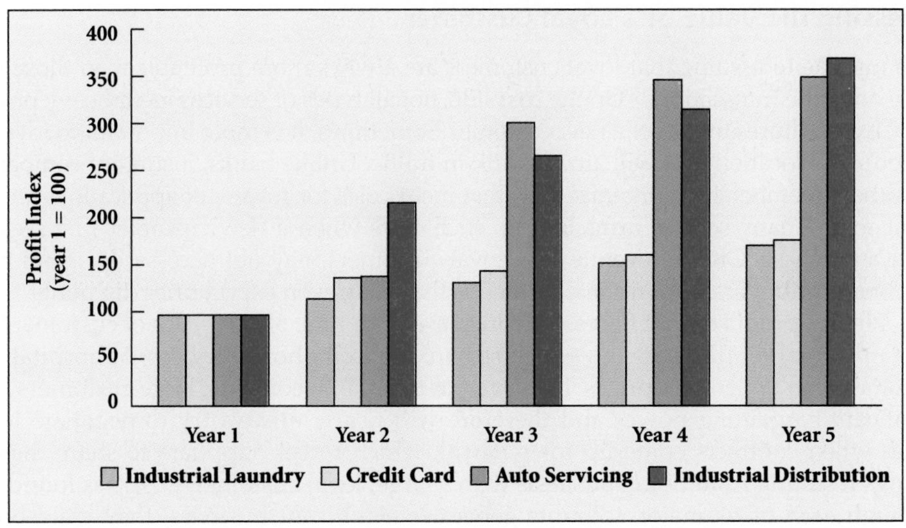

FIGURE 12.2 How Much Profit a Customer Generates over Time

Source: Reprinted by permission of *Harvard Business Review* from Frederick J. Reichheld and W. Earl Sasser Jr. "Zero Defections: Quality Comes to Services" Harvard Business Review 73 (Sept-Oct 1990),p 108.

also make fewer mistakes when involved in operational processes, thus contributing to greater productivity.

3. ***Profit from referrals to other customers.*** Positive word-of-mouth recommendations are like free sales and advertising, saving the firm from having to invest as much money in these activities.
4. ***Profit from price premium.*** New customers often benefit from introductory promotional discounts; long-term customers are more likely to pay regular prices when they are highly satisfied and tend to be less price sensitive.[6] Moreover, customers who trust a supplier may be more willing to pay higher prices at peak periods or for express work.

Furthermore, the upfront costs of attracting these buyers can be amortized over many years. These customer acquisition costs can be substantial and can include sales commissions, advertising and promotions costs, administrative costs of setting up an account, and sending out welcome packages and sign-up gifts.

Figure 12.3 shows the relative contribution of each of these different factors over a seven-year period, based on an analysis of 19 different product categories (both goods and services). Reichheld argues that the economic benefits of customer loyalty noted above often explain why one firm is more profitable than a competitor.

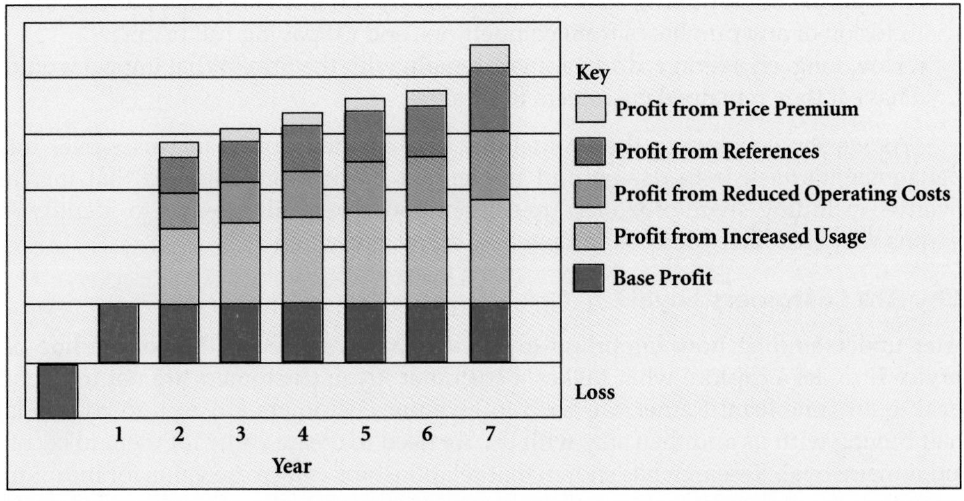

FIGURE 12.3 Why Customers Are More Profitable over Time

Source: Why Customers Are More Profitable Over Time from Frederick J. Reichheld and W. Earl Sasser Jr. "Zero Defections: Quality Comes to Services," Harvard Business Review 73 (Sep.–Oct. 1990): p. 108. Reprinted by permission of Harvard Business School.

Assessing the Value of a Loyal Customer

It's a mistake to assume that loyal customers are always more profitable than those who make one-time transactions.[7] On the cost side, not all types of services incur heavy promotional expenditures to attract a new customer. Sometimes, it is more important to invest in a good retail location that will attract walk-in traffic. Unlike banks, insurance companies, and other "membership" organizations that incur costs for review of applications and account setup, many service firms face no such costs when a new customer first seeks to make a purchase. On the revenue side, loyal customers may not necessarily spend more than one-time buyers, and in some instances, they may even expect price discounts.

Finally, profits do not necessarily increase with time for all types of customers.[8] In most mass market B2C services—such as banking, cell phone services, or hospitality—customers can't negotiate prices. However, in many B2B contexts, large customers have significant bargaining power and therefore will nearly always try to negotiate lower prices when contracts come up for renewal, which forces suppliers to share the cost savings resulting from doing business with a large, loyal customer. DHL has found that although each of its major accounts generates significant business, they yield below average margins. In contrast, DHL's smaller, less powerful accounts, provide significantly higher profitability.[9]

Recent studies have also shown that the profit impact of a customer can vary dramatically depending on the stage of a service's product lifecycle. For instance, referrals by satisfied customers and negative word of mouth from "defected" customers have a much greater effect on profit impact in the early stages of the service product's lifecycle—when the name of the game is acquisition of new customers—than in later stages when the focus is on generating cash flow from the existing customer base.[10]

One of the challenges you will probably face in your work is determining the costs and revenues associated with serving customers to different market segments at different points in their customer lifecycles and predicting future profitability. For insights on how to calculate customer value, see "Worksheet for Calculating Customer Lifetime Value."[11]

The Gap between Actual and Potential Customer Value

For profit-seeking firms, the potential profitability of a customer should be a key driver in marketing strategy. As Alan Grant and Leonard Schlesinger declare: "Achieving the full profit potential of each customer relationship should be the fundamental goal of every business.... Even using conservative estimates, the gap between most companies' current and full potential performance is enormous."[12] They suggest analysis of the following gaps between the actual and potential value of customers:

- What is the current purchasing behavior of customers in each target segment? What would be the impact on sales and profits if they exhibited the ideal behavior profile of (1) buying all services offered by the firm, (2) using these to the exclusion of any purchases from competitors, and (3) paying full price?
- How long, on average, do customers remain with the firm? What impact would it have if they remained customers for life?

As we showed earlier, the profitability of a customer often increases over time. Management's task is to design and implement marketing programs that increase loyalty—including share-of-wallet, up-selling, and cross-selling—and to identify the reasons why customers defect and then take corrective action.

Why Are Customers Loyal?

After understanding how important loyal customers can be for the bottom line of a service firm, let's explore what makes a customer loyal. Customers are not inherently loyal to any one firm! Rather, we need to give our customers a reason to consolidate their buying with us and then stay with us. We need to create value for them to become and remain loyal. Research has shown that relationships can create value for individual consumers through such factors as inspiring greater confidence, offering social benefits, and providing special treatment (see Research Insights 12.1).

WORKSHEET
CALCULATING CUSTOMER LIFETIME VALUE

Calculating customer value is an inexact science that is subject to a variety of assumptions. You may want to try varying these assumptions to see how it affects the final figures. Generally speaking, revenues per customer are easier to track on an individualized basis than are the associated costs of serving a customer, unless (1) no individual records are kept and/or (2) the accounts served are very large and all account-related costs are individually documented and assigned.

Acquisition Revenues Less Costs

If individual account records are kept, the initial application fee paid and initial purchase (if relevant) should be found in these records. Costs, by contrast, may have to be based on average data. For instance, the marketing cost of acquiring a new client can be calculated by dividing the total marketing costs (advertising, promotions, selling, etc.) devoted toward acquiring new customers by the total number of new customers acquired during the same period. If each acquisition takes place over an extended period of time, you may want to build in a lagged effect between when marketing expenditures are incurred and when new customers come on board. The cost of credit checks—where relevant—must be divided by the number of new customers, not the total number of applicants, because some applicants will probably fail this hurdle. Account set-up costs will also be an average figure in most organizations.

Annual Revenues and Costs

If annual sales, account fees, and service fees are documented on an individual-account basis, account revenue streams (except referrals) can be easily identified. The first priority is to segment your customer base by the length of its relationship with your firm. Depending on the sophistication and precision of your firm's records, annual costs in each category may be directly assigned to an individual account holder or averaged for all account holders in that age category.

Value of Referrals

Computing the value of referrals requires a variety of assumptions. To get started, you may need to conduct surveys to determine (1) what percentage of new customers claim that they were influenced by a recommendation from another customer and (2) what other marketing activities also drew the firm to that individual's attention. From these two items, estimates can be made of what percentage of the credit for all new customers should be assigned to referrals. Additional research may be needed to clarify whether "older" customers are more likely to be effective recommenders than "younger" ones.

Net Present Value

Calculating net present value (NPV) from a future profit stream will require choice of an appropriate annual discount figure. (This could reflect estimates of future inflation rates.) It also requires assessment of how long the average relationship lasts. The NPV of a customer, then, is the sum of the anticipated annual profit on each customer for the projected relationship lifetime, suitably discounted each year into the future.

ACQUISITION			YEAR 1	YEAR 2	YEAR 3	YEAR n
Initial Revenue		*Annual Revenues*				
Application fee[a]	____	Annual account fee[a]	____	____	____	____
Initial purchase[a]	____	Sales	____	____	____	____
		Service fees[a]	____	____	____	____
		Value of referrals[b]	____	____	____	____
Total Revenues	____		____	____	____	____
Initial Costs	____	*Annual Costs*				
Marketing	____	Account management	____	____	____	____
Credit check[a]	____	Cost of sales	____	____	____	____
Account setup[a]	____	Write-offs (e.g., bad debts)	____	____	____	____
Less total costs	____		____	____	____	____
Net Profit (Loss)	____		____	____	____	____

[a]If applicable.

[b]Anticipated profits from each new customer referred (could be limited to the first year or expressed as the net present value of the estimated future stream of profits through year n); this value could be negative if an unhappy customer starts to spread negative word of mouth that causes existing customers to defect.

RESEARCH INSIGHTS 12.1

HOW CUSTOMERS SEE RELATIONAL BENEFITS IN SERVICE INDUSTRIES

What benefits do customers see themselves receiving from an extended relationship with a service firm? Researchers seeking answers to this question conducted two studies. The first consisted of in-depth interviews with 21 respondents from a broad cross-section of backgrounds. Respondents were asked to identify service providers they used on a regular basis and were invited to identify and discuss any benefits they received as a result of being a regular customer. Among the comments were:

- I like him [hair stylist]... He's really funny and always has lots of good jokes. He's kind of like a friend now.
- I know what I'm getting—I know that if I go to a restaurant that I regularly go to, rather than taking a chance on all of the new restaurants, the food will be good.
- I often get price breaks. The little bakery that I go to in the morning, every once in a while, they'll give me a free muffin and say, "You're a good customer, it's on us today."
- You can get better service than drop-in customers... We continue to go to the same automobile repair shop because we have gotten to know the owner on a kind of personal basis, and he... can always work us in.
- Once people feel comfortable, they don't want to switch to another dentist. They don't want to train or break a new dentist in.

After evaluating and categorizing the comments, the researchers designed a second study in which they collected 299 survey questionnaires. The respondents were told to select a specific service provider with whom they had a strong, established relationship. Then the questionnaire asked them to assess the extent to which they received each of 21 benefits (derived from analysis of the first study) as a result of their relationship with the specific provider they had identified. Finally, they were asked to assess the importance of these benefits for them.

A factor analysis of the results showed that most of the benefits that customers derived from relationships could be grouped into three categories. The first, and most important, group involved what the researchers labeled confidence benefits, followed by social benefits and special treatment.

- *Confidence benefits* included feelings by customers that in an established relationship there was less risk of something going wrong, confidence in correct performance, ability to trust the provider, lowered anxiety when purchasing, knowing what to expect, and receipt of the firm's highest level of service.
- *Social benefits* embraced mutual recognition between customers and employees, being known by name, friendship with the service provider, and enjoyment of certain social aspects of the relationship.
- *Special treatment benefits* included better prices, discounts on special deals that were unavailable to most customers, extra services, higher priority when there was a wait, and faster service than most customers.

Source: Kevin P. Gwinner, Dwayne D. Gremler, and Mary Jo Bitner, "Relational Benefits in Services Industries: The Customer's Perspective," *Journal of the Academy of Marketing Science*, 26, No. 2, 1998, 101–114.

UNDERSTANDING THE CUSTOMER-FIRM RELATIONSHIP

Before exploring how we can actively improve customer loyalty, let's understand the different types of relationships customers can have with their service providers. There's a fundamental distinction between strategies intended to produce a single transaction and those designed to create extended relationships with customers.

Transactional Marketing

A *transaction* is an event during which an exchange of value takes place between two parties. One transaction or even a series of transactions don't necessarily constitute a relationship, which requires mutual recognition and knowledge between the parties. When each transaction between a customer and a supplier is essentially discrete and anonymous, with no long-term record kept of a customer's purchasing history, and little or no mutual recognition between the customer and employees, then no meaningful marketing relationship can be said to exist. This is true for many services, ranging from passenger transport to food service or visits to a movie theater, in which each purchase and use is a separate event.

Relationship Marketing

The term *relationship marketing* has been widely used to describe the type of marketing activity designed to create extended relationships with customers, but until recently it was only loosely defined. Research by Nicole Coviello, Rod Brodie, and Hugh Munro suggests at least three distinct categories of what they call relational marketing: *database marketing, interaction marketing*, and *network marketing*.[13]

DATABASE MARKETING. In database marketing, the focus is still on the market transaction but now it includes information exchange. Marketers rely on information technology, usually in the form of a database, to form a relationship with targeted customers and retain their patronage over time. However, the nature of these relationships often is not a close one, with communication driven and managed by the seller. Technology is used to (1) identify and build a database of current and potential customers, (2) deliver differentiated messages based on consumers' characteristics and preferences, and (3) track each relationship to monitor the cost of acquiring the consumer and the lifetime value of the resulting purchases.[14] Although technology can be used to personalize the relationship, relations often remain somewhat distant. Utility services such as electricity, gas, and cable TV are good examples.

INTERACTION MARKETING. A close relationship often exists in face-to-face interactions between customers and representatives of the supplier (or "ear-to-ear" interaction by phone). Although the service itself remains important, value is added by people and social processes. Interactions may include negotiations and sharing of insights in both directions. This type of relationship exists in many local service markets, ranging from community banks to dentistry, in which buyer and seller know and trust each other. It is also commonly found in many B2B services. Both the firm and the customer are prepared to invest resources to develop a mutually beneficial relationship. This investment may include time spent sharing and recording information.

As service companies grow larger and make increasing use of technologies such as interactive websites and self-service technology, maintaining meaningful relationships with customers becomes a significant marketing challenge. Firms with large customer bases find it increasingly difficult to build and maintain meaningful relationships through call centers, websites, and other mass-delivery channels (see Figure 12.4).

NETWORK MARKETING. We often say that someone is a "good networker" because he or she is able to put individuals in touch with others who have a mutual interest. In a B2B context, marketers work to develop a network of relationships with customers, distributors, suppliers, the media, consultants, trade associations, government agencies, competitors, and even their customers' customers. Often, a team of individuals within the supplier's firm collaborate to provide effective service to a parallel team within the customer's organization.

The four types of marketing of transactional, database, interaction, and network marketing are not necessarily mutually exclusive. A firm may have transactions with some customers who have neither the desire nor the need to make future purchases, while working hard to move others up the loyalty ladder.[15] Evert Gummesson identified no fewer than 30 types of relationships. He advocates *total relationship marketing*, describing it as:

> . . . marketing based on relationships, networks, and interaction, recognizing that marketing is embedded in the total management of the networks of the selling organization, the market, and society. It is directed to long-term, win-win relationships with individual customers, and value is jointly created between the parties involved.[16]

FIGURE 12.4 Building and Maintaining Relationships through Call Centers Is a Challenge

Creating "Membership" Relationships

The nature of the current relationship with customers can be analyzed by asking first: Does the supplier enter into a formal "membership" relationship with customers, as with telephone subscriptions, banking, and the family doctor? Or is there no defined relationship? Second: Is the service delivered on a continuous basis, as in insurance, broadcasting, and police protection? Or is each transaction recorded and charged separately? Table 12.1 shows the matrix resulting from this categorization, with examples in each category. A *membership relationship* is a formalized relationship between the firm and an identifiable customer that often provides special benefits to both parties.

Discrete transactions, in which each use involves a payment to the service supplier by an essentially "anonymous" consumer, are typical of services like transport, restaurants, cinemas, and shoe repairs. The problem for marketers of such services is that they tend to be less informed than their counterparts in membership-type organizations about who their customers are and how each customer uses the service. Managers in businesses that sell discrete transactions have to work a little harder to establish relationships.

In small businesses such as hair salons, frequent customers are (or should be) welcomed as "regulars" whose needs and preferences are remembered. Keeping formal records of customers' needs, preferences, and purchasing behavior is useful even for small firms, because it helps employees avoid having to ask the same questions on each service occasion, allows them to personalize the service given to each customer, and enables the firm to anticipate future needs.

In large companies with substantial customer bases, transactions can still be transformed into relationships by offering extra benefits to customers who choose to register with the firm (loyalty programs for hotels, airlines, and car rental firms fall into this category). Having a loyalty program in place enables a firm to know who its current customers are and to capture their service transactions and preferences. This is valuable information for service delivery, for allowing customization and personalization, and for segmentation purposes. For transaction-type businesses,

TABLE 12.1 Relationships with Customers

	Type of Relationship Between the Service Organization and Its Customers	
Nature of Service Delivery	**Membership Relationship**	**No Formal Relationship**
Continuous delivery of service	Insurance Cable TV subscription College enrollment Banking	Radio station Police protection Lighthouse Public highway
Discrete transactions	Long-distance calls from subscriber phone Theater series subscription Travel on commuter ticket Repair under warranty Health treatment for HMO member	Car rental Mail service Toll highway Pay phone Movie theater Public transportation Restaurant

loyalty reward programs become a necessary enabler for implementing the strategies in the Wheel of Loyalty (discussed in the next section).

In addition to using loyalty programs, selling the service in bulk (for instance, a theater series subscription or a commuter ticket on public transport) can also transform discrete transactions into membership relationships. We will next discuss how we can systematically think about creating value propositions for our customers to become loyal.

THE WHEEL OF LOYALTY

Building customer loyalty is difficult. Just try to think of all the service firms you are loyal to. Most people cannot think of more than perhaps a handful of firms they truly like (i.e., give a high share-of-heart) and to whom they are committed to going back (i.e., give a high share-of-wallet). This shows that although firms put enormous amounts of money and effort into loyalty initiatives, they often are not successful in building true customer loyalty. We use the Wheel of Loyalty shown in Figure 12.5 as an organizing framework for thinking about how to build customer loyalty. It comprises three sequential strategies.

- First, the firm needs a solid foundation for creating customer loyalty that includes targeting the right portfolio of customer segments, attracting the right customers, tiering the service, and delivering high levels of satisfaction.
- Second, to truly build loyalty, a firm needs to develop close bonds with its customers that either deepen the relationship through cross-selling and bundling or add value to the customer through loyalty rewards and higher level bonds.
- Third, the firm needs to identify and eliminate the factors that result in "churn"—the loss of existing customers and the need to replace them with new ones.

We discuss each of the components of the Wheel of Loyalty in the sections that follow.

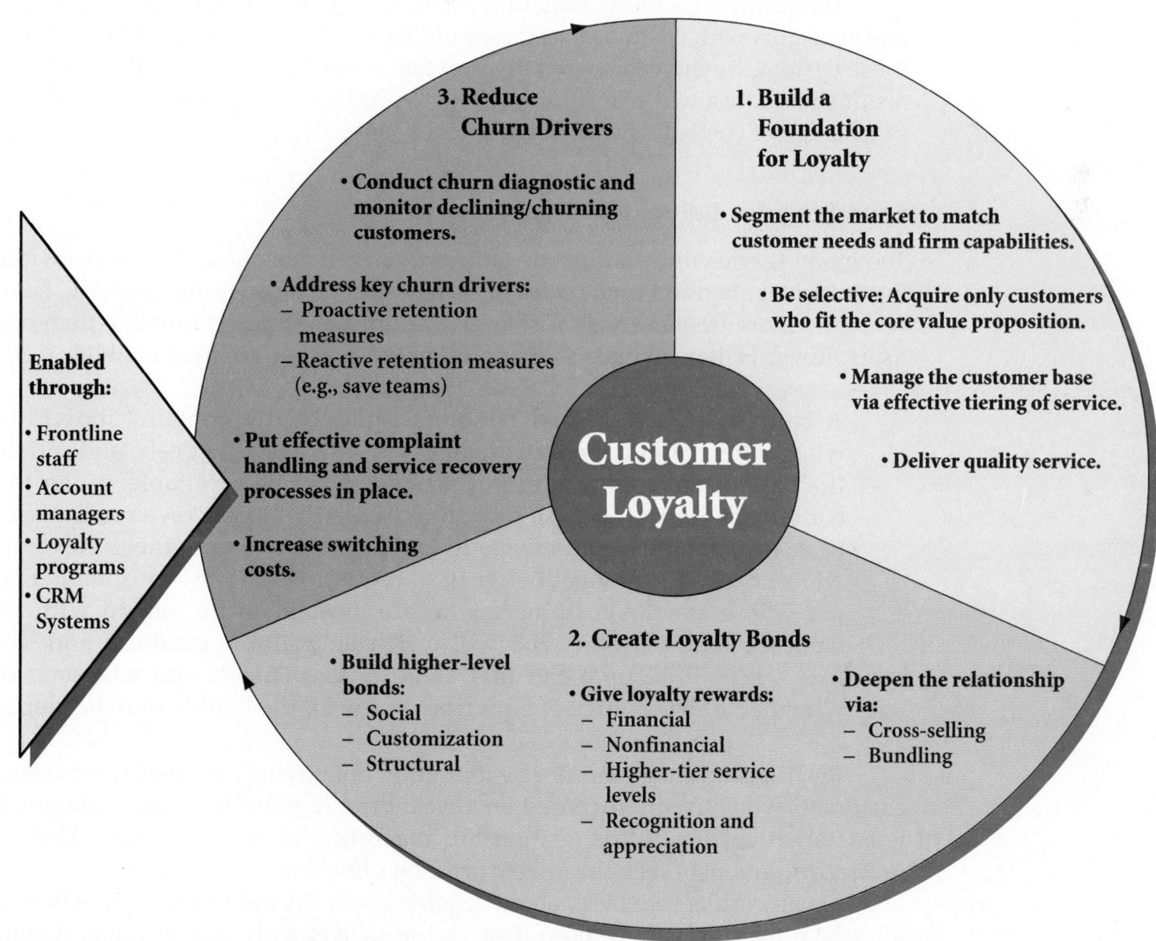

FIGURE 12.5 The Wheel of Loyalty

BUILDING A FOUNDATION FOR LOYALTY

Many elements are involved in creating long-term customer relationships and loyalty. In Chapter 3, we discussed segmentation and positioning. In this section, we emphasize the importance of focusing on serving a portfolio of several desirable customer segments, and then taking pains to build and maintain their loyalty through well-conceived relationship marketing strategies.

Targeting the Right Customers

Loyalty management starts with segmenting the market to match customer needs and firm capabilities, in short, identify and target the right customers. "Who should we be serving?" is a question that every service business needs to raise periodically. Customers often differ widely in terms of needs. They also differ in terms of the value they can contribute to a company. Not all customers offer a good fit with the organization's capabilities, delivery technologies, and strategic direction.

Companies need to be selective about the segments they target if they want to build successful customer relationships. This means focusing on acquiring customers who fit the core value proposition! Matching customers to the firm's capabilities is vital. Managers must think carefully about how customer needs relate to such operational elements as speed and quality, the times when service is available, the firm's capacity to serve many customers simultaneously, and the physical features and appearance of service facilities. They also need to consider how well their service personnel can meet the expectations of specific types of customers, in terms of both personal style and technical competence.[17] Finally, they need to ask themselves whether their company can match or exceed competing services directed at the same types of customers.

The result of carefully targeting customers by matching the company capabilities and strengths with customer needs should be a superior service offering in the eyes of those customers who value what the firm has to offer. As Frederick Reichheld said, "the result should be a win-win situation, where profits are earned through the success and satisfaction of customers, and not at their expense."[18]

Searching for Value, Not Just Volume

Too many service firms still focus on the *number* of customers they serve without giving sufficient attention to the *value* of each customer.[19] Generally speaking, heavy users who buy more frequently and in larger volumes are more profitable than occasional users. Roger Hallowell makes this point nicely in a discussion of banking:

> A bank's population of customers undoubtedly contains individuals who either cannot be satisfied, given the service levels and pricing the bank is capable of offering, or will never be profitable, given their banking activity (their use of resources relative to the revenue they supply). Any bank would be wise to target and serve only those customers whose needs it can meet better than its competitors in a profitable manner. These are the customers who are most likely to remain with that bank for long periods, who will purchase multiple products and services, who will recommend that bank to their friends and relations, and who may be the source of superior returns to the bank's shareholders.[20]

Relationship customers are by definition not buying commodity services. Service customers who buy strictly based on lowest price (a minority in most markets) are not good target customers for relationship marketing in the first place. They are deal prone, continuously seek the lowest price on offer, and switch easily.

Loyalty leaders are picky about acquiring only the right customers, which are those for whom their firms have been designed to deliver truly special value. Acquiring the right customers can bring in long-term revenues, continued growth from referrals, and enhanced satisfaction from employees whose daily jobs are improved when they can deal with appreciative customers. Attracting the wrong customers typically results in costly churn, a diminished company reputation, and disillusioned employees. Ironically, it is often the firms that are highly focused and selective in their acquisition—rather than those that focus on unbridled acquisition—that grow fast over long periods.[21] Best Practice in

BEST PRACTICE IN ACTION 12.1

Vanguard Discourages the Acquisition of "Wrong" Customers

The Vanguard Group is a growth leader in the mutual fund industry that built its $1 trillion in managed assets by painstakingly targeting the right customers for its business model. Its share of new sales, which was around 25 percent, reflected its share of assets or market share. However, it had a far lower share of redemptions, which gave it a market share of net cash flows of 55 percent (new sales minus redemptions), and made it the fastest-growing mutual fund in its industry.

How did Vanguard achieve such low redemption rates? The secret was in its careful acquisition, and its product and pricing strategies, which encouraged the acquisition of the "right" customers.

John Bogle, Vanguard's founder, believed in the superiority of index funds and that their lower management fees would lead to higher returns over the long run. He offered Vanguard's clients unparalleled low management fees through a policy of not trading (its index funds hold the market they are designed to track), not having a sales force, and spending only a fraction of what its competitors did on advertising. Another important part of keeping its costs low was its aim to discourage the acquisition of customers who were not long-term index holders.

Bogle attributes the high customer loyalty Vanguard has achieved to a great deal of focus on customer defections, which are called redemptions in the fund context. "I watched them like a hawk," he explained, and analyzed them more carefully than new sales to ensure that Vanguard's customer acquisition strategy was on course. Low redemption rates meant that the firm was attracting the right kind of loyal, long-term investors. The inherent stability of its loyal customer base has been key to Vanguard's cost advantage. Bogle's pickiness became legendary. He scrutinized individual redemptions with a fine-tooth comb to see who let the wrong kind of customers on board. When an institutional investor redeemed $25 million from an index fund bought only nine months earlier, he regarded the acquisition of this customer a failure of the system. He explained, "We don't want short-term investors. They muck up the game at the expense of the long-term investor." At the end of his chairman's letter to the Vanguard Index Trust, Bogle reiterated: "We urge them [short-term investors] to look elsewhere for their investment opportunities."

This care and attention to acquiring the right customers became legendary. For example, Vanguard turned away an institutional investor who wanted to invest $40 million because Vanguard suspected that the customer would churn the investment within the next few weeks, creating extra costs for existing customers. The potential customer complained to Vanguard's CEO, who not only supported the decision, but also used it as an opportunity to reinforce to his teams why they needed to be selective about the customers they accept.

Furthermore, Vanguard introduced a number of changes to industry practices that discouraged active traders from buying its funds. For example, Vanguard did not allow telephone transfers for index funds, redemption fees were added to some funds, and the standard practice subsidizing new accounts at the expense of existing customers was rejected because the practice was considered disloyal to its core investor base. These product and pricing policies in effect turned away heavy traders, but made the fund unequivocally attractive for the long-term investor.

Finally, Vanguard's pricing was set up to reward loyal customers. For many of its funds, investors pay a one-time fee upfront, which goes into the funds to compensate all current investors for the administrative costs of selling new shares. In essence, this fee subsidizes long-term investors and penalizes short term investors. Another novel pricing approach was the creation of its Admiral shares for loyal investors, which carried an expense fee of one-third less than ordinary shares (0.12 percent per year instead of 0.18 percent).

Source: © 2009 Vanguard Inc.

Source: Adapted from Frederick F. Reichheld, *Loyalty Rules! How Today's Leaders Build Lasting Relationships.* Boston, MA: Harvard Business School Press, 2001, 24–29, 84–87, 144–145; www.vanguard.com, accessed June 10, 2009.

Action 12.1 shows how Vanguard Group, a leader in the mutual funds industry, designed its products and pricing to attract and retain the right customers for its business model.

Different segments offer different value for a service firm. Like investments, some types of customers may be more profitable than others in the short term, but others may have greater potential for long-term growth. Similarly, the spending patterns of some customers may be stable over time, while those of others may be more cyclical, spending heavily in boom times but cutting back sharply in recessions. A wise marketer seeks a mix of segments in order to reduce the risks associated with volatility.[22]

In many cases, David Maister emphasizes, marketing is about getting *better* business, not just *more* business.[23] For instance, the caliber of a professional firm is measured by the type of clients it serves and the nature of the tasks on which it works. Volume alone is no measure of excellence, sustainability, or profitability. In professional services, such as consulting firms or legal partnerships, the mix of business attracted may play an important role in both defining the firm and in providing a suitable mix of assignments for staff members at different levels in the organization.

Finally, managers shouldn't assume the "right customers" are always big spenders. Depending on the service business model, the right customers may come from a large group of people that no other supplier is doing a good job of serving. Many firms have built successful strategies on serving customers segments that had been neglected by established players, which didn't perceive them as sufficiently "valuable." Examples include: Enterprise Rent-A-Car, which targets customers who need a temporary replacement car, avoiding the more traditional segment of business travelers who are pursued by its principal competitors; Charles Schwab, which focuses on retail stock buyers; and Paychex, which provides small businesses with payroll and human resource services.[24]

Managing the Customer Base through Effective Tiering of Service

Marketers should adopt a strategic approach to retaining, upgrading, and even ending relationships with customers. Customer retention involves developing long-term, cost-effective links with customers for the mutual benefit of both parties, but these efforts need not necessarily target all the customers in a firm with the same level of intensity. Research has confirmed that customer profitability and return on sales can be increased by focusing a firm's resources on top-tier customers.[25] Furthermore, different customer tiers often have quite different service expectations and needs. According to Valarie Zeithaml, Roland Rust, and Katharine Lemon, it's critical for service firms to understand the needs of customers within different profitability tiers and adjust their service levels accordingly.[26]

Just as service product categories can be tiered to reflect the level of value included (e.g., first, business, and economy class in air travel; see Chapter 4, pp. 102) so can groups of customers. In the latter instance, service tiers can be developed around different levels of profit contribution of different groups of customers and their needs (including sensitivities to variables such as price, comfort, and speed) and identifiable personal profiles such as demographics. Zeithaml, Rust, and Lemon illustrate this principle through a four-level pyramid (Figure 12.6).

- *Platinum.* These customers constitute a very small percentage of a firm's customer base, but they are heavy users and contribute a large share of the firm's profits. This segment typically is less price sensitive but expects highest service levels, and it is likely to be willing to invest in and try new services.
- *Gold.* The gold-tier includes a larger percentage of customers than the platinum, but individual customers contribute less profit than platinum customers. They tend to be slightly more price sensitive and less committed to the firm.
- *Iron.* These customers provide the bulk of the customer base. Their numbers give the firm economies of scale. Hence, they often are important so that a firm can build and

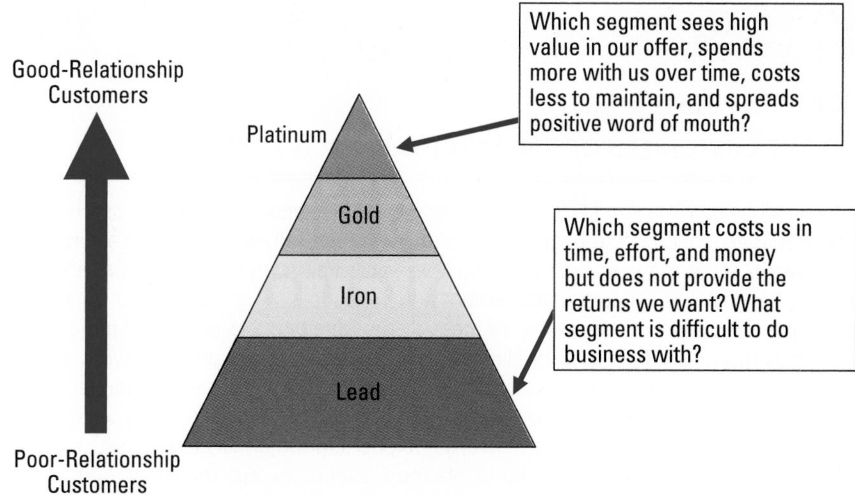

FIGURE 12.6 The Customer Pyramid

Source: Valerie A. Zeithaml, Roland T. Rust & Katharine N. Lemon "The Customer Pyramid: Creating and Serving Profitable Customers" California Management Review 43, no. 4, Summer 2001, Figure 1, pp. 118–142. Copyright © 2001 by The Regents of the University of California. Reprinted by permission of The Regents for electronic posting add "All rights reserved. This article is for personal viewing by individuals accessing this site. It is not to be copied, reproduced, or otherwise disseminated without written permission from the California Management Review. By viewing this document, you hereby agree to these terms. For permission or reprints, contact: cmr@haas.berkeley.edu.

maintain a certain capacity level and infrastructure, which often is needed for serving gold and platinum customers well. However, iron customers often are only marginally profitable. Their level of business is not sufficient to warrant special treatment.

- *Lead.* Customers in this tier tend to generate low revenues for a firm but often require the same level of service as iron customers, turning them into a loss-making segment from a firm's perspective.

The precise characteristics of customer tiers vary, of course, from one type of business to another and even from one firm to another. Service Perspective 12.1 provides an illustration from the marketing research industry.

Customer tiers typically are based on profitability and their service needs. Rather than providing the same level of service to all customers, each segment receives a service level that is customized based on its requirements and value to the firm. For example, the platinum tier is provided some exclusive benefits not available to other segments. The benefit levels for platinum and gold customers often are designed with retention in mind, because these customers are the ones competitors would like to entice to switch.

Marketing efforts can be used to encourage an increased volume of purchases, upgrading the type of service used, or cross-selling additional services to any of the four tiers. However, these efforts have different thrusts for the different tiers, as their needs, usage behaviors, and spending patterns usually are very different. Among segments for which the firm already has a high share-of-wallet, the focus should be on nurturing, defending, and retaining these customers, possibly by use of loyalty programs.[27]

For lead-tier customers, the options are to either migrate them to the iron segment or to terminate them. Migration can be achieved via a combination of strategies, including up-selling, cross-selling, and setting base fees and price increases. For example, imposing a minimum fee that is waived when a certain level of revenue is generated may encourage customers who use several suppliers to consolidate their transactions with a single provider. There may also be opportunities to cut service costs to those customers. Customer behavior can be shaped in ways that reduce the cost of serving them; for instance, transaction charges for electronic channels may be priced lower

SERVICE PERSPECTIVE 12.1

TIERING THE CUSTOMERS OF A MARKET RESEARCH AGENCY

Tiering its clients helped a leading U.S. market research agency understand its customers better. The agency defined *platinum clients* as large accounts that were not only willing to plan a certain amount of research work during the year, but were also able to commit to the timing, scope, and nature of their projects, which made capacity management and project planning much easier for the research firm. The acquisition costs for projects sold to these clients were only 2–5 percent of project values (as compared to as much as 25 percent for clients who required extensive proposal work and project-by-project bidding). Platinum accounts were also more willing to try new services and to buy a wider range of services from their preferred provider. These customers generally were very satisfied with the research agency's work and were willing to act as references for potential new clients.

Gold accounts had a similar profile to platinum clients, except that they were more price sensitive and were more inclined to spread their budgets across several firms. Although these accounts had been clients for many years, they were not willing to commit their research work for a year in advance even though the research firm would have been able to offer them better quality and priority in capacity allocation.

Iron accounts spent moderate amounts on research and commissioned work on a project basis. Selling costs were high, as these firms tended to send out requests-for-proposals (RFPs) to a number of firms for all their projects. They sought the lowest price and often did not allow for sufficient time for the research firm to perform a quality job.

Lead accounts sought only isolated, low-cost projects that tended be "quick and dirty" in nature, with little opportunity for the research firm to add value or to apply its skill sets appropriately. Sales costs were high as the client typically invited several firms to quote. Furthermore, because these firms were inexperienced in conducting research and in working with research agencies, selling a project often took several meetings and required multiple revisions to the proposal. Lead accounts also tended to be high maintenance because they did not understand research work well; they often changed project parameters, scope, and deliverables midstream and then expected the research agency to absorb the cost of any rework, thus further reducing the profitability of the engagement.

Source: Adapted Valarie A. Zeithaml, Roland T. Rust, and Katharine N. Lemon, "The Customer Pyramid: Creating and Serving Profitable Customers," *California Management Review; Berkeley*, 43, No. 4, Summer 2001, 127–128.

than for people-intensive channels. Another option is to create an attractively priced, low-cost platform. In the cell phone industry, for example, low-use mobile users are directed to prepaid packages that do not require the firm to send out bills and collect payments, which also eliminates the risk of bad debts on such accounts.

Divesting, or terminating, customers comes as a logical consequence of the realization that not all existing customer relationships are worth keeping.[28] Some relationships may no longer be profitable for the firm, because they may cost more to maintain than the contributions they generate. Some customers no longer fit the firm's strategy either, because that strategy has changed or because the customers' behavior and needs have changed.

Occasionally customers are "fired" outright (although concern for due process is still important). ING Direct is the fast-food model of consumer banking—it is about as no-frills as it gets. It only has a handful of basic products, and it lures low-maintenance customers with high-interest rates (its Orange savings account paid 3.8 percent in January 2006—several times the industry average) (see Figure 12.7). To offset that generosity, its business model pushes its customers toward online transactions, and the bank routinely fires customers who don't fit its business model. When a customer calls too often (the average customer phone call costs the bank $5.25 to handle) or wants too many exceptions to the rule, the banks sales associates basically say: "Look, this doesn't fit you. You need to go back to your community bank and get the kind of contact you're comfortable with." As a result, ING Direct's cost per account is only one-third of the industry average.[29]

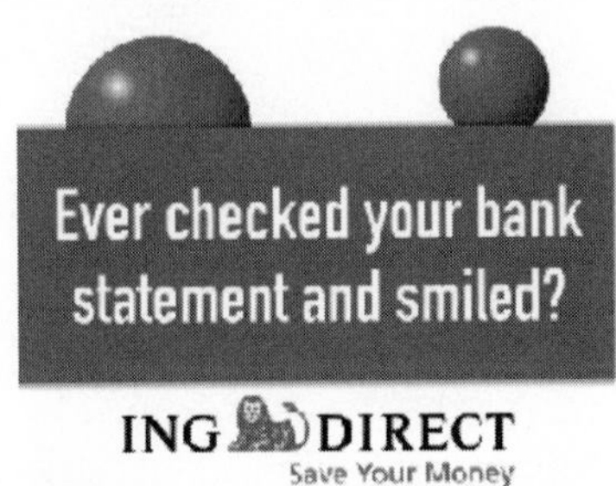

FIGURE 12.7 ING Direct Can Offer High Interest Rates Because Its Costs to Service Customers Are Kept Low

Source: Courtesy of ING Bank.

Other examples where customers get fired include students caught cheating in examinations or country club members who consistently abuse the facilities or other people. In some instances, termination may be less confrontational. Banks wishing to divest themselves of certain types of accounts that no longer fit with corporate priorities have been known to sell them to other banks (one example is credit card holders who receive a letter in the mail telling them that their account has been transferred to another card issuer).

Just as investors need to dispose of poor investments and banks may have to write off bad loans, each service firm needs to regularly evaluate its customer portfolio and consider ending unsuccessful relationships. Legal and ethical considerations, of course, will determine how to take such actions. For example, a bank may introduce a minimum monthly fee for accounts with a low balance (e.g., below $1,000), but for social responsibility considerations waive this fee for customers on social security.

Customer Satisfaction and Service Quality Are Prerequisites for Loyalty

The foundation for true loyalty lies in customer satisfaction, for which service quality is a key input. Highly satisfied or even delighted customers are more likely to become loyal apostles of a firm,[30] consolidate their buying with one supplier, and spread positive word of mouth. Dissatisfaction, in contrast, drives customers away and is a key factor in switching behavior. Recent research has even demonstrated that increases in customer satisfaction lead to increases in stock prices (see Research Insights 12.2).

The satisfaction-loyalty relationship can be divided into three main zones: Defection, indifference, and affection (see Figure 12.8). The *zone of defection* occurs at low satisfaction levels. Customers will switch unless switching costs are high or

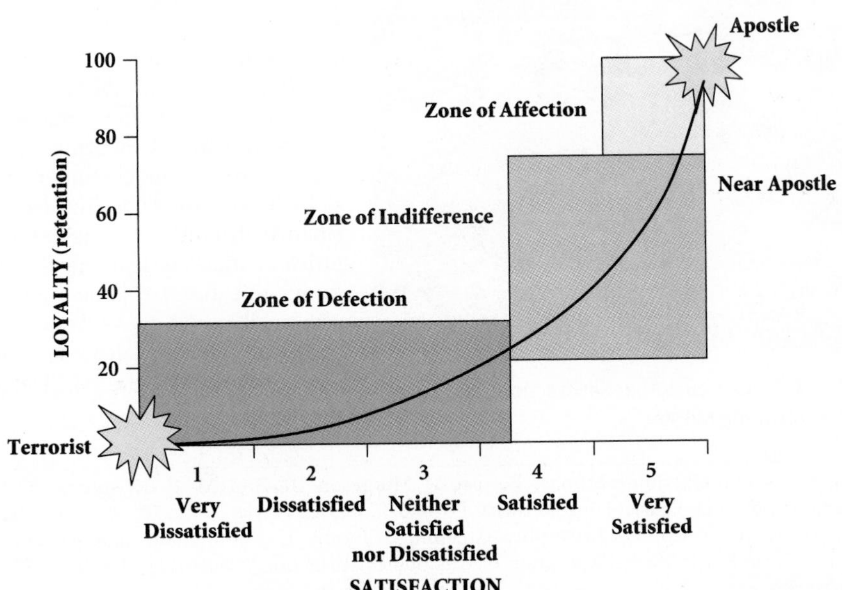

FIGURE 12.8 The Customer Satisfaction-Loyalty Relationship

Source: Reprinted by permission of Harvard Business Review from Thomas O. Jones and W. Earl Sasser, Jr., "Why Satisfied Customers Defect," Harvard Business Review, November-December 1995, p. 91.

RESEARCH INSIGHTS 12.2

CUSTOMER SATISFACTION AND WALL STREET—HIGH RETURNS AND LOW RISK!

Does a firm's customer satisfaction levels have anything to do with its stock price? This was the intriguing research question Claes Fornell and his colleagues wanted to answer. More specifically, they examined whether investments in customer satisfaction lead to excess stock returns (see Figure 12.9), and if so, whether these returns were associated with higher risks as would be predicted by finance theory.

The researchers built two stock portfolios, one hypothetical back-dated portfolio and a real-world portfolio. Both portfolios exclusively consisted of firms that did well in terms of their customer satisfaction ratings (as measured by the American Customer Satisfaction Index (ACSI). The ACSI-based portfolios were rebalanced once a year on the day when the annual ACSI results were announced. Only firms in the top 20 percent in terms of customer satisfaction ratings were included (firms were either retained if they already were in the top 20 percent last year, or firms that improved their satisfaction ranking into the top 20 percent were added to the portfolio). Firms that fell below the 20 percent cut-off were sold.

The return and risk of both portfolios were measured and their risk-adjusted returns were then compared to broad market indices such as the S&P 500 and NASDAQ. The findings were striking for managers and investors alike. Fornell and his colleagues discovered that the ACSI-based portfolio generated significantly higher risk-adjusted returns than their market benchmark indices. Changes in the ACSI ratings of individual firms were significantly related to their future stock price movement. However, simply publishing the latest data on the ACSI index did not immediately move share prices as efficient market theory would have predicted. Rather, share prices seemed to adjust slowly over time as firms published other results (perhaps earnings data or other "hard" facts that may lag customer satisfaction), and excess stock returns were generated as a result. This return represents a stock market imperfection, but it is consistent with research in marketing, which holds that satisfied customers improve the level and the stability of cash flow.

In a later study, Lerzan Aksoy and her colleagues build on these findings and confirmed that a portfolio based on ACSI data outperformed the S&P 500 index over a 10-year period and delivered risk-adjusted abnormal returns.

For marketing managers, the findings of both studies confirm that investments (or "expenses"—if you talk to accountants) in managing customer relationships and the cash flows they produce are fundamental to the firm's and therefore shareholders' value creation.

FIGURE 12.9 Can Customer Satisfaction Data Help to Outperform the Market?

Although the results are convincing, be careful should you want to exploit this apparent market inefficiency and invest in firms that show high increases in customer satisfaction in future ACSI releases—your finance friends will tell you that efficient markets learn fast! You will know this has happened when you see stock prices move as a response of future ACSI releases. You can learn more about the ACSI at www.theacsi.org.

Sources: Claes Fornell, Sunil Mithas, Forrest V. Morgeson III, and M. S. Krishnan, "Customer Satisfaction and Stock Prices: High Returns, Low Risk, *Journal of Marketing*, 70, January 2006, 3–14; Lerzan Aksoy, Bruce Cooil, Christopher Groening, Timothy L. Keiningham, and Atakan Yalçin, "The Long-Term Stock Market Valuation of Customer Satisfaction," *Journal of Marketing*, 72, No. 4, 2008, 105–122.

there are no viable or convenient alternatives. Extremely dissatisfied customers can turn into "terrorists," providing an abundance of negative feedback about the service provider.[31] The *zone of indifference* is found at intermediate satisfaction levels. Here, customers are willing to switch if they find a better alternative. Finally, the *zone of affection* is located at very high satisfaction levels, where customers may have such high attitudinal loyalty that they do not look for alternative service providers. Customers who praise the firm in public and refer others to the firm are described as "apostles." High satisfaction levels lead to improved future business performance.[32]

STRATEGIES FOR DEVELOPING LOYALTY BONDS WITH CUSTOMERS

Having the right portfolio of customer segments, attracting the right customers, tiering the service, and delivering high levels of satisfaction are a solid foundation for creating customer loyalty as shown in the Wheel of Loyalty in Figure 12.5. However, firms can do more to "bond" closely with their customers. Specific strategies include (1) deepening the relationship through cross-selling and bundling; (2) creating loyalty rewards; and (3) building higher level bonds such as social, customization, and structural bonds.[33] We will discuss each of these three strategies next.

Deepening the Relationship

To tie customers closer to the firm, deepening the relationship through bundling and/or cross-selling services is an effective strategy. For example, banks like to sell as many financial products as possible into an account or household. Sophisticated analytical software makes it possible to adopt microsegmentation strategies targeted at small groups of customers who share certain relevant characteristics at a specific point in time and who are seen as potential targets for cross-selling or up-selling campaigns (note the strategy employed by the Royal Bank of Canada, as described in Best Practice in Action 12.2). Once a family has a checking account, credit card, savings account, safe deposit box, car loan, mortgage, and so on with the same bank, the relationship is so deep that switching becomes a major exercise and is unlikely, unless of course, customers are extremely dissatisfied with the bank.

Customers can benefit from consolidating their purchasing of various services from the same provider. One-stop shopping typically is more convenient and less hassle than buying individual services from different providers. When having many services with the same firm, the customer may achieve a higher service tier and receive better service, and sometimes service bundles do come with price discounts.

Encouraging Loyalty through Financial and Nonfinancial Rewards

Few customers buy from only one supplier. This is especially true in situations where service delivery involves separate transactions (such as a car rental) rather than being continuous in nature (as with insurance coverage). In many instances, consumers are loyal to several brands (sometimes described as "polygamous loyalty") but avoid others. In such instances, the marketing goal becomes strengthening the customer's preference for one brand over the others and gaining a greater share of the customer's spending on that service category (also referred to as increasing share-of-wallet). Well-designed loyalty programs can achieve increased share-of-wallet, reward-based bonds.[34] Incentives that offer rewards based on the frequency of purchase, value of purchase, or a combination of both represent a basic level of customer bonding. Rewards can be *financial* or *nonfinancial* in nature.

FINANCIAL REWARDS. Financial rewards are customer incentives that have a financial value (also called "hard benefits"), such as discounts on purchases and loyalty program rewards such as frequent flier miles or the cash-back programs provided by some credit card issuers.

BEST PRACTICE IN ACTION 12.2

Database Marketing at the Royal Bank of Canada

At least once a month, Toronto-based analysts at the Royal Bank of Canada (the country's largest bank) use data modeling to segment its base of 10 million customers. The segmentation variables include credit risk profile, current and projected profitability, life stage, likelihood of leaving the bank, channel preference (i.e., whether customers like to use a branch, self-service machines, the call center, or online banking), product activation (how quickly customers actually use a product they have bought), and propensity to purchase another product (i.e., cross-selling potential). Says a senior vice president, "Gone are the days when we had mass buckets of customers that would receive the same treatment or same offer on a monthly basis. Our marketing strategy is [now] much more personalized. Of course, it's the technology that allows us to do that."

The main source of data is the marketing information file, which records what products customers hold with the bank, the channels they use, their responses to past campaigns, transactional data, and details of any restrictions on soliciting customers. Another source is the enterprise data warehouse, which stores billing records and information from every document a new or existing customer fills out.

Royal Bank analysts run models based on complex algorithms that can slice the bank's massive customer database into tightly profiled microsegments that are based on simultaneous use of several variables, including the probability that target customers will respond positively to a particular offer. Customized marketing programs can then be developed for each of these microsegments, giving the appearance of a highly personalized offer. The data can also be used to improve the bank's performance on unprofitable accounts by identifying these customers and offering them incentives to use lower-cost channels.

An important goal of Royal Bank's segmentation analysis is to maintain and enhance profitable relationships. The bank has found that customers who hold packages of several services are more profitable than those who don't. These customers also stay with the bank an average of three years longer. As a result of the sophisticated segmentation practices at Royal Bank, the response rates to its direct marketing programs have jumped from an industry average of only 3 percent to as high as 30 percent.

Source: Meredith Levinson, "Slices of Lives," *CIO Magazine,* August 15, 2000.

Besides airlines and hotels, more and more service firms ranging from retailers (such as department stores, supermarkets, book shops, and petrol stations), telecommunications providers, and café chains to courier services and cinema chains have or are launching similar rewards programs in response to the increasing competitiveness of their markets. Although some provide their own rewards—such as free merchandise, vehicle upgrades, or free hotel rooms at vacation resorts—many firms denominate their awards in miles that can be credited to a selected frequent flyer program. In short, air miles have become a form of promotional currency in the service sector.[35]

Recent research in the credit card industry suggests that financial rewards-based loyalty programs strengthen the customers' perception of the value proposition and lead to increased revenues due to fewer defections and higher usage levels.[36] To assess the potential of a loyalty program to alter normal patterns of behavior, Grahame Dowling and Mark Uncles argue that marketers need to examine three psychological effects:[37]

- *Brand loyalty versus deal loyalty.* To what extent are customers loyal to the core service (or brand) rather than to the loyalty program itself? Marketers should focus on loyalty programs that directly support the value proposition and positioning of the product in question.
- *How buyers value rewards.* Several elements determine a loyalty program's value to customers: (1) the cash value of the redemption rewards (if customers had to purchase them); (2) the range of choice among rewards—for instance, a selection of gifts rather than just a single gift; (3) the aspirational value of the rewards—something exotic that the consumer would not normally purchase may have greater appeal than a cash-back offer; (4) whether the amount of usage required

to obtain an award places it within the realm of possibility for any given consumer; (5) the ease of using the program and making claims for redemption; and (6) the psychological benefits of belonging to the program and accumulating points.

- *Timing.* How soon can benefits from participating in the rewards program be obtained by customers? Deferred gratification tends to weaken the appeal of a loyalty program. One solution is to send customers periodic statements of their account status, indicating progress toward reaching a particular milestone and promoting the rewards that might be forthcoming when that point is reached.

Of course, well-designed rewards programs alone will not suffice to retain a firm's most desirable customers. If you and other customers are dissatisfied with the quality of service or believe better value can be obtained from a less expensive service, you may quickly become disloyal. No service business that has instituted a rewards program for frequent users can ever afford to lose sight of its broader goals of offering high-service quality and good value relative to the price and other costs incurred by customers.[38] Furthermore, one of the risks associated with a focus on strengthening relationships with high-value customers is that a firm may allow service to other customers to deteriorate.

Finally, customers can even get frustrated especially with financial rewards-based programs, so that rather than creating loyalty and goodwill they then breed dissatisfaction! Examples include when customers feel they are excluded from a reward program because of low balances or volume of business, if they cannot redeem their loyalty points because of black-out dates during high demand periods, if the rewards are seen as having little or no value, and if redemption processes are too cumbersome and time consuming.[39] And some customers already have so many loyalty cards in their wallet that they simply are not interested in adding more cards to that pile, especially if customers see them as only marginally valuable.

NONFINANCIAL REWARDS. Nonfinancial rewards (also called "soft benefits") provide benefits that cannot be translated directly into monetary terms. Examples include giving priority to loyalty program members on reservations waitlists and virtual queues in call centers. Some airlines provide benefits such as higher baggage allowances, priority upgrading, access to airport lounges, and the like to its frequent flyers, even when they are only flying in economy class. Informal loyalty rewards, sometimes found in small businesses, may take the form of periodically giving regular customers a small treat as a way of thanking them.

Important intangible rewards include special recognition and appreciation. Customers tend to value the extra attention given to their needs and appreciate the implicit service guarantee offered by high-tier loyalty program memberships, including efforts to meet their occasional special requests. Many loyalty programs also deliver significant status benefits to customers in the top-tiers who feel part of an elite group and enjoy special treatment.[40] Tiered loyalty programs in particular can provide powerful incentives and motivation for customers to achieve the next higher level of membership that often leads to higher share-of-wallet for the preferred provider.

Nonfinancial rewards, especially if linked to higher tier service levels, are typically more powerful than financial ones as the former can create tremendous value for customers. Unlike financial rewards, nonfinancial rewards directly relate to the firm's core service and directly enhance the customers' experience and value perception. In the hotel context, for example, redeeming loyalty points for free gifts does nothing to enhance the guest experience. However, getting priority for reservations, early check-in, late check-out, upgrades, and receiving special attention and appreciation make your stay more pleasant, leave you with the fuzzy warm feeling that this firm appreciates your business, and makes you want to come back.

Best Practice in Action 12.3 describes how British Airways has designed its Executive Club effectively by combining financial and nonfinancial loyalty rewards.

Building Higher-Level Bonds

One objective of loyalty rewards is to motivate customers to consolidate their purchases with one provider or at least make it the preferred provider. However, reward-based loyalty programs are relatively easy for other suppliers to copy and rarely provide a sustained competitive advantage. In contrast, higher level bonds tend to offer a more sustained competitive advantage. We discuss next the three main types of higher level bonds: (1) social, (2) customization, and (3) structural.

SOCIAL BONDS. Have you ever noticed how your favorite hairdresser addresses you by name when you go for a haircut or how she asks why she hasn't seen you for a long time and hopes everything went well while you were away on a long business trip? Social bonds typically are based on personal relationships between providers and customers. Alternatively, they may reflect pride or satisfaction in holding membership in an organization (e.g., a prestigious university alumni club). Although social bonds are more difficult to build than financial bonds and may require considerable time to achieve, for that same reason they are also harder for competitors to replicate for that same customer. A firm that has created strong social bonds with its customers has a better chance of retaining them for the long term. When social bonds extend to shared relationships or experiences between customers, such as in country clubs or educational settings, they can be a major loyalty driver for the organization.[41]

CUSTOMIZATION BONDS. Customization bonds are built when the service provider succeeds in providing customized service to its loyal customers. For example, Starbucks' employees are encouraged to learn their regular customers' preferences and customize

BEST PRACTICE IN ACTION 12.3

Rewarding Value of Use, Not Just Frequency, at British Airways

Unlike some frequent flyer programs, in which customer usage is measured simply in miles, British Airways' (BA) Executive Club members receive both *air miles* toward redemption of air travel awards and *points* toward silver or gold tier status for travel on BA. With the creation of the OneWorld airline alliance with American Airlines, Qantas, Cathay Pacific, and other carriers, Executive Club members have been able to earn miles (and sometimes points) by flying these partner airlines, too.

As shown in Table 12.2, silver and gold cardholders are entitled to special benefits, such as priority reservations and a superior level of on-the-ground service. For instance, even if a gold cardholder is only traveling in economy class, he or she will be entitled to first-class standards of treatment at check-in and in the airport lounges. However, whereas miles can be accumulated for up to three years (after which they expire), tier status is valid for only 12 months beyond the membership year in which it was earned. In short, the right to special privileges must be re-earned each year. The objective of awarding tier status is to encourage passengers who have a choice of airlines to concentrate their travel on British Airways, rather than to join several frequent flyer programs and collect mileage awards from all of them. Few passengers travel with such frequency that they will be able to obtain the benefits of gold tier status (or its equivalent) on more than one airline.

Points given also vary according to the class of service. Longer trips earn more points than shorter ones (a domestic or short haul European trip in economy class generates 15 points, a transatlantic trip 60 points, and a trip from the UK to Australia earns 100 points.) However, tickets at deeply discounted prices may earn fewer miles and no points at all.

To reward purchase of higher-priced tickets, passengers earn points at double the economy rate if they travel in club (business class) and at triple the rate in first class. To encourage gold and silver cardholders to remain loyal, BA offers incentives for Executive Club members to retain their current tier status (or to move up from silver to gold). Silver cardholders receive a 25 percent bonus on all air miles, regardless of class of service, and gold cardholders receive a 50 percent bonus. In other words, it doesn't pay to spread the miles among several frequent-flyer programs!

TABLE 12.2 Benefits Offered by British Airways to Its Most Valued Passengers

Benefit	Silver Tier Members	Gold Tier Members
Reservations	Dedicated silver phone line	Dedicated gold phone line
Reservation assurance	If flight is full, guaranteed seat in economy when booking full fare ticket at least 24 hours in advance and checking in at least one hour in advance	If flight is full, guaranteed seat in economy when booking full fare ticket at least 24 hours in advance, and checking in at least one hour in advance
Priority waitlist and standby	Higher priority	Highest priority
Advance notification of delays over 4 hours from US or Canada	Yes	Yes
Check-in desk	Club (regardless of travel class)	First (regardless of travel class)
Lounge access	Club departure lounges for passenger and one guest regardless of class of travel	First class departure lounge for passenger and one guest, regardless of travel class; use of arrivals lounges; lounge access anytime, and allowing use of lounges even when not flying BA intercontinental flights
Preferred boarding	Board aircraft at leisure	Board aircraft at leisure
Special services assistance		Problem solving beyond that accorded to other BA travelers
Bonus air miles	+25%	+50%
Upgrade for two		Free upgrade to next cabin for member and companion after earning 2,500 tier points in one year, another upgrade for two after 3,500 points in same year. Award someone else with a Silver Partner card on reaching 4,500 points within membership year

Although the airline makes no promises about complimentary upgrades, members of BA's Executive Club are more likely to receive such invitations than other passengers. Tier status is an important consideration. Unlike many airlines, BA tends to limit upgrades to situations in which a lower class of cabin is overbooked. They do not want frequent travelers to believe that they can plan on buying a less expensive ticket and then automatically receive an upgraded seat.

Source: British Airways Executive Club, www.britishairways.com/travel/ecbenftgold/public/en_us accessed April 27, 2009.

their service accordingly (see Figure 12.10). One-to-one marketing is a specialized form of customization in which each individual is treated as a segment by itself.[42] Many large hotel chains capture the preferences of their customers through their loyalty program databases, so that when customers arrive at their hotel, they find their individual needs have already been anticipated—from preferred drinks and snacks in the minibar to the kind of pillow they like and the newspaper they want to read in the morning. When a

FIGURE 12.10 Starbucks' Employees Are Encouraged to Learn Their Customers' Preferences

customer becomes used to this special service, he or she may find it difficult to adjust to another service provider who is not able to customize the service (at least not immediately, as it takes time for the new provider to learn someone's needs).[43]

STRUCTURAL BONDS. Structural bonds are frequently seen in B2B settings and aim to stimulate loyalty through structural relationships between the provider and the customer. Examples include joint investments in projects and sharing of information, processes, and equipment. Structural bonds can be created in a B2C environment, too. For instance, some airlines have introduced short message service (SMS) check-in, and SMS or email alerts for flight arrival and departure times so that travelers do not have to waste time waiting at the airport in the case of delays. Some car rental companies offer travelers the opportunity to create customized pages on the firm's website where they can retrieve details of past trips, including pick-up and return locations, types of cars, insurance coverage, billing address, credit card details, and so forth. This simplifies and speeds the task of making new bookings. Once customers have integrated their way of doing things with the firm's processes, structural bonds are created that link the customer to the firm and make it more difficult for competition to draw them away.

Have you noticed that while all these bonds tie a customer closer to the firm, combined they also deliver the confidence, social, and special treatment benefits customers desire (refer back to Research Insights 12.1)? In general, bonds will not work well unless they also generate value for the customer!

STRATEGIES FOR REDUCING CUSTOMER DEFECTIONS

So far, we discussed drivers of loyalty and strategies to tie customers more closely to the firm. A complementary approach is to understand the drivers for customer defections, or customer churn, and work on eliminating or reducing those drivers.

Analyze Customer Defections and Monitor Declining Accounts

The first step is to understand the reasons for customer switching. Susan Keveaney conducted a large-scale study across a range of services and found several key reasons why customers switch to another provider[44] (Figure 12.11). Core service failures were mentioned by 44 percent of respondents as a reason for switching; dissatisfactory service encounters by 34 percent; high, deceptive, or unfair pricing by 30 percent; inconvenience in terms of time, location, or delays by 21 percent, and poor response to service failure by 17 percent. Many respondents described a decision to switch as resulting from interrelated incidents, such as a service failure followed by an unsatisfactory service recovery.

Many service firms regularly conduct *churn diagnostics.* This includes the analysis of data on churned and declining customers, exit interviews (call center staff often have a short set of questions they ask when a customer cancels an account to gain a better understanding of why customers defect), and in-depth interviews of former customers by a third-party research agency that typically yield a more detailed understanding of churn drivers.[45]

Some firms even try to predict churn of individual accounts. For example, cell phone service providers use *churn alert systems* that monitor the activity in individual customer accounts with the objective of predicting impending customer switching.

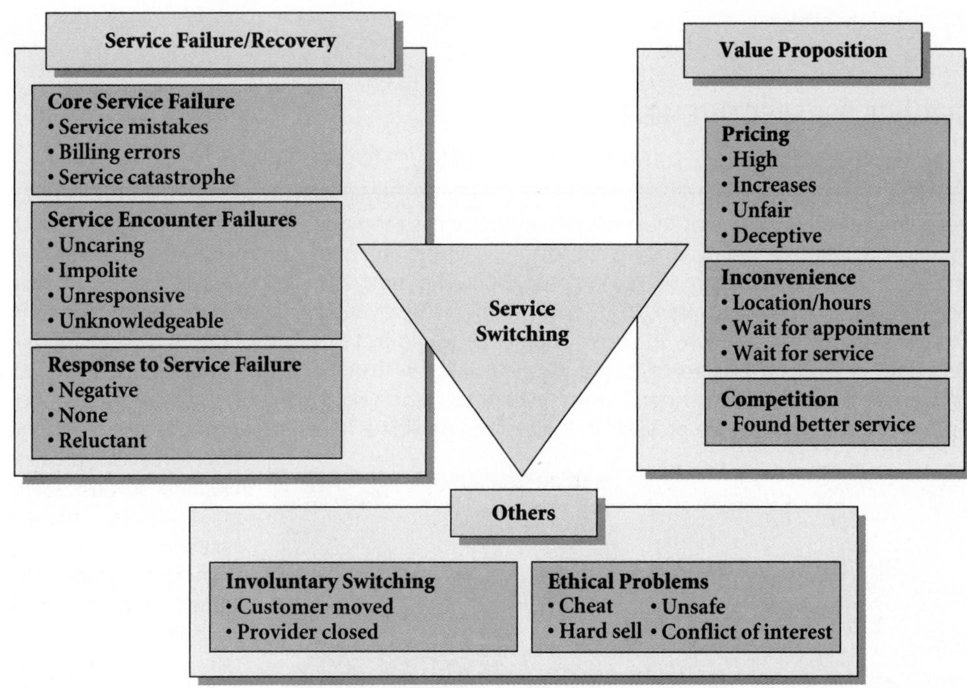

FIGURE 12.11 What Drives Customers to Switch Away from a Service Firm?

Source: Adapted from Susan M. Keaveney, "Customer Switching Behavior in Service Industries: An Exploratory Study," Journal of Marketing 59 (April 1995), 71-82. Copyright © 1995. Reprinted with permission from Journal of Marketing. Published by the American Marketing Association.

Important accounts at risk are flagged and trigger proactive retention efforts such as sending a voucher and/or having a customer service representative call the customer to check on the health of the customer relationship and initiate corrective action if needed.

Address Key Churn Drivers

Keaveney's findings underscore the importance of addressing some generic churn drivers by delivering quality service (see Chapter 14), minimizing inconvenience and other nonmonetary costs, and offering fair and transparent pricing (Chapter 6). In addition to these generic drivers, industry-specific drivers exist as well. For example, handset replacement is a common reason for cell phone service subscribers to discontinue an existing relationship, as new subscription plans typically come with heavily subsidized, brand-new handsets. To prevent handset-related churn, many providers now offer proactive handset replacement programs in which their current subscribers are offered heavily discounted handsets at regular intervals. Some providers even provide handsets for free to high-value customers or against redemption of loyalty points.

In addition to such proactive retention measures, many firms use reactive measure as well. These include specially trained call center staff, so-called *save teams*, who deal with customers who intend to cancel their accounts. The main job of save team employees is to listen to customer needs and issues and to try to address them with the key focus of retaining the customer. However, save teams should be rewarded carefully—see Service Perspective 12.2.

Implement Effective Complaint Handling and Service Recovery Procedures

Effective complaint handling and excellent service recovery are crucial to keeping unhappy customers from switching providers. That includes making it easy for customers to voice their problems with the firm and then responding with a strong service recovery. We will discuss in depth on how to do this effectively in Chapter 13.

SERVICE PERSPECTIVE 12.2

HOLD ON TO THAT CUSTOMER! THE SOCIAL NETWORK WAY...

Retaining customers is one of the most critical challenges for mobile operators, who must work to establish key strategies in minimizing churn and achieving optimum customer loyalty and retention strategies. A recent launch of a relationship-building program by Malaysia's leading mobile operator, Maxis Communications Bhd., negates the generally held belief that increasing agents in the call center is the only way to curb customer churn. In fact, if you take into consideration the call center costs, such as telecom costs and repeat calls, on customer churn, it does have an impact on the overall operational cost and stress level of workforce management. Maxis is the first mobile communications service provider in Malaysia to provide a full range of mobile services to the top three social networking services (SNS) in Malaysia, namely Facebook, Twitter, and Friendster. With the launch of a new service called "fb2mobile," Maxis connects its mobile subscribers to Facebook and Twitter via SMS and MMS. Maxis had previously launched the Friendster Alert service in May 2009, allowing subscribers to receive updates on their Friendster accounts via SMS.

In providing added options to its customers, Maxis will also be looking to include other major social networking services such as Yahoo and MSN Messenger. Fb2mobile is a major leap toward positively managing the churning of mobile subscribers in Malaysia. Other telecom operators will definitely follow suit. Fb2mobile is developed locally, based on the technology and platform called "Mobile@Play" for mobile social information technology company nPlay Sdn Bhd.

Source: http://mytechnews.info.

Increase Switching Costs

Another way to reduce churn is to increase switching barriers.[46] Many services have natural switching costs (e.g., it is a lot of work for customers to change their primary banking account, especially when many direct debits, credits, and other related banking services are tied to that account, plus many customers are reluctant to learn about the products and processes of a new provider).[47]

Switching costs can also be created by instituting contractual penalties for switching, such as the transfer fees levied by some brokerage firms for moving shares and bonds to another financial institution. However, firms need to be cautious so they are not perceived as holding their customers hostage. A firm with high switching barriers and poor service quality is likely to generate negative attitudes and bad word of mouth. "At some point, the last straw is reached and a previously inert customer will have had enough" and switch the service provider.[48]

CRM: CUSTOMER RELATIONSHIP MANAGEMENT

Service marketers have understood for some time the power of customer relationship management, and certain industries have applied it for decades. Examples include the corner grocery store, the neighborhood car repair shop, and providers of banking services to high net-worth clients. Mention the term CRM, however, and costly, complex IT systems and infrastructure, and CRM vendors such as SAP and Siebel immediately come to mind. But CRM actually signifies the whole process by which relations with customers are built and maintained.[49] It should be seen as an enabler of the successful implementation of the Wheel of Loyalty. Let's first look at CRM systems before we move to a more strategic perspective.

Common Objectives of CRM Systems

Many firms have large numbers of customers (sometimes millions), many different touchpoints (for instance, tellers, call-center staff, self-service machines, and websites), at multiple geographic locations. At a single large facility, it's unlikely that a customer will be served by the same frontline staff on two consecutive visits. In such situations, managers historically lacked the tools to practice relationship marketing. Today however, CRM systems act as an enabler, capturing customer information and delivering it to the various touchpoints.

From a customer perspective, well-implemented CRM systems can offer a unified customer interface that delivers customization and personalization. This means that at each transaction, the relevant account details, knowledge of customer preferences and past transactions, or history of a service problem are at the fingertips of the person serving the customer. This can result in a vast service improvement and increased customer value.

From a company perspective, CRM systems allow the company to better understand, segment, and tier its customer base, better target promotions and cross-selling, and even implement churn alert systems that signal if a customer is in danger of defecting.[50] Service Perspective 12.3 highlights some common CRM applications.

SERVICE PERSPECTIVE 12.3

COMMON CRM APPLICATIONS

- **Data collection**—The system captures customer data such as contact details, demographics, purchasing history, service preferences, and the like.
- **Data analysis**—The data captured is analyzed and categorized by the system according to criteria set by firm. This is used to tier the customer base and tailor service delivery accordingly.
- **Sales force automation**—Sales leads, cross-sell and up-sell opportunities can be effectively identified and processed, and the entire sales cycle from lead generation to close of sales and after sales service can be tracked and facilitated through the CRM system.
- **Marketing automation**—Mining of customer data enables the firm to target its market. A good CRM system enables the firm to achieve one-to-one marketing and cost savings, often in the context of loyalty and retention programs. This results in increasing the ROI on its marketing expenditure. CRM systems also enable the assessment of the effectiveness of marketing campaigns through the analysis of responses.
- **Call center automation**—Call center staff have customer information at their fingertips and can improve their service levels to all customers. Furthermore, caller ID and account numbers allow call centers to identify the customer tier the caller belongs to and to tailor the service accordingly. For example, platinum callers get priority in waiting loops.

What Does a Comprehensive CRM Strategy Encompass?[51]

Rather than viewing CRM as a technology, we subscribe to a more strategic view of CRM that focuses on the profitable development and management of customer relationships. Figure 12.12 provides an integrated framework of five key processes involved in a CRM strategy:

1. ***Strategy development*** involves the assessment of business strategy (including articulation of the company's vision, industry trends, and competition). The business strategy typically is the responsibility of top management. Once determined, the business strategy should be guiding the development for the customer strategy, including the choice of target segments, customer base tiering, the design of loyalty bonds, and churn management (as discussed in the Wheel of Loyalty; see Figure 12.5).
2. ***Value creation*** translates the business and customer strategies into specific value propositions for customers and the firm. The value created for customers includes all the benefits delivered through priority-tiered services, loyalty rewards, and customization and personalization. The value created for the firm needs to include reduced customer acquisition and retention costs and increased share-of-wallet.

   Core of CRM is the concept of dual creation of value—customers need to participate in CRM (e.g., through volunteering information) so they can reap value from the firm's CRM initiatives. For instance, only if your driver's license, billing address, credit card details, and car and insurance preferences are stored in a car rental's CRM system, then you benefit from the increased convenience of not having to provide those data for each reservation.

   Firms can even create value through information drawn from one customer for others (e.g., Amazon's analysis of which other books customers have bought with a profile similar to yours and customer ratings of books). CRM seems most successful when there is a win-win situation for the firm and its customers.[52]

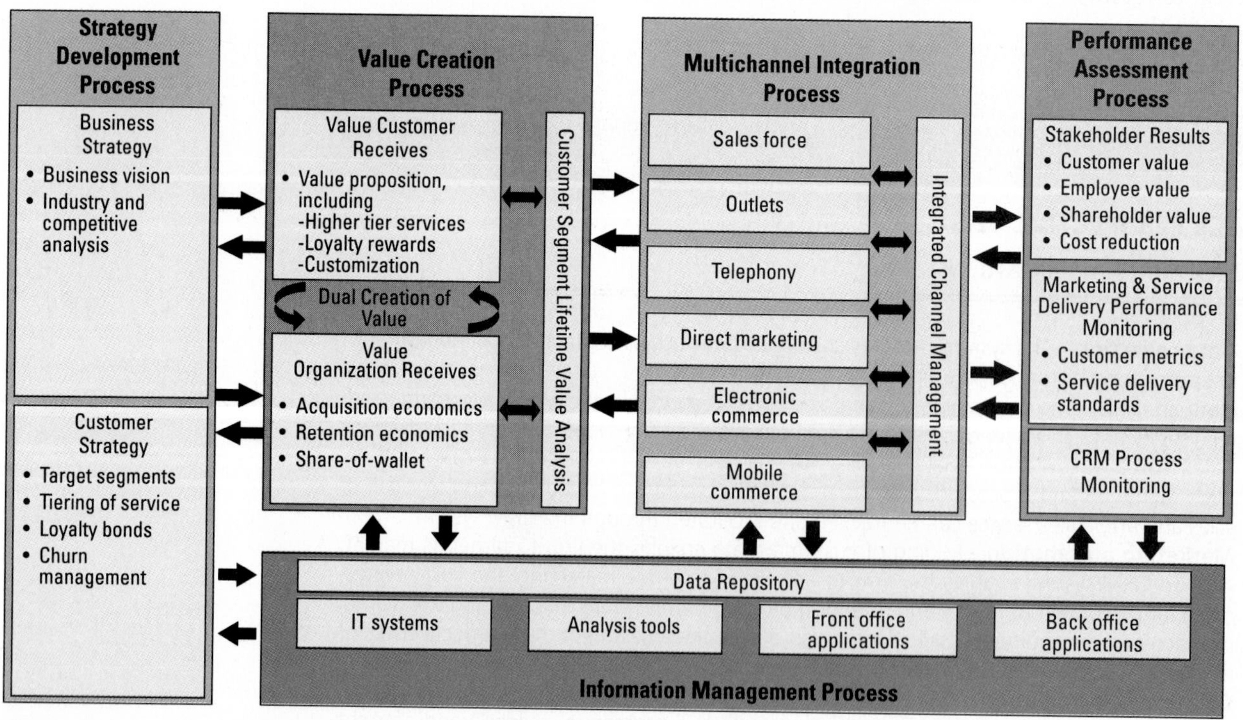

FIGURE 12.12 An Integrated Framework for CRM Strategy

Source: Adapted from Adrian Payne and Paine Frow "A Strategic Framework for Customer Relationship Management." *Journal of marketing* 69 (October 2005), 167–176. Copyright © 2005 Journal of Marketing. Reprinted with permission from the American Marketing Association.

3. ***Multichannel integration.*** Most service firms interact with their customers through a multitude of channels, and it has become a challenge to serve customers well across these many potential interfaces and offer a unified customer interface that delivers customization and personalization. CRM's channel integration addresses this challenge.
4. ***Information management.*** Service delivery across many channels relies on the firm's ability to collect customer information from all channels, integrate it with other relevant information, and make the relevant information available to the front line (or to the customer in a self-service context) at the various touchpoints. The information management process encompasses the data repository (which contains all the customer data), IT systems (which encompasses the IT hardware and software), analytical tools (which include data mining software, and more specific application packages such as campaign management analysis, credit assessment, customer profiling, churn alert systems, and even customer fraud detection and management), front office applications (which support activities that involve direct customer contact, including sales force automation and call centre management applications), and back office applications (which support internal customer related processes including logistics, procurement, and financial processing).
5. ***Performance assessment*** must address three critical questions. First, is the CRM strategy creating value for its key stakeholders (i.e., customers, employees, and shareholders)? Second, are the marketing objectives (ranging from customer acquisition, share-of-wallet, retention to customer satisfaction) and service delivery performance objectives (e.g., call center service standards such as call waiting and first-time resolution rates) being achieved? Third, is the CRM process itself performing up to expectations (e.g., are the relevant strategies being set, is customer and firm value being created, is the information management process working effectively, and is integration across customer service channels being achieved effectively)? The performance assessment process should drive the continuous improvement of the CRM strategy itself.

Common Failures in CRM Implementation

Unfortunately, the majority of CRM implementations have failed in the past. According to the Gartner Group, the implementation failure rate is 55 percent, and Accenture claims it is around 60 percent. A key reason for this high failure rate is that firms often equate installing CRM systems with having a customer relationship strategy. They forget that the system is just a tool to enhance the firm's customer servicing capabilities and is not the strategy itself.

Furthermore, CRM cuts across many departments and functions (e.g., from customer contact centers, online services, and distributions to branch operations, employee training, and IT departments), programs (ranging from sales and loyalty programs to launching of new services and cross-selling initiatives), and processes (e.g., from credit-line authorization all the way to complaint handling and service recovery). The wide-ranging scope of CRM implementation and the unfortunate reality that it is often the weakest link that determines the success of an implementation, shows the challenge of getting it right. Common reasons for CRM failures include:[53]

- **Viewing CRM as a technology initiative.** It's easy to let the focus shift toward technology and its features, with the result that the IT department—rather than top management or marketing—takes the lead in devising CRM strategy. This often results in a lack of strategic direction and understanding of customers and markets during implementation.
- **Lack of customer focus.** Many firms implement CRM without the ultimate goal to enable consistent service delivery for valued customers across all customer service processes and delivery channels.
- **Insufficient appreciation of customer lifetime value (LTV).** The marketing of many firms is not sufficiently structured around the vastly different profitability of different customers. Furthermore, servicing costs for different customer

segments are often not captured well (e.g., using activity-based costing as discussed in Chapter 6).

- **Inadequate support from top management.** Without ownership and active involvement of top management, the CRM strategic intent will not survive the implementation intact.
- **Failing to re-engineer business processes.** It is virtually impossible to implement CRM successfully without redesigning customer service and back-office processes. Many implementations fail because CRM is fitted into existing processes rather than redesigning the processes to fit a customer-centric CRM implementation. Redesigning also requires effective change management and employee engagement and support, which often are lacking.
- **Underestimating the challenges in data integration.** Firms frequently fail to integrate customer data, which often are scattered all over the organization. A key to unlocking the full potential of CRM is to make customer knowledge available in real time to all employees who need it.

In the long run, firms can put their CRM strategies at substantial risk if customers believe that CRM is used in a way detrimental to them.[54] Examples include perceptions of not being treated fairly (including existing customers who are not offered attractive pricing or promotions that are offered, for example, to new accounts) and potential privacy concerns (see Service Perspective 12.4). Being aware and actively avoiding these pitfalls is a first step toward a successful CRM implementation.

How to Get CRM Implementation Right

In spite of the many horror stories of millions of dollars sunk into unsuccessful CRM projects, more and more firms are getting it right. "No longer a black hole, CRM is becoming a basic building block of corporate success," argue Darrell Rigby and Dianne Ledingham.[55] Even CRM systems that have been implemented but have not yet shown results can be well positioned for future success. Seasoned McKinsey consultants recommend taking a step back and studying how to build customer loyalty, rather than focusing on the technology itself.[56] Instead of using CRM to transform entire businesses through the wholesale implementation of the CRM model advanced in Figure 12.12, successful implementations focus on clearly defined problems within their customer relationship cycle. These narrow CRM strategies often reveal additional opportunities for further improvements that, taken together, can evolve into broad CRM implementation extending across the entire company.[57] Likewise, Rigby, Reichheld, and Schefter recommend focusing on the customer strategy and not the technology, posing the question:

> If your best customers knew that you planned to invest $130 million to increase their loyalty...how would they tell you to spend it? Would they want you to create a loyalty card or would they ask you to open more cash registers and keep enough milk in stock? The answer depends on the kind of company you are and the kinds of relationships you and your customers want to have with one another.[58]

Among the key issues managers should debate when defining their customer relationship strategy for a potential CRM system implementation are:

1. How should our value proposition change to increase customer loyalty?
2. How much customization or one-to-one marketing and service delivery is appropriate and profitable?
3. What is the incremental profit potential of increasing the share-of-wallet with our current customers? How much does this vary by customer tier and/or segment?
4. How much time and resources can we allocate to CRM right now?

SERVICE PERSPECTIVE 12.4

CRM EXTREME—A GLIMPSE INTO ORDERING PIZZA IN 2015?

Operator: "Thank you for calling Pizza Delight. Linda speaking. How may I help you?"

Customer: "Good evening, can I order . . ."

Operator: "Sir, before taking your order, could I please have the number of your multi-purpose smart card?"

Customer: "Hold on. . . . it's. . . . um. . . 4555 1000 9831 3213."

Operator: "Thank you! Can I please confirm you're Mr. Thompson, calling from 10940 Wilford Boulevard? You are calling from your home number 432-3876, your cell phone number is 992-4566, and your office number is 432-9377."

Customer: "How in the world did you get my address and all my numbers?"

Operator: "Sir, we are connected to the Integrated Customer Intimacy System."

Customer: "I would like to order a large seafood pizza. . ."

Operator: "Sir, that's not a good idea."

Customer: "Why?!?"

Operator: "According to your medical records, you have very high blood pressure and a far too high cholesterol level, Sir."

Customer: "What?. . . What do you recommend then?"

Operator: "Try our Low Fat Soybean Yoghurt Pizza. You'll like it."

Customer: "How do you know?"

Operator: "You borrowed the book *Popular Soybean Dishes* from the City Library last week, Sir."

Customer: "OK, I give up. . . Get me three large ones then. How much will that be?"

Operator: "That should be enough for your family of 8, Sir. The total is $47.85."

Customer: "Can I pay by credit card?"

Operator: "I'm afraid you'll have to pay us cash, Sir. Your credit card is over the limit and your checking account has an overdue balance of $2,435.88. That's excluding the late payment charges on your home equity loan, Sir."

Customer: "I guess I'll have to run to the ATM and withdraw some cash before your guy arrives."

Operator: "You can't do that, Sir. Based on the records, you've reached your daily machine withdrawals limit for today."

Customer: "Never mind. Just send the pizzas, I'll have the cash ready. How long is it gonna take?"

Operator: "About 45 minutes Sir, but if you don't want to wait you can always come and collect it on your Harley, registration number L.A.6468. . ."

Customer: "#@$#@%^%%@!"

Operator: "Sir, please watch your language. Remember, on April 28, 2014, you were convicted of using abusive language at a traffic warden. . ."

Customer: (speechless)

Operator: "Is there anything else, Sir?"

Source: This story was adapted from various sources, including www.lawdebt.com/gazette/nov2004/nov2004.pdf (accessed January 2006) and a video created by the American Civil Liberties Union (ACLU), available at www.aclu.org/pizza. This video aims to communicate the privacy threats that CRM poses to consumers. The ACLU is a nonprofit organization that campaigns against government's and corporations' aggressive collection of information on people's personal life and habits.

5. If we believe in customer relationship management, why haven't we taken more steps in that direction in the past? What can we do today to develop customer relationships without spending a lot on technology?[59]

Answering these questions may lead to the conclusion that a CRM system may currently not be the best investment or highest priority, or that a scaled down version may suffice to deliver the intended customer strategy. In any case, we emphasize that the system is merely a tool to drive the strategy and thus must be tailored to deliver that strategy.

CONCLUSION

Many elements are involved in gaining market share, increasing share-of-wallet, cross-selling other products and services to existing customers, and creating long-term loyalty. We used the Wheel of Loyalty as an organizing framework, which starts with identifying and targeting the right customers, then learning about their needs, including their preferences for various forms of service delivery. Translating this knowledge into service delivery, tiered service levels, and customer relationship strategies are the key steps toward achieving customer loyalty.

Marketers need to pay special attention to those customers who offer the firm the greatest value, as they purchase its products with the greatest frequency and spend the most on premium services. Loyalty programs provide rewards to high-value customers and facilitate tiered service delivery. These programs also enable marketers to track the behavior of high-value customers in terms of where and when they use the service, what service classes or types of product they buy, and how much they spend.

Customer relationship management is a key enabler for the strategies discussed in the Wheel of Loyalty and often is integrated with loyalty programs. From a customer perspective, CRM can result in vast service improvements and increased customer value (e.g., through customization and increased convenience).

Chapter Summary

LO1 Customer loyalty is an important driver of a service firm's profitability. The profits derived from loyal customers come from (1) increased purchases, (2) reduced operation costs, (3) referral of new customers, and (4) price premiums. Also, customer acquisition costs can be amortized over a longer period of time.

LO2 However, it is not true that loyal customers are always more profitable. They may expect price discounts for staying loyal. To truly understand the profit impact of the customers, firms need to learn how to calculate the *LTV* of their customers. LTV calculations need to include (1) acquisition costs, (2) revenue streams, (3) account-specific servicing costs, (4) expected number of years the customer will stay with the firm, and (5) discount rate for future cash flows.

LO3 Customers are only loyal if it benefits them. Common benefits customers see include:

- *Confidence benefits*, including feeling that there is less risk of something going wrong, ability to trust the provider, and receipt of the firm's highest level of service.
- *Social benefits*, including being known by name, friendship with the service provider, and enjoyment of certain social aspects of the relationship.
- *Special treatment benefits*, including better prices, extra services, and higher priority.

LO4 There is a fundamental difference between relationship marketing and transactional marketing.

- *Relationship marketing* includes the not mutually exclusive approaches of (1) database marketing, (2) interaction marketing, and (3) network marketing.
- Businesses that sell *discrete transactions* have to work harder to build relationships. Offering loyalty programs that track customer purchases across outlets and time are an effective tool for many of such firms.

LO5 It is not easy to build customer loyalty. The *Wheel of Loyalty* offers a systematic framework that guides firms on how to do so. The framework has three components that follow a sequence:

- First, firms need to build a *foundation for loyalty* without which loyalty cannot be achieved. The foundation delivers confidence benefits to its loyal customers.
- Once the foundation is laid, firms can then create *loyalty bonds* to strengthen the relationship. Loyalty benefits deliver social and special treatment benefits.
- Finally, besides focusing on loyalty, firms also have to work on reducing *customer churn.*

To build the foundation for loyalty, firms need to:

LO6 Segment the market and *target the "right" customers.* Firms need to choose their target segments carefully and match them to what the firm can do best. Firms need to focus on customer value, instead of just going for customer volume.

LO7 Manage the customer base via *service tiering*, which divides the customer base into different value tiers (e.g., platinum, gold, iron, and lead). It helps to tailor strategies to the different service tiers. The higher tiers offer higher value for the firm, but also expect higher service levels. For the lower tiers, the focus should be on increasing profitability through building volume, increasing prices, cutting servicing costs, and as a last resort even ending unprofitable relationships.

LO8 Understand that the foundation for loyalty lies in *customer satisfaction*. The satisfaction loyalty relationship can be divided into three main zones: defection, indifference, and affection. Only highly satisfied or delighted customers in the zone of affection will be truly loyal.

Loyalty bonds are used to build relationships with customers. There are three different types of customer bonds:

LO9 Cross-selling and bundling *deepen relationships* that make switching more difficult and often increase convenience through one-stop shopping.

LO10 Loyalty programs aim at building share-of-wallet through *financial rewards* (e.g., loyalty points) and *nonfinancial rewards* (e.g., higher-tier service levels and recognition and appreciation).

LO11 Higher level bonds include *social, customization, and structural bonds*. These bonds tend to be more difficult to copy by competition than reward-based bonds.

LO12 The final step in the Wheel of Loyalty is to understand what causes customers to leave and then systematically reduce these *churn drivers*.

- Common causes for customers to switch include core service failures and dissatisfaction, perceptions that pricing is deceptive and unfair, inconvenience, and poor response to service failures.
- To prevent customers from switching, firms should analyze and address key reasons why their customers leave them, have good complaint handling and service recovery processes in place, and potentially increase customers' switching costs.

LO13 Finally, *CRM systems* should be seen as enabling the successful implementation of the Wheel of Loyalty. CRM systems are particularly useful when firms have to serve large numbers of customers across many service delivery channels. An effective CRM strategy includes five key processes:

- Strategy development, including choice of target segments, tiering of service, and design of loyalty rewards.
- Value creation, including delivering benefits to customers through tiered services and loyalty programs (e.g., priority waitlisting and upgrades).
- Multichannel integration to provide a unified customer interface across many different service delivery channels (e.g., from the website to the branch office).
- Information management, which includes the data repository, analytical tools (e.g., campaign management analysis and churn alert systems), and front and back office applications.
- Performance assessment, which has to address the three questions of:
  (1) Is the CRM creating value for customers and the firm?
  (2) Are its marketing objectives being achieved?
  (3) Is the CRM system itself performing according to expectations?
- Performance assessment should lead to continuous improvement of the CRM strategy and system.

Review Questions

1. Why is customer loyalty an important driver of profitability for service firms?
2. Why is targeting the "right customers" so important for successful customer relationship management?
3. How can you estimate a customer's lifetime value (LTV)?
4. Explain what is meant by a customer portfolio. How should a firm decide the most appropriate mix of customers to have?
5. What is tiering of services? Explain why it is used and its implications for firms and their customers.
6. How do the various strategies described in the Wheel of Loyalty relate to one another?
7. Identify some key measures that can be used to create customer bonds and encourage long-term relationships with customers?
8. What are the arguments for spending money to keep existing customers loyal?
9. What is the role of CRM in delivering a customer relationship strategy?

Application Exercises

1. Identify three service businesses you patronize on a regular basis. For each business, complete the following sentence: "I am loyal to this business because…"
2. What conclusions do you draw about (a) yourself as a consumer and (b) the performance of each of the businesses in Exercise 1? Assess whether any of these businesses managed to develop a sustainable competitive advantage through the way it won your loyalty.
3. Identify two service businesses you used several times but have now ceased to patronize (or plan to stop patronizing soon) because you were dissatisfied. Complete the sentence: "I stopped using (or will soon stop using) this organization as a customer because…"
4. Again, what conclusions do you draw about yourself and the firms in Exercise 3? How would each of these firms potentially avoid your defection? What could each of these firms do to avoid defections in the future of customers with a profile similar to yours?
5. Evaluate the strengths and weaknesses of two frequent user programs, each one from a different service industry. Assess how each program could be improved further.
6. Design a questionnaire and conduct a survey asking about two loyalty programs. The first is about a membership/loyalty program your classmates or their families like best and keep them loyal to that firm. The second should be about a loyalty program that is not well perceived and does not seem to add value to the customer. Use open-ended questions such as "What motivated you to sign up in the first place?" "Why are you using this program?" "Has participating in the program changed your purchasing/usage behavior in any way?" "Has it made you less likely to use competing suppliers?" "What do you think of the rewards available?" "Did membership in the program lead to any immediate benefits in the use of the service?" "What are the three things you like best about this loyalty membership program?" "What did you like least?" and "What are some suggested improvements?" Analyze what features make loyalty/membership programs successful and what features do not achieve the desired results. Use frameworks such as the Wheel of Loyalty to guide your analysis and presentation.
7. Approach service employees in two or three firms with implemented CRM systems. Ask the employees about their experience interfacing with these systems and whether or not the CRM systems (a) help them understand their customers better and/or (b) lead to improved service experiences for their customers. Ask them about potential concerns and improvement suggestions they may have about their organizations' CRM systems.

Endnotes

1. Frederick F. Reichheld and Thomas Teal, *The Loyalty Effect.* Boston: Harvard Business School Press, 1996.
2. Ruth Bolton, Katherine N. Lemon, and Peter C. Verhoef, "The Theoretical Underpinnings of Customer Asset Management: A Framework and Propositions for Future Research," *Journal of the Academy of Marketing Science*, 32, No. 3, 2004, 271–292.
3. Frederick F. Reichheld and W. Earl Sasser, Jr., "Zero Defections: Quality Comes to Services," *Harvard Business Review*, October 1990, 105–111.
4. Ibid.
5. Frederick F. Reichheld and Phil Schefter, "E-Loyalty—Your Secret Weapon on the Web," *Harvard Business Review*, July–August 2002, 105–113.
6. Christian Homburg, Nicole Koschate, and Wayne D. Hoyer, "Do Satisfied Customers Really Pay More? A Study of the Relationship Between Customer Satisfaction and Willingness to Pay," *Journal of Marketing*, 69, April 2005, 84–96.
7. Grahame R. Dowling and Mark Uncles, "Do Customer Loyalty Programs Really Work?" *Sloan Management Review*, Summer 1997, 71–81; Werner Reinartz and V. Kumar, "The Mismanagement of Customer Loyalty," *Harvard Business Review*, July 2002, 86–94.
8. Werner J. Reinartz and V. Kumar, "On the Profitability of Long-Life Customers in a Noncontractual Setting: An Empirical Investigation and Implications for Marketing," *Journal of Marketing*, 64, October 2000, 17–35.
9. Jochen Wirtz, Indranil Sen, and Sanjay Singh, "Customer Asset Management at DHL in Asia," in Jochen Wirtz and Christopher Lovelock, eds., *Services Marketing in Asia—A Case Book.* Singapore: Prentice Hall, 2005, 379–396.
10. John E. Hogan, Katherine N. Lemon, and Barak Libai, "What is the True Cost of a Lost Customer?" *Journal of Services Research*, 5, No. 3, 2003, 196–208.
11. For a discussion on how to evaluate the customer base of a firm, see Sunil Gupta, Donald R. Lehmann, and Jennifer Ames Stuart, "Valuing Customers," *Journal of Marketing Research*, 41, No. 1, 2004, 7–18.
12. Alan W. H. Grant and Leonard H. Schlesinger, "Realize Your Customer's Full Profit Potential," *Harvard Business Review*, 73, September–October 1995, 59–75. See also Nicolas Glady and Christophe Croux, "Predicting

Customer Wallet Without Survey Data," *Journal of Service Research*, 11, No. 3, 2009, 219–231.

13. Nicole E. Coviello, Roderick J. Brodie, and Hugh J. Munro, "Understanding Contemporary Marketing: Development of a Classification Scheme," *Journal of Marketing Management*, 13, No. 6, 501–522.
14. J. R. Copulsky and M. J. Wolf, "Relationship Marketing: Positioning for the Future," *Journal of Business Strategy*," 11, No. 4, 1990, 16–20.
15. Johnson and Selnes proposed a typology of exchange relationships that included "strangers," "aquaintances," "friends," and "partners" and derived implications for customer portfolio management. For details see Michael D. Johnson and Fred Selnes, "Customer Portfolio Management: Towards a Dynamic Theory of Exchange Relationships," *Journal of Marketing*, 68, No. 2, 2004, 1–17.
16. Evert Gummesson, *Total Relationship Marketing*. Oxford: Butterworth-Heinemann, 1999, 24.
17. It has even been suggested to let "chronically dissatisfied customer go to allow front-line staff focus on satisfying the 'right' customers," see Ka-shing Woo and Henry K. Y. Fock, "Retaining and Divesting Customers: An Exploratory Study of Right Customers, 'At-Risk' Right Customers, and Wrong Customers," *Journal of Services Marketing*, 18, No. 3, 2004, 187–197.
18. Frederick F. Reichheld, *Loyalty Rules—How Today's Leaders Build Lasting Relationships*. Boston, MA: Harvard Business School Press, 2001, 45.
19. Yuping Liu, "The Long-Term Impact of Loyalty Programs on Consumer Purchase Behavior and Loyalty," *Journal of Marketing*, 71, No. 4, October 2007, 19–35.
20. Roger Hallowell, "The Relationships of Customer Satisfaction, Customer Loyalty, and Profitability: An Empirical Study," *International Journal of Service Industry Management*, 7, No. 4, 1996, 27–42.
21. Frederick F. Reichheld, *Loyalty Rules – How Today's Leaders Build Lasting Relationships*. Boston, MA: Harvard Business School Press, 2001, 43, 84–85.
22. Ravi Dhar and Rashi Glazer, "Hedging Customers," *Harvard Business Review*, 81. May 2003, 86–92.
23. David H. Maister, *True Professionalism*. New York: The Free Press, 1997 (see especially Chapter 20).
24. David Rosenblum, Doug Tomlinson, and Larry Scott, "Bottom-Feeding for Blockbuster Business," *Harvard Business Review*, March 2003, 52–59.
25. Christian Homburg, Mathias Droll, and Dirk Totzek, "Customer Prioritization: Does it Pay Off, and How Should It Be Implemented?" *Journal of Marketing*, 72. No. 5, 2008, 110–130.
26. Valarie A. Zeithaml, Roland T. Rust, and Katharine N. Lemon, "The Customer Pyramid: Creating and Serving Profitable Customers," *California Management Review*, 43, No. 4, Summer 2001, 118–142.
27. Werner J. Reinartz and V. Kumar, "The Impact of Customer Relationship Characteristics on Profitable Lifetime Duration," *Journal of Marketing*, 67, No. 1, 2003, 77–99.
28. Vikras Mittal, Matthew Sarkees, and Feisal Murshed, "The Right Way to Manage Unprofitable Customers," *Harvard Business Review*, April 2008, 95–102.
29. Elizabeth Esfahani, "How to Get Tough with Bad Customers," *ING Direct*, October 2004, and http://home.ingdirect.com, accessed January 19, 2006.
30. Not only is there a positive relationship between satisfaction and share of wallet, but the greatest positive impact is seen at the upper extreme levels of satisfaction. For details, refer to Timothy L. Keiningham, Tiffany Perkins-Munn, and Heather Evans, "The Impact of Customer Satisfaction on Share of Wallet in a Business-to-Business Environment," *Journal of Service Research*, 6, No. 1, 2003, 37–50.
31. Florian v. Wangenheim, "Postswitching Negative Word of Mouth," *Journal of Service Research*, 8, No. 1, 2005, 67–78.
32. Neil A. Morgan and Lopo Leotte Rego, "The Value of Different Customer Satisfaction and Loyalty Metrics in Predicting Business Performance," *Marketing Science*, 25, No. 5, September–October 2006, 426–439.
33. Leonard L. Berry and A. Parasuraman, "Three Levels of Relationship Marketing," *Marketing Services - Competing through Quality*. New York: The Free Press, 1991, 136–142; Valarie A. Zeithaml, Mary Jo Bitner, and Dwayne D. Gremler, *Services Marketing*, 4th edn. New York: McGraw-Hill, 2006, 196–201.
34. Michael Lewis, "The Influence of Loyalty Programs and Short-Term Promotions on Customer Retention," *Journal of Marketing Research*, 41, August 2004, 281–292; Jochen Wirtz, Anna S. Mattila, and May Oo Lwin, "How Effective are Loyalty Reward Programs in Driving Share of Wallet?" *Journal of Service Research*, 9, No. 4, 2007, 327–334.
35. Katherine N. Lemon and Florian V. Wangenheim, "The Reinforcing Effects of Loyalty Program Partnerships and Core Service Usage," *Journal of Service Research*, 11, No. 4, 2009, 357–370.
36. Ruth N. Bolton, P. K. Kannan, and Matthew D. Bramlett, "Implications of Loyalty Program Membership and Service Experience for Customer Retention and Value," *Journal of the Academy of Marketing Science*, 28, No. 1, 2000, 95–108; Michael Lewis, "The Influence of Loyalty Programs and Short-Term Promotions on Customer Retention," *Journal of Marketing Research*, 41, No. 3, 2004, 281–292.
37. Grahame R. Dowling and Mark Uncles, "Do Customer Loyalty Programs Really Work?" *Sloan Management Review* 38, Summer 1997, 71–82.
38. See for example Iselin Skogland and Judy Siguaw, "Are Your Satisfied Customers Loyal?" *Cornell Hotel and Restaurant Administration Quarterly*, 45, No. 3, 2004, 221–234.
39. Bernd Stauss, Maxie Schmidt, and Adreas Schoeler, "Customer Frustration in Loyalty Programs," *International Journal of Service Industry Management*, 16, No. 3, 2005, 229–252.
40. On the perception of design of loyalty tiers see Xavier Drèze and Joseph C. Nunes, "Feeling Superior: The Impact of Loyalty Program Structure on Consumers' Perceptions of Status," *Journal of Consumer Research*, 35, No. 6, 2009, 890–905.
41. Mark S. Rosenbaum, Amy L. Ostrom, and Ronald Kuntze, "Loyalty Programs and a Sense of Community," *Journal of Services Marketing*, 19, No. 4, 2005, 222–233; Isabelle Szmigin, Louise Canning, and Alexander E. Reppel, "Online Community: Enhancing the Relationship Marketing Concept Through Customer Bonding," *International Journal of Service Industry Management*, 16, No. 5, 2005, 480–496; Inger Roos, Anders Gustafsson, and Bo Edvardsson, "The Role of Customer Clubs in Recent Telecom Relationships," *International Journal of Service Industry Management*, 16, No. 5,

2005, 436–454; Dennis Pitta, Frank Franzak, and Danielle Fowler, "A Strategic Approach to Building Online Customer Loyalty: Integrating Customer Profitability Tiers," *Journal of Consumer Marketing*, 23, No. 7, 2006, 421–429.

42. Don Peppers and Martha Rogers, *The One-to-One Manager.* New York: Currency/Doubleday, 1999.
43. Rick Ferguson and Kelly Hlavinka, "The Long Tail of Loyalty: How Personalized Dialogue and Customized Rewards Will Change Marketing Forever," *Journal of Consumer Marketing*, 23, No. 6, 2006, 357–361.
44. Susan M. Keaveney, "Customer Switching Behavior in Service Industries: An Exploratory Study," *Journal of Marketing*, 59, April 1995, 71–82.
45. For a more detailed discussion of situation-specific switching behavior, refer to Inger Roos, Bo Edvardsson, and Anders Gustafsson, "Customer Switching Patterns in Competitive and Noncompetitive Service Industries," *Journal of Service Research*, 6, No. 3, 2004, 256–271.
46. Jonathan Lee, Janghyuk Lee, and Lawrence Feick, "The Impact of Switching Costs on the Consumer Satisfaction-Loyalty Link: Mobile Phone Service in France," *Journal of Services Marketing*, 15, No. 1, 2001, 35–48; Shun Yin Lam, Venkatesh Shankar, M. Krishna Erramilli, and Bvsan Murthy, "Customer Value, Satisfaction, Loyalty, and Switching Costs: An Illustration from a Business-to-Business Service Context," *Journal of the Academy of Marketing Science*, 32, No. 3, 2004, 293–311; Michael A. Jones, Kristy E. Reynolds, David L. Mothersbaugh, and Sharon Beatty, "The Positive and Negative Effects o Switching Costs on Relational Outcomes, "*Journal of Service Research*, 9, No. 4, 2007, 335–355.
47. Moonkyu Lee and Lawrence F. Cunningham, "A Cost/Benefit Approach to Understanding Loyalty," *Journal of Services Marketing*, 15, No. 2, 2001, 113–130; Simon J. Bell, Seigyoung Auh, and Karen Smalley, "Customer Relationship Dynamics: Service Quality and Customer Loyalty in the Context o Varying Levels of Customer Expertise and Switching Costs," *Journal of the Academy of Marketing Science*, 33, No. 2, 2005, 169–183.
48. Lesley White and Venkat Yanamandram, "Why Customers Stay: Reasons and Consequences of Inertia in Financial Services," *International Journal of Service Industry Management*, 14, No. 3, 2004, 183–194.
49. For an excellent book on CRM see V. Kumar and Werner J. Reinartz, *Customer Relationship Management: A Database Approach.* Hoboken, NJ: John Wiley & Sons, 2006.
50. Kevin N. Quiring and Nancy K. Mullen, "More Than Data Warehousing: An Integrated View of the Customer," in: John G. Freeland, ed., *The Ultimate CRM Handbook—Strategies & Concepts for Building Enduring Customer Loyalty & Profitability.* New York: McGraw-Hill, 2002, 102–108.
51. This section is adapted from Adrian Payne and Pennie Frow, "A Strategic Framework for Customer Relationship Management," *Journal of Marketing*, 69, October 2005, 167–176.
52. William Boulding, Richard Staelin, Michael Ehret, and Wesley J. Johnston, "A Customer Relationship Management Roadmap: What is Known, Potential Pitfalls, and Where to Go," *Journal of Marketing*, 69, No. 4, 2005, 155–166.
53. This section is largely based on Sudhir H. Kale, "CRM Failure and the Seven Deadly Sins," *Marketing Management*, September/October 2004, 42–46.
54. William Boulding, Richard Staelin, Michael Ehret, and Wesley J. Johnston, "A Customer Relationship Management Roadmap: What is Known, Potential Pitfalls, and Where to Go," *Journal of Marketing*, 69, No. 4, 2005, 155–166.
55. Darrell K. Rigby and Dianne Ledingham, "CRM Done Right," *Harvard Business Review*, November 2004, 118–129.
56. Manuel Ebner, Arthur Hu, Daniel Levitt, and Jim McCrory, "How to Rescue CRM?" *The McKinsey Quarterly*, 4, Technology, 2002.
57. Darrell K. Rigby and Dianne Ledingham, "CRM Done Right," *Harvard Business Review*, November 2004, 118–129.
58. Darrell K. Rigby, Frederick F. Reichheld, and Phil Schefter, "Avoid the Four Perils of CRM," *Harvard Business Review*, February 2002, 108.
59. Darrell K. Rigby, Frederick F. Reichheld, and Phil Schefter, "Avoid the Four Perils of CRM," *Harvard Business Review*, February 2002, 108.

CHAPTER 13

Complaint Handling and Service Recovery

One of the surest signs of a bad or declining relationship is the absence of complaints from the customer. Nobody is ever that satisfied, especially not over an extended period of time.

THEODORE LEVITT

To err is human; to recover, divine.

CHRISTOPHER HART, JAMES HESKETT, AND EARL SASSER

(*PARAPHRASING 18TH CENTURY POET ALEXANDER POPE*)

LEARNING OBJECTIVES (LOs)

By the end of this chapter, the reader should be able to:

LO1 Recognize the actions customers may take in response to service failures.

LO2 Understand why customers complain.

LO3 Know what customers expect from the firm when they complain.

LO4 Understand how customers respond to effective service recovery.

LO5 Know the principles of effective service recovery systems.

LO6 Be familiar with the guidelines for frontline employees on how to handle complaining customers and recover from a service failure.

LO7 Recognize the power of service guarantees.

LO8 Understand how to design effective service guarantees.

LO9 Know when firms should not offer service guarantees.

LO10 Be familiar with the seven groups of jaycustomers and understand how to manage them effectively.

Too Little, Too Late—Jetblue's Service Recovery[1]

It was a terrible ice storm on the East Coast of the United States. Hundreds of passengers were trapped for 11 hours inside JetBlue planes at the John F. Kennedy International Airport in New York. These passengers were furious. No one from JetBlue did anything to get the passengers off the planes. On top of that, JetBlue cancelled more than 1,000 flights over six days, leaving even more passengers stranded. This incident cancelled out much that JetBlue had done right to become one of the strongest customer service brands in the United States. JetBlue was going to be ranked number four by *Business Week* in a list of top 25 customer service leaders, but because of this incident it was pulled from the rankings. What happened?

No service recovery plan was in place. No one—not the pilot, flight attendants, or station manager—had the authority to get the passengers off the plane. JetBlue's offer of refunds and travel vouchers did not seem to reduce the anger of the passengers, who had been stranded for so many hours. David Neeleman, JetBlue's CEO, sent a personal email to all customers in the company's database to explain what caused the problem, apologized profusely, and detailed its service recovery efforts. He even appeared on late-night television to apologize and admitted that the company should have had better contingency planning—but the airline still had a long way to go to repair the damage to its reputation.

Slowly, the airline rebuilt its name, starting with its new Customer Bill of Rights, which required the airline to provide vouchers or refunds in certain situations when flights were delayed. Neeleman also changed information systems to keep track of the locations of its crew, upgraded the website to allow online rebooking, and trained staff at headquarters to help out at the airport when needed. All these activities were aimed at climbing its way back up to the heights it fell from.

FIGURE 13.1 JetBlue's New Customer Bill of Rights and Publicity Campaigns Involving the Simpsons Were Measures Taken to Win Customers Back

CUSTOMER COMPLAINING BEHAVIOR

The first law of service quality and productivity might be: Do it right the first time. But we can't ignore the fact that failures continue to occur, sometimes for reasons outside the organization's control such as the ice storm that caused the JetBlue incident in our opening vignette. Many "moments of truth" in service encounters are vulnerable to breakdowns. Such distinctive service characteristics as real-time performance, customer involvement, and people as part of the product greatly increase the chance of service failures to occur. How well a firm handles complaints and resolves problems frequently determines whether it builds customer loyalty or watches its customers take their business elsewhere.

Customer Response Options to Service Failures

Chances are, you're not always satisfied with at least some of the services you receive. How do you respond to your dissatisfaction with these services? Do you complain informally to an employee, ask to speak to the manager, or file a complaint? Or, perhaps you just mutter darkly to yourself, grumble to your friends and family, and choose an alternative supplier the next time you need a similar type of service.

If you are among those who do not complain about poor service, you are not alone. Research around the globe has shown that most people will not complain, especially if they think it will do no good. Figure 13.2 depicts the courses of action a

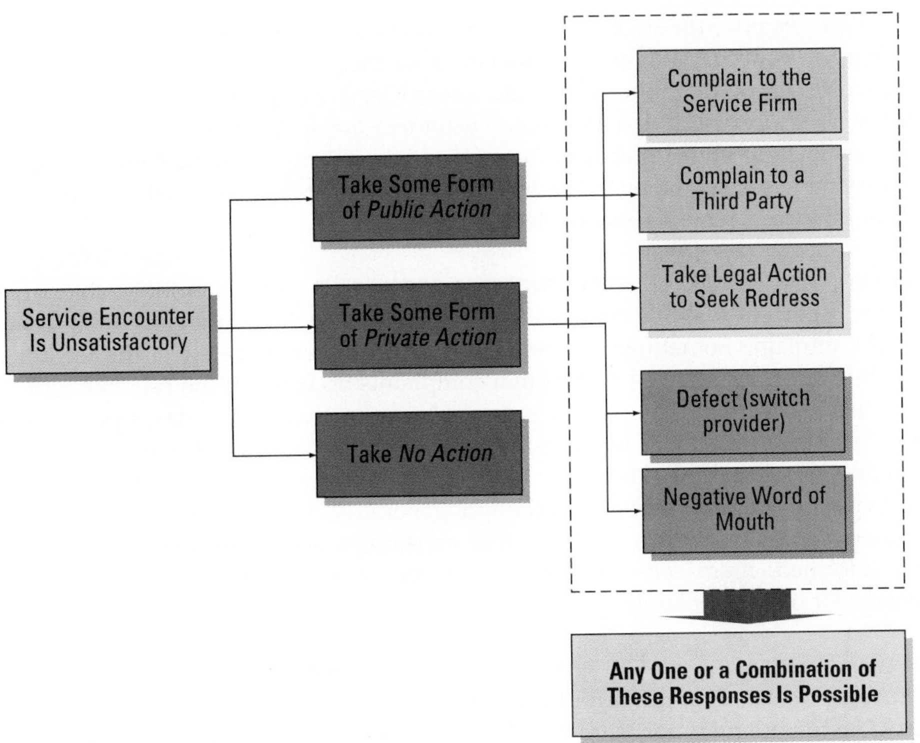

FIGURE 13.2 Customer Response Categories to Service Failures

customer may take in response to a service failure. This model suggests at least three major courses of action:

1. Take some form of public action (including complaining to the firm or to a third party, such as a customer advocacy group, a consumer affairs or regulatory agency, or even civil or criminal court).
2. Take some form of private action (including abandoning the supplier).
3. Take no action.

It's important to remember that a customer can pursue any one or a combination of alternatives. Managers need to be aware that the impact of a defection can go far beyond the loss of that person's future revenue stream. Angry customers often tell many other people about their problems.[2] The Internet allows unhappy customers to reach thousands of people by posting complaints on bulletin boards or setting up their own websites to publicize their bad experiences with specific organizations.[3] A popular strategy in the past when creating such sites was to add a derogatory suffix (such as "sucks") to the name of the offending company.

Understanding Customer Complaining Behavior

To be able to deal effectively with dissatisfied and complaining customers, managers need to understand key aspects of complaining behavior, starting with the questions posed below.

WHY DO CUSTOMERS COMPLAIN? In general, studies of consumer complaining behavior have identified four main purposes for complaining:

1. *Obtain restitution or compensation.* Consumers often complain to recover some economic loss by seeking a refund, compensation, and/or have the service performed again.[4]
2. *Vent their anger.* Some customers complain to rebuild self-esteem and/or to vent their anger and frustration. When service processes are bureaucratic and unreasonable, or when employees are rude, deliberately intimidating, or apparently uncaring, the customers' self-esteem, self-worth, or sense of fairness can be negatively affected. They may become angry and emotional.

3. *Help to improve the service.* When customers are highly involved with a service (e.g., at a college, an alumni association, or their main banking connection), they give feedback to try and contribute toward service improvements.
4. *For altruistic reasons.* Finally, some customers are motivated by altruistic reasons. They want to spare other customers from experiencing the same shortcomings, and they may feel bad if they fail to draw attention to a problem that will raise difficulties for others if it remains uncorrected.

WHAT PROPORTION OF UNHAPPY CUSTOMERS COMPLAIN? Research shows that on average, only 5 percent to 10 percent of customers who have been unhappy with a service actually complain.[5] Sometimes the percentage is far lower. A review of the records of a public bus company showed that formal complaints occurred at the rate of about three complaints for every million passenger trips. Assuming two trips a day, a person would need 1,370 years (roughly 27 lifetimes) to make a million trips. In other words, the rate of complaints was incredibly low, especially since public bus companies are rarely known for service excellence. However, although generally only a minority of dissatisfied customers complain, there's evidence that consumers across the world are becoming better informed, more self-confident, and more assertive about seeking satisfactory outcomes for their complaints.

WHY DON'T UNHAPPY CUSTOMERS COMPLAIN? TARP, a customer satisfaction and measurement firm, has identified a number of reasons why customers don't complain.[6] Customers may not want to take the time to write a letter, send an email, fill in a form, or make a phone call, particularly if they don't see the service as worth the effort. Many customers see the payoff as uncertain and believe that no one would be concerned about their problem or would be willing to resolve it. In some situations, people simply don't know where to go or what to do. Also, many people feel that complaining is unpleasant (Figure 13.3). They may be afraid of confrontation, especially if the complaint involves someone whom the customer knows and may have to deal with again.

Complaining behavior can be influenced by role perceptions and social norms. Customers are less likely to voice complaints in service situations in which they perceive they have "low power" (ability to influence or control the transaction).[7] This is particularly true when the problem involves professional service providers such as doctors, lawyers, or architects; because of their perceived expertise, social norms tend to discourage customer criticism of such individuals.

FIGURE 13.3 Customers Often View Complaining as Difficult and Unpleasant

Source: Courtesy of Images.com

WHO IS MOST LIKELY TO COMPLAIN? Research findings consistently show that people in higher socioeconomic levels are more likely to complain than those in lower levels. Their better education, higher income and greater social involvement give them the confidence, knowledge, and motivation to speak up when they encounter problems.[8] Further, those who complain also tend to be more knowledgeable about the product in question.

WHERE DO CUSTOMERS COMPLAIN? Studies show that the majority of complaints are made at the place where the service was received. One of the authors of this book recently completed a consulting project developing and implementing a customer feedback system and found that more than 99 percent of customer feedback was given face-to-face or over the phone to customer service representatives. Less than 1 percent of all complaints were submitted via email, letters, customer feedback cards, or the firm's website. A survey of airline passengers found that only 3 percent of respondents who were unhappy with their meal actually complained about it, and they all complained to the flight attendant. None complained to the company's headquarters or to a consumer affairs office.[9] Also, customers tend to use noninteractive channels to complain (e.g., email or letters) when they mainly want to vent their anger and frustration, but resort to interactive channels such as face-to-face or the telephone when they want a problem to be fixed or redressed.[10] In practice, even when customers do complain, managers often don't hear about the complaints made to frontline employees. Without a formal customer feedback system, only a tiny portion of the complaints may reach corporate headquarters.[11]

What Do Customer Expect Once They Have Made a Complaint?

Whenever a service failure occurs, people expect to be adequately compensated in a fair manner. However, recent studies show that many customers feel they have not been treated fairly nor received adequate recompense. When this happens, their reactions tend to be immediate, emotional, and enduring.[12]

Stephen Tax and Stephen Brown found that as much as 85 percent of the variation in the satisfaction with a service recovery was determined by three dimensions of fairness (see Figure 13.4):[13]

- ***Procedural justice*** concerns policies and rules that any customer has to go through to seek fairness. Customers expect the firm to assume responsibility, which is the key to the start of a fair procedure, followed by a convenient and responsive recovery process. That includes flexibility of the system and consideration of customer inputs into the recovery process.
- ***Interactional justice*** involves employees of the firm who provide the service recovery and their behavior toward the customer. Giving an explanation for the failure and making an effort to resolve the problem are very important. However, the recovery effort must be perceived as genuine, honest, and polite.
- ***Outcome justice*** concerns compensation a customer receives as a result of the losses and inconveniences incurred because of a service failure. This includes compensation for not only the failure but also time, effort, and energy spent during the process of service recovery.

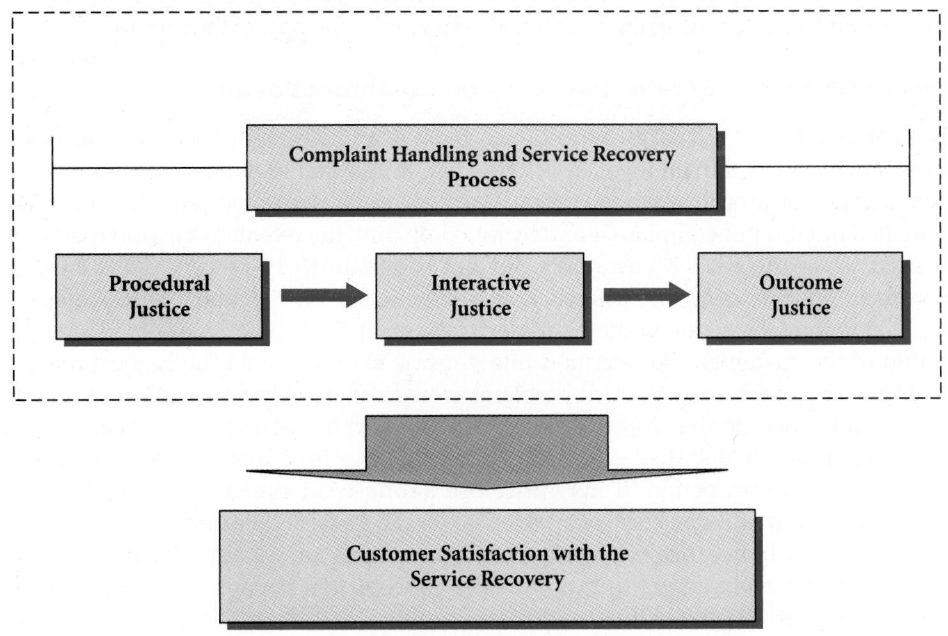

Source: Adapted from Stephen S. Tax and Stephen W. Brown, "Recovering and Learning from Service Failure," Sloan Management Review 49, no. 1 (Fall 1998), 75–88. Copyright © 1998 by Massachusetts Institute of Technology. All rights reserved.

FIGURE 13.4 Three Dimensions of Perceived Fairness in Service Recovery Processes

CUSTOMER RESPONSES TO EFFECTIVE SERVICE RECOVERY

"Thank Heavens for Complainers" was the provocative title of an article about customer complaining behavior, which also featured a successful manager exclaiming, "Thank goodness I've got a dissatisfied customer on the phone! The ones I worry about are the ones I never hear from."[14] Customers who do complain give a firm the chance to correct problems (including some the firm may not even know it has), restore relationships with the complainer, and improve future satisfaction for all.

Service recovery is an umbrella term for systematic efforts by a firm to correct a problem following a service failure and to retain a customer's goodwill. Service recovery efforts play a crucial role in achieving (or restoring) customer satisfaction and loyalty.[15] In every organization, things may occur that have a negative impact on relationships with customers. The true test of a firm's commitment to satisfaction and service quality isn't in the advertising promises, but in the way it responds when things go wrong for the customer. Success in this area includes employee training and motivation. Simon Bell and James Luddington have found that although complaints generally tend to have a negative effect on service personnel's commitment to customer service, employees with a positive attitude toward service and their own jobs may be more likely to view complaints as a potential source of improvement and to explore additional ways in which they can help customers.[16]

Effective service recovery requires thoughtful procedures for resolving problems and handling disgruntled customers. It is critical for firms to have effective recovery strategies, because even a single service problem under the following conditions can destroy a customer's confidence in a firm:

- The failure is totally outrageous (e.g., blatant dishonesty on the part of the supplier).
- The problem fits a pattern of failure rather than an isolated incident.
- The recovery efforts are weak, serving to compound the original problem rather than correct it.[17]

The risk of defection is high, especially when a variety of competing alternatives is available. One study of customer switching behavior in service industries found that close to 60 percent of all respondents who reported changing suppliers did so because of a service failure: 25 percent cited failures in the core service, 19 percent reported an unsatisfactory encounter with an employee, 10 percent reported an unsatisfactory response to a prior service failure, and 4 percent described unethical behavior on the part of the provider.[18]

Impact of Effective Service Recovery on Customer Loyalty

When complaints are satisfactorily resolved, there is a much higher chance that the customers involved will remain loyal. TARP research found that intentions to repurchase for different types of products ranged from 9 percent to 37 percent when customers were dissatisfied but did not complain. For a major complaint, the retention rate increased from 9 percent when dissatisfied customers did not complain to 19 percent if the customer complained and the company offered a sympathetic ear but was unable to resolve the complaint to the satisfaction of the customer. If the complaint could be resolved to the satisfaction of the customer, the retention rate jumped to 54 percent. The highest retention rate, 82 percent, was achieved when problems were fixed quickly—typically on the spot.[19]

We can conclude that complaint handling should be seen as a profit center, not a cost center. When a dissatisfied customer defects, the firm loses more than just the value of the next transaction. It may also lose a long-term stream of profits from that customer and from anyone else who switches suppliers or is deterred from doing business with that firm, because of negative comments from an unhappy friend. However, many organizations have yet to buy into the concept that it pays to invest in service recovery designed to protect those long-term profits.

The Service Recovery Paradox

The *service recovery paradox* refers to the effect that customers who experience a service failure and then have it resolved are sometimes more satisfied than customers who have had no problem in the first place.[20] Research has shown that the service recovery paradox is far from universal.[21] For example, a study of repeated service failures in a retail banking context showed that the service recovery paradox held for the first service failure that was recovered to customers' full satisfaction.[22] However, if a second service failure occurred, the paradox disappeared. It seems that customers may forgive a firm once, but become disillusioned if failures recur. Furthermore, the study also showed that customers' expectations were raised after they experienced a very good recovery; thus, excellent recovery becomes the standard they expect for dealing with future failures.

Whether a customer comes out delighted from a service recovery probably may also depend on the severity and "recoverability" of the failure—no one can replace spoiled wedding photos, a ruined holiday, or eliminate the consequences of a debilitating injury caused by service equipment. In such situations, it's hard to imagine anyone being truly delighted even when a most professional service recovery is conducted. Contrast these examples with a lost hotel reservation for which the recovery is an upgrade to a better room—or even a suite. When poor service is recovered by delivery of a superior product, you're usually delighted and probably hope for another lost reservation in the future.

The best strategy, of course, is to do it right the first time. As Michael Hargrove puts it, "Service recovery is turning a service failure into an opportunity you wish you never had."[23] Unfortunately, empirical evidence shows that some 40 percent to 60 percent of customers reported dissatisfaction with the service recovery processes they experienced.[24]

PRINCIPLES OF EFFECTIVE SERVICE RECOVERY SYSTEMS

Recognizing that current customers are a valuable asset base, managers need to develop effective procedures for service recovery following unsatisfactory experiences. Unfortunately, as already discussed, many service recoveries fail and some of the common causes for failure are shown in Service Perspective 13.1.

SERVICE PERSPECTIVE 13.1

COMMON SERVICE RECOVERY MISTAKES

Here are some typical service recovery mistakes made by many organizations:

- *Managers disregard evidence that shows how service recovery provides a significant financial return.* In recent years, many organizations have focused on cost cutting, paying only lip service to retaining their most profitable customers. On top of that, they have also lost sight of the need to respect all their customers.
- *Companies do not invest enough in actions that would prevent service issues.* Ideally, service planners address potential problems before they become customer problems. Although preventive measures don't eliminate the need for good service recovery systems, they greatly reduce the burden on frontline staff and the service recovery system in its entirety.
- *Customer service employees fail to display good attitudes.* The three most important things in service recovery are attitude, attitude, and attitude. No matter how well designed and well planned the service recovery system is, it won't work well without the friendly and proverbial smile-in-the-voice attitude from frontline staff.
- *Organizations fail to make it easy for customers to complain or give feedback.* Although some improvement can be seen, such as hotels and restaurants offering comment cards, little is done to communicate their simplicity and value to customers. Research shows that a large proportion of customers are unaware of the existence of a proper feedback system that could help them get their problems solved.

Source: Adapted from Rod Stiefbold, "Dissatisfied Customers Require Service Recovery Plans," *Marketing News*, 37, No. 22, October 27, 2003, 44–45.

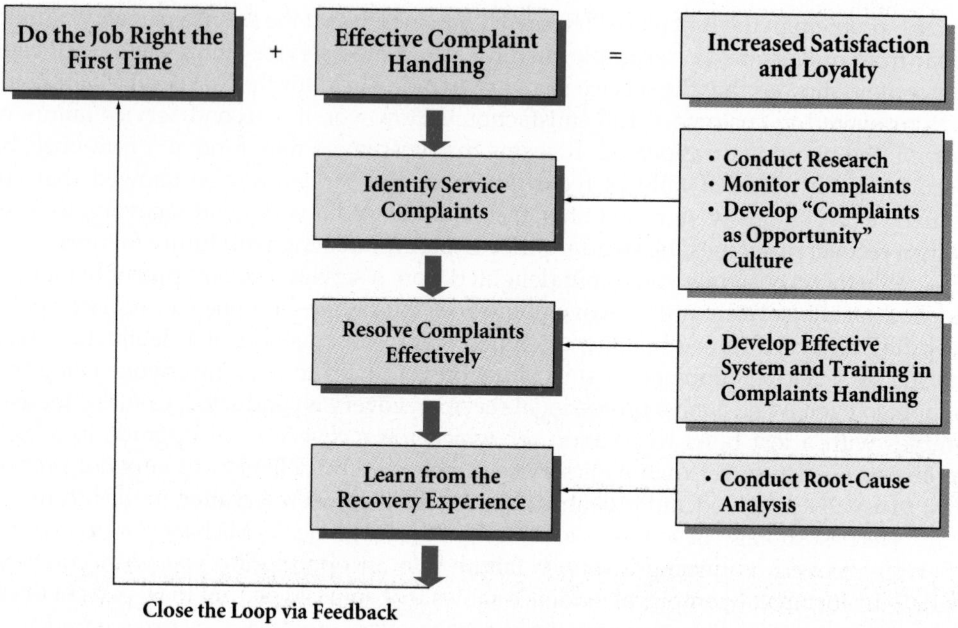

Do the Job Right the First Time + Effective Complaint Handling = Increased Satisfaction and Loyalty

- Identify Service Complaints ← • Conduct Research • Monitor Complaints • Develop "Complaints as Opportunity" Culture
- Resolve Complaints Effectively ← • Develop Effective System and Training in Complaints Handling
- Learn from the Recovery Experience ← • Conduct Root-Cause Analysis

Close the Loop via Feedback

FIGURE 13.5 Components of an Effective Service Recovery System

Source: Adapted from Christopher H. Lovelock, Paul G. Patterson, and Rhett Walker, *Services Marketing: An Asia-Pacific and Australian Perspec- tive*, 4th edition (Sydney: Prentice Hall Australia, 2007), p. 388.

Next, we discuss three guiding principles for how to get it right: (1) make it easy for customers to give feedback, (2) enable effective service recovery, and (3) establish appropriate compensation levels. A fourth principle, learning from customer feedback and driving service improvements, will be discussed in Chapter 14 in the context of customer feedback systems. The components of an effective service recovery system are shown in Figure 13.5.[25]

Make It Easy for Customers to Give Feedback

How can managers overcome unhappy customer's reluctance to complain about service failures? The best way is to address the reasons for their reluctance directly. Table 13.1 gives an overview of potential measures that can be taken to overcome those reasons we identified earlier in this chapter. Many companies have improved their complaint-collection procedures by adding special toll-free phone lines, links on

TABLE 13.1 Strategies to Reduce Customer Complaint Barriers

Complaint Barriers for Dissatisfied Customers	Strategies to Reduce These Barriers
Inconvenience • Difficult to find the right complaint procedure • Effort, e.g., writing and mailing a letter	Make feedback easy and convenient: • Print customer service hotline numbers, email website and/or postal addresses on all customer communications materials (letters, bills, brochures, website, phone book and yellow pages listings, etc.)
Doubtful payoff • Uncertain whether any or what action will be taken by the firm to address the issue the customer is unhappy with	Reassure customers that their feedback will be taken seriously and will pay off: • Have service recovery procedures in place and communicate this to customers, e.g., in customer newsletter and web site. • Feature service improvements that resulted from customer feedback.
Unpleasantness • Fear of being treated rudely • Fear of being hassled • Feeling embarrassed	Make providing feedback a positive experience: • Thank customers for their feedback (can be done publicly and in general by addressing the entire customer base). • Train service employees not to hassle and to make customers feel comfortable. • Allow for anonymous feedback.

their websites, prominently displayed customer comment cards in their branches, or even providing video terminals for recording complaints. In their customer newsletters, some companies feature service improvements that were the direct result of customer feedback under the motto "You told us, and we responded."

Enable Effective Service Recovery

Recovering from service failures takes more than just pious expressions of determination to resolve any problems that may occur. It requires commitment, planning, and clear guidelines. Specifically, effective service recovery procedures should be (1) proactive, (2) planned, (3) trained, and (4) empowered.

SERVICE RECOVERY SHOULD BE PROACTIVE. Service recovery needs to be initiated on the spot, ideally before customers have a chance to complain (see Best Practice in Action 13.1). Service personnel should be sensitized to signs of dissatisfaction and ask

BEST PRACTICE IN ACTION 13.1

Effective Service Recovery in Action

The lobby is deserted. It's not hard to overhear the conversation between the night manager at the Marriott Long Wharf Hotel in Boston and the late-arriving guest.

"Yes, Dr. Jones, we've been expecting you. I know you are scheduled to be here for three nights. I'm sorry to tell you, sir, but we are booked solid tonight. A large number of guests we assumed were checking out did not. Where is your meeting tomorrow, sir?"

The doctor told the clerk where it was.

"That's near the Omni Parker House! That's not very far from here. Let me call them and get you a room for the evening. I'll be right back."

A few minutes later, the desk clerk returned with the good news.

"They're holding a room for you at the Omni Parker House, sir. And, of course, we'll pick up the tab. I'll forward any phone calls that come here for you. Here's a letter that will explain the situation and expedite your check-in, along with my business card so you can call me directly here at the front desk if you have any problems."

The doctor's mood was moving from exasperation toward calm. But the desk clerk was not finished with the encounter. He reached into the cash drawer. "Here are two $10 bills. That should more than cover your cab fare from here to the Parker House and back again in the morning. We don't have a problem tomorrow night, just tonight. And here's a coupon that will get you a complimentary continental breakfast on our concierge level on the fifth floor tomorrow morning. . . and again, I am so sorry this happened."

As the doctor walks away, the night manager turns to the desk clerk, "Give him about 15 minutes and then call to make sure everything went okay."

A week later when it was still a peak period for hotels in that city, the same guest who had overheard the exchange is in a taxi, en route to the same hotel. Along the way, he tells about the great service recovery episode he had witnessed the week before. The two travelers arrive at the hotel and make their way to the front desk, ready to check in.

They are greeted with unexpected news: "I am so sorry, gentlemen. I know you were scheduled here for two nights. But we are booked solid tonight. Where is your meeting scheduled tomorrow?"

The would-be guests exchange a rueful glance as they give the desk clerk their future plans. "That's near the Méridien. Let me call over there and see if I can get you a room. It won't but take a minute." As the clerk walks away, the tale teller says, "I'll bet he comes back with a letter and a business card."

Sure enough, the desk clerk returns to deliver the solution; it's not a robotic script but all the elements from the previous week's show are on display. What the tale teller thought was pure desk-clerk initiative the previous week, he now realizes was planned, a spontaneous yet predetermined response to a specific category of service problem.

Source: Ron Zemke and Chip R. Bell, *Knock Your Socks Off Service Recovery.* New York: AMACOM, 2000, 59–60.

whether customers might be experiencing a problem. For example, the waiter may ask a guest who has only eaten half of his dinner, "Is everything all right, sir?" The guest may say, "Yes, thank you, I am not very hungry," or "The steak is well done, but I had asked for medium rare, plus it is very salty." The latter response then gives the waiter a chance to recover the service, rather than have an unhappy diner leave the restaurant and potentially not return.

RECOVERY PROCEDURES NEED TO BE PLANNED. Contingency plans have to be developed for service failures, especially for those that can occur regularly and cannot be designed out of the system.[26] Revenue management practices in the travel and hospitality industries often result in overbooking, and travelers are denied boarding or hotel guests are "walked" even though they had confirmed seats or reservations. To simplify the task of frontline staff, firms should identify the most common service problems such as overbooking and develop predetermined solution sets for employees to follow. In contact centers, the customer service representatives have prepared scripts to guide them in a service recovery situation.

RECOVERY SKILLS MUST BE TAUGHT. As a customer, you may quickly feel insecure at the point of service failure because things are not turning out as anticipated. So you look to an employee for assistance. But are they willing and able to help you? Effective training builds confidence and competence among frontline staff, enabling them to turn distress into delight.[27]

RECOVERY REQUIRES EMPOWERED EMPLOYEES. Service recovery efforts should be flexible, and employees should be empowered to use their judgment and communication skills to develop solutions that will satisfy complaining customers.[28] This is especially true for out-of-the-ordinary failures for which a firm may not have developed and trained potential solution sets on. Employees need to have the authority to make decisions and spend money in order to resolve service problems promptly and recover customer goodwill. At the Ritz-Carlton and Sheraton hotels, employees are given the freedom to be proactive, rather than reactive. They take ownership of the situation and help resolve the customers' problems to the best of their ability.

How Generous Should Compensation Be?

Clearly, vastly different costs are associated with possible recovery strategies. How much compensation should a firm offer when there has been a service failure? Or would an apology be sufficient instead? The following rules of thumb can help managers to answer these questions:

- **What is the positioning of your firm?** If a firm is known for service excellence and charges a high premium for quality, then customers will expect service failures to be rare, so the firm should make a demonstrable effort to recover the few failures that do occur and be prepared to offer something of significant value. In a more downscale, mass market business, customers are likely to consider something quite modest, such as a free coffee or dessert as fair compensation.
- **How severe was the service failure?** The general guideline is "Let the punishment fit the crime." Customers expect little for minor inconveniences, but a much more significant compensation if major damage in terms of time, effort, annoyance, or anxiety was created by the failure.
- **Who is the affected customer?** Long-term customers and those who spend heavily at a service provider expect more, and it is worth making an effort to save their business. One-time customers tend to be less demanding and have less economic importance to the firm. Hence, compensation can be less, but should still be fair.

There is always the possibility that a first-time user will become a repeat customer if he or she is treated well.

The overall rule of thumb for compensation at service failures should be "well dosed generosity." Being perceived as stingy adds insult to injury, and the firm will probably be better off apologizing rather than offering a minimal compensation.

Doing too much is also not advisable. Overly generous compensation is not only expensive, customers may even interpret such a response negatively raising questions in their minds about the soundness of the business and leading them to become suspicious about the underlying motives. Customers may worry about the implications for the employee as well as for the business. Also, overgenerosity does not seem to result in higher repeat purchase rates than simply offering a fair compensation.[29] There is a risk, too, that a reputation for overgenerosity may encourage dishonest customers to actively "seek" service failures.

Dealing with Complaining Customers

Both managers and frontline employees must be prepared to deal with distressed customers, including jaycustomers who become confrontational in unacceptable ways and sometimes behave in insulting ways toward service personnel who aren't at fault in any way. Service Perspective 13.2 provides specific guidelines for effective problem resolution, designed to help calm upset customers and to deliver a resolution they will see as fair and satisfying.

SERVICE GUARANTEES

One way for particularly customer-focused firms to institutionalize professional complaint handling and effective service recovery is service guarantees. In fact, a growing number of companies offer customers a service guarantee, promising that if service delivery fails to meet predefined standards, the customer will be entitled to one or more forms of compensation, such as an easy-to-claim replacement, refund, or credit. A well-designed service guarantee not only facilitates effective service recovery, but also institutionalizes learning from service failures and subsequent system improvements.[30]

The Power of Service Guarantees

Christopher Hart declares that service guarantees are powerful tools for both promoting and achieving service quality for the following reasons:[31]

1. Guarantees force firms to focus on what their customers want and expect in each element of the service.
2. Guarantees set clear standards, telling customers and employees alike what the company stands for. Payouts to compensate customers for poor service cause managers to take guarantees seriously, because they highlight the financial costs of quality failures.
3. Guarantees require the development of systems for generating meaningful customer feedback and acting on it.
4. Guarantees force service organizations to understand why they fail and encourage them to identify and overcome potential fail points.
5. Guarantees build "marketing muscle" by reducing the risk of the purchase decision and building long-term loyalty.

From the customer's perspective, the primary function of service guarantees is to lower the perceived risks associated with purchase.[32] The presence of a guarantee may also make it easier for customers to complain and more likely that they will do so, because they will anticipate that frontline employees will be prepared to resolve the problem and provide appropriate compensation. Sara Björlin Lidén and Per Skålén found that even when dissatisfied customers were unaware that a service guarantee existed

SERVICE PERSPECTIVE 13.2

GUIDELINES FOR THE FRONT LINE: HOW TO HANDLE CUSTOMER COMPLAINTS

1. ***Act fast.*** If the complaint is made during service delivery, then time is of the essence to achieve a full recovery. When complaints are made after the fact, many companies have established policies of responding within 24 hours, or sooner. Even when full resolution is likely to take longer, fast acknowledgment remains very important.
2. ***Acknowledge the customer's feelings.*** Do this either tacitly or explicitly (for example, "I can understand why you're upset"). This action helps to build rapport, the first step in rebuilding a bruised relationship.
3. ***Don't argue with customers.*** The goal should be to gather facts to reach a mutually acceptable solution, not to win a debate or prove that the customer is an idiot. Arguing gets in the way of listening and seldom diffuses anger.
4. ***Show that you understand the problem from each customer's point of view.*** Seeing situations through the customers' eyes is the only way to understand what they think has gone wrong and why they're upset. Service personnel should avoid jumping to conclusions with their own interpretations.
5. ***Clarify the truth and sort out the cause.*** A failure may result from inefficiency of service, misunderstanding by customers, or the misbehavior of a third party. If you've done something wrong, apologize immediately. The more the customer can forgive you, the less he or she will expect to be compensated. Don't be defensive; acting defensively may suggest that the organization has something to hide or is reluctant to explore the situation fully.
6. ***Give customers the benefit of the doubt.*** Not all customers are truthful and not all complaints are justified. However, customers should be treated as though they have a valid complaint until clear evidence to the contrary emerges. If a lot of money is at stake (as in insurance claims or potential lawsuits), careful investigation is warranted. If the amount involved is small, it may not be worth haggling over a refund or other compensation. However, it's still a good idea to check records to see if there is a past history of dubious complaints by the same customer.
7. ***Propose the steps needed to solve the problem.*** When instant solutions aren't possible, telling customers how the organization plans to proceed shows that corrective action is being taken. It also sets expectations about the time involved (so firms should be careful not to overpromise).
8. ***Keep customers informed of progress.*** Nobody likes being left in the dark. Uncertainty breeds anxiety and stress. People tend to be more accepting of disruptions if they know what's going on and receive periodic progress reports.
9. ***Consider compensation.*** When customers do not receive the service outcomes they believe they have paid for or have suffered serious inconvenience and/or loss of time and money because the service failed, either a monetary payment or an offer of equivalent service in kind is appropriate. This type of recovery strategy may also reduce the risk of legal action by an angry customer. Service guarantees often lay out in advance what such compensation will be, and the firm should ensure that all guarantees are met.
10. ***Persevere to regain customer goodwill.*** When customers have been disappointed, one of the biggest challenges is to restore their confidence and preserve the relationship for the future. Perseverance may be required to defuse customers' anger and to convince them that actions are being taken to avoid a recurrence of the problem. Truly exceptional recovery efforts can be extremely effective in building loyalty and referrals.
11. ***Check the service delivery system and pursue eminence.*** After the customer has left, you should check to determine whether the service failure was caused by accidental mistakes or system defects. Take advantage of every complaint to perfect the whole service system. Even if the complaint is found to be a result of a misunderstanding by customer, this implies that some part of your communication system is ineffective.

before making their complaint, they were positively impressed to learn that the company has a preplanned procedure for handling failures and to find that their complaints were taken seriously.[33]

The benefits of service guarantees can be seen clearly in the case of Hampton Inn's "100% Hampton Guarantee" ("If you're not 100% satisfied, you don't pay"—see Figure 13.6), which has now been extended to Embassy Suites, and Homewood Suites.[34] As a business-building program, Hampton's strategy of offering to refund the cost of the room to a guest who expresses dissatisfaction has attracted new customers and also served as a powerful retention device. People choose to stay at a Hampton Inn because they are confident they will be satisfied. At least as important, the guarantee has become a vital tool to help managers identify new opportunities for quality improvement.

In discussing the impact on staff and managers, the vice president of marketing for Hampton Inn stated, "Designing the guarantee made us understand what made guests satisfied, rather than what *we thought* made them satisfied." It became imperative that everyone from reservationists and frontline employees, to general managers and personnel at corporate headquarters, listen carefully to guests, anticipate their needs to the greatest extent possible, and remedy problems quickly so that guests were satisfied with the solution. Viewing a hotel's function in this customer-centric way had a profound impact on the way the firm conducted business.

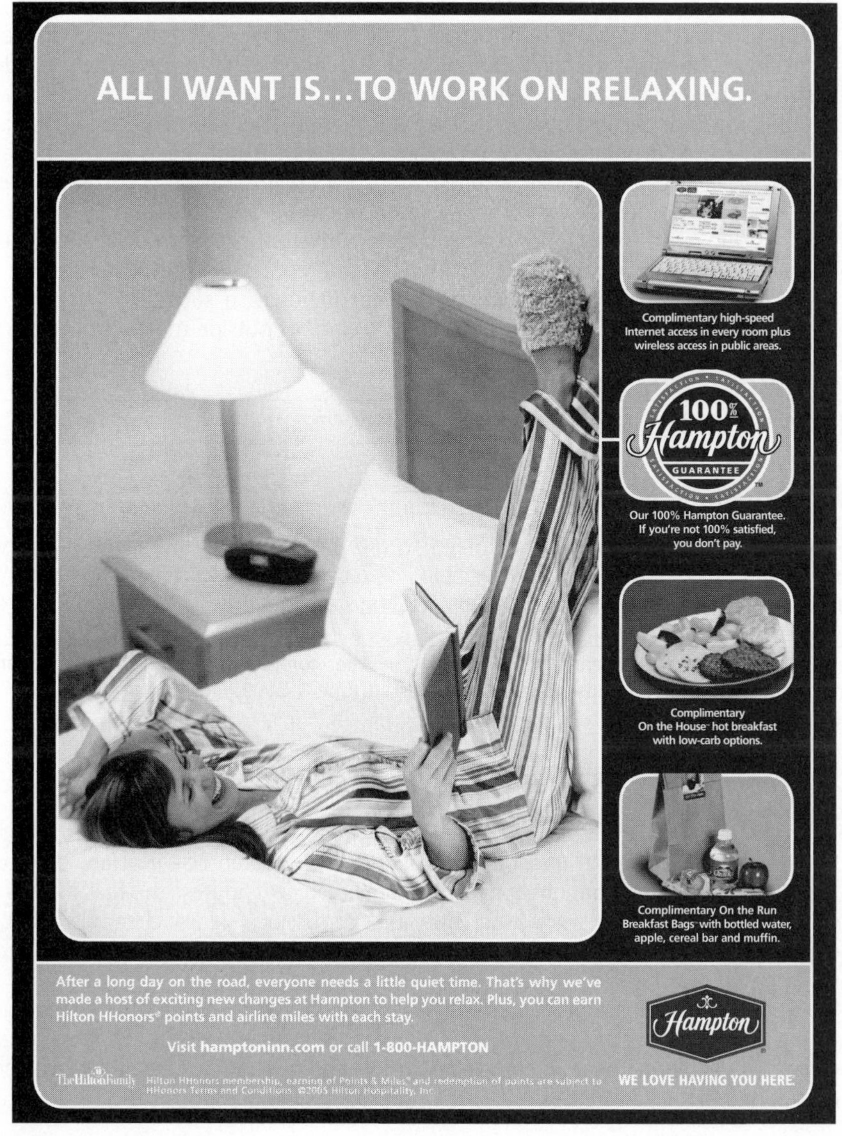

Source: Courtesy of Hilton.

FIGURE 13.6 Hampton Inn Includes Its "100% Satisfaction Guarantee" in Its Advertising

The guarantee "turned up the pressure in the hose," as one manager put it, showing where "leaks" existed and providing the financial incentive to plug them. As a result, the guarantee has had an important impact on product consistency and service delivery across the Hampton Inn chain. Finally, studies have shown a dramatically positive effect of the "100% Hampton Guarantee" on financial performance.

How to Design Service Guarantees

Some guarantees are simple and unconditional. Others appear to have been written by lawyers and contain many restrictions. Compare the examples in Service Perspective 13.3 and ask yourself which guarantees instill trust and confidence in you and would make you like to do business with that firm.

SERVICE PERSPECTIVE 13.3

EXAMPLES OF SERVICE GUARANTEES

United States Postal Service Express Mail Guarantee

Service Guarantee: Express Mail international mailings are not covered by this service agreement. Military shipments delayed due to customs inspections are also excluded. If the shipment is mailed at a designated USPS Express Mail facility on or before the specified deposit time for overnight delivery to the addressee, delivery to the addressee or agent will be attempted before the applicable guaranteed time. Signature of the addressee's agent, or delivery employee is required upon delivery. If a delivery attempt is not made by the guaranteed time and the mailer files a claim for a refund, the USPS will refund the postage unless the delay was caused by: proper retention for law enforcement purposes; strike or work stoppage; late deposit of shipment; forwarding, return, incorrect address, or incorrect ZIP code; delay or cancellation of flights; governmental action beyond the control of the Postal Service or air carriers; war, insurrection, or civil disturbance; breakdowns of a substantial portion of the USPS transportation network resulting from events or factors outside the control of the Postal Service or Acts of God.

Source: Printed on back of Express Mail receipt, January 2006.

L.L. Bean's Guarantee

Our Guarantee. Our products are guaranteed to give 100 percent satisfaction in every way. Return anything purchased from us at any time if it proves otherwise. We do not want you to have anything from L.L. Bean that is not completely satisfactory.

Source: Printed in all L.L. Bean catalogs and on the company's website, www.llbean.com/customerService/aboutLLBean/guarantee.html, accessed June 1, 2009.

MFA Group Inc. (a Professional Recruitment Agency)

We "put our money where our mouth is" in two ways, not just one:

1. Money back: We offer an unconditional money back guarantee—if at any point during the search process you are unhappy with progress, simply address the fact with us and if you are still not 100 percent satisfied after that discussion, we will cheerfully and unconditionally refund every cent you have paid as a retainer. No quibble, no hassle, guaranteed period.
2. Twelve-month candidate guarantee: All candidates placed by us are guaranteed for a full 12 months. If, during this period they leave your firm, for any reason whatsoever, we will conduct an additional search, completely free of charge, until a suitable replacement has been found.

Source: MGA Group's website, http://www.mfagroup.com/recruiting.htm, accessed June 1, 2009.

Excerpt from the "Quality Standard Guarantees" from an Office Services Company

- We guarantee six-hour turnaround on documents of two pages or less. . . (does not include client subsequent changes or equipment failures).
- We guarantee there will be a receptionist to greet you and your visitors during normal business hours. . . (short breaks of less than five minutes are not subject to this guarantee).
- You will not be obligated to pay rent for any day on which there is not a manager on site to assist you (lunch and reasonable breaks are expected and not subject to this guarantee).

Source: Reproduced in Eileen C. Shapiro, *Fad Surfing in the Boardroom.* Reading, MA: Addison-Wesley, 1995, 18.

The Bugs Burger Bug Killer Guarantee (a Pest Control Company)

- You don't owe us a penny until all the pests on your premises have been eradicated.
- If you're ever dissatisfied with the BBBK's service, you will receive a refund for as much as 12 months of service—plus fees for another exterminator of your choice for the next year.
- If a guest spots a pest on your premises, the exterminator will pay for the guest's meal or room, send a letter of apology, and pay for a future meal or stay.
- If your premises are closed down because of the presence of roaches or rodents, BBBK will pay any fines, as well as all lost profit, plus $5,000.

Source: Reproduced in Christopher W. Hart, "The Power of Unconditional Service Guarantees," *Harvard Business Review*, July–August 1990.

All three guarantees—from L.L. Bean, MFA Group, and BBBK—are powerful, unconditional, and instill trust. The other two are weakened by the many conditions. The United States Postal Service has added six new conditions in recent years. Hart argues that service guarantees should be designed to meet the following criteria:[35]

1. **Unconditional**—Whatever is promised in the guarantee must be totally unconditional, and there should not be any element of surprise for the customer.
2. **Easy to understand and communicate** to the customer so that he is clearly aware of the benefits that can be gained from the guarantee.
3. **Meaningful to the customer** in that the guarantee is for something important to the customer, and the compensation should be more than adequate to cover the service failure.[36]
4. **Easy to invoke**—It should be easy for the customer to invoke the guarantee.
5. **Easy to collect on**—If a service failure occurs, the customer should be able to easily collect on the guarantee without any problems.
6. **Credible**—The guarantee should be believable.

Is Full Satisfaction the Best You Can Guarantee?

Full satisfaction guarantees generally have been considered the best possible design. However, it has been suggested that the ambiguity associated with such guarantees can lead to discounting of their perceived value. Customers may raise questions such as "What does full satisfaction mean?" or "Can I invoke a guarantee when I am dissatisfied, although the fault does not lie with the service firm?"[37] The *combined guarantee* addresses this issue by combining the wide scope of a full satisfaction guarantee with the low uncertainty of specific performance standards.[38] The type of guarantee has been shown to be superior to the pure full satisfaction or attribute-specific guarantee designs. Specific performance standards are guaranteed (e.g., on-time delivery), but should the consumer be dissatisfied with any other element of the service, the full-satisfaction coverage of the combined guarantee applies. Table 13.2 shows examples of the various types of guarantees.

TABLE 13.2 Types of Service Guarantees

Term	Guarantee Scope	Example
Single attribute-specific guarantee	One key attribute of the service is covered by the guarantee.	"Any of three specified popular pizzas is guaranteed to be served within 10 minutes of ordering on working days between 12 A.M. and 2 P.M. If the pizza is late, the customer's next order is free."
Multiattribute-specific guarantee	A few important attributes of the service are covered by the guarantee.	Minneapolis Marriott's guarantee: "Our quality commitment to you is to provide: • A friendly, efficient check-in • A clean, comfortable room, where everything works • A friendly efficient check-out If we, in your opinion, do not deliver on this commitment, we will give you $20 in cash. No questions asked. It is your interpretation."
Full-satisfaction guarantee	All aspects of the service are covered by the guarantee. There are no exceptions.	Lands' End's guarantee: "If you are not completely satisfied with any item you buy from us, at any time during your use of it, return it and we will refund your full purchase price. We mean every word of it. Whatever. Whenever. Always. But to make sure this is perfectly clear, we've decided to simplify it further. GUARANTEED. Period."
Combined guarantee	All aspects of the service are covered by the full-satisfaction promise of the guarantee. Explicit minimum performance standards on important attributes are included in the guarantee to reduce uncertainty.	Datapro Information Services guarantees "to deliver the report on time, to high quality standards, and to the contents outlined in this proposal. Should we fail to deliver according to this guarantee, *or should you be dissatisfied with any aspect of our work,* you can deduct any amount from the final payment which is deemed as fair."

Source: Adapted from Jochen Wirtz and Doreen Kum, "Designing Service Guarantees—Is Full Satisfaction the Best You Can Guarantee?" *Journal of Services Marketing,* 15, no. 4 (2001): 282–299.

Is It Always Appropriate to Introduce a Service Guarantee?

Managers should think carefully about their firm's strengths and weaknesses when deciding whether or not to introduce a service guarantee. Amy Ostrom and Christopher Hart identified a number of situations in which a guarantee may be inappropriate:[39]

- Companies that already have a strong reputation for service excellence may not need a guarantee. In fact, it might even be incongruent with their image to offer one as it might even confuse the market.[40] Rather, best in class service firms will be expected to do what is right without offering a service guarantee.
- In contrast, a firm whose service currently is poor must first work to improve quality to a level above what is guaranteed. Otherwise, too many customers will invoke the guarantee with serious cost implications.
- Service firms whose quality is truly uncontrollable because of external forces would be foolish to consider a guarantee. For example, when Amtrak realized that it was paying out substantial refunds because it lacked sufficient control over its railroad infrastructure, it was forced to drop a service guarantee that included reimbursement of fares in the event of unpunctual train service.
- In a market in which consumers see little financial, personal, or physiological risk associated with purchasing and using a service, a guarantee adds little value but still costs money to design, implement, and manage.

Furthermore, in markets where little perceived difference exists in service quality among competing firms, the first firm to institute a guarantee may be able to obtain a first mover advantage and create a valued differentiation for its services. If more than one competitor already has a guarantee in place, offering a guarantee may become a qualifier for the industry, and the only real way to make an impact is to launch a highly distinctive guarantee beyond what is already offered by competitors.[41]

DISCOURAGING ABUSE AND OPPORTUNISTIC CUSTOMER BEHAVIOR

Throughout this chapter, we advocate that firms should welcome complaints and invocations of service guarantees and even encourage them. But while we discussed the importance of professional complaint handling and service recovery, we have to acknowledge that not all complaints are honest. When firms have generous service recovery policies or offer guarantees, there is always the fear that some customers may take advantage. Also, not all complaining customers are right or reasonable in their behavior, and some may actually be the cause of complaints by other customers. We refer to such people as *jaycustomers.*

Visitors to North America from other English-speaking countries often are puzzled by the term "jaywalker," that distinctively American word used to describe people who cross streets at unauthorized places or in a dangerous manner. The prefix "jay" comes from a nineteenth-century slang term for a stupid person. We can create a whole vocabulary of derogatory terms by adding the prefix "jay" to existing nouns and verbs. How about "jaycustomer," for example, to denote someone who "jayuses" a service or "jayconsumes" a physical product (and then "jaydisposes" of it afterward)? We define a jaycustomer as someone who acts in a thoughtless or abusive way, causing problems for the firm, its employees, and other customers.

Customers who act in uncooperative or abusive ways are a problem for any organization. However, they have even more potential for mischief in service businesses, particularly those in which many other customers are present in the service factory. As you know from your own experience, other people's behavior can affect your enjoyment of a service. If you like classical music and attend symphony concerts, you expect audience members to keep quiet during the performance, not spoiling the experience for others by talking, coughing loudly, or failing to turn off their cell phones. By contrast, a silent audience would be deadly during a rock concert or team sports event, where active audience participation adds to the excitement. There's a fine line, however, between spectator enthusiasm and abusive behavior by supporters of rival sports teams. Firms that fail to deal effectively with customer misbehaviors risk damaging their relationships with all the other customers they'd like to keep.

Every service has its share of jaycustomers, but opinions on this topic seem to polarize around two opposing views of the situation. One is denial: "the customer is king and can do no wrong." The other view sees the marketplace of customers as positively overpopulated with nasty people who cannot be trusted to behave in ways that self-respecting service providers should expect and require. The first viewpoint has received wide publicity in gung-ho management books and in motivational presentations to captive groups of employees. But the second view often appears dominant among cynical managers and employees who have been burned at some point by customer misbehaviors. As with so many opposing viewpoints in life, there are important grains of truth in both perspectives, however, it is clear that no self-respecting firm wants an ongoing relationship with an abusive customer.

Every service has its share of jaycustomers. Jaycustomers are undesirable. At best, a firm should avoid attracting them in the first place, and at worst, a firm needs to control or prevent their abusive behavior. Let us first describe the main types of jaycustomers before we discuss how to deal with them.

Seven Types of Jaycustomers[42]

Defining a problem is the first step in resolving it, so let's start by considering the different types of jaycustomers. We've identified seven broad categories and given them generic names, but many customer contact personnel have come up with their own special terms.

THE CHEAT. There are many ways in which customers can cheat service firms. Cheating ranges from writing compensation letters with the sole purpose of exploiting service recovery policies and cheating on service guarantees, to inflating or faking insurance claims and "wardrobing" (e.g., using an evening dress or tuxedo for an evening and then returning it back to the retailer).[43] The following quotes describe the thinking of these customers nicely:

> On checking in to a hotel I noticed that they had a 100 percent satisfaction or your money back guarantee, I just couldn't resist the opportunity to take advantage of it, so on checking out I told the receptionist that I wanted a refund as the sound of the traffic kept me awake all night. They gave me a refund, no questions asked. These companies can be so stupid they need to be more alert.[44]

> I've complained that service was too slow, too quick, too hot, too cold, too bright, too dark, too friendly, too impersonal, too public, too private... it doesn't matter really, as long as you enclose a receipt with your letter, you just get back a standard letter and gift coupon.[45]

Firms cannot easily check whether a customer is faking dissatisfaction or truly is unhappy. At the end of this section, we will discuss how to deal with this type of consumer fraud.

THE THIEF. The thief jaycustomer has no intention of paying and sets out to steal goods and services (or to pay less than full price by switching price tickets, or contesting bills on baseless grounds). Shoplifting is a major problem in retail stores. What retailers euphemistically call "shrinkage" is estimated to cost them huge sums of money in annual revenues. Many services lend themselves to clever schemes for avoiding payment. For those with technical skills, it's sometimes possible to bypass electricity meters, access telephone lines free of charge, or circumvent normal cable TV feeds. Riding free on public transportation, sneaking into movie theaters, or not paying for restaurant meals are also popular. And we mustn't forget the use of fraudulent forms of payment such as using stolen credit cards or checks drawn on accounts without any funds. Finding out how people steal a service is the first step in preventing theft or catching thieves and, where appropriate, prosecuting them. However, managers should try not to alienate honest customers by degrading their service experiences. And provision must be made for honest but absent-minded customers who forget to pay.

THE RULEBREAKER. Just as highways need safety regulations (including "Don't Jaywalk"), many service businesses need to establish rules of behavior for employees and customers to guide them safely through the various steps of the service encounter. Some of these rules are imposed by government agencies for health and safety reasons. The sign found in many restaurants that states "No shirt, no shoes, no service" demonstrates a health-related regulation. And air travel provides one of the best of examples of rules designed to ensure safety—there are few other environments outside prison where healthy, mentally competent, adult customers are quite so constrained (albeit for good reason).

In addition to enforcing government regulations, suppliers often impose their own rules to facilitate smooth operations, avoid unreasonable demands on employees, prevent misuse of products and facilities, protect themselves legally, and discourage individual customers from misbehaving. Ski resorts, for instance, are getting tough on careless skiers who pose risks to both themselves and others. Collisions can cause serious injury and even kill. So ski patrol members must be safety-oriented and sometimes take on a policing role. Just as dangerous drivers can lose their licenses, so can dangerous skiers lose their lift tickets.

At Vail and Beaver Creek in Colorado, ski patrollers once revoked nearly 400 lift tickets in just a single weekend. At Winter Park, Colorado, skiers who lose their passes for dangerous behavior may have to attend a 45-minute safety class before they can get their passes back. Ski patrollers at Vermont's Okemo Mountain may issue warnings to reckless skiers by attaching a bright orange sticker to their lift tickets. If pulled over again for inappropriate behavior, such skiers may be escorted off the mountain and banned for a day or more. "We're not trying to be Gestapos on the slopes," says the resort's marketing director, "just trying to educate people."

How should a firm deal with rulebreakers? Much depends on which rules have been broken. In the case of legally enforceable ones—theft, bad debts, trying to take guns on aircraft—the courses of action need to be laid down explicitly to protect employees and to punish or discourage wrongdoing by customers.

Company rules are a little more ambiguous. Are they really necessary in the first place? If not, the firm should get rid of them. Do they deal with health and safety? If so, educating customers about the rules should reduce the need for taking corrective action. The same is true for rules designed to protect the comfort and enjoyment of all customers. There are also unwritten social norms such as "thou shalt not cut in line" (although this is a much stronger cultural expectation in the United States or Canada than in many countries, as any visitor to Paris or Hong Kong Disneyland can attest). Other customers often can be relied upon to help service personnel enforce rules that affect everybody else; they may even take the initiative in doing so.

There are risks attached to making lots of rules. They can make an organization appear bureaucratic and overbearing. And they can transform employees—whose orientation should be to serve customers—into police officers who see (or are told to see) their most important task as enforcing all the rules. The fewer the rules, the more explicit the important ones can be.

THE BELLIGERENT. You've probably seen him (or her) in a store, at the airport, in a hotel, or restaurant—red in the face and shouting angrily or perhaps icily calm and mouthing off insults, threats, and obscenities. Things don't always work as they should: machines break down, service is clumsy, customers are ignored, a flight is delayed, an order is delivered incorrectly, staff are unhelpful, a promise is broken. Or perhaps the customer in question is expressing resentment at being told to abide by the rules. Service personnel often are abused, even when they are not to blame. If an employee lacks authority to resolve the problem, the belligerent may become madder still, even to the point of physical attack. Unfortunately, when angry customers rant at service personnel, the latter sometimes respond in kind, thus escalating the confrontation and reducing the likelihood of resolution (Figure 13.7).

Drunkenness and drug abuse add extra layers of complication. Organizations that care about their employees go to great efforts to develop skills in dealing with these difficult situations. Training exercises that involve role-playing help employees develop the self-confidence and assertiveness they need to deal with upset, belligerent customers (sometimes referred to as "irates"). Employees also need to learn how to defuse anger, calm anxiety, and comfort distress (particularly when there is good reason for the customer to be upset with the organization's performance).

"We seem to live in an age of rage," declare Stephen Grove, Raymond Fisk, and Joby John, noting a general decline in civility.[46] They suggest that rage behaviors are learned via socialization as appropriate responses to certain situations. Research by Roger Bougie and his colleagues determined that anger and dissatisfaction are qualitatively different emotions. Whereas dissatisfied customers had a feeling of unfulfillment or "missing out" and wanted to find out who or what was responsible for the event, angry customers were thinking how unfair the situation was, sought to get back at the organization, and wanted to hurt someone.[47]

The problem of "Air Rage" has attracted particular attention in recent years because of the risks it poses to innocent people (see Service Perspective 13.4). Blair Berkley and Mohammad

FIGURE 13.7 Confrontations between Customers and Service Employees Can Easily Escalate

SERVICE PERSPECTIVE 13.4

AIR RAGE: UNRULY PASSENGERS POSE A CONTINUING PROBLEM

Joining the term "road rage"—coined in 1988 to describe angry, aggressive drivers who threaten other road users—is "air rage," describing the behavior of violent, unruly passengers who endanger flight attendants, pilots, and other passengers. Incidents of air rage are perpetrated by only a tiny fraction of all airline passengers—reportedly about 5,000 times a year—but each incident in the air may affect the comfort and safety of hundreds of other people.

Although terrorism is an ongoing concern, out-of-control passengers pose a serious threat to safety, too. On a flight from Orlando to London, a drunken passenger smashed a video screen and began ramming a window, telling fellow passengers they were about to "get sucked out and die." The crew strapped him down, and the aircraft made an unscheduled landing in Bangor, Maine, where U.S. marshals arrested him. Another unscheduled stop in Bangor involved a drug smuggler flying from Jamaica to the Netherlands. When a balloon filled with cocaine ruptured in his stomach, he went berserk, pounding a bathroom door to pieces and grabbing a female passenger by the throat.

On a flight from London to Spain, a passenger who was already drunk at the time of boarding became angry when a flight attendant told him not to smoke in the lavatory and then refused to serve him another drink. Later, he smashed her over the head with a vodka bottle before being restrained by other passengers (she required 18 stitches to close the wound). Other dangerous incidents have included throwing hot coffee at flight attendants, head-butting a copilot, trying to break into the cockpit, throwing a flight attendant across three rows of seats, and attempting to open an emergency door in flight. On a U.S. domestic flight with a tragic outcome, a violent passenger was restrained and ultimately suffocated by other passengers after he kicked through the cockpit door of an airliner 20 minutes before it was scheduled to land in Salt Lake City.

A growing number of carriers are taking air rage perpetrators to court. Northwest Airlines permanently blacklisted three violent travelers from flying on its aircraft. British Airways gives out "warning cards" to any passenger getting dangerously out of control. Celebrities are not immune to air rage. Rock star Courtney Love blamed her "potty mouth" after being arrested on arrival in London for disruptive behavior on board a flight from Los Angeles. Some airlines carry physical restraints to subdue out-of-control passengers until they can be handed over to airport authorities.

In April 2000, U.S. Congress increased the civil penalty for air rage from $1,100 to $25,000 in an attempt to discourage passengers from misbehaving. Criminal penalties—a $10,000 fine and up to 20 years in jail—can also be imposed for the most serious incidents. Some airlines have been reluctant to publicize this information for fear of appearing confrontational or intimidating. However, the visible implementation of antiterrorist security precautions have made it more acceptable to tighten enforcement of procedures designed to control and punish air rage.

What causes air rage? Psychological feelings of a loss of control or problems with authority figures may be causal factors for angry behavior in many service settings. Researchers suggest that air travel, in particular, has become increasingly stressful as a result of crowding and longer flights; the airlines themselves may have contributed to the problem by squeezing rows of seats more tightly together and failing to explain delays. Findings suggest that risk factors for air travel stress include anxiety and an anger-prone personality; they also show that traveling on unfamiliar routes is more stressful than traveling on a familiar one. Another factor may be restrictions on smoking. However, alcohol abuse underlies a majority of incidents.

Airlines are training their employees to handle violent individuals and to spot problem passengers before they start causing serious problems. Some carriers offer travelers specific suggestions on how to relax during long flights. And some airlines have considered offering nicotine patches to passengers who are desperate for a smoke but are no longer allowed to light up. Increased security in the air may be curtailing rage behavior on board flights, but concern continues to grow about passenger rage on the ground. An Australian survey of airport employees found that 96 percent of airport staff had experienced air rage at work: 31 percent of agents experienced some form of air rage daily, and 15 percent of agents reported they had been physically touched or assaulted by a passenger.

Sources: Based on information from multiple sources, including Daniel Eisenberg, "Acting Up in the Air," *Time*, December 21, 1998; "Air Rage Capital: Bangor Becomes Nation's Flight Problem Drop Point," *The Baltimore Sun*, syndicated article, September 1999; Melanie Trottman and Chip Cummins, "Passenger's Death Prompts Calls for Improved 'Air Rage' Procedures," *The Wall Street Journal*, September 26, 2000; Blair J. Berkley and Mohammad Ala, "Identifying and Controlling Threatening Airline Passengers, *Cornell Hotel and Restaurant Administration Quarterly*, 42 August–September 2001, 6–24, www.airsafe.com/issues/rage.htm, accessed January 16, 2006; Australian Services Union, www.asu.asn.au/media/airlines_general/20031021_airrage.html, accessed January 16, 2006.

Ala note that violent passengers were considered the number one security concern in the airline industry.[48]

What should an employee do when an aggressive customer brushes off attempts to defuse the situation? In a public environment, one priority should be to move the person away from other customers. Sometimes supervisors may have to arbitrate disputes between customers and staff members; at other times, they need to stand behind the employee's actions. If a customer has physically assaulted an employee, then it may be necessary to summon security officers or the police. Some firms try to conceal such events, fearing bad publicity. Others however, feel obliged to make a public stand on behalf of their employees, like the Body Shop manager who ordered an ill-tempered customer out of the store, telling her: "I won't stand for your rudeness to my staff."

Telephone rudeness poses a different challenge. Service personnel have been known to hang up on angry customers, but that action doesn't resolve the problem. Bank customers, for instance, tend to get upset upon learning that checks have been returned because the account is overdrawn (which means they've broken the rules) or that a request for a loan has been denied. One approach for handling customers who continue to berate a telephone-based employee is for the latter to say firmly: "This conversation isn't getting us anywhere. Why don't I call you back in a few minutes when you've had time to digest the information?" In many cases, a break for reflection is exactly what's needed.

THE FAMILY FEUDERS. People who get into arguments with members of their own family (or worse, with other customers)—make up a subcategory of belligerents we call family feuders. Employee intervention may calm the situation or actually make it worse. Some situations require detailed analysis and a carefully measured response. Others, such as customers starting a food fight in a nice restaurant (yes, such things do happen), require almost instantaneous response. Service managers in these situations need to be prepared to think on their feet and act fast.

THE VANDAL. The level of physical abuse to which service facilities and equipment can be subjected is truly astonishing. Soft drinks are poured into bank cash machines; graffiti are scrawled on both interior and exterior surfaces; burn holes from cigarettes scar carpets, tablecloths, and bedcovers; bus seats are slashed and hotel furniture broken; telephone handsets are torn off; customers' cars are vandalized; glass is smashed and fabrics are torn. The list is endless. Customers don't cause all of the damage, of course. Bored or drunk young people are the source of much exterior vandalism. And disgruntled employees have been known to commit sabotage. But much of the problem does originate with paying customers who choose to misbehave. Alcohol and drugs are sometimes the cause, at other times psychological problems may contribute, and carelessness can play a role. On some occasions, unhappy customers, feeling mistreated by the service provider, try to take revenge in some way.

The best cure for vandalism is prevention. Improved security discourages some vandals. Good lighting helps, as does open design of public areas. Companies can choose pleasing yet vandal-resistant surfaces, protective coverings for equipment, and rugged furnishings. Educating customers on how to use equipment properly (rather than fighting with it) and providing warnings about fragile objects can reduce the likelihood of abuse or careless handling. And there are economic sanctions: security deposits or signed agreements in which customers agree to pay for any damage they cause.

What should managers do if prevention fails and damage is done? If the perpetrator is caught, they should first clarify whether there are any extenuating circumstances (because accidents do happen). Sanctions for deliberate damage can range from a warning to prosecution. As far as the physical damage itself is concerned, it's best to fix it fast (within any constraints imposed by legal or insurance considerations). The general manager of a bus company had the right idea when he said: "If one of our buses is vandalized, whether it's a broken window, a slashed seat, or graffiti on the ceiling, we take it out of service immediately, so nobody sees it. Otherwise, you just give the same idea to five other characters who were too dumb to think of it in the first place!"

THE DEADBEAT. Leaving aside those individuals who never intended to pay in the first place (our term for them is "the thief"), there are many reasons why customers fail to pay for services they have received. Once again, preventive action is better than a cure. A growing number of firms insist on prepayment. Any form of ticket sale is a good example of this. Direct marketing organizations ask for your credit card number as they take your order, as do most hotels when you make a reservation. The next best thing is to present the customer with a bill immediately on completion of service. If the bill is to be sent by mail, the firm should send it fast, while the service is still fresh in the customer's mind.

Not every apparent delinquent is a hopeless deadbeat. Perhaps there's good reason for the delay, and acceptable payment arrangements can be worked out. A key question is whether such a personalized approach can be cost justified, relative to the results obtained by purchasing the services of a collection agency. There may be other considerations, too. If the client's problems are only temporary, what is the long-term value of maintaining the relationship? Will it create positive goodwill and word-of-mouth to help the customer work things out? These decisions are judgment calls, but if creating and maintaining long-term relationships is the firm's ultimate goal, they bear exploration.

Consequences of Dysfunctional Customer Behavior

Lloyd Harris and Kate Reynolds emphasize that dysfunctional customer behavior has consequences for frontline staff, other customers, and the organization itself.[49] Abused employees may not only find their mood or temper negatively affected in the short run, but also may eventually suffer long-term psychological damage. Their own behavior, too, may take on negative dimensions, such as taking revenge on abusive customers. Staff morale can be hurt, with implications for both productivity and quality.

The consequences for customers can take both positive and negative forms. Other customers may rally to the support of an employee whom they perceive as having been abused; however, bad behavior can also be contagious, leading a bad situation to escalate as others join in. More broadly, being exposed to negative incidents can spoil the consumption experience for many customers, even leading them to terminate their use of the service in question. Companies suffer financially when demotivated employees no longer work as efficiently and effectively as before, or when employees are forced to take medical leave. There may also be direct financial losses from restoring stolen or damaged property, legal costs, and paying fraudulent claims.

As suggested in the earlier discussion of air rage, the nature of jaycustomer behavior is likely to be shaped by the characteristics of the service industry in which it occurs. Research Insights 13.1 reports on a study of jaycustomers in the hospitality industry.

Dealing with Consumer Fraud

Dishonest customers can take advantage of generous service recovery strategies, service guarantees, or simply a strong customer orientation in a number of ways. For example, they may steal from the firm, refuse to pay for the service, fake dissatisfaction, purposefully cause service failures to occur, or overstate losses at the time of

RESEARCH INSIGHTS 13.1

CATEGORIZING JAYCUSTOMERS IN HOTELS, RESTAURANTS, AND BARS

To learn more about dysfunctional customer behavior in the hospitality industry, Lloyd Harris and Kate Reynolds developed a research project to identify and categorize different types of misconduct. Open-ended interviews, typically lasting one hour (but sometimes longer) were conducted with 31 managers, 46 frontline employees, and 29 customers. These interviews took place in 19 hotels (all of which had restaurants and bars), 13 restaurants, and 16 bars. A purposive sampling plan was employed, with the goal of selecting informants with extensive participation in and insights of service encounters. All informants had encountered—or had perpetrated—what could be considered as jaycustomer behavior and were invited to give details of specific incidents. In total, the 106 respondents generated 417 critical incidents.

Based on analysis of these incidents, Harris and Reynolds codified eight types of behavior:

1. *Compensation letter writers* who deliberately and fraudulently wrote to centralized customer service departments with largely unjustified complaints in anticipation of receiving a check or gift voucher.
2. *Undesirable customers* whose behavior fell into three subgroups: (a) irritating behavior by "jaykids" and "jayfamilies;" (b) criminal behavior, typically involving drug sales or prostitution; and (c) homeless individuals who used an organization's facilities and stole other customers' refreshments.
3. *Property abusers* who vandalized facilities and stole items—most often to keep as souvenirs.
4. *[Off-duty] service workers* who know how to work the system to their own advantage as customers and deliberately disrupt service encounters, either for financial gain or simply to cause problems for frontline staff.
5. *Vindictive customers* who are violent toward people or property, possibly because of some perceived injustice.
6. *Oral abusers* include professional complainers seeking compensation and "ego hunters" who take pleasure in offending frontline staff and other customers.
7. *Physical abusers* who physically harm frontline staff.
8. *Sexual predators*—often acting in groups—who engage in sexual harassment of frontline personnel either verbally or behaviorally.

Some of these behaviors, such as letter writing and property abuse, are covert in nature (that is, not evident to others at the time they are committed). Certain underlying causes assert themselves across multiple categories; they include desire for personal gain, drunkenness, personal psychological problems, and negative group dynamics.

Table 13.3 shows the percentage of employees and customers reporting incidents within each category. Rather remarkably, with the exception of the "undesirable customers" category, the incidents in the customer column are all self-reports of the respondents' own misbehavior.

The verbatim reports of jaycustomer behavior recorded in this study make somber—even scary—reading. In particular, they demonstrate especially the challenges posed to management and staff by manipulative customers seeking personal financial gain and by the abusive behavior of individuals, sometimes acting in groups and fueled by alcohol, who appear unconstrained by traditional societal norms.

TABLE 13.3 Percentage of Respondents Reporting Incidents by Category

Category	Employees	Customers
Compensation letter writers	30%	20%
Undesirable customers	39	47
Property abusers	51	20
[Off-duty] service workers	11	11
Vindictive customers	30	22
Oral abusers	92	70
Physical abusers	49	20
Sexual predators	38	0

Source: From Lloyd C. Harris and Kate L. Reynolds, "Jaycustomer Behavior: An Exploration of Types and Motives in the Hospitality Industry," Journal of Services Marketing 18, No. 5, 2004, 339–357. Copyright © 2004 Emerald Group Publishing Ltd.

genuine service failures. What steps can a firm take to protect itself against opportunistic customer behavior?

Treating customers with suspicion is likely to alienate them, especially in situations of service failure. The president of TARP notes:

> Our research has found that premeditated rip-offs represent 1 to 2 percent of the customer base in most organizations. However, most organizations defend themselves against unscrupulous customers by... treating the 98 percent of honest customers like crooks to catch the 2 percent who *are* crooks.[50]

Using this knowledge, the working assumptions should be "if in doubt, believe the customer." However, as Service Perspective 13.5 shows, it's crucial to monitor the invocations of service guarantees or repeated compensation payments to the same customer. For example, one Asian airline found that the same customer lost his suitcase on three consecutive flights. The chances of this truly happening are probably lower than winning the national lottery, so frontline staff were made aware of this individual. The next time he checked in his suitcase, the check-in staff videotaped the suitcase almost from check-in to pickup in the baggage claim at the traveler's destination. It turned out that a companion collected the suitcase and took it away while the traveler again made his way to the lost baggage counter to report his missing suitcase. This time, the police were waiting for him and his friend.

In another example, Continental Airlines consolidated 45 separate customer databases into a single data warehouse to improve service and to detect customer fraud. The airline found one customer who received 20 bereavement fares in

SERVICE PERSPECTIVE 13.5
TRACKING DOWN GUESTS WHO CHEAT

As part of its guarantee tracking system, Hampton Inn has developed ways to identify guests who appeared to be cheating—using aliases or various dissatisfaction problems to invoke the guarantee repeatedly in order to get the cost of their room refunded. Guests showing high invocation trends receive personalized attention and follow-up from the company's Guest Assistance Team. Wherever possible, senior managers telephone these guests to ask about their recent stays. The conversation might go as follows: "Hello, Mr. Jones. I'm the director of guest assistance at Hampton Inn, and I see that you've had some difficulty with the last four properties you've visited. Since we take our guarantee very seriously, I thought I'd give you a call and find out what the problems were."

The typical response is dead silence. Sometimes the silence is followed with questions of how headquarters could possibly know about their problems. These calls have their humorous moments as well. One individual, who had invoked the guarantee 17 times in what appeared to be a trip that took him across the U.S. and back, was asked, innocuously, "Where do you like to stay when you travel?" "Hampton Inn," came the enthusiastic response. "But," said the executive making the call, "our records show that the last seventeen times you have stayed at a Hampton Inn, you have invoked the 100 percent Satisfaction Guarantee." "That's why I like them!" proclaimed the guest (who turned out to be a long-distance truckdriver).

Source: Christopher W. Hart and Elizabeth Long, *Extraordinary Guarantees.* New York: AMACOM, 1997.

12 months, off the same dead grandfather. To be able to effectively detect consumer fraud, maintaining a central data warehouse of all compensation payments, service recoveries, returned goods, and any other benefits given to customers based on special circumstances are needed (i.e., such transactions cannot be retained only at the local or branch level, but must be captured in a centralized system), and it is important to merge customer data across silos and channels for detecting unusual transactions and the systems that allow them.[51]

Recent research shows that the amount of a guarantee payout (e.g., whether it is a 10 percent or 100 percent money-back guarantee) had no effect on consumer cheating. However, repeat purchase intention significantly reduced cheating intent. These findings suggest important managerial implications: (1) Managers can implement and thus reap the bigger marketing benefits of 100 percent money-back guarantees without worrying that the large payouts would increase cheating; and (2) guarantees can be offered to regular customers or as part of a membership program, because repeat customers are unlikely to cheat on service guarantees. A further finding was that customers were also reluctant to cheat if the service quality provided was truly high than when it was just satisfactory. This implied that truly excellent services firms have less to worry about cheating than the average provider.[52]

CONCLUSION

Encouraging customer feedback provides an important means of increasing customer satisfaction and retention. It is an opportunity to get into the hearts and minds of the customer. In all but the worst instances, complaining customers are indicating that they want to continue their relationship with the firm, but they are also indicating that all is not well and that they expect the company to make things right. Here, service firms need to develop effective strategies to recover from service failures so they can maintain customer goodwill. That is vital for the long-term success of the company.

Having professional and generous service recovery systems does not mean "the customer is always right" and that the firm is open to customer abuse. Rather, it is important for the benefit of all (i.e., other customers, service employees, and the service firm) to effectively deal with jaycustomers.

Chapter Summary

LO1 When customers are dissatisfied, they have several alternatives. They can take some form of:

- Public action (e.g., complain to the firm, a third party, or even take legal action).
- Private action (e.g., switch to another provider and/or spread negative word of mouth).
- Take no action.

LO2 To effectively recover from a service failure, firms need to understand customer complaining behavior and motivations and what customers expect in response.

- Customers typically complain for any combination of the following four reasons. They want: (1) restitution or compensation, (2) to vent their anger, (3) help to improve the service, and (4) to spare other customers from experiencing the same problems (i.e., they complain for altruistic reasons).
- In practice, most dissatisfied customers do not complain as they may not know where to complain, they find it too much effort and unpleasant, and they perceive the payoffs of their effort uncertain.
- The people most likely to complain tend to be better educated, have higher incomes, and be more socially involved.

LO3 Once customers make a complaint, they expect firms to deal with them in a fair manner along three dimensions of fairness:

- Procedural fairness—customers expect the firm to have a convenient, responsive, and flexible service recovery process.
- Interactional justice—here, customers expect an honest explanation, a genuine effort to solve the problem, and polite treatment.
- Outcome justice—customers expect a compensation that reflects the loss and inconvenience suffered as a result of the service failure.

LO4 Effective service recovery can in many cases avoid customer switching and restore confidence in the service firm. When customers complain, they give the firm a chance to correct problems, restore the relationship with the complainer, and improve future satisfaction. Service recovery is therefore an important opportunity to retain a valued customer.

LO5 Effective service recovery systems should:

- Make it easy for customers to give feedback (e.g., provide hotline numbers and email addresses on all communications materials) and encourage them to provide feedback.
- Enable effective service recovery by making it (1) proactive, (2) preplanned, (3) trained, and (4) empowered.
- Establish appropriate compensation levels. Compensation should be higher if a firm is known for service excellence, if the service failure is serious, and if the customer is important to the firm.

LO6 The guidelines for frontline employees to effectively handle customer complaints and service recovery include:

- (1) act fast; (2) acknowledge the customer's feelings; (3) don't argue with the customer; (4) show you understand the problem from the customer's point of view; (5) clarify the truth and sort out the cause; (6) give customers the benefit of the doubt; (7) propose the steps needed to solve the problem; (8) keep customers informed of progress; (9) consider compensation; (10) persevere to regain customer goodwill; and (11) check the service delivery system and improve it.

LO7 Service guarantees are a powerful way to institutionalize professional complaint handling and service recovery. Service guarantees set clear standards for the firm, and they also reduce customers' risk perceptions and can build long-term loyalty.

LO8 Service guarantees should be: (1) unconditional, (2) easy to understand and communicate, (3) meaningful to the customer, (4) easy to invoke, (5) easy to collect on, and (6) credible.

LO9 Not all firms stand to gain from service guarantees. Specifically, firms should be careful offering service guarantees when: (1) they already have a reputation for service excellence; (2) service quality is too low and has to be improved first; (3) aspects of service quality are uncontrollable because of external factors (e.g., weather); and (4) customers perceive low risk when buying the service.

LO10 Not all customers are honest, polite, and reasonable. Some may want to take advantage of service recovery situations and others may inconvenience and stress frontline employees and other customers alike. Such customers are called jaycustomers.

- There are seven groups of jaycustomers: (1) the cheat, (2) the thief, (3) the rule breaker, (4) the belligerent, (5) the family feuders, (6) the vandal, and (7) the deadbeat.
- The different types of jaycustomers cause different problems for firms and may spoil the service experience of other customers. Hence, firms need to manage their behavior, even if that means, for example, keeping track of how often a customer invokes a service guarantee, or as a last resort, blacklisting them from using the firm's facilities.

Review Questions

1. How do customers typically respond to service failures?
2. Why don't many more unhappy customers complain? And what do customers expect the firm to do once they filed a complaint?
3. Why would a firm prefer its unhappy customers to come forward and complain?
4. What is the service recovery paradox? Under what conditions is this paradox most likely to hold? Why is it best to deliver the service as planned, even if the paradox does hold in a specific context?
5. What can a firm do to make it easy for dissatisfied customers to complain?
6. Why should a service recovery strategy be proactive, planned, trained, and empowered?
7. How generous should compensations related to service recovery be?

8. How should service guarantees be designed? What are the benefits of service guarantees over and above a good complaint handling and service recovery system?
9. Under what conditions is it not suitable to introduce a service guarantee?
10. What are the different types of jaycustomers, and how can a service firm deal with such customers?

Application Exercises

1. Think about the last time you experienced a less-than-satisfactory service experience. Did you complain? Why? If you did not complain, explain why not.
2. When was the last time you were truly satisfied with an organization's response to your complaint. Describe in detail what happened and what made you satisfied.
3. What would be an appropriate service recovery policy for a wrongly bounced check for (a) your local savings bank, (b) a major national bank, and (c) a private bank for high net-worth individuals? Please explain your rationale, and compute the economic costs of the alternative service recovery policies.
4. Design an effective service guarantee for a service with high perceived risk. Explain (a) why and how your guarantee would reduce perceived risk of potential customers and (b) why current customers would appreciate this guarantee even though they are already a customer of that firm and therefore likely to perceive lower levels of risk.
5. How generous should compensation be? Review the following incident and comment. Then evaluate the available options, comment on each, select the one you recommend, and defend your decision.

   "The shrimp cocktail was half frozen. The waitress apologized and didn't charge me for any of my dinner," was the response of a very satisfied customer about the service recovery he received. Consider the following range of service recovery policies a restaurant chain could set, and try to establish the costs for each policy:

   Option 1: Smile and apologize, defrost the prawn cocktail, return it, smile, and apologize again.
   Option 2: Smile and apologize, replace the prawn cocktail with a new one, and smile and apologize again.
   Option 3: Smile, apologize, replace the prawn cocktail, and offer a free coffee or dessert.
   Option 4: Smile, apologize, replace the prawn cocktail, and waive the bill of $80 for the entire meal.
   Option 5: Smile, apologize, replace the prawn cocktail, waive the bill for the entire dinner, and offer a free bottle of champagne.
   Option 6: Smile, apologize, replace the prawn cocktail, waive the bill for the entire dinner, offer a free bottle of champagne, and give a voucher valid for another dinner, to be redeemed within three months.
6. Identify the possible behavior of jaycustomers for a service of your choice. How can the service process be designed to minimize or control the behavior of jaycustomers?

Endnotes

1. "An Extraordinary Stumble at JetBlue," *Business Week*, March 5, 2007, http://www.businessweek.com/magazine/content/07_10/b4024004.htm, accessed June 11, 2009; J. Tschohl, "Too Little, Too Late: Service Recovery Must Occur Immediately—As JetBlue Discovered," Service Quality Institute, May 2007, available: http://www.customer-service.com, accessed April 2008.
2. Roger Bougie, Rik Pieters, and Marcel Zeelenberg, "Angry Customers Don't Come Back, They Get Back: The Experience and Behavioral Implications of Anger and Dissatisfaction in Service," *Journal of the Academy of Marketing Science*, 31, No. 4, 2003, 377–393; Florian v. Wangenheim, "Postswitching Negative Word of Mouth," *Journal of Service Research*, 8, No. 1, 2005, 67–78.
3. Bernd Stauss, "Global Word of Mouth," *Marketing Management* 6, Fall 1997, 28–30.
4. For research on cognitive and affective drivers of complaining behavior, see Jean-Charles Chebat, Moshe Davidow, and Isabelle Codjovi, "Silent Voices: Why Some Dissatisfied Consumers Fail to Complain," *Journal of Service Research*, 7, No. 4, 2005, 328–342.
5. Stephen S. Tax and Stephen W. Brown, "Recovering and Learning from Service Failure," *Sloan Management Review*, 49, No. 1, Fall 1998, 75–88.
6. Technical Assistance Research Programs Institute (TARP), *Consumer Complaint Handling in America; An Update Study, Part II*. Washington, DC: TARP and US Office of Consumer Affairs, April 1986; Nancy Stephens and Kevin P. Gwinner,

"Why Don't Some People Complain? A Cognitive-Emotive Process Model of Consumer Complaining Behavior," *Journal of the Academy of Marketing Science,* 26, No. 3, 1998, 172–189.

7. Cathy Goodwin and B. J. Verhage, "Role Perceptions of Services: A Cross-Cultural Comparison with Behavioral Implications," *Journal of Economic Psychology,* 10, 1990, 543–558.
8. Nancy Stephens, "Complaining," in Teresa A. Swartz and Dawn Iacobucci, eds., *Handbook of Services Marketing and Management.* Thousand Oaks, CA: Sage Publications, 2000, 291.
9. John Goodman, "Basic Facts on Customer Complaint Behavior and the Impact of Service on the Bottom Line," *Competitive Advantage,* June 1999, 1–5.
10. Anna Mattila and Jochen Wirtz, "Consumer Complaining to Firms: The Determinants of Channel Choice," *Journal of Services Marketing,* 18, No. 2, 2004, 147–155; Kaisa Snellman and Tiina Vihtkari, "Customer Complaining Behavior in Technology-based Service Encounters," *International Journal of Service Industry Management,* 14, No. 2, 2003, 217–231; Terri Shapiro and Jennifer Nieman-Gonder, "Effect of Communication Mode in Justice-Based Service Recovery," *Managing Service Quality,* 16, No. 2, 2006, 124–144.
11. Technical Assistance Research Programs Institute (TARP), *Consumer Complaint Handling in America; An Update Study, Part II.* Washington, DC: TARP and US Office of Consumer Affairs, April 1986.
12. Kathleen Seiders and Leonard L Berry, "Service Fairness: What it is and Why it Matters," *Academy of Management Executive,* 12, No. 2, 1990, 8–20. See also Klaus Schoefer and Adamantios Diamantopoulos, "The Role of Emotions in Transating Perceptions of (In)Justice into Postcomplaint Behavioral Responses," *Journal of Service Research,* 11, No. 1, 2008, 91–103; Yany Grégoire and Robert J. Fisher, "Customer Betrayal and Retaliation: When Your Best Customers Become Your Worst Enemies," *Journal of the Academy of Marketing Science,* 36, No. 2, 2008, 247–261.
13. Stephen S. Tax and Stephen W. Brown "Recovering and Learning from Service Failure," *Sloan Management Review,* 49, No. 1, Fall 1998, 75–88; See also Stephen S. Tax and Stephen W. Brown, "Service Recovery: Research, Insight and Practice," in Teresa A. Swartz and Dawn Iacobucci, eds., *Handbook of Services Marketing and Management.* Thousand Oaks, CA: Sage Publications, 2000, 277; Tor Wallin Andreassen, "Antecedents of Service Recovery," *European Journal of Marketing,* 34, No. 1 and 2, 2000, 156–175; Ko de Ruyter and Martin Wetzel, "Customer Equity Considerations in Service Recovery," *International Journal of Service Industry Management,* 13, No. 1, 2002, 91–108; Janet R. McColl-Kennedy and Beverley A. Sparks, "Application of Fairness Theory to Service Failures and Service Recovery," *Journal of Service Research,* 5, No. 3, 2003, 251–266; Jochen Wirtz and Anna Mattila, "Consumer Responses to Compensation, Speed of Recovery and Apology After a Service Failure," *International Journal of Service Industry Management,* 15, No. 2, 2004, 150–166.
14. Oren Harari, "Thank Heavens for Complainers," *Management Review* 86, March 1997, 25–29.
15. Clyde A. Warden, Tsung-Chi Liu, Chi-Tsun Huang, and Chi-Hsun Lee, "Service Failures Away from Home: Benefits in Intercultural Service Encounters," *International Journal of Service Industry Management,* 14, No. 4, 2003, 436–457; Anna S. Mattila and Paul G. Patterson, "Service Recovery and Fairness Perceptions in Collectivist and Individualist Contexts," *Journal of Service Research,* 6, No. 4, 2004, 336–346; Tom DeWitt, Doan T. Nguyen, and Roger Marshall, "Exploring Customer Loyalty Following Service Recovery," *Journal of Service Research,* 10, No. 3, 2008, 269–281.
16. Simon J. Bell and James A. Luddington, "Coping with Customer Complaints," *Journal of Service Research,* 8, No. 3, February 2006, 221–233.
17. Leonard L. Berry, *On Great Service: A Framework for Action.* New York: The Free Press, 1995, 94.
18. Susan M. Keveaney, "Customer Switching Behavior in Service Industries: An Exploratory Study," *Journal of Marketing,* 59, April 1995, 71–82.
19. Technical Assistance Research Programs Institute (TARP), *Consumer Complaint Handling in America; An Update Study, Part II.* Washington DC: TARP and US Office of Consumer Affairs, April 1986.
20. Celso Augusto de Matos, Jorge Luiz Henrique, and Carlos Alberto Vargas Rossi, "Service Recovery Paradox: A Meta-Analysis," *Journal of Service Research,* 10, No. 1, 2007, 60–77; Stefan Michel, "Analyzing Service Failures and Recoveries: A Process Approach," *International Journal of Service Industry Management,* 12, No. 1, 2001, 20–33; Chihyung Ok, Ki-Joon Back, and Carol W. Shankin, "Mixed Findings on the Service Recovery Paradox," *The Service Industries Journal,* 27, No. 5, 2007, 671–686.
21. Stefan Michel and Matthew L. Meuter, "The Service Recovery Paradox: True but Overrated?" *International Journal of Service Industry Management,* 19, No. 4, 2008, 441–457. Other studies also confirmed that the service recovery paradox does not hold universally; Tor Wallin Andreassen, "From Disgust to Delight: Do Customers Hold a Grudge?" *Journal of Service Research,* 4, No. 1, 2001, 39–49; Michael A. McCollough, Leonard L. Berry, and Manjit S. Yadav, "An Empirical Investigation of Customer Satisfaction after Service Failure and Recovery," *Journal of Service Research,* 3, No. 2, 2000, 121–137; James G. Maxhamm III, "Service Recovery's Influence on Consumer Satisfaction, Positive Word-of-Mouth, and Purchase Intentions," *Journal of Business Research,* 54, 2001, 11–24.
22. James G. Maxham III and Richard G. Netemeyer, "A Longitudinal Study of Complaining Customers' Evaluations of Multiple Service Failures and Recovery Efforts," *Journal of Marketing,* 66, No. 4, 2002, 57–72.
23. Michael Hargrove, cited in Ron Kaufman, *Up Your Service!* Singapore: Ron Kaufman Plc. Ltd., 2005, 225.
24. Steven S. Tax and Steven W. Brown, "Recovering and Learning from Service Failure" *Sloan Management Review,* 49, No. 1, Fall 1998, 75–88; Stephen S. Tax, Stephen W. Brown, and Murali Chandrashekaran, "Customer Evaluation of Service Complaint Experiences: Implications for Relationship Marketing," *Journal of Marketing,* 62, No. 2, Spring 1998, 60–76; for a study in the online environment see Betsy B. Holloway and Sharon E. Beatty, "Service Failure in Online Retailing: A Recovery Opportunity," *Journal of Service Research,* 6, No. 1, 2003, 92–105.

25. For a discussion on how to quantify complaint management profitability see Bernd Stauss and Andreas Schoeler, "Complaint Management Profitability: What do Complaint Managers Know?" *Managing Service Quality*, 14, No. 2/3, 2004, 147–156, and for a comprehensive treatment of all aspects of effective complaint management see Bernd Stauss and Wolfgang Seidel, *Complaint Management: The Heart of CRM*. Mason, OH: Thomson, 2004; Janelle Barlow and Claus Møller, *A Complaint is a Gift*, 2nd edn. San Francisco, CA: Berrett-Koehler Publishers, 2008.
26. Christian Homburg and Andreas Fürst, "How Organizatonal Complaint Handling Drives Customer Loyalty: An Analysis of the Mechanistic and the Organic Approach," *Journal of Marketing*, 69, July 2005, 95–114.
27. Ron Zemke and Chip R. Bell, *Knock Your Socks Off Service Recovery*. New York: AMACOM, 2000, 60.
28. Barbara R. Lewis, "Customer Care in Services," in W. J. Glynn and J. G. Barnes, eds., *Understanding Services Management*. Chichester:, Wiley, 1995, 57–89. Prior rapport between employees and customers has also been shown to improve service recovery satisfaction, see Tom DeWitt and Michael K. Brady, "Rethinking Service Recovery Strategies: The Effect of Rapport on Customer Responses to Service Failure," *Journal of Service Research*, 6, No. 2, 2003, 193–207.
29. Rhonda Mack, Rene Mueller, John Crotts, and Amanda Broderick, "Perceptions, Corrections and Defections: Implications for Service Recovery in the Restaurant Industry," *Managing Service Quality*, 10, No. 6, 2000, 339–346; Randi Priluck and Vishal Lala, "The Impact of the Recovery Paradox on Retailer-Customer Relationships," *Managing Service Quality*, 19, No. 1, 2009, 42–59.
30. For an excellent review of extant academic literature on service guarantees see Jens Hogreve and Dwayne D. Gremler, "Twenty Years of Service Guarantee Research," *Journal of Service Research*, 11, No. 4, 2009, 322–343.
31. Christopher W. L. Hart, "The Power of Unconditional Service Guarantees," *Harvard Business Review* 66, July–August 1988, 54–62.
32. L. A. Tucci and J. Talaga, "Service Guarantees and Consumers' Evaluation of Services," *Journal of Services Marketing*, 11, No. 1, 1997, 10–18; Amy Ostrom and Dawn Iacobucci, "The Effect of Guarantees on Consumers' Evaluation of Services," *Journal of Services Marketing*, 12, No. 5, 1998, 362–378.
33. Sara Bjőrlin Lidén and Per Skålén, "The Effect of Service Guarantees on Service Recovery," *International Journal of Service Industry Management*, 14, No. 1, 2003, 36–58.
34. Christopher W. Hart and Elizabeth Long, *Extraordinary Guarantees*. New York: AMACOM, 1997.
35. Christopher W. L. Hart, "The Power of Unconditional Service Guarantees," *Harvard Business Review*, July–August 1988, 54–62.
36. For a scientific discussion on the optimal guarantee payout amount see Tim Baker and David A. Collier, "The Economic Payout Model for Service Guarantees," *Decision Sciences*, 36, No. 2, 2005, 197–220.
37. Gordon H. McDougall, Terence Levesque, and Peter VanderPlaat, "Designing the Service Guarantee: Unconditional or Specific?" *Journal of Services Marketing*, 12, No. 4, 1998, 278–293; Jochen Wirtz, "Development of a Service Guarantee Model," *Asia Pacific Journal of Management*, 15, No. 1, 1998, 51–75.
38. Jochen Wirtz and Doreen Kum, "Designing Service Guarantees – Is Full Satisfaction the Best You can Guarantee?" *Journal of Services Marketing*, 15, No. 4, 2001, 282–299.
39. Amy L. Ostrom and Christopher Hart, "Service Guarantee: Research and Practice," in T. Schwartz and D. Iacobucci, eds., *Handbook of Services Marketing and Management*. Thousand Oaks, CA: Sage Publications, 2000, 299–316.
40. Jochen Wirtz, Doreen Kum, and Khai Sheang Lee, "Should a Firm with a Reputation for Outstanding Service Quality Offer a Service Guarantee?" *Journal of Services Marketing*, 14, No. 6, 2000, 502–512.
41. For a decision support model and whether to have a service guarantee, and if yes, on how to design and implement it, see Louis Fabien, "Design and Implementation of a Service Guarantee," *Journal of Services Marketing*, 19, No. 1, 2005, 33–38.
42. This section is adapted and updated from Christopher Lovelock, *Product Plus*. New York: McGraw-Hill, 1994, Chapter 15.
43. Lloyd C. Harris and Kate L. Reynolds, "The Consequences of Dysfunctional Customer Behavior," *Journal of Service Research*, 6, No. 2, 2003, 144–161; Jochen Wirtz and Doreen Kum, "Consumer Cheating On Service Guarantees," *Journal of the Academy of Marketing Science*, 32, No. 2, 2004, 159–175; Accenture Inc., "One-Fourth of Americans Say It's Acceptable to Defraud Insurance Companies, Accenture Survey Finds," press release, February 12, 2003, available at http://newsroom.accenture.com/article_display.cfm?article_id=3970, accessed April 29, 2009; Chu Wujin, Eitan Gerstner, and James D. Hess, "Managing Dissatisfaction: How to Decrease Customer Opportunism by Partial Refunds," *Journal of Service Research*, 1, No. 2, 1998, 140–155.
44. Kate L. Reynolds and Lloyd C. Harris, "When Service Failure is Not Service Failure: An Exploration of the Forms and Motives of 'Illegitimate' Customer Complaining," *Journal of Services Marketing*, 19, No. 5, 326.
45. Lloyd C. Harris and Kate L. Reynolds, "Jaycustomer Behavior: An Exploration of Types and Motives in the Hospitality Industry," *Journal of Services Marketing*, 18, No. 5, 2004, 339.
46. Stephen J. Grove, Raymond P. Fisk, and Joby John, "Surviving in the Age of Rage," *Marketing Management* 13, March/April 2004, 41–46.
47. Roger Bougie, Rik Pieters, and Marcel Zeelenberg, "Angry Customers Don't Come Back, They Get Back: The Experience and Behavioral Implications of Anger and Dissatisfaction in Services," *Journal of the Academy of Marketing Science*, 31, No. 4, 2003, 377–393.
48. Blair J. Berkley and Mohammad Ala, "Identifying and Controlling Threatening Airline Passengers," *Cornell Hotel and Restaurant Administration Quarterly*, 42, August–September 2001, 6–24.
49. Lloyd C. Harris and Kate L. Reynolds, "The Consequences of Dysfunctional Customer Behavior," *Journal of Service Research*, 6, November 2003, 144–161; Lloyd C. Harris and

Kate L. Reynolds, "Jaycustomer Behavior: An Exploration of Types and Motives in the Hospitality Industry," *Journal of Services Marketing*, 18, No. 5, 2004, 339–357.

50. John Goodman, quoted in "Improving Service Doesn't Always Require Big Investment," *The Service Edge* (July–August, 1990): 3

51. Jill Griffin, "What Your Worst Customers Teach You About Loyalty," January 24, 2006, http://www.marketingprofs.com/6/griffin5.asp, accessed June 6, 2009.

52. Jochen Wirtz and Doreen Kum, "Consumer Cheating on Service Guarantees," *Journal of the Academy of Marketing Science*, 32, No. 2, 2004, 159–175.

CHAPTER 14

Improving Service Quality and Productivity

Not everything that counts can be counted, and not everything that can be counted, counts.

ALBERT EINSTEIN

Our mission remains inviolable: Offer the customer the best service we can provide; cut our costs to the bones; and generate a surplus to continue the unending process of renewal.

JOSEPH PILLAY FORMER CHAIRMAN, SINGAPORE AIRLINES

LEARNING OBJECTIVES (LOs)

By the end of this chapter, the reader should be able to:

LO1 Understand how quality and productivity relate to each other in a services context.

LO2 Be familiar with the different perspectives and dimensions of service quality.

LO3 Know how to use the gaps model for diagnosing and addressing service quality problems.

LO4 Understand the difference between hard and soft measures of service quality.

LO5 Explain the key objectives of effective customer feedback systems.

LO6 Be familiar with key customer feedback collection tools.

LO7 Be familiar with hard measures of service quality and control charts.

LO8 Understand important tools to analyze service problems.

LO9 Appreciate the financial implications of quality improvements.

LO10 Know how to define and measure service productivity.

LO11 Understand the difference between productivity, efficiency, and effectiveness.

LO12 Be familiar with the key methods to improve service productivity.

LO13 Know how productivity improvements impact quality and value.

LO14 Understand how TQM, ISO 9000, the Malcolm-Baldrige Approach, and Six Sigma relate to managing and improving service quality and productivity.

Improving Service Quality in a Ferry Company[1]

Sealink British Ferries, whose routes linked Britain to Ireland and several European countries, was a poor service quality provider. Sealink used a top-down, military-style structure that focused on the operational aspects of ship movements. The quality of customers' experiences received only secondary consideration. Sealink was then acquired by the Swedish company, Stena Line, which is today one of the world's largest car-ferry operators.

Sealink's managerial weaknesses included lack of attention to growing competition from other companies whose new, high-speed ferries offered customers a faster and more comfortable ride. Its top management exercised tight control, issuing directives and applying companywide standards across all divisions, rather than customizing policies to the needs of individual routes. All decisions were subject to head office review. Divisional managers were separated by two management levels from the functional teams engaged in the actual operation. This organizational structure led to conflicts, slow decision making, and inability to respond quickly to market changes.

Stena's philosophy was very different. It operated a decentralized structure, believing that each management function should be responsible for its own activities and accountable for the results. Stena wanted management decisions in the British subsidiary to be taken by people close to the market who understood local competition and demand. Some central functions were moved out to the divisions, including much responsibility for marketing activities. New skills and perspectives came from retraining, transfers, and outside hiring.

Prior to the merger, Sealink had not given priority to punctual or reliable operations. Ferries often were late, standard excuses were used in reports, customer complaints were ignored, and there was little pressure from customer service managers to improve the situation. After the takeover, things started to change. The challenge of late departures and arrivals was resolved through concentration on individual problem areas. On one route, for instance, the port manager involved all operational staff and gave each person "ownership" of a specific aspect of the improvement process. They kept detailed records of each sailing, together with reasons for late departures, and monitored competitors' performance. This participative approach created a close liaison among staff members in different job positions and helped customer service staff to learn from experience. Within two years, the Stena ferries on this route were operating at close to 100 percent punctuality.

On-board service was another area singled out for improvement. Historically, customer service managers did what was convenient for staff rather than customers, including scheduling meal breaks at times when customer demand for service was greatest. As one observer noted, "customers were ignored during the first and last half hour on board, when facilities were closed.... Customers were left to find their own way around [the ship].... Staff only responded to customers when [they] initiated a direct request and made some effort to attract their attention." So Stena required personnel from each on-board functional area to choose a specific area for improvement and work in small groups to achieve this. Initially, some teams were more successful than others, resulting in inconsistent levels of service and customer orientation from one ship to another. Subsequently, managers shared ideas, reviewed experiences, and made adaptations for individual ships. Key changes during the first two years (Table 14.1) contributed to eventual success in achieving consistent service levels on all sailings and all ferries.

By 2009, Stena Line had 35 ships sailing on 18 routes (of which seven served UK ports), carrying some 16 million passengers and 3 million vehicles annually. They included three of the world's largest fast ferries. A leader in all its markets, Stena emphasizes constant service and product improvement. According to the company's website:

FIGURE 14.1 Stena Line's Leading Status Is Attributed to Its On-Board Service Excellence

> The phrase Making Good Time summarises the core of the Stena Line business in three words: fast, enjoyable and efficient sea travel.... Today's customers are looking for more. Basic factors such as punctuality, safety,

clean and well-equipped ferries with good service are now taken for granted, so at Stena Line we're trying even harder to give guests that little extra so they'll want to travel with us again. A way of meeting these new demands is to develop new products and services, and to further customize our offers to suit different requirements. Our ambition is that everyone should find a travel offer in our selection that they like.

TABLE 14.1 Improving Service Quality and Productivity at Sealink After the Takeover

	Inherited Situation	Situation After Two Years
External Context	Inactive competition—"share" market with one competitor	Aggressive competitive activity (two competitors, one operating new, high-speed ferries)
	Static market demand	Growing market
Internal Context	Centralized organization Centralized decision making	Decentralized organization Delegation to specialized decision-making units
	Top management directives	Key manager responsible for each unit team
Managerial Competencies		
• Knowledge	General to industry rather than specific to local markets	Understand both industry and local market
• Experience	Operational and tactical General, industry-based Noncompetitive environment	Operational and decision making Functional management responsibility Exposed to competitive environment
• Expertise	Vague approach to judging situations Short-term focus Generalist competencies	Diagnostic judgmental capabilities Longer-term focus Specific skills for functional tasks
Marketing Decision Making		
• Planning	React to internal circumstances and external threats	Proactive identification of problems
	Minimal information search or evaluation of alternatives	Collect information, consider options
	Focus on tactical issues	Choose among several options
	Inconsistent with other marketing activites	Consistent with other marketing activities
• Actions	Follow top management directives Look to next in line for responsibility Minimal or intermittent communication between functions	Delegation of responsibility Responsibility and ownership for activity Liaison between functions
Marketing Efforts		
• Prepurchase	Mostly media advertising	Advertising plus promotions and informational materials
• Service delivery	Slow, manual booking system Focus on tangible aspects of on-board customer service (e.g., seating, cabins, food, bar)	New, computerized reservation system Better tangibles, sharply improved staff/customer interactions
	Little pressure on operations to improve poor punctuality	Highly reliable, punctual service
	Poor communications at ports and on board ships	Much improved signage, printed guides, electronic message boards, public announcements
	Reactive approach to problem solving	Proactive approach to welcoming customers and solving their problems

Source: Adapted from Audrey Gilmore, "Service Marketing Management Competencies: A Ferry Company Example," *International Journal of Service Industry Management*, 9, No. 1, 1998, 74–92, www.stenaline.com, accessed June 2, 2009.

INTEGRATING SERVICE QUALITY AND PRODUCTIVITY STRATEGIES

The Stena Line success story in the opening vignette is an excellent example that shows how improving service quality and productivity can turn around a failing business. We will learn in this chapter that quality and productivity are twin paths to creating value for both customers and companies.

In broad terms, quality focuses on the benefits created for the customer's side of the equation, and productivity addresses the financial costs incurred by the firm. If not properly integrated, these two foci can be in conflict. For example, making service processes more efficient does not necessarily result in a better quality experience or benefits for customers. In addition, getting service employees to work faster may sometimes be welcomed by customers, but may make them feel rushed and unwanted at other times. Likewise, implementing marketing strategies designed to improve customer satisfaction can prove costly and disruptive if the implications for operations and human resources have not been carefully thought through. The bottom line: Quality and productivity improvement strategies must be considered jointly rather than in isolation. This means that marketing, operations, and human resource managers need to collaborate to ensure they can deliver quality experiences more efficiently to improve the long-term profitability of the firm.

Service Quality, Productivity, and Marketing

Marketing's interest in service quality is obvious: Poor quality places a firm at a competitive disadvantage, potentially driving away dissatisfied customers. Recent years have witnessed a veritable explosion of discontent with service quality at a time when the quality of many manufactured goods has been improving. The 2005 American Customer Satisfaction Index (ACSI) aggregate results for manufactured products, private sector services, and government services in the United States shows clearly that the service sector lags significantly behind manufacturing in terms of quality provided.

Surprisingly, as shown in Figure 14.2, private sector services had only marginally higher scores than federal government services. Claes Fornell concluded that "Citizens have generally low expectations of public sector services, much lower than their expectations with the private sector. The reason behind this is difficult to determine, but possibly emanates from American's general skepticism towards government."[2] These findings show that there is much scope for improving service quality for both private and public sector services.

Improving productivity is important to marketers for several reasons. First, it helps to keep costs down. Lower costs either mean higher profits or the ability to hold

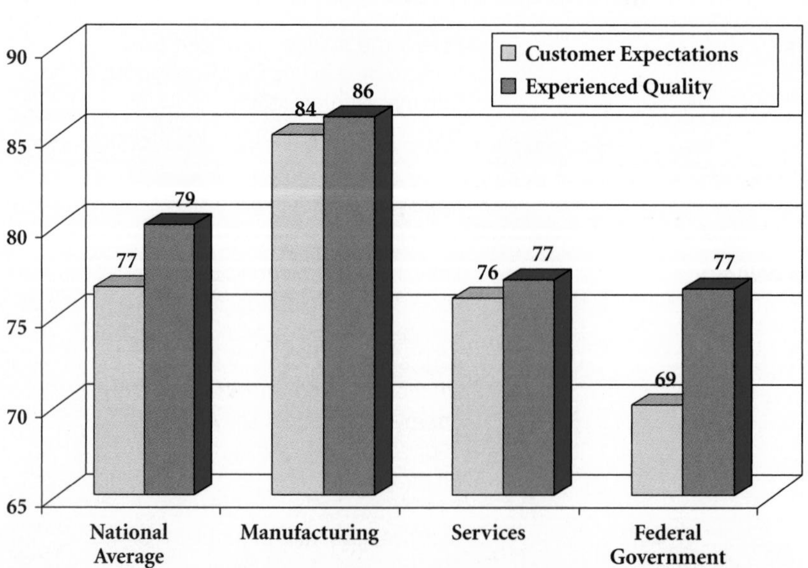

FIGURE 14.2 Services Have Lower Quality than Manufactured Goods

Source: Claes Fornell, "ACSI Commentary: Federal Government Scores." Special Report: Government Satisfaction Scores, Michigan: CFI Group, December 15, 2005, published on www.theacsi.com, accessed on 21 January 2006.

down prices. The company with the lowest costs in an industry has the option to position itself as the low-price leader—usually a significant advantage among price-sensitive market segments. Second, firms with lower costs also generate higher margins, giving them the option of spending more than the competition in marketing activities, and on improving customer service and supplementary services. Such firms may also be able to offer higher margins to attract and reward the best distributors and intermediaries. Third is the opportunity to secure the firm's long-term future through investments in new service technologies and in research to create superior new services, improved features, and innovative delivery systems. Finally, efforts to improve productivity often affect customers. Marketers are responsible for ensuring that negative impacts are avoided or minimized and that new procedures are carefully presented to customers. Positive impacts can be promoted as a new advantage.

FIGURE 14.3 Service Quality Is Difficult to Manage

Historically, services have lagged behind manufacturing in productivity growth, but research by the McKinsey Global Institute shows that five of the seven largest contributors to labor productivity growth in the United States since 2000 have been service industries, including retail and wholesale trade, finance and insurance, administrative support, and scientific and technical services.[3] In conclusion, quality and productivity are twin paths to creating value for both customers and service firms. Let's next examine service quality and how to improve it before we turn to productivity.

WHAT IS SERVICE QUALITY?

What do we mean when we speak of service quality? Company personnel need a common understanding to address issues such as the measurement of service quality, the identification of causes of service quality shortfalls, and the design and implement of corrective actions. As suggested humorously by the restaurant illustration in Figure 14.3, service quality can be difficult to manage, even when failures are tangible in nature.

Different Perspectives of Service Quality

The word *quality* means different things to people according to the context. Common perspectives on quality include.[4]

1. *The transcendent view* of quality is synonymous with innate excellence: a mark of uncompromising standards and high achievement. This viewpoint often is applied to the performing and visual arts. It argues that people learn to recognize quality only through the experience gained from repeated exposure. From a practical standpoint, however, suggesting that managers or customers will know quality when they see it is not very helpful.
2. *The manufacturing-based approach* is supply based and concerned primarily with engineering and manufacturing practices. (In services, we would say that quality is operations driven.) It focuses on conformance to internally developed specifications that often are driven by productivity and cost-containment goals.
3. *User-based definitions* start with the premise that quality lies in the eyes of the beholder. These definitions equate quality with maximum satisfaction. This subjective, demand-oriented perspective recognizes that different customers have different wants and needs.

4. *Value-based definitions* define quality in terms of value and price. By considering the trade-off between performance (or conformance) and price, quality comes to be defined as "affordable excellence."

These different views of quality sometimes lead to disagreements between managers in different functional departments. Furthermore, researchers argue that the nature of services requires a distinctive approach to defining and measuring service quality. The intangible, multifaceted nature of many services makes it harder to evaluate the quality of a service compared to a good. Because customers often are involved in service production, a distinction needs to be drawn between the *process* of service delivery (what Christian Grönroos calls functional quality) and the actual *output* (or outcome) of the service (what he calls technical quality).[5] Grönroos and others also suggest that the perceived quality of a service is the result of an evaluation process in which customers compare their perceptions of service delivery and its outcome to what they expect. Therefore, we define service quality from the user's perspective as consistently meeting or exceeding customer expectations.

Dimensions of Service Quality

Valarie Zeithaml, Leonard Berry, and A. Parasuraman have conducted intensive research on service quality and identified 10 dimensions used by consumers in evaluating service quality (Table 14.2). In subsequent research, they found a high degree of correlation between several of these variables and so consolidated them into five broad dimensions:

- *Tangibles* (appearance of physical elements)
- *Reliability* (dependable and accurate performance)
- *Responsiveness* (promptness and helpfulness)
- *Assurance* (credibility, security, competence, and courtesy)
- *Empathy* (easy access, good communications, and customer understanding)[6]

IDENTIFYING AND CORRECTING SERVICE QUALITY PROBLEMS

After understanding what service quality is, let's explore a model that allows us to identify and correct service quality problems.

The Gaps Model in Service Design and Delivery

Valarie Zeithaml, A. Parasuraman, and Leonard Berry identify four potential gaps within the service organization that may lead to a fifth and most serious final gap—the difference between what customers expected and what they perceived was delivered.[7] Figure 14.4 extends and refines their framework to identify a total of six types of gaps that can occur at different points during the design and delivery of a service performance. Let's explore the six gaps in more detail:

- ***Gap 1—The Knowledge Gap*** is the difference between what senior management believes customers expect and customers' actual needs and expectations.
- ***Gap 2—The Policy Gap*** is the difference between management's understanding of customers' expectations and the quality standards established for service delivery. We call it the policy gap because the management made a policy decision not to deliver what they think customers expect. Reasons for setting standards below customer expectations typically include cost and feasibility considerations.
- ***Gap 3—The Delivery Gap*** is the difference between specified service delivery standards and the delivery teams' and service operations' actual performance on these standards.

TABLE 14.2 Generic Dimensions Used by Customers to Evaluate Service Quality

Dimensions	Characteristics	Queries
Tangibles	Appearance of physical facilities, equipment, personnel, and communication materials	Are the hotel's facilities attractive? Is my accountant dressed appropriately? Is my bank statement easy to understand?
Reliability	Ability to perform the promised service dependably and accurately	Does my lawyer call me back when promised? Is my telephone bill free of errors? Is my TV repaired right the first time?
Responsiveness	Willingness to help customers and provide prompt service	When there is a problem, does the firm resolve it quickly? Is my stockbroker willing to answer my questions? Is the cable TV company willing to give me a specific time when the instaler will show up?
Assurance		
• *Credibility*	Trustworthiness, believability, honesty of the service provider	Does the hospital have a good reputation? Does my stockbroker refrain from pressuring me to buy? Does the repair firm guarantee its work?
• *Security*	Freedom from danger, risk, or doubt	Is it safe for me to use the bank's ATMs at right? Is my credit card protected against unauthorized use? Can I be sure that my insurance policy provides complete coverage?
• *Competence*	Possession of the skills and knowledge required to perform the service	Can the bank teller process my transaction without fumbling around? Is my travel agent able to obtain the Information I need when I call? Does the dentist appear to be competent?
• *Courtesy*	Politeness, respect, consideration, and friendliness of contact personnel	Does the fight attendant have a pleasant demeanor? Are the telephone operators consistently polite when answering my calls? Does the plumber take off muddy shoes before stepping on my carpet?
Empathy		
• *Access*	Approachability and ease of contact	How easy is it for me to talk to a supervisor when I have a problem? Does the airline have a 24-hour toll-free phone number? Is the hotel conveniantly located?
• *Communication*	Listening to customers and keeping them informed in a language they can understand	When I have a complaint, is the manager willing to listen to me? Does my doctor avoid using technical jargon? Does the electrician call when he or she is unable to keep a scheduled appointment?
• *Understanding the customer*	Making the effort to know customers and their needs	Does someone in the hotel recognize me as a regular customer? Does my stockbroker try to determine my specific financial objectives? Is the moving company willing to accommodate my schedule?

- ***Gap 4—The Communications Gap*** is the difference between what the company communicates and what it actually delivers to its customers. This gap is caused by two sub-gaps.[8] First, the internal communications gap is the difference between what the company's advertising and sales personnel think are the product's features, performance, and service quality level and what the company actually is able to deliver. Second, the overpromise gap that can be caused by advertising and sales personnel assessed by the sales they generate can lead them to overpromise.

- *Gap 5—The Perceptions Gap* is the difference between what is, in fact, delivered to the customer and what customers perceive they have received (because they are sometimes unable to accurately evaluate service quality).
- *Gap 6—The Service Quality Gap* is the difference between what customers expect to receive and their perceptions of the service that actually is delivered.

In this model, gaps 1, 5, and 6 represent external gaps between the customer and the organization. Gaps 2, 3, and 4 are internal gaps occurring between various functions and departments within the organization.

Core Strategies to Address Gaps in Service Quality

Gaps at any point in service design and delivery can damage relationships with customers. The service quality gap (number 6) is the most critical; hence, the ultimate goal in improving service quality is to close or narrow this gap as much as possible. However, to achieve this, service organizations usually need to work on closing the other five gaps depicted in Figure 14.4. Improving service quality requires identifying the specific causes of each gap and then developing strategies to close them.

The strength of the gaps model is that it offers generic insights and solutions that can be applied across industries. We summarized a series of generic prescriptions for closing the six quality gaps in Table 14.3. These prescriptions are a good starting point to think about how to close specific gaps in an organization. But of course, each firm must develop its own customized approach to ensure that service quality becomes and remains a key objective.

MEASURING AND IMPROVING SERVICE QUALITY

We now understand the gaps model and the general prescriptions on how to close the six quality gaps. Let's next discuss how to use measurement to guide our service

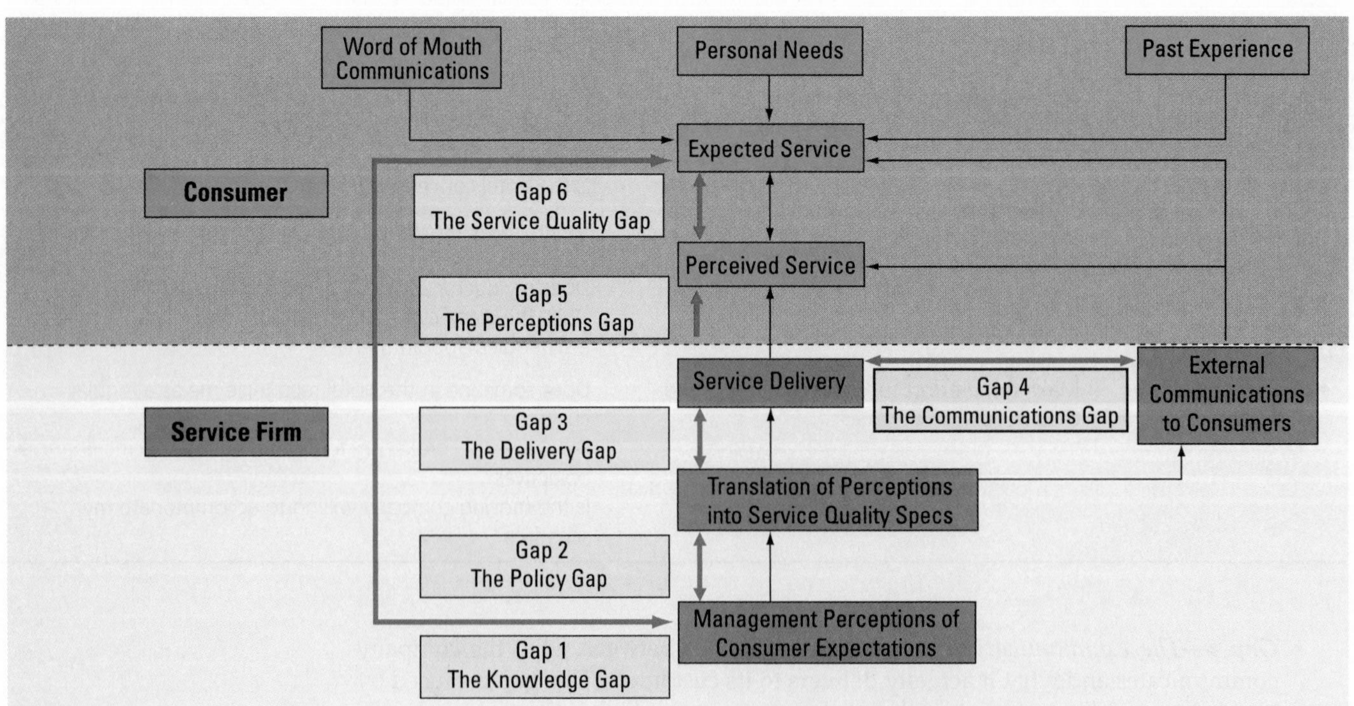

FIGURE 14.4 The Gaps Model

Source: Adapted from the original 5-gaps model developed by Parasuraman, A., Zeithaml, V. A., & Berry, L. L. (1985). A conceptual model of service quality and its implications for future research. *Journal of Marketing* 49, (Fall), pp. 41–50; Zeithaml, V. A., Bitner, M. J., & Gremler, D. (2006). *Services Marketing: Integrating Customer Focus Across the Firm* (p. 46). NY: McGraw Hill/Irwin. A further gap (Gap 5) was added by Christopher Lovelock (1994), Product Plus (p. 112). New York: McGraw Hill.

quality improvement efforts. It is commonly said that "what is not measured is not managed." Without measurement, managers cannot be sure whether service quality gaps exist, let alone what types of gaps, where they exist, and what potential corrective actions should be taken. And, of course, measurement is needed to determine whether goals for improvement are met after changes have been implemented.

Soft and Hard Service Quality Measures

Customer-defined standards and measures of service quality can be grouped into two broad categories: soft and hard. *Soft measures* cannot easily be observed and must be collected by talking to customers, employees, or others. As noted by Valarie Zeithaml and Mary Jo Bitner, "Soft standards provide direction, guidance and feedback to employees on ways to achieve customer satisfaction and can be quantified by measuring customer perceptions and beliefs."[9] SERVQUAL (see Appendix 14.1) is an example of a sophisticated soft measurement system.

Hard measures and standards, in contrast, are characteristics and activities that can be counted, timed, or measured through audits. Such measures might include the number of telephone calls that dropped while the customers were on hold, how many orders were filled correctly, the time required to complete a specific task, how many minutes customers had to wait in line at a particular stage in the service delivery, the number of trains that arrived late, and the number of bags lost. Standards often are set with reference to the percentage of occasions on which a particular measure is achieved. The challenge for service marketers is to ensure that operational measures of service quality reflect customer input.

Organizations known for excellent service make use of both soft and hard measures. These organizations are good at listening to both their customers and their customer-contact employees. The larger the organization, the more important it is to create formalized feedback programs using a variety of professionally designed and implemented customer feedback and research procedures.

We will provide a comprehensive overview of soft measures in the next section on customer feedback, followed later by a section on hard measures.

LEARNING FROM CUSTOMER FEEDBACK[10]

How can companies measure their performance against soft standards of service quality? According to Leonard Berry and A. Parasuraman:

> [C]ompanies need to establish ongoing listening systems using multiple methods among different customer groups. A single service quality study is a snapshot taken at a point in time and from a particular angle. Deeper insight and more informed decision making come from a continuing series of snapshots taken from various angles and through different lenses, which form the essence of systematic listening.[11]

In this section, we discuss how customer feedback can be systematically collected, analyzed, and disseminated via an institutionalized customer feedback system (CFS) to achieve customer-driven learning and service improvements.[12]

Key Objectives of Effective Customer Feedback Systems

"It is not the strongest species that survive, nor the most intelligent, but the ones most responsive to change" wrote Charles Darwin. Similarly, many strategists have concluded that in increasingly competitive markets, the ultimate competitive advantage for a firm is to learn and change faster than the competition.[13] Effective customer feedback systems (CFSs) facilitate fast learning. Specific objectives of effective customer feedback systems typically fall into three main categories:

1. **Assessment and Benchmarking of Service Quality and Performance.** The objective is to answer the question "How satisfied are our customers?" This

TABLE 14.3 Prescriptions for Closing Service Quality Gaps

Types of Quality Gap	Proposed Solutions
Gap 1—The Knowledge Gap	*Educate Management About What Customers Expect* • Sharpen market research procedures, including questionnaire and interview design, sampling, and field implementation, and repeat research studies once in a while • Implement an effective customer feedback system that includes satisfaction research, complaint content analysis, and customer panels • Increase interactions between customers and management • Facilitate and encourage communication between front-line employees and management
Gap 2—The Policy Gap	*Establish the Right Service Processes and Specify Standards* • Get the customer service processes right: ○ Use a rigorous, systematic, and customer-centric process for designing and redesigning customer service processes. ○ Standardize repetitive work tasks to ensure consistency and reliability by substituting hard technology for human contact and improving work methods (soft technology). • Develop tiered service products that meet customer expectations: ○ Consider premium, standard, and economy-level products to allow customers to self-segment according to their needs, or ○ Offer customers different levels of service at different prices • Set, communicate, and reinforce measurable customer-oriented service standards for all work units: ○ Establish for each step in service delivery a set of clear service quality goals that are challenging, realistic, and explicitly designed to meet customer expectations. ○ Ensure that employees understand and accept goals, standards, and priorities
Gap 3—The Delivery Gap	*Ensure that Performance Meets Standards* • Ensure that customer service teams are motivated and able to meet service standards: ○ Improve recruitment with a focus on employee-job fit; select employees for the abilities and skills needed to perform their job well. ○ Train employees on the technical and soft skills needed to perform their assigned tasks effectively, including interpersonal skills, especially for dealing with customers under stressful conditions. ○ Clarify employee roles and ensure that employees understand how their jobs contribute to customer satisfaction; teach them about customer expectations, perceptions and problems. ○ Build cross-functional service teams that can offer customer-centric service delivery and problem resolution. ○ Empower managers and employees in the field by pushing decision-making power down the organization. ○ Measure performance: provide regular feedback and reward customer service team performance as well as individual employees and managers on attaining quality goals. • Install the right technology, equipment, support processes, and capacity: ○ Select the most appropriate technologies and equipment for enhanced performance. ○ Ensure that employees working on internal support jobs provide good service to their own internal customer, the front-line personnel. ○ Balance demand against productive capacity. • Manage customers for service quality. ○ Educate customers so that they can perform their roles and responsibilities in service delivery effectively.

objective includes learning about how well a firm performed in comparison to its main competitor(s), how it performed in comparison to the previous year (or quarter, or month), whether investments in certain service aspects have paid off in terms of customer satisfaction, and where the firm wants to be the following year. Often, a key objective of comparison against other units (branches, teams,

Types of Quality Gap	Suggest Solutions

Gap 4—The Communications Gap	*Close the Internal Communications Gap by Ensuring that Communications Promises are Realistic and Correctly Understood by Customers*
	• Educate managers responsible for sales and marketing communications about operational capabilities:
	  ° Seek inputs from front-line employees and operations personnel when new communications programs are being developed.
	  ° Let service providers preview advertisements and other communications before customers are exposed to them.
	  ° Get sales staff to involve operations stall in face-to-face meetings with customers.
	  ° Develop internal educational and motivational advertising campaigns to strengthen understanding and integration among the marketing, operations, and human resource functions, and to standardize service delivery across different locations.
	• Ensure that communications content sets realistic customer expectations.
	• Be specific with promises and manage customers' understanding of communication content:
	  ° Pretest all advertising, brochures, telephone scripts, and website content prior to external release to see if target audience interpret them as the firm intends [if not, revise and retest]. Make sure that the advertising content reflects those service characteristics that are most important to customers. Let customers know what is not possible and why.
	  ° Identity and explain in real time the reasons for shortcomings in service performance, highlighting those that cannot be controlled by the firm.
	  ° Document beforehand the tasks and performance guarantees that are included in an agreement or contract. After the completion of the work, explain what work was performed in relation to a specific billing statement.

Gap 5—The Perception Gap	*Tangibilize and Communicate the Service Quality Delivered*
	• Make service quality tangible and communicate the service quality delivered:
	  ° Develop service environments and physical evidence cues that are consistent with the level of service provided.
	  ° For complex and credence services, keep customers informed during service delivery on what is being done, and give debriefings after the delivery so that customers can appreciate the quality of service they received.
	  ° Provide physical evidence (e.g., for repairs, show customers the damaged components that were removed).

Gap 6—The Service Quality Gap	Close Gaps 1 to 5 to consistently meet Customer Expectations. Gap 6 is the accumulated outcome of all the preceding gaps. It will be closed when Gaps 1 to 5 have been addressed.

Adapted and extended from Zeithaml, V. A., Parasuraman, A., & Berry, L. L. (1990). *Delivering service quality: Balancing customer perceptions and expectations.* New York: The Free Press; Zeithaml, V. A., Bitner, M. J., & Gremler, D. (2006). *Services marketing: Integrating customer focus across the firm* (5th ed.). New York: McGraw-Hill, 2009, Chapter 2. The remaining prescriptions were developed by the authors.

service products, competitors) is to motivate managers and service staff to improve performance, especially when the results are linked to compensation.

Benchmarking does not only have to be with companies from the same industry. Southwest Airlines benchmarked Formula One pit stops for speedy turnaround of aircraft; Pizza Hut benchmarked Federal Express for on-time package delivery; and Ikea examined the military for excellence in coordination and logistics management.

2. **Customer-Driven Learning and Improvements.** Here, the objective is to answer the questions, "What makes our customers happy or unhappy?" and "What are our strengths we want to cement, and what are our weaknesses we need to improve?" For this, more specific or detailed information on processes and products is required to guide a firm's service improvement efforts and to pinpoint areas with potentially high returns for quality investment.
3. **Creating a Customer-Oriented Service Culture.** This objective is concerned with focusing the organization on customer needs and customer satisfaction, and rallying the entire organization toward a service quality culture.

Of the three objectives just discussed, firms seem to be doing well on the first, but often are missing great opportunities in the other two. Neil Morgan, Eugene Anderson, and Vikas Mittal concluded in their research on the customer satisfaction information usage (CSIU) the following:

> Many of the firms in our sample do not appear to gain significant customer-focused learning benefits from their CS [customer satisfaction] systems, because they are designed to act primarily as a control mechanism [i.e., our assessment or benchmarking].... [Firms] may be well served to reevaluate how they deploy their existing CSIU resources. The majority of CSIU resources... are consumed in CS data collection. This often leads to too few resources being allocated to the analysis, dissemination, and utilization of this information to realize fully the potential payback from the investment in data collection.[14]

Use a Mix of Customer Feedback Collection Tools

Reene Fleming, soprano and America's beautiful voice, once said: "We singers are unfortunately not able to hear ourselves sing. You sound entirely different to yourself. We need the ears of others—from outside...." Likewise, firms need to listen to the voice of the customer. Table 14.4 gives an overview of typically used feedback tools and their ability to meet various requirements. Recognizing that different tools have different strengths and weaknesses, service marketers should select a mix of customer feedback collection tools that jointly deliver the needed information. As Leonard Berry and "Parsu" Parasuraman observed, "Combining approaches enables a firm to tap the strengths of each and compensate for weaknesses."[15]

TOTAL MARKET, ANNUAL, AND TRANSACTIONAL SURVEYS. *Total market surveys* and *annual surveys* typically measure satisfaction with all major customer service processes and products.[16] The level of measurement usually is at a high level, with the objective of obtaining a global index or indicator of overall service satisfaction for the entire firm. This could be based on indexed (e.g., using various attribute ratings) and/or weighted data (e.g., weighted by core segments and/or products).

Overall indices such as these tell how satisfied customers are, but not why they are happy or unhappy. There are limits to the number of questions that can be asked about each individual process or product. For example, a typical retail bank has some 30 to 50 key customer service processes (e.g., from car loan applications to cash deposits at the teller). Because of the sheer number of processes, many surveys have room for only one or two questions per process (e.g., how satisfied are you with our ATM services?) and cannot address issues in greater detail.

In contrast, *transactional surveys*, also called intercept surveys, typically are conducted after customers have completed a specific transaction (Figure 14.5). At this point, if time permits, they may be queried about this process in some depth. In the case of the bank, all key attributes and aspects of ATM services could be included in the survey, including some open-ended questions such as "liked best," "liked least,"

TABLE 14.4 Strengths and Weaknesses of Key Customer Feedback Collection Tools

	Level of Measurement							
Collection Tools	**Firm**	**Process**	**Transaction Specific**	**Actionable**	**Representative, Reliable**	**Potential for Service Recovery**	**First-Hand Learning**	**Cost-Effectiveness**
Total market survey (including competitors)	●	○	○	○	●	○	○	○
Annual survey on overall satisfaction	●	◑	○	○	●	○	○	○
Transactional survey	●	●	◑	◑	●	○	○	○
Service feedback cards	◑	●	●	◑	◑	●	◑	●
Mystery shopping	○	◑	●	●	○	○	◑	○
Unsolicited feedback (e.g., complaints)	○	◑	●	●	○	●	◑	●
Focus group discussions	○	◑	●	●	○	◑	●	◑
Service reviews	○	◑	●	●	○	●	●	◑

Legend: ● meets requirements fully; ◑ moderately; ○ hardly at all.

Source: Adapted from Jochen Wirtz and Monica Tomlin, "Institutionalizing Customer-driven Learning through Fully Integrated Customer Feedback Systems," Managing Service Quality 10 (no. 4, 2000) 210. Copyright © 2000 MCB UP Ltd. Used with permission from Emerald Publishing Group.

and "suggested improvements." Such feedback is more actionable, can tell the firm why customers are happy or unhappy with the process, and usually yields specific insights on how to improve customer satisfaction.

All three survey types are representative and reliable when designed properly. Representativeness and reliability are required for:

1. Accurate assessments of where the company, a process, branch, team, or individual stands relative to quality goals (having a representative and reliable sample means that observed changes in quality scores are not the result of sample biases and/or random errors).
2. Evaluations of individual service employees, service delivery teams, branches, and/or processes, especially when incentive schemes are linked to such measures. The methodology has to be water-tight if staff are to trust and buy into the results, especially when surveys deliver bad news.

The potential for service recovery is important and should, if possible, be designed into feedback collection tools. However, many surveys promise anonymity, making it impossible to identify and respond to dissatisfied respondents. In personal encounters or telephone surveys, interviewers can be instructed to ask customers whether they would like the firm to get back to them on dissatisfying issues.

FIGURE 14.5 Transactional Surveys Are Typically Conducted Following Service Delivery

SERVICE FEEDBACK CARDS. This powerful and inexpensive tool involves giving customers a feedback card (or an online pop-up form, email, or SMS) following completion of a major service process and inviting them to return it by mail or other means to a central customer feedback unit. For example, a feedback card can be attached to each housing loan approval letter or to each hospital invoice. These cards are a good indicator of process quality and yield specific feedback on what works well and what doesn't. However, customers who are delighted or very dissatisfied are likely to be overrepresented among the respondents, which affects the reliability and representativeness of this tool.

MYSTERY SHOPPING. Service businesses often use "mystery shoppers" to determine whether frontline staff are displaying desired behaviors (see Service Perspective 14.1). Banks, retailers, car rental firms, and hotels are among the industries making active use of mystery shoppers. For example, the central reservation offices of a global hotel chain contracts for a large-scale monthly mystery caller survey to assess the skills of individual associates in relation to the phone sales process. Such actions as correctly positioning of the

SERVICE PERSPECTIVE 14.1

CUSTOMER AS QUALITY CONTROL INSPECTORS?

Mystery shopping is a good method for checking whether frontline employees display the desired and trained behaviors and follow the specified service procedures, but don't use customer surveys for this. Ron Kaufman, founder of Up Your Service! College, describes a recent service experience:

"We had a wonderful ride in the hotel car from the airport. The driver was so friendly. He gave us a cold towel and a cool drink. He offered a choice of music, talked about the weather, and made sure we were comfortable with the air conditioning. His smile and good feelings washed over us, and I liked it!"

"At the hotel, I signed the guest registration and gave my credit card. Then the counter staff asked me to complete another form." It read:

LIMOSINE SURVEY

To consistently ensure the proper application of our quality standards, we value your feedback on our limousine service:

1. Were you greeted by our airport representative?	YES/NO
2. Were you offered a cold towel?	YES/NO
3. Were you offered cold water?	YES/NO
4. Was a selection of music available?	YES/NO
5. Did the driver ask you about the air conditioning?	YES/NO
6. Was the driver driving at a safe speed?	YES/NO

Room Number: ________ Limo Number: ________ Date: ________

Kaufman continued: "As I read the form, all the good feelings fell away. The driver's enthusiasm suddenly seemed a charade. His concern for our well-being became just a checklist of actions to follow. His good mood was merely an act to meet the standard, not a connection with his guests. I felt like the hotel's 'quality control inspector,' and I did not like it. If the hotel wants my opinion, make me an advisor not an inspector. Ask me: What did you enjoy most about your ride from the airport? (I'd told them about their wonderful driver). What else could we do to make your ride even more enjoyable? (I'd have recommended offering the use of a cell phone)."

Source: Copyright © 2009 Ron Kaufman. Used with permission.

various products, up-selling and cross-selling, and closing the deal are measured. The survey also assesses the quality of the phone conversation on such dimensions as "a warm and friendly greeting" and "establishing rapport with the caller." Mystery shopping gives highly actionable and in-depth insights for coaching, training, and performance evaluation.

Because the number of mystery calls or visits typically is small, no individual survey is reliable or representative. However, if a particular staff member performs well (or poorly) month after month, managers can infer with reasonable confidence that this person's performance is good (or poor).

UNSOLICITED CUSTOMER FEEDBACK. Customer complaints, compliments, and suggestions can be transformed into a stream of information that can be used to help monitor quality and highlight improvements needed to the service design and delivery. Complaints and compliments are rich sources of detailed feedback on what makes customers unhappy and what delights them.

Like feedback cards, unsolicited feedback is not a reliable measure of overall customer satisfaction, but it is a good source of ideas for improvement. If the objective of collecting feedback is mainly to get feedback on what to improve (rather than for benchmarking and/or assessing staff), reliability and representativeness are not needed, and more qualitative tools—such as complaints/compliments or focus groups—generally suffice.

Detailed customer complaint and compliment letters, recorded telephone conversations, and direct feedback from employees can serve as an excellent tool for communicating internally what customers want and enable employees and managers at all levels to "listen" to customers first hand. Such learning is much more powerful for shaping the thinking and customer orientation of service staff than using "clinical" statistics and reports.

For example, Singapore Airlines prints excerpts from complaint and compliment letters in its monthly employee magazine, *Outlook*. Southwest Airlines shows videos containing footage of customers providing feedback in their training sessions to service staff. Seeing actual customers giving comments about their service (positive and negative) leaves a much deeper and lasting impression on staff than any statistical analysis.

For complaints, suggestions, and inquiries to be useful as research input, they have to be funneled into a central collection point, logged, categorized, and analyzed.[17] That requires a system for capturing customer feedback where it is made and then reporting it to a central unit. Some firms use a simple Intranet site to record all feedback received by any staff member. Coordinating such activities is not a simple matter, because of the many entry points, including the firm's own frontline employees who may be in contact with customers face-to-face, by telephone, or via mail or email, intermediary organizations acting on behalf of the original supplier, and managers who normally work backstage but are contacted by a customer seeking higher authority.

FOCUS GROUP DISCUSSIONS AND SERVICE REVIEWS. Both tools give great specific insights on potential service improvements and ideas. Typically, focus groups are organized by key customer segments or user groups to drill down on the needs of these users. Service reviews are in-depth, one-on-one interviews, usually conducted once a year with a firm's most valuable customers. Usually, a senior executive of the firm visits the customers and discusses issues such as how well the firm performed the previous year and what should be maintained or changed. That senior person then goes back to the organization and discusses the feedback with his or her account managers, and then both write a letter back to the client detailing how the firm will respond to that customer's service needs and how the account will be managed the following year.

Apart from providing an excellent learning opportunity (especially when the reviews across all customers are compiled and analyzed), service reviews focus on retention of the most valuable customers and get high marks for service recovery potential.

Analysis, Reporting, and Dissemination of Customer Feedback

Choosing the relevant feedback tools and collecting customer feedback is meaningless if the company is unable to disseminate the information to the relevant parties to take action. Hence, to drive continuous improvement and learning, a reporting system needs to deliver feedback and its analysis to frontline staff, process owners, branch or department managers, and top management.

The feedback loop to the frontline should be immediate for complaints and compliments, as is practiced in a number of service businesses where complaints, compliments, and suggestions are discussed with staff during a daily morning brief. In addition, we recommend three types of service performance reports to provide the information necessary for service management and team learning:

1. A monthly *Service Performance Update* provides process owners with timely feedback on customer comments and operational process performance. Here, the verbatim feedback is provided to the process manager who can in turn discuss them with his or her service delivery teams.
2. A quarterly *Service Performance Review* provides process owners and branch or department managers with trends in process performance and service quality.
3. An annual *Service Performance Report* gives top management a representative assessment of the status and long-term trends relating to customer satisfaction with the firm's services.

These reports should be short and reader-friendly, focusing on key indicators and providing an easily understood commentary for the people in charge to act on.

HARD MEASURES OF SERVICE QUALITY

Having learned about the various tools for collecting soft service quality measures, let's explore hard measures in more detail. Hard measures typically refer to operational processes or outcomes and include such data as uptime, service response times, failure rates, and delivery costs. In a complex service operation, multiple measures of service quality will be recorded at many different points. In low-contact services in which customers are not deeply involved in the service delivery process, many operational measures apply to backstage activities that have only a second-order effect on customers.

FedEx was one of the first service companies to understand the need for a firm-wide index of service quality that embraced all the key activities that affect customers. By publishing a single, composite index on a frequent basis, senior managers hoped that all FedEx employees would work toward improving quality. The firm recognized the danger of using percentages as targets, because they might lead to complacency. In an organization as large as FedEx, which ships millions of packages a day, even delivering 99 percent of packages on time or having 99.9 percent of flights arrive safely would lead to horrendous problems. Instead, the company decided to approach quality measurement from the baseline of zero failures. As noted by one senior executive:

> It's only when you examine the types of failures, the number that occur of each type, and the reasons why, that you begin to improve the quality of your service. For us the trick was to express quality failures in absolute numbers. That led us to develop the Service Quality Index or SQI [pronounced "sky"], which takes each of 12 different events that occur every day, takes the numbers of those events and multiplies them by a weight... based on the amount of aggravation caused to customers—as evidenced by their tendency to write to FedEx and complain about them.[18]

The design of this "hard" index reflected the findings of extensive "soft" customer research. Looking at service failures from the customer's perspective, the Service Quality Index (SQI) measures daily the occurrence of 12 different activities likely to lead to customer dissatisfaction. The index is composed by taking the raw number of each event and multiplying it by a weighting that highlights the seriousness of that event for customers—to give a point score for each item. The points are then added up to generate that day's index (see Best Practice in Action 14.1). Like a golf score, the lower the index,

BEST PRACTICE IN ACTION 14.1

FedEx's Approach to Listening to the Voice of the Customer

"We believe that service quality must be mathematically measured" declares Frederick W. Smith, Chairman, President, and CEO of FedEx Corporation. The company has a commitment to clear quality goals, followed up with continuous measurement of progress against those goals. This practice forms the foundation for its approach to quality.

FedEx initially set two ambitious quality goals: 100 percent customer satisfaction for every interaction and transaction, and 100 percent service performance on every package handled. Customer satisfaction was measured by the percentage of on-time deliveries, which referred to the number of packages delivered on time as a percentage of total package volume. However, as things turned out, percentage of on-time delivery was an internal standard that was not synonymous with customer satisfaction.

Since FedEx had systematically cataloged customer complaints, it was able to develop what CEO Smith calls the "Hierarchy of Horrors," which referred to the eight most common complaints by customers: (1) wrong day delivery, (2) right day, late delivery, (3) pick-up not made, (4) lost package, (5) customer misinformed, (6) billing and paper work mistakes, (7) employee performance failures, and (8) damaged packages. This list was the foundation on which FedEx build its customer feedback system.

FedEx refined the list of "horrors" and developed the Service Quality Indicator (SQI), a 12-item measure of satisfaction and service quality from the customers' viewpoint. Weights have been assigned to each item based on its relative importance in determining overall customer satisfaction. All items are tracked daily, so that a continuous index can be computed (see Table 14.5).

In addition to the SQI, which has been modified over time to reflect changes in procedures, services, and customer priorities, FedEx uses a variety of other ways to capture feedback.

Customer Satisfaction Survey—This telephone survey is conducted on a quarterly basis with several thousand randomly selected customers, stratified by its key segments. The results are relayed to senior management on a quarterly basis.

Targeted Customer Satisfaction Survey—This survey covers specific customer service processes and is conducted on a semiannual basis with clients who have experienced one of the specific FedEx processes within the last three months.

FedEx Center Comment Cards—Comment cards are collected from each FedEx storefront business center. The results are tabulated twice a year and relayed to managers in charge of the centers.

On-line Customer Feedback Surveys—FedEx has commissioned regular studies to get feedback for its online services, such package tracking, as well as ad hoc studies on new products.

The information from these various customer feedback measures has helped FedEx to maintain a leadership role in its industry and played an important role in enabling it to receive the prestigious Malcolm Baldrige National Quality Award.

TABLE 14.5 Composition of FedEx's Service Quality Index (SQI)

Failure Type	Weighting Factor x No. of Incidents = Daily Points
Late delivery—right day	1
Late delivery—wrong day	5
Tracing requests unanswered	1
Complaints reopened	5
Missing proofs of delivery	1
Invoice adjustments	1
Missed pickups	10
Lost packages	10
Damaged packages	10
Aircraft delays (minutes)	5
Overgoods (packages missing labels)	5
Abandoned calls	1
Total failure points (SQI)	XXX,XXX

Source: Reproduced from "The Six Sigma Way," Peter Pande, Robert P. Neuman and Ronald R. Cavanagh. Copyright © 2000 McGraw-Hill Companies, Inc. Used with permisison.

Sources: "Blueprints for Service Quality: The Federal Express Approach," *AMA Management Briefing*, New York: American Management Association, 1991, 51–64; Linda Rosencrance, "BetaSphere Delivers FedEx Some Customer Feedback," *Computerworld*, 14, No. 14, 2000, 36.

the better the performance. However, unlike golf, the SQI involves substantial numbers—typically six figures—reflecting the huge number of packages shipped daily. An annual goal is set for the average daily SQI, based on reducing the occurrence of failures over the previous year's total. To ensure a continuing focus on each separate component of the SQI, FedEx established 12 Quality Action Teams, one for each component. The teams were charged with understanding and correcting the root causes underlying the observed problems. In the light of new research insights, the SQI components and their weights have been modified slightly over time from the version shown here.

How can we show performance on hard measures? For this, *control charts* offer a simple method of displaying performance on hard measures over time against specific quality standards. The charts can be used to monitor and communicate individual variables or an overall index. Because they are visual, trends are easily identified. Figure 14.6 shows an airline's performance on the important hard standard of on-time departures. The trends displayed suggest that this issue needs to be addressed by management, because performance is erratic and not very satisfactory. Of course, control charts are only as good as the data on which they are based.

TOOLS TO ANALYZE AND ADDRESS SERVICE QUALITY PROBLEMS

After having assessed service quality using soft and hard measures, how can we now drill deeper to identify common causes of quality shortfalls and take corrective actions? When a problem is caused by controllable, internal forces, there's no excuse for allowing it to recur. In fact, maintaining customers' goodwill after a service failure depends on keeping promises made to the effect that "we're taking steps to ensure that it doesn't happen again!" With prevention as a goal, let's look briefly at some tools for determining the root causes of specific service quality problems.

Root Cause Analysis: The Fishbone Diagram

Cause-and-effect analysis employs a technique first developed by the Japanese quality expert, Kaoru Ishikawa. Groups of managers and staff brainstorm all the possible reasons that might cause a specific problem. The resulting factors are then categorized into one of five groups—equipment, manpower, material, procedures, and other—on a cause-and-effect chart, popularly known as a *fishbone diagram* because of its shape. This technique has been used for many years in manufacturing and, more recently, also in services.

To sharpen the value of the analysis for use in service organizations, we show an extended framework that comprises eight rather than five groupings.[19] "People" has been broken into front-stage personnel and back-stage personnel to highlight that front-stage service problems often are experienced directly by customers, whereas back-stage failures

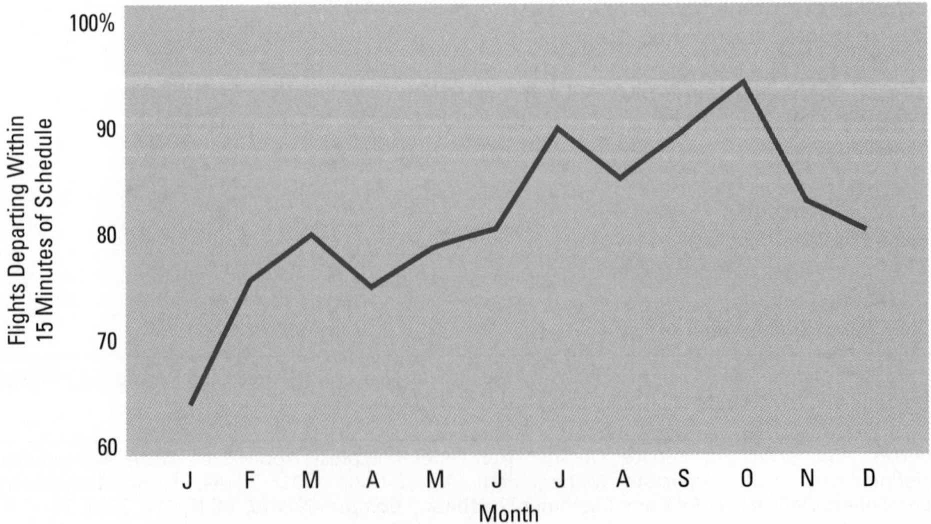

FIGURE 14.6 Control Chart for Departure Delays Showing Percentage of Flights Departing within 15 Minutes of Schedule

tend to show up more obliquely, through a ripple effect. "Information" has been split out from "Procedures," recognizing that many service problems result from information failures often by front-stage personnel to tell customers what to do and when.

In manufacturing, customers have little effect on day-to-day operational processes, but in a high-contact service they are involved in front-stage operations. If they don't play their own roles correctly, they may reduce service productivity and cause quality problems for themselves and other customers. For instance, an aircraft can be delayed if a passenger tries to board at the last minute with an oversized suitcase, which then has to be loaded into the cargo hold. An example of the extended fishbone is shown in Figure 14.7, displaying 27 possible reasons for late departures of passenger aircraft.[20]

Once all the main potential causes have been identified, it's necessary to assess how much impact each cause has on actual delays. This can be established using frequency counts in combination with Pareto analysis, discussed next.

Pareto Analysis

Pareto analysis (named after the Italian economist who first developed it) seeks to identify the principal causes of observed outcomes. This type of analysis underlies the so-called 80/20 rule, because it often reveals that around 80 percent of the value of one variable (in this instance, number of service failures) is accounted for by only 20 percent of the causal variable (i.e., number of possible causes) as identified by the fishbone diagram. Combining the fishbone diagram and Pareto analysis serves to highlight the main causes of service failure.

In the airline example, analysis showed that 88 percent of the company's late departing flights from the airports it served were caused by only four (15 percent) of all the possible factors. In fact, more than half the delays were caused by a single factor: acceptance of late passengers (situations when the staff held a flight for one more passenger who was checking in after the official cutoff time).

On such occasions, the airline made a friend of that late passenger—possibly encouraging a repeat of this undesirable behavior on a future occasion—but risked

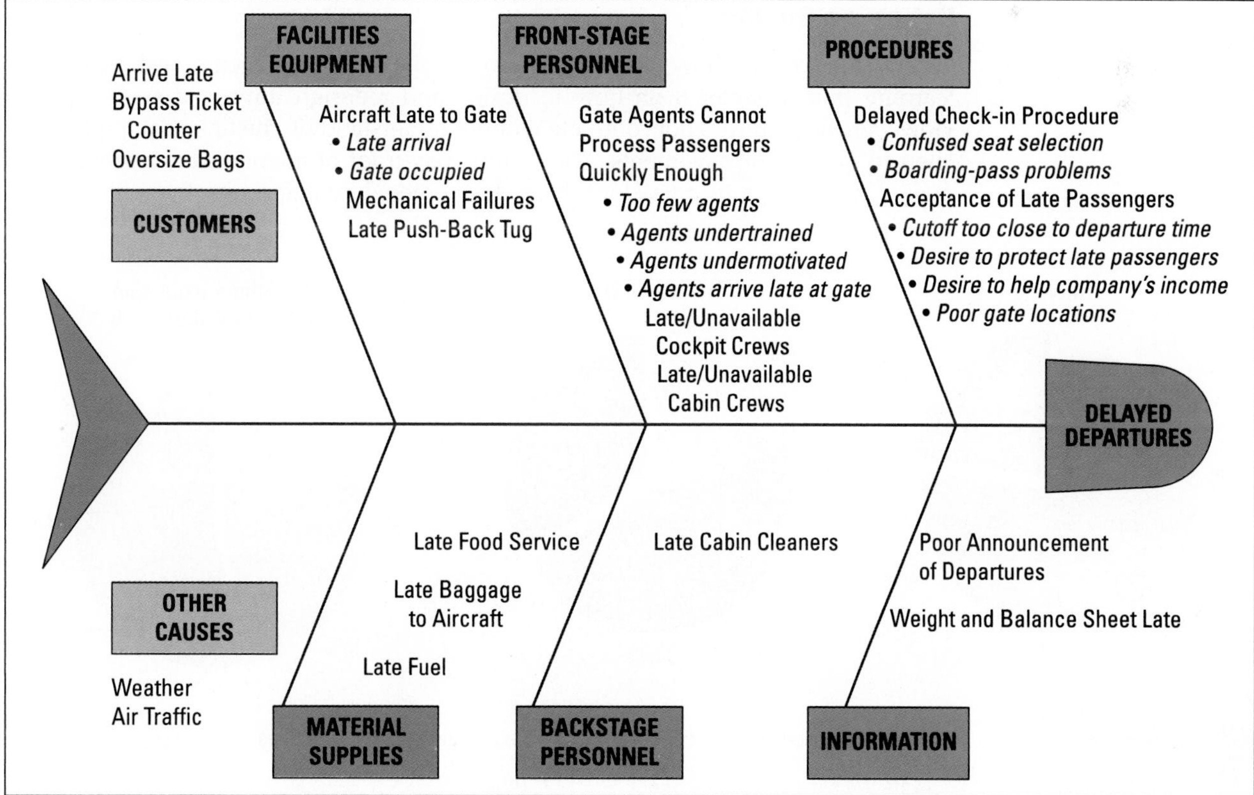

FIGURE 14.7 Cause-and-Effect Chart for Flight Departure Delays

alienating all the other passengers who were already onboard, waiting for the aircraft to depart. Other major delays included waiting for pushback (a vehicle must arrive to pull the aircraft away from the gate), waiting for fueling, and delays in signing the weight and balance sheet (a safety requirement relating to the distribution of the aircraft's load that the captain must observe on each flight). Further analysis, however, showed some significant variations in reasons from one airport to another (see Figure 14.8).

Blueprinting—A Powerful Tool for Identifying Fail Points

Fishbone diagrams and Pareto analyses tell us the causes and importance of quality problems. Blueprints allow us to drill down further to identify where exactly in a service process the problem was caused. As described in Chapter 8, a well-constructed blueprint enables us to visualize the process of service delivery by depicting the sequence of front stage interactions that customers experience as they encounter service providers, facilities, and equipment, together with supporting backstage activities, which are hidden from the customers and are not part of their service experience.

Blueprints can be used to identify the potential fail points where failures are most likely to occur, and they help us to understand how failures at one point (such as incorrect entry of an appointment date) may have a ripple effect later in the process (the customer arrives at the doctor's office and is told the doctor is unavailable). By adding frequency counts to the fail points in a blueprint, managers can identify the specific types of failures that occur most frequently and thus need urgent attention.

One desirable solution is to design fail points out of the system (see Chapter 8 for a discussion of the poka-yokes technique on how to approach this). In the case of failures that cannot easily be designed out of a process or are not easily prevented (such as problems related to weather or the public infrastructure), solutions may revolve around development of contingency plans and service recovery guidelines. Knowing what can go wrong and where is an important first step in preventing service quality problems. (Review Chapter 8 for a more detailed discussion of blueprints and how they can be used to design and redesign customer service processes.)

Return on Quality

We now understand how to drill down to specific quality problems, and we can use the learning from Chapter 8 on how to design and redesign improved service processes. However, the picture is not complete without understanding the financial implications related to quality improvements. Many firms pay a lot of attention to improving service quality, however, quite a few have been disappointed by the results. Even firms that have

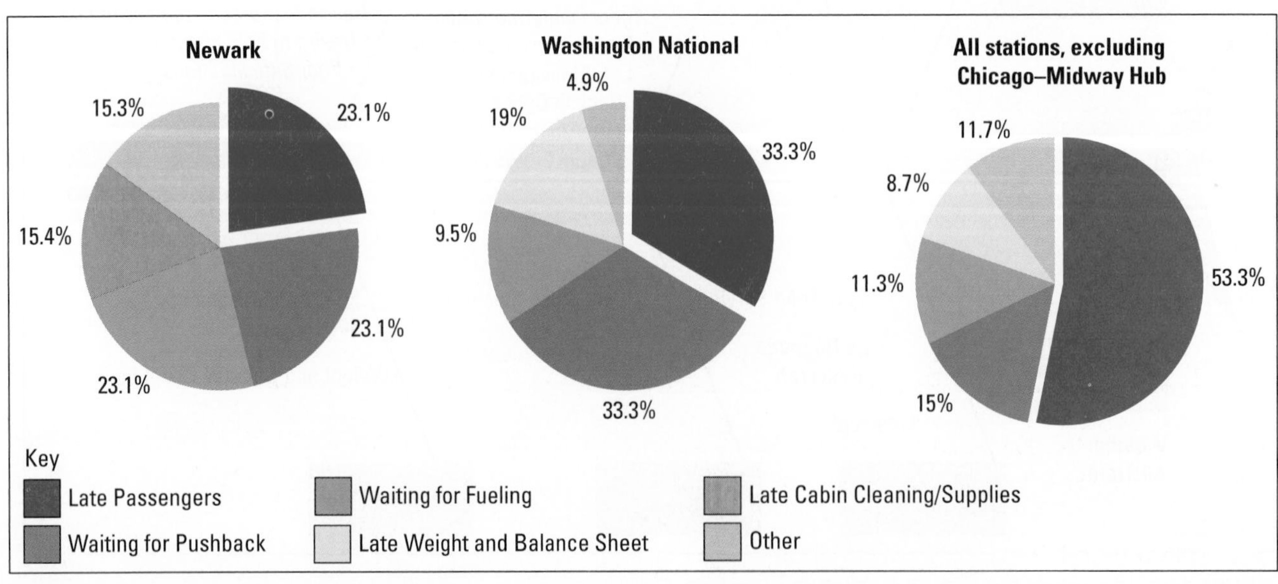

FIGURE 14.8 Analysis of Causes of Flight Departure Delays

been recognized for service quality efforts have sometimes run into financial difficulties, in part because they spent too lavishly on quality improvements. In other instances, such outcomes reflect poor or incomplete execution of the quality program itself.

ASSESS COSTS AND BENEFITS OF QUALITY INITIATIVES. Roland Rust, Anthony Zahonik, and Timothy Keiningham argue for a return on quality (ROQ) approach, based on the assumptions that (1) quality is an investment, (2) quality efforts must be financially accountable, (3) it is possible to spend too much on quality, and (4) not all quality expenditures are equally valid.[21] Hence, expenditures on quality improvement must be related to anticipated increases in profitability. An important implication of the ROQ perspective is that quality improvement efforts may benefit from being coordinated with productivity improvement programs.

To determine the feasibility of new quality improvement efforts, they must be carefully costed in advance and then related to anticipated customer response. Will the program enable the firm to attract more customers (e.g., through word-of-mouth), increase share-of-wallet, and/or to reduce defections? If so, how much additional net income will be generated?

With good documentation, it is sometimes possible for a firm that operates in multiple locations to examine past experience and determine whether a relationship exists between service quality and revenues (see Research Insights 14.1).

RESEARCH INSIGHTS 14.1

QUALITY OF FACILITIES AND ROOM REVENUES AT HOLIDAY INN

To determine the relationship between product quality and financial performance in a hotel context, Sheryl Kimes analyzed three years of quality and operational performance data from 1,135 franchised Holiday Inn hotels in the United States and Canada.

Indicators of product quality came from the franchisor's quality assurance reports. These reports were based on unannounced, semi-annual inspections by trained quality auditors who rotated among different regions and who spent about a day inspecting and rating 19 different areas of each hotel. Twelve of these areas were included in the study: two relating to the guest rooms (bedroom and bathroom) and 10 relating to so-called commercial areas (e.g., exterior, lobby, public restrooms, dining facilities, lounge facilities, corridors, meeting area, recreation area, kitchen, back of house). Each area typically included 10 to 12 individual items that could be passed or failed. The inspector noted the number of defects for each area and the total number for the entire hotel.

Holiday Inn Worldwide also provided data on revenue per available room (RevPAR) at each hotel. To adjust for differences in local conditions, Kimes analyzed sales and revenue statistics obtained from thousands of U.S. and Canadian hotels and reported in the monthly Smith Travel Accommodation Reports (a widely used service in the travel industry). These data enabled Kimes to calculate the RevPAR for the immediate mid-scale competitors of each Holiday Inn hotel. The resulting information was then used to normalize the RevPARs for all Holiday Inns in the sample so that they were now truly comparable. The average RevPAR at the time was about $50.

The analysis was conducted using six-month intervals over a three-year period. For the purposes of the research, if a hotel had failed at least one item in an area, it was considered "defective" in that area. A comparison was then made, on an area by area basis, of the average normalized RevPAR for hotels that were defective in an area against those that were "non-defective."

The findings showed that as the number of defects in a hotel increased, the RevPAR decreased. Hotel areas that showed a particularly strong impact on RevPAR were the exterior, the guest room, and the guest bathroom. Even a single deficiency resulted in a statistically significant reduction in RevPAR, but the combination of deficiencies in all three areas showed an even larger effect on RevPAR over time. Kimes calculated that the average annual revenue impact on a defective hotel was $204,400.

Using an ROQ perspective, the implication was that the primary focus of increased expenditures on housekeeping and preventive maintenance should be the hotel exterior, the guest bedrooms, and guest bathrooms.

Source: Sheryl E. Kimes, "The Relationship between Product Quality and Revenue per Available Room at Holiday Inn," *Journal of Service Research*, 2, November 1999, 138–144.

DETERMINE THE OPTIMAL LEVEL OF RELIABILITY. How far should we go in improving service quality? A company with poor service quality often can achieve big jumps in reliability with relatively modest investments in improvements. As illustrated in Figure 14.9, initial investments in reducing service failure often bring dramatic results, but at some point diminishing returns set in as further improvements require increasing levels of investment, even becoming prohibitively expensive. What level of reliability should we target?

Typically, the cost of service recovery is lower than the cost of an unhappy customer. This suggests a strategy of increasing reliability up to the point that the incremental improvement equals the cost of service recovery or the cost of failure. Although this strategy results in a service less than 100 percent failure free, the firm can still aim to satisfy 100 percent of its target customers by ensuring that either they receive the service as planned or, if a failure occurs, they obtain a satisfying service recovery (see Chapter 13).

DEFINING AND MEASURING PRODUCTIVITY

We highlighted in the introduction of this chapter that we need to look at quality and productivity improvement strategies together rather than in isolation. A firm needs to ensure that it can deliver quality experiences more efficiently to improve its long-term profitability. Let us first discuss what productivity is and how it can be measured.

Defining Productivity in a Service Context

Simply defined, productivity measures the amount of output produced relative to the amount of inputs used. Hence, improvements in productivity require an increase in the ratio of outputs to inputs. An improvement in this ratio might be achieved by cutting the resources required to create a given volume of output or by increasing the output obtained from a given level of inputs.

What do we mean by "input" in a service context? Input varies according to the nature of the business, but may include labor (both physical and intellectual), materials, energy, and capital (consisting of land, buildings, equipment, information systems, and financial assets). The intangible nature of service performances makes it more difficult to measure the productivity of service industries than that of manufacturing. The problem is especially acute for information-based services.

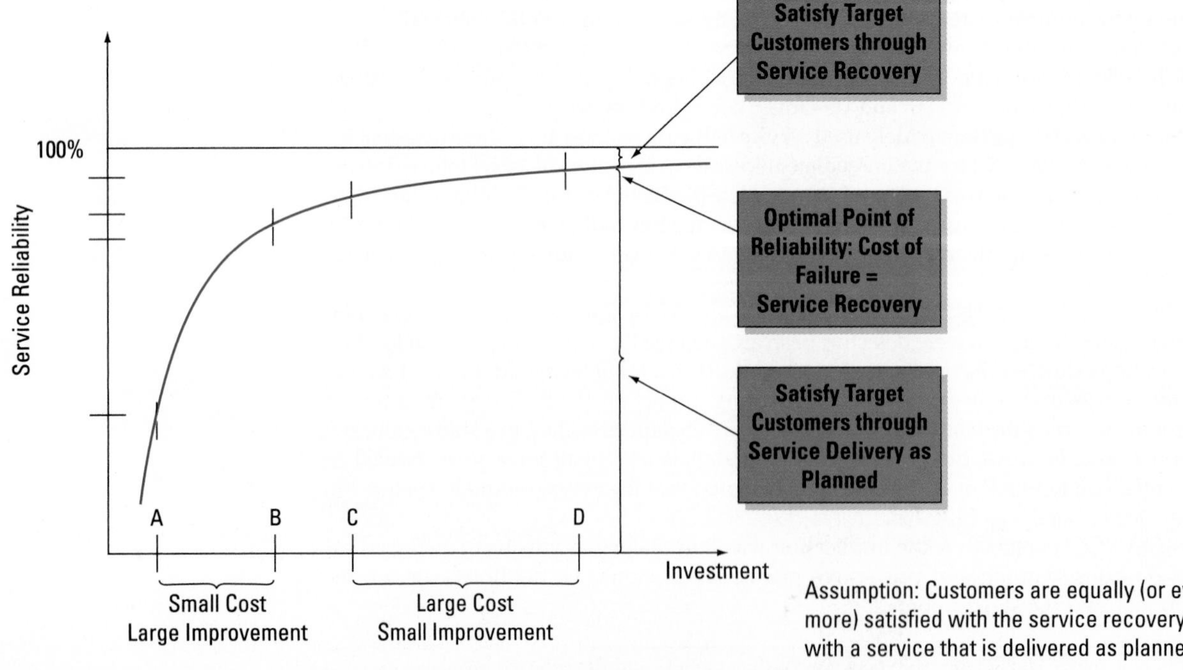

FIGURE 14.9 When Does Improving Service Reliability Become Uneconomical?

Measuring Productivity

Measuring productivity is difficult in services as the output is frequently difficult to define. In a people-processing service, such as a hospital, we can look at the number of patients treated in the course of a year and at the hospital's "census" or average bed occupancy. But how do we account for the various types of interventions performed, such as removal of cancerous tumors, treatment of diabetes, or setting of broken bones? What about differences between patients? How do we evaluate the inevitable difference in outcomes? Some patients get better, some develop complications, and sadly, some even die. Relatively few standardized medical procedures offer highly predictable outcomes.

The measurement task is perhaps simpler in possession-processing services, because many are quasi-manufacturing organizations, performing routine tasks with easily measurable inputs and outputs. Examples include garages that change a car's oil and rotate its tires, or fast-food restaurants that offer limited and simple menus. However, the task gets more complicated when the garage mechanic has to find and repair a water leak, or when we are dealing with a French restaurant known for its varied and exceptional cuisine. What about information-based services? How should we define the output of a bank or a consulting firm?

Service Productivity, Efficiency, and Effectiveness

When we look at the issue of productivity, we need to distinguish among productivity, efficiency, and effectiveness.[22] *Productivity* involves financial valuation of outputs to inputs. *Efficiency* involves comparison to a standard, which usually is time-based—such as how long it takes for an employee to perform a particular task relative to a predefined standard. *Effectiveness,* by contrast, can be defined as the degree to which an organization is meeting its goals, that is, the outcomes it achieves.

Classical techniques of productivity measurement focus on *outputs* rather than *outcomes,* stressing efficiency but neglecting effectiveness. Another major problem in measuring service productivity concerns variability. As James Heskett points out, traditional measures of service output tend to ignore variations in the quality or value of service, thus ignoring effectiveness. In freight transport, for instance, a ton-mile of output for freight delivered late is treated the same for productivity purposes as a similar shipment delivered on time.[23]

Another approach—counting the number of customers served per unit of time—suffers from the same shortcoming. What happens when an increase in customer throughput is achieved at the expense of perceived service quality? Suppose a hairdresser serves three customers per hour and finds she can increase her output to one every 15 minutes by using a faster but noisier hairdryer, reducing conversation with the customer, and rushing her customers. Even if the haircut itself is just as good, the delivery process may be perceived as functionally inferior, leading customers to rate the overall service experience less positively. In this example, productivity and efficiency have been achieved, but not effectiveness (Figure 14.10).

In the long run, organizations that are effective in consistently delivering outcomes desired by customers should be able to command higher prices for their output and build a loyal and profitable customer base. The need to emphasize effectiveness and outcomes suggests that issues of productivity cannot be divorced from those of quality and value.

FIGURE 14.10 Productivity Improvements for the Firm May Result in Customer Frustration if They Cannot Easily Talk to Service Personnel
Source: © Randy Glasbergen

IMPROVING SERVICE PRODUCTIVITY

Intensive competition in many service sectors pushes firms to continually seek ways to improve their productivity.[24] This section discusses potential approaches to and sources of productivity gains.

Generic Productivity Improvement Strategies

Traditionally, operations managers have been in charge of improving service productivity, whose approach typically has centered on such actions as:

- Carefully controlling costs at every step in the process.
- Reducing waste of materials and labor.
- Matching productive capacity to average levels of demand rather than peak levels, so that workers and equipment are not underemployed for extended periods.
- Replacing workers by automated machines and customer-operated self-service technologies (SSTs).
- Providing employees with equipment and data bases that enable them to work faster and/or to a higher level of quality.
- Teaching employees how to work more productively (faster is not necessarily better if it leads to mistakes or unsatisfactory work that has to be redone).
- Broadening the array of tasks that a service worker can perform (which may require revised labor agreements) so as to eliminate bottlenecks and wasteful downtime by allowing managers to deploy workers wherever they are needed most.
- Installing expert systems that allow paraprofessionals to take on work previously performed by more experienced individuals earning higher salaries.

Although improving productivity can be approached incrementally, major gains often require redesigning customer service processes. For example, it's time for service process redesign when customers face unbearably long wait times as happens often in healthcare (e.g., see Figure 14.11). We discussed service process redesign in depth in Chapter 8.

Customer-Driven Approaches to Improve Productivity

In situations in which customers are deeply involved in the service production process, operations managers should also be examining how customer inputs can be made more productive. Marketing managers should be thinking about what marketing strategies should be used to influence customers to behave in more productive ways. Some of these strategies include:

- **Change the Timing of Customer Demand.** By encouraging customers to use a service outside peak periods and offering them incentives to do so, managers can make better use of their productive assets and provide better service. The issues that relate to managing demand in capacity-constrained service businesses is discussed in detail in Chapter 9; revenue management strategies are explored in Chapter 6.
- **Encourage Use of Alternative Service Delivery Channels and Self-Service.** Shifting delivery to more cost-effective service delivery channels such as the

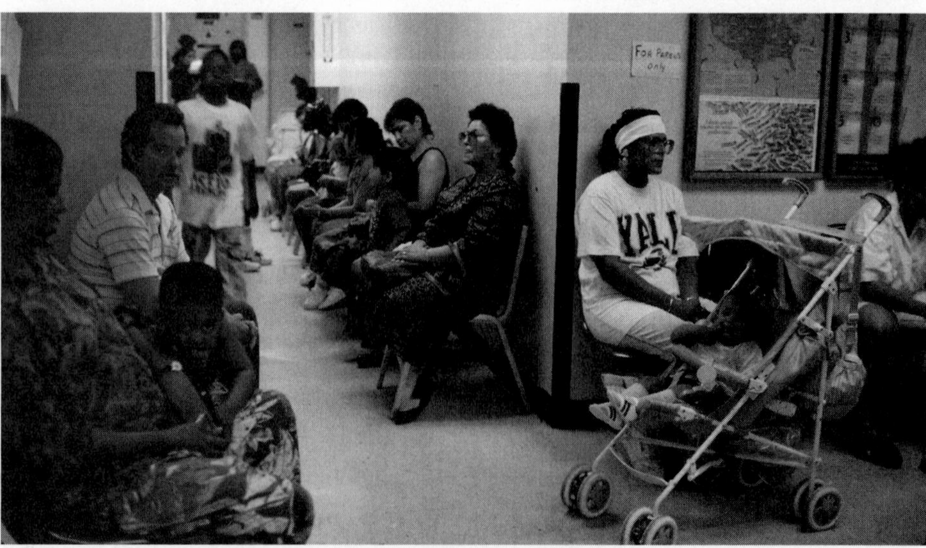

FIGURE 14.11 Long Waiting Times Often Indicate a Need for Service Process Redesign

Internet or self-service machines improve productivity plus facilitate demand management by reducing the pressure on employees and certain types of physical facilities at peak hours. Many technological innovations are designed to get customers to perform tasks previously undertaken by service employees (e.g., see Figure 14.12). The issues related to customers playing a more active role as co-producers of the service are discussed in detail in the context of service process design in Chapter 8.

- **Ask Customers to Use Third Parties.** In some instances, managers may be able to improve service productivity by delegating one or more marketing support functions to third parties. Specialist intermediaries may enjoy economies of scale, enabling them to perform the task more cheaply than the core service provider, allowing the latter to focus on quality and productivity in its own area of expertise. Some intermediaries are identifiable local organizations, such as insurance brokers or travel agencies, which customers can visit in person. Others, such as hotel reservations centers, often subjugate their own identity to that of the client service company. We discussed the use of intermediaries in detail in Chapter 5 in the context of distribution.

FIGURE 14.12 Self-Service Pumps with Credit Card Readers Have Increased Gas Station Productivity

How Productivity Improvements Impact Quality and Value

Managers would do well to examine productivity enhancements from the broader perspective of the business processes used to transform resource inputs into the outcomes desired by customers—especially for processes that not only cross departmental and sometimes geographic boundaries, but also link the back-stage and front-stage areas of the service operation. Hence, as firms make productivity improvements, they need to examine the impact on the customer experience.

FRONT-STAGE EFFORTS TO IMPROVE PRODUCTIVITY. In high-contact services, many productivity enhancements are quite visible. Some changes simply require passive acceptance by customers, while others require customers to adopt new patterns of behavior in their dealings with the organization. If substantial changes are proposed, then it makes sense to conduct market research first to determine how customers may respond. Failure to think through effects on customers may result in a loss of business and cancel out anticipated productivity gains. Refer back to Chapter 8 on how to manage and overcome customers' reluctance to change in service processes.

HOW BACKSTAGE CHANGES MAY IMPACT CUSTOMERS. The marketing implications of back-stage changes depend on whether they affect or are noticed by customers. If airline mechanics develop a procedure for servicing jet engines more quickly, without incurring increased wage rates or material costs, the airline has obtained a productivity improvement that has no impact on the customer's service experience.

Other back-stage changes, however, may have a ripple effect that extends front-stage and affects customers. Marketers should keep abreast of proposed back-stage changes, not only to identify such ripples but also to prepare customers for them. At a bank, for instance, the decision to install new computers and printer peripherals may be driven by plans to improve internal quality controls and reduce the cost of preparing monthly statements. However, this new equipment may change the appearance of bank statements and the time of the month when they are posted. If customers are likely to notice such changes, an explanation may be warranted. If the new statements are easier to read and understand, the change may be worth promoting as a service enhancement.

A CAUTION ON COST REDUCTION STRATEGIES. In the absence of new technology, most attempts to improve service productivity tend to center on efforts to eliminate waste and reduce labor costs. Cutbacks in front-stage staffing mean either that the remaining employees have to work harder and faster, or that there are insufficient personnel to serve customers promptly at busy times. Although employees may be able to work faster for a brief period of time, few can maintain a rapid pace for extended periods: they become exhausted, make mistakes, and treat customers in a cursory manner. Workers trying to do two or three things at once—serving a customer face-to-face while simultaneously answering the telephone and sorting papers, for example—may do a poor job of each task. Excessive pressure breeds discontent and frustration, especially among customer contact personnel who are caught between trying to meet customer needs and attempting to achieve management's productivity goals.

A better way is to search for service process redesign opportunities that lead to drastic improvements in productivity and at the same time increase service quality. Biometrics is set to become a new technology that may allow both—see Service Perspective 14.2.

SERVICE PERSPECTIVE 14.2

BIOMETRICS—THE NEXT FRONTIER IN DRIVING PRODUCTIVITY AND SERVICE QUALITY?

Intense competitive pressure and razor-thin margins in many service industries do not allow firms the luxury of increasing costs to improve quality. Rather, the trick is to constantly seek ways to simultaneously achieve leaps in service quality as well as productivity, something Wirtz and Heracleous call *cost-effective service excellence*. The Internet has in the past allowed many firms to do just that and has redefined industries including financial services, book and music retailing, and travel agencies. Biometrics may be the next major technology driving further service and productivity enhancements.

Biometrics is the authentication or identification of individuals based on a physical characteristic or trait. Physical characteristics include fingerprints, facial recognition, hand geometry, or iris configuration; traits include signature formation, keystroke patterns and voice recognition. Biometrics, as something you are, is both more convenient and more secure than something you know (passwords or pieces of personal information) or something you have (card keys, smart cards, or tokens). There is no risk of forgetting, losing, copying, loaning, or getting your biometrics stolen (Figure 14.13).

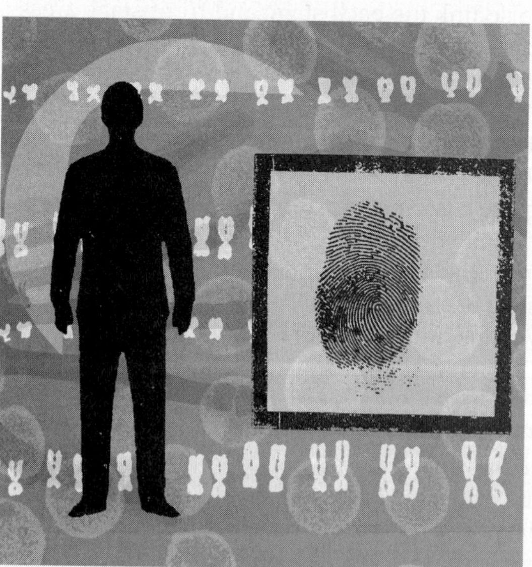

FIGURE 14.13 Customers Cannot Forget or Lose Their Biometrics!

Applications of biometrics range from controlling access to service facilities (used by Disneyworld to provide access to season pass holders), voice recognition at call centers (used by the Home Shopping Network and Charles Schwab to enable fast and hassle-free client authentication), self-service access to safe deposit vaults at banks (used by the Bank of Hawaii and First Tennessee Bank), and cashing checks in supermarkets (used by Kroger, Food 4 Less, and BI-LO).

Sources: Jochen Wirtz and Loizos Heracleous, "Biometrics Meets Services," *Harvard Business Review*, February 2005, 48–49; Loizos Heracleous and Jochen Wirtz, "Biometrics—The Next Frontier in Service Excellence, Productivity and Security in the Service Sector," *Managing Service Quality*, 16, No. 1, 2006.

CONCLUSION

Enhancing service quality and improving service productivity often are two sides of the same coin, offering powerful potential to improve value for both customers and the firm. It is a key challenge for any service business to deliver service quality and satisfaction to its customers in ways that are cost-effective for the firm. Strategies to improve service quality and productivity should reinforce rather than counteract each other. In a world of continuous innovation and competitive markets, only few businesses can afford to spend more money (i.e., allow lower productivity) for better quality. Therefore, the name of the game is to seek improvements that offer quantum leaps in service quality and productivity at the same time.

Chapter Summary

LO1 Quality and productivity are twin paths for creating value for customers and the firm. Quality focuses on the benefits created for customers, and productivity affects the financial costs to the firm.

LO2 There are different definitions of service quality. In this book, we adopt the user-based definition where quality means consistently meeting or exceeding customer expectations.

Customers' perceived service quality consists of five main dimensions: (1) tangibles, (2) reliability, (3) responsiveness, (4) assurance, and (5) empathy.

LO3 The gaps model is an important tool to diagnose and address service quality problems. We identified six gaps that can be the cause of quality shortfalls:

- Gap 1—the knowledge gap.
- Gap 2—the policy gap.
- Gap 3—the delivery gap.
- Gap 4—the communications gap.
- Gap 5—the perceptions gap.
- Gap 6—the service quality gap. It is the most important gap. In order to close Gap 6, all other five gaps have to be closed first.

We summarized a series of potential causes for each of the gaps and provided generic prescriptions for addressing the causes and thereby closing the gaps.

LO4 There are both soft and hard measures of service quality. *Soft measures* are usually based on perceptions of and feedback from customers and employees.

LO5 Feedback from customers should be systematically collected via a *customer feedback system* (*CFS*). The key objectives of a CFS are:

- Assessment and benchmarking of service quality and performance.
- Customer-driven learning and improvement.
- Creating a customer-oriented service culture.

LO6 Firms can use a variety of tools to collect customer feedback, including: (1) total market surveys, (2) annual surveys on overall satisfaction, (3) transactional surveys, (4) service feedback cards, (5) mystery shopping, (6) unsolicited customer feedback, (7) focus group discussions, and (8) service reviews.

A reporting system is needed to channel feedback and its analysis to the relevant parties to take action.

LO7 *Hard measures* relate to operational processes and outcomes and can be counted, timed, or observed. *Control charts* are a simple method of displaying performance on hard measures over time against specific quality standards.

LO8 Key tools analyze and address important service quality problems:

- *Fishbone diagrams* identify the causes of quality problems.
- *Pareto analysis* assesses the frequency of quality problems.
- *Blueprinting* allows drilling down to exactly determine the location of fail points in a customer service process and then help to redesign the process.

LO9 There are financial implications related to service quality improvements. A *return on quality* (*ROQ*) approach assesses the costs and benefits of quality initiatives.

LO10 Besides quality, productivity is another important path to increase value.

LO11 It is important to differentiate these three concepts:

1. *Productivity* involves the financial valuation of outputs relative to inputs (e.g., input/output ratio).
2. *Efficiency* involves comparison to a standard such as industry average (e.g., speed of delivery).
3. *Effectiveness* refers to the degree a goal, such as customer satisfaction, is being met.

Productivity and efficiency cannot be divorced from effectiveness. Firms that strive to be more productive, efficient, and effective in consistently delivering customer satisfaction will be more successful.

LO12 Generic methods to improve productivity include (1) cost control; (2) reduction of waste of materials and labor; (3) matching capacity to demand; (4) replacing labor with machines and SSTs; (5) providing employees with equipment and information that enables them to work faster and better; (6) training employees to work more productively; (7) broadening the job scope of employees to reduce bottlenecks and downtime; (8) using expert systems so that paraprofessionals can do the work previously done by higher-paid experts.

The customer-driven methods to improve productivity include (1) changing the timing of customer demand; (2) encouraging the use of alterative service delivery channels and self-service; (3) getting customers to use third parties for parts of the service delivery.

LO13 When improvements are made to productivity, firms need to bear in mind that both front-stage and backstage improvements could have an impact on service quality and the customer experience.

LO14 TQM, ISO 9000, Malcolm-Baldrige Approach, and Six Sigma are systematic and often complementary approaches to managing and improving service quality and productivity.

Review Questions

1. Explain the relationships between service quality, productivity, and profitability.
2. Identify the gaps that can occur in service quality and the steps that service marketers can take to prevent them.
3. Why are both soft and hard measures of service quality needed?
4. What are the main objectives of an effective customer feedback system?
5. What are the key customer feedback collection tools? What are the strengths and weaknesses of each of these tools?
6. What are the main tools service firms can use to analyze and address service quality problems?
7. Why is productivity more difficult to measure in service than in manufacturing firms?
8. What are the key tools for improving service productivity?
9. How do concepts such as TQM, ISO 9000, Malcolm-Baldrige Approach, and Six Sigma relate to managing and improving service quality and productivity? (Refer to the appendix)

Application Exercises

1. Review the five dimensions of service quality. What do they mean in the context of (a) an industrial repair shop, (b) a retail bank, (c) a Big 4 accounting firm?
2. How would you define "excellent service quality" for an enquiry/information service provided by your phone or electricity company? Call a service organization, and go through a service experience and evaluate it against your definition of "excellence."
3. Collect a few customer feedback forms and tools (customer feedback cards, questionnaires, and online forms), and explain how the information gathered with those tools can be used to achieve the main objectives of effective customer feedback systems.
4. Consider your own recent experiences as a service consumer. On which dimensions of service quality have you most often experienced a large gap between your expectations and your perceptions of the service performance? What do you think the underlying causes might be? What steps should management take to improve quality?
5. In what ways can you, as a consumer, help to improve productivity for at least three service organizations that you patronize? What distinctive characteristics of each service make some of these actions possible?
6. What key measures could be used for monitoring service quality, productivity, and profitability for a large pizza restaurant chain? Specifically, what measures would you recommend to such a firm to use, taking administrative costs into consideration? Who should receive what type of feedback on the results, and why? On which measures would you base a part of the salary scheme of branch level staff and why?
7. Do a literature search, and identify the critical factors for a successful implementation of ISO 9000, the Malcolm-Baldrige Model, and Six Sigma in service firms. (Refer to the Appendix 14.3)

APPENDIX 14.1

MEASURING SERVICE QUALITY USING SERVQUAL

To measure customer satisfaction with various aspects of service quality, Valarie Zeithaml and her colleagues developed a survey instrument called SERVQUAL.[25] It's based on the premise that customers can evaluate a firm's service quality by comparing their perceptions of its service with their own expectations. SERVQUAL is seen as a generic measurement tool that can be applied across a broad spectrum of service industries. In its basic form, the scale contains 21 perception items and a series of expectation items, reflecting the five dimensions of service quality described in Table 14.6.

TABLE 14.6 The SERVQUAL Scale

The SERVQUAL scale includes five dimensions: tangibles, reliability, responsiveness, assurance, and empathy. Within each dimension, several items are measured on a 7-point scale, from *strongly agree* to *strongly disagree*, for a total of 21 items.

SERVQUAL questions

Note: For actual survey respondents, instructions are also included, and each statement is accompanied by a seven-point scale ranging from "strongly agree = 7" to "strongly disagree = 1." Only the end points of the scale are labeled; there are no words above the numbers 2 through 6.

Tangibles

- Excellent banks (refer to cable TV companies, hospitals, or the appropriate service business throughout the questionnaire) will have modern-looking equipment.
- The physical facilities at excellent banks will be visually appealing.
- Employees at excellent banks will be neat in appearance.
- Materials (e.g., brochures or statements) associated with the service will be visually appealing in an excellent bank.

Reliability

- When excellent banks promise to do something by a certain time, they will do so.
- When customers have a problem, excellent banks will show a sincere interest in solving it.
- Excellent banks will perform the service right the first time.
- Excellent banks will provide their services at the time they promise to do so.
- Excellent banks will insist on error-free records.

Responsiveness

- Employees of excellent banks will tell customers exactly when service will be performed.
- Employees of excellent banks will give prompt service to customers.
- Employees of excellent banks will always be willing to help customers.
- Employees of excellent banks will never be too busy to respond to customer requests.

Assurance

- The behavior of employees of excellent banks will instill confidence in customers.
- Customers of excellent banks will feel safe in their transactions.
- Employees of excellent banks will be consistently courteous with customers.
- Employees of excellent banks will have the knowledge to answer customer questions.

Empathy

- Excellent banks will give customers individual attention.
- Excellent banks will have operating hours convenient to all their customers.
- Excellent banks will have employees who give customers personal attention.
- The employees of excellent banks will understand the specific needs of their customers.

Source: Adapted from A. Parasuraman, Valarie A. Zeithaml, and Leonard Berry, "SERVQUAL: A Multiple Item Scale for Measuring Consumer Perceptions of Service Quality." *Journal of Retailing,* 64 (1988): 12–40.

Respondents complete a series of scales that measure their expectations of companies in a particular industry on a wide array of specific service characteristics. Subsequently, they are asked to record their perceptions of a specific company whose services they have used. When perceived performance ratings are lower than expectations, this is a sign of poor quality. The reverse indicates good quality.

LIMITATIONS OF SERVQUAL

SERVQUAL has been widely used, but there are a number of limitations of this measure.[26] Therefore, the majority of researchers using SERVQUAL omits from, adds to, or changes the list of statements purporting to measure service quality.[27] Other research suggests that SERVQUAL mainly measures two factors: intrinsic service quality (resembling what Grönroos termed functional quality) and extrinsic service quality (which refers to the tangible aspects of service delivery and resembles to what Grönroos referred to as technical quality").[28]

These different findings don't undermine the value of Zeithaml, Berry, and Parasuraman's achievement in identifying some of the key underlying constructs in service quality. Rather, they highlight the difficulty of measuring customer perceptions of quality and the need to customize dimensions and measures to the research context.

APPENDIX 14.2

MEASURING SERVICE QUALITY IN ONLINE ENVIRONMENTS

SERVQUAL was developed to measure service quality mostly in a face-to-face service encounter context. In today's online environment, different service quality dimensions with new measurement items become relevant. To measure electronic service quality on websites, Parasuraman, Zeithaml, and Malhotra created a 22-item scale called E-S-QUAL, reflecting the four key dimensions of *efficiency* (i.e., is navigation easy? can transactions be completed quickly? and does the website load fast?), *system availability* (i.e., is the site always available? does it launch right away? and is it stable and does not crash?), *fulfillment* (i.e., are orders delivered as promised, and offerings are described truthfully), and *privacy* (i.e., information privacy is protected and personal information is not shared with other sites).[29] Research Insights 14.2, "New Thinking on Defining and Measuring E-Service Quality," offers the latest perspectives on this topic and addresses the challenge of integrating service quality measures across both virtual and physical channels.

RESEARCH INSIGHTS 14.2

NEW THINKING ON DEFINING AND MEASURING E-SERVICE QUALITY

"To managers of companies with a Web presence," say Joel Collier and Carol Bienstock, "an awareness of how customers perceive service quality is essential to understanding what [they] value in an online-service transaction." E-service quality involves more than just interactions with a website, described as process quality, and extends to outcome quality and recovery quality. And each must be measured. The separation of customers from providers during online transactions highlights the importance of evaluating how well a firm handles customers' questions, concerns, and frustrations when problems arise.

- **Process Quality.** Customers initially evaluate their experiences with an e-retailing website against five process quality dimensions: *privacy, design, information, ease of use,* and *functionality*. This last construct refers to quick page loads, links that don't dead-end, payment options, accurate execution of customer commands, and ability to appeal to a universal audience (including the disabled and those who speak other languages).
- **Outcome Quality.** Customers' evaluations of process quality have a significant effect on their evaluation of outcome quality, made up of *order timeliness, order accuracy,* and *order condition.*
- **Recovery Quality.** In the event of a problem, customers evaluate the recovery process against *interactive fairness* (ability to locate and interact with technology support for a web site, including telephone-based assistance), *procedural fairness* (policies, procedures, and responsiveness in the complaint process), and *outcome fairness.* How the company responds has a significant effect on the customer's satisfaction level and future intentions.

Multichannel Issues

Going one step further, Rui Sousa and Christopher Voss note that many services offer customers a choice of both virtual and physical delivery channels. Customers' evaluations of service quality are formed across all points of contact they have with the firm. In a multichannel setting, researchers must measure *physical quality, virtual quality,* and *integration quality*—the ability to provide customers with a seamless service experience across multiple channels. Achieving consistency across such interactions is particularly relevant when a firm adds new virtual channels, accompanied by specialist support systems that often are poorly integrated with existing systems. To avoid such fragmentation and achieve consistent service quality, Sousa and Voss call for explicit links between the firm's marketing and operations functions.

Sources: Joel E. Collier and Carol C. Bienstock, "Measuring Service Quality in E-Retailing," *Journal of Service Research*, 8, February 2006, 260–275; Rui Sousa and Christopher A. Voss, "Service Quality in Multichannel Services Employing Virtual Channels," *Journal of Service Research*, 8, May 2006, 356–371.

APPENDIX 14.3

SYSTEMATIC APPROACHES TO QUALITY AND PRODUCTIVITY IMPROVEMENT AND PROCESS STANDARDIZATION

Many of the thinking, tools, and concepts introduced in this chapter originate from Total Quality Management (TQM), ISO 9000, Six Sigma, and the Malcolm-Baldrige Model. We discuss each of these approaches and relate them back to the service quality and productivity context in the following sections.

TOTAL QUALITY MANAGEMENT

Total Quality Management (TQM) concepts were originally developed in Japan. They are widely used in manufacturing and more recently in service firms, including educational institutions (see Service Perspective 14.3). TQM can help organizations to attain service excellence, increase the productivity of service delivery processes, and be a continued source of value creation through the feeding of innovative processes for the firm.[30]

Some concepts and tools of TQM can be directly applied to services. As discussed in this chapter, TQM tools such as control charts, flow charts, fish bone diagrams are being used by service firms with great results for monitoring service quality and determining the root causes of specific problems.

Sureshchander et al. identified 12 critical dimensions for successful implementation of TQM in a service context: (1) top management commitment and visionary leadership; (2) human resource management; (3) technical system, including service process design and process management; (4) information and analysis system; (5) benchmarking; (6) continuous improvement; (7) customer focus; (8) employee satisfaction; (9) union intervention and employee relations; (10) social responsibility; (11) servicescapes; and (12) service culture.[31]

ISO 9000 CERTIFICATION

More than 90 countries are members of ISO (the International Organization for Standardization based in Geneva, Switzerland), which promotes standardization and quality to facilitate international trade. ISO 9000 comprises requirements, definitions, guidelines, and related standards to provide an independent assessment and certification of a firm's quality management system. The official ISO 9000 definition of quality is: "The totality of features and characteristics of a product or service that bear on its ability to satisfy a stated or implied need. Simply stated, quality is about meeting or exceeding your customer's needs and requirements." To ensure quality, ISO 9000 uses many TQM tools and internalizes their use in participating firms.

Service firms adopted ISO 9000 standards later than manufacturing firms. Major service sectors that have adopted ISO 9000 certification include wholesale and retail firms, IT service providers, health care providers, consultancy firms, and educational institutions. By adopting ISO 9000 standards, service firms, especially small ones, can not only ensure that their services conform to customer expectations but also achieve improvements in productivity.

MALCOLM BALDRIGE MODEL

The Malcolm Baldrige National Quality Award (MBNQA) was developed by the National Institute of Standards and Technology (NIST) with the goal of promoting best practices in quality management and recognizing and publicizing quality achievements

SERVICE PERSPECTIVE 14.3

TQM IN EDUCATIONAL INSTITUTIONS

Higher educational institutions are increasingly competing for talented students and have started to accept that they have to be more customer-centric in their approach to increase student satisfaction. What is the meaning of service quality in a higher educational institution? Sakthivel, Rajendran, and Raju proposed a TQM model with five variables that measure different dimensions of service quality in an institution of higher learning, and they suggest that these variables will increase student satisfaction.

- ***Commitment of Top Management.*** Top management has to "walk the walk" and make sure that what is preached in terms of educational excellence and service quality is really being practiced.
- ***Course Delivery.*** While institutions of higher learning hire people with expert knowledge, there is a need that such expert knowledge can be transmitted expertly, with passion.
- ***Campus Facilities.*** Attention needs to be focused on having excellent infrastructure and facilities for student learning as well as their extracurricular activities. These facilities also have to be properly maintained.
- ***Courtesy.*** This is a positive attitude toward students that will create a friendly learning environment.
- ***Customer Feedback and Improvement.*** Continuous feedback from students can lead to improvements.

FIGURE 14.14 Higher Learning Increasingly Focuses on Service Quality and TQM

The researchers studied engineering students from a mix of ISO and non-ISO institutions. They found that ISO 9001:2000 certified institutions were adopting TQM faster and offered a better quality education than non-ISO institutions.

Furthermore, their findings showed that while all five variables together did predict student satisfaction, two variables were more important in affecting student satisfaction. The variables were commitment of top management and campus facilities. Top management needs to be committed to quality assurance in making sure the other variables are in place to improve the student experience.

Source: P. B. Sakthivel, G. Rajendran, and R. Raju, "TQM Implementation and Students' Satisfaction of Academic Performance," *The TQM Magazine*, 17, No. 6, 2005, 573–589.

among U.S. firms. Countries other than the United States have similar quality awards that follow the MBNQA model.

While the framework is generic and does not distinguish between manufacturing and service organizations, the award has a specific service category, and the model can be used to create a culture of ongoing service improvements. Major services firms that have won the award include Ritz-Carlton, FedEx, and AT&T. Research has confirmed that employing this framework can improve organizational performance.[32]

The Baldrige Model assesses firms on seven areas:

1. Leadership commitment to a service quality culture.
2. Planning priorities for improvement, including service standards, performance targets, and measurement of customer satisfaction, defects, cycle-time, and productivity.

3. Information and analysis that will aid the organization to collect, measure, analyze, and report strategic and operational indicators.
4. Human resources management that enables the firm to deliver service excellence, ranging from hiring the right people, to development, involvement, empowerment, and motivation.
5. Process management, including monitoring, continuous improvement, and process redesign.
6. Customer and market focus that allows the firm to determine customer requirements and expectations.
7. Business results.[33]

SIX SIGMA

The Six Sigma approach was originally developed by Motorola to improve product quality and reduce warranty claims and was soon adopted by other manufacturing firms to reduce defects in a variety of areas.

Subsequently, service firms embraced various Six Sigma strategies to reduce defects, reduce cycle times, and improve productivity.[34] As early as 1990, GE Capital applied Six Sigma methodology to reduce the backroom costs of selling consumer loans, credit card insurance, and payment protection. Its president and COO Denis Nayden said,

> Although Six Sigma was originally designed for manufacturing, it can be applied to transactional services. One obvious example is in making sure the millions of credit card and other bills GE sends to customer are correct, which drives down our costs of making adjustments. One of our biggest costs in the financial business is winning new customers. If we treat them well, they will stay with us, reducing our customer-origination costs.[35]

Statistically, Six Sigma means achieving a quality level of only 3.4 defects per million opportunities (DPMO). To understand how stringent this target is, consider mail deliveries. If a mail service delivers with 99 percent accuracy, it misses 3,000 items out of 300,000 deliveries. But if it achieves a Six Sigma performance level, only one item out of this total will go astray.

Over time, Six Sigma has evolved from a defect reduction approach to an overall business improvement approach. As defined by Pande, Neuman, and Cavanagh:

> Six Sigma is a comprehensive and flexible system for achieving, sustaining and maximizing business success. Six Sigma is uniquely driven by close understanding of customer needs, disciplined use of facts, data and statistical analysis, and diligent attention to managing, improving, and reinventing business processes.[36]

Two strategies, process improvement and process design/redesign, form the cornerstone of the Six Sigma approach. Process improvement strategies aim at identifying and eliminating the root causes of the service delivery problems, thereby improving service quality. Process design/redesign strategies act as a supplementary strategy to improvement strategy. If a root cause can't be identified or effectively eliminated within the existing processes, either new processes are *designed* or existing process are *redesigned* to fully or partially address the problem.

The most popular Six Sigma improvement model for analyzing and improving business processes is the DMAIC model, shown in Table 14.7. DMAIC stands for **D**efine the opportunities, **M**easure key steps/inputs, **A**nalyze to identify root causes, **I**mprove performance, and **C**ontrol to maintain performance.

WHICH APPROACH SHOULD A FIRM ADOPT?

As there are various approaches to systematically improving a service firm's service quality and productivity, the question arises: Which approach should be adopted—TQM, ISO9000, the Malcolm Baldrige Model, or Six Sigma? TQM can be applied at

TABLE 14.7 Applying the DMAIC Model to Process Improvement and Redesign

	Six Sigma Methodology to Improve and Redesign Processes	
	Process Improvement	**Process Design/Redesign**
Define	Identify the problem Define requirements Set goals	Identify specific or broad problems Define goal/change vision Clarify scope and customer requirements
Measure	Validate problem/process Refine problem/goal Measure key steps/inputs	Measure performance to requirements Gather process efficiency data
Analyze	Develop causal hypothesis Identify "vital few" root causes Validate hypothesis	Identify best practices Assess process design • Value/non–value–adding • Bottlenecks/disconnects • Alternative paths Refine requirements
Improve	Develop ideas to remove root causes Test solutions Standardize solution/measure results	Design new process • Challenge assumptions • Apply creativity • Workflow principles Implement new process, structures, systems
Control	Establish standard measures to maintain performance Correct problems as needed	Establish measures and reviews to maintain performance Correct problems as needed

Source: Reproduced from Peter Pande, Robert P. Neuman, and Ronald R. Cavanagh, *The Six Sigma Way*. New York: McGraw-Hill, 2000.

differing levels of sophistication, and basic tools such as flowcharting, frequency charts, and fishbone diagrams probably should be adopted by almost any type of service firm. ISO 9000 seems to offer the next level of commitment and complexity, followed by the Malcolm Baldrige Model and finally Six Sigma.

Any one of these approaches can be a useful framework for understanding customer needs, analyzing processes, and improving service quality and productivity. Firms can choose a particular program, depending on their own needs and desired level of sophistication. Each program has its own merits, and firms can adopt more than one. For example, the ISO 9000 program can be used for standardizing the procedures and process documentation, which can lead to reduction in variability. Six Sigma and Malcolm Baldrige programs can be used to improve processes and to focus on performance improvement across the organization.

The key success factor of any of these programs depends on how well a specific quality improvement program is integrated with the overall business strategy. Firms that adopt a program because of peer pressure or just as a marketing tool are less likely to succeed than firms that view these programs as useful development tools.[37] Service champions make best practices in service quality management a core part of their organizational culture.[38]

The National Institute of Standards and Technology (NIST), which organizes the Malcolm Baldrige Award program, tracked a hypothetical stock index called the "Baldrige Index" of award winners. It was observed that winners consistently outperformed the S&P 500 index.[39] Ironically however, the two-time winner of the award and Six Sigma pioneer, Motorola had been suffering financially and losing market share, in part through failure to keep up with new technology. Success cannot be taken for granted—and implementation, commitment, and constant adaptation to changing markets, technologies, and environments are keys to sustained success.

Endnotes

1. Adapted from Audrey Gilmore, "Service Marketing Management Competencies: A Ferry Company Example," *International Journal of Service Industry Management*, 9, No. 1, 1998, 74–92, www.stenaline.com, accessed June 2, 2009.
2. Claes Fornell, "ACSI Commentary: Federal Government Scores," *Special Report: Government Satisfaction Scores*, Michigan: CFI Group, December 15, 2005, published on www.theacsi.com, accessed January 21, 2006.
3. Martin Neil Baily, Diana Farrell, and Jaana Remes, "Where US Productivity is Growing," *The McKinsey Quarterly*, No. 2, 2006, 10–12.
4. David A. Garvin, *Managing Quality*. New York: The Free Press, 1988, especially Chapter 3.
5. Christian Grönroos, *Service Management and Marketing*, 3rd edn. Chichester, NY: Wiley, 2007.
6. Valarie A. Zeithaml, A. Parasuraman, and Leonard L. Berry, *Delivering Quality Service*. New York: The Free Press, 1990.
7. A. Parasuraman, Valarie A. Zeithaml, and Leonard L. Berry, "A Conceptual Model of Service Quality and Its Implications for Future Research," *Journal of Marketing*, 49, Fall 1985, 41–50; Valarie A. Zeithaml, Leonard L. Berry, and A. Parasuraman, "Communication and Control Processes in the Delivery of Services," *Journal of Marketing*, 52, April 1988, 36–58.
8. The sub-gaps in this model are based on the 7-gaps model. C. Lovelock, *Product Plus*. New York: McGraw-Hill, 1994, 112.
9. Valarie A. Zeithaml, Mary Jo Bitner, and Dwayne D. Gremler, *Services Marketing*, 4th edn. New York: McGraw-Hill, 2006, 292.
10. This section is based partially on Jochen Wirtz and Monica Tomlin, "Institutionalizing Customer-driven Learning Through Fully Integrated Customer Feedback Systems," *Managing Service Quality*, 10, No. 4, 2000, 205–215.
11. Leonard L. Berry and A. Parasuraman, "Listening to the Customer—The Concept of a Service Quality Information System," *Sloan Management Review* 38, Spring 1997, 65–76.
12. Customer listening practices have been shown to affect service performance, growth and profitability, see William J. Glynn, Sean de Búrca, Teresa Brannick, Brian Fynes, and Sean Ennis, "Listening Practices and Performance in Service Organizations," *International Journal of Service Industry Management*, 14, No. 3, 2003, 310–330.
13. W. E. Baker and J. M. Sinkula, "The Synergistic Effect of Market Orientation and Learning Orientation on Organizational Performance," *Journal of the Academy of Marketing Science*, 27, No. 4, 1999, 411–427.
14. Neil A. Morgan, Eugene W. Anderson, and Vikas Mittal, "Understanding Firms' Customer Satisfaction information Usage," *Journal of Marketing*, 69, July 2005, 131–151.
15. Leonard L. Berry and A. Parasuraman provide an excellent overview of all key research approaches discussed in this section plus a number of other tools in their paper, "Listening to the Customer – The Concept of a Service Quality Information System," *Sloan Management Review* 38, Spring 1997, 65–76.
16. For a discussion on suitable satisfaction measures, see Jochen Wirtz and Lee Meng Chung, "An Examination of the Quality and Context-Specific Applicability of Commonly Used Customer Satisfaction Measures," *Journal of Service Research*, 5, May 2003, 345–355.
17. Robert Johnston and Sandy Mehra, "Best-Practice Complaint Management," *Academy of Management Executive*, 16, No. 4, 2002, 145–154.
18. Comments by Thomas R. Oliver, then senior vice president, sales and customer service, Federal Express; reported in Christopher H. Lovelock, *Federal Express: Quality Improvement Program*. Lausanne: International Institute for Management Development, 1990.
19. Christopher Lovelock, *Product Plus: How Product + Service = Competitive Advantage*. New York: McGraw-Hill, 1994, 218.
20. These categories and the research data that follow have been adapted from information in D. Daryl Wyckoff, "New Tools for Achieving Service Quality," *Cornell Hotel and Restaurant Administration Quarterly* 42, August–September 2001, 25–38.
21. Roland T. Rust, Anthony J. Zahonik, and Timothy L. Keiningham, "Return on Quality (ROQ): Making Service Quality Financially Accountable," *Journal of Marketing*, 59, April 1995, 58–70; Roland T. Rust, Christine Moorman, and Peter R. Dickson, "Getting Return on Quality: Revenue Expansion, Cost Reduction, or Both?" *Journal of Marketing*, 66, October 2002, 7–24.
22. Kenneth J. Klassen, Randolph M. Russell, and James J. Chrisman, "Efficiency and Productivity Measures for High Contact Services," *The Service Industries Journal*, 18, October 1998, 1–18.
23. James L. Heskett, *Managing in the Service Economy*. New York: The Free Press, 1986.
24. For a more in-depth discussion on service productivity, refer to Cynthia Karen Swank, "The Lean Service Machine," *Harvard Business Review*, 81, No. 10, 2003, 123–129.
25. A. Parasuraman, Valarie A. Zeithaml, and Leonard Berry, "SERVQUAL: A Multiple Item Scale for Measuring Consumer Perceptions of Service Quality," *Journal of Retailing*, 64, 1988, 12–40.
26. See, for instance, Francis Buttle, "SERVQUAL: Review, Critique, Research Agenda," *European Journal of Marketing*, 30, No. 1, 1996, 8–32; Simon S. K. Lam and Ka Shing Woo, "Measuring Service Quality: A Test-Retest Reliability Investigation of SERVQUAL," *Journal of the Market Research Society*, 39, April 1997, 381–393; Terrence H. Witkowski and Mary F. Wolfinbarger, "Comparative Service Quality: German and American Ratings Across Service Settings," *Journal of Business Research*, 55, 2002, 875–881; Lisa J. Morrison Coulthard, "Measuring Service Quality: A Review and Critique of Research Using SERVQUAL," *International Journal of Market Research*, 46, Quarter 4, 2004, 479–497.
27. Anne M. Smith, "Measuring Service Quality: Is SERVQUAL Now Redundant?" *Journal of Marketing Management*, 11, January/February/April 1995, 257–276.
28. Gerhard Mels, Christo Boshoff, and Denon Nel, "The Dimensions of Service Quality: The Original European Perspective Revisited," *The Service Industries Journal*, 17, January 1997, 173–189.

29. A. Parasuraman, Valarie A. Zeithaml, and Arvind Malhotra, "E-S-QUAL: A Multiple-Item Scale for Assessing Electronic Service Quality," *Journal of Service Research*, 7, No. 3, 2005, 213–233.
30. C. Mele and M. Colurcio, "The Evolving Path of TQM: Towards Business Excellence and Stakeholder Value," *International Journal of Quality and Reliability Management*, 23, No. 5, 2006, 464–489; C. Mele, "The Synergic Relationship Between TQM and Marketing in Creating Customer Value," *Managing Service Quality*, 17, No. 3, 2007, 240–258.
31. G. S. Sureshchandar, Chandrasekharan Rajendran, and R. N. Anantharaman, "A Holistic Model for Total Service Quality," *International Journal of Service Industry Management*, 12, No. 4, 2001, 378–412.
32. Susan Meyer Goldstein and Sharon B. Schweikhart, "Empirical Support for the Baldrige Award Framework in U.S. Hospitals," *Health Care Management Review*, 27, No. 1, 2002, 62–75.
33. Allan Shirks, William B. Weeks, and Annie Stein, "Baldrige-Based Quality Awards: Veterans Health Administration's 3-Year Experience," *Quality Management in Health Care*, 10, No. 3, 2002, 47–54; National Institute of Standards and Technology, "Baldrige FAQs," http://www.nist.gov/public_affairs/factsheet/baldfaqs.htm, accessed June 12, 2009.
34. Jim Biolos, "Six Sigma Meets the Service Economy," *Harvard Business Review* 80, November 2002, 3–5.
35. Mikel Harry and Richard Schroeder, *Six Sigma—The Breakthrough Management Strategy Revolutionizing the World's Top Corporations*. New York: Currency, 2000, 232.
36. Peter S. Pande, Robert P. Neuman, and Ronald R. Cavanagh, *The Six Sigma Way: How GE, Motorola, and Other Top Companies Are Honing their Performance*. New York: McGraw-Hill, 2000.
37. Gavin Dick, Kevin Gallimore, and Jane C. Brown, "ISO9000 and Quality Emphasis: An Empirical Study of Front-Room and Back Room Dominated Service Industries," *International Journal of Service Industry Management*, 12, No. 2, 2001, 114–136; Adrian Hughes and David N. Halsall, "Comparison of the 14 Deadly Diseases and the Business Excellence Model," *Total Quality Management*, 13, No. 2, 2002, 255–263.
38. Cathy A. Enz and Judy A. Siguaw, "Best Practices in Service Quality," *Cornell Hotel and Restaurant Administration Quarterly* 41, October 2000, 20–29.
39. "Eight NIST Stock Investment Study," USA: Gaithersburg, National Institute of Standards and Technology, March 2002.

CHAPTER 15

Striving for Service Leadership

Marketing is so basic that it cannot be considered a separate function.... It is the whole business seen from the point of view of its final result, that is, from the customer's point of view. Concern and responsibility for marketing must, therefore, permeate all areas of the enterprise.

PETER DRUCKER[1]

[T]he more short-term a company's focus becomes, the more likely the firm will be to engage in behavior that actually destroys value.

DON PEPPERS AND MARTHA ROGERS

LEARNING OBJECTIVES (LOs)

By the end of this chapter, the reader should be able to:

LO1 Understand the implications of the Service-Profit Chain for service management.

LO2 Appreciate that the marketing, operations, and human resource management functions need to be closely integrated in service businesses, and understand how this can be achieved.

LO3 Be familiar with the four levels of service performance.

LO4 Understand what actions are required to move a service firm from service loser to service leader.

LO5 Explain what human leadership involves in a services context.

LO6 Appreciate the qualities needed in effective leaders in service firms.

LO7 Understand the role leaders, at all levels within their organization, play in building service success.

LO8 Understand the relationship between service leadership, culture, and climate.

Leadership and Company Culture at IKEA North America[2]

IKEA North America was listed in *Fortune* magazine's list of 100 Best Companies to work for in 2007. Who was leading this company? Pernille Spiers-Lopez, a native of Denmark, joined IKEA North America in 1990 as the marketplace manager for its West Coast stores and then worked her way up and became President in 2001. Pernille Spiers-Lopez has certain personal values that have influenced the culture at IKEA North America.

IKEA has a strong culture of caring for its employees. Spiers-Lopez expects employees at IKEA to make their families the number one priority in their lives, and she leads by example and tries to keep regular hours at work and avoid business travel on weekends. Recognizing her caring for the family lives of her employees, Spiers-Lopez was given the Family Champion Award by *Working Mother*. Under her leadership, IKEA North America also provided benefits offered by few retail stores in the United States. For example, even part-timers who worked 20 hours a week had full medical and dental insurance for their partners and children. Recognizing her strong leadership skills, Spiers-Lopez was promoted to head IKEA's global human resources in 2009 where she will oversee 135,000 employees in 24 countries. What, according to Spiers-Lopez, are characteristics of effective service leadership?

- Being authentic and not afraid to face mistakes and change one's mind.
- Trusting the people around, and being trusted.
- Self-examination and personal values.

THE SERVICE-PROFIT CHAIN

In our opening vignette, Spiers-Lopez showed a strong focus on the welfare of her employees. Yet other service leaders focus on customers. "Businesses succeed by getting, keeping, and growing customers," state respected consultants and authors Don Peppers and Martha Rogers.[3] Arguing that Wall Street's ongoing obsession with current-period revenue and earnings can actually destroy value, they declare:

> Investors today want executives to demonstrate that their companies can make money and grow, the old-fashioned way—by earning it from the value proposition they offer customers. They want a firm's customers to buy more, to buy more often, and to stay loyal longer. They want a firm to show that it can go out and get more customers. . . .

Growth fuels innovation and creativity, generating new ideas and initiatives, and stimulating managers in all areas to "think outside the box." Growth keeps a company vibrant and alive, making it a good place to work—a place that provides employees with economic benefits and opportunities for advancement.[4]

Throughout this book, we've examined how to manage service businesses to achieve customer satisfaction and profitable performance. One focus has been on marketing, the only function that actually generates operating revenues for a business. However, we've consistently emphasized that the array of marketing activities in service organizations, embracing each of the 7 Ps, extends beyond the responsibilities assigned to a traditional marketing department. Hence, both planning and implementation of service marketing strategies require active collaboration with operations and human resources management.

What is the link between Spiers-Lopez's focus on employees and Peppers and Rogers' focus on customers? In fact, both are crucially important, and success in one area rubs off on the other. This is clearly shown in the Service-Profit Chain model we will discuss next, where we draw together themes and insights from earlier chapters, particularly those on managing employees, building customer loyalty, and improving service quality and productivity, as we examine the challenging task of leading a service business that seeks to be customer focused and market oriented.

Important Links in the Service-Profit Chain

James Heskett and his colleagues at Harvard argue that when service companies put employees and customers first, a radical shift occurs in the way they manage and measure success. They relate profitability, customer loyalty, and customer satisfaction to the value created by satisfied, loyal, and productive employees:

> Top-level executives of outstanding service organizations spend little time setting profit goals or focusing on market share.... Instead they understand that in the new economics of service, frontline workers and customers need to be the center of management concern. Successful service managers pay attention to the factors that drive profitability....investment in people, technology that supports frontline workers, revamped recruiting and training practices, and compensation linked to performance for employees at every level....
>
> The service-profit chain, developed from analyses of successful service organizations, puts "hard" values on "soft" measures. It helps managers target new investments to develop service and satisfaction levels for maximum competitive impact, widening the gap between service leaders and their merely good competitors.[5]

The Service-Profit Chain, shown in Figure 15.1, displays a series of hypothesized links in a managerial process that can lead to success in service businesses.

Table 15.1 provides a useful summary, highlighting the behaviors required of service leaders in order to manage their organizations effectively. Working backwards from the desired end results of revenue growth and profitability, links 1 and 2 focus on customers and include an emphasis on identifying and understanding customer needs, investments to ensure customer retention, and a commitment to adopting new performance measures that track such variables as satisfaction and loyalty among both customers and employees. Link 3 focuses on the value for customers created by the service concept and highlights the need for investments to continually improve both service quality and productivity.

Another set of service leadership behaviors (links 4–7) relate to employees and include organizational focus on the frontline, supporting the design of jobs that offer greater latitude for employees and investing in the development of promising managers. Also included in this category is the concept that paying higher wages actually decreases labor costs after reduced turnover, higher productivity, and higher quality are taken into account. Underlying the chain's success (link 8) is top management leadership.

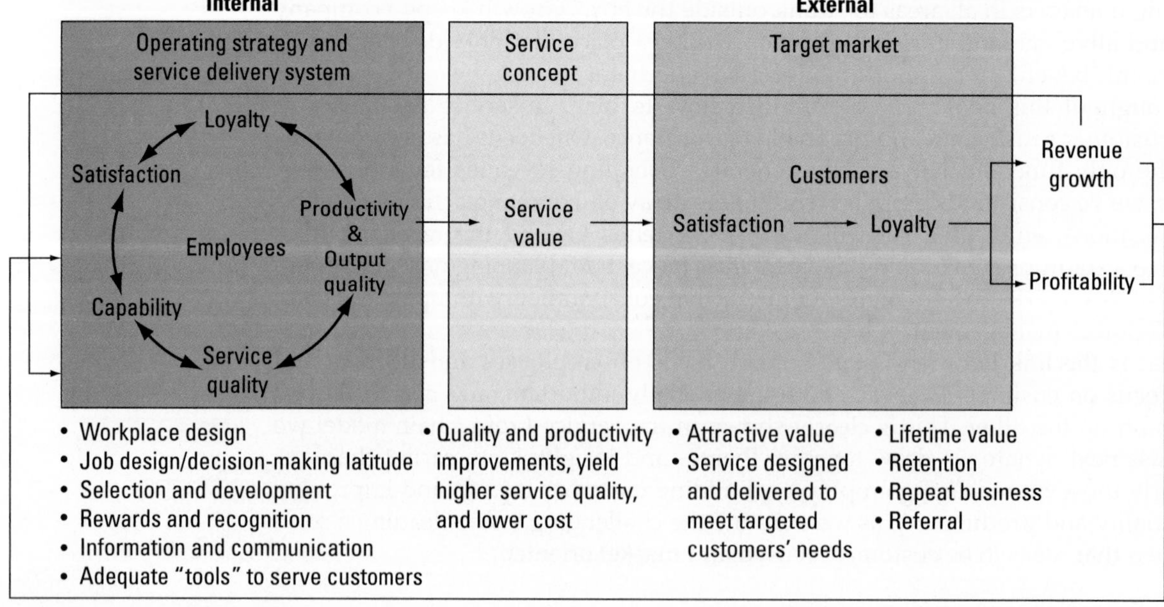

FIGURE 15.1 The Service-Profit Chain

Source: Reprinted by permission of Harvard Business Review. From "Putting the service-profit chain to work." By Heskett, J.L., Jones, T.O., Loveman, G.W., Sasser Jr., W.E., & Schlesinger, L.A. (March–April), p. 166.

TABLE 15.1 Links in the Service-Profit Chain

1. Customer loyalty drives profitability and growth
2. Customer satisfaction drives customer loyalty
3. Value drives customer satisfaction
4. Quality and productivity drive value
5. Employee loyalty drives service quality and productivity
6. Employee satisfaction drives employee loyalty
7. Internal quality drives employee satisfaction
8. Top management leadership underlies the chain's success

Source: James L. Heskett et al., "Putting the Service Profit Chain to Work," *Harvard Business Review*, March April 1994; James L. Heskett, W. Earl Sasser, and Leonard L. Schlesinger, *The Service Profit Chain*, Boston: Harvard Business School Press, 1997.

Getting the Service-Profit Chain Right Creates Shareholder Value

For firms that do it right, success is ultimately rewarded by an increase in the value attached to the organization itself, expressed in public companies by their stock price. As demonstrated by ACSI research, most service industries demonstrate a strong relationship between customer satisfaction—what everyone in the firm should be working to achieve—and shareholder value (Figure 15.2). An important distinction between service leaders and firms in other categories is how they approach value creation. The former seek to create value creation through customer satisfaction and its antecedents, whereas the others often aim to boost shareholder value through tactical measures to increase sales, short-term cost cutting, unlocking asset value through selected sell-offs, and taking advantage of financial market dynamics.

INTEGRATING MARKETING, OPERATIONS, AND HUMAN RESOURCES

The themes and relationships underlying the Service-Profit Chain illustrate compellingly the mutual dependency among marketing, operations, and human resources in meeting the needs of service customers: marketing, operations, and

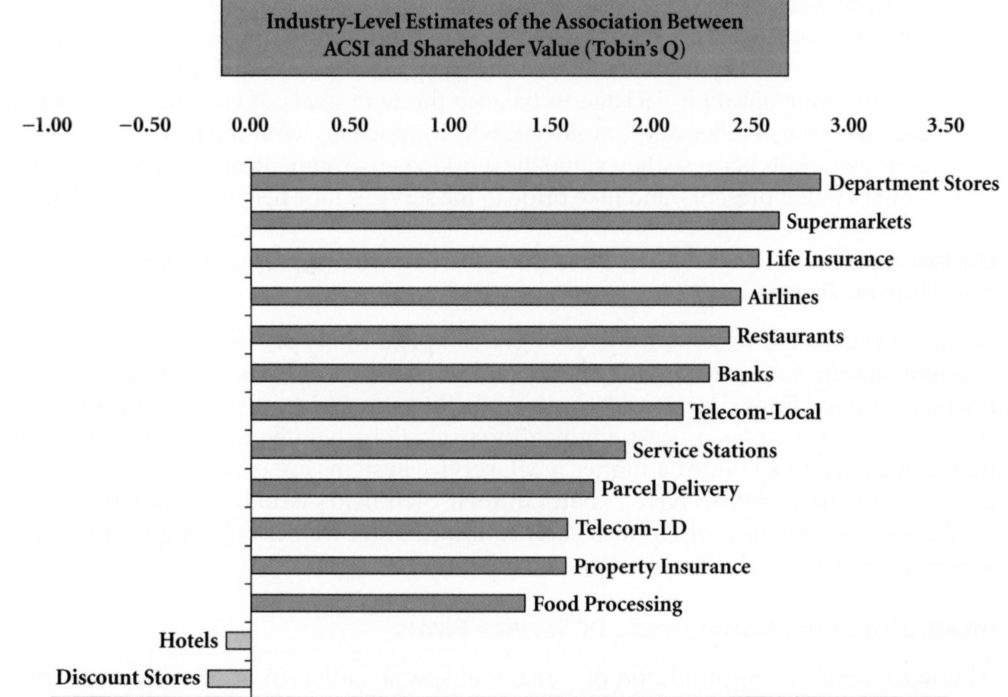

Source: Claes Fornell et al., "The American Customer Satisfaction Index at Ten Years." ACSI, 2005: 42

FIGURE 15.2 Customer Satisfaction is Closely Linked to Shareholder Value in Most Service Industries human resources (HR). Figure 1.16 in Chapter 1 on page 51 shows how the departments depend on each other.

How Are Marketing, Operations, and Human Resources Linked?

In what ways do the departments depend on each other? As we have seen, many service firms, especially those involving people-processing services, actually are "factories in the field." Customers enter whenever they need the service in question. When customers are actively involved in production and the service output is consumed as it is produced, the services marketing function is entwined with—and dependent on—the procedures, personnel, and facilities managed by operations. In a high-contact service, competitive outcomes may live or die on the basis of the caliber of service personnel recruited and trained by HR. Service organizations can't afford to have HR specialists who don't understand customers and their needs. When employees understand and support the goals of their organization, have the skills and training needed to succeed in their jobs, and recognize the importance of creating and maintaining customer satisfaction, both marketing and operations activities should be easier to manage.

Each of the three functions should have requirements and goals that relate to customers and contribute to the mission of the firm. They can be expressed generally as follows:

- **The Marketing Function**. To target specific types of customers whom the firm is well equipped to serve and create ongoing relationships with them by delivering a carefully defined service product in return for a price that offers value to customers and the potential for profits to the firm. Customers will recognize this value proposition as one of consistent quality that delivers solutions to their needs and is superior to competing alternatives.
- **The Operations Function**. To create and deliver the specified service product to targeted customers by selecting those operational techniques that allow the firm to consistently meet customer-driven quality, schedule, and cost and productivity goals and enable the business to reduce its costs through continuing improvements in productivity. The chosen operational methods will match skills that employees and intermediaries or contractors currently possess or can be trained to develop. The firm will have the resources to support these operations with the necessary facilities, equipment, and technology while avoiding negative impacts on employees and the broader community.
- **The Human Resources Function**. To recruit, train, and motivate frontline employees, service delivery team leaders, and managers who can work well together for a realistic compensation package to balance the twin goals of customer satisfaction and operational efficiency. Employees will want to stay with the firm and enhance their own skills because they value the working environment, appreciate the opportunities that it presents, and take pride in the services they help to create and deliver.

Do We Need Additional Skill Sets Besides Marketing, Operations, and Human Resources?

Services systems are becoming increasingly complex. Many services are crucially dependent on information technology and communications infrastructures (e.g., in global financial service firms), large and complex facilities (e.g., in integrated airport infrastructures), and complex process engineering (e.g., globally integrated supply chains in B2B contexts), and so on. At a higher level, service systems are evolving into a science in which it is necessary to have experts in their own fields who have knowledge that cuts across the different disciplines such as information technology, engineering, and service management (see Service Perspective 15.1).

Integrating Functional Areas in Service Firms

Although there's a long tradition of functional specialization in business, narrow perspectives get in the way of effective service management. One of the challenges facing senior managers in any type of organization is to avoid creating what are sometimes

SERVICE PERSPECTIVE 15.1

IBM'S SERVICE SCIENCE INITIATIVE

Organizations have many functional departments such as marketing, logistics, and research that work independently, rather than jointly together. Even business schools train their graduates in specific disciplines such as accounting, finance, marketing, and operations management but often lack the knowledge about how to integrate across functions. Furthermore, they tend to know even less about other important disciplines, such as information technology or process engineering, that are also necessary for designing and managing complex service systems well.

IBM recognized this problem and has been leading the world in its initiative on service science, which IBM termed Service Science, Management and Engineering (SSME). SSME combines knowledge in computer science, operations research, engineering, business strategy, management science, social and cognitive science and legal science, so that the necessary skills are developed for the service economy. IBM has been mobilizing universities and research centers to collaborate with them.

Today, service science has become a part of the curriculum in many universities around the world. These universities focus on interdisciplinary research and teaching so that they are able to produce "T" graduates—those who not only have in-depth knowledge in one specialized area, but also have sufficient knowledge that cuts across several disciplines so that experts from these various disciplines can work together well.

Service science is an approach to enable us to study, design, and manage effective service systems that create value for our customers. Companies that recognize this will hire graduates with the necessary knowledge and skills in service science so that they can have an edge in the competitive service economy. By studying services marketing, you have made a first step toward becoming familiar with service science, but you need to be aware that all these other disciplines are also important and you should work on picking up the key concepts in those fields too.

Sources: "Are We Ready for 'SERVICE'?" ThinkTank, October 10, 2005, www.research.ibm.com/ssme/20051010_services.shtml, accessed April 29, 2009; M. M. Davis and I. Berdrow, "Service Science: Catalyst for Change in Business School Curricula," *IBM Systems Journal*, 47, No. 1, 2008, 29–39; R. C. Larson, "Service Science: At the Intersection of Management, Social, and Engineering Sciences," *IBM Systems Journal*, 47, No. 1, 2008, 41–51; Paul P. Maglio and Jim Spohrer, "Fundamentals of Service Science," *Journal of the Academy of Marketing Science*, 36, No. 1, 2008, 18–20.

referred to as "functional silos" in which each function exists in isolation from the others, jealously guarding its independence.

As service firms place more emphasis on developing a strong market orientation and serving customers well, there's increased potential for conflict among the three functions, especially between marketing and operations. How comfortably can the three functions coexist in a service business, and how are their relative roles perceived? Sandra Vandermerwe makes the point that high-value creating enterprises should be thinking in term of *activities*, not functions.[6]

Yet in many firms, we still find individuals from marketing and operations backgrounds at odds with each other. Marketers may see their role as one of continually adding value to the product offering, enhancing its appeal to customers and stimulating sales. Operations managers, by contrast, may see their job as paring back "extras" to reflect the reality of service constraints—such as staff and equipment—and the need for cost containment. After all, they may argue, no value will be created if we operate at a loss. Conflicts may also occur between human resources and the other two functions, especially where employees are in boundary spanning roles that require them to balance customer satisfaction against operational efficiency.

Changing traditional organizational perspectives doesn't come readily to managers who have been comfortable with established approaches. However, as long as a service business continues to be organized along functional lines (and still many are), achieving the necessary coordination and strategic synergy requires that top management establish clear imperatives for each function. Each imperative should relate to customers and define how a specific function contributes to the overall mission. Part of the challenge of service management is to ensure that each of these three functional imperatives is compatible with the others and that all are mutually reinforcing.

Potential ways to reduce interfunctional conflict and break down the cultural barriers between departments include:

1. Interfunctional transfers of individuals who will develop a more holistic perspective and be able to view issues from the different perspectives of the various departments.
2. Establishing integrating project teams (e.g., for new service development or customer service process redesign).
3. Having interfunctional service delivery teams.
4. Appointing formally designated individuals whose job it is to integrate specific objectives, activities, and processes between departments. For example, Robert Kwortnik and Gary Thompson suggest forming a department in charge of "service experience management" that integrates marketing and operations.[7]
5. Internal marketing and training (see Chapter 11).
6. Finally, top management commitment that ensures the overarching objectives of all departments are integrated (see section on human leadership later in this chapter).

CREATING A LEADING SERVICE ORGANIZATION

So far, we have discussed the Service-Profit Chain, which prescribes best practice management thinking about how to run a service firm and the need for integration across functions and discipline. Let's next explore what it takes to move a firm from a service loser to a service leader.

From Losers to Leaders: Four Levels of Service Performance

Service leadership is not based on outstanding performance within a single dimension. Rather, it reflects excellence across multiple dimensions. In an effort to capture this performance spectrum, we need to evaluate the organization within each of the three functional areas described earlier—marketing, operations, and human resources. Table 15.2 modifies and extends an operations-oriented framework proposed by Richard Chase and Robert Hayes.[8] It categorizes service performers into four levels: loser, nonentity, professional, and leader. At each level, there is a brief description of a typical organization across 12 dimensions.

Under the marketing function, we look at the role of marketing, competitive appeal, customer profile, and service quality. Under the operations function, we consider the role of operations, service delivery (front stage), back-stage operations, productivity, and introduction of new technologies. Finally, under the human resources function, we consider the role of human resources management, the workforce, and frontline management. Obviously, there are overlaps between these dimensions and across functions. Additionally, there may be variations in the relative importance of some dimensions in different industries and across different delivery systems. For instance, human resource management tends to play a more prominent strategic role in high contact services. The goal of this overall service performance framework is to generate insights into how service leaders perform so well and what needs to be changed in organizations that are not performing as well as they might.

If you want to do an in-depth appraisal of a company in a specific industry, you may find it useful to view Table 15.2 as a point of departure, modifying some of the elements to create a customized framework for analysis.

SERVICE LOSERS. Service losers are at the bottom of the barrel from both customer and managerial perspectives, getting failing grades in marketing, operations, and HRM. Customers patronize them for reasons other than performance, typically, because there is no viable alternative, which is one reason why service losers continue to survive. Managers of such organizations may even see service delivery as a necessary evil. New technology is only introduced under duress, and the uncaring workforce is a negative constraint on performance. The cycle of failure presented earlier in Chapter 11 (Figure 11.5, p. 309 describes how such organizations behave in relation to employees and what the consequences are for customers.

SERVICE NONENTITIES. Although their performance still leaves much to be desired, service nonentities have eliminated the worst features of losers. As shown in Table 15.2, nonentities are dominated by a traditional operations mindset, typically based on achieving cost savings through standardization. Their marketing strategies are unsophisticated, and the roles of human resources and operations might be summed up, respectively, by the philosophies "adequate is good enough" and "if it ain't broke, don't fix it." Consumers neither seek out nor avoid such organizations. Managers may spout platitudes about improving quality and other goals but are unable to set clear priorities, chart a clear course, or command the respect and commitment of their subordinates (Figure 15.3). Several such firms often can be found competing in lackluster fashion within a given marketplace, and you might have difficulty distinguishing one from the others. Periodic price discounts tend to be the primary means of trying to attract new customers. The cycle of mediocrity (Figure 11.7, p. 311) portrays the human resources environment of many such organizations and its consequences for customers.

SERVICE PROFESSIONALS. Service professionals are in a different league from nonentities and have a clear market positioning strategy. Customers within the target segments seek out these firms based on their sustained reputation for meeting expectations. Marketing is more sophisticated, using targeted communications and pricing based on value to the customer. Research is used to measure customer satisfaction and obtain ideas for service enhancement. Operations and marketing work together to introduce new delivery systems and recognize the tradeoff between productivity and customer-defined quality. There are explicit links between back-stage and front-stage activities and a much more proactive, investment-oriented approach to HRM than is found among nonentities. The Cycle of Success (Figure 11.8, p. 312) highlights the HR strategies that lead to a high level of performance by most employees of organizations in the service professionals category (and by all who work for service leaders), together with its positive impact on customer satisfaction and loyalty.

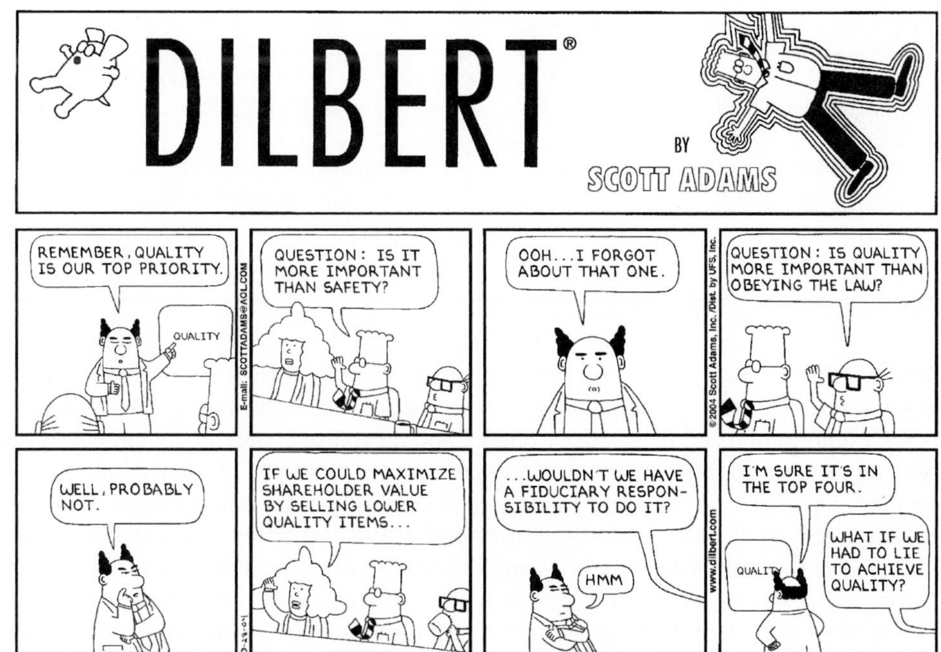

FIGURE 15.3 Dilbert's Boss Loses Focus—and His Audience

Source: DILBERT: © Scott Adams/Dist. by permission of United Syndicate, Inc.

TABLE 15.2 Four Levels of Service Performance

Level	1. Loser	2. Nonentity
	Marketing Function	
Role of marketing	Tactical role only; advertising and promotions lack focus; no involvement in product or pricing decision	Uses mix of selling and mass communication, using simple segmentation strategy; makes selective use of price discounts and promotions; conducts and tabulates basic satisfaction surveys
Competitive appeal	Customers patronize firm for reasons other than performance	Customers neither seek nor avoid the firm
Customer profile	Unspecified; a mass market to be served at a minimum cost	One or more segments whose basic needs are understood
Service quality	Highly variable, usually unsatisfactory. Subservient to operations priorties	Meets some customer expectations; consistent on one or two key dimensions, but not all
	Operations Function	
Role of operations	Reactive; cost oriented	The principal line management function: creates and delivers product, focuses on standardization as key to productivity, defines quality from internal perspective
Service delivery (front-stage)	A necessary evil. Locations and schedules are unrelated to preferences of customers, who are routinely ignored	Sticklers for tradition; "If it ain't broke, don't fix it"; tight rules for customers; each step in delivery run independently
Backstage operations	Divorced from front-stage; cogs in a machine	Contributes to individual front-stage delivery steps but organized separately; unfamiliar with customers
Productivity	Undefined; managers are punished for failing to stick within budget	Based on standardization; rewarded for keeping costs below budget
Introduction of new technology	Late adopter, under duress, when necessary for survival	Follows the crowd when justified by cost savings
	Human Resources Function	
Role of human resources	Supplies low-cost employees who meet minimum skill requirements for the job	Recruits and trains employees who can perform competently
Workforce	Negative constraint: poor performers, do not care, disloyal	Adequate resource, follows procedures but uninspired; turnover often high
Frontline management	Controls workers	Controls the process

SERVICE LEADERS. Service leaders are the *crème de la crème* of their respective industries. Whereas service professionals are good, service leaders are outstanding. Their company names are synonymous with service excellence and an ability to delight customers. Service leaders are recognized for their innovation in each functional area of management as well as for their superior internal communications and coordination among these three functions—often the result of a relatively flat organizational structure and extensive use of teams. As a result, service delivery is a seamless process organized around the customer.

Marketing efforts by service leaders make extensive use of customer relationship (CRM) systems that offer strategic insights about customers, who are often addressed on a one-to-one basis. Concept testing, observation, and contacts with lead customers are

3. Professional	4. Leader
Marketing Function	
Has clear positioning strategy against competition; uses focused communications with distinctive appeals to clarify promises and educate customers; pricing is based on value; monitors customer usage and operates loyalty programs; uses a variety of research techniques to measure customer satisfaction and obtain ideas for service enhancements; works with operations to introduce new delivery systems	Innovative leader in chosen segments, known for marketing skills; brands at product/process level; conducts sophisticated analysis of relational databases as inputs to one-to-one marketing and proactive account management; uses state-of-the art research techniques; uses concept testing, observation, and use of lead customers as inputs to new-product development; close to operations/HR
Customers seek out the firm, based on its sustained reputation for meeting customer expectations	Company's name is synonymous with service excellence; its ability to delight customers raises expectations to levels that competitors can't meet
Groups of individuals whose variation in needs and value to the firm are clearly understood	Individuals are selected and retained based on their future value to the firm, including their potential for new service opportunities and their ability to stimulate innovation
Consistently meets or exceeds customer expectations across multiple dimensions	Raises customer expectations to new levels; improves continuously
Operations Function	
Plays a strategic role in competitive strategy; recognizes trade off between productivity and customer-defined quality; willing to outsource; monitors competing operations for ideas, threats	Recognized for innovation, focus, and excellence; an equal partner with marketing and HR management; has in-house research capability and academic contacts; continually experimenting
Driven by customer satisfaction, not tradition; willing to customize, embrace new approaches; emphasis on speed, convenience, and comfort	Delivery is a seamless process organized around the customer; employees know whom they are serving; focuses on continuous improvement
Process is explicitly linked to front-stage activities; sees role as serving "internal customers," who in turn serve external customers	Closely integrated with front-stage delivery, even when geographically far apart, understands how own role relates to overall process of serving external customers; continuing dialog
Focuses on reengineering backstage processes; avoids productivity improvements that will degrade customers' service experience; continually refining processes for efficiency	Understands concept of return on quality; actively seeks customer involvement in productivity improvement; ongoing testing of new processes and technologies
An early adopter when IT promises to enhance service for customers and provide a competitive edge	Works with technology leaders to develop new applications that create first-mover advantage; seeks to perform at levels competitors cannot match
Human Resources Function	
Invests in selective recruiting, ongoing training; keeps close to employees, promotes upward mobility; strives to enhance quality of working life	Sees quality of employees as strategic advantage; firm is recognized as outstanding place to work; HR helps top management to nurture culture
Motivated, hard working, allowed some discretion in choice of procedures, offers suggestions	Innovative and empowered; very loyal, committed to firm's values and goals; creates procedures
Listens to customers; coaches and facilitates workers	Source of new ideas for top management; mentors, workers to enhance career growth, value to firm

employed in the development of new, breakthrough services that respond to previously unrecognized needs. Operations specialists work with technology leaders around the world to develop new applications that will create a first mover advantage and enable the firm to perform at levels that competitors cannot hope to reach for a long time to come. Senior executives see quality of employees as a strategic advantage. HRM works with them to develop and maintain a service-oriented culture and to create an outstanding working environment that simplifies the task of attracting and retaining the best people.[9] Service leaders typically perfected and integrated the cycle of success. The employees are committed to the firm's values and goals. Because they are engaged, empowered, and quick to embrace change, they are an ongoing source of new ideas.

FIGURE 15.4 Microsoft's Up Your Service! College Certified Course Leaders Are Ready to Train Their Colleagues and Help to Build a Sizzling Service Culture

Moving to a Higher Level of Performance

Firms can move either up or down the performance ladder. Once-stellar performers can become complacent and sluggish. Organizations devoted to satisfying their current customers may miss important shifts in the marketplace and find themselves turning into have-beens. These businesses may continue to serve a loyal but dwindling band of conservative customers, but they are unable to attract demanding new consumers with different expectations. Companies whose original success was based on mastery of a specific technological process may find that, in defending their control of that process, they have encouraged competitors to find higher-performing alternatives. And organizations whose management has worked for years to build up a loyal workforce with a strong service ethic may find that such a culture can be quickly destroyed as a result of a merger or acquisition that brings in new leaders who emphasize short-term profits. Unfortunately, senior managers sometimes delude themselves into thinking that their company has achieved a superior level of performance when, in fact, the foundations of that success are crumbling.

In most markets, we can also find companies moving up the performance ladder through conscious efforts to coordinate their marketing, operations, and HRM functions to establish more favorable competitive positions and better satisfy their customers. For example, Microsoft has recognized that the customer and partner experience is increasingly important to earn high levels of satisfaction and loyalty. Microsoft is now shifting the organization from developer-centric to a more customer-focused culture using a companywide initiative called Customer and Partner Experience (CPE). CPE's objective is to monitor, manage, and improve every perception point customers and partners encounter as they try, buy, download, use, integrate and upgrade Microsoft's software. Several programs drive CPE, and one of them is UP Your Service! College, a program for customer service training and building a superior service culture and service excellence mindset (Figure 15.4).

Leading Change Toward a Higher Performance Level

Transformation of an organization and moving it up the performance ladder can take place in two different ways: evolution or turnaround. *Evolution* in a business context involves continual mutations designed to ensure the survival of the fittest. Top management must proactively evolve the focus and strategy of the firm to take advantage of changing conditions and the advent of new technologies. Without a continuing series of mutations, it's unlikely a firm can remain successful in a dynamic marketplace. A different type of transformation occurs in turnaround situations in which leaders (usually new ones) seek to bring distressed organizations back from the brink of failure and set them on a healthier course.

Chan Kim and Renée Mauborgne, both professors at INSEAD, have identified four hurdles leaders face in reorienting and formulating strategy.[10]

- *Cognitive hurdles* are present when people cannot agree on the causes of current problems and the need for change.
- *Resource hurdles* exist when the organization is constrained by limited funds.
- *Motivational hurdles* prevent a strategy's rapid execution when employees are reluctant to make needed changes.
- *Political hurdles* take the form of organized resistance from powerful vested interests seeking to protect their positions.

Turning around an organization that has limited resources requires concentrating those resources where the need and the likely payoffs are greatest. And John Kotter, perhaps the best-known authority on leadership, argues that in most successful change management processes, those in leadership roles must navigate through eight complicated and often time-consuming stages:[11]

- Creating a sense of urgency to develop the impetus for change.
- Putting together a team strong enough to direct the process.
- Creating an appropriate vision of where the organization needs to go.
- Communicating that new vision broadly.
- Empowering employees to act on that vision.
- Producing sufficient short-term results to create credibility and counter cynicism.
- Building momentum and using that to tackle the tougher change problems.
- Anchoring the new behaviors in the organizational culture.

According to noted author Rosabeth Moss Kanter, it can be advantageous in turnaround situations to bring in a new CEO from outside the organization.[12] Such individuals, she argues, are better able to disentangle system dynamics because they were not previously caught up in them, and to voice problems and change habits. New CEOs may also have more credibility in representing and respecting customers. Exemplary turnaround leaders, she says, understand the powerful, unifying effect of focusing on customers. This focus can facilitate the difficult task of obtaining collaboration across departments and divisions. In addition to breaking down barriers between marketing, operations, and human resources or between various product or geographic divisions, turnaround CEOs may also need to reorient financial priorities to enable collaborative groups to tackle new business opportunities.

IN SEARCH OF HUMAN LEADERSHIP

So far, we have discussed how we can move a firm from a service loser to a service leader. However it still requires human leaders to take them in the right direction, set the right strategic priorities, and ensure that the relevant strategies are implemented throughout the organization. We will address the following questions in the next sections: "What is leadership?" "What are leadership qualities?" and "What is the role leaders have in shaping a culture and climate for service excellence?"

LEADERSHIP VERSUS MANAGEMENT. *Leadership* relates to the development of vision and strategies and the empowerment of people to overcome obstacles and made the vision happen. *Management*, by contrast, involves keeping the current situation operating through planning, budgeting, organizing, staffing, controlling, and problem solving. Says Kotter:

> Leadership works through people and culture. It's soft and hot. Management works through hierarchy and systems. It's harder and cooler . . . The fundamental purpose of management is to keep the current system functioning. The fundamental purpose of leadership is to produce useful change, especially nonincremental change. It's possible to have too much or too little of either. Strong leadership with no management risks chaos; the organization might walk right off a cliff. Strong management with no leadership tends to entrench an organization in deadly bureaucracy.[13]

Leadership is an essential and growing aspect of managerial work because the rate of change has been increasing. Reflecting both competition and technological advances, new services or service features are introduced at a faster rate and tend to have shorter lifecycles. In the meantime, the competitive environment shifts continually as a result of international firms entering new geographic markets, mergers and acquisitions, and the exit of former competitors. The process of service delivery has speeded up, with customers demanding faster service and faster responses when things go wrong. As a result, declares Kotter, effective top executives may now spend up to 80 percent of their time leading—double the figure required not that long ago. Even those at the bottom of the management hierarchy may spend at least 20 percent of their time on leadership.

SETTING DIRECTION VERSUS PLANNING. People often confuse the activities of planning and setting direction. *Planning*, according to Kotter, is a management process designed to produce orderly results, not change. *Setting a direction*, by contrast, is more inductive than deductive. Leaders look for patterns, relationships, and linkages that help to explain things and suggest future trends. Direction setting creates visions and strategies that describe a business, technology, or corporate culture in terms of what it should become over the long term and that articulate a feasible way of achieving this goal. Effective leaders have a talent for simplicity in communicating with others who may not share their background or knowledge; they know their audiences and are able to distill their messages, conveying even complicated concepts in just a few phrases.[14]

Many of the best visions and strategies are not brilliantly innovative; rather, they combine some basic insights and translate them into a realistic competitive strategy that serves the interests of customers, employees, and stockholders. Some visions, however, fall into the category that Gary Hamel and C. K. Pralahad describe as "stretch"—a challenge to attain new levels of performance and competitive advantage that might at first sight seem beyond the organization's reach.[15] Stretching to achieve such bold goals requires creative reappraisal of traditional ways of doing business and leverage of existing resources through partnerships (see Service Perspective 15.2). It also requires creating the energy and the will among managers and employees to perform at higher levels than they believe they are able to do.

Individual Leadership Qualities

Many commentators have written on the topic of leadership. It has even been described as a service in its own right. The late Sam Walton, founder of the Wal-Mart retail chain, highlighted the role of managers as "servant leaders."[16] There are many definitions of leadership, but the various definitions tend to contain three common elements: (1) it involves a group as leadership cannot exist without the cooperation of the employees; (2) it is goal-directed whereby leaders influence their followers toward the achievement of certain goals and visions; and (3) there tends to be hierarchy in the group. Sometimes, the hierarchy is one where the leader is clearly at the top while at other times, it is informal.[17] The following are some qualities that effective leaders in a service organization should have:

- Love for the business. Excitement about the business will encourage individuals to teach the business to others and to pass on to them the art and secrets of operating it.
- Service leaders need to see service quality as the foundation for competing.[18]
- Recognizing the key part played by employees in delivering service, service leaders need to believe in the people who work for them and pay special attention to communicating with employees.
- Many outstanding leaders are driven by a set of core values they pass on in the organization.[19] For example, in the opening vignette, Pernille Spiers-Lopez puts her family as top priority. This is also the culture at IKEA, North America, where there is a strong stress on work-life balance.
- Effective leaders have a talent for communicating with others in a way that is easy to understand. They know their audiences and are able to communicate even complicated ideas in simple terms accessible to all.[20] Effective communication is probably a leader's most important skill to inspire an organization to create success.
- Effective leaders are able to ask great questions and get answers from the team, rather than just rely on themselves to dominate the decision-making process.[21]
- The best CEOs are able to reset their goals and will not stick to decisions that were right for yesterday, but not for tomorrow.[22]
- Effective leaders need to know the purpose of the existence of the company and formulate and implement strategy, watching over it daily and living with it over time.[23]

Rakesh Karma warns against excessive emphasis on charisma in selecting CEOs, arguing that it leads to unrealistic expectations.[24] He notes that unethical behavior may occur when charismatic but unprincipled leaders induce blind obedience in their followers and cites the illegal activities stimulated by the leadership of Enron, which eventually led to the company's collapse. Jim Collins concludes that a leader does not

SERVICE PERSPECTIVE 15.2

CAN CIRQUE DU SOLEIL STRETCH FURTHER?

Who would have believed in the mid-1980s that Le Club des Talons Hauts (The High Heels Club), a small band of French-speaking street performers who walked on stilts and lived in a youth hostel near Quebec City, Canada, would one day become the world-famous Cirque du Soleil? With its unique mix of music, dance, and acrobatics, the Cirque du Soleil (Circus of the Sun) has created a new category of live entertainment, packaged in a variety of distinctive shows, attended by millions around the world (Figure 15.5). "People said we reinvented the circus—we didn't reinvent the circus," declares president Guy Laliberté:

> We repackaged a way of presenting the circus show in a much more modern way . . . We took an art form that was known, that had a lot of dust on it, where people had forgotten it could be something other than what they knew, and we organized for ourselves a new creative platform.

FIGURE 15.5 Cirque du Soleil Advertises Its Mystère Show in Las Vegas

(continued)

To achieve its present eminence, featuring six touring shows and six permanent shows in conjunction with partnering resorts—five with Las Vegas casino hotels and one at Walt Disney World resort in Florida—the *Cirque* has had to face and resolve financial, managerial, and artistic challenges. For the well-paid performers, who include many former Olympic athletes, the notion of stretch (both physically and metaphorically) is central to their professional lives. "Creative people always need new challenges," says COO Daniel Lamarre. Organizations, by contrast, sometimes find it easier to rest on their laurels. However, such an approach could contain the seeds of failure for the *Cirque*.

Cirque du Soleil faces new competitors today, including two that have emerged from its home turf, *Cirque Éloize* and *Cirque Éos*, both spawned by the growing supply of graduates from two recently formed circus schools in Quebec. Cirque copycats have also sprung up in France and Argentina. An even greater challenge comes from the U.S. company, Feld Enterprises, that owns the famous Ringling Bros and Barnum & Bailey Circus. Feld has created a new production, Barnum's Kaleidoscope, that replaces the traditional circus performers with a mix of acrobatic performers and live music at much higher admission prices.

Cirque du Soleil has grown in recent years by adding new shows with new partner resorts. In 2006, it launched *Love*, a show based on the music of the Beatles, making the Mirage casino its fifth partner in Las Vegas. But a key question for Cirque is where future growth will come from as its core market becomes more crowded. Not only is new competition driving up the cost of finding and retaining top performers, but it is unclear how much longer the privately held Canadian company can continue filling 1000-seat theaters at high admission prices with what some critics view as essentially variations on the same product. Continued evolution will be required.

Source: Robert J. David and Amir Motamedi, "Cirque du Soleil: Can It Burn Brighter?" *Journal of Strategic Management Education*, 1, No. 2, 2004, 369–382, www.cirquedusaoleil.com, accessed June 2, 2009.

require a larger-than-life personality. Leaders who aspire to take a company to greatness, he says, need to have personal humility blended with intensive professional will, ferocious resolve, and a willingness to give credit to others while taking the blame themselves.[25] Such a leadership approach is exemplified by His Highness Sheikh Mohamed bin Zayed Al Nahyan, Crown Prince of Abu Dhabi, in the re-branding of Abu Dhabi as a luxury tourist destination (Service Perspective 15.3).

Finally, in hierarchical organizations, structured on a military model, it's often assumed that leadership at the top is sufficient. However, as Sandra Vandermerwe points out, forward-looking service businesses need to be more flexible. Today's greater emphasis on using teams within service businesses means that

> [L]eaders are everywhere, disseminated throughout the teams. They are found especially in the customer facing and interfacing jobs in order that decision-making will lead to long-lasting relationships with customers... leaders are customer and project champions who energize the group by virtue of their enthusiasm, interest, and know-how.[26]

Role Modeling Desired Behavior

One of the traits of successful leaders is their ability to role model the behavior they expect of managers and other employees. Often, this requires the approach known as "management by walking around," popularized by Thomas Peters and Robert Waterman in their book *In Search of Excellence*.[27] When Herb Kelleher was CEO of Southwest Airlines, no one was surprised to see him turn up at a Southwest maintenance hanger at 2 a.m. or even to encounter him working an occasional stint as a flight attendant. Walking around involves regular visits, sometimes unannounced, to various areas of the company's operation. This approach provides insights into both back-stage and

SERVICE PERSPECTIVE 15.3

ABU DHABI—BUILDING A PLACE BRAND

The Emirate of Abu Dhabi is the federal capital of the seven emirates of the United Arab Emirates. The Office of the Brand of Abu Dhabi (OBAD) was established in 2007. Its key purpose is to define the brand identity of the Emirate of Abu Dhabi and to design a comprehensive strategy that would guard and act as a patron of this brand identity. Creating a tourist brand in the national context is not easy. It needs to reflect the values of its people, identify with the values of its tourists and visitors, and yet be distinctive in a very competitive global tourism market.

This task was undertaken through identification of "cultural seekers" in the luxury tourism market using face-to-face workshops in the UK, Germany, and France, some of the key source markets. They distilled the values these tourists seek through the brand pyramid. The essence of the brand emerged in a single word: respect. This concept is inherent throughout the population of Abu Dhabi, which not only takes pride in and respects its heritage and customs but also its international guests. It is manifested through its policies that respect, encourages and protects business endeavors. It is translated in the events it supports like the Abu Dhabi Grand Prix '09/Ferrari team, which has a history of tradition.

The brand is visually represented by a Dhow, a traditional sailboat that reinforces the rich roots of its people. To reinforce this identity, OBAD sponsors an annual photography competition to see Abu Dhabi through the eyes of its residents. The agency arranged workshops and consultations to ensure that the brand is used appropriately in logos, corporate campaigns, and advertisements. This requires constant leadership and supervision, which is managed through its team. To ensure that the team can work seamlessly with both public and private companies, the team reports directly to His Highness Sheikh Mohamed bin Zayed Al Nahyan, Crown Prince of Abu Dhabi and Chairman of the Executive Council.

Sources: The Office of the Brand of Abu Dhabi (2009), http://brand.abudhabi.ae/; Branding Abu Dhabi Brand, http://brand.abudhabi.ae/.

front-stage operations, the ability to observe and meet both employees and customers, and an opportunity to see how corporate strategy is implemented at the frontline.

Periodically, this approach may lead to a recognition that changes are needed in a firm's strategy. Encountering the CEO on such a visit can also be motivating for service personnel. It also provides an opportunity for role modeling good service. Best Practice in Action 15.1 describes how the CEO of a major hospital learned the power of role modeling early in his tenure.

Turning around an organization that has limited resources requires concentrating those resources where the need and the likely payoffs are greatest. As an example of effective leadership under such conditions, Kim and Mauborgne highlight the work of William Bratton, who achieved fame during a 20-year police career in Boston and New York. Bratton believed in putting his key managers face-to-face with the problems that were of greatest concern to the public. When he became chief of the New York Transit Police, Bratton found that none of the senior staff officers rode the subway. So he required all transit police officials, including himself, to ride the subway to work and to meetings, even at night, instead of traveling in cars provided by the city. In that way, senior officials were exposed to the reality of the problems faced by millions of ordinary citizens and by police officers who strove to keep order.

Bratton's predecessors had lobbied for money to increase the number of subway cops, believing the only way to stop muggers was to have officers ride every subway line and patrol each of the system's 700 exits and entrances. By contrast, Bratton had his staff analyze where subway crimes were committed. Finding that the vast majority occurred at

BEST PRACTICE IN ACTION 15.1

A Hospital President Learns the Power of Role Modeling

During his 30-year tenure as president of Boston's Beth Israel Hospital (now Beth Israel Deaconess Medical Center), Mitchell T. Rabkin, MD, was known for regularly spending time making informal visits to all parts of the hospital. "You learn a lot from 'management by walking around,'" he said. "And you're also seen. When I visit another hospital and am given a tour by its CEO, I watch how that CEO interacts with other people, and what the body language is in each instance. It's very revealing. Even more, it's very important for role modeling." To reinforce that point, Dr. Rabkin liked to tell the following story:

> People learn to *do* as a result of the way they see you and others *behave*. An example from Beth Israel that's now almost apocryphal—but *is* true—is the story of the bits of litter on the floor.
>
> One of our trustees, the late Max Feldberg, head of the Zayre Corporation, asked me one time to take a walk around the hospital with him and inquired, "Why do you think there are so many pieces of paper scattered on the floor of this patient care unit?"
>
> "Well, it's because people don't pick them up," I replied.
>
> He said, "Look, you're a scientist. We'll do an experiment. We'll walk down this floor and we'll pick up every other piece of paper. And then we'll go upstairs, there's another unit, same geography, statistically the same amount of paper, but we won't pick up anything."
>
> So this 72-year-old man and I went picking up alternate bits of the litter on one floor and nothing on the other. When we came back 10 minutes later, virtually all the rest of the litter on the first floor had been removed and nothing, of course, had changed on the second.
>
> And "Mr. Max" said to me, "You see, it's not because *people* don't pick them up, it's because *you* don't pick them up. If you're so fancy that you can't bend down and pick up a piece of paper, why should anybody else?"

Source: Christopher Lovelock, *Product Plus: How Product + Service = Competitive Advantage.* New York: McGraw-Hill, 1994.

only a few stations and on a couple of lines, the chief redeployed his officers to focus on the problem areas and shifted a number of uniformed officers into plain clothes. Coupled with time-saving innovations in arrest-processing procedures, this dramatic reallocation of resources resulted in a significant reduction in subway crime without new investment in resources.

There is a risk, of course, that prominent leaders may become too externally focused at the risk of their internal effectiveness. A CEO who enjoys an enormous income (often through exercise of huge stock options), maintains a princely lifestyle, and basks in widespread publicity may even turn off low-paid service workers at the bottom of the organization.

Leadership, Culture, and Climate

To close this chapter, we take a brief look at a theme that runs throughout the book: the leader's role in nurturing an effective culture within the firm.[28] *Organizational culture* can be defined as including:

- Shared perceptions or themes regarding what is important in the organization.
- Shared values about what is right and wrong.
- Shared understanding about what works and what doesn't work.
- Shared beliefs and assumptions about *why* these beliefs are important.
- Shared styles of working and relating to others.

John Hamm believes that effective communication is a leader's most critical tool for the essential task of inspiring the organization to take responsibility for creating a better future. The most effective leaders, he says, ask themselves, "What needs to happen today to get where we want to go? What vague belief or notion can I clarify or debunk?" Those CEOs who can communicate precisely will best be able to align the organization's commitment and energy with well-understood vision of the firm's real goals and opportunities.[29]

Transforming an organization to develop and nurture a new culture along each of these five dimensions is no easy task for even the most gifted leader. It's doubly difficult when the organization is part of an industry that prides itself on deeply rooted traditions, including many different departments run by independent-minded professionals in different fields who are very attuned to how they are perceived by fellow professionals in the same field at other institutions. This situation often is found in such pillars of the nonprofit world as colleges and universities, major hospitals, and large museums. Service Perspective 15.4 describes the challenges faced by a new director in transforming Boston's Museum of Fine Arts at a low point in its history.

Organizational climate represents the tangible surface layer on top of the organization's underlying culture. Among six key factors that influence an organization's working environment are its *flexibility* (how free employees feel to innovate); their sense of *responsibility* to the organization; the level of *standards* people set; the perceived aptness of *rewards*; the *clarity* people have about mission and values; and the level of *commitment* to a common purpose.[30]

Once the values of the organization are part of the hearts and minds of its employees, they can work independently and yet be collaborative as they are all thinking with the mission and goals.[31] From an employee perspective, this climate is directly related to managerial policies and procedures, especially those associated with human resource management. In short, climate represents the shared perceptions of employees about the practices, procedures, and types of behaviors that get rewarded and supported in a particular setting.

Because multiple climates often exist simultaneously within a single organization, a climate must relate to something specific—for instance, service, support, innovation, or safety. A climate for service refers to employee perceptions of those practices, procedures, and behaviors that are expected with regard to customer service and service quality and that get rewarded when performed well. Essential features of a service-oriented culture include clear marketing goals and a strong drive to be the best in delivering superior value or service quality.[32]

Leaders are responsible for creating cultures and the service climates that go along with them. Transformational leadership may require changing a culture that has become dysfunctional in the context of what it takes to be successful. Why are some leaders more effective than others in bringing about a desired change in climate? As presented in Research Insights 15.1, research suggests that it may be a matter of style.

Creating a new climate for service, based on an understanding of what is needed for market success, may require a radical rethink of human resource management activities, operational procedures, and the firm's reward and recognition policies. Newcomers to an organization must quickly familiarize themselves with the existing culture, otherwise they will find themselves being led by it, rather than leading through it and, if necessary, changing it.

CONCLUSION

The Service-Profit Chain highlights a set of relationships that directly links profits and growth to not only customer satisfaction and loyalty but also to employee satisfaction, loyalty, and productivity. This model draws together the themes and insights from the earlier chapters in this book, particularly those on managing employees, building customer loyalty, and improving service quality and productivity. In this chapter, we examined the

SERVICE PERSPECTIVE 15.4

REVERSING COURSE AT THE MUSEUM OF FINE ARTS, BOSTON

Boston's venerable Museum of Fine Arts, founded in 1870, had been going downhill for several years when the board recruited a new director in June 1994. Their choice was art historian Malcolm Rogers, then deputy director of the National Portrait Gallery in London. Arriving in Boston, Rogers found a dispirited institution. Reflecting financial difficulties and recent staff cutbacks, morale was low. Corporate memberships had slumped and attendance had declined.

One of the new director's first acts was to host a breakfast for the entire staff and introduce what would become a central theme:

> *We are one museum, not a collection of departments. The museum consists of security guards, curators, technicians, benefactors, volunteers, public relations personnel. We all have our individual professional expertise. And by working cooperatively with colleagues, we all have areas that can be improved.*

Rogers' "one museum" theme, repeated at frequent intervals, sent the message that the director's agenda took precedence over that of the traditionally independent curators who operated the museum's many different art departments and set priorities for acquisitions and exhibitions. One curator quickly resigned. While he was recognized for his good humor and friendly, outgoing manner, the new director showed that he could be blunt and decisive. He took a tough line with expenditures and began a program to cut staff size by 20 percent. However, his cutbacks did not extend to services for museum visitors. Instead, he set about creating a more welcoming environment. Said Rogers:

> *I'm firmly committed to the idea that museums are here to serve the community, and that's going to be one of the keynotes of my work here in Boston—to encourage the MFA to turn out toward its public and to satisfy as broad a constituency as possible.*

He soon reopened the main entrance on Huntington Avenue, which had been closed to save money, and reversed the trend of curtailing admission hours, another of his predecessor's cost-cutting initiatives. Daily schedules were extended and seven-day operations instituted. Three nights a week, the museum remained open until 10 p.m. On "Community Days," three Sundays a year, the MFA was open free of charge.

Each successive year, Rogers launched activities to improve the museum's facilities and image, including new exterior lighting to better display the MFA's imposing facade at night, extending the main restaurant, and opening a new rooftop terrace. Making the MFA an evening destination, especially for people living in or close to the city, was another objective. The broader variety of exhibitions (to encourage multiple visits per year), upgraded restaurants, and improved museum atmosphere all played a role. An ambitious $500 million capital campaign was launched, part of which would fund construction of a major building expansion.

Externally, Rogers enjoyed a much higher public profile than his predecessors. Said Pat Jacoby, then deputy director of marketing and development: "Malcolm personifies marketing: He's accessible, he's an advocate of PR, he cares about the visitors, and he believes the MFA can set the standard for other museums." Rogers declared:

> *Marketing is central to the life of a great museum that's trying to get its message out. It's part of our educational outreach, our social outreach. Unfortunately, certain people don't like the word "marketing." What I see out there—and also to a certain extent inside the museum—is a very conservative culture that cannot accept that institutions previously considered "elite" should actually be trying to attract a broader public and also listening to what the public is saying. But it's all to do with fulfilling your mission.*
>
> *Clearly part of a museum's mission is guardianship of precious objects, but unless we're communicating those objects to people effectively and our visitors are enjoying them—and the ambiance of the setting in which they are displayed and*

interpreted—then we're only operating at 50% effectiveness or less. Having said this, I want to stress that the mission comes first and that marketing is absolutely the servant of our mission. We're not just in the business of finding out what people want and then giving it to them.

Rogers sought to pick a mix of exhibitions that combined high scholarly content with popular appeal. His view, shared by the senior staff and supported by the board, was that one show in five should be of a "blockbuster" nature, which meant hosting such an exhibition at least once every two years. He also sought to display art from the MFA's permanent collection to best advantage, including small revolving shows. Paintings in the 15 European galleries were rehung in innovative ways designed to stimulate the audience and engage them more actively. However, there was much criticism among the art community when 27 Impressionist paintings from the MFA's celebrated Monet collection were loaned (for a reported $1 million fee) to a gallery at the Bellagio casino in Las Vegas, where they were seen by 450,000 visitors.

In 2002, the MFA board adopted a long-term strategic plan, titled *One Museum—Great Museum—Your Museum.* It was organized around 10 strategic goals (Table 15.3), each supported by a set of initiatives and over 200 detailed action plans.

By mid-2006, many of these initiatives were well underway. The fundraising drive for the new extension had passed $335 million mark. Attendance had begun to grow again, after slumping nationwide following 9/11. The MFA continued its strategy of periodically exhibiting nontraditional art forms and art collections, including *Speed, Style and Beauty: Cars from the Ralph Lauren Collection,* featuring 16 classic European cars owned by the fashion designer. Rogers argued that these vehicles were as much works of art as furniture, long an accepted component of many art museums' collections. Despite such criticisms as the *New York Times* review headlined "Art with Lousy Mileage but Shiny Celebrity Gloss," attendance exceeded its goals and met an important objective of attracting a much higher proportion of male visitors than usually came to the museum.

TABLE 15.3 Ten Strategic Goals for the MFA

Collections	1. Continue to improve quality of the collection
	2. Improve management, care, and knowledge of the collection
	3. Provide and promote worldwide electronic access to the collection
Experiencing	4. Engage, educate, and delight visitors
	5. Retain and expand audiences by understanding their needs
	6. Schedule an exhibition program that meets a variety of objectives
Facilities	7. Enlarge and improve the physical plant
Financial	8. Pursue fundraising required by the Master Site plan and other strategic goals
	9. Ensure fiscal stability
Organization	10. Adopt an audience-aware, results-oriented experimental attitude and realign the organization to support these activities

Sources: Christopher Lovelock, "Museum of Fine Arts, Boston," *Services Marketing,* 4th ed. Upper Saddle River, NJ: Prentice Hall, 2001, 625–638; V. Kasturi Rangan and Marie Bell, "Museum of Fine Arts Boston," Harvard Business School Case 9-506-027; Museum of Fine Arts website, www.mfa.org, accessed June 14, 2009.

challenges of moving a business toward service leadership, both from an organizational perspective and from the perspective of the individuals leading this journey.

Transforming an organization and maintaining service leadership is no easy task for even the most gifted leader. We hope that having worked through this book will help you to become a more effective marketer and leader in any service organization. We also hope we not only managed to equip you with the necessary knowledge, understanding, and insights but also with the beliefs and attitudes about what propels a firm to service leadership.

RESEARCH INSIGHTS 15.1

THE IMPACT OF LEADERSHIP STYLES ON CLIMATE

Daniel Goleman, an applied psychologist at Rutgers University, is known for his work on emotional intelligence—the ability to manage ourselves and our relationships effectively. Having earlier identified six styles of leadership, he investigated how successful each style has proved to be in affecting climate or working atmosphere, based on a major study of the behavior and impact on their organizations of thousands of executives.

Coercive leaders demand immediate compliance ("Do what I tell you") and were found to have a negative impact on climate. Goleman comments that this controlling style, often highly confrontational, has value only in a crisis or in dealing with problem employees. *Pacesetting leaders* set high standards for performance and exemplify these through their own energetic behavior; this style can be summarized as "Do as I do, now." Somewhat surprisingly it, too, was found to have a negative impact on climate. In practice, the pacesetting leader may destroy morale by assuming too much, too soon, of subordinates—expecting them to know already what to do and how to do it. Finding others to be less capable than expected, the leader may lapse into obsessing over details and micromanaging. This style is likely to work only when seeking to get quick results from a highly motivated and competent team.

The research found that the most effective style for achieving a positive change in climate came from *authoritative leaders* who have the skills and personality to mobilize people toward a vision, building confidence and using a "Come with me" approach. The research also found that three other styles had quite positive impacts on climate: *affiliative leaders* who believe that "People come first," seeking to create harmony and build emotional bonds; *democratic leaders* who forge consensus through participation ("What do you think?"); and *coaching leaders* who work to develop people for the future and whose style might be summarized as "Try this."

Source: Daniel Goleman, "Leadership that Gets Results," *Harvard Business Review*, 78, March–April 2000, 78–93.

Chapter Summary

LO1 The Service-Profit Chain shows that service leadership in an industry requires high performance in several related areas:

- Customer relationships must be managed effectively and there must be strategies to build and sustain loyalty.
- Value must be created and delivered to the target customers in ways that lead them to see the firm's offering as superior to competing offerings.
- Service quality and productivity must be continuously improved.
- Service employees must be enabled and motivated.
- Top management's leadership needs to drive and support all the components of the Service-Profit Chain.

LO2 To be successful, the marketing, operations, and human resource management functions need to be tightly integrated and work closely together in well coordinated ways.

- Integration means that the key deliverables and objectives of the various functions are not only compatible but also mutually reinforcing.
- Ways to improve integration include (1) internal transfers across functional areas, (2) cross-functional project teams, (3) internal marketing and training, and (4) management commitment that ensures the overarching objectives of all functions are integrated.

LO3 There are four levels of service performance, and only the last two follow the Service-Profit Chain's principles. They are:

- ***Service losers.*** They follow the cycle of failure and are poor performers in marketing, operations, and HRM. Service losers survive because monopoly situations give customers little choice but to buy from them.
- ***Service nonentities.*** Their performance still leaves much to be desired, but they have eliminated the worst features of losers. They typically function in the cycle of mediocrity.
- ***Service professionals.*** They have a clear market position, and customers in target segments seek them out based on their sustained reputation for meeting expectations. They typically function in the cycle of success.

- *Service leaders.* They are the crème de la crème of their respective industries. They typically perfect and internalize the cycle of success for their service business.

LO4 We contrasted the description and actions of a service leader against professionals, nonentities, and losers along the three functional areas in Table 15.2 on page 446.

- Service leadership requires high performance across a number of dimensions, including managing and motivating employees, continuously improving service quality and productivity, creating and delivering a superior value proposition to target customers, and developing strategies for building and sustaining customer loyalty.

No organization can hope to move up the performance ladder and achieve enduring success without change, which can be in the form of evolutionary change or turnaround change.

- The primary force behind effective change management is human leadership.
- Senior management needs to communicate a vision and at the same time set the strategic goals, develop the strategies to achieve those goals, and then ensure the successful implementation of that strategy.
- One of the challenges for top management is to create a culture that encourages employees to take risks, share ideas, and be willing to try new approaches.
- To overcome barriers for change, leadership must navigate through eight stages for successful change management, starting with the creation of a sense of urgency to develop the impetus for change and ending with anchoring the new behaviors in the organizational culture.

LO5 Human leadership is needed for strategy development and its implementation. These tasks make leading different from managing, with the latter focusing on keeping the current situation going. Leadership is a growing part of managerial work.

LO6 The qualities leaders in service organizations at all levels should have include:

- Love for the business.
- The perspective that service quality is a key foundation for success.
- A strong belief in the people who work for them and recognition of the importance of the frontline.
- A set of core values they pass on to the organization.
- Effective communication skills, which is probably a leader's most important skill to inspire an organization or a team to create success.
- Ability to ask great questions and get answers from their team.
- Understand the purpose and existence of the company and reset their goals for change when needed.
- Ability to role model the behaviors they expect of others.

LO7 Exemplary leaders understand the powerful, unifying effect of focusing on customers and creating a culture for service. It is therefore an important role of leaders to develop a strong organizational culture so that its employees have shared:

- Perceptions of what is important to the company and why it is important.
- Values about what is right and wrong.
- Understanding of what works and what does not.
- Beliefs and assumptions about why these beliefs are important.
- Shared styles of working and relating to others.

LO8 Organizational climate is the surface layer on top of the culture. Climate represents the shared perceptions of employees about the practices and behaviors that get rewarded in an organization. An essential feature of a service-oriented culture is a strong drive to be the best in delivering superior value and service excellence.

Review Questions

1. What are the implications of the Service-Profit Chain for service management?
2. Supporters of the Service-Profit Chain argue that strong links connect employee satisfaction and loyalty, service quality and productivity, value, and customer satisfaction and loyalty. Do you think these same relationships would prevail in low-contact environments in which customers use self-service technology? Why or why not?
3. Why do the marketing, operations, and human resource management functions need to be closely coordinated in service organizations?
4. What are the causes of tension among the marketing, operations, and human resource functions? Provide specific examples of how these tensions might vary from one service industry to another.

5. How are the four levels of service performance defined? Based on your own service experiences, provide an example of a company for each category.
6. What is the difference between leadership and management? Illustrate with examples.
7. What is meant by transformational leadership? Explain how the challenges differ between an organization undergoing evolutionary change and one that requires a turnaround.
8. "Exemplary turnaround leaders understand the powerful, unifying effect of focusing on customers." Comment on this statement. Is focusing on customers more likely to have a unifying effect within a company under turnaround conditions than at other times?
9. Why is role modeling a desirable quality in leaders?
10. What is the relationship among leadership, climate, and culture?

Application Exercises

1. Analyze a service firm along the key aspects of the Service-Profit Chain. Assess how well the firm is performing at the various components of the Service-Profit Chain, and make specific suggestions for improvements.
2. Contrast the roles of marketing, operations, and human resources in (1) a gas station chain, (2) a Web-based brokerage firm, and (3) an insurance company.
3. Select a company you know well, and obtain additional information from a literature review, website, company publication, blog, and so on. Evaluate the company on as many dimensions of service performance as you can, identifying where you believe it fits on the service performance spectrum shown in Table 15.2.
4. What is the role of senior management in moving a firm toward consistently delivering service excellence?
5. Profile an individual whose leadership skills have played a significant role in the success of a service organization, identifying personal characteristics you consider important.
6. Based on all you've learned working throughout this book, what do you believe are the key drivers of success for service organizations? Try and develop an integrative causal model that explains the important drivers of success for a service organization.

Endnotes

1. Peter Drucker did not regard himself as a marketer, yet his writing has had profound impact on the marketing field and discipline. The opening quote is discussed further in Frederick E. Webster Jr., "Marketing IS Management: The Wisdom of Peter Drucker," *Journal of the Academy of Marketing Science*, 37, No. 1, 2009, 20–27.
2. Fortune, "100 Best Companies to Work for 2007," http://money.cnn.com/magazines/fortune/bestcompanies/2007/, accessed June 3, 2009; Knowledge@Wharton, "IKEA: Furnishing Good Employee Benefits Along with Dining Room Sets," http://knowledge.wharton.upenn.edu/article.cfm?articleid=959, accessed June 3, 2009; J. Wang, "Learning From the Best: Speaker Profiles for August 8 Women's Leadership Exchange Conference," *Long Beach Business Journal*, July 2006, 3–4. For an excellent book on IKEA and its values see Bo Edvardsson and Bo Enquist, *Values-based Service for Sustainable Business: Lessons from Ikea*. New York: Routledge, 2009.
3. Don Peppers and Martha Rogers, *Return on Customer*. New York: Currency Doubleday, 2005, 1
4. Don Peppers and Martha Rogers, *Return on Customer*. New York: Currency Doubleday, 2005, 7–8.
5. James L. Heskett, Thomas O. Jones, Gary W. Loveman, W. Earl Sasser Jr., and Leonard A. Schlesinger, "Putting the Service Profit Chain to Work," *Harvard Business Review* 72, March/April 1994; James L. Heskett, W. Earl Sasser, Jr., and Leonard A. Schlesinger, *The Service Profit Chain*. New York: The Free Press, 1997.
6. Sandra Vandermerwe, *From Tin Soldiers to Russian Dolls*. Oxford: Butterworth-Heinemann, 1993, 82.
7. Robert J. Kwortnik Jr. and Gary M. Thompson, "Unifying Service Marketing and Operations With Service Experience Management," *Journal of Service Research*, 11, No. 4, 2009, 389–406.
8. Richard B. Chase and Robert H. Hayes, "Beefing Up Operations in Service Firms," *Sloan Management Review* 33, Fall 1991, 15–26.
9. Claudia H. Deutsch, "Management: Companies Scramble to Fill Shoes at the Top," nytimes.com, November 1, 2000.
10. W. Chan Kim and Renée Mauborgne, "Tipping Point Leadership," *Harvard Business Review*, 81, April 2003, 61–69.
11. John P. Kotter, *What Leaders Really Do*. Boston: Harvard Business School Press, 1999, 10–11.

12. Rosabeth Moss Kanter, "Leadership and the Psychology of Turnaround," *Harvard Business Review*, 81, June 2003, 58–67.
13. John P. Kotter, *What Leaders Really Do*. Boston: Harvard Business School Press, 1999, 10–11.
14. Deborah Blagg and Susan Young, "What Makes a Leader?" *Harvard Business School Bulletin*, February 2001, 31–36.
15. Gary Hamel and C. K. Prahlahad, *Competing for the Future*. Boston: Harvard Business School Press, 1994.
16. Leonard L. Berry, Venkatesh Shankar, Janet Turner Parish, Susan Cadwallader, and Thomas Dotzel, "Creating New Markets Through Service Innovation,"*MIT Sloan Management Review*, 47, Winter 2006, 56–63.
17. James L. Heskett, W. Earl Sasser Jr., and Leonard A. Schlesinger, *The Service Profit Chain*. New York: The Free Press, 1997, 236.
18. A. Nahavandi, *The Art and Science of Leadership*. Upper Saddle River, NJ: Pearson Education Inc., 2006.
19. Leonard L. Berry, *On Great Service:– A Framework for Action*. New York: The Free Press, 1995, 9.
20. Leonard L. Berry, *Discovering the Soul of Service*. New York: The Free Press, 1999, 44, 47. See also D. Micheal Abrashoff, "Retention Through Redemption," *Harvard Business Review* 79, February 2001, 136–141, which provides a fascinating example on successful leadership in the U.S. Navy.
21. D. Blagg and S. Young, "What Makes a Leader?" *Harvard Business School Bulletin*, February 2001, 31–36.
22. J. Hamm, "The Five Messages Leaders Must Manage," *Harvard Business Review* 84, May 2006, 115–123.
23. D. A. Nadler, "The CEO's 2nd Act," *Harvard Business Review* 85, January 2007, 66–72.
24. C. A. Montgomery, "Putting Leadership Back into Strategy," *Harvard Business Review* 86, January 2008, 54–60.
25. Rakesh Karma, "The Curse of the Superstar CEO," *Harvard Business Review*, 80, September 2002, 60–66.
26. Jim Collins, "Level 5 Leadership: The Triumph of Humility and Fierce Resolve," *Harvard Business Review* 79, January 2001, 66–76.
27. Sandra Vandermerwe, *From Tin Soldiers to Russian Dolls*. Oxford: Butterworth-Heinemann, 1993, 82.
28. Thomas J. Peters and Robert H. Waterman, *In Search of Excellence*. New York: Harper & Row, 1982, 122.
29. This section is based, in part, on Benjamin Schneider and David E. Bowen, *Winning the Service Game*. Boston: Harvard Business School Press, 1995; David E. Bowen, Benjamin Schneider, and Sandra S. Kim, "Shaping Service Cultures through Strategic Human Resource Management," in T. Schwartz and D. Iacobucci, eds., *Handbook of Services Marketing and Management*. Thousand Oaks, CA: Sage Publications, 2000, 439–454.
30. John Hamm, "The Five Messages Leaders Must Manage," *Harvard Business Review*, 84, May 2006, 114–123.
31. Daniel Goleman, "Leadership that Gets Results," *Harvard Business Review*, 78, March–April 2000, 78–93.
32. Rosabeth Moss Kanter, "Transforming Giants," *Harvard Business Review* 86, January 2008, 43–52.
33. Hans Kasper, "Culture and Leadership in Market-oriented Service Organisations," *European Journal of Marketing*, 36, No. 9/10, 2002, 1047–1057; Ronald A. Clark, Michael D. Hartline, and Keith C. Jones, "The Effects of Leadership Style on Hotel Employees' Commitment to Service Quality," *Cornell Hospitality Quarterly*, 50, No. 2, 2009, 209–231.

CASE 1 Sullivan Ford Auto World

CHRISTOPHER LOVELOCK

A young health care manager unexpectedly finds herself responsible for running a family-owned car dealership that is in trouble. She is very concerned about the poor performance of the service department and wonders whether a turnaround is possible.

Viewed from Wilson Avenue, the Sullivan Ford Auto World dealership presented a festive sight. Flags waved and strings of triangular pennants in red, white, and blue fluttered gaily in the late afternoon breeze. Rows of new model cars and trucks gleamed and winked in the sunlight. Geraniums graced the flowerbeds outside the showroom entrance. A huge rotating sign at the corner of Wilson Avenue and Victoria Street sported the Ford logo and identified the business as Sullivan's Auto World. Banners below urged "Let's Make a Deal!'

Inside the handsome, high-ceilinged showroom, four of the new model Fords were on display—a dark-green Explorer SUV, a red Mustang convertible, a white Focus sedan, and a red Ranger pickup truck. Each car was polished to a high sheen. Two groups of customers were chatting with salespeople, and a middle-aged man sat in the driver's seat of the convertible, studying the controls.

Upstairs in the comfortably furnished general manager's office, Carol Sullivan-Diaz finished running another spreadsheet analysis on her laptop. She felt tired and depressed. Her father, Walter Sullivan, had died four weeks earlier at the age of 56 of a sudden heart attack. As executor of his estate, the bank had asked her to temporarily assume the position of general manager of the dealership. The only visible changes that she had made to her father's office were installing an all-in-one laser printer, scanner, copier, and fax, but she had been very busy analyzing the current position of the business.

Sullivan-Diaz did not like the look of the numbers on the printout. Auto World's financial situation had been deteriorating for 18 months, and it had been running in the red for the first half of the current year. New car sales had declined, dampened in part by rising interest rates. Margins had been squeezed by promotions and other efforts to move new cars off the lot. Reflecting rising fuel prices, industry forecasts of future sales were discouraging, and so were her own financial projections for Auto World's sales department. Service revenues, which were below average for a dealership of this size, had also declined, although the service department still made a small surplus.

Had she had made a mistake last week, Carol wondered, in turning down Bill Froelich's offer to buy the business? Admittedly, the amount was substantially below the offer from Froelich that her father had rejected two years earlier, but the business had been more profitable then.

The Sullivan Family

Walter Sullivan had purchased a small Ford dealership in 1983, renaming it Sullivan's Auto World, and had built it up to become one of the best known in the metropolitan area. Six years back, he had borrowed heavily to purchase the current site at a major suburban highway intersection, in an area of town with many new housing developments.

There had been a dealership on the site, but the buildings were 30 years old. Sullivan had retained the service and repair bays, but torn down the showroom in front of them, and replaced it by an attractive modern facility. On moving to the new location, which was substantially larger than the old one, he had renamed his business Sullivan's Ford Auto World.

Everybody had seemed to know Walt Sullivan. He had been a consummate showman and entrepreneur, appearing in his own radio and television commercials, and was active in community affairs. His approach to car sales had emphasized promotions, discounts, and deals in order to maintain volume. He was never happier than when making a sale.

Carol Sullivan-Diaz, aged 28, was the eldest of Walter and Carmen Sullivan's three daughters. After obtaining a bachelor's degree in economics, she had gone on to earn an MBA degree and had then embarked on a career in health care management. She was married to Dr. Roberto Diaz, a surgeon at St. Luke's Hospital. Her 20-year-old twin sisters, Gail and Joanne, both students at the local university, lived with their mother.

In her own student days, Sullivan-Diaz had worked part-time in her father's business on secretarial and bookkeeping tasks, and as a service writer in the service department, so she was quite familiar with the operations of the dealership. At business school, she had decided on a career in health care management. After graduation, she had worked as an executive assistant to the president of St. Luke's, a large teaching hospital. Two years later, she joined Metropolitan Health Plan, a large multi-hospital facility that also provided long-term care, as assistant director of marketing, a position she had now held for almost three years. Her responsibilities included designing new services, complaint handling, market research, and introducing an innovative day care program for hospital employees and neighborhood residents.

Carol's employer had given her a six-week leave of absence to put her father's affairs in order. She doubted that she could extend that leave much beyond the two weeks still remaining. Neither she nor other family members were interested in making a career of running the dealership. However, she was prepared to take time out from her health care career to work on a turnaround if that seemed a viable proposition. She had been successful in her present job and believed it would not be difficult to find another health management position in the future.

The Dealership

Like other car dealerships, Sullivan's Ford Auto World operated both sales and service departments, often referred to in the trade as "front end" and "back end," respectively. Both new and used vehicles were sold, since a high proportion of new car and van purchases involved trading in the purchaser's existing vehicle. Auto World would also buy well-maintained used cars at auction for resale. Purchasers who decided that they could not afford a new car would often buy a "preowned" vehicle instead, while shoppers who came in looking for a used car could sometimes be persuaded to buy a new one. Before being put on sales, used vehicles were carefully serviced, with parts replaced as needed. They were then thoroughly cleaned by a detailer whose services were hired as required. Dents and other blemishes were removed at a nearby body shop and occasionally the vehicle's paintwork was resprayed, too.

The front end of the dealership employed a sales manager, seven salespeople, an office manager, and a secretary. One of the salespeople had given notice and would be leaving at the end of the following week. The service department, when fully staffed, consisted of a service manager, a parts supervisor, nine mechanics, and two service writers. The Sullivan twins often worked part-time as service writers, filling in at busy periods, when one of the other writers was sick or on vacation, or when—as currently—there was an unfilled vacancy. The job entailed scheduling appointments for repairs and maintenance, writing up each work order, calling customers with repair estimates, and assisting customers when they returned to pick up the cars and pay for the work that had been done.

Sullivan-Diaz knew from her own experience as a service writer that it could be a stressful job. Few people liked to be without their car, even for a day. When a car broke down or was having problems, the owner was often nervous about how long it would take to get it fixed and, if the warranty had expired, how much the labor and parts would cost. Customers were quite unforgiving when a problem was not fixed completely on the first attempt and they had to return their vehicle for further work.

Major mechanical failures were not usually difficult to repair, although the parts replacement costs might be expensive. It was often the "little" things, like water leaks and wiring problems, that were the hardest to diagnose and correct, and it might be necessary for the customer to return two or three times before such a problem was resolved. In these situations, parts and materials costs were relatively low, but labor costs mounted up quickly, often costing $75 an hour. Customers could often be quite abusive, yelling at service writers over the phone or arguing with service writers, mechanics, and the service manager in person.

Turnover in the service writer job was high, which was one reason why Carol—and more recently her sisters—had often been pressed into service by their father to "hold the fort" as he described it. More than once, she had seen an exasperated service writer respond sharply to a complaining customer or hang up on one who was being abusive over the telephone. Gail and Joanne were currently taking turns to cover the vacant position, but there were times when both of them had classes and the dealership had only one service writer on duty.

By national standards, Sullivan's Auto World stood toward the lower end of medium-sized dealerships, selling around 1,100 cars a year, equally divided between new and used vehicles. In the most recent year, its revenues totaled $26.6 million from new and used car sales and $2.9 million from service and parts—down from $30.5 million and $3.6 million, respectively, in the previous year. Although the unit value of car sales was high, the margins were quite low, with margins for new cars substantially lower than for used ones. Industry guidelines suggested that the contribution margin (known as the departmental selling gross) from car sales should be about 5.5 percent of sales revenues, and from service, around 25 percent of revenues. In a typical dealership, 60 percent of the selling gross came from sales and 40 percent from service, but the balance was shifting from sales to service. The selling gross was then applied to fixed expenses, such as administrative salaries, rent or mortgage payments, and utilities.

For the most recent 12 months at Auto World, Sullivan-Diaz had determined that the selling gross figures were 4.6 and 24 percent, respectively, both of them lower than in the previous year and insufficient to cover the dealership's fixed expenses. Her father had made no mention of financial difficulties and she had been shocked to learn from the bank after his death that Auto World had been two months behind in mortgage payments on the property. Further analysis also showed that accounts payable had also risen sharply in the previous six months. Fortunately, the dealership held a large insurance policy on Sullivan's life, and the proceeds from this had been more than sufficient to bring mortgage payments up to date, pay down all overdue accounts, and leave some funds for future contingencies.

Outlook

The opportunities for expanding new car sales did not appear promising, given declining consumer confidence and recent layoffs at several local plants that were expected to hurt the local economy. However, recent promotional incentives had reduced the inventory to manageable levels. From discussions with Larry Winters, Auto World's sales manager, Sullivan-Diaz had concluded that costs could be cut by not replacing the departing sales representative, maintaining inventory at current reduced level, and trying to make more efficient use of advertising and promotion. Although Winters did not have Walter's exuberant personality, he had been Auto World's leading sales representative before being promoted and had shown strong managerial capabilities in his current position.

As she reviewed the figures for the service department, Sullivan-Diaz wondered what potential might exist for improving its sales volume and selling gross. Her father had never been very interested in the parts and service business, seeing it simply as a necessary adjunct of the dealership. "Customers always seem to be miserable back there," he had once remarked to her. "But here in the front end, everybody's happy when someone buys a new car." The service facility, hidden behind the showroom, was not easily visible from the main highway. Although the building was old and greasy, the equipment itself was modern and well maintained. There was sufficient capacity to handle more repair work but a higher volume would require hiring one or more new mechanics.

Customers were required to bring cars in for servicing before 8:30 a.m. After parking their cars, customers entered the service building by a side door and waited their turn to see the service writers who occupied a cramped room with peeling paint and an interior window overlooking the service bays. Customers stood while work orders for their cars were prepared. Ringing telephones frequently interrupted the process. Filing cabinets containing customer records and other documents lined the far wall of the room.

If the work were of a routine nature, such as an oil change or tune up, the customer was given an estimate immediately. For more complex jobs, they would be called with an estimate later in the morning once the car had been examined. Customers were required to pick up their cars by 6:00 p.m. on the day the work was completed. On several occasions, Carol had urged her father to computerize the service work order process, but he had never acted on her suggestions, so all orders continued to be handwritten on large yellow sheets, with carbon copies below.

The service manager, Rick Obert, who was in his late forties, had held the position since Auto World opened at its current location. The Sullivan family considered him technically skilled, and he managed the mechanics effectively. However, his manner with customers could be gruff and argumentative.

Customer Survey Results

Another set of data that Sullivan-Diaz had studied carefully were the results of the customer satisfaction surveys that were mailed to the dealership monthly by a research firm retained by the Ford Motor Company.

Purchasers of all new Ford cars were sent a questionnaire by mail within 30 days of making the purchase and asked to use a five-point scale to rate their satisfaction with the dealership sales department, vehicle preparation, and the characteristics of the vehicle itself.

The questionnaire asked how likely the purchaser would be to recommend the dealership, the salesperson, and the manufacturer to someone else. Other questions asked if the customers had been introduced to the dealer's service department and been given explanations on what to do if their cars needed service. Finally, there were some classification questions relating to customer demographics.

A second survey was sent to new car purchasers nine months after they had bought their cars. This questionnaire began by asking about satisfaction with the vehicle and then asked customers if they had taken their vehicles to the selling dealer for service of any kind. If so, respondents were then asked to rate the service department on 14 different attributes—ranging from the attitudes of service personnel to the quality of the work performed—and then to rate their overall satisfaction with service from the dealer.

Customers were also asked about where they would go in the future for maintenance service, minor mechanical and electrical repairs, major repairs in those same categories, and bodywork. The options listed for service were selling dealer, another Ford dealer, "some other place," or "do-it-yourself." Finally, there were questions about overall satisfaction with the dealer sales department and the dealership in general as well as the likelihood of their purchasing another Ford product and buying it from the same dealership.

Dealers received monthly reports summarizing customer ratings of their dealership for the most recent month and for several previous months. To provide a comparison with how other Ford dealerships performed, the reports also included regional and national rating averages. After analysis, completed questionnaires were returned to the dealership; since these included each customer's name, a dealer could see which customers were satisfied and which were not.

In the 30-day survey of new purchasers, Auto World achieved better than average ratings on most dimensions. One finding that puzzled Carol was that almost 90 percent of respondents answered "yes" when asked if someone from Auto World had explained what to do if they needed service, but less than a third said they had been introduced to someone in the service department. She resolved to ask Larry Winters about this discrepancy.

The nine-month survey findings disturbed her. Although vehicle ratings were in line with national averages, the overall level of satisfaction with service at Auto World was consistently low, placing it in the bottom 25 percent of all Ford dealerships. The worst ratings for service concerned promptness of writing up orders, convenience of scheduling the work, convenience of service hours, and appearance of the service department. On length of time to complete the work, availability of needed parts, and quality of work done ("was it fixed right?"), Auto World's rating was close to the average. For interpersonal variables such as attitude of service department personnel, politeness, understanding of customer problems, and explanation of work performed, its ratings were relatively poor.

When Sullivan-Diaz reviewed the individual questionnaires, she found a wide degree of variation between customers' responses on these interpersonal variables, ranging all the way across a five-point scale from "completely satisfied" to "very dissatisfied." Curious, she had gone to the service files and examined the records for several dozen customers who had recently completed the nine-month surveys. At least part of the ratings could be explained by which service writers the customer had dealt with. Those who had been served two or more times by her sisters, for instance, gave much better ratings than those who had dealt primarily with Jim Fiskell, the service writer who had recently quit.

Perhaps the most worrisome responses were those relating to customers' likely use of Auto World's service department in the future. More than half indicated they would use another Ford dealer or "some other place" for maintenance service (such as oil change, lubrication, or tune-up) or for minor mechanical and electrical repairs. About 30 percent would use another source for major repairs. The rating for overall satisfaction with the selling dealer after nine months was below average and the customer's likelihood of purchasing from the same dealership again was a full point below that of buying another Ford product.

Options

Sullivan-Diaz pushed aside the spreadsheets she had printed out and shut down her laptop. It was time to go home for dinner. She saw the options for the dealership as basically twofold: either prepare the business for an early sale at what would amount to a distress price, or take a year or two to try to turn it around financially. In the latter instance, if the turnaround succeeded, the business could subsequently be sold at a higher price than it presently commanded, or the family could install a general manager to run the dealership for them.

Bill Froelich, owner of another nearby dealership, had offered to buy Auto World for a price that represented a fair valuation of the net assets, according to Auto World's accountants, plus $250,000 in goodwill. However, the rule of thumb when the auto industry was enjoying good times was that goodwill should be valued at $1,200 per vehicle sold each year. Carol knew that Froelich was eager to develop a network of dealerships in order to achieve economies of scale. His prices on new cars were very competitive, and his nearest dealership clustered several franchises—Ford, Lincoln Mercury, Volvo, and Jaguar—on a single large property.

An Unwelcome Disturbance

As Carol left her office, she spotted the sales manager coming up the stairs leading from the showroom floor. "Larry," she said, "I've got a question for you."

"Fire away!" replied the sales manager.

"I've been looking at the customer satisfaction surveys. Why aren't our sales reps introducing new customers to the folks in the Service Department? It's supposedly part of our sales protocol, but it only seems to be happening about one-third of the time!"

Larry Winters shuffled his feet. "Well, Carol, basically I leave it to their discretion. We tell them about service, of course, but some of the guys on the floor feel a bit uncomfortable taking folks over to the service bays after they've been in here. It's quite a contrast, if you know what I mean."

Suddenly, the sound of shouting arose from the floor below. A man of about 40, wearing a windbreaker and jeans, was standing in the doorway yelling at one of the salespeople. The two managers could catch snatches of what he was saying, in between various obscenities:

"... three visits... still not fixed right... service stinks... who's in charge here?" Everybody else in the showroom had stopped what they were doing and had turned to look at the newcomer.

Winters looked at his young employer and rolled his eyes. "If there was something your dad couldn't stand, it was guys like that, yelling and screaming in the showroom and asking for the boss. Walt would go hide out in his office! Don't worry, Tom'll take care of that fellow and get him out of here. What a jerk!"

"No," said Sullivan-Diaz, "I'll deal with him! One thing I learned when I worked at St. Luke's was that you don't let people yell about their problems in front of everybody else. You take them off somewhere, calm them down, and find out what's bugging them."

She stepped quickly down the stairs, wondering to herself, "What else have I learned in health care that I can apply to this business?"

EXHIBIT 1: Marketing Cars is a Different Proposition to Marketing Services for the Same Vehicles

Study Questions

1. How does marketing cars differ from marketing services for those same vehicles?
2. Compare and contrast the sales department and the service department at Auto World.
3. From a consumer perspective, what useful parallels do you see between running a car sales and service dealership and managing health care services?
4. What advice would you give to Carol on future strategy for the business?

CASE 2 Four Customers in Search of Solutions

Christopher Lovelock

Four telephone subscribers from suburban Toronto call their telephone company to complain about a variety of problems. How should the company respond in each instance?

Among the many customers of Bell Canada in Toronto, Ontario, are four individuals living on Willow Street in a middle-class suburb of the city. Each of them has a telephone-related problem and decides to call the company about it.

Winston Chen

Winston Chen grumbles constantly about the amount of his home telephone bill (which is, in fact, in the top 2 percent of all household phone bills in Ontario). There are many calls to countries in Southeast Asia on weekday evenings, almost daily calls to Kingston (a smaller city not far from Toronto) around midday, and calls to Vancouver, British Columbia, most weekends. Mr. Chen uses the same company for his telephone and internet broadband needs. One day, Mr. Chen receives a telephone bill which is even larger than usual. On reviewing the bill, he is convinced that he has been overcharged, so he calls the phone company to complain and request an adjustment.

Marie Portillo

Marie Portillo has missed several important calls recently because the caller received a busy signal. She phones the customer service department to determine possible solutions to this problem. Ms. Portillo's telephone bill is at the median level for a household subscriber. (The median is the point at which 50 percent of all bills are higher and 50 percent are lower.) Most of the calls from her house are local, but there are occasional international calls to Mexico or to countries in South America. She does not subscribe to any value-added services.

Eleanor Vanderbilt

During the past several weeks, Mrs. Vanderbilt has been distressed to receive a series of obscene telephone calls. It sounds like the same person each time. She calls the telephone company to see if they can put a stop to this harassment. Her phone bill is in the bottom 10 percent of all household subscriber bills and almost all calls are local.

Richard Robbins

For more than a week, the phone line at Rich Robbins' house has been making strange humming and crackling noises, making it difficult to hear what the other person is saying. After two of his friends comment on these distracting noises, Mr. Robbins calls to report the problem. His guess is that it is caused by the answering machine, which is getting old and sometimes loses messages. Mr. Robbins' phone bill is in the 75th percentile for a household subscriber. Most calls are made to locations within Canada, usually at evenings and weekends, although there are a few calls to the United States, too. He studied for his undergraduate degree at NYU and he likes to keep in touch with some of his former classmates.

Study Questions

1. Based strictly on the information in the case, how many possibilities do you see to segment the telecommunications market?
2. As a customer service rep, how would you address each of the problems and complaints reported?
3. As a marketing manager, do you see any marketing opportunities for the telephone company in any of these complaints?

CASE 3 Dr. Beckett's Dental Office

LAUREN K. WRIGHT

A dentist seeks to differentiate her practice on the basis of quality. She constructs a new office and redesigns the practice to deliver high quality to her patients and to improve productivity though increased efficiency. However, it's not always easy to convince patients that her superior service justifies higher fees that are not always covered by insurance.

Management Comes to Dentistry

"I just hope the quality differences are visible to our patients," mused Dr. Barbro Beckett as she surveyed the office that housed her well-established dental practice. She had recently moved to her current location from an office she felt was too cramped to allow her staff to work efficiently—a factor that was becoming increasingly important as the costs of providing dental care continued to rise. While Dr. Beckett realized that productivity gains were necessary, she did not want to compromise the quality of service her patients received.

The classes Dr. Beckett took in dental school taught her a lot about the technical side of dentistry but nothing about the business side. She received no formal training in the mechanics of running a business or understanding customer needs. In fact, professional guidelines discouraged marketing or advertising of any kind. That had not been a major problem 22 years earlier, when Dr. Beckett started her practice, since profit margins had been good then. But the dental care industry had changed dramatically. Costs rose as a result of labor laws, malpractice insurance, and the constant need to invest in updating equipment and staff training as new technologies were introduced. Dr. Beckett's overhead was now between 70 and 80 percent of revenues before accounting for her wages or office rental costs.

At the same time provider overhead was rising, there was a movement in the United States to reduce health care costs to insurance companies, employers, and patients by offering "managed health care" through large health maintenance organizations (HMOs). The HMOs set the prices for various services by putting an upper limit on the amount that their doctors and dentists could charge for various procedures. The advantage to patients was that their health insurance covered virtually all costs. But the price limitations meant that HMO doctors and dentists would not be able to offer certain services that might provide better quality care but were too expensive. Dr. Beckett had decided not to become an HMO provider because the reimbursement rates were only 80–85 percent of what she normally charged for treatment. She felt that she could not provide high-quality care to patients at these rates.

These changes presented some significant challenges to Dr. Beckett, who wanted to offer the highest level of dental care rather than being a low-cost provider. With the help of a consultant, she decided her top priority was differentiating the practice on the basis of quality. She and her staff developed an internal mission statement that reflected this goal.

The mission statement (prominently displayed in the back office) read, in part: *It is our goal to provide superior dentistry in an efficient, profitable manner within the confines of a caring, quality environment.*

Since higher quality care was more costly, Dr. Beckett's patients often had to pay fees for costs not covered by their insurance policies. If the quality differences weren't substantial, these patients might decide to switch to an HMO dentist or another lower-cost provider.

Redesigning the Service Delivery System

The move to a new office gave Dr. Beckett a unique opportunity to rethink almost every aspect of her service. She wanted the work environment to reflect her own personality and values as well as providing a pleasant place for her staff to work.

Facilities and Equipment

Dr. Beckett first looked into the office spaces available in the Northern California town where she practiced. She didn't find anything she liked, so she hired an architect from San Francisco to design a contemporary office building with lots of light and space. This increased the building costs by $100,000, but Dr. Beckett felt it would be a critical factor in differentiating her service.

Dr. Beckett's new office was Scandinavian in design (reflecting her Swedish heritage and attention to detail). The waiting room and reception area were filled with modern furniture in muted shades of brown, grey, green, and purple. Live plants and flowers were abundant, and the walls were covered with art. Classical music played softly in the background. Patients could enjoy a cup of coffee or tea and browse through the large selection of current magazines and newspapers while they waited for their appointments.

The treatment areas were both functional and appealing. There was a small conference room with toys for children and a DVD player that was used to show patients educational films about different dental procedures. Literature was available to explain what patients needed to do to maximize the benefits of their treatment outcomes.

The chairs in the examining rooms were covered in leather and very comfortable. Each room had a large window that allowed patients to watch birds eating at the feeders that were filled each day. There were also attractive mobiles hanging from the ceiling to distract patients from the unfamiliar sounds and sensations they might be experiencing. Headphones were available with a wide selection of music.

The entire "back office" staff (including Dr. Beckett) wore uniforms in cheerful shades of pink, purple, and blue that matched the office décor. All the technical equipment looked very modern and was spotlessly clean. State-of-the-art computerized machinery was used for some procedures. Dr. Beckett's dental degrees were prominently displayed in her office, along with certificates from various programs that she and her staff had attended to update their technical skills (Exhibit 1).

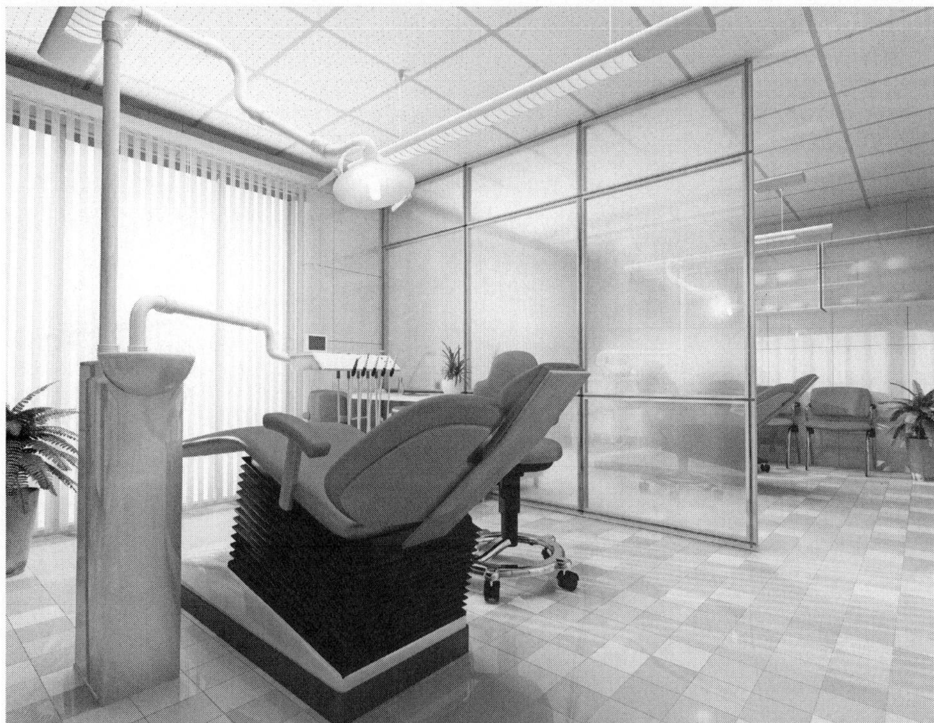

EXHIBIT 1: A Modern, State-of-the-Art Treatment Room Projects a Professional Image to Visiting Patients

Service Personnel

There were eight employees in the dental practice, including Dr. Beckett (who was the only dentist). The seven staff members were separated by job function into "front office" and "back office" workers. Front office duties (covered by two employees) included receptionist and secretarial tasks and financial/budgeting work. The back office was divided into hygienists and chair side assistants.

The three chair side assistants helped the hygienists and Dr. Beckett with treatment procedures. They had specialized training for their jobs but did not need a college degree. The two hygienists handled routine exams and teeth cleaning plus some treatment procedures. In many dental offices, hygienists had a tendency to act like "prima donnas" because of their education (a bachelor's degree plus specialized training) and experience. According to Dr. Beckett, such an attitude could destroy any possibility of teamwork among the office staff. She felt very fortunate that her hygienists viewed themselves as part of a larger team that worked together to provide quality care to patients.

Dr. Beckett valued her friendships with staff members and understood that they were a vital part of the service delivery. "90 percent of patients' perceptions of quality come from their interactions with the front desk and the other employees—not from the staff's technical skills," she stated. When Dr. Beckett began to redesign her practice, she discussed her goals with the staff and involved them in the decision-making process. The changes meant new expectations and routines for most employees, and some were not willing to adapt. There was some staff turnover (mostly voluntary) as the new office procedures were implemented. The current group worked very well as a team.

Dr. Beckett and her staff met briefly each morning to discuss the day's schedule and patients. They also had longer meetings every other week to discuss more strategic issues and resolve any problems that might have developed. During these meetings, employees made suggestions about how to improve patient care. Some of the most successful staff suggestions include: "thank you" cards to patients who referred other patients; follow-up calls to patients after major procedures; a "gift" bag to give to patients after they've had their teeth cleaned that contains a toothbrush, toothpaste, mouthwash and floss; buckwheat pillows and blankets for patient comfort during long procedures; coffee and tea in the waiting area; and a photo album in the waiting area with pictures of staff and their families (Exhibit 2).

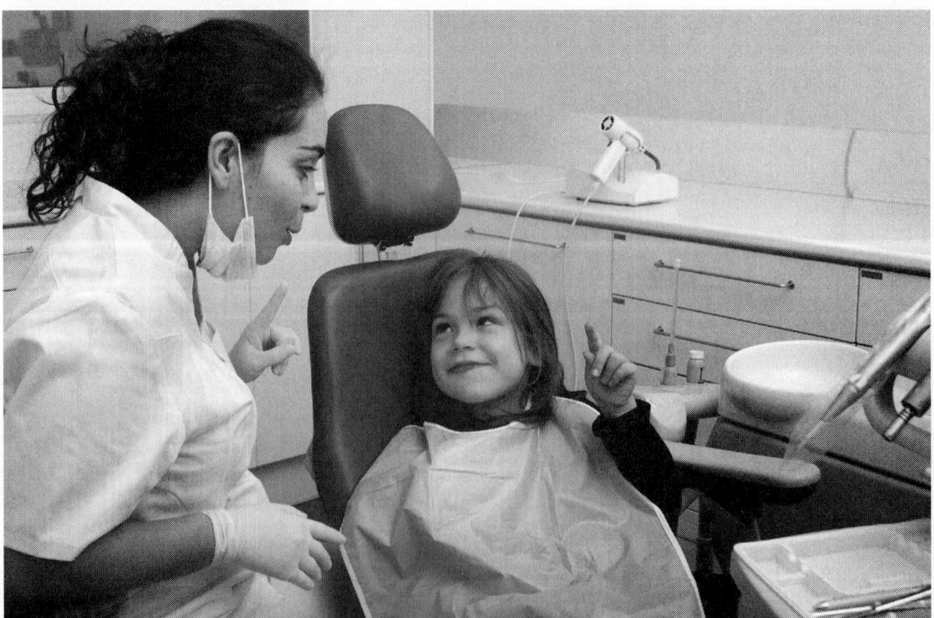

EXHIBIT 2: Service Delivery Is Enhanced through Customized Interaction with Patients Both Young and Old

The expectations for staff performance (in terms of both technical competence and patient interactions) were very high. But Dr. Beckett provided her employees with many opportunities to update their skills by attending classes and workshops. She also rewarded their hard work by giving monthly bonuses if business had been good. Since she shared the financial data with her staff, they could see the difference in revenues if the schedule was slow or patients were dissatisfied. This provided an extra incentive to improve service delivery. The entire office also went on trips together once a year (paid for by Dr. Beckett); spouses were welcome to participate but had to cover their own trip expenses. Past destinations for these excursions had included Hawaii and Washington, D.C.

Procedures and Patients

With the help of a consultant, all the office systems (including billing, ordering, lab work, and patient treatment) were redesigned. One of the main goals was to standardize some of the routine procedures so that error was reduced and all patients would receive the same level of care. Specific times were allotted for each procedure and the staff worked very hard to see that these times were met. Office policy specified that patients should be kept waiting no longer than 20 minutes without being given the option to reschedule, and employees often called patients in advance if they knew there would be a delay. They also attempted to fill in cancellations to make sure office capacity was maximized. Staff members substituted for each other when necessary or helped with tasks not specifically in their job descriptions in order to make things run more smoothly.

Dr. Beckett's practice included about 2,000 "active" patients (and many more who came infrequently). They were mostly white-collar workers with professional jobs (university employees, health care workers, and managers/owners of local establishments.) She did no advertising; all of her new business came from positive word of mouth by current patients. Dr. Beckett's practice was so busy that patients often had to wait 3–4 months for a routine cleaning and exam (if they didn't have their appointments automatically scheduled every 6 months), but they didn't seem to mind the delay.

The dentist believed that referrals were a real advantage because new patients didn't come in "cold." She did not have to sell herself because they had already been told about her service by friends or family. All new patients were required to have an initial exam so that Dr. Beckett could do a needs assessment and educate them about her service. She believed this was the first indication to patients that her practice was different from others they had experienced.

The Biggest Challenge

"Redesigning the business was the easy part," Dr. Beckett sighed. "Demonstrating the high level of quality to patients is the hard job." She said this task was especially difficult since most people disliked going to the dentist or felt that it was an inconvenience and came in with a negative attitude. Dr. Beckett tried to reinforce the idea that quality dental care depended on a positive long-term relationship between patients and the dental team. This philosophy was reflected in a section of the patient mission statement hanging in the waiting area: *We are a caring, professional dental team serving motivated, quality-oriented patients interested in keeping healthy smiles for a lifetime. Our goal is to offer a progressive and educational environment. Your concerns are our focus.*

Although Dr. Beckett enjoyed her work, she admitted it could be difficult to maintain a positive attitude. The job required precision and attention to detail, and the procedures were often painful for patients. She often felt as though she were "walking on eggshells" because she knew patients were anxious and uncomfortable, which made them more critical of her service delivery. It was not uncommon for patients to say negative things to Dr. Beckett even before treatment began (such as, "I really hate going to the dentist—it's not you, but I just don't want to be here!"). When this happened, she reminded herself that she was providing quality service whether patients appreciated it or not. "The person will usually have to have the dental work done anyway," she

EXHIBIT 3: A Team of Closely-Knit Professionals Working Under the Guidance of a Clear, Common Mission Statement Can Help Overcome the Most Negative Preconceived Notions About Visiting the Dentist

remarked, "so I just do the best job I can and make them as comfortable as possible." Even though patients seldom expressed appreciation for her services, she hoped that she made a positive difference in their health or appearance that would benefit them in the long run.

Study Questions

1. Which of the seven elements of the Services Marketing Mix are addressed in this case? Give examples of each "P" you identify.
2. Why do people dislike going to the dentist? Do you feel Dr. Beckett has addressed this problem effectively?
3. How do Dr. Beckett and her staff educate patients about the service they are receiving? What else could they do?
4. What supplementary services are offered? How do they enhance service delivery?
5. Contrast your own dental care experiences with those offered by Dr. Beckett's practice. What differences do you see? Based on your review of this case, what advice would you give (a) to your current or former dentist, and (b) to Dr. Beckett?

CASE 4 Banyan Tree Hotels & Resorts

Jochen Wirtz

Banyan Tree Hotels and Resorts had become a leading player in the luxury resort and spa market in Asia. As part of its growth strategy, Banyan Tree had launched new brands and brand extensions that included resorts, spas, residences, destination club memberships, retail outlets, and even museum shops. Now, the company was preparing to aggressively grow its global footprint in the Americas, Caribbean, Europe and the Middle East while preserving its distinctive Asian identity and strong brand image of Banyan Tree.

A brand synonymous with private villas, tropical garden spas, and retail galleries promoting traditional craft, Banyan Tree Hotels and Resorts received its first guest in 1994 in Phuket, Thailand. Since then, it had grown into a leading manager and developer of niche and premium resorts, hotels and spas in Asia Pacific. Despite having minimal advertising, Banyan Tree achieved global exposure and a high level of brand awareness through the company's public relations and global marketing programs. Much interest was also generated by the company's socially responsible business values and practices caring for the social and natural environments. With a firm foothold in the medium-sized luxury resorts market, the company introduced a new and contemporary brand Angsana in 2000 to gain a wider customer base. As the resorts market became increasingly crowded with similar competitive offerings, lured by the success of Banyan Tree, the company had to contemplate about expanding its business and preserving its distinct identity. Banyan Tree and Angsana resorts were expanding geographically outside of Asia and also into the urban hotel market in major cities throughout the world. With around 34 hotels and resorts scheduled to open over the next three years, Banyan Tree faced the challenge of translating and maintaining the success of a niche Asian hospitality brand into various market segments on a global scale.

Company Background

By early 2009, Banyan Tree Hotels and Resorts (BTHR) managed and/or had ownership interests in 25 resorts and hotels, 68 spas, 65 retail galleries, and two golf courses in 55 locations in 23 countries. Since its establishment in 1994, the company's flagship brand, Banyan Tree, had won some four hundred international tourism, hospitality, design, and marketing awards, some of which included the "Best Resort Hotel in Asia-Pacific" (Phuket) for four consecutive years from Business Traveller Awards since 2002, "Seychelles' Best Resort" and "Seychelles' Best Spa" from World Travel Awards (2003), "Best Hotels for Rooms" (Bangkok) from UK Conde Nast Traveller (2006), "Best Hotel (Luxury)" (Lijiang) from Hospitality Design Awards (2007), and "PATA Gold Award—Ecotourism Project Category" (Bintan) from Pacific Asia Travel Association Gold Awards (2008).[1]

BTHR was founded by Ho Kwon Ping, a travel enthusiast and former journalist, and his wife Claire Chang, a strong advocate of corporate social responsibility. Prior to entering the hotels and resorts business, Ho spent some 15 years managing the family business, which was into everything imaginable, such as commodities, food products, consumer electronics, and property development, competing mainly on cost, and was

---

Jochen Wirtz is Associate Professor of Marketing and Academic Director of the UCLA—NUS Executive MBA Program at the National University of Singapore.

The support and feedback of the management of Banyan Tree Hotels & Resorts in the writing of this case is gratefully acknowledged.

[1]The complete list of awards won by Banyan Tree can be found on the company's website at www.banyantree.com.

not dominant in any particular country or industry, while Chang was deeply involved in sociology and social issues. The closing of a factory in Thailand one year after its opening—because it lost out to other low-cost producers in Indonesia—was the last straw for Ho, who then realized that a low-cost strategy was not only difficult to follow but would also lead nowhere. Determined to craft out something proprietary that would allow the company to become a price maker rather than a price taker, Ho decided that building a strong brand was the only way for him to maintain a sustainable competitive advantage.

The idea of entering the luxury resorts market was inspired by the gap in the hotel industry that giant chains such as the Hilton and Shangri-La could not fill. There existed a market segment that wanted private and intimate accommodation without the expectation of glitzy chain hotels. This was fueled by the sharp price gap between the luxurious Aman Resorts and other resorts in the luxury resorts market. For example, the Amanpuri in Thailand, one of Aman's resorts, charged in 2004 a rack rate for its villas ranging from $650 to more than $7,000 a night, whereas the prices of other luxury resorts, such as the Shangri-La Hotel and Phuket Arcadia Beach Resort by Hilton in Thailand, were priced below $350. Noticing the big difference in prices between Aman Resorts and the other resorts in the luxury resorts market, Ho saw potential for offering an innovative niche product that could also bridge the price gap in this market. Seasoned travelers themselves, Ho and Chang backpacked throughout the world in their youth. Their extensive experiences are evident in their nonconforming beliefs that resorts should provide more than just accommodation. Ho and Chang hit upon the idea of building a resort comprising individual villas, local-inspired architectural design, and positioned as a romantic and intimate escapade for guests. Banyan Tree had moved up its positioning into the higher end of the luxury market, and by 2008 its rack rates were typically between $1,200 and $7,000 for the resort in Phuket, and between Euros 1,500 and Euro 4,200 for the resort in the Seychelles.

Operations at Banyan Tree began with only one resort in Phuket, situated on a former mining site once deemed too severely ravaged to sustain any form of development by a United Nations Development Program planning unit and the Tourism Authority of Thailand. It was a bold decision, but the company, together with Ho, Chang, and Ho's brother Ho Kwon Cjan, restored it after extensive rehabilitation works costing a total of $250 million. So successful was Banyan Tree Phuket when it was finally launched that the company worked quickly to build two other resorts, one at Bintan Island in Indonesia and the other at Vabbinfaru Island in the Maldives. The company never looked back. Even though Asia's travel industry experienced periodic meltdowns such as the Asian Economic Crisis in 1997–1998, the September 11 attacks on the World Trade Center in 2001, the dot.com crisis in 2001–2002, severe acute respiratory syndrome (SARS) in 2003, and the Tsunami on December 26, 2004, no employee was retrenched and room rates at Banyan Tree rose steadily.

Brand Origins

Known as Yung Shue Wan in the local dialect, Banyan Tree Bay was a fishing village on Lamma Island in Hong Kong, where Ho and his wife Chang lived for three idyllic years before he joined the family business. Despite the village's modest and rustic setting, they remember it to be a sanctuary of romance and intimacy. The large canopies of the Banyan Tree also showed semblance of the shelter afforded by Asia's tropical rainforests. Ho and Chang thus decided to name their resort Banyan Tree and position it as a sanctuary for the senses.

The Service Offering

Unlike most other resorts then, Banyan Tree resorts comprised individual villas that came with a private pool or spa treatment room, each designed to offer guests exclusivity and utmost privacy. For example, a guest could skinny-dip in the private pool within his villa without being seen by other guests, putting him in a world of his own (see Exhibit 1).

EXHIBIT 1: World of Privacy in a Double Pool Villa at Banyan Tree Phuket

All Banyan Tree hotels and resorts were designed around the concept of providing "a sense of place" to reflect and enhance the culture and heritage of the destination. This is reflected in the architecture, furnishings, landscape, vegetation, and service offers. To create a sense of exotic sensuality and ensure the privacy of its guests, the resorts are designed to blend into the natural landscape of the surrounding environment and use the natural foliage and boulders as the privacy screen (see Exhibit 2 showing Banyan Tree Seychelles). The furnishings of Banyan Tree villas were deliberately native to convey the exoticism of the destination with its rich local flavor and luxurious feel. The spa pavilions in Seychelles were constructed around the large granite boulders and lush foliage to offer an outdoor spa experience in complete privacy. The resorts' local flavor was also reflected in the services offered, some of which were unique to certain resorts. Employees were allowed to vary the service delivery process according to local culture and practices, as long as these were consistent with the brand promise of romance and intimacy. Thus, in Phuket, for instance, a couple could enjoy dinner on a traditional Thai long tail boat accompanied by private Thai musicians while cruising instead of dining in a restaurant. Banyan Tree Phuket also offered wedding packages in which couples were blessed by Buddhist monks. In the Maldives, wedding ceremonies could be conducted underwater among the corals. Guests could also choose to dine in a castaway sandbank with only their private chefs and the stars for company and watch the sunset toasting champagne on a Turkish gullet returning from a trip watching a school of spinner dolphins.

EXHIBIT 2: Banyan Tree Seychelles Blends Well into Its Natural Environment

Products and services were conceived with the desired customer experience in mind. One such product was the "Intimate Moments" package, specially created for couples. This was presented as a surprise when guests returned to find their villas

EXHIBIT 3: Banyan Tree Spa Pavilion with a View

decorated with lit candles, incense oil lamps burning, flower petals spread throughout the room, satin sheets on the decorated bed, a chilled bottle of champagne or wine, and tidbits placed next to the outdoor bath which is decorated with flowers, candles, and bath oils. The couple was presented with a variety of aromatic massage oils to further inspire those intimate moments.

Another draw of the resorts was the Banyan Tree Spa, found at every Banyan Tree property. The pioneer of the tropical garden spas concept, Banyan Tree Spas offered a variety of aromatic oil massages, and face and body beauty treatments using traditional Asian therapies, with a choice of indoors or outdoors treatment. The spa products used were natural, indigenous products, made from local herbs and spices. Nonclinical in concept, Banyan Tree Spas relied mainly on the "human touch" instead of energy-consuming, high-tech equipment. The spa experience was promoted as a sensorial, intimate experience that would rejuvenate the "body, mind, and soul," and was mainly targeted at couples who would enjoy their treatments together.

In line with Banyan Tree's ethos of conserving local culture and heritage and promoting cottage crafts, Chiang founded the Banyan Tree Gallery, a retail outlet showcasing indigenous crafts. Banyan Tree Gallery outlets were set up in each resort. Items sold were made by local artisans and included traditionally woven handmade fabrics, garments, jewelery, handicrafts, tribal art, and spa accessories such as incense candles and massage oils that guests could use at home to recreate the Banyan Tree experience.

Embarking on projects to support the various communities in the locations Banyan Tree resorts are situated, Banyan Tree Gallery worked closely with village cooperatives and nonprofit craft marketing agents to provide gainful employment to the artisans. While acting as a marketing channel for Asian crafts like basket weaving, hill tribe cross-stitching and lacquerware, Banyan Tree Gallery also educated its customers about the crafts with an accompanying write-up. In the course of Banyan Tree Gallery's operations, the community outreach extended from across Thailand to Laos, Cambodia, India, Nepal, Sri Lanka, Indonesia, Malaysia, and Singapore.

The result of Banyan Tree's efforts was "a very exclusive, private holiday feeling," as described by one guest. Another guest commented, "It's a treat for all the special occasions like honeymoons and wedding anniversaries. It's the architecture, the sense of place, and the promise of romance."

EXHIBIT 4: A Contemporary Asian Shopping Experience with a Strong Sense of Corporate Responsibility at Banyan Tree Gallery

Marketing Banyan Tree

In the first two years after Banyan Tree was launched, the company's marketing communications was managed by an international advertising agency. The agency also designed the Banyan Tree logo (shown in Exhibit 5), and together with the management came up with the marketing tagline: "Sanctuary for the Senses."

Though furnished luxuriously, Banyan Tree resorts were promoted as providing romantic and intimate "smallish" hotel experiences, rather than luxurious accommodation as touted by most competitors then. "Banyan Tree Experiences" was marketed as intimate private moments. The resorts saw themselves as setting the stage for guests to create those unforgettable memories.

When Banyan Tree was first launched, extensive advertising was carried out for a short period of time to gain recognition in the industry. Subsequently, the company scaled down on advertising and kept it minimal, mainly in high-end travel magazines in key markets. The advertisements were visual in nature with succinct copy or showcased the awards and accolades won. Exhibit 6 shows a Banyan Tree advertisement highlighting the award-winning Banyan Tree Spa.

EXHIBIT 5: Banyan Tree Logo

Brand awareness for Banyan Tree was generated largely through public relations and global marketing programs. For example, relationships with travel editors and writers were cultivated to encourage visits to the resorts. This helped increase editorial coverage on Banyan Tree, which management felt was more effective in conveying the "Banyan Tree Experience" from an impartial third-party perspective. Its website, www.banyantree.com, increasingly drove online bookings and provided vivid information about the latest offerings of Banyan Tree's fast growing portfolio.

The management of marketing activities was centralized at the Singapore headquarters for consistency in brand building. BTHR appointed a few key wholesalers in each targeted market and worked closely with them to promote sales. Rather than selling through wholesale and retail agents that catered to the general market, BTHR chose to work only with agents specializing in exclusive luxury holidays targeted at wealthy customers. Global exposure was also achieved through Banyan Tree's membership in the Small Luxury Hotels and Leading Hotels of the World. Targeting high-end consumers, they represent various independent exclusive hotels and have sales offices in major cities around the world.

The end of 2007 marked a new stage of Banyan Tree's global expansion, with the launch of its own GDS code "BY." GDS is a global distribution system used by travel providers to process airline, hotel, and car rental reservations across 640,000 terminals of travel agents and other distribution partners around the world. Prior to BY, Banyan Tree was represented by its marketing partners, Leading Hotels of the World (LW) and Small Luxury Hotels (LX). Now, Banyan Tree had its unique identity on the GDS, further strengthening its brand presence and customer ownership. Banyan Tree now has enough critical mass to ensure the economic feasibility of a GDS private label. The acquisition of its own GDS code meant that Banyan Tree was transitioning from a relatively small regional player to a global brand in the eyes of the travel industry.

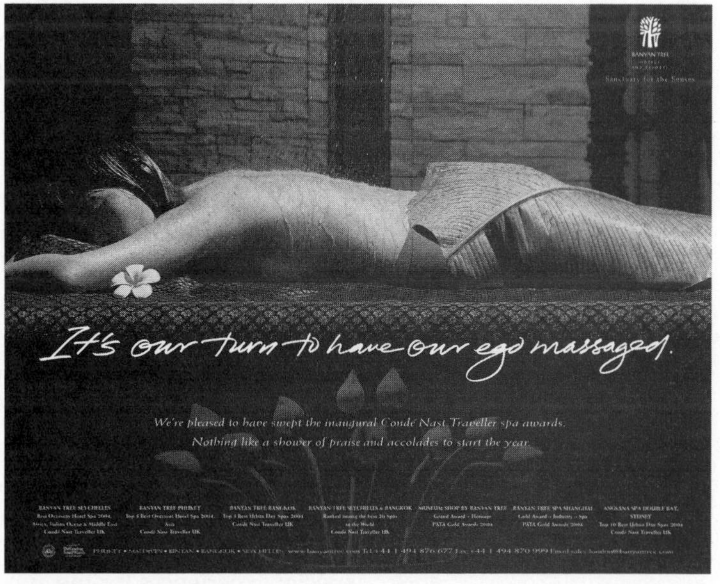

EXHIBIT 6: Advertisement Showcasing "Spa of the Year" Award from Conde Nast Traveller

Brand Values

Banyan Tree embraced certain values, such as actively caring for the natural and human environment and revitalizing local communities, which in turn created pride and respect among staff. The company hoped to build the brand on values that employees and customers could identify with and support as part of their own life values. A dedicated corporate social responsibility committee, headed by Chang and featuring general managers and valued associates from each resort, was formed to focus on these issues simultaneously with both a regional overview and local perspectives. Thus, the company worked actively to preserve, protect, and promote the natural and human environments in which Banyan Tree resorts were located.

Preserving the Environment

Resorts were built using local materials as much as possible and at the same time minimizing the impact on the environment. At Banyan Tree Bintan, for example, the 70 villas located in a rainforest were constructed around existing trees, cutting down as few trees as possible, to minimize the impact the resort had on the natural environment. The villas were built on stilts and platforms to avoid cutting trees and possible soil erosion. At Banyan Tree Maldives Vabbinfaru and Banyan Tree Seychelles, fresh water supply was obtained by the more expensive method of desalination, instead of extracting water from the underground water table, which risked long-term disruption of the ecological system. Toiletries such as shampoo, hair conditioner, bath foam, and body lotion provided by the resorts were nontoxic and biodegradable and filled in reusable containers made from celadon or ceramic. Refuse was recycled where possible and treated through an in-house incinerator system. Wastewater was also treated and recycled in the irrigation of resort landscapes.

Through the retail arm Banyan Tree Gallery, the human environment efforts were evident in the active sourcing of traditional crafts from indigenous tribes to provide gainful employment. These employment opportunities provided a source of income for the tribes and, at the same time, preserved their unique heritage.

In line with the Banyan Tree Group's Green Imperative initiative, Banyan Tree Gallery constantly used ecofriendly and recycled materials in the development of its merchandise. Examples included photo frames made using discarded telephone directories, elephant dung paper stationary, and lead-free celadon and ceramic spa amenities. Unique collections like the black resin turtles stationary range and leaf-inspired merchandise were created to promote environmental awareness and were accompanied by a write-up to educate the consumer on the targeted conservation campaign. In support of animal rights, the galleries did not carry products made from shell or ivory.

Besides trying to conduct business in an environmentally responsible manner, BTHR actively pursued a number of key initiatives, including its Greening Communities program. Greening Communities was launched as a challenge to seven participating resorts. It planted 28,321 trees in the first two years of the program. Banyan Tree Lijiang, for example, planted some 20,000 fruit trees to create additional income for families of the supporting community. While trees will absorb carbon and improve the quality of the environment, the main goal of this program was to engage local communities, associates, and guests to share the causes of climate change and actions that can reduce our collective carbon footprint.

Creating Brand Ownership Among Employees

All employees were trained in the basic standards of five-star service establishments, which included greeting guests, remembering their first names, and anticipating their needs. In addition, some employees got a taste of the "Banyan Tree Experience" as part of their training. The management believed that the stay would help employees better understand what guests will experience, and, in return, enhance their delivery of special experiences for the guests.

Although management imposed strict rules in the administration of the resorts, employees were empowered to exercise creativity and sensitivity. For example, the housekeeping teams were not restricted by a standard bed decoration. Rather, they were given room for creativity although they had general guidelines for turning the bed to keep in line with the standards of a premium resort. Banyan Tree invested liberally in staff welfare: employees were taken to and from work in air-conditioned buses and had access to various amenities, including high-quality canteens, medical services, and child care facilities. Staff dormitories had televisions, telephones, refrigerators, and attached bathrooms. The company's generous staff welfare policies apparently paid off. Ho said, "The most gratifying response is the sense of ownership that our staff began to have. It's not a sense of financial ownership, but they actually care about the property. In our business, service and service standards do not always mean the same thing as in a developed country, where standards are measured by efficiency and productivity, by people who are already quite well-versed in a service culture. We operate in places that, sometimes, have not seen hotels. People come from villages. What we need—more than exact standards—is for them to have a sense of hospitality, a sense that the guest is an honored person who, by virtue of being there, is able to give a decent livelihood to the people who work. This creates a culture in which everybody is friendly and helpful.

Involving Guests in Environmental Conservation

Part of the company's corporate social responsibility initiatives were designed to encourage environmental conservation and help ecological restoration. To create greater environmental awareness, Banyan Tree organized activities that involved interested guests in their research and environmental preservation work. In the Maldives, for instance, guests were invited to take part in the coral transplantation program (see Exhibit 7 for a picture of guest involvement in the long-running coral planting program). Guests who participated in the program were then encouraged to return several years later to see the progress of their efforts. Guests were also offered free marine biology sessions allowing them to learn more about the fascinating marine life and its conservation. Guests also had an opportunity to take part in the Green Sea Turtle Headstarting Projects. The response from guests was tremendously positive.

In 2002, Banyan Tree established the Green Imperative Fund (GIF) to further support community-based and environmental initiatives in the regions where it has a presence. Guests were billed $2 per room night at Banyan Tree properties and $1 at Angsana properties (of which they could opt out if they wished) and the company matched dollar for dollar. Details of the program were communicated to guests through various methods, including sand-filled turtles and in-villa turndown gifts.

Guests generally were happy to know that their patronage contributed to meaningful causes, like the construction of new schools for the local community, the restoration of coral reefs, and the longevity of local village crafts.

EXHIBIT 7: Guests Participate in Planting Corals at Banyan Tree Maldives and Angsana Ihuru

Involving the Local Community

In addition to engaging local craftsmen to produce indigenous art and handicrafts for sale at its galleries, Banyan Tree also involved the local community in all aspects of its business, even as the resorts were being built. Villas were constructed with as much indigenous material as possible, most of which was supplied by local traders. Traditional arts and handicrafts that complemented the villas' aesthetics were also purchased from local artisans.

The company believed in building profitable resorts that would benefit the surrounding environment and contribute to local economies through the creation of employment and community development projects. Thus, besides providing employment for the local community, the company brought business to the local farmers and traders by making it a point to purchase fresh produce from them. Whenever possible, the company supported other regional tourism ventures that would benefit the wider local community and enhance the visitor's experience. The Banyan Tree Maldives Marine Laboratory is a prime example: it is the first fully equipped private research facility to be fully funded and operated by a resort. The lab seeks to lead conservation efforts in the Maldives to protect and regenerate coral and marine life for the future of the tourism industry as well as to promote awareness and education of this field to the local community.

Recognizing that the disparity in lifestyles and living standards between guests and the local community might create a sense of alienation within the local community, a community relations department was set up to develop and manage community outreach programs. After consultations with community stakeholders, a number of funding scholarships for needy children were given, a school and child care center were built, lunches and parties for the elderly were hosted, and local cultural and religious activities were supported.

One of BTHR's formalized programs was Seedlings, which aimed to help young adults from local communities and motivate them and provide the means for completing their education to successfully enter the labor force as adults. This program benefitted the community at large as it provided the next generation with educational opportunities and to break the poverty cycle.[2]

Growing Banyan Tree

In 2002, BTHR took over the management of a city hotel in the heart of Bangkok from Westin Hotel Company. The hotel was rebranded as Banyan Tree Bangkok, after extensive renovation works were completed to upgrade the hotel's facilities and build new additional spa amenities and a Banyan Tree Gallery. This was the first Banyan Tree hotel to be located in the city, unlike the other beachfront Banyan Tree properties. Banyan Tree planned to open city hotels in Seoul, Beijing, Shanghai, and Hangzhou, and Angsana expanded into Dubai and London.

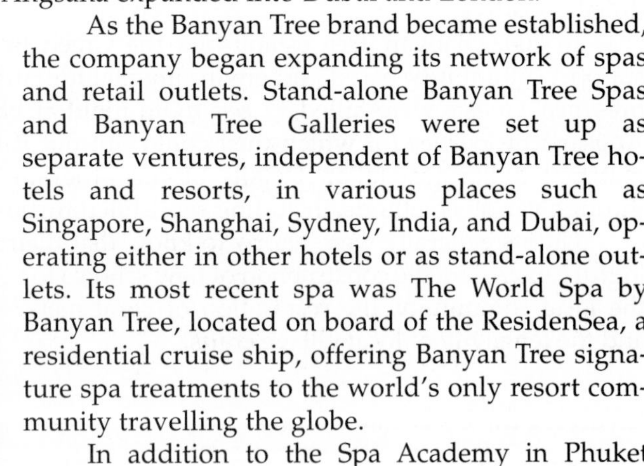

As the Banyan Tree brand became established, the company began expanding its network of spas and retail outlets. Stand-alone Banyan Tree Spas and Banyan Tree Galleries were set up as separate ventures, independent of Banyan Tree hotels and resorts, in various places such as Singapore, Shanghai, Sydney, India, and Dubai, operating either in other hotels or as stand-alone outlets. Its most recent spa was The World Spa by Banyan Tree, located on board of the ResidenSea, a residential cruise ship, offering Banyan Tree signature spa treatments to the world's only resort community travelling the globe.

EXHIBIT 8: Extending the Banyan Tree Maldives Experience Onboard the Banyan Velaa

In addition to the Spa Academy in Phuket opened in 2001, and to support its fast-growing spa business, in 2007 Banyan Tree opened two new spa academies in Lijiang, China and Bangkok, Thailand.

After establishing a foothold in the luxury resorts market, BTHR introduced the Angsana brand in response to demand from hotel operators in Asia that were keen to introduce spa services in their hotels. As the positioning of these hotels did not fit that of Banyan Tree, the company decided to launch a

[2]Detailed information on BTHR's CSR activities can be found at http://www.banyantree.com/csr.

new brand, Angsana, a more contemporary and affordable brand than Banyan Tree, to run as stand-alone spa businesses in other hotels.

The first Angsana Spa was opened in 1999 at Dusit Laguna, one of several hotels at Laguna Phuket, an integrated resort development with shared facilities located at Bang Tao Bay in Thailand. The Angsana Spa was so well received that the company quickly set up five other such spas in various hotels in Thailand. In 2000, BTHR opened its first Angsana Resort & Spa, complete with an Angsana Gallery, located less than one kilometer away from Banyan Tree Bintan in Indonesia.

In 2003, Banyan Tree launched The Museum Shop by Banyan Tree—a joint partnership with Singapore's National Heritage Board to showcase Asia's rich and diverse cultural heritage through unique museum-inspired merchandise. Designed to inspire and educate shoppers, The Museum Shop by Banyan Tree makes history more accessible and approachable to the layperson. By 2008, Banyan Tree had in total 65 retail outlets, ranging from Banyan Tree Galleries, Banyan Tree Spa Galleries, The Museum Shop by Banyan Tree, Elements Jewelry by Banyan Tree, and Angsana Galleries to Angsana Spa Galleries.

Banyan Tree Galleries are the retail outlets supporting the hotels, while Banyan Tree Spa Galleries support the spa outlets, selling more spa-focused merchandise such as signature aromatherapy amenities, essential oils, candles, and body care products. The Museum Shop by Banyan Tree is located in various museums in Singapore and the merchandise sold will be inspired by the artifacts exhibited in the respective museums. The Elements Jewelery by Banyan Tree sells specialized merchandise such as jewelry and fashion items.

The Road Ahead

To diversify its geographic spread, Ho had started to venture into locations in South America (the first resort in Mexico opened in 2009), Southern Europe, and the Middle East where he hoped to replicate Banyan Tree's rapid success. However, given the higher costs of doing business in the Americas and Europe, would the same strategy that had brought fame and success to Banyan Tree in Asia be workable in the rest of the world? Ho's ultimate vision was "to string a necklace of Banyan Tree Resorts around the world; not quantity, but a number of jewels that form a chain around the world." In 2008 alone, Banyan Tree had signed management contracts that would expand its operations to at least an additional 50 Banyan Tree and Angsana properties by 2011. Of the properties under development, the majority were resorts and/or integrated resorts, and approximately 10 were city hotels.

While expanding the company's network of hotels and resorts, spas, and retail outlets, Ho had to be mindful of the brands' focus and be careful not to dilute the brands. He also had to consider the strategic fit of the company's portfolio of brands, which comprised Banyan Tree and Angsana.

Banyan Tree certainly stood out among its competitors in the resorts industry when it was first launched. Since then, its success had attracted various competitors

EXHIBIT 9: Angsana Maldives Ihuru

who offer similar products and services. Thus, it was imperative that Banyan Tree retained its competitive advantage to prevent losing its distinctive position in the market.

Study Questions

1. What are the main factors that contributed to Banyan Tree's success?
2. Evaluate Banyan Tree's brand positioning and communications strategies. Can Banyan Tree maintain its unique positioning in an increasingly overcrowded resorts market?
3. Discuss whether the brand portfolio of Banyan Tree and Angsana, as well as the product portfolio of beach resorts and city hotels, spas, galleries, and museum shops fit as a family. What are your recommendations to Banyan Tree for managing these brands and products in future?
4. What effect does the practice of corporate social responsibility have on brand equity?
5. What potential problems do you foresee bringing Banyan Tree to the Americas, Europe, and the Middle East? How could Banyan Tree address those issues?

CASE 5 Giordano: Positioning for International Expansion

JOCHEN WIRTZ

As it looks to the future, a successful Asian retailer of casual apparel must decide whether to maintain its existing positioning strategy. Management wonders what factors will be critical to success and whether the firm's competitive strengths in merchandise selection and service are readily transferable to new international markets.

To make people "feel good" and "look great."

GIORDANO'S CORPORATE MISSION

In mid-2009, Giordano, a Hong Kong-based retailer of casual clothes targeted at men, women, and children through its five company brands—Giordano, Giordano Concepts, Giordano Ladies, Giordano Junior, and Blue Star Exchange—was operating more than 1,800 retail stores and counters in some 30 markets worldwide. Its main markets were mainland China, Hong Kong, Japan, Korea, Singapore, and Taiwan. Other countries in which it had a presence were Australia, Indonesia, Malaysia, the Middle East, and North America. In September 2008, there were 1,757 Giordano and Giordano Junior stores, 46 Giordano Ladies stores, 29 Giordano Concept stores, and 111 Blue Star Exchange stores. Sales had grown to HK$4,950 million (U.S.$561 million) by 2007 (see Exhibit 1). Giordano stores were located in retail shopping districts with good foot traffic. Views of a typical storefront and store interior are shown in Exhibit 2. In most geographic markets serviced by Giordano, the retail clothing business was deemed extremely competitive.

The board and top management team were eager to maintain Giordano's success in existing markets and to enter new markets, especially in mainland China. Several issues were under discussion. First, in what ways, if at all, should Giordano change its current positioning in the marketplace? Second, would the factors that had contributed to Giordano's success in the past remain equally critical over the coming years, or were new key success factors emerging? Finally, as Giordano sought to enter new markets around the world, were its competitive strengths readily transferable to other markets?

Company Background

Giordano was founded in Hong Kong by Jimmy Lai in 1980. In 1981, it opened its first retail store in Hong Kong and began to expand its market by distributing Giordano merchandise in Taiwan through a joint venture. In 1985, it opened its first retail outlet in Singapore.

Responding to slow sales, in 1987 Giordano changed its positioning strategy. Until 1987, it had sold exclusively men's casual apparel. When Lai and his colleagues realized that an increasing number of female customers were attracted to their stores, he repositioned the chain as a retailer of value-for-money merchandise, selling discounted casual unisex apparel, with the goal of maximizing unit sales instead of margins. This shift in strategy was successful, leading to a substantial increase in turnover. In 1994, Peter Lau Kwok Kuen succeeded Lai and became chairman of the company.

Management Values and Human Resource Policies

A willingness to try new and unconventional ways of doing business and to learn from past errors was part of Lai's management philosophy and soon became an integral part of Giordano's culture. Lai saw the occasional failure as a current limitation that

EXHIBIT 1: Giordano Financial Highlights

	2008 (6 Months ended 30 June)	2007	2006	2005	2004	2003	2002	2001	2000	1999	1998
Turnover (million HK$)	2,342	4,950	4,372	4,413	4,003	3,389	3,588	3,479	3,431	3,092	2,609
Turnover increase (percent)	11.6	13.2	(0.01)	0.10	18.1	(5.5)	3.1	1.4	11.0	18.5	(13.4)
Profit after tax and minority interests (million HK$)	206	304	218	431	393	266	328	377	416	360	76
Profit after tax and minority interests increase over previous year (percent)	32.9	39.4	(49.4)	9.6	47.7	(18.9)	(13.0)	(9.4)	15.3	373.7	11.8
Shareholders' fund (million HK$)	1,928	1,927	1,987	2,122	1,954	1,799	1,794	1,695	1,558	1,449	1,135
Working capital (million HK$)	716	736	862	1,029	1,004	961	861	798	1,014	960	725
Total debt to equity ratio	0.45	0.47	0.45	0.36	0.35	0.4	0.3	0.4	0.3	0.3	0.3
Inventory turnover on sales (days)	28	33	35	31	30	24	26	30	32	28	44
Return on total assets (percent)	7	10.3	7.3	15.2	14.9	10.7	13.7	16.8	20.7	21.5	5.3
Return on average equity (percent)	10.8	15.1	10.0	19.9	20.9	14.8	18.8	23.2	27.7	27.9	6.9
Return on sales (percent)	8	6	4.7	9.2	9.8	7.8	9.1	10.8	12.1	11.6	2.9
Earning per share (cents)	13.9	19.8	13.8	27.5	27.20	18.50	22.80	26.30	29.30	25.65	5.40
Cash dividend per share (cents)	6.5	21.5	26.5	26.5	23.00	21.00	19.00	14.00	15.25	17.25	2.25

Source: Annual Reports 1998 through 2008, Giordano International

EXHIBIT 2: Typical Giordano Storefront

indirectly pointed management to the right decision in the future. To demonstrate his commitment to this philosophy, Lai took the lead by being a role model for his employees, adding,

> *... Like in a meeting, I say, look, I have made this mistake. I'm sorry for that. I hope everybody learns from this. If I can make mistakes, who... do you think you are that you can't make mistakes?*

He also believed strongly that empowerment would minimize mistakes—that if everyone was allowed to contribute and participate, mistakes could be minimized.

Another factor that contributed to the firm's success was its dedicated, ever-smiling sales staff of over 11,000. Giordano considered frontline workers its customer-service heroes. Charles Fung, executive director and general manager (Taiwan), remarked:

> *Even the most sophisticated training program won't guarantee the best customer service. People are the key. They make exceptional service possible. Training is merely a skeleton of a customer service program. It's the people who deliver that give it form and meaning.*

Giordano had stringent selection procedures to make sure the candidates selected matched the desired employee profile. Selection continued into its training workshops, which tested the service orientation and character of a new employee.

Giordano's philosophy of quality service could be observed not only in Hong Kong but also in its overseas outlets. The company had been honored by numerous service awards over the years (see Exhibit 3). Fung described its obsession with providing excellent customer service in the following terms:

> *The only way to keep abreast with stiff competition in the retail market is to know the customers' needs and serve them well. Customers pay our pay checks; they are our bosses... Giordano considers service to be a very important element [in trying to draw customers]... service is in the blood of every member of our staff.*

EXHIBIT 3: Selected Awards Giordano Received

Award	Awarding organization	Category	Year(s)
Mystery Shoppers Award	Singapore Retailers Association (SRA)	—	2006
Top Service Award	Next Magazine Taiwan	Chain Stores of Fashion & Accessories	2006
Service and Courtesy – Supervisory Level	Hong Kong Retail Management	Fashion & Accessories	2006
Best Service Performance Brand; Best Service Performance	Department of Economic Development of Dubai	Large Business; Service Performance	2006
The Wall Street Journal Asia 200 Survey	The Wall Street Journal Asia	Most admired publicly traded companies in Asia	2007
Dubai Service Excellence Performance Award	Dubai Department of Economic Development	Customer Service	2007
4th Premier Asian Licensing Award	Hong Kong Trade Development Council and the International Licensing Industry Merchandiser's Association	Best Licensee	2007
Top Service Award 2008	Next Magazine	Chain Store of Fashion & Accessories	2008
Hong Kong Brands Awards 2008	American Chamber of Commerce Hong Kong	Fashion and Apparel	2008
2008 Service and Courtesy Award	Hong Kong Retail Management Association (HKRMA)	Junior Frontline Level and the Supervisor Level	2008
Caring Company 2008/2009	Hong Kong Council of Society Service (HKCSS)	Corporate Social Responsibility	2009

Giordano believed and invested heavily in employee training and has been recognized for its commitment to training and developing its staff by such awards as the Hong Kong Management Association Certificate of Merit for Excellence in Training and the People Developer Award from Singapore, among others. Fung explained:

> *Training is important. However, what is more important is the transfer of learning to the store. When there is a transfer of learning, each dollar invested in training yields a high return. We try to encourage this [transfer of learning] by cultivating a culture and by providing positive reinforcement, rewarding those who practice what they learned.*

Giordano offered what Fung claimed was "an attractive package in an industry where employee turnover is high." Giordano motivated its people through a base salary that probably was below market average, but added attractive performance-related bonuses. These initiatives and Giordano's emphasis on training had resulted in a lower staff turnover rate.

Giordano was only too aware that managing its human resources (HR) became a major challenge when it decided to expand into global markets. To replicate its high-service-quality positioning, Giordano knew it needed to consider the HR issues involved in setting up retail outlets in unfamiliar territory. For example, the recruitment, selection, and training of local employees required modifications to its formula for success in its current markets owing to differences in the culture, education, and technology of the new countries. Labor regulations also affected HR policies such as compensation and welfare benefits.

Focusing Giordano's Organizational Structure on Simplicity and Speed

Giordano maintained a flat organizational structure. The company's decentralized management style empowered line managers, and at the same time encouraged fast and close communication and coordination. For example, top management and staff had desks located next to each other, separated only by shoulder panels. This closeness allowed easy communication, efficient project management, and speedy decision making, which were all seen as critical ingredients to success amid fast-changing consumer tastes and fashion trends. This kept Giordano's product development cycle short. The firm made similar demands on its suppliers.

In addition, the company kept its operations lean to focus on what it considered its competitive advantage: service. One of their main strategic objectives was to disengage from manufacturing to focus on retailing. This was implemented by reducing its interest in their joint ventures with key manufacturers. This allowed the group to channel its resources from the Garment Trading & Manufacturing Division to the more profitable Retail & Distribution Division.[1]

Service

Giordano's commitment to service began with its major Customer Service Campaign in 1989. In that campaign, yellow badges bearing the words "Giordano Means Service" was worn by every Giordano employee, and its service philosophy had three tenets: "We welcome unlimited try-ons; we exchange—no questions asked; and we serve with a smile." As a result, the firm started receiving its numerous service-related awards over the years. It had also been ranked number one for eight consecutive years by the *Far Eastern Economic Review* for being innovative in responding to customers' needs. Furthermore, proving its expansion success in the Middle East, in 2006, Giordano received double awards for exceptional service and customer centricity from the Government of Dubai.

Management had launched several creative, customer-focused campaigns and promotions to extend its service orientation. For instance, in Singapore, Giordano asked its customers what they thought would be the fairest price to charge for a pair of jeans and charged each customer the price they were willing to pay. This one-month campaign was immensely successful, with some 3,000 pairs of jeans sold everyday during the promotion. In another service-related campaign, over 10,000 free T-shirts were given to customers for giving feedback and criticizing Giordano's services.

To ensure customer service excellence, performance evaluations were conducted frequently at the store level as well as for individual employees. Internal competitions were designed to motivate employees and store teams to do their best in serving customers. Every month, Giordano awarded the "Service Star" to individual employees, based on nominations provided by shoppers. In addition, every Giordano store was evaluated every month by mystery shoppers. Based on the combined results of these evaluations, the "Best Service Shop" award was given to the top store. Customer feedback cards were available at all stores and were collected and posted at the office for further action. Increasingly, customers were providing feedback via the firm's corporate website.

In late 2006, Giordano opened Giordano University, located at Dongguan in China. At its initial stage, the University trained staff located in Hong Kong and Mainland China with plans to offer training to its other markets and even franchisees and authorized dealers. Giordano's efforts on staff training and development reaped results as was shown by the many service awards it clinched.

Value for Money

Lai explained the rationale for Giordano's value-for-money policy.

> Consumers are learning a lot better about what value is. So we always ask ourselves how can we sell it cheaper, make it more convenient for the consumer to buy and deliver faster today than [we did] yesterday. That is all value, because convenience is value for the consumer. Time is value for the customer.

---

[1]Management Discussion and Analysis, *Interim Financial Report 2008,* Giordano International, 30.
Giordano to dispose of their interest in garment manufacturing subsidiary (accessed via http://www.giordano.com.hk/web/HK/investors/news/2008-06-30_Placita%20Disposal_E.pdf, on March 9, 2009)

Giordano was able to sell value-for-money merchandise consistently through careful selection of suppliers, strict cost control, and by resisting the temptation to increase retail prices unnecessarily. For instance, to provide greater shopping convenience to customers, Giordano started to open kiosks in subway and train stations in 2003 aimed at providing their customers with a "grab and go" service.

Inventory Control

In order to maximize use of store space for sales opportunities, a central distribution center replaced the function of a back storeroom in its outlets. Information technology (IT) was used to facilitate inventory management and demand forecasting. When an item was sold, the barcode information—identifying size, color, style, and price—was recorded by the point-of-sale cash register and transmitted to the company's main computer. At the end of each day, the information was compiled at the store level and sent to the sales department and the distribution center. The compiled sales information became the store's order for the following day. Orders were filled during the night and were ready for delivery by early morning, ensuring that before a Giordano store opened for business, new inventory was already on the shelves.

Another advantage of its IT system was that information was disseminated to production facilities in real time. Such information allowed customers' purchase patterns to be understood, and this provided valuable input to its manufacturing operations, resulting in less problems and costs related to slow-moving inventory. The use of IT also afforded more efficient inventory holding. Giordano's inventory turnover on sales was reduced from 58 days in 1996 to merely 28 days in 2008. Its excellent inventory management reduced costs and allowed reasonable margins, while still allowing Giordano to reinforce its value-for-money philosophy. All in all, despite the relatively lower margins as compared to its peers, Giordano was still able to post healthy profits. Such efficiency became a crucial factor when periodic price wars were encountered.

Product Positioning

Fung recognized the importance of limiting the firm's expansion and focusing on one specific area. Simplicity and focus were reflected in the way Giordano merchandised its goods. Its stores featured no more than 100 variants of 17 core items, whereas competing retailers might feature 200 to 300 items. He believed that merchandising a wide range of products made it difficult to react quickly to market changes.

Giordano's willingness to experiment with new ideas and its perseverance despite past failures could also be seen in its introduction of new product lines. It ventured into mid-priced women's fashion with the label "Gio Ladies"—featuring a line of smart blouses, dress pants, and skirts—targeted at executive women. Reflecting retailer practices for such clothing, Giordano enjoyed higher margins on upscale women's clothing—typically 50–60 percent of selling price as compared to 40 percent for casual wear.

Here, however, Giordano ran into some difficulties as it found itself competing with more than a dozen seasoned players in the retail clothing business, including Esprit. Initially, the firm failed to differentiate its new Giordano Ladies line from its mainstream product line and even sold both through the same outlets. In 1999, however, Giordano took advantage of the boom that followed the Asian currency crisis in many parts of Asia, to aggressively relaunch its "Giordano Ladies" line, which subsequently met with great success.

As of September 2008, the reinforced "Giordano Ladies" focused on a select segment—the "office ladies, dressier" market with 46 "Giordano Ladies" shops in Hong Kong, Taiwan, Singapore, Malaysia, Indonesia, and China, offering personalized and exceptional service as one of its core offerings. Among other things, the employees were trained to memorize names of regular customers and recall their past purchases.

During the late 1990s, Giordano had begun to reposition its brand by emphasizing differentiated, functionally value-added products clothes and broadening its appeal by improving on visual merchandising and apparel. In 1999, the firm launched Blue Star

EXHIBIT 4: Giordano's First BSX Store in Hong Kong

Exchange (BSE), a new line of casual clothing for the price conscious customer. A typical storefront and store layout are shown in Exhibit 2. Giordano's relatively mid-priced positioning worked well—inexpensive, yet contemporary-looking outfits appealed to Asia's frugal customers, especially during a period of economic slowdown. However, over time, this positioning became inconsistent with the brand image that Giordano had tried hard to build over the years. As one senior executive remarked, "The feeling went from 'this is nice and good value' to 'this is cheap.'" As such, Giordano started to focus on establishing clear brand images and creating distinct identities between its brands. In September 2006, Giordano announced that it would be rebranding Bluestar Exchange. As explained by Peter Lau,

> The apparel retail market is getting increasingly competitive, regardless of whether you are talking about the high end or the mass market. In order to succeed, you must achieve meaningful differentiation from your competitors or else you risk becoming lost in the crowd. We believe it is time to give Bluestar Exchange a makeover to sharpen its image, and decided to go outside the company to get a fresh perspective.[2]

The newly revamped brand, now known as BSX (see Exhibit 4), was unveiled at the launch of its first flagship store in Hong Kong in April 2007. The shift saw BSX evolve from price to "fun sell," targeting the key youth demographic.[3] Expansion plans to bring BSX to other countries were made, following careful review and tweaking after its Hong Kong debut.

Additionally, having earned success in its value-for-money lines, Giordano now wanted to penetrate the "upper-premium" segment. This was done via the introduction of Giordano Concepts and its existing Giordano Ladies range. The lines focused on quality lifestyle and targeted the fashion-conscious consumer in the affluent market segment. In contrast to its unisex Giordano stores that carried a majority of items for women, Concept stores carry 60 percent of items catering to males.

---

[2]Giordano Re-brand Bluestar exchange article (accessed via http://www.giordano.com.hk/web/HK/investors/news/Bluestar%20Rebranding.html on January 2008).

[3]Bluestar shifts from price to fun sell, James Murphy, *Asia's Media & Marketing Newspaper*; March 11, 2006, p. 11.

To create alignment between the new up-market positioning and brand image, Giordano Concepts and Giordano Ladies stores were distinctly different from its mainstream stores. This included a revamp in store interiors and staff image to exude exclusivity, induce curiosity, and more importantly appeal to an affluent target group. For instance, to enhance its "white"-themed summer collection of 2006, flagship Concept stores in Hong Kong and Taiwan were dressed in abstract wall patterns and modern images.

Giordano gradually remarketed its core brand in ways that sought to create the image of a trendier label. To continue connecting with customers, Giordano launched several promotions. Among its successes was the "World without Strangers" slogan. First launched in South Asia as a means to raise funds for the Tsunami victims in Phuket, it gained quick favor with its other markets and in 2005 was launched across the region. The slogan extends to a range of T-shirts and rubber wristbands that promote international friendship. The products came in a variety of colors and brought across the message through words like: "Strength, Explore, Listen, Believe, Imagine and Accept."[4] Ishwar Chugani, Executive Director for Giordano Middle East, explained:

> The words are designed to be personal watchwords, such as "have strength in your convictions", or "explore the world around you", almost reminders to live outside the box and experience the variety of life. . . . The shirts are a sign of solidarity for fellow humans, spreading a message of peace, acceptance and open-mindedness, which is something we can all use from time to time.[5]

In light of international crises and at times fragile cross-border friendships, "World without Strangers" served as a mediator and avenue for which customers could express themselves. The company has been able to act as a mouthpiece for society, championing various themes from environmentalism to community work and even the economy. An example would be the "Cheer U Up" collection, produced in collaboration with Mr. Jim Chim Sui-man aimed to lift the spirits of the people in the financial turmoil during the 2009 world economic crisis. Thus, the firm's skills in executing innovative and effective promotional strategies helped the retailer to gain public favor and approval.

Giordano's Competitors

To beat the intense competition prevalent in Asia—especially in Hong Kong—founder Jimmy Lai believed that Giordano had to develop a distinctive competitive advantage. So he benchmarked Giordano against best-practice organizations in four key areas: (1) computerization (from The Limited), (2) a tightly controlled menu (from McDonald's), (3) frugality (from Wal-Mart), and (4) value pricing (as implemented at the British retail chain Marks & Spencer). The emphasis on service and the value-for-money concept had proven successful.

Giordano's main competitors in the value-for-money segment had been Hang Ten, Bossini, and Baleno, and at the higher end, Esprit. Exhibit 5 shows the relative positioning of Giordano and its competitors: The Gap, Bossini, Hang Ten, Baleno, and Esprit. Hang Ten and Bossini were generally positioned as low-price retailers offering reasonable quality and service. The clothes emphasized versatility and simplicity. But while Hang Ten and Baleno were more popular among teenagers and young adults, Bossini had a more general appeal. Their distribution strategies were somewhat similar, but they focused on different markets. For instance, while Hang Ten was mainly strong in Taiwan, Baleno increasingly penetrated mainland China and Taiwan. On the other hand, Bossini was very strong in Hong Kong and relatively strong in China. The

[4]Al-Bawaba News, Giordano world without strangers spreading goodwill, October 11, 2005 (accessed via Factiva on December 2007).

[5]Al-Bawaba News, Giordano world without strangers spreading goodwill, October 11, 2005 (accessed via Factiva on December 2007).

EXHIBIT 5: Market Positioning of Giordano and Principal Competitors

Firms	Positioning	Target market
Giordano (www.giordano.com.hk)	Value for money Mid-priced but trendy fashion	Unisex casual wear for all ages (under different brands)
The Gap (www.gap.com)	Value for money Mid-priced but trendy fashion	Unisex casual wear for all ages (under different brands)
Esprit (www.esprit-intl.com)	More up-market than Giordano Stylish, trendy	Ladies' casual, but also other specialized lines for children and men
Bossini (www.bossini.com)	Value for money (comparable to Giordano)	Unisex, casual wear, both young and old
Baleno (www.baleno.com.hk)	Value for money Trendy, young age casual wear	Unisex appeal, young adults
Hang Ten (www.hangten.com)	Value for money Sporty lifestyle	Casual wear and sports wear, teens and young adults

company planned to make its business in China into the group's largest turnover and profit contributor. The geographic areas in which Giordano, The Gap, Espirit, Bossini, Baleno, and Hang Ten operate are shown in Exhibit 6.

Esprit was an international fashion lifestyle brand. Esprit promoted a lifestyle image, and its products were strategically positioned as good quality and value—a

EXHIBIT 6: Geographic Presence of Giordano and Its Principal Competitors

Country	Giordano	The Gap	Esprit	Bossini	Baleno	Hang Ten
Asia						
Hong Kong/Macau	X	—	X	X	X	X
Singapore	X	X	X	X	X	X
South Korea	X	X	X	X	—	X
Taiwan	X	—	X	X	X	X
China	X	X	X	X	X	X
Malaysia	X	X	X	X	X	X
Indonesia	X	X	X	X	X	—
Philippines	X	—	X	X	—	X
Thailand	X	—	X	X	X	—
Japan	X	X	—	—	—	X
Middle East	X	X	X	X	X	X
World						
U.S. and Canada	X	X	X	X	—	X
Europe	—	X	X	X	—	—
Australia	X	—	X	—	—	—
Total	**1,585**	**3,117**	**9,751**	**827**	**1,160**	**NA**

Note: "X" indicates presence in the country/region; "—" indicates no presence.

Sources: *Giordano International Limited*, retrieved March 9, 2009 from http://www.giordano.com.hk/web/HK/ourCompany.html; Annual Report 2007, *Gap Inc.*, retrieved March 9, 2009 from http://media.corporate-ir.net/media_files/IROL/11/111302/AR07.pdf; *Esprit*; Retrieved March 9 2009, from http://www.esprit.com/index.php?command=Display&navi_id=104; *Bossini International Holdings Limited*, Retrieved March 9, 2009, from http://www.bossini.com/bossini/html/eng/common/global.jsp ; *Baleno*, Retrieved March 9, 2009 from http://www.baleno.com.hk/EN/stores_list_map.asp; *Hang Ten*, retrieved March 9, 2009, 2005 from *http://www.hangten.com.hk/countryLink.do*

EXHIBIT 7: Competitive Financial Data for Giordano, The Gap, Esprit, and Bossini

	Giordano	The Gap	Esprit	Bossini
Turnover (US$ million)	639	15,736	4,403	298
Profit after tax and minority interests (US$ million)	39.2	833	832	8.2
Return on total assets (percentage)	7.0	10.6	33.1	6.97
Return on average equity (percentage)	10.8	19.5	46.0	9.71
Return on sales (percentage)	8.0	5.3	20.7	3.8
Number of employees	12,100	154,000	10,541	4,300
Sales per employee (US$ '000)	52.81	102.18	457.43	69.02

Note: The Gap reports its earnings in US$. All reported figures have been converted into US$ at the following exchange rate (as of Mar 2009): US$1 = HK$7.75.

Sources: *Annual Report 2007*, Giordano International; *Annual Report 2007*, The Gap; II 2007 *Annual Report*, Esprit International; *Financial Report 2007/8*, Bossini International Holdings Limited; *Annual Report 2007/08*.

position that Giordano was occupying. By 2008, Esprit had a distribution network of over 12,000 stores and outlets in more than 40 countries in Europe, Asia, America, the Middle East, and Australia. The main markets were in Europe, which accounted for approximately 86.7 percent of sales. The Esprit brand products were principally sold via directly managed retail outlets, wholesale customers (including department stores, specialty stores, and franchisees), and by licensees for products manufactured under license, principally through the licensees' own distribution networks.

Although each of these firms had slightly different positioning strategies, they competed in a number of areas. For example, all firms heavily emphasized advertising and sales promotion—selling fashionable clothes at attractive prices. Almost all stores were also located primarily in good ground-floor areas, drawing high-volume traffic and facilitating shopping, browsing, and impulse buying. However, none had been able to match the great customer value offered by Giordano.

A threat from U.S.–based The Gap was also looming. The Gap had already entered Japan. After 2005, when garment quotas were largely abolished, imports into the region had become more cost effective for this U.S. competitor. Through franchise partners such as FJ Benjamin Holdings Ltd, The Gap expanded its international presence with franchises in Bahrain, Greece, Indonesia, Korea, Kuwait, Oman, Qatar, Malaysia, Russia, Saudi Arabia, Philippines, Singapore, Turkey, and the United Arab Emirates. Financial data for Giordano, Esprit, The Gap, and Bossini, are shown in Exhibit 7.

Giordano's Growth Strategy

Early in its existence, Giordano's management had realized that regional expansion was required to achieve substantial growth and economies of scale. By 2007, Giordano had over 1,800 stores in more than 30 markets. Exhibit 8 shows the growth achieved across a number of dimensions from 1998 to 2007. Despite a drop in profits in 2006 due to the unforeseen warm winter as well as the astounding rise in rental expenses in Hong Kong, Giordano showed relatively consistent growth over the years as profits rebounded in 2007 with a 39.4 percent increase.

Driven in part by its desire for growth and in part by the need to reduce its dependence on Asia in the wake of the 1998 economic meltdown, Giordano set its sights on markets outside Asia. Australia was an early target and the number of retail outlets increased from four in 1999 to 56 in 2008. Although the Asian financial crisis had caused Giordano to rethink its regional strategy, it was still determined to enter and

EXHIBIT 8: Operational Highlights for Giordano's Retail and Distribution Division

	2007	2006	2005	2004	2003	2002	2001	2000	1999	1998
Number of retail outlets										
— directly managed by the Group	1000	962	914	811	550	473	456	367	317	308
— franchised	895	805	780	774	813	783	703	553	423	370
Total number of retail outlets	1,895	1,767	1,694	1,585	1,363	1,256	1,159	920	740	678
Retail floor area directly managed by the Group (in '000 sq. ft.)	995	957	918	846	650	599	597	465	301	358
Sales per square foot (HK$)	4,975	4,568	4,807	4,300	4,200	4,500	5,100	7,400	8,400	6,800
Number of employees	12,100	11,000	11,000	9,000	7,900	8,000	8,287	7,166	6,237	6,319
Comparable store sales Increase/ (decrease) (percentage)	2	(3)	(1)	7	(9)	(2)	(4)	4	21	(13)
Number of sales associates	N.A	N.A.	N.A.	N.A.	3,200	2,900	2,603	2,417	2,026	1,681

Source: Annual Report 2007, Giordano International; N.A. = not available.

further penetrate new Asian markets. This determination led to successful expansion in mainland China (see Exhibit 9), where the number of retail outlets grew from 253 in 1999 to 881 by 2008. Giordano's management foresaw both challenges and opportunities arising from the People's Republic of China's accession to the World Trade Organization.

Giordano opened more stores in Indonesia, bringing its total in that country to 100 stores. In Malaysia, Giordano planned to refurnish its outlets and intensify its local promotional campaigns to consolidate its leadership position in the Malaysian market. To improve store profitability, Giordano had already converted some of its franchised Malaysian stores into company-owned stores.

Having gained a foothold in the far eastern region, Giordano began expansion into India in 2006 and North America and the Middle East in 2007. In June, 2007, Giordano unveiled its first franchised store in Cairo, Egypt. Since the launch of its first store in Chennai, Giordano increased its presence in India to nine stores in five cities.[6]

The senior management team knew that Giordano's future success in such markets would depend on a detailed understanding of consumer tastes and preferences for fabrics, colors, and advertising. In the past, the firm had relied on maintaining a consistent strategy across different countries, including such elements as positioning, service levels, information systems, logistics, and human resource policies. However, implementation of such tactical elements as promotional campaigns usually was left mostly to local managers. A country's overall performance in terms of sales, contribution, service levels,

EXHIBIT 9: Giordano's Flagship Store in Shanghai

[6]Giordano opens three new stores in India, November 20, 2008 http://www.giordano.com.hk/web/HK/investors/IR2008/2008-11-20%20Pune%20+%20Mumbai.pdf (accessed March 9, 2009).

and customer feedback was monitored by regional headquarters (for instance, Singapore for Southeast Asia) and the head office in Hong Kong. Weekly performance reports were distributed to all managers.

As the organization expanded beyond Asia, it was becoming clear that different strategies had to be developed for different regions or countries. For instance, to enhance profitability in mainland China, the company recognized that better sourcing was needed to enhance price competitiveness. Turning around the Taiwan operation required refocusing on basic designs, streamlining product portfolio, and implementing their micromarketing strategy more aggressively. In Europe, Giordano was investigating a variety of market entry opportunities.

Decisions Facing the Senior Management Team

Although Giordano had been extremely successful, it faced a number of challenges. A key issue was how the Giordano brand should be positioned against the competition in both new and existing markets. Was a repositioning required in existing markets, and would it be necessary to follow different positioning strategies for different markets (e.g., Hong Kong versus Southeast Asia)?

A second issue was the sustainability of Giordano's key success factors. Giordano had to carefully explore how its core competencies and the pillars of its success were likely to develop over the coming years. Which of its competitive advantages were likely to be sustainable and which ones were likely to be eroded?

A third issue was Giordano's growth strategy in Asia as well as across continents. Would Giordano's competitive strengths be readily transferable to other markets? Would strategic adaptations to its strategy and marketing mix be required, or would tactical moves suffice?

Study Questions

1. Describe and evaluate Giordano's product, business and corporate strategies.
2. Describe and evaluate Giordano's current positioning strategy. Should Giordano reposition itself against its competitors in its current and new markets, and should it have different positioning strategies for different geographic markets?
3. What are Giordano's key success factors and sources of competitive advantage? Are its competitive advantages sustainable, and how would they develop in the future?
4. Could Giordano transfer its key success factors to new markets as it expanded both in Asia and the other parts of the world?
5. How do you think Giordano had/would have to adapt its marketing and operations strategies and tactics when entering and penetrating your country?
6. What general lessons can be learned from Giordano for other major clothing retailers in your country?

CASE 6 Distribution at American Airlines

BENJAMIN EDELMAN

American Airlines sought to reduce the fees it pays to global distribution services (GDSs) to distribute its air travel services to travel agents. But GDSs held significant tactical advantages. For example, GDSs had signed long-term exclusive contracts with the corporate customers who were American's best customers. Furthermore, travel agents tended to favor whichever GDS offered the highest commissions— impeding price competition among GDSs. Against this backdrop, American considered how best to cut its GDS costs.

The GDS Negotiation Team at American Airlines faced the formidable task of reducing American's ticket distribution costs. Ticket distribution was increasingly electronic—with more than 95 percent of tickets existing only in a database, never printed on paper or "distributed" in the physical sense. Yet American continued to pay hundreds of millions of dollars per year to Global Distribution System's (GDS's) intermediaries that let travel agents book and confirm flights on American. If American simply refused to pay these costs, it would disappear from GDS listings—disrupting relationships with the travel agents whose corporate accounts were American's most profitable customers. But paying top dollar for database services was equally untenable, particularly as American struggled with rising fuel prices and increased competition from new entrants.

American had a proposed response to high GDS fees: a Source Premium Policy that would force travel agents to pay the extra cost incurred by American as a result of the agency's choice of GDS. This policy would reduce American's GDS expense, but travel agents were up in arms. If American pushed forward with the Source Premium Policy, travel agents might steer passengers elsewhere—leaving American even worse off than under GDS's high fees.

The Structure and History of Airline Ticket Distribution

American Airlines' operations grew rapidly after World War II. In 1921, American's corporate predecessor had just five small airplanes for transporting airmail. But expansion was brisk: In 1946, American ordered 220 new planes.

Early logistics proved challenging, and even taking reservations could be complex. Initially, passenger listings were stored on paper records in reservations offices at each point of departure. To request a reservation, a passenger would call American or visit a "city ticket office" retail location. American staff would use telephone or teletype to check with the departure city to assure that space was available on the specified flight on the specified day. A 1967 HBS teaching case described American's Chicago reservations office:

> A large cross-hatched board dominates one wall, its spaces filled with cryptic notes. At rows of desks sit busy men and women who continually glance from thick reference books to the wall display while continuously talking on the telephone and filling out cards. One man sitting in the back of the room is using field glasses to examine a change that has just been made on the display board. The chatter of teletype and sound of card sorting equipment fills the air.[1]

As American's network grew and passenger volume increased, paper passenger lists and telephone confirmations proved inadequate. American in 1952 introduced the

Professor Benjamin Edelman prepared this case. HBS cases are developed solely as the basis for class discussion. Cases are not intended to serve as endorsements, sources of primary data, or illustrations of effective or ineffective management.

Magnetronic Reservisor to help automate inventory control. Using a mechanical console installed on each desk, an agent pushed buttons to indicate the desired date and flight. If space was available, a light on the console would be illuminated. When a flight sold out, a staff person removed a wire from the master control board, breaking the circuit and disabling the agent's light on any future requests for that flight. The Reservisor offered major productivity improvements: A trial in the Boston reservations office served an additional 200 passengers daily, with 20 fewer reservations staff. Yet reservations remained complex: Processing a typical round-trip ticket required the efforts of 12 different people, taking up to three hours from start to finish. With so many steps, errors were widespread, and reservation agent productivity was decreasing as itineraries became more complex.[2]

An improved alternative came from a chance meeting between American Airlines then-president C. R. Smith and IBM then-president Thomas Watson, Jr. on an American Airlines flight in 1956. Aviation historian Robert Serling recounts their conversation:

> "What line of business are you in?" CR asked.
> "Business machines, computers. How about you?"
> "Airlines. This one, as a matter of fact."
> "You must be having all sorts of problems these days. What's your biggest one?"
> "Answering the goddamned telephone."[3]

American and IBM collaborated on the design of an improved inventory management system, ultimately called the Semi-Automated Business Reservations Environment (SABRE). IBM provided the hardware, while AA and IBM jointly built the software. The initial investment was comparable to half a dozen Boeing 707 jet airplanes.[4]

Despite SABRE's cost, American viewed the program as a success. Customers would still call or visit American staff to book flights, but SABRE eliminated time-consuming checks with departurecity reservation lists. American reported that SABRE allowed a 30 percent reduction in reservation staff.

In a 1976 innovation, American's marketing department began providing SABRE terminals to interested travel agencies. American anticipated strategic advantages from travel agents use of the terminals: SABRE would make it particularly easy for agents to browse and confirm American flights. SABRE was installed at 130 travel agents locations within the first year, and hundreds more the next.[5] American reported that the first 200 travel agent installations of SABRE yielded $20.1 million of annual incremental passenger revenue, a 500 percent return on investment.[6] Seeing American's success, competing airlines scrambled to implement similar systems of their own: United offered travel agents Apollo, while TWA offered PARS, DELTA offered DATAS II, and Eastern offered System One.

The Rise of Competing Global Distribution Systems

Most travel agencies chose computer terminals from a single provider: Each terminal used different commands to perform the same tasks, and installing multiple providers added complexity, particularly in duplication of accounting records. Travel agencies therefore sought systems that could book flights on multiple airlines. In response, airlines upgraded their offerings to allow bookings on competing carriers. For example, a travel agent with American Airlines' SABRE could use SABRE to book flights on United, while an agent with United's Apollo could equally book flights on American. This multi-carrier approach was initially called a Customer Reservation System (CRS), later a Global Distribution System (GDS).

The rise of the GDS created the prospect of opportunistic behavior. For example, if an airline owned a GDS, it could configure the GDS to show the airline's own flights first—even if others offered a lower fare or a more direct routing. Furthermore, airlines that owned GDS's could charge other airlines for preferred placement in GDS listings. From 1983 to 1987, a series of cases challenged these "display bias" tactics, and in 1984 the Department of Transportation established a set of regulations to standardize GDS operations. In particular, regulations forbade GDS's from using ranking flights based on carrier identity, e.g., ranking some flights higher merely because they were operated by a preferred carrier. Additional rules prohibited GDS's from charging discriminatory booking fees or from unreasonably limiting travel agents' ability to switch GDS's or use multiple GDS's. Finally, GDS's owned by airlines had to provide non-owner airlines with information and capabilities as accurate and reliable as those provided to the owner. Conversely, in a rule often referred to as "mandatory participation," airlines that owned GDS's had to offer service in all other GDS's also. Exhibit 1 presents excerpts of these rules.

Initially, travel agents were of limited importance, for travelers directly contacted whatever airline they wished to fly. But the 1978 deregulation of US air travel brought major changes: Airlines could set their own schedules, fares, and routes without government oversight. Suddenly, travel agents played a key role in helping travelers find the best choices in an increasingly competitive marketplace. By 1989, more than 80 percent of tickets were booked through travel agents.[7]

Payments and Competition under Global Distribution Systems

Initially airlines had paid all the costs of the GDS's they created. But as airlines and GDS's began to keep each other at arms length, they formalized the fee structure charged to airline participants. In particular, when a GDS issued a ticket on an airline, the GDS would charge the airline a fee for each flight segment in the passenger's itinerary. In 2002, on average an airline paid a GDS $4.25 per flight segment. The average ticket includes more than one segment, and the average booking fee per ticket was $11. At United Airlines, GDS fees totaled 3.3 percent of revenue for tickets sold through GDS's.[8]

GDS's in turn spent a portion of this fee on payments to travel agents: The more a GDS offered a travel agent, the more likely that travel agent was to choose that GDS rather than a competitor. By 2002, fewer than half of travel agencies paid monthly fees for GDS services, and 60 percent of travel agents received a signing bonus for joining a GDS. In addition, GDS's paid travel agents "incentive payments" of $1 to $1.70 per segment.[9]

EXHIBIT 1: Regulation of GDS Relationships (as of 2002) (excerpted)

§255.7—System owner participation in other systems.

(a) Each system owner shall participate in each other system (to the extent that such owner participates in such an enhancement in its own system) if the other system offers commercially reasonable terms for such participation. Fees shall be presumed commercially reasonable if: (1) They do not exceed the fees charged by the system of such system owner in the United States, or (2) They do not exceed the fees being paid by such system owner to another system in the United States.

(b) Each system owner shall provide complete, timely, and accurate information on its airline schedules, fares, and seat availability to each other system in which it participates on the same basis and at the same time that it provides such information to the system that it owns, controls, markets, or is affiliated with. If a system owner offers a fare or service that is commonly available subscribers to its own system, it must make that fare or service equally available for sale through other system in which it participates.

§255.8—Contracts with subscribers.

(a) No subscriber contract may have a term in excess of five years. No system may offer subscriber or potential subscriber a subscriber contract with a term in excess of three years unless system simultaneously offers such subscriber or potential subscriber a subscriber contract with a no longer than three years. No contract may contain any provision that automatically extends contract beyond its stated date of termination, whether because of the addition or deletion equipment or because of some other event.

§255.9—Use of third-party hardware, software and databases.

(a) No system may prohibit or restrict, directly or indirectly, the use of:

(1) Third-party computer hardware or software in conjunction with CRS services, except necessary to protect the integrity of the system, or

(2) A CRS terminal to access directly any other system or database providing information airline services, unless the terminal is owned by the system.

(b) This section prohibits, among other things, a system's:

(1) Imposition of fees in excess of commercially reasonable levels to certify third-party equipment;

(2) Undue delays or redundant or unnecessary testing before certifying such equipment. . .

§255.10—Marketing and booking information.

(a) Each system shall make available to all U.S. participating carriers on nondiscriminatory terms all marketing, booking, and sales data relating to carriers that it elects to generate from its system. The data made available shall be as complete and accurate as the data provided a system owner.

Source: 14 CFR Ch. 11

A European Commission diagram[10] summarized the resulting payment flow:

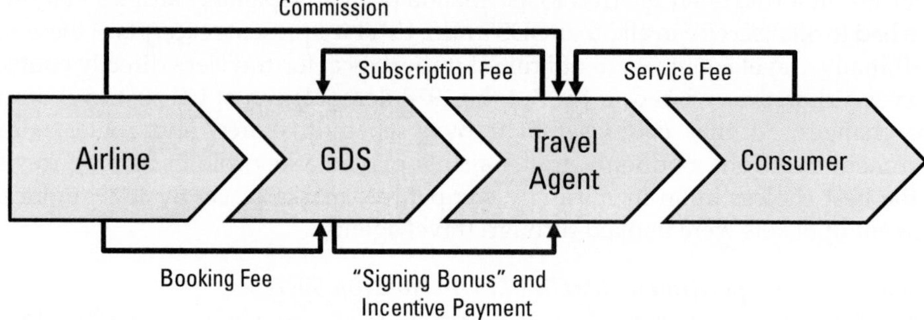

Because travel agents did not pay booking fees, they had no direct incentive to use the system that charged airlines the lowest fees. Instead, a travel agent would typically choose whichever GDS offered the travel agent the largest incentive payment.

Most travel agents still used only one GDS. Accessing multiple GDS required more training, more equipment, and considerable accounting complexity.

In general, airlines participated in all four GDS's. Airlines recognized that each travel agent could access only one GDS, and no airline wanted to turn away travel agents that might book its tickets.

US GDS Deregulation

By 2000, comprehensive GDS regulation was increasingly viewed as unnecessary. Although major airlines still obtained 58 percent of their bookings from "brick-and-mortar" travel agencies, 10 percent of bookings came from airlines' own web sites, and these bookings did not need to pass through a GDS. Furthermore, 15 percent of bookings came from new online travel agencies such as Expedia and Travelocity. These bookings did use GDS's. (For example, Travelocity used SABRE, and Expedia and Orbitz used Worldspan.) But a new set of "direct connect" systems were expected to let online travel agencies bypass GDS's to work directly with airlines.[11]

Meanwhile, by 2002, American had sold SABRE and United had sold Apollo. Airlines' divestitures of their GDS's reduced concerns about a GDS favoring its parent airline.

After a series of consultations, the Department of Transportation in 2002 decided to remove most regulation of GDS's. After a brief transition period, the regulations shown in Exhibit 1 would no longer apply; instead, airlines and GDS's could negotiate privately to establish the parameters of their relationship. These changes went into effect in January 2004.[12]

In 2003, on the eve of full deregulation, airlines and GDS's entered their first round of comprehensive negotiations. Thanks to revised regulations, airlines were no longer required to submit all their fares to all GDS's. Thus, some airlines introduced "web fares"—lower prices available only to customers who booked tickets directly with an airline, typically on the airline's web site. However, GDS's wanted to provide airlines' lowest prices to their travel agents and to their travel agents' passengers. If an airline guaranteed to provide a GDS with access to all of its fares, as of 2003 a GDS typically offered the airline discounts (averaging 12 percent) on the GDS's fees.[13] The Department of Transportation applauded this result: "As we predicted, the airlines' control over access to their webfares has led some of the [GDS] systems to offer airlines discounted booking fees in return for the ability to sell those fares."[14]

Exhibit 2 presents GDS market shares as of 2003.

Booking Travel after GDS Deregulation

Despite lowered prices from GDS's, not all airlines used GDS's. As of 2004, Southwest participated only in SABRE. Furthermore, Southwest offered limited functions (for example, no immediate booking confirmations), and SABRE could sell only Southwest's highest fares. JetBlue also limited its use of GDS's. For example, in 2004 JetBlue withdrew from SABRE, reporting that most of its customers did not require GDS services.[15] In lieu of GDS's, these airlines encouraged passengers to book directly, e.g., by telephone or online.[16]

In contrast, other airlines still obtained most of their bookings through GDS's. For example, as of 2004, 70 percent of American's tickets were booked through travel

EXHIBIT 2: GDS Market Shares (as of 2003)

	USA/Canada	Central/South America	Europe/Middle East	Asia/Pacific	Worldwide
Amadeus	9%	38%	49%	15%	26%
Galileo	21%	6%	31%	15%	22%
SABRE	42%	50%	13%	4%	24%
Worldspan	28%	6%	8%	4%	24%
Abacus				19%	4%
Topas				4%	1%
Infini				4%	1%
TravelSky				36%	8%

Source: Adapted from MetaGroup estimates based on interviews with GDS's and airlines.

agents.[17] See Exhibit 3, tabulating distribution channel prevalence by year. American's 2001 operations included 112,400,000 flight segments booked through GDS's; for these bookings, American paid more than $424 million of GDS fees.[18] GDS's in turn earned high profits compared with airlines. See Exhibit 4, comparing profits at SABRE and Amadeus with profits at American and United.

For leisure customers, direct web-based bookings were increasingly common. But business customers continued to favor bookings through travel agencies. Many companies required that their employees use travel agents in order to assure compliance with corporate travel policies, facilitate streamlined payment and accounting, and receive personalized assistance with complicated or changing trips.

The 2006 GDS Negotiations

In 2006, American Airlines faced the impending expiration of its 2003 three-year contracts with the four then-existing GDS's. American had achieved some cost reductions in 2003, but it still considered GDS's fees excessive. American sought to reduce fees considerably through 2006 contracts.

By July, American had reached agreements with Worldspan and Galileo. Under these agreements, Worldspan and Galileo would offer additional services to travel agents: "Worldspan Super Access" and "Galileo Content Continuity." If a travel agent chose one of these new services, it would be able to view and book all of American's fares. However, by entering one of these agreements, the agent would accept a reduction or elimination of its incentive payment from the GDS. For example, a Galileo Content Continuity travel agent would give up $0.80 of its GDS GDS incentive payment.[19] At the same time, for tickets booked through these new services, American's GDS payment would be approximately $0.60 per segment. In contrast, SABRE and Amadeus held firm in charging American GDS fees of more than $4 per segment.*

On July 12, 2006, American announced its Source Premium Policy. Effective September 1, American would charge travel agents a $3.50 "source premium" fee per segment, for all segments booked through GDS's other than those AA designated as "competitive booking sources." Worldspan Super Access and Galileo Content

EXHIBIT 3: Distribution Channel Prevalence

	1999	2002	2005
Airline web sites	3%	13%	38%
Airline call centers	26%	24%	
Online travel agents	4%	17%	
Traditional travel agents	67%	46%	

Source: Adapted from "Airline Ticketing: Impact of Changes in the Airline Ticket Distribution Industry." General Accounting Office. July 2003. "Consultation Paper on the Possible Revision of Regulation 2299/89 on a Code of Conduct for Computerised Reservation Systems." European Commission Directorate-General for Energy and Transport. February 23, 2007.

*American did not disclose specific fees, but publicly available sources provide some information. See e.g. note 18.

EXHIBIT 4: Profits at Airlines and GDS's—Net Profit Before Special Items

Year	American Airlines	United Airlines	US Airlines Collectively	SABRE	Amadeus
1999	$985	$1,235	$5,400	$331	$117
2000	$813	$50.0	$2,500	$144	$129
2001	($1,800)	($2,145)	($8,300)	$31.1	$110
2002	($3,500)	($3,212)	($11,300)	$214	$156
2003	($1,200)	($2,808)	($3,600)	$83.3	$200
2004	($751)	($1,721)	($9,100)	$190	$294
2005	($857)		($1,143)	$172	

Source: SEC 10-K filings of American Airlines, United Airlines, and SABRE. IATA Economics Briefing, December 7, 2005. Amadeus financial statements.
Note: Amounts in millions of dollars of profit and (loss). Amadeus values converted from Euros to Dollars as of corresponding years.

Continuity were designated as competitive, hence not subject to the fee. Any travel agent that chose one of these services would not pay the source premium fee. However, the source premium would apply to all SABRE and Amadeus bookings, and to all Worldspan and Galileo bookings other than through the Super Access and Content Continuity programs. Exhibit 5 gives excerpts of the Source Premium Policy.

Travel Agents' Response

Some travel agents reacted negatively to American's proposed policy. Just one day after American's announcement, the American Society of Travel Agents issued a press release condemning American's approach. ASTA CEO Kathryn Sudeikis complained, "American's announcement tells every travel agency in America: if you want to sell us, run your business the way we tell you or you'll be forced to pay us for the privilege of booking our services. This policy of shifting still more costs off of American's financial statements onto the backs of travel agents and their customers is unconscionable. American is trying to use its market power to impose its costs on other market players, as a condition to providing what travel agents clearly require to do business efficiently."[20]

EXHIBIT 5: Source Premium Policy (as of August 31, 2006)

American Airlines wishes to provide all agencies access to full schedule, fare and inventory content through the distribution source of their choice, on terms that allow American to compete with its low cost rivals.

To achieve this end, American has negotiated full content access deals with many distribution providers that offer new, cost-effective products. These products are referred to as "Competitive Booking Sources." Travel agencies that use Competitive Booking Sources to create bookings will have access to full American content.

American recognizes that some travel agencies or corporate travel departments may value the use of certain GDS providers that do not qualify as Competitive Booking Sources. Accordingly, American currently intends to preserve flexibility for these agencies and corporations by providing full content access through other presently available providers, referred to as "Other Booking Sources," although these sources are more expensive to American. In exchange for the flexibility to choose Other Booking Sources, agencies that use these sources will be required to bear a portion of the cost of content distribution via these sources. Also, American, consistent with any applicable contractual obligations, may eventually withhold content from Other Booking Sources, particularly if an Other Booking Source fails to display American content on neutral terms as compared with other airlines.

		Source Premium per Net Booked Segment
Competitive Booking Sources	Worldspan Super Access Product Galileo Content Continuity Program All G2 Switchworks GDS Products All Farelogix GDS Products	NONE
Other Booking Sources	Any Amadeus GDS Product Any SABRE Product Any Other Worldspan Product Any Other Galileo/Apollo Program	$3.50

The Source Premium will be applied to all Other Booking Source net bookings originated or changed on or after September 1, 2006.

Source: American Airlines—http://www.aa.com/agency.

Travel agents objected to the Source Premium Policy in part because GDS incentive payments were the major remaining form by which airlines paid most travel agents. By 2002, airlines had largely eliminated ordinary travel agent commissions. Without GDS payments, most travel agents would receive no payments from the airlines whose tickets they sold—making it increasingly difficult for travel agents to offer services to customers without a separately-itemized charge. (However, most travel agents had already begun to charge customers for each ticket issued.)

Travel agents also suggested that American's move was improper, unjustified, or even unfair. Airlines had always paid GDS's to distribute airlines' tickets, and most travel agents saw little reason for change. American's surcharges on SABRE-issued tickets were particularly hard for travel agents to understand because American had created SABRE and because American had previously encouraged travel agents to install and rely on SABRE terminals.

Travel agents who specialized in expensive corporate tickets thought they were not getting appropriate credit for the high revenues they provided. "Whether the fare is $1,800 or $180, a roundtrip of non-stops booked through one of AA's non-preferred channels still would generate a $7 fee," commented travel industry newsletter *The Beat*, citing industry sources.[21]

Additional complications came from travel agents' long-term contracts with GDS's. American's July announcement offered just seven weeks until implementation. But most travel agents had long-term contracts with GDS's; the average such contract lasted three years.[22] So, even if a travel agent wanted to move to a different GDS at American's suggestion, the travel agent would need some time to do so. Travel agents faced further complications from their relationships with many airlines: If each airline came to favor a different GDS, a travel agent might be forced to pay extra fees no matter which GDS it chose.

Those critical of American's Source Premium Policy often cited Northwest's August 2004 Shared GDS Fee. Northwest had proposed to charge travel agencies $7.50 for each round-trip ticket and $3.75 for each one-way ticket issued via a GDS.[23] Northwest's fee prompted an uproar from travel agents and GDS's, and Northwest dropped the fee just two weeks later.[24]

Travelers' Perspective

The Business Travel Coalition, an association of companies buying air travel, weighed in largely against GDS fees. The BTC's key concern was obtaining access to all fares, without exclusion of airlines' lowest fares.

The BTC also expressed concern about the overall secrecy of airlines' dealings with travel agents. The BTC claimed that corporate travel managers "have been somewhat in the dark about the depth of the financial arrangements between the GDSs and TMCs," adding that "never has there been a process involving industry structural change that has been so cloaked in secrecy."[25]

American's Approach

Despite these challenges, American staff insisted that the Source Premium Policy was the right way forward. "We need to help travel agents understand how expensive some channels can be," explained Cory Garner, Manager of Distribution Strategy. "Right now, an agency chooses a GDS and the airline pays the bill. If an agency is protected from the financial consequences of its choice of GDS, how can it be expected to make the most economical decision on behalf of the customer?"

Seeing the struggle between American, GDS's, and travel agents, one source called the negotiation a "poker game."[26] Another industry insider pondered the competitive implications, particularly at American hub cities: "What if the other carriers say nothing until after September. [L]ook for market share swings, especially in O'Hare and Dallas/Fort Worth, not to mention other big AA markets?"[27]

By mid-August, American had largely reached agreement on key pricing terms with remaining GDS's SABRE and Amadeus. But American's Charlie Sultan, Managing Director of Sales, Planning and Analysis, explained that other issues remained unresolved. Particularly controversial were potential future agreements in which American might seek to communicate directly with travel agents or large customers, without routing bookings through a GDS. Sultan told *The Beat*: "We were not willing to sign up for [an agreement] that said, 'We cannot sit down with our travel agency partners or corporate partners and figure out how the two of us can do business if it involves potentially not booking through SABRE.' That is not pro-consumer, or pro-agency or pro-supplier. That is only pro-SABRE."[28]

As September 1 neared, Charlie Sultan and co-lead negotiator Chris Degroot had a choice to make. American could follow through in implementing the Source Premium Policy—reducing GDS expenses, but risking losing business as travel agents encouraged customers to choose other carriers. Or American could cancel the Source Premium Policy—preserving travel agent relationships, but making little headway on distribution costs.

Study Questions

1. American Airlines could distribute directly via the Internet and its own call centers in a highly cost-effective manner. Why then should American Airlines sell via travel agents at all?
2. American Airlines spends hundreds of millions of dollars on GDS fees. In the end, who is paying for these costs? How are the economic costs paid for in this channel?
3. From a GDS perspective, what techniques can it use to retain and protect is current business model?
4. Should American Airlines implement the Source Premium Policy?

Endnotes

1. R.F. Meyer. "American Airlines SABRE (A)." Harvard Business School Case No. EA-C 768 (1967).
2. Copeland, Duncan, Richard Mason, and James McKenney. "SABRE: The Development of Information-Based Competence and Execution of Information-Based Competition." *IEEE Annals of the History of Computing*. Vol. 17, No. 3, 1995.
3. Serling, Robert, 1985. "Eagle: The Story of American Airlines." New York: St. Martin's Press.
4. Copeland, et al. Id.
5. Copeland, et al. Id.
6. US District Court, Central District of California. "Memorandum from T.G. Plaskett to A.V. Casey." American Airlines documents AA080713-AA080714, January 17, 1977.
7. Labich, Kenneth. "Should Airlines Be Reregulated?" *Fortune*. June 19, 1989.
8. CRS Regulations, Final Rule, RIN 2105-AC65, January 7, 2004. Citing United Reply Comments.
9. CRS Regulations, Final Rule, RIN 2105-AC65, January 7, 2004. Citing SABRE Comments. See also, Promedia.travel. "The Evolving Managed Travel Distribution Chain in 2006." http://www.thebeat.travel/blog/ downloads/promedia-GDS-guide.pdf .
10. "Consultation Paper on the Possible Revision of Regulation 2299/89 on a Code of Conduct for Computerised Reservation Systems." European Commission Directorate-General for Energy and Transport. February 23, 2007.
11. CRS Regulations, Final Rule, RIN 2105-AC65, January 7, 2004. Citing Galileo Comments and Guerin-Calvert, Jernigan & Hurdle Declaration.
12. CRS Regulations, Final Rule, RIN 2105-AC65, January 7, 2004.
13. Alamardi, Fariba, 2006. "The Future of Airline Distribution." *Journal of Air Transport Management* 12 (2006) 122–134.
14. 67 FR 69381.
15. Kontzer, Tony. "JetBlue Pulls Out of SABRE, As Web Sales Rise." *Information Week*. December 20, 2004.
16. CRS Regulations, Final Rule, RIN 2105-AC65, January 7, 2004. Citing SABRE comments.
17. CRS Regulations, Final Rule, RIN 2105-AC65, January 7, 2004. Citing American comments.

18. See e.g. George Nicoud III, American Airlines, "Follow-Up to July 12, 2002 Testimony," available at http://govinfo.library.unt.edu/ncecic/other_testimony/american_letter.pdf.
19. "Interview: Travelport SVP Kurt Ekert." *The Beat*. July 31, 2006.
20. "American Airlines Announcement Threatens to Throw Industry into Chaos, Says ASTA." American Society of Travel Agents. July 13, 2006.
21. "Galileo Reveals Incentive Cut Amid AAngst." *The Beat*. July 13, 2006.
22. CRS Regulations, Final Rule, RIN 2105-AC65, January 7, 2004.
23. "Northwest Airlines to Charge for GDS Bookings." *M-Travel Travel Distribution News*. August 24, 2004.
24. Karantzavelou, Vicky. "ACTA Welcomes Northwest Decision to Drop Shared GDS Fees." *Travel Daily News*. September 6, 2004.
25. "BTC Attacks Airlines, Cites AA-SABRE PNR Issue." *The Beat*. August 9, 2006.
26. "80 Cent: Galileo Matches SABRE Number in Fee, Not Cut." *The Beat*. July 14, 2006.
27. "Galileo Reveals Incentive Cut Amid AAngst." *The Beat*. July 13, 2006.
28. "Interview: AA Exec Details SABRE Impasse." *The Beat*. August 10, 2006.

CASE 7 The Accra Beach Hotel: Block Booking of Capacity During a Peak Period

SHERYL E. KIMES, JOCHEN WIRTZ, AND CHRISTOPHER LOVELOCK

Cherita Howard, sales manager for the Accra Beach Hotel, a 141-room hotel on the Caribbean island of Barbados, was debating what to do about a request from the West Indies Cricket Board. The Board wanted to book a large block of rooms more than six months ahead during several of the hotel's busiest times and was asking for a discount. In return, it promised to promote the Accra Beach in all advertising materials and television broadcasts as the host hotel for the upcoming West Indies Cricket Series, an important international sporting event.

The Hotel

The Accra Beach Hotel and Resort had a prime beachfront location on the south coast of Barbados, just a short distance from the airport and the capital city of Bridgetown. Located on $3^1/_2$ acres of tropical landscape and fronting one of the best beaches on Barbados, the hotel featured rooms offering panoramic views of the ocean, pool, or island.

The centerpiece of its lush gardens was the large swimming pool, which had a shallow bank for lounging plus a swim-up bar. In addition, there was a squash court and a fully equipped gym. Golf was also available only 15 minutes away at the Barbados Golf Club, with which the hotel was affiliated.

The Accra Beach had two restaurants and two bars as well as extensive banquet and conference facilities. It offered state-of-the-art conference facilities to local, regional, and international corporate clientele and had hosted a number of large summits in recent years. Three conference rooms, which could be configured in a number of ways, served as the setting for large corporate meetings, training seminars, product displays, dinners, and wedding receptions. A business center provided guests with Internet access, faxing capabilities, and photocopying services.

EXHIBIT 1: Beach View of the Accra Beach Hotel

The hotel's 122 standard rooms were categorized into three groups—Island View, Pool View, and Ocean View—and there were 13 Island View Junior Suites and 6 Penthouse Suites, each decorated in tropical pastel prints and handcrafted furniture. All rooms were equipped with cable/satellite TV, air conditioning, ceiling fans, a hair dryer, a coffee maker, direct-dial telephone, a bathtub/shower, and a balcony.

Standard rooms were configured with either a king-size bed or two twin beds in the Island and Ocean View categories, while the Pool Views had two double beds. The six Penthouse Suites, which all offered ocean views, contained all the features listed for the standard rooms plus added comforts. They were built on two levels, featuring a living room with a bar area on the third floor of the hotel and a bedroom accessed by an internal stairway on the fourth floor. These suites also had a bathroom containing a Jacuzzi, shower stall, double vanity basins, and a skylight.

Note: Certain data have been disguised.

EXHIBIT 2: Pool View of the Accra Beach Hotel

The 13 Junior Suites were fitted with a double bed or two twin beds, plus a living room area with a sofa that converted into another bed.

Hotel Performance

The Accra Beach enjoyed a relatively high occupancy rate, with the highest occupancy rates achieved from January through March and the lowest generally during the summer (Exhibit 3). Their average rate followed a similar pattern, with the highest room rates ($150–$170) achieved from December through March but relatively low rates ($120) during the summer months (Exhibit 4). The hotel's RevPAR (revenue per available room—a product of the occupancy rate times the average room rate) showed even more variation, with RevPARs exceeding $140 from January through March but falling to less than $100 from June through October (Exhibit 5). The rates on the Penthouse suites ranged from $310 to $395, while those on the Junior Suites ranged from $195 to $235. Guests had to pay Barbados Value-Added Tax (VAT) of 7.5 percent on room charges and 15 percent on meals.

The hotel has traditionally promoted itself as a resort destination, but in the last few years, it has been promoting its convenient location and has attracted many business customers. Cherita works extensively with tour operators and corporate travel managers. The majority of hotel guests were corporate clients from companies such as Barbados Cable & Wireless and the Caribbean International Banking Corporation (Exhibit 6). The composition of hotel guests had changed drastically over the past few years. Traditionally, the hotel's clientele had been dominated by tourists from the UK and Canada, but during the past few years, the percentage of corporate customers had increased dramatically. The majority of corporate customers come for business meetings with local companies.

Sometimes, guests who were on vacation (particularly during the winter months) felt uncomfortable finding themselves surrounded by businesspeople. As one vacationer put it, "There's just something weird about being on vacation and going to the beach and then seeing suit-clad businesspeople chatting on their cell phones." However, the hotel achieved a higher average room rate from business guests than

EXHIBIT 3: Accra Beach Hotel: Monthly Occupancy Rate

Year	Month	Occupancy (%)
2 Years Ago	January	87.7
2 Years Ago	February	94.1
2 Years Ago	March	91.9
2 Years Ago	April	78.7
2 Years Ago	May	76.7
2 Years Ago	June	70.7
2 Years Ago	July	82.0
2 Years Ago	August	84.9
2 Years Ago	September	64.7
2 Years Ago	October	82.0
2 Years Ago	November	83.8
2 Years Ago	December	66.1
Last Year	January	87.6
Last Year	February	88.8
Last Year	March	90.3
Last Year	April	82.0
Last Year	May	74.7
Last Year	June	69.1
Last Year	July	76.7
Last Year	August	70.5
Last Year	September	64.7
Last Year	October	71.3
Last Year	November	81.7
Last Year	December	72.1

vacationers and had found the volume of corporate business much more stable than that from tour operators and individual guests.

The West Indies Cricket Board

Cherita Howard, the hotel's sales manager, had been approached by the West Indies Cricket Board (WICB) about the possibility of the Accra Beach Hotel serving as the host hotel for next spring's West Indies Cricket Home Series, an important international sporting event among cricket-loving nations. The location of this event rotated among several different Caribbean nations and Barbados would be hosting the next one, which would feature visiting teams from India and New Zealand.

Cherita and Jon Martineau, general manager of the hotel, both thought the marketing exposure associated with hosting the teams would be very beneficial for the hotel but were concerned about accepting the business because they knew from past experience that many of the desired dates were usually very busy days for the hotel. They were sure the rate that the WICB was willing to pay would be lower than the average rate of $140–$150 they normally received during these times. In contrast to regular guests, who could usually be counted on to have a number of meals at the hotel, team members and officials would probably be less likely to dine at the hotel because they would be on a per diem budget. On average, both corporate customers and vacationers spend about $8 per person for breakfast and about $25 per person for dinner (per person including VAT). The contribution margin on food and beverage is approximately 30 percent. About 80 percent of all guests have breakfast at the hotel and approximately 30 percent of all guests dine at the hotel (there are many other attractive restaurant options nearby). Martineau thought only about 25 percent of the cricket group would have breakfast at the hotel and maybe only about 10 percent would dine at the hotel. Also, they worried about how the hotel's other guests might react to the presence of the cricket teams. Still, the marketing potential

EXHIBIT 4: Accra Beach Hotel: Average Daily Room Rate

Year	Month	Average Room Rate (U.S.$)
2 Years Ago	January	159.05
2 Years Ago	February	153.73
2 Years Ago	March	157.00
2 Years Ago	April	153.70
2 Years Ago	May	144.00
2 Years Ago	June	136.69
2 Years Ago	July	122.13
2 Years Ago	August	121.03
2 Years Ago	September	123.45
2 Years Ago	October	129.03
2 Years Ago	November	141.03
2 Years Ago	December	152.87
Last Year	January	162.04
Last Year	February	167.50
Last Year	March	158.44
Last Year	April	150.15
Last Year	May	141.79
Last Year	June	136.46
Last Year	July	128.49
Last Year	August	128.49
Last Year	September	127.11
Last Year	October	132.76
Last Year	November	141.86
Last Year	December	151.59

Note: Average room rate is inclusive of VAT.

for the hotel was substantial. The WICB had promised to list the Accra Beach as the host hotel in all promotional materials and during the televised matches.

The West Indies Home Series was divided into three parts, and each would require bookings at the Accra Beach Hotel. The first part pitted the West Indies team against the Indian team and would run from April 24 to May 7. The second part featured the same two teams and would run from May 27 to May 30. The final part showcased the West Indies team against the New Zealand team and would run from June 17 to June 26.

The WICB wanted 50 rooms (including two suites at no additional cost) for the duration of each part and was willing to pay $130 per night per room. Both breakfast and VAT were to be included, and each team had to be housed on a single floor of the hotel. In addition, the WICB insisted that laundry service for team uniforms (cricket teams typically wear all-white clothing) and practice gear be provided at no additional charge for all team members. Cherita estimates that it will cost the hotel about $20 per day if they can do the laundry in-house, but about $200 per day if they have to send it to an outside source.

Cherita called Ferne Armstrong, the reservations manager of the hotel, and asked her what she thought. Like Cherita, Ferne was concerned about the possible displacement of higher-paying customers, but offered to do further investigation into the expected room sales and associated room rates for the desired dates. Since the dates were more than six months in the future, Ferne had not yet developed forecasts. But she was able to provide data on room sales and average room rates from the same days of the previous year (Exhibit 7).

Soon after Cherita returned to her office to analyze the data, she was interrupted by a phone call from the head of the WICB wanting to know the status of his request. She promised to have an answer for him before the end of the day. As soon as she hung up, Martineau called and chatted about the huge marketing potential of being the host hotel.

Cherita shook her head and wondered, "What should I do?"

EXHIBIT 5: Accra Beach Hotel: Revenue per Available Room (RevPAR)

Year	Month	Revenue per Available Room (in U.S.$)
2 Years Ago	January	139.49
2 Years Ago	February	144.66
2 Years Ago	March	144.28
2 Years Ago	April	120.96
2 Years Ago	May	110.45
2 Years Ago	June	96.64
2 Years Ago	July	100.15
2 Years Ago	August	102.75
2 Years Ago	September	79.87
2 Years Ago	October	105.80
2 Years Ago	November	118.18
2 Years Ago	December	101.05
Last Year	January	141.90
Last Year	February	148.67
Last Year	March	143.02
Last Year	April	123.12
Last Year	May	105.87
Last Year	June	94.23
Last Year	July	98.55
Last Year	August	90.59
Last Year	September	82.24
Last Year	October	94.62
Last Year	November	115.89
Last Year	December	109.24

Note: RevPAR refers to revenue per available room and is computed by multiplying the room occupancy rate (see Exhibit 1) with the average room rate (Exhibit 2). Revenue per available room is inclusive of VAT.

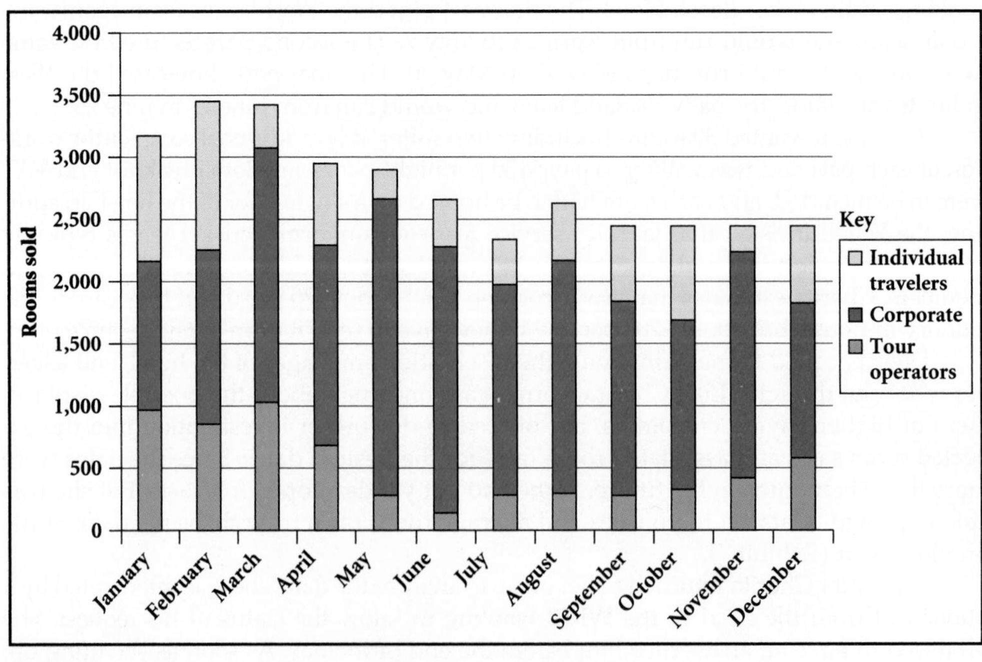

EXHIBIT 6: Market Segments as per Last Year

EXHIBIT 7: Room Sales and Average Daily Room Rates for Same Periods in Previous Year

Date of WICB Home Series	Rooms Sold in Last Year during the Same Period	Average Daily Room Rate (ADR) in U.S.$
Part 1		
4/24	141	129
4/25	138	120
4/26	135	128
4/27	134	135
4/28	123	133
4/29	128	124
4/30	141	119
5/1	141	124
5/2	141	121
5/3	139	122
5/4	112	118
5/5	78	126
5/6	95	130
5/7	113	138
Part II		
5/27	99	131
5/28	114	132
5/29	114	136
5/30	125	136
Part III		
6/17	124	125
6/18	119	122
6/19	112	126
6/20	119	111
6/21	125	110
6/22	116	105
6/23	130	106
6/24	141	101
6/25	141	110
6/26	125	115

Note: ADR excludes VAT.

Study Questions

1. What factors lead to variations in demand for rooms at a hotel such as the Accra Beach?
2. Indentify the various market segments currently served by the hotel. What are the pros and cons of seeking to serve customers from several segments?
3. What are the key considerations facing the hotel as it reviews the booking requests from the West Indies Cricket Board[2]?
4. What action should Cherita Howard take and why?

[2] For simplification of calculations, assume that each room will hold only one occupant, that is, 50 rooms equate to 50 cricket players.

CASE 8 Revenue Management of Gondolas: Maintaining the Balance Between Tradition and Revenue

Sheryl E. Kimes

A ride on a gondola, one of the historical black boats of Venice, is considered by many part of the quintessential Venice experience. However, while demand for gondolas is extremely high, the number of boats has dropped from several thousand gondolas in the eighteenth century to about 400 today. In addition, there is pressure to maintain some of the traditions associated with the gondolas, so increasing revenue is tricky. The question now is how can a balance between tradition and revenue be maintained?

Although Venice is considered one of the most beautiful and romantic cities in the world, modern Venice has faced many challenges, including a loss of population to other parts of Italy and physical damage from flooding, pollution, and age. The basis of the Venetian economy is tourism, and the beauty of the architecture and canals and the many art and cultural attractions draw 20 million visitors per year from around the world.

Venice is set on over 100 islands interconnected by about 150 canals. All transportation within the city is either by boat or on foot. A ride on a gondola, one of the historical black boats of Venice, is considered by many part of the quintessential Venice experience. Although the demand for gondola rides is extremely high, the number of boats has dropped from several thousand gondolas in the eighteenth century to about 400 today. Gondolas are regulated by the City of Venice and there is a strong desire to maintain their tradition; but at the same time, the economic impact on the city and its population is considerable. The question is how to best balance the maintenance of tradition with the economic impact on the gondolier and the city.

Tourism in Venice

Venice receives over 20 million tourists per year of which less than half (8.7 million) spend the night. About 80 percent of the tourists come from outside of Italy. Venice has one of the highest ratios of tourists to local residents (89 visitors for every 100 Venetians—the highest in Europe). During busy periods (the summer, over Christmas, and during Carnivale), more than 40,000 people per day enter the city. Since 2004, there has been a 30 percent increase in the number of overnight stays. Americans represent the largest proportion of overnight tourists. The number of Japanese tourists dropped by 7 percent in 2006; but the number of Russians increased by 31 percent; Spanish by 18 percent, and French by 11 percent.

The Gondola

The first mention of the gondola was in 1094, but gondolas became popular during the fifteenth century and helped people better maneuver around the canals of Venice. Gondolas are designed to navigate the shallow, narrow canals of Venice and are strictly bound by tradition. The gondolas are 36 feet (11 m) long, 4.5 feet (1.4 m) wide, and weigh about 1102 pounds (500 kg). The left side is higher than the right side by 9.45 inches (24 cm) and the bottoms are flat so that they can function in the very shallow water (sometimes much less than a meter deep). The gondolas are constructed of 280 pieces of eight different types of wood and only have metal in the head and stem of the boat. Gondolas traditionally are black and take about 3–6 months to build at a cost of approximately 20,000 to 30,000 Euros.

EXHIBIT 1: Gondolas Moored at San Marco, Venice

Gondoliers. Gondolas are owned and steered by gondoliers. Their numbers have dropped from several thousand in the eighteenth century to only 425 today. Gondoliers are usually male and must be born in Venice. Traditionally, being a gondolier was passed from one generation to the next, but in recent years, this has changed because many young people have decided to take more lucrative and less physically demanding jobs. To become a gondolier, potential applicants take a test that measures their boat-handling skills, their language ability, their knowledge of the city, and their ability to work with tourists.

Gondoliers are divided into 10 traghetti (or ferry stations). Each traghetto elects representatives (called barcali) who represent the traghetto to the government. Gondola rides are available at about eight stazi (ferry stations) throughout the city.

EXHIBIT 2: Venetian Gondolier Dressed in Traditional Outfit

The Role of Gondolas in Tourism

Gondolas were once the primary source of transportation in Venice, but with the advent of faster and less expensive motorboats and vaporetti (a form of water-based bus), they have become more of a tourist activity than a source of transportation.[1] During the 1920s, it was thought that gondolas would disappear, and a lively debate ensued with even Mussolini chiming in that the gondola tradition needed to be preserved. Even by the late nineteenth century, Mark Twain had commented that gondolas were little more than an anachronism.

As mass tourism increased, the design and operation of gondolas were altered in order to be able to accommodate more tourists and generate additional revenue. The boats were lengthened and narrowed, and a more elaborate oar link was developed so that the gondola could be steered by one oarsman. These modifications, along with a few other design changes, provided more space for passengers. In addition, as the amount of motorized boat traffic has increased, it has become more difficult to safely maneuver the gondolas through the narrow canals.

Pricing and Distribution. By 1930, tour guides such as Baedeker's listed gondola prices by the hour and by the trip, and by 1945, the gondola trips were based more on the experience rather than actual transportation to a destination.

Since World War II, the tourist demand for gondola rides has been extremely high, and the posted rates have increased accordingly. Whereas the posted rate was $0.42 for 50 minutes in 1930; it reached $1.00 by 1945, $5.00 by 1965; and had climbed to $70 by 1999.

The price of gondola rides is regulated by the city. Day rates are 80 Euros for 40 minutes for a maximum of six passengers, while night rates (7 p.m.–8 a.m.) are 20 Euros higher. Although the rates are regulated, they are not always followed, and many prices are set through negotiation. Due to the popularity of gondola rides, it is quite possible to share the gondola with strangers.

Gondolas typically are booked in one of three ways: either directly with the gondolier, through a hotel, or through a third-party travel agency. Hotels and travel agencies often package the gondola ride with other services, such as a dinner or music, and take a sizable commission.

About 80 percent of gondola business comes from tour operators. Typically, tour operators either package the gondola ride with other travel options such as hotel rooms, bus tours, and transfers or sell them separately. In the former case, customers do not even know the cost of the gondola ride because it is included in the package price.

Even when customers can see the price, it generally is on a per person basis, so the price does not seem exorbitant. That being said, the rates are based on six people per gondola. Given that tour operator rates range from 35 Euros to over 70 Euros per person, the revenue associated with one 50-minute gondola ride is substantial. The tour operator passes along some of this revenue to the stazi who in turn distribute it to the gondolas, but still is able to maintain a very good profit margin even after covering costs.

The gondoliers seem to like working with the tour operators because of the guaranteed and steady stream of business. In addition, much of the tour operator business arrives en masse which makes it easier and more efficient to fill and dispatch gondolas. Still, the tour operator profit margin is high and there may be opportunities for the stazi to increase revenue.

Carovane (caravans) of multiple gondolas (sometimes up to 30) often are used to keep groups together and to increase efficiency. Sometimes an accordionist and singer are provided for the entire carovana (at a cost of about 150 Euros). Sending out a large carovana requires a great deal of coordination because of the need to quickly load and unload customers. Gondolas are not the most stable of boats for customers to board, and retired gondoliers are assigned to assist with loading and unloading.

---

[1]Much of the discussion on the next two pages is taken from Robert C. Davis and Garry R. Marvin, 2004, *Venice: The Tourist Maze.* Berkeley, CA: University of California Press.

The carovane follow a set route and can easily return to the dock within 50 minutes for the next group of passengers. Each of the stazi has different routes that are designed to ensure a smooth flow and to avoid traffic tie-ups with vaparettos and other commercial boats.

Demand and Revenue. Firm statistics on the number of gondola rides do not exist, but it is estimated that about one-quarter of all tourists take a gondola ride. In 2004, it was estimated that there were at least 3 million gondola rides. Even with a rate of $20 per person, this is a sizable business.

Gondolas generate income for not only the gondoliers, the ganzeri (usually retired gondoliers who help with the boats) and the group leaders of the stazi but also for the boat construction trade (including the boatyard, the oar markers, the smiths, and the gilders), but also provide jobs and revenue for hat makers and tailors (who supply the traditional gondolier uniform) and generate a sizable amount of souvenir sales.

The Dilemma

Although the demand for gondola rides is extremely high, capacity issues seem to be constraining the number of rides that can be offered. This, combined with the pressure to maintain some of the tradition associated with the gondolas, makes increasing revenue tricky. Still, the revenue provided by the gondola industry is substantial and plays an important role in the Venice economy. How should they proceed?

Interesting Websites on Gondolas

http://www.gondolaonline.org/03.html

http://www.gondolavenezia.it/history_tariffe.asp?Pag=43

http://www.venicewelcome.com/servizi/tour-ing/venicewalktours.htm

http://researchnews.osu.edu/archive/venice.htm

Study Questions

1. What can be done to increase the capacity of gondolas? What revenue impact would this have?
2. How can you balance revenue maximization with the maintenance of cultural heritage? Is it possible? If so, what would you recommend?
3. Consider the pricing structure of the gondolas. What sort of changes would you recommend? How would customers react? What revenue impact would your recommendations have?

CASE 9 Aussie Pooch Mobile

CHRISTOPHER LOVELOCK AND LORELLE FRAZER

After creating a mobile service that washes dogs outside their owners' homes, a young entrepreneur has successfully franchised the concept. Her firm now has more than 100 franchises in many parts of Australia, as well as a few in other countries. She and her management team are debating how best to plan future expansion.

Elaine and Paul Beal drew up in their 4 × 4 outside 22 Ferndale Avenue, towing a bright blue trailer with red and white lettering. As Aussie Pooch Mobile franchisees whose territory covered four suburbs of Brisbane, Australia, they were having a busy day. It was only 1:00 p.m., and they had already washed and groomed 16 dogs at 12 different houses. Now they were at their last appointment—a 'pooch party' of ten dogs at number 22, where five other residents of the street had arranged to have their dogs washed on a biweekly basis.

Prior to their arrival outside the house, there had been ferocious growling and snarling from a fierce-looking Rottweiler. But when the animal caught sight of the brightly colored trailer, he and two other dogs in the yard bounded forward eagerly to the chain link fence, in a flurry of barking and wagging tails.

Throughout residential areas of Brisbane and in a number of other Australian cities, dogs of all shapes and sizes were being washed and groomed by Aussie Pooch Mobile franchisees. By early 2002, the company had grown to over 100 franchisees and claimed to be "Australia's largest mobile dog wash and care company." A key issue facing its managing director, Christine Taylor, and members of the management team was how to plan and shape future expansion.

Compound

Located in Burpengary, Queensland, just north of Brisbane, Aussie Pooch Mobile Pty. Ltd. (APM) was founded in 1991 by Christine Taylor, then aged 22. Taylor had learned customer service early, working in her parents' bait and tackle shop from the age of 8. Growing up in an environment with dogs and horses as pets, she knew she wanted to work with animals and learned dog grooming skills from working in a local salon. At 16, Chris left school and began her own grooming business on a part-time basis, using a bathtub in the family garage. Since she was still too young to drive, her parents would take her to pick up the dogs from their owners. She washed and groomed the animals at home and then returned them.

Once Taylor had learned to drive and bought her own car, she decided to take her service to the customers. So she went mobile, creating a trailer in which the dogs could be washed outside their owners' homes and naming the fledgling venture "The Aussie Pooch Mobile." Soon, it became a full-time job. Eventually, she found she had more business than she could handle alone, so she hired assistants. The next step was to add a second trailer. Newly married, she and her husband, David McNamara, ploughed their profits into the purchase of additional trailers and gradually expanded until they had six mobile units.

The idea of franchising came to Taylor when she found herself physically constrained by a difficult pregnancy: "David would go bike riding or head to the coast and have fun with the jet ski and I was stuck at home and felt like I was going nuts, because I'm a really active person. I was hungry for information on how to expand the business, so I started researching other companies and reading heaps of books and came up with franchising as the best way to go, since it would provide capital and also allow a dedicated group of small business people to help expand the business further."

As existing units were converted from employees to franchisee operations, Taylor noticed that they quickly became about 20 percent more profitable. Initially, APM focused on Brisbane and the surrounding region of southeast Queensland. Subsequently, it expanded into New South Wales and South Australia in 1995, into Canberra, Australian Capital Territory (ACT), in 1999, and into Victoria in 2000 (Exhibit 1). Expansion into

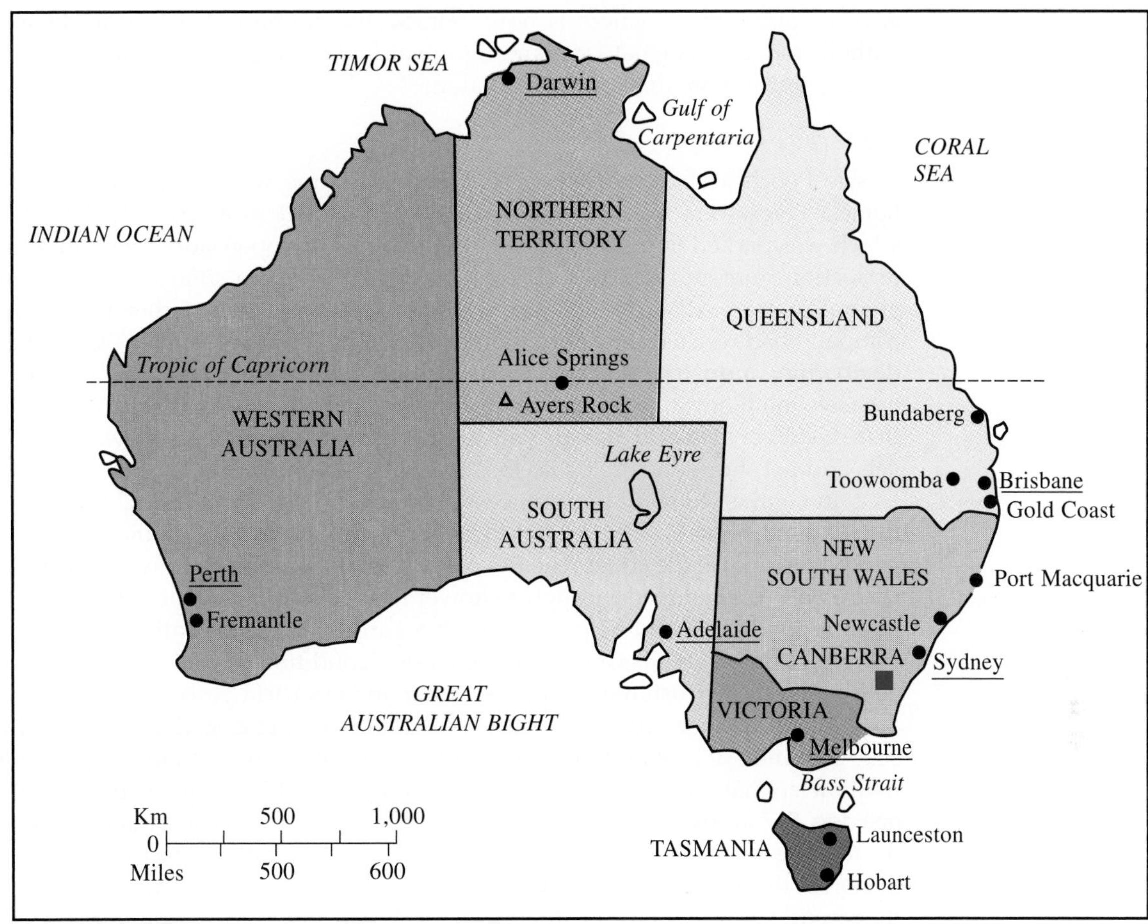

EXHIBIT 1: Map of Australia

Western Australia was expected in mid-2002. In 1996, a New Zealand division of the firm was launched in Tauranga, a small city 200 km southeast of Auckland, under the name Kiwi Pooch Mobile. In 2001, Aussie Pooch Mobile launched into the United Kingdom, beginning with a town in northern England. Soon, there were four operators under a master franchisee. The following year saw the official launch of The Pooch Mobile Malaysia, also under a master franchisee.

By early 2002, the company had 125 mobile units in Australia, of which 55 were located in Queensland, 42 in New South Wales, eight in ACT, 12 in South Australia, and eight in Victoria. In addition, representatives operated another six company-owned units. The company bathed more than 20,000 dogs each month and had an annual turnover of approximately $3 million.[1] APM was a member of the Franchise Council of Australia and complied with the Franchising Code of Conduct. The management team consisted of Chris Taylor as managing director and David McNamara as director responsible for overseeing trailer design and systems support. Each state had its own manager and training team. The central support office also housed staff who provided further assistance to managers and franchisees.

Expansion had benefitted from the leverage provided by several master franchisees, who had obtained the rights to work a large territory and sell franchises within it. Said Taylor: "I look at the business as if it's my first child. I see it now starting to get into those early teens where it wants to go alone, but it still needs me to hold its hand a little bit, whereas initially it needed me there the whole time. With the support staff we

[1]Financial data are in Australian dollars. Exchange rates at the time of publication were: A$1.00 = US$0.57 = €0.58.

have in place, the business is now gaining the support structure it needs to work without me. This is what I am aiming towards. I appreciate that a team of people can achieve much more than one person alone."

The Service Concept

Aussie Pooch Mobile specialized in bringing its dog washing services to customers' homes. Dogs were washed in a hydrobath installed in a specially-designed trailer, which was parked in the street. The trailer had partly open sides and a roof to provide protection from sun and rain (Exhibit 2). Apart from flea control products and a few grooming aids, APM did not attempt to sell dog food and other pet supplies. The company had resisted the temptation to diversify into other fields. "Our niche is in the dog bathing industry," declared Chris Taylor: "I don't want us to be a jack of all trades because you'll never be good at anything. We now have an exclusive range of products that customer demand has driven us to providing, but we still work closely with vets and pet shops and are by no means a pet shop on wheels."

In contrast to retail pet service stores, where customers brought their animals to the store or kennel, APM brought the service to customers' homes, with the trailer parked outside on the street. The use of hydrobath equipment, in which warm, pressurized water was pumped through a shower head, enabled operators to clean dogs more thoroughly than would be possible with a garden hose. The bath was designed to rid the dog of fleas and ticks and improve its skin condition as well as to clean its coat and eliminate smells. Customers supplied water and electrical power.

The fee paid by customers varied from $15–$30 per dog, depending on breed and size, condition of coat and skin, behaviour, and geographic location, with discounts for multiple animals at the same address. On average, regular customers paid a fee of $25 for one dog, $47 for two, and $66 for three. At "pooch parties," a concept developed at APM, the homeowner acting as host typically received one complimentary dogwash at the discretion of the operator. Additional services, for which an extra fee was charged, included the recently introduced aromatherapy bath ($2.50) and blow drying of the animal's coat for $5–$10 (on average, $8). Blow drying was especially recommended in cool weather to prevent the animal from getting cold. Operators also offered free advice to customers

EXHIBIT 2: The Aussie Pooch Mobile Trailer

about their dogs' diet and health care, including such issues as ticks and skin problems. They encouraged customers to have their dogs bathed on a regular basis. The most commonly scheduled frequencies were once every two or four weeks.

A Satisfied User

The process of bathing a dog involved a sequence of carefully coordinated actions, as exemplified by Elaine Beal's treatment of Zak, the Rottweiler. "Hello my darling, who's a good boy?" crooned Elaine as she patted the enthusiastic dog, placed him on a leash, and led him out through the gate to the footpath on this warm, sunny day. Paul busied himself connecting hoses and electrical cords to the house, while Elaine began back-combing Zak's coat in order to set it up for the water to get underneath. She then led the now placid dog to the hydrobath inside the trailer, where he sat patiently while she removed his leash and clipped him to a special collar in the bath for security. Meanwhile the water had been heating to the desired temperature.

Over the next few minutes, Elaine bathed the dog, applied a medicated herbal shampoo to his coat, and rinsed him thoroughly with the pressure driven hose (Exhibit 3). After releasing Zak from the special collar and reattaching his leash, she led him out of the hydrobath and onto the footpath, where she wrapped him in a chamois cloth and dried him. Next, she cleaned the dog's ears and eyes with disposable baby wipes, all the time continuing to talk soothingly to him. She checked his coat and skin to ensure there were no ticks or skin problems, gave his nails a quick clip, and sprayed a herbal conditioner and deodorizer onto Zak's now gleaming coat and brushed it in. Returning Zak to the yard and removing the leash, Elaine patted him and gave him a large biscuit, specially formulated to protect the animal's teeth.

EXHIBIT 3: A Labrador Retriever Receives a Bath in a Aussie Pooch Mobile Hydrobath

The Australian Market

Australia's population of 19.3 million in 2001 was small in relation to the country's vast land area of 7.7 million km^2 (almost three million square miles). By contrast, the United States had a population 15 times that of Australia on a land area, including Alaska and Hawaii, of 9.2 million km^2. A federal nation, Australia was divided into six states—New South Wales (NSW), Victoria, Queensland, South Australia, Western Australia, and the island of Tasmania—plus two territories: the large but thinly populated Northern Territory and the small Australian Capital Territory (ACT) which contained the federal capital, Canberra, and its suburbs and was an enclave within NSW. The average annual earnings for employed persons was $35,000.

With much of the interior of the continent uninhabitable and many other areas inhospitable to permanent settlement, most of the Australian population was concentrated in a narrow coastal band running clockwise from Brisbane on the southeast coast through Sydney and Melbourne to Adelaide, the capital of South Australia. Some 2,700 km (1,600 miles) to the west lay Perth, known as the most isolated city in the world. A breakdown of the population by state and territory is shown in Exhibit 4. The northern half of the country was in the tropics, Brisbane and Perth enjoyed a subtropical climate, and the remaining major cities had a temperate climate (Exhibit 5). Melbourne was known for its sharp fluctuations in temperature.

There were about four million domestic dogs in the country and approximately 42 percent of the nation's 7.4 million households owned at least one. Ownership rates were slightly above average in Tasmania, the Northern Territory, and Queensland and somewhat below average in Victoria and the ACT. In 1995, it was estimated that

EXHIBIT 4: Population of Australia by State and Territory, June 2001

State/Territory	Population (000)
New South Wales	6,533
Victoria	4,829
Queensland	3,628
South Australia	1,502
Western Australia	1,910
Tasmania	470
Australian Capital Territory	314
Northern Territory	198
Australia Total	*19,387*

Source: Australian Bureau of Statistics 2001.

Australians spent an estimated $1.3 billion on dog-related goods and services, of which 46 percent went to dog food, 22 percent to veterinary services, 12 percent to dog products and equipment, and 11 percent to other services, including washing and grooming (Exhibit 6).

Franchising in Australia

By the beginning of the twenty-first century, the Australian franchising sector had reached a stage of early maturity. McDonald's, KFC, and Pizza Hut opened their first outlets in Australia in the 1970s. These imported systems were followed by many home-grown business format franchises such as Just Cuts (hairdressing), Snap Printing, Eagle Boys Pizza, and VIP Home Services, all of which grew into large domestic systems and then expanded internationally, principally to New Zealand and Southeast Asia.

In 2002, Australia boasted approximately 700 business format franchise systems holding over 50,000 outlets. Although the United States had many more systems and outlets, Australia had more franchisors per capita, reflecting the relative ease of entry into franchising in this country. Most of the growth in franchising had occurred in business format franchising as opposed to product franchising. Business format franchises provided franchisees with a full business system and the rights to operate under the franchisor's brand name, whereas product franchises merely allowed independent operators to supply a manufacturer's product, such as car dealerships or soft-drink bottlers. Typically, franchisees were required to pay an upfront franchise fee (averaging $30,000 in service industries and $40,000 in retailing) for the right to operate under the franchise system within a defined geographic area. This initial fee was included in the total start-up cost of the business (ranging from around $60,000 in the service sector to more than $200,000 in the retail industry). In addition, franchisees paid a royalty on all

EXHIBIT 5: Average Temperatures for Principal Australian Cities (in Degrees Celsius)*

	July (Winter)		January (Summer)	
	High	Low	High	Low
Adelaide, SA	14.9	6.9	27.9	15.7
Brisbane, Qld	20.6	9.5	29.1	20.9
Cariberra, ACT	11.5	0.0	28.5	13.6
Darwin, NT	30.7	19.7	32.4	25.2
Hobart, Tas	12.3	4.0	22.3	11.9
Melbourne, Vic	12.9	5.2	26.0	13.5
Perth, WA	17.7	8.1	31.5	16.9
Sydney, NSW	16.9	6.9	26.3	18.6

Source: Australian Bureau of Meteorology, www.bom.gov.au.

*Celsius to Fahrenheit Conversion: 0°C = 32°F, 10°C = 50°F, 20°C = 68°F, 30°C = 86°F.

EXHIBIT 6: Distribution of Consumer Expenditures on Dog-Related Goods and Services, 1995

Product/Service	Allocation
Dog food	46%
Vet charges	21%
Dog products	10%
Dog equipment	2%
Dog services	11%
Pet purchases	5%
Other expenses	4%
Total dog-related expenditures	*$1.3 billion*

Source: BIS Shrapnell Survey 1995.

sales and an ongoing contribution toward advertising and promotional activities designed to build brand awareness and preference. Would-be franchisees who lacked sufficient capital might be able to obtain bank financing against personal assets such as property or an acceptable guarantor.

Franchising Trends

The rapid growth of franchising had been stimulated in part by demographic trends, including the increase in dual-income families, which had led to greater demand for outsourcing of household services such as lawn mowing, house cleaning, and pet grooming. Some franchise systems offered multiple concepts under a single corporate brand name. For instance, VIP Home Services had separate franchises available in lawn mowing, cleaning, car washing, and rubbish removal. Additional growth came from conversion of existing individual businesses to a franchise format. For instance, Eagle Boys Pizza had often approached local pizza operators and offered them the opportunity to join this franchise. Almost half the franchise systems in Australia were in retail trade (32 percent nonfood and 14 percent food). Another large and growing industry was the property and business services sector (20 percent), as shown in Exhibit 7. Most franchisees were former white-collar workers or blue-collar supervisors who craved independence and a lifestyle change.

EXHIBIT 7: Distribution of Franchise Systems in Australia by Industry, 1999

Industry	Percentage
Retail trade—non-food	31
Property and business services	20
Retail trade—food	14
Personal and other services	7
Construction and trade services	6
Accommodation, cafes and restaurants	4
Education	4
Cultural and recreation services	4
Unclassified	3
Manufacturing and printing	3
Finance and insurance	2
Transport and storage	1
Communication services	1
Total—all industries	*100%*

Source: Lorelle Frazer and Colin McCosker, *Franchising Australia 1999*, Franchise Council of Australia/University of Southern Queensland, Toowoomba, 1999, p. 39.

Over the years, Australia's franchising sector had experienced a myriad of regulatory regimes. Finally in 1998, in response to perceived problems in many franchising systems, the federal government introduced a mandatory Franchising Code of Conduct, administered under the Trade Practices Act. Among other things, the Code required that potential franchisees be given full disclosure about the franchisor's background and operations prior to signing a franchise agreement. In contrast, the franchising sector in the United States faced a patchwork of regulations that varied from one state to another. Yet in the United Kingdom, there were no specific franchising regulations beyond those applying to all corporations operating in designated industries.

Master franchising arrangements had become common in Australian franchise systems. Under master franchising, a local entrepreneur was awarded the rights to subfranchise the system within a specific geographic area, such as an entire state. Because of Australia's vast geographic size, it was difficult for a franchisor to monitor franchisees who were located far from the head office. The solution was to delegate to master franchisees many of the tasks normally handled by the franchisor itself, making them responsible for recruiting, selecting, training, and monitoring franchisees in their territories as well as overseeing marketing and operations.

Not all franchisees proved successful and individual outlets periodically failed. The main reasons for failure appeared to be poor choice of location or territory and a franchisee's own shortcomings. In addition to the obvious technical skills required in a given field, success often hinged on possession of sales and communication abilities. Disputes in franchising were not uncommon, but could usually be resolved internally without recourse to legal action. The causes of conflict most frequently cited by franchisees related to franchise fees and alleged misrepresentations made by the franchisor. By contrast, franchisors cited conflicts based on lack of adherence to the system by franchisees.

Australia was home to a number of internationally known franchise operators, including Hertz Rent-a-Car, Avis, McDonald's, KFC, Pizza Hut, Subway, Kwik Kopy and Snap-on Tools. By contrast, most Burger King outlets operated under the name Hungry Jack's, an acquired Australian chain with significant brand equity.

Jim's Group

One of Australia's best known locally developed franchisors was Melbourne-based Jim's Group, which described itself as one of the world's largest home service franchise organizations. The company had originated with a mowing service started by Jim Penman in Melbourne in 1982 when he abandoned ideas of an academic career after his PhD thesis was rejected. In 1989, Penman began franchising the service, now known as Jim's Mowing, as a way to facilitate expansion. The business grew rapidly, using master franchisees in different regions to recruit and manage individual franchisees. The company's dark green trucks, displaying a larger-than-life logo of Penman himself, bearded and wearing a hat, soon became a familiar sight on suburban streets around Melbourne. Before long, the franchise expanded to other parts of Victoria and then to other states.

Over the following years, an array of other home-related services were launched under the Jim's brand, including Jim's Trees, Jim's Paving, Jim's Cleaning, Jim's Appliance Repair, and Jim's Floors. Each service featured the well-recognized logo of Jim Penman's face on a different colored background. Jim's Dogwash made its debut in 1996, employing a bright red, fully enclosed trailer emblazoned by a logo that had been amended to show Jim with a dog. By early 2002, Jim's Group comprised more than two dozen different service divisions, over 90 master franchisees, and some 1,900 individual franchisees. In many instances, master franchisees were responsible for two or more different service divisions within their regions. Jim's Group's philosophy was to price franchises according to local market conditions. If work in a prospective territory were easy to find but franchisees hard to attract, the price might be lowered somewhat, but not too much; otherwise, the company felt there would be insufficient commitment.

In recent years, Jim's Group had expanded overseas. In New Zealand, it had six master franchisees and 232 franchisees and offered mowing, tree work, cleaning, and dog washing services. It had also established a significant presence for Jim's Mowing in the Canadian province of British Columbia. But attempts to launch Jim's Mowing in the United States had failed due to difficulty in finding good operators.

Jim's Dogwash had over 60 franchises operating in Australia (primarily in Victoria) and New Zealand. This firm's experience had shown that growth was hampered by the shortage of suitable franchisees, since operators needed to be dog lovers with a background in dog care.

Franchising Strategy at Aussie Pooch Mobile

New APM franchisees were recruited through newspaper advertisements and "advertorials" as well as by word of mouth. The concept appealed to individuals who sought to become self-employed but wanted the security of a proven business system rather than striking out entirely on their own. Interested individuals were invited to meet with a representative of the company to learn more. If they wished to proceed further, they had to complete an application form and submit a deposit of $250 to hold a particular area for a maximum of four weeks, during which the applicant could further investigate the characteristics and prospects of the designated territory. This fee was credited to the purchase cost of the franchise if the applicant decided to proceed or returned if the applicant withdrew. A new franchise cost $24,000 (up from $19,500 in 1999). An additional 10 percent had to be added to this fee to pay the recently introduced federal goods and services tax (GST). Exhibit 8 identifies how APM costed out the different elements.

Selection Requirements for Prospective Franchisees

The company had set a minimum educational requirement of passing Year 10 of high school (or equivalent). Taylor noted that successful applicants tended to be outdoors people who shared four characteristics:

"They are self motivated and outgoing. They love dogs, and they want to work for themselves. Obviously, being great with dogs is one part of the business—our franchisees understand that the dog's even an extended member of the customer's family—but it's really important that they can handle the bookwork side of the business as well, because that's basically where your bread and butter is made."

Other desirable characteristics included people skills and patience, plus a good telephone manner. Would-be franchisees also had to have a valid driver's license, access to a vehicle that was capable of towing a trailer, and the ability to do this type of driving in an urban setting. Originally, Taylor had expected that most franchisees would be relatively young, with parents willing to buy their children a franchise and set them up with a job,

EXHIBIT 8: Aussie Pooch Mobile: Breakdown of Franchise Purchase Cost, 2002 vs. 1999

Item	1999		2002	
	$	$	$	$
Initial training		2,200.00		2,200.00
Initial franchise fee		4,021.50		6,173.00
Guaranteed income		5,000.00		N/A
Exclusive territory plus trailer registration		N/A		6,600.00
Fixtures, fittings, stock, insurance etc:				
Aussie Pooch Mobile trailer and hydrobath	4,860.00		5,340.00	
Consumables (shampoo, conditioner, etc.)	160.00		230.00	
Trade equipment and uniforms	920.00		881.65	
Insurance	338.50	6,278.50	575.35	7,027.00
Initial advertising		2,000.00		2,000.00
*Total franchise cost**		*$19,500.00*		*$24,000.00*

*Total franchise costs excludes 10% GST, introduced in July 2000.

but in fact only about half of all franchisees were aged 21–30; 40 percent were aged 31–40 and 10 percent were in their forties or fifties. About 60 percent were female.

Potential franchisees were offered a trial work period with an operator to see if they liked the job and were suited to the business, including not only skills with both animals and people but also sufficient physical fitness.

In return for the franchise fee, successful applicants received the rights to a geographically defined franchise, typically comprising about 12,000 homes. Franchisees also obtained an APM trailer with all necessary products and solutions to service the first 100 dogs, plus red uniform shirts and cap, advertising material, and stationery. The trailer was built to industrial grade standards and its design included many refinements developed by APM in consultation with franchisees to simplify the process of dog washing and enhance the experience for the animal. Operators were required to travel with a mobile phone, which they had to pay for themselves.

In addition to franchised territories, APM had six company-owned outlets. These were operated by representatives who leased the territory and equipment and in return paid APM 25 percent of the gross weekly revenues (including GST). Taylor had no plans to increase the number of representatives. The reps generally were individuals who either could not currently afford the start-up cost or who were evaluated by the company for their suitability as franchisees. Typically, reps either became franchisees within about six months or left the company.

Assisting New Franchisees

The franchisor provided two weeks' pre-opening training for all new franchisees and representatives also spent about 10 hours with each one to help them open their new territories. Training topics included operational and business procedures, effective use of the telephone, hydrobathing techniques, dog grooming techniques, and information on dog health and behavior. Franchisees were given a detailed operations manual containing 104 pages of instructions on running the business in accordance with company standards.

To help new franchisees get started, APM placed advertisements in local newspapers for a period of 20 weeks. It also prepared human interest stories for distribution to these newspapers. Other promotional activities at the time of launch included distributing pamphlets in the territory and writing to local vets and pet shops to inform them of the business. APM guaranteed new franchisees a weekly income of $600 for the first 10 weeks and paid for a package of insurance policies for six months, after which the franchisee became responsible for the coverage.

Fees and Services

Ongoing support by the franchisor included marketing efforts, monthly newsletters, a telephone hotline service for advice, an insurance package, regular (but brief) field - visits, and additional training. If a franchisee fell sick or wished to take a vacation, APM would offer advice on how to best deal with this situation, in many cases organizing a trained person to help out. It also organized periodic meetings for franchisees in the major metropolitan areas at which guest presenters spoke on topics relating to franchise operations. Previous guest speakers included veterinarians, natural therapists, pharmacists, and accountants. More recently, APM had offered one-day seminars, providing more team support and generating greater motivation than the traditional meeting style. In return for these services, franchisees paid a royalty fee of 10 percent of their gross weekly income, plus an advertising levy of an additional 2.5 percent. Income was reported on a weekly basis and fees had to be paid weekly. In addition to these fees, operating costs for a franchisee included carrelated expenses, purchase of consumable products such as shampoo, insurance, telephone, and stationery. Exhibit 9 shows the average weekly costs that a typical franchisee might expect to incur.

Franchisees included several couples, like the Beals, but Taylor believed that having two operators work together was not really efficient, although it could be companionable. Paul Beal, a retired advertising executive, had other interests and did not always accompany Elaine. Some couples split the work, with one operating three days a week and the other three or even four days. All franchisees were required to be

EXHIBIT 9: Average Annual Operating Expenses for an Aussie Pooch Mobile Franchisee, 1999 vs. 2002

Expense	1999 $	2002 $
Consumable products	3,552	2,880
Car registration	430	430
Car insurance	500	500
Fuel	2,400	3,360
Insurances	642	1,151
Repairs and maintenance	1,104	1,104
Phones, stationery, etc.	1,440	1,920
Communication levy	624	624
Franchise royalties	4,416	5,583
Advertising levy	1,104	1,395
Total	*$16,212*	*$18,947*

substantially involved in the hands-on running of the business; some had more than one territory and employed additional operators to help them.

To further support individual franchisees, APM had formed a Franchise Advisory Council, composed of a group of experienced franchisees who had volunteered their time to help other franchisees and the system as a whole. Each franchisee was assigned to a team leader, who was a member of the FAC. The Council facilitated communications between franchisees and the support office, meeting with the managers every three months to discuss different issues within the company.

Marketing and Competition

The company advertised Aussie Pooch Mobile service in the Yellow Pages as well as paying for listings in the White Pages of local phone directories. It promoted a single telephone number nationwide in Australia, staffed by an answering service 24 hours a day, seven days a week. Customers paid only a local call charge of 25 cents to access this number. They could leave their name and telephone number, which would then be electronically sorted and forwarded via alphanumeric pagers to the appropriate franchisee who would then return the call to arrange a convenient appointment time. APM also offered expert advice on local advertising and promotions and made promotional products and advertising templates available to franchisees. Other corporate communications activities included maintaining the website, www.hydrobath.com; distributing public relations releases to the media; and controlling all aspects of corporate identity such as trailer design, business cards, and uniforms.

"I try to hold the reins pretty tightly on advertising matters," said Taylor, noting that the franchise agreement required individual franchisees to submit their plans for promotional activities for corporate approval. She shook her head as she remembered an early disaster, involving an unauthorized campaign by a franchisee who had placed an offer of a free dog wash in a widely distributed coupon book. Unfortunately, this promotion had set no expiration date or geographic restriction, with the result that customers were still presenting the coupon more than a year later across several different franchise territories.

With APM's approval, some franchisees had developed additional promotional ideas. For example, Elaine and Paul Beal wrote informative articles and human interest stories about dogs for their local newspaper. When a client's dog died, Elaine sent a sympathy card and presented the owner with a small tree to plant in memory of the pet.

Developing a Territory

Obtaining new customers and retaining existing ones was an important aspect of each franchisee's work. The brightly colored trailer often attracted questions from passersby and presented a useful opportunity to promote the service. Operators could ask satisfied customers to recommend the service to their friends and neighbors. Encouraging owners to increase the frequency of washing their dogs was another way to build business. Knowing that a dog might become lonely when its owner was absent and was liable to develop behavior problems, Elaine Beal sometimes recommended the acquisition of a "companion pet." As Paul remarked, "Having two dogs is not twice the trouble, it halves the problem!"

However, to maximize profitability, franchisees also had tooperate as efficiently as possible, minimizing time spent in nonrevenue-producing activities such as travel, set up, and socializing. As business grew, some franchisees employed additional operators to handle the excess workload, so that the trailer might be in service extended hours, seven days a week. Eventually, a busy territory might be split, with a portion sold off to a new franchisee.

APM encouraged this practice. The company had found that franchisees reached a comfort zone at about 80 dogs a week and then their business stopped growing because they could not physically wash any more dogs. Franchisees could set their own price when selling all or part of a territory and APM helped them to coordinate the sale. When a territory was split, a franchisee usually was motivated to rebuild the remaining half to its maximum potential.

Competition

Although many dog owners had traditionally washed their animals themselves (or had not even bothered), there was a growing trend toward paying a third party to handle this task. Dog washing services fell into two broad groups. One consisted of fixed-site operations to which dog owners brought their animals for bathing. The location of these businesses included retail sites in suburban shopping areas, kennels, and service providers' own homes or garages. The second type of competition, which had grown in popularity in recent years, consisted of mobile operations that traveled to customers' homes.

With few barriers to entry, there were numerous dog washing services in most major metropolitan areas. Many of these services included the word "hydrobath" in their names. In Brisbane, for example, the Yellow Pages listed 19 mobile suppliers in addition to APM and 26 fixed-site suppliers, a few of which also washed other types of animals (Exhibit 10). The majority of dog washing services in Australia were believed to be standalone operations, but there were other franchisors in addition to Aussie Pooch Mobile. Of these, the most significant appeared to be Jim's Dogwash and Hydrodog.

Jim's Dogwash (part of Melbourne-based Jim's Group) had nine master franchisees and 52 franchises in Australia and four masters and nine franchisees in New Zealand (Exhibit 11). Jim's expansion strategy had been achieved in part by creating smaller territories than APM and pricing them relatively inexpensively, in order to stimulate recruitment of new franchisees. A territory, typically encompassing about 2,000 homes, currently sold for $10,000 (comprising an initial franchise fee of $6,000, $3000 for the trailer, and $1,000 for other equipment) plus 10 percent GST. Jim's fee for washing a dog, including blow drying, ranged from $28 to $38. However, the firm did not offer aromatherapy or anything similar.

Another franchised dog washing operation was Hydrodog, based on the Gold Coast in Queensland with 49 units in Queensland, nine in New South Wales, eight in Western Australia, and one each in Victoria, South Australia, and the Northern Territory. Hydrodog began franchising in 1994. By 2002, a new franchise unit cost $24,950 (including GST), of which $10,800 was accounted for by the initial franchise fee for a 10,000-home territory. In addition to their dog grooming services, which included blowdrying and ranged in price from $15 to $40, Hydrodog franchisees sold dog food products, including dry biscuits and cooked or raw meats (chicken, beef, or kangaroo). They did not offer aromatherapy.

Developing a Strategy for the Future

Managing continued expansion presented an ongoing challenge to the directors of Aussie Pooch Mobile. However, as Chris Taylor pointed out, "You can be the largest but you may not be the best. Our focus is on doing a good job and making our franchisees successful."

EXHIBIT 10: Competing Dog Washing Services in the Greater Brisbane Area, 2002

(A) Services including the word "mobile" in their names

A & Jane's Mobile Dog Wash
A Spotless Dog Mobile Hydrobath
Akleena K9 Mobile Hydrobath
Alan's Mobile Dog and Cat Wash
Fancy Tails Mobile Hydrobath
Fido's Mobile Dog Wash and Clipping
Go-Go's Mobile Pet Parlour
Happy Pets Mobile Hydrobath
Itch-Eeze Mobile Dog Grooming and Hydrobath Service
James' Mobile Pet Grooming and Hydrobath
My Pets Mobile Hydrobath
Paw Prints Mobile Dog Grooming
Preen A Pooch-Mobile
Rainbow Mobile Dog Wash
Redlands Mobile Pet Grooming and Hydrobath
Sallie's Mobile Dogwash
Scrappy Doo's Mobile Hydrobath
Superdog Mobile Hydrobath
Western Suburbs Mobile Dog Bath

(B) Other listings containing the words "bath," "wash," 'hydro," or similar allusions

Aussie Dog Hydrobath
Budget K9 Baths
Conmurra Hydrobaths
Dandy Dog Hydrobath
Dial A Dogwash
Doggy Dunk
Flush-Puppy
Heavenly Hydropet
Helen's Hydrobath
Herbal Dog Wash
Home Hydrobath Service
Hydro-Hound
Jo's Hydrowash
K9 Aquatics
K9 Kleeners
Keep Em Kleen
Maggie's Shampooch
Nome's Turbo Pet Wash
P.R. Turbo Pet Wash
Paws in More Hydrobath and Pet Care Services
Puppy Paws Dog Wash
Splish Splash Hydrobath
Scrubba Dub Dog
Soapy Dog
Super Clean Professional Dog Wash
Tidy Tim's Hydrobath

Source: Yellow Pages Online, March 2002 under "Dog & Cat Clipping & Grooming" (excludes services delivered only to cats).

EXHIBIT 11: Profile of Jim's Group Franchisees

Location	All Master Franchisees	Master Dogwash Franchisees	Individual Dogwash Franchisees
Victoria	41	6	36
New South Wales + ACT	8	1	7
Queensland	13	—	—
Western Australia	13	—	3
South Australia	6	1	4
Tasmania	1	—	—
Northern Territory	1	1	2
Australia	83	9	52
New Zealand	6	4	9
Canada	1	—	—
Grand Total	*90*	*13*	*61*

Source: Jim's Group website, www.jims.net, accessed January 2002.

To facilitate expansion outside its original base of southeast Queensland, APM had appointed a franchise sales manager in Sydney for the New South Wales market and another in Melbourne for both Victoria and South Australia. One question was whether to adopt a formal strategy of appointing master franchisees. Currently, there were master franchises on the Gold Coast (a fast-growing resort and residential area southeast of Brisbane), in the ACT, and in the regional cities of Toowoomba and Bundaberg in Queensland and in Newcastle and Port Macquarie in New South Wales. For years, Taylor had been attracted by the idea of expanding internationally. In 1996, the company had licensed a franchisee in New Zealand to operate a subsidiary named Kiwi Pooch Mobile. However, there was only one unit operating by early 2002 and she wondered how best to increase this number. Another subsidiary had been established as a master franchise in the French province of New Caledonia, a large island northeast of Australia. Launched in late 2000 under the name of La Pooch Mobile; it had one unit. Another master franchise territory had been established in Malaysia in late 2001, and there were two units operating in 2002.

In 2001, APM had granted exclusive rights for operation in the United Kingdom to a British entrepreneur who operated under the name The Pooch Mobile. Thus far, four units were operating in the English county of Lincolnshire, 200 km (125 miles) north of London. This individual noted that English people traditionally washed their dogs very infrequently, often as little as once every two to three years, but once they had tried The Pooch Mobile, they quickly converted to becoming monthly clients, primarily for the hygiene benefits.

As the company grew, the directors knew it was likely to face increased competition from other providers of dog washing services. But as one successful franchisee remarked: "Competition keeps us on our toes. It's hard being in the lead and maintaining the lead if you haven't got anybody on your tail."

Study Questions

1. How did Christine Taylor succeed in evolving the local dog washing service she developed as a teenager into an international franchise business?
2. Compare and contrast the tasks involved in recruiting new customers and recruiting new franchisees.
3. From a franchisee's perspective, what are the key benefits of belonging to the APM franchise in (a) the first year and (b) the third and subsequent years?
4. In planning for future expansion, what strategy should Taylor adopt for APM and why?

CASE 10 Shouldice Hospital Limited (Abridged)

JAMES HESKETT AND ROGER HALLOWEEL

Two shadowy figures, enrobed and in slippers, walked slowly down the semidarkened hall of the Shouldice Hospital. They did not notice Alan O'Dell, the hospital's managing director, and his guest. Once they were out of earshot, O'Dell remarked good naturedly, "By the way they act, you'd think our patients own this place. And while they're here, in a way they do." Following a visit to the five operating rooms, O'Dell and his visitor once again encountered the same pair of patients still engrossed in discussing their hernia operations, which had been performed the previous morning.

History

An attractive brochure that was recently printed, although neither dated nor distributed to prospective patients, described Dr. Earle Shouldice, the founder of the hospital: Dr. Shouldice's interest in early ambulation stemmed, in part, from an operation he performed in 1932 to remove the appendix from a seven-year-old girl and the girl's subsequent refusal to stay quietly in bed. In spite of her activity, no harm was done, and the experience recalled to the doctor the postoperative actions of animals upon which he had performed surgery. They had all moved about freely with no ill effects.

By 1940, Shouldice had given extensive thought to several factors that contributed to early ambulation following surgery. Among them were the use of a local anesthetic, the nature of the surgical procedure itself, the design of a facility to encourage movement without unnecessarily causing discomfort, and the post operative regimen. With these things in mind, he began to develop a surgical technique for repairing hernias[1] that was superior to others; word of his early success generated demand.

Dr. Shouldice's medical license permitted him to operate anywhere, even on a kitchen table. However, as more and more patients requested operations, Dr. Shouldice created new facilities by buying a rambling 130-acre estate with a 17,000-square foot main house in the Toronto suburb of Thornhill. After some years of planning, a large wing was added to provide a total capacity of 89 beds.

Dr. Shouldice died in 1965. At that time, Shouldice Hospital Limited was formed to operate both the hospital and clinical facilities under the surgical direction of Dr. Nicholas Obney. In 1999, Dr. Casim Degani, an internationally recognized authority, became surgeon-in-chief. By 2004, 7,600 operations were performed per year.

The Shouldice Method

Only external (versus internal) abdominal hernias were repaired at Shouldice Hospital. Thus most first-time repairs, "primaries," were straightforward operations requiring about 45 minutes. The remaining procedures involved patients suffering recurrences of

---

Professor James Heskett prepared the original version of this case, "Shouldice Hospital Limited," HBS No. 683-068. This version was prepared jointly by Professor James Heskett and Roger Hallowell (MBA 1989, DBA 1997). HBS cases are developed solely as the basis for class discussion. Cases are not intended to serve as endorsements, sources of primary data, or illustrations of effective or ineffective management.

[1]Most hernias, knows as external abdominal hernias, are protrusions of some part of the abdominal contents through a hole or slit in the muscular layers of the abdominal wall which is supposed to contain them. Well over 90 percent of these hernias occur in the groin area. Of these, by far the most common are inguinal hernias, many of which are caused by a slight weakness in the muscle layers brought about by the passage of the testicles in male babies through the groin area shortly before birth. Aging also contributes to the development of inguinal hernias. Because of the cause of the affliction, 85% of all hernias occur in males.

hernias previously repaired elsewhere.[2] Many of the recurrences and very difficult hernia repairs required 90 minutes or more.

In the Shouldice method, the muscles of the abdominal wall were arranged in three distinct layers, and the opening was repaired, each layer in turn, by overlapping its margins as the edges of a coat might be overlapped when buttoned. The end result reinforced the muscular wall of the abdomen with six rows of sutures (stitches) under the skin cover, which was then closed with clamps that were later removed. (Other methods might not separate muscle layers, often involved fewer rows of sutures, and sometimes involved the insertion of screens or meshes under the skin.)

A typical first-time repair could be completed with the use of pre-operative sedation (sleeping pill) and analgesic (pain killer) plus a local anesthetic, an injection of Novocain in the region of the incision. This allowed immediate postoperative patient ambulation and facilitated rapid recovery.

The Patients' Experience

Most potential Shouldice patients learned about the hospital from previous Shouldice patients. Although thousands of doctors had referred patients, doctors were less likely to recommend Shouldice because of the generally regarded simplicity of the surgery, often considered a "bread and butter" operation. Typically, many patients had their problem diagnosed by a personal physician and then contacted Shouldice directly. Many more made this diagnosis themselves.

The process experienced by Shouldice patients depended on whether or not they lived close enough to the hospital to visit the facility to obtain a diagnosis. Approximately 10 percent of Shouldice patients came from outside the province of Ontario, most of these from the United States. Another 60 percent of patients lived beyond the Toronto area. These out-of-town patients often were diagnosed by mail using the Medical Information Questionnaire shown in Exhibit 1. Based on information in the questionnaire, a Shouldice surgeon would determine the type of hernia the respondent had and whether there were signs that some risk might be associated with surgery (for example, an overweight or heart condition, or a patient who had suffered a heart attack or a stroke in the past six months to a year, or whether a general or local anesthetic was required). At this point, a patient was given an operating date and sent a brochure describing the hospital and the Shouldice method. If necessary, a sheet outlining a weight-loss program prior to surgery was also sent. A small proportion was refused treatment, either because they were overweight, represented an undue medical risk, or because it was determined that they did not have a hernia.

Arriving at the clinic between 1:00 p.m. and 3:00 p.m. the day before the operation, a patient joined other patients in the waiting room. He or she was soon examined in one of the six examination rooms staffed by surgeons who had completed their operating schedules for the day. This examination required no more than 20 minutes, unless the patient needed reassurance. (Patients typically exhibited a moderate level of anxiety until their operation was completed.) At this point, it occasionally was discovered that a patient had not corrected his or her weight problem; others might be found not to have a hernia at all. In either case, the patient was sent home.

After checking administrative details, about an hour after arriving at the hospital, a patient was directed to the room number shown on his or her wrist band. Throughout the process, patients were asked to keep their luggage (usually light) with them.

All patient rooms at the hospital were semiprivate, containing two beds. Patients with similar jobs, backgrounds, or interests were assigned to the same room to the extent possible. Upon reaching their rooms, patients busied themselves unpacking, getting acquainted with roommates, shaving themselves in the area of the operation, and changing into pajamas.

---

[2] Based on tracking of patients over more than 30 years, the gross recurrence rate for all operations performed at Shouldice was 0.8 percent. Recurrence rates reported in the literature for these types of hernia varied greatly. However, one text stated, "In the United States, the gross rate of recurrence for groin hernias approaches 10 percent."

At 4:30 p.m., a nurse's orientation provided the group of incoming patients with information about what to expect, including the need for exercise after the operation and the daily routine. According to Alan O'Dell, "Half are so nervous they don't remember much." Dinner was then served, followed by further recreation, and tea and cookies at 9:00 p.m. Nurses emphasized the importance of attendance at that time because it provided an opportunity for preoperative patients to talk with those whose operations had been completed earlier that same day.

Patients to be operated on early were awakened at 5:30 a.m. to be given pre-op sedation. An attempt was made to schedule operations for roommates at approximately the same time. Patients were taken to the pre-operation room where the circulating nurse administered Demerol, an analgesic, 45 minutes before surgery. A few minutes prior to the first operation at 7:30 a.m., the surgeon assigned to each patient administered Novocain, a local anesthetic, in the operating room. This was in contrast to the typical hospital procedure in which patients were sedated in their rooms prior to being taken to the operating rooms.

Upon completion of the operation, during which a few patients were "chatty" and fully aware of what was going on, patients were invited to get off the operating table and walk to the post operation room with the help of their surgeons. According to the Director of Nursing:

> "Ninety-nine percent accept the surgeon's invitation. While we use wheelchairs to return them to their rooms, the walk from the operating table is for psychological as well as physiological [blood pressure, respiratory] reasons. Patients prove to themselves that they can do it, and they start their all-important exercise immediately."

Throughout the day after their operation, patients were encouraged to exercise by nurses and housekeepers alike. By 9:00 p.m. on the day of their operations, all patients were ready and able to walk down to the dining room for tea and cookies, even if it meant climbing stairs, to help indoctrinate the new "class" admitted that day. On the fourth morning, patients were ready for discharge.

During their stay, patients were encouraged to take advantage of the opportunity to explore the premises and make new friends. Some members of the staff felt that the patients and their attitudes were the most important element of the Shouldice program. According to Dr. Byrnes Shouldice, son of the founder, a surgeon on the staff, and a 50 percent owner of the hospital:

> Patients sometimes ask to stay an extra day. Why? Well, think about it. They are basically well to begin with. But they arrive with a problem and a certain amount of nervousness, tension, and anxiety about their surgery. Their first morning here they're operated on and experience a sense of relief from something that's been bothering them for a long time. They are immediately able to get around, and they've got a three-day holiday ahead of them with a perfectly good reason to be away from work with no sense of guilt. They share experiences with other patients, make friends easily, and have the run of the hospital. In summer, the most common aftereffect of the surgery is sunburn.

The Nurses' Experience

Thirty four full-time-equivalent nurses staffed Shouldice each 24-hour period. However, during nonoperating hours, only six full-time-equivalent nurses were on the premises at any given time. While the Canadian acute-care hospital average ratio of nurses to patients was 1:4, at Shouldice the ratio was 1:15. Shouldice nurses spent an unusually large proportion of their time in counseling activities. As one supervisor commented, "We don't use bedpans." According to a manager, "Shouldice has a waiting list of nurses wanting to be hired, while other hospitals in Toronto are short-staffed and perpetually recruiting."

The Doctors' Experience

The hospital employed 10 full-time surgeons and eight part-time assistant surgeons. Two anesthetists were also on site. The anesthetists floated among cases except when

EXHIBIT 1: Medical information Questionnaire

FAMILY NAME (Last Name) | FIRST NAME | MIDDLE NAME

STREET & NUMBER (or Rural Route or P.O. Box) | Town/City | Province/State

County | Township | Zip or Postal Code | Birthdate: Month Day Year

Telephone
Home .... if none, give
Work .... neighbour's number ....
| Married or Single | Religion

NEXT OF KIN: Name | Address | Telephone #

INSURANCE INFORMATION: Please give name of Insurance Company and Numbers. | Date form completed

HOSPITAL INSURANCE: (Please bring hospital certificates)
O.H.I.P. Number ________ BLUE CROSS Number ________

OTHER HOSPITAL INSURANCE
Company Name ________
Policy Number ________

SURGICAL INSURANCE: (Please bring insurance certificates)
O.H.I.P. Number ________ BLUE SHIELD Number ________

OTHER SURGICAL INSURANCE
Company Name ________
Policy Number ________

WORKMEN'S COMPENSATION BOARD
Claim No. | Approved Yes No | Social Insurance (Security) Number

Occupation | Name of Business | Are you the owner?††If Retired – Former Occupation
Yes No

How did you hear about Shouldice Hospital? (If referred by a doctor, give name & address)

Are you a former patient of Shouldice Hospital? Yes No Do you smoke? Yes No

Have you ever written to Shouldice Hospital in the past? Yes No

What is your preferred admission date? (Please give as much advance notice as possible)
No admissions Friday, Saturday or Sunday.

FOR OFFICE USE ONLY

Date Received | Type of Hernia | Weight Loss lbs.

Consent to Operate ☐
Heart Report ☐
| Special Instructions | Approved

Referring Doctor Notified | Operation Date

SHOULDICE HOSPITAL

7750 Bayview Avenue
Box 379, Thornhill, Ontario L3T 4A3 Canada
Phone (418) 889-1125

(Thornhill - One Mile North Metro Toronto)

MEDICAL

INFORMATION

Patients who live at a distance often prefer their examination, admission and operation to be arranged all on a single visit — to save making two lengthy journeys. The whole purpose of this questionnaire is to make such arrangements possible, although, of course, it cannot replace the examination in any way. Its completion and return will not put you under any obligation.

Please be sure to fill in both sides.

This information will be treated as confidential.

(continued on next page)

EXHIBIT 1: *(Continued)*

THIS CHART IS FOR EXPLANATION ONLY

Ordinary hernias are mostly either at the navel ("belly-button") - or just above it

or down in the groin area on either side

An "Incisional hernia" is one that bulges through the scar of any other surgical operation that has failed to hold - wherever it may be.

Right Groin Left Groin

THIS IS YOUR CHART – PLEASE MARK IT!

(MARK THE POSITION OF EACH HERNIA YOU WANT REPAIRED WITH AN "X")

Right Groin Left Groin

APPROXIMATE SIZE...
Walnut (or less) ☐ ☐
Hen's Egg or Lemon ☐ ☐
Grapefruit (or more) ☐ ☐

ESSENTIAL EXTRA INFORMATION

Use only the sections that apply to your hernias and put a ✓ in each box that seems appropriate.

NAVEL AREA (AND JUST ABOVE NAVEL) ONLY	Yes	No
Is this navel (bellybutton) hernia your FIRST one?	☐	☐
If it's NOT your first, how many repair attempts so far?	☐	

GROIN HERNIAS ONLY	RIGHT GROIN Yes	RIGHT GROIN No	LEFT GROIN Yes	LEFT GROIN No
Is this your FIRST GROIN HERNIA ON THIS SIDE?	☐	☐	☐	☐

How many hernia operations in this groin already? Right ☐ Left ☐

DATE OF LAST OPERATION ☐

INCISIONAL HERNIAS ONLY (the ones bulging through previous operation scars)
Was the original operation for your Appendix? ☐ , or Gallbladder? ☐ ,
or Stomach? ☐ , or Prostate? ☐ ☐ , or Hysterectomy? , or Other?..............................

....

How many attempts to repair the hernias have been made so far? ☐

PLEASE BE ACCURATE!: Misleading figures, when checked on a admission day, could mean postponement of your operation till your weight is suitable.

HEIGHT.............ft..............ins. WEIGHT...........lbs. Nude or just pyjamas Recent gain?...........lbs. Recent loss?............lbs.

Waist (muscles relaxed)........................ins. Chest (not expanded).......................ins.

GENERAL HEALTH

Age.............years is your health now GOOD ☐ , FAIR ☐ , or POOR ☐

Please mention briefly any severe past illness – such as a "heart attack" or a "stroke", for example, from which you have now recovered (and its approximate date).................
....

We need to know about other present conditions, even though your admission is NOT likely to be refused because of them.

Please tick ☑ any condition for which you are having regular treatment:		Name of any prescribed pills, tablets or capsules you take regularly -
Blood Pressure	☐	
Excess body fluids	☐	
Chest pain ("angina")	☐	
Irregular Heartbeat	☐	
Diabetes	☐	
Asthma & Bronchitis	☐	
Ulcers	☐	
Anticoagulants (to delay blood-clotting or to "thin the blood")	☐	
Other..		

Did you remember to MARK AN "X" on your body chart to show us where each of your hernias is located?

general anesthesia was in use. Each operating team required a surgeon, an assistant surgeon, a scrub nurse, and a circulating nurse. The operating load varied from 30 to 36 operations per day. As a result, each surgeon typically performed three or four operations each day.

A typical surgeon's day started with a scrubbing shortly before the first scheduled operation at 7:30 a.m. If the first operation was routine, it usually was completed by 8:15 a.m. At its conclusion, the surgical team helped the patient walk from the room and summoned the next patient. After scrubbing, the surgeon could be ready to operate again at 8:30 a.m. Surgeons were advised to take a coffee break after their second or third operation. Even so, a surgeon could complete three routine operations and a fourth involving a recurrence and still be finished in time for a 12:30 p.m. lunch in the staff dining room.

Upon finishing lunch, surgeons not scheduled to operate in the afternoon examined incoming patients. A surgeon's day ended by 4:00 p.m. In addition, a surgeon could expect to be on call one weekday night in ten and one weekend in ten. Alan O'Dell commented that the position appealed to doctors who "want to watch their children grow up. A doctor on call is rarely called to the hospital and has regular hours." According to Dr. Obney:

> When I interview prospective surgeons, I look for experience and a good education. I try to gain some insight into their domestic situation and personal interests and habits. I also try to find out why a surgeon wants to switch positions. And I try to determine if he's willing to perform the repair exactly as he's told. This is no place for prima donnas.
>
> Dr. Shouldice added:
>
> Traditionally a hernia is often the first operation that a junior resident in surgery performs. Hernia repair is regarded as a relatively simple operation compared to other major operations. This is quite wrong, as is borne out by the resulting high recurrence rate. It is a tricky anatomical area and occasionally very complicated, especially to the novice or those doing very few hernia repairs each year. But at Shouldice Hospital a surgeon learns the Shouldice technique over a period of several months. He learns when he can go fast and when he must slow down. He develops a pace and a touch. If he encounters something unusual, he is encouraged to consult immediately with other surgeons. We teach each other and try to encourage a group effort. And he learns not to take risks to achieve absolute perfection. Excellence is the enemy of good.

Chief Surgeon Degani assigned surgeons to an operating room on a daily basis by noon of the preceding day. This allowed surgeons to examine the specific patients they were to operate on. Surgeons and assistants were rotated every few days. Cases were assigned to give doctors a nonroutine operation (often involving a recurrence) several times a week. More complex procedures were assigned to more senior and experienced members of the staff. Dr. Obney commented:

> If something goes wrong, we want to make sure that we have an experienced surgeon in charge. Experience is most important. The typical general surgeon may perform 25 to 50 hernia operations per year. Ours perform 750 or more.

The 10 full-time surgeons were paid a straight salary, typically $144,000.[3] In addition, bonuses to doctors were distributed monthly. These depended on profit, individual productivity, and performance. The total bonus pool paid to the surgeons in a recent year was approximately $400,000. Total surgeon compensation (including benefits) was approximately 15 percent more than the average income for a surgeon in Ontario.

---

[3]All monetary references in the case are to Canadian dollars. $1 US equaled $1.33 Canadian on February 23, 2004.

Training in the Shouldice technique was important because the procedure could not be varied. It was accomplished through direct supervision by one or more of the senior surgeons. The rotation of teams and frequent consultations allowed for an ongoing opportunity to appraise performance and take corrective action. Wherever possible, former Shouldice patients suffering recurrences were assigned to the doctor who performed the first operation "to allow the doctor to learn from his mistake." Dr. Obney commented on being a Shouldice surgeon:

> A doctor must decide after several years whether he wants to do this for the rest of his life because, just as in other specialties—for example, radiology—he loses touch with other medical disciplines. If he stays for five years, he doesn't leave. Even among younger doctors, few elect to leave.

The Facility

The Shouldice Hospital contained two facilities in one building—the hospital and the clinic. On its first level, the hospital contained the kitchen and dining rooms. The second level contained a large, open lounge area, the admission offices, patient rooms, and a spacious glass-covered Florida room. The third level had additional patient rooms and recreational areas. Patients could be seen visiting each others' rooms, walking up and down hallways, lounging in the sunroom, and making use of light recreational facilities ranging from a pool table to an exercycle. Alan O'Dell pointed out some of the features of the hospital:

> The rooms contain no telephone or television sets. If a patient needs to make a call or wants to watch television, he or she has to take a walk. The steps are designed specially with a small rise to allow patients recently operated on to negotiate the stairs without undue discomfort. Every square foot of the hospital is carpeted to reduce the hospital feeling and the possibility of a fall. Carpeting also gives the place a smell other than that of disinfectant.
>
> This facility was designed by an architect with input from Dr. Byrnes Shouldice and Mrs.W. H. Urquhart (the daughter of the founder). The facility was discussed for years, and many changes in the plans were made before the first concrete was poured. A number of unique policies were also instituted. For example, parents accompanying children here for an operation stay free. You may wonder why we can do it, but we learned that we save more in nursing costs than we spend for the parent's room and board.

Patients and staff were served food prepared in the same kitchen, and staff members picked up food from a cafeteria line placed in the very center of the kitchen. This provided an opportunity for everyone to chat with the kitchen staff several times a day and the hospital staff to eat together. According to O'Dell, "We use all fresh ingredients and prepare the food from scratch in the kitchen." The Director of Housekeeping pointed out:

> I have only three on my housekeeping staff for the entire facility. One of the reasons for so few housekeepers is that we don't need to change linens during a patient's four-day stay. Also, the medical staff doesn't want the patients in bed all day. They want the nurses to encourage the patients to be up socializing, comparing notes [for confidence], encouraging each other, and walking around, getting exercise. Of course, we're in the rooms straightening up throughout the day. This gives the housekeepers a chance to josh with the patients and to encourage them to exercise.

The clinic housed five operating rooms, a laboratory, and the patient-recovery room. In total, the estimated cost to furnish an operating room was $30,000. This was considerably less than for other hospitals which require a bank of equipment with which to administer anesthetics for each room. At Shouldice, two mobile units were used by the anesthetists when needed. In addition, the complex had one "crash cart" per floor for use if a patient should suffer a heart attack or stroke.

Administration

Alan O'Dell described his job:

> We try to meet people's needs and make this as good a place to work as possible. There is a strong concern for employees here. Nobody is fired. [This was later reinforced by Dr. Shouldice, who described a situation involving two employees who confessed to theft in the hospital. They agreed to seek psychiatric help and were allowed to remain on the job.] As a result, turnover is low.
>
> Our administrative and support staff are nonunion, but we try to maintain a pay scale higher than the union scale for comparable jobs in the area. We have a profit-sharing plan that is separate from the doctors'. Last year the administrative and support staff divided up $60,000.
>
> If work needs to be done, people pitch in to help each other. A unique aspect of our administration is that I insist that each secretary is trained to do another's work and in an emergency is able to switch to another function immediately. We don't have an organization chart. A chart tends to make people think they're boxed in jobs.[4] I try to stay one night a week, having dinner and listening to the patients, to find out how things are really going around here.

Operating Costs

The 2004 budgets for the hospital and clinic were close to $8.5 million[5] and $3.5 million, respectively.[6]

The Market

Hernia operations were among the most commonly performed operations on males. In 2000, an estimated 1,000,000 such operations were performed in the United States alone. According to Dr. Shouldice:

> When our backlog of scheduled operations gets too large, we wonder how many people decide instead to have their local doctor perform the operation. Every time we've expanded our capacity, the backlog has declined briefly, only to climb once again. Right now, at 2,400, it is larger than it has ever been and is growing by 100 every six months.

The hospital relied entirely on word-of-mouth advertising, the importance of which was suggested by the results of a poll carried out by students of DePaul University as part of a project (Exhibit 3 shows a portion of these results). Although little systematic data about patients had been collected, Alan O'Dell remarked that "if we had to rely on wealthy patients only, our practice would be much smaller."

Patients were attracted to the hospital, in part, by its reasonable rates. Charges for a typical operation were four days of hospital stay at $320 per day, and a $650 surgical fee for a primary inguinal (the most common hernia). An additional fee of $300 was assessed if general anesthesia was required (in about 20 percent of cases). These charges compared to an average charge of $5,240 for operations performed elsewhere. Round-trip fares for travel to Toronto from various major cities on the North American continent ranged from roughly $200 to $600.

---

[4]The chart in Exhibit 2 was prepared by the case writer, based on conversations with hospital personnel.
[5]This figure included a provincially mandated return on investment.
[6]The latter figure included the bonus pool for doctors.

EXHIBIT 2: Organization Chart

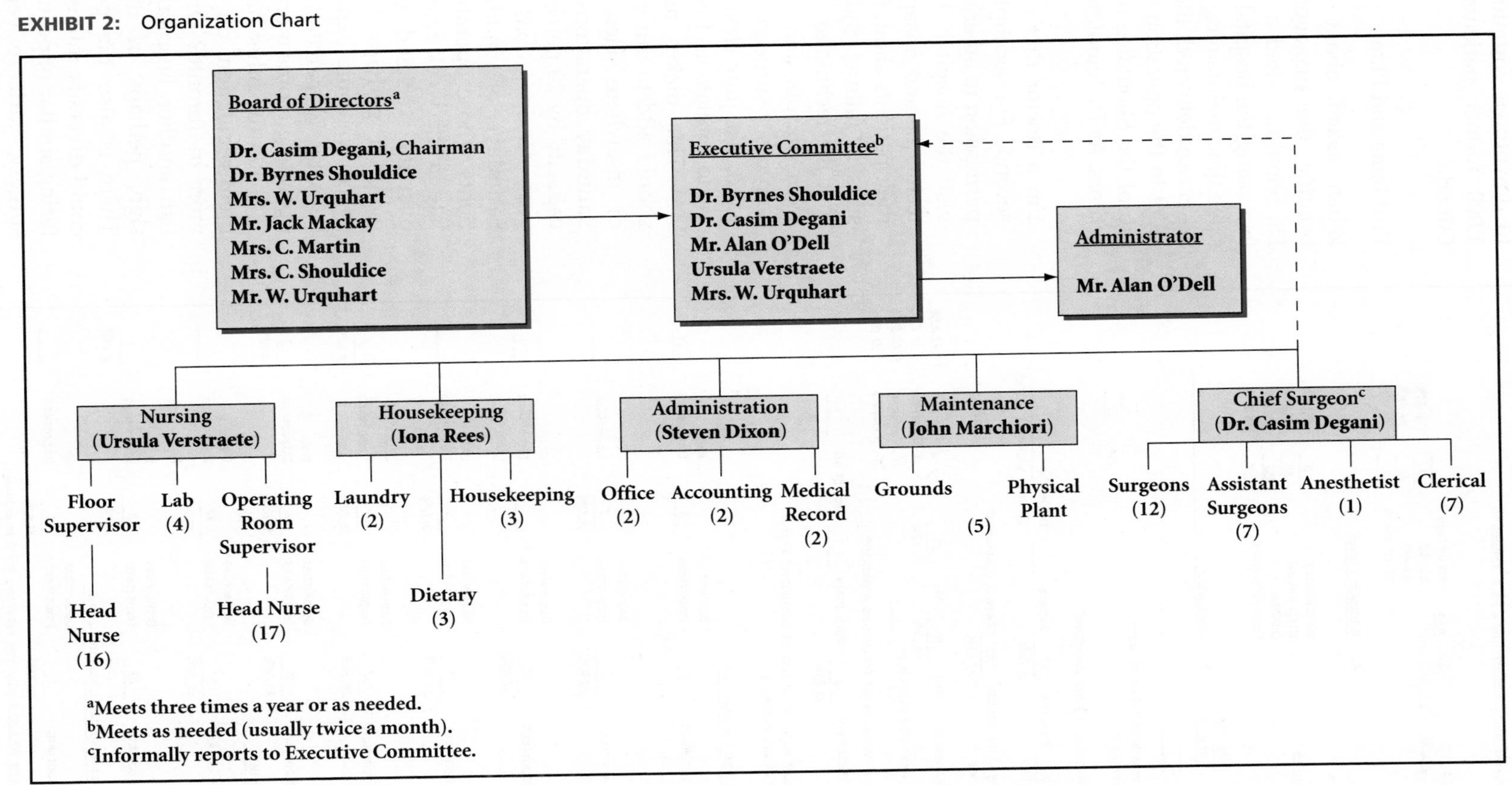

The hospital also provided annual checkups to alumni, free of charge. Many occurred at the time of the patient reunion. The most recent reunion, featuring dinner and a floor show, was held at a first-class hotel in downtown Toronto and was attended by 1,000 former patients, many from outside Canada.

Direction: For each question, please place a check mark as it applies to you.

1. Sex

Male	41	95.34%
Female	2	4.65%

2. Age

20 or less		
21–40	4	9.30%
41–60	17	39.54%
61 or more	22	51.16%

3. Nationality

Directions: Please place a check mark in nation you represent and please write in your province, state or country where it applies.

Canada	38	Province	88.37%
America	5	State	11.63%
Europe		Country	
Other			

4. Education level

Elementary	5	11.63%
High School	18	41.86%
College	1980	30.23%
Graduate work	7	16.28%

5. Occupation ______

6. Have you been overnight in a hospital other than Shouldice before your operation? Yes 31 No 12

7. What brought Shouldice Hospital to your attention?

Friend 23 (53.49%) Doctor 9 (20.93%) Relative 7 (16.28%) Article ___ Other 4 (Please explain) 9.30%

8. Did you have a single 25 (58.14%) or double 18 (41.86%) hernia operation?

9. Is this your first Annual Reunion? Yes 20 (46.51%) No 23 (53.49%)

If no, how many reunions have you attended? ___

2-5 reunions - 11 47.63%
6-10 reunions - 5 21.73%
11-20 reunions - 4 12.39%
21-36 reunions - 3 13.05%

10. Do you feel that Shouldice Hospital cared for you as a person?

Most definitely 37 (86.05%) Definitely 6 (13.95%) Very little ___ Not at all ___

11. What impressed you the most about your stay at Shouldice? Please check one answer for each of the following.

	Very Important	Important	Somewhat Important	Not Important
A. Fees charged for operation and hospital stay	10	3	6	24
B. Operation Procedure	33 (76.74%)	9 (20.93%)	1 (2.33%)	
C. Physician's Care	31 (72.10%)	12 (27.90%)	-	-
D. Nursing Care	28 (65.12%)	14 (32.56%)	1 (2.32%)	
E. Food Service	23 (53.48%)	11 (25.59%)	7 (16.28%)	2 (4.65%)
F. Shortness of Hospital Stay	17 (39.53%)	15 (34.88%)	8 (18.60%)	3 (6.98%)
G. Exercise; Recreational Activities	17 (39.53%)	14 (32.56%)	12 (27.91%)	-
H. Friendships with Patients	25 (58.15%)	10 (23.25%)	5 (11.63%)	3 (6.98%)
I. "Shouldice Hospital hardly seemed like a hospital at all."	25 (58.14%)	13 (30.23%)	5 (11.63%)	

12. In a few words, give the MAIN REASON why you returned for this annual reunion.

EXHIBIT 3: Shouldice Hospital Annual Patient Reunion Data

Problems and Plans

When asked about major questions confronting the management of the hospital, Dr. Shouldice cited a desire to seek ways of increasing the hospital's capacity while at the same time maintaining control over the quality of service delivered, the future role of government in the operation of the hospital, and the use of the Shouldice name by potential competitors. As Dr. Shouldice put it:

> I'm a doctor first and an entrepreneur second. For example, we could refuse permission to other doctors who want to visit the hospital. They may copy our technique and misapply it or misinform their patients about the use of it. This results in failure, and we are concerned that the technique will be blamed. But we're doctors, and it is our obligation to help other surgeons learn. On the other hand, it's quite clear that others are trying to emulate us. Look at this ad.
>
> This makes me believe that we should add to our capacity, either here or elsewhere. Here, we could go to Saturday operations and increase our capacity by 20 percent. Throughout the year, no operations are scheduled for Saturdays or Sundays, although patients whose operations are scheduled late in the week remain in the hospital over the weekend. Or, with an investment of perhaps $4 million in new space, we could expand our number of beds by 50 percent, and schedule the operating rooms more heavily.
>
> On the other hand, given government regulation, do we want to invest more in Toronto? Or should we establish another hospital with similar design, perhaps in the United States? There is also the possibility that we could diversify into other specialties offering similar opportunities such as eye surgery, varicose veins, or diagnostic services (e.g. colonoscopies).
>
> For now, we're also beginning the process of grooming someone to succeed

Dr. Degani when he retires. He's in his early 60s, but at some point we'll have to address this issue. And for good reason, he's resisted changing certain successful procedures that I think we could improve on. We had quite a time changing the schedule for the administration of Demerol to patients to increase their comfort level during the operation. Dr. Degani has opposed a Saturday operating program on the premise that he won't be here and won't be able to maintain proper control.

Alan O'Dell added his own concerns:

How should we be marketing our services? Right now, we don't advertise directly to patients. We're even afraid to send out this new brochure we've put together, unless a potential patient specifically requests it, for fear it will generate too much demand. Our records show that just under 1 percent of our patients are medical doctors, a significantly high percentage. How should we capitalize on that? I'm also concerned about this talk of Saturday operations. We are already getting good utilization of this facility. And if we expand further, it will be very difficult

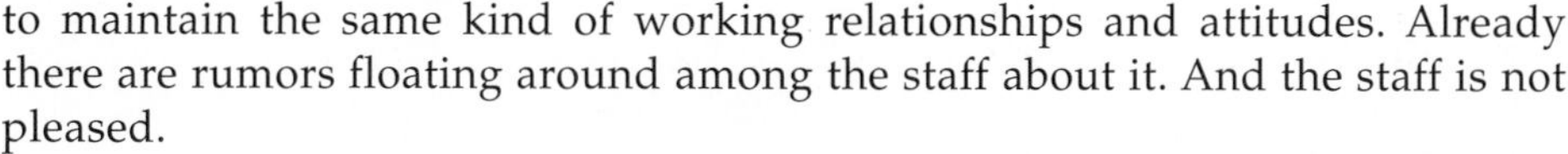

to maintain the same kind of working relationships and attitudes. Already there are rumors floating around among the staff about it. And the staff is not pleased.

The matter of Saturday operations had been a topic of conversation among the doctors as well. Four of the older doctors were opposed to it. While most of the younger doctors were indifferent or supportive, at least two who had been at the hospital for some time were particularly concerned about the possibility that the issue would drive a wedge between the two groups. As one put it, I'd hate to see the practice split over the issue.

The Canadian Hernia Clinic

Hernias (Ruptures) Required Under local anesthesia as by Canadian method.

No Overnight Hospital Stay.

Consultations Without Charge

23061 St. Rd. 7
BOCA RATON, FLA. 33433
482-7755

EXHIBIT 4: Advertisement by a Shouldice Competitor

EXHIBIT 5: The Shouldice Hospital Grounds Are a Haven for Rest and Recuperation

Study Questions

1. What is the market for this service? How successful is Shouldice Hospital?
2. Define the service model for Shouldice. How does each of its elements contribute to the hospital's success?
3. As Dr. Shouldice, what actions, if any, would you like to take to expand the hospital's capacity, and how would you implement such changes?

CASE 11 Red Lobster

Christopher Lovelock

A peer review panel of managers and service workers from a restaurant chain must decide whether or not a waitress has been unfairly fired from her job.

"It felt like a knife going through me!" declared Mary Campbell, 53, after she was fired from her waitressing job at a restaurant in the Red Lobster chain. But instead of suing for what she considered unfair dismissal after 19 years of service, Campbell called for a peer review, seeking to recover her job and three weeks of lost wages.

Three weeks after the firing, a panel of employees from different Red Lobster restaurants was reviewing the evidence and trying to determine whether the server had, in fact, been unjustly fired for allegedly stealing a guest comment card completed by a couple of customers whom she had served.

Peer Review at Darden Industries

Red Lobster was owned by Darden Industries, which also owned other restaurant chains like Olive Garden, Bahama Breeze, Smokey Bones Barbeque, and Grill and Seasons 52. The company, which has more than 65,000 employees, had adopted a policy of encouraging peer review of disputed employee firings and disciplinary actions several years earlier. The company's key objectives were to limit worker lawsuits and ease workplace tensions.

Advocates of the peer review approach, which had been adopted at several other companies, believed it was a very effective way of channeling constructively the pain and anger that employees felt after being fired or disciplined by their managers. By reducing the incidence of lawsuits, a company could also save on legal expenses.

A Darden spokesperson stated that the peer review program had been "tremendously successful" in keeping valuable employees from unfair dismissal. Each year, about 100 disputes ended up in peer review, with only 10 subsequently resulting in lawsuits. Red Lobster managers and many employees also credited peer review with reducing racial tensions. Ms. Campbell, who said she had received dozens of calls of support, chose peer review over a lawsuit not only because it was much cheaper, but "I also liked the idea of being judged by people who know how things work in a little restaurant."

The Evidence

The review panel included a general manager, an assistant manager, a server, a hostess, and a bartender, who had all volunteered to review the circumstances of Mary Campbell's firing. Each panelist had received peer review training and was receiving regular wages plus travel expenses. The instructions to panelists were simply to do what they felt was fair.

Campbell had been fired by Jean Larimer, the general manager of the Red Lobster in Marston, where the former worked as a restaurant server. The reason given for the firing was that Campbell had asked the restaurant's hostess, Eve Taunton, for the key to the guest comment box and stole a card from it. The card had been completed by a couple of guests whom Campbell had served and who seemed dissatisfied with their experience at the restaurant. Subsequently, the guests learned that their comment card, which complained that their prime rib of beef was too rare and their waitress was "uncooperative," had been removed from the box.

 This case is based on information in a story by Margaret A. Jacobs in the *Wall Street Journal.* Real names have been disguised.

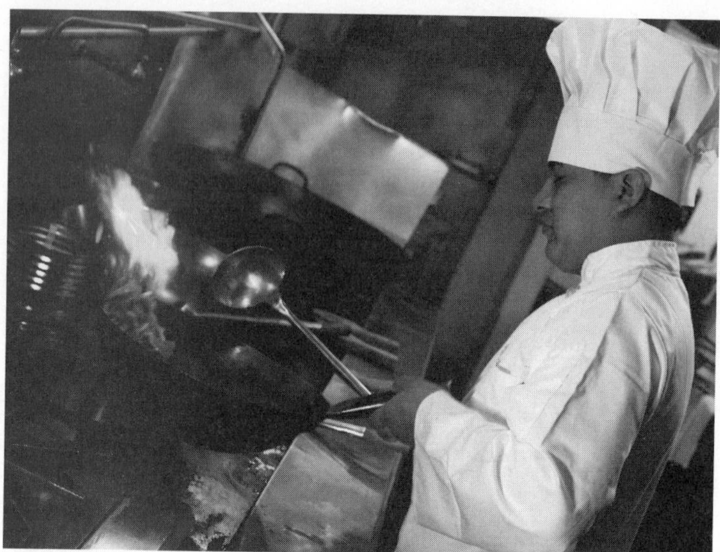

EXHIBIT 1: The Restaurant Scene Becomes the Testing Ground for the Validity of Peer Review

Jean Larimer's Testimony. Larimer, who supervised 100 full- and part-time employees, testified that she had dismissed Campbell after one of the two customers complained angrily to her and her supervisor. "She [the guest] felt violated," declared the manager, "because her card was taken from the box and her complaint about the food was ignored." Larimer drew the panel's attention to the company rule book, pointing out that Campbell had violated the policy that forbade removal of company property.

Mary Campbell's Testimony. Campbell testified that the female customer had requested that her prime rib be cooked "well done" and then subsequently complained that it was fatty and undercooked. The waitress told the panel that she had politely suggested that "prime rib always has fat on it," but arranged to have the meat cooked some more. However, the woman still seemed unhappy; she poured some steak sauce over the meat, but then pushed away her plate without eating all the food. When the customer remained displeased, Campbell offered her a free dessert. But the guests decided to leave, paid the bill, filled out the guest comment card, and dropped it in the guest comment box.

Admitting she was consumed by curiosity, Campbell asked Eve Taunton, the restaurant's hostess, for the key to the box. After removing and reading the card, she pocketed it. Her intent, she declared, was to show the card to Ms. Larimer, who had been concerned earlier that the prime rib served at the restaurant was overcooked, not undercooked. However, she forgot about the card and later, accidentally, threw it out.

Eve Taunton's testimony. At the time of the firing, Taunton, a 17-year old student, was working at Red Lobster for the summer. "I didn't think it was a big deal to give her [Campbell] the key," she said. "A lot of people would come up to me to get it."

The Panel Deliberates

Having heard the testimony, the members of the review panel had to decide whether Ms. Larimer had been justified in firing Ms. Campbell. The panelists' initial reactions to the situation were split by rank, with the hourly workers supporting Campbell and the managers supporting Larimer. But then the debate began in earnest in an effort to reach consensus.

Study Questions

1. What are the marketing implications of this situation?
2. Evaluate the concept of peer review. What are its strengths and weaknesses? What type of environment is required to make it work well?
3. Review the evidence. Do you believe the testimony presented?
4. What decision would you make and why?

CASE 12 Menton Bank

Christopher Lovelock

Problems arise when a large bank, attempting to develop a stronger customer service orientation, enlarges the tellers' responsibilities to include selling activities.

"I'm concerned about Karen," said Margaret Costanzo to David Reeves. The two bank officers were seated in the former's office at Menton Bank. Costanzo was a Vice President of the bank and manager of the Victory Square branch, the third largest in Menton's large branch network. She and Reeves, the branch's Customer Service Director, were having an employee appraisal meeting. Reeves was responsible for the customer service department, which coordinated the activities of the Customer Service Representatives (CSRs, formerly known as tellers) and the Customer Assistance Representatives (CARs, formerly known as new accounts assistants).

Costanzo and Reeves were discussing Karen Mitchell, a 24-year-old customer service representative, who had applied for the soon-to-be-vacant position of head CSR. Mitchell had been with the bank for three and a half years. She had applied for the position of what had then been called head teller a year earlier, but the job had gone to a candidate with more seniority. Now, that individual was leaving—his wife had been transferred to a new job in another city—and the position was once again open. Two other candidates had also applied for the job.

Both Costanzo and Reeves agreed that, against all criteria used in the past, Karen Mitchell would have been the obvious choice for head teller. She was both fast and accurate in her work, presented a smart and professional appearance, and was well liked by customers and her fellow CSRs. However, the nature of the teller's job had been significantly revised nine months earlier to add a stronger marketing component. CSRs were now expected to offer polite suggestions that customers use Automated Teller Machines (ATMs) for simple transactions. They were also required to stimulate customer interest in the broadening array of financial services offered by the bank. "The problem with Karen," as Reeves put it, "is that she simply refuses to sell."

The New Focus on Customer Service at Menton Bank

Although it was the largest bank in the region, Menton had historically focused on corporate business, and its share of the retail consumer banking business had declined in the face of aggressive competition from other financial institutions. Three years earlier, the Board of Directors had appointed a new Chief Executive Officer (CEO) and given him the mandate of developing a stronger consumer orientation at the retail level. The goal was to seize the initiative in marketing the ever-increasing array of financial services now available to retail customers. The CEO's strategy, after putting in a new management team, was to begin by ordering an expansion and speed-up of Menton's investment in electronic delivery systems, which had fallen behind the competition. To achieve this strategy, a new banking technology team had been created.

During the past 18 months, the bank had tripled the number of ATMs located inside its branches, replacing older ATMs with the latest models featuring color touch screens and capable of a broader array of transactions. Menton was already a member of a several ATM networks, giving its customers access to freestanding 24-hour booths in shopping centers, airports, and other high-traffic locations. The installation of new ATMs was coupled with a branch renovation program, designed to improve the physical appearance of the branches. A pilot program to test the impact of these "new look" branches was already underway. In the longer term, top management intended to redesign the interior of each branch. As more customers switched to electronic banking from remote locations, the bank planned to close a number of its smaller branches.

Another important move had been to introduce automated telephone banking, which allowed customers to check account balances and to move funds from one account to another by touching specific keys on their phone in response to the instructions of a computerized voice. This service was available 24/7, and utilization was rising steadily. Customers could also call a central customer service office to speak with a bank representative concerning service questions or problems with their accounts as well as to request new account applications or new checkbooks, which would be sent by mail. This office currently operated on weekdays from 8:00 a.m. to 8:00 p.m. and on Saturdays from 8:00 a.m. to 2:00 p.m., but Menton was evaluating the possibility of expanding the operation to include a broad array of retail bank services, offered on a 24-hour basis.

The technology team had completely redesigned the bank's website to make it possible to offer what were described as the region's most "user-friendly" Internet banking services. Customers had online access to their accounts and could also obtain information about bank services, branch locations and service hours, location of ATMs, as well as answers to commonly asked questions. Finally, the bank had recently started issuing new credit cards containing chips imbued with radio-frequency identification (RFID), which speeded transactions by allowing customers to wave their cards close to a special reader rather than having to swipe them in the traditional way. All these actions seemed to be bearing fruit. In the most recent six months, Menton had seen a significant increase in the number of new accounts opened, as compared to the same period of the previous year; and quarterly survey data showed that Menton Bank was steadily increasing its share of new deposits in the region.

Customer Service Issues

New financial products had been introduced at a rapid rate. But the bank found that many existing "platform" staff—known as new accounts assistants—were ill-equipped to sell these services because of lack of product knowledge and inadequate training in selling skills. As Costanzo recalled: "The problem was that they were so used to sitting at their desks waiting for a customer to approach them with a specific request, such as a mortgage or car loan, that it was hard to get them to take a more positive approach that involved actively probing for customer needs. Their whole job seemed to revolve around filling out forms or responding to prompts on their computer screens. We were way behind most other banks in this respect."

As the automation program proceeded, the mix of activities performed by the tellers started to change. A growing number of customers were using the ATMs, the website, and automated telephone banking for a broad array of transactions, including cash withdrawals and deposits (from the ATMs), transfers of funds between accounts, and requesting account balances. The ATMs at the Victory Square branch had the highest utilization of any of Menton's branches, reflecting the large number of students and young professionals served at that location, Costanzo noted that customers who were older or less educated seemed to prefer being served by "a real person, rather than a machine." They were particularly reluctant to make deposits via an ATM.

A year earlier, the head office had selected three branches, including Victory Square, as test sites for a new customer service program, which included a radical redesign of the branch interior. The Victory Square branch was in a busy urban location, about one mile from the central business district and less than 10-minutes' walk from the campus of a large university. The branch was surrounded by retail stores and close to commercial and professional offices. The other test branches were among the bank's larger suburban offices in two different metropolitan areas and were located in a shopping mall and next to a big hospital, respectively.

As part of the branch renovation program, each of these three branches had previously been remodeled to include no fewer than four ATMs (Victory Square had six), which could be closed off from the rest of the branch so they would remain accessible to customers 24 hours a day. Further remodeling was then undertaken to locate a customer service desk near the entrance; close to each desk were two electronic information terminals, featuring color touch screens that customers could activate to obtain information on a variety of bank services. The teller stations were redesigned to provide two levels of service: an express station for simple deposits and for cashing of approved checks as well as regular stations for the full array of services provided by tellers. The number of stations open at a given time was varied to reflect the volume of anticipated business and staffing arrangements were changed to ensure that more tellers were on hand to serve customers during the busiest periods. Finally, the platform area in each branch was reconstructed to create what the architect described as "a friendly, yet professional appearance."

Human Resources

With the new environment came new training programs for the staff of these three branches and new job descriptions and job titles: customer assistance representatives (for the platform staff), customer service representatives (for the tellers), and customer service director (instead of assistant branch manager). The head teller position was renamed head CSR. Details of the new job descriptions are shown in the Appendix at the end of this case. The training programs for each group included sessions designed to develop improved knowledge of both new and existing retail products. (CARs received more extensive training in this area than did CSRs.) The CARs also attended a 15-hour course, offered in three separate sessions, on basic selling skills. This program covered key steps in the sales process, including building a relationship, exploring customer needs, determining a solution, and overcoming objections.

The sales training program for CSRs, by contrast, consisted of just two 2-hour sessions designed to develop skills in recognizing and probing customer needs, presenting product features and benefits, overcoming objections, and referring customers to CARs. All staff members in customer service positions participated in sessions designed to improve their communication skills and professional image: clothing and personal grooming and interactions with customers were all discussed. The trainer said, "Remember, people's money is too important to entrust to someone who doesn't look and act the part!"

CARs were instructed to rise from their seats and shake hands with customers. Both CARs and CSRs were given exercises designed to improve their listening skills and their powers of observation. All employees working in places where they could be seen by customers were ordered to refrain from drinking soda and chewing gum while on the job. (Smoking by both employees and customers had been banned some years earlier under the bank's smoke-free office policy.)

Although Menton Bank's management anticipated that most of the increased emphasis on selling would fall to the CARs, they also foresaw a limited selling role for the customer service representatives, who would be expected to mention various products and facilities offered by the bank as they served customers at the teller windows. For instance, if a customer happened to say something about an upcoming vacation, the CSR was supposed to mention traveler's checks. If the customer complained about bounced checks, the CSR should suggest speaking to a CAR about opening a personal line of credit that would provide an automatic overdraft protection. If the customer mentioned investments, the CSR was expected to refer him or her to a CAR who could provide information on money market accounts, certificates of deposit, or Menton's discount brokerage service. All CSRs were supplied with their own business cards. When making a referral, they were expected to write the customer's name and the product of interest on the back of a card, give it to the customer and send that individual to the customer assistance desks.

In an effort to motivate CSRs at the three branches to sell specific financial products, the bank experimented with various incentive programs. The first involved cash bonuses for referrals to CARs that resulted in sale of specific products. During a one-month period, CSRs were offered a $50 bonus for each referral leading to a customer opening a personal line of credit account. The CARs received a $20 bonus for each account they opened, regardless of whether or not it came as a referral or simply a walk-in. Eight such bonuses were paid to CSRs at Victory Square, with three each going to just two of the full-time CSRs, Jean Warshawski and Bruce Greenfield. Karen Mitchell was not among the recipients. However, this program was not renewed, since it was felt that there were other, more cost-effective means of marketing this product. In addition, Reeves, the Customer Service Director, had reason to believe that Bruce Greenfield had colluded with one of the CARs, his girlfriend, to claim referrals which he had not, in fact, made. Another test branch reported similar suspicions of two of its CSRs. A second promotion followed and was based on allocating credits to the CSRs for successful referrals. The value of the credit varied according to the nature of the product—for instance, a debit card was worth 500 credits—and accumulated credits could be exchanged for merchandise gifts. This program was deemed ineffective and discontinued after three months. The basic problem seemed to be that the value of the gifts was seen as too low in relation to the amount of effort required. Other problems with these promotional schemes included lack of product knowledge on the part of the CSRs and time pressures when many customers were waiting in line to be served.

The bank had next turned to an approach which, in David Reeves' words, "used the stick rather than the carrot." All CSRs had traditionally been evaluated half-yearly on a variety of criteria, including accuracy, speed, quality of interactions with customers, punctuality of arrival for work, job attitudes, cooperation with other employees, and professional image. The evaluation process assigned a number of points to each criterion, with accuracy and speed the most heavily weighted. In addition to appraisals by the Customer Service Director and the branch manager, with input from the head CSR, Menton had recently instituted a program of anonymous visits by what was popularly known as the "mystery client." Each CSR was visited at least once a quarter by a professional evaluator posing as a customer. This individual's appraisal of the CSR's appearance, performance, and attitude was included in the overall evaluation. The number of points scored by each CSR had a direct impact on merit pay raises and on selection for promotion to the head CSR position or to platform jobs.

To encourage improved product knowledge and "consultative selling" by CSRs, the evaluation process was revised to include points assigned for each individual's success in sales referrals. Under the new evaluation scheme, the maximum number of points assignable for effectiveness in making sales—directly or through referrals to CARs—amounted to 30 percent of the potential total score. Although CSR-initiated sales had risen significantly in the most recent half-year, Reeves sensed that morale had dropped among this group, in contrast to the CARs, whose enthusiasm and commitment had risen significantly. He had also noticed an increase in CSR errors. One CSR had quit, complaining about too much pressure.

Karen Mitchell

Under the old scoring system, Karen Mitchell had been the highest-scoring teller/CSR for four consecutive half-years. But after two half-years under the new system, her ranking had dropped to fourth out of the seven full-time tellers. The top-ranking CSR, Mary Bell, had been with Menton Bank for 16 years, but had declined repeated invitations to apply for a head teller position, saying she was happy where she was, earning at the top of the CSR scale, and did not want "the extra worry and responsibility." Mitchell ranked first on all but one of the operationally related criteria (interactions with customers, where she ranked second), but sixth on selling effectiveness (Exhibit 1). Costanzo and Reeves had spoken to Mitchell about her performance and expressed disappointment. Mitchell had informed them, respectfully but firmly, that she saw the most important aspect of her job as giving customers fast, accurate, and courteous service, telling the two bank officers:

> I did try this selling thing but it just seemed to annoy people. Some said they were in a hurry and couldn't talk now; others looked at me as if I were slightly crazy to bring up the subject of a different bank service than the one they were currently transacting. And then, when you got the odd person who seemed interested, you

EXHIBIT 1: Performance Scores of the CSRs

Menton Bank: Summary of performance evaluation scores for customer service representatives at Victory Square branch during latest two half-year periods

		Operational Criteria[1] (max.: 70 points)		Selling Effectiveness[2] (max.: 30 points)		Total Score	
CSR Name[3]	**Length of Full-Time Bank Service**	**1st Half**	**2nd Half**	**1st Half**	**2nd Half**	**1st Half**	**2nd Half**
Mary Bell	16 years, 10 months	65	64	16	20	81	84
Scott Dubois	2 years, 3 months	63	61	15	19	78	80
Bruce Greenfield	12 months	48	42	20	26	68	68
Karen Mitchell	3 years, 7 months	67	67	13	12	80	79
Sharon Rubin	1 year, 4 months	53	55	8	9	61	64
Swee Hoon Chen	7 months	—	50	—	22	—	72
Jean Warshawski	2 years, 1 month	57	55	21	28	79	83

Note: 1. Totals based on sum of ratings points against various criteria, including accuracy, work production, attendance, and punctuality, personal appearance, organization of work, initiative, cooperation with others, problem-solving ability, and quality of interaction with customers.

2. Points awarded for both direct sales by CSR (e.g., traveler's checks) and referral selling by CSR to CAR (e.g., debit card, certificates of deposit, personal line of credit).

3. Full-time CSRs only (part-time CSRs were evaluated separately).

could hear the other customers in the line grumbling about the slow service.

"Really, the last straw was when I noticed on the computer screen that this woman had several thousand in her savings account so I suggested to her, just as the trainer had told us, that she could earn more interest if she opened a money market account. Well, she told me it was none of my business what she did with her money, and stomped off. Don't get me wrong, I love being able to help customers, and if they ask for my advice, I'll gladly tell them about what the bank has to offer."

Selecting a New Head CSR

Two weeks after this meeting, it was announced that the head CSR was leaving. The job entailed some supervision of the work of the other CSRs (including allocation of work assignments and scheduling part-time CSRs at busy periods or during employ vacations), consultation on—and, where possible, resolution of—any problems occurring at the teller stations, and handling of large cash deposits and withdrawals by local retailers (see position description in the Appendix at the end of this case). When not engaged on such tasks, the head CSR was expected to operate a regular teller window.

The pay scale for a head CSR ranged from $10.00–$15.00 per hour, depending on qualifications, seniority, and branch size, as compared to a range $8.40–$12.00 per hour for CSRs. The pay scale for CARs ranged from $9.20–$13.50. Full-time employees (who were not unionized) worked a 40-hour week, including some evenings until 6:00 p.m. and certain Saturday mornings. Costanzo indicated that the pay scales were typical for banks in the region, although the average CSR at Menton

EXHIBIT 2: Bank Tellers Today Are Expected to Shoulder Wider Job Responsibilities to Meet the Demand for Greater Customer Service Orientation

was better qualified than those at smaller banks and therefore higher on the scale. Karen Mitchell was currently earning $10.80 per hour, reflecting her education, which included a diploma in business administration, three-and-a-half years' experience, and significant past merit increases. If promoted to head CSR, she would qualify for an initial rate of $12.50 an hour. When applications for the positions closed, Mitchell was one of three candidates. The other two candidates were Jean Warshawski, 42, another CSR at the Victory Square branch; and Curtis Richter, 24, the head CSR at one of Menton Bank's small suburban branches, who was seeking more responsibility.

Warshawski was married with two sons in school. She had started working as a part-time teller at Victory Square some three years previously, switching to full-time work a year later in order, as she said, to put away some money for her boys' college education. Warshawski was a cheerful woman with a jolly laugh. She had a wonderful memory for people's names, and Reeves had often seen her greeting customers on the street or in a restaurant during her lunch hour. Reviewing her evaluations over the previous three years, Reeves noted that she had initially performed poorly on accuracy and at one point, when she was still a part-timer, had been put on probation because of frequent inaccuracies in the balance in her cash drawer at the end of the day. Although Reeves considered her much improved on this score, he still saw room for improvement. The Customer Service Director had also on occasion reprimanded her for tardiness during the past year. Warshawski attributed this to health problems with her elder son who, she said, was now responding to treatment.

Both Reeves and Costanzo had observed Warshawski at work and agreed that her interactions with customers were exceptionally good, although she tended to be overly chatty and was not as fast as Karen Mitchell. She seemed to have a natural ability to size up customers and to decide which ones were good prospects for a quick sales pitch on a specific financial product. Although slightly untidy in her personal appearance, she was very well organized in her work and was quick to help her fellow CSRs, especially new hires. She was currently earning $10.20 per hour as a CSR and would qualify for a rate of $12.10 as head CSR. In the most recent six months, Warshawski had ranked ahead of Mitchell as a result of being very successful in consultative selling (Exhibit 1).

Richter, the third candidate, was not working in one of the three test branches, and so had not been exposed to the consultative selling program and its corresponding evaluation scheme. However, he had received excellent evaluations for his work in Menton's small Longmeadow branch, where he had been employed for three years. A move to Victory Square would increase his earnings from $11.20 to $12.10 per hour. Reeves and Costanzo had interviewed Richter and considered him intelligent and personable. He had joined the bank after dropping out of college midway through his third year, but had recently started taking evening courses in order to complete his degree. The Longmeadow branch was located in an older part of town, where commercial and retail activities were rather stagnant. This branch (which was rumored to be under consideration for closure) had not yet been renovated and had no ATMs, although there was an ATM accessible to Menton customers one block away. Richter supervised three CSRs and reported directly to the branch manager who spoke very highly of him. Since there were no CARs in this branch, Richter and another experienced CSR took turns to handle new accounts and loan or mortgage applications.

Costanzo and Reeves were troubled by the decision that faced them. Prior to the bank's shift in focus, Mitchell would have been the natural choice for the head CSR job which, in turn, could be a stepping stone to further promotions, including CAR, Customer Service Director, and, eventually, Manager of a small branch or a management position in the head office. Mitchell had told her superiors that she was interested in making a career in banking and that she was eager to take on further responsibilities.

Compounding the problem was the fact that the three branches testing the improved branch design and new customer service program had just completed a full year of the test. Costanzo knew that sales and profits were up significantly at all three branches, relative to the bank's performance as a whole. She anticipated that top management would want to extend the program systemwide after making any modifications that seemed desirable.

Study Questions

1. Identify the steps taken by Menton Bank to develop a stronger customer orientation in its retail branches.
2. Compare and contrast the jobs of CAR and CSR. How important is each (a) to bank operations and (b) to customer satisfaction?
3. Evaluate the strengths and weaknesses of Karen Mitchell and the other candidates for head CSR.
4. What action do you recommend for filling the head CSR position?

Appendix

Menton Bank: Job Descriptions for Customer Service Staff in Branches

Previous Job Description for Teller

FUNCTION: Provides customer services by receiving, paying out, and keeping accurate records of all money involved in paying and receiving transactions. Promotes the bank's services.

Responsibilities

1. Serves customers:
   - Accepts deposits, verifies cash and endorsements, and gives customers their receipts.
   - Cashes checks within the limits assigned or refers customers to supervisor for authorization.
   - Accepts savings deposits and withdrawals, verifies signatures, and posts interest and balances as necessary.
   - Accepts loan, credit card, utility, and other payments.
   - Issues money orders, cashier's checks, traveler's checks, and foreign currency.
   - Reconciles customer statements and confers with bookkeeping personnel regarding discrepancies in balances or other problems.
   - Issues credit card advances.
2. Prepares individual daily settlement of teller cash and proof transactions.
3. Prepares branch daily journal and general ledger.
4. Promotes the bank's services:
   - Cross-sells other bank services appropriate to customer's needs.
   - Answers inquiries regarding bank matters.
   - Directs customers to other departments for specialized services.
5. Assists with other branch duties:
   - Totals receipts at night and mail deposits.
   - Reconciles ATM transactions.
   - Provides safe deposit services.
   - Performs secretarial duties.

New Job Description for Customer Service Representative

FUNCTION: Provides customers with the highest quality services, with special emphasis on recognizing customer need and cross-selling appropriate bank services. Plays an active role in developing and maintaining good relations.

Responsibilities

1. Presents and communicates the best possible customer service:
   - Greets all customers with a courteous, friendly attitude.
   - Provides fast, accurate, friendly service.
   - Uses customer's name whenever possible.
2. Sells bank services and maintains customer relations:
   - Cross-sells retail services by identifying and referring valid prospects to a CAR or customer service director. When time permits (no other customers waiting in line), should actively cross-sell retail services.
   - Develops new business by acquainting noncustomers with bank services and existing customers with additional services they are not currently using.
3. Provides a prompt and efficient operation on a professional level:
   - Receives cash and/or checks for checking accounts, savings accounts, taxes withheld, loan payments, Mastercard and Visa, mortgage payments, money orders, traveler's checks, cashier's checks.
   - Verifies amount of cash and/or checks received, being alert to counterfeit or fraudulent items.

- Cashes checks in accordance with bank policy. Watches for stop payments and holds funds per bank policy.
- Receives payment of collection items, safe deposit rentals, and other miscellaneous items.
- Confers with head CSR or Customer Service Director on nonroutine situations.
- Sells traveler's checks, money orders, monthly transit passes, and cashier's checks and may redeem coupons and sell or redeem foreign currency.
- Prepares coin and currency orders as necessary.
- Services, maintains, and settles ATMs as required.
- Ensures only minimum cash exposure, necessary for efficient operation, is kept in cash drawer; removes excess cash immediately to secured location.
- Prepares accurate and timely daily settlement of work.
- Performs bookkeeping and operational functions as assigned by Customer Service Director.

New Job Description for Head Customer Service Representative

FUNCTION: Supervises all CSRs in the designated branch office, ensuring efficient operation and the highest-quality service to customers. Plays an active role in developing and maintaining good customer relations. Assists other branch personnel on request.

Responsibilities

1. Supervises the CSRs in the branch:
   - Allocates work, coordinates work flow, reviews and revises work procedures.
   - Ensures teller area is adequately and efficiently staffed with well-trained, qualified personnel.
   - Assists CSRs with more complex transactions.
   - Resolves routine personnel problems, referring more complex situations to Customer Service Director.
   - Participates in decisions concerning performance appraisal, promotions, wage changes, transfers, and termination of subordinate CSR staff.
2. Assumes responsibility for CSRs' money:
   - Buys and sells money in the vault, ensuring adequacy of branch currency and coin supply.
   - Ensures CSRs and cash sheets are in balance.
   - Maintains necessary records, including daily branch journal and general ledger.
3. Accepts deposits and withdrawals by business customers at the commercial window.
4. Operates teller window to provide services to retail customers (see Responsibilities for CSRs).

New Job Description for Customer Assistance Representative

FUNCTION: Provides services and guidance to customers/prospects seeking banking relationships or related information. Promotes and sells needed products and responds to special requests by existing customers.

Responsibilities

1. Provides prompt, efficient, and friendly service to all customers and prospective customers:
   - Describes and sells bank services to customers/prospects who approach them directly or via referral from customer service reps or other bank personnel.
   - Answers customers' questions regarding bank services, hours, etc.
2. Identifies and responds to customers' needs:
   - Promotes and sells retail services and identifies any existing cross-sell opportunities.
   - Opens new accounts for individuals, businesses, and private organizations.
   - Prepares temporary checks and deposit slips for new checking/NOW accounts.
   - Sells checks and deposit slips.
   - Interviews and takes applications for and pays out on installment/charge card accounts and other credit-related products.

- Certifies checks.
- Handles stop payment requests.
- Responds to telephone mail inquiries from customers or bank personnel.
- Receives notification of name or address changes and takes necessary action.
- Takes action on notification of lost passbooks, credit cards, ATM cards, collateral, and other lost or stolen items.
- Demonstrates ATMs to customers and assists with problems.
- Coordinates closing of accounts and ascertains reasons.

3. Sells and services all retail products:
   - Advises customers and processes applications for all products covered in CAR training programs (and updates).
   - Initiates referrals to the appropriate department when a trust or corporate business need is identified.

New Job Description for Customer Service Director

FUNCTION: Supervises CSRs, CARs, and other staff as assigned to provide the most effective and profitable retail banking delivery system in the local marketplace. Supervises sales efforts and provides feedback to management concerning response to products and services by current and prospective banking customers. Communicates goals and results to those supervised and ensures operational standards are met in order to achieve outstanding customer service.

Responsibilities

1. Supervises effective delivery of retail products:
   - Selects, trains, and manages CSRs and CARs.
   - Assigns duties and work schedules.
   - Completes performance reviews.
2. Personally, and through those supervised, renders the highest level of professional and efficient customer service available in the local marketplace:
   - Provides high level of service while implementing most efficient and customer-sensitive staffing schedules.
   - Supervises all on-the-job programs within office.
   - Ensures that outstanding customer service standards are achieved.
   - Directs remedial programs for CSRs and CARs as necessary.
3. Develops retail sales effectiveness to the degree necessary to achieve market share objectives:
   - Ensures that all CSRs and CARs possess comprehensive product knowledge.
   - Directs coordinated cross-sell program within office at all times.
   - Reports staff training needs to branch manager and/or regional training director.
4. Ensures adherence to operational standards:
   - Oversees preparation of daily and monthly operational and sales reports.
   - Estimates, approves, and coordinates branch cash needs in advance.
   - Oversees ATM processing function.
   - Handles or consults with CSRs/CARs on more complex transactions.
   - Ensures clean and business-like appearance of the branch facility.
5. Informs branch manager of customer response to products:
   - Reports customer complaints and types of sales resistance encountered.
   - Describes and summarizes reasons for account closings.
6. Communicates effectively the goals and results of the bank to those under supervision:
   - Reduces office goals into a format which translates to goals for each CSR or CAR.
   - Reports sales and cross-sell results to all CSRs and CARs.
   - Conducts sales- and service-oriented staff meetings with CSRs/CARs on a regular basis.
   - Attends all scheduled customer service management meetings organized by regional office.

CASE 13 Dr. Mahalee Goes to London: Global Client Management

CHRISTOPHER LOVELOCK

A senior account officer at an international bank is about to meet a wealthy Asian businessman who seeks funding for a buyout of his company. The prospective client has already visited a competing bank.

It was a Friday in mid-February and Dr. Kadir Mahalee, a wealthy businessman from the southeast Asian nation of Tailesia, was visiting London on a trip that combined business and pleasure. Mahalee, who held a doctorate from the London School of Economics and had earlier been a professor of international trade and government trade negotiator, was the founder of Eximsa, a major export company in Tailesia. Business brought him to London every two to three months. These trips provided him with the opportunity to visit his daughter, Leona, the eldest of his four children, who lived in London. Several of his 10 grandchildren were attending college in Britain, and he was especially proud of his grandson, Anson, who was a student at the Royal Academy of Music. In fact, he had scheduled this trip to coincide with a violin recital by Anson at 2:00 p.m. on this particular Friday.

The primary purpose of Mahalee's visit was to resolve a delicate matter regarding his company. He had decided to retire and wished to make arrangements for the company's future. His son, Victor, was involved in the business and ran Eximsa's trading office in Europe. However, Victor was in poor health and unable to take over the firm. Mahalee believed that a group of loyal employees were interested in buying his company, if the necessary credit could be arranged.

Before leaving Tailesia, Mahalee discussed the possibility of a buyout with his trusted financial adviser, Lee Siew Meng, who recommended that he talk to several banks in London because of the potential complexity of the business deal:

> *The London banks are experienced in buyouts. Also, you need a bank that can handle the credit for the interested buyers in New York and London, as well as Asia. Once the buyout takes place, you'll have significant cash to invest. This would be a good time to review your estate plans as well.*

Referring Mahalee to two competitors, The Trust Company and Global Private Bank, Lee added:

> *I've met an account officer from Global who called on me several times. Here's his business card; his name is Miguel Kim. I've never done any business with him, but he did seem quite competent. Unfortunately, I don't know anyone at the Trust Company, but here's their address in London.*

After checking into the Savoy Hotel in London the following Wednesday, Mahalee telephoned Kim's office. Since Kim was out, Mahalee spoke to the account officer's secretary, described himself briefly, and arranged to stop by Global's Lombard Street office around mid-morning on Friday.

On Thursday, Mahalee visited The Trust Company. The two people he met were extremely pleasant and had spent some time in Tailesia. They seemed very knowledgeable about managing estates and gave him some good recommendations about handling his complex family affairs. However, they were clearly less experienced in handling business credit, his most urgent need.

EXHIBIT 1: Receiving a Client on Short Notice Would Require a Bank's Vice President to Rely on All Her Expertise and Experience to Clinch the Deal

The next morning, Mahalee had breakfast with Leona. As they parted, she said, "I'll meet you at 1:30 p.m. in the lobby of the Savoy, and we'll go to the recital together. We mustn't be late if we want to get front-row seats."

On his way to Global Private Bank, Mahalee stopped at Mappin & Webb's jewelry store to buy his wife a present for their anniversary. His shopping was pleasant and leisurely; he purchased a beautiful emerald necklace that he knew his wife would like. When he emerged from the jewelry store, he was caught in an unexpected snow flurry. He had difficulty finding a taxi and his arthritis started acting up, making walking to the nearest tube station out of the question. At last, he caught a taxi and arrived at the Lombard Street location of Global Bancorp about noon. After going into the street-level branch of Global Retail Bank, he was redirected by a security guard to the Private Bank offices on the second floor.

He arrived at the Private Bank's nicely appointed reception area at 12:15 p.m. The receptionist greeted him and contacted Miguel Kim's secretary, who came out promptly to see Mahalee, and declared:

> *Mr. Kim was disappointed that he couldn't be here to welcome you, Dr. Mahalee, but he had a lunch appointment with one of his clients that was scheduled over a month ago. He expects to return at about 1:30. In the meantime, he has asked another senior account officer, Sophia Costa, to assist you.*

Sophia Costa, 41, was a vice president of the bank and had worked for Global Bancorp for 14 years (two years longer than Miguel Kim). She had visited Tailesia once, but had not met Mahalee's financial adviser nor any member of the Mahalee family. An experienced relationship manager, Costa was knowledgeable about offshore investment management and fiduciary services. Miguel Kim had looked into her office at 11:45 a.m. and asked her if she would cover for him in case a prospective client, a Dr. Mahalee, whom he had expected to see earlier, should happen to arrive. He told Costa that Mahalee was a successful Tailesian businessman planning for his retirement, but that he had never met the prospect personally, then rushed off to lunch.

The phone rang in Costa's office, and she reached across the desk to pick it up. It was Kim's secretary. "Dr. Mahalee is in reception, Ms. Costa."

Study Questions

1. Prepare a flowchart of Dr. Mahalee's service encounters.
2. Putting yourself in Mahalee's shoes, how do you feel (both physically and mentally) after speaking with the receptionist at Global? What are your priorities right now?
3. As Sophia Costa, what action would you take in your first five minutes with Mahalee?
4. What would constitute a good outcome of the meeting for both the client and the bank? How should Costa try to bring about such an outcome?

CASE 14 Hilton HHonors Worldwide: Loyalty Wars

JOHN DEIGHTON AND STOWE SHOEMAKER

Hilton Hotels regards frequent guest programs as the lodging industry's most important marketing tool, serving to direct promotional and customer service efforts at the heavy user. How should management of Hilton's international guest rewards program respond when Starwood, a competing hotel group operating several brands, ups the ante in the loyalty stakes?

Jeff Diskin, head of Hilton HHonors® (Hilton's guest reward program), opened *The Wall Street Journal* on February 2, 1999, and read the headline, "Hotels Raise the Ante in Business-Travel Game." The story read, "Starwood Hotels and Resorts Worldwide Inc. is expected to unveil tomorrow an aggressive frequent-guest program that it hopes will help lure more business travelers to its Sheraton, Westin and other hotels. Accompanied by a $50 million ad campaign, the program ratchets up the stakes in the loyalty-program game that big corporate hotel companies, including Starwood and its rivals at Marriott, Hilton and Hyatt are playing."[1]

Diskin did not hide his concern: "These guys are raising their costs, and they're probably raising mine too. They are reducing the cost-effectiveness of the industry's most important marketing tool by deficit spending against their program. Loyalty programs have been at the core of how we attract and retain our best customers for over a decade. But they are only as cost-effective as our competitors let them be."

Loyalty Marketing Programs

The idea of rewarding loyalty had its origins in coupons and trading stamps. First in the 1900s and again in the 1950s, America experienced episodes of trading-stamp frenzy that became so intense that congressional investigations were mounted. Retailers would give customers small adhesive stamps in proportion to the amount of their purchases, to be pasted into books and eventually redeemed for merchandise. The best-known operator had been the S&H Green Stamp Company. Both episodes had lasted about 20 years, declining as the consumer passion for collecting abated and vendors came to the conclusion that any advantage they might once have held had been competed away by emulators.

Loyalty marketing in its modern form was born in 1981 when American Airlines introduced the AAdvantage frequent-flyer program, giving "miles" in proportion to miles traveled, redeemable for free travel. It did so in response to the competitive pressure that followed airline deregulation. The American Airlines program had no need of stamps, because it took advantage of the data warehousing capabilities of computers. Soon program administrators realized that they had a tool that did not merely reward loyalty but identified by name and address the people who accounted for most of aviation's revenues and made a one-to-one relationship possible.

Competing airlines launched their own programs, but, unlike stamp programs, frequent-flyer programs seemed to survive emulation. By 1990, almost all airlines offered

Professor John Deighton of Harvard Business School and Professor Stowe Shoemaker of the William F. Harrah College of Hotel Administration, University of Nevada, Las Vegas, prepared this case. HBS cases are developed solely as the basis for class discussion. Cases are not intended to serve as endorsements, sources of primary data, or illustrations of effective or ineffective management. The case reflects the status of Hilton Hotels Corporation and Hilton HHonors Worldwide as of January 1999. Hilton has made numerous changes since that time, including Hilton Hotels Corporation's acquisition of Promus Hotel Corporation.

them. In the late 1990s, Delta Airlines and United Airlines linked their programs together, as did American and US Airways in the United States. Internationally, United Airlines and Lufthansa combined with 11 other airlines to form Star Alliance, and American, British Airways, and four others formed an alliance called Oneworld. In these alliances, qualifying flights on any of the member airlines could be credited to the frequent-flyer club of the flyer's choice.

As the decade ended, computer-based frequency programs were common in many service industries, including car rentals, department stores, video and book retailing, credit cards, movie theaters, and the hotel industry.

The Hotel Industry

Chain brands were a major factor in the global hotel market of 13.6 million rooms.[2] The chains supplied reservation services, field sales operations, loyalty program administration, and the management of hotel properties under well-recognized names such as Hilton and Marriott. (See Exhibit 1 for details of the seven largest U.S. hotel chains competing in the business-class hotel segment.)

While the brands stood for quality, there was less standardization of operations in hotel chains than in many other services. The reason was that behind a consumer's experience of a hotel brand might lie any of many methods of control. A branded hotel might be owned and managed by the chain, but it might be owned by a third party and managed by the chain, or owned by the chain and managed by a franchisee,

EXHIBIT 1: The U.S. Lodging Industry

	Countries	Properties	Rooms	Owned Properties	Franchised Properties	Management Contracts
Marriott International[a]	53	1,764	339,200	49	936	776
Bass Hotels and Resorts[b]	90	2,700	447,967	76	2,439	185
Hilton Hotels Corp.[c]	11	272	91,060	39	207	16
Starwood Hotels and Resorts Worldwide, Inc.[d]	72	695	212,950	171	291	233
Hyatt[e]	45	246	93,729	NA	NA	NA
Carlson[f]	50	581	112,089	1	542	38
Hilton International[g]	50	224	62,941	154	0	70
Promus[h]	11	1,398	198,526	160	1,059	179

[a]Includes Marriott Hotels, Resorts and Suites; Courtyard, Residence Inn, TownePlace Suites, Fairfield Inn, SpringHill Suites, Marriott Vacation Club International; Conference Centers, Marriott Executive Residences, Ritz-Carlton, Renaissance, Ramada International.

[b]Includes Inter-Continental, Forum, Crowne Plaza, Holiday Inn, Holiday Inn Express, Staybridge.

[c]Includes Hilton Hotels, Hilton Garden Inns, Hilton Suites, Hilton Grand Vacation Clubs, and Conrad International.

[d]Includes St. Regis, Westin Hotels and Resorts, Sheraton Hotels and Resorts, Four Points, Sheraton Inns, The W Hotels. Does not include other Starwood-owned hotels, flagged under other brands (93 properties for 29,322 rooms).

[e]Includes Hyatt Hotels, Hyatt International, and Southern Pacific Hotel Corporation (SPHC). Because it is a privately held corporation, it will not divulge the breakdown of rooms between ownership, franchise, and management contract.

[f]Includes Radisson Hotels Worldwide, Regent International Hotels, Country Inns and Suites.

[g]A wholly owned subsidiary of what was once known as the Ladbroke Group. In spring 1999, Ladbroke changed their name to Hilton Group PLC to reflect the emphasis on hotels.

[h]Includes such brands as Doubletree, Red Lion, Hampton Inn, Hampton Inn & Suites, Embassy Suites, and Homewood Suites.

Source: World Trade Organization and company information.

or, in some cases, owned and managed by the franchisee. Occasionally chains managed one another's brands, because one chain could be another's franchisee. Starwood, for example, ran hotels under the Hilton brand as Hilton's franchisee. Information about competitors' operating procedures therefore circulated quite freely in the industry.

Consumers

For most Americans, a stay in a hotel was a relatively rare event. Of the 74 percent of Americans who traveled overnight in a year, only 41 percent used a hotel, motel, or resort. The market in which Hilton competed was smaller still, defined by price point and trip purpose and divided among business, convention, and leisure segments.

The **business** segment accounted for one-third of all room nights in the market that Hilton served. About two-thirds of these stays were at rates negotiated between the guest's employer and the chain, but since most corporations negotiated rates with two and sometimes three hotel chains, business travelers had some discretion to choose where they would stay. About one-third of business travelers did not have access to negotiated corporate rates and had full discretion to choose their hotel.

The **convention** segment, comprising convention, conference, and other meeting-related travel, accounted for another third of room nights in Hilton's competitive set. The choice of hotel in this instance was in the hands of a small number of professional conference organizers, typically employees of professional associations and major corporations.

The **leisure** segment accounted for the final third. Leisure guests were price sensitive, often making their selections from among packages of airlines, cars, tours, and hotels assembled by a small group of wholesalers and tour organizers at rates discounted below business rates.

Although the chains as a whole experienced demand from all segments, individual properties tended to draw disproportionately from one segment or another. Resort hotels served leisure travelers and some conventioneers, convention hotels depended on group and business travel, and hotels near airports were patronized by guests on business, for example. These segmentation schemes, however, obscured the fact that the individuals in segments differentiated by trip purpose and price point were often the same people. Frequent travelers patronized hotels of various kinds and price segments, depending, for example, on whether a stay was a reimbursable business expense, a vacation, or a personal expense.

Competition

Four large global brands dominated the business-class hotel market (Table A). Each competed at more than one price point. (Exhibit 2 shows the price points in the industry, and Exhibit 3 shows the distribution of brands across price points.)

STARWOOD Beginning in 1991, Barry Sternlicht built Starwood Hotels and Resorts Worldwide from a base in a real estate investment trust. In January 1998, Starwood bought Westin Hotels and Resorts, and a month later it bought ITT Corporation, which included Sheraton Hotels and Resorts, after a well-publicized battle with Hilton Hotels

TABLE A

Marriott International	339,200 rooms
Starwood Hotels and Resorts	212,900 rooms
Hyatt Hotels	93,700 rooms
Hilton Hotels	91,100 rooms
Hilton International	62,900 rooms

Source: Company records.

EXHIBIT 2: Price Segments in the Lodging Industry

- Luxury: Average rack rate over $125, full-service hotels with deluxe amenities for leisure travelers and special amenities for business and meeting markets. Chains in this segment include Four Seasons, Hilton, Hyatt, Inter-Continental (a Bass Hotels and Resorts brand), Marriott Hotels and Resorts, Renaissance (a Marriott International brand), Ritz-Carlton (also a Marriott International brand), Sheraton (a Starwood Hotels and Resorts brand), and Westin (also a Starwood Hotels and Resorts brand).
- Upscale: Average rack rate between $100 and $125, full-service hotels with standard amenities. Includes most all-suite, non-extended-stay brands. Crowne Plaza (a Bass Hotels and Resorts brand), Doubletree Guest Suites (a Promus Hotel Corp. brand), Embassy Suites (also a Promus Hotel Corp. brand), Radisson (a Carlson Worldwide Hospitality brand), Hilton Inn, and Clarion (a Choice Hotels brand) are all examples of chains in this segment.
- Midmarket with food and beverage (F&B): Average rack rate between $60 and $90, full-service hotels with lower service levels and amenities than the upscale segment. Examples include Best Western, Courtyard (a Marriott International brand), Garden Inn (a Hilton brand), Holiday Inn (a Bass Hotels and Resorts brand), and Howard Johnson (a Cendant brand).
- Midmarket without F&B: Average rack rate between $45 and $70, with limited-service and comparable amenities to the midmarket with F&B segment. Examples of chains in this segment include Hampton Inns (a Promus brand), Holiday Inn Express (a Bass Hotels and Resorts brand), and Comfort Inn (a Choice Hotels brand).
- Economy: Average rack rate between $40 and $65, with limited service and few amenities. Fairfield Inn (a Marriott International brand), Red Roof Inn, Travelodge, and Days Inn of America (a Cendant brand) are examples of economy chains.
- Budget: Average rack rate between $30 and $60, with limited service and basic amenities. Motel 6, Super 8, and Econo Lodge are the best-known chains in this segment.
- Extended stay: Average rack rate between $60 and $90, targeted to extended-stay market and designed for extended length of stay. Marriott International has the following two brands in this market: Residence Inn by Marriott and TownePlace Suites. Other chains include Homewood Suites (a Bass Hotels and Resorts brand), Summerfield Suites, and Extended Stay America.

Source: U.S. lodging chains segmented by RealTime Hotel Reports Inc., authors of the 1998 Lodging Survey.

Corporation. By year-end, Starwood had under unified management the Westin, Sheraton, St. Regis, Four Points, and Caesar's Palace brands. Starwood had recently announced plans to create a new brand, W, aimed at younger professionals.

MARRIOTT Marriott International operated and franchised hotels under the Marriott, Ritz-Carlton, Renaissance, Residence Inn, Courtyard, TownePlace Suites, Fairfield Inn, SpringHill Suites, and Ramada International brands. It also operated conference centers and provided furnished corporate housing. A real estate investment trust, Host Marriott, owned some of the properties operated by Marriott International, as well as some Hyatt, Four Season, and Swissotel properties.

HYATT The Pritzker family of Chicago owned Hyatt Corporation, the only privately owned major hotel chain. Hyatt comprised Hyatt Hotels, operating hotels and resorts in the United States, Canada, and the Caribbean; and Hyatt International, operating overseas. Hyatt also owned Southern Pacific Hotel Group, a three- and four-star hotel chain based primarily in Australia. Although the companies operated independently, they ran joint marketing programs.

The 1990s had been a time of consolidation and rationalization in the lodging industry, partly due to application of information technologies to reservation systems

EXHIBIT 3: Segments Served by the Major Chains

	Luxury	Upscale	Mid-Market with Food and Beverage	Mid-Market without Food and Beverage	Economy	Budget	Extended Stay
Hilton	X	X	X	X			
Hyatt	X						
Marriott	X	X	X		X		X
Starwood	X	X	X				X

Source: Company records.

and control of operations. Diskin reflected on the trend: "Historically, bigger has been better because it has led to economies of scale and bigger and better brands to leverage. Historically, big players could win even if they did not do a particularly good job on service, performance, or programs. Now [after the Starwood deal] there's another big player. It would have been nice if it had been Hilton that was the largest hotel chain in the world, but biggest is not the only way to be best."

Marketing the Hilton Brand

The Hilton brand was controlled by two entirely unrelated corporations, Hilton Hotels Corporation (HHC), based in Beverley Hills, California, and Hilton International (HIC), headquartered near London, England. In 1997, however, HHC and HIC agreed to reunify the Hilton brand worldwide. They agreed to cooperate on sales and marketing, standardize operations, and run the Hilton HHonors loyalty program across all HHC and HIC hotels. At the end of 1998, HHC divested itself of casino interests and announced "a new era as a dedicated hotel company."

The exit from gaming, the reunification of Hilton's worldwide marketing, and the extension of the brand into the middle market under the Hilton Garden Inns name were initiatives that followed the appointment in 1997 of Stephen F. Bollenbach as president and chief executive officer of Hilton. Bollenbach had served as chief financial officer of Marriott and most recently as chief financial officer of Disney, and he brought to Hilton a passion for branding. To some members of the Hilton management team, the focus on brand development was a welcome one. "Hilton's advantage has been a well-recognized name, but a potentially limiting factor has been a widely varying product and the challenge of managing customer expectation with such a variety of product offerings. Since Hilton includes everything from world-renowned properties like The Waldorf-Astoria and Hilton Hawaiian Village to the smaller middle-market Hilton Garden Inns, it's important to give consumers a clear sense of what to expect from the various types of hotels," observed one manager.

In mid-1999, the properties branded as Hilton hotels comprised:

1. 39 owned or partly owned by HHC in the United States
2. 207 franchised by HHC to third-party managers in the United States
3. 16 managed by HHC in the United States on behalf of third-party owners
4. 10 managed internationally under HHC's Conrad International brand
5. 220 managed by HIC in over 50 countries excluding the U.S.

The executives at Hilton HHonors worked for these 492 hotels and their 154,000 rooms. The previous year had been successful. Revenues had been in the region of $158 per night per guest, and occupancy had exceeded break-even. Hotels like Hilton's tended to cover fixed costs at about 68 percent occupancy, and 80 percent of all revenue at higher occupancy levels flowed to the bottom line. Advertising, selling, and other marketing costs (a component of fixed costs) for this group of hotels were not published, but industry norms ran at about $750 per room per year.[3]

Hilton HHonors Program

Hilton HHonors was the name Hilton gave to its program designed to build loyalty to the Hilton brand worldwide. Hilton HHonors Worldwide (HHW) operated the program, not as a profit center but as a service to its two parents, HHC and HIC. It was required to break even each year and to measure its effectiveness through a complex set of program metrics. Diskin ran the limited liability corporation with a staff of 30, with one vice president overseeing the program's marketing efforts and one with operational and customer service oversight. (Exhibit 4 shows the income statement for HHW.)

Membership in the Hilton HHonors program was open to anyone who applied, at no charge. Members earned points toward their Hilton HHonors account whenever they stayed at HHC or HIC hotels. When Hilton HHonors members accumulated enough points in the program, they could redeem them for stays at HHonors hotels, use them

EXHIBIT 4: Hilton HHonors Worldwide: 1998 Income Statement

(While these data are broadly reflective of the economic situation, certain competitively sensitive information has been masked.)

	$ (THOUSANDS)	
Revenue		
Contributions from hotels		
Domestic	$39,755	
International	$10,100	
Strategic partner contributions	$18,841	
Membership fees[a]	$1,141	
Total		**$69,837**
Expense		
Redemptions		
Cash payments to hotels	$12,654	
Deferred liability[b]	$9,436	
Airline miles purchases	$17,851	
Member acquisition expenses	$7,273	
Member communication expenses	4,236	
Program administration expenses	$17,988	
Total		**$69,438**
Net Income		**$399**

[a]From members of the Hilton Senior HHonors program only. The Senior HHonors program invited people over 60 to receive discounted stays in exchange for a membership fee. Regular HHonors members do not pay a membership fee.

[b]More points were issued than redeemed. From the outstanding balance a deferred liability was charged to HHW's income statement, based on estimating the proportion of points that would ultimately be redeemed.

Source: Company records (masked). For purposes of consistency in calculation among class members, assume an average nightly revenue of $158 per room. Assume that airline miles are purchased from the airline by Hilton at 1 cent per mile.

to buy products and services from partner companies, or convert them to miles in airline frequent-flyer programs. (Exhibit 5 shows how points in the program flowed among participants in the program, as detailed in the text that follows.)

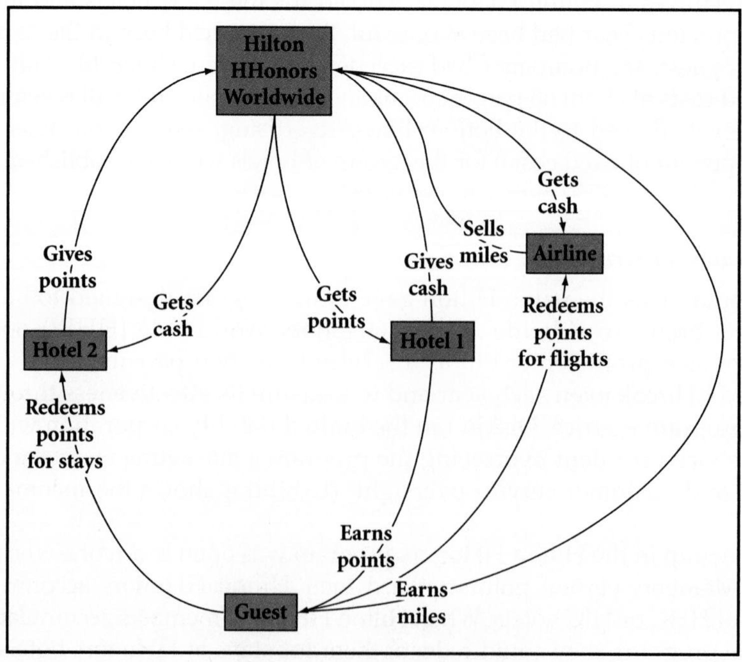

EXHIBIT 5: How the Hilton HHonors Program Works *Source:* Company.

There were four tiers of membership—Blue, Silver, Gold, and Diamond. The program worked as follows at the Blue level in 1998.

- When a member stayed at a Hilton hotel and paid a so-called business rate,[4] the hotel typically paid HHW 4.5 cents per dollar of the guest's folio (folio is the total charge by the guest before taxes). HHW credited the guest's Hilton HHonors account with 10 points per eligible dollar of folio.
- Hilton guests could earn mileage in partner airline frequent-flyer programs for the same stay that earned them HHonors points, a practice known as Double Dipping. (Hilton was the only hotel chain to offer double dipping; other chains with frequency programs required guests to choose between points in the hotel program or miles in the airline program.) If the member chose to double dip, HHW bought miles from the relevant airline and credited the guest's airline frequent-flyer account at 500 miles per stay.
- If the guest used points to pay for a stay, HHW reimbursed the hosting hotel at more than the costs incremental to the cost of leaving the room empty but less than the revenue from a paying guest. The points needed to earn a stay depended on the class of hotel and fell when occupancy was low. As illustration, redemption rates ranged from 5,000 points to get 50 percent off the $128 cost of a weekend at the Hilton Albuquerque, to 25,000 points for a free weekend night at the $239 per night Hilton Boston Back Bay. A number of exotic rewards were offered, such as a two-person, seven-night diving adventure in the Red Sea for 350,000 points, including hotel and airfare.
- Members earned points by renting a car, flying with a partner airline, using the Hilton Credit Card from American Express, or buying products promoted in mailings by partners such as FTD Florists and Mrs. Field's Cookies. Members could buy points at $10 per thousand for up to 20% of the points needed for a reward.
- Members had other benefits besides free stays. They had a priority-reservation telephone number. Check-in went faster because information on preferences was on file. Members were favored over nonmembers when they asked for late checkout. If members were dissatisfied, they were guaranteed a room upgrade certificate in exchange for a letter explaining their dissatisfaction. Points could be exchanged for airline miles and vice versa and to buy partner products such as airline tickets, flowers, Mrs. Field's Cookies products, Cannondale bicycles, AAA membership, Princess Cruises trips, and car rentals.

Members were awarded Silver VIP status if they stayed at HHonors hotels four times in a year. They earned a 15 percent bonus on base points, received a 5,000-point bonus after seven stays in a quarter, and received a 10,000-point discount when they claimed a reward costing 100,000 points. They were given a certificate for an upgrade to the best room in the hotel after every fifth stay.

Members were awarded Gold VIP status if they stayed at HHonors hotels 16 times or for 36 nights in a year. They earned a 25 percent bonus on base points, received a 5,000-point bonus after seven stays in a quarter, and received a 20,000-point discount when they claimed a reward costing 100,000 points. They were given a certificate for an upgrade to the best room in the hotel after every fifth stay and were upgraded to best available room at time of check-in.

The top 1 percent of members were given Diamond VIP status. This level was not mentioned in promotional material, and no benefits were promised. Diskin explained, "Our goal at the time was to underpromise and overdeliver. If you stay a lot, we say thank you, and as a reward we want to give you Diamond VIP status. We get a lot more bang, more affinity, more vesting from the customer if we do something unexpected. As an industry, we should never overpromise. It leads the public to decide that this is all smoke and mirrors, and it makes it harder for us to deliver genuine value." Table B shows HHW's member activity in 1998.

A further 712,000 stays averaging 2.4 nights were recorded in 1998 for which no Hilton HHonors membership card was presented but instead airline miles were

TABLE B Members' Paid Activity in 1998

	Members (000)	Members Active in 1998 (000)	Stays for Which Members Paid (000)	Nights for Which They Paid (000)	Spending on Which They Earned Points ($000)	Stays per Active Member in 1998	Nights per Active Member in 1998	Reward Claimed by Member
Diamond	24	20	310	521	$62,000	15.5	26.1	27,000
Gold	220	84	1,110	1,916	$266,000	13.2	22.8	34,200
Silver	694	324	1,023	1,999	$341,000	3.2	6.2	70,200
Blue	1,712	992	1,121	2,579	$439,000	1.1	2.6	48,600
Total	2,650	1,420	3,564	7,015	$1,108,000	2.5	4.9	180,000

Source: Company records (certain competitively sensitive information has been masked).

claimed and airline membership numbers were captured, so that the guest could be given a unique identifier in the Hilton database. Spending on these stays totaled $327 million.

Guests identified by their HHonors or airline membership numbers occupied 22.5 percent of all the rooms occupied in the Hilton Hotels and Hilton International network in a year. They were a much smaller proportion of all the guests who stayed with Hilton in a year because they tended to be frequent travelers. Hilton's research found that Hilton HHonors members spent about $4.6 billion on accommodation per year, not all of which was with Hilton. The industry estimated that members of the frequent-stayer programs of all the major hotel chains represented a market worth $11.1 billion and that the average member belonged to 3.5 programs.

Rationales for the Program

1. Revenue and Yield Management

Hotel profitability was acutely sensitive to revenue. A trend in the industry was to appoint a "revenue manager" to each property to oversee the day-to-day decisions that affected hotel revenue. Yield management models were probabilistic algorithms that helped this manager set reservations policy. He or she used past history and other statistical data to make continuously updated recommendations regarding hotel booking patterns and what price to offer a particular guest. Simulation studies had shown that when booking was guided by a good yield management model, a company's revenue increased by 20 percent over a simple "first come, first served, fixed price" policy.

In the hotel industry, effectively managing yield meant utilizing a model to predict that a room was highly likely to come available due to cancellation or no-show, as well as driving business to higher-paying or longer-staying guests. Variable pricing meant that the rate charged for a room depended not only on its size and fittings but also on the day of booking, the day of occupation, the length of stay, and customer characteristics. Of these factors, customer characteristics were the most problematic.

Customer characteristics were needed by the model to estimate "walking cost," the cost of turning a customer away. That cost in turn depended on the customer's future lifetime value to the chain, a function of their willingness to pay, and past loyalty to the chain. These were considered "soft" variables, notoriously difficult to estimate. The better the historical information on a customer, however, the better the estimate. As Adam Burke, HHonors' senior director of marketing for North America, put it, "Who gets the room—the person paying $20 more that you may never see again, or the guy spending thousands of dollars in the system? If we have the right data, the model can be smart enough to know the difference." Some in the hotel industry argued that a benefit of a frequent-guest program was to let the reservations system make those distinctions.

2. Collaborating with Partners

HHW partnered with 25 airlines, three car rental firms, and a number of other firms. Burke explained, "Why is Mrs. Field's Cookies in the program? We have several objectives—regional relevance to consumers, access to partners' customers, making it easier for members to attain rewards. A franchisee may say, 'Why are we doing something with FTD Florists?' We point out that their investment keeps costs down and gives a broader range of rewards to our members."

Burke explained why Hilton offered double dipping: "We have 2.5 million members. The airline frequent-flyer programs have 20, 30, 40 million members who aren't HHonors members and do travel a lot. Airlines don't mind us talking to their members because—through double dipping—we don't compete with their programs. In fact, we complement them by allowing our joint customers to earn both currencies."

3. Working with Franchisees

The Hilton HHonors program was a strong factor in persuading hotel owners to become Hilton franchisees or give Hilton a management contract to run their property. Franchisees tended to be smaller hotels, more dependent on "road warrior" business than many of Hilton's convention hotels, resort hotels, and flagship properties. They saw value in a frequent-guest program to attract business, and HHW's program cost was comparable with or lower than its competitors'. The program's ability to drive business, however, remained its biggest selling point. Diskin elaborated, "Seven or eight years ago some operators were concerned about the cost of the program. We took a bunch of the most vocal, critical guys and we put them in a room for two days with us to discuss the importance of building long-term customer loyalty, and they came out saying, 'We need to spend more money on the program!'"

4. Relations with Guests

The program let the most valuable guests be recognized on-property. Diskin explained:

> In a sense, the loyalty program is a safe haven for the guest. If there is a problem and it is not taken care of at the property level, the guest can contact our customer service team. It's a mechanism to make sure we hear about those problems. We also do outbound after-visit calling, and we call HHonors members because they're the best database and the most critical guests we have. They have the most experience and the highest expectations. We do feedback groups with members in addition to focus groups and quantitative research. We invite a bunch of members in the hotel down for dinner, and we say we want to talk about a subject. I get calls from people that are lifelong loyalists, not because of any changes we've made, but because once we invited them and asked them their opinion. People care about organizations that care about them.

Hilton customized a guest's hotel experience. Diskin explained, "We build guest profiles that keep track of preferences, enabling the hotel to provide customized services. For instance, consider the guest that always wants a room that is for nonsmokers and has a double bed. This information can be stored as part of the member's record so that when she or he makes a reservation, the guest will receive this type of room without having to ask, no matter where the guest is staying."

HHW used direct mail to cultivate the relationship between members and the Hilton brand. Diskin explained, "Certainly you want to focus much of your effort on your highest-revenue guests, but there are also opportunities to reach out and try to target other customer segments. For example, we worked with a nontravel partner to overlay data from their customer files onto our total membership base and identified segments that might like vacation ownership, others who would be great for the casinos, and some that might like the business and teleconferencing services we offer."

Diskin was concerned that some travelers spread their hotel patronage among several chains and did not receive the service to which their total expenditure entitled them. He noted, "Our research suggests that a quarter of the frequent travelers are members of loyalty programs but don't have true loyalty to any one brand. They never get to enjoy the benefits of elite-program status because they don't consolidate their business with one chain. They typically don't see the value in any of the loyalty schemes because they haven't changed their stay behavior to see the benefits."

5. Helping Travel Managers Gain Compliance

A significant proportion of Hilton's business came from contracts with large corporate clients. Hilton offered discounted rates if the corporation delivered enough stays. Burke explained:

> If you are a corporate travel manager, you want employees to comply with the corporate travel policy. You negotiated a rate by promising a volume of stays. While some travel managers can tell employees that they have to follow the company policy if they want to get reimbursed, many others can only recommend. What if someone is a very loyal Marriott customer, yet Marriott is not one of that company's preferred vendors? A travel office is going to have a real hard time getting that guy to stay at Hilton if they can't mandate it.

We respond with a roster of offerings to give that Marriott traveler a personal incentive to use us, the preferred vendor. Our overall objective is to use the program as a tool that can help the travel manager with compliance to their overall travel policy.

Member Attitudes

HHW made extensive use of conjoint analysis to measure what members wanted from the Hilton HHonors program. Burke explained:

> Members come in for an hour-and-a-half interview. They're asked to trade off program elements, including services and amenities in the hotel, based on the value they place on those attributes relative to their cost. The results help us determine the appropriate priorities for modifying the program. We find that different people have different needs. Some people are service oriented. No amount of miles or points is ever going to replace a warm welcome and being recognized by the hotel as a loyal customer. Other people are games players. They go after free stays, and they know the rules as well as we do. We've been in feedback groups where these people will educate us on how our program works! And, of course, many people are a combination of both.

Using a sample that was broadly representative of the program's upper-tier membership categories, program research found that Hilton HHonors members had an average of over 30 stays in all hotel chains per year, staying 4.2 nights per stay. Between 1997 and 1998, Hilton experienced a 17.5 percent increase in member utilization of HHonors hotels globally. Despite this improvement, more than half of HHonors member stays went to competing chains annually—this was primarily attributable to Hilton's relatively limited network size and distribution. The conjoint analysis suggested that roughly one in five HHonors member stays were solely attributable to their membership in the program—making these stays purely incremental.

The study found that the most important features of a hotel program were room upgrades and airline miles, followed by free hotel stays and a variety of on-property benefits and services. Members wanted a streamlined reward-redemption process and points that did not expire. These findings led to refinements in the terms of membership for 1999, but Diskin was exploring more innovative approaches to the rewards program.

Diskin recognized that in their market research studies, consumers tended to describe an ideal program that was simply a version of the programs with which they were familiar. He was looking for more radical innovation:

> Hilton and Marriott tend to attract "games players." We want to compete effectively on the reward elements but also introduce them to the more high-touch, high-feel kind of guest experience as well. The customer base that we have accumulated comprises games players primarily. So we've got to deliver that benefit but still go further.
>
> We've been on a mission to dramatically improve the stay experience for members of the upper-tier ranks of the program. That is the key to competitive distinctiveness. That's not something that anybody can imitate. We want our best customers to feel that when they go to Hilton, they know Hilton knows they're the best customer and they're treated special. We want them to think, "I'm going to have the kind of room I want, I'm going to have the kind of stay I like, and if I have a problem, they're going to take care of it." We want the staff to know who's coming in each day and make sure that these guests get a personal welcome. Our new customer reservation system will get more information down to the hotel. We'll know a lot more about our incoming guests. We will have a guest manager in the hotel whose job it is to make you feel special and to address any concerns you may have.

The Starwood Announcement

The Wall Street Journal of February 2, 1999, announced the birth of the Starwood Preferred Guest Program, covering Westin Hotels Resorts, Sheraton Hotels Resorts, The Luxury Collection, Four Points, Caesar's, and Starwood's new W brand hotels, representing more than 550 participating properties worldwide. It became clear that Starwood was adding program features that might be expensive to match. Four features in particular were of concern.

No blackout dates All frequent guest and airline programs until now had ruled that members could not claim free travel during the very height of seasonal demand and when local events guaranteed a hotel full occupancy. Starwood was saying that if there was a room to rent, points were as good as money.

No capacity control Programs until now had let hotel properties limit the number of rooms for free stays. Starwood was telling hotels that all unreserved rooms should be available to guests paying with points.

Paperless rewards Guests had had previously to exchange points for a certificate and then use the certificate to pay for an authorized stay. Under Starwood's system, individual properties would be able to accept points to pay for a stay.

Hotel reimbursement Now that blackout dates were abolished, a property, particularly an attractive vacation destination, might have to contend with many more points-paying guests than before. Starwood therefore raised the rate at which it reimbursed hotels for these stays. To meet the cost, it charged participating hotels 20 percent to 100 percent more than its competitors on paid stays.

Starwood was pledging to invest $50 million in advertising to publicize the program—significantly more than HHW had historically spent on program communications.

EXHIBIT 6: Membership Offerings of the Four Major Business-Class Hotel Chains in 1998

Chain	Membership Restrictions[a]	Point Value	Eligible Charges	New Member Bonus	Airline Mileage Accrual
Starwood	One stay per year to remain active—basic; 10 stays or 25 room nights per year—medium; 25 stays or 50 room nights	2 Starpoints = $1 basic; 3 Starpoints = $1 medium or premium	Room rate, F&B, laundry/valet, phone, in-room movies	Periodically	Starpoints earned can be converted to miles 1:1; cannot earn both points and miles for the same stay
Hilton	One stay per year to remain active—Blue; 4 stays per year or 10 nights—medium; 16 stays per year or 36 nights—premium; 28 stays or 60 nights—top	10 pts. = $1—Blue; +15% bonus on points earned—medium; +25% bonus on points earned—premium; +50% bonus on points earned—top	Room rate, F&B, laundry, phone	Periodically	500 miles per qualifying stay in addition to point earnings
Hyatt	One stay per year to remain active—basic; 5 stays or 15 nights per year—medium 25 stays or 50 nights per year—premium	5 pts. = $1; +15% bonus on points earned—medium; +30% bonus on points earned—premium	Room rate, F&B, laundry, phone	Periodically	500 miles per stay; not available if earning points
Marriott	No requirements for basic; 15 nights per year—medium; 50 nights per year—premium	10 pts. = $1; +20% bonus on points earned—medium; +25% bonus on points earned—premium	Room rate, F&B, laundry, phone	Double points first 120 days	3 miles per dollar spent at full-service hotels; 1 mile per dollar spent at other hotels; not available if earning points

[a]Most programs run three tiers. For ease of comparison, the three levels are named basic, medium, and premium. HHonors has four tiers.

(Exhibit 6 compares the loyalty programs of the four major business-class hotel chains after the Starwood announcement.)

Diskin's Dilemma

Without any doubt, Starwood had raised the ante in the competition for customer loyalty. Diskin had to decide whether to match or pass. He mused:

> Do we have to compete point for point? Or do we want to take a different positioning and hold on to our loyal members and differentiate HHonors from Starwood and other competitors? We're in a cycle where for 10 years the cost to our hotels of our frequent-guest program as a percent of the folio has been cycling down. Yet activation, retention, and member spend per visit all have improved. If we can deliver the same amount of business to the Hilton brand and it costs less, Hilton makes more margin. That attracts investors, franchise ownership, new builders. That's another reason why they buy the Hilton flag.

As Diskin saw it, Starwood's Preferred Guest announcement was a solution to a problem Hilton did not have, arising from its recent purchases of the Sheraton and Westin chains:

> They are trying to develop the Starwood brand with the Starwood Preferred Guest Program. They are targeting the most lucrative part of the business, the individual business traveler, where Sheraton and Westin independently have

EXHIBIT 6: (*Continued*)

Chain	Affinity Credit Card Point Accurual	Point Purchase	Bonus Threshold Rewards	Exchange Hotel Points for Airline Miles	Hotel Rewards
Starwood	1,000 hotel pts. first card use; 1 hotel pt. = $1 spent; 4 hotel points = $1 spent at Starwood hotels	NA	NA	1:1 conversion except JAL, KLM, Ansett, Qantas, Air New Zealand; 5,000 bonus miles when you convert 20,000 hotel points; minimum 2,000 Starpoints—basic; minimum 15,000—medium; no minimum for premium	5 categories; 1 free night category 1 is 3,000 Starpoints; 1 free night category 5 is 12,000 Starpoints
Hilton	5,000 hotel pts. for application; 2,500 hotel points first card use; 2 hotel pts. = $1 spent; 3 hotel pts. = $1 spent at HHonors Hotels	$10 = 1,000 pts. up to 20% of the total points of the reward	2,000 pts. = 4 stays per quarter	10,000 pts. = 1,500 miles; 20,000 pts. = 3,500 miles; 50,000 pts. = 10,000 miles; minimum 10,000 hotel points exchange, can also exchange airline miles for hotel points	5 categories: free weekend night 10,000 lowest; 35,000 highest
Hyatt	None	$10 = 500 pts. up to 10% of the total points of the reward	None basic	3 pts. = 1 mile; minimum 9,000-point exchange	Weekend night no category: 8,000 pts.; if pre mium time there is an additional 5,000 pts.; come with partner awards
Marriott	5,000 hotel pts. first card use; 1 hotel pt. = $1 spent; 3 hotel points = $1 spent at Marriott Rewards hotels	$10 =1,000 pts. up to 10% of the total points of the reward	None basic	10,000 pts. = 2,000 miles; 20,000 pts. = 5,000 miles; 30,000 pts. = 10,000 miles; minimum = 10,000 hotel point exchange	2 categories: 20,000 free weekend low category, and 30,000 high category

Source: Assembled by the casewriters from the promotional materials of each hotel chain in 1999.

never been as effective as Marriott, Hyatt, and Hilton. Sheraton's frequent-guest program wasn't very effective. They changed it every few years; they used to have members pay for it. Westin never had enough critical mass of properties for it to be important for enough people. So now, together they can address Westin's critical-mass problem and Sheraton's relevance.

But if frequent-guest programs were a good idea, perhaps bigger programs were an even better idea. Diskin reflected: "Hotel properties routinely pay 10 percent commission to a travel agent to bring them a guest. Yet they continually scrutinize the cost of these programs. Of course, they're justified in doing so, but the return on investment clearly justifies the expenditure. And our competitors certainly seem to see a value in increasing their investment in their programs."

Diskin tried to predict Hyatt's and Marriott's response to the Starwood announcement. The industry was quite competitive enough. He thought back to his early years at United Airlines and recalled the damage that price wars had done to that industry.

Study Questions

1. What are the strengths and weaknesses of the Hilton HHonors program from the standpoints of:
   a. Hilton Hotels Corp and Hilton International
   b. member properties (franchised hotels)
   c. guests
   d. corporate travel departments
2. How does the value generated to Hilton by the program compare to its cost?
3. What is Starwood attempting to do and how should Jeff Diskin respond?

Endnotes

1. The Wall Street Journal, February 2, 1999, p. B1.
2. World Trade Organization.
3. For the purpose of consistency in calculation among class members, assume an occupancy of 70 percent. The information in this paragraph has been masked. No data of this kind are publicly available, and these data are not to be interpreted as indicative of information private to either HHC or HIC.
4. Hilton distinguished three kinds of rate. "Business rates" were higher than "leisure rates," which in turn were higher than "ineligible rates," which referred to group tour wholesale rates, airline crew rates, and other deeply discounted rates.

CASE 15 Massachusetts Audubon Society

CHRISTOPHER LOVELOCK

A nonprofit environmental organization that operates more than 40 wildlife sanctuaries seeks to develop a strategy to increase the loyalty and involvement of its current members. A task force is focusing on developing a communications strategy for the existing membership, with the primary objective being to increase member value. Findings from a survey of its members may offer some insights.

> FROM THE STRATEGIC PLAN 2000–2010
> We embrace a vision of Massachusetts in which people appreciate and understand native plants and animals and their habitats and work together to ensure that they are truly protected. From the barrier beaches, heathlands, and salt marshes of the coast; to the vernal pools, red maple swamps, and forests of the interior; all the way to the fens and mountaintops of the Berkshire highlands, the Commonwealth's natural splendor encompasses an abundance of scenic and ecological treasures. But unless and until the public develops a conservation ethic that incorporates a love and respect for nature with a willingness to act on its behalf, we are in danger of losing this natural wealth forever.

Several pairs of cardinals were fluttering around the bird feeder outside the Audubon Shop at Drumlin Farm Wildlife Sanctuary; the scarlet and crimson plumage of the males stood out vividly against the bare trees. Nearby, under the watchful eyes of their teachers and a sanctuary naturalist, a group of schoolchildren were chattering excitedly as they walked down the path toward the enclosure where the farm animals were located.

Despite the chill in the air on this November day, several people were lined up in the reception area to gain admission to the sanctuary. The staff member on duty was explaining sympathetically to two visitors from New York that their membership in the National Audubon Society did not, unfortunately, entitle them to free admission at Massachusetts Audubon Society sanctuaries, since the two organizations had no formal relationship.

Steven Solomon and Susannah Caffry watched the bright red birds from the warm interior of the shop as they put on their jackets. Solomon was vice president of Mass Audubon's resources division and Caffry was director of marketing and communication. They had been meeting with the store manager and were now about to return to the nearby mansion that served as the Society's headquarters. Both were scheduled to participate in a task force discussion of how to develop a new communications strategy targeted at existing members. "The key to success," Solomon told Caffry as they stepped outside, "lies in finding ways to engage our members more actively in Mass Audubon."

History of the Audubon Movement

In the late 19th century, there were no laws in the United States to control the hunting of birds and animals. Entire species went into decline and two birds, the great auk and Carolina parakeet, were exterminated. Migratory fowl were killed in immense numbers, with hunters traveling to the coastal marshes of Massachusetts from as far away as Ohio.

Among those who spoke up against this slaughter was George Bird Grinnell, editor of the magazine *Forest and Stream*. In 1886, he created the nation's first bird preservation organization, which he named the Audubon Society after the great

Note: Certain data in this case have been disguised.

American naturalist and wildlife painter, John James Audubon (1785–1851). Within three months, more than 38,000 people had joined the society. But Grinnell was unable to cater to such a large, geographically dispersed group and had to disband the society after a couple of years.

The Audubon Societies

In 1896, two socially prominent cousins from Boston's Back Bay, Harriet Hemenway and Minna Hall, galvanized public support and formed the Massachusetts Audubon Society, which soon had 900 members. Refusing to wear hats and clothing decorated with plumes or other bird parts, they lobbied politicians and newspaper editors for protection of birds. Several months later, the Pennsylvania Audubon Society was founded, and by 1899 another 15 states had established Audubon societies.

In 1901, several local Audubon Societies for med the National Association of Audubon Societies for the Protection of Wild Birds and Animals. Both this association and local societies worked for passage of bird protection laws. An early priority included state bans on selling the plumes of native birds. National legislation included the Federal Migratory Bird Treaty Act of 1918 and creation of a National Wildlife Refuge system where birds would be safe from hunters. Over the years, additional state societies affiliated or merged with the National Association (later renamed the National Audubon Society). By 2001, the Massachusetts Audubon Society was one of only a handful of state societies remaining unaffiliated with the national society.

Other Players in the Environmental Movement

There were literally hundreds of environmental organizations in the U.S., with most being local or regional in nature. Some pursued a broad agenda; others focused on a specific goal, such as the Rails-to-Trails Conservancy, which sought to convert thousands of miles of unused railroad corridors into trails for recreation and nature appreciation. National players included Friends of the Earth, National Audubon Society, Sierra Club, The Nature Conservancy, and the Wilderness Society. Several of these organizations had chapters or offices in Massachusetts. The Appalachian Mountain Club was regional, with chapters throughout the Northeast U.S. By contrast, Mass Audubon, the Trustees of Reservations and MASSPIRG confined their activities to Massachusetts. (See the Appendix at the end of this case for brief profiles.)

Although organizations sometimes worked in coalitions to advocate specific political agenda, they also competed for funding and, to some extent, for members. On occasion, some of them had even competed for the same piece of environmentally sensitive property. The Nature Conservancy protected 17,000 acres (70 km^2) in the state, Mass Audubon held 29,000 acres (120 km^2), and The Trustees of Reservations had more than 45,000 acres (180 km^2). Many other nonprofit organizations operated individual sanctuaries and nature centers or preserved land from development through land trusts.

In the public sector, preservation and conservation agencies included the National Park Service, which was best known in Massachusetts for the 43,600-acre (176-km^2) Cape Cod National Seashore. The Commonwealth of Massachusetts preserved land for recreational purposes through a number of state parks, and many towns and cities had parks and conservation land trusts of their own. The motivations ranged from keeping attractive vistas and recreational areas out of the hands of developers to preserving habitats for threatened animal and plant species and protecting local water supplies.

Evolution of Mass Audubon

From its initial focus on bird protection, the Massachusetts Audubon Society (MAS) embraced a variety of conservation issues, including the protection of land and habitat, especially wetlands. In 1916, it created America's first private wildlife sanctuary at Moose Hill, 20 miles (32 km) southwest of Boston, later adding many other sanctuaries. It became known for its lectures, guided nature walks, and educational programs for children. MAS created the first environmental summer camp for children and one of the first natural history travel programs to offer guided nature tours and birding trips overseas. It also opened one of the first stores to focus on natural history merchandise.

In 1952, Louise Ayer Hathaway bequeathed to MAS her Drumlin Farm estate in Lincoln, 15 miles north of Boston. Her will stipulated that this working New England farm was to serve as a sanctuary for wildlife and as a model farm to show young city dwellers how food was grown. The accompanying mansion became the Society's new headquarters.

Under the presidency of Gerard Bertrand (1980–1998), MAS acquired many threatened locations through gift or purchase. It also helped landowners to obtain conservation restrictions that offered tax benefits and then assumed management of their properties. These strategies were made possible by active fundraising and a growing membership.

Bertrand also re-emphasized the Society's historical commitment to the study, observation, and protection of birds. Like the renowned ornithologist, Roger Tory Peterson, he recognized that birds were an "ecological litmus paper." Because of their rapid metabolism and wide geographic range, bird populations were quick to reflect changes in the environment. Hence a documented decline in bird numbers provided an early warning of environmental deterioration. Key initiatives during this period included plans for two urban sanctuaries to better serve the needs of city dwellers, especially urban children. Completion of the new Boston Nature Center, constructed on the 67-acre grounds of a former state mental hospital, was scheduled for fall 2002.

Membership grew from 26,600 in 1980 to 67,000 in 1998, while the area of land protected by the Society rose from 11,600 to 28,000 acres (Exhibit 1). The number of research studies and educational programs also increased substantially. Following the Centennial celebrations of 1996 and completion of a $34 million capital campaign, Bertrand left to chair Bird Life International; later he was also named vice chairman of the National Audubon Society's board of directors.

New Leadership

Although proud of the amount of wildlife habitat now protected by the Society, some board members and staff were concerned by the absence of a comprehensive plan to guide future direction. They worried that years of rapid growth were affecting Mass Audubon's ability to do the best possible job of managing the many properties it had acquired. As Bancroft Poor, VP–Operations, recalled: "The Society was really stretched by the years of expansion and some of the infrastructure was near the breaking point."

In January 1999, the board appointed Laura Johnson as the Society's new president. Johnson came to MAS from a 16-year career with The Nature Conservancy (TNC), an international environmental organization that maintained the largest private system of nature sanctuaries in the world. A native of Massachusetts and a lawyer by training, Johnson had initially worked on legal issues for TNC but soon switched over

EXHIBIT 1: Massachusetts Audubon Society: Key Statistics, 1980–2001

YEAR	# MEMBERS (000)	# ACRES PROTECTED[1] (000)	OPERATING REVENUE ($000)	OPERATING GIFTS/GRANTS ($000)	ENDOWMENT[2] ($ MILLION)
1980	26.6	11.6	2,529	362	10.9
1985	31.0	12.4	4,180	490	22.8
1990	48.0	18.1	6,955	1,017	35.2
1995	55.1	23.9	9,042	1,486	57.1
2000	67.6	28.6	13,791	2,584	92.3
2001	65.4	29.1	14,113	2,863	89.2

[1]1,000 acres = approximately 400 hectares (ha) or 4 square kilometers (km^2).

[2]Endowment is shown at market value except for land, which is valued at either its original purchase price or at $1 if donated as a gift (based on the Society's intention never to sell).

Source: MAS records.

to management, eventually being placed in charge of 12 states as eastern regional director. Reflecting on her time with TNC, she noted that it was a very focused organization with a culture of measurement. In particular, she said, the Conservancy offered a clear and compelling message about its goal of identifying important landscapes for protection, purchasing them, and protecting them. People could readily understand that their donations made a difference and thus feel a part of the enterprise.

A key motivation for Johnson was to be involved in creating an overall conservation ethic in Massachusetts, a task that she believed MAS performed better than any other organization. She was very concerned that modern lifestyles tended to separate people, especially children, from the natural environment. "Kids today are not outside, they're indoors playing on their computers," she said, "Or if they are outside, it's to play in a soccer game. Parents are afraid to let them wander." In Johnson's view, simply protecting land would be insufficient if in the future people forgot why the land in question was important, did not feel connected to it, and had no stake in it.

Johnson soon articulated a need to sharpen the Society's focus and develop a clear sense of direction. Despite a strong "feel good" sentiment towards the organization, relatively few members, she discovered, had a sense of the array of activities in which it was engaged and made assumptions that tended to mirror how they had come to join the organization. For instance, birders thought MAS was about birds, young families from the Boston area thought in terms of Drumlin Farm, and individuals who cared about public policy perceived the Society in terms of lobbying activities on Beacon Hill, site of the Massachusetts state government. So the first question Johnson asked was: "What are we and what do we want to be?"

Developing a Strategic Plan for 2000–2010

Over a six-month period in 1999, Johnson led and guided a comprehensive strategic planning effort. Its goals were to assess MAS strengths and resources, to evaluate the status of the Massachusetts environment and the impact of widespread changes, and to clearly define critical conservation issues. This assessment would enable MAS to define its own specific role relative to other conservation organizations. McKinsey & Co., the international consulting firm, gave pro bono support to the project.

A strong consensus emerged that biological conservation—that is, maintaining sustainable populations of the state's native biological diversity—lay at the heart of the Society's work. In looking toward the future, staff, the board, volunteers, and members reaffirmed their belief, passionately in many cases, that all of the Society's efforts should be directed toward protecting the nature of Massachusetts. From this belief emerged a common vision (reproduced at the beginning of this case) and a specific role for the Society:

> The Massachusetts Audubon Society serves both as a leader and as a catalyst for conservation, by acting directly to protect the nature of Massachusetts and by stimulating individual and institutional action through education, advocacy, and habitat protection.

The phrase, "Protecting the Nature of Massachusetts," which had been used sporadically up to this point, was adopted as the organization's signature and appeared beneath the Society's name on publications and stationery.

The strategic plan identified five major threats to biodiversity: loss of habitat to development; fragmentation of wildlife habitat; disruption of natural ecological cycles and processes through human alterations; the crowding out of native plants and animals by invasive species; and incompatible land use, such as using open space for recreational activities that damaged plants and threatened wildlife.

Following board approval of the plan, Johnson launched an in-depth examination of educational activities at MAS. In addition, the board directed a science review committee, composed of distinguished educators and scientists, to examine scientific activities at Mass Audubon. It also commissioned a study of information technology needs.

Education Plan

Discussions with staff members revealed that existing education programs, while high quality and well respected, lacked a common focus and connection to Mass Audubon themes and mission. Johnson acknowledged that the biggest challenge was to identify the most effective ways to use education to stimulate conservation action:

> We needed to find the best way to leverage our unique strengths—our sanctuary system, our scientific expertise, our advocacy capability, and our tremendously passionate staff—so that Mass Audubon could be a catalyst for conservation. We do thousands of programs, so there's plenty of activity to measure and we could say great things in terms of the number of programs held and the number of school children involved. But none of those measures would identify what the activities accomplished in terms of making a difference.
>
> Our teacher naturalists do a wonderful job with our programs, but it's a very expensive business model. And not every visitor to our sanctuaries wants to enroll in a program for a day or even a couple of hours. So we decided to explore an array of activities to get the message across. Our education director said at one point that we have this cultural bias at Mass Audubon that if we can just open up people's heads and dump into their heads what we know, they'll become just like us! But it doesn't work that way. We now have this paradigm from "caring to knowledge to action." When people act, that's the impact.

The education master plan emphasized the importance of creating significant outdoor experiences that might bring about transformations in people's environmental attitudes and values. Research showed that among children, shared family experiences in nature had the greatest influence in forming their attitudes as adults. To meet varied learning styles, the plan called for a mix of live programs, nature center exhibits, and self-guided trails at sanctuaries, plus opportunities for learning through publications, audiovisual media, interactive pages on the MAS website, and articles in local newspapers.

Organization

By this time, MAS was operating 58 wildlife sanctuaries across the Commonwealth, of which 41 were open to the public and 23 were staffed (Exhibit 2). They ranged in size

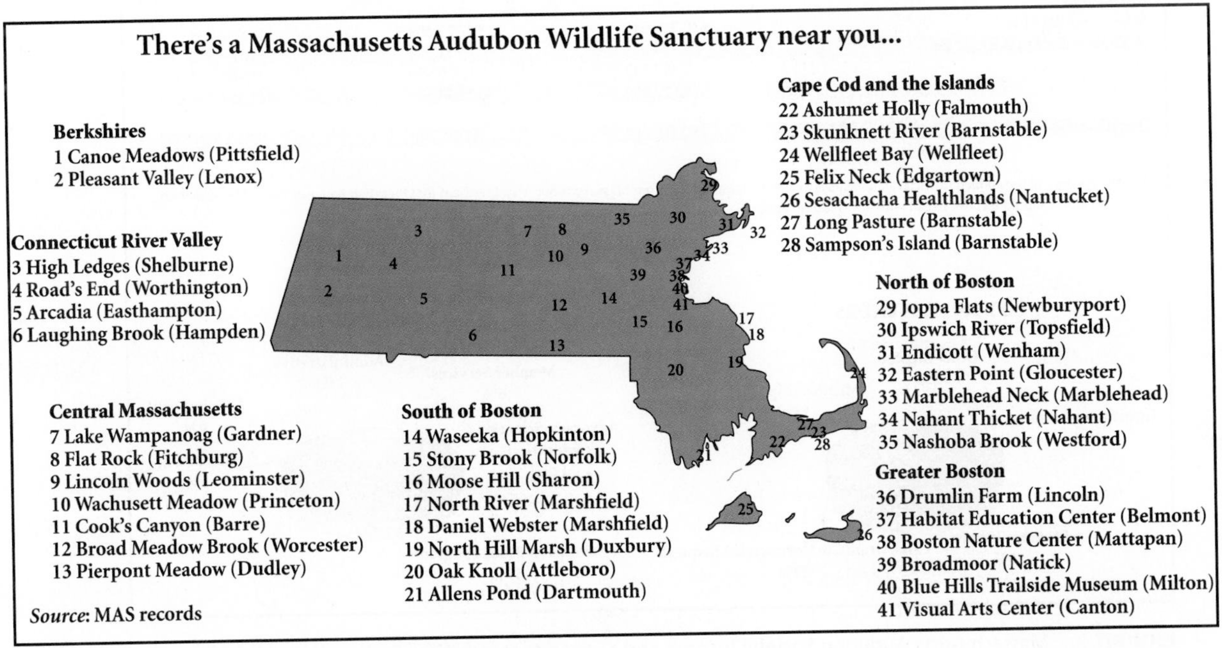

EXHIBIT 2: Map of Massachusetts Showing Location of Sanctuaries *Source:* MAS records.

from the 4-acre (1.5-ha) Nahant Thicket, a magnet for migrating songbirds on an otherwise rocky peninsula, to Ipswich River which comprised 2,265 acres (917 ha) of forests, meadows, and wetlands. There were 511,000 visits to the sanctuaries in the most recent year, including some 145,000 schoolchildren. The five most popular sanctuaries—Blue Hills Trailside Museum on the western edge of Greater Boston, Daniel Webster and North River on the South Shore, Wellfleet Bay on Cape Cod, and Drumlin Farm in Lincoln—jointly accounted for 70 percent of all visitation.

Historically, some sanctuaries had operated with a high degree of independence from MAS headquarters, targeting local residents, schools, and vacationers. Their directors were often well known in the communities they served. Sanctuaries were under considerable pressure to increase program revenues each year to help balance the budget. However, the result was often what one director described as "a hodgepodge of programs, many of which have little to do with the society's mission."

MAS was one of only two environmental organizations that monitored the Massachusetts state government and promoted a specific environmental agenda. Although some members were invested in these statewide advocacy efforts, others saw Mass Audubon simply in terms of their local sanctuary. Declared one staff member, "In our members' eyes, we can be as big as a major advocacy issue or as small as a favorite trail."

For the most recent fiscal year, MAS had an operating income of $14.6 million and generated a small surplus—as it had done for the past three years. Gifts, grants and unrestricted bequests totaled $3.3 million and membership dues, $2.7 million; income from programs and investments each amounted to $4.2 million; and revenues from all other sources, including profits from the Audubon shop, a Mass Audubon credit card, and the Society's Natural History Travel program came to $0.2 million (Exhibit 3). Salaries and benefits accounted for more than 70 percent of all expenses.

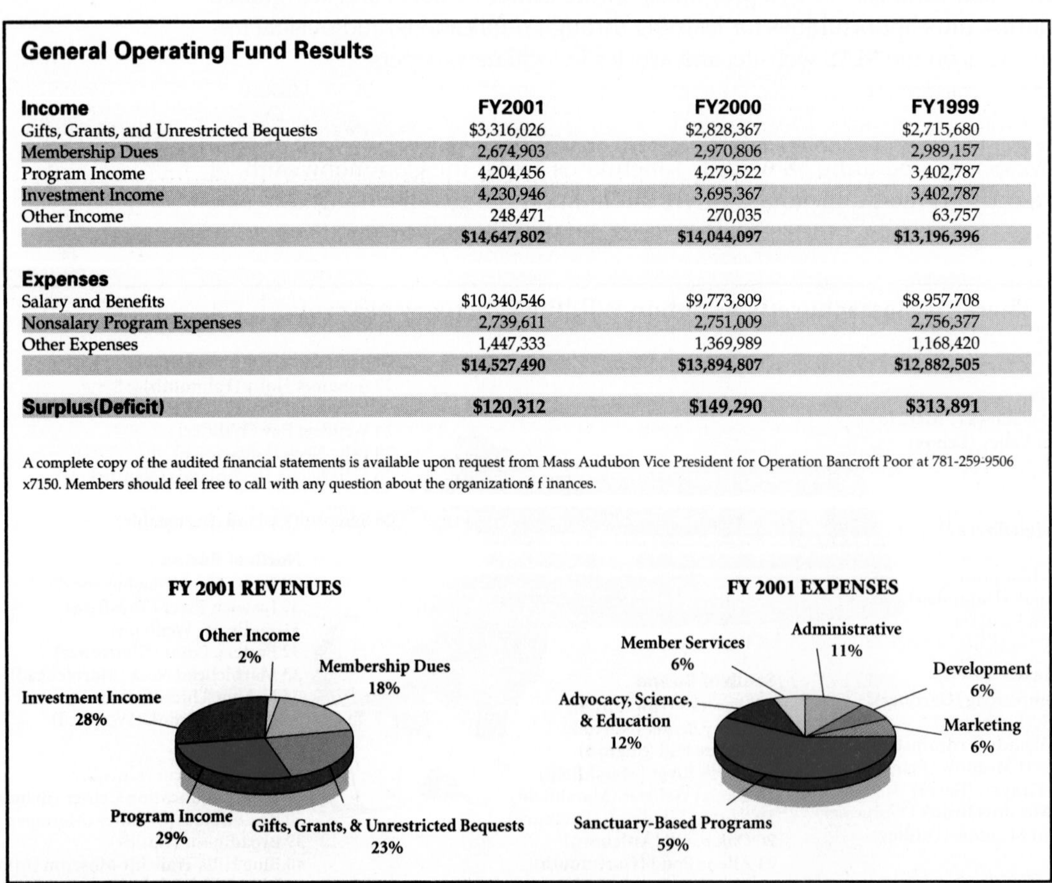

General Operating Fund Results

Income	FY2001	FY2000	FY1999
Gifts, Grants, and Unrestricted Bequests	$3,316,026	$2,828,367	$2,715,680
Membership Dues	2,674,903	2,970,806	2,989,157
Program Income	4,204,456	4,279,522	3,402,787
Investment Income	4,230,946	3,695,367	3,402,787
Other Income	248,471	270,035	63,757
	$14,647,802	**$14,044,097**	**$13,196,396**
Expenses			
Salary and Benefits	$10,340,546	$9,773,809	$8,957,708
Nonsalary Program Expenses	2,739,611	2,751,009	2,756,377
Other Expenses	1,447,333	1,369,989	1,168,420
	$14,527,490	**$13,894,807**	**$12,882,505**
Surplus(Deficit)	**$120,312**	**$149,290**	**$313,891**

A complete copy of the audited financial statements is available upon request from Mass Audubon Vice President for Operation Bancroft Poor at 781-259-9506 x7150. Members should feel free to call with any question about the organizations̓ f inances.

EXHIBIT 3: Massachusetts Audubon Society: Income and Expenditures for Year Ending June 30, 2001
Source: MAS records.

Restructuring

MAS was governed by a 27-member board of directors, who elected from among their number a chair, three vice-chairs, and a treasurer. Providing additional expertise and support was a board-appointed council, whose 75 members were drawn from across the state, often being recommended by staff members at HQ or the sanctuaries. This governance structure, adopted in 1999, replaced an unwieldy 80-member board with different categories of directors, which lacked clear roles and expectations for its members and had no term limits.

One outcome of the strategic planning process was changes to the design of the MAS organization. The revised structure in place in 2001 consisted of four divisions, each of which was each headed by a vice president reporting to Laura Johnson (Exhibit 4).

Conservation Science and Ecological Management was formerly within Programs, but in response to the findings of the Science Review Committee was established as a separate division in order to sharpen its focus and raise its stature. It included a bird conservation department, GIS/data management, and employed five scientists with responsibilities for each of the three regions, the education department, and advocacy.

Operations was headed by Bancroft Poor, chief financial officer (CFO), whose responsibilities included administrative and financial operations, capital assets and planning, human resources, and information technology. The *Programs* division incorporated advocacy, education, land protection, the sanctuaries, and the Society's overnight summer camp. Finally, the *Resources* division was created to integrate fundraising, membership, and marketing activities and to raise their visibility.

The Resources Division

To head the new Resources Division, Johnson hired Steven L. Solomon, previously vice president of resources at the Museum of Science in Boston. Earlier, he had also worked for the Boston Symphony Orchestra and the Museum of Fine Arts, as well as Harvard's Graduate School of Design. Solomon was attracted by the changes that were taking place at MAS and shared Johnson's belief that development and marketing should be linked. He declared:

> There are a lot of organizations that have separate marketing and development divisions, but in fact they have so many interlocking elements that they need to

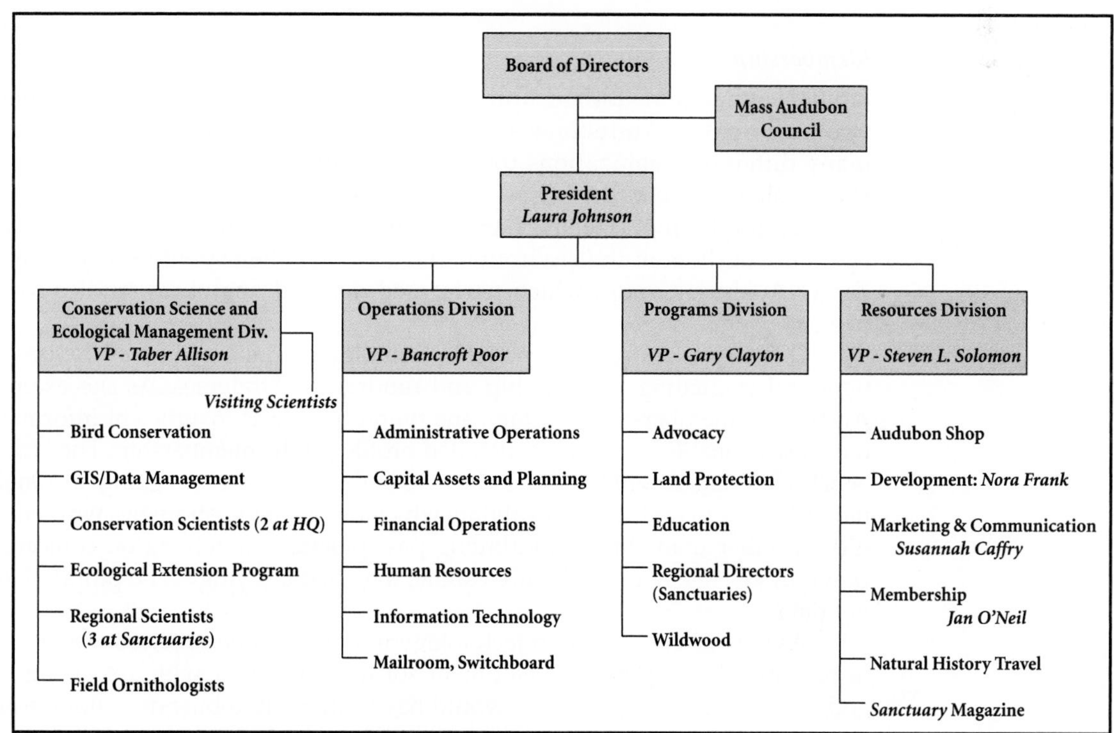

EXHIBIT 4: Organization Chart *Source:* MAS records.

> work closely together. When you're working in development at the level we are, it's based almost entirely on relationships. We want to be like Britain's RSBP [Royal Society for the Protection of Birds], which has a very clearly defined philosophy: "Membership is everybody's job."

The new division included the directors of development, marketing and communication, and membership; the editor of *Sanctuary*, the Society's bimonthly magazine; the manager of Natural History Travel, which organized naturalist-led tours (particularly for birders) to destinations around the world; and the manager of the Audubon Shop.

Development

Development activities embraced an annual fund to raise unrestricted gifts and capital campaigns to finance specific projects. All members were urged to contribute to the annual appeal; most were contacted by mail although major donors might be solicited personally. Capital campaigns ran over a period of several years. They usually involved intensive advance planning and early solicitation of major gifts. Several campaigns were currently in progress: $4 million for new facilities at the Wellfleet sanctuary; $2 million for new information technology; $6 million for Drumlin Farm; and $1.2 million for Wildwood, the new residential summer camp.

Nora Frank, director of development, had joined Mass Audubon as manager of major gifts after working in admissions, development, and marketing for a residential school. She believed strongly in the need to keep donors and members involved and informed:

> One way to engage people is to let them know what we are doing and what their money is supporting. Right now, we don't have any common vehicle outside of solicitation that tells people what we are doing with their money, applauds them for helping to make a difference, and tells them how they can get further involved. Money comes in every time we use *Sanctuary* to highlight a specific need, even when we don't specifically ask for it. People do want to get involved but we haven't been letting them know what's happening.

Membership

Jan O'Neil had joined Mass Audubon 18 months earlier as director of membership. "Coming to Mass Audubon was a great opportunity to transition from dealing with many different organizations to focusing on one that I'd been a member of almost my whole life," remarked O'Neil. Her prior experience included 12 years with the New Boston Group, a telemarketing firm that made fundraising calls for nonprofits, many of them in the environmental area. She then spent two years working for Target Analysis Group, which performed detailed analytical studies for nonprofit clients.

O'Neil was a strong proponent of employing reliable data as the basis for planning and evaluating membership and fundraising strategies. As she examined Mass Audubon's membership program, she found there was insufficient information in the database to enable her to create detailed profiles of the membership. The lack of reliable benchmark data meant that it was hard to document what was going on. One of her initial tasks was to find ways to validate which membership strategies worked and which didn't, rather than simply continuing past practices or relying on conjecture. At her previous job, she remarked with a smile, they had a saying, "The plural of anecdote is not data."

As part of the $2 million technology initiative, some $400,000 was being invested in new membership and development software, together with associated installation and training. The new software would have extremely robust data storage and reporting capabilities, greatly enhancing the membership department's ability to profile and track members.

Between 1997 and 1999, MAS membership had surged from 54,400 to 67,400 households, spurred by the $34 million Centennial fundraising campaign, which included a $400,000 advertising campaign involving radio, billboards, and press. But it had since fallen back to around 65,000 household members. Like many nonprofits, MAS experienced churn in its membership, with about 20% turning over each year. Although that was less than in most organizations, there was still a continuing need to recruit new members. Although regular household membership cost $47 ($37 for individuals), new members could join initially for only $25. Forty-five percent of new members were recruited at the sanctuaries and 42 percent through direct mail solicitation. The balance joined as a result of visiting Mass Audubon's website, word-of-mouth recommendations, or other encounters.

Admission charges to the sanctuaries for non-members ranged from $3 for adults and $2 for children up to $6/$4 at Drumlin Farm. As one aspect of their pitch, admissions staff were trained to point out the savings associated with joining immediately and then being able to make this and future visits for the next year free of charge. It had proved a particularly compelling sell for families.

Direct mail solicitation involved purchase of mailing lists from brokers or swapping of membership lists with other nonprofits. Some 500,000–700,000 letters were mailed each year, at an average cost of $0.39 each, and typically yielded a response rate of around 1 percent. A recent mailing came in a colorful envelope bearing the slogan "Coming soon to a neighborhood near you" and a picture of a bird standing on a for-sale sign in open countryside. The letter inside was headed "Massachusetts Is Disappearing!" and warned that every day the state lost 44 acres of land to development. It then described Mass Audubon's conservation, education, and advocacy efforts and promoted the benefits of membership. New members received a welcome package of materials. The unit cost to MAS was about $3.25, exclusive of any premiums offered as inducements.

O'Neil noted that only 55 percent of first-year members would renew their membership, but this figure compared favorably to comparable national organizations, where renewal rates were typically only 30–35 percent. The estimated annual printing and mailing costs for renewals was $195,000. Although some members remained loyal for life, a board member with expertise in marketing estimated that the average duration of a member relationship that was renewed after the first year was eight years. In general, said O'Neil, "The longer someone has been a member, the more likely they are to stay a member." Added Solomon: "Members who are happily engaged are much more likely to renew."

At renewal time, members were encouraged to migrate to higher levels of membership: Supporting ($60), Defender ($75), Donor ($100), Protector ($150), Sponsor ($250), Patron ($500), and Leadership Friend ($1,250). Dues for the last-named category had been raised from $1,000 the previous year. Members of this group received a number of benefits, including invitations to exclusive events, meetings with Mass Audubon scientists and sanctuary directors, and special outings such as naturalist-led hikes or canoe trips. A small fee was sometimes charged for outings in order to preserve the full tax deductibility of the membership contribution. O'Neil and her colleagues in the Resources Division had been discussing the possibility of developing supplementary benefits for members enrolled in some of the other levels.

In addition to free admission to the sanctuaries, all members received six issues of *Sanctuary* magazine each year, discounts on MAS courses, lectures, programs, and day camps, and savings on purchases from the sanctuary shops. Depending on location, they might also receive newsletters from their nearest sanctuary. O'Neil estimated the annual printing and mailing costs associated with serving members at $330,000. This did not include the cost of staff time.

Premiums, such as day packs or tote bags bearing the Mass Audubon logo, were often used as inducements to renew at a higher level. The unit cost of purchasing and mailing such a premium was about $5. Former members were contacted for up to ten years in an effort to get them to rejoin. Exhibit 5 shows the division of membership between the different levels at the end of the 2000–2001 fiscal year. About 70 percent of members renewed at the same rate, 20 percent upgraded, and 10 percent downgraded.

EXHIBIT 5: MAS Membership by Contribution Level, June 30, 2001

LEVEL	DUES	NUMBER
Introductory	$25	12,093
Student	$20	460
Individual	$37	9,224
Family	$47	28,908
Supporting	$60	6,366
Defender	$75	2,152
Donor	$100	3,335
Protector	$150	1,092
Sponsor	$250	433
Patron	$500	205
Leadership Friend	$1,000	584
Complimentary		520
TOTAL		**65,372**

Source: MAS Membership Department.

Marketing and Communication

Susannah Caffry had worked for Mass Audubon for two years. After leaving college, she entered the telecommunications industry, but found the work increasingly unrewarding. A keen outdoorswoman, she took a three-month sabbatical during which she went on an intensive canoeing trip with Outward Bound. Her experience convinced her that she wanted to work in the nonprofit sector and she accepted an offer from Outward Bound to join their Boston operation as director of admissions, later being promoted to vice president of marketing and public relations. In addition to communications, her work included recommendations on design, scheduling, and pricing of courses and programs.

MAS had earlier employed a director of marketing to manage communication activities associated with the Society's Centennial. As these activities wound down, the position was expanded to include development activities, but the attention given to marketing dwindled due to the more pressing needs of fundraising. The incumbent left at the same time the Resources Division was created and Caffry was recruited by Steve Solomon for the newly defined position of director of marketing and communication.

Caffry said she was attracted to Mass Audubon by the commitment to marketing among the leadership, but had found that not everyone in the organization understood or appreciated the value of a marketing perspective. More than once, she admitted, somebody had told her, "We don't like the M-word!" An important task involved marketing Wildwood, the Society's new summer camp for children. Because some staff members assumed that marketing activities only involved communication tasks such as signage and development of brochures, it took her some time, she admitted, to become involved in decisions on scheduling, pricing, and service features at the camp, all of which she saw as critical to success.

Caffry spent her first few months gathering information and learning how people on the staff, board, and council felt about marketing-related issues at Mass Audubon. She encountered passionately held views that were often widely divergent. There were, for instance, those who loved *Sanctuary* magazine because they saw it as "pure" and free from overt marketing and promotion of Mass Audubon's programs and agenda. Others, by contrast, regarded it as "elitist" and "arrogant," noting that the stories presupposed a level of technical understanding of the environment beyond that held by nonspecialists. Similar variations in viewpoint surrounded the newsletters published by the individual sanctuaries and also the website. Summarizing the situation, Caffry remarked:

> There was no holistic approach as to how we were communicating. We had many different vehicles but they weren't held to any consistent message. I found a lot of conflicting opinions concerning the objectives of Mass Audubon's different

> communications activities. For instance there was no consensus at all as to what the purpose of *Sanctuary* magazine was. I also discovered that our annual report was not meeting the needs of our development office. This is a fundamental, critical communication effort for nonprofits.
>
> I see our overall objective as bringing together the communications activities without undermining the strengths of the organization—an important one being the commitment and feeling of ownership demonstrated by the sanctuary directors and other program staff.

Communication Strategy Task Force

Prior to Solomon's arrival, there had been no explicit strategy for coordinating all the Society's communications efforts. As a board member, Alfred (Appy) Chandler had long been concerned about the fragmentation of communication efforts, with each group, such as advocacy, attending to its own portfolio and operating relatively independently of the others. *Sanctuary* magazine, the Society's primary periodical for members, was started, he declared, "not as a mouthpiece of Mass Audubon but almost as an independent journal that would carry articles about the Society's mission as opposed to stories about Mass Audubon itself."

In addition to an in-house publishing effort that produced books and field guides, a variety of staff members across the organization wrote press releases, and there were various public relations efforts by the development office, such as staffing a booth at a flower show or other event. Many of the individual sanctuaries published their own newsletters, but they lacked a coordinated formatting and often failed to convey any real sense of being part of a larger, statewide organization. Chandler promoted the need for an integrated communication strategy to pull all the pieces together, so that the Society could speak with a single voice.

As president, Laura Johnson facilitated a meeting of MAS Council members to define the challenges that the Society faced with regard to its communications strategy. Among the key themes that emerged were a need for greater clarity in terms of "what, why, when, and to whom?" and a sense that the Society was not doing a good enough job of telling the MAS story to either its members or the general public. Break-out reports emphasized the need to find ways to strengthen the "brand" and to understand members and their preferences better. A range of opinions was expressed about *Sanctuary;* while most agreed that it was a high-quality magazine, many argued that it needed to clarify its purpose.

The following month, the board approved creation of a communication strategy task force to work with a consulting firm and MAS staff. Its purpose was to "oversee a review and analysis of current external communication activities and preparation of a communication plan for the Society, including recommendations for long-term strategy." Its scope extended to membership, education, public relations, advocacy, marketing, sanctuary activities, and publications. The task force was composed of board and council members who either had marketing and communications expertise or who represented a consumer point of view. Chandler was named as chair. Commenting on the role of the consultant, EMI Strategic Marketing, Caffry observed:

> The consultant was very useful. There were so many sacred cows at Mass Audubon, so many personal feelings, and so many emotions that the consultant could ask questions that I, frankly, could not. There's a certain amount of skepticism in some quarters about the work related to communications and marketing. Not everybody is eager to see change and we have joked that there's a great deal of "anticipointment" related to the communication plan.

Focus and Objectives

After some debate, the task force decided to focus on developing a communications strategy for the existing membership, with the primary objective to increase member value. This would be achieved through better education of members about Mass Audubon's mission, by engaging them actively in "protecting the nature of

Massachusetts, increasing their support for MAS programs, and growing their financial contributions."

Additional objectives were (1) to reinforce MAS's role and positioning as the leader in conservation, environmental education, and advocacy within Massachusetts, thus differentiating it from other environmental organizations; (2) to establish a clear, distinctive, contemporary image for the Society, portraying it as dynamic, current, and important; and (3) to communicate more cost effectively through better use of all available media and channels. The work of the task force included reviewing Mass Audubon's existing communications, undertaking a competitive audit of those organizations whose activities and appeal overlapped MAS in some measure (see the Appendix at the end of this case), and conducting a detailed survey.

Member Survey

Recognizing that existing knowledge of members' interests and perceptions was largely anecdotal, the task force decided to conduct a large-scale survey of members. It sought to identify channels for future communications, understand how members perceived MAS, and determine the relative importance they placed on its mission and programs. Additional goals included gauging the degree of membership overlap between MAS and other organizations and determining whether there were meaningful differences between demographic groups in their reactions to MAS communications and content.

Working with the consultant, the task force developed a mail questionnaire that was bound around the cover of an issue of *Sanctuary* magazine and mailed to 62,000 members. More than 8,000 completed questionnaires were returned and promptly reviewed to gather any handwritten comments. Work on manually keying, coding, and cleaning the quantitative data concluded after 4,448 questionnaires, which was viewed as more than enough responses for the proposed statistical analysis.

Following a review of the preliminary tabulations (Exhibit 6), cross-tabs were run to determine how member views and priorities related to member characteristics on a wide array of segmentation variables. One aspect of this analysis involved segmenting members according to their most important reason for joining Mass Audubon. The top three reasons, accounting for 90 percent of respondents, were "believe in the organization and mission" (34 percent), "to protect the environment" (30 percent), and "to visit the sanctuaries" (26 percent).

Analysis showed that, compared to the first two groups, those who joined primarily to visit the sanctuaries tended to be younger and were more likely to have children under 18 in their households. Over 90 percent had visited a sanctuary within the past year, compared to about three-fourths of those in the other segments. They were somewhat less likely to have made a gift to the Society, and a higher proportion of them belonged at the $47 (or lower) membership levels. Although they were less likely to read *Sanctuary* magazine in depth, they expressed more interest than the other groups in receiving a newsletter that listed MAS programs, classes, and events.

Creating a New Communications Program

After returning to the headquarters building from their visit to the Audubon Shop, Solomon and Caffry joined other members of the task force in the board room. The topic for discussion involved drawing some preliminary conclusions from the survey results and the competitive audit and relating these insights to current communication efforts. Within the next few weeks, the task force was expected to present the board with recommendations for a new communications program.

EXHIBIT 6: Responses to Selected Questions on Member Survey, September 2001 (*N* = 4,448)

Why did you become a member of Mass Audubon? Please rank importance:

	# 1	# 2	# 3
Believe in organization and mission	34%	35%	12%
Protect the environment	30	29	15
Visit the sanctuaries	26	21	25
Participate in programs, classes, events	6	8	10
Participate in birding related events, seminars	3	3	5
Get *Sanctuary* magazine	1	4	9

How important are the following aspects of Mass Audubon's mission to you?
(5-point scale: 5 = extremely important, 4 = very important)

	5	4
Protecting the environment for wildlife	81%	14%
Saving land from development	75	15
Providing nature preserves to walk/hike, enjoy birds/wildlife	60	29
Educating kids about the natural world/environment	60	27
Being an advocate for legal actions to protect environment	55	24

How often have you visited a Mass Audubon sanctuary or site in the past year?

Not visited	21%
1 visit	17
2–3 visits	24
>3 visits	38

What do you know about the relationship between National Audubon and Mass Audubon?

Same group	1%
MAS local branch	21
Separate organizations	48
Don't know	30

Do you read *Sanctuary* magazine?
Yes: 96% No: 4%

If yes, how frequently?
Always: 43% Frequently: 27% Sometimes: 18% Skim: 12%

Do you read the newsletter from your local sanctuary?
Yes: 78% No: 16% No response: 6%

If yes, how frequently?
Always: 50% Frequently: 26% Sometimes: 14% Skim: 10%

How interested would you be in a newsletter that listed MA programs, classes, and events across the state?
Extremely: 9% Very: 20% Somewhat: 51% Not at all: 20%

If interested, how often would you want to receive this listing?
Bimonthly: 15% Quarterly: 56% Two times per year: 29%

Do you have an e-mail address for personal mail?
Yes: 74% No: 26%

If yes, would you be interested in learning about MA events by e-mail?
Yes: 46% No: 54%

If yes, how often would you like to receive e-mails?
Weekly: 12% Monthly: 61% Quarterly: 27%

What types of things would you like to be informed about via e-mail?

Calendars of events at sanctuaries	72%
News about important public legislation/policy in Mass.	58

(Continued)

EXHIBIT 6: *(Continued)*

Mass Audubon activities to protect the nature of Mass.	57
Environment-related events in Mass.	55
News about the sanctuaries	48
News about your local sanctuary only	24

Have you ever visited our Web site?

Yes: 18% No: 82%

Have you ever visited other environmental Web sites?

Yes: 38% No: 62%

If yes, how often do you visit environmental Web sites in a month?

Once: 53% 2–3 times: 29% 4–10 times: 13% 11 or more: 5% (Mean = 2.8)

Would you come to the Mass Audubon Web site to sign up for events?

Yes: 63% No: 37%

Would you go to interesting Mass Audubon events more than 20 miles from home?

Yes: 63% No: 37%

If yes, how many miles would you travel?

20 miles: 5% 30 miles: 28% 50 miles: 49% 100 + miles: 18%

To which environmental organizations do you belong? Are you a member of any of these?

Mass Audubon	100%	PBS/WGBH	83%
The Nature Conservancy	38	Museum of Fine Arts	42
Trustees of Reservations	27	WBUR	36
Appalachian Mountain Club	18	Museum of Science	25
World Wildlife	15	New England Aquarium	15
National Audubon	15	Franklin Park Zoo	8
Other	27		

Source: MAS records. Note that certain data have been disguised.

Appendix

Profiles of Selected Environmental Organizations

Appalachian Mountain Club (www.outdoors.org)

Founded in 1876 and headquartered in Boston, the AMC had some 94,000 members and described itself as "America's oldest conservation and recreation organization." Membership cost $40 for an individual and $65 for a family. AMC's mission statement emphasized "protection, enjoyment, and wise use of the mountains, rivers, and trails of the Northeast." Its 125th Anniversary Capital Campaign had a target of $30 million. AMC had 12 chapters extending from Maine to Washington, DC, including four in Massachusetts that collectively accounted for some 32,000 members. The Club's active publication program included *AMC Outdoors,* an award-winning monthly member magazine dedicated to recreation and conservation in the Northeast; *Appalachia,* described as "America's longest-running journal of mountaineering and conservation;" many trail and field guides; and a variety of recreation-oriented "how-to" books. AMC offered environmental education programs and sought to develop the skills and understanding needed to enjoy, protect, and advocate for the backcountry. Outdoor recreation services included group trips, trail maintenance, and provision of a network of camps, campgrounds, lodges, and cabins, plus a chain of high-mountain huts for hikers and climbers along the New Hampshire segments of the Appalachian Mountain Trail.

Friends of the Earth (www.foe.org)

FoE was founded in 1972 by a former president of the Sierra Club, who felt that the latter organization was insufficiently vigorous in its defense of the environment. Based in Washington, DC, it was a national nonprofit advocacy organization with affiliates in 66 countries, "dedicated to protecting the planet from environmental degradation; preserving biological, cultural, and ethnic diversity; and empowering citizens to have an influential voice in decisions affecting the quality of the environment—and their lives." In the U.S., FoE worked to preserve clean air and water, advocate public health protection, and examine the root causes of environmental degradation. It researched government policies and tax programs, and engaged in lobbying and legal action. FoE's "Economics for the Earth" program focused on the economics of protecting the environment and included the "Green Scissors" campaign—an alliance of environmentalists and conservative taxpayer organizations dedicated to cutting government subsidies that resulted in environmental damage. Its legal program to ensure enforcement of, and compliance with, U.S. environmental laws was located in FoE's Northeast office in Burlington, Vermont. Membership could be obtained for a donation of $25 or more. Members received a quarterly newsletter, *EarthFocus,* and the biweekly *EarthFocus Online*. They were also entitled to discounts on FoE publications and merchandise.

National Audubon Society (www.audubon.org)

Based in New York, NAS boasted 550,000 members, 508 chapters, and 100 sanctuaries and nature centers from coast to coast, including eight in Connecticut and two in Maine, but none in Massachusetts. Dedicated to the preservation of birds, other wildlife, and habitat, it employed more than 300 staff members and had assets of some $170 million. Expenses in 2000 totaled $58 million, of which $8.7 million was devoted to marketing and communications and $23 million to field operations. Membership cost $35, but new members could enroll for only $20. Benefits included membership in the local chapter (which usually organized a variety of activities) and receipt of the widely praised bimonthly magazine *Audubon,* which had won many awards in fields such as nature photography, essays, and design. NAS's 1995 strategic plan committed it to decentralize activities, with a goal of moving from nine regional offices to, ultimately, 50 state programs. In pursuit of this goal, the president had actively encouraged independent state Audubon societies to join or affiliate themselves with NAS. By 2001, the only states in which NAS lacked offices or chapters were Massachusetts, New Hampshire, and Rhode Island, each of which had its own state society. NAS lobbied actively in Washington on issues that were central to its mission, including improved funding of the National Wildlife Refuge system. Chapters worked at the state and local levels. Seeking to protect migratory birds, NAS was also active in Bermuda, the U.S. Virgin Islands, many Central American countries, and parts of South America. The Society was actively engaged in a major rebranding program, including a revised logo, and was now promoting itself simply as "Audubon."

Sierra Club (www.sierraclub.org)

Based in San Francisco, the Sierra Club took its name from California's Sierra Nevada range and was founded in 1892 by the famous naturalist, writer, and conservationist John Muir. From its early days, it combined organization of group excursions in the mountains with political activity to create national parks and forest reserves. Over subsequent decades it was often successful in fighting proposals for damming of wild and scenic rivers across large areas of the western United States. It gradually evolved into a national organization, with a strong presence in Washington, using education, lobbying, and litigation to achieve its environmental goals. From the 1970s onwards, it broadened its emphasis to fight for clean air and water and extended its anti-dam crusade to other countries, including Canada and Brazil. Its mission emphasized enjoyment, exploration, and preservation of the "wild places of the earth," promoting responsible use of resources, and education to protect and restore the quality of both the natural and human environment. By 2001, it had some 700,000 members and chapters in many states, including Massachusetts. The club organized more than 300 national and international outings in addition to the numerous outings organized by local chapters. Members received a monthly environmental newsletter, *The Planet,* and an attractive glossy bimonthly magazine, *Sierra.*

The Trustees of Reservations (www.thetrustees.org)

Founded in 1891, this Massachusetts organization maintained 91 reservations representing many of the state's most scenic, ecologically rich, and historically important landscapes. Its landholdings, which also included several historic buildings, protected some 45,000 acres (180 km^2) through ownership or conservation restrictions. Collectively, the reservations provided a wide range of recreational opportunities. The organization also offered function rentals at the large Crane Estate in Ipswich and bed-and-breakfast accommodation at this and one other property. Basic membership cost $40 for individuals or $60 for couples and families. Benefits included a free guidebook, a 50 percent discount off admission charges at TTOR reservations, discounts in its shops, and receipt of a quarterly newsletter.

MASSPIRG (www.masspirg.org)

The Massachusetts Public Interest Research Group was one of 26 independent, state-based research groups advocating for the public interest in their home states. In 1983, an alliance of state-based PIRGs created US PIRG (www.uspirg.org) to share ideas and resources and, where appropriate, coordinate regional or national efforts. MASSPIRG sought to uncover threats to public health or well-being and fight to end them, using investigative research, media exposés, grassroots organizing, advocacy, and litigation. Its stated goal was to deliver persistent, results-oriented, public interest activism that protected the environment, encouraged a fair and sustainable economy, and fostered responsive, democratic government. Among the six programs it was pursuing in Massachusetts were the environment (open space, recycling, clean water, and toxics), energy (efficiency and clean, renewable power), and transportation (efficient and environmentally sound). Each program director worked with many different constituencies in support of specific goals. Located in Boston close to the Massachusetts State House, the organization had a full-time attorney on its staff. Members received MASSPIRG MASSCITIZEN, a quarterly report of activities.

The Nature Conservancy (www.nature.org)

Founded in 1951, TNC defined its mission as preserving "the plants, animals, and natural communities that represent the diversity of life on Earth by protecting the lands and waters they need to survive." Its approach was to protect carefully chosen portfolios of land and water within scientifically defined ecoregions, in order to ensure the survival of each region's biological diversity. TNC had a reputation as a very focused organization that used a nonconfrontational approach to achieve its goals. By 2002, it had successfully protected 12.6 million acres (50,000 km^2) in the United States and an additional 80.2 million acres (325,000 km^2) across Canada, the Asia-Pacific Region, the Caribbean, and Latin America. It had 1,400 preserves, one million members, and had launched a $1 billion campaign—the largest private conservation campaign ever undertaken—to save 200 of the world's "Last Great Places." TNC's approaches employed outright purchase and management of land under partnerships or conservation easements. A few of its properties, principally in the western U.S., offered accommodation and excursions, but none of those in Massachusetts did. TNC was based in Arlington, Virginia, and published *Nature News,* an interactive newsletter for members sent once or twice monthly by email, as well as *Nature Conservancy* magazine, which had recently been revamped and was offered free of charge to members enrolled at the $50 or higher level. Basic membership was $25 a year.

The Wilderness Society (www.wilderness.org)

Founded in 1935, TWS worked to develop a nationwide network of wild lands through public education, scientific analysis, and advocacy. Its goal was "to ensure that future generations will enjoy the clean air and water, wildlife, beauty, and opportunities for recreation, and renewal that pristine forests, rivers, deserts, and mountains provide." Headquartered in Washington, TWS had eight regional offices across the country, including one in Boston. The activities of the northeast region focused on the Great Northern Forest—"the largest and last continuous wild forest east of the Mississippi River"—which stretched from northern New York state, across the northern Green and White Mountains, to the remote wetlands of eastern Maine. In return for a contribution of $30 or more, members received the Society's annual full-color publication *Wilderness Year,* a quarterly color newsletter, and member alerts.

Study Questions

1. How is MAS currently positioned against other environmental organizations in Massachusetts?
2. What is a new member potentially worth to MAS? (Hint: Use customer lifetime value analysis.) Beyond the financial issue, why is membership important to MAS?
3. What approaches should MAS use to retain members and to persuade them to upgrade their membership levels?
4. As a participant in the Task Force on Member Communications Strategy, what actions would you recommend to the board?

CASE 16 TLContact: CarePages Service (A)

CHRISTOPHER LOVELOCK

An Internet start-up company has successfully developed a Web-based service that enables hospital patients to stay in touch with family and friends through the medium of individualized home pages. Three years after launch, the company is finally becoming profitable and the founder and CEO is reviewing strategies for future growth.

Eric Langshur, CEO of TLContact, Inc. (TLC), was pleased as he drafted the company's latest quarterly activity update. The news was encouraging on almost all fronts.

TLC's primary product, CarePages, was a Web-based service that enabled patients to stay in touch with family members and friends through the medium of individualized home pages. Utilization of CarePages was accelerating among existing customers, primarily acute care hospitals in the United States and Canada, and the company continued its record of 100 percent renewals. New sales were up dramatically, individual users continued to be delighted with the service, and new enhancements had been well received. Press coverage and word-of-mouth had been phenomenal; the latest Google search of "tlcontact" had yielded more than 400 entries. Meanwhile, competitors were stumbling and one had just shut down. Eric predicted that consolidated annual revenues would reach about $3 million, up sharply over the previous year.

Then he shook his head as he looked again at the $3 million figure. Fifteen years earlier, at age 25 and fresh out of an MBA program, he had been running a $25 million business. And prior to launching TLContact in 2000 with his wife, Sharon, a physician, he had been president of a large division of a multinational aerospace company. Were challenge and reward directly proportional to scale? He didn't think so.

The activity update on which he was working would make pleasant reading, he reflected, for the firm's board of directors in advance of their upcoming meeting. But Eric wanted to avoid any sense of complacency, because the firm's very success could still attract viable competition. Despite having some prestigious clients, TLC had only penetrated a small percentage of what was potentially a very large market. The firm offered a trusted and valued access to hospital patients, with potential for hospitals and other sponsors to use it as a customized communication channel. Yet TLC also offered access to a vastly larger audience of health-oriented consumers. Might other sponsors, in addition to hospitals, be interested in the potential synergies?

The Company

Located in Chicago and created at the height of the dot.com boom, TLC was among the small percentage of Internet start-ups that had survived after the bubble burst. The management team consisted of Eric Langshur, CEO; Charlyn Slade, RNC, president; Raul Vasquez, chief technical officer; Lindsay Paul, VP–business development–healthcare; JoAnne Resnic, VP–health care services; and Sharon Langshur, MD, medical director. In addition, the company employed a technical team of four consisting of a graphic designer, a customer service manager, and two software engineers. The Sales and Business Development team comprised Slade and Resnic, both former nurse administrators, and Paul, a Harvard MBA with an extensive background in healthcare consulting.

During 2002, TLC had a net loss of $0.7 million. The company was privately held by the founders and 20 private investors. Initial financing had involved an initial investment in 2000 of $3 million by what Eric described as "angel" investors, and an additional investment of $900,000 plus $1.7 million of convertible loans, again from private investors in 2002. At the end of the first quarter of 2003, monthly revenues were meeting operational expenses.

The TLC Service Concept

On behalf of sponsoring hospitals and other in-patient healthcare facilities in North America, TLC created personalized homepages for patients that linked them to family and friends during hospitalization and extended care, including maternity. Typically, the homepage, which TLC branded as a CarePage, was accessed through the healthcare organization's own website, but TLC also offered the option of access through the company's website. In both instances, all hosting took place on TLC's servers. The CarePage enabled family and friends to stay up to date on the patient's condition and to communicate messages of support (for an example, see Exhibit 1).

A CarePage was usually created when a patient was first admitted, although maternity patients often requested it be set up before their due dates. In most instances, a friend or family member agreed to act as CarePage manager and was provided with simple procedures for creating a page and updating content. The manager then informed the patient's family and friends of the address and the password required for access. Two levels of security were offered, with the higher level requiring additional screening to ensure that only specified visitors could gain access. Visitors, known as "members," could leave short messages on the site for all to read.

The service was offered free to patients and visitors, being presented as an added benefit of patronizing the sponsoring healthcare organization. The fee paid by the sponsor varied according the size of the institution, level of use, and premium options selected, but in 2003 averaged about $20,000 a year. TLC was exploring an alternative business model in which a third-party corporate sponsor paid the fee on behalf of the institution and received cobranding recognition on the CarePages.

The basic offering included such features as sending automatic email notification of an update on the patient's condition to all registered visitors to a specific CarePage, the ability to order gifts and flowers, and a guestbook tracking all visitors to the site,

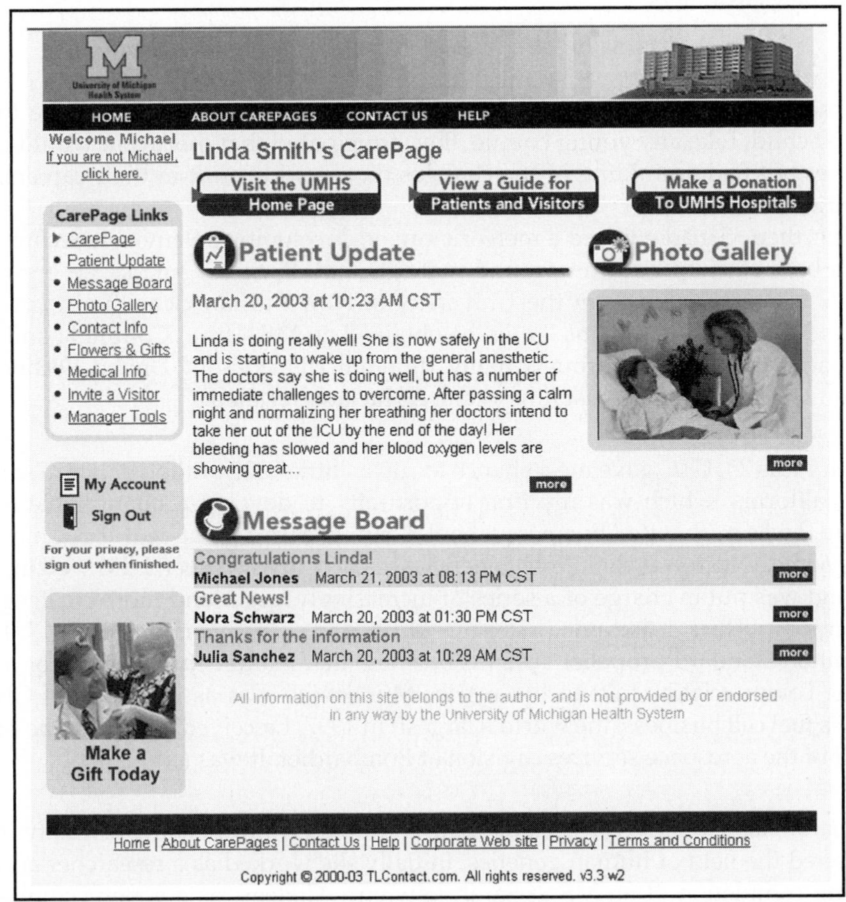

EXHIBIT 1: Sample CarePage

plus the options of posting photos and creating links to relevant background medical information.

TLC was currently testing a new feature that enabled visitors to make a donation to the healthcare institution serving the patient. For an additional fee, sponsors could also obtain feedback on usage patterns, conduct surveys of visitors, post a hospital CEO welcome message, link to the hospital gift shop, and feature a customized inbox. Spanish-language CarePages were also available for an extra fee. The company had documented different patterns of CarePage use, showing that it varied according to the nature of the patient's situation. On average, a CarePage remained "up" for 85 days and attracted 50 members, each of whom visited 15 times. However, the average hospital stay in the United States, across all categories, was only 5.2 days.

TLC's procedures ensured privacy protection, meeting the provisions of the Health Information Privacy and Accountability Act (HIPAA). Its website displayed the TRUSTe Privacy Seal, a consumer branded symbol certifying that the site met stringent requirements of notice, choice, access, security, and redress.

Operations

TLContact's service operated on three company-owned servers positioned at a remote facility, an arrangement termed co-location. These servers were connected to TLC's offices across a high-speed T1 line, which allowed almost all administrative and backup tasks to be achieved remotely. TLC had invested heavily in technology, primarily its custom-built software, as part of a continuing effort to improve the usability of the service. This process benefited considerably from having a development team that, by necessity of the company's small size, spent part of their time providing customer support. Direct contact with users' problems and questions provided a constant stream of ideas for improvements to the site. In general, a new version of the software was released every six to eight weeks, incorporating newly developed ideas as well as the needs of new customers.

History: Genesis of an Idea

In February 1998, Eric and Sharon Langshur were looking forward to the birth of their first child. Like any young couple, they anticipated that this event would change their lives but had no inkling of the changes that would result in their careers, especially Eric's.

Eric, then 35, had enjoyed a meteoric career, developing an enviable record for his skills in both start-up and turnaround management. Born in Canada, he grew up in Montreal and graduated from the University of New Brunswick with a degree in finance and information systems. Later, he obtained an MBA from Columbia and began a fast-paced progression through many different divisions of United Technologies Corporation in the space of just nine years. As he later recalled,

> When I was 25, UTC gave me a chance to run a "little" $25 million entity in southern California, which was my first opportunity to develop a quantifiable track record. I was fresh out of business school. I had to learn a great deal about managing people, which was definitely beneficial so early in my career. I did well in that job and was put in charge of a series of increasingly larger and more challenging businesses. Then I became vice president and general manager of UTC's Hamilton Standard propeller systems business that manufactures props for most of the commercial aircraft in the world. My last job was as president of ONSI, UTC's fuel cell business, the world's largest. In 1997, I received an offer to be president of the aerospace services division at Bombardier. It was a dream job.

Sharon, also a native of Canada, had graduated from McGill University in 1986 and entered the field of human genetics. Initially she worked as a researcher and then, following completion of an MS at Sarah Lawrence College, as a genetic counselor in clinical human genetics. Deciding to pursue a career in medicine, she enrolled in medical school at the University of Connecticut and received her MD in 1997, achieving honors in all clinical rotations and serving as class valedictorian. During her pregnancy, she continued her one-year academic fellowship in anatomic pathology.

Eric's new job with Bombardier—a prominent Canadian manufacturer whose products included aircraft, rail transit systems, and recreational vehicles—involved a move from Connecticut to Chicago in September 1997. The plan was for him to commute for several months while Sharon remained in Hartford to await the birth of their baby.

On February 25, Sharon gave birth to a son, whom they named Matthew. But complications became evident almost immediately and within days, a pediatric cardiologist had diagnosed the baby's heart as missing a left ventricle, a potentially fatal condition that would have been untreatable only a decade earlier. Facing the prospect of a series of complex operations on Matthew's heart, involving surgical procedures that only a handful of hospitals in the nation were qualified to perform, the Langshurs decided to complete their move to Chicago and have the baby treated at the University of Michigan Medical Center in Ann Arbor. The first surgery took place five days later.

It was a desperately worrying time for everyone. "When Sharon was pregnant," Eric remembered, "I wanted our child to be smart, handsome, athletic, outgoing, and with all the social graces. After he was diagnosed, I just wanted him to live." The couple's extended family and large circle of friends were deeply concerned and anxious for news.

Out on the West Coast, Sharon's younger brother, Mark Day, was completing his PhD in mechanical engineering at Stanford. Feeling isolated, knowing nothing about the heart, and wanting to do something useful, Mark turned to the Internet, which was just beginning to hit its stride. His search turned up a lot of information from the American Heart Association and an array of medical sources. Within a few weeks, he had created a simple website that family and friends could access. He edited the information he had gathered and loaded it on the site, together with bulletins on Matthew's condition and how the baby was responding to treatment. Sharon sent him regular updates on Matthew's progress and additional medical information. "It was a very simple site," Mark declared later. "If I had paid somebody else to do it for me, it probably wouldn't have cost more than a few hundred dollars." To minimize the need for emailing, Mark added a bulletin board so that people could send messages to Sharon and Eric.

To everyone's surprise, the site proved exceptionally popular. News spread by word-of-mouth and the site recorded hundreds of daily visitors, with more than 200 different people leaving messages for the family. People who had never before used the Internet found a way to access the site, follow Matthew's progress, and send messages.

The Langshurs were overwhelmed by this outpouring of support but also deeply grateful for the way in which the website enabled them to avoid having to spend massive amounts of time responding to phone calls and repeating the same information time and time again. The site remained up for two years, during which time Matthew successfully underwent three surgeries to repair his heart and eventually developed into a happy, healthy toddler.

Creation of TLContact.com

The success of Matthew's website convinced the Langshurs that there was a market opportunity for an Internet-based company to deliver similar information services for patients and their families, potentially on a national basis. They were inspired not only by the business opportunities this venture presented, but also by a desire to help other families enjoy the same benefits that they had received.

In late 1999, Eric and Sharon made the decision to quit their jobs (Sharon was a pediatric resident at Children's Memorial Hospital) and start their own company. "It was the height of the Internet boom," Eric recalled, "and a very heady time when millions of dollars could be raised on the basis of a short business plan." The Langshurs soon succeeded in raising $3 million from several "angel" investors.

Meantime, Mark was enjoying a long-planned hiking and climbing tour of several countries in Asia and Africa. Having recently obtained his PhD, he had decided against pursuing an academic career and was debating what to do next. He and a group of friends celebrated New Year's Eve by climbing Mount Kilimanjaro, a dramatic extinct volcano in Kenya and, at 19,340 feet (5,896 m), the highest mountain in Africa. When the party returned to civilization, Mark found a message waiting for him from his sister and brother-in-law: Would he like to join their new start-up as chief technology officer?

Mark flew into Chicago on the day of the Super Bowl, the freezing temperatures of the upper Midwest contrasting sharply with the tropical heat of Kenya. But it was an intoxicating atmosphere for dot.com entrepreneurs and investors. Business news stories that day described the huge amounts of money that an array of Internet-based companies were spending on TV advertising during the Super Bowl broadcast.

The business model for the new venture followed the B2C approach that dominated most Internet start-ups. The goal was to market directly to patients' families and to prospective parents, charging a fee per page. The company needed a name and, in keeping with its consumer orientation, the Langshurs wanted to call it 4U.com, which they saw as simple and memorable. However, a search revealed that this domain name, although not in use, was already registered. Eric laughed as he recalled what happened next.

> When we contacted the owner, he indicated that he was willing to sell the rights to the URL for $2 million. The lunacy of the times was further highlighted when one of our early investors urged us to just go ahead and buy it! But we didn't think that was a prudent use of $2 million.

Instead, they selected the name TLContact.com, a play on the common abbreviation of "tender loving care." Each patient site was named a "CarePage," and procedures were devised to control access and ensure patient confidentiality.

Initial Start-Up

In addition to Eric as CEO, Sharon as director of medical services, and Mark as CTO, the team was expanded to include a president with an extensive healthcare operations background, a VP–business development, and a VP–health care services, as well as administrative support staff. Mark began to build a technology team to create the website and its supporting systems. Meantime, an advisory board was formed to help shape the new company's strategy, monitor progress, and provide an objective perspective. TLC also benefited from advice provided by Sharon's father, George Day, an internationally recognized marketing professor at the Wharton School of the University of Pennsylvania. She noted that he had taught them the importance of listening to the market, understanding the needs of target customers, and finding ways to avoid or circumvent strategic obstacles.

Eric found himself making a sharp transition in his professional lifestyle, moving from the president's office of a multimillion business to a second-floor office above a storefront. At Bombardier's aerospace division, and prior to that at UTC, he had had thousands of employees. After a few months, TLC's payroll (including himself, Sharon, Mark, and technical staff) was up to $50,000 per month. However, he conceded that this situation did not prevent him from continuing to think big. There were 6,000 acute-care hospitals in the U.S., 17,000 nursing homes, and over 3,000 hospices. The number of patients treated each year was estimated at 40 million. Everyone was convinced that huge rewards awaited the firm that could move quickly to penetrate this market.

Quickly recognizing the difficulties and expense of trying to market directly to individual patients, TLC soon shifted its sales focus to a hospital-based approach. With competition between hospitals becoming increasingly heated, enhancing patient satisfaction had become a strategic imperative at many institutions. Offering patients access to TLC seemed like a logical service enhancement to its proponents. But, despite early support from the pediatric cardiology group at the University of Michigan Medical Center (where Matthew had been treated), selling to hospitals proved much more difficult than expected.

TLC's original business model anticipated being in hundreds of hospitals within a year or so. The company was in a hurry to build a strong market base before competitors could do so. Already, there were a number of competing organizations, all of them quite small and each started by individuals who had created a website to keep family and friends informed of developments relating to somebody's health. They included Baby Press Conference, targeted at prospective parents; TheStatus, run as a sideline of a Web design company in Anchorage, Alaska; VisitingOurs, a rather basic service that outsourced the Web technology; and another rather basic service called CaringBridge, operated by a nonprofit organization.

To their dismay, the Langshurs and their colleagues soon realized that selling to hospitals was going to be a slow and difficult task. Sharon observed:

> We found the difficulties of selling to hospitals to be myriad. Based on my experience as a physician, we initially felt that we could sell to docs on the basis of helping them to enhance the quality of the patient experience. We knew they cared about patients and wanted to do the best for them. But after several months of barking up that tree, we realized that physicians didn't have the time to listen or the budget to purchase and were usually just too busy with delivery of medical care.
>
> So after six months or so, we shifted our efforts to PR and marketing departments, which did have a budget and were more likely to be able to see the advantages for their hospitals in terms of increased patient satisfaction.

However, hospital administrators didn't like the idea of having to ask their patients to pay for the service—after all, there were no charges for television and other nonmedical services designed to enhance satisfaction—so the discussion then shifted to the possibility of the hospital itself purchasing the basic service and making the option available to all patients who requested it. Yet many administrators failed to grasp the appeal of the service for patients or the advantages to the hospital of offering it. So TLC had to adopt a missionary approach, pointing out that advantages for the hospital included not only more satisfied patients but also fewer demands on hospital staff as families and friends replaced telephone requests for information by a simple search of the website.

In its sales efforts, TLC also cited the findings of a national study on patient satisfaction by the Picker Institute, which found that when asked about problems encountered during their hospital stays, 27 percent of the 23,763 patients surveyed reported lack of emotional support, 28 percent cited inadequate information and education, and 23 percent complained about insufficient involvement of family and friends. The survey data showed that patients receiving inadequate emotional support during their hospital stay were up to ten times more likely to say that they would not return to that hospital or recommend it.

Meantime, Mark and his technology team were hard at work on systems design. He emphasized that this task was vastly different in cost and complexity from the simple website that he had designed earlier for his nephew.

> A key question at the outset had been whether to contract with someone to build the website or do it ourselves. It wasn't entirely clear whether it was worth the extra cost of outsourcing to gain the advantage of speed, although we were under tremendous pressure to move quickly since there was a level of paranoia about the risk that competitors might get a jump on us and dominate what was seen as a very lucrative market. On the other hand, if we did it ourselves, we would retain the intellectual capital and would find it easier to undertake future updates and expansions. Having had the experience of creating the initial website and seen its functionality, I had a very clear idea of how I wanted this thing built, which gave us a running start.
>
> In February 2000, the dot.com boom was just about at its peak and outsourcing was wildly expensive—we were quoted $400,000 for just a scoping study! So

> we hired some consultants who could really help us set up the initial architecture and help achieve some of our key goals, especially flexibility. During the same period, I hired several people full time. We took a deliberate approach to hire very skilled people. After a couple of months we had a technical team of about 10, including a programming group, a graphic design team, and a support group whose work included content design. The total cost was in the range of four to five hundred thousand dollars to achieve a functioning website.
>
> It's very difficult to create a piece of software that's really user friendly. It takes an incredible amount of skill, effort, and time to develop something that's usable, functional, and scalable—meaning that it can be expanded and built upon without failing. For enterprise-wide applications you have to support the server with an operating system. We chose to go open source, which significantly reduced the cost because the source code is freely available. We launched in early August.

An additional round of "angel" financing was obtained during the summer of 2000, which enabled TLC to enhance the functionality of the service and add optional features. By late 2000, TLC had completed proof-of-concept prototype and alpha testing of the service. It had secured launch customers in three targeted market segments: acute care, long-term care, and hospice. Recognizing two distinct needs, it had created two distinct products, Acute CarePage and Baby CarePage. The latter was targeted at parents who were expecting a baby.

An Evolving Marketing Strategy

TLC's market strategy evolved into a threefold thrust. The first strategic component was to continue offering a stand-alone service, positioned as an e-business patient satisfaction solution that offered important benefits for hospitals and health systems. Among patients and their families, TLC planned to rely on a "viral" marketing effect through word-of-mouth referrals, thus limiting the need for mass media advertising. Although the number of users was still small, feedback had been exceptionally positive. The second component involved outsourcing direct sales to a national distribution partner that had established relationships with hospitals and health facilities. The third component involved licensing TLC software and its functionality to trusted third-party vendors and consultants. These partners could then bundle TLC's service as a "feature" to enhance their own product offerings, in return for royalties and other payments.

Sales Activities

By early 2001, sales discussions were in progress at more than two dozen hospitals and health systems. Despite validation of TLC service by a number of leading healthcare providers, the sales process was proving very slow. Hospital acceptance required the buy-in of numerous constituents, including administration, marketing, patient services, IT, legal, and physicians. But some could still not see the value of the service. As Sharon put it, "They had difficulty thinking outside the box." Budgetary constraints were a major reason for saying no. A few large hospitals with significant endowments declined on the grounds that they might want to develop their own services in house.

However, TLC met its sales target for the first quarter by signing contracts with the University of Michigan Health System, New York Presbyterian Hospital, and Children's Memorial Hospital in Chicago. The first two hospitals specified that CarePages had to be fully branded under their own names and employ their own distinctive color schemes, although the tag line, "Powered by TLContact" would appear as a subscript.

Each branded product required the customization of over 70 Web pages and 400 images, but TLC soon developed this capability, which it believed offered a significant competitive advantage. Other enhancements included an option for user feedback, addition of an email notification tool to announce updated news on a CarePage, and inclusion of software logic to automatically fix common mistakes that visitors might make in CarePage names, thereby reducing the volume of customer service enquires.

Eric had always been very cost conscious, so planning at TLC had emphasized the need to rush toward cash flow positive status. However, with the dot.com bubble now burst and sales progress proving sluggish, the Langshurs realized that TLC had to slow its burn rate by making significant cutbacks in staff numbers. It was a painful decision.

TLC continued to refine its sales approach so that it could address the specific concerns of the different decision makers at a hospital. It also refined its pricing policy, which Eric admitted had been rather unsophisticated, and began customizing it to the characteristics and needs of individual hospitals. On average, hospitals paid about $20,000 a year for the service. One encouraging development was that the lead time for concluding a sales agreement with a hospital was getting shorter, dropping from an average of nine months in early 2001 to only three months by the end of 2002. Eric remarked:

> We've learned a great deal about how to communicate our value proposition succinctly and to simplify our sales process. Most importantly, with every new account we sign, market acceptance of the product grows and the sales cycle shortens.

An important contributing factor was the exceptionally positive nature of the feedback received from CarePage users (see Exhibit 2 for a representative sample). Competitors, however, did not seem to be faring as well. BabyPressConference had shut down in 2002. TLC considered purchasing its assets but decided that this would not be a worthwhile investment. None of the remaining three appeared as active in the marketplace.

EXHIBIT 2: Recent Feedback

- "TLContact has been the lifeline of many of the families on my unit and keeps the support network of family and friends alive and thriving. I cannot stress enough how important this website is to families in crisis or enduring a chronic illness. Thank you. Thank you. Thank you!" (Theresa, Child Life Specialist, C.S. Mott Children's Hospital)
- "This is a prime example of why Children's [Hospital] has the world-class reputation it does. Thanks for caring enough about your patients and their families to continually strive to keep Children's 'a cut above.'"
- "What a wonderful service to provide to your patients and their families. . . . This can only help to enhance the patient's rate of recovery and help everyone cope with the hospitalization experience."
- "I cannot express what an incredible blessing this website was. We could update everyone at the same time without anything getting misconstrued. To go to the site and see so many folks sending well wishes and prayers and was so uplifting and helpful. We received so many comments from family and friends that the site was fabulous! Please keep this service!"
- "I want you to know that this is a brilliant idea. It helps immeasurably to humanize the difficulties of communication surrounding hospitalization."
- "What a great concept! For someone that is not a family member, but a close friend, this is a great way to communicate on the schedule of the patient's family. I'm really impressed. . . . I'm going to forward this link to my pastor, I'm sure he will find it useful."
- "My daughter's illness was sudden and life threatening. We were transferred from one hospital to a children's hospital. Everyone had thought the worst when they couldn't find us in our hometown hospital. Our only connection was your service. It saved me, mom, from intense stress as everyone wanted to know hour-by-hour updates. In some cases it was the ONLY information our families received. Your service is a godsend for the patients and the families. Because of your service churches around the US gathered to pray for our little girl. Those prayers wouldn't have happened if we didn't have the internet connection that you and the hospital gave to us. Now we celebrate that our little girl made it and people like you helped us."
- "Excellent service, and such a help at such a stressful time in our lives. Not having to make multiple phone calls, and everyone hearing information 'firsthand.' is such a huge help. We've often logged on in the middle of the night, from the ICU, in the middle of our stressful life-and-death dance as the baby fights to live, to read all the kind words of encouragement our family & friends have left for us. The baby's been in and out of the hospital many times now in his short 6 months so far, and words cannot express what a difference it makes, to know that everyone's out there pulling for us, and praying for us. Thanks so much!"
- "This web service is perfect for our situation. My 19-year-old son suffered a severe head injury. The hospital he was transferred to is 3 hours from our home. We live in a very small, tight community. We have lots and lots of concerned family and friends. Our son will have ongoing treatment and progress that our family & friends want to stay informed of. It's a wonderful tool and I have had nothing but positive feedback from the users. Thank you."
- "You have a truly done a wonderful thing with this CarePage, and the pictures, updates, and message board help friends and family all keep in contact, all at the same place—it's just remarkable! Thank you so much for providing this service. It's great for those of us who cannot afford to be there in person, but whose hearts are there to support our friends and family. It's people like you who make a difference in this world! May God Richly Bless You All in your continued efforts to help those in need!"

Although continuing to add individual hospitals to its client base and target new ones, TLC now recognized that prospects for significant sales growth centered on achieving distribution agreements with large systems. Its first success in what was seen as a long-lead-time sale came with a distribution agreement with CHCA, a buying consortium for 38 leading children's hospitals. A direct-to-hospice co-marketing initiative was launched with the National Hospice and Palliative Care Organization, which represented 2,100 of the nation's 3,140 hospices. Subsequently, the firm began a paid pilot program with Tenet Corporation, operator of 116 acute-care hospitals.

Continued innovation in CarePages functionality included creation of a Spanish-language option, developed in collaboration with a Mexican hospital system, which would be offered to U.S. hospitals for an extra fee. Also under development was refinement of procedures for surveying members after they had completed a certain number of visits. Other new features in development included a Nurses Hall of Fame, allowing members to pay tribute to exceptional healthcare workers, thereby improving nursing hiring and retention; a Message Inbox, allowing hospitals to deliver targeted messages to members; and a "Send a Prayer" feature which provided a functional link to a faith-based prayer group. Eric believed that each of these features demonstrated that the product had great acceptance as a trusted channel to the healthcare consumer.

In June 2002, Mark Day left the company to enroll in the MBA program at Wharton. Having transitioned from a technical role to one more deeply involved with marketing, sales, and fund raising, Mark now sought to build a more fundamental understanding of these areas through his MBA studies.

Research Insights

Working with researchers and a sponsoring institution, TLC had conducted a survey of CarePages visitors and managers. In September 2002, it added a new feature to the Children's Hospital Boston site, an online survey capability. This was tested during a two-week period in the pediatric cardiology unit. One version was offered to CarePages managers, who were automatically presented with the survey at their fifth log-in, and another to CarePages visitors who first saw the survey at their third log-in. During a two-week period, 27 managers (90 percent) and 636 visitors (79 percent) responded. A majority (63 percent) of all respondents were female. The results, presented in Exhibit 3, showed that the service was highly valued. The majority of users reported that the service improved their opinion of the Children's Hospital, made them more likely to recommend it, led them to visit the hospital's website, and increased their likelihood of donating to the hospital foundation.

A second project involved the launch of pilot donation programs at C.S. Mott Children's Hospital in Michigan and Children's Memorial Hospital in Chicago. When visitors were asked about their willingness to make a donation, 11 percent stated that they were willing to make a donation immediately and another 22 percent requested the opportunity to do so later.

Eric was very excited about this finding, since it suggested that TLC could be presented to nonprofit hospitals as a self-financing service. But he recognized the importance of continuing to employ what some experts had described as "permission marketing."

> We're a mission-driven organization. We created this company to serve patients, their families, and their support networks. We understand the importance of the contract that we make with our members and we like to think of it as a moral contract. However, we recognize that the service we deliver to our members doesn't provide sufficient revenue to our customers, the hospitals. Added value items are what persuade hospitals to buy. So in certain respects we've commercialized the reach that we offer to the hospitals, but we try to do it in a way that we regard as "noble."
>
> We wouldn't do anything that would adversely impact the integrity of our service delivery. So we ask permission from our users to give their names to the hospital foundation for mailing—they can choose to opt in. If a hospital's CarePages service is sponsored by a third party, then a similar, permission-based approach might be used to give members the opportunity to receive information from that sponsor.

EXHIBIT 3: Executive Summary: Children's Hospital Boston Online Survey Results

In September 2002, TLContact added a new feature to the Children's Hospital Boston branded site: an online survey, with one version offered to CarePage Managers (who are first presented with the survey at their 5th log-in) and another to CarePages Visitors (who first see the survey after their 3rd log-in).

The TLContact Online Survey garnered an outstanding response rate. The initial test period ran from August 29 to September 13, 2002, and was targeted at patient families of the 50- bed cardiovascular unit of CHB. During the initial test period, surveys were completed by 27/30 (90%) of Managers and 636/806 (79%) of Visitors. There were a total of 663 respondents, most (63%) of whom were female. As detailed in the following section, virtually all Managers and Visitors highly value the CarePages service. Moreover, the majority of people who used the service report that it improved their opinion of the hospital, made them more likely to recommend the hospital, led them to visit the hospital's website, and increased their likelihood of donating to the hospital foundation.

Questions Asked of Both Managers and Visitors (27 Managers + 636 Visitors = 663 total)

	Number of Responses	Percent
1. How are you related to the patient?		
I am a friend:	466	72%
I am a family member or guardian:	169	26%
I am a caregiver or care provider:	14	2%
I am the patient:	2	0%
2. Would you recommend the CarePage service to other people?		
Yes:	641	99%
No:	5	1%
3. Do you think that CarePages are an important service for hospitals to offer?		
Yes:	643	99%
No:	6	1%
4. Did your experience with Children's Hospital Boston's CarePage service. . .		
	# Yes	% Yes
Improve your opinion of the hospital?	528	91%
Make you more likely to recommend this hospital?	503	86%
Cause you to visit Children's Boston Web site?	319	55%
Make you more likely to make a charitable gift to the hospital foundation?	298	53%

The questions that were asked only of Managers indicated that most learned of the CarePages service via hospital materials. The item in which Managers rated hospital service (see #2 below) indicates the value of increasing adoption of the CarePages service, perhaps though personal messages from hospital staff. These "real-time" service ratings offer clear and significant opportunities for improving service and satisfaction.

Questions Asked Only of Managers (27 total)

1. How did you learn about the CarePage service?

	Number of Responses	Percent
Materials in the hospital	11	46%
Hospital staff member	7	29%
Friend or family member	6	25%
Hospital physician	0	0%
The Internet	0	0%
Ad or story in the media	0	0%

2. Please rate the following. . .

	Poor	Fair	Good	VeryGood	Excellent
	(%Based On 21 Responses To This Item)				
Overall quality of patient care:	0%	0%	0%	14%	86%
Doctor courtesy and attentiveness:	0%	5%	5%	19%	71%
Staff courtesy and attentiveness:	0%	0%	0%	33%	67%
Communication about patient care:	0%	0%	5%	43%	52%
Admissions process:	5%	5%	20%	30%	40%
Cleanliness of room:	0%	10%	14%	38%	38%
Food:	5%	10%	29%	38%	19%

(Continued)

EXHIBIT 3: *(Continued)*

Questions Asked Only of Visitors (442 Responses of 636 Total)

1. Please rate your overall impression of Children's Hospital Boston. . .

	% N/A	% Poor	% Good	% Excellent
Quality of care:	55%	0%	9%	36%
Commitment to patient satisfaction:	51%	0%	11%	38%
Staff courtesy and attention:	60%	0%	9%	31%
		Valid Percent (based on responses other than N/A)		
Quality of care:		0%	20%	80%
Commitment to patient satisfaction:		0%	22%	78%
Staff courtesy and attention:		0%	23%	77%

2. Which of the following areas of health education are of interest to you?

	Number of Responses	Percent of Respondents*
Heart disease	153	47%
Cancer screening and treatment	120	37%
Women's health issues	122	37%
Health and fitness	121	37%
Weight control and obesity	96	29%
Common aging concerns	84	26%
Allergies and asthma	77	24%
Depression	75	23%
Diabetes	69	21%
Pain management	58	18%
Growth and development	51	16%
Behavioral problems	45	14%
Common childhood illnesses	41	13%
Clinical trials	21	6%
Immunization	17	5%
"Other"	28	9%

*The total percentage for all items is greater than 100% because the 326 people who answered this question offered multiple responses (i.e., they were interested in more than one area). Responses to the Visitors' question regarding hospital service reflect what they hear from the CarePage Managers, as well as general impressions and personal experience. The item regarding interest in health education provides a sense of topics about which respondents desire more information, suggesting an opportunity for TLContact's partners.

The Current Situation

The first quarter of 2003 saw a rapid acceleration of revenues as more hospitals signed up for TLC service, existing customers renewed their contracts, and the number of CarePages at each institution continued to grow. Unlike new sales, renewals involved almost no additional cost for TLC and increasing utilization generated higher revenues from existing customers. TLC now served 40 hospitals; they were predominantly academic medical centers and included several of the most prestigious institutions in the United States and Canada. There were additional prospects in the sales pipeline. However, the company did not yet have any customers among nursing homes and hospices.

Existing competitors no longer seemed to pose a threat. VisitingOurs had recently shut down, and a comparison of the service features offered by TLC and the two remaining players, TheStatus and CaringBridge, showed that TLC's CarePages service had substantial advantages (Exhibit 4). Moreover, the prospect that some hospitals might attempt to create their own service offerings appeared increasingly unlikely. A large, well-endowed children's hospital, which had previously declared its intention to develop a similar service in-house, had recently decided to adopt TLC

EXHIBIT 4: Patient Communication Service Feature Comparison

	TLCONTACT	THESTATUS	CARINGBRIDGE
Customer Service			
Toll-free phone support	✓	✓	
Email support	✓	✓	✓
Spanish-language support	✓		
Comprehensive online help	✓	✓	
Features for Healthcare Facilities			
Custom Services			
Welcome message	✓		
Active survey system	✓		
Active donation system	✓		
Custom links to hospital's web site	✓	✓	
Unit specification	✓		
Spanish-language version	✓		
Baby-specific version	✓	✓	✓
Detailed usage reports	✓	✓	
Branding			
Co-branded patient page	✓	✓	✓
Entire web site co-branded	✓		
Customized colors and graphics	✓		
Features for Patients			
Patient Updates/News	✓	✓	✓
Email notification	✓		
Ability to edit	✓	✓	
Adjustable time zones	✓	✓	
Sorting and paging	✓		
Printer-friendly version	✓	✓	
Message Board	✓	✓	✓
Ability to reply to messages	✓		
Printer-friendly version	✓	✓	

instead, admitting that internal analysis had revealed that going it alone would be not only be very time consuming but also prohibitively expensive.

Planning the Agenda for the Board Meeting

Having completed the quarterly activity update, Eric turned to the task of creating an agenda for the upcoming board meeting. He started to rough out some thoughts. Under FUTURE GROWTH, he jotted down: "How fast? What directions? Key targets as selling priorities? Opportunities for revenues from new added-value services? Launch stripped-down version of TLC service at much lower price?"

The next heading was COMPETITION. He wrote "VisitingOurs folds. Comparison chart of TLC vs TheStatus, Caring Bridge. Future threats??" Eric paused, holding his pen in the air. He recognized that at some point a major player in the trillion-dollar healthcare market might be tempted to replicate TLC's CarePages technology and service features. However, he was reassured that it would require an extensive investment of money and time. A further barrier to competition was patent protection. Ultimately, however, strategic partnerships, continued growth, product enhancements, and maintenance of exceptional customer satisfaction levels constituted the most complete defense. Lowering the pen to paper, he added: "Would competition hurt us? Can we competition-proof TLC?"

An important issue for the board to discuss concerned the role of future partnerships between TLC and other industry players. Recently, one large supplier of medical equipment and services had expressed interest in taking a minority financial stake in the company. POSSIBLE FINANCIAL PARTNERSHIP, he wrote, and below it: "Finance for accelerated growth? Market leverage? Pros and cons? Timing—now vs. later?"

Eric smiled. With an agenda like this, he anticipated a stimulating discussion at the board meeting. Then his face took on a more serious look. "WE ARE A MISSION-DRIVEN ORGANIZATION" he printed carefully, and underlined it twice.

Study Questions

1. Evaluate the evolution of TLC and identify the key decisions that kept it afloat and underpinned its subsequent success.
2. How does TLC create value for (a) patients and (b) hospitals?
3. Review the four topics on Eric Langshur's draft of the agenda for the board meeting. As a board member, what position would you take on each topic and why?

CASE 17 The Accellion Service Guarantee

Jochen Wirtz and Jill Klein

A high-technology company introduces what it considers to be a bold service quality guarantee to communicate its commitment to service excellence to customers, prospects, and its own employees.

Accellion was a young, high-technology firm with leading-edge technology in the distributed file storage, management, and delivery market space. Still new to the industry, the firm aimed to become the global backbone for the next generation of Internet-based applications.

Accellion's main value proposition to the world's largest enterprises ("the Global 2000"), as well as to Internet-based providers of premium content, was to allow them to serve their users faster, increase operational efficiencies, and lower total costs. Specifically, Accellion customers could improve the access time for downloading and uploading files by more than 200 percent. This performance improvement was achieved by locating an intelligent storage and file management system at the "edges of the Internet" and thereby delivering content from regions located closer to the end-user. The typical time-consuming routing through many servers and hubs could be avoided using Accellion's infrastructure.

The need for an Internet infrastructure to deliver high bandwidth content to end-users had never been greater. There was a trend toward multimedia and personalized Web content, all of which could not be delivered efficiently by existing infrastructure, which routed data through the congested network of servers that form the backbone of the Internet. This prompted Accellion to develop and launch a new service: distributed file storage, management, and delivery. Accellion provided an applications platform that resided on independent servers, which were directly connected to the users' Internet Service Providers (ISPs), thereby avoiding the congested "centers" of the Internet. This decreased access time and allowed Accellion to distribute specialized content and applications more efficiently.

To effectively market Accellion's value proposition, Warren J. Kaplan, Accellion's CEO, and S. Mohan, its Chief Strategist and Founder, felt that in addition to its leading-edge technology, key success factors for Accellion's aggressive growth strategy were excellence in service delivery and high customer satisfaction. They envisioned that customers would prefer to leverage Accellion's technology and partnerships instead of having to manage the details of deploying, maintaining, and upgrading their own storage infrastructure for distributed Internet applications. To build a customer-driven culture and to communicate service excellence credibly to the market, Accellion aimed to harness the power of service guarantees.

Cost-effective services for improving performance and reliability were becoming critical, as the widespread use of multimedia and other large files increased exponentially. The value proposition was clearly attractive, but how could Accellion convince prospective clients that its technology and service actually could deliver what they promised?

Mohan felt that a Quality of Service (QoS) Guarantee would be a powerful tool to make its promises credible and, at the same time, push his team to deliver what has been promised. Mark Ranford, Accellion's Director for Product Management, and Mohan spearheaded the development of the QoS Guarantee. They finally launched the QoS Guarantee (shown in Exhibit 1) stating that "it is a revolutionary statement of our

This case is an updated version of a case previously in the INSEAD case series. The authors gratefully acknowledge the invaluable support by S. Mohan, Accellion's Chief Strategist, for his assistance and feedback to earlier versions of this case.

EXHIBIT 1: Accellion's Service Guarantee

QUALITY OF SERVICE GUARANTEE

The Accellion Quality of Service Guarantee defines Accellion's assurance and commitment to providing the Customer with value-added Service and is incorporated into Accellion's Customer Contract. The definition of terms used herein is the same as those found in the Customer Contract.

1. **Performance Guarantee**
   Accellion guarantees that the performance of the Network in uploading and downloading content, as a result of using the Accellion Service, will be no less than 200 percent of that which is achieved by a benchmark origin site being accessed from the edges of the Internet. For all purposes herein, performance measurement tests will be conducted by Accellion.

2. **Availability Guarantee**
   Accellion guarantees 100 percent service availability, excluding *force majeure* and scheduled maintenance for customers who have opted for our replication services.

3. **Customer Service Guarantee**
   Should Accellion fail to meet the service levels set out in Sections 1 and 2 above, Accellion will credit the customer's account with one (1) month's service fee for the month affected when the failure(s) occurred, provided the customer gives written notice to Accellion of such failure within five (5) days from the date such failure occurred. The customer's failure to comply with this requirement will forfeit the customer's right to receive such credit.

   Accellion will notify the customer no less than 48 hours (2 days) in advance of scheduled maintenance. If the service becomes unavailable for any other reason, Accellion will promptly notify the customer and take all necessary action to restore the service.

   Accellion maintains a 24-hour support center and will provide the customer with a response to any inquiry in relation to the service no more than 2 hours from the time of receipt of such query by customer service.

4. **Security and Privacy Policy**
   Accellion has complete respect for the customer's privacy and that of any customer data stored in Accellion servers. The Accellion service does not require customers to provide any end-user private details for the data stored on the servers. All information provided to Accellion by the customer is stored for the customer's sole benefit. Accellion will not share, disclose, or sell any personally identifiable information to which it may have access and will ensure that the customer's information and data [are] kept secure.

   Disclosure of customer's information or data in Accellion's possession shall only be made where such disclosure is necessary for compliance with a court order, to protect the rights or property of Accellion and to enforce the terms of use of the service as provided in the contract.

   Accellion will ensure that the customer's information and data [are] kept secure and protected from unauthorized access or improper use, which includes taking all reasonable steps to verify the customer's identity before granting access.

EXHIBIT 2: Email to All Accellion Staff Announcing the Launch of the QoS Guarantee

Dear Team,

I am pleased to forward to everyone our industry's leading Quality of Service guarantee (QoS). Please read it over very carefully. You will find it to be very aggressive, and it puts the ownership on everyone in this company to deliver. Customers don't want a Service Level Agreement (SLA); they just want their network up and running all the time. That is why we have created this no questions asked guarantee. This type of guarantee has proven successful in other industries where service is key to success (e.g., Industry Leaders such as Gartner Group, LL Bean, Nordstrom, etc.).

As a member of the Accellion team, you are key to our client's satisfaction.

Thanks in advance for your support in making our clients and ourselves successful.

commitment to the customer to do whatever it takes to ensure satisfaction." The official launch of the guarantee was announced to all staff by email (Exhibit 2).

Their QoS Guarantee, however, was just part of Accellion's push for operational excellence. Many factors worked together to keep the company focused on its clients and providing the best possible service, so that the staff could create a large and loyal customer base for their innovative product. Thus, it was very important to raise awareness for Accellion's unique value proposition and convince the early adopters of the advantages.

Accellion's customers reacted positively. One customer stated, "Hey look at this. I haven't seen anything like it. No one offers 100 percent availability. That's tremendous." Another customer exclaimed, "You must really be confident in your service. This really is risk free now, isn't it?" Accellion was committed to its guarantee and strongly believed that having the best network and technology partners would enable it to deliver on its promise.

EXHIBIT 3: Accellion's QoS 100 Percent Availability Guarantee Instills Client Confidence in Their Internet-Based File Storage and Management Services

Study Questions

1. What is the marketing impact of a well-designed service guarantee?
2. Evaluate the design of Accellion's guarantee shown in Exhibit 1. How effective will it be in communicating service excellence to potential and current customers? Would you recommend any changes to its design or implementation?
3. Will the guarantee be successful in creating a culture for service excellence within Accellion? What else may be needed for achieving such a culture?
4. Do you think customers might take advantage of this guarantee and "stage" service failures to invoke the guarantee? If yes, how could Accellion minimize potential cheating on its guarantee?

CASE 18 Starbucks: Delivering Customer Service

YOUNGME MOON AND JOHN QUELCH

Starbucks, the dominant specialty-coffee brand in North America, must respond to recent market research indicating that the company is not meeting customer expectations in terms of service. To increase customer satisfaction, the company is debating a plan that would increase the amount of labor in its stores and theoretically increase speed-of-service. However, the impact of the plan (which would cost $40 million annually) on the company's bottom line is unclear.

In mid-2002, Christine Day, Starbucks' senior vice president of administration in North America, sat in the seventh-floor conference room of Starbucks' Seattle headquarters and reached for her second cup of *toffee nut latte*. The handcrafted beverage—a buttery, toffee-nut flavored espresso concoction topped with whipped cream and toffee sprinkles—had become a regular afternoon indulgence for Day ever since its introduction earlier that year.

As she waited for her colleagues to join her, Day reflected on the company's recent performance. While other retailers were still reeling from the post-9/11 recession, Starbucks was enjoying its 11th consecutive year of 5 percent or higher comparable store sales growth, prompting its founder and chairman, Howard Schultz, to declare: "I think we've demonstrated that we are close to a recession-proof product."[1]

Day, however, was not feeling nearly as sanguine, in part because Starbucks' most recent market research had revealed some unexpected findings. "We've always taken great pride in our retail service," said Day, "but according to the data, we're not always meeting our customers' expectations in the area of customer satisfaction."

As a result of these concerns, Day and her associates had come up with a plan to invest an additional $40 million annually in the company's 4,500 stores, which would allow each store to add the equivalent of 20 hours of labor a week. "The idea is to improve speed-of-service and thereby increase customer satisfaction," said Day.

In two days, Day was due to make a final recommendation to both Schultz and Orin Smith, Starbucks' CEO, about whether the company should move forward with the plan. "The investment is the EPS [earnings per share] equivalent of almost seven cents a share," said Day. In preparation for her meeting with Schultz and Smith, Day had asked one of her associates to help her think through the implications of the plan. Day noted, "The real question is, do we believe what our customers are telling us about what constitutes 'excellent' customer service? And if we deliver it, what will the impact be on our sales and profitability?"

Company Background

The story of how Howard Schultz managed to transform a commodity into an upscale cultural phenomenon had become the stuff of legends. In 1971, three coffee fanatics—Gerald Baldwin, Gordon Bowker, and Ziev Siegl—opened a small coffee shop in Seattle's Pike Place Market. The shop specialized in selling whole arabica beans to a niche market of coffee purists.

In 1982, Schultz joined the Starbucks marketing team; shortly thereafter, he traveled to Italy, where he became fascinated with Milan's coffee culture, in particular, the

---

Professors Youngme Moon and John Quetch prepared this case. HBS cases are developed solely as the basis for class discussion. Cases are not intended to serve as endorsements, sources of primary data, or illustrations of effective or ineffective management.

role the neighborhood espresso bars played in Italians' everyday social lives. Upon his return, the inspired Schultz convinced the company to set up an espresso bar in the corner of its only downtown Seattle shop. As Schultz explained, the bar became the prototype for his long-term vision:

> The idea was to create a chain of coffeehouses that would become America's "third place." At the time, most Americans had two places in their lives—home and work. But I believed that people needed another place, a place where they could go to relax and enjoy others, or just be by themselves. I envisioned a place that would be separate from home or work, a place that would mean different things to different people.

A few years later, Schultz got his chance when Starbucks' founders agreed to sell him the company. As soon as Schultz took over, he immediately began opening new stores. The stores sold whole beans and premium-priced coffee beverages by the cup and catered primarily to affluent, well-educated, white-collar patrons (skewed female) between the ages of 25 and 44. By 1992, the company had 140 such stores in the Northwest and Chicago and was successfully competing against other small-scale coffee chains such as Gloria Jean's Coffee Bean and Barnie's Coffee & Tea.

That same year, Schultz decided to take the company public. As he recalled, many Wall Street types were dubious about the idea: "They'd say, 'You mean, you're going to sell coffee for a dollar in a paper cup, with Italian names that no one in America can say? At a time in America when no one's drinking coffee? And I can get coffee at the local coffee shop or doughnut shop for 50 cents? Are you kidding me?'"[2]

Ignoring the skeptics, Schultz forged ahead with the public offering, raising $25 million in the process. The proceeds allowed Starbucks to open more stores across the nation.

By mid-2002, Schultz had unequivocally established Starbucks as the dominant specialty-coffee brand in North America. Sales had climbed at a compound annual growth rate (CAGR) of 40 percent since the company had gone public, and net earnings had risen at a CAGR of 50 percent. The company was now serving 20 million unique customers in well over 5,000 stores around the globe and was opening on average three new stores a day. (See Exhibits 1–3 for company financials and store growth over time.)

What made Starbucks' success even more impressive was that the company had spent almost nothing on advertising to achieve it. North American marketing primarily consisted of point-of-sale materials and local-store marketing and was far less than the industry average. (Most fast-food chains had marketing budgets in the 3 percent to 6 percent range.)

For his part, Schultz remained as chairman and chief global strategist in control of the company, handing over day-to-day operations in 2002 to CEO Orin Smith, a Harvard MBA (1967) who had joined the company in 1990.

The Starbucks Value Proposition

Starbucks' brand strategy was best captured by its "live coffee" mantra, a phrase that reflected the importance the company attached to keeping the national coffee culture alive. From a retail perspective, this meant creating an "experience" around the consumption of coffee, an experience that people could weave into the fabric of their everyday lives.

There were three components to this experiential branding strategy. The first component was the coffee itself. Starbucks prided itself on offering what it believed to be the highest-quality coffee in the world, sourced from the Africa, Central and South America, and Asia-Pacific regions. To enforce its exacting coffee standards, Starbucks controlled as much of the supply chain as possible—it worked directly with growers in various countries of origin to purchase green coffee beans, it oversaw the custom-roasting process for the company's various blends and single-origin coffees, and it controlled distribution to retail stores around the world.

The second brand component was service, or what the company sometimes referred to as "customer intimacy." "Our goal is to create an uplifting experience every

EXHIBIT 1: Starbucks' Financials, FY 1998 to FY 2002 ($ in millions)

	FY 1998	FY 1999	FY 2000	FY 2001	FY 2002
Revenue					
Co-Owned North American	1,076.8	1,375.0	1,734.9	2,086.4	2,583.8
Co-Owned Int'l (UK, Thailand, Australia)	25.8	48.4	88.7	143.2	209.1
Total Company-Operated Retail	1,102.6	1,423.4	1,823.6	2,229.6	2,792.9
Specialty Operations	206.1	263.4	354.0	419.4	496.0
Net Revenues	**1,308.7**	**1,686.8**	**2,177.6**	**2,649.0**	**3,288.9**
Cost of Goods Sold	578.5	747.6	961.9	1,112.8	1,350.0
Gross Profit	**730.2**	**939.2**	**1,215.7**	**1,536.2**	**1,938.9**
Joint-Venture Income[a]	1.0	3.2	20.3	28.6	35.8
Expenses:					
Store Operating Expense	418.5	543.6	704.9	875.5	1,121.1
Other Operating Expense	44.5	54.6	78.4	93.3	127.2
Depreciation & Amortization Expense	72.5	97.8	130.2	163.5	205.6
General & Admin Expense	77.6	89.7	110.2	151.4	202.1
Operating Expenses	**613.1**	**785.7**	**1,023.8**	**1,283.7**	**1,656.0**
Operating Profit	**109.2**	**156.7**	**212.3**	**281.1**	**310.0**
Net Income	**68.4**	**101.7**	**94.5**	**181.2**	**215.1**
% Change in Monthly Comparable Store Sales[b]					
North America	5%	6%	9%	5%	7%
Consolidated	5%	6%	9%	5%	6%

Source: Adapted from company reports and Lehman Brothers, November 5, 2002.

[a]Includes income from various joint ventures, including Starbucks' partnership with the Pepsi-Cola Company to develop and distribute Frappuccino and with Dreyer's Grand Ice Cream to develop and distribute premium ice creams.

[b]Includes only company-operated stores open 13 months or longer.

EXHIBIT 2: Starbucks' Store Growth

	FY 1998	FY 1999	FY 2000	FY 2001	FY 2002
Total North America	**1,755**	**2,217**	**2,976**	**3,780**	**4,574**
Company-Operated	1,622	2,038	2,446	2,971	3,496
Licensed Stores[a]	133	179	530	809	1,078
Total International	**131**	**281**	**525**	**929**	**1,312**
Company-Operated	66	97	173	295	384
Licensed Stores	65	184	352	634	928
Total Stores	**1,886**	**2,498**	**3,501**	**4,709**	**5,886**

Source: Company reports.

[a]Includes kiosks located in grocery stores, bookstores, hotels, airports, and so on.

EXHIBIT 3: Additional Data, North American Company-Operated Stores (FY2002)

	AVERAGE
Average hourly rate with shift supervisors and hourly partners	$9.00
Total labor hours per week, average store	360
Average weekly store volume	$15,400
Average ticket	$3.85
Average daily customer count, per store	570

Source: Company reports.

time you walk through our door," explained Jim Alling, Starbucks' senior vice president of North American retail. "Our most loyal customers visit us as often as 18 times a month, so it could be something as simple as recognizing you and knowing your drink or customizing your drink just the way you like it."

The third brand component was atmosphere. "People come for the coffee," explained Day, "but the ambience is what makes them want to stay." For that reason, most Starbucks had seating areas to encourage lounging and layouts that were designed to provide an upscale yet inviting environment for those who wanted to linger. "What we have built has universal appeal," remarked Schultz. "It's based on the human spirit, it's based on a sense of community, the need for people to come together."[3]

Channels of Distribution

Almost all of Starbucks' locations in North America were company-operated stores located in high-traffic, high-visibility settings such as retail centers, office buildings, and university campuses.[4] In addition to selling whole-bean coffees, these stores sold rich-brewed coffees, Italian-style espresso drinks, cold-blended beverages, and premium teas. Product mixes tended to vary depending on a store's size and location, but most stores offered a variety of pastries, sodas, and juices, along with coffee-related accessories and equipment, music CDs, games, and seasonal novelty items. (About 500 stores even carried a selection of sandwiches and salads.)

Beverages accounted for the largest percentage of sales in these stores (77 percent); this represented a change from 10 years earlier, when about half of store revenues had come from sales of whole-bean coffees. (See Exhibit 4 for retail sales mix by product type; see Exhibit 5 for a typical menu board and price list.)

Starbucks also sold coffee products through noncompany-operated retail channels; these so-called "Specialty Operations" accounted for 15 percent of net revenues. About 27 percent of these revenues came from North American food-service accounts, that is, sales of whole-bean and ground coffees to hotels, airlines, restaurants, and the like. Another 18 percent came from domestic retail store licenses that, in North America, were only granted when there was no other way to achieve access to desirable retail space (e.g., in airports).

The remaining 55 percent of specialty revenues came from a variety of sources, including international licensed stores, grocery stores and warehouse clubs (Kraft Foods handled marketing and distribution for Starbucks in this channel), and online and mail-order sales. Starbucks also had a joint venture with Pepsi-Cola to distribute bottled Frappuccino beverages in North America, as well as a partnership with Dreyer's Grand Ice Cream to develop and distribute a line of premium ice creams.

Day explained the company's broad distribution strategy:

> Our philosophy is pretty straightforward—we want to reach customers where they work, travel, shop, and dine. In order to do this, we sometimes have to establish relationships with third parties that share our values and commitment to quality. This is a particularly effective way to reach newcomers with our brand. It's a lot less intimidating to buy Starbucks at a grocery store than it is to walk into one of our coffeehouses for the first time. In fact, about 40 percent of our new coffeehouse customers have already tried the Starbucks brand before they walk through our doors. Even something like ice cream has become an important trial vehicle for us.

EXHIBIT 4: Product Mix, North American Company-Operated Stores (FY2002)

	Percent of Sales
Retail Product Mix	
Coffee Beverages	77%
Food Items	13%
Whole-Bean Coffees	6%
Equipment & Accessories	4%

Source: Company reports.

EXHIBIT 5: Typical Menu Board and Price List for North American Company-Owned Store

Espresso Traditions Classic Favorites	Tall	Grande	Venti
Toffee Nut Latte	2.95	3.50	3.80
Vanilla Latte	2.85	3.40	3.70
Caffe Latte	2.55	3.10	3.40
Cappuccino	2.55	3.10	3.40
Caramel Macchiato	2.80	3.40	3.65
White Chocolate Mocha	3.20	3.75	4.00
Caffe Mocha	2.75	3.30	3.55
Caffe Americano	1.75	2.05	2.40

Espresso	Solo	Doppio
Espresso	1.45	1.75

Extras	
Additional Espresso Shot	.55
Add flavored syrup	.30
Organic milk & soy available upon request	

Frappuccino Ice Blended Beverages	Tall	Grande	Venti
Coffee	2.65	3.15	3.65
Mocha	2.90	3.40	3.90
Caramel Frappuccino	3.15	3.65	4.15
Mocha Coconut (limited offering)	3.15	3.65	4.15

Crème Frappuccino Ice Blended Crème	Tall	Grande	Venti
Toffee Nut Crème	3.15	3.65	4.15
Vanilla Crème	2.65	3.15	3.65
Coconut Crème	3.15	3.65	4.15

Tazo Tea Frappuccino Ice Blended Teas	Tall	Grande	Venti
Tazo Citrus	2.90	3.40	3.90
Tazoberry	2.90	3.40	3.90
Tazo Chai Crème	3.15	3.65	4.15

Brewed Coffee	Tall	Grande	Venti
Coffee of the Day	1.40	1.60	1.70
Decaf of the Day	1.40	1.60	1.70

Cold Beverages	Tall	Grande	Venti
Iced Caffe Latte	2.55	3.10	3.50
Iced Caramel Macchiato	2.80	3.40	3.80
Iced Caffe Americano	1.75	2.05	3.40

Coffee Alternatives	Tall	Grande	Venti
Toffee Nut Crème	2.45	2.70	2.95
Vanilla Crème	2.20	2.45	2.70
Caramel Apple Cider	2.45	2.70	2.95
Hot Chocolate	2.20	2.45	2.70
Tazo Hot Tea	1.15	1.65	1.65
Tazo Chai	2.70	3.10	3.35

Whole Beans: Bold Our most intriguing and exotic coffees	1/2 lb	1 lb
Gold Coast Blend	5.70	10.95
French Roast	5.20	9.95
Sumatra	5.30	10.15
Decaf Sumatra	5.60	10.65
Ethiopia Sidame	5.20	9.95
Arabian Mocha Sanani	8.30	15.95
Kenya	5.30	10.15
Italian Roast	5.20	9.95
Sulawesi	6.10	11.65

Whole Beans: Smooth Richer, more flavorful coffees	1/2 lb	1 lb
Espresso Roast	5.20	9.95
Decaf Espresso Roast	5.60	10.65
Yukon Blend	5.20	9.95
Café Verona	5.20	9.95
Guatemala Antigua	5.30	10.15
Arabian Mocha Java	6.30	11.95
Decaf Mocha Java/SWP	6.50	12.45

Whole Beans: Mild The perfect introduction to Starbucks coffees	1/2 lb	1 lb
Breakfast Blend	5.20	9.95
Lightnote Blend	5.20	9.95
Decaf Lightnote Blend	5.60	10.65
Colombia Narino	5.50	10.45
House Blend	5.20	9.95
Decaf House Blend	5.60	10.65
Fair Trade Coffee	5.95	11.45

Source: Starbucks location: Harvard Square, Cambridge, Massachusetts, February 2003.

Starbucks Partners

All Starbucks employees were called "partners." The company employed 60,000 partners worldwide, about 50,000 in North America. Most were hourly-wage employees (called *baristas*) who worked in Starbucks retail stores. Alling remarked, "From day one, Howard has made clear his belief that partner satisfaction leads to customer satisfaction. This belief is part of Howard's DNA, and because it's been pounded into each and every one of us, it's become part of our DNA too."

The company had a generous policy of giving health insurance and stock options to even the most entry-level partners, most of whom were between the ages of 17 and 23. Partly as a result of this, Starbucks' partner satisfaction rate consistently hovered in the 80 percent to 90 percent range, well above the industry norm,[5] and the company had recently been ranked 47th in the *Fortune* magazine list of best places to work, quite an accomplishment for a company with so many hourly-wage workers.

In addition, Starbucks had one of the lowest employee turnover rates in the industry—just 70 percent, compared with fast-food industry averages as high as 300 percent. The rate was even lower for managers, and as Alling noted, the company was always looking for ways to bring turnover down further: "Whenever we have a problem store, we almost always find either an inexperienced store manager or inexperienced baristas. Manager stability is key—it not only decreases partner turnover, but it also enables the store to do a much better job of recognizing regular customers and providing personalized service. So our goal is to make the position a lifetime job."

To this end, the company encouraged promotion from within its own ranks. About 70 percent of the company's store managers were ex-baristas, and about 60 percent of its district managers were ex-store managers. In fact, upon being hired, all senior executives had to train and succeed as baristas before being allowed to assume their positions in corporate headquarters.

Delivering on Service

When a partner was hired to work in one of Starbucks' North American retail stores, he or she had to undergo two types of training. The first type focused on "hard skills" such as learning how to use the cash register and learning how to mix drinks. Most Starbucks beverages were handcrafted, and to ensure product quality, there was a prespecified process associated with each drink. Making an espresso beverage, for example, required seven specific steps.

The other type of training focused on "soft skills." Alling explained:

> In our training manual, we explicitly teach partners to connect with customers—to enthusiastically welcome them to the store, to establish eye contact, to smile, and to try to remember their names and orders if they're regulars. We also encourage partners to create conversations with customers using questions that require more than a yes or no answer. So for example, "I noticed you were looking at the menu board—what types of beverages do you typically enjoy?" is a good question for a partner to ask.

Starbucks' "Just Say Yes" policy empowered partners to provide the best service possible, even if it required going beyond company rules. "This means that if a customer spills a drink and asks for a refill, we'll give it to him," said Day. "Or if a customer doesn't have cash and wants to pay with a check (which we aren't supposed to accept), then we'll give her a sample drink for free. The last thing we want to do is win the argument and lose the customer."

Most barista turnover occurred within the first 90 days of employment; if a barista lasted beyond that, there was a high probability that he or she would stay for three years or more. "Our training ends up being a self-selection process," Alling said. Indeed, the ability to balance hard and soft skills required a particular type of person, and Alling believed the challenges had only grown over time:

> Back in the days when we sold mostly beans, every customer who walked in the door was a coffee connoisseur, and it was easy for baristas to engage in chitchat while

> ringing up a bag. Those days are long gone. Today, almost every customer orders a handcrafted beverage. If the line is stretching out the door and everyone's clamoring for their coffee fix, it's not that easy to strike up a conversation with a customer.

The complexity of the barista's job had also increased over time; making a *venti tazoberry and crème*, for instance, required 10 different steps. "It used to be that a barista could make every variation of drink we offered in half a day," Day observed. "Nowadays, given our product proliferation, it would take 16 days of eight-hour shifts. There are literally hundreds of combinations of drinks in our portfolio."

This job complexity was compounded by the fact that almost half of Starbucks' customers customized their drinks. According to Day, this created a tension between product quality and customer focus for Starbucks:

> On the one hand, we train baristas to make beverages to our preestablished quality standards—this means enforcing a consistent process that baristas can master. On the other hand, if a customer comes in and wants it their way—extra vanilla, for instance—what should we do? Our heaviest users are always the most demanding. Of course, every time we customize, we slow down the service for everyone else. We also put a lot of strain on our baristas, who are already dealing with an extraordinary number of sophisticated drinks.

One obvious solution to the problem was to hire more baristas to share the workload; however, the company had been extremely reluctant to do this in recent years, particularly given the economic downturn. Labor was already the company's largest expense item in North America (see Exhibit 3), and Starbucks stores tended to be located in urban areas with high wage rates. Instead, the company had focused on increasing barista efficiency by removing all nonvalue-added tasks, simplifying the beverage production process, and tinkering with the facility design to eliminate bottlenecks.

In addition, the company had recently begun installing automated espresso machines in its North American cafés. The *verismo* machines, which decreased the number of steps required to make an espresso beverage, reduced waste, improved consistency, and had generated an overwhelmingly positive customer and barista response.

Measuring Service Performance

Starbucks tracked service performance using a variety of metrics, including monthly status reports and self-reported checklists. The company's most prominent measurement tool was a mystery shopper program called the "Customer Snapshot." Under this program, every store was visited by an anonymous mystery shopper three times a quarter. Upon completing the visit, the shopper would rate the store on four "Basic Service" criteria:

- ***Service***—Did the register partner verbally greet the customer?
  Did the barista and register partner make eye contact with the customer?
  Say thank you?
- ***Cleanliness***—Was the store clean?
  The counters?
  The tables?
  The restrooms?
- ***Product quality***—Was the order filled accurately?
  Was the temperature of the drink within range?
  Was the beverage properly presented?
- ***Speed of service***—How long did the customer have to wait?
  The company's goal was to serve a customer within three minutes, from back-of-the-line to drink-in-hand. This benchmark was based on market research which indicated that the three-minute standard was a key component in how current Starbucks customers defined "excellent service."

In addition to Basic Service, stores were also rated on "Legendary Service," which was defined as "behavior that created a memorable experience for a customer, that inspired a customer to return often and tell a friend." Legendary Service scores were based on secret shopper observations of service attributes such as partners initiating conversations with customers, partners recognizing customers by name or drink order, and partners being responsive to service problems.

During 2002, the company's Customer Snapshot scores had increased across all stores (see Exhibit 6), leading Day to comment, "The Snapshot is not a perfect measurement tool, but we believe it does a good job of measuring trends over the course of a quarter. In order for a store to do well on the Snapshot, it needs to have sustainable processes in place that create a well-established pattern of doing things right so that it gets 'caught' doing things right."

Competition

In the United States, Starbucks competed against a variety of small-scale specialty coffee chains, most of which were regionally concentrated. Each tried to differentiate itself from Starbucks in a different way. For example, Minneapolis-based Caribou

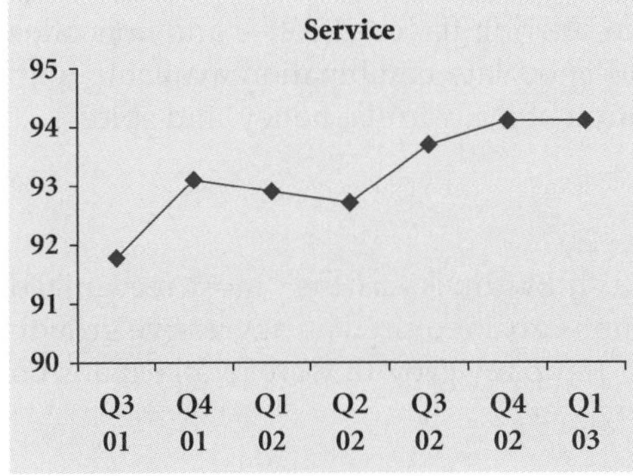

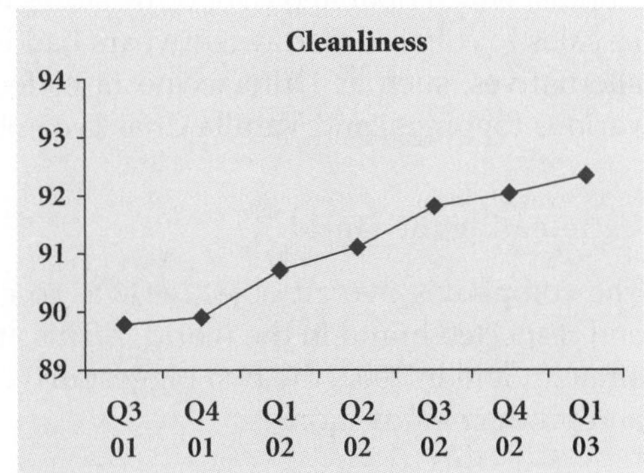

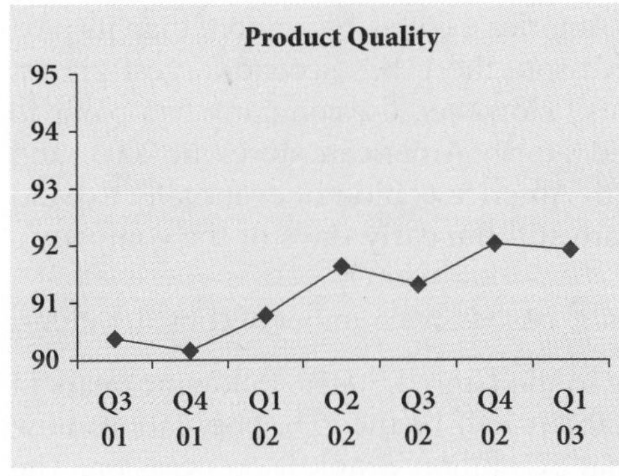

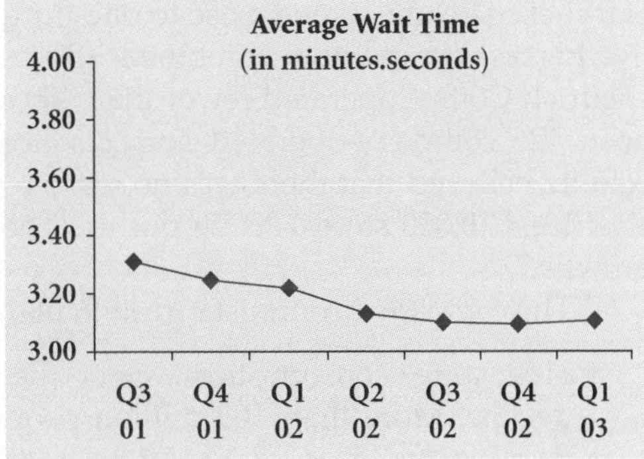

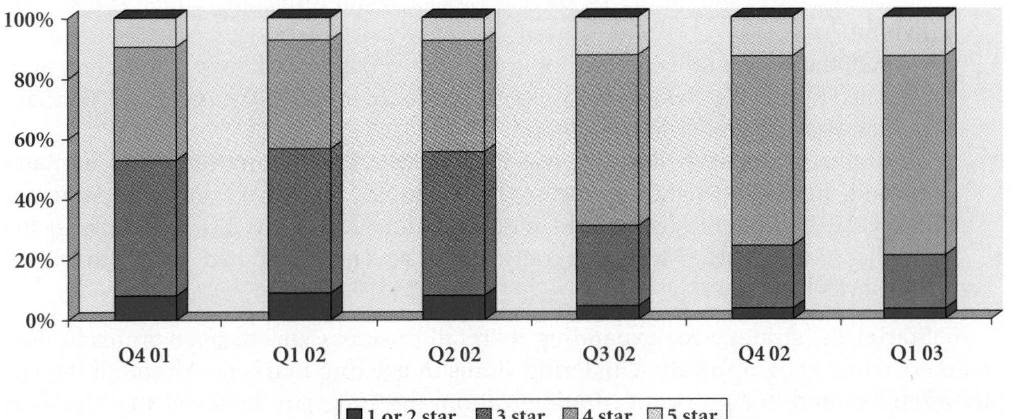

EXHIBIT 6: Customer Snapshot Scores (North American Stores) *Source:* Company information.

Coffee, which operated more than 200 stores in nine states, differentiated itself on store environment. Rather than offer an upscale, pseudo-European atmosphere, its strategy was to simulate the look and feel of an Alaskan lodge, with knotty-pine cabinetry, fireplaces, and soft seating. Another example was California-based Peet's Coffee & Tea, which operated about 70 stores in five states. More than 60 percent of Peet's revenues came from the sale of whole beans. Peet's strategy was to build a super-premium brand by offering the freshest coffee on the market. One of the ways it delivered on this promise was by "roasting to order," that is, by hand roasting small batches of coffee at its California plant and making sure that all of its coffee shipped within 24 hours of roasting.

Starbucks also competed against thousands of independent specialty coffee shops. Some of these independent coffee shops offered a wide range of food and beverages, including beer, wine, and liquor; others offered satellite televisions or Internet-connected computers. Still others differentiated themselves by delivering highly personalized service to an eclectic clientele.

Finally, Starbucks competed against donut and bagel chains such as Dunkin Donuts, which operated over 3,700 stores in 38 states. Dunkin Donuts attributed half of its sales to coffee and in recent years had begun offering flavored coffee and noncoffee alternatives, such as Dunkaccino (a coffee and chocolate combination available with various toppings) and Vanilla Chai (a combination of tea, vanilla, honey, and spices).

Caffeinating the World

The company's overall objective was to establish Starbucks as the "most recognized and respected brand in the world."[6] This ambitious goal required an aggressive growth strategy, and in 2002, the two biggest drivers of company growth were retail expansion and product innovation.

Retail Expansion

Starbucks already owned close to one-third of America's coffee bars, more than its next five biggest competitors combined. (By comparison, the U.S.'s second-largest player, Diedrich Coffee, operated fewer than 400 stores.) However, the company had plans to open 525 company-operated and 225 licensed North American stores in 2003, and Schultz believed that there was no reason North America could not eventually expand to at least 10,000 stores. As he put it, "These are still the early days of the company's growth."[7]

The company's optimistic growth plans were based on a number of considerations:

- First, coffee consumption was on the rise in the United States, following years of decline. More than 109 million people (about half of the U.S. population) now drank coffee every day, and an additional 52 million drank it on occasion. The market's biggest growth appeared to be among drinkers of specialty coffee,[8] and it was estimated that about one-third of all U.S. coffee consumption took place outside of the home, in places such as offices, restaurants, and coffee shops. (See Exhibit 7.)
- Second, there were still eight states in the United States without a single company-operated Starbucks; in fact, the company was only in 150 of the roughly 300 metropolitan statistical areas in the nation.
- Third, the company believed it was far from reaching saturation levels in many existing markets. In the Southeast, for example, there was only one store for every 110,000 people (compared with one store for every 20,000 people in the Pacific Northwest). More generally, only seven states had more than 100 Starbucks locations.

Starbucks' strategy for expanding its retail business was to open stores in new markets while geographically clustering stores in existing markets. Although the latter often resulted in significant cannibalization, the company believed that this was more than offset by the total incremental sales associated with the increased store

EXHIBIT 7: Total U.S. Retail Coffee Market (includes both in-home and out-of-home consumption)

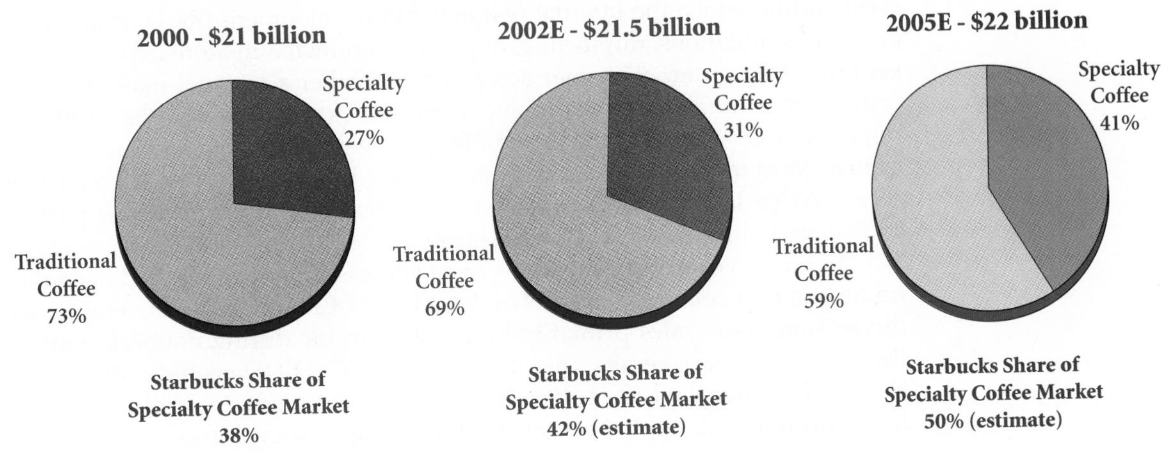

Starbucks Share of Specialty Coffee Market 38%

Starbucks Share of Specialty Coffee Market 42% (estimate)

Starbucks Share of Specialty Coffee Market 50% (estimate)

Other estimates[a] for the U.S. retail coffee market in 2002:

- In the home, specialty coffee[b] was estimated to be a $3.2 billion business, of which Starbucks was estimated to have a 4% share.
- In the food-service channel, specialty coffee was estimated to be a $5 billion business, of which Starbucks was estimated to have a 5% share.
- In grocery stores, Starbucks was estimated to have a 7.3% share in the ground-coffee category and a 21.7% share in the whole-beans category.
- It was estimated that over the next several years, the overall retail market would grow less than 1% per annum, but growth in the specialty-coffee category would be strong, with compound annual growth rate (CAGR) of 9% to 10%.
- Starbucks' U.S. business was projected to grow at a CAGR of approximately 20% top-line revenue growth.

Source: Adapted from company reports and Lehman Brothers, November 5, 2002.

[a]The value of the retail coffee market was difficult to estimate given the highly fragmented and loosely monitored nature of the market (i.e., specialty coffeehouses, restaurants, delis, kiosks, street carts, grocery and convenience stores, vending machines, etc.).

[b]Specialty coffee includes espresso, cappuccino, latte, café mocha, iced/ice-blended coffee, gourmet coffee (premium whole bean or ground), and blended coffee.

concentration. As Schultz readily conceded, "We self-cannibalize at least a third of our stores every day."[9]

When it came to selecting new retail sites, the company considered a number of criteria, including the extent to which the demographics of the area matched the profile of the typical Starbucks drinker, the level of coffee consumption in the area, the nature and intensity of competition in the local market, and the availability of attractive real estate. Once a decision was made to move forward with a site, the company was capable of designing, permitting, constructing, and opening a new store within 16 weeks. A new store typically averaged about $610,000 in sales during its first year; same-store sales (comps) were strongest in the first three years and then continued to comp positively, consistent with the company average.

Starbucks' international expansion plans were equally ambitious. Starbucks already operated over 300 company-owned stores in the United Kingdom, Australia, and Thailand, in addition to about 900 licensed stores in various countries in Asia, Europe, the Middle East, Africa, and Latin America. (Its largest international market was Japan, with close to 400 stores.) The company's goal was to ultimately have 15,000 international stores.

Product Innovation

The second big driver of company growth was product innovation. Internally, this was considered one of the most significant factors in comparable store sales growth, particularly since Starbucks' prices had remained relatively stable in recent years. New products were launched on a regular basis; for example, Starbucks introduced at least one new hot beverage every holiday season.

The new product development process generally operated on a 12- to 18-month cycle, during which the internal research and development (R&D) team tinkered with product formulations, ran focus groups, and conducted in-store experiments and market tests. Aside from consumer acceptance, whether a product made it to market depended on a number of factors, including the extent to which the drink fit into the "ergonomic flow" of operations and the speed with which the beverage could be handcrafted. Most importantly, the success of a new beverage depended on partner acceptance. "We've learned that no matter how great a drink it is, if our partners aren't excited about it, it won't sell," said Alling.

In recent years, the company's most successful innovation had been the 1995 introduction of a coffee and noncoffee-based line of Frappuccino beverages, which had driven same-store sales primarily by boosting traffic during nonpeak hours. The bottled version of the beverage (distributed by PepsiCo) had become a $400 million[10] franchise; it had managed to capture 90 percent of the ready-to-drink coffee category, in large part due to its appeal to noncoffee-drinking 20-somethings.

Service Innovation

In terms of nonproduct innovation, Starbucks' stored-value card (SVC) had been launched in November 2001. This prepaid, swipeable smart card—which Schultz referred to as "the most significant product introduction since Frappuccino"[11]—could be used to pay for transactions in any company-operated store in North America. Early indications of the SVC's appeal were very positive: After less than one year on the market, about 6 million cards had been issued, and initial activations and reloads had already reached $160 million in sales. In surveys, the company had learned that cardholders tended to visit Starbucks twice as often as cash customers and tended to experience reduced transaction times.

Day remarked, "We've found that a lot of the cards are being given away as gifts, and many of those gift recipients are being introduced to our brand for the first time. Not to mention the fact that the cards allow us to collect all kinds of customer-transaction data, data that we haven't even begun to do anything with yet."

The company's latest service innovation was its T-Mobile HotSpot wireless Internet service, which it planned to introduce in August 2002. The service would offer high-speed access to the Internet in 2,000 Starbucks stores in the United States and Europe, starting at $49.99 a month.

Starbucks' Market Research: Trouble Brewing?

Interestingly, although Starbucks was considered one of the world's most effective marketing organizations, it lacked a strategic marketing group. In fact, the company had no chief marketing officer, and its marketing department functioned as three separate groups—a market research group that gathered and analyzed market data requested by the various business units, a category group that developed new products and managed the menu and margins, and a marketing group that developed the quarterly promotional plans.

This organizational structure forced all of Starbucks' senior executives to assume marketing-related responsibilities. As Day pointed out, "Marketing is everywhere at Starbucks—it just doesn't necessarily show up in a line item called 'marketing.' Everyone has to get involved in a collaborative marketing effort." However, the organizational structure also meant that market- and customer-related trends could sometimes be overlooked. "We tend to be great at measuring things, at collecting market data," Day noted, "but we are not very disciplined when it comes to using this data to drive decision making." She continued:

> This is exactly what started to happen a few years ago. We had evidence coming in from market research that contradicted some of the fundamental assumptions we had about our brand and our customers. The problem was that this evidence was all over the place—no one was really looking at the "big picture." As a result, it took awhile before we started to take notice.

TABLE A Qualitative Brand Meaning: Independents vs. Starbucks

Independents:

- Social and inclusive
- Diverse and intellectual
- Artsy and funky
- Liberal and free-spirited
- Lingering encouraged
- Particularly appealing to younger coffeehouse customers
- Somewhat intimidating to older, more mainstream coffeehouse customers

Starbucks:

- Everywhere—the trend
- Good coffee on the run
- Place to meet and move on
- Convenience oriented; on the way to work
- Accessible and consistent

Source: Starbucks, based on qualitative interviews with specialty coffeehouse customers.

Starbucks' Brand Meaning

Once the team did take notice, it discovered several things. First, despite Starbucks' overwhelming presence and convenience, there was very little image or product differentiation between Starbucks and the smaller coffee chains (other than Starbucks' ubiquity) in the minds of specialty coffeehouse customers. There *was* significant differentiation, however, between Starbucks and the independent specialty coffeehouses (see Table A).

More generally, the market research team discovered that Starbucks' brand image had some rough edges. The number of respondents who strongly agreed with the statement "Starbucks cares primarily about making money" was up from 53 percent in 2000 to 61 percent in 2001, while the number of respondents who strongly agreed with the statement "Starbucks cares primarily about building more stores" was up from 48 percent to 55 percent. Day noted, "It's become apparent that we need to ask ourselves, 'Are we focusing on the right things? Are we clearly communicating our value and values to our customers, instead of just our growth plans?'" (see Table B).

The Changing Customer

The market research team also discovered that Starbucks' customer base was evolving. Starbucks' newer customers tended to be younger, less well-educated, and in a lower income bracket than Starbucks' more established customers. In addition, they visited the stores less frequently and had very different perceptions of the Starbucks brand compared to more established customers (see Exhibit 8).

Furthermore, the team learned that Starbucks' historical customer profile—the affluent, well-educated, white-collar female between the ages of 24 and 44—had expanded. For example, about half of the stores in southern California had large numbers of Hispanic customers. In Florida, the company had stores that catered primarily to Cuban-Americans.

TABLE B The Top Five Attributes Consumers Associate with the Starbucks Brand

- Known for specialty/gourmet coffee (54% strongly agree)
- Widely available (43% strongly agree)
- Corporate (42% strongly agree)
- Trendy (41% strongly agree)
- Always feel welcome at Starbucks (39% strongly agree)

Source: Starbucks, based on 2002 survey.

EXHIBIT 8: Starbucks' Customer Retention Information

% of Starbucks' customers who first started visiting Starbucks...	
In the past year	27%
1–2 years ago	20%
2–5 years ago	30%
5 or more years ago	23%

Source: Starbucks, 2002. Based on a sample of Starbucks' 2002 customer base.

	New Customers (first visited in past year)	Established Customers (first visited 5 + years ago)
Percent female	45%	49%
Average age	36	40
Percent with college degree +	37%	63%
Average income	$65,000	$81,000
Average # cups of coffee/week (includes at home and away from home)	15	19
Attitudes toward Starbucks:		
High-quality brand	34%	51%
Brand I trust	30%	50%
For someone like me	15%	40%
Worth paying more for	8%	32%
Known for specialty coffee	44%	60%
Known as the coffee expert	31%	45%
Best-tasting coffee	20%	31%
Highest-quality coffee	26%	41%
Overall opinion of Starbucks	**25%**	**44%**

Source: Starbucks, 2002. "Attitudes toward Starbucks" measured according to the percent of customers who agreed with the above statements.

Customer Behavior

With respect to customer behavior, the market research team discovered that, regardless of the market—urban versus rural, new versus established—customers tended to use the stores the same way. The team also learned that, although the company's most frequent customers averaged 18 visits a month, the typical customer visited just five times a month (see Figure A).

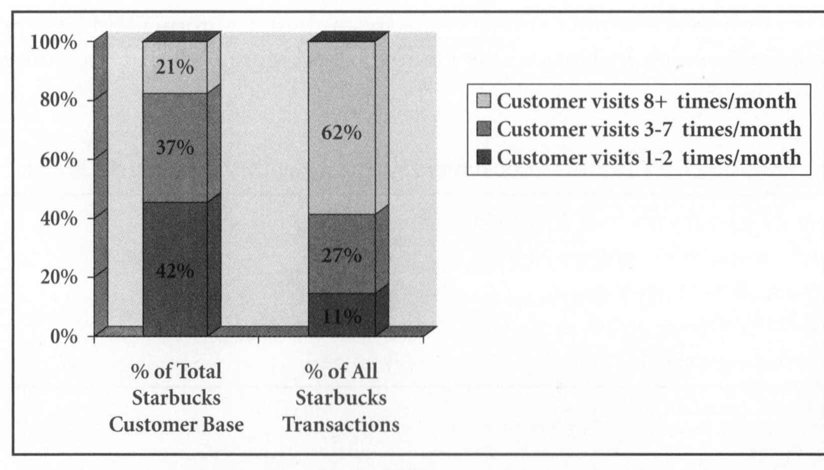

FIGURE A: Customer Visit Frequency

EXHIBIT 9: Starbucks' Customer Behavior, by Satisfaction Level

	Unsatisfied Customer	Satisfied Customer	Highly Satisfied Customer
Number of Starbucks Visits/Month	3.9	4.3	7.2
Average Ticket Size/Visit	$3.88	$4.06	$4.42
Average Customer Life (Years)	1.1	4.4	8.3

Source: Self-reported customer activity from Starbucks survey, 2002.

Measuring and Driving Customer Satisfaction

Finally, the team discovered that, despite its high Customer Snapshot scores, Starbucks was not meeting expectations in terms of customer satisfaction. The satisfaction scores were considered critical because the team also had evidence of a direct link between satisfaction level and customer loyalty (see Exhibit 9 for customer satisfaction data).

While customer satisfaction was driven by a number of different factors (see Exhibit 10), Day believed that the customer satisfaction gap could primarily be attributed to a *service gap* between Starbucks scores on key attributes and customer expectations. When Starbucks had polled its customers to determine what it could do to make them feel more like valued customers, "improvements to service"—in particular, speed-of-service—had been mentioned most frequently (see Exhibit 11 for more information).

EXHIBIT 10: Importance Rankings of Key Attributes in Creating Customer Satisfaction
Source: Self-reported customer activity from Starbucks survey, 2002.

To be read: *83% of Starbucks' customers rate a clean store as being highly important (90+ on a 100-point scale) in creating customer satisfaction.*

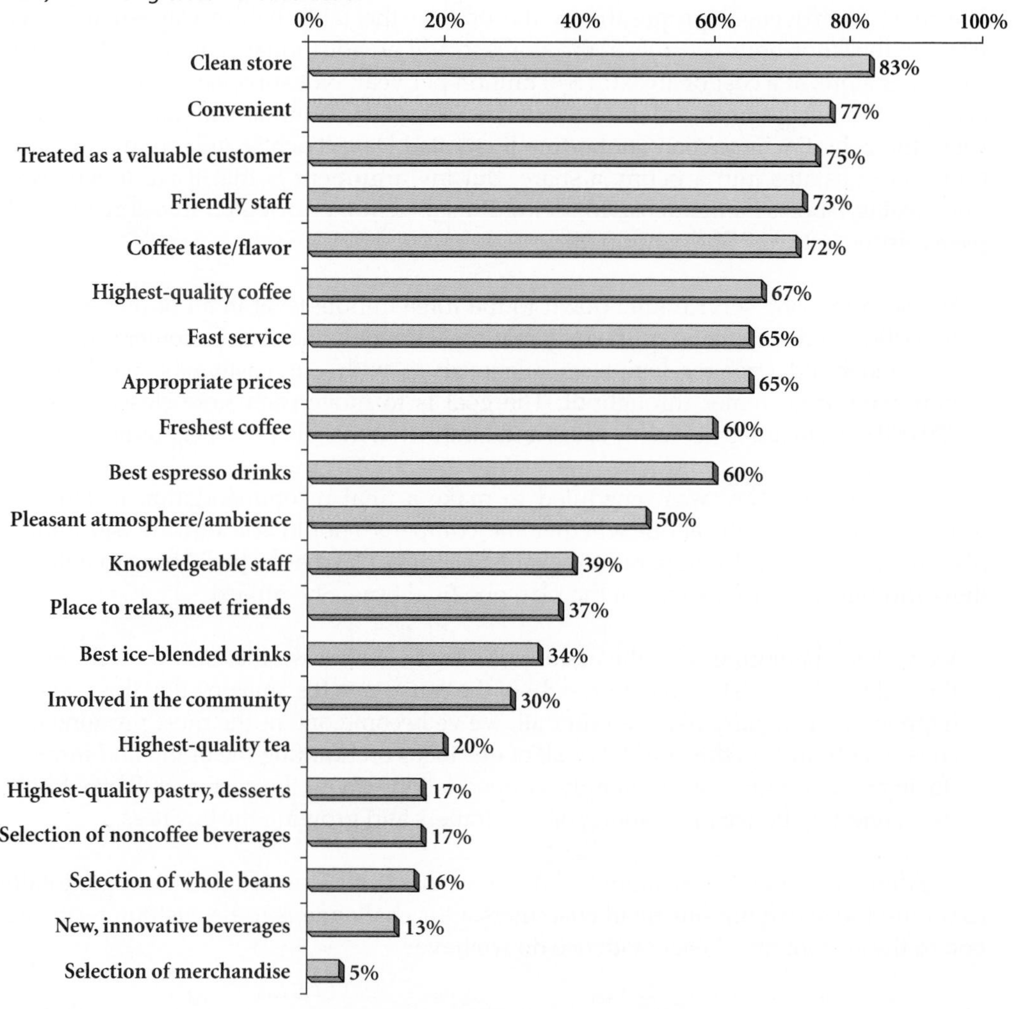

EXHIBIT 11: Factors Driving "Valued Customer" Perceptions

How could Starbucks make you feel more like a valued customer?	% Responses
Improvements to Service (total)	**34%**
Friendlier, more attentive staff	19%
Faster, more efficient service	10%
Personal treatment (remember my name, remember my order)	4%
More knowledgeable staff	4%
Better service	2%
Offer Better Prices/Incentive Programs (total)	**31%**
Free cup after X number of visits	19%
Reduce prices	11%
Offer promotions, specials	3%
Other (total)	**21%**
Better quality/Variety of products	9%
Improve atmosphere	8%
Community outreach/Charity	2%
More stores/More convenient locations	2%
Don't Know/Already Satisfied	**28%**

Source: Starbucks, 2002. Based on a survey of Starbucks' 2002 customer base, including highly satisfied, satisfied, and unsatisfied customers.

Rediscovering the Starbucks Customer

Responding to the market research findings posed a difficult management challenge. The most controversial proposal was the one on the table before Day—it involved relaxing the labor-hour controls in the stores to add an additional 20 hours of labor, per week, per store, at a cost of an extra $40 million per year. Not surprisingly, the plan was being met with significant internal resistance. "Our CFO is understandably concerned about the potential impact on our bottom line," said Day. "Each $6 million in profit contribution translates into a penny a share. But my argument is that if we move away from seeing labor as an expense to seeing it as a customer-oriented investment, we'll see a positive return." She continued:

> We need to bring service time down to the three-minute level in all of our stores, regardless of the time of day. If we do this, we'll not only increase customer satisfaction and build stronger long-term relationships with our customers, we'll also improve our customer throughput. The goal is to move each store closer to the $20,000 level in terms of weekly sales, and I think that this plan will help us get there.

In two days, Day was scheduled to make a final recommendation to Howard Schultz and Orin Smith about whether the company should roll out the $40 million plan in October 2002. In preparation for this meeting, Day had asked Alling to help her think through the implications of the plan one final time. She mused:

> We've been operating with the assumption that we do customer service well. But the reality is, we've started to lose sight of the consumer. It's amazing that this could happen to a company like us—after all, we've become one of the most prominent consumer brands in the world. For all of our focus on building the brand and introducing new products, we've simply stopped talking about the customer. We've lost the connection between satisfying our customers and growing the business.

Alling's response was simple: "We know that both Howard and Orin are totally committed to satisfying our retail customers. Our challenge is to tie customer satisfaction to the bottom line. What evidence do we have?"

Study Questions

1. What factors accounted for Starbucks' success in the early 1990s and what was so compelling about its value proposition? What brand image did Starbucks develop during this period?
2. Why have Starbucks' customer satisfaction scores declined? Has the company's service declined or is it simply measuring satisfaction the wrong way?
3. How has Starbucks changed since its early days?
4. Describe the ideal Starbucks customer from a profitability standpoint. What would it take to ensure that this customer is highly satisfied? How valuable to Starbucks is a highly satisfied customer?
5. Should Starbucks make the $40 million investment in labor in the stores? What's the goal of this investment? Is it possible for a mega-brand to deliver customer intimacy?

Endnotes

1. Jake Batsell, "A Grande Decade for Starbucks," *The Seattle Times*, June 26, 2002.
2. Batsell.
3. Batsell.
4. Starbucks had recently begun experimenting with drive-throughs. Less than 10 percent of its stores had drive-throughs, but in these stores, the drive-throughs accounted for 50 percent of all business.
5. Industrywide, employee satisfaction rates tended to be in the 50 percent to 60 percent range. Source: Starbucks, 2000.
6. Starbucks 2002 Annual Report.
7. Dina ElBoghdady, "Pouring It On: The Starbucks Strategy? Locations, Locations, Locations," *The Washington Post*, August 25, 2002.
8. National Coffee Association.
9. ElBoghdady.
10. Refers to sales at retail. Actual revenue contribution was much lower due to the joint-venture structure.
11. Stanley Holmes, "Starbucks' Card Smarts," *BusinessWeek*, March 18, 2002.

GLOSSARY OF SERVICE MARKETING AND MANAGEMENT TERMS

This glossary defines key terms used in this book and more generally in service marketing and management. For a broader coverage of marketing terms, see the glossaries in marketing management texts such as Philip Kotler and Kevin Lane Keller, *Marketing Management*, 13th ed. (Upper Saddle River, NJ: Prentice Hall, 2008) or consult the American Marketing Association's online *Dictionary of Marketing Terms* (www.marketingpower.com/mg-dictionary.php).

You should be aware that not everyone attaches precisely the same meaning to the same term. That's why it's important that you know and can clarify your own understanding when using a particular word or phrase. As often happens in an evolving field, the same terms sometimes get defined and used in different ways by academics and practitioners and among managers in different industries. Even individual companies may attach distinctive meanings to specific terms.

Words and phrases may also mean entirely different things when applied in nonmanagerial contexts. This situation is, of course, typical of language in general. The 3,750-page *Shorter Oxford English Dictionary*, 5th ed. (Oxford, UK, and New York: Oxford University Press, 2003) contains no less than 31 definitions of the word "service," embracing applications from domestic work, waiting in restaurants, and military duty to tennis, legal procedures, and the breeding of farm animals!

A

activity-based costing (ABC): an approach to costing based on identifying the activities performed and then determining the resources that each consumes.

adequate service: the minimum level of service a customer will accept without being dissatisfied.

advertising: any paid form of nonpersonal communication by a marketer to inform, educate, or persuade members of target audiences.

arm's length transactions: interactions between customers and service suppliers in which mail or telecommunications minimize the need to meet face to face.

attitude: a person's consistently favorable or unfavorable evaluations, feelings, and action tendencies toward an object or idea.

auction: a selling procedure managed by a specialist intermediary in which the price is set by allowing prospective purchasers to bid against each other for a product offered by a seller.

augmented product: a core product (a good or a service) plus supplementary elements that add value for customers.

B

backstage (or technical core): those aspects of service operations hidden from customers.

balking: a decision by a customer not to join a stand in line (queue) because the wait appears too long.

banner ads: small, rectangular boxes on websites that contain text and perhaps a picture to support a brand.

benchmarking: the process of comparing an organization's products and processes to those of competitors or leading firms in other industries to find ways to improve performance, quality, and cost effectiveness.

benefit: an advantage or gain that customers obtain from performance of a service or use of a physical good.

benefit-driven pricing: the strategy of relating the price to that aspect of the service that directly creates benefits for customers.

blog: a publicly accessible "web log" containing frequently updated pages in the form of journals, diaries, news listings, etc.; authors—known as bloggers—typically focus on specific topics.

blueprint: a visual map of the sequence of activities required for service delivery that specifies front-stage and back-stage elements and the linkages between them.

boundary spanning positions: jobs that straddle the boundary between the external environment, where customers are encountered, and the internal operations of the organization.

brand: a name, phrase, design, symbol, or some combination of these elements that identifies a company's services and differentiates it from competitors.

C

chain stores: two or more outlets under common ownership, control and brand name, selling similar goods and services.

chase demand strategy: adjusting the level of capacity to meet the level of demand at any given time.

churn: loss of existing customer accounts and the need to replace them with new ones.

clicks and mortar: a strategy of offering service through both physical stores and virtual storefronts via websites on the Internet.

competition-based pricing: the practice of setting prices relative to those charged by competitors.

competitive advantage: a firm's ability to perform in one or more ways that competitors cannot or will not match.

complaint: a formal expression of dissatisfaction with any aspect of a service experience.

complaint log: a detailed record of all customer complaints received by a service provider.

conjoint analysis: a research method for determining the utility values consumers attach to varying levels of a product's attributes.

consumption: the purchase and use of a service or good.

control charts: charts that graph quantitative changes in service performance on a specific variable relative to a predefined standard.

control model of management: an approach based on clearly defined roles, top-down control systems, a hierarchical organizational structure, and the assumption that management knows best.

core competency: a capability that is a source of competitive advantage.

corporate culture: the shared beliefs, norms, experiences, and stories that characterize an organization.

corporate design: the consistent application of distinctive colors, symbols, and lettering to give a firm an easily recognizable identity.

cost leader: a firm that bases its pricing strategy on achieving the lowest costs in its industry.

cost-based pricing: the practice of relating the price charged to the costs associated with producing, delivering, and marketing a product.

credence attributes: product characteristics that customers may not be able to evaluate even after purchase and consumption.

critical incident: a specific encounter between customer and service provider in which the outcome has proved especially satisfying or dissatisfying for one or both parties.

critical incident technique (CIT): a methodology for collecting, categorizing, and analyzing critical incidents that have occurred between customers and service providers.

CRM system: IT systems and infrastructure that support the implementation and delivery of a customer relationship management strategy.

customer churn: customers canceling a contractual agreement who then sign a new contract, with either the same service provider or a new provider.

customer contact personnel: service employees who interact directly with individual customers, either in person or through mail and telecommunications.

customer equity: the total combined customer lifetime values of the company's entire customer base.

customer interface: all points at which customers interact with a service organization.

customer lifetime value (CLV): the net present value of the stream of future contributions or profits expected over each customer's purchases during his or her anticipated lifetime as a customer of the organization.

customer relationship management (CRM): the overall process of building and maintaining profitable customer relationships by delivering superior customer value and satisfaction.

customer satisfaction: a short-term emotional reaction to a specific service performance.

customer training: formal training courses offered by service firms to teach customers about complex service products.

customization: tailoring service characteristics to meet each customer's specific needs and preferences.

cyberspace: a term used to describe the absence of a definable physical location where electronic transactions or communications occur.

D

data mining: the extracting of useful information about individuals, trends, and segments from a mass of customer data.

data warehouse: a comprehensive database containing customer information and transaction data.

database marketing: the process of building, maintaining, and using customer databases and other databases for contacting, selling, cross-selling, up-selling, and building customer relationships.

defection: a customer's decision to transfer brand loyalty from a current service provider to a competitor.

delivery channels: the means by which a service firm (sometimes assisted by intermediaries) delivers one or more product elements to its customers.

demand curve: a curve that shows the number of units the market will buy at different prices.

demand cycle: a period of time during which the level of demand for a service will increase and decrease in a somewhat predictable way before repeating itself.

demographic segmentation: dividing the market into groups based on demographic variables such as age, gender, family lifecycle, family size, income, occupation, education, religion, and ethnic group.

desired service: the "wished for" level of service quality that a customer believes can and should be delivered.

discounting: a strategy of reducing the price of an item below the normal level.

dynamic pricing: a technique, employed primarily by e-tailers, to charge different customers different prices for the same products, based on information collected about their purchase history, preferences, and price sensitivity.

E

e-commerce: buying, selling, and other marketing processes supported by the Internet (*see also* **e-tailing**).

emotional labor: the act of expressing socially appropriate (but sometimes false) emotions toward customers during service transactions.

empowerment: authorizing employees to find solutions to service problems and make appropriate decisions about responding to customer concerns without having to ask a supervisor's approval.

enablement: providing employees with the skills, tools, and resources they need to use their own discretion confidently and effectively.

enhancing supplementary services: supplementary services that may add extra value for customers.

e-tailing: retailing through the Internet instead of through physical stores.

excess capacity: an organization's capacity to create service output is not fully utilized.

excess demand: demand for a service at a given time exceeds the organization's ability to meet customer needs.

expectations: internal standards that customers use to judge the quality of a service experience.

experience attributes: product performance features that customers can evaluate only during service delivery.

expert systems: interactive computer programs that mimic a human expert's reasoning to draw conclusions from data, solve problems, and give customized advice.

F

facilitating supplementary services: supplementary services that aid in the use of the core product or are required for service delivery.

fail point: a point in a process where there is a significant risk of problems that can damage service quality.

financial outlays: all monetary expenditures incurred by customers in purchasing and consuming a service.

fishbone diagram: a chart-based technique that relates specific service problems to different categories of underlying causes (also known as a cause-and-effect chart).

fixed costs: costs that do not vary with production or sales revenue.

flat-rate pricing: the strategy of quoting a fixed price for a service in advance of delivery.

flowchart: a visual representation of the steps involved in delivering service to customers (*see also* **blueprint**).

Flower of Service: a visual framework for understanding the supplementary service elements that surround and add value to the product core.

focus: the provision of a relatively narrow product mix for a particular market segment.

focus groups: groups of six to ten people carefully selected on certain characteristics (e.g., demographics, psychographics, or product ownership) who are convened by researchers for in-depth, moderator-led discussions on specific topics.

franchise: a contractual association between a franchiser (typically a manufacturer, wholesaler, or service organization) and independent businesspeople (franchisees) who buy the right to own and operate one or more units in the franchise system.

frequency programs (FPs): programs designed to reward customers who buy frequently and in substantial amounts.

front stage: those aspects of service operations and delivery that are visible or otherwise apparent to customers.

G

geographic segmentation: dividing a market into different geographical units such as countries, regions, or cities.

global industry: an industry in which the strategic positions of competitors in major geographic or national markets are fundamentally affected by their overall global positions.

goods: physical objects or devices that provide benefits for customers through ownership or use.

H

halo effect: the tendency for consumer ratings of one prominent product characteristic to influence ratings for many other attributes of that same product.

high-contact services: services that involve significant interaction among customers, service personnel, and equipment and facilities.

human resource management (HRM): the coordination of tasks related to job design, employee recruitment, selection, training, and motivation; it also includes planning and administering other employee-related activities.

I

image: a set of beliefs, ideas, and impressions held regarding an object.

impersonal communications: one-way communications directed at target audiences not in personal contact with the message source (including advertising, promotions, and public relations).

information processing: intangible actions directed at customers' assets.

information search: the stage of the buyer decision-making process in which the consumer searches for information to help make a purchase decision.

information-based services: all services in which the principal value comes from the transmission of data to customers (includes both mental stimulus processing and information processing).

in-process wait: a wait that occurs during service delivery.

inputs: all resources (labor, materials, energy, and capital) required to create service offerings.

intangibility: a distinctive characteristic of services that makes it impossible to touch or hold on to them in the same manner as physical goods.

intangible: something experienced that cannot be touched or preserved.

integrated marketing communications (IMC): a concept in which an organization carefully integrates and coordinates its many communications channels to deliver a clear, consistent, and compelling message about the organization and its products.

internal communications: all forms of communication from management to employees in a service organization.

internal customers: employees who receive services from an internal supplier (another employee or department) as a necessary input to performing their own jobs.

internal marketing: marketing by a service firm directed at its employees to train and motivate them and instill a customer focus.

internal services: service elements within any type of business that facilitate creation of, or add value to, its final output.

Internet: a large public web of computer networks that connects users from around the world to each other and to a vast information repository.

inventory: for *manufacturing*, physical output stockpiled after production for sale at a later date; for *services*, future output not yet reserved in advance, such as the number of hotel rooms still available for sale on a given day.

involvement model of management: an approach based on the assumption that employees are capable of self-direction and—if properly trained, motivated, and informed—can make good decisions concerning service operations and delivery.

iTV: (interactive television) procedures that allow viewers to alter the viewing experience by controlling TV program delivery (e.g., TiVo, video on demand) and/or content.

J

jaycustomer: a customer who acts in a thoughtless or abusive way, causing problems for the firm, its employees, and other customers.

L

levels of customer contact: the extent to which customers interact directly with elements of the service organization.

low-contact services: services that require minimal or no direct contact between customers and the service organization.

loyalty: a customer's commitment to continue patronizing a specific firm over an extended period of time.

M

market focus: the extent to which a firm serves few or many markets.

market segmentation: the process of dividing a market into distinct groups within which all customers share relevant characteristics that distinguish them from customers in other segments and who respond in a similar way to a given set of marketing efforts.

marketing communications mix: the full set of communication tools (both paid and unpaid) available to marketers, including advertising, sales promotion, events, public relations and publicity, direct marketing, and personal selling.

marketing implementation: the process that turns marketing plans into projects and ensures that such projects are executed in a way that accomplishes the plan's stated objectives.

marketing research: the systematic design, collection, analysis, and reporting of customer and competitor data and findings relevant to a specific marketing situation facing an organization.

marketplace: a physical location where suppliers and customers meet to do business.

mass customization: offering a service with some individualized product elements to a large number of customers at a relatively low price.

maximum capacity: the upper limit to a firm's ability to meet customer demand at a particular time.

medium-contact services: services that involve only a limited amount of contact between customers and elements of the service organization.

membership relationship: a formalized relationship between the firm and a specified customer the may offer special benefits to both parties.

mental intangibility: difficulty for customers in visualizing an experience in advance of purchase and understanding the process and even the nature of the outcome (*see also* **physical intangibility).**

mental stimulus processing: intangible actions directed at people's minds.

mission statement: succinct description of what the organization does, its standards and values, whom it serves, and what it intends to accomplish.

molecular model: a framework that uses a chemical analogy to describe the structure of service offerings.

moment of truth: a point in service delivery where customers interact with service employees or self-service equipment and the outcome may affect perceptions of service quality.

mystery shopping: a research technique that employs individuals posing as ordinary customers in order to obtain feedback on the service environment and customer-employee interactions.

N

needs: subconscious, deeply felt desires that often concern long-term existence and identity issues.

net value: the sum of all perceived benefits (gross value) minus the sum of all perceived outlays.

nonfinancial outlays: (*see* **nonmonetary costs**).

nonmonetary costs: the time expenditures, physical and mental effort, and unwanted sensory experiences associated with searching for, buying, and using a service.

O

opportunity cost: the potential value of the income or other benefits foregone as a result of choosing one course of action instead of other alternatives.

optimum capacity: the point beyond which a firm's efforts to serve additional customers will lead to a perceived decline in service quality.

organizational climate: employees' shared perceptions of the practices, procedures, and types of behaviors that get rewarded and supported in a particular setting.

organizational culture: shared values, beliefs, and work styles based on an understanding of what is important to the organization and why.

OTSU ("opportunity to screw up"): (*see* **fail point**).

outputs: the final outcomes of the service delivery process as perceived and valued by customers.

P

Pareto analysis: an analytical procedure to identify what proportion of problem events is caused by each of several different factors.

people: customers and employees involved in service production.

people processing: services that involve tangible actions to people's bodies.

perception: the process in which individuals select, organize, and interpret information to form a meaningful picture of the world.

perceptual map: a visual illustration of how customers perceive competing services.

permission marketing: a marketing communications strategy that encourages customers to volunteer permission to a company to communicate with them through specific channels so they may learn more about its products and continue to receive useful information and specific offers of value to them.

personal communications: direct communications between marketers and individual customers that involve two-way dialog (including face-to-face conversations, phone calls, and email).

personal selling: two-way communications between service employees and customers designed to directly influence the purchase process.

physical effort: undesired consequences to a customer's body resulting from involvement in the service delivery process.

physical evidence: visual or other tangible clues that provide evidence of service quality.

physical intangibility: service elements not accessible to examination by any of the five sense; elements that cannot be touched or preserved by customers.

place, cyberspace, and time: management decisions about when, where, and how to deliver services to customers.

positioning: establishing a distinctive place in the minds of customers relative to competing products.

possession processing: tangible actions to goods and other physical possessions belonging to customers.

postencounter stage: the final stage in the service purchase process where customers evaluate the service experienced and form their satisfaction/dissatisfaction judgment with the service outcome.

postprocess wait: a wait that occurs after service delivery has been completed.

posttransaction surveys: techniques to measure customer satisfaction and perceptions of service quality while a specific service experience is still fresh in the customer's mind.

predicted service: the level of service quality a customer believes a firm will actually deliver.

preprocess wait: a wait before service delivery begins.

prepurchase stage: the first stage in the service purchase process where customers identify alternatives, weigh benefits and risks, and make a purchase decision.

price and other user outlays: expenditures of money, time, and effort that customers incur in purchasing and consuming services.

price bucket: an allocation of service capacity (for instance, seats) for sale at a particular price.

price bundling: the practice of charging a base price for a core service plus additional fees for optional supplementary elements.

price elasticity: the extent to which a change in price leads to a corresponding change in demand in the opposite direction. (Demand is described as "price inelastic" when changes in price have little or no impact on demand.)

price leader: a firm that takes the initiative on price changes in its market area and is copied by others.

process: a particular method of operations or series of actions, typically involving steps that need to occur in a defined sequence.

product: the core output (either a service or a manufactured good) produced by a firm.

product attributes: all features (both tangible and intangible) of a good or service that can be evaluated by customers.

product elements: all components of the service performance that create value for customers.

productive capacity: the extent of the facilities, equipment, labor, infrastructure, and other assets available to a firm to create output for its customers.

productivity: how efficiently service inputs are transformed into outputs that add value for customers.

promotion and education: all communication activities and incentives designed to build customer preference for a specific service or service provider.

psychographic segmentation: dividing a market into different groups based on personality characteristics, social class, or lifestyle.

psychological burdens: undesired mental or emotional states experienced by customers as a result of the service delivery process.

public relations: efforts to stimulate positive interest in a company and its products by sending out news releases, holding press conferences, staging special events, and sponsoring newsworthy activities put on by third parties.

purchase process: the stages a customer goes through in choosing, consuming, and evaluating a service.

Q

quality: the degree to which a service satisfies customers by meeting their needs, wants, and expectations.

queue: a line of people, vehicles, other physical objects, or intangible items waiting their turn to be served or processed.

queue configuration: the way in which a waiting line is organized.

R

rate fences: techniques for separating customers so that segments for whom the service offers high value are unable to take advantage of lower priced offers.

reciprocal marketing: a marketing communications tactic in which an online retailer allows its paying customers to receive promotions for another online retailer and vice versa, at no up-front cost to either party.

reengineering: the analysis and redesign of business processes to create dramatic performance improvements in such areas as cost, quality, speed, and customers' service experiences.

relationship marketing: activities aimed at developing long-term, cost-effective links between an organization and its customers for the mutual benefit of both parties.

reneging: a decision by a customer to leave a queue before reaching its end because the wait is longer or more burdensome than originally anticipated.

repositioning: changing the position a firm holds in a consumer's mind relative to competing services.

retail displays: presentations in store windows and other locations of merchandise, service experiences, and benefits.

retail gravity model: a mathematical approach to retail site selection that involves calculating the geographic center of gravity for the target population and then locating a facility to optimize customers' ease of access.

return on quality: the financial return obtained from investing in service quality improvements.

revenue management: a pricing and product design strategy based on charging different prices to different segments in order to maximize the revenue that can be derived from a firm's available capacity at any specific period of time (*also known as yield management*).

role: a combination of social cues that guides behavior in a specific setting or context.

role congruence: the extent to which both customers and employees act out their prescribed roles during a service encounter.

S

S-D Logic: (*see* **Service Dominant Logic**).

sales promotion: a short-term incentive offered to customers and intermediaries to stimulate quicker or greater purchase.

satisfaction: a person's feelings of pleasure or disappointment resulting from a consumption experience when comparing a product's perceived performance or outcome in relation to his or her expectations.

scripts: learned sequences of behaviors obtained through personal experience or communications with others.

search attributes: product characteristics that consumers can readily evaluate prior to purchase.

segment: a group of current or prospective customers who share common characteristics, needs, purchasing behavior, or consumption patterns.

sensory burdens: negative sensations experienced through a customer's five senses during the service delivery process.

service: an economic activity offered by one party to another, most commonly employing time-based performances to bring about desired results in recipients or in objects or other assets for which purchasers have responsibility. In exchange for their money, time, and effort, service customers expect to obtain value from access to goods, labor, professional skills, facilities, networks, and systems; but they do not normally take ownership of any of the physical elements involved.

service blueprint: (*see* **blueprint, flowchart**).

service delivery system: the part of the total service system where final "assembly" of the elements takes place and the product is delivered to the customer; it includes the visible elements of the service operation.

Service Dominant Logic: advocates that all products (goods and services) are valued for the service they provide and that value is co-created. For example, a razor ultimately provides a barbering service that is co-created with the user, and the value is derived by the service and not the good itself.

service encounter: a period of time during which customers interact directly with a service.

service encounter stage: the second stage in the service purchase process where the service delivery takes place through interactions between customers and the service provider.

service factory: the physical site where service operations take place.

service failure: a perception by customers that one or more specific aspects of service delivery have not met their expectations.

service focus: the extent to which a firm offers few or many services.

service guarantee: a promise that if service delivery fails to meet predefined standards, the customer is entitled to one or more forms of compensation.

service marketing system: the part of the total service system where the firm has any form of contact with its customers, from advertising to billing; it includes contacts made at the point of delivery.

service model: an integrative statement that specifies the nature of the service concept (what the firm offers, to whom, and through what processes), the service blueprint (how the concept is delivered to target customers), and the accompanying business model (how revenues will be generated sufficient to cover costs and ensure financial viability).

service operations system: the part of the total service system where inputs are processed and the elements of the service product are created.

service preview: a demonstration of how a service works to educate customers about the roles they are expected to perform in service delivery.

service-profit chain: a strategic framework that links employee satisfaction to performance on service attributes to customer satisfaction, then to customer retention, and finally to profits.

service quality: customers' long-term, cognitive evaluations of a firm's service delivery.

service quality information system: an ongoing service research process that provides timely, useful data to managers about customer satisfaction, expectations, and perceptions of quality.

service recovery: systematic efforts by a firm after a service failure to correct a problem and retain a customer's goodwill.

Service Science, Management and Engineering (SSME): combines management sciences (including services marketing), computer science, operations research, industrial engineering, social and cognitive sciences, legal sciences, and others to innovate and design complex service systems.

service sector: the portion of a nation's economy represented by services of all kinds, including those offered by public and nonprofit organizations.

services marketing mix: seven strategic elements, each beginning with P, in the services marketing mix, representing the key ingredients required to create viable strategies for meeting customer needs profitably in a competitive marketplace.

servicescape: the design of any physical location where customers come to place orders and obtain service delivery.

SERVQUAL: a pair of standardized 22-item scales that measure customers' expectations and perceptions concerning five dimensions of service quality.

Seven (7) Ps: (*see* **services marketing mix).**

social marketing: makes use of social networks to increase a firm's online presence, ranging from advertising on social networking sites to viral marketing and providing social networking sites focused around the service promoted.

SSME: (*see* Service Science, Management and Engineering).

standardization: reducing variation in service operations and delivery.

stickiness: a website's ability to encourage repeat visits and purchases by providing users with easy navigation and problem-free execution of tasks and by keeping its audience engaged with interactive communication presented in an appealing fashion.

sustainable competitive advantage: a position in the marketplace that can't be taken away or minimized by competitors in the short run.

T

tangible: capable of being touched, held, or preserved in physical form over time.

target market: a part of the qualified available market with common needs or characteristics that a company decides to serve.

target segments: segments selected because their needs and other characteristics fit well with a specific firm's goals and capabilities.

third-party payments: payments to cover all of part of the cost of a service or good made by a party other than the user (who may or may not have made the actual purchase decision).

three-stage model of service consumption: a framework depicting how consumers move from a prepurchase stage (in which they recognize their needs, search for and evaluate alternative solutions, and make a decision) to a service encounter search (in which they obtain service delivery) and a postencounter stage (in which they evaluate service performance against expectations).

time expenditures: time spent by customers during all aspects of the service delivery process.

total costs: the sum of the fixed and variable costs for any given level of production.

transaction: an event during which an exchange of value takes place between two parties.

Twitter: a social networking and microblogging service that allows its users to send and read other users' updates, which are up to 140 characters in length and send and receive via the Twitter website, Short Message Service (SMS), or external applications.

U

undesirable demand: requests for service that conflict with the organization's mission, priorities, or capabilities.

V

value chain: The series of departments within a firm or external partners and subcontractors that carry out value-creating activities to design, produce, market, deliver, and support a product or service offering.

value exchange: transfer of the benefits and solutions offered by a seller in return for financial and other value offered by a purchaser.

value net (*or* value network): a system of partnerships and alliances a firm creates to source, augment, and deliver its service offering.

value proposition: the full set of benefits a company promises to deliver.

value-based pricing: the practice of setting prices based on what customers are willing to pay for the value they believe they will receive.

variability: a lack of consistency in inputs and outputs during the service production process.

variable costs: costs directly dependent on the volume of production or service transactions.

viral marketing: using the Internet to create word-of-mouth effects to support marketing efforts.

W

Wheel of Loyalty: a systematic and integrated approach to targeting, acquiring, developing, and retaining a valuable customer base.

word of mouth: positive or negative comments about a service made by one individual (usually a current or former customer) to another.

Y

yield: the average revenue received per unit of capacity offered for sale.

yield management: (*see* **revenue management**).

Z

zone of tolerance: the range within which customers are willing to accept variations in service delivery.

CREDITS

Chapter 1, p. 29: Shutterstock; p. 42: Shutterstock; p. 48: Getty Images, Inc.– Taxi; p. 48: Shutterstock.

Chapter 2, p. 58: Shutterstock; p. 61: istockphoto.com; p. 64: Juniper Unlimited; p. 65: Shutterstock; p. 68: Shutterstock; p. 76: © godfer/Fotolia.com.

Chapter 3, p. 82: Shutterstock; p. 89: istockphoto.com.

Chapter 4, p. 105: © GV Images/Alamy; p. 110: Shutterstock; p. 113: iphotostock.com; p. 119: Shutterstock.

Chapter 5, p. 142: Courtesy of www.firstdirect.com; p. 144: Kathy Ringrose; p. 148: Reprinted with permission of DHL International Ltd.

Chapter 6, p. 158: Shutterstock; p. 161: Shutterstock.

Chapter 7, p. 186: Courtesy of Westin Hotels & Resorts a registered trademark of Starwood Hotels & Resorts Worldwide, Inc.; p. 200: www.easyjet.com/EN/Abut/photgaller.html. © easyJet airline company limited; p. 201: Getty Images, Inc. – Agence France Presse; p. 205: Wikipedia, The Free Encyclopedia.

Chapter 8, p. 219: Shutterstock; p. 222: Stockbyte RF/Getty Images, Inc.; p. 231: istockphoto.com; p. 239: Getty Images, Inc.– Photodisc/Royalty Free; p. 243: Shutterstock.

Chapter 9, p. 250: © Fingal/Fotolia.com; p. 253: Shutterstock; p. 259 © moodboard/Fotolia.com.

Chapter 10, p. 276: Shutterstock; p. 278: istockphoto.com; p. 279: Courtesy of ORBIT Hotel & Hostel in Los Angeles, orbithotel.com; p. 279: Starwood Hotel & Resorts Worldwide, Inc.; p. 287: Getty Images/Digital Vision; p. 289: Malaysia Tourism Promotion Board; p. 290: Panos Pictures; p. 292: Getty Images Inc. – Image Bank; p. 292: Angus Oborn © Rough Guides.

Chapter 11, p. 301: istockphoto.com; p. 304: Photo Researchers, Inc.; 308 © Jagadeesh/Reuters/CORBIS All Rights Reserved; p. 318: PhotoEdit Inc.; p. 321: Shutterstock.

Chapter 12, p. 337: © Ashley Cooper/Alamy; p. 344: Shutterstock; p. 352: AP Wide World Photos; p. 358: AP Wide World Photos, p. 360: © fotoliaguy/Fotolia.com.

Chapter 13, p. 372: Shutterstock; p. 389: PhotoEdit Inc.

Chapter 14, p. 402: Shutterstock; p. 405: Getty Images Inc.– Stone Allstock; p. 413: The Image Works; p. 424: Randy Matusow; p. 425: Getty Images/Digital Vision; p. 426: Randy Matusow.

Chapter 15, p. 448: Courtesy of Ron Kaufman/www .UPYourService.com.

Case 1, p. 467: istockphoto.com.

Case 3, p. 471–472, 474: istockphoto.com.

Case 5, p. 487: Giordano International Limited; p. 491: GIORDANO GROUP.

Case 7, p. 506, 507: Banyan Tree Hotels and Resorts.

Case 8, p. 513: Shutterstock.

Case 11, p. 542: Shutterstock.

Case 12, p. 547: istockphoto.com.

Case 13, p. 554: istockphoto.com.

Case 17, p. 601: istockphoto.com.

Cover: © BC photography/Alamy.

NAME INDEX

C

F

G

K

L

X

Y

Z

SUBJECT INDEX

D

E

F

G

H

S

T